AN

ARABIC-ENGLISH LEXICON

AN

ARABIC-ENGLISH LEXICON

BY

EDWARD WILLIAM LANE

IN EIGHT PARTS

PART 8 ي - ن

القاموس

AN

ARABIC-ENGLISH LEXICON,

DERIVED FROM THE BEST AND THE MOST COPIOUS EASTERN SOURCES;

COMPRISING A VERY LARGE COLLECTION
OF WORDS AND SIGNIFICATIONS OMITTED IN THE ḲÁMOOS,
WITH SUPPLEMENTS TO ITS ABRIDGED AND DEFECTIVE EXPLANATIONS,
AMPLE GRAMMATICAL AND CRITICAL COMMENTS,
AND EXAMPLES IN PROSE AND VERSE:

COMPOSED BY MEANS OF THE MUNIFICENCE OF THE MOST NOBLE

ALGERNON,

DUKE OF NORTHUMBERLAND, K.G.,

ETC. ETC. ETC.,

AND THE BOUNTY OF

THE BRITISH GOVERNMENT:

BY EDWARD WILLIAM LANE,

HON. DOCTOR OF LITERATURE OF THE UNIVERSITY OF LEYDEN, CORRESPONDENT OF THE INSTITUTE OF FRANCE, ETC.

IN TWO BOOKS:

THE FIRST CONTAINING ALL THE CLASSICAL WORDS AND SIGNIFICATIONS COMMONLY KNOWN
TO THE LEARNED AMONG THE ARABS:
THE SECOND, THOSE THAT ARE OF RARE OCCURRENCE AND NOT COMMONLY KNOWN.

BOOK I.—PART 8.

ن — ى

AND SUPPLEMENT.

EDITED BY STANLEY LANE-POOLE.

KALPAZ

ISBN: 978-93-5128-813-8(Set)
ISBN: 978-93-5128-822-0(HB)

First Published in 1893
Indian Reprint in 2017

Published by

Kalpaz Publications
C-30, Satyawati Nagar,
Delhi – 110052
E-mail: kalpaz@hotmail.com
Website: kalpazpublications.com
Ph.: +91-9212142040

Cataloging in Publication Data—DK

Courtesy: D.K. Agencies (P) Ltd. <docinfo@dkagencies.com>

Lane, Edward William, 1801-1876, **author.**

Madd al-qa˜mu˜s = An Arabic-English lexicon : derived from the best and the most copious eastern sources, comprising a very large collection of words and significations omitted in the Kamoos, with supplements to its abridged and defective explanations, ample grammatical and critical comments, and examples in prose and verse : composed by means of the munificence of the most noble algernon, Duke of Northumberland, K. G., etc. etc. etc., and the bounty of the British Government / by Edward William Lane.

volumes cm

English and Arabic.

Parts 6-8 edited with a memoir by Stanley Lane Poole.

"First published in 1863"—Title page verso.

"In two books: the first containing all the words and significations commonly known to the learned among the Arabs : the second, those that are of rare occurrence and not communly known."

ISBN 9789351288138 (set :

1. Arabic language—Dictionaries—English. 2. English language—Dictionaries—Arabic. I. Lane-Poole, Stanley, 1854-1931, editor. II. Title. III. Title: Arabic-English lexicon.

PJ6640.L36 2017 DDC 492.7321 23

ن

The twenty-fifth letter of the alphabet; called نُونٌ: it is one of the class termed ذَلْقِيَّةٌ [or *liquids*]; and is a letter of augmentation. — نّ with teshdeed, and preceded by a fat-ḥah, is sometimes redundantly affixed to a word at the end of a verse: see an ex. *voce* تُو. — ن, the sign of the dual, with ḍamm, in one dial., instead of kesr, see خَشِيفٌ. — See also صَادٌ. — As a numeral, it denotes *fifty*.

نأ

R. Q. 1. نَأْنَأَهُ *He fed him,* or *nourished him, well.* (Ḳ.) ═ *He restrained him,* or *turned him back,* (El-Umawee, Ṣ, Ḳ,) *from a thing that he desired to do.* (El-Umawee, Ṣ.) ═ نَأْنَأَ فِى الرَّأْيِ, inf. n. نَأْنَأَةٌ and مُنَأْنَأَةٌ; [the latter an unusual form of inf. n.;] and ↓ تَنَأْنَأَ; *He was weak,* (M, Ḳ,) or *confused;* (Ṣ;) *and not firm* or *sound,* (Ṣ, M, Ḳ,) *in his judgment,* or *opinion.* (Ṣ, M, Ḳ.) — نَأْنَأَ فِى الأَمْرِ *He was weak in the affair.* (Ṣ.) — نَأْنَأَ عَنْهُ, and ↓ تَنَأْنَأَ, *He was unable to do it.* (Ḳ.) — نَأْنَأَ, inf. n. نَأْنَأَةٌ; (AA;) and ↓ تَنَأْنَأَ; (Ṣ;) — *He was weak, feeble,* or *remiss.* (AA, Ṣ, TA.)

R. Q. 2: see R. Q. 1 in three places.

نَأْنَأٌ and ↓ نَأْنَاءٌ (Ṣ, Ḳ) and ↓ نُؤْنُوءٌ and ↓ مُنَأْنَأٌ *Weak; cowardly.* (Ṣ, Ḳ.) — نَأْنَأٌ *One who frequently turns about,* or *rolls, the pupil,* or *black part, of his eye.* (Ḳ.)

نَأْنَأَةٌ: see the verb. — *Weakness.* (AA, Ṣ.) — طُوبَى لِمَنْ مَاتَ فِى النَّأْنَأَةِ [*Good betide him who hath died in (the time of) weakness!*] i. e., in the first of El-Islám, before it acquired strength, (Ṣ,) and its adherents and assistants multiplied. (TA.)

نَأْنَآءٌ, نُؤْنُوءٌ, and مُنَأْنَأٌ: see نَأْنَأٌ.

نأت

1. نَأَتَ, aor. ـِ, (Ṣ, Ḳ,) contr. to analogy, like يَرْجِعُ, (TA,) and ـَ, (Ḳ,) agreeably with analogy, (TA,) inf. n. نَئِيتٌ, (Ṣ, Ḳ,) of the measure فَعِيلٌ, because it signifies a sound, like أَنِينٌ, (TA,) and نَأْتٌ, (Ḳ,) contr. to analogy, because the verb is intrans., (TA,) *He* (a man, Ṣ) *moaned;* or *breathed violently,* or *with moaning;* or *uttered his voice or breath with moaning;* syn. أَنَّ, (Ṣ, TA) and نَهَتَ: (Ṣ, Ḳ:) or it signifies *he uttered a louder sound than such as is termed* أَنِينٌ. (Ḳ.) ═ نَأَتَهُ *He envied him;* (Ḳ;) [as also نَأَدَهُ.] ═ نَأَتَ, inf. n. نَأْتٌ, *He walked,* or *went, at a slow pace.* (L.)

نَآتٌ i.q. نَهَّاتٌ: (Ṣ:) النَّآتُ *The lion.* (Ḳ.)

نأج

1. نَأَجَ فِى الأَرْضِ, aor. ـَ, inf. n. نُؤُوجٌ, *He went, went away, departed,* or *set forth journeying, through the land, or earth.* (Ṣ, Ḳ.) — نَأَجَ الخَبَرُ *The news, tidings,* or *information, went,* or *went away, through the land.* (T.) — نَأَجَتِ الرِّيحُ, aor. ـَ, inf. n. نَئِيجٌ, *The wind became in a state of commotion: blew with a swift course, and with a sound.* (Ṣ, Ḳ.) — نَأَجَتِ الرِّيحُ المَوْضِعَ *The wind passed swiftly over the place.* (TA.) — نُئِجَ القَوْمُ (like عُنِىَ [pass. in form but neut. in signification] TA) *The people experienced,* or *suffered, a swift and sounding wind.* (Ṣ, Ḳ.) [See an ex. voce مَنْأَجٌ.] — نَأَجَتِ الإِبِلُ فِى سَيْرِهَا [*The camels were swift in their pace*]. (TA.) — نَأَجَتِ الرَّائِحَةُ i.q. عَجَّتْ, [app., *The odour diffused itself strongly* or *powerfully*]. (TA.) ═ نَأَجَ, (aor. ـَ, inf. n. نَأْجٌ, TA,) *It (an owl) uttered a moaning cry;* or *hooted;* syn. نَأَمَ: (Ḳ:) and in like manner a man. (TA.) — نَأَجَ, (aor. ـَ and ـِ, inf. n. نَأْجٌ and نُؤَاجٌ, TA,) *He (a bull) lowed.* (Ḳ.) — نَأَجَ إِلَى اللّٰهِ, (aor. ـَ, TA,) *He humbled,* or *abased, himself, with earnestness,* in supplication, *to God.* (Ṣ, Ḳ.) ═ نَئِجَ *He ate weakly,* or *feebly.* (Ḳ.)

رِيحٌ نَؤُوجٌ *Wind in a state of commotion:* (Ṣ, Ḳ:) *swift in its course, and making a sound:* pl. نَوَائِجُ. (TA.)

نَأَّجٌ *Quick; swift.* (TA.) — النَّأَّجُ *The lion:* (Ḳ:) so called because of his quick leaping, or springing. (TA.) ═ نَأَّجٌ A bull *that lows much.* (TA.) — A man *having a high voice.* (TA.)

نَائِجَاتٌ [Birds of the kind called] هَام *uttering cries.* (Ṣ, L, Ḳ.) [In the CḲ, for هَام is put هَوَامّ. See an ex. voce مَنْأَجٌ.] — Also, *Winds blowing violently:* (TA:) pl. نَوَائِجُ. (A.)

أُدْعُ رَبَّكَ بِأَنْأَجِ مَا تَقْدِرُ عَلَيْهِ *Supplicate thy Lord with the utmost humility,* or *abasement, and earnestness, of which thou art capable.* (TA, from a trad.)

مَنْأَجٌ [*A place where a wind blows with a swift course and with a sound*]. Ex.

• وَتَنْأَجُ الرُّكْبَانُ كُلَّ مَنْأَجِ •
• بِهِ نَئِيجُ كُلِّ رِيحٍ سَيْهَجِ •

(Ṣ.) — [*A place where birds of the kind called* هَام *utter their cries*]. Ex.

• وَاتَّخَذَتْهُ النَّائِجَاتُ ↓ مَنْأَجَا •

(TA [but quoted in the Ṣ as an ex. of مَنْأَج in the former sense].)

حَدِيثٌ مَنْؤُوجٌ i.q. مَعْطُوفٌ [app. *A distorted story*]: (Ḳ:) so explained by ISk, as occurring in the following verse:

• قَدْ عَلِمَ الأَحْمَآءُ وَالأَزَاوِيجْ •
• أَنْ لَيْسَ عَنْهُنَّ حَدِيثٌ مَنْؤُوجْ •

(TA.)

نأد

1. نَأَدَتْهُ دَاهِيَةٌ, (aor. ـَ, A, inf. n. نَأْدٌ, L,) *A calamity befell him:* (Ḳ:) or *pressed heavily upon him, and distressed him.* (A.) — See نَأَتَ.

نَأْدٌ and ↓ نَأْدَى (Ṣ, L, Ḳ) and ↓ نَؤُودٌ (L, Ḳ) *A calamity:* (Ṣ, L, Ḳ:) pl. of the second, نَآئِدُ.

(L.) — دَاهِيَةٌ نَآدٌ, and ▼ نَآدَى, and ▼ نَؤُودٌ, (A, L,) *A calamity that presses heavily, and distresses.* (A.)

نَآدَى : see نَآدٌ.

نَؤُودٌ : see نَآدٌ.

ناش

1. نَاشَهُ, aor. ـُ, (Ṣ,) inf. n. نَوْشٌ, (Ṣ, A, Ḳ,) *He postponed, delayed,* or *retarded, it,* syn. أَخَّرَهُ; (Ṣ, M, A,* Ḳ,*) namely, an affair. (Ṣ, M.) — *He made it* (a thing) *to be distant,* or *remote; put it at a distance; put it,* or *sent it, away,* or *far away.* (TA.) ═ نَوْشٌ also signifies The *taking,* or *reaching,* [a thing,] *absolutely,* or *with the hand,* or *with the extended hand;* (A, Ḳ;) and so ▼ تَنَاوُشٌ, (Mṣb,) and تَنَاؤُشٌ, (Mṣb, Ḳ,) and نَوْشٌ: (IDrd, TA:) or ▼ تَنَاؤُشٌ, with ء, signifies the *taking from a distant place;* and without ء, the taking from a near place. (Th, TA.) You say, نُشْتُهُ, inf. n. نَوْشٌ, *I took it,* or *reached it, absolutely,* or *with my hand,* or *with my extended hand.* (TA.) And it is said in the Ḳur, [xxxiv. 51,] ▼ وَأَنَّى لَهُمُ ٱلتَّنَاوُشُ, and التَّنَاؤُشُ, with and without ء, accord. to different readers: (TA:) with ء, the word is from التَّنَوُّشُ, the و being changed to ء because of the ḍammeh; [so that the meaning is, *But how shall the attaining* of belief *be possible to them?*] (Zj, Bḍ;*) or from نَأَشْتُ as signifying تَأَخَّرْتُ [see 6 below]; so that the meaning is *the reaching* [or *attaining*] *from afar:* (Bḍ:) or from نَئِيشٌ, meaning, "motion in a state of slowness or tardiness:" (Zj:) or it is from نَأَشْتُ الشَّىْءَ, (Bḍ,) inf. n. نَأْشٌ, (IB, TA,) signifying *I sought,* or *sought for* or *after, the thing:* (IB, Bḍ:) [so that the above phrase in the Ḳur. may be rendered *But how shall the seeking* of belief *be possible to them?*] — It also signifies, (namely نَوْشٌ,) The *taking* [a thing]: and *seizing violently:* (A, Ḳ:) or *taking in a violent seizure:* you say, نَاشَهُ, inf. n. نَوْشٌ, *he took him,* or *it, in a violent seizure.* (TA.)

6. تَنَاءَشَ *He,* or *it, became,* or *remained, behind; became delayed,* or *retarded; it became postponed;* syn. تَأَخَّرَ; (Ṣ;) and so ▼ نَاشَ, said of a man; (Bḍ, xxxiv. 51;) and ▼ انتأش, (Ṣ, TA,) said of an affair. (Ṣ.) — *He,* or *it, became distant,* or *remote;* or *he went, removed, retired,* or *withdrew himself, to a distance,* or *far away;* (Ṣ, TA;) as also ▼ انتأش. (TA.) ═ See also 1, in three places.

8: see 6, in two places.

نَؤُوشٌ *Strong; overcoming;* or *prevailing;* (Ḳ;) *possessing might* or *strength, courage, valour,* or *prowess.* (TA.) You say also, قَدَرٌ نَؤُوشٌ *An overcoming decree;* as also نَوَّاشٌ. (TA.) See also art. نوش.

فَعَلَهُ نَئِيشًا *He did it lastly,* or *latterly,* or *last of all.* (Ṣ, A, Ḳ.) And جَآءَ نَئِيشًا *He came lastly,* or *latterly,* or *last of all:* (A:) or *slowly, tardily,* or *late.* (TA.) And لَحِقَنَا نَئِيشًا مِنَ النَّهَارِ *He overtook us after the day had declined;* (Ibn-'Abbád, Ḳ;) i.e., he held back from us, and then followed us in haste, fearing escape. (TA.) — نَئِيشٌ also signifies *Motion in a state of slowness* or *tardiness.* (Zj.) ═ Th also explains نَئِيشٌ as signifying *Distant* or *remote.* (TA.)

[ناط, &c.

See Supplement.]

نب

1. نَبَّ, aor. ـِ, inf. n. نَبِيبٌ (Ṣ, Ḳ) and نَبٌّ and نُبَابٌ; and ▼ نَبْنَبَ; *He* (a goat) *uttered a sound,* or *cry,* [or *rattled,*] *and was excited by desire of the female:* (Ṣ:) or *uttered a sound,* or *cry,* [or *rattled,*] *when excited by desire of the female,* (Ḳ,) or *at rutting-time.* (TA.) لَا تَنِبُّوا عِنْدِى نَبِيبَ التُّيُوسِ † *Do not cry out* [*in my presence like as he-goats rattle at rutting-time*]. Said by 'Omar to some persons who had come to make a complaint to him. (TA.) — [Hence,] نَبَّ † *He desired sexual intercourse.* (TA.) — نَبَّ عَتُودُهُ † *He was proud,* or *behaved proudly, and magnified himself.* (Ḳ.)

2. نَبَّبَ, inf. n. تَنْبِيبٌ, *It* (a plant) *produced a knotted stem.* (Ḳ.) — إِنِّى أَرَى الشَّرَّ نَبَّبَ † [*Verily I see evil,* or *the evil, to have grown, like a plant producing knotted stems*]. (TA.)

4. انبهُ طُولُ العُزْبَةِ † [*Length of celibacy made him to be desirous of sexual intercourse*]. (TA.) — انبَّ, inf. n. إِنْبَابٌ, if not a mistake for انبت, inf. n. انبات, meaning "he became pubescent," probably signifies *He was excited, and uttered libidinous sounds, with the desire of sexual intercourse.* (TA.) See R. Q. 1.

5. تنبّب *It* (water) *was made to flow;* or *was set a flowing.* (Ḳ.)

R. Q. 1: see 1. — نَبْنَبَ ‡ *He* (a man, TA) *talked nonsense,* (*and uttered libidinous sounds,* TA,) *in concubitu:* (Ḳ:) implying his acting like a he-goat at rutting-time. (TA.) — *He prolonged his work, to do it well.* (Ḳ.)

نَبَّةٌ *A disagreeable,* or *abominable, smell.* (Ḳ.) Probably a mistake for بَنَّةٌ; and therefore not mentioned by the leading lexicographers. (TA.)

نُبِّيٌّ *A table* (مَائِدَة) *made of palm-leaves.* (Ḳ, voce بُنِّيٌّ, q.v.)

أُنْبَبٌ or أَنْبُبٌ : see أُنْبُوبٌ and أُنْبُوبَةٌ.

أُنْبُوبٌ see أُنْبُوبَةٌ. — أُنْبُوبُ قَرْنٍ † *That part of a horn that is above the knotty portion, to the extremity:* [i.e., *the smooth part*]. (TA.) — أُنْبُوبٌ ‡ *The spout,* or *tube, of a jug.* (TA.) — † *A pipe* of a tank, or cistern, *through which the water flows:* either from تَنَبَّبَ, or from أُنْبُوبٌ as signifying "an internodal portion" of a reed, or cane. (TA.) — أَنَابِيبُ الرِّئَةِ ‡ *The* [*bronchi,* or] *air-passages of the lungs.* (Ḳ.) ▼ أُنْبَبٌ or أَنْبُبٌ is said to signify the same, in an instance mentioned by IAạr, in which a poet speaks of the substance resembling lights which a camel in heat protrudes from his mouth, and which is called غِيلَة, as coming forth بَيْنَ الأَنْبُبِ: in which case, the word, if أَنْبُبٌ, may be a pl., regularly أَنُبٌّ, of which the sing. is نَبٌّ; or, if with ḍammeh to the hemzeh, it may be a contraction of أُنْبُوبٌ, used as a coll. gen. n., in a pl. sense. (TA.) — أُنْبُوبٌ *A way,* or *road.* (Ḳ.) [Ex.] اِلْزَمِ الأُنْبُوبَ *Keep to the way,* or *road.* (Aṣ.) — أُنْبُوبُ جَبَلٍ ‡ *A track,* or *streak,* (طَرِيقَةٌ,) *in a mountain,* (Ḳ,) *appearing distinctly therein:* of the dial. of Hudheyl: (TA:) Ex. ذَهَبَ فِى كُلِّ انبوب [*He went along every track of the mountain,* or *mountains*]. (TA.) [As a coll. gen. n., used in the pl. sense: ex.] Málik Ibn-Khálid El-Khuzá'ee says,

* فِى رَأْسِ شَاهِقَةٍ أُنْبُوبُهَا خَضِرُ *

[*On the top of a lofty mountain, the streaks of which are green*]. (TA.) — أُنْبُوبٌ ‡ *A row of trees* (Ḳ) &c. (TA.) [See أُسْكُوبٌ.] — أُنْبُوبٌ *An elevated tract of land:* (Ḳ:) *one that is fine* (رقيق) *and elevated:* pl. أَنَابِيبُ. (TA.)

أُنْبُوبَةٌ *An internodal portion* of a reed or cane; *such a portion* thereof *as intervenes between two joints,* or *knots:* (Lth, Ṣ:) i.q. كَعْبٌ, [which signifies as above, and also *a joint,* or *knot,*] with reference to a reed, or cane, or a spear-shaft: (Ḳ:) as also ▼ أُنْبُوبٌ (Lth, Ḳ) and ▼ أُنْبُبٌ, which latter is probably a contraction: (Ḳ:) [see below:] or the pl. of انبوبة is أُنْبُوبٌ and أَنَابِيبُ: (Ṣ:) [or انبوب is a coll. gen. n., of which the n. un. is انبوبة, and the pl. انابيب: see also art. انب]. — [Hence,] اِجْعَلِ الأَمْرَ أُنْبُوبَةً وَاحِدَةً *Make thou the affair,* or *case,* [*uniform,* or] *one uniform thing.* (Fr. in TA in art. بأج.) — [Also, *A sheath* of a plant. See أُمْصُوخَةٌ.] — And *Any kind of tube.* See قَصَبٌ.]

نبأ

1. نَبَأَ, (Ḳ,) inf. n. نَبْءٌ, (TA,) *He uttered a low voice,* or *sound:* or *he* (a dog) *cried,* or *barked.* (Ḳ.) [See نبح.] ═ نَبَأَ, aor. ـَ, inf. n. نَبْءٌ and نُبُوءٌ, *He was exalted,* or *elevated.* ═ نَبَأَ عَلَيْهِمْ, (Ḳ,) inf. n. نَبْءٌ and نُبُوءٌ, (Ṣ,) *He assaulted them;*

came forth upon them: (K:) like نَبَعَ and نَبَهَ: *he came upon them.* (AZ, Ṣ.) [See also نَابِئٌ.] — نَبَأَ *He went forth* from a land to another land. (Ṣ, K.) [See نَابِئٌ.] — نَبَأَتْ بِهِ الأَرْضُ i. q. جَآءَتْ بِهِ, *The land brought,* or *led him:* (Ṣ, L:) [accord. to Golius, *The land brought,* or *produced, it:* but it is a phrase well known to the learned among the Arabs in the present day, as similar to نَادَاهُ تُرَابُهُ "his dust, or earth, (i. e. the place of his burial,) called him:" and the explanation which I have given is confirmed by the citation, in the Ṣ, of the following verse, of Ḥanash Ibn-Málik, immediately after نبأت به in the sense of جاءت به:]

فَنَفْسَكَ أَحْرِزْ فَإِنَّ الحُتُو
فَ يَنْبَأْنَ بِالمَرْءِ فِي كُلِّ وَادْ

[*Then take good care of thyself; for deaths* (of various kinds) *bring* (or *lead*) *a man into every valley* (or *place*): i. e., fate brings him to the place where he is destined to be buried, wherever it be]. (Ṣ.) — نَبَأَ, aor. ـَ: see 4.

2. نَبَّأَ: see 4.

3. نَابَأَهُ *He acquainted* or *informed him, and the latter did the same.* (K.) — Also, simply, *He acquainted* or *informed him.* (TA.) — نَابَأَهُمْ *He quitted their neighbourhood; withdrew to a distance from them.* (K.) [See also art. نبو.]

4. انبأهُ إِيَّاهُ, and بِهِ, (and عَنْهُ, Ṣ, K, art. كود;) and ▼ نَبَّأَهُ (Ṣ,* K) and ▼ نَبَّأَهُ, (Ṣ,* TA,) each followed by اياه or به; (TA;) *He informed him,* or *told him, of it:* (K:) or these verbs, followed by اياه, signify *he made him to know it;* and followed by به, *he informed him,* or *told him, of it.* (TA.) — Es-Semeen says, that انبأ and ▼ نبّأ and اخبر and خبّر, when they convey the meaning of knowledge, are triply transitive, or may govern three objective complements, the greatest number that any verb can govern: (TA:) [ex. أَنْبَأْتُ زَيْدًا عَمْرًا قَائِمًا *I acquainted Zeyd that 'Amr was standing*]. — It is also said, that ▼ نبّأ has a more intensive signification than انبأ: ex. مَنْ أَنْبَأَكَ هٰذَا قَالَ نَبَّأَنِىَ العَلِيمُ الخَبِيرُ [*Who hath acquainted thee with this? He said, The Knowing, the Intelligent* (God), *hath apprized me:* Kur, lxvi. 3]. (TA.) — Sb has mentioned أَنَا أَنْبُؤُكَ [for انا أُنْبِئُكَ] as used for the sake of conformity in sound with a preceding word. (M, TA.) [See art. جوأ.] = رَمَى فَأَنْبَأَ *He cast,* or *shot, but did not split,* or *cleave,* or *make a slight cut,* or *scratch:* (Ṣ, K:) or, *did not penetrate.* (K.)

5. تَنَبَّأَ, (Ṣ, K,) said to have been pronounced with ء universally; (Sb, Ṣ;) but in the L, تنبّى; (TA;) *He arrogated to himself the gift of prophecy,* or *office of a prophet.* (L, K.)

10. استنبأ النَّبَأَ *He sought,* or *searched after, information,* or *news.* (K.) — وَيَسْتَنْبِئُونَكَ أَحَقٌّ هُوَ (in the Kur, x. 54) means *And they will ask thee to inform them,* [saying,] *Is it true?* (Bḍ.)

نَبَأٌ *Information; a piece of information; intelligence; an announcement; news; tidings; a piece of news; an account; a narrative,* or *narration; a story:* or *what is related from another or others:* syn. خَبَرٌ: (Ṣ, Mṣb, K:) it is generally held to be syn. with خبر; but accord. to Er-Rághib, signifies *an announcement of great utility, from which results either knowledge or a predominance of opinion, and true:* (TA:) pl. أَنْبَآءٌ. (K.) — النَّبَأُ العَظِيمُ [Kur, lxxviii. 2,] accord. to some, *The Kur-án:* others say, *the resurrection:* and others, *the case of the Prophet.* (TA.) — الأَنْبَآءُ, in the Kur, xxviii. 66, (فَعَمِيَتْ عَلَيْهِمُ الأَنْبَآءُ,) signifies *The allegations, pleas,* or *excuses.* (TA.)

نَبْأَةٌ *An eminence,* or *protuberance, in the earth,* or *ground.* (TA.) — نَبْأَةٌ *A low voice,* or *sound:* (Ṣ, K:) or the *cry,* or *barking, of dogs.* (K.)

نَبِىْءٌ, (Ṣ, K,) pronounced with ء in the dial. of the people of Mekkeh, (Ṣ,) whose pronunciation of it is disapproved by Sb on account of its uncommonness; (TA;) by others, نَبِىٌّ, without ء; (Ṣ, K, TA;) *A prophet:* (TA:) of the measure فَعِيلٌ used in the sense of the measure مُفْعَلٌ [i. e. مُفْعَلٌ or مُفْعِلٌ] (IB) or فَاعِلٌ (Ṣ, Es-Sunoosee) or مَفْعُولٌ; (Es-Sunoosee) i. e., *who acquaints* or *informs mankind,* (Ṣ, K, TA,) or *who is acquainted* or *informed, respecting God and things unseen:* or accord. to some, it is derived from نُبُوَّةٌ and نَبَاوَةٌ signifying "elevation;" (see art. نبو;) in which case it is originally without ء: or, accord. to others, from نَبِىْءٌ in a sense given below; that of "a conspicuous way." (TA.) It is a less special word than رَسُولٌ [when thereby is meant an apostle of God]; for every رسول is a نبىّ, but not every نبىّ is a رسول. (TA.) Pl. أَنْبِيَآءُ (Ṣ, K, without ء, because the ء is changed into ى in the sing., Ṣ,) and نُبَآءُ (Ṣ, K, like كُرَمَآءُ [pl. of كَرِيمٌ] TA,) and أَنْبَآءٌ [K, these two preserving the original radical ء] and نَبِيُّونَ, (K,) without ء: (TA:) but some pronounced the first and last of these pls., in the Kur-án, with ء; though the more approved pronunciation is without ء. (TA.) The dim. is نُبَيِّئٌ, (Ṣ, K,) with those who make the pl. نُبَآءُ [or أَنْبَآءٌ]; but with those who make the pl. أَنْبِيَآءُ, it is نُبَيٌّ. (K.) — An Arab of the desert said to Mohammad, يَا نَبِىْءَ ٱللّٰهِ, and the latter disapproved of his pronouncing نبىء in this case with ء, because, as it signifies *An emigrant,* he meant thereby to call him an emigrant from Mekkeh to El-Medeeneh. (Ṣ, K, TA.) — نَبِىْءٌ *A conspicuous, an evident,* or *a clear, way.* (K.) Hence, accord. to some, the apostle [or rather prophet] is so called, because he is the conspicuous, evident, way, that conducts to God. (MF.) — نَبِىْءٌ and ▼ نَابِئٌ *An elevated,* or *a protuberant,* or *gibbous, place.* (K.) — Hence it is said in a trad., لَا تُصَلُّوا عَلَى النَّبِىْءِ [*Pray not upon the place that is elevated,* or *protuberant*]. (K.)

نُبُوْءَةٌ, (K, in the CK نُبُوَّةٌ) in which the ء is sometimes softened in pronunciation, and sometimes [or rather generally] changed into و which is incorporated into the preceding و so that the word is written and pronounced نُبُوَّةٌ, (TA,) *Prophecy;* the *gift of prophecy;* the *office,* or *function, of a prophet.* (MA, K.) Dim. نُبَيِّئَةٌ. (Ṣ, K.)

نَابِئٌ act. part. n. of نَبَأَ. — A bull [app. a ثَوْرٌ وَحْشِىٌّ] *that goes forth from one land* or *country to another.* (TA.) — A torrent *that comes forth from another land* or *tract.* (Ṣ.) — A man *coming forth unexpectedly from an unknown quarter.* (Ṣ, A.) — [See also نَبِىْءٌ.]

هَلْ عِنْدَكُمْ نَابِئَةُ خَبَرٍ, i. q. جَائِبَةُ خَبَرٍ, [*Have ye any current news?* or—*news from a distant place?* &c.: see جائبة]. (A.)

نبت

1. نَبَتَ, (Ṣ, M, K,) aor. ـُ, inf. n. نَبْتٌ and نَبَاتٌ; [which two ns. see mentioned as substs.;] and ▼ تنبّت; (M;) and ▼ انبت; (Fr, Ṣ, K;) [respecting which last see below;] *It* (a thing, M, or a leguminous [or other] plant, Ṣ, K,) *grew; grew forth; sprouted; vegetated;* or *germinated.* (Ṣ, M, K.) Aṣ disallows ▼ انبت in this sense; but AO allows it, alleging the words of Zuheyr, حَتَّى إِذَا أَنْبَتَ ▼ البَقْلُ [*Until, when the leguminous plants grew*]. نَبَتَ and ▼ أَنْبَتَ are said to be like مَطَرَتِ السَّمَآءُ and أَمْطَرَتْ. In the Kur, xxiii. 20, Ibn-Ketheer, Aboo-'Amr and El-Hadremee read تُنْبِتُ: others, تَنْبُتُ: but ISd says, that, accord. to the former reading, some hold ب, which follows تُنْبِتُ, to be redundant; and others hold that مَا تُنْبِتُ is understood after تُنْبِتُ. Fr holds them to be syn. (TA.) — نَبَتَ عَلَى حَالَةٍ حَسَنَةٍ *He,* or *it, grew in a good manner, condition,* or *state.* (L.) — نَبَتَ, inf. n. نُبُوتٌ, ‡ *It* (a girl's breast) *became swelling, prominent,* or *protuberant.* (K.) — نَبَتَتِ الأَرْضُ, and ▼ أَنْبَتَت, *The land produced,* or *gave growth to, plants,* or *herbage.* (Ṣ, K.)

2. نبّت, inf. n. تَنْبِيتٌ, ‡ *He fed* or *nourished,* or *reared* or *brought up,* a child: (Ṣ, K:) *he nourished* a girl, *and nursed* her up *well, hoping that she might profit excellently.* (TA.) — نَبِّتْ أَجَلَكَ بَيْنَ عَيْنَيْكَ [‡ *Plant the term of thy life before* (lit. between) *thine eyes;* i. e., keep it ever before thee]. (Ṣ.) — نبّت, inf. n. تَنْبِيتٌ, *He planted* a tree. (M, Ṣ, K.) — *He sowed* seed, (M,) or grain. (A.)

4. انبتهُ, (Ṣ, Ḳ,) inf. n. إِنْبَاتٌ [for which نَبَاتٌ occurs, as shown below], (TA,) *He* (God) *caused it, or made it,* (a plant) *to grow, vegetate, or germinate.* (Ṣ, Ḳ.) — انبت, inf. n. إِنْبَاتٌ; for which inf. n. نَبَاتٌ occurs in the Ḳur, iii. 32; and lxxi. 16; ‡ *He* (God) *caused* a child *to grow.* (TA.) — See 1. — انبت *His* (a boy's) *hair of the pubes grew forth;* (Ṣ, Ḳ;) *he having nearly attained the age of puberty.* (TA.) *He* (a boy) *became hairy:* and in like manner a girl. (Mṣb.)

5 : see 1.

10. استنبتهُ [*He endeavoured to make it grow, or vegetate, or germinate*]. (TA, art. بلس.) استنبتهُ بِالبَذْرِ [*He grew it, or raised it, by means of seed*], and بِالنَّوَى [*by means of date-stones*], and بالغرس [*by means of planting*]. (Mgh, art. حرث.)

نَبْتٌ and ▼ نَبَاتٌ [properly coll. gen. ns.] are syn., (Ṣ, Ḳ,) [signifying *A plant, a herb:* and *plants, herbs, or herbage:*] *whatever God causes to grow, vegetate, or germinate, in the earth:* (Lth:) the latter is an inf. n. used as a subst.: (Lth:) or it is a subst. which is used in the place of an inf. n. of أَنْبَتَ: (Fr:) n. un. of the former نَبْتَةٌ; (AḤn;) [and of the latter نَبَاتَةٌ of which the pl. نَبَاتَاتٌ is mentioned in the Ḳ in this art., and frequently occurs in other works]. — أَهْلُ بَيْتٍ وَأَهْلُ نَبْتٍ *A people of* the highest *rank, or nobility, and a people whose property has grown* to the most flourishing state *by means of their own exertions.* (L, from a trad.)

نِبْتَةٌ The *manner, form, state, or condition, in which a thing grows, or germinates.* (L.) — إِنَّهُ لَحَسَنُ النِّبْتَةِ *Verily he,* or *it, is of a goodly manner, &c., of growth.* (L.)

نَبَاتٌ: see نَبْتٌ. — سُكَّر نَبَات [*Sugar-candy;* so called in the present day;] *an admirable kind of sugar, of which are made pieces resembling crystal, intensely white and lustrous:* app. Persian, and post-classical. (MF.)

خَبِيثٌ نَبِيتٌ *Vile, and contemptible, or despicable:* (Lḥ, Ḳ:) said of a man, and of a thing. (TA.) In some copies of the Ḳ, and in the L, instead of حَقِيرٌ, we read فَقِيرٌ, [accord. to which, the meaning is *vile, and poor*]. (TA.)

نَبِيتَةٌ sing. of نَبَائِتُ, which latter signifies the *ridges that are raised along the edges of rivulets such as are called* فُلْجَان (in the CḲ, فلحان) *to retain the water:* النبائت being expl. by أَعْضَادُ الفُلْجَانِ: so in the L, &c.: in several copies of the Ḳ we read, in the place of اعضاد, اغصان: but this is a mistake. (TA.)

نَابِتُ كُلِّ شَىْءٍ *What is fresh, or new, of anything, when it is growing forth small.* (TA.) نَبَتَتْ لَهُمْ نَابِتَةٌ *There grew up unto them young offspring,* (Ṣ, Ḳ,) *that became conjoined to the old, and increased their number.* (TA.) Dim. نُوَيْبِتَةٌ. (L.) — إِنَّ بَنِى فُلَانٍ لَنَابِتَةُ شَرٍّ [*Verily the sons of such a one are an evil offspring*]. (Ṣ.) — مَا أَحْسَنَ نَابِتَةَ بَنِى فُلَانٍ *How good is the manner, condition, or state, in which grow* (مَا تَنْبُتُ عَلَيْهِ, see 1,) *the camels &c.,* (أَمْوَال) *and children of the sons of such a one!* — نَابِتَةٌ (TA) and نَوَابِتُ [pl. of the former] (Ṣ, Ḳ) *Inexperienced young men.* (Ṣ, Ḳ.) You say, هٰذَا قَوْلُ النَّابِتَةِ, and النَّوَابِتِ, *This is the saying of inexperienced young men.* (TA.) — النَّوَابِتُ *The name of a certain sect who introduced strange innovations in El-Islám.* (A, TA.) El-Jáḥidh couples them with the رَافِضَة. (MF.)

مَنْبِتٌ: see مَنْبَتٌ.

مَنْبِتٌ ‡ *Origin,* or *race,* [from which a man springs;] syn. أَصْلٌ. (L.) So in the phrase إِنَّهُ لَفِى مَنْبِتِ صِدْقٍ ‡ *Verily he belongs to an excellent race;* is *of an excellent origin*]: and so in the phrase فِى أَكْرَمِ المَنَابِتِ [*of the most generous of origins, or races.*] (TA.) — مَنْبَتٌ *A place in which plants, or herbs, grow:* (Ṣ, Ḳ:) dev. from the constant course of speech: analogically it should be ▼ مَنْبِتٌ: (Ḳ:) as the aor. of the verb from which it is derived is not يَنْبِتُ, with kesreh: but there are other examples like it; as مَسْجِدٌ and مَطْلِعٌ &c.: ▼ مَنْبَتٌ, however, also sometimes occurs. (TA.) [Pl. مَنَابِتُ.]

أَرْضٌ مِنْبَاتٌ [*Land abounding with plants, or herbage*]. (Ḳ, voce رَحْبَةٌ, &c.)

مَنْبُوتٌ (contr. to analogy, Ṣ, [for مُنْبَتٌ,]) *A plant caused to grow, or germinate.* (Ṣ, Ḳ.)

مُتَنَبِّتٌ *Firmly rooted;* syn. مُتَأَصِّلٌ. (TA.)

تَنْبِيتٌ and ▼ تِنْبِيتٌ, (Ḳ,) the latter so written, not as being so originally, but for the sake of agreement in sound [with respect to the first and second vowels], (AḤei,) a subst., signifying *What grows, or germinates, of slender* (i. e. small, TA,) *trees,* [or *shrubs,*] *and large:* (Ḳ:) ex.,

بَيْدَاءُ لَمْ يَنْبُتْ بِهَا تَنْبِيتُ

[*A desert in which there grew not aught of shrubs or of large trees*]: (TA:) *young shoots of palm-trees:* (IḲṭṭ:) the *prickles and branches that are cut off from a palm-tree, to lighten it.* (AḤn, as from 'Eesa Ibn-'Omar.) — *Pieces of the hump of a camel.* (L.)

تِنْبِيتٌ: see تَنْبِيتٌ.

يَنْبُوتٌ [coll. gen. n.] *A certain species of trees:* (Ṣ:) *poppy-plants;* syn. شَجَرُ الخَشْخَاشِ: and *other trees of a large kind:* or the *trees called* خَرُّوب [see below]: (Ḳ:) or *a kind of thorny trees, having branches and leaves, with a fruit of the kind called* جَرْو, i. e., *round; called in 'Omán* غَاف: n. un. with ة: AḤn says that there are two species of ينبوت; one of these is *a kind of thorny and short trees, also called* خُرُّوب [q. v.] *having a fruit resembling a bubble, in which are red grains, having an astringent effect upon the bowels, used as a medicine;* the other species is *a large species of trees:* ISd says, An Arab of the desert, of the tribe of Rabeea, described to me the ينبوتة as [*a tree*] *resembling a large apple-tree, the leaves of which are smaller than those of the apple, having a fruit smaller than the* زُعْرُور, *intensely black and intensely sweet, with grains,* or *stones, which are put into scales, or balances:* [evidently meaning the *carob,* or *locust-tree,* (see خُرُّوب,) whence our term "carob," applied to a small weight, the twenty-fourth part of a grain]. (L [See غاف and قُرْقُور].)

نبث

1. نَبَثَ, aor. ـُ, inf. n. نَبْثٌ; (and ▼ انتبث, Ḳ;) *i. q.* نَبَشَ; (AZ, Ṣ, Ḳ;) i. e., *He dug with the hand.* (AZ, Ṣ.) — نَبَثَ, aor. ـِ, inf. n. نَبْثٌ, *He took forth, or dug out, dust, or earth, from a well or a river.* (L.) — نَبَثُوا عَنِ الأَمْرِ ‡ *They searched, or sought, for, or after, the thing; inquired respecting it; sought for information respecting it; searched into, inquired into, investigated, scrutinized, or examined, it.* (TA.) = نَبِثَ, [aor. ـَ,] inf. n. نَبَثٌ, ‡ *He was angry.* (Ḳ.)

6. تَنَابَثُوا عَنِ الأَسْرَارِ ‡ *They searched into each other's secrets.* (A.)

8. انتبث: see 1. — *He took; received into his hand.* (Ḳ.) — *He tucked up the skirts of his shirt, or the like, when sitting on the ground.* (Ḳ.) — *It* (سَوِيق or the like) *increased in size* (رَبَا) *in the water:* (Ḳ:) as also انتبذ. (TA.)

10. استنبث أَخَاهُ عَنْ سِرِّهِ ‡ *He examined his brother respecting his secret.* (A.)

نَبْثٌ *A trace, vestige, or mark:* (Ḳ:) *a trace, or mark, of digging:* (A:) pl. أَنْبَاثٌ. (TA.) — مَا رَأَيْتُ لَهُ عَيْنًا وَلَا نَبْثًا *I saw not the man himself, or the thing itself, nor any trace of him, or it.* (L.) — See نَبِيثٌ.

نَبِيثٌ The *dust that an animal digs up with its feet in running.* (IAạr.) — ▼ نَبِيثَةٌ (Ṣ, Ḳ) and نَبِيثٌ and ▼ نَبْثٌ (L) The *dust, or earth, that is taken forth, or dug out, from a well or a river:* (Ṣ, L, Ḳ:) pl. of the first, نَبَائِثُ. (A.) — نَبِيثٌ and ▼ مَنْبُوثٌ *Earth, or dust, taken forth, or dug out, from a well or a river.* (L.) — ▼ نَبِيثَةٌ سَبْعٍ

Flesh-meat buried by a beast of prey against the time of want. (IAth, from a trad.) ═ نَبِيثٌ *A species of sea-fish*; accord. to IAar; but it is also said, on his authority, that it is called يَنْبِيثٌ; therefore it seems that one of these two words is a mistake for the other, or that they are two dial. forms. See also يَنْبِيثٌ, in art. بنث. (TA.) ═ خَبِيثٌ نَبِيثٌ ‡ *Very bad, evil, wicked, or corrupt*: (K:) applied to a man: (TA:) the latter word is an imitation sequent to the former. (S, and some copies of the K.) ═ أَبْدَى نَبِيثَةَ القَوْمِ, and نَبَائِثَهُمْ, ‡ [*He revealed the elicited secret of the people, and their elicited secrets*]. (A.) — بَيْنَهُمْ شَحْنَآءُ وَنَبَائِثُ ‡ [*Between them are enmity and secrets elicited*]. (A.)

نَبِيثَةٌ: see نَبِيثٌ.

أُنْبُوثَةٌ *A certain game* (*played by children*, TA,) *in which something is buried in a hole dug in the ground, and he who takes it forth wins the game.* (K.)

مَنْبُوثٌ: see نَبِيثٌ.

ظَهَرَتْ مَنَابِثُهُمْ وَلَمْ تَخْفَ خَبَائِثُهُمْ ‡ [*The occasions for the scrutiny of their conduct appeared, and their evil qualities were not hidden*]. (A.)

نبج

1. نَبَجَ, aor. ِ, inf. n. نَبِيجٌ, *He uttered a loud, or vehement voice, or cry.* (TA.) — نَبَجَ, inf. n. نُبَاجٌ, *Pepedit, certo modo*: (TA:) inf. n. نَبْجٌ, *crepitum ventris emisit; pepedit.* (S, K.) — نَبَجَ, inf. n. نَبِيجٌ and نُبَاجٌ, *He* (a dog) *barked*; i.q. نَبَحَ. (S, K.) ═ نَبَجَ *He mixed up*, or beat up, fresh milk, *with a* نَبَّاجَة, *until it became froth, in which state it is eaten with dates, taken up with three fingers.* Only the Benoo-Asad did this. (IKh.) — نَبَجَ *He mixed up* سَوِيق &c. (TA.)

نَبِيجٌ and ✝ مَنْبُوجٌ Milk *mixed up, or beaten up, in the manner explained voce* نَبَجَ. (IKh.) — نَبِيجٌ and ✝ نَابِجَةٌ *A kind of food of the Arabs in the time of paganism, (in seasons of dearth, or famine*, TA,) *made by mixing up, and beating up, soft camel's hair* (وَبَر) *with milk.* (K.)

نُبَاجٌ *Loud, or vehement, in voice, or cry.* (S, K.) — نَبَّاجٌ and ✝ نُبَاجِيٌّ *A dog that barks much*; (K;) *a loud-barking dog.* (S.) [See نُبَاحٌ.] ═ نَبَّاجٌ [The *wooden implement called*] *a* مِجْدَح, *for* [*mixing up*] سَوِيق (K) &c.; (TA;) also called مِخْوَض and مِزْهَف. (El-Mufaddal.) [See also نَبَّاجَة.]

النَّبَّاجَةُ *The anus*; syn. الاِسْتُ. (S, K.) — كَذَبَتْ نَبَّاجَتُهُ *Pepedit.* (S.) — نَبَّاجَةٌ *A wooden implement at the end of which is a thing resembling a* فَلْكَة [or the round head of a spindle], with which fresh milk is mixed up, or beaten up, *in the manner explained voce* نَبَجَ. (IKh.) [See also نَبَّاجٌ.]

نَبَّاجٌ: see نُبَاجِيٌّ.

نَبِيجٌ: see نَابِجَةٌ.

أَنْبَجٌ and ✝ أَنْبِجٌ The *fruit of a certain Indian tree*, (K,) *which is preserved*, or *made into a confection, with honey*; *in form like the peach, with the head edged* (مُحَرَّف); [but this seems rather to apply to a kind mentioned below, resembling the almond;] *it is brought to El-'Irák; and has within it a stone like that of the peach*: (L:) an arabicized word, from [the Persian] أَنْبَ [or أَنْبْ]. (K.) — Hence ✝ أَنْبِجَاتٌ, (L,) with kesreh to the ب, *Medical confections*: app. an arabicized word: (S:) or *confections, or preserves, made with honey, of the* أُتْرُجّ *and* إِهْلِيلَج *and the like.* (L.) — Accord. to AHn, انبج is the name of *Certain trees abounding in Arabia, in the districts of 'Omán; planted; they are of two kinds; one of these has a fruit resembling the almond, which is sweet from the commencement of its growth; the other has a fruit in appearance like the Damask plum* (إِجَّاص), *is at first sour, and then becomes sweet when ripe: each has a stone, and has a sweet odour: the fruit of the sour kind is pressed down in jars, or earthern pots,* [حِبَاب: so I read for جباب:] *while fresh, and kept until it attains to a ripe state, when it becomes as though it were the banana, in its odour and taste: the tree grows great so as to become like the walnut* (جَوْز), *which it resembles also in its leaves: and when it attains to perfection, the sweet* [fruit] *is yellow; and the bitter,* [or *sour*,] *red.* (L.)

أَنْبِجٌ: see أَنْبَجٌ.

أَنْبَجَانٌ Dough *that has become in a state of fermentation, and inflated, or swollen*, (S, K,) *and sour*: (TA:) in some books written with خ; but heard from the Arabs with ج, accord. to Aboo-Sa'eed and Abu-l-Ghowth and others: (S:) there is no word like it except أُرْوَنَانٌ. (S, K.)

مَنْبَجَانِيٌّ: see أَنْبَجَانِيٌّ. — Also, A mess of broken, or crumbled, bread, (ثَرِيد,) *in which is* [*some degree of*] *heat.* (K.)

كِسَآءٌ مَنْبَجَانِيٌّ, (S, K,) the latter word being formed after the manner of مَخْبَرَانِيٌّ and مَنْظَرَانِيٌّ, (S,) and ✝ أَنْبَجَانِيٌّ, rel. ns. of مَنْبِج, each with fet-hah to the ب, contr. to analogy, (K,) the latter disallowed by IKt, but occurring in a trad. and in poetry, and not to be disallowed because contr. to analogy, since there are many such rel. ns., as مَرْوَزِيٌّ and رَازِيٌّ &c., (TA,) *A certain kind of* كِسَآء, *so called in relation to a place named* مَنْبِج: (S, K, &c.:) or كِسَآءٌ أَنْبَجَانِيٌّ, and أَنْبِجَانِيٌّ, which latter form is related by IAth as the one retained in the memory, *a certain kind of* كِسَآء, *so called in relation to a place named* انبجان; *of wool, having a nap*, or *pile, without a border; one of the meanest kinds of coarse garments*: its أ, accord. to some, is an augmentative letter. (TA.)

مَنْبُوجٌ: see نَبِيجٌ.

نبح

1. نَبَحَ, aor. ِ and َ, [the former of which, accord. to the Msb, seems to be more common,] inf. n. نَبْحٌ and نَبِيحٌ and نُبَاحٌ and نِبَاحٌ (S, K) and نُبُوحٌ (L,) and تَنْبَاحٌ, (K,) the last having an intensive and frequentative signification, (TA,) *He* (a dog, S, L, K) *barked.* (L.) — Also, (sometimes, S,) ‡ said of a gazelle, (T, S, K,) when he has advanced in years, and his horns have branched forth: (T:) and ‡ of a he-goat, (K,) in coupling-time: (L:) and ‡ of a serpent; (K;) meaning *he uttered a cry, or sound*: (L:) also ‡ of a hoopoe, (هُدْهُد,) inf. n. نُبَاحٌ, signifying *it uttered a harsh cry, by reason of age*: (L:) and ‡ of a lion, inf. n. نُبَاحٌ, signifying *he uttered a cry* (L, K) *like the barking of a whelp.* (Aboo-Kheyreh, L.) — نَبَحَ عَلَيْهِ and نَبَحَهُ الكَلْبُ, (T, Msb,) and ✝ نَابَحَهُ, (T,) *The dog barked at him.* (Msb.) — فُلَانٌ لَا يُعْوَى وَلَا يُنْبَحُ † [*Such a one is not howled at nor barked at*]: i.e., by reason of his weakness, no account is taken of him, and neither good nor evil is said to him. (L.) — نَبَحَ ‡ *He* (a poet) *satirized.* (A.) — نَبَحَتْنِي كِلَابُكَ ‡ *Thy revilings reached, or overtook, me.* (L.)

3: see 1.

4. انبحهُ and ✝ استنبحهُ, *He made him* (a dog) *to bark*: (S, K:) استنبح ✝ الكَلْبَ *he excited*, or *induced, the dog to bark*: said of a man when, having lost his way, he imitates the bark of that animal, in order that a dog may hear him, and, imagining him to be a dog, may bark, and so guide him. (L.) Said also of a guest, [or one who would be a guest, and who desires to guide himself to a place of entertainment]. (A.) [See an ex. cited, from the poet El-Akhtal, voce إِرْدَبٌّ.]

10: see 4.

نُبُوحٌ ‡ The *clamour, confused noise*, or *mixture of voices, of a tribe*, (S,) or *of a people*, (K,) *and the barkings of their dogs*, (S, K,) *and the cries of their other animals.* (A.) — Subsequently put in the place of ‡ *Multitude, and might*, or *power*: (S:) and signifying ‡ *a numerous assembly.* (K.) El-Akhtal says,

إِنَّ العَرَارَةَ وَالنُّبُوحَ لِدَارِمٍ

[*Verily strength, or eminence, or lordship, and multitude, and might, or power, belong to Dárim*]. (Ṣ.)

نَبَّاحٌ A dog *that barks much.* (A.) — نَبَّاحٌ A man (L) *having a vehement,* or *loud, voice.* (L, Ḳ.) — ▾ نُبَاحٌ, with ḍammeh, (Ḳ,) or نُبَّاحٌ (as in the L) ‡ *A hoopoe* (هُدْهُد) *that coos* (يُقَرْقِر) *much.* (IAạr, Ḳ.) — نَبَّاحٌ ‡ A gazelle *that cries much,* or *often:* (IAạr:) and ▾ نَبَّاحَةٌ *the same* applied to the female. (AA, Ḳ.) == نَبَّاحٌ *White, small* [*shells such as are called*] صَدَف: (TA:) *small, white* [*shells such as are called*] مَنَاقِف, *of Mekkeh,* (T, Ḳ, TA,) i.e. *brought from Mekkeh:* (TA:) *put into* [*necklaces such as are called*] قَلَائِد (Ḳ, TA) *and* وُشُح, *and used for repelling the* [*evil*] *eye:* (TA:) n. un. with ة. (Ḳ.)

نُبَاحٌ: see نَبَّاحٌ.

نُبَّاحِىٌّ A dog *having a loud bark.* (Lḥ.)

كَلْبٌ نَابِحٌ *A barking dog:* pl. كِلَابٌ نَوَابِحُ, and نُبَّحٌ, and نُبُوحٌ. (L.)

نَبَّاحَةٌ: see نَبَّاحٌ.

رَجُلٌ مَنْبُوحٌ *A man likened to a dog.* (L.) — ‡ *A man reviled.* (L.)

نبخ

4. انبخ *He sowed in a land such as is called* نَبْخَاء. (Ḳ, TA.)

نَبْخٌ The *small-pox;* (Ṣ;) in an absolute sense: (TA:) or the *small-pox of sheep or goats &c.,* (Ḳ,) — Also, (Ṣ, Ḳ,) and ▾ نَبَخٌ, (Ḳ,) *Blisters,* or *pustules that fill with water, on the hand,* (Ṣ, Ḳ,) *occasioned by work:* (Ḳ:) when they break, or dry up, the hand becomes callous by work: [a coll. gen. n.:] n. un. with ة. (TA.) — Also ▾ نَبَخٌ *Marks of fire,* [*or blisters occasioned by burning,*] *upon the body.*

نَبَخٌ: see نَبْخٌ.

نَبْخَاءُ *A hill, or mound, such as is called* أَكَمَةٌ: (Ṣ:) or *elevated ground:* (TA:) or *elevated and loose ground, not consisting of sand, but of hard and stony earth:* (Th, Ḳ:) pl. نَبَاخِىُّ: (Ḳ:) it has a broken pl. of the class proper to substs. because it is an epithet in which the quality of a subst. predominates. (TA.)

نَابِخَةٌ *A proud, a haughty,* or *an imperious, man:* (Ṣ, Ḳ:) pl. نَوَابِخُ. (Ṣ.) — *A speaker.* (Ḳ.)

أَنْبَخُ *Rude, coarse, rough, gross;* (Ḳ;) an epithet applied to a man. (TA.) — تُرَابٌ أَنْبَخُ *Dust of a dusky colour, and abundant.* (L, Ḳ.) [See an ex. voce هَبَيَّخ, art. هبخ.]

نبذ

1. نَبَذَهُ, aor. ِ, inf. n. نَبْذٌ, (Ṣ, L, Mṣb, Ḳ,) *He cast, threw,* or *flung, it away, as a thing esteemed of no account* or *importance:* this is the original signification; and in this sense it is mostly used in the Ḳur-án: (Er-Rághib:) *he cast, threw,* or *flung, it* (Ṣ, A, L, Mṣb, Ḳ) *from his hand,* (Ṣ, L,) *before him* or *behind him:* (L, Ḳ:) and *he cast, threw,* or *flung, it far away,* or *to a distance:* (L:) and (so in the L; but in the Ḳ, or) *he cast, threw,* or *flung it in any manner:* (L, Ḳ:) ▾ نبّذ, has teshdeed given to it to denote frequency, or repetition, of the action, or its application to many objects. (Ṣ, A, L.) — نَبَذَ خَاتَمَهُ *He threw his signet from his hand.* (L, from a trad.) — فَنَبَذُوهُ وَرَآءَ ظُهُورِهِمْ (Ḳur, iii. 184) ‡ [lit., *And they cast it behind their backs;*] means *and they did not observe it;* (namely, their covenant;) *they disregarded it.* (Beyḍ.) — نَبْذٌ is both by act and by word; having for its objects both substances and accidents: (L:) you say نَبَذَ العَهْدَ ‡ *He dissolved the league,* or *covenant, and cast it from him to him with whom he had made it:* (A, L, Mṣb:*) and نَبَذَ كُلُّ فَرِيقٍ مِنْهُمَا إِلَى صَاحِبِهِ العَهْدَ الَّذِى تَهَادَنَا عَلَيْهِ ‡ [*Each party of them cast from him, to the other, the league,* or *covenant, by which they had made a truce;* i. e., *each party of them rejected it,* or *renounced it, to the other*]: (T:) and نَبَذَ إِلَى العَدُوِّ, and ▾ نابذه, ‡ *He cast from him the league,* or *covenant, to the enemy, and dissolved it:* and ▾ تَنَابَذُوا ‡ *They mutually cast from themselves the league,* or *covenant, and dissolved it.* (A.) See also 3. — نَبَذَ أَمْرِى وَرَآءَ ظَهْرِهِ ‡ [lit., *He cast my affair behind his back;* meaning,] *he did not perform my affair;* (A;) *he neglected it.* (Mṣb.) — نَبَذَتْ فُلَانَةُ قَوْلًا مَلِيحًا ‡ *Such a woman threw out a goodly, beautiful,* or *pretty, saying.* (A.) — نَبَذْتُ إِلَيْهِ السَّلَامَ, and التَّحِيَّةَ, ‡ *I threw to him the salutation.* (A.) — نُبِذْتُ بِكَذَا ‡ [*I had such a thing* as it were *thrown to me; I had it thrown in my way;*] *I had it offered,* or *presented, to me, the meeting with it being appointed,* or *prepared;* as also رُمِيتُ بِهِ. (A.) — لِلّٰهِ أُمٌّ نَبَذَتْ بِكَ ‡ *To God* (*be attributed the excellence of*) *the mother that brought thee forth!* (A.) — نَبَذَ *He threw forth* earth or dust [in digging a hole &c.]; as also نَبَثَ. (A.) See also نَبِيذَةٌ. — نَبَذَ *He threw* dates or raisins *into a bag or skin, and poured water upon them, and left the liquor until it fermented and became intoxicating:* (T:) [or, simply, *he steeped* dates or raisins *in water;* for the beverage thus made, called نَبِيذ, was not always left until it became intoxicating, as is shown by several trads.] — نَبَذَ نَبِيذًا, (Ṣ, L, Ḳ, &c.,) the most usual form of the verb, (Ḳz,) aor. ِ, only; (MF;) and ▾ نبّذه, (A, L, Ḳ,) and ▾ انبذه, (L, Ḳ,) a form used by the vulgar, (S, IDrst,) and rejected by Th and others, but mentioned, on the authority of Er-Ruásee, by Fr, who says that he had not heard it from the Arabs, but that the authority of its transmitter is worthy of reliance, (TA,) and ▾ انتبذه; (L, Ḳ;) ‡ *He made beverage of the kind called* نَبِيذ. (Ṣ, A, L, Ḳ.) — Also, نَبَذَ تَمْرًا, (Lḥ, IAth, L,) and عِنَبًا, (IAth, L,) and ▾ انبذه, but this is seldom used, (Ḳuṭr, Lḥ, ISk, and others, and L,) and ▾ انتبذه, (L,) ‡ *He made, of the dates, and of the grapes, beverage of the kind called* نَبِيذ; (Lḥ, L;) *he left the dates, and the grapes, in water, that it might become beverage of the kind so called.* (IAth, L.) — Also, ▾ انتبذ ‡ *He made for himself that beverage.* (A.) — فُلَانٌ يَنْبِذُ عَلَىَّ ‡ *Such a one boils against me like* [*the beverage called*] نَبِيذ. (A.) == نَبَذَ, [aor. ِ,] (Ṣ, L, Ḳ,) inf. n. نَبْذٌ (L, Ḳ) and نَبَذَانٌ, (Ṣ, Ḳ,) *It* (a vein) *pulsed;* (L, Ḳ;) a dial. form of نَبَضَ. (Ṣ, L.)

2: see 1.

3. نابذهُ, inf. n. مُنَابَذَةٌ, *He bargained with him by saying, Throw thou to me the garment,* or *piece of cloth,* (A'Obeyd, L, Ḳ,) or *other article of merchandise,* (A'Obeyd, L,) or *I will throw it to thee, and the sale shall become binding,* or *settled,* or *concluded, for such a sum:* (A'Obeyd, L, Ḳ:) or, *by throwing to another a garment,* or *piece of cloth, the other doing the like:* (Lḥ, L, Ḳ:) or, *by saying, When thou throwest thy commodity,* or *when I throw my commodity, the sale is binding,* or *settled,* or *concluded, for such a sum:* (Mṣb:) or, *by saying, When I throw it to thee,* or *when thou throwest it to me, the sale is binding,* or *settled,* or *concluded:* (Mgh, art. لمس:) or, *by saying, When I throw the pebble* (L, Ḳ) *to thee,* (L,) *the sale is binding,* or *settled,* or *concluded:* (L, Ḳ:) or *by another's throwing a pebble to him:* (L:) بَيْعُ المُنَابَذَةِ and بَيْعُ الحَصَاةِ and بَيْعُ إِلْقَاءِ الحَجَرِ signify the same; (Mgh;) as also بَيْعُ الإِلْقَاءِ: (A:) such bargaining is forbidden. (L.) — نابذوا, inf. n. مُنَابَذَةٌ; and ▾ انتبذوا; ‡ *They retired,* each of the two parties, *apart,* in war. (L, Ḳ.) — نَابَذَهُمُ الحَرْبَ, and نَبَذَ إِلَيْهِمُ الحَرْبَ, *He retired from them to a place aside,* or *apart, in war, for a just purpose,* (لِلْحَقِّ, in the 'Eyn *for war,* لِلْحَرْبِ, TT,) *they doing the like:* (Lth, T, L:) or these two phrases, followed by عَلَى سَوَآءٍ, are used when there is between two parties at variance a covenant, or league, or a truce, after fighting, and they desire to dissolve the league, or covenant, and each party casts it from him (يَنْبِذُهُ) to the other: thus, فَانْبِذْ إِلَيْهِمْ عَلَى سَوَآءٍ, in the Ḳur, [viii. 60, lit., *cast thou from thee, to them,* their league, or covenant, *in an equitable,* or *just, manner,*] means, announce thou to them that thou hast dissolved the league between thee and them, so that they may have equal knowledge with thee of the dissolving thereof and of the returning to war:

(T, L:) على سواء here signifies على الحَقِّ وَالعَدْلِ: (Lh:) نَابَذَهُ الحَرْبَ also signifies *he made war with him openly;* (Ṣ, L, Mṣb;) and is syn. with نَبَذَ إِلَيْهِ الحَرْبَ: (L:) and نَابَذُوهُمْ عَلَى سَوَآءٍ *they made war with them openly, in an equitable manner, declaring their hostile intention, so that it was equally known to their enemies and themselves.* (L.) See also 1. — نَابَذْتُهُمْ ‡ *I acted contrarily to, or differently from, or adversely to, them; or was, or became, contrary to, or different from, or adverse to, them;* syn. خَالَفْتُهُمْ. (Mṣb.)

4: see 1.

6: see 1.

8. انتبذ ‡ *He went, withdrew, or retired, aside, or apart, from others; separated himself from others.* (Ṣ, A, L, Ḳ.) — انتبذت مَكَانًا (Ḳur, xix. 16,) ‡ *She withdrew, or retired, to a place apart from her family,* (L, Mṣb,) *far away.* (Mṣb.) — إِنْتَبَذَ عَنْ قَوْمِهِ *He withdrew, or retired, from his people.* (M.) — إنتبذ نَاحِيَةً *He went aside.* (T.) See 1. — And see إِنْتَبَثَ in art. نبث.

نَبْذٌ ‡ *A little; a small quantity;* (Ṣ, A, L, Ḳ;) مِنَ المَالِ *of wealth, or property;* (Ṣ, A, L;) as also ↓ نُبْذَةٌ [which is a word much used though I find it explained in few lexicons]; (L, TA;) because what is little is thrown away, and disregarded: (A:) and in like manner, of herbage, and of rain, and of hoariness or hoary hair, (Ṣ, A, L,) &c.: (L:) and *a small number* of men: (A, L:) and the latter word, *a piece,* or *portion,* of a thing, such as a perfume: (L:) pl. of the former, أَنْبَاذٌ: (L, Ḳ:) [and of the latter, نُبَذٌ.] — أَنْبَاذٌ مِنَ النَّاسِ (Ḳ,* TA) ‡ *The refuse of the people;* (TA;) *mixed people of the baser sort.* (Ḳ, TA.)

— بَيْنَنَا وَبَيْنَ بَنِى فُلَانٍ نَبْذَةٌ: see جَذْبَةٌ. — جَلَسَ نَبْذَةً, and ↓ نُبْذَةً, ‡ *He sat aside, or apart.* (Ṣ, A, L, Mṣb, Ḳ.)

نُبْذَةٌ: see نَبْذٌ: — and نَبْذَةٌ.

نَبِيذٌ *Cast, thrown, or flung,* [&c.; see 1;] (Ḳ;) *i. q.* ↓ نَبِيذَةٌ.مَنْبُوذٌ (L.) But see below. — *The earth or dust that is thrown forth from a hole or the like that is dug;* as also نَبِيثَةٌ: pl. نَبَائِذُ. (A,* L.) Yaḳoob asserts, that the ذ is a substitute for ث. (L.) — نَبِيذٌ ‡ *A kind of beverage, made of dates, and of raisins;* i. e., *must; and of honey;* i. e., *mead; and of wheat, and of barley, &c.;* i. e. *wort:* (L:) or *made of dates, or of raisins, which one throws* (يَنْبِذُ, i. e. يَطْرَحُ, whence its appellation,) *into a vessel or skin of water, and leaves until it ferments* (يَفُورُ, T, L, or يَغْلِى, Mgh) *and becomes intoxicating, or not so long as to become intoxicating:* before it has become so, it is a lawful beverage: (T, L:) whether intoxicating or not, it is thus called: (L:) or it is thus called because it is left (يُنْبَذُ, i. e., يُتْرَكُ,) until it becomes strong; (Mṣb;) being *expressed juice, or the like, that is left* (نُبِذَ) [*for a time to acquire strength*]: (L, Ḳ:) it is said that this word is originally of the measure فَعِيلٌ in the sense of the measure مَفْعُولٌ, but that it has become obsolete in this latter sense, and, applied to the beverage, is used as though it were a primitive substantive, as is shown by the form of its pl., (M, F,) which is أَنْبِذَةٌ; (Ṣ, L, MF;) for a word of the measure فعيل in the sense of the measure مفعول has not this form of pl.: (MF:) *wine expressed from grapes* is also called نَبِيذٌ, like as نبيذ is also called خَمْرٌ: [نَبِيذٌ is a coll. gen. n., and its n. un. is with ة:] نَبِيذَةٌ signifies *some* نَبِيذ; lit., *a portion thereof.* (Mṣb, art. خمر.) See also مِزْرٌ. (L.)

نَبِيذَةٌ: see نَبِيذٌ, and مَنْبُوذٌ.

نَبَّاذٌ [One *who throws things away often,* or *quickly*]. See أَخَّاذٌ. — نَبَّاذٌ [One *who makes, or sells, the beverage called* نَبِيذ]. (Ṣ, Ḳ, art. سكر.)

مِنْبَذَةٌ *A pillow, or cushion;* (Lh, Ṣ, A, L, Ḳ;) *upon which one reclines, or sits:* so called because it is thrown upon the ground to be sat upon: (L:) pl. مَنَابِذُ. (A.) Ex. تَرَبَّعُوا عَلَى المَنَابِذِ [*They sat cross-legged upon the pillows, or cushions*]. (A.)

مَنْبُوذٌ *A child cast out by its mother* (T, Ṣ, L, Mṣb, Ḳ) *in the road,* (T, Ṣ, L, Ḳ,) *on the occasion of her bringing it forth, and which a Muslim picks up and maintains; whether a bastard or lawfully begotten;* (T, L;) *a foundling:* (L, Ḳ:) such may not be called a bastard because its kin may be established: (T, L:) also, † *a bastard;* (L, Ḳ;) because such is cast away in the road: (L:) fem. مَنْبُوذَةٌ (L) and ↓ نَبِيذَةٌ: (A, L:) pl. masc. مَنْبُوذُونَ and مَنَابِذَةٌ; (L;) and pl. of مَنْبُوذَةٌ, and نبيذة, نَبَائِذُ. (A.) — ↓ نَبِيذَةٌ † *A ewe or other animal* (L) *that is not eaten, by reason of its leanness:* (L, Ḳ:) so called because it is cast away. (L.) — صَلَّى عَلَى قَبْرٍ مَنْبُوذٍ *He* (Moḥammad) *prayed upon the tomb of a foundling:* or, accord. to another reading, على قَبْرٍ مَنْبُوذٍ, meaning, *upon a tomb apart,* (L,) or *distant,* (Ḳ,) *from other tombs;* (L, Ḳ;) like an expression occurring in another trad., مَرَّ بِقَبْرٍ مُنْتَبِذٍ ↓ *he passed by a tomb apart from other tombs.* (L.)

هُوَ مُنْتَبِذُ الدَّارِ ‡ *He is far from his house.* (A.) — مُنْتَبِذٌ and ↓ مُتَنَبِّذٌ [A man &c.,] *aside, or apart, or separate, from others;* (L;) [See also مَنْبُوذٌ: and see a verse of Lebeed, voce أَصْلٌ.]

مُتَنَبِّذٌ: see مُنْتَبِذٌ.

نبر

1. نَبَرَ, (T, Ṣ, A, Ḳ,) aor. ِ, (Ṣ, Ḳ,) inf. n. نَبْرٌ, (Ṣ,) *He,* (a man, Ṣ, A,) or *it,* (anything, T,) *raised,* or *elevated,* a thing: (T, Ṣ, A, Ḳ:) or نَبْرٌ signifies specially the *raising of the voice:* (MF, from the first part of the Keshsháf:) or the *rising of the voice;* so with the Arabs; and one says نَبَرَ الرَّجُلُ, inf. n. نَبْرَةٌ, meaning, *the man spoke in a high tone:* (IAmb:) and نَبَرَ, inf. n. نَبْرَةٌ, *he* (a man) *uttered a sound:* (A:) and [the inf. n.] نَبْرَةٌ, signifies the *crying out,* or *shouting, from fright, or fear:* (T, Ḳ:) and نَبْرَةُ المُغَنِّى, *the singer's raising his voice from a low to a high pitch.* (Ṣ, Ḳ.) — نَبَرَ الحَرْفَ, (Ṣ, M, A, Ḳ,) aor. ِ, (M, Ḳ,) inf. n. نَبْرٌ, (Ṣ, M,) *He pronounced the letter with hemz* (هَمَزَ). (Ṣ, M, A, Ḳ.) قُرَيْشٌ لَا تَنْبِرُ [*The tribe of Ḳureysh*] *do not pronounce with hemz.* (Ṣ.) A man said to the Prophet, يَا نَبِىْءَ اللّٰهِ [*O Prophet of God*]; and he said لَا تَنْبِرْ بِاسْمِى, i. e. *Pronounce not thou my name with hemz:* (M:) for the tribe of Ḳureysh did not pronounce with hemz. (TA.) And when El-Mahdee performed the pilgrimage, he preferred El-Kisáee to recite the prayers in El-Medeeneh, and the people of that city disapproved of his pronouncing with hemz, asking him wherefore he did so in reciting the Ḳur-án in the mosque of the Apostle of God. (TA.)

8. انتبر *It* (a heap of wheat) *rose,* by additions. (T.) — *It* (the body, M, Ḳ, and a wound, T, A) *swelled; became swollen.* (T, M, A, Ḳ.) — *It* (the mouth, TA,) *became blistered,* or *vesicated.* (Ḳ, TA.) And انتبرت يَدُهُ *His arm, or hand, became blistered.* (Ṣ, A.) — *He* (the أَمِير, M, and the خَطِيب, Ḳ) *ascended the* مِنْبَر [*or pulpit*]. (M, Ḳ.)

نِبْرٌ sing. of أَنْبَارٌ, (T, Ṣ,) which signifies *Heaps,* syn. أَكْدَاسٌ, (M, Ḳ,) or *a collection,* (M, Ṣ,) of طَعَام, (Ṣ, M, Ḳ, MṢ,) meaning of wheat, and of barley, [or other corn,] and of dates: (MṢ:) or [in the TA, and] *granaries* (أَهْرَآء) of طعام: (in the present day, *a granary:*] what is called هُرْىٌ being also called نِبْرٌ because the طعام, when poured in its place, rises: and the pl. pl. [i. e. pl. of انبار] is أَنَابِيرُ. (T.) — أَنْبَارٌ also signifies *A merchant's magazine, or chamber,* (بَيْتٌ,) *in which he puts together, in order, or piles up, his goods.* (M, Ḳ.) [In the Ḳ, it is added, that the sing. is نِبْرٌ: but this addition seems to be misplaced: for انبار in the last of the senses here explained, as well as when applied to a granary, and to a collection of طعام, appears to be a pl. without a sing.]

نَبْرَةٌ *Anything rising from a thing.* (M, A, Ḳ.) — *A swelling in the body.* (M, Ḳ.) — *I. q.* هَمْزَةٌ [meaning the *sound,* or the *character,* so called]. (T, Ṣ, Ḳ.)

مِنْبَرٌ The *pulpit of the* خَاطِب [*in a mosque*]: (M, TA:) so called because of its height: (Ṣ, M, A, Ḳ:) [pl. مَنَابِرُ.]

مُنَبَّرٌ: see مَنْبُورٌ.

الْمَسْأَلَةُ الْمِنْبَرِيَّةُ: see the first paragraph of art. عول.

مَنْبُورٌ *Pronounced with hemz* (هَمْز). (T.) قَصَائِدُ مَنْبُورَةٌ, and ↓ مُنَبَّرَةٌ, *i. q.* مَهْمُوزَةٌ [i. e. *Poems of which the verses end with hemz*].

نبز

1. نَبَزَهُ, aor. ـِ , inf. n. نَبْزٌ, *He called him, or named him, by a by-name, surname, or nickname; he by-named him, surnamed him, or nicknamed him;* syn. لَقَّبَهُ; (Ṣ, Mṣb, Ḳ;) mostly signifying *he called him, or named him, by a nickname, a name of reproach, or an opprobrious appellation;* (TA;) as also ↓ نَبَّزَهُ: (Ḳ:) or the latter is with teshdeed to denote muchness, or frequency, or repetition, of the action, or its application to many objects: you say, فُلَانٌ يُنَبِّزُ ↓ بِالصِّبْيَانِ *Such a one by-names, surnames, or* [rather] *nicknames, the children;* syn. يُلَقِّبُهُمْ. (Ṣ.) — النَّبْزُ is also *syn. with* اللَّمْزُ; (Ḳ;) or is *like the latter:* (TA;) [i.e., نَبَزَهُ also signifies *He upbraided, or reproached, him; or the like.*]

2: see 1, in two places.

6. تَنَابَزُوا, (Mṣb, Ḳ,*) or تَنَابَزُوا بِالْأَلْقَابِ, (Ṣ,) *They called one another by by-names, surnames, or* [rather] *nicknames:* (Ṣ, Mṣb,* Ḳ:) *or they upbraided, reproached, or reviled, one another;* (Ḳ, TA;) *calling one another by names of reproach.* (TA.) So in the Ḳur, xlix. 11; where the doing so is forbidden. (TA.)

نَبَزٌ, [or, accord. to the Mṣb, it seems to be نَبْزٌ, for it is there said to be an inf. n. used as a subst., but this form I have never met with elsewhere,] *A by-name; or surname; or nickname;* syn. لَقَبٌ; (Ṣ, Mṣb, Ḳ;) mostly, *the latter;* i. e., *a name of reproach; an opprobrious appellation:* (TA:) but Kh, [makes it, contr. to common usage, to signify *a proper name;* for he] says, that names are of two kinds; أَسْمَآءُ نَبَزٍ, such as زَيْدٌ and عَمْرٌو; and أَسْمَآءُ عَامٍّ, such as فَرَسٌ and رَجُلٌ and the like: (TA:) pl. أَنْبَازٌ. (Ṣ.)

نِبْزٌ *Ignoble, or mean,* (Ṣgh, Ḳ,) *in his grounds of pretension to respect, or his rank or quality, and in his natural disposition.* (Ḳ.)

رَجُلٌ نُبَزَةٌ *A man who is much accustomed to call others by by-names, surnames, or* [rather] *nicknames.* (Ḳ.)

نبش

1. نَبَشَ, aor. ـُ , (Ṣ, Mgh, Mṣb,) inf. n. نَبْشٌ, (Ṣ, A, Mgh, Mṣb, Ḳ) *He took, drew, or pulled, out, or forth,* (Mgh, Mṣb, Ḳ,) a thing, (Mṣb, TA,) [as] a leguminous plant, (Ṣ,) or a thing buried, (Mgh,) or a thing *after burial,* (TA,) [as] a corpse; (Ṣ, TA;) whence نَبَّاشٌ, q. v.: (Ṣ, Mgh:) *he made* a thing that was concealed or covered *to come out or forth, or to become apparent.* (A, Ḳ.) — [Hence,] هُوَ يَنْبُشُ لِعِيَالِهِ, (A, TA,) inf. n. as above, (Ḳ, TA,) ‡ *He draws forth sustenance hence and thence for his family, or household:* (A:) or ‡ *he gains, or earns, or seeks sustenance, for them.* (Ḳ,* TA.) — And هُوَ يَنْبُشُ الْأَسْرَارَ, (A, TA,) and الْحَدِيثَ, inf. n. as above, (Ḳ, TA,) ‡ *He draws forth, or elicits, secrets,* and *discourse, narration, or information:* (Ḳ,* TA:) or نَبَشْتُ السِّرَّ signifies † *I divulged the secret.* (Mṣb.) — And ↓ إِنْتَبَشَ الْعُرُوقَ ‡ *He drew forth, or extracted, the veins.* (A.) — Also, *He removed,* a thing from over another thing which it covered or concealed; (A, Mṣb,* Ḳ;) and earth from a thing beneath it: (A, Mṣb:*) whence نَبَّاشٌ, q. v. (Mṣb, Ḳ.) — And hence, نَبَشَ الْقَبْرَ [*He uncovered, or he rifled, or ransacked, the grave*]. (A, Mgh, Mṣb.) = Also, *He dug with the hand;* as also نَبَثَ. (AZ, in Ṣ, art. نبث.)

5. هُوَ يَتَنَبَّشُ عَنِ الْأَسْرَارِ [app. † *He endeavours to draw forth or elicit, or he searches out, secrets*]. (TA.)

8: see 1.

نِبَاشَةٌ The *trade, or occupation, of the* نَبَّاش. (TA.)

[نَبِيشَةٌ *Earth extracted* from a well or burrow or the like. Hence,] نَبِيشَةُ الْيَرْبُوعِ [*The earth extracted by the jerboa* in making its burrow]. (T in art. دمر.)

نَبَّاشٌ *One who rifles, or ransacks, graves; who takes forth the dead from them; or who uncovers graves.* (Mgh, Mṣb.) See 1, in two places.

أُنْبُوشٌ *A thing that is taken, drawn, or pulled, out, or forth:* (Lḥ:) *the lower part of leguminous plants taken, drawn, or pulled, out, or forth:* (Ṣ, Ḳ:) *or trees pulled out by the trunk and roots:* (Ḳ:) as also ↓ أُنْبُوشَةٌ: (TA:) or ↓ both signify *what is torn out by the rain:* (AHeyth:) pl. أَنَابِيشُ, (Ṣ, Ḳ,) the pl. of both the above words. (AHeyth.) — Also, *Full-grown unripe dates that are pierced with thorns in order that they may ripen.* (TA.) — And the pl. signifies *Small arrows.* (Ṣgh.) Some say that this pl. has no singular. (MF.)

أُنْبُوشَةٌ: see أُنْبُوشٌ, in two places.

نبض

1. نَبَضَ, aor. ـِ , inf. n. نَبْضٌ and نَبَضَانٌ (Ṣ, A, Ḳ) and نَبِيضٌ, (so in a copy of the Ṣ,) *It* (a vein, or an artery,) *pulsed, or beat,* (TA,) [or *throbbed;*] *was, or became, in a state of motion, or agitation.* (Ṣ, A, Ḳ.) — [Hence,] مَا نَبَضَ لَهُ عِرْقُ عَصَبِيَّةٍ ‡ [*No party-spirit, or zeal in the cause of his party, became roused, or excited, in him;*] *he did not aid his people, or party, against oppression; was not angry, or zealous, for them, and did not defend them.* (A, TA.) — And نَبَضَ ↓ نَابِضُهُ ‡ *His anger became roused, or excited.* (A, TA.) — [Hence also,] نَبَضَتِ الْأَمْعَآءُ, aor. as above, (in the L, written ـُ, but this is doubtless a mistake,] † *The bowels became in a state of commotion.* (TA.) — And نَبَضَ الْبَرْقُ † *The lightning flashed lightly, or slightly,* (Ḳ, TA,) *like the* نَبْض *of a vein or an artery.* (TA.) = See also 4.

2: see 4, in two places.

4. أَنْبَضَتِ الْحُمَّى عِرْقَهُ *The fever made his vein, or artery, to pulse, beat,* (TA,) [*throb,*] or *become in a state of motion or agitation.* (A, TA.*) — انبض القَوْسَ, (T, Ṣ, M, A, Mgh,) like أَنْضَبَهَا, (Lth, T, M,) but the former is the more approved; (Lth, 'Eyn;) and انبض عَنْهَا; (A, Mgh;) or انبض فِيهَا; (AḤn, Ḳ;) and نَبَّضَ ↓ فِيهَا, inf. n. تَنْبِيضٌ; (AḤn, TA;) in the Ḳ, نَبَضَ ↓ فِيهَا, which is a mistake; (TA;) [*He twanged the bow;*] *he made the bow to give a sound:* (AḤn, Ḳ:) or *he put the string of the bow in motion,* [*or made it to vibrate,*] (A, Ḳ,) or *pulled it,* (T, Ṣ, M, Mgh,) *and then let it go,* (Ṣ, Mgh,) *in order that it might twang,* (Ṣ, Ḳ,) or *produce a sound:* (T, M, Mgh:) and انبض بِالْوَتَرِ (Ṣ, A, Mgh) signifies the same: (Ṣ, Mgh:) or *he took the string of the bow with the ends of his two fingers, and then let it go so that it might fall against the handle of the bow:* (Jm:) and انبض الْوَتَرَ *he pulled the string of the bow without an arrow, and then let it go:* (Yaạḳoob:) or *he pulled the string of the bow, and then let it go so that he heard it give a sound.* (Lḥ.) Hence the proverb, إِنْبَاضٌ بِغَيْرِ تَوْتِيرٍ, (Ṣ,) or مِنْ غَيْرِ تَوْتِيرٍ, (A,) [*Twanging* the bow *without fastening, or binding, or bracing, the string;* meaning ‡ *threatening without the means of execution*]: applied to him who pretends to that which he has not the means of performing. (A, TA.) [See also art. وتر.] And a poet says,

لَأَرْمِيَنَّكَ رَمْيًا غَيْرَ تَنْبِيضِ ↓

[*I will assuredly shoot thee with a shooting, not a mere twanging*]: meaning, my pulling [of the bow] shall not be a threatening, but execution. (TA.) — You say also, أَنْبَضَ النَّدَّافُ مِنْبَضَتَهُ [*The separater and loosener of cotton by means of the bow and mallet made his mallet to cause the string of the bow to vibrate*]. (A, TA.)

نَبْضٌ [an inf. n. used as a subst., signifying The *pulse*]. — Also, *A pulsing vein, or artery:*

as in the saying جَسَّ الطَّبِيبُ نَبْضَهُ [*The physician felt his pulsing vein, or artery: or his pulse*]: but it is more chaste to say ▼ مَنْبِضَهُ q.v. (TA.) — See also نَبْضٌ. — [It is also used as an epithet. You say,] فُؤَادٌ نَبْضٌ, as also ▼ نَبِضٌ, and ▼ نَبُضٌ, (Ṣgh, Ḳ,) and ▼ نَبِيضٌ, (A, TA,) ‡ *A heart that is sharp in intellect, clever, acute,* (A, Ṣgh, Ḳ,) *and very brisk* or *lively* or *sprightly* or *prompt.* (A, TA.)

حَبَضٌ مَا بِهِ حَبَضٌ وَلَا نَبَضٌ, (IDrd, Ṣ, Ḳ,) and ▼ ولا نَبْضٌ, (Ṣgh,) *There is not in him any motion:* (Ṣ, Ṣgh, Ḳ:) or *sound,* or *voice, nor pulsation:* (AA, in Ṣ, art. حبض:) or *strength:* (IDrd:) with fet-ḥ to the second letter, only used in a negative phrase: (L:) Aṣ says, I know not what is الحَبَضُ, (Ṣ in art. حبض,) or النَّبَضُ. (TA.) — فُؤَادٌ نَبَضٌ: see نَبْضٌ.

نَبِضٌ: see نَبْضٌ.

نَبْضَةٌ [*A single pulsation*]. You say, رَأَيْتُ وَمْضَةَ بَرْقٍ كَنَبْضَةِ عِرْقٍ [*I saw a slight flash of lightning, like a single pulsation of an artery*]. (A, TA.)

نَبِيضٌ: see نَبْضٌ.

نَابِضٌ [part. n. of 1]. You say, مَا دَامَ فِىَّ عُرَيْقٌ نَابِضٌ لَمْ أَخْذُلْكَ [*As long as there remains in me a little artery pulsing, I will not abstain,* or *hold back, from aiding thee*]; i.e., ‡ *as long as I remain alive.* (A, TA.) — [Hence,] ‡ *Anger.* (Lth, A, Ḳ.) See 1, where an ex. is given. — † *An archer:* lit. *one who has a twanging.* (Mgh.)

مَنْبِضُ القَلْبِ *The place where one sees the heart pulsing,* (TA,) or *in motion;* (A, Ḳ;) *and where one perceives the gentle sound of its* [*pulsation,* or] *motion.* (A, O.) You say, جَسَّ الطَّبِيبُ مَنْبِضَهُ [*The physician felt his place of pulsation*], and مَنَابِضَهُمْ [*their places of pulsation*]. (A, TA.) مَا يَعْرِفُ لَهُ مَنْبِضَ عَسَلَةٍ means ‡ *He has no origin* [*known*]; like مَضْرِبَ عَسَلَةٍ; (A, TA;) *nor any people* [*to whom he belongs*]. (TA.)

وَجَعٌ مُنْبِضٌ [*A pain causing pulsation,* or *throbbing*]. (L, TA.)

مِنْبَضٌ, (Ṣ, Ḳ,) or ▼ مِنْبَضَةٌ, (A,) The *wooden mallet with which one separates and loosens cotton by striking with it the string of a bow;* syn. مِنْدَفٌ, like مِحْبَضٌ; (Ṣ;) or مِنْدَفَةٌ: (A, Ḳ:) مَنَابِضُ is said by Kh to occur in poetry as [its pl.,] meaning مَنَادِفُ. (Ṣ.)

مِنْبَضَةٌ: see what next precedes.

نبط

1. نَبَطَ, aor. ـُ and ـِ, inf. n. نُبُوطٌ (Ṣ, Ḳ) and نَبْطٌ, (Ḳ,) *It* (water) *welled,* or *issued forth.* (Ṣ, Ḳ.) ═ See also 4.

2: see 4.

3: see 10.

4. انبط *He* (a digger) *reached the water:* (AA, Ṣ:) or *reached the first that appeared of the water of a well,* (Ḳ, TA,) and *produced it,* or *fetched it out, by his labour.* (TA.) And انبط فِى غَضْرَآءَ *He produced,* or *fetched out, by labour, water from good clay,* or *from clay containing no sand.* (TA.) ═ [It is also trans.: you say,] انبط الرَّكِيَّةَ; and ▼ استنبطها; (M, Ḳ;) and ▼ نَبَّطَهَا; (IAạr, M, TA;) in the Ḳ ▼ تَنَبَّطَهَا; (TA;) and ▼ نَبَطَهَا, (M, Ḳ [in the CḲ with teshdeed to the ب]) aor. ـُ, (TA,) inf. n. نَبْطٌ; (M;) *He produced,* or *fetched out, by his labour* [*in digging*], *the water of the well;* syn. أَمَاهَهَا; (M, Ḳ;) and of the first, (TA,) and last, (TA,) [or rather of all,] استخرج مَآءَهَا. (Ḳ, TA.) And انبط المَآءَ, inf. n. إِنْبَاطٌ; and ▼ استنبطهُ; *He* (a digger [of a well]) *produced,* or *fetched out, by his labour,* or *work, the water.* (Mṣb.) — See also 10, in five places. ═ إِنْبَاطٌ also signifies The *producing an effect,* or *making an impression;* syn. تَأْثِيرٌ. (Ibn-'Abbád, Ṣgh, Ḳ.)

5: see 4: — and 10. ═ تنبّط also signifies *He affected to be like,* or *imitated, the* نَبَط [or *Nabathæans*]: or *he asserted himself to be related to them.* (Ḳ, TA.) [Compare 10, in the last of the senses assigned to it below.]

8: see 10.

10. استنبط: see 4, in two places: its primary signification is [that mentioned above,] from نَبَطٌ signifying the "water that comes forth from a well when it is first dug." (Zj.) — And hence, (Zj,) *He drew out,* or *forth; extracted; educed; produced; elicited; fetched out by labour* or *art; got out;* or *extorted;* syn. اِسْتَخْرَجَ; (Zj, Ṣ;) a thing: (Zj:) and † *He made* anything *to appear after occultation;* as also ▼ انبط; (B;) [i.e. *he brought it to light:*] and اُسْتُنْبِطَ † *it* (anything) *was made apparent, after occultation;* as also ▼ أُنْبِطَ: (Ḳ:) or the latter, [simply,] † *it was made apparent.* (L.) And [hence] ‡ *He* (a lawyer) *elicited* (استخرج) *an occult,* or *esoteric, doctrine of law, by his intelligence, and his labour,* or *study:* (Ḳ, TA:) or you say استنبطهُ, meaning † *he elicited it* (استخرجهُ), namely a judicial sentence, *by labour,* or *study;* as also ▼ انبطهُ, inf. n. إِنْبَاطٌ: (Mṣb:) or † *he searched out the knowledge of it.* (Jel. iv. 85.) And استنبط مِنْهُ عِلْمًا, and خَبَرًا, and مَالًا, ‡ *He drew forth, elicited,* or *extorted,* (استخرج,) *from him knowledge,* and *good,* or *wealth,* and *property.* (TA.) And ▼ نِبَاطٌ [app. an inf. n. of نَابَطَ] signifies the same as إِسْتِنْبَاطُ حَدِيثٍ † The *drawing forth,* or *eliciting,* (إِسْتِخْرَاجُ) *of discourse.* (TA.) And ▼ تنبّط الكَلَامَ, accord. to the Ḳ, or, accord. to Ṣgh, on the authority of Ibn-'Abbád, ▼ انتبطهُ, (TA,) † *He drew forth,* or *elicited,* (استخرج,) *speech.* (Ibn-'Abbád, Ṣgh, Ḳ.) And ▼ انبط العِلْمَ ‡ *He revealed knowledge, and spread it among men.* (TA.) — استنبط الفَرَسَ † *He sought to obtain offspring from the mare:* occurring in a trad.: but accord. to one relation, it is إِسْتَبْطَنَهَا, meaning, "he sought what was in her belly." (TA.) ═ *He* (a man) *became a* [*naturalized*] نَبَطِىّ [or *Nabathæan*]. (Ṣ,* TA.) It is said by Eiyoob Ibn-El-Ḳirreeyeh, أَهْلُ عُمَانَ عَرَبٌ ٱسْتَنْبَطُوا وَأَهْلُ البَحْرَيْنِ نَبِيطٌ ٱسْتَعْرَبُوا [*The people of 'Omán are Arabs who became naturalized Nabathæans, and the people of El-Baḥreyn are Nabathæans who became naturalized Arabs*]. (Ṣ, TA.) [See also 5.]

نَبَطٌ *What first appears of the water of a well* (IDrd, Ḳ) *when it is dug;* (IDrd;) as also ▼ نُبْطَةٌ: (Ḳ:) or *the water that comes forth from a well when it is first dug:* (Zj:) or the *water that issues forth from the bottom of a well when it is dug;* (Ṣ, accord. to one copy;) or this is termed ▼ نَبِيطٌ: (Ṣ, accord. to another copy; and TA:) pl. [of pauc.] أَنْبَاطٌ and [of mult.] نُبُوطٌ. (TA.) — [Hence the saying,] فُلَانٌ قَرِيبُ الثَّرَى بَعِيدُ النَّبَطِ † *Such a one's promising is near,* [but] *his fulfilling is remote:* i.e. *he promises, but does not fulfil.* (IAạr.) And فُلَانٌ لَا يُدْرَكُ نَبَطُهُ, (TA,) and لَا يُدْرَكُ لَهُ نَبَطٌ, (ISd, TA,) ‡ *Such a one's depth is not known,* (Ḳ,* TA,) and *the extent of his knowledge:* (TA:) or *such a one's depth is not known;* meaning that he is cunning, or possessing intelligence mixed with craft and forecast. (ISd, TA.) And فُلَانٌ لَا يُنَالُ نَبَطُهُ † *Such a one is invincible, and inaccessible to his enemy.* (TA.) — نَبَطٌ also signifies *A well of which the water has been produced,* or *fetched out, by labour* [*of the digger*]. (Ṣ, TA.) — And *What oozes,* or *exudes, from a mountain, as though it were sweat, coming forth from the sides of the rock.* (TA.) ═ النَّبَطُ, (Ṣ, Mgh, Mṣb, Ḳ,) and ▼ النَّبِيطُ, (Ṣ, Mṣb, Ḳ,) and الأَنْبَاطُ, (Ḳ,) the last is a pl. (AAF, Ṣ, Mṣb) of the first, (AAF,) and the second is [a quasi-pl. n.] like كَلِيبٌ, (AAF, L,) [*The Nabathæans;*] *a people who alight and abide in the* بَطَائِح [see أَبْطَحُ] *between the two 'Iráḳs:* (Ṣ, Ḳ:) or *a people* (T, M, Mgh, Mṣb) *who alight and abide,* (T, TA,) or *who used to alight and abide,* (Mṣb,) *in the* سَوَاد (T, M, Mgh, Mṣb) *of El-'Iráḳ:* (M, Mgh, Mṣb:) afterwards applied to *mixed people;* or *people of the lowest* or *basest* or *meanest sort;* or *the refuse of men;* and *the vulgar sort thereof:* (Mṣb:) the people to whom these appellations properly apply were called نَبَط because of their fetching out by labour (لِٱسْتِنْبَاطِهِمْ) what comes forth from the lands: (TA:) [for they were distinguished for agriculture; and hence their proper appellations are used as equivalent to "clowns," or "boors:" but a derivation commonly obtaining with us is that from Nebaioth the son of Ishmael:] the n. un. is ▾نَبَاطِىٌّ, (Yaạḳoob, IAạr, Ṣ, Mgh, Mṣb, Ḳ,) and ▾نَبَاطِىٌّ, (IAạr, Ṣ, Mṣb, Ḳ,) like يَمَانِىٌّ, (Ṣ,) and ▾نِبَاطِىٌّ, (Ḳ,) and ▾نَبَاطٍ, (Ṣ, Ḳ,) like يَمَانٍ, (Ṣ,) and ▾نَبَطِىٌّ, (Ṣ, Ḳ,) like يَمَنِىٌّ, (Ṣ,) but this is disallowed by IAạr, (Mgh, TA,) and, accord. to Lth, ▾نَبَطَانِىٌّ, but this [also] is disallowed by IAạr. (Mṣb.)

نُبْطَةٌ:
نَبَطِىٌّ:
نَبَطَانِىٌّ:
نَبَاطٍ:
نَبِيطٌ: and ٱلنَّبِيطُ:
نَبَاطِىٌّ and نُبَاطِىٌّ and نِبَاطِىٌّ:
} see نَبَطٌ.

[نبع, &c.

See Supplement.]

نبهرج

نَبَهْرَجٌ *i. q.* بَهْرَجٌ, q. v. (TA). [The place in which it is mentioned in the Ḳ shows that F regards the ن as a radical letter; and though it is said in the TA that its being so is doubtful, he is right accord. to those who hold that every letter of an arabicized word is to be regarded as a radical if it, or a letter for which it is substituted, is found in the original.]

[نبو,

See Supplement.]

نت

1. نَتَّ, [aor. ـِ,] inf. n. نَتِيتٌ, *i. q.* كَتَّ, inf. n. كَتِيتٌ; (Ḳ;) and نَفَتَ, inf. n. نَفِيتٌ: (L, Ḳ:) [*It* (a cooking-pot) *boiled:* &c.] — نَتَّ مَنْخِرُهُ غَضَبًا *His nostril became inflated,* or *swollen, by reason of anger.* (Ḳ.)

2. نَتَّتَ *He explained* news, tidings, or a report. (Ḳ.)

5. See R. Q. 1.

R. Q. 1. تَنَتْنَتَ (in a MS. copy of the Ḳ ▾تَنَتَّتَ, [and so in the CḲ,] but the former is the more correct, TA) *He* (a man, L) *became dirty* (تقذّر) *after having been clean.* (IAạr, L, Ḳ.)

نُتَّةٌ *A small hollow,* or *cavity, in* [*stones of the kind called*] صَفْوَانٌ, (Ḳ,) in which the rain-water collects. (TA.)

نتأ

1. نَتَأَ, aor. ـَ, inf. n. نَتْءٌ and نُتُوْءٌ, (Ṣ, Ḳ,) *It swelled; swelled up; rose; grew up.* (Ḳ.) Said of a plant, &c. (Ṣ.) — نَتَأَ, (Ṣ, Ḳ,) inf. n. نُتُوْءٌ, (TA,) *It protruded,* or *projected, from its place, without becoming separated.* (Ṣ, Ḳ.) — نَتَأَ *It* (an ulcer, or a wound,) *swelled.* (Ṣ, Ḳ.) — *It* (a girl's breast) *swelled forth,* or *became prominent,* or *protuberant.* (TA.) — نَتَأَتْ *She* (a girl) *grew up,* (Ṣ,) *and became marriageable.* (Ṣ, Ḳ.) — نَتَأَ عَلَيْهِمْ, inf. n. نَتْءٌ, *He rose,* or *exalted himself, above them.* (TA.) — [You say,] تَحْقِرُهُ وَيَنْتَأُ *Thou despisest him, and he riseth,* or *exalteth himself:* (Ṣ:) or — *he emulateth thee:* or — *he becometh great.* A proverb, said of him who does not manifest his character or design by outward appearance, but keeps it secret: or of him who advances and exalts himself by his cunning, while thou thinkest him senseless, or negligent. Accord. to some, it is تحقره وينتو, without ء: see art. نتو. (TA.) = نَتَأَ *He went up* from one country or land to another. (TA.) = نَتَأَ عَلَيْهِمْ *He came upon them;* syn. إِطَّلَعَ. (Ṣ, Ḳ.)

8. انتتأ *He rose,* or *exalted himself.* (Ḳ.) — انتتأ لَهُ *He encountered him; met him; opposed himself to him.* (Ḳ, TA: the verb is explained in the Ḳ by إِنْبَرَى.)

نتب

1. نَتَبَ, aor. ـُ, inf. n. نُتُوبٌ, *It swelled forth; became prominent,* or *protuberant.* (Ṣ, Ḳ.) Said of a girl's breast. (Ṣ.)

نتج

1. نَتَجَ, (Ṣ, Ḳ, &c.,) aor. ـِ, (as in the L, [but I believe this to be a mistake,]) or ـَ, (accord. to the Mṣb, MṢ, MF,) inf. n. نَتْجٌ; (Ṣ;) and ▾انتج; (A;) *He assisted* a she-camel, (Ṣ, K, &c.,) [and a mare, see نُتِجَتْ,] and a ewe or she-goat (Mṣb) [or other quadruped], *in bringing forth; delivered her of her young one; acting to her as a midwife does to a woman.* (T, Mṣb, &c.) The original form of expression is نَتَجَهَا وَلَدًا *He assisted her in bringing forth a young one; delivered her of a young one.* (Mṣb.) El-Kumeyt has used the form ▾اِنْتَتَجَ in the sense of نَتَجَ: but it is not commonly current in Arabic. (TA.) AḤn mentions the saying إِذَا نَآءَتِ ٱلْجَبْهَةُ نَتَّجَ ▾ٱلنَّاسُ وَوَلَّدُوا وَٱجْتُنِىَ أَوَّلُ ٱلْكَمْأَةِ [*When El-Jebhah* (the tenth of the Mansions of the Moon) *sets anti-heliacally,* (for the setting, not the rising, is here meant, and this it did, about the commencement of the era of the Flight, in central Arabia, on the 11th of February,) *the people assist their beasts, much,* or *frequently, in bringing forth, and deliver them, and the first of the truffles are gathered*]. Thus he relates the saying, with teshdeed to the ت of نتج, to denote frequency of the act. (L.) — نُتِجَتْ, pass. in form, [but neut. in signification,] inf. n. نِتَاجٌ (Ṣ, Ḳ, &c.) and نَتْجٌ; (TA;) and ▾أُنْتِجَتْ, (Ḳ,) also pass. in form; and some say نَتَجَتْ, but this is rare, and not heard by IAạr; (TA;) and some, also, say ▾أَنْتَجَتْ, (Lth, Kr,) but Az holds this to be a mistake; (TA;) *She* (a camel, IAạr, Ṣ, Ḳ, &c., and a mare, IAạr, and a sheep or goat or other quadruped, Mṣb) *brought forth:* (T, Mṣb, TA:) or one does not say نُتِجَتِ ٱلشَّاةُ unless a man assist at the bringing forth. (Lth.) Thus one suppresses the objective complement of the verb. And one also says نُتِجَتِ ٱلنَّاقَةُ وَلَدًا *The she-camel brought forth a young one:* and in like manner one says of a ewe or a she-goat: and sometimes, with the same meaning, نَتَجَت الناقة ولدا, in the act. form. (Mṣb.) One also says ▾تَنَاتَجَتِ ٱلْإِبِلُ *The camels brought forth.* (A.) [You say,] نُتِجَ ٱلْقَوْمُ, (Lth,) and ▾أَنْتَجَ, (L,) *The people's camels* or *sheep* or *goats brought forth:* (Lth, L:) or ▾أَنْتَجُوا *they had pregnant camels bringing forth.* (Ḳ.) One may also say نُتِجَ ٱلْوَلَدُ, meaning *The young one of a she-camel* &c., [see نُتِجَتْ, above,] *was brought forth,* or *born.* (Mṣb.) See 4. — [Hence,] ٱلرِّيحُ تَنْتِجُ ٱلسَّحَابَ ‡ [*The wind assists the clouds in the discharging of their rain;* i. e., *draws forth the rain from the clouds.* (A, L.) — [نُتِجَ *It was produced, it resulted,* or *was a natural consequence.*]

2: see 1.

4. أَنْتَجَتْ *She* (a camel, Ṣ, and a mare, Ṣ, Ḳ, or other solid-hoofed animal, Mṣb,) *became pregnant:* (T:) and so ▾نَتَجَتْ, said of a she-camel, (Mṣb,) or other beast; but this is rare: (Es-Saraḳustee, Mṣb:) or *attained to the time of bringing forth:* (Ṣ, Ḳ:) or *became evidently pregnant:* (Yaạḳoob, Ṣ, Mṣb:) accord. to IAạr, أُنْتِجَتْ, in the pass. form, signifies *she* (a mare, and a camel,) *became near to the time of bringing forth;* and he had not heard أَنْتَجَتْ, in the act. form. (TA.) — See 1 and 8. — أَنْتَجَ or أُنْتِجَ (?) ‡ *It produced a thing as its fruit,* or *result.* Ex. ٱلْعَجْزُ وَٱلتَّوَانِى تَزَاوَجَا فَأَنْتَجَا ٱلْفَقْرَ *Impotence and remissness combined together, and produced, as*

their result, poverty. (A, L.) And هٰذِهِ المُقَدِّمَةُ لَا تُنْتِجُ نَتِيجَةً صَادِقَةً *This preamble will not produce a praiseworthy result.* (A.)

5. تَنَتَّجَتْ *She* (a camel) *breathed hard* (تزحّرت) *that her young one might come forth.* (K.)

6: see 1.

8. اِنْتَتَجَتْ (L, K, TA: in the CK أَنْتَجَتْ) *She* (a camel) *went away at random, and brought forth in a place unknown:* (K:) or *she brought forth by herself, unassisted by any one;* (Yaakoob, L;) as also ✱ أَنْتَجَتْ. (L.)

نِتَاجٌ: see نُتِجَتْ. — [Also, an inf. n. in the sense of a pass. part. n., like حَمْلٌ in the sense of مَحْمُولٌ, &c., *What is brought forth* by a camel &c.; and *what are brought forth* by camels &c., collectively; *a brood* thereof; its, or their, *increase,* or *offspring;* as is plainly shown in the lexicons &c., in many passages: for ex., see شَرْخٌ, and دِفْءٌ: also applied, in the TA art. بطن, to the *young* in the belly of a mare].

نَتُوجٌ, (AZ, S, K,) a rare form of epithet from a verb of the measure أَفْعَلَ, (Kr,) and ✱ مُنْتِجٌ, (AZ, TA,) or the latter is not allowable, (S, K,) and ✱ نَتِيجٌ, (Kr,) A she-camel, (S, Kr,) or a mare, (S, K,) or other solid-hoofed animal, (Msb,) *pregnant:* (Lth:) or *that has attained to the time of bringing forth:* (S, K:) or *evidently pregnant:* (Yaakoob, S, Msb:) or *near to the time of bringing forth, and big-bellied.* (AZ.) — [See also مَنْتُوجَةٌ.]

نَتِيجٌ: see نَتُوجٌ.

نَتِيجَةٌ *A young one* of a she-camel &c. [see نَتَجَ and نُتِجَتْ] *brought forth.* (Msb.) — نَتِيجَةٌ † *Any produce, fruit, result,* or *natural consequence,* of a thing: (KL:) [the *sum* of a speech or saying: *a necessary inference:* the *conclusion* of an argument or of a syllogism: pl. نَتَائِجُ.] You say, هٰذِهِ نَتِيجَةٌ مِن نَتَائِجِ كَرَمِكَ ‡ [*This is one of the fruits,* or *results, of thy generosity*]. (A.) [For another ex. see 4.] — هُمَا نَتِيجَةٌ *They are both of one age:* said of two sheep. (Yoo, S.) غَنَمُ فُلَانٍ نَتَائِجُ *The sheep,* or *goats, of such a one are of one age.* (S, K.) هٰذَا الوَلَدُ نَتِيجُ وَلَدِى ‡ *This child is one born in the same month,* or *year, as my child.* (A.)

نَاتِجٌ A man *assisting* a she-camel &c. [see نَتَجَ] *in bringing forth; delivering* her; or *one who assists* her *in bringing forth; who delivers her.* (Msb, TA.)

مَنْتِجٌ The *time at which a she-camel,* (S,) or *a mare,* (K,) *brings forth.* (S, K.) Ex. أَتَتِ النَّاقَةُ عَلَى مَنْتِجِهَا *The she-camel arrived at the time of her bringing forth.* (S.)

مُنْتِجٌ: see نَتُوجٌ. — قَعَدَ مُنْتِجًا ‡ *He sat accomplishing a want of nature.* (A.)

مَنْتَجَةٌ The *anus;* syn. اِسْتٌ; as also مِنْتَجَةٌ. (K.)

مَنْتُوجَةٌ A she-camel &c., [see نَتَجَ] *assisted in bringing forth; delivered.* (Msb, TA.) — Also, A she-camel [&c., see نُتِجَتْ,] *bringing forth;* (T;) and so, accord. to Kr, ✱ نَتُوجٌ, which, he says, is the only epithet of this measure from a verb of the measure فُعِلَ, except بَتُولٌ: (TA:) pl. مَنَاتِيجُ: ex. نُوقٌ مناتيج *she-camels bringing forth.* (A.)

نتح

1. نَتَحَ, aor. ـِ, inf. n. نَتْحٌ, *He,* or *it, sweated.* (L.) — نَتَحَ, aor. ـِ, inf. n. نَتْحٌ and نُتُوحٌ, *It* (a leathern vessel, or skin,) *sweated,* or *exuded moisture,* (S, L,) as when a skin sweats with the butter that is in it. (L.) — نَتَحَ, aor. ـَ, inf. n. نَتْحٌ and نُتُوحٌ, *It* (sweat) *exuded* (S, L, K) from the skin, (L, K,) or from the roots of the hair; (T, L;) and grease, from a skin; and moisture, from the soil. (L, K.) — [And said of moisture, *It percolated:* see an ex. voce عَرِقَ.] — فُلَانٌ يَنْتِحُ نَتِيحَ الحَمِيتِ ‡ [*Such a one sweats like a butter-skin*]: said of one who is fat. (A.) — نَتَحَتْ ذِفْرَى البَعِيرِ عَرَقًا *The camel's protuberance behind his ear dripped with sweat,* by reason of his journeying during a vehemently hot summer-day. (L.) — نَتَحَتِ الدُّمُوعُ, inf. n. نَتْحٌ, † *The tears flowed.* (MF.) — نَتَحَهُ *It* (heat, L, K, and some other thing, L,) *made him to sweat.* (L, K.) [Its aor. seems to be يَنْتَحُ; and MF thinks that, in an instance which follows, it may be written with ا after the ت by poetic licence.] F observes, that J has fallen into three errors with respect to اِنْتَاحَ; [saying that الاِنْتِيَاحُ (in the place of which is put, in some copies of the S, الاِنْتِبَاحُ, as is mentioned in the TA,) is like النَّتْحُ,] and citing these words of Dhu-r-Rummeh, describing a camel making his voice to reciprocate in the شِقْشِقَة,

[✱ رَقْشَاءَ تَنْتَاحُ اللُّغَامَ المُزْبِدَا ✱]

first, because the root of the present art. is sound, so that الانتياح has no place in it; secondly, because this word has no meaning (in this art. TA); and thirdly, because the [correct] reading is تَمْتَاحُ, meaning "casts forth" the froth of the mouth. Neither IB nor IM has animadverted on J in this case. MF, however, observes, that one relation of a verse &c., does not impugn the correctness of another relation that differs from it; and that perhaps the ن of تنتاح is a substitute for م; such substitution being frequent; [as in the case of اِنْتَتَحَ;] or that the ا is what is termed أَلِفُ إِشْبَاعٍ, and added for the sake of the metre. (TA.)

8. اِنْتَتَحَ: see اِمْتَتَحَ, in art. متح.

نَتْحٌ *Sweat.* (K.) — See what follows.

نُتُوحٌ The *gums of trees:* (S, K:) one should not say نُتُوعٌ, (S,) as is commonly said: (TA:) it is doubtful whether its sing. be نَتْحٌ, or of some other form. (MF.)

نِحْىٌ نَتَّاحٌ *A butter-skin that sweats much.* (A.)

مَنْتَحَةٌ The *podex:* or the *anus:* syn. اِسْتٌ. (L, K.)

يَنْتُوحٌ *A certain bird,* (L, K,) *bald-headed, found in sandy tracts.* (L.)

مَنَاتِحُ العَرَقِ *The pores through which the sweat exudes.* (S.)

نتخ

1. نَتَخَ, (S, L, K,) aor. ـِ, (K, JK,) or ـُ, (L, JK,) inf. n. نَتْخٌ, (S, L,) *He pulled* a thing *out,* or *up,* or *off; removed* it *from its place; displaced* it. (S, L, K.) *He extracted,* or *pulled out,* a tooth: (S, L:) and, a thorn from his foot (S, L) with an instrument called مِنْتَاخٌ, or مِنْتَاخَانِ: (L:) or *he extracted* in a general sense. (L.) *It* (a hawk, or falcon, L, K, and a vulture, L,) *pulled off,* or *tore off,* or *snatched away,* flesh (S, L, K) with its bill: (S, L:) and a raven, or crow, in like manner, a sore upon the back of a camel. (L.) — نُتِخَ مِنْ أَصْحَابِهِ ‡ *He was removed,* or *taken away, from his companions.* (A.) نَتَخَتْهُ المَنِيَّةُ مِنْ بَيْنِ قَوْمِهِ ‡ *Death removed him from among his people.* (A.) — See also نَخَتَ.

مِنْتَاخٌ *An instrument with which thorns are extracted from the foot;* syn. مِنْقَاشٌ: (S, L, K:) مِنْتَاخَانِ the *same, having two extremities.* (Az, L.) See مِنْقَاشٌ.

نتر

1. نَتَرَ, aor. ـُ, (S, M, A, Msb,) inf. n. نَتْرٌ, (S, M, Msb, K,) *He pulled* a thing, (S, M, Msb, K,✱) [as, for instance,] a garment, or piece of cloth, (A,) and his ذَكَر, which a man is required to do three times after بَوْل, (S, TA,) *hard,* or *with vehemence.* (S, M, A, Msb, K.) — *He drew* a bow *vehemently:* (K,✱ TA:) *he drew* the bow-string *strongly;* (TA;) or *so that the bow nearly broke.* (A.) — *He rent* a

garment, or piece of cloth, *with his fingers* or *with his teeth*. (M, Ḳ.) And [in like manner,] نَتَرَتِ القِسِىُّ أَوْتَارَهَا *The bows broke their strings.* (IḲṭṭ.) — *He snatched* a thing *unawares.* (Ḳ,* TḲ.) — *He acted ungently, roughly, harshly,* or *violently,* (Ḳ,* TA,) in an affair. (TA.) — نَتَرَ فِى مَشْيِهِ, (T, M,) inf. n. as above, (T,) *He* (a man) *was as though he were pulling, in his walking:* (T:) *he leaned in his walking;* as also ▾ انتتر. (M.)

8. انتتر *It became pulled* (M, Ḳ) *hard,* or *with vehemence.* (M.) — See also 1, last signification.

10. استنتر مِنْ بَوْلِهِ *He pulled his* ذَكَر *so as to express the remains of his* بَوْل, in purifying himself in the manner termed إِسْتِنْجَآء; (M,* A, Ḳ,*) being earnestly desirous and careful to perform this act [fully]. (A, Ḳ.)

طَعْنٌ نَتْرٌ *A thrusting,* or *piercing, in which extraordinary force or energy is exerted,* (M, Ḳ,) *as though pulling vehemently that by which the weapon passes in the person thrust,* or *pierced:* app. an inf. n. used as an epithet: (M:) or *a thrusting,* or *piercing, that is like a snatching unawares.* (ISk, T, Ṣ.) The saying of 'Alee, recorded in a trad., إِطْعَنُوا النَّتْرَ has been explained as meaning *Thrust ye,* or *pierce ye, with extraordinary force* or *energy:* and *as though snatching unawares.* (TA.) [See art. سعر.] Accord. to IAạr, (T,) طَعْنَةٌ نَتْرَةٌ signifies *A thrust that passes through.* (T, Ḳ.)

نَتْرَةٌ *A hard,* or *vehement, pull:* (Mṣb:) pl. نَتَرَاتٌ. (Ṣ, Mṣb.) — See نَتْرٌ.

قَوْسٌ نَاتِرَةٌ *A bow that breaks its string, by reason of its hardness:* (Ṣ, Ḳ:) pl. نَوَاتِرُ: (Ṣ:) or قِسِىٌّ نَوَاتِرُ signifies *bows having the strings broken.* (M.)

[مُنَاتِرَةٌ, in the Ḳ, I suspect to be a mistake for مُنَابِرَةٌ.]

نتش

1. نَتَشَ, (Ṣ, A, Ḳ,) aor. ـِ, inf. n. نَتْشٌ, (A, Ḳ,) *He extracted;* or *drew,* or *pulled, out,* or *forth;* (Ṣ, A, Ḳ;) a thing, (Ṣ,) or a thorn, (A, Ḳ,) and the like, (Ḳ,) and hair, (TA,) with the مِنْتَاش: (Ṣ, A, Ḳ, TA:) *he plucked out* hair or the like. (IDrd, Ḳ.) — *He plucked,* or *pulled,* flesh, and the like, *by pinching* it *with his fingers,* (Lth, Ḳ,) and *by taking hold upon it with his teeth.* (Lth, TA.) — نَتَشَ الجَرَادُ الأَرْضَ, aor. and inf. n. as above, *The locusts ate the herbage of the earth.* (TA.) — مَا نَتَشْتُ مِنْ فُلَانٍ شَيْئًا *I did not obtain,* (Ṣ,) or *take,* (A,) *from such a one anything.* (Ṣ, A.) — هُوَ يَنْتِشُ لِعِيَالِهِ, (Lḥ, TA,) inf. n. as above, (Ḳ,) ‡ *He gains,* or *earns,* or *seeks sustenance, for his family,* or *house-hold.* (Lḥ, Ḳ,* TA.) — هُوَ يَنْتِشُ مِنْ كُلِّ عِلْمٍ † *He takes* [or *acquires*] *of every science.* (A,* TA.)

مَا أَخَذَ إِلَّا نَتْشًا *He took not save a little.* (TA.)

مِنْتَاشٌ [*A kind of tweezers;*] *an instrument with which one extracts,* or *draws* or *pulls out* or *forth,* (Ṣ, A, Ḳ,) *a thing* (Ṣ,) or *a thorn,* (A, Ḳ,) and *the like,* (Ḳ,) and *hair;* (TA;) *i. q.* مِنْقَاشٌ. (Ṣ, Ḳ.)

[نتض &c.,

see Supplement.]

نث

1. نَثَّ, [aor. ـِ,] inf. n. نَثٌّ, *It* (a bone) *distilled,* or *let flow, the oily matter that was in it:* (TA:) [as also مَثَّ.] — نَثَّ, aor. ـِ, inf. n. نَثِيثٌ (Ṣ, Ḳ,) and نَثٌّ; (Ṣ;) and ▾ نَثْنَثَ; (Ḳ;) *It* (a skin) *exuded* (Ṣ, Ḳ) *the clarified butter that was in it:* like مَثَّ. (TA.) — وَأَنْتَ تَنِثُّ نَثِيثَ الحَمِيتِ (accord. to one reading, نَثَّ الحميت, TA) *And thou sweatest like the butter-skin.* (Ṣ, from a trad.) — نَثَّ, aor. ـِ, inf. n. نَثِيثٌ, *He sweated by reason of fatness, and appeared as though he were anointed:* as also مَثَّ: (TA:) or *he sweated by reason of his bigness, and his abundance of flesh.* (A'Obeyd.) — نَثَّ, (so in the TA,) [aor. ـُ,] or ▾ نَثْنَثَ, (so in the Ḳ,) *He wiped* his hand (Ḳ) with a napkin: as also مَثَّ. (TA.) — نَثَّ, [aor. ـُ,] *He anointed* a wound: as also مَثَّ. (TA.) — نَثَّ, aor. ـُ, (Ṣ, M, L, Ḳ,) and ـِ, (M, L, Ḳ,) the latter [which deviates from a constant rule] thought by MF to be a mistake, he not knowing any authority for it except the Ḳ, and disallowed by the T, (TA,) inf. n. نَثٌّ; (Ṣ;) and ▾ نَثَّثَ, inf. n. تَنْثِيثٌ; (TA;) *He divulged,* (Ṣ, Ḳ,) or *spread, dispersed, disseminated,* (TA,) news, tidings, or information, (Ḳ,) or what was talked of: (Ṣ, TA:) like بَثَّ: or *he spread* what should rather be concealed than spread. (TA.) [See also نَثَا.]

2: see 1.

R. Q. 1. نَثْنَثَ *He sweated much.* (Ḳ.) — See 1.

نَثٌّ A wall (حَائِط) that is *moist,* or *damp,* (Ḳ,) *and flaccid.* (TA.)

كَلَامٌ غَثٌّ نَثٌّ [*Very bad,* or *corrupt speech*]: نَثٌّ is here an imitative sequent to غَثٌّ. (Ḳ.)

نِثَاثٌ *Ointment with which a wound is anointed.* (Ḳ.)

نَثِيثَةٌ The *moisture exuded by a skin, such as is called* زِقّ or سِقَآء. (Ḳ.)

نَثَّاثٌ and ▾ مِنَثٌّ [A man *who is in the habit of divulging,* or *spreading, dispersing,* or *disseminating, news, tidings,* or *information,* or *what is talked of,* or *what should rather be concealed*]. (Th.)

نَاثٌّ One *who traduces the Muslims behind their backs, but saying of them what is true, and mentioning their vices,* or *faults:* pl. نُثَّاثٌ: (AA:) [the pl. only is mentioned in the Ḳ, and explained as signifying persons *who traduce others behind their backs, but saying of them what is true*].

نَثَّاثٌ: see مِنَثٌّ.

مِنَثَّةٌ *A small portion of wool with which one anoints* (Ḳ) *a wound.* (TA.)

نثت

نَثِتَ, aor. ـَ, [inf. n. نَثَتٌ,] *It* (flesh-meat) *became changed,* or *altered, and stank:* formed by transposition from نَتِثَ: (Ḳ:) and so a wound. (TA.)

لِثَةٌ نَثِتَةٌ *A gum that is flabby and bleeding:* and in like manner شَفَةٌ, *a lip:* (TA:) [as also نَتِثَةٌ].

نثر

1. نَثَرَ, aor. ـُ, (Ṣ, M, A, Mṣb, Ḳ,) and ـِ, (M, Mṣb, Ḳ,) inf. n. نَثْرٌ (Ṣ, M, A, Mṣb, Ḳ) and نِثَارٌ, (M, Ḳ,) or the latter is a simple subst., (Ṣ, A, Mṣb,) *He scattered* a thing, *sprinkled* it, *strewed* it, *dispersed* it, or *threw* it *dispersedly,* (Lth, T, M, A, Mṣb, Ḳ, TA,) *with his hand;* (Lth, T;) as, for instance, grain, (Lth, T,) and fruit and the like, (Mṣb,) walnuts and almonds and sugar, (Lth, T,) and pearls, &c.; (A;) as also ▾ نثّر, (M, Ḳ,) inf. n. تَنْثِيرٌ; (TA;) [or the latter is with teshdeed to denote muchness, or frequency, or repetition, of the action; or its application to many objects: see مَنْثُورٌ.] — نَثَرَتِ النَّخْلَةُ ‡ *The palm-tree* [*scattered* or] *shook off its unripe dates.* (A.) — وَجَأَهُ فَنَثَرَ أَمْعَآءَهُ ‡ *He smote him with a knife and scattered his intestines*]. (M, A.) — لَأَنْثُرَنَّكَ نَثْرَ الكَرِشِ ‡ [*I will assuredly scatter thine intestines like as one scatters the contents of the stomach of a ruminant beast*]: said in threatening. (A.) — نَثَرَ وَلَدًا ‡ *He* (a man, M) *had many children born to him.* (M, Ḳ, TA.) And نَثَرَتِ المَرْأَةُ بَطْنَهَا, (T, A, Mgh TA,) and كَرِشَهَا, (A, in art. كرش,) ‡ *The woman brought forth many children;* (T, A, in art. كرش;) *scattered children* لِلزَّوْجِ *to the husband.* (Mgh.) — نَثَرَ الكَلَامَ ‡ *He spoke,* or *talked, much.* (M, Ḳ, TA.) — نَثَرَ قِرَآءَتَهُ

‡ *He hastened*, or *was quick, in his reading*, or *reciting*. (A.) —— نَثَرَ, aor. ـِ, inf. n. نَثِيرٌ, ‡ *He* (a beast of carriage, M, Ḳ, and a camel, M, and an ass, T) *sneezed* [app. *so as to scatter the moisture in his nostrils*]: (T, M, Ḳ, TA:) or *did with his nose what is like sneezing*: (T:) *he* (an ass, and a sheep or goat) *sneezed, and expelled what annoyed* or *hurt him, from his nose*: (A:) or نَثَرَتْ *she* (a ewe or goat) *ejected from her nose what annoyed* or *hurt her*. (Ṣ.) And نَثَرَ, (Fr, T, IAth, Mgh, Mṣb,) aor. ـِ, (T, IAth,) inf. n. نَثْرٌ (T, Mgh) [and app. نَثِيرٌ, as above], ‡ *He* [a man] *blew his nose; ejected the mucus from his nose*; syn. اِمْتَخَطَ; (IAth;) as also ▼ استنثر: (Ṣ, Ḳ, art. مخط:) and *he ejected what was in his nose, of mucus*, and *of that which annoyed* or *hurt him, in performing the ablution termed* وُضُوء; (Ṣgh, TA;) as also ▼ أَنْثَرَ, accord. to some: (TA:) or ▼ أَنْثَرَ signifies *he ejected what was in his nose*; or *he emitted his breath from his nose*; or *he introduced the water into his nose*; as also ▼ انتثر and ▼ استنثر: (Ḳ:) but this last explanation is outweighed in authority; the form ▼ انثر is disallowed by the leading lexicologists; and the author of the Ḳ, in respect of this form, follows Ṣgh, without due consideration: (TA:) [accord. to the more approved opinion,] نَثَرَ signifies *he scattered what was in his nose by the breath*; as also ▼ انتثر and ▼ استنثر: (Ṣ:) or, as some of the learned say, *he snuffed up water, and then ejected what was in it, of anything annoying* or *hurting*, or *of mucus*; as also ▼ استنثر: (IAạr, T, Mgh:) or ▼ استنثر (T, M, IAth, Ḳ) and ▼ انتثر, (Ḳ,) *he snuffed up water, and then ejected it* (T, M, IAth, Ḳ) *by the breath of the nose*: (T, M, Ḳ:) accord. to some, نَثَرَ and ▼ استنثر signify *he* (a person performing وُضُوء) *snuffed up water*: but others say that the latter signifies *he ejected what was in his nose, of mucus &c.*; agreeably with a trad. to be cited below: (Mṣb:) IAạr says, that ▼ استنثر signifies *he snuffed up water, and put in motion the* نَثْرَة, or *end of the nose*, in purification: (T [in the Mgh, this explanation is ascribed to Fr:]) and Fr, that نَثَرَ and ▼ انتثر and ▼ استنثر signify *he put in motion the* نَثْرَة, in purification. (T.) It is said of Moḥammad, كَانَ يَسْتَنْشِقُ ثَلَاثًا فِى كُلِّ مَرَّةٍ يَسْتَنْثِرُ [*He used to snuff up water three times, every time ejecting it*; &c.] and this indicates that ▼ استنثر differs from استنشق. (T, Mgh, Mṣb.) And it is said in a trad., إِذَا ٱسْتَنْشَقْتَ فَٱنْثُرْ, (Ṣ, Mṣb,) and فَٱنْثِرْ, with the conjunctive ا, and with ḍamm and kesr to the ث, (Mṣb,) *When thou snuffest up water, scatter what is in thy nose by the breath*; (Ṣ;) or *eject what is in thy nose, of mucus, &c.*: (Mṣb:) or, as A'Obeyd relates it, ▼ فَأَنْثِرْ; inf. n. إِنْثَارٌ: (Mṣb:) or, as he relates it إِذَا تَوَضَّأْتَ فَأَنْثِرْ, with the disjunctive ا; and he does not explain it; but the lexicologists do not allow ▼ أَنْثَرَ, from الإِنْثَارُ; one only says, نَثَرَ and ▼ انتثر and ▼ استنثر. (T.) No instance of ▼ استنثر used transitively has been heard, except in a trad. of El-Ḥasan Ibn-'Alee, ▼ اِسْتَنْثَرَ أَنْفَهُ [*He ejected the contents of his nose*; or *he blew his nose*]; as though the root [نَثَرَ] were regarded in it, or as though it were made to import the meaning of نَقَّى. (Mgh.)

2: see 1, first signification.

3. [نَاثَرَهُ *He contended with him in scattering, strewing*, or *dispersing*, a thing or things. And hence,] —— ‡ رَأَيْتُهُ يُنَاثِرُهُ الدُّرَّ [lit., *I saw him contending with him in scattering pearls*: meaning,] ‡ *I saw him holding a disputation*, or *colloquy, with him, in beautiful*, or *elegant, language*. (A.)

4. انثر as syn. with نَثَرَ and استنثر and انتثر: see 1, latter half. ═ انثرهُ ‡ *He made his nose to bleed*; syn. أَرْعَفَهُ. (Ṣ, A, Ḳ.) You say, طَعَنَهُ فَأَنْثَرَهُ ‡ [*He pierced him and made his nose to bleed*]: (Ṣ:) and ضَرَبَهُ فَأَنْثَرَهُ [*He smote him and made his nose to bleed*]. (A.) —— ‡ *He threw him down upon his* نَثْرَة, (M, A, TA,) i. e., (TA,) [*upon the end of his nose*: or] *upon his* خَيْشُوم. (Ḳ, TA.) You say, طَعَنَهُ فَأَنْثَرَهُ عَنْ فَرَسِهِ ‡ [*He pierced him and threw him down upon the end of his nose from his horse*]. (M, A.*)

5: } see 8.
6: }

8. انتثر (Ṣ, M, A, Mṣb, Ḳ) and ▼ تناثر (Ṣ, M, A, Ḳ) and ▼ تنثّر (M, Ḳ) *It became scattered, strewn, dispersed*, or *thrown dispersedly*: (Ṣ,* M, A, Mṣb, Ḳ:) [or the second more properly signifies *it became scattered*, &c., *by degrees, gradually*, or *part after part*; resembling تَسَاقَطَ &c.: and the third, being quasi-pass. of 2, denotes muchness, or frequency, or repetition, of the action; or its application to many things.] You say, انتثرت الكَوَاكِبُ † *The stars became dispersed*: or *became scattered like grain*. (TA.) And انتثروا and ▼ تنثّروا ‡ [*They* (meaning men) *became as though they were scattered by the hand*]. (A.) [And ▼ تناثر الشَّعَرُ, and الوَرَقُ, † *The hair*, and *the leaves, fell off, and became scattered, by degrees*.] And ▼ تناثر القَوْمُ ‡ *The people fell sick and died* [*one after another*]: (M, Ḳ:*) or you say مَرِضُوا فَتَنَاثَرُوا ▼ مَوْتًا [*they fell sick and became separated by death, one after another*]. (A.) ═ See also 1, latter half, throughout.

10: see 1, latter half, throughout.

نَثْرٌ ‡ [*Prose*: so accord. to general usage: and] *rhyming prose*: *contr. of* نَظْمٌ: so called as being likened to [scattered pearls, or] scattered grain. (TA.)

نَثْرٌ: see نُثَارٌ: and نِثَارٌ: and مُنْتَثِرٌ. ═ ‡ *Loquacity*, (M, TA,) *and the divulging of secrets*. (TA.)

نَثِرٌ ‡ *Loquacious*; *one who talks much*: as also ▼ مِنْثَرٌ (M, Ḳ) and ▼ نَيْثَرَانٌ: (Ṣgh, Ḳ:) or *vainly* or *frivolously loquacious, and a divulger of secrets*: (A:) fem. نَثِرَةٌ only. (M.)

نَثْرَةٌ [*A single act of scattering, strewing, dispersing*, or *throwing dispersedly, with the hand*. And hence,] —— ‡ *A sneeze*: (Ḳ:) or the *like thereof*; peculiar to a beast of carriage (Ṣ) [or other beast, and a fish, as appears from what here follows.] It is said in a trad. (A, TA) of Kaạb, (TA,) الجَرَادُ نَثْرَةُ حُوتٍ (A, TA) ‡ *The locust is* [produced by] *the sneeze of a fish*: or, as in a trad. of I'Ab, نَثْرَةُ الحُوتِ *the sneeze of the fish*. (TA.) [From this it is inferred that the locust is, like fish, lawful to be captured by one in a state of إِحْرَام.] ═ ‡ The *end of the nose*: (IAạr, T:) or *i.q.* خَيْشُومٌ: (A:) or the خيشوم *with what is next to it*: (M, Ḳ:) and (M, A; but in the Ḳ, or) the *interstice that is between the two mustaches*, (Ṣ, M, A, Ḳ,) *against the partition between the two nostrils*: (Ṣ, M, Ḳ:) so [in a man and] in the lion: (Ṣ, M:) or the *nose* of the lion. (M.) —— Hence, (T, &c.,) النَّثْرَةُ, (T, Ṣ, M, Ḳ,) and نَثْرَةُ الأَسَدِ, (T, A,) ‡ *Two stars, between which is the space of a span*, (شِبْرٌ, [said in several law-books to be the twelfth part of a رُمْح, and therefore twenty-two minutes and a half, accord. to modern usage; but there is reason to believe that ancient usage differed from the modern with respect to both these measures, and was not precise nor uniform;]) *and in* [or *between*] *which is a particle* (لَطْخ) *of white, as though it were a portion of cloud*; it is *the nose of Leo*, [which the Arabs extended far beyond the limits which it has upon our globes, (see الذِّرَاعُ,)] (Ṣ, Ḳ,) and is *a Mansion of the Moon*: (Ṣ:) [app. *the Aselli*; *Asellus Boreus and Asellus Australis*; *two small stars in Cancer, between which is a little cloud or nebula, called Præsepe*: (see Pliny, l. xviii. c. 35:)] *a certain star or asterism, which is of the stars* or *asterisms of Leo, and which is a Mansion of the Moon*: (M:) [app. meaning *the same*, or *Præsepe*:] or *a certain star in the sky, as though it were a particle* (لَطْخ) *of cloud, over against two small stars, in the science of astronomy pertaining to the sign of Cancer* [*though accord. to the Arabs belonging to Leo*]: (T:) [app. *Præsepe*; the two small stars adjacent to it being the Aselli:] *a certain star, as though it were a particle* (لَطْخ) *of cloud*; so called because it appears as though the lion had ejected it from his nose: (A:) [app. meaning the same:] in the Megista [of Ptolemy] it is mentioned by the name of *the manger* [i. e., *Præsepe*], and the name of the two small [for المنيرة in my copy of Ḳzw, I read الصغيرة,] stars is the two asses [i. e., the Aselli]: (Ḳzw, Description of Cancer:) or *the nose and nostrils of the lion, consisting of three obscure stars, near together:* الطَّرْفُ is [*before them, and is*] *the two eyes of the lion, consisting of two stars, before which is* الجَبْهَةُ, *consisting of four stars:* (AHeyth:) [app. meaning *the Aselli together with Præsepe:*] *three stars, near together; the nose of the lion;* [app. meaning the same;] *which compose the Eighth Mansion of the Moon:* (Ḳzw, Description of the Mansions of the Moon:) [these descriptions apply to this Mansion of the Moon accord. to those who make النَّوْء to signify "the heliacal rising:" see مَنَازِلُ القَمَرِ, in art. نزل:] or *the bright star* [app. meaning β] *in Cancer:* (Ḳzw, Description of Cancer:) [this agrees with the place of the Eighth Mansion of the Moon accord. to those who make النَّوْء to signify "the anti-heliacal setting:" see again مَنَازِلُ القَمَرِ] The Arabs say إِذَا طَلَعَتِ النَّثْرَةُ قَنَأَتِ البُسْرَةُ, meaning, *When* النثرة *rises* [heliacally], *the unripe date begins to have its redness intermixed with blackness:* its rising is very soon after that of الشِّعْرَى [or Sirius: about the epoch of the Flight, it rose heliacally, in central Arabia, on the 17th of July, O. S.; and Sirius, on the 13th of the same month]. (M.)

نُثَارٌ *What becomes scattered, strewn, or dispersed, of, or from, a thing;* (Ṣ, Mṣb;) as also ▼ نُثَارَةٌ, (M, Ḳ,) and ▼ نَثَرٌ, (Ḳ, [but see مُنْتَثِرٌ,]) and, as some say, ▼ نِثَارٌ: (Mṣb:) so the ▼ نُثَارَة of wheat, and of barley, and the like: (Lḥ, M:) or نُثَارٌ signifies the *crumbs of bread,* and *of every-thing, that become scattered around the table:* (T:) or the *crumbs* of the table *that become scattered around;* as also ▼ نُثَارَةٌ: (A:) or this last, *what becomes scattered from the table, and is eaten in the hope of obtaining a recompense* [*for preventing its being thrown away* or *trodden under foot*]. (Lḥ, M, Ḳ.*)

نِثَارٌ, with kesr, a subst. from نَثَرَ, (Ṣ, A, Mṣb,) signifying The *act of scattering, strewing, dispersing,* or *throwing dispersedly,* [anything,] (Lth, T, A, Mṣb,) [and particularly fruits and the like, such as] walnuts and almonds and sugar [and money, &c., on festive occasions,] and grain. (Lth, T.) You say شَهِدْتُ نِثَارَ فُلَانٍ *I was present at,* or *I witnessed, such a one's scattering* (Lth, T, A) of fruits, &c. (Lth, T.) And كُنَّا فِى نِثَارِهِ *We were at his scattering.* (A.) — Also, *What is scattered, strewn, dispersed,* or *thrown dispersedly,* (A, Mṣb, TA,) of such things as sugar and fruits and the like, (A, TA,) [and money, &c., on festive occasions;] a subst., (A, TA,) in the sense of مَنْثُورٌ, (A, Mṣb, TA,) like كِتَابٌ in the sense of مَكْتُوبٌ; (Mṣb;) as also ▼ نَثَرٌ. (A, TA.) [See also مُنْتَثِرٌ.] You say أَصَبْتُ مِنَ النِّثَارِ *I obtained* [somewhat] *of the scattered* [sugar or fruits &c.]. (Mṣb.) And مَا أَصَبْنَا مِنْ نَثَرِ فُلَانٍ شَيْئًا *We did not obtain aught of such a one's scattered things,* such as sugar and fruit. (TA.) — Accord. to some, i. q. نُثَارٌ in the first of the senses explained above. (Mṣb.)

نَثُورٌ ‡ A female, (Ṣ, Ḳ,) or woman, (M,) *having numerous offspring:* (Ṣ, M, A, Ḳ:) and so a male, (M,) or man. (TA.) — ‡ A ewe, or she-goat, (TA,) *having a wide orifice to the teat:* (Ḳ, TA:) as though she scattered the milk. (TA.) — See also نَاثِرٌ.

نَثِيرٌ: see مَنْثُورٌ.

نُثَارَةٌ: see نُثَارٌ, in three places.

نَاثِرٌ (A) and ▼ مِنْثَارٌ (A, Ḳ) ‡ A palm-tree (نَخْلَةٌ) *that shakes off its unripe dates:* (A:) or *of which the unripe dates become scattered.* (Ḳ.) — And the former, ‡ A sheep or goat *that coughs, so that something becomes scattered from its nose;* as also نَافِرٌ: (Aṣ, Ṣ:) or a sheep or goat *that ejects from its nose what resembles worms;* as also ▼ نَثُورٌ: (M, Ḳ:) or *that sneezes, and ejects from its nose what annoys* or *hurts it, resembling worms.* (TA.)

نَيْثَرَانٌ: } see نَثْرٌ.
مَنْثَرٌ: }

دُرٌّ مُنْتَثِرٌ *Pearls scattered,* or *strewn, much.* (Ṣ, TA.) See مَنْثُورٌ.

مِنْثَارٌ: see نَاثِرٌ.

دُرٌّ مَنْثُورٌ, and ▼ نَثِيرٌ, *Pearls scattered, strewn, dispersed,* or *thrown dispersedly, with the hand.* (A,* TA.) See also مُنْتَثِرٌ, and مَنْثَرٌ. You say كَأَنَّ لَفْظَهُ الدُّرُّ النَّثِيرُ [*As though his speech were scattered pearls*]. (A.) — لَهُ كَرِشٌ مَنْثُورَةٌ ‡ *He has* [*numerous*] *young children.* (A, art. كرش.) — Also مَنْثُورٌ *A kind of sweet-smelling flower;* (TA;) [the *gilliflower:* so called in the present day: see also خِيرِىٌّ:] — See also خَشْخَاشٌ.

مُنْتَثِرٌ *In a scattered* or *strewn state; in a state of dispersion;* (M;) as also ▼ مُتَنَاثِرٌ, (TA,) and ▼ نَثَرٌ, which last is applied to a thing and to things. (M.) See also نِثَارٌ, and نُثَارٌ, and مَنْثُورٌ. You say ▼ دُرٌّ مُتَنَاثِرٌ [*Pearls in a scattered state*]. (TA.)

مُتَنَاثِرٌ: see مُنْتَثِرٌ.

[نثط, &c.

See Supplement.]

نج

1. نَجَّ, aor. ـُ, inf. n. نَجِيجٌ (Ṣ, Ḳ) and نُجٌّ, (TA,) *It* (a wound, or an ulcer) *flowed with its contents* [namely *purulent matter,* or *blood*]: (Aṣ, Ṣ, Ḳ:) or *exuded its contents:* and in like manner, *it* (the back of a beast) *flowed with purulent matter:* and *it* (the ear) *flowed with blood and purulent matter.* (TA.) = نَجَّ and مَجَّ, (in the TA, art. مج, it is said مَجَّ and نَجَّ,) accord. to IAạr, are syn. (TA) نَجَّ الشَّىْءَ مِنْ فِيهِ, inf. n. نَجٌّ, signifies i. q. مَجَّهُ. (TA.)

R. Q. 1. نَجْنَجَ الأَمْرَ, (inf. n. نَجْنَجَةٌ, Ṣ,) *He agitated the thing,* or *affair, to and fro, in his mind,* (Ṣ,) *and did not execute it;* (TA;) *he thought upon the thing,* or *affair, but did not determine upon it.* (Ṣ, Ḳ.) See R. Q. 2. — نَجْنَجَ الإِبِلَ *He drove back the camels from the water:* (L:) or *he drove them back time after time to the tank,* or *cistern;* expl. by رَدَّدَهَا على الحَوْضِ: (Ṣ, Ḳ:) [but عَلَى, meaning here *to,* seems to be a mistake for عَنْ, *from*]. Dhu-r-Rummeh says,

• حَتَّى إِذَا لَمْ يَجِدْ وَغْلًا وَنَجْنَجَهَا •
• مَخَافَةَ الرَّمْىِ حَتَّى كُلُّهَا هِيمُ •

[*Until, when he finds not a place of refuge, and drives them back from the water,* (accord. to the explanation in the L,) *fearing to be shot at, so that all of them are thirsting*]. (Ṣ.) — نَجْنَجَ *He moved about* [a thing; in the Ṣ, on the authority of A'Obeyd, a man], (Ṣ, Ḳ,) *and turned over and over.* (TA.) — One says, نَجْنِجْ أَمْرَكَ فَلَعَلَّكَ تَجِدُ إِلَى الخُرُوجِ سَبِيلًا [*Turn the thing over and over in thy mind, and perhaps thou wilt find a way of egress,* or *escape*]. (TA.) — نَجْنَجَ, (inf. n. نَجْنَجَةٌ, Ṣ,) *He went round about in fright,* or *fear.* (Ṣ, Ḳ.) — نَجْنَجَ اللُّقْمَةَ *He moved the morsel to and fro* in his mouth, *and did not swallow it;* like لَجْلَجَ. (Aboo-Turáb.)

R. Q. 2. تَنَجْنَجَ *He was in a state of commotion,* or *agitated, and confounded, perplexed,* or *amazed.* (Ḳ.) — تنجنج فِى رَأْيِهِ, and ▼ نَجْنَجَ فِيهِ, *He was confounded,* or *perplexed, and agitated, in his judgment,* or *opinion.* (TA.) — تَنَجْنَجَ لَحْمُهُ *His flesh became much and flabby.* (Ṣ.) Accord. to F, this is a mistake for تَبَجْبَجَ; but Hr agrees herein with J. (TA.)

نجأ

1. نَجَأَهُ, aor. ـَ, (Ṣ, Ḳ,) inf. n. نَجْءٌ (so in the Ṣ: in the TA, نَجْأَةٌ: [but this I think a mistake:]); and ▼ انتجاه (Lḥ, Ḳ) and ▼ تنجّاه; (Ṣ, Ḳ;) *He affected him,* or *it, by an evil,* or *a malignant, eye.* (Ṣ, Ḳ.)

5 and 8: see 1.

نَجِىُّ ▼ العين, and نَجُوءُ العين, and نَجُو العَيْنِ, and نَجِىُّ العين, *Having an evil*, or *a malignant, eye*; (Fr, Ṣ, Ḳ;) *and powerfully affecting therewith.* (Ḳ.)

نَجُوءُ العَيْنِ see نَجُوءٌ; and نَجِىٌّ; and نَجِىٌّ.

نَجْأَةٌ *An affecting with an evil*, or *a malignant, eye*: (Ks:) *force*, or *eagerness, of look*: (Ks, IAth, Ṣ:) *lust*, or *desire*, or *a hankering after a thing.* (Ks, Ḳ.) Ex. رُدُّوا نَجْأَةَ السَّائِلِ بِاللُّقْمَةِ (Ṣ) *Avert the beggar's evil eye*; (Ks;) or *the force*, or *eagerness, of his look at thy food*, or *at thee*; (Ṣ;) or *his lust*; or *accomplish his desire, and avert his eye from thy food, in compassion for him*; (TA;) do this *by giving him a morsel.* (Ṣ.) — رُدَّ عَنْكَ نَجْأَةَ هٰذَا الشَّىْءِ *Avert from thee the desire of this thing.* (TA.)

نجب

1. نَجَبَ الشَّجَرَةَ, aor. ـُ and ـِ, inf. n. نَجْبٌ, *He took off the bark of the stem*, or *trunk, of the tree*: (Ṣ:) or نَجَبَهُ, aor. and inf. n. as above; and ▼ نَجَّبَهُ, inf. n. تَنْجِيبٌ; and ▼ انتجبه; *He took off its bark; barked it.* (ISd, Ḳ.) See نَجَبٌ. — نَجُبَ, aor. ـُ, inf. n. نَجَابَةٌ, *He was generous, noble*, or *liberal*, *&c.*: [see نَجِيبٌ]. (Mṣb, Ḳ.) *He*, or *it, was excellent*, or *choice.* (MA.) [Said of a horse and the like, *He was generous, excellent, strong, light*, or *swift.*] — نَاجَبَهُ فَنَجَبَهُ: see 3.

2: see 1.

3. ▼ نَاجَبَهُ فَنَجَبَهُ [*He vied with him*, or *strove to surpass him, in generosity, nobleness*, or *liberality; and he surpassed him therein.*] (TA, art. خير.)

4. انجب *He begot a generous, noble*, or *liberal, child; such as is termed* نَجِيبٌ. (Ṣ.) [This verb, being coupled in the Ḳ with نَجُبَ, might be imagined syn. therewith; but this, accord. to the TA, is not the case.] El-Aashà says,

أَنْجَبَ أَزْمَانَ وَالِدَاهُ بِهِ

إِذْ نَجَلَاهُ فَنِعْمَ مَا نَجَلَا

(Ṣ) *He begot a generous son in the times when his parents (rejoiced) in him, when they produced him; and excellent was that which they produced.* Accord. to one reading, the second word is أَيَّامَ: and أَيَّامَ وَالِدَيْهِ is also read in place of ازمان والداه; in which case, ايّام is fig. the agent of انجب. (TA.) — انجبت is said of a woman, in the same sense. (TA.) See also انخب. — انجب [as also انخب] *He begot a cowardly child*: (from نَجَبٌ, the "bark" of a tree: TA:) thus the verb bears two contr. significations: (Ḳ:) or the two significations are not necessarily contr.; for a courageous man may be not generous, or liberal; and a generous, or liberal, man may be not courageous. (MF.)

8. انتجبهُ *He selected him; chose him*; (Ṣ;) *preferred him above others.* (TA.) See also انتخب. — See 1. — ذَهَبَ يَنْتَجِبُ *He went to collect* [*the kind of bark called*] نَجَبٌ. (TA.) — A poet says,

يَا أَيُّهَا الزَّاعِمُ أَنِّى أَجْتَلِبْ

وَأَنَّنِى غَيْرَ عِضَاهِى أَنْتَجِبْ

meaning, *O thou who assertest that I take the verses of other poets and appropriate them to myself, and*, and as it were, *take the bark of other trees than my own 'idáh*, to tan therewith . . . (TA.) [See عِضَاهٌ.]

نَجْبٌ: see نَجِيبٌ.

نَجَبٌ The *bark* (لِحَآء) of trees: (Ṣ, Ḳ:) or the *rind of the roots* thereof: or *of what is hard* thereof. (Ḳ.) The soft peel of branches is not thus called; nor is the rind of roots called قِشْر, but نجب: n. un. نَجَبَةٌ. (TA.)

نُجْبَةُ نَمْلَةٍ *A bite of an ant.* So in a trad., accord. to one reading: accord. to another reading, it is نُخْبَةٌ. Both these words are given by IAth on the authority of Z. (TA.)

نُجَبَةٌ and نُجْبَةٌ: see نَجِيبٌ.

نَجِيبٌ A *generous, noble, liberal*, man; (Ṣ, Ḳ;) one *distinguished by rank* or *quality, nobility* or *eminence, reputation* or *note* or *consideration*; (Ḳ;) *excellent*; *of great worth in his kind*; one who is *like his father in generosity and actions*: (TA:) as also ▼ نَجْبٌ (Ḳ) [explained as signifying "liberal, generous"] and ▼ نُجَبَةٌ: (Ṣ, Ḳ:) or you call a man نجيب when he is generous, noble, or liberal; but when he is unequalled among his people in generosity, &c., you say هُوَ نُجَبَةُ ▼ قَوْمِهِ, in measure like حُلَمَةٌ: (El-'Alam Es-Sakhâwee:) [but MF doubts the correctness of this measure; and seems to think that the correct word is ▼ نُجْبَة:] هو نُجَبَةُ ▼ القَوْمِ is said of a man when he is the man, among them, who is distinguished by generosity, &c.: (Ṣ:) pl. نُجَبَآءُ and أَنْجَابٌ and نُجُبٌ. (Ḳ.) — نَجِيبٌ *Excellent*, as an epithet applied to any animal; (IAth;) a *generous, excellent*, camel or horse; one *of high breed*; (ISd;) a *strong, light, swift*, camel: (TA:) you say نَاقَةٌ نَجِيبَةٌ as well as نَاقَة نَجِيبٌ: (Ḳ:) pl. نَجَائِبُ (Ṣ, Ḳ) and نُجُبٌ. (Ṣ.) — نَجَائِبُ القُرْآنِ *The most excellent, and the purest, parts of the Ḳur-án.* Of such is the سُورَةُ الأَنْعَامِ. (TA.) In like manner, ▼ نَوَاجِبُهُ *The heart thereof* that has [as it were] no نَجَب [or bark] upon it: or *the best*, or *most excellent, thereof.* (Ḳ.)

نَوَاجِبُ: see what next precedes.

مُنْجِبٌ A man *who begets generous, noble*, or *liberal, children; such as are termed* نُجَبَآء. (Ḳ.) In like manner, اِمْرَأَةٌ مُنْجِبَةٌ, and ▼ مِنْجَابٌ: (Ṣ, Ḳ:) pl. of the latter مَنَاجِيبُ. (Ṣ.) — ▼ منجاب also signifies A woman *who has generous, noble*, or *liberal, children; such as are termed* نجباء. (TA.)

مِنْجَابٌ A *weak* man: (Ṣ, Ḳ:) pl. مَنَاجِيبُ. (TA.) See مُنْجِبٌ, and also مِنْخَابٌ. — مِنْجَابٌ An arrow *that has neither feathers nor head*; (A'Obeyd, Ṣ;) *that is trimmed, shaped*, or *pared, but has neither feathers nor head.* (Aṣ, A'Obeyd, Ḳ.) — مِنْجَابٌ *An iron with which a fire is stirred.* (Ḳ.)

مَنْجُوبٌ A vessel that is *capacious within*: (Ḳ:) a *capacious* vessel of the kind called قَدَحٌ: (Ṣ:) or *wide*, or *capacious, in the bottom*: i.q. مَنْجُوفٌ, which, accord. to ISd, is the correct word; but others say that the ب and ف may be interchangeable. (TA.) — جِلْدٌ مَنْجُوبٌ *A hide tanned with the bark of the trunk of the* طَلْح. (Ṣ.) — سِقَآءٌ منجوبٌ *A skin tanned with the same*: (Ṣ, Ḳ:) or *with* [*the kind of bark called*] نَجَبٌ: (Ḳ:) as also نَجَبِىٌّ (Ṣ, Ḳ) and مُنْجَبٌ: (Aboo-Mis-ḥal, Ḳ:) but the last is disapproved by ISd, because it is of the measure مُفْعَلٌ, which is not used in the sense of the measure مَفْعُولٌ. (TA.)

مُنْتَجَبٌ *Select; chosen; choice*: (Ḳ:) an epithet applied to anything. (TA.)

نجث

1. نَجَثَ, aor. ـُ, inf. n. نَجْثٌ; and ▼ تنجّث; (TA;) and ▼ انتجث and ▼ استنجث; (Ḳ;) *He extracted, drew out*, or *caused to come forth*, (Ḳ, TA,) a thing: apparently more especially used with reference to what is talked of, or news, tidings, or the like. (TA.) — نَجَثَ عَنْهُ, aor. ـُ, (and ▼ نَجَّثَ, inf. n. تَنْجِيثٌ, TA,) and ▼ تَنَجَّثَ; *He searched*, or *sought, for*, or *after, it*; *inquired respecting it; sought for information respecting it; searched into, inquired into, investigated, scrutinized*, or *examined, it*; i. e. an affair. (Aṣ.) — نَجَثَ قَبْرًا, [aor. ـُ,] inf. n. نَجْثٌ, *He dug up the contents of a grave.* (TA, from a trad.) — فُلَانٌ يَنْجُثُ بَنِى فُلَانٍ, (inf. n. نَجْثٌ, L,) *Such a one seduces, misleads*, or *leads astray*, (يَسْتَغْوِى, Fr, Ṣ, Ḳ, or, accord. to A'Obeyd, يَسْتَغْوِى, with the unpointed

ع م, i.e., *summons, by a cry, to sedition, or the like,* Ṣ,) *and implores aid of, the sons of such a one.* (Fr, Ṣ, Ḳ.) [See 10 in art. عو.]

5. تنجّث الأَخْبَارَ *He searched, or sought, for, or after, news, or tidings.* (TA.) [See also 1.]

6. تَنَاجَثُوا [*They revealed secrets, one to another*]: تَنَاجُثٌ signifies the *same as* تَبَاثٌّ, (Ḳ,) and تَبَاحُثٌ. (TA.) — تناجثوا [*They searched, investigated, scrutinized, or examined, together*]: تَنَاجُثٌ signifies the same as تَبَاحُثٌ. (TA.)

8. انتجث *He, or it, became inflated.* (Ḳ.) — انتجث *His fatness became apparent.* (Ḳ.) One says انتجثت الشَّاةُ *The ewe became fat.* (TA.) — See also 1.

10. استنجث شَيْئًا *He exposed himself to a thing; or ventured upon it:* (Ṣ, Ḳ, TA:) *he devoted himself eagerly to it, and set about it, or commenced it.* (TA.) — See also 1.

نَجْثٌ and ▼ نُجُثٌ *A coat of mail;* syn. دِرْعٌ. (Ḳ.) — Also, (or ▼ نُجُثٌ, Ṣ,) The *pericardium;* syn. غِلَافُ القَلْبِ: (Ṣ, Ḳ:) pl. أَنْجَاثٌ. (Ṣ.) — The *house* (بَيْت) of a man: pl. أَنْجَاثٌ. (Ḳ.)

نَجَّاثٌ: see نَجِثٌ.

نُجُثٌ: see نُجُثٌ.

نَجِيثٌ ‡ *A hidden secret.* (Ḳ.) — See نَجِيثَةٌ. — بَدَا نَجِيثُ القَوْمِ *The secret of the people, which they concealed, became apparent, or revealed.* (Fr, Ṣ.) — أَتَانَا نَجِيثُ القَوْمِ *The affair of the people, which they kept secret, came to our knowledge.* (TA.) — See نَجِيثَةٌ. — نَجِيثٌ *What attains its utmost aim* (ما بلغ), *of praise, or of an encomium.* (TA.) — نَجِيثٌ *A butt at which one shoots, or casts, consisting of earth collected together:* (Ṣ, Ḳ:) *or earth that is taken forth, and of which a butt is constructed, to shoot at, or cast at.* (TA.) — أَمْرٌ لَهُ نَجِيثٌ *An affair that has an evil end, conclusion, issue, or result.* (TA.) — نَجِيثٌ *A certain leguminous plant.* (Ḳ.) — نَجِيثٌ *Slow; tardy.* (Ḳ.) [See نَبِيثٌ.]

نَجِيثَةٌ (and ▼ نَجِيثٌ, TA) The *dust, or earth, that is taken forth, or dug out, from a well;* (Ṣ;) *i. q.* نَبِيثَةٌ. (Ṣ, Ḳ.) — نَجِيثَةٌ *What has become apparent, or manifest, of that which is foul, or disgraceful, of news, tidings, or information.* (Ṣ, Ḳ.) — نَجِيثَةٌ *Endeavour; effort:* (Ḳ:) as also نَكِيثَةٌ. (TA.) So in the phrase بَلَغَتْ نَجِيثَتُهُ [*His utmost endeavour, or effort, was exerted, or employed*]. (Ḳ.)

نَجَّاثٌ and ▼ نَجِثٌ One *who is in the habit of searching, or seeking, for, or after, things; of inquiring respecting them; of seeking for information respecting them; searching into, inquiring into, investigating, scrutinizing or examining, them:* (Ḳ:) a man *who searches after news, diligently, or with labour, or perseverance, or time after time, and elicits it;* (Aṣ;) as also نَجَّاثٌ عَنِ الأَخْبَارِ. (TA.)

نجح

1. نَجَحَتِ الحَاجَةُ, (Ṣ, Mṣb, Ḳ,) aor. ـَ; and ▼ انجحت, (Mṣb, Ḳ,) inf. n. إِنْجَاحٌ; (Mṣb;) *The want, or thing wanted, became attained, or accomplished.* (Ṣ, Mṣb, Ḳ.) — نَجَحَ, aor. ـَ; (Mṣb;) and ▼ انجح, (Ṣ, Mṣb, Ḳ,) inf. n. إِنْجَاحٌ; (Mṣb;) *He succeeded; he attained, or accomplished, his want, or wants, or the thing, or things, that he wanted.* (Ṣ, Mṣb, Ḳ.) — [You say,] مَا أَفْلَحَ فُلَانٌ وَلَا ▼ أَنْجَحَ *Such a one did not prosper, or succeed, nor attain, or accomplish, his want, or wants.* (Ṣ.) — نَجَحَ أَمْرُهُ *His affair became easy.* (Ṣ, Ḳ.)

4: See 1. — أَنْجَحْتُ حَاجَتَهُ, (Ṣ,) and أَنْجَحْتُهَا لَهُ, (TA,) *I accomplished for him his want.* (Ṣ, TA.) أَنْجَحَ اللّٰهُ حَاجَتَهُ *God accomplished for him his want:* (Ḳ:) or, *helped him to attain, or accomplish, it.* (TA.) — [So, أَنْجَحَ اللّٰهُ سَعْيَهُ *God made, or may God make, his work to succeed, prosper, or have a good issue or result.*] — انجح بِهِ *He, or it, overcame him.* (Ḳ.) Ex. إِذَا رُمْتَ البَاطِلَ أَنْجَحَ بِكَ ‡ *If thou seek what is vain, it will overcome thee.* (A.)

5. تنجّح الحَاجَةَ, and ▼ استنجحها, *He sought, asked, or demanded, the accomplishment of the want, or thing needed, from him who had promised him;* syn. تَنَجَّزَهَا. (Ṣ, Ḳ.) — ▼ استنجح اللّٰهَ [*He sought, or begged, of God, success, or the accomplishment of his want*]. (A.) See an ex. voce عَمَلٌ.

6. تَنَاجَحَتْ أَحْلَامُهُ, (Ṣ, A, Ḳ,) تناجحت عَلَيْهِ احلامه (ISd) ‡ *His dreams followed one another with truth:* (Ṣ, Ḳ:) *or the truth of his dreams was continuous:* (ISd:) *or he had consecutive true dreams.* (A, L.)

10: see 5.

نُجْحٌ and ▼ نَجَاحٌ, (Ṣ, Mṣb, Ḳ,) two substs., the former from نَجَحَ and the latter from أَنْجَحَ, (Mṣb,) *Success; or the attainment, or accomplishment, of one's wants,* (Ṣ, Mṣb,) *or, of a thing.* (Ḳ.) [See an ex. voce سَرَاحٌ.]

نَجَاحٌ: see نُجْحٌ.

رَأْىٌ نَجِيحٌ *Right counsel, advice, or opinion.* (Ṣ, Ḳ.) — سَيْرٌ نَجِيحٌ, (Ṣ, Ḳ,) and ▼ نَاجِحٌ, (Ḳ,) ‡ *A vehement pace:* (Ḳ:) *a quick pace.* (Ṣ.) — مَكَانٌ نَجِيحٌ, and ▼ نَاجِحٌ, † *A near place;* syn. وَشِيكٌ. (L.) — نَهْضٌ نَجِيحٌ ‡ *An energetic rising, or raising of one's self.* (L.) [You say,] نَهَضَ فِي هٰذَا الأَمْرِ نَهْضًا نَجِيحًا ‡ *He rose quickly to employ himself in this affair.* (A.) — See مُنْجِحٌ.

نَجَاحَةٌ *Patience.* (Ḳ.)

نَفْسٌ نَجِيحَةٌ *A patient mind.* (Ḳ.) — مَا نَفْسِى عَنْهُ بِنَجِيحَةٍ *My mind does not patiently refrain from it.* (L.)

أَمْرٌ نَاجِحٌ *An easy affair.* (Ṣ, Ḳ.) — See نَجِيحٌ.

مُنْجِحٌ A man *who attains, or accomplishes, his want, or wants;* pl. مَنَاجِحُ and مَنَاجِيحُ: (Ṣ, Ḳ:) as also ▼ نَجِيحٌ. (L, Ḳ.)

مَنَاجِحُ [a pl. of which the sing. is app. مَنْجَحَةٌ, meaning, acc. to analogy, *A cause of success, or of the attainment, or accomplishment, of one's wants, or of a thing:* see an ex. voce مَبَاجِحُ.] (A, TA, art. بجح.)

نجد

1. نَجَدَهُ, aor. ـُ, (Ṣ, L,) inf. n. نَجْدٌ, (L, Ḳ,) *He overcame, conquered, subdued, overpowered, prevailed over, or surpassed, him.* (AO, Ṣ, L, Ḳ.) — نَجَدَ رَأْيُهُ فِى الأُمُورِ, inf. n. نَجْدٌ, *He exerted his judgment in affairs.* (Sh, L.) — نَجُدَ, (Ṣ, M, &c.,) [aor. ـُ,] inf. n. نَجَادَةٌ (M, L, Ḳ) and نَجْدَةٌ, (Ḳ,) or the latter is a simple subst., (M, L,) *He* (a man, Ṣ, L,) *was, or became, courageous,* (Ṣ, M, L, Mṣb, Ḳ,) *and sharp, or vigorous and effective, in those affairs which others lack power or ability to accomplish:* (M, L, Ḳ:) or, *very valiant:* or, *quick in assenting to that which he was called or invited to do, whether it were good or evil.* (M, L.) See also 10, and 4. — نَجِدَ, aor. ـَ, inf. n. نَجَدٌ; (Ṣ, L;) or نُجِدَ, like عُنِىَ, inf. n. نَجْدٌ; (Ḳ;) *He became* [*overcome,*] *afflicted, distressed, or oppressed, by sorrow, grief, or anxiety.* (Ṣ, L, Ḳ.) — نَجِدَ, aor. ـَ, (Ṣ, L,) and ـِ, which is extr., (L,) [or properly the aor. of نَجُدَ,] inf. n. نَجَدٌ, (Ṣ, L,) *He* (a man, Ṣ) *sweated, by reason of work, or of sorrow, grief, or anxiety:* (Ṣ, L:) and ▼ أُنْجِدَ *he* (a man, TA) *sweated.* (Ḳ.) — نُجِدَ عَرَقًا, (Ḳ,) نَجِدَ عَرَقًا, (L,) *He,* (L,) or *it,* namely the body, (Ḳ,) *flowed with sweat.* (L, Ḳ.) — نَجِدَ, aor. ـَ, (TA,) inf. n. نَجَدٌ (Ḳ) *He was, or became, stupid, dull, wanting in intelligence; not penetrating, sharp, vigorous, or effective, in the performing of affairs; soft, without strength, or sturdiness, and without endurance: and weary, or fatigued.* (Ḳ, TA.) — نَجِدَ *He became*

terrified, or *frightened*. (L.) — نَجَدَ, (aor. ـُ, L,) inf. n. نُجُودٌ, *It* (a thing, or an affair,) *was*, or *became, apparent, manifest, plain*, or *evident*. (L, Ḳ.) — نَجَدَ, aor. ـُ, inf. n. نُجُودٌ, *It* (a road) *was*, or *became, apparent, manifest, conspicuous*, or *plain*. (L.) — أَعْطَاهُ الأَرْضَ بِمَا نَجَدَ مِنْهَا *He gave him the land with what came forth from it*. (L.)

2. نَجَّدَهُ الدَّهْرُ, (inf. n. تَنْجِيدٌ, Ḳ,) *Time*, or *habit*, or *fortune, tried*, or *proved, him, and taught him*, (Ṣ, L,) *and rendered him expert*, or *experienced, and well informed*, (L,) or *firm*, or *sound, in judgment*: (Ḳ:) as also نَجَذَهُ, which is more approved. (L.) — نَجَّدَ, inf. n. تَنْجِيدٌ, *He ran*; syn. عَدَا. (Ḳ.) — نَجَّدَ, inf. n. تَنْجِيدٌ, *He ornamented*, or *decorated*, a house or tent (بيت) *with the articles of furniture called* نُجُود, pl. of نَجْدٌ: (Ṣ,* L, Ḳ:*) [and, accord. to present usage, *he manufactured beds and the like, and pillows; and teased, separated*, or *loosened*, cotton, for stuffing beds, &c., *with the bow and mallet*: see also إِنْجَادٌ].

3. ناجدهُ *He went forth to him to fight*, or *combat*. (A.) — ناجدت الإِبِلَ *She* (a camel) *vied with the other camels in abundance of milk*: *she yielded abundance of milk when the other camels had little*. (L, Ḳ.*) — See 4.

4. انجد, (Ṣ, L, Mṣb, Ḳ,) inf. n. إِنْجَادٌ; (L;) and ▾ نَجَدَ, aor. ـُ; (Mṣb;) and ▾ ناجد, inf. n. مُنَاجَدَةٌ; (Ṣ, L;) *He aided*, or *assisted*, another: (Ṣ, L, Mṣb, Ḳ;) *he succoured* him. (L.) — انجدهُ عَلَيْهِ *He aided*, or *assisted, him against him*. (L.) — انجد الدَّعْوَةَ (Ṣ, L, Ḳ) *He answered*, or *complied with, the call, prayer*, or *invitation*. (L, Ḳ.) And انجدهُ الدَّعْوَةَ *He answered*, or *complied with, his call, prayer*, or *invitation*. (M, L.) — انجد *He was*, or *became*, or *drew, near to his family*, or *wife*; expl. by قَرُبَ مِنْ أَهْلِهِ. (Lḥ, ISd, Ḳ.) — انجدت السَّمَآءُ *The sky became clear*. (Ḳ.) — انجد (L, Ḳ) and ▾ تنجّد (Ḳ) *He*, or *it*, (a person, or thing, L, both said of such a thing as a mountain, TA,) *became high*, or *lofty*. (L, Ḳ.) — غَارَ وَأَنْجَدَ † *He became famous in the low countries and in the high*. (A.) — انجد, (inf. n. إِنْجَادٌ, L,) *He entered upon the country of Nejd*: (Ṣ, L:) or *he came to Nejd*, or *to high land or country*: (L, Ḳ:) or *he went thither*: (L:) or *he went forth to*, or *towards, it*. (Lḥ, ISd, L, Ḳ.) — أَنْجَدَ مَنْ رَأَى حَضَنًا, a proverb, *He enters Nejd who sees Ḥadan*, which is the name of a mountain; i. e., in going up from El-Ghowr, or El-Ghór. (Ṣ, L.)

5. تنجّد: see 4. — *He swore a big oath*. (L.)

10. استنجدهُ *He asked*, or *desired, of him aid*, or *assistance*, (Ṣ, L, Ḳ,*) *and succour*. (L.) — استنجد *He* (a man) *became strong after having been weak*, (Ṣ, L, Ḳ,) or *sick*. (TA.) — استنجد عَلَيْهِ, (Ṣ, L,) and بِهِ, (L, TA,) *He became emboldened against him*, (Ṣ, L, Ḳ,) *and clave to him*, (L,) *after having regarded him with awe*, or *fear*. (Ṣ, L, Ḳ.) — استنجد *He became courageous after having been cowardly*. (A.) See also نَجُدَ.

نَجْدٌ *High*, or *elevated, land* or *country*: (Ṣ, L, Mṣb, Ḳ:) or *hard, and rugged, and elevated*, or *high, table-land*: only *stony and rugged*, or *hard, elevated land, like a mountain, standing over against one and intercepting his view of what is behind it, but not very high*, is thus called: (L:) pl. أَنْجُدٌ, (Ṣ, L, Ḳ,) a pl. of pauc., (TA,) and أَنْجَادٌ, (L, Ḳ,) [also a pl. of pauc.,] and نِجَادٌ and نُجُودٌ (Ṣ, L, Ḳ) and نُجُدٌ; (IAạr, L, Ḳ;) and pl. of نُجُودٌ, أَنْجِدَةٌ; [another pl. of pauc.;] (Ṣ, Ḳ;) or this is a mistake, and it is pl. of نِجَادٌ, like as أَحْمِرَةٌ is pl. of حِمَارٌ; or it is a pl. deviating from common rule. (IB, L.) You say أُعْلُ هَاتِيكَ النِّجَادَ *Ascend thou these high lands*; and هَاذَاكَ النِّجَادَ *this high land*, making it singular. (L.) — نَجْدٌ, (Ṣ, L, Ḳ, &c.,) and نَجُدٌ, (Ḳ,) the latter of the dial. of Hudheyl, (Akh,) of the masc. gender, [*The high land*, or *country*;] *a division of the country of the Arabs; opposed to* الغَوْر, [or the low country,] i. e., Tihámeh; *all the high land from Tihámeh to the land of El-'Irák*; (Ṣ, L;) *above it are Tihámeh and El-Yemen, and below it El-'Irák and Esh-Shám*; (Ḳ;) *it begins, towards El-Ḥijáz, at Dhát-'Irḳ*, (Mṣb, Ḳ,) *and ends at Sawád of El-'Irák*, and hence it is said to form no part of El-Ḥijáz: (Mṣb:) or *it comprises all that is beyond the moat*, or *fosse, which Kisrà made to the Sawád of El-'Irák until one inclines to the Ḥarrah* (الحَرَّة), *when he is in El-Ḥijáz*; (El-Báhilee, T, L, Mṣb;) *and it extends to the east of El-Ghowr*, or *El-Ghór*; which is all the tract of which the torrents flow westwards: Tihámeh extends from Dhát-'Irḳ to the distance of two days' journey beyond Mekkeh: the tract beyond this, westward, is Ghowr, or Ghór; and beyond this, southwards, is Es-Saráh, as far as the frontiers of El-Yemen: (El-Báhilee, L:) or, as the Arabs of the desert have been heard to say, *the country which one enters when, journeying upwards, he leaves behind him 'Ijliz, which is above El-Ḳaryateyn, and which he quits when he descends from the mountain-roads of Dhát-'Irḳ, where he enters Tihámeh, and when he meets with the stony tracts termed* حِرَار *in Nejd, where El-Ḥijáz commences*: (Aṣ, L:) or *the high country from Baṭn-er-Rummeh to the mountain-roads of Dhát-'Irḳ*: (ISk, L:) or *the country from El-'Odheyb to Dhát-'Irḳ, and to El-Yemámeh, and to El-Yemen, and to the two mountains of Ṭeiyi, and from El-Mirbed to Wejreh*: Dhát-'Irḳ is the beginning of Tihámeh, extending to the sea and Juddeh: El-Medeeneh is not of Tihámeh nor of Nejd, but of El-Ḥijáz, higher than El-Ghowr, or El-Ghór, and lower than Nejd. (IAạr, L.) — نَجْدٌ *An elevated road*: (Ṣ:) or *an elevated and conspicuous road*. (L, Ḳ.) *A road in a mountain*. (L.) [Hence طَلَّاعُ الأَنْجُدِ, expl. below, and in art. طلع.] — هَدَيْنَاهُ النَّجْدَيْنِ [Kur, xc. 10] *We have shown him the two ways*; the way of good and that of evil: (Beyḍ, Jel, L:) or *the two conspicuous ways*: (L:) — or *We have given him the two breasts*; (Beyḍ, L;) for نَجْدٌ also signifies *a woman's breast*; (L, Ḳ;) the belly beneath it being like the [country called] غَوْر. (TA.) — أَمَا وَنَجْدَيْهَا مَا فَعَلْتَ ذٰلِكَ *Now, by her two breasts, didst thou not that?* A form of oath of the Arabs. (MF.) — نَجْدٌ and ▾ نَاجِدٌ A thing, or an affair, *apparent, manifest, plain*, or *evident*. (L.) — طَلَّاعُ أَنْجِدَةٍ and هُوَ طَلَّاعُ أَنْجُدٍ, (Ṣ, L, Ḳ,) and طَلَّاعُ نِجَادٍ, (L, Ḳ,) and الأَنْجُدِ, (Ḳ, art. طلع,) and النِّجَادِ, (L, Ḳ,) ‡ *He is one who surmounts difficult affairs*: (A:) or *he is one who manages affairs thoroughly*, (L, Ḳ,) *and masters them*: (L:) or *he is a man expert in affairs, who surmounts and masters them by his knowledge and experience and excellent judgment*: or, *who aims at lofty things*: (Ḳ, art. طلع:) or *he is one who rises to eminences, or to lofty things or circumstances, or to the means of attaining such things*: (Ṣ:) as also طَلَّاعُ الثَّنَايَا. (Ṣ, Ḳ, art. طلع.) See نَجِدٌ, and مُنَاجِدٌ. — نَجْدٌ, sing. of نُجُودٌ (A'Obeyd, Ṣ, L, Ḳ) and of نِجَادٌ, (L, Ḳ,) which signify *The articles of household furniture and the like* (مَتاع) *with which a house or tent* (بيت) *is ornamented*, or *decorated*; (A'Obeyd, Ṣ, L;) *the carpets and beds or other things that are spread, and the pillows, used for that purpose*: (L, Ḳ:) *the cloths or stuffs used for this purpose, with which the walls are hung, and which are spread*; (L;) *the curtains which are hung upon the walls*: (A:) and أَنْجَادٌ, pl. of نَجْدٌ, *household furniture, consisting of such things as are spread, and pillows, and curtains*. (L.) — نَجْدٌ *A skilful*, or *an expert*, guide of the way. (L, Ḳ.) — نَجْدٌ, (Ḳ,) or ▾ نُجُدٌ, (L,) *A place in which are no trees*. (L, Ḳ.) — نَجْدٌ *A kind of tree resembling the* شُبْرُم (L, Ḳ) *in its colour and manner of growth and its thorns*. (L.)

نَجْدٌ *Sweat*, (Ṣ, L, Ḳ,) *by reason of work*, or *of sorrow, grief*, or *anxiety*, &c. (L.) — النَّجَدَاتُ *A certain sect of the Khárijees*, (Ṣ, L,) *of those called the Ḥarooreeyeh*; (L;) *the companions*, (Ṣ, Ḳ,) or *followers*, (L,) *of Nejdeh Ibn-'Ámir* (Ṣ, L, Ḳ) *El-Ḥarooree* (L) *El-Ḥanafee*, (Ṣ, L, Ḳ,) *of the Benoo-Ḥaneefeh*; (TA;) *also called* ▾ النَّجْدِيَّةُ. (TA.)

نَجُدٌ : see نَجِدٌ.

نَجْدٌ and ▼ نَجُدٌ and ▼ نَجِيدٌ (Ṣ, M, L, Ḳ) and ▼ نَجْدٌ (M, L, Ḳ) A *courageous man,* (Ṣ, M, L, Ḳ,) *sharp,* or *vigorous and effective, in those affairs which others lack power* or *ability to accomplish:* (M, L, Ḳ:) or *courageous and strong:* (Mṣb:) or *very valiant:* or *quick in assenting to that which he is called* or *invited to do, whether it be good* or *evil:* (M, L:) pl. of نَجْد, أَنْجَادٌ, like as أَيْقَاظٌ is pl. of يَقُظٌ; (Ṣ, L;) or this is pl. of نَجْدٌ and نَجِدٌ; (Sb, M, L;) and not of نَجِيدٌ: (M, L:) the pl. of this last is نُجُدٌ and نُجَدَآءُ. (Ṣ, L.) — ▼ النَّجِيدُ *The lion:* (Ḳ:) so called because of his courage. (TA.) — نَجْدٌ فِى الحَاجَةِ A man *quick in accomplishing that which is wanted,* or *needed.* (Ṣ, L.) — نَجِدٌ and ▼ مَنْجُودٌ (L) and ▼ نَجِيدٌ (TA) and ▼ نَاجِدٌ, in which last the ا is perhaps inserted by poetic licence, (L,) *Sweating, by reason of work,* or *of sorrow, grief,* or *anxiety, &c.* (L, TA.) See also مَنْجُودٌ.

نَجُدٌ : see نَجْدٌ.

نَجْدَةٌ, a simple subst. (M, L,) *Courage,* (Ṣ, M, L, Mṣb, Ḳ,) *and sharpness,* or *vigour and effectiveness, in those affairs which others lack power* or *ability to accomplish:* (M, L:) or *courage with steadiness, and calmness in awaiting fearlessly death, victory,* or *martyrdom:* (Esh-Shiháb [El-Khafájee]:) or *great valour:* or *quickness in assenting to that which one is called* or *invited to do, whether it be good* or *evil.* (M, L.) — ذُو نَجْدَةٍ A man *possessing valour.* (Ṣ, L.) See مُنَاجِدٌ. — نَجْدَةٌ *Fight; combat; battle.* (L, Ḳ.) — *Terror; fright.* (L, Ḳ.) — *Difficulty; distress; affliction; adversity:* (Lḥ, Ṣ,* L, Mṣb,* Ḳ:*) pl. نَجَدَاتٌ (Mṣb.) Ex. لَاقَى فُلَانٌ نَجْدَةً *Such a one experienced difficulty, distress, trouble,* or *adversity.* (Lḥ, Ṣ, L.) — See also a saying of Ṣakhr-el-Ghei, and a citation from a trad., voce رِسْلٌ. — نَجْدَةٌ *Aid; assistance.* (Mṣb.) — هُوَ آبْنُ نَجْدَتِهَا ‡ *He is ignorant thereof:* contr. of هو ابن بَجْدَتِهَا. By نجدة is meant an allusion to Nejdeh El-Ḥarooree. (A.) See نَجْدٌ.

نِجْدَةٌ, with kesr, *Trial,* or *affliction,* (بَلَآءٌ) [*experienced*] *in wars.* (Esh-Shiháb [El-Khafájee] and TA.)

النَّجْدِيَّةُ : see نَجْدٌ.

نِجَادٌ The *suspensory cords* or *strings of a sword:* (Ṣ, Ḳ:) or the *part thereof that lies upon the shoulder.* (L.) — طَوِيلُ النِّجَادِ [lit., *Having long suspensory cords* or *strings to his sword,*] means ‡ a man *of tall stature:* for when a man is tall his نجاد must be long. (L.)

نَجُودٌ, applied to a she-ass, and to a she-camel, *Long-necked:* (L, Ḳ:) or, so applied, (Ḳ,) or specially to a she-ass, (L,) or to a wild she-ass, (Ṣ,) *that does not become pregnant:* (Ṣ, L, Ḳ:) but Sh says, that this meaning is disapproved; and that the correct meaning is *tall,* applied to a she-ass: (L:) or *tall; overpeering:* (Ṣ, L:) or *high and great:* from نَجْدٌ [signifying "high or elevated land"]: (Aṣ, L:) pl. نُجُدٌ. (Ṣ, L, Ḳ.) — Also, applied to a she-camel, *Sharp; spirited; vigorous:* (L, Ḳ:) a correct meaning thus applied: (Sh:) or *strong:* (R:) one *that precedes,* or *outgoes, others:* (L, Ḳ:) or *strong in spirit:* (L:) pl. as above. (Ḳ.) — Also, so applied, *Abounding with milk:* (L, Ḳ:) and, *that vies with the other camels in abundance of milk,* (L, Ḳ,) *and surpasses them therein,* (L,) or *yields abundance when they have little:* (Ḳ:) [but for اذا غَرُزْنَ, in the copies of the Ḳ in my hands, meaning "when they yield abundance of milk," I read اذا غَرَزْنَ:] pl. as above. (Ḳ.) — Also, so applied, *That lies down upon a high,* or *elevated, place:* (Ḳ:) or *that will not lie down save upon high ground:* (L:) pl. as above. (Ḳ.) — Also, An *intelligent* woman; *sharp,* or *quick, in intellect:* (Ḳ:) *possessing judgment;* as though she exerted her judgment in affairs: a strange meaning in which the word is used in a trad.: (Sh, L:) pl. as above. (Ḳ.) — See مَنْجُودٌ, and مُنَاجِدٌ. — نَجُودٌ *One who works in shaking and spreading and stuffing and arranging* [*those articles of household furniture which are called*] نُجُود [pl. of نَجْدٌ]. (M, L.) See also نَجَّادٌ.

نَجِيدٌ : see نَجْدٌ, and مَنْجُودٌ.

نَجَّادٌ *One who manufactures* (يُعَالِجُ) *beds and the like, and pillows; and sews them:* (Ṣ, L, Ḳ:) [and, accord. to present usage, *who teases, separates,* or *loosens, cotton, for stuffing beds &c., with the bow and mallet:* as also ▼ مُنَجِّدٌ:] *one who ornaments,* or *decorates, houses, and beds and the like, and carpets.* (AHeyth, L.) See also نَجُودٌ.

نَاجِدٌ and ▼ مَنْجُودٌ *Stupid, dull, wanting in intelligence; not penetrating, sharp, vigorous,* or *effective, in the performing of affairs; soft, without strength,* or *sturdiness, and without endurance: and weary,* or *fatigued.* (TA.) — See نَجِدٌ.

نَاجِدَةٌ, sing. of نَوَاجِدُ (L,) which signifies *Streaks of fat* (L, Ḳ) upon the shoulders of a camel: occurring in a trad.: so called because of their elevation. (L.)

نَاجُودٌ *Wine:* (Aṣ, L, Ḳ:) or *excellent wine:* or the *first wine that comes forth when the clay is removed from the mouth of the jar:* (Aṣ, L:) of the masc. gender. (L.) — *A wine-vessel:* (Ḳ:) *any vessel into which wine is put,* (A'Obeyd, Ṣ, Ḳ,*) *such as a* بَاطِيَة, (L,) or *a* جَفْنَة *&c.:* (A'Obeyd, Ṣ, L:) or *a wine-cup,* or *a cup of wine;* syn. كَأْسٌ: (L:) or *a vessel in which wine is cleared;* (A;) *a clarifier,* or *strainer for wine;* syn. رَاوُوقٌ; (Lth, L;) which last is the meaning that most assign to the word. (TA.) — *Saffron.* (Aṣ, L, Ḳ.) — *Blood.* (Aṣ, L, Ḳ.)

مِنْجَدٌ *A small mountain* (Ḳ, [in the CḲ, for جُبَيْل is put حُبَيْل,]) *overlooking a valley.* (TA.) — مِنْجَدٌ *A kind of ornament,* (L, Ḳ,) *worn by women,* (L,) *adorned with gems,* or *jewels,* (L, Ḳ,) *one over another:* (L:) *a necklace of pearls and gold,* or *of cloves, a span in breadth, extending from the neck to the part beneath the breasts, and lying upon the place of the* نِجَاد; (L, Ḳ;) i. e. of the نجاد of a man's sword: from نَجَّدَ البَيْتَ: (L:) pl. مَنَاجِدُ. (L, Ḳ.)

مِنْجَدَةٌ *A light staff* or *stick with which a beast of carriage is urged on.* (Ḳ.) — *A stick,* or *wooden instrument, with which wool is teased,* or *separated, i. q.* مِنْدَفٌ (?) (TA,) *and with which the* حَقِيبَة *of a camel's saddle is stuffed.* (Ḳ, TA.)

مِنْجَادٌ A man *who aids,* or *assists, much* or *well.* (Lḥ, L.)

مَنْجُودٌ *Overcome; conquered; subdued; overpowered:* and *fatigued.* (L.) — مَنْجُودٌ and ▼ نَجِيدٌ (and ▼ نَجُودٌ applied to a female, R,) *Afflicted, distressed,* or *oppressed, by sorrow, grief* or *anxiety.* (Ṣ, L, Ḳ.) See also نَجِدٌ. — مَنْجُودٌ *In a state of perishing* or *destruction.* (L, Ḳ.) — See نَاجِدٌ.

مُنَجَّدٌ, as also مُنَجِّدٌ, (Ṣ, L,) which latter is the more approved, (L,) A man *tried and strengthened by experience; expert,* or *experienced;* (Ṣ, L, Ḳ;) *who has had experience in affairs, and has estimated and understood them, and become well informed.* (L.)

مُنَجِّدٌ : see نَجَّادٌ.

مُنَاجِدٌ *A fighter; a combatant.* (Ṣ, L, Ḳ.) — *An aider; an assistant;* (Ḳ;) [and so, app., ▼ نَجْدٌ and ▼ نَجْدَةٌ and ▼ نَجُودٌ, mentioned in the A].

نجذ

1. نَجَذَهُ, aor. ـِ, (TK,) [or ـُ, accord. to the rule of the Ḳ,] inf. n. نَجْذٌ, (L, Ḳ,) *He bit him,* or *it,* (L, Ḳ,) *with the* نَاجِذ, which is the *tooth next behind the canine tooth:* [but see this word:] (L:) or, *with the* نَوَاجِذ. — نَجَذَهُ (inf. n. نَجْذٌ, TḲ,) ‡ *He importuned him in asking:* نَجْذٌ signifies also *vehement speaking.* (Ḳ.)

2. نجّذه † *It* (experience) *strengthened him:*

(A:) or *tried and strengthened him.* (Ṣ, L.) Suheym Ibn-Wetheel says,

• وَنَجَّذَنِى مُدَاوَرَةُ الشُّؤُونِ •

[*And the applying myself to the management of affairs has tried and strengthened me*]. (Ṣ, L.) See 3, in art. دور. And see نجد.

ناجذ sing. of نَوَاجِذُ, which signifies The *furthest of the* أَضْرَاس [or *molar teeth*], (Ṣ, A, L, Mṣb, Ḳ,) of a man; (Ṣ, Mṣb;) which are four in number, (Ṣ, L, Mṣb, Ḳ,) next after the أَرْحَآء; (L;) also called أَضْرَاسُ الحُلُمِ, [or the *teeth of puberty*, and أَضْرَاسُ العَقْلِ, or the *wisdom-teeth*,] (Ṣ, Mgh, L, Mṣb,) because they grow after the attaining to puberty, and the completion of the intellectual faculties: (Ṣ, L, Mṣb:) or all the اضراس [or *molar-teeth*]: or the *teeth next behind the canine teeth:* (L, Mṣb, Ḳ:) *altogether four in number:* (L, Mṣb:) or the *canine teeth:* (L, Mṣb, Ḳ:) which last, accord. to Th, (L, Mṣb,) or the last but one, accord. to IAth, (L,) is the signification meant in the trad. (respecting Mohammad, L.) ضَحِكَ حَتَّى بَدَتْ نَوَاجِذُهُ [*He laughed so that his* نواجذ *appeared*]; (L, Mṣb;) because Mohammad's utmost laugh was slight; or this is a hyperbolical expression, not meant to be literally understood; for the signification of نواجذ most commonly obtaining is the first of those given above: (L:) the phrase also signifies *he laughed violently,* or *immoderately:* (Ṣ, L:) the term نواجذ is also sometimes used in relation to the horse, (Ṣ, L,) or a solid-hoofed animal, as well as man; (Bári', Mṣb;) and they are [termed] the أَنْيَاب in a soft-footed animal such as the camel; and the سَوَالِغ in a cloven-hoofed animal. (Ṣ, L.) See also سِنّ. — عَضُّوا عَلَيْهَا بِالنَّوَاجِذِ ‡ *They held her fast, as one holds fast in biting with all his grinders.* (L, from a trad.) — أَبْدَى نَاجِذَهُ † *He was immoderate in his laughter:* and, *in his anger.* (A.) — عَضَّ عَلَى نَاجِذِهِ † *He attained to the age of puberty;* or *of manly vigour;* or *of firmness,* or *soundness, of judgment:* (A, L, Ḳ:*) and *he became patient, and firm, vigorous,* or *hardy, in the management of affairs.* (L.) — بَلَغَ فِى العِلْمِ وَغَيْرِهِ بِنَاجِذِهِ † *He made his knowledge, &c., sound,* or *firm.* (A.) — بَدَتْ نَوَاجِذُهُ *His* نواجذ *appeared* by reason of anger or of laughter. (L.)

مُنَجَّذٌ † A man (Ṣ, L) *tried and strengthened by experience; expert,* or *experienced:* (T, Ṣ, L, Ḳ:) or (so in the L; in the Ḳ, and) *who has experienced probations, trials,* or *calamities,* (Lḥ, L, Ḳ,) *and thus become a vigorous manager of affairs.* (TA.) See also مُنَجَّدٌ.

مَنَاجِذُ [*Moles*]: used as pl. of جُلْذٌ, (L, Ḳ,) and of خُلْدٌ. (L, Ḳ, &c., art. خلد.)

نجر

نَجَرَ, (Ṣ, A, Mṣb,) aor. ـُ, (Ṣ, Mṣb,) inf. n. نَجْرٌ, (Ṣ, A, Mṣb, Ḳ,) *He worked* wood *as a carpenter; cut* or *hewed it; formed* or *fashioned it by cutting; cut it out; hewed it out; shaped it out;* syn. نَحَتَ; (Lth, Ṣ, A, Ḳ;) or, as some say, قَطَعَ. (TA.) — نَجَرَتْ, (TA,) [aor. as above, accord. to the rule of the Ḳ,] inf. n. نَجْرٌ, (Ḳ,) *She* (a woman) *made,* or *prepared, the kind of food called* نَجِيرَة, (Ḳ,* TA,) for her children, and her pastors. (TA.)

نَجْرٌ † The *shape,* or *form,* of a man [or beast]; his *appearance,* or *external state* or *condition:* (TA:) † *species; distinctive quality* or *property;* syn. لَوْنٌ; as also ▾ نِجَارٌ and ▾ نُجَارٌ: (Ṣ, TA:) ‡ *nature; natural* or *native disposition* or *temper* or *other quality* or *property;* (A, TA;) of a man [&c.]; as also ▾ نِجَارٌ or ▾ نُجَارٌ: (A [in my copy of the A written erroneously نَجَارٌ:]) his *place of growth;* as also نجار: (A:) *origin;* syn. أَصْلٌ; as also ▾ نِجَارٌ and ▾ نُجَارٌ: (Ṣ,* Ḳ:) *grounds of pretension to respect; rank* or *quality, nobility, honourableness,* or *estimableness;* syn. حَسَبٌ; (Ṣ,* TA;) as also ▾ نِجَارٌ (Ṣ,* Mṣb, TA) and ▾ نُجَارٌ: (Ṣ, TA:) *generosity of mind* or *spirit* (A.) It is said in the prov.,

• كُلُّ نِجَارٍ إِبِلٍ نِجَارُهَا ▾ •
• وَنَارُ إِبِلِ العَالَمِينَ نَارُهَا •

Every species of camels is their species: (Ṣ:) or *every origin* &c.: (Ḳ:) [*and every mark of the camels of the various peoples of the world is their mark:* (the latter hemistich is omitted in the Ṣ, Ḳ, but inserted in the TA:)] the camels here mentioned by the poet were stolen from among a variety of camels, and comprised every species [with every mark]. (TA.) The proverb is applied to him who confounds things; (Ṣ;) and means, he has in him every sort of disposition, and has no opinion in which he is settled. (A'Obeyd, Ṣ, Ḳ.) [See Freytag's Arab. Prov., ii. 317. See also نَارٌ.]

نَجْرَانٌ The *piece of wood in which is the foot of a door:* (Ḳ:) or the *piece of wood upon which the foot of a door turns:* (Ṣ:) or the *foot of a door, upon which it turns:* (A:) or the دَرْوَنْد [a Persian word signifying a *bolt,* and a *hook,*] *of a door.* (IAạr, TA.) [Chald. נִגְרָא vectis, pessulus: (Golius:) which suggests that the original signification may be that assigned by IAạr: but the first and second and third are alone agreeable with the following verse.] AO, cites this ex.:

• صَبَبْتُ المَآءَ فِى النَّجْرَانِ حَتَّى •
• تَرَكْتُ البَابَ لَيْسَ لَهُ صَرِيرُ •

[*I poured water into,* or *upon, the* نجران, *so that I made the door to have no creaking*]. (Ṣ.)

نُجَارٌ and نِجَارٌ: see نَجْرٌ, throughout.

نُجَارَةٌ [*Cuttings, chips, parings, shavings,* or *the like, of wood;*] *what is cut,* or *hewn,* (Ḳ, TA,) *from wood,* (TA,) *when it is worked by the carpenter.* (TA.)

نِجَارَةٌ The *art of carpentry.* (Mṣb, Ḳ.)

نَجِيرَةٌ *Milk mixed with flour:* or *with clarified butter:* (Ḳ:) or, accord. to Abu-l-Ghamr El-Kilábee, *fresh milk to which clarified butter is added.* (Ṣ.) See خَزِيرَةٌ.

نَجَّارٌ *A carpenter.* (Ṣ, A, Mṣb, Ḳ.)

أَنْجَرٌ The *anchor of a ship,* (A, Ḳ,) *composed of pieces of wood,* (Ḳ, TA,) *which are put with their heads in contrary directions, and the middles of which are bound together in one place, after which,* (TA,) *molten lead is poured between them, so that they become like a rock;* (Ḳ, TA;) *the heads of the pieces of wood project, and to these are tied ropes; then it is lowered in the water,* (TA,) *and when it becomes fast, the ship becomes fast:* (Ḳ, TA:) it is a Persian word, (TA,) arabicized, from لَنْگَر: (Ḳ, TA:) [or from the Greek ἄγκυρα:] accord. to the T, a word of the dial. of El-'Irák. (TA.) You say هُوَ أَثْقَلُ مِنْ أَنْجَرٍ *He is heavier than an anchor.* (A.)

إِنْجَارٌ: see إِنْجَازٌ.

مَنْجُورٌ *Wood worked, cut, hewed, formed,* or *fashioned by the carpenter.* (A.)

نجز

1. نَجِزَ, aor. ـَ, (Ṣ, Ḳ,) inf. n. نَجَزٌ; (Ṣ;) and نَجَزَ, aor. ـُ, (Ḳ,) inf. n. نَجْزٌ; (TḲ;) *It* (a thing, Ṣ, TA,) *came to an end; came to nought; perished, passed away:* (Ṣ, Ḳ, TA:) in these senses, the former is the more chaste, and has been so generally used that the latter has been said to be not allowable; but both have been heard. (TA.) *It* (a speech or discourse) *finished,* (Ḳ, TA,) *and became complete.* (TA.) *He* (a man) *died:* (Ṣ:) occurring in a verse of En-Nábighah Edh-Dhubyánee: as related by J, نَجِزَ; but as related by A'Obeyd, نَجَزَ. (TA.) — نَجَزَ الوَعْدُ, (A, Mgh, Mṣb, Ḳ,) aor. ـُ, (Mṣb, Ḳ,) inf. n. نَجْزٌ; (Mṣb;) and نَجِزَ, aor. ـَ, (Ḳ;) inf. n. نَجَزٌ; (TḲ;) *The promise came to pass, and was accomplished:* (A, Mgh:) or *the promise was prompt,* or *quick, in taking effect:* (Mṣb:) or *the thing promised* (TḲ) *came, arrived,* or *became present:* (Ḳ, TA:) in this sense, the former is the more chaste; but both have been heard. (TA.) — نَجَزَ is also trans.: see 4, in four places.

2: see 4.

3. نَاجَزَهُ, (Mgh,) or نَاجَزَهُ القِتَالَ, (A,) inf. n. مُنَاجَزَةٌ, (Ṣ, A, Mgh, Ḳ,) *He fought him:* (Ḳ:) or *he went,* or *came, out,* or *forth, in the field, to fight him,* (Ṣ, Mgh, Mṣb,) *and fought him:* (Ṣ, Mgh:) or *he* (a horseman) *went,* or *came, out,* or *forth, into the field, to fight him,* (another horseman,) *and they strove together until each of them slew the other,* or *until one of them was slain:* (TA:) and ▼ تَنَاجَزُوا signifies the same as مُنَاجَزَةٌ: (Ḳ:) you say, تَنَاجَزَ القَوْمُ, meaning, *The people contended together in the mutual shedding of blood;* as though they hastened in doing so. (TA.) [Hence the saying,] إِنْ رُمْتَ المُحَاجَزَةَ فَقَبْلَ المُنَاجَزَةِ [*If thou desire the reciprocal prevention of fighting, and the making of peace, let it be before fighting*]: (A:) or المُحَاجَزَةُ قَبْلَ المُنَاجَزَةِ (Ṣ, Ḳ) [*the reciprocal prevention of fighting, and*] *the making of peace,* [should be] *before the striving together,* (المُعَالَجَة, as in the CḲ,) or *hastening,* (المُعَاجَلَة, as in some copies of the Ḳ and in the TA, and, accord. to the latter, المُسَارَعَة,) *in fighting:* (Ḳ, TA:) a proverb: (Ṣ, TA:) relating to the prudence of him who hastens to flee from him whom he has not power to withstand: (Ḳ:) or applied to him who seeks peace after fighting. (A'Obeyd, Ḳ.) —— Also, *He contended with him in an altercation; disputed with him; litigated with him.* (TA.)

4. انجز حَاجَتَهُ, (Ḳ,) inf. n. إِنْجَازٌ; (TA;) and ▼ نَجَزَهَا, (ISk, Ṣ, Ḳ,) aor. ـُ, inf. n. نَجْزٌ (ISk, Ṣ) and نَجَازٌ, or this is a subst. in the sense of إِنْجَازٌ, like عَطَآءٌ in that of إِعْطَآءٌ; (Ḥar, p. 326;) *He accomplished his want:* (ISk, Ṣ, Ḳ:) and ▼ نَجَزْتُهُ حَاجَتَهُ *I accomplished for him his want.* (A.) —— انجز الوَعْدَ, (A, Mgh, CḲ,) and ▼ نَجَزَهُ, (Ṣ,) *He fulfilled,* or *performed, the promise:* (Ṣ,* A,* Mgh, CḲ:) or *he made the promise to be prompt,* or *quick, in taking effect.* (Mṣb.) You say also, انجز عَلَىَّ المَوْعِدَ *He fulfilled to me the promise;* (Ḳ, accord. to the TA;) as also ▼ نَجَزَ: (TA:) and ▼ نَجَزْتُهُ بِهِ *I made it to be prompt,* or *quick in taking effect to him.* (Mṣb.) [Hence the saying,] أَنْجَزَ حُرٌّ مَا وَعَدَ (Ṣ, Ḳ) *An ingenuous man fulfils what he promises:* a proverb: (TA:) alluding to the fulfilment of a promise: and sometimes, to the asking, or demanding, the fulfilment thereof: El-Ḥárith the son of 'Amr said to Ṣakhr the son of Nahshal, "Shall I guide thee to booty and one fifth of it be for me?" and he answered, "Yes:" so he guided him to some people from El-Yemen, and Ṣakhr made a sudden attack upon them, and engaged with them in conflict, and overcame, and obtained booty; and when he turned back, El-Ḥárith said to him the above words, and Ṣakhr fulfilled his promise to him. (Ḳ.) —— انجز عَلَى القَتِيلِ *He hastened and completed,* or *made certain, the slaughter of the slain man; i. q.* أَجْهَزَ عَلَيْهِ. (Abu-l-Miḳdám Es-Sulamee and Ḳ.)

5: see 10, in five places.

6: see 3.

10. استنجز حَاجَتَهُ, and ▼ تنجّزها, *He sought,* or *asked,* or *demanded, the accomplishment of his want, from him who had promised him;* (Mṣb;) syn. إِسْتَنْجَحَهَا. (Ṣ, Ḳ.) And استنجز الوَعْدَ, and ▼ تنجّزها, (Mgh,) or العِدَةَ, (Ḳ,) *He sought,* or *asked,* or *demanded, the fulfilment of the promise:* (Mgh, Ḳ:) and العِدَةَ ▼ تنجّزه *he asked of him the fulfilment of the promise.* (TA.) Hence, ▼ تَنَجُّزُ البَرَاآتِ *The demanding and receiving of immunities.* (Mgh.) You say also, إِسْتَنْجَزْتُ مِنْهُ كِتَابًا, and تَنَجَّزْتُهُ, [app. meaning, *I sought,* or *asked,* or *demanded, of him the finishing,* or *completion, of a writing,* or *letter,* or *book.*] (A.)

نَجْزٌ and ▼ نُجْزٌ are syn. You say, أَنْتَ عَلَى نَجْزِ حَاجَتِكَ, and ▼ نُجْزِ حَاجَتِكَ, *Thou art on the point of accomplishing thy want.* (Ṣ, Ḳ.)

نُجْزٌ: see نَجْزٌ.

نَجِيزٌ: see نَاجِزٌ, in three places.

نَجِيزَةٌ *A recompense.* You say, لَأَنْجِزَنَّ نَجِيزَتَكَ *I will assuredly pay thy recompense.* (TA.)

نَاجِزٌ *Coming to an end; coming to nought; perishing; passing away.* (TA.) —— [*Complete: accomplished.*] —— A promise *that has been fulfilled;* as also ▼ نَجِيزٌ: (TA:) or *that has come to pass, and is accomplished.* (A, Mgh.) —— *Present; ready;* (Ṣ, Mṣb, Ḳ, TA;) as also ▼ نَجِيزٌ: (Ḳ:) and ▼ both, *promptly,* or *quickly, done,* or *given.* (TA.) You say, بِعْتُهُ نَاجِزًا بِنَاجِزٍ (Ṣ, A, Mgh, Mṣb) [*I sold it,* or *I sold to him,*] *present,* or *ready,* [merchandise,] *for present,* or *ready,* [money,] (TA,) like يَدًا بِيَدٍ, (Ṣ, A, Mgh, Mṣb,) i. e., تَعْجِيلًا بِتَعْجِيلٍ. (Ṣ.) And لَا يُبَاعُ غَائِبٌ بِنَاجِزٍ, meaning, *A debt to be paid at a future time shall not be sold for ready money.* (Mgh.) And نَاجِزٌ بِنَاجِزٍ is a proverb, [meaning *Ready* merchandise *with ready* money,] like يَدٌ بِيَدٍ, and عَاجِلٌ بِعَاجِلٍ. (TA.) It is said in a trad., بِيعُوا حَاضِرًا بِنَاجِزٍ [*Sell ye present merchandise for ready money*]. (Ṣ.) And a poet ('Abeed Ibn-El-Abraṣ, TA, art. كلأ,) says,

وَإِذَا تُبَاشِرُكَ الهُمُو •
مُ فَإِنَّهَا كَالٍ وَنَاجِزْ •

(Ṣ, TA, ubi supra;) [*And when griefs attend thee,* know that] *they are, some, debts to be payed at future periods, and some, payments in ready money.* (TA, ubi supra.) The saying [of 'Abd-Allah Ibn-'Ámir El-Ḳurashee, owner of a horse named Esh-Shamoos, (TA, art. شمس,)]

جَرْىَ الشَّمُوسِ نَاجِزًا بِنَاجِزِ •

[app. meaning, Quickly *as the running of Esh-Shamoos; ready with ready,* or *prompt with prompt;*] is explained by IAạr, as meaning, Thou hast given an evil recompense and I have recompensed thee in like manner: or, as he says in one place, this is said when one does a thing and thou dost the like thereof; he not being able to go beyond thee in word or in deed. (TA.) [Respecting this saying, Freytag says, in his Arab. Prov., i. 305, (where, for نَاجِزًا we find نَاجِزٌ,) that it applies to him who is equal to the execution of the things which he undertakes, as well good as bad: and that جَرَى is to be supplied before جَرْىَ.]

نجس

1. نَجِسَ, aor. ـَ; (Ṣ, Mṣb, Ḳ;) and نَجَسَ, aor. ـُ; (Mṣb;) and نَجُسَ, aor. ـُ, (Ḳ,) accord. to some, but the books of good repute are silent respecting this last; (Mṣb;) inf. n. نَجَسٌ, (Ṣ, Mṣb, TA,) of the first; (Mṣb;) and نَجَاسَةٌ, (TA,) or this last is a simple subst. [as the verb نَجُسَ to which by rule it should belong is not of good authority]; (Mṣb;) *It was,* or *became, unclean, dirty, filthy,* or *impure;* (Mṣb;) [i. e.,] *contr. of* طَهِرَ, or طَهُرَ: (Mṣb, Ḳ:*) نَجَاسَةٌ is of two kinds; one kind is perceived by sense; and one kind is perceived by the mind; of which latter kind is that which is attributed, in the Ḳur, ix. 28, to those who assert God to have associates: (Er-Rághib, B:) but in this latter sense, it is said by Z, to be tropical. (TA.) [See also نَجَاسَةٌ below.] You also say, (of a garment, A, Mṣb,) ▼ تنجّس, meaning, *It was,* or *became, rendered unclean, dirty, filthy,* or *impure.* (A, Mṣb, Ḳ.) —— نَجَّسَ, [app. an inf. n. of which the verb is نَجَسَ,] The *making a child's* عُوذَة [or *amulet, of any of the kinds described below, voce* تَنْجِيسٌ]. (TA.)

2. نجّسهُ, (Ṣ, A, Mṣb, Ḳ,) inf. n. تَنْجِيسٌ, (TA,) *He rendered him,* or *it, unclean, dirty, filthy,* or *impure;* (A, Mṣb, Ḳ;) and ▼ انجسهُ signifies the same. (Ṣ, A, Ḳ.) El-Ḥasan said of a man who married a woman with whom he had committed fornication, هُوَ أَنْجَسَهَا ▼ فَهُوَ أَحَقُّ بِهَا [*He defiled her, therefore he is most worthy of her*]. (A, TA.*) —— نَجَّسَتْهُ الذُّنُوبُ ‡ [*Sins,* or *crimes, defiled him*]. (A, TA.) —— نَجَّسَ لَهُ, and نَجَّسَهُ, *He charmed him;* or *fortified him by a charm* or *an amulet* [*of any of the kinds described below, voce* تَنْجِيسٌ, q.v.]; syn. عَوَّذَهُ. (TA.)

4: see 2, in two places.

5. تنجّس: see نَجِسَ. —— *He did a deed whereby to become free from uncleanness, dirt, filth,* or *impurity;* (Ḳ;) like as you say تَأَثَّمَ and تَحَرَّجَ and تَحَنَّثَ, meaning, he did a deed whereby to become free from crime, sin, &c. (TA.)

نَجْسٌ : ⎫
نِجْسٌ : ⎬ see نَجِسٌ.
نَجَسٌ : ⎪
نَجُسٌ : ⎭

نَجَسٌ and ▼ نَجِسٌ (Ṣ, A, O, Mṣb, Ḳ) and ▼ نَجُسٌ and ▼ نَجْسٌ and ▼ نِجْسٌ (A, O, Ḳ) *Unclean, dirty, filthy,* or *impure:* (A, Mṣb, Ḳ:) the last of these is only used when the word is preceded or followed by رِجْسٌ: (ISd:) or only when it is preceded by رِجْسٌ: (Fr, Ṣ,* and Ḥar in the Durrat-el-Ghowwáṣ:) but this remark correctly applies only to the greater number of instances: (M, F:) the second of the above five forms is an inf. n. used as an epithet; (A, Mṣb;) and is [therefore] used as sing. and dual. and pl. and masc. and fem., without variation: (TA:) [and the first and last are also used as pls., as will be seen below; but when so used, I suppose قَوْمٌ or some other coll. gen. n. to be understood:] the pl. [of every one of the other forms] is أَنْجَاسٌ (A, Mṣb, TA) and [of the fourth and fifth, and perhaps of the first and third also, though I do not remember similar instances,] نِجْسَةٌ. (TA.) [See also نَجَاسَةٌ, below.] نَجَسٌ and ▼ نَجِسٌ [&c.], applied to a man, signify *Unclean,* &c., [both properly and tropically]. (TA.) [The two following examples are said in the A to be tropical.] ‡ اَلنَّاسُ أَجْنَاسٌ وَأَكْثَرُهُمْ أَنْجَاسٌ [*Men are of several kinds, and most of them are unclean.*] (A, TA.) And ‡ إِنَّمَا ٱلْمُشْرِكُونَ نَجَسٌ [*Verily the associaters of others with God are but unclean*], said in the Ḳur, [ix. 28,] (Ṣ, A, TA,) or نَجِسٌ, or ▼ نِجْسٌ, accord. to certain readers. (TA.) — Also, all the above forms, A man *having an incurable disease.* (TA.) — See also نَاجِسٌ.

نُجُسٌ : see مُنَجِّسٌ.

نِجَاسٌ : see تَنْجِيسٌ.

نَجِيسٌ : see نَاجِسٌ.

نَجَاسَةٌ : see 1: *Uncleanness, dirtiness, filthiness,* or *impurity.* (Mṣb.) — In the conventional language of the law, *A particular uncleanness, of such a kind as renders prayer invalid; as urine,* and *blood,* and *wine.* (Mṣb.)

نَجِسٌ and ▼ نَجِيسٌ (Ṣ, A, Ḳ) and ▼ نَجِسٌ and دَآءٌ نَاجِسٌ (TA) *An incurable disease:* (Ṣ, Ḳ, TA:) or *a disease that baffles the* مُنَجِّسُون. (A.) See مُنَجِّسٌ.

أَنْجَسُ [*More,* and *most, unclean, dirty, filthy,* or *impure*]. You say, لَا تَرَى أَنْجَسَ مِنَ ٱلْكَافِرِ ‡ [*Thou wilt not see any one more unclean than the unbeliever*]. (A, TA.)

تَنْجِيسٌ The *name of a thing, either something unclean,* or *bones of the dead,* or *a menstruous rag, which used to be hung upon him for whom there was a fear of the jinn's,* or *genii's, being attached to him:* (Ḳ:) or the *hanging of some such thing upon such a person, as a child* or *any other; for they used to say that the jinn would not approach those things:* (TA:) or *a thing which the Arabs used to do, as an amulet, to drive away thereby the* [*evil*] *eye:* (Ṣ:) ▼ مُنَجِّسَةٌ also is the name of *a kind of amulet:* (IAạr:) and ▼ نِجَاسٌ is syn. with تَعْوِيذٌ; [by which may be meant either that it signifies *an amulet,* or that it is a quasi-inf. n. of 2; for it is said that] it is app. a subst. from نَجَّسَ لَهُ, or نَجَّسَهُ, as signifying عَوَّذَهُ. (IAạr.) See also 2.

مُنَجِّسٌ One *who hangs, upon him for whom there is fear, unclean things, such as bones of the dead, and the like, to drive away the jinn,* or *genii; because these beings shun such things;* (Ṣ,* A, TA;) one *who fortifies by charms* or *amulets* [*of the kinds above mentioned*]; syn. مُعَوِّذٌ: (Ḳ:) pl. مُنَجِّسُونَ: (A:) and ▼ نُجُسٌ [a pl. of which the sing. is not mentioned] is syn. with مُعَوِّذُونَ. (IAạr.) — Also, *A little piece of skin that is put upon the notch* [*which is the place*] *of the bow-string.* (TA.)

مُنَجِّسَةٌ : see تَنْجِيسٌ.

نجش

1. نَجَشَ, aor. ـُ, (Ṣ, Mṣb,) inf. n. نَجْشٌ, (Ṣ, Mṣb, Ḳ,) *He concealed himself.* (Mṣb.) — [And hence, *He pursued* game, or objects of the chase: (see نَاجِشٌ:) or] *he roused* game, or objects of the chase, (Ṣ, Mgh, Ḳ,) *and scared them from place to place.* (TA.) You say also, نَجَشُوا عَلَيْهِ ٱلصَّيْدَ, meaning, *They scared the chase,* or *game, towards him, and drove and collected it to him.* (TA.) — *He searched after* a thing, *and roused* it. (Sh, A'Obeyd, Ḳ.) This, accord. to Sh, is the primary signification: [but accord. to Fei, the primary signification is the first given above:] and hence the saying in a trad., لَا تَطْلُعُ ٱلشَّمْسُ حَتَّى تَنْجُشَهَا ثَلَثُمِائَةٍ وَسِتُّونَ مَلَكًا *The sun does not rise until three hundred and sixty angels rouse it.* (TA.) — *He drew forth, educed,* or *elicited.* (Ḳ.) — *He collected together* (Ṣ, Ḳ) camels [&c.] *after a state of dispersion.* (Ṣ.) — *He drove vehemently.* (TA.) — نَجَشَ, aor. ـُ, (Mṣb, TA,) inf. n. نَجْشٌ (Ṣ, A, Mgh, Mṣb, Ḳ) and نَجَشٌ, [which is the form generally used by the professors of practical law,] (ISh, Mgh, Ṣgh, TA,) or this is a simple subst., (Mṣb,) *He demanded the sale of an article of merchandise for more than its price,* (A, Mgh, Mṣb,) *not meaning to purchase it,* (Mgh, Mṣb,) *in order that another might see him and fall into the snare thus laid for him:* and in like manner it is used with respect to marriage, [i.e., with respect to dowers,] and other things: (A, Mgh, Mṣb:) and the doing thus is forbidden: (Mgh:) it is from نَجَشَ signifying "he roused" game: (Mgh:) or from the same verb signifying "he concealed himself;" because he who does so conceals his intention: (Mṣb:) or *he augmented the price of an article of merchandise, not desiring to purchase it, but in order that another might hear him and augment in the same manner:* (A'Obeyd, L:) or *he outbade in a sale, in order that another might fall into a snare, he himself not wanting the thing:* (Ṣ:) or *he augmented the price of an article of merchandise,* or *praised it, in order that another might see that, and be deceived by him:* (Ibráheem El-Ḥarbee:) or *he praised an article of merchandise belonging to another in order that he might sell it,* or *dispraised it in order that it might not be easy for him to sell it:* (ISh:) or *he concurred with a man desiring to sell a thing, by praising him:* (Abu-l-Khaṭṭáb, Ḳ:) or *he bargained with a man desiring to sell a thing, offering him a large price, in order that another might see him and fall into a snare:* or *he scared people from one thing to another:* (Ḳ:) also, *he praised a thing;* or *praised it exceedingly,* or *for that which was not in it,* or *excessively and falsely;* syn. مَدَحَ شَيْئًا and أَطْرَاهُ: and *he invented,* or *forged, a lie.* (TA.) It is said in a trad., (Ṣ,) ▼ لَا تَنَاجَشُوا, (Ṣ, Mgh, Mṣb,) i.e., *Ye shall not practise* نَجْش, or نَجَش: (Mgh, Mṣb:) or ▼ تَنَاجُشٌ signifies the *bidding one against another, successively increasing their offers, in a sale, or other case;* (Ḳ;) for it sometimes signifies the doing so *in the case of a dowry, in order that the doing so may be heard, and the amount may consequently be augmented:* (TA:) and Sh mentions, with respect to ▼ تَنَاجُشٌ, on the authority of Aboo-Sa'eed, another thing, which is allowable, namely, [that it signifies the *conspiring to promote the marrriage of*] *the woman who has been married and divorced time after time;* and [*the sale of*] *the article of merchandise that has been bought time after time and then sold.* (TA.)

6: see 1, last part.

نَجَشٌ, said to be a subst. from نَجَشَ: see 1.

نَجُوشٌ : ⎫
نَجِيشٌ : ⎭ see نَاجِشٌ.

اَلنَّجَاشِىُّ — see نَاجِشٌ. نَجَاشِىٌّ and اَلنَّجَاشِىُّ, (Ṣ, Mgh, Ḳ,) the form preferred by El-Fárábee, (Mgh,) and اَلنَّجَاشِىُّ, (Mgh, Mṣb, Ḳ,) which is the more common, (Mṣb,) but the former is the more chaste, (Ṣgh, Ḳ,) and [اَلنِّجَاشِىُّ and اَلنِّجَاشِى] with kesr to the ن, which is said to be the more chaste, (Ḳ,) and is preferred by Th, (TA,) but teshdeed of the ج is a mistake, (Mgh, MF,) *The name of the King of the Abyssinians;* (IDrd, Ṣ;) *like as one says* كِسْرَى *and* قَيْصَرُ; an Abyssinian word: (IDrd:) or *a certain King of the Abyssinians, whose name was* أَصْحَمَةُ; (Mgh, Mṣb, Ḳ;) [as is commonly said; but authors differ respecting his name;] and IḲt says, that النجاشى is in Coptic اصحمة, meaning "a gift:" (TA:) or originally the proper name of an individual, and afterwards a common title. (MF.)

نَجَّاشٌ: see نَاجِشٌ, in four places.

نَجَّاشِىٌّ: see نَاجِشٌ, in two places.

نَاجِشٌ *A pursuer,* or *capturer,* or *insnarer, of game,* or *objects of the chase;* (Mṣb;) as also ▾ نَجِيشٌ and ▾ نَجَّاشٌ; (Ibn-'Abbád, Ḳ;) because he conceals himself: (Mṣb:) or [نَاجِشٌ and] ▾ نَجُوشٌ and ▾ نَجَّاشٌ signify *one who rouses the game,* or *objects of the chase;* (Az, TA;) and so ▾ مِنْجَشٌ and ▾ مِنْجَاشٌ: (L:) or نَاجِشٌ and ▾ نَجَاشِىٌّ (Akh, Ḳ) [and ▾ نَجَاشِىٌّ accord. to some copies of the Ḳ] and ▾ مِنْجَاشٌ (Az, Ḳ) *one who rouses them in order that they may pass by the pursuer,* or *capturer,* or *insnarer, thereof:* (Akh, Az, Ḳ:) or نَاجِشٌ signifies *one who scares them towards him, and drives and collects them to him:* (Ṣ, A, TA:) and ▾ نَجَّاشٌ *one who drives vehemently;* (TA;) or *one who urges camels;* (A;) or *who collects them after a state of dispersion:* (Ṣ:) and ▾ نَجَّاشِىٌّ [with teshdeed to the ج as well as to the ى,] *one who drives,* or *urges, travelling-camels and other beasts of carriage, in the market-place, to elicit their qualities of pace:* (AA, TA:) and this last also signifies [absolutely] *one who draws forth,* or *elicits, a thing.* (A'Obeyd, TA.) ═ Also, *One who practises* نَجْشٌ, or نَجَشٌ, *in an affair of buying and selling:* (Mṣb, TA:*) [see 1:] and ▾ نَجَّاشٌ *one who does so much, or often.* (Mṣb.)

مِنْجَشٌ: } see نَاجِشٌ; the latter, in two
مِنْجَاشٌ: } places.

قَوْلٌ مَنْجُوشٌ *A saying drawn forth,* or *elicited:* (TA:) and *a forged saying, in which is falsehood.* (IAạr, TA.)

نجص

إِنْجَاصٌ: see art. أجص.

[نجع, &c.
See Supplement.]

نح

1. نَحَّ, aor. ـُ, inf. n. نَحِيحٌ, *He* (a man) *reiterated a sound,* or *made it to reciprocate,* (رَدَّدَهُ,) *in his inside:* (Ṣ, L:) or *his voice was reiterated,* or *made to reciprocate,* (تَرَدَّدَ,) *in his inside;* as also ▾ نَحْنَحَ and ▾ تَنَحْنَحَ: (Ḳ:) [each of these verbs, of which the last seems to be the most common, signifies, as is implied in the L &c., and accord. to present usage, *he made a reiterated humming in his throat, like a slight coughing,* or, as some say, *more violent than coughing;* as is often done by a niggard when he is asked for a thing:] التَّنَحْنُحُ is well known, (Ṣ,) and النَّحْنَحَةُ is like it; (Lth, Ṣ;) it is [*the making a sound,* or *sounds, in the throat,*] *slighter than coughing;* and is the pretence of the niggard: (Lth:) *or it is more violent than coughing;* as also النَّحِيحُ. (L.) See also جرة. — [Hence, from the sound employed,] نَحَّ, aor. ـُ, *He incited,* or *urged on,* a camel. (Ḳ.)

R. Q. 1. See نَحَّ. — نَحْنَحَهُ *He repulsed him* (namely an asker, or a beggar, L) *in a foul,* or *an abominable, manner.* (L, Ḳ.)

R. Q. 2: see نَحَّ.

نَحَاحَةٌ *Niggardliness; avarice.* (Ḳ.) — Also, contr., *Liberality; bounty; munificence; generosity.* (Ḳ.)

شَحِيحٌ نَحِيحٌ [*Very niggardly,* or *avaricious*]: the latter word is an imitative sequent: (Ṣ, Ḳ:) or it is a corroborative syn. of the former: (MF:) as though meaning one who when asked for something, disliking to give it, has recourse to a pretence, and makes a reiterated breathing [or humming in his throat] as a feint to hide his unwillingness. (L.) [See also نَحَانِحَةٌ.]

نَحْنَحٌ: see نَحَانِحَةٌ.

نَحَانِحَةٌ *Niggardly,* or *avaricious,* men: *base, ungenerous, mean,* or *sordid,* men, *who make a reiterated humming in the throat* (يَتَنَحْنَحُونَ) *when they are asked for something:* (A:) pl. of ▾ نَحْنَحٌ: or a pl. having no sing. (TA.) [See also نَحِيحٌ.]

نحب

1. نَحَبَ, aor. ـُ, inf. n. نَحْبٌ; (Ṣ, A, Ḳ;) and ▾ نَحَّبَ, inf. n. تَنْحِيبٌ; (A;) *He vowed; made a vow;* (Ṣ, Ḳ;) *put himself under an obligation to do a thing.* (A.) — نَحَبَ, aor. ـُ, inf. n. نَحْبٌ, *He laid a bet,* or *wager; betted,* or *wagered.* (Ḳ.) [The explanation of the inf. n. by مُرَاهَنَةٌ, in the Ḳ, seems to imply that it is the same as 3; but this appears to be doubtful.] ═ نَحَبَ, aor. ـِ, (Ṣ, Mṣb,) or ـُ, (Ḳ,) inf. n. نَحِيبٌ, (Ṣ, Ḳ,) or this is a subst., (Mṣb,) and نَحْبٌ; (Ḳ;) and ▾ انتحب; (Ṣ, Ḳ;) ‡ *He raised his voice with weeping,* or *wailing; wept,* or *wailed, loud;* (Ṣ;) *wept,* or *wailed, most violently;* (M, Ḳ;) *wept,* or *wailed, with prolonged voice.* (TA.) — نَحَبَ, aor. ـِ, (Ṣ, Ḳ,) inf. n. نُحَابٌ (Ṣ) and نَحْبٌ (Ḳ) *He* (a camel, Ṣ) *had a cough,* or *coughed.* (Ṣ, Ḳ.) ═ نَحَبَ, [aor. ـُ,] inf. n. نَحْبٌ, *He went, travelled,* or *journeyed, at a quick pace:* (AA, Ṣ, Ḳ:) or *with a light pace:* (Ḳ:) *with much exertion and perseverance.* (TA.) [The inf. n. only is mentioned, and said, in the Ṣ, to be syn. with نَعْبٌ.]

2: see 1. ═ نَحَّبوا, inf. n. تَنْحِيبٌ, ‡ *They strove,* or *exerted themselves, in their work; worked with energy:* (AA, Ṣ, Ḳ:) or *they went on, travelled,* or *journeyed,* (*with energy,* TA,) *until they came near to the water:* (Ḳ:) *they made a hard journey by night, in order to arrive at the water on the morrow.* (Ṣ.) — نَحَّبْنَا سَيْرَنَا *We pursued our journey laboriously,* or *with energy.* (TA.) — نحّب السَّفَرُ فُلَانًا † *The journey harassed such a one,* (Ḳ,) *being long.* (TA.) — نحّب عَلَى أَمْرٍ, and فِى أَمْرٍ, ‡ *He applied himself to a thing,* or *set about it, and adhered to it.* (TA.)

3. ناحبهُ, (inf. n. مُنَاحَبَةٌ, TA,) *He laid a bet,* or *wager, with him,* (Ḳ,) عَلَى أَمْرٍ *respecting a thing.* (TA.) — نَاحَبْتُهُ إِلَى فُلَانٍ *I cited him,* or *invited him, to submit our case to such a one as judge; I cited him before such a one as judge.* (Ṣ, Ḳ.) — ناحبه *I contended with him,* or *disputed with him, for glory,* or *honour,* or *superiority in glorious* or *honourable qualities and the like,* (Ḳ,) *before a judge,* or *umpire.* (TA.) — Talḥah said to Ibn-'Abbás, هَلْ لَكَ فِى أَنْ أُنَاحِبَكَ وَتَرْفَعَ النَّبِىَّ (Ṣ) [or تَرْفَعُ النبى: for I find it stated in the margin of a copy of the Ṣ, that J left the final letter of ترفع without a vowel point, either fet-ḥah or ḍammeh:] *Wilt thou that I contend with thee,* or *dispute with thee, for glory,* or *honour,* and that thou enumerate thine excellencies and the honour which thou derivest from thine ancestors &c., I doing the like, *and that thou put the Prophet out of the question,* not mentioning thy relationship to him, since this excellence is conceded to thee? (AM.)

6. تناحبوا *They appointed together a time,* لِلْقِتَالِ *for fighting;* and sometimes for other purposes. (Ḳ.)

8: see 1. — *He sighed vehemently;* (Ḳ;) *wept and sighed vehemently.* (TA.)

نَحْبٌ *A vow.* (Ṣ, Ḳ.) — قَضَى نَحْبَهُ *He died:* or *he was slain in an expedition undertaken for the sake of God's religion:* originally meaning *he accomplished his vow:* see Ḳur, xxxiii. 23: (Mṣb:) as though he had constrained himself [by a vow] to fight until he died: (TA:) or it signifies *he ended his term,* or *period of life; ended his days:* (Fr, Zj:) [or *he finished his time:* (as implied in the Ṣ): or *he yielded his soul:* or *he accomplished his want:*] from significations given below. (TA.) — نَحْبٌ *A great bet, or wager:* syn. خَطَرٌ عَظِيمٌ. (Ḳ.) So in the following verse of Jereer:

• بِطِخْفَةَ جَالَدْنَا المُلُوكَ وَخَيْلُنَا •
• عَشِيَّةَ بِسْطَامٍ جَرَيْنَ عَلَى نَحْبِ •

[*In Tikhfeh we contended with the sword with the kings; and our horses, in the evening of Bisṭám, ran for a great bet*]. (TA.) — نَحْبٌ *A proof; a demonstration; an evidence:* syn. بُرْهَانٌ. (Ḳ.) — *A necessity; want; needful thing; an object of want or need:* syn. حَاجَةٌ. (Ḳ.) See قَضَى نَحْبَهُ. — ‡ *Death.* (Ḳ.) See قَضَى نَحْبَهُ, above. — *A term; fixed period;* the *period of life.* (Ḳ.) See قَضَى نَحْبَهُ, above. — The *soul:* syn. نَفْسٌ. (AO, Ḳ.) — *Mind; purpose; aspiration; desire; ambition:* syn. هِمَّةٌ. (Ḳ.) ═ خِمْسٌ نَحْبٌ *A laborious journey:* syn. دَائِبٌ. (Ṣ.) — سَيْرٌ نَحْبٌ, (TA,) and ▼ سير مُنَحِّبٌ (Ḳ) ‡ *A quick pace,* or *journey.* (Ḳ, TA.) — The same epithets are likewise applied, in the same sense, to a man. (TA.) — نَحْبٌ *A quick* (or *light,* Ḳ,) *pace,* or *mode of going, travelling,* or *journeying,* (AA, Ṣ, Ḳ,) *with much exertion and perseverance.* (TA.) — سَارَ فُلَانٌ عَلَى نَحْبٍ *Such a one went on; travelled,* or *journeyed, with energy;* [lit., *for a great bet,* or *wager;*] as though he had laid a [great] bet, and therefore strove, or exerted himself. (Ṣ.) — نَحْبٌ *Length.* (AA, Ḳ.) — يوم نحب [so in the TA: perhaps, يَوْمُ نَحْبٍ, but more probably يَوْمٌ نَحْبٌ] *A long day.* (Er-Riyáshee.) — نَحْبٌ *A space of time: a time.* (Ṣ, Ḳ.) See قَضَى نَحْبَهُ, above. — *Sleep:* syn. نَوْمٌ. (L, Ḳ: in some copies of the Ḳ, يَوْمٌ. TA.) — *Fatness.* (Ḳ.) — I.q. شِدَّةٌ [*Vehemence; violence; &c.:* or *distress; difficulty; adversity; &c.*]. (Ḳ.) — *A game of hazard:* syn. قِمَارٌ. (Ḳ.) ═ A *great* camel. (Ḳ.) Perhaps a mistake for نَجْبٌ. (TA.)

نُحْبَةٌ ‡ i.q. قُرْعَةٌ [*A lot* used in sortilege: or *lots* collectively: or *sortilege* itself;] (Ḳ;) from نَاحَبَهُ "he cited him before a judge;" "he contended with him for glory;" and "he laid a bet, or wager, with him;" because it is, as it were, a judge, or that which decides, in a case of sortilege. (TA.) — لَوْ عَلِمَ النَّاسُ مَا فِي الصَّفِّ الأَوَّلِ لَاقْتَتَلُوا عَلَيْهِ وَمَا تَقَدَّمُوا إِلَّا بِنُحْبَةٍ [*If men knew what* advantage *is attained by being in the first row of* the congregation in the mosque, *they would fight for it, and not advance but by lot*]. (TA, from a trad.)

نُحَابٌ *A cough that attacks camels:* as also نُحَازٌ and قُحَابٌ. (As from AZ.) See 1.

نَاحِبَةٌ ‡ *A weeping,* or *wailing, woman:* pl. نَوَاحِبُ. (TA.)

سَارَ سَيْرًا مُنَحِّبًا *He proceeded,* or *journeyed, in a direct course, not desiring* [*to pursue*] *any other:* as though he had made a vow to do so. El-Kumeyt says,

• تَخِذْنَ بِنَا عَرْضَ الفَلَاةِ وَطُولَهَا •
• كَمَا صَارَ عَنْ يُمْنَى يَدَيْهِ المُنَحِّبُ •

By المنحّب is meant the man. ISd says, Th cites this verse, and says in explanation of it, This was a man who swore, saying, If I do not overcome, I will cut off my hand. He seems to consider it as implying the signification of vowing. So in the L. But it requires consideration. (TA.) — سِرْنَا إِلَيْهَا ثَلَاثَ لَيَالٍ مُنَحِّبَاتٍ *We proceeded,* or *journeyed, thither during three nights of laborious travelling.* (TA.)

نحت

1. نَحَتَ, aor. ـَ, (Ṣ, L, Ḳ,) contr. to analogy, (TA,) and ـِ, (L, Ḳ,) which is the form preferred by IJ, because of the guttural letter, but this is disputed by MF, (TA,) and ـُ, (Ḳ,) which is the form of weakest authority, (TA,) inf. n. نَحْتٌ, (Ṣ,) *He cut,* or *hewed; formed,* or *fashioned, by cutting; cut out, hewed out,* or *shaped out; chipped:* syn. بَرَى: (Ṣ, Ḳ:) *he worked* wood and the like *as a carpenter;* syn. نَجَرَ: *he pared, peeled, barked,* or *deprived of its outer covering by paring, abrasure,* or *wearing away the exterior: he sawed.* (L.) [See also نَكَتَ.] Accord. to some, the operation termed نحت is only performed upon something hard and strong, as stone and wood and the like. (MF.) [▼ انتحت seems to signify *He cut, &c., for himself:*] you say, اِنْتَحِتْ مِنَ الخَشَبِ مَا يَكْفِيكَ لِلْوَقُودِ [*Cut,* or *hew, for thyself, of the wood, what will suffice thee for fuel*]. (A.) — نَحَتَ بَيْتًا فِي الجَبَلِ, aor. ـِ and ـَ, inf. n. نَحْتٌ, *He cut out,* or *hewed out, a house in the mountain.* In the Ḳur, xv. 82, El-Ḥasan [El-Baṣree] reads يَنْحَتُونَ. (Mṣb.) [Accord. to the Ḳ, his reading is يَنْحَاتُونَ, (in the CḲ, تَنْحَاتُونَ,) but this I find nowhere else, and I believe it to be a mistake.] — نُحِتَ عَلَى الكَرَمِ ‡ [*He was fashioned after the model of generosity; made by nature generous*]. (A.) — نَحَتَ *Inivit* puellam: (Ḳ:) as also نَكَتَ; but the latter is the better known. (TA.) — نَحَتَ, inf. n. نَحْتٌ, ‡ *He beat, struck,* or *smote,* him with a staff, or stick: (TA:) [as also نَكَتَ]. — نَحَتَ *He threw* him *down prostrate.* (Ḳ.) — نَحَتَ بِلِسَانِهِ ‡ *He blamed; reprehended; reviled* a man. (L.) [See also نَكَتَ.] — نَحَتَ ‡ *It* (a journey, or travel,) *emaciated* a camel: (Ḳ:) *it made* a man *less; made him thin,* or *slender.* (TA.) — نَحَتَ, (TA,) [aor. ـِ and ـَ?] inf. n. نَحِيتٌ and نَحِيتَةٌ, *He sighed aloud:* the inf. ns. syn. with نَئِيتٌ and زَحِيرٌ. (Ḳ.)

8: see 1. — انتحت ‡ *It* (wood or the like) *was* [*cut,* or *hewn; formed,* or *fashioned, by cutting; cut out, hewed out,* or *shaped out; chipped;*] *worked* by a carpenter: [*pared, peeled, barked,* or *deprived of its outer covering: sawn*]. (L.) — انتحت مَنَاسِمُهُ ‡ *His* (a camel's) مناسم [i.e. *toes* or *feet*] *were worn, abraded, wasted, lessened,* or *attenuated.* (L.)

نَحْتٌ and ▼ نُحَاتٌ (Ḳ) and ▼ نَحِيتَةٌ (Ṣ, Ḳ) ‡ *Nature; natural,* or *native, disposition, temper,* or *other property;* (Ṣ, Ḳ;) *a particular cast,* or *fashion, of constitution, after which a man is* [*as it were*] *cut out* [*by the Creator*]: (TA:) and the first, the *source,* or *origin, from which one is* [*as it were*] *cut out:* [see also ▼ مَنْحَتٌ]. (Lḥ.) — الكَرَمُ مِنْ نَحْتِهِ *Generosity is* [*a part*] *of his nature;* or, [*derived*] *from his source,* or *origin.* (Lḥ.) — هُوَ عَجِيبُ النَّحْتِ *He is of a wonderful nature.* (TA.) — هُوَ كَرِيمُ ▼ النَّحِيتَةِ *He is generous in nature,* or *disposition.* (AZ.) ═ بَرْدٌ نَحْتٌ *Unmixed* [i.e. *severe*] *cold:* (Ḳ:) but this is said to be a corruption of بَحْتٌ. (TA.) [See also نُحَاتٌ.]

نَحِيتٌ *A comb:* syn. مُشْطٌ or مِشْطٌ. (So in different copies of the Ḳ.) ═ حَافِرٌ نَحِيتٌ *A hoof of which the edges have gone* [or *become abraded, been worn away*]; (Ṣ, Ḳ;) [and so ▼ حافر مَنْحُوتٌ, occurring in the Ḳ in art. حلك, where, in its place in the Ṣ, we find حافر نَحِيتٌ.] — نَحِيتٌ ‡ An *emaciated* camel: (Ḳ:) a camel *whose feet are worn, abraded,* or *wasted.* (L.) — ▼ نَحِيتَةٌ *A* [*portion of the*] *trunk of a tree, which is hewn out, and hollowed, in the form of a jar such as is called* حُبٌّ, *for bees:* pl. نُحُتٌ. (L.) — نَحِيتٌ Anything *bad;* what is *bad* of anything. (L.) ═ نَحِيتٌ One *who introduces himself among a people, and lives with them, not being of their race.* (Ṣ, Ḳ.)

نُحَاتٌ: see نَحْتٌ.

نُحَاتَةٌ *Cuttings, chips, parings, and the like,* (Ṣ, Ḳ,) of wood [&c.]. (TA.)

نَحِيتَةٌ: see نَحْتٌ and نَحِيتٌ.

مَنْحَتٌ ‡ The *source,* or *origin,* of a man, [from which he is, as it were, cut out]: pl. مَنَاحِتُ. (TA.) See also نَحْتٌ. — هُوَ مِنْ مَنْحَتِ صِدْقٍ *He is of an excellent source,* or *origin.* (A.) — هُمْ كِرَامُ المَنَاحِتِ *They are of generous sources,* or *origins.* (A.)

مِنْحَتٌ (Ṣ, Ḳ) and ▼ مِنْحَاتٌ (Mṣb, TA) *An implement with which one performs the operation of cutting, hewing, and the like;* (Ṣ, Ḳ, L;) *an adz, or addice.* (Mṣb.)

مِنْحَتٌ : see مِنْحَاتٌ.

فَرَسٌ مُنْحَتُ الحَوَافِرِ [*A horse having the hoofs much worn.*] (IDrd, Ḳ, art. حلك.)

مَنْحُوتٌ : see نَحِيتٌ. — *A word compounded of two* [or *more*] *words;* such as بَسْمَلَ, حَمْدَلَ, حَسْبَلَ, حَوْقَلَ, &c. (Mṣb, TA, art. بسمل.)

نحث

نَحِيثٌ dial. form of نَحِيفٌ: (Kr:) ISd thinks the ث to be a substitute for ف. (TA.)

نحر

1. نَحَرَ, (A, Mṣb, Ḳ,) aor. ـَ, (Mṣb, Ḳ,) inf. n. نَحْرٌ (Ṣ, Mṣb, Ḳ) and مَنْحَرٌ (Mṣb) and تَنْحَارٌ [an intensive form], (Ḳ,) *He stabbed, or stuck,* (A, Ḳ,) a camel, (A, TA,) or a beast, (Mṣb,) [but generally the former,] *in his* نَحْر, (A,) or *in his* مَنْحَر, (TA,) *where the windpipe* (حُلْقُوم) *commences in the uppermost part of the breast;* (Ḳ, TA;) [i.e., *in the* لَبَّة; for] نَحْرٌ in the لَبَّة is like ذَبْحٌ in the throat. (Ṣ.) [Hence,] يَوْمُ النَّحْرِ [*The day of the stabbing of the camels &c.*]; (Ḳ;) and عِيدُ النَّحْرِ [*the festival of the stabbing of the camels &c.*]; (Mṣb;) *the tenth of* [*the month*] *Dhu-l-Ḥijjeh;* (Ḳ;) because then the camels and cows and bulls brought as offerings to Mekkeh, for sacrifice, are stabbed. (TA.) — *He slew.* (TA.) — نَحَرَهُ, aor. and inf. ns. as above, *He hit, or hurt, his* نَحْر. (Ḳ.) You say نَحَرْتُ الرَّجُلَ *I hit, or hurt, the* نَحْر *of the man.* (Ṣ.) — [Hence,] نَحَرَ الأُمُورَ عِلْمًا ‡ [*He mastered affairs, or the affairs, by knowledge, or science*]: (A): *he knew affairs soundly, or thoroughly.* (Ḥar, 2nd ed. of Paris, p. 95, Com.) And يَنْحَرُ العِلْمَ نَحْرًا ‡ [*He masters knowledge, or science, indeed*]. (A, Ḳ.) Jereer was asked respecting the Islámee poets, and answered, نَبْعَةُ الشُّعَرَآءِ لِلْفَرَزْدَقِ [meaning, "The bow," or "the arrow, of the poets belongs to El-Farezdaḳ;" applying the term نبعة in this manner because bows and arrows were made of the tree called نَبْع]: so it was said, "Then what hast thou left for thyself?" and he answered, أَنَا نَحَرْتُ الشِّعْرَ نَحْرًا ‡ [*I have mastered poetry indeed*]. (A.) You say also, نَحَرْتُ الشَّىْءَ عِلْمًا † *I knew the thing thoroughly, or superlatively well;* as also قَتَلْتُهُ عِلْمًا. (Bḍ in iv. 156.) — [Hence also,] نَحَرَ الصَّلَاةَ ‡ *He performed, or recited, the prayer in the first part of its time.* (TA.) — نَحَرَهُمُ اللّٰهُ, occurring in a trad., may mean either † *May God hasten to do them good,* or *may God slay them.* (IAth.) — [Hence also,] نَحَرْتُ الرَّجُلَ, (Ṣ, A,) inf. n. نَحْرٌ, (A,) ‡ *I became opposite to the man;* syn. صِرْتُ فِى نَحْرِهِ. (Ṣ;) *I faced, or fronted, him;* syn. قَابَلْتُهُ. (A, TA.) And نَحَرَ الدَّارُ الدَّارَ, [or نَحَرَتْ,] (Ḳ,) aor. ـَ, (TA,) ‡ *The house faced, or fronted, the house;* (Ḳ, TA;) as also ▼ نَاحَرَتْ. (TA.) And دِيَارُهُمْ تَنْحَرُ الطَّرِيقَ ‡ *Their houses face, or front, the road.* (A.) [See also 6.] And Abu-l-Gheyth says, that the last night of the month, with its day, is called النَّحِيرَةُ for this reason, لِأَنَّهَا تَنْحَرُ الشَّهْرَ الَّذِى بَعْدَهَا, i.e., *Because it becomes opposite to the month that is after it:* or *because it reaches the first part of the month that is after it.* (Ṣ.)

3: see 1, near the end.

6. تَنَاحَرُوا فِى القِتَالِ (Ṣ, TA) *They stabbed one another in the* نَحْر, or *slew one another, in fight.* Here the verb is used in its proper sense. (TA.) — [Hence,] تَنَاحَرَ القَوْمُ عَلَى الأَمْرِ, (A, Ḳ,) and ▼ انتحروا عَلَيْهِ, (Ṣ, A, Ḳ,) ‡ *The people were mutually niggardly,* or *tenacious,* or *avaricious, of the thing,* (Ṣ, A, Ḳ,) *so that they almost slew one another.* (Ḳ,* TA.) — الدَّارَانِ تَتَنَاحَرَانِ ‡ *The two houses face, or front, each other.* (Ḳ.) [The like is also said in the A.] Fr. says, I have heard some of the Arabs say مَنَازِلُهُمْ تَنَاحَرُ, [for تَتَنَاحَرُ,] ‡ *Their places of abode face, or front, one another; this is opposite to this.* (TA.)

8. انتحر *He* (a man, Ṣ) *stabbed himself in the* نَحْر, (Ṣ,) or *slew himself.* (Ḳ.) It is said in a proverb, سُرِقَ السَّارِقُ فَٱنْتَحَرَ [*The robber was robbed, and in consequence slew himself*]: (Ṣ:) or سَرَقَ السَّارِقُ فَٱنْتَحَرَ [app. meaning, ‡ *The robber robbed, and so occasioned his own slaughter:* for it is said that the verb is here used tropically]. (TA; and so in a copy of the Ṣ, and of the A.) [The former reading, which I prefer, is given in Freytag's Arab. Prov., q.v., vol. i. p. 618.] — ‡ *It* (a cloud) *burst with much water.* (A.) — See also 6.

النَّحْرُ, (Ṣ, Mṣb,) or نَحْرُ الصَّدْرِ, (A, Ḳ,) *The uppermost part of the breast, or chest;* (A, Ḳ;) as also ▼ المَنْحَرُ: (Sb, IB, Ḳ:) or *the place of the collar or necklace:* (A, Ḳ:) or *that part of the breast or chest which is the place of the collar or necklace;* (Ṣ, Mṣb;) so accord. to A'Obeyd: (TA, art. ترب:) which is also called ▼ المَنْحَرُ: (Ṣ:) or *the breast or bosom or chest itself:* (TA:) or النُّحُورُ, the pl., is also applied to *the breasts or chests:* (Mṣb:) and النَّحْرُ, (A,) or ▼ المَنْحَرُ, (Ṣ, A, Mṣb, Ḳ, TA,) also signifies *the part in which a camel is stabbed, or stuck;* (A, TA; *where the windpipe* (حُلْقُوم) *commences, in the uppermost part of the breast:* (TA:) or *the place where the* هَدْى [or *animal brought as an offering to Mekkeh or to the Kaabeh or to the Ḥaram, such as a camel, cow, bull, sheep, or goat, to be sacrificed,*] *&c., is stabbed, or stuck:* (Ṣ, Ḳ:) or *the place, in the throat, where a beast is stabbed, or stuck:* (Mṣb:) نَحْرٌ is masc., (Lḥ, Ḳ,) only: (Lḥ:) [or sometimes fem.: see an ex., voce تَرِبَ:] its pl. is نُحُورٌ, (A, Mṣb, Ḳ,) only: (TA:) and the pl. of ▼ مَنْحَرٌ is مَنَاحِرُ. (A.) — نَحْرٌ also signifies ‡ *The first, the first part,* or *the commencement,* of the day; (Ṣ, Ḳ;) and of the month, (Ḳ,) as also ▼ نَاحِرٌ; (TA;) and of the ظَهِيرَة, which is when the sun has reached its highest point, [especially in summer,] as though it had reached the نَحْر, as also ▼ نَاحِرَةٌ: (TA:) pl. نُحُورٌ. (Ḳ.) You say جَآءَ فِى نَحْرِ النَّهَارِ, &c., ‡ *He came in the first part of the day, &c.* (TA.) See also نَحِيرَةٌ. — Also, قَعَدَ فُلَانٌ فِى نَحْرِ فُلَانٍ ‡ *Such a one sat in front of such a one; facing him; opposite to him.* (A.) And صَارَ فِى نَحْرِهِ [‡ *He, or it, became in front of, or opposite to, him, or it*]. (Ṣ.) And هٰذَا بِنَحْرِ هٰذَا ‡ *This is in front of, facing, or opposite to, this.* (Fr, TA.)

نِحْرٌ : see نِحْرِيرٌ.

لَقِيتُهُ صَحْرَةَ بَحْرَةَ نَحْرَةَ, with tenween, † *I met him in open view.* (Ṣgh, Ḳ.) See بَحْرَةٌ and صَحْرَةٌ.

نِحْرِيرٌ (Ṣ, A, Ḳ) and ▼ نِحْرٌ (Ḳ) ‡ *Soundly, or thoroughly, learned;* (Ṣ;) or *skilled* or *skilful, intelligent, experienced,* (A, Ḳ, TA,) or, as some say, (TA,) *sound in what he does, skilful and intelligent, knowing and skilful in everything:* because he masters (يَنْحَرُ) knowledge or science: (A, Ḳ, TA:) pl. of the former, نَحَارِيرُ. (A.)

نَحِيرٌ A camel [or other beast] *stabbed, or stuck,* (Ḳ, TA,) *in the* مَنْحَر, (TA,) *where the windpipe* (حُلْقُوم) *commences, in the uppermost part of the breast;* (Ḳ, TA;) and ▼ مَنْحُورٌ signifies [the same: and] *slaughtered:* (TA:) the former is masc. and fem., and the fem. is also نَحِيرَةٌ: (TA:) pl. of نَحِير, (Ḳ,) and of نَحِيرَة, (TA,) نَحْرَى and نَحَائِرُ and نُحَرَآءُ. (Ḳ, TA.) — ‡ A son *devoted to be sacrificed:* of the measure فَعِيلٌ in the sense of the measure مَفْعُولٌ. (Mgh.) — ▼ النَّحِيرَةُ ‡ *The first day of the month;* [as also, app., ▼ نَحِيرَتُهُ, ▼ نَاحِرَتُهُ, and ▼ نَحْرُ الشَّهْرِ:] or *the last thereof;* (Ḳ;) as also ▼ النَّاحِرُ: (TA:) or *the last night thereof;* (Ṣ, Ḳ;) as also ▼ النَّحِير: (Ḳ:) or *the last night thereof with its day* [i.e. the day immediately following]; as also ▼ النَّاحِرَةُ; because it becomes opposite to that which is next after it, or because it reaches to the first part thereof [or of the following month]: (Abu-l-Gheyth, Ṣ:) pl. نَوَاحِرُ (Ṣ, Ḳ) and نَاحِرَاتٌ, (Ḳ,) both extr. [as pls. of نَحِيرَةٌ, but reg. as pls. of نَاحِرَةٌ], (TA,) [and app. نَحَائِرُ, being agreeable with rule as pl. of نَحِيرَةٌ: or] نَحَائِرُ الشَّهْرِ signifies *i.q.* نُحُورُهُ: see نَحْرٌ. (TA.) You say also جَآءَ فِى نَحْرِ الشَّهْرِ, and نَاحِرَتِهِ, and نَحِيرَتِهِ, ‡ [app. signifying *He came on the first day of the month.*] And مَا أَرَاهُ إِلَّا فِى نُحُورِ الشُّهُورِ, and نَوَاحِرِهَا, and نَحَائِرِهَا, ‡ [app., *I see him not save on the first days of the months.*] (A.)

نَحِيرَةٌ: see نَحِيرٌ.

نَحَّارٌ: see مِنْحَارٌ.

نَاحِرٌ and نَاحِرَةٌ: see نَحْرٌ and نَحِيرٌ. — نَوَاحِرُ الأَرْضِ, [pl. of نَاحِرَةٌ,] ‡ *The parts facing, in front of,* or *opposite to, the earth* or *land.* (TA.)

المَنْحَرُ: see النَّحْرُ, in two places.

مِنْحَارٌ an intensive epithet applied to a man, [*A great slaughterer of camels;* as also ↓ نَحَّارٌ:] and signifying † *Liberal; bountiful; munificent;* or *generous.* (Ṣ, TA.) You say إِنَّهُ لَمِنْحَارٌ بَوَائِكَهَا *Verily he is a* [*great*] *slaughterer of the fat camels:* (Ṣ, Ḳ:) and هُمْ نَحَّارُونَ لِلْجُزُرِ [*They are great slaughterers of camels*]. (A.)

مَنْحُورٌ: see نَحِيرٌ. — ‡ *Faced,* or *fronted.* (TA.)

المَنْحُورُ: see النَّحْرُ.

[نحز,
See Supplement.]

نحس

1. نَحَسَ, aor. ـُ; (Ṣ, A, Ḳ;) and نَحِسَ, aor. ـَ; (Ḳ;) and نَحُسَ, like [its contr.] سَعُدَ; (Bḍ, xvii. 30;) inf. n. [of the first] نَحْسٌ and [of the second] نُحُوسَةٌ; (TA;) *He,* or *it, was,* or *became, unprosperous, unfortunate, inauspicious,* or *unlucky:* (Ṣ, A, Ḳ:) said of a man, (A, Bḍ,) and of a star, (TA,) or other thing. (Ṣ, TA.)

4. أَنْحَسَتِ النَّارُ *The fire had much* نُحَاس, i.e., *smoke.* (IḲṭṭ.)

6: see 8.

8. انتحس *He became overthrown,* or *subverted;* as also ↓ تناحس. And the former is also said of a man's جَدّ [or good fortune]. (A, TA.)

نَحْسٌ *Unprosperousness, unfortunateness, inauspiciousness,* or *unluckiness; contr. of* سَعْدٌ; (Ṣ, A, Ḳ;) of stars, and of other things: pl. [of pauc.] أَنْحُسٌ and [of mult.] نُحُوسٌ; (TA;) and مَنَاحِسُ is an irreg. pl. of the same, (TA,) syn. with مَشَائِمُ, (IDrd, Ḳ, TA,) which is in like manner an irreg. pl. of شُؤْمٌ. (TA.) [In Ḥar, p. ٣٧٥, a doubt is expressed respecting مَنَاحِس, as to its being a pl. of نَحْسٌ; but only from ignorance of their being any authority for its being so: it may, however, be pl. of مَنْحَسَةٌ, and not of نَحْسٌ.] In the Ḳur, [liv. 19,] some read, فِى يَوْمِ نَحْسٍ [*In a day of unprosperousness*]: others read نحس as an epithet. (Ṣ.) See نَحِسٌ. — Also, *Difficulty, distress, trouble,* or *fatigue; harm, injury,* or *evil state* or *condition;* syn. جَهْدٌ and ضُرٌّ: pl. أَنْحُسٌ. (TA.)

نَحِسٌ (Ṣ, A, Ḳ) and ↓ نَحْسٌ (Ṣ, A) and ↓ مَنْحُوسٌ (A, TA) and ↓ نَحُوسٌ and ↓ نَحِيسٌ (TA) *Unprosperous, unfortunate, inauspicious,* or *unlucky.* (Ṣ, A, Ḳ.) You say, رَجُلٌ نَحِسٌ and نَحْسٌ (A) and مَنْحُوسٌ (A, TA) [*An unprosperous man*]: pl. of the last, مَنَاحِيسُ. (TA.) And يَوْمٌ نَحْسٌ (Ṣ, A, TA) [and نَحِسٌ] and نَحُوسٌ (A, TA) and نَحِيسٌ and مَنْحُوسٌ (TA) [*An unprosperous day*]: and in the pl., أَيَّامٌ نَحْسٌ, [which seems to indicate that نَحْسٌ is originally an inf. n.,] (TA,) and نَحِسَةٌ, and نَحِسَاتٌ, which is pl. of نَحِسَةٌ, (Az, TA,) and نَحْسَةٌ, (Ḳ,) and [its pl.] نَحْسَاتٌ, (Ṣ, TA,) and نَحِيسَةٌ, (Ḳ,) [and app. ↓ نَاحِسَةٌ,] and [its pl.] نَوَاحِسُ. (TA.) In the Ḳur, [liv. 19,] some read, ↓ فِى يَوْمٍ نَحِسٍ [*In an unprosperous day*], as well as فِى يَوْمِ نَحْسٍ: (Ṣ, TA:) and AA reads [in the Ḳur, xli. 15,] فِى أَيَّامٍ نَحْسَاتٍ: and نَحِسَاتٍ is another reading. (TA.) You also say, ↓ عَامٌ نَاحِسٌ and ↓ نَحِيسٌ, meaning, ‡ *A year of dearth* or *drought* or *sterility:* (IDrd, Ḳ:) so they assert. (IDrd.) And ↓ النَّحْسَانِ is an appellation of *The two planets Saturn and Mars:* (Ibn-'Abbád, Ḳ:) like as [the contr.] السَّعْدَانِ is applied to Venus and Mercury. (Ibn-'Abbád.)

نَحَاسٌ: see نُحَاسٌ: — and نِحَاسٌ.

نُحَاسٌ (Ṣ, Ḳ, &c.) and ↓ نِحَاسٌ (Fr, Ḳ) and ↓ نَحَاسٌ, (Ḳ,) the last, (TA,) or all, (Ḳ,) on the authority of Abu-l-'Abbás El-Kawáshee, (Ḳ,) a word of well-known meaning; (Ṣ;) *Copper:* and *brass;* syn. قِطْرٌ: (Ḳ:) or صُفْرٌ: (Ibn-Buzurj:) or *a species of* صُفْر *intensely red:* (TA:) a chaste Arabic word. (TA.) — Also, *Fire:* (IF, Ḳ:) and the *sparks that fall from brass* (صُفْر), or *from iron, when it is beaten* (AO, Ḳ) *with the hammer:* (TA:) or نُحَاسٌ signifies *smoke:* so in the Ḳur, lv. 35: (Fr, Az, Bḍ, and others; accord. to Az, all the interpreters of the Ḳur.; and it is wonderful that the author of the Ḳ has omitted this signification: TA:) but some say that it is ↓ نِحَاسٌ signifies the *smoke of* صُفْر; and نُحَاسٌ signifies صُفْر itself: (Ibn-Buzurj:) or the latter signifies *smoke in which is no flame:* (Ṣ, Jel:) or *smoke that rises high, and of which the heat is weak, and which is free from flame:* (AḤn:) or *molten* صُفْر: (Bḍ:) and some read نُحُسٌ, which is the pl. (Bḍ.) — See also نِحَاسٌ.

نِحَاسٌ (Ṣ, A, Ḳ) and ↓ نُحَاسٌ (Ṣ, Ḳ) and ↓ نَحَاسٌ (Ḳ, but excluded by the TA) *Nature; natural,* or *native, disposition* or *temper* or *other quality* or *property:* (Ṣ, A, Ḳ, TA:) and *origin:* (Ṣ, A, TA:) or *that to which the origin of a thing reaches.* (IAạr, Ḳ.) You say, فُلَانٌ كَرِيمُ النِّحَاسِ, (Ṣ, A,) and ↓ النُّحَاسِ, (Ṣ,) *Such a one is generous of nature,* &c., *and origin.* (Ṣ, A.) — See also نُحَاسٌ, in two places.

نَحُوسٌ: } see نَحِسٌ, throughout.
نَحِيسٌ: }

[نَحَّاسٌ *A worker of copper* or *brass:* a coppersmith.]

نَاحِسٌ: see نَحِسٌ, in two places.

مَنْحَسٌ *A place of unprosperousness, unfortunateness, inauspiciousness,* or *unluckiness:* pl. مَنَاحِسُ. (Ḥar, p. ٣٧٣.)

مَنْحَسَةٌ [*A cause of unprosperousness, unfortunateness, inauspiciousness,* or *unluckiness:* pl., accord. to rule, مَنَاحِسُ]. (A, TA, art. تعس.)

مَنْحُوسٌ: see نَحِسٌ, in three places.

مَنَاحِسُ: see نَحْسٌ, مَنْحَسٌ, and مَنْحَسَةٌ.

[نحص, &c.,
See Supplement.]

نخ

1. نَخَّ, [aor., accord. to analogy, ـُ,] inf. n. نَخٌّ; (Ṣ, Ḳ;) and ↓ نَخْنَخَ; (IAạr, Ḳ;) *He went,* or *journeyed, vehemently.* (IAạr, Ṣ, Ḳ.) — نَخَّ, aor. ـُ, (L,) inf. n. نَخٌّ, (Ṣ, L,) *He drove, and urged, and chid,* camels: (L:) *he drove vehemently.* (Th, Ṣ.) — نَخَّ بِالإِبِلِ, (Lth,) [aor. ـُ,] inf. n. نَخٌّ; (Lth, Ḳ;) and ↓ نَخْنَخَ بِهَا; (AM;) and نَخْنَخَهَا; (Lth;) *He chid the camels by the cry of* إِخّ إِخّ (or إِخْ إِخْ, as in the CḲ and a MS. copy of the Ḳ: in the L written once اِخ اخ, and twice اِخ اخ:) *in order that they might lie down upon their breasts, with folded legs:* (Lth, AM, L, Ḳ:) you say نَخَّ بِهَا نَخًّا شَدِيدًا, and نَخَّةً شَدِيدَةً, *he did so vehemently.* (Lth.) — Also, ↓ نخنخ, (inf. n. نَخْنَخَةٌ, Lth,) *He made a camel to lie down upon its breast, with folded legs.* (IAạr, Lth, Ṣ, Ḳ.) — نَخَّ الإِبِلَ, and نَخَّ بِهَا, [aor. ـُ,] inf. n. نَخٌّ, *He made the camels to lie down near by the collector of the alms required by*

the law, called صَدَقَة, *that he might take them in payment of those alms.* (L.)

R. Q. 1: see 1.

R. Q. 2. تَنَخْنَخَ *It* (a camel) *lay down upon its breast, with its legs folded.* (Lth, Ṣ, Ḳ.) — Also, تنخنخت *She,* (a camel,) *lying upon her breast, with her legs folded, raised her breast from the ground.* (L.)

نُخٌّ, [originally an inf. n., then used in the sense of a pass. part. n.,] *Camels that are made to lie down near by the collector of the alms required by the law, called* صَدَقَة, *that he may take them in payment of those alms.* (Ṣ, Ḳ.)

نُخٌّ and ▼ نُخَاخَةٌ (in the CḲ نَخاخَةٌ) *i. q.* مُخٌّ [*Marrow, &c.*]. (Ḳ.) — هٰذَا مِنْ نُخِّ قَلْبِى, and نخاخة ▼ قلبى, *i. q.* من مخّ قلبى, and مُخَّتِهِ, q. v. (TA.)

نَخَّةٌ or ▼ نُخَّةٌ or ▼ نِخَّةٌ, as occurring in the following words of a trad., لَيْسَ فِى النَّخَّةِ صَدَقَةٌ, [*No alms are required by the law in the case of* . . . . ,] is variously explained. (TA.) It is said that نَخَّةٌ signifies *Slaves,* (AO, Az, Ṣ, Ḳ,) *men and women:* (AO, Az:) also, *a* [single] *male slave:* (ISh:) also, *working bulls* or *cows;* (Ṣ, Ḳ;) and so نُخَّةٌ: (Ḳ:) Th says that this is the correct meaning, because it is from نَخٌّ, signifying the "act of driving vehemently;" and Ks says that this is its meaning, but that it is only نُخَّةٌ, with damm: (Ṣ:) also, *asses,* حُمُرٌ, [in the CḲ, حُمْرٌ,] (IAạr, L, Ḳ,) collectively; (L;) and so نُخَّةٌ (L, Ḳ) and نِخَّةٌ: (Ḳ:) also, [*animals*] *reared in houses or tents:* (Ḳ:) also, *whatever are employed in labour, of camels, and bulls or cows, and asses, and slaves;* as also نُخَّةٌ: (Aboo-Sa'eed:) also, *pastors;* and so نُخَّةٌ: also, *drivers, leaders, or attendants, of camels:* (Ḳ:) also, the *taking of a deenár for himself by the collector of the alms required by the law, called* صَدَقَة, (Ṣ, Ḳ,) *after he has finished receiving those alms:* (Ṣ:) also, the *deenár itself so taken is thus called.* (Ḳ.) In all these senses the word نخّة is explained in the above trad. (TA.)

نُخَّةٌ and نِخَّةٌ: see نَخَّةٌ throughout.

نُخَاخَةٌ: see نُخٌّ.

نخب

1. نَخَبَ, (Ṣ, Ḳ,) aor. ـُ, (Ṣ,) or ـِ, (Ḳ,) inf. n. نَخْبٌ; (Ṣ, Ḳ;) and ▼ انتخب; (Ṣ;) *He drew, or took, out, or forth:* (Ṣ, Ḳ:) syn. of the latter verb, انتزع, (Ṣ,) in a trans. sense. (TA.) — نَخَبَ الصَّيْدَ *He* (a hawk) *tore out the heart of the game.* (TA.) — نَخَبَ, aor. ـِ and ـُ, (Ḳ,) inf. n. نَخْبٌ, (Ṣ, Ḳ,) *Inivit feminam:* (Ṣ, Ḳ:) so accord. to some, in an absolute sense: (ISd:) or *inivit feminam peculiari quodam modo.* (ISd, Ḳ.) — نَخَبَ, aor. ـُ, inf. n. نَخْبٌ, *It* (an ant, or a louse, TA) *bit.* (Ḳ.) ═ نُخِبَ *He was cowardly, and his intellect quitted him;* syn. هُبِتَ. (Ṣ, art. هبت.) — كَلَّمْتُهُ فَنُخِبَ عَنِّى *I spoke to him, and he was unable to reply to me:* syn. كَلَّ عَنْ جَوَابِى. (TA.)

4. انخب (as also انجب, TA) *He begot a cowardly son:* (Ḳ:) from مَنْخُوبٌ. (TA.) — انخب *He begot a brave, or courageous, son:* (Ḳ:) from نُخْبَةٌ. (TA.) Thus the verb bears two contr. significations. (Ḳ.) See also انجب.

5: see 8.

8. See 1. — انتخبهُ [and ▼ تَنَخَّبَهُ, as is shown by a verse cited in art. سقب, conj. 4,] *He chose, selected,* or *preferred, him,* or *it.* (Ṣ, Ḳ.) Ex. انتخب مِنَ القَوْمِ مِائَةَ رَجُلٍ *He chose,* or *selected, from the people a hundred men.* (TA, from a trad.)

10. استنخبت *Congressum viri concupivit femina.* (El-Umawee, Ṣ, Ḳ.)

نَخْبٌ, (Ḳ,) or ▼ نَخْبَةٌ, (L, confirmed by the citation of two examples in verse,) and ▼ مَنْخَبَةٌ (Ḳ) and يَنْخُوبَةٌ (L) *The podex:* syn. إِسْتٌ. (L, Ḳ.) — نَخْبٌ *Foramen vulvæ feræ:* syn. خرق الثفر. (TA.) — نَخْبَةٌ *Foramen pudendi:* syn. خرق الجلد. (Nh.) ═ نَخْبٌ *Cowardice; weakness of heart.* (TA.) See نَخِبٌ. ═ نَخْبٌ *A large draught;* i. q. Pers. دُوسْتكَانِى [dóst-kánee]. (Ḳ.)

نُخَبٌ: see نُخْبَةٌ.

نَخِبٌ (Ṣ, Ḳ) and ▼ نَخْبٌ and ▼ نَخَبَةٌ (so accord. to the TA: in the CḲ نُخْبَةٌ:) and ▼ نُخَبَةٌ (in the CḲ ▼ نُخْبَةٌ) and ▼ نِخَبٌ and ▼ نَخِيبٌ (Ḳ) and ▼ نَخِيبٌ and ▼ مَنْخُوبٌ and ▼ مُنْتَخَبٌ (Ṣ, Ḳ) and ▼ يَنْخُوبٌ, (Ḳ,) to which the CḲ adds ▼ نُخْبٌ, *A cowardly* man; *a coward;* as though his heart were drawn out; (Ṣ;) i. e., *having no heart.* (TA.) ▼ قَلْبٌ نَخِيبٌ [*A cowardly heart*]: نخيب signifies *a coward, who has no heart:* or, accord. to some, one *who acts corruptly.* (TA.) Pl. (of ▼ نخيب, TA,) نُخُبٌ: (Ḳ:) of ▼ منخوب, مَنْخُوبُونَ, and sometimes, in poetry, accord. to IAth, مَنَاخِبُ: and Aboo-Bekr mentions نخبات as a pl. of نخبة. (TA.)

نُخْبَةٌ: see نَخْبٌ and نَخِبٌ. ═ نَخْبَةُ نَمْلَةٍ, and نَجْبَةُ نملة, q. v., *A bite of an ant.* Both these modes of writing the word are mentioned by IAth on the authority of Z.

نُخَبَةٌ: see نَخِبٌ and نُخْبَةٌ.

نُخْبَةٌ (Aṣ, Ṣ, Ḳ) and ▼ نُخَبَةٌ (AM, Ḳ), the former the more approved word, (TA,) *Chosen; choice; select; preferred; excellent; best:* or *what is chosen, &c.:* (Ḳ:) *i. q.* نُجْبَةٌ, q. v.: (Ṣ:) pl. of the former نُخَبٌ. (Ṣ.) Ex. جَاءَ فِى نُخَبِ أَصْحَابِهِ *He came with the best of his companions.* (Ṣ.) نخبة المَتَاعِ *The choice part of the goods,* or *utensils, &c.;* *what was drawn,* or *taken, out from them.* (TA.) — *A company,* or *troop, chosen,* or *selected, and drawn out, from the men.* Ex., from a trad., خَرَجْنَا فِى النُّخْبَةِ *We went forth with the chosen band.* (TA.) — See نَخِبٌ.

نِخَبٌ and نَخِبٌ and نَخِيبٌ: see نَخِبٌ.

نِخَابٌ *The skin of the heart.* (TA.)

مَنْخَبَةٌ: see نَخْبٌ.

مِنْخَابٌ syn. with مِنْجَابٌ; (TA;) *A weak man, in whom is no good:* (Ḳ:) pl. مَنَاخِيبُ, and sometimes, in poetry, مَنَاخِبُ. (TA.)

مَنْخُوبٌ *Lean; meagre; emaciated.* (Ḳ.) — See نَخِبٌ.

مُنْتَخَبٌ: see نَخِبٌ.

يَنْخُوبٌ: see نَخِبٌ.

يَنْخُوبَةٌ: see نَخْبٌ.

نخت

1. نَخَتَ, inf. n. نَخْتٌ, *He pecked,* or *picked up, and pulled off,* or *tore off, and snatched away, with his beak;* syn. نَقَرَ and نَتَخَ, (Ḳ,) formed by transposition. (TA.) — نَخَتَ, [aor. ـُ,] inf. n. نَخْتٌ, *He took a date, or two dates, from a bag or other receptacle for travelling-provisions &c.* (Ḳ.) — نَخَتَ, [aor. ـُ,] inf. n. نَخْتٌ, *He plucked out;* syn. نَتَفَ. (IAth, L.) ═ See 2.

2. نخّت لِفُلَانٍ, as also سخّت لهُ, *He went to the utmost length* (استقصى) *in speaking to such a one.* So in the Nawádir. (Az, L.) [Accord. to the Ḳ, ▼ نَخَتَ, inf. n. نَخْتٌ.]

نَخْتَةُ نَمْلَةٍ *A bite of an ant.* So in a trad., accord. to one reading: accord. to another reading, it is نَخْبَةٌ [q. v.]. (L.)

نخج

1. نَخَجَ الدَّلْوَ, (Ṣ, Ḳ,) and نَخَجَ بِهَا, (TA,) aor. ـَ, inf. n. نَخْجٌ, (Ḳ,) *He agitated, or moved about, the bucket;* (Ṣ, Ḳ;) a dial. form of مَخَجَ; (Ṣ;) or, accord. to Yaạkoob, its ن is substituted for م: *he moved about the bucket in the well in order that it might fill.* (TA.) — نَخَجَ, (Ṣ, Ḳ,) aor. ـَ (Ḳ) and ـُ, (L,) inf. n. نَخْجٌ, (Ḳ,) *Inivit feminam.* (Ṣ, Ḳ.)

نَخِيجَةٌ, (ISk, Ṣ, Ḳ,) or, accord. to some, نَخِيجٌ, without ة, (TA,) or, as some say, نُخَيْجَةٌ, and (says J) I know not which is right, (Ṣ,) *Thin butter which comes forth from the skin when it is carried on a camel, after the first butter has been taken forth.* (Ṣ, Ḳ.)

نخر

1. نَخَرَ, (Ṣ, A, Mṣb, Ḳ,) aor. ـُ (Ṣ, Mṣb, Ḳ) and ـِ, (Ṣ, Ḳ,) inf. n. نَخِيرٌ, (Ṣ, A, Mṣb, Ḳ,) and نَخْرٌ, (CḲ, but omitted in MS. copies of the Ḳ,) said of a horse, (Aṣ, TA,) and of an ass, (A, TA,) and of a man, (TA,) [*He snorted;* and *he snored;*] *he made a sound, or noise, with the nose;* (Ṣ;) *he made a sound, or noise, from his nose; he prolonged the breath from the* خَيَاشِيم [or *air-passages of the nose*]; (Mṣb;) *he made a sound, or noise, from his* خياشيم, *as though it were a musical note issuing convulsively;* (TA;) *he uttered a prolonged sound, or noise, from his* خياشيم: (A, Ḳ:) the sound which horses make, termed نَخِيرٌ, is *from the nostrils;* that termed شَخِيرٌ, from the mouth; and that termed كَرِيرٌ, from the chest. (Aṣ, in TA, art. شخر.) You also say of a woman نَخَرَتْ, aor. ـُ and ـِ, (L,) or ـِ, (so in the TA,) meaning, *She made the same noise,* [i. e., *she snorted,*] *in the act of concubitus, as though she were possessed.* (L, TA.) ═ نَخِرَ, (Ṣ, Mṣb, Ḳ,) aor. ـَ, (Mṣb, Ḳ,) inf. n. نَخَرٌ, (Mṣb,) *It* (a thing, Ṣ, or a bone, Mṣb, TA, and wood, TA) *became old and wasted and crumbling;* (Ṣ, Mṣb, Ḳ;) *it became old and wasted and soft, crumbling when touched.* (TA.)

نَخِرٌ (Ṣ, Mṣb, Ḳ) and ↓ نَاخِرٌ (Mṣb, Ḳ) A bone, (Ṣ, Mṣb,) and wood, (TA,) *old and wasted and crumbling;* (Ṣ, Mṣb, Ḳ;) *old and wasted and soft, crumbling when touched:* (TA:) fem. of each with ة: (Ḳ:) or the former signifies a bone *old and wasted:* (Ḳ:) and the latter, a *hollow* bone, *having a hole passing through it,* (Ḳ, TA,) *whence comes, when the wind blows, a sound like that which is termed* نَخِير; [see نَخَرَ;] (TA;) a bone *into which the wind enters and whence it then issues with the sound so termed;* (Ṣ;) a bone, and wood, *in which the wind makes the sound so termed.* (A.) Of the two readings, in the Ḳur, [lxxix. 11,] عِظَامًا نَخِرَةً and عِظَامًا نَاخِرَةً, Fr prefers the former, as agreeable in form with the words ending the other verses; and he says that نَاخِرَة and نَخِرَة are the same in meaning, like طَمِعٌ and طَامِعٌ. (TA.)

نُخْرَةٌ ‡ *A vehement blowing* of the wind. (Ṣ, A, Ḳ.) ═ Also, (Ṣ, A, Ḳ,) and ↓ نُخَرَةٌ, (Ṣ,) The *fore part* of the nose, (Ṣ, Ḳ,) i. e., the *head* thereof, [or the *flexible part,*] of a man, (TA,) and of a horse, and of an ass, and of a pig, (Ṣ,) and of a sheep or goat, and of a she-camel: (TA:) or the *hole* thereof; (Ḳ;) i. q. ↓ مَنْخِرٌ: (A:) or the *part between the two nostrils:* or the *end,* or *tip,* of the nose: (Ḳ:) or, as some say, the *nose* itself: (A, TA:) whence the saying, (TA,) هشم نُخْرَتَهُ *He broke his nose.* (Ṣ, TA.)

نُخَرَةٌ: see نُخْرَةٌ.

نَاخِرٌ *Making the sound termed* نَخِير: see 1. (TA.) — مَا بِهَا نَاخِرٌ, (Ṣ, Ḳ,) i. e., بِالدَّارِ, (A,) ‡ *There is not any one in it,* (El-Báhilee, Yaạḳoob, Ṣ, Ḳ,) i. e., *in the house.* (A.) ═ See also نَخِرٌ.

مَنْخُرٌ, مُنْخُرٌ, مِنْخِرٌ, and مُنْخُورٌ: see مَنْخِرٌ.

مَنْخِرٌ, [the most common form,] originally, The *place of the sound termed* نَخِير. See 1. (Mṣb.) — And hence, (Mṣb,) The *hole of the nose;* the *nostril;* (Ṣ, Mṣb, Ḳ;) as also ↓ مِنْخِرٌ, (T, Ṣ, Mṣb, Ḳ,) with kesr to the م to agree with the vowel of the خ, like as they say مِنْتِنٌ [for مُنْتِنٌ], (Ṣ, Mṣb,) both of which words are extr., as مِفْعِلٌ is not one of the [regular] measures, (Ṣ,) and it is said that there is no word of this measure beside these two, (Mṣb,) or ↓ مِنْخِرٌ is for ↓ مِنْخِيرٌ, and in like manner مِنْتِنٌ is for مِنْتِينٌ, which is the original form, (T, TA,) and ↓ مَنْخُرٌ and ↓ مُنْخُرٌ (Ḳ) and ↓ مُنْخُورٌ, (Ṣ, Mṣb, Ḳ,) like عُصْفُورٌ (Mṣb) and مُلْمُولٌ, (Ḳ, [in the CḲ, erroneously, مَلْمُول,]) which last is [said to be] of the dial. of Ṭeiyi, (Mṣb,) and said to occur in a verse of Gheylán, but IB says that the right reading is مُنْحُور, with ح, syn. with نَحْر: (Ṣgh, in art. نحر; and L, in the present art.) pl. مَنَاخِر and مَنَاخِير; (Mṣb;) [the latter irreg., unless pl. of مِنْخِير or مُنْخُور.]

مِنْخَارٌ A man *who makes the sound termed* نَخِير [see نَخَرَ] *in the act of concubitus:* (TA:) and a woman *who does so in that act, as though she were possessed.* (Ḳ.)

مُنْخُورٌ: } see مَنْخِرٌ.
مِنْخِيرٌ: }

نخرب

Q. 1. نَخْرَبَ *It* (a canker-worm) *pierced holes in,* or *eroded,* a tree. (Ḳ.) IJ derives this verb from خَرَابٌ, (TA,) q. v.

نُخْرُوبٌ; (Ṣ, Ḳ;) mentioned in the Ḳ without description of its measure because there is no Arabic word of the measure فُعْلُولٌ; but some prefer it being written نُخْرُوبٌ, [as it is in the CḲ,] asserting its ن to be augmentative, so that its measure is نُفْعُولٌ, as IAạr holds, asserting it to be derived from خَرَابٌ; (TA;) *A fissure,* or *cleft,* in a stone. (Ṣ, Ḳ.) — Also, [so in the TA: in the CḲ and a MS. copy, or,] *A hole, perforation,* or *bore,* in anything. (Ḳ.) Pl. نَخَارِيبُ. (Ṣ.) — Also, the pl., The *holes,* or *cells, prepared with wax for the bees to deposit their honey therein:* (Ḳ:) *holes like the cells of wasps.* (L.)

نَخْرَبُوتٌ [i. q. تَخْرَبُوتٌ] An *excellent, nimble,* or *agile,* she-camel. Some say that its ن is augmentative, and its radical letters are خرب; but its derivation from خَرَابٌ is not apparent; therefore its ن should be considered as radical. (AḤei.)

مُنَخْرَبَةٌ, and شَجَرَةٌ مُنَخْرِبَةٌ, *A tree that is old and pierced with holes.* (Ḳ.)

نخس

1. نَخَسَهُ, aor. ـُ, (Ṣ, A, Mṣb, Ḳ,) and ـَ, (Lḥ, Ṣ, A, Mgh, Ḳ,) and ـِ, (Lḥ, TA,) inf. n. نَخْسٌ, (Ṣ, Mgh, Mṣb,) *He goaded,* or *pricked,* him, namely, a beast, (A, Mgh, Mṣb, Ḳ,) with a stick (Ṣ, Mgh, Mṣb, Ḳ,) or the like, (A, Mgh, Mṣb, Ḳ,) *in the hinder part,* or *the side,* (A, Ḳ,) *so that he became excited.* (Mṣb.) — نَخَسَ بِهِ *He goaded his beast.* (Mgh.) — نَخَسُوا بِهِ, (A, L, TA,) or نَخَسُوهُ, (Ḳ,) *They goaded his* (a man's) *beast, and drove him* (the man) *away;* (A, L, TA;) *they drove him away, goading his camel with him.* (Ḳ.) — And نَخَسَ بِالرَّجُلِ † *He excited,* or *roused, the man, and disquieted,* or *disturbed, him.* (L, TA.) — You say also, ↓ أَنْخَسَ بِهِ, meaning, أَبْعَدَهُ ‡ [*He put him, or sent him, away,* or *far away*]. (A, TA.) [Or perhaps the right reading is إِنْخَسْ بِهِ, meaning, أَبْعِدْهُ [*Put thou him,* or *send thou him, away,* or *far away:* as seems to be indicated by what immediately follows in those two works and here.] And تَكَلَّمَ فَنَخَسُوا بِهِ ‡ [app. meaning, *He spoke, and they put him away*]. (A, TA.)

4: see 1.

نِخَاسَةٌ and نَخَاسَةٌ The *trade of selling beasts:* and the *trade of selling slaves.* (Ḳ.)

نَخَّاسٌ *A goader of beasts.* (Mṣb.) — And hence, (Ṣ,* A,* Mṣb,) *A seller of beasts;* (Ḳ;) *one who acts as a broker for the sale of beasts* (Mgh, Mṣb) *and the like:* (Mṣb:) and *a seller of slaves;* (Ḳ;) sometimes used in the latter sense: (TA:) a genuine Arabic word. (IDrd.)

[نخش, &c.

See Supplement.]

ند

1. نَدَّ, aor. ـِ, inf. n. نَدٌّ (Ṣ, M, A, &c.,) and نِدَادٌ and نُدُودٌ (Ṣ, M, L, Ḳ) and نَدِيدٌ; (M, L, Mṣb, Ḳ;) and ↓ تَنَادَّ; (M, L;) *He* (a camel) *took fright, or shied, and fled, or ran away at random,* or *became refractory, and went away at random;*

or *ran away*, or *broke loose, and went hither and thither by reason of his sprightliness.* (Ṣ, M, A, L, Mṣb, Ḳ.) See also 6, below. — Also نَدَّ, contr., *It* (a people) *assembled.* ('Ináyeh, MF.) — نَدَّ *It* (a word) *deviated from the constant course of speech*; like شَذَّ; as some say; as mentioned by El-Fárisee: but it is not of good authority, nor agreeable with the usage of Sb. (M, L.)

2: see 4. — نَدَّدَ, inf. n. تَنْدِيدٌ, *He raised his voice.* (L.) — نَدَّدَ *He raised his voice in saying of another that which he* (the latter) *disliked.* (Lth, in L, art. شيد.) See 4 in art. شيد. — نَدَّدَ بِهِ, (inf. n. تَنْدِيدٌ, L.) *He declared*, or *exposed, his vices*, or *faults*; (M, L, Ḳ;) in verse or prose; (M, L;) *he rendered him notorious*, or *infamous.* (AZ, Ṣ, L.) — *He made him to hear what was bad, evil, abominable*, or *foul*: (AZ, T, M, L, Ḳ.) *he reviled him.* (AZ, T, L.)

3. نَادَّهُ *He opposed him, oppugned him.* (L, Ḳ.)

4. انَدَّ and ✝ نَدَّدَ *He dispersed* camels. (M, L, Ḳ.)

6. تَنَادُّوا *They dispersed themselves, and betook themselves away.* (Ḳ.) [See also 1.] Hence, يَوْمُ التَّنَادِّ (Ṣ, M, L, Ḳ,) [*The day of men's dispersing themselves, and betaking themselves in different directions*], applied to the day of resurrection: (M, L:) so in the Ḳur, [xl. 34,] accord. to the reading of some; (Ṣ, M, L, Ḳ;) namely El-'Abbás and others: (Ḳ:) Az says, accord. to the reading of Ed-Ḍaḥḥák only: (L:) others read التَّنَادِ; which may also be from نَدَّ; one of the dáls being changed into ى, and being then elided: (T, L:) or this may be from النِّدَآء: (M:) or يوم التنادّ may mean *the day of men's assembling themselves together*, from نَدَّ signifying "it (a people) assembled." ('Ináyeh MF.)

نَدٌّ (and ✝ نِدٌّ, M, L,) *A certain kind of perfume*, (Ṣ, M, L, Ḳ,) well known, (Ḳ,) *with which one fumigates*: (Lth, M, L:) *a certain wood with which one fumigates*: (Mṣb:) or, as some say, *i. q.* غَالِيَةٌ: or, as Z says, in the Rabeeạ el-Abrár, *a compound of aloes-wood aromatized with musk and ambergris and* بَان: (TA:) or (accord. to Aboo-'Amr Ibn-El-'Alà, T, L) ambergris, عَنْبَرٌ: (T, L:) or عَبِيرٌ [i. e., either *saffron*, or *a certain mixture of perfumes*: so in the copy of the T used by the author of the TT, if correctly transcribed by him:] it is not Arabic: (Ṣ:) or is thought by IDrd to be not genuine Arabic: (M, L,) many of the lexicologists, however, hold it to be genuine Arabic; and it occurs in verses of old poets; (MF;) but this does not prove that it is not an arabicized word. (TA.) — نَدٌّ *A high hill*; (Ḳ;) *a hill rising high into the sky*: (Ṣ, L:) of the dial. of El-Yemen: (L:) *a great hill* (أَكَمَة) *of clay or loam.* (Ḳ.)

نِدٌّ and ✝ نَدِيدٌ and ✝ نَدِيدَةٌ *A like* (Ṣ, L, Ḳ) of a person or thing: (L:) or *a like* of a thing *by participation of substance*; a more special term than مِثْلٌ, which signifies "a like by participation of anything:" (the ḳáḍee Zekereeyà, MF:) or *a thing which does*, or *may, supply, the place of another thing*: (TA:) or *a like that is contrary*, or *opposed, to another thing*; (Mṣb;) *that opposes it* (يُنَادُّهُ, i. e., يُخَالِفُهُ,) *in its circumstances*; (L;) *syn. with* ضِدٌّ and شِبْهٌ: (Akh:) and hence the first is applied to *an idol*; *a thing taken as an object of worship instead of the true God*: (L:) pl. of the first, أَنْدَادٌ; (L, Mṣb, Ḳ;) and of the second, نُدَدَآءُ; and of the third, نَدَائِدُ. (Ḳ.) You say, هُوَ نِدُّ فُلَانٍ, and نَدِيدُهُ, and نَدِيدَتُهُ, *He is the like of such a one*: (L:) and هِىَ نِدُّ فُلَانَةَ, (ISh, L, Ḳ,) *She is the like of such a female*; (ISh, L;) but not نِدُّ فُلَانٍ. (ISh, L, Ḳ.) You also say هُوَ نِدِّى, and نَدِيدِى, meaning *He is my opponent with respect to the course that I would pursue, contending with me for a different course.* (AHeyth, T, L.) — See نَدٌّ.

نَدُودٌ A she-camel *wont to take fright*, or *shy, and run away, at random*; *&c.*: see 1. (M, L.)

نَدِيدٌ and نَدِيدَةٌ: see نِدٌّ.

نَادٌّ, act. part. n. of نَدَّ, A camel *taking fright*, or *shying, and running away, at random*; *&c.*: pl. نَوَادُّ: (Mṣb, TA:) and quasi pl. n. نَدَدٌ; (L;) signifying camels *in a state of dispersion.* (L, Ḳ.) — لَيْسَ لَهُ نَادٌّ *He has not any means of subsistence*: (Ḳ:) app. meaning live stock; from نَدَّ, said of a camel. (TA.) — [See also شَادٌّ, and أَشَدُّ.]

طَيْرٌ أَنَادِيدُ, and يَنَادِيدُ, *Birds in a state of dispersion*: (M, L:) [like أَبَادِيدُ and يَبَادِيدُ or تَبَادِيدُ: see an ex. in art. بد.] — ذَهَبُوا أَنَادِيدَ, and يَنَادِيدَ, (L, and some copies of the Ḳ,) or تَنَادِيدَ, (as in other copies of the Ḳ,) *They* (a people, L) *became dispersed in every direction.* (L, Ḳ.)

مُنِدٌّ A voice *raised high in calling.* (L.)

ندأ

1. نَدَأَ, aor. ـَ, *He hated* a thing: or it is a mistake for بَذَأَ. (Aṣ, Ṣ, Ḳ.) — نَدَأَ, (Ṣ, Ḳ,) aor. ـَ, inf. n. نَدْءٌ (TA) *He cast* flesh-meat *into the fire*: (Ḳ:) or *he buried it*, (Ṣ, Ḳ,) or a cake of bread, (Ṣ,) *in hot ashes*, (Ṣ, Ḳ, TA,) that it might become thoroughly cooked, or baked. (Ṣ.) — نَدَأَ, (Ḳ,) inf. n. نَدْءٌ, (TA,) *He frightened.* (Ḳ.) — نَدَأَ *He cast* a person *upon the ground.* (Ḳ.) — نَدَأَ عَلَيْهِمْ *He came forth upon them.* (Ḳ.) — نَدَأَ المَلَّةَ *He made*, or *prepared, the kind of fire called* مَلَّة. (Ḳ.)

Q. Q. 1. نَوْدَأَ, inf. n. نَوْدَأَةٌ, *He ran, with a slack pace*: syn. عَدَا. (Ḳ.)

نَدْأَةٌ: see نُدْأَةٌ.

نُدْأَةٌ and ✝ نَدْأَةٌ *Abundance of wealth*, or *of camels*, or *sheep &c.*: (Ṣ, Ḳ:) like نُدْهَةٌ and نَدْهَةٌ: (Ṣ:) by some explained as consisting of *twenty sheep* or *goats.* (MF.) — Also, both words, The *rainbow*: (Ṣ, Ḳ:) also called ✝ نَدِىءٌ. (Ḳ.) — Also, both words, *A redness in the clouds towards the setting* or *rising of the sun*: (Ḳ:) or *a redness by the side of the sun at its rising* or *setting*: (TA:) or, *by the side of the place of its rising* or *setting*: (T:) also called ✝ نَدِىءٌ. (Ḳ.) — Also, both words, *A halo*, or *circle, round the sun* or *moon.* (Ḳ.) — Also, the former word, نُدْأَةٌ, ‡ *A streak in flesh-meat, differing in colour from the rest*: (Ḳ:) *such a streak in the flesh of a slaughtered camel*: (T:) and, in the dual, *two streaks inside the two thighs, having over them a thin, white, sinewy substance, resembling a spider's web, divided, one from the other, by a single muscle, and thus appearing like two muscles*: asserted by more than one to be tropical. (TA.) — *What is above the navel*, in a horse. (Ḳ.) — *A woollen thing*, (TA,) also called دُرْجَة, *which is stuffed into the tuel of a she-camel*, [*and into her vulva*, as explained voce دُرْجَة,] *and which is afterwards taken out when she has taken a liking for another camel's colt*, (Ḳ,) or *for the stuffed skin of a camel's colt prepared for her.* (IAạr.) [See دُرْجَة for a more full explanation.] — *One of several parts* or *portions of scattered herbage*: (like نُفَاْة: (TA:) also called ✝ نُدَاَة: pl. نُدَأٌ. (Ḳ.)

نُدَأَةٌ: see preceding sentence.

نَدِىءٌ, a subst., like طَبِيخٌ, [or rather an epithet in which the quality of a substantive predominates,] *Flesh-meat*, or *bread, cooked*, or *baked, by being buried in hot ashes.* (IAth, Ṣ.) لَحْمٌ نَدِىءٌ *Flesh-meat cooked*, or *baked, &c.* (TA.) — [See also نُدْأَةٌ, in two places.]

ندب

1. نَدَبَهُ لِلْأَمْرِ, (Ṣ,) or إِلَى الأَمْرِ, aor. ـُ, (Mṣb, Ḳ,) inf. n. نَدْبٌ; (Mṣb, TA;) and ✝ انتدبه للامر; this latter verb being used transitively as well as intransitively; (Mṣb;) *He*, or *it, called, summoned*, or *invited, him to the thing*; (Ṣ, Mṣb, Ḳ;) *and instigated, incited*, or *urged, him to it*: (Ḳ.) i. e., to war, succour, &c. (TA.) — [You say,] مَا نَدَبَنِى إِلَى مَا فَعَلْتُ إِلَّا النُّصْحُ لَكَ ‡ *Nothing incited me to do what I have done but sincerity towards thee.* (TA.) — نَدَبَهُ إِلَى أَمْرٍ, [and لِأَمْرٍ;] and ✝ نَدَّبَهُ; (see مَنْدُوبٌ;)] *He sent him to do a thing.* (Ḳ.) — نَدَبَ المَيِّتَ, (aor. ـُ, inf. n. نَدْبٌ, Ṣ,) ‡ *He*

wailed for, wept for, or *deplored the loss of, the dead man, and enumerated his good qualities and actions.* (Ṣ, Ḳ.) نَدَبَتِ المَيِّتَ ‡ *She* (a wailing woman) *called upon the dead man, praising him, and saying* وَافُلَانَاهْ *and* وَاهَنَاهْ, *Alas for such a one! and Alas for thee!* (M) or *she, as it were, called upon the dead man, enumerating his good qualities and actions, as though he heard her.* (Mṣb.) It is said that the action is peculiarly that of women; and that the verb is derived from نَدَبَهُ, "he called him" to do a thing; or from نَدَبٌ, "a scar," because the wailer mentions the memorials of him who has gone; or perhaps from نَدْبٌ, "lightness, or activity." (MF.) ═ نَدِبَ, aor. ـَ, (inf. n. نَدَبٌ, TA;) and ↓ اندب; *It* (a wound) *had a hardened scar, such as is termed* نَدَبَة. (Ḳ.) — نَدِبَ, aor. ـَ, inf. n. نَدْبٌ [so accord. to the TA, agreeably with analogy; but in the CḲ and a MS. copy, نَدَبٌ; whence, and from the form of the latter of the two inf. ns. here following, it seems not improbable that the verb may be also written نَدَبَ;] and نُدُوبَةٌ and نُدُوبٌ, *It* (the back) *had upon it scars, such as are termed* نُدُوب. (Ḳ.) ═ نَدُبَ, aor. ـُ, inf. n. نَدَابَةٌ, TA,) *He was light,* or *active,* (and quick, TA,) *in the accomplishment of affairs,* or *wants: he was clever, ingenious,* or *acute in mind; excellent.* (Ḳ.)

2. ندّب *He took, got,* or *won, a bet, wager,* or *stake.* (L.) — See 1.

4. اندبهُ *It* (a wound) *made,* or *left, a scar upon him.* (Ḳ.) — *He made a scar upon his skin.* (TA.) — See نَدِبَ. — اندب بِظَهْرِهِ, and فِى ظهره, *He,* or *it, left scars* (نُدُوب) *upon his back.* (TA.) — أَنْدَبَتْهُ الحَاجَةُ إِنْدَابًا شَدِيدًا ‡ *The thing,* or *want, made a severe impression upon him.* (TA.) — اندب نَفْسَهُ, and بِنَفْسِهِ, *He exposed himself to peril.* (Ḳ.) ═ See 1.

8. انتدب لَهُ *He answered,* or *complied with,* or *obeyed, his call, summons,* or *invitation,* (Ṣ,) *and hastened to him,* when called to war, succour, &c. (TA.) — انتدب اللّٰهُ لِمَنْ خَرَجَ فِى سَبِيلِهِ (occurring in a trad., TA,) *God answereth his prayer for forgiveness* [*who goeth forth to fight for the sake of his religion*]: or *is surety,* or *guarantee, for him:* or *hasteneth to grant him a good recompense:* or *graciously maketh his completion of that* [*recompense*] *to him necessary and sure.* (Ḳ.) — انتدبوا إِلَيْهِ *They hastened to him,* either at his call, or summons, or of their own accord. (TA.) — خُذْ مَا انتدب *Take thou what is easily attainable; what offers itself without difficulty:* (AA, Ḳ:) as also ما انتدم. (TA.) — See 1 ═ انتدب لَهُ *He opposed him in his speech.* (Ḳ.) ═ إِيَّاكُمْ وَرِضَاعَ السَّوْءِ فَإِنَّهُ لَا بُدَّ مِنْ أَنْ يَنْتَدِبَ *Beware of giving your children to a bad nurse; for it* [that is the evil consequence, or the bad qualities that will be acquired,] *will inevitably appear* some day. Said by 'Omar. (TA.)

نَدْبٌ A man who is *light,* or *active,* (and quick, TA,) *in the accomplishment of an affair,* or *a want;* (Ṣ, Ḳ;) as also ↓ مِنْدَبِىٌّ (Ḳ) and ↓ مِنْدِبِىٌّ: (TA:) a man *who, when he is sent to accomplish a great,* or *an important, affair, finds it light to him:* (A:) *clever, ingenious,* or *acute in mind; excellent:* pl. نُدُوبٌ and نُدَبَاءُ: (Ḳ:) the former agreeable with analogy; the latter formed from the imaginary sing. نَدِيبٌ; like سُمَحَاءُ, pl. of سَمْحٌ. (TA.) — نَدْبٌ, as applied to a horse, *Sharp-spirited;* (Lth, Ṣ;) contr. of بَلِيدٌ (Lth) *excellent.* (TA.) — نَدْبٌ *Lightness,* or *activity.* (MF.) — أَرَاكَ نَدْبًا فِى الحَوَائِجِ [*I see thee to be clever in accomplishing affairs,* or *wants.* (A.) ═ See نَدَبٌ.

نَدَبٌ, (Ṣ, Ḳ,) and, by poetical licence, ↓ نَدْبٌ, (MF,) The *scar,* (Ṣ,) or *scars,* (Ḳ,) *of a wound,* (Ṣ, Ḳ,) *not rising above the surrounding skin:* (Ṣ:) accord. to the Ḳ, pl. نَدَبَةٌ [which is written in several MS. copies of the Ḳ نُدْبَةٌ; and so in the CḲ; but this, accord. to the TA, is incorrect;] but it is a coll. gen. n., of which the n. un. is نَدَبَةٌ, like as شَجَرَةٌ is that of شَجَرٌ: (MF:) pl. أَنْدَابٌ and نُدُوبٌ: (Ḳ:) the former of نَدَبٌ agreeably with analogy: the latter dev. with respect to analogy; or pl. of نَدْبٌ. (MF.) — نَدَبٌ is also applied, in a trad., to the ‡ *Marks* made by Moses' smiting the stone [from which, thereupon, water flowed forth]; these marks being thus likened to the scars of wounds. (TA.) — نَدَبٌ is also employed to signify ‡ *Scars* upon men's reputation. A poet says,

قَوْمٌ سَأَتْرُكُ فِى أَعْرَاضِهِمْ نَدَبَا

A people upon whose reputation I will leave scars, the effects of my satires. (TA.) ═ نَدَبٌ The *direction in which one shoots an arrow* or *arrows:* syn. رِشْقٌ. (So in the Ṣ and the CḲ and several MS. copies of the Ḳ: in other copies, رَشْقٌ The *act of shooting an arrow* or *arrows.* Both these readings are correct accord. to the TA. See below.) إِرْتَمَى نَدَبًا أَوْ نَدَبَيْنِ *He shot an arrow* or *arrows in one direction* or *in two directions:* syn. وَجْهًا أَوْ وَجْهَيْنِ. (TA.) — نَدَبُنَا يَوْمَ كَذَا (said by those who are to contend at a shooting-match, TA,) *The day of our commencing shooting shall be such a day.* (Ḳ.) This confirms the assertion in the TA, that نَدَبٌ is syn. with رَشْقٌ, as well as with رِشْقٌ. In the Turk. Ḳ, in the place of يَوْمَ ٱبْتِدَائِنَا, we find يوم ٱنْتِدَابِنَا; and Freytag adopts the latter reading; but I find no other authority for it.] — نَدَبٌ *A bet, wager, stake,* or *thing wagered; what is staked at a shooting-match,* or *a race, and taken by the winner:* (Ṣ,* Ḳ,* L:) pl. أَنْدَابٌ. (Mṣb.) So in the following phrases. — بَيْنَهُمْ نَدَبٌ [*Between them is a bet,* or *wager*]. — أَقَامَ فُلَانٌ عَلَى نَدَبٍ [*Such a one stood to a bet, wager,* or *stake*]. (TA.) — 'Orweh says,

أَيَهْلِكُ مُعْتَمٌّ وَزَيْدٌ وَلَمْ أَقُمْ
عَلَى نَدَبٍ يَوْمًا وَلِى نَفْسُ مُخْطِرِ

[*Shall Moątemm and Zeyd perish, and I not stand to a stake, some day, when I have the soul of one who makes his life a stake to his adversary and sallies forth against him?*] These two were his ancestors. (Ṣ.) Or, accord. to Az, who reads أَتَهْلِكُ, they were two tribes. (TA.)

نَدُبٌ: see نَدِيبٌ.

نَدَبَةٌ [a fem. epithet] Any camel's foot, or hoof, [meaning any camel, or hoofed beast,] *that does not remain in one state.* (Ḳ.)

نُدْبَةٌ, a subst., *A call; a summons; an invitation to do a thing.* (Mṣb.) — نُدْبَةٌ: a subst., ‡ The *act of wailing for, weeping for, lamenting,* or *deploring the loss of, one who is dead, as described in the explanations of* نَدَبَ المَيِّتَ, and نَدَبَتْهُ. (Ṣ, Ḳ, M, Mṣb.) — هَاءُ النُّدْبَةِ [*The* ه *of lamentation*]. ═ عَرَبِىٌّ نُدْبَةٌ *An Arabian of chaste speech;* (Ḳ;) *eloquent.* (TA.)

نَدِيبٌ, (Ḳ,) or ↓ نَدِبٌ, (L,) A back *having upon it scars, such as are termed* نُدُوب: (L, Ḳ:) the former epithet is also applied in the same sense to a wound: and, so applied, is also explained by the word مَنْدُوبٌ: (TA:) [app. meaning *that will be wailed for,* or *deplored;* i.e., *fatal*].

نَادِبَةٌ ‡ *A wailing woman;* or *one wailing for, weeping for,* or *deploring the loss of, one who is dead, as described in the explanations of* نَدَبَ المَيِّتَ, and نَدَبَتْهُ: (M, Mṣb:) pl. نَوَادِبُ. (Mṣb.)

النَّدَّابَتَانِ a name given to *Two bad marks in horses.* (TA.)

مَنْدَبٌ *A place to which one is called, summoned,* or *invited.* Hence بَابُ المَنْدَبِ [The Strait Báb el-Mendeb, or *The Strait of the Place of Summons:*] so called because a certain king summoned a number of men to break through the mountain there, which originally opposed a barrier to the sea, in order to drown his enemy; and this they did, thus overwhelming with the waters many cities and towns with their inhabitants, and forming the sea which intervenes between El-Yemen and Abyssinia, and which extends to 'Eydháb and Ḳuṣeyr [&c.]. (Yaąkoot.) This king was Alexander the Greek! (TA.) [It is probable that the appearance of the Strait gave rise to this story, and thus to its name: but it is also probable that the name may signify *The Strait of the Place of Wailing for the Dead*; as many perish who go forth from it.]

مِنْدَبَى and مِنْدِبَى : see نَدْبٌ.

مَنْدُوبٌ : see مُنَدَّبٌ.

مَنْدُوبٌ One *sent to do a thing; a messenger; an envoy; an ambassador.* (TA.) — فُلَانٌ مَنْدُوبٌ لِأَمْرٍ عَظِيمٍ, and ▾ لَهُ مُنَدَّبٌ, *Such a one is sent to do a great thing; or to perform an important affair.* (A.) — ▾ مُنَدِّبَةٌ an appellation, given by the people of Mekkeh to their *Envoys, or ambassadors, to the palace of the Khaleefeh.* (TA.) — مَنْدُوبٌ *Desired; sought; sought after;* as the name of a certain horse it is thus explained: from نَدَبٌ, as signifying "a pledge that is given on the occasion of a race." (L.) — مَنْدُوبٌ: see نَدَبَ المَيِّتَ: A thing *bewailed,* [or *complained of as painful,*] *with the exclamation of* يَا or وَا, *O!* or *Alas!* (KT.) [The name of the thing thus bewailed, or complained of, has always an ا of prolongation and ه annexed to it, or the ا only.] — مَنْدُوبٌ, originally مَنْدُوبٌ إِلَيْهِ, A thing *to the performance of which one is called, summoned,* or *invited:* (Mṣb:) [hence,] *approved:* (Ḳ:) a signification verified by the doctors of practical law: (TA:) a thing *the doing of which is more excellent than the leaving it undone, in the eye of the prescriber of the law, but which it is allowable to leave undone.* (KT.) [Freytag, in quoting the original words, omits فِعْلُهُ before رَاجِحًا.]

ندح

1. نَدَحَهُ, aor. ـَ, (A, Ḳ,) inf. n. نَدْحٌ; and ▾ نَدَّحَهُ, (A,) inf. n. تَنْدِيحٌ; (TA;) *He made it* (a place, A) *spacious, roomy, wide, or ample.* (A, Ḳ.) — Hence the saying of Umm-Selemeh to 'Áïsheh, (when she desired to go forth to El-Baṣrah, TA,) قَدْ جَمَعَ القُرْآنُ ذَيْلَكِ فَلَا تَنْدَحِيهِ, i.e., [*The Ḳur-án hath drawn together, or contracted, thy skirt; therefore*] *do not widen it,* (Ṣ, L, Ḳ,) or *do not spread it abroad,* (L,) by thy going forth to El-Baṣrah: (Ṣ, L, Ḳ:) the pronoun ه refers to the word ذيل: the speaker alluded to the words of the Ḳur-án, [xxxiii. 33,] وَقَرْنَ فِي بُيُوتِكُنَّ وَلَا تَبَرَّجْنَ. (L.) Accord. to one relation, the last words are لَا تَبْدَحِيهِ, i.e., do not open it. (Ṣ.) — نَدَحَتِ النَّعَامَةُ أُدْحُوحَةً *The ostrich excavated and made wide a hollow place for her eggs.* (A.) — أَتْرَبَ فَنَدَحَ *He became possessed of wealth like the dust, and enlarged his mode of life, and scattered his property.* A proverb. (MF, from Meyd.)

2: see 1.

3. نادحهُ *He vied with him, or contended with him for superiority, in multitude, or abundance.* (R.)

5. تَنَدَّحَتِ الغَنَمُ مِنْ مَرَابِضِهَا, (Ṣ, Ḳ,) or فِي مَرَابِضِهَا, (A, L, &c.,) and ▾ انتدحت, (TA,) *The sheep, or goats, became dispersed from,* (Ṣ, Ḳ,) or *in,* (A, L, &c.,) *their nightly resting-places, and became distended by repletion.* (Ṣ, A, L, Ḳ.)

8: see 5.

9. إِنْدَحَّ بَطْنُهُ, inf. n. إِنْدِحَاحٌ, *His belly became distended by reason of repletion.* (Ṣ.) This, says IB, is its proper art., not art. دح. (TA, art. دح, in which J also mentions it.) F says, that J is in error in mentioning this verb, as also in mentioning إِنْدَاحَ بَطْنُهُ, inf. n. إِنْدِيَاحٌ, in the present art.; the proper place of the former being in art. دح; and that of the latter, in art. دوح: but MF says, that J has merely mentioned them here because of the resemblance of their radical letters and significations to the radical letters and significations belonging to this art. (TA.)

نَدْحٌ and ▾ نُدْحٌ (Ḳ) and ▾ مَنْدُوحَةٌ and ▾ مُنْتَدَحٌ (Ṣ) *Spaciousness; roominess; width; ampleness* (L, Ḳ.) = Also, ▾ نُدْحٌ (Ṣ, Ḳ) and نَدْحٌ and ▾ مُنْتَدَحٌ and ▾ مَنْدُوحَةٌ and ▾ نُدْحَةٌ and ▾ نَدْحَةٌ (Ḳ) *A spacious, roomy, wide, or ample, tract of land;* (Ṣ, Ḳ;) as also أَرْضٌ مَنْدُوحَةٌ: (L:) and ▾ مُنْتَدَحٌ *a spacious, roomy, wide, or ample, place:* (Ṣ:) pl. (of the first and second words, TA) أَنْدَاحٌ; (Ṣ, Ḳ;) and pl. of مندوحة, مَنَادِيحُ, and by poetic licence مَنَادِحُ; (TA;) which is allowable also in other cases than those of poetical licence: (MF;) and it (منادح) also signifies *deserts; or waterless deserts.* (Ṣ.) — Also ▾ وَادٍ نَادِحٌ *A wide valley.* (L.) — ▾ لَكَ فِي هٰذِهِ الدَّارِ مُنْتَدَحٌ *Thou hast ample space, or room, in this house.* (A.) — لِي عَنْ هٰذَا الأَمْرِ مَنْدُوحَةٌ ▾, and ▾ مُنْتَدَحٌ, *I have ample scope, freedom, or liberty, to avoid this thing, or affair:* (Ṣ, L:) or *I have that which renders me in no need of this thing, or affair.* (L.) — إِنَّ فِي المَعَارِيضِ لَمَنْدُوحَةً ▾ عَنِ الكَذِبِ [a trad.,] *Verily, in oblique, indirect, ambiguous, or equivocal, modes of speech, is ample scope, freedom, or liberty, to avoid lying:* (Ṣ, L:) or, *that which renders one in no need of lying:* (L:) one should not say مُنْدُوحَةٌ, (TA,) nor مَمْدُوحَةٌ. (Ṣ.) — نَدْحٌ and ▾ نُدْحٌ also signify *Multitude; copiousness; abundance.* (L, Ḳ.) — Also, The *face of a mountain, or part which faces the spectator, above its foot, or base;* (Ḳ;) *its side, or extremity,* which inclines to width: (TA:) pl. أَنْدَاحٌ. (Ḳ.)

نِدْحٌ *A heavy thing;* syn. ثِقْلٌ. (Ḳ.) — Also, *A thing that one sees from afar.* (Ḳ.)

نُدْحَةٌ, نَدْحَةٌ, نَادِحٌ, مَنْدُوحَةٌ, مُنْتَدَحٌ: see نَدْحٌ.

أُنْدُوحَةٌ *A wide hollow place excavated by an ostrich for her eggs.* (A.)

ندر

1. نَدَرَ, (T, Ṣ, M, &c.,) aor. ـُ, (Ṣ, M, Mṣb,) inf. n. نَدْرٌ, (Ṣ,) or نُدُورٌ, (M, Mṣb, Ḳ,) [which latter is the more common, if not the only right, form,] *It fell,* (T, M, Mṣb, Ḳ,) or *went, or came, out, or forth, from another thing,* or *from other things,* (Mṣb,) or *from amid a thing,* (T,) or *from the inside of a thing,* (T, M, Ḳ,) or *from among things, so as to be apparent,* or *standing out to view;* (M, Ḳ;) *it fell, and became apart, fell off, fell out,* or *went, or came, out, or forth, from the generality of things,* or *the general assemblage, main body, bulk, or common mass, to which it pertained,* or *from other things:* (Ṣ, TA:) or, [in some cases,] simply, *it fell,* or *dropped.* (TA.) — نَدَرَ مِنْ قَوْمِهِ *He went forth* [*and became separated*] *from his people.* (Mṣb.) And نَدَرَ مِنْ بَيْتِهِ *He went forth from his house or tent.* (A.) I heard one say to his wife, أُنْدُرِي [*Go thou forth and be separate:* app. meaning, *be thou divorced*]. (Z, in the A, immediately following what here immediately precedes.) — نَدَرَ العَظْمُ, (A,) or نَدَرَ مِنْ مَوْضِعِهِ, (Mṣb,) *The bone became dislocated* or *displaced.* (A, Mṣb.) It is said of a man, in a trad., عَضَّ يَدَ آخَرَ فَنَدَرَ ثَنِيَّتُهُ [or, accord. to another relation, نَدَرَتْ, meaning, *He bit the arm, or hand, of another, and his central incisor dropped out*]. (TA.) — نَدَرَ طَائِرٌ عَنْ شَجَرَةٍ *A bird dropped and alighted from a tree.* (TA.) — نَدَرَ نَادِرٌ مِنَ الجَبَلِ *A prominence projected,* or *jutted out, from the mountain.* (A.) — أَصَابَ المَطَرُ الحَشِيشَ فَنَدَرَ الرُّطْبُ *The rain fell upon the dry herbage and the fresh herbage came forth.* (A.) And نَدَرَ النَّبَاتُ *The plant put forth its leaves* (M, Ḳ) *from its uppermost branches.* (M.) And نَدَرَتِ الشَّجَرَةُ *The tree produced its* خُوصَة [q. v.]; (M, Ḳ;) which is the case when the camels are able to pasture upon them: (M:) or *became green.* (Ṣgh, Ḳ.) — نَدَرَ فِي عِلْمٍ, or فَضْلٍ, (IḲṭṭ,) and فِي فَضْلِهِ, (Mṣb,) ‡ *He outwent others* [or *became extraordinary*] (IḲṭṭ, Mṣb) *in knowledge or science,* or *in excellence,* (IḲṭṭ,) and *in his excellence.* (Mṣb.) — نَدَرَ الكَلَامُ, ‡ inf. n. نَدَارَةٌ, (Mṣb, TA,) ‡ *The speech, or language, was extraordinary* or *strange,* [with respect to usage or analogy or both]: (TA:) *it was the contr. of chaste:* (Mz, 13th نَوْع:) [but this explanation requires restriction; for what is extraordinary with respect to usage is the contr. of chaste; but many a word that is extraordinary with respect to analogy is more chaste than a cognate word agreeable with analogy: hence the above phrase is also explained as signifying] *the speech,* or *language, was chaste and good.* (Mṣb.)

4. اندرهُ, trans. of نَدَرَ, *He made it to fall,* or *to go,* or come, out, or *forth, from another thing,*

or *from other things*; [&c.: see 1:] (Mṣb:) *he made it to fall.* (Ṣ, Ḳ.) You say, ضَرَبَ يَدَهُ بِالسَّيْفِ فَأَنْدَرَهَا [*He struck his arm,* or *hand, with the sword, and made it to fall.*] (Ṣ.) And أَنْدَرَ مِنَ الحِسَابِ كَذَا † [*He made such a thing to fall out, he threw it out, from the reckoning*]. (Ṣ.) And أَنْدَرَ البِكَارَةَ فِى الدِّيَةِ † *He threw out,* or *rejected, the young camels in the mulct for homicide.* (A.) [See also 6.] And أَنْدَرَ عَنْهُ مِنْ مَالِهِ كَذَا † *He took forth* (أَخْرَجَ) *from him, of his property, such a thing.* (M, Ḳ, TA.) And أَنْدَرْتُ يَدَ فُلَانٍ عَنْ مَالِى † *I caused* [*the hand of*] *such a one to cease from freely disposing of my property.* (A.) — اندر *He said,* or *did, something extraordinary,* or *strange.* (IḲṭṭ.)

6. تنادروا [*They mutually threw out,* or *rejected, a thing from a reckoning*]. A poet (namely Aboo-Kebeer El-Hudhalee, TA) says,

وَإِذَا الكُمَاةُ تَنَادَرُوا طَعْنَ الكُلَى
نَدْرَ البِكَارَةِ فِى الجَزَآءِ المُضْعَفِ

[*When the courageous men covered with arms mutually threw out from the reckoning the piercing of the kidneys, as the young camels fall out from the reckoning in the doubled compensation*]: he says, that their blood is suffered to be shed unrevenged, like as the young camels are thrown out from the account in the mulct for homicide: (Ṣ, TA:) meaning, that the pierced kidneys are thrown out from the reckoning, like as the young camel is thrown out, and not reckoned, in the mulct for homicide that is doubled time after time. (IB, TA.) — فُلَانٌ يَتَنَادَرُ عَلَيْنَا (A, TA) † *Such a one comes to us* [*rarely,* or] *sometimes.* (TA.)

10. استندرت الإِبِلُ *The camels sought after the leaves that had come forth upon the uppermost branches of the plants, to eat them, and applied themselves diligently to them:* (M:) [or you say,] استندرت النَّبَاتَ *they sought after the plants, to eat them, and applied themselves diligently to them.* (TA.) And المَالُ يَسْتَنْدِرُ الرُّطْبَ [*The camels*] *seek after the fresh herbage leisurely, and by degrees,* or *repeatedly.* (A.) [The original signification of استندر seems to be *He desired to find a thing* or *things in a separate* or *scattered state*; or *to single out.*] — استندروا أَثَرَهُ † *They tracked his footsteps.* (A.)

نَدْرَةٌ and ▾ نُدْرَةٌ, with fet-ḥ and ḍamm, are substs. from نَدَرَ, [signifying The *state of being apart from,* or *out of, the generality,* or *main body*; &c.: — and hence, † *Extraordinariness*; *rareness.*] (Mṣb.) You say, لَا يَكُونُ ذٰلِكَ إِلَّا فِى النَّدْرَةِ, or ▾ فِى النُّدْرَةِ, and ▾ الَّا نَادِرًا, (Mṣb,) and لَا يَقَعُ ذٰلِكَ إِلَّا فِى النَّدْرَةِ, (A,) † *That will not be,* (Mṣb,) and *that will not happen,* (A,) *save* [*extraordinarily*; *or rarely*; or *once*] *in,* or *during, the space of* [*several*] *days*; syn. فِيمَا بَيْنَ الأَيَّامِ. (Mṣb.) And إِنَّمَا يَكُونُ ذٰلِكَ فِى النَّدْرَةِ بَعْدَ النَّدْرَةِ † *That is,* or *will be, only once in whiles.* (TA.) And لَقِيَهُ نَدْرَةً, (M, Ḳ,) and فِى النَّدْرَةِ, (Ṣ, M, Ḳ,) and ▾ فِى النَّدِيرَةِ, (Ṣ, TA,) and ▾ فِى النُّدْرَةِ, (TA,) and ▾ نَدْرَى (M, Ḳ) and فِى نَدْرَى, (Ṣ, Ḳ,) and النَّدْرَى, (M, Ḳ,) and فِى النَّدْرَى, (Ṣ, M, Ḳ,) † *He met him* [*once*] *in,* or *during, the space of* [*several*] *days*; syn. بَيْنَ الأَيَّامِ, (M, Ḳ,) or فِيمَا بَيْنَ الأَيَّامِ. (Ṣ.) — Also نَدْرَةٌ *A piece of gold,* (Ḳ,) and *of silver,* (TA,) *found in the mine.* (Ḳ.) See also شَذْرٌ.

نُدْرَةٌ : } see نَدْرَةٌ.
نَدَرَةٌ :

نَدْرَى : see نَدْرَةٌ. — نَقَدَهُ مِائَةً نَدْرَى *He produced* [or *payed*] *to him a hundred out of his property.* (M, Ḳ.)

نَدِيرَةٌ : see نَدْرَةٌ.

نَادِرٌ [act. part. n. of نَدَرَ; *Falling,* or *going,* or *coming, out,* or *forth, from another thing*; &c.: see 1]. — *A wild ass going,* or *coming, forth from the mountain.* (TA.) — *A prominence,* or *projecting part,* of a mountain. (A,* Mṣb.) — [*What remains here and there upon the ground, of rain,* i. e., *of rain-water*: n. un. with ة: pl. of the latter, نَوَادِرُ.] You say, شَرِبَتِ الإِبِلُ مِنْ نَادِرِ, and نَوَادِرِهِ المَطَرِ, [*The camels drank of what remained here and there upon the ground, of the water of the rain.*] (A.) — † *Extraordinary*; *strange*; *rare*; *unusual*; applied to speech or language [and to a word and any other thing: fem. and n. un. with ة: pl. of the latter as above: see نَدَرَ, and نَدَرَ]: (A:) or *very extraordinary, strange, rare,* or *unusual,* applied to speech or language; and in like manner نَادِرَةٌ [as an epithet in which the quality of a subst. predominates] applied to a word: pl. of the latter as above: (Mz, 13th نوع: [see also مُطَّرِدٌ:]) or نَوَادِرُ الكَلَامِ signifies *what deviate from the generality of words* or *speech* or *language.* (Ṣ,* M, Ḳ.) You say also, فُلَانٌ نَادِرَةُ الزَّمَانِ, meaning, † *Such a one is the unequalled of the age.* (Ḳ,* TA.) [And نَادِرَةٌ, used in this manner as a subst., signifies † Any *extraordinary, strange, rare,* or *unusual, thing,* or *saying*: pl. as above.] See مُضْحِكَاتٌ. — لَا يَكُونُ ذٰلِكَ إِلَّا نَادِرًا : see نَدْرَةٌ.

أَنْدَرُ i. q. بَيْدَرٌ [*A place in which wheat* or *grain is trodden out*]; (Ṣ, M, Ḳ;) in the dial. of the people of Syria: (Ṣ, M:) or, (Ḳ,) accord. to Kr, (M,) *reaped wheat collected together*; or *wheat collected together in the place where it is trodden out*: (M, Ḳ:) pl. أَنَادِرُ. (Ṣ, Ḳ.)

[ندس, &c.,
See Supplement.]

نذر

1. نَذَرَ عَلَى نَفْسِهِ, (Yoo, Akh, T, Ṣ, M, A,* Ḳ,) aor. ِ and ُ, (M, Ḳ,) inf. n. نَذْرٌ (Yoo, Akh, Ṣ, M, Ḳ,) and نُذُورٌ, (M, Ḳ,) [*He made a vow*; *imposed upon himself a vow*; أَنْ يَفْعَلَ كَذَا *that he would do such a thing*; either *absolutely,* or *conditionally,* as will be explained below;] *he made* [a future action] *binding,* or *obligatory, on himself*; (T, M, A, Ḳ;) as also ▾ انتذر. (Ḳ.) And ▾ انتذر نَذْرًا signifies the same as نَذَرَ [*He vowed a vow*]. (Ṣgh.) You say also نَذَرْتُ مَالِى, aor. ُ [and ِ as implied in the Ḳ] inf. n. نَذْرٌ, [*I vowed my property*; *made a vow to give it.*] (Yoo, Akh, Ṣ, Ḳ.*) And نَذَرْتُ لِلّٰهِ كَذَا, (Ṣ, Mṣb, Ḳ,) aor. ُ and ِ, (Ṣ, Mṣb,) inf. n. نَذْرٌ, (Mṣb,) *I made it binding,* or *obligatory, on myself,* [i. e., *I vowed,*] *of my own free will, to do* or *to give such a thing to God*; namely, some religious service, or an alms, &c.: (TA:) or نَذْرٌ signifies the *promising conditionally*; as when one says, "*Such a thing shall be obligatory on me if God restore to health my sick* [*son* or *other*]:" this is termed نَذْرٌ: but the saying "I impose upon myself the giving a deenár as alms," is not so termed. (Ḳ.) The doing this is repeatedly forbidden in traditions: but what is meant thereby is, one's doing so in the belief that he may attain by it something which God has not decreed to betide him, or that he may divert from himself something decreed to befall him: yet if he do so, fulfilment is obligatory on him. (IAth.) You say also, نَذَرَ الوَلَدَ, (M, Ḳ,) and نَذَرَتْهُ, (M,) *He* (the father, M, Ḳ) and *she* (the mother, M) *appointed the child* [*by a vow*] *to be a minister* or *servant to the church,* (M, Ḳ,) or *to a place appropriated to religious services* or *exercises,* or *acts of devotion*: (TA:) so in the Ḳur, iii. 31. (M.) — نَذِرَ بِالشَّىْءِ, aor. َ, (M, IḲṭṭ, Mṣb, Ḳ,) inf. n. نَذَرٌ (M, IḲṭṭ) and نَذَارَةٌ and نِذَارَةٌ, (IḲṭṭ,) or, as some assert, it has no inf. n., like عَسَى &c., the Arabs being content to use in its stead أَنْ followed by the verb, as is said in the 'Ináyeh, on the Ḳur, chap. xiv., (MF,) *He knew of the thing*: (Mṣb:) or *he knew of the thing and was cautious of it* or *on his guard against it* or *in fear of it.* (M, Ḳ.) You say also نَذِرَ القَوْمُ بِالعَدُوِّ (Ṣ, A) *The people knew of the enemy*: (Ṣ:) or *knew of the enemy and prepared themselves for them*: (A:) or *knew of the enemy and were cautious of them* or *on their guard against them* or *in fear of them.* (TA.) And it is said in a trad., إِنْذَرِ القَوْمَ *Have thou knowledge of the people and be cautious of them* or *on thy guard against them* or *in fear of them.* (TA.)

4. انذرته الشَّىْءَ, أَنْذَرْتُهُ بِالأَمْرِ, (M, Ḳ,) and (Mṣb,) inf. n. إِنْذَارٌ (T, Ṣ, M, Mṣb, Ḳ) and نُذْرٌ (M, Ḳ) the latter accord. to Kr, but correctly it is a simple subst., (M,) and نُذُرٌ, (T, Ḳ,) or this is pl. of نَذِيرٌ, (T,) and نُذْرٌ, (Ḳ,) accord. to Lḥ and Kr, (TA,) [but this is properly a simple subst.,] and نَذِيرٌ, (M, Ḳ,) accord. to Zj, (M,) or Ez-Zejjájee, (TA,) but this should rather be regarded as a simple subst., (T, M,) *I informed him*, or *advised him, of the thing*: (M, Ḳ, TA:) this is the primary signification: (TA:) and [*I warned him of the thing*;] *I cautioned him*, or *put him on his guard, against the thing, and put him in fear*, (M,* Ḳ,) *in my communication* or *announcement*: (Ḳ:) in this sense the verb is used in the Ḳur, xl. 18: (M, TA:) or *I announced to him the thing*, (Ṣ,* Mṣb,) generally in a case of *putting in fear the person addressed*, or *frightening him*, (Mṣb,) or never otherwise than in such a case: (Ṣ:) and thus the verb is used in the Ḳur, ubi supra., وَأَنْذِرْهُمْ يَوْمَ الآزِفَةِ [*And warn them and put them in fear of the day of the approaching event*, the day of resurrection] meaning, put them in fear of its punishment: (Mṣb:) and أَنْذَرْتُهُ بِكَذَا *I informed him*, or *advised him, of such a thing*. (Mṣb.) انذره also signifies *He* (a spy) *informed him*, or *advised him, of the state of the enemy*: in the copies of the Ḳ, نَذَرَهُ; but this is a mistake. (TA.) And you say, أَنْذَرْتُ القَوْمَ مَسِيرَ العَدُوِّ إِلَيْهِمْ *I informed the people of the march of the enemy towards them, to put them on their guard*. (T.) And أَنْذَرْتُهُمُ العَدُوَّ, and أَنْذَرْتُ القَوْمَ بِالعَدُوِّ, signify the same. (A.) It is said in a proverb, قَدْ أَعْذَرَ مَنْ أَنْذَرَ, meaning, *He hath become excused*, and averted from himself the blame of men, *who hath warned* thee that he will punish thee for a future evil deed proceeding from thee, if thou then do the evil deed and he punish thee. (T.) See also أَعْذَرَ, in two places: and see عُذْرٌ.

6. تنادر القَوْمُ *The people warned*, or *cautioned, one another*, or *put one another in fear*, (M, Ḳ,) of a terrifying evil. (TA.) You say تنادر القومُ كَذَا *The people warned one another*, (Ṣ,) *and put one another in fear, of such a thing*. (Ṣ, A.) A poet says, (Ṣ,) namely, En-Nábighah, (T, TA,) describing a serpent, (T,) and his being threatened by En-Noamán so that he passed the night as though he had been stung, turning over and over upon his bed, (TA,)

تَنَاذَرَهَا الرَّاقُونَ مِنْ سُوْءِ سَمِّهَا •
تُطَلِّقُهُ طَوْرًا وَطَوْرًا تُرَاجِعُ •

[*Of which the charmers have warned one another, and put one another in fear, on account of the evil nature of its poison, which it discharges one time and one time draws back*]. (T, Ṣ, TA.)

8: see نَذَرَ, in two places.

10. استنذر إِلَيْهِ *He offered warning to him* (A, TA, art. عذر.) See استعذر.

نَذْرٌ *A vow, which a man makes to be binding*, or *obligatory, on himself*; (T, M,* Ḳ,* TA;) [either *absolutely*, or *conditionally*: (see نَذَرَ:)] pl. نُذُورٌ: (Ṣ, M, Ḳ:*) and in the following verse of Ibn-Aḥmar, some say that نُذُرٌ is pl. of نَذْرٌ, like as رُهُنٌ is pl. of رَهْنٌ; but others say that it is pl. of نَذِيرٌ in the sense of مَنْذُورٌ:

كَمْ دُونَ لَيْلَى مِنْ تَنُوفِيَّةٍ •
لَمَّاعَةٍ تُنْذَرُ فِيهَا النُّذُرْ •

[*How many a waterless desert glistening with the mirage, in which vows*, or *things vowed, are vowed, lie in the way to Leylà!*]. (Ṣ.) —— Also, ‡ *The mulct for an intentional wound*; used in this sense by Esh-Sháfi'ee, (T, TA,) and of the dial. of El-Ḥijáz; (TA;) *i.q.* أَرْشٌ, (T, A, Ḳ, TA,) which is of the dial. of the people of El-'Irák: (T, TA:) pl. نُذُورٌ: (T, A, Ḳ:) said by Aboo-Nahshal to be *only for wounds, small and great*. (T, Ḳ.*) You say, عِنْدَ فُلَانٍ, (T, TṢ, L,) or لِى قِبَلَ فُلَانٍ نَذْرٌ, (Ḳ,) ‡ *A mulct for a wound is owed to me*. (T, Ḳ, &c.) And أَعْطَيْتُهُ نَذْرَ جُرْحِهِ ‡ *I gave him the mulct for his wound*. (A.) Aboo-Sa'eed Ed-Dareer says that it is thus called لِأَنَّهُ نُذِرَ فِيهِ, i. e., because it is made binding, or obligatory, for it; [namely, for the wound;] from the phrase نَذَرْتُ على نَفْسِي. (T, TA.) —— [*A votive offering*]. —— See also نُذُرٌ.

نُذْرٌ (M) and ▼ نُذُرٌ (T, Ṣ, Ḳ) [and ▼ نَذْرٌ (see 4)] and ▼ نَذِيرٌ (Ṣ, M) and ▼ نَذِيرَةٌ (M) and ▼ نَذَارَةٌ (Esh-Sháfi'ee, Ḳ) and ▼ نُذْرَى (Ḳ) are substs. in the sense of إِنْذَارٌ [meaning *An informing*, or *advising, of a thing*: and *a warning*, or *cautioning, and putting one on his guard, against a thing, and putting one in fear of a thing*; &c.: (see 4:)] (T, Ṣ, M, Ḳ:) or *a putting one in fear in announcing a thing*. (TA.) عُذْرًا أَوْ نُذْرًا and عُذْرًا أَوْ نُذُرًا, accord. to different readings, in the Ḳur, lxxvii. 6, put in the accus. case as causal complements, signify لِلْإِعْذَارِ وَالْإِنْذَارِ [*For excusing and warning*]. (Zj, T.) [See also art. عذر.] And in like manner, ▼ نُذُرٌ, in the Ḳur, liv. 16, &c., signifies إِنْذَارِى. (Ṣ, Ḳ.) And so ▼ نَذِيرٌ, in the Ḳur, lxvii. 17. (T, M.) Hence also the saying of the Arabs, عُذْرَاكَ لَا نُذْرَاكَ, meaning, أَعْذِرْ وَلَا تُنْذِرْ [i. e. *Do thou that for which thou wilt be excused*, by inflicting punishment when it is deserved, *and do not* merely *warn and put in fear*]. (TA.)

نُذُرٌ : } see نُذْرٌ.
نُذْرَى :

نَذِيرٌ *i. q.* ▼ مُنْذِرٌ, (T, Ṣ, M, A, Mṣb, Ḳ,) as also ▼ نَذِيرَةٌ; (M;) i. e. [One *who gives information*, or *advice, of a thing*, or *things*: and one *who warns*;] one *who cautions*; (M, TA;) *and who puts in fear*: (TA:) one *who gives notice to a people of an enemy*, or *other thing, that has come upon them*; (TA;) *a spy who gives notice, to a people, of an enemy, to put them on their guard*; (A;) and in like manner ▼ نَذِيرَةٌ, *a spy who informs an army of the state of the enemy*: (T, Ḳ:) نَذِيرٌ is of the measure فَعِيلٌ in the sense of the measure مُفْعِلٌ: (M, L:) or its verb was نَذَرَ, but this has become obsolete: (T:) its pl. is نُذُرٌ; (M, Mṣb, Ḳ;) occurring in the Ḳur, liv. 23, [&c.]. (TA.) —— [Hence,] ابو مُنْذِرٍ *The cock* (Ḥar. p. 644). —— [And also,] النَّذِيرُ *The apostle*: (M, Ḳ:) so in the Ḳur, xxxv. 34, accord. to Th: (M:) *the prophet* Moḥammad: (T, Ḳ:) so, accord. to most of the expositors, in that verse of the Ḳur. (T.) —— *Hoariness*, or *whiteness of the hair*: (T, M, Ḳ:) so, accord. to some, in the verse of the Ḳur, last referred to: (T, M:) but the explanation immediately preceding is more probable. (T.) —— *The sound of a bow*: (AḤn, M, Ḳ:) because it warns, or frightens, (يُنْذِرُ,) that which is shot at. (AḤn, M.) —— *I. q.* مَنْذُورٌ [i. e. *Vowed*]: pl. نُذُرٌ. (Ṣ.) See نَذَرَ. —— See also نُذْرٌ.

نَذَارَةٌ : see نُذْرٌ.

نَذِيرَةٌ [*A votive gift*;] *that which he gives who makes a vow*. (M, Ḳ.) —— *A child appointed by the father* (M, Ḳ) *and mother* (M) [*by a vow*] *to be a minister*, or *servant to the church*, (M, Ḳ,) or *to a place appropriated to religious services*, or *exercises*, or *acts of devotion*: (T:) pl. نَذَائِرُ. (T.) —— See also نَذِيرٌ, in two places. —— And see نُذْرٌ.

نَاذِرٌ : see مُنْذِرٌ.

مُنْذِرٌ : } see نَذِيرٌ.
مَنْذُورٌ :

فُلَانٌ مُنْذِرٌ إِلَىَّ بِعَيْنِهِ, and ▼ نَاذِرٌ, *Such a one is looking at me hard* or *intently, and making his eye prominent*. (T, in TA, art. زنر.)

مُتَنَاذَرٌ [A thing *of which people warn* or *caution one another*, or *of which they put one another in fear*]: applied to a disease [&c.]. (TA, art. خبر voce خَيْبَرِى.) —— [Hence,] † المُتَنَاذَرُ *The lion*. (Ṣgh, Ḳ.)

نذل

1. نَذُلَ, inf. n. نَذَالَةٌ, *He was*, or *became, low, base, vile, ignoble, mean, sordid*, or *contemptible*, (Ṣ, Ḳ,) *in all his circumstances*. (Ḳ.)

نَذْلٌ A man *vile*, or *mean, and despised in all his circumstances*. (Ḳ.)

نرب

Q. Q. 1. نَيْرَبَتِ الرِّيحُ التُّرَابَ فَوْقَهُ, or عَلَى الأَرْضِ, (TA,) inf. n. نَيْرَبَةٌ, (TA,) *The wind lays the dust upon it*, or *upon the ground, in cross, wavy lines*: syn. تَنْسِجُهُ. (Ḳ.) Hence نَيْرَبَ الكَلَامَ. (TA.) —— It has been asserted that ن and ر do not come together in any [pure] Arabic word; and F has said the same in art. نرش; [or rather he has there said that ر does not occur in an Arabic word with ن before it;

(meaning a radical ن;)] yet he has here mentioned this word as though it were pure Arabic. So says MF. To this it may be replied, that ى is inserted to separate the ن and ر, as remarked in the L. (TA.) — نَيْرَبَ *He forged* [speech, or language]: syn. نَسَجَ. (Ḳ.) You say هُوَ يُنَيْرِبُ القَوْلَ. (TA.) — نَيْرَبَ *He mixed*, or *confounded*, *speech*, [*introducing what was false with that which was true*]. (Ḳ.) — نَيْرَبَ *He uttered a malicious and mischievous misrepresentation, a calumny*, or *slander*. (Ḳ.)

نَيْرَبٌ (Ṣ, Ḳ) and ▼ نَيْرَبَةٌ (as in several copies of the Ḳ, [and I am inclined to think that this is the correct reading, as it may certainly be correctly used in the sense here given, being properly an inf. n., agreeably with analogy,] or ▼ مَنْرَبَةٌ (as in others, which is said in the TA to be the correct word, and to be given on the authority of AA, [but it exhibits an incongruity of letters: see 1:]) *Mischief; malicious and mischievous misrepresentation, calumny*, or *slander*. (Ṣ, Ḳ.) — نَيْرَبٌ, fem. with ة; and ذُو نَيْرَبٍ; *A mischievous* man; (Ḳ;) one *who utters malicious and mischievous misrepresentations, calumnies*, or *slanders*. (TA.) — نَيْرَبٌ *A strong man.* (Ḳ.)

نَيْرَبَى *A calamity; a misfortune.* (Ḳ.)

نَيْرَبَةٌ and مَنْرَبَةٌ: see نَيْرَبٌ.

نرج

1. نَرَجَ *He thrashed* wheat, or corn, *with a* نَوْرَج. (TA.)

نَوْرَجٌ (L, Ḳ) and ▼ نَيْرَجٌ and ▼ نُورَجٌ, the last of the dial. of El-Yemen, and a word of which there is not the like in Arabic, (L,) *A thrashing-instrument*, or *that with which heaps of wheat*, or *corn, are thrashed, whether of wood* or *of iron*; (L, Ḳ;) or, *of iron and wood*; (Sifr es-Sa'ádeh;) [*a kind of drag, used, in Egypt and Arabia and some other countries of Western Asia, for the purpose of separating the grain of wheat and barley &c. and cutting the straw, which serves as fodder; it is a machine in the form of a chair fixed upon a sledge, which moves upon small iron wheels, or thin circular plates, generally eleven, fixed to three thick axle-trees, four to the foremost, the same number to the hindmost, and three to the intermediate axle-tree: this machine is drawn, in a circle, by a pair of cows or bulls, their driver being seated upon it, over the corn*: pl. [of the first and last words] نَوَارِجُ. (TA.) — Also, the first and second, *A ploughshare.* (Ḳ.)

نُورَجٌ and نَيْرَجٌ: see نَوْرَجٌ.

نَارَنْجٌ *A well-known fruit;* [the *orange; citrus aurantium; of which there are two species common in the gardens of the East, one sweet, and the other bitter*:] an arabicized word, from [the Persian] نَارَنْگ [also called نَارِنج]. (Ḳ.)

نرجس

نَرْجِسٌ and نِرْجِسٌ [*The Narcissus*]: see art. رجس. The former is mentioned by ISd in art. رجس: the latter, in the present art. (TA.)

نرد

نَرْدٌ [The *game of tricktrack, backgammon*, or *tables*: and, app., *a pair of tables and other apparatus with which that game is played*:] *a certain thing with which one plays*; (M, L;) *well known*: (M, L, Ḳ:) a Persian word, (M, L,) arabicized: (M, L:) also called نَرْدَشِيرُ, (M, L, Ḳ,) because invented (as some say, TA) by Ardasheer the son of Bábak, (Ḳ,) a Persian king. (TA.) It is said in a trad., that he who plays at this game is as though he plunged his hand into the flesh and blood of the pig. (L.)

نرز

نَوْرُوزٌ: see what follows.

نَيْرُوزٌ, an arabicized word, (Ṣ, A, Mṣb,) from نَوْرُوزْ, (A, Ḳ,) which in Persian; meaning "new day;" (TA;) and ▼ نَوْرُوزٌ; but the former, which is of the measure فَيْعُولٌ, is the better in repute, because فَوْعُولٌ is not the measure of an Arabic word; (Mṣb;) The *first day of the year; New-year's-day*: (A, Mṣb, Ḳ:) *with the Persians, when the sun enters Aries*: and *with the Copts, the first of* [*the month*] *Toot* [*the ancient Thoth*, or the tenth of September, N.S., excepting when immediately following their leap-year, which is when our next ensuing year is a leap-year]. (Mṣb, TA.) The word نيروز is said to have been first used in the time of the 'Abbásee Khaleefehs; but it is related to have been used in the time of 'Alee. (TA.)

نز

1. نَزَّتِ الأَرْضُ, (A, Mṣb, Ḳ,) aor. ـِ, inf. n. نَزٌّ; (Mṣb;) and ▼ انزّت, (Ṣ, A, Mṣb,) *The ground*, or *land, had water exuding*, or *oozing, from it*: (Ṣ, Ḳ:) or *had much flowing moisture*: (Mṣb:) or *became* [*abundant in*] مَنَابِع [or *places welling forth water*], as in the TṢ and the Ḳ, or مَنَاقِع [or *places of stagnant water*] *by reason of the* نَزّ. (TA.) — [نَزَّتْ بِهِ البِطْنَةُ: see بِطْنَةٌ.] — نَزَّ, aor. ـِ, inf. n. نَزِيزٌ, *He* (an antelope, Ṣ,) *ran*: (Ṣ, Ḳ:) or *he* (an ostrich, and an antelope,) *leaped, jumped, sprang*, or *bounded*. (A.) — *He* (an antelope, Ṣ,) *uttered a cry*, or *cries*. (Ibn-El-Jarráḥ, Ks, Ṣ, Ḳ.)

4: see 1, first signification.

نَزٌّ and ▼ نِزٌّ *Water that exudes*, or *oozes, from the ground*: (Ṣ, Ḳ:) or *flowing moisture*: (Mṣb:) the latter is the better word; and is [said to be] Persian, arabicized: (TA:) the former is an inf. n. used as a subst. (Mṣb.) — [The pl. is نُزُوزٌ, occurring in the TA in art. عذو.] — [The former is also used as an epithet: fem. with ة. You say,] أَرْضٌ نَزَّةٌ *Ground*, or *land, having water exuding*, or *oozing, from it*; syn. ذَاتُ نَزٍّ; as also ▼ نَازَّةٌ. (Lḥ, TA.) — [Hence, perhaps,] نَزٌّ also signifies † *liberal, bountiful*, or *munificent*. (Ṣgh, Ḳ.) — Also, نَزٌّ *Much*, or *many*. (Ḳ.) — A man (A'Obeyd, Ṣ) *light*, or *active*, (A'Obeyd, Ṣ, Ḳ,) or *light in spirit*, (TA,) *sharp in mind*, (A'Obeyd, Ṣ, Ḳ,) *clever*, or *ingenious*, (A'Obeyd, Ḳ,) *and intelligent*. (A'Obeyd, TA.) — *Light, inconstant, fickle*, or *unsteady*: (Ḳ:) an epithet of dispraise. (TA.) — A man (TA) *much*, or *often, in motion*; as also ▼ مِنَزٌّ: (Ḳ:) a man, (A,) and an ostrich, (Ṣ, Ḳ, TA,) *that does not remain still in one place*: (Ṣ, A, Ḳ:) or *that is quick*, or *swift, and does not remain still in one place*: (TA:) or an ostrich, and an antelope, *that leaps, jumps, springs*, or *bounds*: (A:) and a *light*, or an *active*, camel; (TA;) and so نَزَّةٌ, applied to a she-camel. (Ṣ, TA.) — *Light* dust. (TA.) — ▼ نِزٌّ, and ▼ نَزِيزَةٌ, *i. q.* لِزٌّ and لَزِيزَةٌ. (TA, art. لز.)

نِزٌّ: see نَزٌّ.

نَزِيزٌ: see نَزٌّ, last sentence.

نَازٌّ: fem. with ة: see نَزٌّ.

مِنَزٌّ *A child's cradle*: (A, Ḳ:) because of its frequent motion. (TA.) — See also نَزٌّ.

نزأ

1. نَزَأَ بَيْنَهُمْ, (Ṣ, Ḳ,) aor. ـَ, inf. n. نَزْءٌ and نُزُوءٌ, (Ṣ,) *He excited discord between them*: (AZ, Ṣ, Ḳ:) like نَزَغَ. (TA.) — نَزَأَهُ عَلَى صَاحِبِهِ *He incited*, or *urged, him against his companion.* (Ḳ,* TA.) — مَا نَزَأَكَ عَلَى هٰذَا *What incited, urged*, or *induced, thee to this?* (Ks, Ṣ.) — نَزَأَ عَلَيْهِ, (Ṣ, Ḳ,) inf. n. نَزْءٌ, (Ṣ,) *He made an attack*, or *assault, upon him*; syn. حَمَلَ. (Ks, Ṣ, Ḳ.) — نَزَأَهُ عَنْ قَوْلِهِ *He turned him back from what he had said.* (Ḳ,* TA.) — نُزِئَ بِهِ, like عُنِىَ, [i.e., pass. in form, but neut. in signification,] *He was addicted*, or *devoted, to it; desirous of it.* (TA.) — إِنَّكَ لَا تَدْرِي عَلَامَ يُنْزَأُ هَرِمُكَ, (Ṣ, Ḳ,) thus thou sayest, addressing thyself, when a man has been pursuing a good or an evil way, and turned from it to another way, or accord. to some copies of the Ṣ, بِمَ instead of عَلَامَ, [which is for عَلَى مَا;] (TA;) *Verily thou knowest not to what thing thy mind will become addicted*, or *devoted*: (ISk, Ṣ, Ḳ:) i. e., to what thy state will come. (Ḳ.) In one copy of the Ḳ, هَرَمُكَ *thine old age*, is put instead of هَرِمُكَ. (TA.)

نَزِىٌّ *An inciter, instigator,* or *exciter.* (TA.)

رَجُلٌ نَزَّآءٌ [*A man much addicted,* or *devoted,* to a thing; *very desirous* of it]. (TA.) [See نَزِىٌّ.]

مَنْزُوٌّ بِهِ *Addicted,* or *devoted, to it; desirous of it.* (Ṣ, Ḳ.)

نزب

1. نَزَبَ, aor. ـِ, inf. n. نَزِيبٌ (Ṣ, Ḳ) and نَزْبٌ and نُزَابٌ (Ḳ) *He* (an antelope) *uttered a cry,* or *sound,* (Ṣ, Ḳ,) *at rutting-time.* (Ṣ.) Used with reference to the buck and the doe; (Ḳ;) or the buck only. (Ṣ, Ḳ.)

6. تنازبوا *i. q.* تنابزوا. (Ḳ.) Accord. to IHsh and others, this verb has not been heard [from the Arabs of the classical ages], but only the subst. نَزَبٌ, which is therefore decided to be a transp. form of نَبَزٌ. (TA.)

نَزَبٌ *A surname; a nickname; a name of reproach; an opprobrious appellation:* syn. لَقَبٌ: (Ḳ:) *i. q.* نَبَزٌ. (TA.) See 6.

نَيْزَبٌ *A buck-antelope;* and *a bull.* (Ḳ.) [By the latter is probably meant the kind of antelope called بَقَرُ الوَحْشِ.]

نزح

1. نَزَحَ, aor. ـِ and ـَ, inf. n. نَزْحٌ and نُزُوحٌ; (Ḳ;) and ↓ انتزح; (TA;) *He,* or *it,* (a thing, TA,) *became distant,* or *remote.* (Ḳ.) — نَزَحَتِ الدَّارُ, inf. n. نُزُوحٌ, *The house,* or *dwelling, became distant,* or *remote.* (Ṣ.) — نُزِحَ بِفُلَانٍ, (Ṣ, Ḳ,) a verb like عُنِىَ, [pass. in form, but neut. in signification,] (Ḳ,) *Such a one became far removed from his dwelling-place.* (Ṣ, Ḳ.) ═ نَزَحَ البِئْرَ, (Ṣ, Mṣb, Ḳ,) aor. ـَ (Mṣb) and ـِ, (TA,) inf. n. نَزْحٌ (Ṣ, Mṣb) and نُزُوحٌ; (Mṣb;) and ↓ أَنْزَحَهَا; (Ḳ;) *He drew forth all the water of the well; exhausted it entirely:* (Ṣ, Mṣb, Ḳ:) or *he drew from it until little water remained in it; nearly exhausted it.* (Ḳ.) — نَزَحَتِ البِئْرُ, (A, Mṣb, Ḳ,) aor. ـَ, (TA,) inf. n. نَزْحٌ (Ḳ) and نُزُوحٌ, (TA,) *The well became entirely exhausted:* (A, Mṣb, Ḳ:) or, *became nearly exhausted.* (Ḳ.) See 4. — قَدْ نَزَحْتَنِى † *Thou hast exhausted me of what I had,* or *possessed.* (L, from a trad.)

4. أَنْزَحَ القَوْمُ, (L, and so in some copies of the Ḳ, [agreeable with analogy,]) or ↓ نَزَحَ, (so in other copies of the Ḳ,) *The people had the water of their wells entirely,* or *nearly, exhausted.* (L, Ḳ.) See 1.

8: see 1.

شَرُّكَ سَرْحٌ وَخَيْرُكَ نَزْحٌ † [*Thy wickedness ranges abroad unrestrained, and*] *thy goodness is little.* (A.)

نَزَحٌ: see نَازِحٌ. — Also, *Turbid water.* (Ḳ.)

نُزُحٌ and نَزُوحٌ and نَزِيحٌ: see نَازِحٌ.

نَازِحٌ and ↓ نَزَحٌ and ↓ نُزُحٌ and ↓ نَزُوحٌ and ↓ نَزِيحٌ *A thing,* (Ḳ,) or dwelling, (TA,) *distant,* or *remote.* (Ḳ.) بَلَدٌ نَازِحٌ *A distant,* or *remote, town,* or *country:* (Ṣ:) and دَارٌ نَازِحَةٌ *a distant,* or *remote, house,* or *dwelling.* (Mṣb.) — ↓ قَوْمٌ مَنَازِيحُ *A distant,* or *remote, people.* (Ṣ, Ḳ.) And إِبِلٌ منازيح *Camels from distant regions.* (A.) ISd says, that it is pl. of ↓ مِنْزَاحٌ, meaning *That comes to the water from a distant place.* (L.) ═ نَازِحٌ and ↓ نَزَحٌ and ↓ نَزُوحٌ *A well entirely exhausted:* or *nearly exhausted:* (Ḳ:) or ↓ بِئْرٌ نَزُوحٌ signifies *a well containing little water:* pl. نُزُحٌ: (Ṣ:) and بِئْرٌ ↓ نَزَحٌ, نَزَحٌ being of the measure فَعَلٌ in the sense of the measure مَفْعُولٌ, *a well containing no water;* and it is allowable to say مَنْزُوحَةٌ: (Mṣb:) or *a well of which the water has been exhausted:* (so in some copies of the Ṣ, and the like in the Nh:) or *a well of which most of the water has been drawn forth.* (So in other copies of the Ṣ, and in the Ḳ.) See an ex., voce مَدَارَةٌ, art. دور.

مِنْزَحَةٌ *A bucket* (Ḳ) *with which water is drawn;* (TA;) and *the like thereof.* (Ḳ.)

مِنْزَاحٌ and مَنَازِيحُ: see نَازِحٌ.

انت بِمُنْتَزَحٍ مِنْ كَذَا † *Thou art far removed from such a thing;* (Ṣ, Ḳ*;) and, by poetic licence, بِمُنْتَزَاحٍ, with أَلِف إِشْبَاع. (Ṣ.) Ex. أَنْتَ مِنَ الذَّمِّ بِمُنْتَزَحٍ † *Thou art far removed from blame.* (A.)

نزر

1. نَزُرَ, aor. ـُ, inf. n. نَزَارَةٌ (Ṣ, A, Mṣb, Ḳ) and نُزُورٌ (Mṣb, Ḳ) and نُزُورَةٌ, (Ḳ,) or نُزْرَةٌ, as in the M and L, and perhaps one of these last two forms is a mistake for the other, (TA,) *It was,* or *became, little,* or *small, in quantity* or *number;* (Ṣ, A, Mṣb, Ḳ;) *paltry, mean, contemptible,* or *inconsiderable.* (Ṣ, TA.) See also 5. — Also, inf. n. نَزَارَةٌ, *He* (a man) *was,* or *became, possessed of little good,* or *little wealth.* (AZ.) — نَزُرَتْ, inf. n. نَزْرٌ, *She* (a camel) *had little milk.* (TA.) ═ نَزَرَهُ, aor. ـُ, (TA,) inf. n. نَزْرٌ, (Ḳ,) *He despised, and deemed little, him,* or *it.* (Ḳ,* TA.) See also 2. — *He smote him with the* [evil] *eye.* (Fr, in TA, art. شزر.) ═ نَزَرَهُ, (Aṣ, A,) aor. ـَ, (Aṣ,) inf. n. نَزْرٌ, (Aṣ, Ḳ,) *He drew forth,* or *got out, what he had, by little and little:* (Aṣ:) *he importuned him,* or *pressed him, in asking* (A, Ḳ) *a matter of science or a gift.* (A.) You say also, فُلَانٌ لَا يُعْطِى حَتَّى يُنْزَرَ, (A, Ḳ,) or ↓ يُنَزَّرَ, (so in two copies of the Ṣ,) *Such a one will not give until he is importuned,* or *pressed,* (A, Ḳ,) *and despised.* (Ṣ, Ḳ, TA.)

2. نزّره, inf. n. تَنْزِيرٌ; (Ḳ;) or ↓ نَزَرَهُ, aor. ـُ, inf. n. نَزْرٌ; (Mṣb;) *He made it little,* or *small, in quantity;* (Mṣb, Ḳ;) namely, a gift; as also ↓ أَنْزَرَهُ. (Ḳ.) — Also نزّره *He gave him a little, small, paltry, mean, contemptible,* or *inconsiderable, gift.* (TA.) [It seems to be implied in the TA, that ↓ أَنْزَرَهُ also has this signification.] ═ See also 1, last signification.

4. انزره: see 2, in two places. — Also, *He* (God) *caused him to be possessed of little good,* or *little wealth.* (AZ.)

5. تنزّر *i. q.* تَقَلَّلَ, (Ḳ,) i. e., *It became diminished,* or *rendered little* or *small in quantity.* (TḲ.) See also نَزُرَ. — *He asserted himself to be related to the tribe of Nizár:* (Ḳ:) or *he made himself like that tribe:* or *he introduced himself among them,* (Ṣ, Ḳ,) *not being one of them.* (TA.)

نَزْرٌ, applied to anything, (TA,) *little,* or *small, in quantity* or *number;* (Ṣ, A, Mṣb;) *paltry, mean, contemptible,* or *inconsiderable:* (Ṣ, TA:) as also ↓ نَزِيرٌ (Mṣb, Ḳ) and ↓ نَزُورٌ (Mṣb) and ↓ مَنْزُورٌ: (Ḳ:) or the last signifies *little,* or *small, in quantity,* applied to a gift, (Ṣ, TA,) and to food; (TA;) or a gift *made little,* or *small, in quantity:* (Mṣb:) and نَزْرٌ and ↓ مَنْزُورٌ a gift *obtained by importunity* or *pressing:* and ↓ غَيْرُ مَنْزُورٍ a gift *given without its being asked for; without importunity* or *pressing.* (TA.) It is also applied to speech: thus the speech of Moḥammad is described as فَصْلٌ لَا نَزْرٌ وَلَا هَذْرٌ [*Distinct;*] *not little,* or *scanty,* so as to indicate impotence, *nor much and corrupt:* (Ḳ:) or *not little nor much.* (TA, art. هذر.) — A man *possessing little,* or *no, good,* or *goodness; little,* or *no, wealth;* and so ↓ مَنْزُورٌ; as also ↓ نَزُورٌ. (AZ.) ═ مَا جِئْتَ إِلَّا نَزْرًا *Thou hast not come otherwise than slowly, tardily,* or *late.* (Ḳ.)

نَزِرَةٌ: see نَزُورٌ.

نِزَارٌ *The quality,* in a she-camel, *of scarcely ever conceiving except against her will.* (TA.)

نَزُورٌ Any thing *little,* or *small, in quantity* or *number.* (Ḳ.) See also نَزْرٌ. — A woman *having few children;* (Ṣ, Ḳ;) and in like manner applied to a bird; (Ṣ, TA;) as also ↓ نَزِرَةٌ, with kesr to the ز, applied to a woman: (Ḳ:) pl. of the former, نُزُرٌ: (TA:) or the former epithet signifies *having little milk;* (Ḳ;) applied in this sense to a she-camel. (TA.) A she-camel *having wide orifices to her teats.* (L, voce فتوح.) — *Of little speech; that speaks not until importuned,* or *pressed.* (En-Naḍr.) — A she-camel *whose young one has died and that affects the young one of another,* (Ḳ

TA,) *but whose milk comes not save scantily.* (TA.) — A she-camel (TA) *that scarcely ever conceives except against her will:* (Ḳ:) a mare *slow to conceive.* (L.)

نَزِيزٌ : } see نَزُّ ; the latter, in five places.
مَنْزُورٌ : }

[نزع, &c.

See Supplement.]

نس

نَسْنَاسٌ (Ṣ, M, Mṣb, Ḳ) and نِسْنَاسٌ (Ḳ) *A kind of creatures* (خَلْق [an appellation often applied particularly to *human beings*]) *whereof* [*every*] *one jumps*, or *hops, upon one leg:* (Ṣ, Mṣb, Ḳ:) it is related in a trad., that a tribe of 'Ád disobeyed their apostle, and that God thereupon transformed them into نَسْنَاس, *every man of them having a* [*single*] *arm and a* [*single*] *leg,* [*consisting*] *of one half* [*of a human being*], *hopping like as the bird hops, and pasturing like as beasts pasture;* (Ḳ;) *and these are found in the islands of China:* (TA:) or, *as some say, these have become extinct;* (Ḳ;) for a transformed being lives not more than three days, as the learned have established; (TA;) *and what exist now, of this make, are a distinct class of creatures:* (Ḳ:) or *they are of three kinds;* نَاسٌ *and* نَسْنَاسٌ *and* نَسَانِسُ ; (Ḳ;) *and the second of these are the baser sort;* (TA;) or *the* نسانس *are the females of them,* (Ḳ,) as Aboo-Sa'eed Ed-Dareer says; (TA;) or *they are of higher rank than the* نسناس, (Ḳ,) as is said in the O: (TA:) or the نسناس are [the *peoples called*] *Yájooj and Májooj:* (IAạr, Mṣb, Ḳ:) or *a certain people of the sons of Adam:* (Ḳ:) or *certain creatures in the form of men,* (M, Ḳ,) *so called because of the weakness of their make,* from نَسْنَسَةٌ, which signifies weakness, (M,) *differing from men in some things, and not of them:* (Ḳ:) or, accord. to what is said [by some], *a certain beast, reckoned among wild animals, that is hunted and eaten, having the form of a man with one eye and leg and arm, and that speaks like man:* (Kr, M:) or *a species of marine animal:* (Mṣb:) or, accord. to El-Mes'oodee, *an animal like a man having one eye, that comes forth from the water, and speaks, and, when it gets a man within its power, kills him:* or, as is related in the مجالسة, on the authority of Ibn-Is-ḥák, *certain creatures* (خَلْق) *in El-Yemen:* ابن الرقيس says, that they are *of the sons of Sám the son of Sám, brothers of 'Ád and Thamood, not possessing reason, living in the salt-water* (الاجاج) *on the coast of the Sea of India: the Arabs hunt them, and speak to them, and they speak the Arabic language, and propagate one with another, and poetize,* or *versify, and name themselves by the names of the Arabs:* (TA:) [in the present day, this appellation is applied to *a pigmy:* and also, to *an ape:*] Es-Suyooṭee says, in the Deewán el-Ḥayawán, as to the animal which the vulgar call نسناس, it is *a species of apes* or *monkeys, not living in water, and the eating of which is unlawful:* but as to the marine animal, some hold it to be lawful; whereas the sheykh Aboo-Ḥámid holds the eating of the نسناس [of any kind] to be unlawful, because it has the form of the sons of Adam. (TA.) It is said in a trad. of Aboo-Hureyreh, ذَهَبَ النَّاسُ وَبَقِىَ النَّسْنَاسُ [*The men have gone, and the* نسناس *remain*]. Being asked who were the نسناس, he answered, *Those who affect to be like men but are not men.* (TA.)

[For the verb نَسَّ, &c.: see Supplement.]

نسأ

1. نَسَأَ, aor. ـَ, (Ṣ, Ḳ,) inf. n. نَسْءٌ; (Ṣ;) and ↓ نَسَّأَ, (Ṣ, Ḳ,) inf. n. تَنْسِئَةٌ, (Ṣ,) *He chid* (Ṣ, Ḳ) a camel (Ṣ) &c. (L) *he urged,* or *drove,* it. (Ṣ, Ḳ.) — نَسَأَ, aor. ـَ, inf. n. نَسْءٌ (Ṣ, Ḳ) and مَنْسَأَةٌ (Ḳ) [and نَسُوْءٌ, mentioned in the TA, art. وضأ;] and ↓ انسأ; (Ṣ, Ḳ;) *He postponed,* or *delayed,* a thing. (Ṣ, Ḳ. Explained in the Ṣ, Ḳ by أَخَّرَ, and in the Ḳ by كَلَأَ, also, both of which words, accord. to the TA, are syn.) [See an ex. of the use of انسا, without a final ء, in art. عقب, voce عُقْبَةٌ.] — نَسَأَ اللّٰهُ فِى أَجَلِهِ, and ↓ انسأ اللّٰهُ أَجَلَهُ, *God postponed the end of his life;* i. e., *prolonged his life:* (so in the Fṣ:) accord. to IḲṭṭ, نسأ اللّٰه اجله, and ↓ انسأ فى اجله. (TA.) All of these four modes of expression are allowable: (MF:) as also ↓ نَسَّأَ اللّٰه اجله: (Z:) and نَسَأَهُ اللّٰهُ فِى اجله, and ↓ أَنْسَأَهُ اللّٰهُ أَجَلَهُ. (Aṣ, Ṣ.) — أُنْسِئَ لَهُ فِى عُمْرِهِ, *His life was prolonged.* (TA, from a trad.) — نَسَأَ الإِبِلَ, inf. n. نَسْءٌ, *He delayed* or *deferred the watering of the camels;* or *kept them from water beyond the accustomed time.* (L.) — نَسَأَ فِى ظِمْءِ الإِبِلِ, (Ṣ, Ḳ,) inf. n. نَسْءٌ, (Ṣ,) *He increased the time between the two drinkings,* or *waterings, of the camels, by a day:* (A:) or *by a day,* or *two days, or more.* (A, L, Ḳ.) — نَسَأَ الإِبِلَ عَنِ الحَوْضِ *He kept back,* or *put back,* or *drove back, the camels from the tank,* or *cistern.* (Ṣ, L, Ḳ.*) — مَالَهُ نَسَأَهُ اللّٰهُ *What aileth him! May God render him ignominious!* (Kr, L,) or *put him backward!* (L.) Whom he puts backward, He renders ignominious. (L.) — نَسَأَ, inf. n. نَسْءٌ, *He sold* a thing *with postponement of the payment;* he *sold it upon credit.* (TA.) — نَسَأَهُ البَيْعَ, and ↓ انسأهُ البيع, *He made the sale to him to be on credit.* (Ṣ, Ḳ.) ↓ انسأهُ البَيْعَ *He postponed for him the period of the payment of the price of the thing sold.* (A.) — نَسَأَ عَنْهُ دَيْنَهُ, inf. n. نَسَاءٌ; (Akh, Ṣ;) and ↓ انسأهُ دينه, (Ṣ,* Ḳ,) and ↓ انسأهُ الدَّيْنَ; (Akh, Ṣ;) *He postponed for him the period of the payment of his debt.* (Ṣ, TA.) — نُسِئَتْ, a verb like عُنِىَ, [i. e., pass. in form, but neut. in sense,] aor. تُنْسَأُ, inf. n. نَسْءٌ, *Her menstrual discharge was later than its usual time, and it was therefore hoped that she was pregnant:* (Kh, Ṣ, Ḳ:) or *her menstrual discharge was later than its usual time, and her pregnancy commenced:* (TA:) or *she began to be pregnant:* (Aṣ, Ṣ:) or *she conceived.* (Aṣ.) = نَسَأَ اللَّبَنَ, (Ṣ, Ḳ,*) inf. n. نَسْءٌ, (TA,) *He mixed the milk with water.* (Ṣ, Ḳ.*) — نسأهُ اللبن, and نسأ لَهُ اللَّبَنَ, *He mixed the milk with water for him.* (TA.) — نَسَأَهُ *He gave him to drink* نَسْء, q. v.; (Ḳ;) i. e. *wine,* or *milk.* (TA.) — نَسَأَتْ *She* (an antelope) *licked* her young one *just after its birth.* (Ḳ.) = نَسَأَ, (Ṣ, Ḳ,) inf. n. نَسْءٌ, (Ṣ,) *It* (a camel, sheep, &c.,) *became fat:* (TA:) or *began to grow fat; when its soft hair* (وَبَر), *after falling off, began to grow again.* (Ṣ, Ḳ.)

2: see 1.

4: see 1. — انسأهُ *He granted him a delay of payment,* or *granted him credit, in a sale,* or *in the case of a debt.* (A.) — أَنْسَأْتُ سُرْبَتِى *I made my way to lead me far off.* (Ṣ.) [See art. سرب.]

5: see 8.

8. انتسأ *It was postponed,* or *delayed;* syn. تَأَخَّرَ. (A.) — انتسأ *He* (a camel, Ṣ,) *went far off* in the pasture. (Ṣ, Ḳ.) — *It* (a party of people) *went far off.* (TA.) — انتسأ عَنْهُ *He retired,* or *withdrew far off, from him* or *it.* (Ṣ.) تَنَسَّؤُوا and اِنْتَسَؤُوا occur in two readings of a trad., for اِنْتَسَؤُوا, (which is the correct reading,) in this sense. (TA.) [Hence it appears that ↓ تنسّأ, accord. to some, also signifies *he retired, &c.*]

10. استنسأهُ *He asked him to postpone* or *to grant him a delay in, the payment of his debt.* (Ṣ, Ḳ.) [See also 1.] — استنسأهُ البَيْعَ *He asked him to make the sale to be on credit,* or *for payment at a future period.* (A.) — استنسأ غَرِيمَهُ *He asked his creditor to grant him a delay in the payment of his debt.* (A.)

نَسْءٌ and ↓ نِسْءٌ and ↓ نَسُوْءٌ *A woman who is supposed to be pregnant;* (Ḳ;) as also ↓ نَسُوْءٌ (A, Ḳ) and ↓ نَسُوْءٌ: (A:) or *in whom pregnancy has appeared:* (Ḳ:) or, نَسْءٌ, (Ḳ) and ↓ نَسُوْءٌ, (TA,) as also ↓ نَسِىءٌ, accord. to J and IM, but this is rejected by F, (TA,) *a woman whose menstrual discharge is later than its usual time, and who is therefore hoped to be pregnant:* (Ṣ, Ḳ:) pl. [of نسء] أَنْسَاءٌ and نُسُوْءٌ: and نِسْوَةٌ نِسَاءٌ is also said; and sometimes the sing. (نَسْءٌ), being originally an inf. n., is used as a pl. (TA.) = نَسْءٌ and ↓ نَسِىءٌ *Thin, watery, milk:* (Ḳ:) or *milk mixed with water.* (T, Ṣ.) [See 1.] — Also, both words, (TA,) or the former only; (Ḳ, MF;) but ↓ نِسِىءٌ is quoted in this sense, from IAạr, who is said to have pronounced it thus, erroneously, for نَسِىءٌ; (TA;) *Wine;*

(IAar;) *drink that dispels the reason.* (Ḳ.) ═ نَسْءٌ *Fatness: or its commencement;* (Ḳ;) its completeness, (consequent upon eating dry food, being called إِقْتِرَارٌ.) (Ṣ.) — جَرَى النَّسْءُ فِى الدَّوَابِّ, (Ṣ,) or مَارَ, (TA,) [*Fatness, or its commencement, ran through the beasts of carriage*].

نِسْءٌ *One who mixes, or converses, with others:* ex. هُوَ نِسْءُ نِسَآءٍ *He is one who mixes, or converses, with women.* (Ḳ.) — See نَسْءٌ.

نُسْءٌ and نُسُوءٌ and نَسُوءٌ and نَسِىٌّ and نِسِىٌّ: see نَسْءٌ.

نَسَآءٌ *Length of life.* (Akh, Ṣ, Ḳ.) — The Fakeeh of the Arabs [El-Ḥárith Ibn-Keledeh, as said in the Mz, close of 39th نوع, where the following is quoted,] says, مَنْ سَرَّهُ النَّسَآءُ وَلَا نَسَآءَ فَلْيُخَفِّفِ الرِّدَآءَ وَلْيُبَاكِرِ الغَدَآءَ وَلْيُؤَخِّرِ العَشَآءَ وَلْيُقِلَّ غِشْيَانَ النِّسَآءِ [*Let him whom length of life rejoiceth* (*but there is no long endurance in life*) *lighten his debts, and make his morning-meal early, and delay his evening-meal, and take little enjoyment in women*]: (Ṣ,* TA:) الرداء here means *debt.* (T, M, TA, in art. ردى, where this saying is cited with some variations.)

نَسِىٌّ, of the measure فَعِيلٌ in the sense of the measure مَفْعُولٌ, (Ṣ,) *A month which the Arabs, in the time of paganism, postponed:* (Ḳ:) the doing of which is forbidden in the Ḳur, ix. 37. (Ṣ.) — Also, as an inf. n. of نَسَأَ, (which it is also said to be in the L,) The *postponing of a month:* i. e., the *postponing of the sacredness of a month; transferring it to another month.* When the Arabs returned from Minà, [after the accomplishment of the pilgrimage,] it was customary for a man of the tribe of Kinάneh to arise and say, أَنَا الَّذِى لَا يُرَدُّ لِى قَضَآءٌ ["I am he whose decree is not to be rejected"]; (Ṣ;) or إِنِّى لَا أُحَابُ وَلَا أُعَابُ وَلَا يُرَدُّ قَوْلِى, or ولا يردّ مَا قَضَيْتُ بِهِ; ["Verily I am not to be accused of a sin, nor am I to be charged with a fault, nor is my saying, (or decree,) to be rejected;"] (TA;) whereupon they would say, أَنْسِئْنَا شَهْرًا ["Postpone for us a month"]; i. e., "Postpone for us the sacredness of El-Moḥarram, and transfer it to Ṣafar:" for they disliked that three months during which they might not make predatory expeditions should come upon them consecutively, as their subsistence was obtained by such expeditions: so he made El-Moḥarram free from restriction to them. (Ṣ.) [But this, as appears from what is said in the Ḳur, ix. 37, was not done every year.] The tribes of Ṭeiyi and Khath'am did not observe the sacred months; therefore the نَاسِئُ (or postponer) proclaimed it lawful to slay them therein, when they were aggressors. (TA.) — [The term نَسِىٌّ appears also to have been applied to The *postponement of the time of the pilgrimage;* which was another custom of the Pagan Arabs, mentioned under this word in the TA.] The Arabs, liking that the day of their return from pilgrimage should always be at one season of the year, postponed it every year eleven days; at the same time keeping sacred the two months in which the pilgrimage took place, and the month next after those two, and also the month of Rejeb, at whatever season this fell. (TA.) [For the same purpose, at one time, they used to intercalate a month in the third and sixth and eighth of every eight years. See Ḳur, ix. 36, where the prohibition of this custom is implied; and Sale's Prel. Disc., § vii.]. — See نَسْءٌ.

نَسِىٌّ — (Ḳ, TA) and ↓ نَسِيْئَةٌ and ↓ نُسْأَةٌ, (Ṣ, Ḳ,) like كُلْأَةٌ, (Ṣ,) *A postponement,* or *delay, as to the time of the payment of a debt,* or *of the price of a thing sold, &c.* (Ṣ, Ḳ, TA.) The first is a subst.; (Ḳ;) and also an inf. n.; (L;) [and each of the others seems to be sometimes used as such]. — بَاعَهُ بِنَسِيْئَةٍ ↓, and ↓ بِنُسْأَةٍ, (as also بِكُلْأَةٍ, Ṣ,) *He sold it on credit; for payment to be made at a future period.* (Ṣ, Ḳ, TA.)

نَسِيْئَةٌ: see نَسِىٌّ. — Also, *A debt of which the payment is deferred by the creditor to a future period.* (TA.) — *A sale upon credit, in which the payment is deferred to a certain, or definite, period.* (TA.)

نَاسِئٌ, pl. نَسَأَةٌ (Ṣ) and نَاسِئُونَ, (TA,) *One whose office it was to perform the act called* نَسِىٌّ; *i. e., the postponing of a month:* (Ṣ, TA:) he was also called قَلَمَّسٌ, pl. قَلَامِسُ. (TA.) ═ نَاسِئٌ Anything *fat:* or *beginning to grow fat:* in the Ḳ it is said, كُلُّ نَاسِئٍ سَمِينٌ: in the L, كلّ سمين ناسئ, which is more proper. (TA.)

مَنْسَأَةٌ: see 1. — صِلَةُ الرَّحِمِ مَثْرَاةٌ فِى المَالِ مَنْسَأَةٌ فِى الأَثَرِ [*Union with kindred is a means of multiplying wealth, a means of prolonging one's memorial*]. (TA, from a trad.) ═ See مِنْسَأَةٌ.

مِنْسَأَةٌ (Ṣ, Ḳ) and ↓ مَنْسَأَةٌ, (Ḳ,) and also without ء, (Ṣ, Ḳ,) *A staff,* or *stick:* so called because a beast is urged or driven with it: (Ḳ:) *a pastor's great staff.* (TA.) For مِنْسَأَتَهُ, in the Ḳur, xxxiv. 13, some read مِنْ سَأَتِهِ; i. e. "from, or of, the end of his staff;" سَأَةٌ originally signifying the "bent part at each end of a bow;" (Fr, TA, &c.;) and being here used tropically. (TA.) This reading is disapproved by the author of the Ḳ. but is supported by good authorities. (TA.)

مُنْتَسَأٌ *An interval; a distance; a space.* (Ṣ.) إِنَّ لِى عَنْكَ لَمُنْتَسَأً *Verily I am far from thee.* (Ṣ.)

نسب

1. نَسَبَهُ, aor. ـُ, (Ṣ, Ḳ,) inf. n. نَسْبٌ and نِسْبَةٌ; (Ṣ;) and aor. ـِ, inf. n. نَسْبٌ and نِسْبَةٌ; (Ḳ, TA;) *He mentioned his* [i. e. another's] *relationship,* [*lineage,* or *genealogy*]; (Ṣ, Ḳ;) saying, *He is such a one, the son of such a one;* or *He is of such a tribe,* or *city;* or *of such an art,* or *such a trade;* and *the like.* (Lb. T.) — نَسَبَهُ, aor. ـُ, inf. n. نَسْبٌ, *He traced up his* [i.e. another's] *lineage to his greatest ancestor.* (TA.) — نَسَبَهُ, [aor. ـُ ?,] *He asked him to mention,* or *tell him, his relationship,* [*lineage,* or *genealogy*]. (Ḳ.) — جَلَسْتُ إِلَيْهِ فَنَسَبَنِى فَٱنْتَسَبْتُ ↓ إِلَيْهِ [*I sat by him, and he asked me to tell him my lineage; so I mentioned my lineage to him*]. (A.) — نَسَبَتْنَا فَٱنْتَسَبْنَا ↓ لَهَا [*She asked us to tell her our lineage; so we mentioned our lineage to her*]. (IAar, from a trad.) — نَسَبَهُ الى فُلَانٍ *He asserted him to be related to such a one:* and *he referred his lineage,* or *origin, to such a one.* — *He referred the origin* or *derivation of his name to such a one.* — *He attributed,* or *ascribed, it to such a one.* See, for ex. كَذَّبَ and صَدَّقَ in the Mṣb. — ‡ نَسَبَهُ إِلَى كَذَا *He referred its origin,* or *the origin* or *derivation of its name, to such a thing.* — *He attributed,* or *ascribed, it to such a thing.* — [نَسَبَهُ إِلَى فُلَانٍ *He named him,* or *called him, in relation,* or *reference, to such a one;* meaning an ancestor: and in like manner, in relation, or reference, to a tribe, a town or district, an art or trade, &c. See نِسْبَةٌ. — ‡ نَسَبَهُ إِلَى كَذَا *He named it,* or *called it, in relation,* or *reference, to such a thing.* — نَسَبَهُ إِلَى كَذَا, and, by inversion, نَسَبَ إِلَيْهِ كَذَا, (see Ṣ and Ḳ, in art. جهل, &c.) ‡ *He attributed* or *imputed to him,* or *charged him with,* or *accused him of, such a thing;* namely, a fault &c. Both phrases are often used as signifying thus by classical writers, and in the present day.] — نَسَبَ بِٱلْمَرْأَةِ, (Ṣ, Ḳ,) aor. ـُ, (Ṣ,) and ـِ, (L,) inf. n. نَسِيبٌ (Ṣ, Ḳ) and نَسَبٌ and مَنْسَبَةٌ, (Ḳ,) *i. q.* شَبَّبَ بِهَا; q. v.; (Ṣ, Ḳ;) *He mentioned the woman in an amatory manner, in the beginning* [or *prelude*] *of a poem:* (TA, voce شَبَّبَ:) *he mentioned the woman in amatory language, in the beginning of a* قَصِيدَة*, and then turned to the object of praise:* [for it is a general rule to commence a قصيدة in praise of a king, or hero, or the like, with نسيب; the transition from this is termed التَّخَلُّص: see also اِقْتَضَبَ:] (IKh:) *he mentioned the woman in his poem, describing her as characterized by beauty and youth &c.:* (Lb:) or *describing her as characterized by good qualities, whether truly* or *falsely.* (Z.) This phrase and نَسَبَ الرَّجُلَ both signify description; the latter signifying "he described the man with relation to his father, or his city or country, or

the like;" and the former phrase, *he described the woman as characterized by beauty and youth and love or affection &c.* (IDrst.) نَسِيبٌ is also employed to signify the *describing of the places where the objects of love have taken up their abode in the season of the* رَبِيع *and at other times, and the lover's longing to meet them and be united with them, and what else is comprised in the signification of the words* تَشْبِيبٌ *and* غَزَلٌ. (MF.) [See غَزِلَ, and غَزَلٌ.]

3. نَاسَبَهُ *He shared with him in relationship.* (TA.) — فُلَانٌ يُنَاسِبُ فُلَانًا *Such a one is related to, or a relation of, such a one.* (Ṣ.) — ناسبه, inf. n. مُنَاسَبَةٌ, ‡ *He, or it, bore relation to, resembled, was similar to, conformable to, analogous to, correspondent to, suitable to, befitted, him or it.* (Ṣ, Ḳ, Mṣb.) See also نِسْبَةٌ.

4. انسبت الرِّيحُ *The wind was violent, and drove along the dust and pebbles:* (Ḳ:) [as also انشبت].

5. تنسّب *He asserted himself to be a relation, or kinsman, or to be related,* [إِلَيْكَ] *to thee.* Hence the proverb, القَرِيبُ مَنْ تَقَرَّبَ لَا مَنْ تَنَسَّبَ: (Ṣ, Ḳ:) i. e. *He is* [*indeed*] *an ally who allies himself by affection and friendship: not he who asserts himself to be a kinsman.* (TA.)

6. تناسبوا ‡ *They were mutually, or reciprocally, related; resembled one another; were similar, conformable, analogous, correspondent, or suitable, one to another; befitted one another.* (TA.) See also نِسْبَةٌ. — [And تناسب *It was suitable in its parts, proportionate, symmetrical, or uniform.*]

8. See 10 and 1. — انتسب إِلَى أَبِيهِ *He asserted his relationship to his father,* whether truly or falsely; (Ṣ;) [*saying, I am the son of such a one:* as was generally done by a champion when he sallied forth to challenge]. — انتسب *It* (a voice) *was attributed, or ascribed, to him.* (TA, art. غنث.)

10. استنسب (Ḳ) and ▾ انتسب (TA) *He mentioned his* [i. e. his own] *relationship,* [*lineage, or genealogy*]. (Ḳ.) One says to a man, in asking him respecting his relationship, &c., إِسْتَنْسِبْ لَنَا أَىْ إِنْتَسِبْ لَنَا حَتَّى نَعْرِفَكَ [*Mention thy relationship, or lineage, to us, that we may know thee*]. (AZ.)

Q. Q. 1. نَيْسَبَ بَيْنَهُمَا, inf. n. نَيْسَبَةٌ, *He went to and fro between them two with malicious and mischievous misrepresentations, calumnies, or slanders, &c.* (L, Ḳ.)

نَسْبٌ: see نَسَبٌ.

نَسَبٌ and ▾ نِسْبَةٌ and ▾ نُسْبَةٌ (Ṣ, Ḳ) *Relationship; relation; kindred; consanguinity;* [*family; race; lineage; parentage; pedigree; genealogy; origin; reputed relationship* or *lineage* or *origin;*] (Ḳ;) *with respect to father and mother;* (ISk;) or *with respect to fathers only:* (Ḳ:) pl. of the first, أَنْسَابٌ; (Ṣ;) of the ▾ second, نِسَبٌ; and of the ▾ third, نُسَبٌ. (Mṣb.) The first, by poetical license, is contracted into ▾ نَسْبٌ. (T.) [You say,] بَيْنَهُمَا نَسَبٌ *Between them is relationship;* said whether they may lawfully marry one another, or not. (Mṣb.) See نَسِيبٌ.

نِسْبَةٌ ‡ *Relation; proportion; comparison;* with respect to quantity, or measure, and the like. See نَسَبٌ. — بِنِسْبَةِ كَذَا *In proportion to such a thing.* — نِسْبَةُ العَشَرَةِ إِلَى المِائَةِ *The proportion of ten to a hundred is* [*that of a tenth*]. (Mṣb.) — [You also say بِالنِّسْبَةِ إِلَى كَذَا *In relation to, or in comparison with, such a thing.*] — نِسْبَةٌ *A name of relation to a father, mother, tribe, town or district, art or trade, &c.:* [as جَوْهَرِىٌّ, مَكِّىٌّ, قُرَشِىٌّ, فَاطِمِىٌّ, عَلَوِىٌّ:] ending with ىّ. A more general name of this kind should precede a more particular one: thus you say القُرَشِىُّ الهَاشِمِىُّ: and it is better that a name of relation to a tribe should precede one of relation to a town or the like: thus you say القُرَشِىُّ المَكِّىُّ. It is said that the Arabs originally called themselves by such names only in relation to tribes; and that, when they took up their abodes in cultivated lands and in cities, they borrowed names of relation to towns and the like from the Persians and Copts. (Mṣb.) — تَنَاسُبٌ (TA) and ▾ مُنَاسَبَةٌ (Ṣ, Ḳ) and ▾ نِسْبَةٌ (TA) ‡ *Resemblance; similarity; conformity; analogy; correspondence; suitableness; fitness.* (Ṣ, Ḳ, TA.) Ex. بَيْنَ الشَّيْئَيْنِ نسبة, and ▾ مناسبة, and ▾ تناسب, *Between the two things is a resemblance, &c.* بَيْنَهُمَا نسبة قَرِيبَةٌ. *Between them two is a near resemblance, &c.* (TA.) [نِسْبَةٌ حُكْمِيَّةٌ *The relation of a predicate to its subject* (in books on logic).]

نُسْبَةٌ: see نَسَبٌ.

نَسِيبٌ i. q. ▾ مُنَاسِبٌ, [*A sharer in relationship; one who becomes a sharer in relationship by marriage*]: (Ḳ:) pl. نُسَبَاءُ and أَنْسِبَاءُ. (TA.) — نَسِيبٌ (Ṣ, Ḳ) and ▾ مَنْسُوبٌ (Ḳ) One *related; a relation; a kinsman.* (Ṣ, Ḳ, TA.) You say فُلَانٌ نَسِيبِى [*Such a one is my relation*]: and هُمْ أَنْسِبَائِى [*They are my relations*]. (TA.) ▾ نَسَبٌ, also, is used for ذُو نَسَبٍ [*A relation, or kinsman*]; and means *a male, or female, relation;* (Jel, xxv. 56;) and for ذَوُو نَسَبٍ [*relations, or kinsmen*]. (Bḍ, ibid.) [See also صِهْرٌ.] — نَسِيبٌ and ▾ مَنْسُوبٌ A man *of rank, or quality,* or *the like, and of family, or lineage.* (TA.) — ▾ نَسِيبٌ نَاسِبٌ [*An elegant amatory mentioning of a woman,* or *of women, in the beginning of a poem*] is a phrase like شِعْرٌ شَاعِرٌ. (Ḳ.) See أَنْسَبُ.

نَسَّابٌ (Ḳ) and ▾ نَسَّابَةٌ (Ṣ, Ḳ) *Skilful in genealogy:* (Ḳ:) [or rather, the former signifies *very skilful in genealogies;* or *a great genealogist:*] the latter, *possessing the utmost knowledge in genealogies;* or *a most skilful genealogist:* [this being of a doubly intensive form;] the ة being annexed to render the epithet one of excessive praise: (Ṣ:) pl. of the former نَسَّابُونَ, and of the latter نَسَّابَاتٌ: (TA:) you say عِنْدِى ثَلَاثَةُ نَسَّابَاتٍ, meaning ثَلَاثَةُ رِجَالٍ نَسَّابَاتٍ. (Ṣ.)

نَسَّابَةٌ: see نَسَّابٌ.

نَاسِبٌ: see نَسِيبٌ.

نَيْسَبٌ *A straight,* or *direct, and conspicuous,* or *open, road,* or *way:* (Ḳ:) or *narrow road,* or *way:* (TA:) as also ▾ نَيْسَبَانٌ: (Ḳ:) some say نيسب, نَيْسَمٌ which is a dial. form: (TA:) or signifies the *traces of a road,* or *way.* (K.) — Also نَيْسَبٌ *Ants that appear like a road;* (Ṣ;) *ants following one another uninterruptedly.* (Ḳ.) Dukeyn Ibn-Rejà says,

* عَيْنًا تَرَى النَّاسَ إِلَيْهَا نَيْسَبَا *

[*A source to which thou seest the people* (*repairing like*) *ants proceeding in uninterrupted succession*]. (Ṣ.) — Also, the *track of ants,* (ISd, Ḳ,) *and of a serpent, and of wild asses going to their watering-places.* (TA.)

نَيْسَبَانٌ: see نَيْسَبٌ.

هٰذَا الشِّعْرُ أَنْسَبُ *This poetry is more,* or *most, elegant in what is termed* نَسِيب. see 2: (Ḳ:) as though they had said شِعْرٌ نَسِيبٌ نَاسِبٌ, like شِعْرٌ شَاعِرٌ, to give intensiveness to the signification, and thence formed the word أَنْسَبُ. (TA.)

خَطٌّ مَنْسُوبٌ [A] *regular* [*hand-writing*]: syn. ذُو قَاعِدَةٍ: (TA:) [properly, *named in relation to its author &c.*] — شِعْرٌ مَنْسُوبٌ *Poetry,* or *a poem, in which is* نَسِيب, [or *an amatory mention of a woman,* or *women, in its beginning*]: pl. مَنَاسِيبُ. (Ḳ.) See نَسِيبٌ.

مُنَاسِبٌ: see نَسِيبٌ.

مُنَاسَبَةٌ and تَنَاسُبٌ: see نِسْبَةٌ.

نسج

1. نَسَجَ, aor. ـِ, inf. n. نَسْجٌ, *He, or it, drew, collected,* or *gathered, together* a thing: *drew and joined,* or *adjoined,* one thing to another. This is the primary signification. (L.) — نَسَجَتِ

الرِّيحُ الوَرَقَ وَالهَشِيمَ *The wind gathered together the leaves and the dry fragments of plants.* Hence, accord. to some, نَسَجَ الثَّوْبَ, because the weaver adjoins the warp to the woof. (TA.) — نَسَجَتِ الرِّيحُ التُّرَابَ ‡ *The wind drew the dust together.* (TA.) — نَسَجَتِ الرِّيحُ المَآءَ, and الرَّمْلَ, and التُّرَابَ, and رَسْمَ الدَّارِ, ‡ *The wind made rippling lines, in cross directions, upon the water, and the sand, and the dust, and [with dust] upon the traces of the dwelling.* (A.) [And so] إِنْتَسَجَتْ ▼ طَرَائِقُ كَالحُبُكِ ‡ *Rippling lines were made, in cross directions,* by the wind, upon the water, (Ṣ,* A,) and the sand, and the dust, and the traces of the dwelling. (A.) — نَسَجَتِ الرِّيحُ الرَّبْعَ ‡ *The wind, blowing in cross directions, obliterated the traces of the place where persons had alighted,* (Ṣ, Ḳ,) [by covering it with dust or sand in such a manner as that it might be likened to a web]. — نَسَجَ ‡ *It* (a spider) *wove, or spun,* its web. (A.) — نَسَجَ الثَّوْبَ, aor. ـِ, and ـُ, (Ṣ, Ḳ,) inf. n. نَسْجٌ, (Ṣ,) *He wove the piece of cloth, or the garment.* (TA, &c.) And نَسَجَ سَيْرًا *He plaited a thong.* (TA, in art. نسع.) — نَسَجَ الشِّعْرَ ‡ *He wove, or composed verses.* (TA.) — نَسَجَ الكَلَامَ ‡ *He* (a liar, TA,) *forged speech.* (Ḳ.) — Also, ‡ *He explained, or expounded, language;* syn. لَخَّصَهُ. (Ḳ.) — نَسَجَتِ النَّاقَةُ فِى سَيْرِهَا ‡ *The she-camel moved her legs quickly in going along.* (TA.)

8. انتسج *It became drawn, collected,* or *gathered, together: became drawn and joined,* or *adjoined,* to another thing. (L.) See 1. — انتسج *It* (a piece of cloth, or a garment,) *became woven.* (TA.)

نَسْجُ العَنْكَبُوتِ ‡ *The spider's web.* (A.) — See نَسِيجٌ.

نُسُجٌ *Prayer-carpets; carpets upon which prayer is performed;* syn. سَجَّادَاتٌ. (IAạr, Th, Ḳ.)

نَسُوجٌ ‡ A she-camel *that moves her legs quickly in going along:* (TA:) or a she-camel *whose load that she carries does not shake about:* (Ḳ:) so in all the copies of the Ḳ; but accord. to more than one of the leading lexicologists, a she-camel *whose load, and saddle, are unsteady upon her, and shaking about:* (TA:) and a she-camel *that makes her load to shift forward to her* كَاهِل, [*or the part of the back next the neck,*] *by reason of the vehemence of her pace.* (ISh, Ḳ.)

نَسِيجٌ and ▼ نَسْجٌ [the latter originally an inf. n.] i. q. مَنْسُوجٌ, *Woven.* (Mṣb, TA.) [And hence both, as substs., signify *A web.*] So ▼ نَسِيجَةٌ *a web, a thing woven.* (Ṣ, Ḳ, art. طرق.) — هُوَ نَسِيجُ وَحْدِهِ (an indeterminate expression, Hishám and Fr, in L, art. وحد, q. v.,) ‡ *He is unequalled, unique,* or *an only one of his kind,* in knowledge &c.: for when a garment, or piece of cloth, is of a high quality, no other is woven of exactly the same kind. (Ṣ, Ḳ, &c.) It is only said in praise of a person. (TA.) [Opposed to عُيَيْرُ وَحْدِهِ.] — ثَوْبُ ▼ نَسْجِ اليَمَنِ *A garment, or piece of cloth, the texture of El-Yemen.* (Mṣb.) — ▼ نَسْجُ الغَيْثِ ‡ [*The texture of the rain*]; meaning the *plants,* or *herbage.* (TA.)

نَسَاجَةٌ *A kind of* مِلْحَفَة, with which a person envelops himself. App. thus called by what is originally an inf. n. (L, from a trad.).

نِسَاجَةٌ The *art of weaving.* (Ṣ, Ḳ.)

نَسِيجَةٌ: see نَسِيجٌ.

نَسَّاجٌ [in some copies of the Ḳ, ▼ نَاسِجٌ, the act. part. n. of نَسَجَ,] *A weaver.* (Ḳ.) — نَسَّاجٌ also, *A manufacturer of coats of mail.* (Ḳ) — نَسَّاجٌ also, ‡ *A liar;* (Ḳ;) *a forger of lies.* (TA.)

نَاسِجٌ: see نَسَّاجٌ.

مَنْسَجٌ and مَنْسِجٌ *A place where the art of weaving is practised.* (Ṣ, Ḳ.) — See مِنْسَجٌ.

مِنْسَجٌ (Ṣ, Ḳ) and مِنْسِجٌ (TA) [*A weaver's loom;*] the *apparatus upon which the web is stretched to be woven;* (Ṣ, Ḳ;) the *wood and apparatus used in the art of weaving, upon which the web is stretched to be woven:* (M:) or, specially, the حَفّ; (TA;) i. e. the *stay of a weaver's loom;* syn. حَفٌّ: (TḲ:) [in the present day, applied to *a frame for weaving:* and to *one for embroidering*]. — مِنْسَجٌ (Ṣ, Ḳ,) and ▼ مَنْسِجٌ (TA) [The *withers* of a horse: or the *lower part thereof:* or the *part below the withers:*] the *prominent part from the branches of the shoulder-blades to the lower part of the neck and to the even part of the back;* as also حَارِكٌ: behind it is the كَاهِل: (A'Obeyd:) or *in a horse, the same as the* كاهل *in a man, and the* حارك *in a camel:* (TA:) or the *part* of a horse *below the* حارك [which latter is the *withers,* or *the upper part thereof*]: (Ṣ, Ḳ:) or the *swelling part of the* كَاثِبَة [or *withers*] of a beast, *at the place where the mane terminates, beneath the pommel of the saddle:* (T:) said to be so called because the sinews of the neck extend towards the back, and those of the back towards the neck, and are woven together upon the shoulder-blades: (TA:) or the *extremity of the mane:* (A:) or the *part between the mane and the place where the shoulder-blades unite:* pl. مَنَاسِجُ. (TA.)

نسح

1. نَسَحَ, aor. ـَ, (inf. n. نَسْحٌ, Ṣ,) *He dispersed and removed* dust; syn. أَذْرَى. (Ḳ, and some copies of the Ṣ.) = نَسِحَ, aor. ـَ, (inf. n. نَسَحٌ, Ṣ,) *He coveted;* syn. طَمِعَ. (Ḳ, and some copies of the Ṣ.)

مِنْسَاحٌ *A thing with which dust is dispersed and removed.* (Ḳ.)

نسخ

1. نَسَخَ, aor. ـَ, (L, Ḳ,) inf. n. نَسْخٌ; and ▼ انتسخ; (L;) *He, or it, annulled, superseded, obliterated, effaced,* or *cancelled,* (L, Ḳ,) a thing, بِشَىْءٍ آخَرَ *by another thing.* (L.) *It annulled,* or *superseded,* a thing, *and took the place of* it. (L.) Ex. نَسَخَتِ الشَّمْسُ الظِّلَّ, and ▼ انتسخته, ‡ *The sun annulled,* or *superseded, the shade,* (Ṣ, L,) *and took the place of it.* (L.) نَسَخَ الشَّيْبُ الشَّبَابَ ‡ *Hoariness took the place of youth.* (A, Mṣb.) Also, نَسَخَ *He annulled, superseded, abolished,* or *made void,* a thing, *substituting for it another thing.* (Ḳ.) Ex. نَسَخَ آيَةً *He* (God) *abrogated, annulled,* or *superseded, the verse* of the Ḳur-án, (Lth, Fr, Ṣ, L,) *substituting for it another;* (Lth, Fr, L;) بِالآيَةِ *by the* [i. e. another] *verse:* (Ṣ:) or *he changed it, by substituting for it another:* نَسْخٌ signifying *he changed* a thing *by substituting for it another thing.* (IAạr, L.) [See also 4.] Legal نَسْخٌ, or abrogation, may respect the letter and the force of command, or one of these; whether the command have been performed, as is generally the case, or have not been performed, as in the case of the sacrifice of Ishmael, [or, as some of the Muslims say, agreeably with the Bible narrative, Isaac,] for Abraham was commanded to sacrifice him, and then the command was abrogated before its execution. (Mṣb.) — Also, نَسَخَ *He, or it, changed,* or *altered,* a thing. (Ḳ.) Ex. نَسَخَتِ الرِّيحُ آثَارَ الدَّارِ *The wind changed,* or *altered,* [or, it may also be rendered, *obliterated,* or *effaced,*] *the traces of the dwelling.* (Ṣ.) — نَسَخَهُ *He transformed him,* or *metamorphosed him, into a worse,* or *more foul,* or *more ugly, shape;* i. q. مَسَخَهُ: (Ḳ:) ex. نَسَخَهُ اللّٰهُ قِرْدًا *God transformed him into an ape.* (Fr, Aboo-Sa'eed.) — [Also, as used in post-classical, and perhaps in classical, times, *He* (God) *caused his soul to pass into the body of another man.*] The *connexion of the soul of a human being, after its departure from the body, with the body of another human being,* is termed نَسْخٌ; with the body of

a beast, مَسْخٌ; with a plant, فَسْخٌ; and with an inanimate and not-increasing body, رَسْخٌ. (Marginal note in a copy of the KT.) [But see 1 (last sentence) in art. فسخ. See also 6.] — نَسَخَ *He transferred* a thing *from one place to another*, it remaining the same: (TA:) *he transferred* what was in a bee-hive *to another* [*hive* or *place*]. (Ḳ.) — نَسَخَ الكِتَابَ, (Ṣ, Mṣb, Ḳ,) aor. ـَ, inf. n. نَسْخٌ; (Mṣb;) and ♦ انتسخهُ, (Ṣ, Mṣb, Ḳ,) and استنسخهُ; (Ṣ, Ḳ;) are syn., (Ṣ,) signifying *He copied*, or *transcribed, the writing*, or *book*, (T, Mṣb, Ḳ,) *letter for letter*. (T.) — مَا نَسَخَهُ وَإِنَّمَا مَسَخَهُ [*He has not copied it, but only corrupted it by changing the diacritical points and altering the meanings*]. (A.) — ♦ نَسْتَنْسِخُ, in the Ḳur, xlv. 28, signifies *We set down, or register, and preserve:* (Jel:) or *We command to be transcribed and to be set down, or registered.* (T.)

3: see 6.

4. انسخ *He* (God) *made* a verse of the Ḳur-án *to be abrogated, annulled*, or *superseded*, by another verse: (Z, MF:) or *found* it *to be so;* like أَحْمَدَهُ "he found him, or it, to be praised, or praiseworthy." (AAF.) In the Ḳur, ii. 100, Ibn-'Ámir reads مَا نُنْسِخْ for مَا نَنْسَخْ. (TA.) [See also 1.]

6. تناسخت الأَشْيَآءُ *The things succeeded one another, one taking the place of another.* (L.) — تناسخت القُرُونُ, (A, Mṣb,) and الأَزْمِنَةُ, (Mṣb, Ḳ,) ‡ *The times succeeded, one in the place of another;* (Mṣb, Ḳ;) *one passing away after another.* (Ḳ.) — تناسخت الوَرَثَةُ, ‡ [*The heirs died, one after another, and so cancelled their rights to inheritance*]. (A.) تَنَاسُخٌ (Ṣ, Ḳ) and ♦ مُنَاسَخَةٌ (Ḳ) in the case of an inheritance, (Ṣ, Ḳ,) or with respect to the fixed primary portions of an inheritance assigned by the Ḳur-án, is The *dying of heirs after other heirs while the original inheritance remains undivided.* (Ṣ, Ḳ.) — تناسخ *It became changed from one state to another.* (L.) — تناسخت الأَرْوَاحُ ‡ [*The souls transmigrated*]. (MF.) تَنَاسُخٌ, [The *transmigration of the soul from one human body to another*, is thus explained;] the *connexion of the soul with the body after its separation from another body, without the intervention* (تَخَلُّل) *of any time between the two connexions, by reason of the essential love subsisting between the soul and the body.* (KT; in some copies of which تحلّل is put for تخلّل.) [See also 1.]

نُسْخَةٌ *A copy*, or *transcript:* (Ṣ, L, Mṣb, Ḳ:) so called because it supplies the place of the original: (L:) pl. نُسَخٌ. (Mṣb.) — Also, *A copy, or an original, from which a transcript is made:* (L:) [pl. as above].

نَسِيخَةٌ: see نُسَيْخِيَّةٌ.

بَلْدَةٌ نَسِيخَةٌ, and ♦ نُسَيْخِيَّةٌ, *A distant town*, or *district*, or *country.* (Ḳ.) — [*A transverse* or *cross wind.* See نَيِّحَة in art. نوح.]

نَاسِخٌ and ♦ مُنْتَسِخٌ *A copier*, or *transcriber, of a writing* or *writings*, or *of a book* or *books.* (L.) — آيَةٌ نَاسِخَةٌ *A verse of the Ḳur-án that abrogates, annuls*, or *supersedes, another verse.* (Ṣ.) [See 1.] [And so,] ♦ آيَةٌ مَنْسُوخَةٌ *A verse of the Ḳur-án that is abrogated, annulled*, or *superseded, by another verse.* (Ṣ.) — [نَاسِخٌ An epithet applied to a particle, (namely, إِنَّ and the like, and مَا and لَا,) or a verb, (namely, the abstract كَانَ and the like, and كَادَ and the like, and ظَنَّ and the like,) *which effects a change of the grammatical form*, or *of the meaning, in a nominal proposition before which it is placed.* الحُرُوفُ النَّاسِخَةُ لِلْاِبْتِدَآءِ *The particles which annul the quality of the inchoative.*]

التَّنَاسُخِيَّةُ (Ḳ) ‡ *The sect which holds the doctrine of* تَنَاسُخُ الأَرْوَاحِ [*or the transmigration of souls*], *and denies the resurrection.* (MF.)

مَنْسُوخٌ and ♦ مُنْتَسَخٌ A writing, or book, *copied*, or *transcribed.* (Mṣb.) — See نَاسِخٌ.

مَنْسُوخٌ: see مُنْتَسَخٌ.

مُنْتَسِخٌ: see نَاسِخٌ.

نسر

1. نَسَرَ, aor. ـِ (Ṣ, M, Ḳ) and ـُ, (M, Ḳ,) inf. n. نَسْرٌ, (Ṣ, M, Ḳ,) *He* (a bird, M, Ḳ, or a hawk or falcon, Ṣ, [or other bird, see نَسْرٌ below,]) *plucked* flesh (Ṣ, M, Ḳ) *with his beak.* (Ṣ, TA.) You say also, نَسَرَهُ بِمِنْسَرِهِ, meaning, *He* (a hawk or falcon [or other bird]) *plucked his flesh with his beak.* (A.) ═ [Hence,] نَسَرَهُ ‡ *He blamed him; found fault with him; spoke evil of him behind his back, or in his absence, saying of him what would grieve him if he heard it.* (A.)

10. استنسر *He* (the بُغَاث [or ignoble bird, or most ignoble of birds,] Ṣ, M) *became a* نَسْر [or *vulture*]: (M:) or *became like the* نَسْر (Ṣ, Ḳ) *in strength.* (Ḳ.) Hence the proverb, إِنَّ البُغَاثَ بِأَرْضِنَا يَسْتَنْسِرُ [*Verily the most ignoble bird, or most ignoble birds, in our land becomes like the vulture, or become like vultures*]: (Ṣ, M:) meaning, the weak among us becomes strong. (Ṣ.) See also art. بغث.

نَسْرٌ (Ṣ, M, Mṣb, Ḳ, &c.) and sometimes ♦ نِسْرٌ [agreeably with the modern general pronunciation] and ♦ نُسْرٌ, (Sheykh-el-Islám Zekereeyá, in his Comm. on the Expos. of Bd,) but this is very strange, (MF,) [The *vulture;* app. any vulture, whatever be its species or variety, known to the Arabs, except the رَخَم, or aquiline vulture; and said to be applied by some of the Arabs to the *eagle;* (see also نُسَارِيَّةٌ;) agreeing with the Hebrew נֶשֶׁר, which is plainly applied to the former bird in Micah, i. 16, and probably in other instances;] *a certain bird*, (Ṣ, M, A, Mṣb, Ḳ,) *well known;* (A, Mṣb;) so called because it plucks (يَنْسُرُ) a thing, and swallows it, (A, and so in some copies of the Ḳ,) or, and pulls it out (so in some copies of the Ḳ,) or, and chases and captures it; (so in some copies of the Ḳ; the various readings being وَيَبْتَلِعُهُ and وَيَقْتَلِعُهُ and وَيَقْتَنِصُهُ;) it is said that *it has no* مِخْلَب [or *talon*], *but only the* ظُفْر [or *nail*], *like that of the domestic cock and hen, and of the crow and the like, and of the* رَخَمَة [*or aquiline vulture*]: (Ṣ:) the *bird called in Persian* كَرْكَسْ, *which eats carcases until it is unable to fly, and is said to live a thousand years:* (Ḳzw:) AḤn asserts, that the نسر is *a bird of the description called* عِتَاق; [which is a term applied to *birds of prey*, and to *noble birds*, (in a sense wider than that in which this appellation is used in English falconry,) and especially to *eagles;*] but [ISd says] I know not how that is: (M:) pl. (of pauc., Ṣ) أَنْسُرٌ and (of mult., Ṣ) نُسُورٌ. (Ṣ, M, Mṣb, Ḳ.) — النَّسْرُ الوَاقِعُ † [*The Falling*, or *Alighting, Vulture*,] and النَّسْرُ الطَّائِرُ † [*The Flying Vulture*,] are *two stars* or *asterisms*, (Ṣ,* M, A, Mṣb, Ḳ,) *well-known*, (M,) *which together are called* النَّسْرَانِ [*the Two Vultures*], (M, A,) *and each of which alone is called* النَّسْرُ (M, Mṣb, Ḳ) *and* نَسْرٌ; (M;) *being likened to the bird so named:* (M:) *the former is the bright star* [α] *in the constellation* الشِّلْيَاقُ [or *Lyra*] *likened by the Arabs to a vulture* (نسر) *that has contracted its wings to itself, as though it had alighted upon something:* and *the latter consists of the three well-known stars* [α and β and γ] *in the constellation* العُقَابُ [or *Aquila*]: (Ḳzw:) [The former rose heliacally, about the epoch of the Flight, in central Arabia, on the 25th of November, O.S., with the Eighteenth Mansion of the Moon, which is α of Scorpio; and the latter, on the 28th of December, O.S.: and both set, together, anti-heliacally, at that period and in that part, on the 24th of July, O.S. See نَوْءٌ, and دَبُور.] ═ نَسْرٌ (Ṣ, M, Mṣb) and النَّسْرُ, (Ṣ, M, Ḳ,) the latter occurring in a verse cited in art. عز, (Ṣ,) *A certain idol*, (Ṣ, M, Mṣb, Ḳ,) *belonging to Dhu-l-Kelaạ*, (Ṣ, Mṣb, Ḳ,) *in the land of Ḥimyer*, (Ṣ, Ḳ,) *as* يَغُوثُ *did to Medhḥij, and* يَعُوقُ *to Hemdán, of the idols of the people of Noah*, (Ṣ,) all of which are mentioned in the Ḳur, lxxii. 22 and 23: (Ṣ, M:) or *a certain good man, who lived between Adam and Noah, and of whom, after his death, was made an image, which, after a long time, became an object of worship;* like وَدّ and سُوَاع and يَغُوث, and يَعُوق, mentioned therewith in the Ḳur, ubi supra. (Bḍ.) ═ Also, نَسْرٌ [The *frog*, or *frush*, of the hoof of a horse or ass or mule; thus called in the present day;] *a portion of tough flesh*, [or rather *a horny substance*,] *in the* بَطْن [or *sole*] *of the solid hoof, as though it were a date-stone*, [which it resembles in substance,] or *a pebble*: (Ṣ:) or the *flesh of the solid hoof, which the poets liken to date-stones*: (T:) or *a portion of flesh*, (Ḳ,) or *of hard flesh*, (M,) *in the* بَاطِن [or *sole*, or *inner part*,] *of the solid hoof*, (M, Ḳ, TA,) *as though it were a pebble*, or *a date-stone*, (TA:) or *what rises in the* باطن *of the hoof of the horse, from*, or *of, the upper part thereof*: (M, Ḳ:) or the باطن *itself of the solid hoof*: (M:) pl. نُسُورٌ, (M, Ḳ,) which Aboo-Sa'eed explains as signifying the *prominences in the* بَطْن [or *sole*] *of the solid hoof, which are likened to date-stones because of their hardness, and which do not touch the ground.* (TA.) Hence the saying, حَافِرٌ صُلْبُ النُّسُورِ [*A solid hoof hard in the frog*: the sing. and pl. being used indiscriminately]. (TA.)

نُسْرٌ : } see نَسْرٌ, first signification.
نِسْرٌ :

نِسْرِينٌ [The *wild rose, dog-rose, eglantine*, or *sweet brier*: so in the present day: and, accord. to Spreng., Hist. Rei Herb., cited by Freytag, the *jonquil*:] *a well-known rose*; (Ḳ;) *a well-known sweet-smelling flower*; (Mṣb;) *a species of sweet-smelling flower*; (M;) a Persian word, (M, Mṣb,) arabicized: (Mṣb:) of the measure فِعْلِيل; and, if so, the [final] ن is radical: or of the measure فِعْلِين; and if so, that letter is augmentative: Az says, I know not whether it be Arabic or not. (Mṣb.)

نُسَارِيَّةٌ The *eagle*; syn. عُقَابٌ: (IAạr, Ḳ:) likened to the نَسْر. (IAạr, TA.) [Hence it appears that, accord. to IAạr, the نسر is not the eagle.]

نَاسُورٌ (also written with ص, Ṣ, Mṣb,) *A certain disease that happens in the inner angles of the eyes*, (Ṣ, Mṣb, Ḳ,) *with an incessant defluxion therefrom*: (Ṣ, TA:) *and sometimes it happens also in the part around the anus*: *and in the gum*: (Ṣ, Mṣb:) or it signifies also *a certain disease in the part around the anus*: and *a certain disease in the gum*: (Ḳ:) and is an arabicized word [from the Persian]: (Ṣ, Mṣb:) نَوَاصِير, pl. of نَاصُور, accord. to certain of the physicians, is a term applied to *deep ulcers in the anus, at the extremity of the gut.* (Mṣb, art. نصر.) —— Also, *A vein constantly becoming recrudescent*, (عِرْقٌ غَبِرٌ,) *with an incessant defluxion*; (Ṣ, Ḳ;) *corrupt within*; *whenever its upper part heals, breaking forth again with corruption.* (TA.) See also غَرَبٌ.

مِنْسَرٌ (Ṣ, A, Mṣb, Ḳ) and ↓ مَنْسِرٌ, (Mṣb, Ḳ,) or the former only, (AZ,) The *beak* of a bird (Ṣ, A, Mṣb, Ḳ) of *prey*; (Ṣ, Mṣb;) or of a hawk or falcon; (A;) that of any other bird being called مِنْقَار. (Ṣ, Mṣb.) ═ [Hence,] ↓ both words also signify † *A portion of an army that goes before the main army*: (Ṣ, Ḳ:) [likened to the beak of a bird of prey; as the side bodies are likened to the wings:] and *a troop of horse or horsemen in number from thirty to forty*: or *from forty to fifty*: or *from forty to sixty*: (M, Ḳ:) or *from a hundred to two hundred*: (M, Mṣb, Ḳ:) or *a troop of horse* or *horsemen*: (El-Farábee, Mṣb:) or *an army that does not pass by anything without snatching it away.* (Mṣb.)

مَنْسِرٌ : see مِنْسَرٌ, throughout.

[نسط, &c.

See Supplement.]

نش

1. نَشَّ, aor. ـِ, (A, TA,) inf. n. نَشِيشٌ (Ṣ, A, Mgh, Mṣb, Ḳ) and نَشٌّ, (TA,) *It* (said of water, Ṣ, Mgh, Mṣb, Ḳ, and of other things, Ṣ, Ḳ, such as wine, and flesh-meat, TA) *made a sound in boiling, estuating*, or *fermenting*: (Ṣ, Mgh, Mṣb, Ḳ:) and *it* (anything) *made a sound like that of boiling, estuating, or fermenting*; or *of beginning to do so*: and *it* (water) *made a sound in pouring forth.* (TA.) You say also, نَشَّتِ القِدْرُ, (TA,) inf. n. نَشِيشٌ; (IDrd, Ḳ;) and ↓ نَشْنَشَتْ, (TA,) inf. n. نَشْنَشَةٌ; (IDrd, Ḳ;) *The cooking-pot made a sound in boiling*: (IDrd, Ḳ:) or *began to boil, and so made a sound.* (TA.) And نَشَّ المَآءُ فِى كُوزٍ جَدِيدٍ [*The water made a sound in a new earthen mug*]: (A:) or نَشَّ الكُوزُ الجَدِيدُ فِى المَآءِ *The new* [earthen] *mug made a sound in the water.* (Mgh.) And ↓ نَشْنَشَ الدِّرْعُ *The coat of mail made a sound*, (Ḳ,) or *clinking.* (Fr.) —— Also, *It* (wine, A, Mgh, or the beverage called نَبِيذ, TA,) *estuated*, or *fermented*: (A, Mgh, TA:) or نَشِيش signifies the *beginning to estuate*, or *ferment*, of the first of expressed juice [of grapes or dates &c.]. (TA.) —— نَشَّتِ اللَّحْمَةُ, inf. n. نَشٌّ, *The piece of flesh-meat dripped.* (Sh, from certain of the Kilábees.) ═ Also نَشَّ, aor. ـِ, inf. n. نَشِيشٌ (Ṣ, Ḳ) and نَشٌّ, (TA,) said of a pool of water left by a torrent, *Its water began to sink into the earth*: (Ṣ, Ḳ:) or *its water dried up, and sank into the earth.* (TA.) *It* (water upon the surface of the ground) *dried up.* (TA.) *It* (a full-grown unripe date) *lost its moisture.* (TA.) ═ نَشَّ الدُّهْنَ بِالرَّيْحَانِ [aor., app., ـُ,] *He infused the oil*, or other *ointment, with perfume, by boiling it with sweet-smelling plants until it made a sound in boiling.* (TA.) [See also سَلِيخَة.] ═ نَشَّ الذُّبَابَ [aor., accord. to analogy, ـُ, but vulgarly, in the present day, ـِ,] *He drove* [or *whisked*] *away the flies.* (TA.)

R. Q. 1. نَشْنَشَ, see 1, in two places. See also شَنْشَنَة.

نَشٌّ The *half of an* أُوقِيَّة [or *ounce*]; (Ṣ, A, Mgh, Mṣb, Ḳ;) i. e., *twenty dirhems*; (Ṣ, Mṣb, Ḳ;) the أوقيّة being forty dirhems; (Ṣ, Mṣb;) and five dirhems being called نَوَاة: (Ṣ:) or the *weight of a date-stone* (نواة) *of gold*: or the *weight of five dirhems*: or the *quarter of an* اوقيّة: (TA:) and the *half* of anything; (IAạr, Sh, Az, Mgh, Mṣb;) as, for instance, of a dirhem, and of a cake of bread. (IAạr, Sh, Az, Mgh.)

نَشَاشَةٌ : see نَشَّاشَةٌ.

أَرْضٌ نَشِيشَةٌ and ↓ نَشَّاشَةٌ *Salt land that produces no herbage.* (IDrd, Ḳ.)

سَبَخَةٌ نَشَّاشَةٌ, (Ṣ, A, Ḳ,) and ↓ نَشَاشَةٌ, (Az, TA,) *A tract of salt land of which the moisture* [or, as in a copy of the A, *the earth*,] *does not dry up, nor its pasture*, or *herbage, grow*: (A, Ḳ:) or *what appears of the water of salt lands, and begins to sink therein, so that it becomes salt.* (Ṣ.)

نَشِيشَةٌ : see نَشَّاشَةٌ.

مَنَشُّ السَّاحِلِ *The part of the shore of a sea or great river from which the water has retired.* (A.)

مِنَشَّةٌ [*A fly-whisk*;] *a thing with which the flies are driven away.* (TA.)

دُهْنٌ مَنْشُوشٌ *Oil*, or other *ointment, infused with perfume*, (Ḳ, TA,) *by boiling it with sweet-smelling plants until it makes a sound in boiling.* (TA.) [See also سَلِيخَة.]

نشأ

1. نَشَأَ, aor. ـَ; and نَشُؤَ, aor. ـُ; inf. n. نَشْءٌ and نُشُوْءٌ and نَشَآءٌ and نَشْأَةٌ and نَشَآءَةٌ; *He lived*; (Ḳ;) *and* (accord. to Sh) *he rose*, or *became elevated*, or *high.* (TA.) —— [*It rose.*] —— النَّشْأَةُ الأُخْرَى, or النَّشَآءَةُ, [Ḳur, liii. 48,] *The resurrection*: [lit., *the other life*]. (TA.) —— النَّشْأَةُ الآخِرَةُ, or النَّشَآءَةُ, [Ḳur, xxix. 19, *the same*: lit., *the latter life*]. (TA.) [See also نَشْأَةٌ below.] —— نَشَأَ, (Ṣ, Ḳ,) inf. n. نَشْءٌ and نَشَآءٌ (TA) and نُشُوْءٌ; (Ṣ;) *He grew up*, (Ḳ,) *and became a youth*, or *young man.* (Ṣ, Ḳ.) [See نَاشِئٌ.] —— نَشَأْتُ فِى بَنِى فُلَانٍ, (Ṣ,) and مَنْشَئِى فى بنى فلان, (TA.) *I grew up, and became a young man, among the sons of such a one.* (Ṣ, TA.) —— نَشَأَ, (Ṣ, Ḳ,) inf. n. نَشْءٌ and نُشُوْءٌ, (TA,) *It* (a cloud) *rose*, (Ṣ, Ḳ,) *and appeared*: said of its first begin-

ning. (TA.) — نَشَأَ *He arose.* (TA.) — [*It became produced; it originated;* عَنْ *from another thing*, See 4.] — *It happened, occurred, or came to pass.* (TA.) — نَشَأَ لَهُ رَأْىٌ [*An opinion occurred to him,* or *arose in his mind*]. (Ṣ, Ḳ, art. بدو.)

2. نَشَّىَ and ♦ أَنْشَىَ are syn., (Ṣ, Ḳ,) [signifying *He was reared, made to grow,* or *grow up, and to become a young man.*] See 4.

4. انشأ *He* (i.e. God) *raised* the clouds. (Ṣ, Ḳ.) — انشأ عَلَمًا *He set up a beacon,* or *sign of the way,* in a desert or highway: (TA:) and so ♦ استنشأ عَلَمًا *He set up a beacon,* or *sign of the way.* (A.) — انشأهُ, inf. n. إِنْشَآءٌ, *He* (i.e. God) *caused him to attain the age of manhood,* or *nearly that age.* (TA.) See 2. — انشأ and ♦ نشأ [so TA: app. نَشَّأَ:] *He* (i.e. God) *created; produced; originated.* (Ṣ.) انشأ اللّٰه الخَلْقَ *God originated the creation.* (TA.) — أَنْشَأْتُهُ *I originated it; brought it into being* or *existence; made it,* or *produced it, for the first time, it not having been before.* (Mṣb.) — انشأ *He founded* or *began to build,* a house [&c.]. (Ḳ.) — *He framed* or *constructed,* a proverb, or phrase. (TA.) — *He composed* language [such as an ode or the like]. (TA.) — *He recited* poetry, or a خُطْبَة, *well.* (IAạr.) — *He forged* a tradition, (Ṣ, Ḳ,) *and attributed* it [to the Prophet]. (Lth) — انشأ, followed by an aor., *He began* (Ṣ, Ḳ) to relate, (Ḳ,) or say, (TA,) or do. (Ṣ.) — انشأ منهُ *He went forth from it.* (Ḳ.) Ex. مِنْ أَيْنَ أَنْشَأْتَ, *Whence hast thou come forth?* (TA.) — انشأت النَّاقَةُ *The she-camel conceived:* (Ḳ:) of the dial. of Hudheyl. (TA.) — انشأ عَلَيْهِ *He came to, advanced to,* or *approached him* or *it.* (TA.)

5. تنشّأ لِحَاجَتِهِ *He rose and went to accomplish his affair,* or *business.* (AA, Ḳ.) — تنشّأ عَادِيًا *He arose and went running to accomplish his affair.* (AA.)

10: see 4. — يَسْتَنْشِئُ الرِّيحَ *He scents the wind:* said of a wolf: (ISk, Ṣ:) and استنشأ الأَخْبَارَ *He sought,* or *searched after, news:* (Ḳ, TA:) in both instances, with and without ء; (Ṣ,* L;) being derived from نَشِيتُ الرِّيحَ (Ṣ, L) and رَجُلٌ نَشْيَانُ لِلْخَبَرِ: [see also مُسْتَنْشِئَةٌ.] (L.) — إِسْتَنْشَأْتُهُ قَصِيدَةً [*I requested him to compose,* or, perhaps, *to recite an ode,* or *the like*]. (A.)

نَشْءٌ and ♦ نَشِئٌ *Risen clouds:* (Ḳ:) or the *first that rises of them:* (Ṣ, Ḳ:) or their *first appearance:* (ex. لِهٰذَا السَّحَابِ نَشْءٌ حَسَنٌ *These clouds have a good first appearance:*) or *clouds when they appear like a piece of drapery* (مُلَآءَة) *spread out.* (TA.) — نَشْءٌ The *exhalation,* or *odour, of wine.* (IAạr.) [See 10.] — See نَاشِئٌ. — Also, The *young ones of camels:* (Kr, Ḳ:) pl. [or rather quasi-pl. n.] نَشَأٌ. (Ḳ.)

نَشْأَةٌ and ♦ نَشَاءَةٌ *A creation; an original production.* (Aboo-'Amr Ibn-El-'Ala, Ṣ) [See also 1.] — See نَشِيئَةٌ.

نَشَاءَةٌ: see what precedes.

نَشِئٌ: see نَشْءٌ.

نَشِيئَةٌ The *first part that is made of a tank,* or *cistern.* (ISk, Ṣ, Ḳ.) — بَادِى النَّشِيئَةِ A tank, or cistern, *of which the water is dried up, and the bottom apparent.* (Ṣ.) — Also, نشيئة The *stone that is placed in the bottom of a tank,* or *cistern.* (A'Obeyd, Ṣ, Ḳ.) — The *earth that is behind the* نَصَائِب, (Ḳ,) *which are the stones that are set up around the tank, the interstices between which stones are filled up with kneaded clay:* (TA:) or it is said to signify *what is constructed round the tank;* also called أَعْضَادٌ. (TA.) — نشيئة البِئْرِ *The earth that is taken forth from the well.* (TA.) — نَشِيئَةٌ *What is fresh and green of the plant which is called, when dry,* طَرِيفَةٌ. (Ḳ,* TA.) — And (which is nearly as above, L,) The *plants* نَصِىّ *and* صِلِّيَان: (L, Ḳ:) or accord. to AḤn, the *plant called* ثَغْرَة, *when it has become a little thick, and high, and is yet fresh and green:* (TA:) or, (as he says on another occasion, TA,) *what has sprung,* or *sprouted up, of any plant, and not yet become thick;* as also ♦ نَشَأَةٌ. (Ḳ). See نَاشِئٌ, at the end.

نَاشِئٌ *A young person past the age of puberty:* (TA:) or *a boy* or *girl past the age of childhood:* (Ṣ, Ḳ:) or *a comely young man:* (IAạr:) or *a youth who has attained the stature of a man:* (AHeyth:) a girl, as well as a boy, is called thus; (TA;) and they also say, جَارِيَةٌ نَاشِئَةٌ. (AA.) Pl. نَشْءٌ and نَشَأٌ (Ṣ, Ḳ [or these two are rather quasi-pl. ns.,] or the ♦ former is an inf. n. used as an epithet, Aboo-Moosa,) and نَاشِئُونَ (AHeyth) and نَوَاشِئُ: (TA:) or the last is a pl. of ناشئ as applied to a girl. (MF.) Lth says that ♦ نَشْءٌ signifies *Young people;* or *youths;* and is used in the sing. also: ex. هُوَ نَشْءُ سَوْءٍ *He is a bad youth:* and he says that he had never heard ناشئ used as an epithet for a girl. Fr says that the ء of the pl. نَشْءٌ is sometimes suppressed, and they say, in the nom. نَشُو صِدْقٍ [*Excellent youths*]; acc., نَشَا صدق; gen. نَشِى صدق. (TA.) — نَاشِئٌ *Clouds not completely collected together.* Hence, it is said, is derived the expression نَشَأَ الصَّبِىُّ; which is therefore tropical. (TA.) — نَاشِئٌ *Whatever happens* (and, perhaps, *appears* TA,) *in the night:* pl. نَاشِئَةٌ; (Ḳ;) a strange form of pl. of a word of the measure فَاعِلٌ: (M, F:) or نَاشِئَةٌ [see Ḳur, lxxiii. 6,] is an inf. n. (Ḳ) in the sense of قِيَامٌ: (TA:) AM says, that نَاشِئَةُ اللَّيْلِ signifies قيام الليل the *rising in the night:* (TA:) or ناشئة الليل signifies the *first part* of the night, and of the day: or the *first of the hours* of the night: (Ṣ, Ḳ:) or *a pious act* of the night; i.e., performed in the night: (Ṣ:) or every *hour* of the night *in which one rises:* (Ḳ:) or every *hour* of the night: (Zj:) or *a rising after a sleeping,* (Ḳ,) *in the first part* of the night; (TA;) as also ♦ نَشِيئَةٌ. (Ḳ.)

مَنْشَأٌ [The *place of origination* of anything, properly and tropically; its *source.*]

مُنْشَأٌ and ♦ مُسْتَنْشَأٌ A beacon, or sign of the way, *raised and pointed.* (Ḳ.) [See the verbs.] — Also, the former, An *elevated* hill. — الجَوَارِى المُنْشَآتُ [Ḳur, lv. 24,] *The ships with elevated sails:* (Mujáhid, Ṣ, Ḳ:) or, accord. to one reading, ♦ المُنْشِئَاتُ, *The ships elevating their sails:* (TA:) or, *advancing and retiring;* or *coming and going:* (Fr:) or, *commencing their courses.* (TA.)

نَاقَةٌ مُنْشِئٌ *A she-camel that has conceived:* (Ḳ:) of the dial. of Hudheyl. (TA.) — See مُنْشَأٌ.

مُسْتَنْشَأٌ: see مُنْشَأٌ.

مُسْتَنْشِئَةٌ, (Ḳ,) also without ء, (TA,) *A female diviner:* (Ḳ:) so called because she seeks, or searches after, news: see the verb: or from انشأ "he originated:" (TA:) or مُسْتَنْشِئَةُ, without tenween, is *the proper name of a certain female diviner,* (T,) *one of the Muwelledehs* (مُوَلَّدَات) *of Ḳureysh, in the time of Moḥammad.* (TA.)

نشب

1. نَشِبَ الشَّىْءُ فِى الشَّىْءِ, aor. َ, inf. n. نُشُوبٌ (Ṣ) and نَشَبٌ (Ḳ, accord. to TA, &c: in the CḲ نَشْبٌ:) and نُشْبَةٌ; (Ḳ;) and ♦ انتشب (Ṣ, Ḳ) [and ♦ تنشّب, q. v.]; *The thing stuck fast in the thing.* (Ṣ.) نَشِبَ العَظْمُ فِيهِ *The bone stuck fast in him,* or *it;* (TA;) *would not pass through.* (Ḳ.) — نَشِبَ, aor. َ, inf. n. نَشَبٌ, *It became caught,* or *entangled,* فِى شَىْءٍ *in a thing;* as game in a net, or snare. (Lth.) — اِشْتَرَيْتُ سِمْسِمًا فَنَشِبَ فِيهِ رَجُلٌ [*I bought some sesame, and a man seized it,* or *laid hold upon it, for himself*]. (TA). نَشِبَتِ الحَرْبُ بَيْنَهُمْ, (Ṣ, A,) inf. n. نُشُوبٌ, (A,) ‡ *The war,* or *fight, became intricate and entangled* (اشتبكت), *between them.* (TA.) — مَا نَشِبْتُ أَفْعَلُ كَذَا ‡ *I ceased not*

to do so. (Ḳ.) — مَا عَلِقْتُ like مَا نَشِبْتُ أَقُولُهُ ‡ I did not cease saying it. (A.) — لَمْ يَنْشَبْ أَنْ فَعَلَ كَذَا ‡ *He did not delay to do so; [he did so without delay].* (A.) — لَمْ يَنْشَبْ وَرَقَةُ أَنْ مَاتَ ‡ *Waraḳah delayed not to die; [died without delay, or immediately;]* lit., did not cling to anything else. Occurring in a trad. (IAth.) — نَشِبَهُ الأَمْرُ *The thing was incumbent upon him:* syn. لَزِمَهُ. (Ḳ.)

2. نَشَّبُوا فِى قَتْلِ عُثْمَانَ [*They set about, or commenced, the slaughter of 'Othmán*]. (TA, from a trad.) — نَشَّمَ i. q. نَشَّبَ فِى الشَّىْءِ: (Ḳ:) mentioned by Lḥ, but as being of weak authority. (TA.) — See 4.

3. ناشبه الحَرْبَ † *He waged open war with him; contended with him therein; [app., with pertinacity].* (Ṣ.) — ناشب عَدُوَّهُ, inf. n. مُنَاشَبَةٌ, ‡ [*He contended with his enemy with pertinacity*]. (A.)

4. أَنْشَبْتُهُ فِيهِ, (Ṣ, Ḳ,) and ↑ نَشَّبْتُهُ, (Ḳ,) *I made it to stick fast in it,* (Ṣ,) *so that it would not pass through.* (Ḳ.) — انشب *He* (a fowler or the like) *had game caught,* or *entangled, in his snare,* or *net.* (Ṣ, Ḳ.) — *He* (a hawk) *fixed his talons into his prey.* (TA.) — انشبت الرِّيحُ i. q. انسبت, *The wind was violent, and drove along the dust and pebbles.* (Ḳ.)

5. تَنَشَّبَ الشَّوْكُ بِالثَّوْبِ *The thorns caught in,* or *to,* or *laid hold upon, the garment.* (Mṣb, art. علق.) — تَنَشَّبَ فِى قَلْبِهِ حُبُّهَا ‡ [*Love of her took fast hold upon,* or *became fixed in, his heart*]. (A.) — See 1.

6. تَنَاشَبُوا حَوْلَهُ *They drew themselves together, cleaving one to another, around him.* (Ḳ,* TA.)

8. See 1. — Also, *He collected fire-wood.* (Ḳ.) — انتشب طَعَامًا *He collected together corn, and made for himself property* (نَشَب) *thereof.* (Ḳ.)

نَشَبٌ (Ṣ, Ḳ) and ↑ نَشَبَةٌ and ↑ مَنْشَبَةٌ *Moveable and immoveable property;* syn. مَالٌ and عَقَارٌ: (A'Obeyd, Ṣ, Mṣb:) or *the latter only:* (Mṣb:) or *fixed property, consisting of animate and inanimate things; [or live stock and land &c.; or land &c. with its live stock;]* lit. vocal and mute, نَاطِق and صَامِت: (Ḳ:) or نشب is a term mostly applied to *immoveable property, such as houses and land;* whereas مال is a term mostly applied to moveable property, such as silver and gold coin, &c.: but this latter term is sometimes applied to all that a man possesses; and sometimes especially, or particularly, to camels. (TA.) See also 8. [You say,] لَكُمْ نَسَبٌ وَمَا لَكُمْ نَشَبٌ مَا أَنْتُمْ إِلَّا خَشَبٌ [*Ye have (good) lineage; but ye have not fixed property: ye are nothing but logs of wood*]. (A, and in a MS. copy of the Ḳ: in the CḲ, with the pron. of the third pers., and with إِنْ in place of the latter ما.) = نَشَبٌ *A certain tree, of which bows are made,* (Ḳ,) *one of the trees of the desert.* (TA.)

كُنْتُ مَرَّةً نُشْبَةً فَصِرْتُ اليَوْمَ عُقْبَةً *I was once such that, when I clung to a man, he experienced evil from me; but now I have reverted from being such through weakness.* (IAạr, Ḳ.*) [See also art. عقب.] A proverb. Said by El-Ḥárith Ibn-Bedr El-Ghudánee. Applied in the case of him who has become abased after having been great or powerful. MF observes, that نشبة as syn. with عَلِقٌ is properly written ↑ نَشَبَةٌ; and that it is altered here to assimilate it to عُقْبَةٌ: but it will be seen that نُشْبَةٌ is explained in the Ḳ, in another instance in this art. in a sense suitable to it in this proverb. (TA.) — نُشْبَةٌ [*A holdfast.* And hence,] ‡ *A man who, when he is involved,* or *engaged, in an affair, can scarcely be extricated,* or *disengaged, from it;* (A, Ḳ;) or *who is unable to accomplish it:* (TA:) *one who, when charged with,* or *accused of, a vice,* or *fault,* or *the like, will scarcely forsake it.* (L.) [See an explanation of a verse cited voce غُضْبٌ.] = نُشْبَةُ a proper name of *The wolf.* (Ḳ.) Imperfectly declinable. (TA.)

نَشَبَةٌ: see نَشَبٌ, and نُشْبَةٌ.

نَشَّابٌ *A maker of arrows.* (Ḳ.) See نَاشِبٌ.

نُشَّابٌ coll. gen. n., *Arrows:* syn. سِهَامٌ, (Ṣ,) or نَبْلٌ: (Ḳ:) n. un. with ة: (Ṣ, Ḳ:) pl. نَشَاشِيبُ: (TA:) from نَشِبَ "it stuck fast" in a thing. (Mṣb.)

نَاشِبٌ *Sticking fast* in a thing. (Mṣb.) — *Possessing arrows.* (Ṣ, Ḳ.) A word of the same kind as لَابِنٌ and تَامِرٌ: (Mṣb:) after the manner of a relative noun; having no corresponding verb from which to be formed. (TA.) قَوْمٌ نَاشِبَةٌ [*A people, or party, possessing arrows*]. (Ṣ.) — Also, قَوْمٌ نَاشِبَةٌ, (TA,) and ↑ نَشَّابَةٌ, (Ḳ,) *A people shooting,* or *who shoot, arrows.* (Ḳ, TA.) — نَاشِبَةُ المَحَالِ *The pulley that sticks fast,* or *will not run.* A poet says,

وَتِلْكَ بَنُو عَدِيّ قَدْ تَأَلَّوْا •
فَيَا عَجَبًا لِنَاشِبَةِ المَحَالِ •

[*And those, the sons of 'Adee, fell short of what they should do, or delayed: and I wonder at the pulley that sticks fast, and will not run!*] He compares them, in their holding back from aiding them, [see art. الو,] to the pulley that will not run. So explained by IAạr, and the L. In the Ḳ explained imperfectly. (TA.)

مَنْشَبٌ *A place whence one cannot extricate himself.* Ex. نَشِبَ مَنْشَبَ سَوْءٍ ‡ *He fell into an evil, or a misfortune, from which he could not deliver, or extricate himself.* (A, Ḳ.)

مِنْشَبٌ [*An instrument by which a thing is made to catch, or stick fast:* pl. مَنَاشِبُ]. [Hence,] مَنَاشِبُ قُفْلٍ [*The catches of a lock*]. (A'Obeyd, in TA, voce فَرَاشٌ, q. v.) — مِنْشَبٌ *Tough,* or *dry, bad, unripe dates;* syn. بُسْرُ الغَشْوِ: pl. مَنَاشِبُ. (Ḳ.) — أَتَوْنَا بِغَشْوٍ مِنْشَبٍ يَأْخُذُ بِالحَلْقِ [*They brought us tough, or dry, bad, unripe dates, that choked, or stuck in the throat*]. (IAạr.)

مَنْشَبَةٌ: see نَشَبٌ.

مُنَشَّبٌ A garment of the kind called بُرْد *figured with the forms of arrows:* (Ḳ:) or *figured with a pattern resembling the notches of arrows.* (A.)

نشج

1. نَشَجَ, aor. ـِ, inf. n. نَشِيجٌ and نُشُوجٌ, *It* (water) *made a sound* [in running] *upon the ground.* (L.) — نَشَجَ, aor. ـِ, inf. n. نَشِيجٌ (Ṣ, Ḳ) and نَشْجٌ, (Ṣ,) *He sobbed:* (L:) *he became choked with weeping, without raising,* or *prolonging, his voice therein:* (Ṣ, Ḳ:) *he wept like a child when he is beaten, when his weeping does not find egress, but is reciprocated in his chest:* (A'Obeyd:) *he became choked with weeping, on an occasion of fright,* or *fear.* (T.) — نَشَجَ, (Ḳ,) or نَشَجَ بِصَوْتِهِ, inf. n. نَشِيجٌ, (Ṣ;) ‡ *He* (an ass) *made his voice to reciprocate* (Ṣ, Ḳ) *in his chest:* (Ṣ:) *he brayed,* (A'Obeyd,) *on an occasion of fright,* or *fear.* (TA.) — نَشَجَ ‡ *It* (a cooking-pot, and a skin, Ṣ, Ḳ, and a jar, or earthen pot, Ṣ) *made a gurgling noise by the motion of its contents, as in boiling.* (Ṣ, Ḳ.) — نَشَجَ, (aor. ـِ, inf. n. نَشِيجٌ, TA.) *He* (a singer) *made a distinction,* or *an interval,* (فَصَلَ,) *between two sounds, and prolonged* [*the same*]. (Ḳ.) — نَشَجَ † *It* (a frog) *made a reciprocating croaking.* (Ḳ.) — نَشَجَتِ الطَّعْنَةُ ‡ *The stab made a* [*gurgling*] *sound within,* on the coming forth of the blood. (TA.) — نَشَجَ, aor. ـِ, inf. n. نَشِيجٌ, *He,* or *it, uttered,* or *made, a sound,* or *noise.* (L.)

نَشْجٌ *A channel in which water flows:* pl. أَنْشَاجٌ. (Ṣ, Ḳ.)

عَبْرَةٌ نَشْجٌ *A weeping that reciprocates in the throat, with sobbing.* (L.)

نَشِيجٌ The *channel of a torrent:* pl. أَنْشَاجٌ. (L.)

نشح

1. نَشَحَ, aor. ـَ, inf. n. نَشْحٌ and نُشُوحٌ, *He drank a little,* (L,) *less than what would satisfy him:* (Ṣ, L, Ḳ:) or, contr., *he drank until he was full:* (L, Ḳ:) as also ↑ انتشح. (L.) — نَشَحَ *He gave his camel a little water to drink:* (L:) *he watered horses so as to allay the vehemence of their thirst.* (T, L, Ḳ.)

8: see 1.

نَشُوحٌ *A little water.* (Ṣ, Ḳ.) Abu-n-Nejm says, describing asses,

حَتَّى إِذَا مَا غَيَّبَتْ نَشُوحَا

(Ṣ, L,) meaning *Until, when they had taken into their bellies a little water:* or نشوح signifies *a drink less than suffices to satisfy.* (L.)

نشد

1. نَشَدَ, (Ṣ, Ḳ, &c.,) aor. ـُ, (Ṣ, Mṣb. &c.,) inf. n. نَشْدٌ (L, Mṣb, Ḳ) and نِشْدَةٌ and نِشْدَانٌ, (Ṣ, M, L, Ḳ,) or these two are simple substs., (Mṣb,) *He raised his voice in seeking for,* or *after,* a stray-beast, or beast that had been lost; *he called out and inquired respecting it*; *he cried it*: (L:) or *he sought for,* or *after,* it: (Lḥ, A'Obeyd, Ṣ, M, L, Mṣb, Ḳ:) and [in like manner] ↓ انشد *he asked,* or *desired, to be directed to* it. (M, L, Ḳ.) — Also, *He made known,* or *gave information of,* a stray-beast, or beast that had been lost; (Lḥ, A'Obeyd, M, L, Mṣb Ḳ;) and so ↓ انشد: (Lḥ, Ṣ, M, IḲṭṭ, L, Mṣb, Ḳ:) thus the latter verb [as well as the former] bears two contr. significations. (M, Ḳ.) See also نَاشِدٌ. — نَشَدَ † *He sought, sought for* or *after,* or *desired, a thing.* (L.) — نَشَدَهُ † *He asked, begged,* or *besought, him.* (L.) — نُشِدَ † *He was asked, begged,* or *besought.* (Ṣ, L.) See 6: and 4. — نَشَدَهُ, (aor. ـُ, L,) inf. n. نِشْدَةٌ [and نَشْدَةٌ (see below)] and نِشْدَانٌ; (L;) and ↓ نَاشَدَهُ, inf. n. مُنَاشَدَةٌ and نِشَادٌ; (M, L, Ḳ;) ‡ *He adjured him.* (M,* L,* Ḳ.) — نَشَدَهُ بِٱللّٰهِ ‡ *He adjured him by God;* (L, Ḳ;*) accord. to most of the grammarians and lexicologists, *with a desire of conciliating him.* (MF.) — نَشَدَهُ, (aor. ـُ, T, Ṣ,) inf. n. نَشْدٌ, ‡ *He said to him* نَشَدْتُكَ ٱللّٰهَ, (Ṣ, L, Ḳ,) which signifies *I conjure, beg,* or *beseech, thee by God;* (Ṣ, A, Mgh, L, Mṣb, Ḳ;) as though thou remindedst him of God, and he remembered; (Ṣ, L;) as also أَنْشُدُكَ ٱللّٰهَ, and بِٱللّٰهِ, (L,) and ↓ نَاشَدْتُكَ ٱللّٰهَ, (A, Mgh, L,) and بِٱللّٰهِ: (Mgh, L, Mṣb:) originally, *I conjure thee by God, raising my voice:* (Et-Towsheeḥ:) or it signifies *I remind thee of God, conjuring;* and originally, *I beseech of thee by God;* the thing for which one conjures being preceded by إِلَّا or what is syn. therewith, [as لَمَّا,] or by an interrogative or imperative or prohibitive: (MF:) or it signifies *I remind thee of God, desiring to conciliate thee;* as also نَشَدْتُكَ بِٱللّٰهِ: (Mṣb:) or نشدتك الله, inf. n. نَشْدَةٌ and نِشْدَةٌ and نِشْدَانٌ, signifies *I adjure thee by God;* as also ↓ أَنْشَدْتُكَ بِٱللّٰهِ; (M, L,) or this latter is erroneous: (Mgh, L:) and so signifies نَشْدَكَ ٱللّٰهَ; (M, L, Ḳ;) in which نَشْدَ is said to be originally نَشْدَةً, an inf. n. put in the place of the verb, or نشدك الله is a phrase of unpremeditated formation, like عَمْرَكَ ٱللّٰهَ and قِعْدَكَ ٱللّٰهَ; or this phrase, which occurs in a trad., may be incorrectly transmitted, and should perhaps be أَنْشُدُكَ ٱللّٰهَ: (IAth, L:) نَشَدْتُكَ بِٱللّٰهِ or نَشَدَهُ signifies *he said to him* وَالرَّحِمِ [*I conjure thee,* or *adjure thee, by God and relationship;* &c.]: (Lth, T, L:) *I beg,* or *beseech, thee by God, and by relationship, raising my voice.* (L.) — نَشَدَ *He remembered* God. (Ṣ, L.) — *He knew,* or *was acquainted with,* a person. (L, Ḳ.) — نَشَدَهُ عَهْدَهُ, aor. ـُ, *He reminded him of his compact, covenant, engagement,* or *promise.* (Mgh.)

3. نَاشَدَهُ الأَمْرَ, and فِى الأَمْرِ, † *He desired and asked of him the thing.* (L.) — See 1.

4. انشدهُ, and انشد لَهُ, † *He answered him; gave him his assent,* or *consent, to that which he asked, begged,* or *besought.* The ا in this case is called أَلِفُ الإِزَالَةِ: as though the verb meant he caused his raising of his voice (نَشِيدَهُ) to cease. (L.) See also 6: and 1. — انشد, (inf. n. إِنْشَادٌ, A, Mṣb,) ‡ *He recited* poetry; (Ṣ,* A, L, Mṣb,* Ḳ;) properly, [*he chanted it,*] *with a high voice;* (L;) for the reciter [usually] raises his voice in reciting: (A:) *he raised it in fame;* as also نَشَدَ. (L.) — أَنْشَدَنِى شِعْرَهُ ‡ *He recited to me his poetry.* (Ṣ,* A.) — انشد ‡ [*He cited,* or *quoted,* a verse, or verses. (The lexicons, &c., passim.)] — انشد بِهِمْ ‡ *He satirized them.* (L, Ḳ.) — انشد † *He gave.* (Ṣ, L.) See 6.

5. تنشّد الأَخْبَارَ ‡ *He sought to learn news* (A, Ḳ) *without others knowing the same.* (A.)

6. تناشدوا ‡ *They recited* [poetry] *one to another.* (L, Mṣb, Ḳ.) — El-Aạshà, in the following verse,

رَبِّى كَرِيمٌ لَا يُكَدِّرُ نِعْمَةً
وَإِذَا تُنُوشِدَ فِى المَهَارِقِ أَنْشَدَا

[*My lord is generous; he does not sully a favour: and when he is asked,* or *begged,* or *besought, in papers, he gives*], means, accord. to AO, that En-Noạmán Ibn-El-Mundhir, when asked, or begged, or besought, to write grants to poets (جَوَائِز), gave: تنوشد is here for نُشِدَ, meaning سُئِلَ. (Ṣ, L.)

10. استنشدهُ الشِّعْرَ (Ṣ, A,* L, Ḳ*) ‡ *He asked or desired him to recite the poetry.* (Ḳ.)

نَشْدَةٌ and ↓ نِشْدَانٌ *Search for,* or *after, a stray-beast.* See also 1. (Mṣb.) Also, *A making known,* or *informing respecting, a stray beast.* See also 1. (Mṣb.) — نِشْدَةٌ *A voice; a cry; a sound.* (Ḳ.)

نِشْدَانٌ: see نِشْدَةٌ.

نَشِيدٌ *Elevation of the voice:* (L, Ḳ:) or the voice itself. (L.) — ‡ *Poetry recited* (Ṣ, A, L, Mṣb, Ḳ) *by people, one to another;* (Ṣ, A, L, Ḳ:) as also ↓ أُنْشُودَةٌ: (Ḳ:) pl. of the former, نَشَائِدُ; (TA;) and of the latter, أَنَاشِيدُ. (A, Ḳ.)

نَاشِدٌ [act. part. n. of نَشَدَ] in the following verse of Aboo-Du-ád,

وَتَصِيخُ أَحْيَانًا كَمَا ٱسْـ
ـتَمَعَ المُضِلُّ لِصَوْتِ نَاشِدْ

[*And she listens sometimes like as he who has lost a beast gives ear to the voice of a* ناشد], signifies *a man making known,* or *giving information of, a stray-beast:* or, as some say, *one seeking for,* or *after, a stray-beast;* for he who has lost a beast desires to find one who, like himself, has lost one, that he may be consoled thereby. (Ṣ, M, L.) See art. صوخ. — نَاشِدُونَ *Men who seek after stray-camels, and take them, and confine them from their owners.* (L.)

أُنْشُودَةٌ: see نَشِيدٌ.

مُتَنَاشَدٌ ‡ Poetry *recited by people, one to another.* (Ṣ, L, Ḳ.)

نشر

1. نَشَرَ, (Ṣ, A, Mṣb,) aor. ـُ, (Ṣ, TA,) inf. n. نَشْرٌ, (Ṣ, A, Mṣb, Ḳ,) *He spread, spread out,* or *open, expanded,* or *unfolded,* (Ṣ, TA,) a garment or piece of cloth (A, Mṣb, TA) or the like, (TA,) goods, &c., (Ṣ,) and a writing; (A;) *contr. of* طَوَى; (A, Ḳ;) as also ↓ نشّر, inf. n. تَنْشِيرٌ: (Ḳ, TA:) [or the latter is with teshdeed to denote muchness, or frequency, or repetition, of the action, or its application to many objects, as is shown by an explanation of its act. part. n., which see below. Hence لَفٌّ وَنَشْرٌ: see art. لف.] — [*He spread out,* or, as we say, *pricked up,* his ears: and hence the saying,] نَشَرَ لِذٰلِكَ الأَمْرِ أُذُنَيْهِ, lit., *He spread out his ears at that thing:* meaning, ‡ *he was covetous of that thing,* or *eager for it.* (Ḥar. p. 206.) [See نَاشِرٌ, below.] — نَشَرَ الخَبَرَ, (Ṣ, A, Ḳ,) aor. ـُ and ـِ, (Ṣ, Ḳ,) inf. n. نَشْرٌ, (Ḳ,) ‡ *He spread,* or *published, the news.* (Ṣ, A, Ḳ.) — Also نَشَرَ, aor. ـُ, (Mṣb,) inf. n. نَشْرٌ; (Mṣb, Ḳ;) [and ↓ نشّر, or this is with teshdeed for the purpose mentioned above;] *He scattered,* or *dispersed,* (Mṣb, Ḳ, TA,) [people, &c.; or] sheep or goats, (Mṣb, TA,) and camels, (TA,) *after confining them in the nightly resting-place.* (Mṣb.) — *He sprinkled* water. (A.) — نَشَرَتِ الرِّيحُ *The wind blew in a misty* or *cloudy day* [*so as to disperse the mist or clouds*]. (IAạr, Ḳ.) — نَشَرَ عَنْهُ, (A, Ḳ,) inf. n. نَشْرٌ; (A;) and ↓ نشّر عنه, (A, L, TA,) inf. n. تَنْشِيرٌ; (Ṣ, A, L, TA;) and in like manner ↓ نَشَرَهُ; (Ṣ, TA;) ‡ *He charmed away*

from him sickness, (Ṣ,* A, L, Ḳ,*) and *diabolical possession,* or *madness,* (L, Ḳ,) *by a* نُشْرَة, i. e., *a charm,* or *an amulet;* (Ṣ, A, L, Ḳ;) *as though he dispersed it from him:* (A:) and in like manner ↑ نشّرهُ *he wrote for him a* نُشْرَة. (Ṣ.) El-Kilábee says, فَإِذَا نُشِرَ المَسْفُوعُ كَانَ كَأَنَّمَا أُنْشِطَ مِنْ عِقَالٍ ‡ [*And when he who is smitten by the evil eye is charmed by a* نُشْرَة, *he is as though he were loosed from a bond*]: i. e., it [the effect of the eye] departs from him speedily. (Ṣ [in two copies of which I find نُشِرَ, as above; but in the TA, ↑ نُشِّرَ.]) And in a trad. it is said, نَشَّرَهُ ↑ بِقُلْ أَعُوذُ بِرَبِّ النَّاسِ ‡ *He charmed away the effect of enchantment from him* [*by the words* "*Say I seek refuge in the Lord of men:*" the commencement of the last chap. of the Ḳur-án]. (Ṣ.) ═ نَشَرَ, (El-Ḥasan, Zj, A, Ḳ,) aor. ـُ, (TA,) inf. n. نَشْرٌ and نُشُورٌ; (Ḳ, TA;) or ↑ أَنْشَرَ; (I'Ab, Fr, Ṣ, A, Mgh, Mṣb;) or both; (A, Ḳ;) ‡ *He* (God, Ṣ, A, &c.) *raised* the dead *to life; quickened* them; *revivified,* or *revived,* them. (Zj, Ṣ, A, Mgh, Mṣb, Ḳ, &c.) I'Ab reads [in the Ḳur, ii. 261,] كَيْفَ نُنْشِرُهَا [*How we will raise them to life*], and adduces in his favour the words [in the Ḳur. lxxx. 22,] ثُمَّ إِذَا شَاءَ أَنْشَرَهُ ↑ ‡ [*Then, when He pleaseth, He raiseth him to life*]: El-Ḥasan reads نَنْشُرُهَا: [and others read نُنْشِزُهَا, with záy:] but Fr says, that El-Ḥasan holds it to refer to unfolding and folding, and that the proper way is to use انشر [in this sense,] transitively, and نَشَرَ intransitively. (Ṣ, TA.) [See also طَوَى, which has the contr. meaning.] — Hence, أَنْشَرَ ↑ الرَّضَاعُ العَظْمَ: *i. q.* أَنْشَزَ, with záy: (Mṣb:) or ‡ *The sucking strengthened the bone.* (Mgh.) ═ نَشَرَ, (Ṣ, A, Mṣb, Ḳ,) aor. ـُ, (Ṣ,) inf. n. نُشُورٌ (Ṣ, A, Mṣb, TA) and نَشْرٌ, (Mṣb,) agreeably with what Fr says, (Ṣ,) signifies ‡ *He* (a dead person) *lived after death; came to life again; revived;* (Ṣ, TA;) or *lived; came to life;* (A, Mṣb;) as also ↑ انتشر. (A.) Hence يَوْمُ النُّشُورِ ‡ *The day of resurrection.* (Ṣ.) — نَشَرَ, (TA,) inf. n. نَشْرٌ, (Ḳ, TA,) ‡ *It* (herbage, or pasturage,) *became green in consequence of rain in the end of summer after it had dried up.* (TA.) — ‡ *It* (a plant) *began to grow forth in the ground.* (Ḳ,* TA.) You say, مَا أَحْسَنَ نَشْرَهَا ‡ *How good is its first growth!* (TA.) — † *It* (a tree) *put forth its leaves.* (Ḳ.) — † *It* (foliage) *spread.* (Ḳ.) — نَشَرَتِ الأَرْضُ, (Ṣ, A, Ḳ,) aor. ـُ, (TA,) inf. n. نُشُورٌ, (Ḳ,) ‡ *The land being rained upon in the end of summer, its herbage,* or *pasturage, became green after it had dried up:* (Ṣ, TA:) or *the land, being watered by the rain called* الرَّبِيع, *put forth its herbage.* (A, Ḳ.) See نَشْرٌ. ═ نَشَرَ, (Ṣ, A, Mṣb,) aor. ـُ, (Ṣ,) inf. n. نَشْرٌ, (Ḳ,) ‡ [*He sawed* wood;] *he cut* (قَطَعَ, Ṣ, or نَحَتَ, Ḳ) wood, (Ṣ, A, Mṣb, Ḳ,) *with a* مِنْشَار. (Ṣ, A, Mṣb.)

2: see 1, in five places, throughout the former half of the paragraph.

3. نَاشَرَهُ الثِّيَابَ [*He spread,* or *unfolded, with him the garments* or *pieces of cloth*]. (A.)

4: see 1, after the middle of the paragraph.

5: see 8, in two places.

6. تَنَاشَرُوا الثِّيَابَ [*They spread,* or *unfolded, one with another, the garments,* or *pieces of cloth*]. (A.)

8. انتشر [quasi-pass. of 1,] *It spread, expanded,* or *unfolded; it became spread, expanded,* or *unfolded;* as also ↑ تنشّر: (Ḳ:) [or the latter, being quasi-pass. of 2, denotes muchness, &c.] — انتشرت النَّخْلَةُ *The branches of the palm-tree spread forth.* (Ḳ.) [And انتشرت الأَغْصَانُ *The branches spread forth:* and *the branches straggled.*] — انتشر الخَبَرُ ‡ *The news spread,* or *became published,* (Ṣ, A, Ḳ,) — And انتشرت فِى النَّاسِ *among the people.* (A.) — الرَّائِحَةُ † [*The odour spread,* or *diffused itself.*] (Ḳ in art. فوح; &c.) — انتشر النَّهَارُ † *The day became long and extended:* (Ḳ:) and so one says of other things. (TA.) — انتشر العَصَبُ † *The sinews,* or *tendons, became inflated,* or *swollen,* (Ḳ,) *by reason of fatigue:* (TA:) إِنْتِشَارٌ is *a state of inflation,* or *swelling, in the sinews,* or *tendons, of a beast, occasioned by fatigue:* (Ṣ:) AO says, that *the sinew,* or *tendon, which becomes inflated,* or *swollen, is the* عُجَايَة, (Ṣ,* TA,) and that what is termed تَحَرُّكُ الشَّظَى is similar to this affection, excepting in its not being so well endured by the horse: by another, or others, it is said, that انتشار of the sinews, or tendons, of a beast, in his fore leg, is *a breaking, and consequent displacement,* of those sinews. (TA.) — انتشر ذَكَرُهُ † *His penis became erect.* (TA.) [And hence,] انتشر الرَّجُلُ ‡ *The man became excited by lust.* (S, Ḳ.) — انتشر المَآءُ [In my copy of the A, استنشر, but this I regard as a mistranscription,] *The water became sprinkled;* as also ↑ تنشّر: (A:) [or the latter signifies *it became much sprinkled.*] — انتشروا فى الأَرْضِ *They became scattered,* or *dispersed,* or *they scattered,* or *dispersed, themselves, in the land,* or *earth.* (A.) — انتشرت الغَنَمُ, (Mṣb, TA,) and الإِبِلُ, (Ḳ, TA,) *The sheep* or *goats* [and *the camels*] *became scattered,* or *dispersed, after having been confined in their nightly resting-place:* (Mṣb:) or *the sheep* or *goats* (TA) and *the camels* (Ḳ, TA) *became scattered,* or *dispersed, through negligence of their pastor.* (Ḳ, TA.) — انتشر الأَمْرُ † *The state of things,* or *affairs, became dissolved, broken up, decomposed, disorganized,* or *unsettled;* syn. تَشَتَّتَ. (TA, art. شت.) ═ See also 1, latter part of the paragraph. — انتشر also signifies *He put himself in motion, and went on a journey.* (TA, in art. بسو.) — انتشر الذِّئْبُ فِى الغَنَمِ *The wolf made an incursion among the sheep* or *goats.* (TA in art. شع.)

10. استنشرهُ *He demanded,* or *desired, of him that he should unfold* (أَنْ يَنْشُرَ) to him (عَلَيْهِ) [a thing]. (A.)

نَشْرٌ used in the sense of an act. part. n.: see نَاشِرٌ. — And in the sense of a pass. or quasi-pass. part. n.: see نَشَرٌ. — *A sweet odour:* (Ṣ, A, Ḳ:) [because it spreads:] or *odour in a more general sense;* (A, Ḳ;) i. e., *absolutely, whether sweet* or *stinking:* (A'Obeyd:) or the *odour of a woman's mouth,* (ADḳ, A, Ḳ,) and *of her nose,* (ADḳ, TA,) and *of her arm-pits* (أَعْطَاف), *after sleep.* (ADḳ, A, Ḳ.) ═ ‡ *Herbage,* or *pasturage, which has dried up and then become green in consequence of rain in the end of summer* or *spring* (see below, and see بِسَمَاك): (Ṣ, Ḳ:) *it is bad for the pasturing animals when it first appears, and men flee from it with their camels &c.;* (Ṣ, TA;) *which it affects with the* [*disease called*] سُهَام *when they pasture upon it at its first appearance:* [see remarks on a verse cited in art. بيض, voce بَاضَ: and see another verse in art. جرب, voce أَجْرَبُ:] AḤn says, that *it does not injure animals with the solid hoof; or if it do so, they leave it until it dries, and then its evil quality departs from it: it consists of leguminous plants and of* [*the herbage termed*] عُشْب; or, as some say, *of the latter only:* (TA:) [an ex. of the word is cited in art. جرب, voce أَجْرَبُ:] or *herbage,* or *pasturage, of which the upper part dries up and the lower part is moist and green:* (Lth:) or *herbage produced by the rain called* الرَّبِيع: (A:) and *what has come forth, of plants,* or *herbage.* (TA.) ═ *Life.* (Ḳ.)

نَشَرٌ is of the measure فَعَلٌ in the sense of the measure مَفْعُولٌ, (Mṣb, TA,) syn. with مَنْشُورٌ, like as قَبَضٌ is with مَقْبُوضٌ, (Mgh,) and syn. with مُنْتَشِرٌ, (Ṣ, Mṣb, Ḳ,) [therefore signifying *Spread, expanded,* or *unfolded: scattered,* or *dispersed,* &c.: and *spreading,* or *being spread,* &c.: *being scattered,* &c.:] and *a thing that one has spread, expanded,* or *unfolded:* &c. (O, voce سَبَلٌ, q. v.) — You say اِكْتَسَى البَازِى رِيشًا نَشَرًا *The hawk,* or *falcon, became clad in spreading and long feathers.* (Ṣ, TA.) — And hence نَشَرٌ is applied to *People in a scattered,* or *dispersed, state, not collected under one head,* or *chief;* (Mṣb, Ḳ;) as also ↑ نَشْرٌ: (Ḳ:) and to *sheep* or *goats in a scattered,* or *dispersed, state, after having been confined in their nightly resting-place:* (Mṣb:) or *sheep* or *goats,* and *camels, in a scattered,* or *dispersed, state, through the negligence of their pastor.* (TA.) You say, رَأَيْتُ القَوْمَ نَشَرًا *I saw the people in a scattered,* or *dispersed, state.* (Ṣ.) And جَآءَ القَوْمُ نَشَرًا *The people came in a scattered,* or *dispersed, state.* (TA.) — Hence also, نَشَرُ المَآءِ *What is sprinkled, of water,* (Mgh, TA,) in the performance of the ablution termed الوُضُوْء. (TA.) It is said in a trad., أَتَمْلِكُ نَشَرَ

الْمَآءِ [*Dost thou possess what is sprinkled of water?*] (Ṣ;) or مَنْ يَمْلِكُ نَشَرَ الْمَآءِ [*Who possesseth what is sprinkled of water?*] (Mgh;) [app. meaning, that it is gone and cannot be recovered.] —— And hence, أَللّٰهُمَّ ٱضْمُمْ نَشَرِى † *O God, compose what is discomposed*, or *disorganized, of my affairs:* (Ḳ,* TA:) a phrase like لُمَّ شَعَثِى. (TA.) 'Áïsheh says, in a trad., describing her father, فَرَدَّ نَشَرَ الإِسْلَامِ عَلَى غَرِّهِ, meaning, † *And he restored what was discomposed*, or *disorganized*, [lit., what was unfolded,] *of El-Islám, to its state in which it was in the time of the Apostle of God*, [lit.. to its fold, or plait;] alluding to cases of apostacy, and her father's sufficiency to treat them. (TA.) ═══ See also نَاشِرٌ.

نُشْرَةٌ ‡ *A charm*, or *an amulet*, (رُقْيَةٌ, Ṣ, L, Ḳ,) *by which a sick person, and one possessed*, or *mad, is cured;* (A,* L, Ḳ;) *by which the malady is* [*as it were*] *dispersed from him.* (L.) Moḥammad, being asked respecting that which is thus termed, answered, that it is of the work of the devil: and El-Ḥasan asserted it to be a kind of enchantment. (TA.)

نَشُورٌ: see نَاشِرٌ.

نُشَارَةٌ ‡ [*Saw-dust;*] *what falls from the* مِنْشَار [or *saw*]; (Ṣ;) *what falls in* نَشْر [or *sawing*]. (Ḳ.)

نَاشِرٌ act. part. n. of نَشَرَ. —— كَانَ يُكَبِّرُ نَاشِرَ الأَصَابِعِ *He* (Moḥammad) *used to say* أَللّٰهُ أَكْبَرُ *spreading*, or *unfolding, his fingers:* said to mean *not making his hand a clenched fist.* (Mgh.) —— جَآءَ نَاشِرًا أُذُنَيْهِ [*He came spreading*, or, as we say, *pricking up, his ears:* meaning,] ‡ *he came in a state of covetousness*, or *eagerness.* (IAạr, L.) [In a copy of the A, طَائِعًا is erroneously put for طَامِعًا.] —— وَٱلنَّاشِرَاتِ نَشْرًا, in the Ḳur., [lxxvii. 3,] signifies *And the angels*, (TA,) or *the winds*, (Jel,) *that do scatter the rain:* (Jel, TA:) or *the winds that do bring rain.* (TA.) And رِيحٌ نَشُورٌ ♦, of which the pl. is رِيَاحٌ نُشُرٌ, signifies *Wind that spreads* [the clouds], or *scatters* [the rain]; (Ṣ; and Bḍ, vii. 55;) نَشُورٌ being syn. with نَاشِرٌ: (Bḍ:) or it signifies *in a scatttered state.* (Jel, vii. 55.) [In the Ḳur, ubi supra,] يُرْسِلُ الرِّيَاحَ نُشُرًا بَيْنَ يَدَىْ رَحْمَتِهِ, and نُشْرًا, and نَشْرًا ♦, and نَشَرًا ♦, [*Sendeth the winds, &c.*,] (Ḳ,* TA,) all these being various readings, (TA,) نُشُرًا is pl. of نَشُورٌ, (Bḍ, Ḳ,) in the sense of نَاشِرٌ; (Bḍ;) or the meaning is, *in a state of dispersion before the rain;* (Jel;) and نُشْرًا is a contraction; (Bḍ, Ḳ;) and the third reading means ‡ *quickening*, or *making to live, by spreading the clouds wherein is the rain*, (Ḳ,) which is the life of everything, (TA,) نَشْرًا ♦ being an inf. n. used as a denotative of state, in the sense of نَاشِرَاتٍ, or as an absolute objective complement [of يرسل], for إِرْسَالٌ and نَشْرٌ are nearly alike; (Bḍ;) and the fourth is extr., (IJ, Ḳ,) and is said to mean مُنْتَشِرَةً نَشَرًا ♦ [which is virtually the same as the third]: [Zj, Ḳ:) another reading is بُشُرًا, pl. of بَشِيرَةٌ, (TA,) or of بَشُورٌ; (TA, in art. بشر;) or بُشْرًا, (Bḍ, Jel,) a contraction of بُشُرًا, (Bḍ,) pl. of بَشِيرٌ. (Bḍ, Jel.) ═══ أَرْضٌ نَاشِرَةٌ ‡ *Land having herbage*, or *pasturage, which has dried up and then become green in consequence of rain in the end of summer:* (Ṣ:) or *having herbage produced by the rain called* الرَّبِيع. (A.) See نَشْرٌ.

الْمَنْشَرُ ‡ *The place of resurrection.* (TA.)

صُحُفٌ مُنَشَّرَةٌ [*Scattered*, or *much scattered, writings* or *the like*] is with teshdeed to denote muchness, or frequency, or repetition, of the action, or its application to many objects. (Ṣ, TA.)

مِنْشَارٌ ‡ [*A saw;*] *a certain instrument for cutting wood.* (Ṣ, Mṣb, Ḳ.) —— Also, [but less commonly], *A wooden implement with prongs*, [lit., fingers,] *with which wheat and the like are winnowed.* (Ḳ.)

مَنْشُورٌ *What is not sealed*, [here meaning *not closed with a seal*,] *of the writings of the Sultán* [or *of a viceroy*]; (Ḳ;) i. e., *what is now commonly known by the name of* فَرْمَان: pl. مَنَاشِيرُ. (TA.) —— † A man *whose state of affairs is disorganised*, or *disordered.* (Ḳ.)

نشز

1. نَشَزَ, aor. ـُ and ـِ, (Ṣ, Mṣb, Ḳ,) inf. n. نَشْزٌ, (Ṣ, Ḳ,) or نُشُوزٌ, (Mṣb,) *He rose*, or *raised himself*, (Ṣ, A, Mṣb, Ḳ,) فِى الْمَكَانِ *in the place*, (Ṣ,) and فِى مَجْلِسِهِ *in his sitting-place*, (TA,) and عَنْ مَكَانِهِ, (A,) or مِنْ مَكَانِهِ, (Mṣb,) *from his place:* (A, Mṣb:) or *he rose a little* in his sitting-place: (TA:) or *he stood up after sitting.* (TA.) Both forms of the aor. occur, accord. to different readings, (the former being the reading of the people of El-Ḥijáz, and the latter that of others, Fr, TA,) in the Ḳur, [lviii. 12,] وَإِذَا قِيلَ ٱنْشُزُوا فَٱنْشُزُوا, (Mṣb, TA,) meaning, accord. to Aboo-Is-ḥáḳ, *And when it is said, Rise ye and stand up, then do ye rise and stand up.* (TA.) Accord. to IḲṭṭ, نَشَزَ الْقَوْمُ فِى مَجْلِسِهِمْ signifies *The people drew themselves together* [*in their sitting-place* to make room] for those sitting with them: and also *they rose from their sitting-place, and stood up.* (TA.) You say also, نَشَزَ بِالْقَوْمِ فِى الْخُصُومَةِ, inf. n. نُشُوزٌ, *He rose with the people for the purpose of contention, altercation*, or *litigation.* (TA.) —— *He, or it, overtopped*, or *overlooked, an elevated piece of ground, and appeared.* (TA.) —— [*It rose; rose from its place; was*, or *became, high* or *elevated, protuberant* or *prominent; it protruded.*] —— نَشَزَتْ نَفْسُهُ ‡ *His soul*, or *spirit;* or *stomach, heaved*, (A, Ḳ,) *by reason of fright.* (A, TA.) ═══ Hence, from نَشْزٌ in the first of the senses explained above, (Mṣb,) or from نَشْزٌ, signifying "high, or elevated, ground," (Aboo-Is-ḥáḳ, TA,) نَشَزَتِ الْمَرْأَةُ, (Ṣ, Ḳ,) or نَشَزَتْ عَلَى زَوْجِهَا, (A, Mgh, TA,) or مِنْ زَوْجِهَا, (Mṣb,) and بِزَوْجِهَا, (TA,) aor. ـُ and ـِ, inf. n. نُشُوزٌ, (Ṣ, Mṣb, Ḳ,) ‡ *The woman*, or *wife, was*, or *became, disobedient to her husband*, (Ṣ, Mgh, Mṣb, Ḳ,) *and exalted herself against him*, (TA,) *and resisted him*, or *withstood him*, (Mṣb,) *and hated him*, (Ṣ, Mgh, Ḳ,) *and deserted him:* (TA:) or *she disliked him*, or *hated him*, (Zj, Mgh, TA,) *and was an evil companion to him.* (Zj, TA.) And نَشَزَ بَعْلُهَا عَلَيْهَا, (Ṣ, A, Ḳ,) or مِنْهَا, aor. ـُ and ـِ, (Mṣb,) inf. n. نُشُوزٌ, (TA,) ‡ *Her husband treated her injuriously, and was unkind to her*, or *estranged himself from her:* (Ṣ, Ḳ:) or *forsook her, and was unkind to her*, or *estranged himself from her:* (Mṣb:) or *disliked her*, or *hated her*, (Zj, Mgh, TA,) *and was an evil companion to her.* (Zj, TA.)

4. انشزهُ *He raised it*, (A, Mṣb, Ḳ,) namely, a place, (Mṣb,) or a thing, (Ḳ,) from its place. (A, Ḳ.) —— [Hence,] انشز عِظَامَ الْمَيِّتِ *He* [God] *raised the bones of the dead to their places, and set them*, or *put them together, one upon another.* (Ṣ, Ḳ.) So in the Ḳur, [ii. 261,] وَٱنْظُرْ إِلَى ٱلْعِظَامِ كَيْفَ نُنْشِزُهَا ثُمَّ نَكْسُوهَا لَحْمًا [*And look thou at the bones* (of thine ass), *how we raise them to their places, &c., then we clothe them with flesh*], accord. to the reading of Zeyd Ibn-Thábit; (Fr, Ṣ,* TA;) but the Koofees read [نُنْشِرُهَا] with rá: the former reading, however, accord. to Th, is preferred. (TA.) [See art. نشر.] —— Hence also, انشر الرَّضَاعُ الْعَظْمَ ‡ *The sucking of the breast increased*, or *augmented, the bone:* as also انشرهُ, with rá. (Mṣb.)

نَشْزٌ and نَشَزٌ ♦ *A high*, or *an elevated, place;* (Ṣ, A, Mgh, Ḳ;) as also نَشَازٌ ♦: (Ṣ, Ḳ:) or *high*, or *elevated, ground:* (Zj, TA:) or *high*, or *elevated, and hard, ground:* (M, TA:) or *what rises from a valley to the* [*adjacent*] *ground, and is not rugged:* (TA:) pl. (of the first, Ṣ, Mṣb) نُشُوزٌ, (Ṣ, Mgh, Mṣb, Ḳ,) and (of the second, Ṣ, TA, or of the first, Mṣb) نِشَازٌ, (Ṣ, Mṣb, Ḳ,) and (of the second, Ṣ, Mṣb,) أَنْشَازٌ. (Ṣ, Mgh, Mṣb, Ḳ.) You say, قَعَدَ عَلَى نَشْزٍ مِنَ الأَرْضِ, and نَشَزٍ, [*He sat upon a high piece of ground.*] (Mṣb.) And أُقْعُدْ على ذٰلِكَ النَّشَازِ *Sit thou upon that high place.* (Ṣ.)

نَشَزٌ: } see نَشْزٌ.
نَشَازٌ: }

نَاشِزٌ *Rising*; or *rising from its place*; *high*, or *elevated*; *protuberant*, or *prominent*; *protruding*. (Ḳ,* TA.) You say, قَلْبٌ نَاشِزٌ *A heart rising from its place by reason of fright*. (Ḳ, TA.) And تَلٌّ نَاشِزٌ *A high*, or *an elevated*, *mound*, or *hill*: pl. [reg. of نَاشِزَةٌ and irreg. of نَاشِزٌ] نَوَاشِزُ. (TA.) And رَكَبٌ نَاشِزٌ *A protuberant*, *high*, *pubes*, or *mons Veneris*. (TA.) And نَحْمَةٌ نَاشِزَةٌ *A piece of flesh elevated*, or *protuberant*, *upon the body*. (TA.) And عِرْقٌ نَاشِزٌ *A vein constantly swollen and pulsating* (A, Ḳ*) in consequence of disease (Ḳ, TA) or from some other cause. (TA.) And رَجُلٌ نَاشِزُ الجَبْهَةِ *A man having a high*, or *prominent*, *forehead*. (TA.) And اِمْرَأَةٌ نَاشِزَةٌ القُصَيْرَى *A woman large in the sides, having the* قصيرى [or *lowest of the ribs*] *with the flesh upon it, prominent*. (IAạr, TA.) — Also, (A, TA,) or نَاشِزَةٌ, (Mgh,) [but the former is the more common,] ‡ A woman *disobedient to her husband*, (Mgh, TA,) *and exalting herself against him*, (TA,) *and hating him*, (Mgh, TA,) *and deserting him*. (TA.) See 1. [The former epithet is also applied in like manner to a husband.]

نشط

1. نَشِطَ, aor. ـَ, inf. n. نَشَاطٌ (Ṣ, Mṣb, Ḳ) and مَنْشَطٌ, (TA,) *He* (a man, Ṣ, TA, and a beast of carriage, TA,) *was*, or *became*, *brisk*, *lively*, *sprightly*, *frisky*, *active*, *agile*, *prompt*, and *quick*; syn. خَفَّ, (Mṣb, TA,) and أَسْرَعَ; (Mṣb;) *contr. of* كَسِلَ; (TA;) or *pleased*, *cheerful*, *happy*, or *willing*; to do work, &c.; (Lth, Ḳ;) or by reason of his work; (Mṣb;) as also ▼ تنشّط, (Ṣ,* Ḳ,) لِأَمْرِ كَذَا [*to do*, or *on account of*, *such a thing*, or *such an affair*]. (Ṣ, TA.) You say also, نَشِطَ إِلَيْهِ [*He betook himself to him*, or *it*, *with briskness*, *liveliness*, *sprightliness*, or *the like*]. (TA.) — [Hence, app.,] نَشِطَتِ الدَّابَّةُ *The beast of carriage became fat*. (Ḳ.) — نَشَطَ, aor. ـُ, inf. n. نَشْطٌ, (Ṣ, Ḳ, TA,) *He went forth* from a place: (Ḳ:) *he passed*, or *crossed*, from one country or the like to another: (TA:) said, for instance, of a wild bull: (AO, IDrd, Ṣ, Ḳ:) and in like manner, a star, [meaning a planet,] from one sign of the zodiac to another. (Ṣ, Ḳ.) And نَشَطَتِ الإِبِلُ, aor. ـُ, inf. n. نَشْطٌ, *The camels went*, either *in a right direction* or *otherwise*. (TA.) — [Hence,] الهُمُومُ تَنْشِطُ بِصَاحِبِهَا (Ṣ, TA) † *Griefs*, or *disquietudes of mind*, *lead forth him who has them* [*from place to place*]. (TA.) Himyán Ibn-Koháfeh says,

• أَمْسَتْ هُمُومِى تَنْشِطُ المَنَاشِطَا •
• أَلشَّامَ بِى طَوْرًا وَطَوْرًا وَاسِطَا •

[meaning تنشط بى الى المناشط, i. e., † *My griefs*, or *disquietudes of mind*, *became such as to lead me forth to the places to which one goes forth*, *to Syria at one time*, *and at one time to Wásit*]. (Ṣ.) You say also of a road, يَنْشِطُ مِنَ الطَّرِيقِ الأَعْظَمِ ‡ *It goes forth from the main road*, to the right, and to the left. (Lth, Ḳ.*) And نَشَطَ بِهِمْ طَرِيقٌ فَأَخَذُوهُ ‡ [*A road led them forth*, *and they took it*]. (TA.) — نَشَطَ الدَّلْوَ, (Ṣ, Ḳ,) aor. ـِ (Ḳ,* TA) and ـُ, (TA,) [inf. n. نَشْطٌ,] *He pulled out the bucket*, (Ṣ, Ḳ,) or *pulled it up*, (TA,) from the well, (Ṣ, TA,) *without a pulley*. (Ṣ, Ḳ.) — And hence, المَلَائِكَةُ تَنْشِطُ الأَرْوَاحَ † *The angels draw forth the souls like as the bucket is drawn forth from the well*: (Zj:) and تَنْشِطُ نَفْسَ المُؤْمِنِ بِقَبْضِهَا (Fr, L, Ḳ [in the CḲ تَقْبِضُهَا]) which means, (Ḳ,) accord. to Ibn-'Arafeh, (TA,) † *they loose the soul of the believer gently*. (Ḳ, TA.) — [Hence also,] one says of a she-camel, [likening the motion of her fore legs to that of the arms of a man pulling up a bucket from a well without a pulley,] حَسَنَ مَا نَشَطَتِ السَّيْرَ, meaning † *Good was her wide stretching out of her fore legs* (Aṣ, Ṣ, TA) *in her going along*. (TA.) — نَشَطَ الحَبْلَ, (Ṣ, Mṣb, Ḳ,) aor. ـُ, (Ḳ, and so in a copy of the Ṣ,) or ـِ, (Mṣb, and so in a copy of the Ṣ,) inf. n. نَشْطٌ, (Ṣ, Mṣb,) *He tied the cord*, or *rope so as to form a knot*; (Ḳ, TA;) as also ▼ نَشَّطَهُ, (Ḳ,) inf. n. تَنْشِيطٌ: (TA:) or *he tied it in a knot such as is termed* أُنْشُوطَةٌ; (AZ, Ṣ, Mṣb;) as also ▼ the latter verb: (Ḥam, p. ٧٥٢:) and نَشَطَ العُقْدَةَ *he tied the knot so as to form what is thus termed*: (Mgh:) and نَشَطَ الأُنْشُوطَةَ *he tied the knot thus termed*. (TA.) [See also 4.] — نَشَطَ, and نُشِطَ مِنْ عِقَالٍ: see 4.

2. نَشَّطَهُ, inf. n. تَنْشِيطٌ, *He*, or *it*, *rendered him* نَشِيط [i. e. *brisk*, *lively*, *sprightly*, *frisky*, &c.]; (Ḳ;) as also ▼ انشطهُ. (Yaạkoob, Ḳ.) — See also 1, last sentence but one, in two places; and see 4.

4. انشط, said of a man, (Ḳ,* TA,) or of a company of men, (S,) *His*, or *their*, *beasts*, (S, Ḳ,) or *family*, (Ḳ,) *were*, or *became*, *in a state of* نَشَاط [i. e. *briskness*, *liveliness*, *sprightliness*, *friskiness*, &c.: see 1]. (S, Ḳ.) — As a trans. v.: see 2. — [Hence, app.,] *It* (herbage) *rendered* a beast *fat*. (S, TA.) — *He loosed*, *untied*, or *undid*, (S, Mgh, Mṣb, Ḳ,) a cord, or rope, (S, Ḳ,) or a knot such as is termed أُنْشُوطَة; (Mgh, Mṣb,) as also ▼ انتشط; and ▼ نَشَطَ; (Mgh;) and in like manner, the bond termed عِقَال; (Mṣb;) and so, perhaps, ▼ نشّط: (Ḥam, p. ٧٥٢:) *he pulled* a cord, or rope, *until*, or *so that*, *it became loosed*, *untied*, or *undone*; (TA;) as also ▼ انتشط: (S, Ḳ, TA,) *he caused* the عقال *to become loosed*, *untied*, or *undone*, *by pulling its* انشوطة: (Ḳ,* TA:) *he loosed*, *untied*, or *undid*, a knot *by a single pull*. (TA.) You say also, انشط البَعِيرَ *He loosed*, *untied*, or *undid*, *the* انشوطة [*of the* عقال] *of the camel*. (TA.) And انشط البَعِيرَ مِنْ عِقَالِهِ *He loosed the camel from his* عِقَال. (Mṣb.) [And hence the saying,] كَأَنَّمَا أُنْشِطَ مِنْ عِقَالٍ *As though he were loosed* [*from a bond such as is called* عِقَال]: (Ṣ,* Mgh, TA:) a proverb, relating to an event's happening quickly; (Mgh;) or said of him who commences any work quickly; and of the sick when he recovers; and of a person who has swooned when he revives; and of a person sent to execute an affair, hastening his determination respecting it: (TA:) it is often related in a different manner, كانما نُشِطَ من عقال; but this is not correct. (IAth, TA.) [But see above, in this paragraph; and see 1, where a similar meaning is assigned to the unaugmented verb.] — *He bound*, or *tied*, *him*, or *it*, *firmly*, *fastly*, or *strongly*: so in the copies of the Ḳ; so that, if this be correct, the verb has two contr. significations. (TA.) — See also 8.

5: see 1, first sentence. — تنشّطت فِى سَيْرِهَا *She* (a camel) *hastened*, or *was quick*, *in her going*, or *pace*. (Ṣ, Ḳ.) — تنشّط المَفَازَةَ ‡ *He passed through*, or *over*, *the desert*, (Ḳ, TA,) *with swiftness*, *and with briskness*, *liveliness*, *sprightliness*, or *activity*. (TA.) And تنشّطهُ † *He traversed it quickly*, or *swiftly*. (IB, in TA, voce جِرْجَابٌ.) And تنشّطت الأَرْضَ † *She* (a camel) *traversed*, or *crossed*, *the land*, *like the* نَاشِط *in her quickness*, or *her aim*, *with briskness*, *liveliness*, or *sprightliness*. (TA.)

8. انتشط *It* (a cord, or rope,) *became loosed*, *untied*, or *undone*. (Ḥar, p. ٣٦١.) — † *He* (a man) *became loosed* from the tie of silence, (Ḥar, p. ٣٦٠; Mgh,) and from that of impotence. (Mgh [in which a doubt is expressed as to its being of classical authority].) — As a trans. v.: see 4, in two places. — *He pulled*, or *drew*, *a thing*. (TA.) — *He seized* a thing, *took it hastily*, or *snatched it unawares*: a meaning wrongly assigned in the Ḳ to ▼ انشط. (TA.) You say also, انتشط المَالُ المَرْعَى, (Sh, Ḳ,) and الكَلَأَ, (Sh,) *The camels*, or *sheep* or *goats*, *pulled up*, or *out*, *the herbage*, with the teeth. (Sh, Ḳ.) — *He scaled* a fish; (Ḳ;) as though meaning *he pulled off the scales* thereof. (TA.)

نُشُطٌ [app. a pl. of ▼ نَاشِطٌ] Persons *untwisting cords*, *or ropes*, *in the time of undoing them for the purpose of their being twisted* or *plaited a second time*. (IAạr, Ḳ.)

نَشْطَةٌ as used in the following saying, (Mgh,) الشُّفْعَةُ كَنَشْطَةِ العِقَالِ *The right termed* شفعة *is like the loosing of the bond called* عقال, in respect of the speediness with which it becomes of no effect, (Mgh, Mṣb,) by delay, (Mṣb,) is of the measure فَعْلَةٌ from أَنْشَطَ, or from نَشَطَ in the sense of انشط; or the meaning is, *like the tying of the* عقال; i. e., it is of short duration; but the former explanation is the more apparently right. (Mgh.)

بِئْرٌ نَشُوطٌ *A well from which the bucket does not come forth until it is much pulled,* (Aṣ, Ṣ, TA,) *by reason of the distance of its bottom;* (TA;) *contr. of* بِئْرٌ أَنْشَاطٌ. (Ḳ.)

نَشِيطٌ (Ṣ, Mṣb, Ḳ) *Brisk, lively, sprightly, active, agile, prompt,* and *quick;* (Mṣb;) or *pleased, cheerful, happy,* or *willing;* to do work &c.; as also ↑ نَاشِطٌ; (Ḳ;) [see نَشِطَ;] applied to a man; (Ṣ, TA;) and to a beast of carriage; fem. with ة: (TA:) pl. نِشَاطٌ (Ḥar, p. 591) [and نَشَاطَى]. — A man (TA) *whose family, or beasts, are in a state of* نَشَاط [i. e. *briskness, liveliness, sprightliness,* &c.: see 1]; as also ↑ مُنْشِطٌ. (Ḳ, TA.)

نَاشِطٌ: see نَشِيطٌ. — In a verse of Eṭ-Ṭirimmáḥ, [see استطرب,] نَاشِطًا is used for شَوْقًا نَازِعًا [*By reason of yearning,* or *longing, desire*]. (Ḳ, in art. دو.) — A wild bull *going forth from land to land,* (Ṣ, Ḳ,) or *from country to country.* (TA.) — Hence, (Ṣ,) النَّاشِطَاتُ, as used in the Ḳur, lxxix. 2, meaning *The stars* [or *planets*] *going forth from one sign of the zodiac to another:* (Ṣ, Ḳ:) or it means *the stars that rise, then set:* (A'Obeyd, TA:) or *the angels that draw forth the souls like as the bucket is drawn forth from the well:* (Zj, TA:) or *the angels that loose the soul of the believer gently:* (Fr,* Ibn-'Arafeh, Ḳ:) or *the believing souls that are brisk, lively, sprightly, or active, at death:* (Ḳ,* TA:) or, as some say, [too fancifully,] *the angels that ratify events;* from نَشَطَ العُقْدَةَ, q. v.; and as this signifies the tying of a knot which is easily undone, the thing's easiness to them is thus notified. (TA.) — ‡ A road *going forth from the main road, to the right,* and *to the left:* (Lth, Ḳ*:) pl. نَوَاشِطُ: (TA:) which latter word is applied in like manner to water-courses (Ḳ, TA) *going forth from the main water-course to the right and left.* (TA.) — See also نُشُطٌ.

بِئْرٌ أَنْشَاطٌ, (Ḳ, and so in a copy of the Ṣ, as on the authority of Aṣ, but in another copy of the Ṣ the ا is without any vowel,) and بِئْرٌ إِنْشَاطٌ, (Ḳ, and, accord. to the TA, on the authority of Aṣ, and mentioned by IB on the authority of A'Obeyd,) *A well of little depth, from which the bucket comes forth by means of a single pull:* (Aṣ, Ṣ, Ḳ:) the latter may be defended on the ground of considering إِنْشَاطٌ as originally an inf. n., of أَنْشَطَ signifying "he loosed, untied, or undid," a knot "by a single pull." (TA.)

أُنْشُوطَةٌ [*A knot tied with a bow,* or *with a double bow, so as to form a kind of slip-knot;* whence, in modern vulgar Arabic, عُقْدَة وَشُنَيْطَة, applied to such a tie; and شُنَيْطَة, applied to a simple slip-knot;] *a knot,* or *tie, which easily becomes undone,* or *untied, like that of the running band of a pair of drawers;* (Ṣ, Mgh, Ḳ;) *a knot,* or *tie, which becomes undone when one of its two ends is pulled.* (Mṣb, TA.) You say, مَا عِقَالُكَ بِأُنْشُوطَةٍ, meaning † *Thy love,* or *affection, is not weak,* or *frail.* (Ṣ.)

مَنْشَطٌ *A thing on account of which, or to do which, one is brisk, lively, sprightly,* or *active;* or *pleased, cheerful,* or *happy; and which one likes,* or *prefers, to do:* opposed to مَكْرَهٌ. (TA.)

[مَنْشَطٌ *A place to which one goes forth:* pl. مَنَاشِطُ. See an ex. of the pl., voce نَشَطَ.]

مُنْشِطٌ: see نَشِيطٌ.

مِنْشَطٌ *Having much* نَشَاط [i. e. *briskness, liveliness, sprightliness, friskiness,* &c.: see 1]. (TA.)

[نشع &c.
See Supplement.]

نص

1. نَصَّ الشَّىْءَ, (Ṣ,) aor. ـُ, (Mgh,) inf. n. نَصٌّ, (Mgh, TA,) *He raised the thing;* syn. رَفَعَهُ [which is here to be understood, like the English equivalent by which I have rendered it, in several senses, as the sequel will show]. (Ṣ, Mgh, TA.) This is the primary signification: (TA:) or, accord. to Aṣ, it is from نَصَّ النَّاقَةَ, q.v. infra. (Ṣ.) You say, نَصَّ العَرُوسَ, (M, Ḳ,) or نَصَّتْهَا, (A, Mgh,) or نَصَّا النِّسَآءَ, (Mṣb,) aor. as above, (A, Mgh,) and so the inf. n., (Mṣb,) *He,* or *she,* or *the women, raised,* (A, Mṣb,) or *seated,* (Ḳ,) or *raised and seated,* (Mgh,) or *showed,* or *displayed,* (M,) *the bride upon the* مِنَصَّة, (M, A, Mṣb, Ḳ,) or *upon the* مَنَصَّة. (Mgh.) And نَصَّتِ الظَّبْيَةُ جِيدَهَا *The doe-antelope raised,* or *elevated, her neck.* (M, TA.) And نُصَّ فُلَانٌ سَيِّدًا ‡ *Such a one was set up as a lord,* or *chief.* (A, TA.) And نَصَّ المَتَاعَ, (M, Ḳ,) inf. n. as above, (M,) *He put the furniture,* or *goods,* or *utensils, one upon another.* (M, Ḳ.) Hence, (TA,) نَصَّ الحَدِيثَ, (M, Mṣb, TA,) or نَصَّهُ إِلَى صَاحِبِهِ, (A,) aor. and inf. n. as above, (M, Mṣb, TA,) ‡ *He traced up,* or *ascribed,* or *attributed, the tradition to the author thereof, resting it on his authority, by mentioning him,* or *mentioning, uninterruptedly, in ascending order, the persons by whom it had been handed down, up to the author;* or *mentioning the person who had related it to him from the author, if only one person intervened;* syn. رَفَعَهُ; (M, TA;) [i.e.] رَفَعَهُ إِلَى مَنْ قَالَهُ: (Mṣb:) IAạr says, (TA,) النَّصُّ signifies الإِسْنَادُ إِلَى الرَّئِيسِ الأَكْبَرِ ‡ [*the tracing up,* or *ascribing,* or *attributing,* a tradition, *in the manner explained above, to the greatest person of authority,* here meaning Moḥammad, or the author of the tradition]; (Ḳ, TA;) [i. e.] نَصُّ الحَدِيثِ signifies إِسْنَادُهُ وَرَفْعُهُ إِلَى الرَّئِيسِ الأَكْبَرِ. (Mgh.) You also say, نَصَّ الحَدِيثَ إِلَيْهِ, (Ḳ,) or إِلَى فُلَانٍ, (Ṣ,) ‡ *He ascribed,* or *attributed,* or *traced up, the tradition to him,* or *to such a one, in the manner explained above;* syn. رَفَعَهُ. (Ṣ, Ḳ.) See also أَنَصَّ. — نَصَّ الشَّىْءَ † *He made the thing apparent, manifest, plain,* or *evident; he showed it, exhibited it, manifested it, evinced it, discovered it,* or *revealed it.* (M,* Ḳ.) [The verb seems to be thus used because a thing is rendered conspicuous by being raised. See نَصَّ العَرُوسَ, above.] — [Hence, نَصَّ عَلَى شَىْءٍ مَّا, aor. and inf. n. as above, ‡ *He,* or *it,* (generally said of a passage in the Ḳur. or a trad.,) *made a statement,* or *a plain, explicit, unequivocal declaration, respecting some,* or *any, particular thing, not capable of application to any other thing:* and *he mentioned something,* or *anything, particularly,* or *specially; he particularized,* or *specified it by words;* very frequently used in these senses: and such we are to understand from the saying] النَّصُّ also signifies التَّوْقِيفُ وَالتَّعْيِينُ عَلَى شَىْءٍ مَّا: (Ḳ:) [for which I would rather read النَّصُّ عَلَى شَىْءٍ مَّا also signifies التَّوْقِيفُ وَالتَّعْيِينُ: adding the observation that التوقيف as syn. with النصّ is restricted in art. وقف in the Ḳ to a special relation to the law: and that النَّصُّ عَلَى الشَّىْءِ is often found explained as signifying تَعْيِينُهُ; as, for instance, in p. ٣٧٧ of Ḥar.:] these significations of النَّصُّ are tropical, from that word as denoting "elevation" and "appearance." (TA.) See also نَصٌّ below. — [From نَصَّهُ signifying "he raised it," and consequently "he made it apparent," are derived several other significations, here following.] — يَنُصُّهُمْ [app. for يَنُصُّ مَا عِنْدَهُمْ] occurs in a trad. respecting Heraclius, meaning † *He elicits, and makes apparent, their opinion:* (TA:) or نَصَّ الرَّجُلَ, (Ṣ, M, &c.,) inf. n. as above, (M,) signifies ‡ *he went to the utmost point in questioning,* or *asking, the man respecting a thing,* (Ṣ, Ḳ,) *so as to elicit what he possessed* [*of information respecting it*]; (Ṣ;) i. e. (TA) ‡ *he importuned the man in questioning,* or *asking, and urged him to tell the utmost that he knew;* (A, TA;) or † *he questioned, or asked, the man respecting a thing so as to elicit the utmost that he possessed* [*of information respecting it*]. (M.) [See also 3.] — [In like manner you say,] نَصَّ النَّاقَةَ, (Ṣ, M, Mgh, Ḳ,) and الدَّابَّةَ, (M, Mṣb,) aor. as above, (M,) and so the inf. n., (Ṣ, M,) *He made the*

she-camel, and *the beast, to exert herself to the full*, or *to the utmost*, or *beyond measure, in going*, or *pace*; or *to go the pace termed* مَرْفُوع; syn. رَفَعَهَا فِى السَّيْرِ: (M, Mgh:) or *he elicited her utmost pace*; (Ḳ, TA;) from النَّصّ as signifying الرَّفْع; for the phrase رَفَعَهَا فِى السَّيْرِ necessarily implies the eliciting the utmost of her celerity of pace: (TA:) or *he went a vehement pace so as to elicit the utmost that she possessed* [*of celerity*]: (Aṣ, Ṣ:) or *he put her in motion so as to elicit her utmost pace*: (A'Obeyd, TA:) or *he urged*, or *incited, her, and elicited her pace*: (Mṣb:) نَصَّ, alone, also occurs in a trad., (M, Mṣb,) as meaning رَفَعَ نَاقَتَهُ: (M:) and ▼نَصْنَصَ نَاقَتَهُ signifies the same as نَصَّهَا. (IḲṭṭ, TA.) You do not say of a camel نَصَّ, making him the agent, and the verb intrans. (O,* TA.) [In the M, however, I find it said, that النَّصّ and النَّصِيصُ signify السَّيْرُ الشَّدِيدُ; app. indicating that they are inf. ns., of which the verb is نَصَّ, aor., accord. to rule, ِ, signifying *He went a vehement pace*, or *vehemently*: and Golius says, as on the authority of Ibn-Maạroof, that this verb is used intransitively, with نَصِيص for its inf. n., as signifying *valide incessit*: but see نَصّ below.] — [Hence, app.,] النَّصّ also signifies The *urging* or *inciting* [a beast]; syn. الحَثّ. (M.) — And نَصَّ الشَّىْءَ, (M, Ḳ,) aor. ُ, inf. n. نَصّ, (TA,) *He moved the thing; put it in motion*, or *into a state of commotion; agitated it; stirred it; shook it*; (M, Ḳ;) as also ▼نَصْنَصَهُ. (Ṣ, M, Ḳ.) Hence the saying, فُلَانٌ يَنُصُّ أَنْفَهُ غَضَبًا (Ḳ, TA [in the CḲ, incorrectly, يَنِصُّ,]) *Such a one moves about his nose by reason of anger*. (TA.) And ▼نَصْنَصَ لِسَانَهُ *He moved about his tongue*; (Ṣ, M;) like نَضْنَضَهُ; (M;) which is a dial. form; (A'Obeyd, Ṣ;) the former being the original; the ص not being, as some assert it to be, substituted for the ض; for these two letters are not of the same kind so as to be commutable. (M.) ═ See also 8.

2: see 3.

3. نَاصَّهُ, (Ḳ,) inf. n. مُنَاصَّةٌ, (TA,) *He* (a man, TA) *went to the utmost length with him*, (namely his creditor,) *in reckoning, so as to omit nothing therein*; (Ḳ, TA;) as also ▼نَصَّصَهُ, (Ḳ,) inf. n. تَنْصِيصٌ. (TA.) *He* (God) *went to the utmost length with him*, (namely a man,) *in questioning and in reckoning*. (TA.) [See also 1.]

6. تَنَاصَّ القَوْمُ *The people*, or *company of men, crowded, thronged*, or *pressed, together*. (TA.)

8. انتصّ *He*, or *it*, (said of a camel's hump, Lth, TA,) *became raised*, or *elevated*, or *high*: (Ḳ, TA:) or (TA) *became even and erect*. (Lth, Ḳ,* TA.) [In a copy of the A, the verb in these senses, and relating to a camel's hump, is written نَصَّ.] You say also, انتصّت العَرُوسُ, (M, Ḳ,) or انتصّت على المِنَصَّةِ, (A,) *The bride became raised*, (A,) or *seated*, (Ḳ,) or *shown* or *displayed*, (M,) *upon the* مِنَصَّة. (M, A, Ḳ.) ═ *He* (a man, TA) *drew himself together; contracted himself*; or *shrank*. (Ibn-'Abbád, Ḳ, TA.)

R. Q. 1. نَصْنَصَ, (Ṣ, M, Ḳ,) inf. n. نَصْنَصَةٌ, (Sh, M,) *He*, or *it, became in motion*, or *in a state of commotion; became agitated, stirred*, or *shaken; moved*, or *moved about*,; *bestirred himself* or *itself; shook*. (Sh.) *He* (a man) *shook* in his walk, *being erect*. (M.) *He* (a camel) *shook*, or *became in a state of commotion, in rising from the ground*. (M.) — [Also,] said of a camel, it is like حَضْحَضَ; (Ṣ;) i.e., it signifies (TA) *He* (the camel) *fixed*, or *made firm* or *steady, his knees upon the ground, and put himself in motion*, or *in a state of commotion, previously to rising*. (Lth, Ḳ, TA.) [See also نَضْنَضَ.] — And *He* (a camel) *made a hollow place in the ground with his breast, in order to lie down*. (M, TA.) ═ نَصْنَصَ used transitively, see 1, latter portion, in three places.

نَصّ The *end*, or *extremity*, of anything; (Az, Ṣ, M;) the *utmost*, or *extreme, extent, term, limit, point*, or *reach*, of a thing: this is the primary signification. (Az, TA.) It is said in a trad., (Ṣ, M,) of 'Alee, (Ṣ,) إِذَا بَلَغَ النِّسَآءُ نَصَّ الحِقَاقِ فَالعَصَبَةُ أَوْلَى بِهَا مِنَ الأُمِّ (Ṣ,* M, Ḳ,*) or نَصَّ الحَقَائِقِ, (Ḳ,* TA,) but the former is that which is commonly known; (TA;) i.e. *When women attain the period of mature intellect*, (Mbr, Ṣ, Ḳ, TA,) *and know the real natures of things*, (Ḳ, art. حق,) [*then the male relations on the father's side have a better right to dispose of her* in marriage *than the mother*;] meaning, *when they attain to that age at which they are qualified to contend for their rights*; [accord. to the former reading;] for this is what is termed الحِقَاق: (Ḳ,* TA:) or *when they attain to puberty*: (Az, TA:) or *when they attain to that period at which they become objects of contention for right; when every one of the guardians asserts himself to have the best right*: (Ḳ:) or الحقاق in the trad. is a metaphorical term, from the same word as applied to camels [when entering upon the fourth year]; (Ḳ,* TA;) and الحقائق, also, in this case, accord. to some, properly signifies the same, being a pl. of حِقَّةٌ; (TA in art. حق;) and the meaning is, *when they attain to the extreme term of childhood*. (M, Ḳ.) ═ In the conventional language of men of science, it signifies ‡ *A thing* [or *statement*] *plainly*, or *explicitly, declared*, or *made manifest, by God*, and *his Apostle*; of the measure فَعْلٌ in the sense of the measure مَفْعُولٌ: (Mṣb:) or a نَصّ of the Ḳur-án, and of the traditions, is *an expression*, or *a phrase*, or *a sentence, indicating a particular meaning, not admitting any other than it*: (TA:) so in the conventional language of the lawyers and the scholastic theologians: (MF, on the خُطْبَة of the Ḳ:) or *a statute*, or *an ordinance, indicated by the manifest* or *plain meaning of words* of the Ḳur-án, and of the Sunneh: from النَّصّ as denoting "elevation" and "appearance:" or, as some say, from نَصَّهُ as signifying "he elicited, and made apparent, his opinion." (TA.) Hence, also, as used by the practical lawyers, it signifies ‡ *An evidence*, or *a proof*: (TA:) [and particularly *a text of the Ḳur-án*, or *of the Sunneh, used as an authority in an argument, for proof of an assertion*.] The pl. [in all these senses] is نُصُوصٌ. (Mṣb.) — [Also, † The *text*, or *very words*, of an author, book, writing, or passage: frequently used in this sense.] ═ *Hardness, difficulty*, or *straitness*, of an affair, or a state, or case. (M, TA.) ═ سَيْرٌ نَصٌّ, and ▼نَصِيصٌ, (Ṣ, Ḳ,) *A vehement pace, in which a beast is made to exert itself to the full*, or *to the utmost*, or *beyond measure*; or *in which the utmost possible celerity is elicited*; [this meaning seems to be indicated, though not expressed, in the Ṣ;] syn. جِدٌّ رَفِيعٌ: (Ḳ:) or, the former, as Az says, in one place, *a kind of swift pace*: or, as he says in another place, the *utmost pace which a beast of carriage is able to attain*: (TA:) or نَصٌّ and ▼نَصِيصٌ signify *a vehement pace* or *going*. (M.) See 1.

نَصِيصٌ: see نَصٌّ, last sentence, in two places.

هُوَ نَصَّاصُ الأَنْفِ *He is one who moves about his nose* [*much*] by reason of anger. (Ibn-'Abbád, Ḳ.)

حَيَّةٌ نَصْنَاصٌ *A serpent that moves about much*. (Ḳ.) [See also نَضْنَاضٌ.]

أَنَصُّ [a comparative and superlative epithet from نَصَّ الحَدِيثَ, q. v.]. 'Amr Ibn-Deenár said, مَا رَأَيْتُ رَجُلًا أَنَصَّ لِلْحَدِيثِ مِنَ الزُّهْرِىِّ *I have not seen a man more skilled in tracing up*, or *ascribing*, or *attributing, a tradition to its author, in the manner explained above*, (voce نَصَّ,) *than Ez-Zuhree*; *i. q.* أَرْفَعَ لَهُ and أَسْنَدَ. (TA.)

مَنَصَّةٌ: see what next follows, throughout.

مِنَصَّةٌ, (Ṣ, M, A, Mṣb, Ḳ,) or ▼مَنَصَّةٌ, (Mgh,) The *thing upon which a bride is raised* (Ṣ,* A, Ḳ) *and seated*, (Mgh,) or *shown* or *displayed*, (M,) or *upon which she stands* (تقف [but this is probably a mistake for تَقْعُدُ, i. e. *sits*,]) *when displayed to the bridegroom*, (Mṣb,) *in order that she may be seen* (M, Mgh) [*and distinguished*] *from among the women*; (Mgh;) being *a chair*, (Mgh, Mṣb, TA,) or *couch*; (TA;) or *consisting of pieces of cloth raised, and carpets laid smoothly for a seat*: (M:) written with kesr (Mṣb, Ḳ) as being an instrument, (Mṣb,) or with fet-ḥ [as being a place]: (Mgh:) accord. to some authorities, مِنَصَّة and

مَنَصَّةٌ seem to signify the same thing: (TA:) or the latter is the حَجَلَة [i.e. *a kind of curtained canopy*] (Ḳ, TA) *over the* مِنَصَّة: (TA:) from نَصَّ المَتَاعَ, q. v. (Ḳ.) It is said in a proverb, وُضِعَ فُلَانٌ عَلَى المِنَصَّةِ † *Such a one was exposed to disgrace and infamy:* (TA:) or *to the utmost disgrace and infamy.* (M.)

نصأ

1. نَصَأَهُ, aor. َ, *He took him by the* نَاصِيَة [or *forelock*]: (Ḳ:) from نَاصِيَةٌ: and therefore regarded by some as improperly mentioned in the Ḳ in this art. (MF.) —— نَصَأَ, aor. َ, (Ṣ, Ḳ,) inf. n. نَصْءٌ, (TA,) *He chid,* (a camel, TA, or she-camel, Ṣ); syn. زَجَرَ. (AZ, Ṣ, Ḳ.) —— نَصَأَ, (Ṣ, Ḳ,) inf. n. as above, (TA,) *He raised,* or *elevated,* a thing: (Ks, AA, Ṣ, Ḳ:) dial. form of نَصَّ. (Ṣ.)

نصب

1. نَصَبَ, aor. ُ, inf. n. نَصْبٌ; (Ṣ, Ḳ;) and ▼ نَصَّبَ; (Ḳ;) *He set up, put up, set upright, erected,* a thing: (Ṣ:) *he elevated, raised, reared,* a thing. (Ḳ.) —— *He set up,* a stone *as a sign,* or *mark.* (Mṣb.) —— نَصَبَ رَأْسَهُ *He raised his head.* (TA.) —— نَصِبَ, aor. َ, inf. n. نَصَبٌ, *He* (a goat) *had erect ears.* (Ṣ: the inf. n. only mentioned.) —— نَصَبْتُ فُلَانًا لِكَذَا *I set,* or *set up, such a one as an obstacle to such a thing,* or *as a butt for such a thing, like the butt of archers.* (TA, art. عرض.) —— نُصِبَ فُلَانٌ لِعِمَارَةِ البَلَدِ ‡ [*Such a one was set up,* or *appointed, for the putting,* or *keeping, of the town,* or *district, in a flourishing* or *prosperous state, with respect to buildings, culture, population, &c.*]. (A.) —— نَصَبَ, aor. ُ, inf. n. نَصْبٌ, (Ṣ, Ḳ,) or نَصَبَ نَصْبَ العَرَبِ, (Ṣ,) † *He sang,* or *chanted, a kind of song,* or *chant, peculiar to the Arabs,* (Ṣ, Ḳ, &c.,) *of the description termed* حُدَاء, (Ḳ,) [*by which camels are urged,* or *excited,*] or *a kind of song* (Ḳ) *resembling what is thus termed,* (Ṣ,) *but finer,* or *more delicate.* (Ṣ, Ḳ.) What is termed نَصْبٌ is The *kind of singing, or chanting, above described:* (Ṣ, Ḳ:) or *a kind of* حُدَاء *resembling singing:* (AA:) or *a kind of modulation:* (Sh:) or *a kind of song, or chant, of the Arabs:* (ISd:) or, *of the Arabs of the desert:* (TA:) or *poetry such as is commonly recited, well regulated and set to an air:* (Nh:) *so called because, in* [*singing or chanting*] *it, the voice is raised,* or *elevated.* (The Fáïḳ.) —— نَصَبَ الحَرْفَ, [aor. ِ, (not ُ,) inf. n. نَصْبٌ,] *He wrote,* or *pronounced, the* [*final*] *letter with* نَصْب; (Ṣ;) *which is, in the case of the final inflection of a word, like* فَتْح *in the non-inflection:* (Ṣ, Ḳ:) [*i.e., he wrote it,* or *pronounced it, with* َ or ً:] so called because the sound of a word of which the final letter is so pronounced rises to the highest cavity of the mouth. (Lth.) A conv. term of grammar. (Ṣ, Ḳ.) نَصَبَ الكَلِمَةَ [*He wrote, or pronounced, the word with* نَصْب, *i.e., making its vowel of inflection* َ or ً &c., *according to the rules of grammar:*] *he made the word to have fet-ḥah as its vowel of inflection.* (Mṣb.) —— نَصَبَ لَهُ الحَرْبَ, (inf. n. نَصْبٌ, TA,) *He made war upon him:* syn. وَضَعَ. (Ḳ.) —— Of anything that is raised, and with which one goes to meet, or encounter, a thing, one says نُصِبَ, and of the agent, نَصَبَ. (M, Ḳ.) —— نَصَبَ لَهُ, aor. ِ, inf. n. نَصْبٌ, ‡ *He acted with hostility,* or *enmity, towards him.* (Ṣ, Ḳ.) See also 3. —— نَصَبْتُ لَهُ رَأْيًا ‡ *I gave him counsel from which he should not deviate.* (A.) —— نَصَبَ, aor. ِ, (inf. n. نَصْبٌ, TA,) *He put down* a thing: syn. وَضَعَ. Thus the verb bears two contr. significations. (Ḳ.) —— [*He set,* or *put,* absolutely: often used in this sense.] —— نَصَبَهُ, aor. ُ; and ▼ انصبه, (inf. n. إِنْصَابٌ, TA,) *It* (disease) *pained him; occasioned him pain.* (Ḳ.) —— نَصَبَ السَّيْرَ, aor. ِ, (inf. n. نَصْبٌ, TA,) † *He strove,* or *exerted himself, unusually in his pace:* (Ḳ:) or نَصَبَ signifies *he pursued his journey with diligence,* or *energy:* (TA:) or *he travelled on all the day, at a gentle pace:* (Ṣ, Ḳ:) or *he journeyed on all the night.* (TA.) En-Naḍr says, النَّصْبُ is the first pace; then, الدَّبِيبُ, [but see وَسَجَ;] then, العَنَقُ; then, التَّزَيُّدُ; then, العَسْجُ; then, الرَّتَكُ; then, الوَخْدُ; then, الهَمْلَجَةُ. (TA.) ═ نَصِبَ, aor. َ, inf. n. نَصَبٌ, *He was fatigued, tired,* or *wearied,* (Ṣ, Ḳ.) —— نَصِبَ, inf. n. نَصَبٌ, *He suffered difficulty, trouble, distress,* or *affliction.* (TA.) —— نَصِبَ *He strove; laboured;* or *toiled.* (Ḳ.) —— فَإِذَا فَرَغْتَ فَانْصَبْ [Ḳur, xciv. 7,] signifies *And when thou shalt have finished* thy prescribed prayers, *fatigue thyself* in supplication: (Ḳatádeh, Jel:) or *when thou shalt have finished* the obligatory prayers, *fatigue thyself* in the performance of the voluntary. (TA.) See نَاصِبٌ.

2. نَصَّبَتِ الخَيْلُ آذَانَهَا *The horses erected their ears often,* or *exceedingly.* The teshdeed is to render the signification frequentative or intensive. (Ṣ.) —— See 1, and 3.

3. ناصبه الشَّرَّ, (inf. n. مُنَاصَبَةٌ, TA,) ‡ *He made an open show of evil conduct, mischief,* or *malevolence, to him;* (Ḳ;) and in like manner, of enmity, (TA,) and of war; (Ṣ, TA;) as also ▼ نَصَبَهُ, (Ḳ,) unaugmented. (TA: in the CḲ, ▼ نَصَّبه.) See also نَصَبَ لَهُ.

4. انصبه *He fatigued, tired,* or *wearied, him:* (Ṣ, Ḳ:) *it* (an affair) *fatigued him, &c.:* (TA:) *it* (grief, or anxiety,) *fatigued, tired,* or *wearied, him;* (CḲ, TA;) as also ▼ نَصَبَ لَهُ; (TA;) and perhaps ▼ نَصَبَهُ is also used in this sense, with reference to grief, or anxiety. (Ḳ.) See 1. ═ انصب الحَدِيثَ إِلَى رَسُولِ اللّٰهِ *He ascribed,* or *attributed, the tradition to the Apostle of God;* syn. أَسْنَدَهُ إِلَيْهِ and رَفَعَهُ. (TA.) ═ انصبه *He assigned him,* or *gave him, a* ▼ نَصِيب; i.e., a *lot,* or *portion.* (Ḳ.) ═ انصب السِّكِّينَ *He made,* or *put, a handle* (نِصَاب) *to the knife.* (Ṣ, Ḳ.)

5. تنصّبتِ الأُتُنُ حَوْلَ الحِمَارِ *The she-asses stood round the he-ass.* (Ṣ, Ḳ.) —— See 8.

6. تناصبوه *They divided it into lots,* or *portions, among themselves.* (TA.)

8. انتصب and ▼ تنصّب, quasi-pass. of نَصَبَ and نَصَّبَ, *He,* or *it, became set up, put up, set upright,* or *erected; stood up,* or *upright,* or *erect; became elevated, raised,* or *reared:* (Ḳ:) *became even and erect.* (TA, art. نص.) —— *He stood erect, raising his head.* (TA.) —— [*It was,* or *became, erect, vertical,* or *perpendicular.*] —— [انتصب شَعْرُهُ *His hair, being full-grown, stood out:* see ▼ مُنْتَصِبٌ.] —— انتصب (TA) and ▼ تنصّب (Ḳ) ‡ *It* (dust) *rose high.* (Ḳ, TA.) —— إِنْتَصِبْ *Set up thy cooking-pot* [*upon the* مِنْصَب, *or trivet,*] *to cook,* said to a cook. (IAạr.) —— انتصبت أَسْنَانُهُ إِلَى قُدَّامٍ [*Its teeth stood out forwards:* see مُنْتَصِبٌ:] said of a mouth. (TA, art. دلق.) —— [إِنْتِصَابٌ is often used absolutely as meaning *An erection of the penis.*] —— انتصب الحَرْفُ *The letter* [meaning the final letter of a word] *was written,* or *pronounced,* with نَصْب: [see نَصَبَ الحَرْفَ]. (Ṣ.)

نَصْبٌ: see نَصَبَ, (of which it is the inf. n.,) throughout. —— نَصْبٌ and ▼ نَصَبٌ and ▼ نُصْبٌ and ▼ نَصِيبَةٌ *A sign,* or *mark, set up to show the way;* or *a standard set up:* syn. عَلَمٌ مَنْصُوبٌ: (Ḳ:) *i.e., set up* [*as a sign*] *to a people:* (TA:) or نُصُبٌ is pl. of نَصِيبَةٌ, like as سُفُنٌ is of سَفِينَةٌ. (Lth, TA.) Also, ▼ نُصْبَةٌ, *A pole,* or *mast;* syn. سَارِيَةٌ; (Ḳ;) *set up to show the way:* (TA:) also, ▼ أَنَاصِيبُ and ▼ تَنَاصِيبُ (pls. which have no sings., TA,) *Signs,* or *marks,* or *stones, set up to show the way;* syn. أَعْلَامٌ and صُوًى: (Ḳ:) *stones set up on the tops of isolated small mountains, whereby travellers are to be directed:* (TA:) also, ▼ يَنْصُوبٌ [pl. يَنَاصِيبُ] signifies *A sign,* or *mark, set up to show the way in a desert.* (Fr.) In the Ḳur, lxx., last verse but one, some read نَصْبٍ, meaning as above: others نُصُبٍ, meaning "idols." (Zj.) —— نَصْبٌ also signifies *A goal; or limit;* syn. غَايَةٌ: (Ḳ:) or rather, some say that it has this signification [in the verse of the Ḳur. above referred to]; but the former meaning, of "a sign, &c.," is the more correct. (TA.) — See also نُصْبٌ and نُصُبٌ, below. — نَصْبٌ, with respect to rhyme in a verse, is The *being free from anything that would mar it*, (Akh, Ḳ,) *when the verse itself is not curtailed*; for when the verse is curtailed, the term نصب is not applicable, though the rhyme be perfect: accord. to an explanation received from the Arabs: not one of the terms of Kh. (Akh.) Derived from الاِنْتِصَابُ, as signifying "the standing erect; being tall; making one's self tall, by stretching the neck;" and therefore not applied to verse that is curtailed. (IJ, ISd.) — نَصْبٌ *One who is set, or set up, as an obstacle* to a thing, or *as a butt* for a thing, *like the butt of archers.* (TA, art. عرض.) See 1. — نَصْبٌ [*A peculiar mode of singing, or chanting: or a peculiar kind of song, or chant*]: (See 1.)

هٰذَا نُصْبُ عَيْنِى, and ↑ نَصْبُ عينى, or the latter is a barbarism, (Ḳ,) disallowed by Ḳt; but it is allowed by Mṭr; and said to have been heard from the Arabs [of the classical ages]; *This is a conspicuous object of my eye; a thing in full view of my eye*: said of a thing that is manifest, or conspicuous, [standing before one,] and even when it is lying, or thrown down. (TA.) — جَعَلْتُهُ نصبَ عينى *I made him, or it, a conspicuous object, or a thing in full view, of my eye.* (TA.) — Mṭr says, that نَصْب, in this case, is an inf. n. used in the sense of a pass. part. n., and means an object [as it were set, or set up,] *conspicuously seen* of the eye, *so as not to be forgotten, nor to be unheeded, nor to be placed behind the back*, or *uncared for*, or *disregarded*. (MF.) — نُصْبٌ (Ṣ, Ḳ) and ↑ نَصْبٌ and ↑ نُصُبٌ (Ḳ) *Evil*; (Ṣ;) *trial; affliction; misfortune*: (Ṣ, Ḳ:) so in the Ḳur, xxxviii., 40: (Ṣ:) *disease*: (Ḳ:) *affliction occasioned by disease*. (Lth.) See also نَصَبٌ.

نِصْبٌ : see نَصِيبٌ.

نَصَبٌ [as a subst.] *Fatigue; weariness; toil.* — *Difficulty; trouble; distress; affliction.* (TA.) See the verb: and see نَصْبٌ.

نَصِبٌ *Diseased; sick; and in pain.* (Ḳ.)

نُصْبٌ : see نَصْبٌ. — نُصُبٌ (Ḳ, Mṣb) and ↑ نُصْبٌ (Ḳ: accord. to the Ṣ, the latter is sometimes written نُصُبٌ: [but it seems that نُصُبٌ is the more common of the two words:]) and ↑ نَصْبٌ (Ṣ, Mṣb) *What is set up and worshipped to the exclusion of*, or *in preference to, the true God*: (Ṣ:) or *anything that is so worshipped*: (Ḳ:) or *a stone that is set up and so worshipped*: (Mṣb:) the pl. of نُصُبٌ is أَنْصَابٌ: (Ṣ, Mṣb:) or نُصُبٌ is a pl. of نَصْبٌ, like as سُقُفٌ is of سَقْفٌ: (Mṣb:) or it is a pl. of which the sing. is نِصَابٌ; and it may be a sing., the pl. of which is أَنْصَابٌ: (Zj:) which last word, accord. to some, is *syn.* with أَصْنَامٌ: but others deny this; because اصنام are figured and sculptured or painted; whereas انصاب are of an opposite description. (Mṣb.) [See a verse cited in art. مور.] — Also, الأَنْصَابُ *Certain stones which were set up around the Kaabeh, over which it was customary for the name of some deity to be pronounced in the killing of animals* (يُهَلُّ عَلَيْهَا), *and upon which victims were slain in sacrifice to another, or others, than the true God*: (ISd, Ḳ:) pl. of نُصُبٌ, as أَعْنَاقٌ is of عُنُقٌ; or of نُصْبٌ, as أَقْفَالٌ is of قُفْلٌ. (TA.) — نُصُبٌ, as occurring in the Ḳur, v. 4, signifies *An idol*; or *a stone which the pagan Arabs set up, to sacrifice*, or *slay animals, before it*, or *by it, and which became red with the blood*: (Ḳt:) or pl. of نِصَابٌ, and signifying *idols*. (Jel.) — أَنْصَابُ الحَرَمِ *The limits of the sacred territory* [*of Mekkeh*]; (Ḳ;) *i.e., signs, or marks, set up there, whereby it might be known.* (TA.) See also نَصْبٌ.

نُصْبَةٌ *A laying of a snare*; meaning *a plot, a stratagem*, or *an artifice*. (TA.)

نُصْبَةٌ : see نَصْبٌ.

نِصَابٌ The *place of sun-set*; مَغِيبُ الشَّمْسِ; (Ḳ;) the *place to which it returns.* (TA.) — See مَنْصِبٌ: and نُصُبٌ. — نِصَابٌ The *handle* of a knife; (Ṣ, Ḳ;) *in which the* سِيلَان *is set*: (TA:) pl. نُصُبٌ. (Ḳ.) — نِصَابٌ, of property, ‡ The *amount which renders it incumbent on the possessor to pay the alms*, or *tax, called* الزَّكَاة: (Ṣ, Ḳ:) as two hundred dirhems, or five camels, (Ṣ,) [or twenty deenárs, or forty sheep or goats. (IbrD.)] So called as being the "source" whence the tax comes. (Mṣb.)

نَصِيبٌ (Ṣ, Ḳ) and ↑ نِصْبٌ (Ḳ) ‡ *A share*, or *portion*, or *lot*, syn. حَظٌّ; (Ṣ, Ḳ;) of a thing; (Ṣ;) or of anything; (TA;) *a set portion*: (A:) [hence it appears to be in the sense of مَنْصُوبٌ *what is set*:] pl. of the former أَنْصِبَآءُ and أَنْصِبَةٌ (Ḳ, Mṣb) [the latter a pl. of pauc.], and نُصُبٌ. (Mṣb.) — نَصِيبٌ *A tank*, or *cistern.* (Ṣ, Ḳ.) — *A snare*, or *fowler's net, set*, or *set up*: (Ṣ, Ḳ:) thus in the sense of مَنْصُوبٌ. (TA.) See also مَنْصُوبَةٌ.

نَصِيبَةٌ, (Ṣ,) or نَصَائِبُ, (Ḳ,) which latter is the pl. of the former, (TA,) *Stones which are set up around a tank, or cistern, and the interstices of which are filled up with kneaded clay.* (Ṣ, Ḳ.) Dhu-r-Rummeh says,

هَرَقْنَاهُ فِى بَادِى النَّشِيئَةِ دَاثِرٍ
قَدِيمٍ بِعَهْدِ المَآءِ بُقْعٍ نَصَائِبُهْ

[*We poured it out into an old cistern of which the water was dried up and the bottom apparent, which for a long time had contained no water, the stones set up around which, having their interstices filled up with kneaded clay, were black and white*]. (Ṣ.) The pron. in هرقناه refers to a large bucket mentioned before. (TA.) — نَصَائِبُ is also explained by A'Obeyd as signifying *Stones that are set up around a tank*, or *cistern, to mark the quantity of water with which the camels will be satisfied.* (TA.) See نَصْبٌ.

هَمٌّ نَاصِبٌ i. q. مُنْصِبٌ, *Grief*, or *anxiety, that fatigues, tires*, or *wearies*: (Ḳ:) after the manner of a rel. n.: (Sb, Ḳ:) meaning ذُو نَصَبٍ; like لَابِنٌ and تَامِرٌ: or ناصب is here an act. part. n. used in the sense of the pass. part. n. [مَنْصُوبٌ] followed by فيه; *i. e.* يُنْصَبُ فِيهِ, *in which one is fatigued, tired*, or *wearied*; like لَيْلٌ نَائِمٌ, meaning يُنَامُ فِيهِ, &c.: (Ṣ:) or the phrase نَصَبَهُ الهَمُّ, in the sense of أَتْعَبَهُ, has been heard; (Ḳ;) and ناصب is its act. part. n. (TA.) — نَصَبٌ نَاصِبٌ is also said to be a phrase of the same kind as مَوْتٌ مَائِتٌ, and شِعْرٌ شَاعِرٌ; [therefore meaning *Severe fatigue*, or *difficulty*, or *trouble, and the like*]. (TA.) — Also عَيْشٌ نَاصِبٌ, and ↑ ذُو مَنْصَبَةٍ, *A fatiguing, laborious*, or *troublesome, life.* (Ḳ.) — النَّوَاصِبُ, and ↑ النَّاصِبِيَّةُ, and أَهْلُ النَّصْبِ, *Appellations of a sect who made it a matter of religious obligation to bear a violent hatred to 'Alee* (Ḳ) *the son of Aboo-Ṭálib*: (TA:) [so called] لِأَنَّهُمْ نَصَبُوا لَهُ because they acted with hostility, or enmity, towards him, (Ḳ,) and openly opposed him: they were a sect of the Khawárij. الخَوَارِج. (TA.)

نَاصِبَةُ الشُّجَاعِ *The eye of the serpent called* شجاع, *which it raises to look.* (TA in art. شجع.) — By the expression كَنَاصِبَةِ الشُّجَاعِ in the following words of the poet,

بَصُرْ كَنَاصِبَةِ الشُّجَاعِ المُرْصِدِ

is meant *Like the eye of the brave man, which he raises* (يَنْصِبُهَا) *to look at, or see, something.* (TA.)

النَّاصِبِيَّةُ : see نَاصِبٌ.

أَنْصَبُ A goat *having erect horns*: (Ṣ, Ḳ:) fem. نَصْبَآءُ. (Ṣ.) — نَصْبَآءُ A she-camel *having an elevated breast.* (Ṣ, Ḳ.) — أُذُنٌ نَصْبَآءُ *An ear that is erect, and approaches the other ear.* (TA.)

مَنْصِبٌ [so accord. to the copies of the Ṣ and Ḳ in my hands, and the Mṣb, which states it to be of the same measure as مَسْجِدٌ, and the TA: written by Golius and Freytag مَنْصَبٌ:] and ↑ نِصَابٌ ‡ *Origin; source*; (Ṣ, Ḳ, Mṣb;) of anything; (TA;) *that to which a person* or *thing is referred, as his* or *its source*; syn.

مَرْجِعٌ; (Ḳ;) *place where*, or *whence, a thing grows;* (Mṣb;) *place where a person* or *thing is set, or set up.* (TA.) Pl. [of the former, مَنَاصِبُ, and] of the latter, نُصُبٌ and أَنْصِبَةٌ. (Az, Mṣb.) — لَهُ مَنْصِبُ صِدْقٍ *He has an excellent origin.* (Mṣb.) — هُوَ يَرْجِعُ إِلَى مَنصِبِ صِدْقٍ and ▾ نِصَابِ صدق, *He traces back his lineage to an excellent origin.* (TA.) — مَنْصِبٌ † *Rank*, or *quality, nobility*, or *eminence, and the like, absolutely*, or *derived from ancestry:* syn. حَسَبٌ and شَرَفٌ: from the same word as signifying "origin, source, &c." (Esh-Shiháb.) — لِفُلَانٍ مَنْصِبٌ *To such a one pertains eminence of rank* or *station.* (Mṣb.) — إِمْرَأَةٌ ذَاتُ مَنصِبٍ *A woman of rank* or *quality &c.*, (حَسَب,) *and of beauty:* or *of beauty* alone; because alone it exalts her. (Mṣb.) — مَنْصِبٌ, in the language of those of post-classical times, [and commonly pronounced, in the present day, مَنْصَب,] † *A post, an office, a function*, or *a magistracy;* as though meaning the place in which a man is set, set up, or elevated; (Shifá el-Ghaleel;) or in which he is set, or set up, to see, or observe, [or supervise]: (MF:) pl. مَنَاصِبُ. (TA.) — [أَرْبَابُ المَنَاصِبِ † *Functionaries; magistrates.*] — See مِنْصَبٌ.

مِنْصَبٌ *An iron thing* (*an iron trivet*, TA,) *upon which a cooking-pot is set up:* (IAạr, Ḳ:) as also ▾ مَنْصِبٌ. (MF.)

مَنْصَبَةٌ *Fatigue, labour*, or *trouble:* [or *a cause of fatigue, &c.*]. (Ḳ.) See نَاصِبٌ.

مَنْصُوبَةٌ, as an epithet, applied to a شَبَكَة or حِبَالَة (*A net* or *snare*) *set*, or *set up.* And hence, as a subst., like دَابَّةٌ and عَجُوزٌ, † *An artifice, a stratagem, a trick, a plot, a resource*, or *an expedient:* or *a stratagem* in the game of chess. You say سَوَّى فُلَانٌ منصوبةً [*Such a one framed a stratagem*, or *plot*]. (Z.)

مُنَصَّبٌ A horse *of which the prevailing characteristic of his whole make is the erect position of his bones, so that he stands erect without needing to bend* [*his joints*]. (TA.) — صَفِيحٌ مُنَصَّبٌ [*Broad and thin stones*] *set up, one upon another.* (Ṣ.) — ثَغْرٌ مُنَصَّبٌ *Teeth*, or *fore teeth, of even growth;* (Ḳ;) *as though set up and made even.* (TA.) [See an ex. in a verse cited voce شَنَبٌ.] — ثَرًى مُنَصَّبٌ, accord. to the Ḳ, *i. q.* مُجَعَّدٌ; but this is a mistake; and the correct word is جَعْدٌ, *Soft moist earth;* as in other books. (TA.)

مُنْتَصِبٌ ‡ Dust *rising high.* (Ṣ.) — † Hair *full grown, and standing out.* (TA, art. سبكر.) — أَسْنَانٌ مُنْتَصِبَةٌ إِلَى خَارِجٍ (Ṣ in art. دفق) or الى قُدَّامٍ (JK in that art.) *Teeth standing out* or *forwards*].

يَنْصُوبٌ:
أَنَاصِيبُ:
تَنَاصِيبُ:
} see نَصْبٌ.

نصت

1\. نَصَتَ, aor. ـِ, (L, Ḳ,) inf. n. نَصْتٌ; (L;) and ▾ انصت, inf. n. إِنْصَاتٌ, (Ṣ, L, Ḳ) which latter is the more approved; (L;) and ▾ انتصت; (L, Ḳ;) *He was silent:* (L, Ḳ:) or *he was silent and listened:* (Ṣ:) or *he was silent to listen:* (L:) or *he was silent as one listening:* (Er-Rághib:) or *he listened:* (Mṣb:) or انتصب signifies *he stood*, or *paused, listening.* (Mṣb.) — أَنْصَتَهُ ▾, and نَصَتَ لَهُ, انصت لَهُ, (Ṣ, Ḳ,) and إِلَيْهِ, (Z,) and (L,) *He was silent, and listened to his speech.* (Ṣ, Ḳ, &c.)

4\. انصتهُ *He made him silent; silenced him.* (Sh, Ḳ.) — انصتهُ عَنِّى *He made him to be silent*, [*and to abstain*] *from* [*speaking of*, or *to*,] *me.* (Aṣ.) — See 1. ═ انصت لِلَّهْوِ *He inclined to play*, or *sport.* (IAạr, Ḳ.)

8: see 1.

10\. استنصتهُ *He asked him*, or *desired him, to be silent:* (Ḳ:) or, *to be silent and to listen to him.* (TA.)

نُصْتَةٌ *Silence:* [or *silence and listening, &c.*] (Ḳ.)

نصح

1\. نَصَحَ لَهُ, and نَصَحَهُ, (Ṣ, Ḳ, &c.,) but the former is the original mode of expression, (Lb,) and is the more chaste, (Ṣ, Mṣb,) and the latter was scarcely ever used by the Arabs, (Fr,) aor. ـَ, inf. n. نُصْحٌ and نَصَاحَةٌ (Ṣ, Ḳ,) and نَصِيحَةٌ, (A, L, Mṣb,) or this last is a simple subst., (Ṣ, Ḳ,) and نِصَاحَةٌ and نَصْحٌ (L) and نُصُوحٌ (TA) and نَصَاحِيَةٌ; (Ḳ;) and ▾ ناصحهُ, inf. n. مُنَاصَحَةٌ; (MF;) *He advised him*, or *counselled him*, [*in an absolute sense,*] *sincerely, honestly*, or *faithfully:* and *he so acted towards him:* (Mṣb:) *he directed him to that which was for his good, by words*, or *speech*, which is the proper signification; or *otherwise*, which is a tropical signification: (Lb:) or *he gave him good advice*, or *counsel; directed him to what was good:* or *he advised him*, or *counselled him, sedulously*, or *earnestly:* or *he acted sincerely*, or *honestly, to him*, (MF,) or *he was benevolent towards him; desired what was good for him.* (Nh, MF.) — نَصَحْتُ لَهُ نَصِيحَتِى, inf. n. نُصُوحٌ, *My advice*, or *counsel*, or *conduct, was sincere, honest*, or *faithful, to him.* (L.) — نَصَحَتْ تَوْبَتُهُ, inf. n. نُصُوحٌ ‡ *His repentance was*, or *became, true*, or *sincere*, [*&c.:* see نَصُوحٌ].

(A.) — جِئْنَاكَ لِلنَّصَاحَةِ لَمْ نَأْتِ لِلرَّقَاحَةِ [*We have come unto Thee for the purpose of sincere worship: we have not come for gain*, or *traffic:* see art. رقح]. (Ṣ, art. رقح.) — نَصَحَ ‡ *It* (anything, Ṣ) *was*, or *became, pure, unadulterated*, or *genuine.* (Ṣ, Ḳ.) ═ نَصَحَ, (Ṣ, Ḳ,) aor. ـَ, inf. n. نَصْحٌ; (Ṣ;) and ▾ تنصّح; (Ḳ;) ‡ *He sewed a* garment, (Ṣ, Ḳ,) or a shirt: (TA:) or *he sewed* it *well.* (A.) ═ نَصَحَ الرِّىَّ, (inf. n. نُصْحٌ, TA,) ‡ *He* (a man, TA,) *drank until he was satisfied.* (Ḳ.) — نَصَحَتِ الإِبِلُ الشُّرْبَ, aor. ـَ, inf. n. نُصُوحٌ, ‡ *The camels drank in good earnest.* (IAạr, Ṣ.) — نَصَحَ الغَيْثُ البَلَدَ, (inf. n. نُصْحٌ, TA,) ‡ *The rain watered the district so that its herbage became close, without any bare part:* (En-Naḍr, Ḳ:) or, *watered it abundantly.* (TA.) ═ نَصَحَ, aor. ـَ, inf. n. نُصْحٌ, *He clarified* honey. (MF.) But this is rejected by the author of the Ḳ in [the work entitled] the Baṣáïr. (TA.)

3\. ناصحهُ, inf. n. مُنَاصَحَةٌ, [*He advised him*, or *counselled him, with sincerity* or *faithfulness, &c., reciprocally:* see also 1]. (A.)

4\. انصح *He watered* camels *so as to satisfy them with drink.* (IAạr, Ṣ, Ḳ.)

5\. تنصّح *He was prodigal of* نُصْح [i. e., *sincere* or *faithful advice or counsel, &c.*] Hence the saying of Aktham Ibn-Ṣeyfee, إِيَّاكُمْ وَكَثْرَةَ التَّنَصُّحِ فَإِنَّهُ يُورِثُ التُّهَمَةَ [*Beware ye of being prodigal of sincere* or *faithful advice* or *counsel, for it occasions doubt*, or *suspicion*, or *evil opinion*]. (L.) — تنصّح *He affected to be like*, or *imitated*, نُصَحَآء [i. e., *those who advise*, or *counsel, sincerely, honestly*, or *faithfully, &c.:* see نَاصِحٌ]. (Ṣ, Ḳ.) — See 1.

6\. تناصحوا [*They advised* or *counselled one another sincerely* or *faithfully, &c.:* see 1]. (A, art. فضح.)

8\. انتصح *He accepted* نَصِيحَة, (Ṣ, Ḳ,*) or نُصْح, (TA,) [i. e., *sincere, honest*, or *faithful, advice or counsel, &c.*]. As an ex. of this signification the following is cited

* يَقُولُ ٱنْتَصِحْنِى إِنَّنِى لَكَ نَاصِحٌ *

[*He says, Accept my sincere advice, for I am to thee a sincere adviser*]: (TA:) and إِنْتَصِحْ كِتَابَ ٱللّٰهِ *Accept the sincere* or *faithful advice* or *counsel of the Book of God.* (A.) But IB says, that the verb in this sense is intrans.; and that, when trans., it signifies *He took* a person *as a* نَصِيح [a *sincere* or *faithful adviser* or *counsellor, &c.*]; whence the saying لَا أُرِيدُ مِنْكَ

لَا أُرِيدُ مِنْكَ أَنْ تَنْصَحَنِى , i. e. نُصْحًا وَلَا ٱنْتِصَاحًا وَلَا أَنْ تَتَّخِذَنِى نَصِيحًا [*I do not desire of thee sincere or faithful advice, nor thy taking me as a sincere or faithful adviser*]. (L.) — See 10.

10. اِسْتَنْصَحَهُ , (Ṣ, L,) and ♦ اِنْتَصَحَهُ , (L,) *He reckoned him*, or *deemed him*, نَصِيح , (Ṣ, L,) i. e., *a sincere, faithful*, or *honest, adviser*, or *counsellor*, or *actor*. (L.)

نِصَاحٌ ‡ *Thread* (Ṣ, Ḳ) *with which one sews:* (Ṣ:) pl. نُصُحٌ (Ḳ, TA; in the CḲ نُصْحٌ ;) and نِصَاحَةٌ : (Ḳ:) the kesreh and ا in the latter are not those which are in the sing., and the ة is added as a fem. sign of the pl. (TA.) [See also خَيْطٌ.]

نِصَاحَاتٌ *Skins.* (Ṣ, Ḳ.) Aṣ cites as an ex. this verse of El-Aạsha,

* فَتَرَى القَوْمَ نَشَاوَى كُلَّهُمْ *
* مِثْلَمَا مُدَّتْ نِصَاحَاتُ الرُّبَحْ *

(Ṣ, &c.) ربح here signifies, accord. to some, a young camel such as is called رُبَعٌ : (Az:) or a lamb, or kid: (ISd:) or the bird called in Persian زاغ. (TA.) [But see what follows.] — Also, (accord. to El-Muürrij, TA.) *Snares*, (as in some copies of the Ḳ, and in the TA) or *cords*; (as in other copies of the Ḳ) *having loops* (حِلَق) *made to them, which are set, and with which apes* (قُرُود) *are caught;* (Ḳ;) *one of these animals being attached to one of the cords to attract others.* (TA.) Agreeably with this signification some explain the verse of El-Aạsha cited above; رُبَحٌ , originally رُبَاحٌ , signifying apes. (TA.)

تَوْبَةٌ نَصُوحٌ ‡ *True*, or *sincere, repentance:* (Ṣ, Ḳ:) from نَصَحَتِ الإِبِلُ الشُّرْبَ : (IAạr, Ṣ:) or [*repentance that mends one's life;*] from نَصَحَ الثَّوْبَ , agreeably with the saying of Moḥammad, "He who traduces the absent rends, and he who begs forgiveness of God mends:" [see رَفَأَ :] (Ṣ:) or *such repentance that one returns not after it to that of which he repents:* (Ḳ:) *sincere repentance, after which one returns not to sin:* so explained by Moḥammad himself: (TA:) or *very sincere, or very honest repentance:* (Zj:) فَعُول being a measure of an intensive epithet, applicable alike to the masc. and fem.: (TA:) or *repentance in which one does not purpose to return* (Ḳ) *to the sin of which he repents.* (TA.) The people of El-Medeeneh read [in the Ḳur, lxvi., 8,] نُصُوحًا : but some read نُصُوحًا , which is an inf. n. (Fr.)

نَصِيحٌ : see نَاصِحٌ .

نَصِيحَةٌ , an inf. n., (L, Mṣb,) or a simple subst., (Ṣ, Ḳ,) *Sincere, honest*, or *faithful, advice*, or *counsel, and conduct:* (Mṣb:) *direction to that which is for the good of the person who is the object, by words*, or *speech*, which is the proper signification; or *otherwise*, which is a tropical signification: (Lb:) or *good advice or counsel; direction to what is good:* or *sedulousness*, or *earnestness, in advice* or *counsel:* or *sincere* or *honest conduct:* (MF:) or *benevolence; desire for what is good for the person who is the object:* (Nh, MF:) [pl. نَصَائِحُ].

نَصَّاحٌ : see نَاصِحٌ .

نَاصِحٌ (act. part. n. of نَصَحَ) and ♦ نَصِيحٌ are syn., (Ṣ, Ḳ,) signifying One *who advises*, or *counsels, sincerely, honestly*, or *faithfully:* and *who so acts:* (Mṣb:) [*who directs another to that which is for the good of the latter, by words*, or *speech;* or *otherwise:* or *who gives good advice*, or *counsel:* or *who advises*, or *counsels, sedulously*, or *earnestly:* or *who acts sincerely*, or *honestly:* or *benevolent; who desires what is good for another:* see نَصَحَ لَهُ :] pl. of the former نُصَّحٌ and نُصَّاحٌ ; (Ḳ;) and of the latter, نُصَحَآءُ . (Ṣ.) — رَجُلٌ نَاصِحُ الجَيْبِ ‡ *A man pure*, or *sincere, of heart;* (Ṣ;) *in whom is no deceit, dishonesty, insincerity*, or *dissimulation:* (Ḳ:) said to be an expression similar to طَاهِرُ الثَّوْبِ [q. v.]. (TA.) [See also art. جيب.] — نَاصِحٌ (Ṣ, Ḳ) and ♦ نَصَّاحٌ and نَاصِحِىٌّ (Ḳ) ‡ *A sewer; a worker with the needle; a tailor.* (Ṣ, Ḳ.) — نَاصِحٌ ‡ *Pure*, or *clear*, honey, (Aṣ, Ṣ, Ḳ,) &c., like نَاصِعٌ (Aṣ, Ṣ). سَقَانِى نَاصِحَ العَسَلِ ‡ *He gave me to drink white honey;* or *fine*, or *thin, white honey.* (A.) — غُيُوثٌ نَوَاصِحُ ‡ *Rains succeeding one another.* (A.)

مِنْصَحٌ and مِنْصَحَةٌ ‡ *A needle, with which one sews.* (L, Ḳ.) If thick, it is called شُغِيزَةٌ . (L.)

مِنْصَاحٌ : see مَنْصُوحٌ .

قَمِيصٌ مَنْصُوحٌ , (A, L,) and ♦ مِنْصَاحٌ , (A,) ‡ *A shirt that is rent* (A) *and sewed.* (L.) [See also مُتَنَصِّحٌ.] — أَرْضٌ مَنْصُوحَةٌ ‡ *A land plentifully watered by rain*, (Ḳ,) *having its herbage closely conjoined*, (ISd, Ḳ,) as though the spaces which were between the several portions of the herbage were closed up by sewing. (ISd.)

مُتَنَصَّحٌ ‡ *Well sewed.* (AA, Ḳ.) [See also مَنْصُوحٌ.] — Also ‡ *A place*, in a garment, *repaired and sewed:* (TA:) *a patched place*, or *place of patching:* (Ḳ:) *a place for sewing;* similar to مُتَرَقَّعٌ , q. v. (TA in art. رقع.)

نصر

1. نَصَرَهُ , (M, A, Ḳ,) aor. ـُ , (M,) inf. n. نَصْرٌ (M, A, Ḳ) and نُصْرَةٌ , (A,) or this is a simple subst., (Ṣ, Mṣb,) and نُصُورٌ , (Ḳ,) [but see the verse of Khidásh in what follows,] *He aided* or *assisted him*, (M, Ḳ,) namely, a person wronged, misused, or treated unjustly or injuriously, (M, A, Ḳ,) *against his enemy:* (TA:) [*he avenged him:* (see the verse here following, and see 8:)] *he supplied his want*, or *somewhat thereof.* (TA.) Kidásh Ibn-Zuheyr says,

* فَإِنْ كُنْتَ تَشْكُو مِنْ خَلِيلٍ مَخَانَةً *
* فَتِلْكَ الجَوَازِى عَقْبُهَا وَنُصُورُهَا *

[*And if thou complain of treachery from a friend, those requitals are its result and its avengers*, or *avengement*]: here نُصُور may be a pl. of نَاصِرٌ , like شُهُودٌ is of شَاهِدٌ ; or it may be an inf. n., like دُخُولٌ and خُرُوجٌ . (M.) You say, نَصَرَهُ مِنْ عَدُوِّهِ , (A,) عَلَى عَدُوِّهِ , (Ṣ, A, Mṣb,) and Mṣb,) aor. ـُ , (Ṣ, Mṣb,) inf. n. نَصْرٌ (Ṣ, A, Mṣb) and نُصْرَةٌ , (A,) or this, as remarked above, is a simple subst., (Ṣ, Mṣb,) *He* (namely, God, Ṣ, A, or a man, Mṣb,) *aided* or *assisted him*, and *strengthened him, against his enemy:* (Mṣb:) [*he avenged him of his enemy.* (See 8.)] And نَصَرَهُ ٱللّٰهُ *God made him to be victorious, to conquer*, or *to overcome:* so in the Ḳur, xxii. 15, where the pronoun relates to Moḥammad. (TA.) In the Ḳur, xlvii. 8, إِنْ تَنْصُرُوا ٱللّٰهَ يَنْصُرْكُمْ means, *If ye aid God's religion and his apostle, He will aid you* against your enemy: (Bḍ, Jel:) or *if ye aid his servants*, &c.: or *if ye keep his ordinances and aid his orders and comply with his commands and shun the things which He hath forbidden*, &c. (El-Baṣáir.) And the trad. أُنْصُرْ أَخَاكَ ظَالِمًا أَوْ مَظْلُومًا is explained as meaning, *Prevent thou thy brother from wronging when he is a wronger, and aid him against his wronger when he is wronged.* (TA.) Also, نَصَرَهُ مِنْهُ , (Ḳ,) inf. n. نَصْرٌ and نُصْرَةٌ , (TA,) [or the latter in this sense, as in the cases above mentioned, is a simple subst.,] *He served* or *preserved him from him* or *it.* (Ḳ.) — نَصَرَ ٱللّٰهُ الأَرْضَ *God gave rain to the earth* or *land.* (A.) And نَصَرَ الغَيْثُ الأَرْضَ , (Ṣ, M, Ḳ,) [aor. ـُ ,] inf. n. نَصْرٌ , (M,) ‡ *The rain aided the earth* or *land:* (Ṣ:) or *watered it:* (M:) or *watered it generally and copiously*, (Ḳ, TA,) *and caused it to produce herbage:* (TA:) and نَصَرَ البَلَدَ ‡ *it assisted the country to produce abundance of herbage:* (TA:) and نُصِرَتِ الأَرْضُ ‡ *the earth* or *land was watered by rain.* (Ṣ.) — Hence, نَصَرَهُ , aor. ـُ , inf. n. نَصْرٌ , ‡ *He gave to him.* (M.) An Arab of the desert [in the A a beggar] accosted a people saying, أُنْصُرُونِى نَصَرَكُمُ ٱللّٰهُ , meaning, ‡ *Give ye to me: may God give to you.*

(M, A.) — نَصَرَهُ ٱللّٰهُ also signifies † *God bestowed upon him the means of subsistence*, or *the like*; syn. رَزَقَهُ. (IKtt.)

2. نَصَّرَهُ, (inf. n. تَنْصِيرٌ, K,) *He made him a Christian.* (S, M, K.) It is said in a trad., [relating to the natural disposition of a child to adopt the true faith,] فَأَبَوَاهُ يُهَوِّدَانِهِ وَيُنَصِّرَانِهِ [*But his two parents make him a Jew* or *make him a Christian*]. (S.)

3. [ناصره *He rendered reciprocal aid to him.* See an ex. voce عَاصَرَ.]

5. تنصّر *He laboured*, or *strove, to aid*, or *assist*; syn. عَالَجَ النَّصْرَ: (M, K:) not of the same category as تَحَلَّمَ [he endeavoured to acquire حِلْم] and تبرّر [he endeavoured to characterize himself by بِرّ]. (M.) — *He became a Christian.* (M, K.)

6. تناصروا *They aided* or *assisted one another*: (S, Msb, TA:) *they assisted one another to aid.* (M, A, K, TA.) — تَنَاصَرَتِ الأَخْبَارُ ‡ *The accounts*, or *tidings, confirmed*, or *verified, one another.* (M, K, TA.)

8. انتصر *He defended himself*: (Bd, Jel, lv. 35:) *he defended himself against his wronger*, or *injurer.* (TA.) — انتصر منْهُ *He exacted*, or *obtained, his right*, or *due, completely, from him, so that each of them became on a par with the other*: (Az, TA:) *he revenged himself upon him.* (Az, S, M,* Msb, K.)

10. استنصر *He asked, sought*, or *desired, aid*, or *assistance.* (M, K.) And استنصره *He asked him to aid him*, (S, Msb, K,) عَلَيْهِ *against him*, (S, K,) i. e. against his enemy. (S, TA.) — ‡ *He begged*; (K;) as though he asked for a gift, which is termed نَصْر. (TA.)

نَصْرٌ [used a subst.,] *Aid* or *assistance*, rendered to another, *especially against an enemy*: [*avengement* of another:] *victory* or *conquest*: (Bd, xxix. 9:) and ↓ نُصْرَةٌ is a subst. from نَصَرَهُ [and therefore signifies the same]: (S, Msb:) or the ↓ latter signifies *good aid*, or *assistance*: (M, K:) and this ↓ same word, when the object is God, signifies *aid of God's servants*; &c.; as explained above: see 1. (El-Basáir.) — *Spoil*; *plunder*; *booty.* (Bd, ubi supra.) — ‡ *Rain*; (A, TA;) as also ↓ نُصْرَةٌ: (TA:) in like manner as it is called فَتْحٌ: (A, TA:) or the ↓ latter signifies *a complete rain.* (IAar.) — [Hence,] ‡ *A gift*: (S, TA:) and نَصَائِرُ *gifts.* (M.) — See also نَاصِرٌ.

نَصْرٌ: see نَاصِرٌ.

نُصْرَةٌ: see نَصْرٌ, in five places.

نَصْرِىٌّ: } see نَصْرَانِىٌّ.
نَصْرَانٌ: }

نَصْرَانِىٌّ, (S, A, Msb, K, &c.) and ↓ نَصْرَانٌ, (M, A,) or this latter has not been used without the addition of the relative ى, (S,) or it has been sometimes used, (M,) and ↓ نَصْرِىٌّ, (M, Msb, K,) but we have not heard this used, (M,) [*A Christian*: or this is a secondary application, and the original meaning is *a Nazarene*:] fem. نَصْرَانِيَّةٌ, (S, A, Msb, K,) and نَصْرَانَةٌ, (S, A, K,) or the latter is used only by poetic licence: (IB:) ↓ نَصَارَى [applied to the *Christians*] is a rel. n. from نَاصِرَةُ, [or Nazareth,] a town of Syria, (S, M, K,) also called نَصْرَانَةُ, (Lth, IDrd, K,) or نَصْرَانُ, (S, Msb,) and نَصُورِيَةُ, (M, Sgh, K,) without teshdeed, accord. to Sgh, (TA,) and نُصْرِىٌّ and نُصْرَى, (as in a copy of the M,) or نَصْرَى and نَصُورَةُ: (TA:) so originally, and then applied to such as hold the religion of its inhabitants: (Msb:) this is the opinion of the lexicologists; but it is of weak authority, though admissible as there are other anomalous rel. ns.: (M:) or [so in K, but in the S, and] نَصَارَى is pl. of نَصْرِىٌّ, (Kh, M, Msb, K,) like as مَهَارَى is pl. of مَهْرِىٌّ; (Msb, K;) or of نَصْرَانٌ (Kh, S, M) and نَصْرَانَةٌ, (S,) like as نَدَامَى is pl. of نَدْمَانٌ (Kh, S, M) and نَدْمَانَةٌ; (S;) but more probably of نَصْرَانٌ, because this word has been sometimes used, whereas we have not heard نَصْرِىٌّ used: (M:) and it is implied in the copies of the K, that أَنْصَارٌ is pl. of نَصْرَانِىٌّ; but correctly, it is a pl. of نَصْرَانٌ, without ى, as is said in the TS, and the L, in both of which is mentioned the saying of the poet,

* لَمَّا رَأَيْتُ نَبَطًا أَنْصَارَا *

[*When I saw Nabatheans, Christians*], meaning نَصَارَى. (TA.)

النَّصْرَانِيَّةُ *The religion of the* نَصَارَى [or *Christians*]. (K, TA.)

نَصُورٌ One *who aids*, or *assists, much* or *well.* (TA in art. عقرب.)

نَصِيرٌ: see نَاصِرٌ. It has the signification of the measure فَاعِلٌ or of the measure مَفْعُولٌ; for أَخَوَانِ نَصِيرَانِ, occurring in a trad., means *Two brothers, aiders of, and aided by, each other.* (TA.)

نَصَارَى: see نَصْرَانِىٌّ.

نَصَائِرُ: see نَصْرٌ.

نَاصِرٌ act. part. n. of نَصَرَ, *An aider* or *assister, especially against an enemy*; &c.; as also ↓ نَصِيرٌ, (S,* M, A, Msb, K,) and ↓ نَصْرٌ: (Sgh, K:) pl. (of نَصِيرٌ, (S, M, Msb, and of نَاصِرٌ, M,) أَنْصَارٌ (S, M, A, Msb, K) and (of نَاصِرٌ, M) نُصَّارٌ, (M, K,) and نُصُورٌ may also be a pl. of the same, as occurring in the verse of Khidásh, cited above: (M:) and أَنَاصِيرُ is a pl. pl., being pl. of أَنْصَارٌ: (TA:) and ↓ نَصْرٌ is used as sing. and pl., (M, K,) being an inf. n. employed as an epithet, like عَدْلٌ. (M.) — الأَنْصَارُ also signifies *The Assistants of the Prophet*; (M, K;) of [the tribes of] El-Ows and El-Khazraj; (TA;) being an epithet applied to them especially, (M, K,) and used as a subst., as though it were the name of a tribe, wherefore the rel. n. أَنْصَارِىٌّ [which is used as sing.] is formed from it. (M.)

نَاسُورٌ: see نَاصُورٌ.

أَنْصَارٌ: see نَصْرَانِىٌّ: — and نَاصِرٌ.

أَنْصَارِىٌّ: see نَاصِرٌ.

مَنْصُورٌ [*Aided* or *assisted, especially against an enemy*, &c.]. — أَرْضٌ مَنْصُورَةٌ ‡ *Land watered by rain*; *rained upon.* (S, A.)

مُسْتَنْصِرٌ [*Asking, seeking*, or *desiring, aid*, or *assistance*]. — ‡ *A beggar.* (M.)

[نصع, &c.

See Supplement.]

نض

1. نَضَّ, aor. ـِ, inf. n. نَضِيضٌ (S, A, Mgh, Msb, K) and نَضٌّ, (K,) *It* (water) *welled* from a source, or spring: (TA:) or *flowed*: (TA:) or *flowed*, (S, Mgh, K,) or *came forth*, (Mgh, Msb,) *by little and little*, (S, A, Mgh, Msb,) from stone or the like; (Mgh;) like بَضَّ: (A:) or *exuded*; or *oozed forth*, (A, K,) [like بَضَّ;] *like as it does from stone.* (TA.) You say also, سَحَابَةٌ تَنِضُّ بِالْمَآءِ *A cloud flowing with water.* (TA.) And رِيحٌ تَنِضُّ بِالْمَآءِ [app. *A wind bringing rain*]. (K.) And نَضَّتِ القِرْبَةُ مِنْ شِدَّةِ المَلْءِ, (K,) aor. ـِ, inf. n. نَضِيضٌ, (TA,) *The water-skin slit*, or *burst*, (K, TA,) *and its water came forth*, (TA,) *in consequence of being very full.* (K, TA.) — [Hence,] نَضَّ إِلَيْهِ مِنْ مَعْرُوفِهِ شَىْءٌ, aor. ـِ, inf. n. نَضٌّ [and نَضِيضٌ], † *Somewhat flowed to him from his bounty*: but the verb is mostly thus used in negative phrases. (TA.) You say also, نَضَّ مِنْ مَعْرُوفِكَ نُضَاضَةٌ † *A little of thy bounty* [*flowed forth*]. (TA.) And نَضَّ لَهُ بِشَىْءٍ † *He did him a small benefit*; as also بَضَّ. (As.) — Hence too, (Mgh,) نَضَّ, (IKoot, S, A, &c.,) aor. ـِ, inf. n. نَضِيضٌ, (K,) also signifies ‡ *It* (a thing, IKoot, Msb, or an affair, K)

was, or became, within the power or *reach*; or *possible*; or *easy of obtainment* or *attainment*; or *prepared*, or *ready*; or *produced*; or *apparent*; or *it presented itself*; syn. أَمْكَنَ; (Ḳ, TA;) and تَيَسَّرَ; (Ṣ, A, Mgh, Mṣb, TA;) and حَصَلَ; (IKooṭ, Mgh, Mṣb, TA;) and ظَهَرَ. (Mgh.) You say, خُذْ مَا نَضَّ ‡ *Take thou*, or *receive thou, what hath become easy of obtainment* or *attainment*: or *prepared*, or *ready*; or *produced*; or *apparent*; or *what hath presented itself*; syn. تَيَسَّرَ; (Ṣ, A, Mgh, Mṣb, TA;) and حَصَلَ; (Mgh, TA;) لَكَ *to thee*, or *for thee*; (Ṣ, A, Mgh, TA;) مِنْ دَيْنٍ *of a debt*; (Ṣ;) or من الدَّيْنِ *of the debt*; (Mṣb;) or من دَيْنِكَ *of thy debt*; (A, Mgh;) or من غَرِيمِكَ *from thy debtor*. (TA.) And it is said in a trad., خُذُوا صَدَقَةَ مَا نَضَّ مِنْ أَمْوَالِهِمْ ‡ *Take ye the poor-rate of what hath appeared, or presented itself, of their possessions*; syn. ظَهَرَ, and حَصَلَ. (Mgh.) You say also, نَضَّ الثَّمَنُ † *The price was*, or *became, produced*, or *apparent*, or *prepared*, or *ready*: *was*, or *became, given in ready money*, or *promptly*, or *quickly*, or *in advance*: syn. حَصَلَ: and تَعَجَّلَ. (Mṣb.) And مَا نَضَّ بِيَدِى مِنْهُ شَىْءٌ, (Ṣ, Mṣb,) i.e. مَا حَصَلَ † [*Nothing became produced*, or *apparent*, &c., *by my hand therefrom*: or, accord. to A'Obeyd, or Aṣ, (see نَاضٌّ,) the verb in this instance seems to have the signification here next following]. (Mṣb.) نَضَّ مَالُهُ also signifies ‡ *His property became converted into money*, or *cash, after it had been a commodity*, or *commodities*. (A, Mgh.*)

2: see **R.Q. 1**, in two places.

4. انضّ *He* (a pastor, Ṣ) *gave lambs or kids to drink a small quantity of milk*. (Ṣ, Ḳ, TA.) —— † *He accomplished* a want. (Ḳ.)

5: see **10**, in two places. —— تَنَضَّضْتُ فُلَانًا † *I excited, incited, urged*, or *instigated, such a one*. (Ṣgh, Ḳ, TA.) [In one copy of the Ḳ, ▼تَنَضْنَضْتُ.]

8: see **10**.

10. استنضّ الثِّمَادَ *He sought repeatedly and perseveringly the* [*small quantities*, or *remains*, termed] ثِمَاد, *of water, and took of them little by little*. (TA [in which, however, الثِّمَارَ is erroneously put for الثِّمَادَ].) —— [Hence,] هُوَ يَسْتَنِضُّ مَعْرُوفًا ‡ *He seeks*, or *demands, bounty*, or *a benefit, as it were drop by drop*; syn. يَسْتَقْطِرُهُ: (Ḳ, TA:) or *extracts*, or *elicits, it*: (TA:) or *seeks*, or *demands, its accomplishment*. (A, TA.) And هُوَ يَسْتَنِضُّ حَقَّهُ, (Ṣ, Ḳ,) or ▼يَنْتَضُّ حقّه, (so in a copy of the Mṣb,) † *He seeks*, or *demands, the accomplishment of his right*, or *due*, (Ṣ, Mṣb, Ḳ,) *and takes*, or *receives*, (Ṣ,) *part after part*, (Ṣ, Mṣb,) مِنْ فُلَانٍ *from such a one*: (Ṣ:) or *extracts*, or *elicits, it, part after part*. (Ḳ.) And ▼تَنَضَّضْتُ مِنْهُ حَقِّى [in one copy of the Ḳ ▼تَنَضْنَضْتُ] † *I took*, or *exacted*, or *received, fully*, or *wholly, from him, my right*, or *due*, (Ḳ, TA.) *part after part*: (TA:) [as also تَبَضَّضْتُهُ منه.] And ▼تَنَضَّضْتُ الحَاجَةَ [in one copy of the Ḳ ▼تَنَضْنَضْتُ] † *I sought*, or *demanded, the accomplishment of the want*. (Ḳ.)

R. Q. 1. نَضْنَضَ, (Ḳ, TA,) or ▼نَضَّضَ, (so in the CḲ,) said of a man, (TA,) † *His* نَاضّ, (Ḳ, TA,) i.e. *what was apparent of his property*, (TA,) *became much*, or *abundant*. (Ḳ, TA.) —— *He moved about* his tongue; as also نَصْنَصَ; but the ض in the former is not a substitute for the ص in the latter, as some assert it to be: (L, TA:) the verb is used in this sense in speaking of a man; (TA;) and of a serpent; (Ṣ*, A, Ḳ;) inf. n. نَضْنَضَةٌ: (Ṣ, but in one copy نَضِيضَةٌ:) and accord. to Ibn-'Abbád, نَضْنَضَةٌ [the inf. n.] signifies *the making*, or *uttering, of a sound*; or *the sound itself*; (صَوْتٌ;) [app. *by a motion of the tongue*;] of the serpent; and hence, [accord. to some,] the epithet نَضْنَاضٌ, as applied to a serpent: (TA:) or this epithet is from the phrase, (IAạr,) نَضْنَضَ فُلَانًا, (IAạr, Ḳ,) ▼نَضَّضَهُ, (so in the CḲ,) *He put such a one in motion*, (IAạr,) and *he disquieted, disturbed*, or *unsettled, him*; or *removed him from his place*. (IAạr, Ḳ.) [In one place, in the TA, اسنضّ منه شَيْئًا is made to signify the same; but this is doubtless a mistake, arising from an omission in transcription.] You say also, نَضْنَضَ البَعِيرُ ثَفِنَاتِهِ *The camel moved about his* ثفنات [q.v.], *and made them to be in contact with the ground*; or this is [نَصْنَصَ,] with ص. (TA.)

R. Q. 2: see **5**: —— and see also **10**, in two places.

نَضٌّ (Ṣ, Mṣb, Ḳ) and ▼نَاضٌّ (Ṣ, A, Mgh, Mṣb, Ḳ) ‡ *Gold and silver coin or money*; or *deenárs and dirhems*: (Ṣ, A, Mgh, Mṣb:) such are called ▼نَاضُّ المَالِ: (A, TA:) or the *dirhem and deenár*: (Ḳ:) of the dial. of El-Ḥijáz: (Aṣ, Ṣ, Mgh, Mṣb:) but accord. to A'Obeyd, (Ṣ, Mṣb,) or Aṣ, (TA,) these are called ▼نَاضٌّ only *when converted into such after having been a commodity*, or *commodities*; (Ṣ, Mṣb, Ḳ;) because one says, مَا نَضَّ بِيَدِى مِنْهُ شَىْءٌ, (Ṣ, Mṣb,) i.e. مَا حَصَلَ: (Mṣb:) نَضٌّ also signifies *what is apparent*, or *produced*, or *prepared*, or *ready*; and so ▼نَاضٌّ, particularly of property: (TA:) and ▼ the latter, *what has continuance*, or *endurance*, of property. (Mṣb.) A man of much property is described as being أَكْثَرُ النَّاسِ ▼نَاضًّا ‡ [*The most abounding of men in gold and silver coin*]. (TA.) —— See also نَضِيضٌ.

نَضَضٌ *Water upon sand beneath which is hard ground, from which whenever any exudes and collects, it is taken*. (TA.)

بِئْرٌ نَضُوضٌ *A well of which the water flows by little and little*: or *oozes forth*. (Ḳ, TA.)

نَضِيضٌ Water *little in quantity*: (Ṣ, O, L, Ḳ:) pl. نِضَاضٌ; (Ṣ, O, L, TA; in the Ḳ, نَضَائِضُ, which is a mistake. TA.) Also, *A small quantity* of milk. (Ṣ, Ḳ.) —— رَجُلٌ نَضِيضُ اللَّحْمِ † *A man having little flesh*; (Ḳ;) as also ▼نَضٌّ, and ▼نُضَاضَةٌ. (TA.) —— جَاؤُوا بِأَقْصَى نَضِيضِهِمْ, and ▼نَضِيضَتِهِمْ, *They came with the most remote of their company*; (O, Ḳ;) from Ibn-'Abbád. (TA.)

نُضَاضَةٌ *A remainder*, (Ṣ, Ḳ,) or *small remainder*, (A,) of water, (Ṣ, A, Ḳ,) &c.: (Ṣ, Ḳ:) the *last* thereof: pl. نَضَائِضُ and نِضَاضٌ. (TA.) [Hence,] نُضَاضَةُ وَلَدِ الرَّجُلِ ‡ *The last of the children of the man*: (AZ, Ṣ, A, Ḳ:) applied alike to the male and female and to two and more; (Ṣ, Ḳ;) like عِجْزَةٌ and كِبْرَةٌ. (Ṣ.) —— ‡ *A small thing*: (A:) *what comes into one's hand*, of a thing: *a small benefit*. (TA.)

نَضِيضَةٌ *A small quantity of rain*: (AA, Ṣ, Ḳ:) or *a weak rain*: or *a weak cloud*: or *one flowing with water*: (TA:) pl. [of pauc.] أَنِضَّةٌ and [of mult.] نَضَائِضُ. (Ṣ, Ḳ.) —— A wind *that brings rain*, (تَنِضُّ بِالْمَآءِ,) *so that it flows*: or a *weak* wind. (A'Obeyd, Ḳ.) —— لَقَدْ تَرَكَتِ الإِبِلُ المَآءَ وَهِىَ ذَاتُ نَضِيضَةٍ, and ذَاتُ نَضَائِضَ, *The camels have left the water, having thirst*; (Ṣ, Ḳ;*) *not having satisfied their thirst*. (Ṣ.) —— *The sound of the roasting of flesh-meat upon heated stones*: pl. نَضَائِضُ: (Ṣ, Ḳ:) ISd, however, says, I think that نَضَائِضُ is a sing., like خُشَارِمُ; but the sing. may be نَضِيضَةٌ. (TA.) [It seems to me not improbable that نَضَائِضُ may be a mis-transcription, for نَضَانِضُ, pl. of the inf. n. نَضْنَضَةٌ used as a subst.] —— See also نَضِيضٌ.

نَضْنَاضٌ: see نَضِيضٌ. —— حَيَّةٌ نَضْنَاضٌ, (IAạr, Ṣ, Ḳ,) and نَضْنَاضَةٌ, (Ṣ, A, Ḳ,) *A serpent that remains not still in a place*, (IAạr, Ḳ,) *by reason of its malignity and liveliness*: (IAạr:) or *that, when it bites, kills immediately*: (Ḳ:) or *that moves about its tongue*, (Ṣ, A, Ḳ,) *having put it forth*; (Ḳ;) as also with ص: [see نَصْنَاصٌ:] (TA:) or *that utters a sound, or sounds*. (TA.) It is said that Dhu-r-Rummeh, being asked respecting the meaning of نَضْنَاضٌ, did nothing more than move about his tongue in his mouth; (Ṣ;) or put forth his tongue, and move it about, (IJ, O,) in his mouth, making a sign with it to him who asked him. (O.)

فَضْفَاضَةٌ : نَضْنَاضَةٌ see فَضْفَاضَةٌ.

نَاضٌّ ‡ A thing, or an affair, *within one's power or reach* [&c.: see 1, of which it is the part. n.]. (Ḳ.) —— See also نَضٌّ in six places.

نضب

1. نَضَبَ, aor. ـُ (Ṣ, Ḳ, &c.) and also ـِ, (Mṣb,) which latter is strange, (MF,) inf. n. نُضُوبٌ; (Ṣ, Ḳ, &c.;) and ↓ نَضْبٌ; (Ḳ;) *It* (water) *sank into the earth; disappeared in the earth:* (Ṣ, M, Ḳ, &c.:) and *became low:* (Ṣ:) *became remote.* (Ṣ, M.) —— نَضَبَ الحَوْضُ, occurring in a verse cited by Th, [*The water of the tank or cistern, sank into the earth*]. (TA.) —— نَضَبَتْ عُيُونُ الطَّائِفِ [*The sources of El-Ṭáïf became dried up*]. (A.) —— مَا نَضَبَ عَنْهُ البَحْرُ وَهُوَ حَىٌّ فَمَاتَ فَكُلُوهُ *That from which the water of the sea has become exhausted, and has dried up, it being alive, and which has then died, eat ye it.* (TA, from a trad.) —— كُنَّا عَلَى شَاطِئِ النَّهْرِ بِالْأَهْوَازِ وَقَدْ نَضَبَ عَنْهُ المَآءُ [*We were on the bank of the river in El-Ahwáz, and the water had sunk, or receded, from it, leaving it dry*]. (TA, from a trad.) —— نَضَبَتْ عَيْنُهُ, (aor. ـُ, inf. n. نُضُوبٌ, TA,) ‡ *His eye sank, or became depressed, in the socket:* or it is only said of the eye of a she-camel. (Ḳ.) —— نَضَبَ *It* (herbage and the like, that had been abundant,) *became little, or scanty:* (Ḳ:) or *failed altogether.* (TA.) —— نَضَبَ is met. used with reference to accidents [as it is properly with respect to substances]: thus it is said in a trad., نَضَبَ عُمْرُهُ ‡ *His life passed away, or ended.* (IAth.) This is what F means by saying نَضَبَ فُلَانٌ signifies مَاتَ, ‡ *Such a one died.* (TA.) —— نَضَبَ خَيْرُهُ, inf. n. نُضُوبٌ, ‡ *His goodness, or beneficence, became little.* (AZ.) —— نَضَبَ مَآءُ وَجْهِهِ ‡ *He was not ashamed.* (TA.) = نَضَبَ, (inf. n. نُضُوبٌ, TA,) ‡ *It* (a desert) *was far-extending.* (Ḳ.) —— نَضَبَ, inf. n. نُضُوبٌ, ‡ *It* (a people, or party,) *was, or became, distant.* (Ṣ.) —— نَضَبَ ‡ *It* (a people, or party,) *strove, or used exertion,* [app., *in a journey.*] (TA.) = نَضَبَ, aor. ـُ, *It* (a thing, TA,) *flowed, and ran.* (Ḳ.) By our saying "a thing," we mean to exclude water, though water is included in the definition of a thing: so that we need not infer from what is said in the Ḳ that the verb bears two contr. significations. (TA.) [But this observation appears to me to be scarcely admissible.] —— نَضَبَتِ الدَّبَرَةُ [in the copies of the Ḳ in my hands, written دُبْرَة] *The sore on the back of a camel &c. became severe.* (Ḳ.) ‡ نَضَبَ الدَّبَرُ ‡ *The scar of the sore became severe and deep in the back.* (A.) = نَضَبَ الثَّوْبَ *He pulled off the garment.* (Mṣb.)

2: see 1 —— نَضَّبَت, inf. n. تَنْضِيبٌ, *She* (a camel) *had little milk; and her flow thereof became slow;* (Ḳ;) *and her milk was long in flowing again into her udder after each previous milking.* (TA.)

4. انضب القَوْسَ *He pulled the string of the bow, in order that it might make a sound:* like أَنْبَضَهَا: (Ḳ:) the former verb is [said to be] an original syn. of the latter; (TA;) [and if so, it has an inf. n., as shown below:] or *he pulled the string of the bow, and then let it go, to make it twang:* or *he pulled the string of the bow without an arrow, and then let it go, to make it twang:* (TA:) or *he caused the bow to make a sound, or twang:* (AḤn, L:) انضب وَتَرَ القَوْسِ *is the same as* أَنْبَضَهُ, of which it is a transp. syn. (Ṣ.) AḤn, gives to it the inf. n. إِنْضَابٌ; and yet asserts it to be formed by transposition: but this is absurd; for verbs so formed have not inf. ns.; as mentioned by Sb and Aboo-'Alee and the rest of the skilful grammarians. (Abu-l-Ḥasan.) See قَلْبٌ.

غَضِيرٌ نَاضِبٌ *A pool of which the water has sunk into the earth.* (A.) —— [So] ↓ عين مَنْضَبَةٌ *A source of which the water has sunk into the earth;* [*a source that has become dried up*]. (A.) —— خَرْقٌ نَاضِبٌ ‡ [*A deep hole:* or *a far extending desert*]: syn. بَعِيدٌ. (Ṣ, TA.) —— إِنَّ فُلَانًا لَنَاضِبُ الخَيْرِ ‡ *Verily such a one is a person of little good,* or *beneficence.* (AZ.) —— نَاضِبٌ ‡ *Distant; remote:* (Aṣ, Ṣ:) an epithet applied to water and anything. (TA.) —— جَرْىٌ نَاضِبٌ † *A far-extending run.* (TA.)

تَنْضُبٌ, a coll. gen. n., [I find it said to have been written with tenween by J himself: but it appears to have been also used as a generic proper name; and as such, having the measure of a verb, it must be written تَنْضُبُ, being imperfectly declinable:] *A certain tree:* the ت is augmentative, because there is no word of the measure فَعْلُلٌ; whereas there are words of the measure تَفْعُلٌ, as تَقْتُلٌ and تَخْرُجٌ: n. un. تَنْضُبَةٌ: (Ṣ:) *a certain tree of El-Ḥijáz:* (Ḳ:) *it grows large, in the form,* or *manner, of the* سَرْح, *having white and thick branches; and folds, such as are called* حَظَائِر, *are made of it:* [this is the only meaning I can assign to the words وهو محتظر به, supposing به to be omitted after محتظر, though يُحْتَظَرُ would be better:] *its leaves are contracted; and it always appears as though it were dry and dusty, though growing:* (TA:) *its thorns are like those of the* عَوْسَج: (Ḳ, TA:) *and it has a fruit* [called مُغْد (L, Ḳ, art. مغد)] *like small grapes, which is eaten, of a reddish colour:* AḤn says, that *its smoke is white, of the colour of dust; and that poets therefore liken dust to it:* and in one place he says, that it is *a large tree, without leaves* [*properly so called*], *which has a trunk, and from which grow thick boughs, with many branches; its leaves* [*if such they may be called*] *being only shoots, which are eaten by the camels and sheep and goats:* Aboo-Naṣr says, that it is *a tree having short thorns: not of the trees that grow on lofty mountains; frequented by chameleons:* [see حِرْبَآءٌ, in art. حرب: and see an ex. in a verse cited voce سَاقٌ:] ISd thinks that it is thus called because of its little sap: AM says, that it is *a large tree, from which are cut tentpoles:* (TA:) and Ibn-Selemeh says, that it is *a tree from which arrows are made.* (Ṣ.) —— نُوقٌ كَقِدَاحِ التَّنْضُبِ [*She-camels like arrows made of the wood of the tendub*]. (TA).

مَنْضَبَةٌ : see نَاضِبٌ.

نضج

1. نَضِجَ, aor. ـَ, inf. n. نُضْجٌ and نَضْجٌ, (Ṣ, Ḳ, &c.,) or these are [properly] simple substs., (the former accord. to the L, and both accord. to the Mṣb,) and the inf. n. is نَضَجٌ, (Mṣb,) *It* (fruit, الثَّمَرُ, Ṣ, Ḳ, [in the CḲ التَّمْر, or dates,] as grapes, and dates, TA, and flesh-meat, Ṣ, Ḳ, whether dried in the sun or roasted, TA, [or cooked in any way,]) *attained to a perfect state of fitness for being used,* or *for being eaten:* it (fruit) *became ripe,* or *mature:* it (flesh-meat) *became thoroughly cooked.* (Ṣ, Ḳ, &c.) See 2. [And *It* (the skin of one tormented in Hell) *became thoroughly burned:* see Ḳur iv. 59.] —— *It* (an ulcer or the like) *became ripe,* or *suppurated.*]

2. نَضَّجَتِ النَّاقَةُ بِوَلَدِهَا, (Ṣ, Ḳ,) and نَضَّجَتْ وَلَدَهَا, (Ḳ,) and ↓ نَضِجَتْ بِهِ, (L,) ‡ *She* (a camel) *exceeded the usual period of gestation by a month, or thereabout:* (L:) or *exceeded the year and did not bring forth:* (Ṣ, Ḳ:) *was pregnant, and exceeded the year, counting from the time when she conceived, and did not bring forth.* (Aṣ.) Th uses the expression نضّجت ولدها as signifying *She* (a woman) *exceeded the usual period of gestation, namely nine months;* or *did so by a month:* in which case the child is more strong for the delay. (TA.) —— نَضَّجَتِ النَّاقَةُ بِلَبَنِهَا ‡ *The she-camel attained the utmost point with her milk:* but ISd thinks it a mistake for نضّجت بولدها. (L.) = See 4.

4. انضج *He rendered* fruit, or flesh-meat, (whether dried in the sun or roasted, TA, [or cooked in any way],) *perfectly fit for being used,* or *for being eaten: rendered ripe,* or *mature: thoroughly cooked:* (Ṣ, Ḳ:) *it* (the proper time) *rendered* fruit *ripe,* or *mature; ripened,* or *matured it.* (TA.) —— AḤn uses this verb in a strange manner, explaining the expression نَبَاتٌ مَهْرُوٌّ by the words الَّذِى قَدْ أَنْضَجَهُ البَرْدُ [meaning, *a plant,* or *herbage, that is nipped, shrunk, shrivelled,* or *blasted, by the cold*]: this is strange because إِنْضَاجٌ is an effect

of heat; not of cold. (M.) [See أَحْرَقَ.] — انْضِجْ رَأْيَكَ ‡ *Mature thy judgment*, or *thine opinion*]. (A.) — لَا يُنْضِجُ الكُرَاعَ, (L,) or لَايَسْتَنْضِجُ ▾ كُرَاعًا, (A,) [*He does not thoroughly cook the slender part of the leg of a sheep*, or the like]: i. e., he is weak, and of no use, or does not possess a competence. (L.) — [انضج also signifies *It matured*, or *caused to suppurate*, an ulcer or the like; as also ▾ نَضَّجَ.]

10: see 4.

نُضْجٌ: see نَضْجٌ.

نَضْجٌ and ▾ نُضْجٌ: see 1. — As simple substs., in relation to fruit, or to flesh-meat, *A perfect state of fitness for being used*, or *for being eaten: ripeness*, or *maturity*: the *state of being thoroughly cooked*. (L, Mṣb.)

نَضِيجٌ and ▾ نَاضِجٌ (Ṣ, Ḳ) and ▾ مُنْضَجٌ (TA) Fruit, and flesh-meat, (whether dried in the sun or roasted, TA, [or cooked in any way,]) *in a perfect state of fitness for being used*, or *for being eaten: ripe*, or *mature: thoroughly cooked*: (Ṣ, Ḳ, &c.:) pl. [of the first, and perhaps of the second also,] نِضَاجٌ. (TA.) — نَضِيجُ الرَّأْيِ ‡ A man *of sound*, [or *mature*] *judgment*. (Ṣ, Ḳ.) — أَمْرٌ مُنْضَجٌ ▾ ‡ [*A matured affair*; *an affair soundly*, or *thoroughly, managed*]. (A.)

نَاضِجٌ: see نَضِيجٌ.

مُنْضَجٌ: see نَضِيجٌ.

مُنْضِجٌ: see what follows.

مُنَضِّجٌ (Ṣ, L, Ḳ) and ▾ مُنْضِجٌ and each with ة (L) ‡ A she-camel *that exceeds the usual period of gestation by a month, or thereabout*: (L:) or *that exceeds the year and does not bring forth*: (Ṣ, Ḳ:) pl. مُنَضِّجَاتٌ (Ṣ) and مُنْضِجَاتٌ. (L.) See an ex. voce قِرَابٌ. — [Also both, but the latter the more common, *A suppurative medicine*.]

مِنْضَاجٌ *An iron instrument for roasting flesh-meat*; syn. سَفُّودٌ. (Ḳ.)

نضح

1. نَضَحَ, aor. ـِ, (Ṣ, Ḳ,) and ـَ, (Mṣb, MF,) inf. n. نَضْحٌ, (Ṣ,) *He sprinkled* a house, or chamber, [with water]: (Ṣ, Ḳ:) or *he sprinkled it lightly*: (TA:) نَضْحٌ is like نَضْخٌ; and sometimes these two words agree, and sometimes they differ: (Lth:) some say that they both signify any sprinkling: (TA:) or the former signifies what is intentional; and the latter, what is unintentional. (IAṭr.) [See نَضَخَ.] — نَضَحْتُ عَلَيْهِ المَآءَ, inf. n. نَضْحٌ, [*I sprinkled water*, or *the water, upon him*]. (Aṣ.) — نَضَحَ, aor. ـِ, and ـَ, inf. n. نَضْحٌ, *He moistened*, or *sprinkled*, a garment, or piece of cloth. (Mṣb.) — أَصَابَهُ نَضْحٌ مِنْ كَذَا [*A sprinkling of such a thing came upon him*]. (TA.) — نَضَحَتْ بِبَوْلِهَا *She* (a camel) *sprinkled her urine*. (TA.) — نَضَحَ عَطَشَهُ, (Ṣ, Ḳ,) aor. ـِ, inf. n. نَضْحٌ, (Ṣ,) ‡ *It* (water, TA,) *moistened* [or *allayed*] *his thirst*, (Ṣ, TA,) *and allayed it*: (Ḳ, TA:) *took it away*: or *almost took it away*: (TA:) also (Ḳ) or نَضَحَ الرِّىَّ, (TA,) *he satisfied his thirst with drink*: (Ḳ:) or *he drank less than what would satisfy his thirst*. (Ṣ, Ḳ.) — نَضَحَ المَآءُ المَالَ *The water took away the thirst of the camels* &c.: or nearly did so. (T.) — نَضَحَ المَآءَ *He* (a camel) *carried water from a river* or *canal* or *well to irrigate standing corn* or *the like*. (Mṣb.) — نَضَحَ *He moistened* a skin, in order that it might not break. — نَضَحَ الجُلَّةَ, aor. ـِ, inf. n. نَضْحٌ, *He sprinkled the palm-leaf date-basket with water, in order that its dates might stick together*: (L:) or *he scattered forth its contents*. (L, Ḳ.) — نَضَحَ (inf. n. نَضْحٌ, Ṣ,) *He watered* palm-trees, (Ḳ,) and standing corn &c., (TA,) *by means of a camel carrying the water*. (Ḳ.) — سُقِىَ الزَّرْعُ نَضْحًا *The standing corn* &c. *was watered by means of buckets*, (غُرُوب and دِلَآء,) *and camels carrying the water*; not by means of a channel opened for that purpose. (TA.) — هٰذِهِ نَخْلٌ تُنْضَحُ *These are palm-trees that are watered* [*by the means above mentioned*]. (Ṣ.) — فُلَانٌ يَسْقِى بِالنَّضْحِ [*Such a one waters* palm-trees &c. *by the means above mentioned*]. (Ṣ.) — يَنْضَحُ عَلَى البَعِيرِ *He drives the camel that carries the water for irrigation, watering palm-trees* [&c.] (Ṣ.) — نَضَحُوهُمْ بِالنَّبْلِ, (inf. n. نَضْحٌ, TA.) ‡ *They shot at them* [or *sprinkled them*] *with arrows*: (Ṣ, Ḳ:) *they scattered arrows among them*, like as water is sprinkled. (TA.) Mohammad said to the archers at the battle of Ohod, انْضَحُوا عَنَّا الخَيْلَ ‡ *Shoot ye at the horses and their riders with arrows* [*and so repel them from us*]. (Ṣ,* TA.) — نَضَحَ فَرْجَهُ, aor. ـِ and ـَ; (TA;) and ▾ انتضح and ▾ استنضح [both of which are thus used as intrans.]; (Ḳ;) *He sprinkled some water upon his pudendum after the ablution called* الوُضُوء: (Ḳ:) as also انْتَفَضَ. (TA.) — نَضَحَ بِالبَوْلِ عَلَى فَخِذَيْهِ *He made* [*a little sprinkling of*] *urine to fall upon his thighs*. (Ḳ.) Hence the saying in a trad., النَّضْحُ مِنَ النَّضْحِ, meaning, that he upon whom falls a little sprinkling of urine, like the heads of needles, as explained by Z, must sprinkle the part with water, and is not required to wash it. (TA.) — نَضَحَتْنَا السَّمَآءُ *The sky rained upon us*. (L.) — نَضَحَ, [aor. ـِ,] *He* (a horse) *sweated*. (Mṣb.) — نَضَحَ بِالعَرَقِ, inf. n. نَضْحٌ and نَضَحَانٌ, *He* (a man, and a horse,) *broke out with sweat*: and in like manner, the protuberance behind a camel's ear; and the arm-pit or the like. (L.) [See an ex. in a verse cited in art. عدو, conj. 3.] — يَنْضَحُ طِيبًا † *He diffuses the odour of perfume*: lit., sweats it. (L, from a trad.) — نَضَحَ *It* (sweat) *exuded*, or *came forth*. (Mṣb.) — نَضَحَتِ القِرْبَةُ, (Ṣ, Ḳ,) and الخَابِيَةُ, (Ṣ,) aor. ـِ, inf. n. نَضْحٌ and تَنْضَاحٌ, (Ṣ, Ḳ,) [the latter of an intensive form,] *The water-skin*, and *the jar*, (*being thin*, TA,) *sweated*, (ISk, Ṣ, Ḳ,) or *exuded its water*. (TA.) — نَضَحَ الجَبَلُ *The mountain sweated water between its masses of rock*. (TA.) — نَضَحَ الشَّجَرُ, inf. n. نَضْحٌ, TA,) ‡ *The trees began to break out with leaves*. (Aṣ, Ṣ, Ḳ.) — نَضَحَ الزَّرْعُ, and ▾ انضح, † *The standing corn became thick in its body*, (TA,) *and began to have the farinaceous substance in its grains, yet moist*, or *succulent*, or *tender*. (Ḳ.) — نَضَحَتِ العَيْنُ, (L, Ḳ,) aor. ـِ, inf. n. نَضْحٌ; (L;) and ▾ انتضحت, (L, Ḳ,) and ▾ تنضّحت; (Ḳ;) *The eye overflowed with tears*: (L, Ḳ:) *the eye filled with tears and then overflowed without stopping*. (L.) — نَضَحَ, aor. ـِ, *It* (a sea, or great river,) *flowed*. (TA, art. تير.) — انْضَحُوا الرَّحِمَ بِبِلَالِهَا: see بِلَالٌ. — نَضَحَ عَنْهُ, and ▾ ناضح عَنْ فُلَانٍ, (Ṣ, Ḳ,) aor. ـِ; (Ṣ;) and ▾ ناضح عنه, (Ḳ,) inf. n. مُنَاضَحَةٌ and نِضَاحٌ; (TA;) ‡ *He repelled from, and defended, such a one*: (Ṣ, Ḳ:) as also مَضَحَ: (Shujáa:) and نَضَحَ الرَّجُلَ *he repelled from the man*. (Kr.) — نَضَحَ عَنْ نَفْسِهِ ‡ *He defended himself with an argument, a plea*, or *an allegation*. (Ṣ.)

3: see 1.

4: see 1. — انضح عِرْضَهُ † *He aspersed his honour*, or *reputation*: (Ḳ:) *marred it*; as also أَمْضَحَهُ: (Shujáa Es-Sulamee:) *made people to carp at it*. (Khaleefeh.)

5: see 1 and 8. — رَأَيْتُهُ يَتَنَضَّحُ مِمَّا قُرِفَ بِهِ ‡ *I saw him deny*, (Ṣ, Ḳ,) *and declare himself clear of*, (Ṣ,) *that of which he was accused*, or *suspected*. (Ṣ, Ḳ.*) — تنضّح مِنْ أَمْرٍ ‡ *He pretended to be clear*, or *quit, of the thing*. (TA.)

8. انتضح عَلَيْهِمُ المَآءُ *The water became sprinkled upon them*. (Ṣ.) — انتضح البَوْلُ عَلَى الثَّوْبِ *The urine became sprinkled upon the garment*. (Mṣb.) — انتضح بِالنَّضُوحِ *He sprinkled himself with the kind of perfume called* نَضُوح. (L.) [And ▾ تنضّح is used in similar sense in art. غسل in the Ḳ.] See 1.

10: see 1.

نَضْخٌ *A rain between two rains; better than what is called* طَلّ; (L;) *i. q.* نَضْخٌ, with respect to rain. (Sh.) —— نَضَخَاتٌ [or نَضْحَاتٌ?] *A slight, or scanty, scattered shower of rain.* (L.) —— Also ▼ نَاضِخٌ *Rain.* (L.) —— نَضْخٌ † *Perfume that is thin, like water:* pl. نُضُوخٌ and أَنْضِخَةٌ: [see also نَضُوخٌ:] what is thick, like خَلُوق and غَالِيَة, is called نَضْخٌ. (L.) —— *A mark left by water, or anything thin, such as vinegar and the like:* differing from نَضْخٌ [q. v.]. (AA, in TA, art. نضح.)

نَضْخٌ and ▼ نَضِيخٌ ‡ *A watering-trough or tank;* or so called because it moistens [or allays] the thirst of camels: (IAar, Ṣ:) or *a small watering-trough* or *tank:* (TA:) or the latter *a watering-trough* or *tank that is near to the well, so as to be filled with the bucket;* and it may be large: (Lth:) pl. of the former أَنْضَاخٌ; and of the latter نُضُخٌ. (Ṣ.) —— نَضْخُ الوُضُوْءِ *What is sprinkled in the performance of the ablution called* الوضوء. (L.) [See نَضْخُ فَرْجِهِ.]

نَضُوخٌ: see نَضِيخَةٌ.

نَضُوخٌ مَزَادَةٌ *A* مزادة *that sweats, or exudes its water.* (TA.) —— نَضُوخٌ ‡ *A certain kind of perfume.* (Ṣ, Ḳ.) [See also نَضْخٌ.] —— قَوْسٌ نَضُوخٌ, and ▼ نَضِيخَةٌ, *A bow that impels the arrow with force, or sends it far, and that scatters the arrows much;* expl. by ▼ طَرُوحٌ نَضَّاخَةٌ بِالنَّبْلِ. (AHn, Ḳ.) —— النَّضُوخُ One of the names of *The bow.* (TA.)

نَضِيخٌ *Sweat.* (Ṣ.) —— See نَضْخٌ.

نَضَّاخٌ He *who drives the camel that carries water from a well &c., for irrigating land,* (Ṣ, Ḳ,) *and waters palm-trees* [&c.]. (Ṣ.) —— See قَوْسٌ نَضُوخٌ.

نَضَّاخَةٌ: see مِنْضَخَةٌ.

نَاضِخٌ ‡ *A camel* (Ṣ) *or an ass* or *a bull* (TA) *upon which water is drawn* (يُسْتَقَى عَلَيْهِ) [*from a well &c.*]: (Ṣ, TA:) *a camel that carries water* (يَحْمِلُ المَآءَ) *from a river* or *canal* or *well to irrigate seed-produce;* so called because it is a means of moistening [or allaying] thirst by the water which it carries: (Mṣb:) the female is called نَاضِخَةٌ (Ṣ, Mṣb) and سَانِيَةٌ [q. v.]: (Ṣ:) pl. نَوَاضِخُ. (Mṣb.) —— Afterwards applied to *Any camel:* as in the following instance, occurring in a trad., أَطْعِمْهُ نَاضِخَكَ *Give him thy camel to eat.* (Mṣb.) —— See نَضْخٌ.

مِنْضَخَةٌ (L, Ḳ) as also مِنْضَخَةٌ, (IAar, L,) vulg. ▼ نَضَّاخَةٌ, (Az,) *i. q.* زَرَّاقَةٌ, (IAar, L, [in some copies of the Ḳ زُرْقَة; in the CḲ زَرَاقَة,] i. e. *An instrument made of copper or brass for shooting forth naphtha* [*into a besieged place:* mentioned in several histories]. (L.)

نضخ

1. نَضَخَهُ, aor. ـَ, [and ـِ, see below], inf. n. نَضْخٌ, *He sprinkled him,* or *it,* [with water &c.]: or *i. q.* نَضَحَهُ: (Ḳ:) AZ says, نَضْخٌ signifies the *act of sprinkling,* like نَضْحٌ; these two words being syn.: you say نَضَخْتُ, aor. أَنْضَخُ: (Ṣ:) or the former signifies less than the latter: (Ḳ:) so most say: (L:) or the former signifies what is unintentional; and the latter, what is intentional: (IAar, L:) Aṣ says, that the latter is the act of man: (L:) and the former, he says, signifies more than the latter, and has no pret. nor aor.: and Aboo-'Othmán Et-Towwazee says, that the former signifies the mark, or effect, that remains upon a garment or other thing, and that the act is termed نَضْحٌ, with ح unpointed: (Ṣ:) Aṣ says, that نَضْخٌ has no verb nor act. part. n.; and A'Obeyd says, that it has no pret. nor aor. ascribed to any authority: or you say نَضَخْتُ الثَّوْبَ, aor. ـِ and ـَ, inf. n. نَضْخٌ, *I wetted the garment;* and it signifies more than نَضَحْتُ. (Mṣb.) نُضِخَتْ مَغَابِنُهَا, inf. n. نَضَخَانٌ, *Her* (a she-camel's) *arm-pits were sprinkled* with pitch. (Ṣ, L, from a verse of El-Ḳaṭámee.) أَصَابَهُ نَضْخٌ مِنْ كَذَا *A sprinkling, more* [or *less*] *than what is termed* نَضْحٌ, *came upon him.* (Aṣ, Ṣ.) —— نَضَخْنَاهُمْ بِالنَّبْلِ, (Yz, Ṣ,) and نضخنا النَّبْلَ فِيهِمْ, (Ḳ,) *i. q.* نضحناهم, (Yz, Ṣ,) *We* [*shot at them and*] *sprinkled them with arrows;* or *scattered arrows among them;* (Yz, Ṣ, Ḳ;) meaning, our enemies. (Ḳ.) —— نَضَخَ, (inf. n. نَضْخٌ, L,) *It* (water) *boiled forth vehemently* (*in gushing,* L,) from its source, (L, Ḳ,) or *boiled up vehemently.* (Aboo-'Alee, L, Ḳ.)

3. ناضخا, inf. n. مُنَاضَخَةٌ and نِضَاخٌ, *They sprinkled each other.* (Ṣ, Ḳ.)

8. انتضخ *It* (water) *became sprinkled.* (Ṣ, Ḳ.)

9. انضخّ and ▼ انضاخّ *It* (water) *poured out,* or *forth.* (TA.)

11: see 9.

نَضْخٌ *A mark,* or *effect, that remains upon a garment* or *other thing,* (Aboo-'Othmán Et-Towwazee, Ṣ, Ḳ,) *as the body,* (TA,) *from perfume,* (Ḳ,) or *mire, or a soil or pollution:* (TA:) or *from blood, and saffron, and mud, and the like:* نَضْحٌ being with water, and with anything thin, such as vinegar and the like. (AA.) [See also نَضْحٌ.]

نَضْخَةٌ *A rain; a shower of rain.* (Ṣ, Ḳ.)

غَيْثٌ نَضَّاخٌ *A copious rain.* (Ṣ, Mṣb, Ḳ.) —— عَيْنٌ نَضَّاخَةٌ *A copious spring of water:* (Ṣ:) or *a spring that boils forth,* or *gushes forth* (Ṣ, Mṣb) *copiously.* (Mṣb.) —— نَضَّاخَةُ الذِّفْرَى A she-camel *that sweats copiously in the part called* ذفرى, *behind the ear.* (L.)

مِنْضَخَةٌ, [in the TA منضخ,] vulgo نَضَّاخَةٌ, *i. q.* زَرَّاقَةٌ: (Ḳ, TA:) [in the CḲ, زَرَاقَة, which is a mistake: see مِنْضَخَةٌ].

نضد

1. نَضَدَ, aor. ـِ, (Ṣ, Ḳ, &c.,) inf. n. نَضْدٌ; (Ṣ, L, Mṣb;) and ▼ نضّد, (L, Ḳ,) inf. n. تَنْضِيدٌ; (Ṣ, L;) or the latter has an intensive signification; (Ṣ, L;) *He put* goods, household-goods, or commodities, (مَتَاع, Ṣ, L, Ḳ,) *one upon another:* (Ṣ, L, Mṣb, Ḳ:) or *put,* or *set,* them *together,* (T, A, L,) *in regular order,* or *piled up:* (A:) both verbs signify the same: (L, Ḳ:) or the latter, *he put* them *one upon another* [or *side by side*] *compactly.* (Ṣ, L.) —— [You say,] نَضَدْتُ اللَّبِنَ عَلَى المَيِّتِ [*I placed the crude bricks in order against the corpse, to support it;* as it is laid upon its right side, or so inclined that the face is towards Mekkeh]. (L.)

2. نضّد, inf. n. تَنْضِيدٌ, *He* [God] *made a person's teeth to be disposed in regular order.* (A.) —— See 1.

5. تَنَضَّدَتِ الأَسْنَانُ *The teeth were disposed in regular order.* (A.)

8. انتضد, [quasi-pass. of 1, *It was put,* or *set, one part upon,* or *beside, another, in regular order; was piled up,* or *became piled up*]. (Ḳ, art. فقر.) —— انتضد ‡ *It* (a people, A) *remained, stayed, abode,* or *dwelt,* in a place; (A, Ḳ;) *and collected* there. (A.)

نَضَدٌ *Goods, household-goods,* or *commodities, put one upon another:* (Ṣ, L, Ḳ:) or, *put,* or *set, together,* (A, L,) *in regular order,* or *piled up:* (A:) or the *best thereof:* (L, Ḳ:) or *such things in general:* but the first meaning is the most appropriate: (L:) pl. أَنْضَادٌ. (Ṣ, L.) —— رَأَيْتُ نَضَدًا مِنَ الثِّيَابِ وَالفُرُشِ *I saw a number of garments,* or *pieces of cloth, and of beds,* or *the like, put together in regular order,* or *piled up.* (A.) —— See نَضِيدَةٌ. —— نَضَدٌ *A couch-frame,* or *a raised couch,* (سرير,) *upon which goods, household-goods, or commodities, are put one upon another,* (Ṣ, L, Ḳ,) or *put,* or *set, together, in regular order,* or *piled up:* (A, L:) or simply, *a couch-frame,* or *raised couch;* (سرير;) so called because the things so termed are generally put upon it: (L, Mṣb:) or *a* مِشْجَب, or *a thing resembling this, upon which garments and household-goods are put, one upon another,* or *together.* (L.) —— نَضَدٌ ‡ *Glory; honour; dignity; might;* or *power;* (A;) *eminence;* or *nobility.* (Ḳ.) ——

نَضَدٌ ‡ *Eminent; or noble:* (L, K:) applied to a man: pl. أَنْضَادٌ. (L.) — Also, (A, L,) and the pl., (S, A, L,) ‡ *A man's paternal and maternal uncles* (S, A, L) *preëminent in nobility.* (S, L.) — Also, the pl., ‡ *The party, or company,* (L, K,) *and number,* (A, L, K,) *and auxiliaries, or assistants,* (A,) of a people, (L, K,) or of a man: (A:) and the sing. and pl., *companies, or congregated bodies, of men.* (A.) — نَضَدٌ ‡ *A fat she-camel;* (K;) likened to a couch-frame, or a raised couch, upon which are the things termed نَضَد; (TA;) as also ▾ نَضُودٌ. (K.) — أَنْضَادٌ, of mountains, *Stones, such as are called جَنَادِل, one upon another.* (S, L, K.) Also, of clouds, *Portions piled up, one above another:* (S, L, K:) sing. نَضَدٌ. (L.)

نَضُودٌ: see نَضَدٌ and نَضِيدٌ.

نَضِيدٌ and ▾ مَنْضُودٌ (Msb, K,) and ▾ مُنَضَّدٌ, [or the last has an intensive signification, as is shewn above,] Goods, household-goods, or commodities, (K,) *put one upon another:* (Msb, K:) [or *put, or set, together, in regular order, or piled up:* and the last, *put one upon another, or side by side, compactly:* see 1]. — طَلْعٌ نَضِيدٌ, in the Kur, [l. 10,] *Spadices of palm-trees [having their flowers] compacted, or compactly disposed;* (L;) *yet in their envelopes;* (Fr, L;) for when they have come forth therefrom they cease to be نضيد. (L.) — ▾ طَلْحٌ مَنْضُودٌ, in the Kur, [lvi. 28,] *Gum-acacias having fruit or leaves closely set, one above another, from bottom to top, without their trunks being apparent below.* (L.) — شَجَرُ الجَنَّةِ نَضِيدٌ مِنْ أَصْلِهَا إِلَى فَرْعِهَا *The trees of paradise are closely set with leaves and fruit, one above another, from bottom to top, without having trunks apparent:* (L, from a trad.:) and similarly ▾ نَضُودٌ (Jel, lvi. 20.)

نَضِيدَةٌ *A pillow:* and *any stuffed article of household furniture:* (L, K:) pl. نَضَائِدُ: and ▾ نَضَدٌ is used as a coll. n. (L.)

مَنْضُودٌ: see نَضِيدٌ.

دُرٌّ مُنَضَّدٌ *Pearls arranged, or put together, in regular order.* (A.) — See نَضِيدٌ.

نضر

1. نَضَرَ, aor. ـُ; (IAar, S, A, Msb, K;) and نَضِرَ, aor. ـَ; and نَضُرَ, aor. ـُ; (IAar, S, A, K;) the last [also] mentioned by A'Obeyd; (S;) inf. n. نَضَارَةٌ, (S, A, Msb, K,) of the first; (S, Msb;) and نُضُورٌ (K) and نَضْرَةٌ, (S, A, K,) of the second, (S,) or this is a simple subst., (Msb,) and نَضَرٌ, (TA,) [also of the second;] and نَضْرٌ, (K;) [of the third;] and ▾ أَنْضَرَ; (IAar, L, K, TA;) *It* (a tree, A, K, and a plant, A, and foliage, TA, and a colour, K, and a face, IAar, S, Msb, K, and anything, TA,) *was, or became, beautiful* (S, Msb, K,) *and bright:* (S* [see نَضْرَةٌ below] or, when said of a face, tropically used, (A,) signifying as above: (TA:) or ‡ *it was, or became, beautiful and fresh:* or *beautiful and fine-skinned, so that the blood appeared [through the skin]:* syn. حَسُنَ وَغَضَّ: (A:) or *pleasant:* (Fr:) and ▾ انضر, said of a tree, *its foliage became green.* (TA.) — [When said of a man, sometimes signifying *He was, or became, in a state of enjoyment,* or *in a plentiful and pleasant and easy state of life;* agreeably with a usage of نَضَرَ and ▾ نَضَّرَ and ▾ أَنْضَرَ to be mentioned below. And in like manner, when said of life, it signifies *It was, or became plentiful and pleasant and easy.*] — نَضَرَهُ اللّٰهُ, (IAar, S, A, Msb, K,) aor. ـُ, (Msb,) inf. n. نَضْرٌ; (TA;) and ▾ نَضَّرَهُ, (S, A, K,) or this has an intensive signification; (Msb;) and ▾ انضره; (IAar, S, A, K;) when the pronoun relates to the face, (IAar, S, A,) in which case it is tropical, (A,) [or to a tree, or colour, as is implied in the K,] *God made it beautiful* (S, A, K,) *and bright.* (S,* TA.) — When the pronoun relates to a man, the meaning (of the first of these three forms, as mentioned by En-Nadr and Sh and in the Mgh and TA, and of the ▾ second, as mentioned by As, and En-Nadr and Sh, &c., and of the ▾ third, as mentioned in the TA,) is *God made him to have enjoyment,* or *plentiful and pleasant and easy life;* syn. نَعَّمَهُ; (S, Mgh, Msb, TA;) or جَعَلَهُ نَاضِرًا [which signifies the same]: (A'Obeyd:) or نَضَرَهُ اللّٰهُ, (El-Azdee, Mgh,) and ▾ نَضَّرَهُ اللّٰهُ, (El-Hasan El-Muäddib, TA,) signifies † *God made his rank,* or *station, good* (El-Azdee, El-Hasan El-Muäddib, Mgh, TA,) *among mankind:* (El-Hasan El-Muäddib, TA:) not relating to beauty of the face; (El-Azdee, El-Hasan El-Muäddib, Mgh, TA:) but is similar to the saying, أُطْلُبُوا الحَوَائِجَ إِلَى حِسَانِ الوُجُوهِ [which see explained in art. وجه]. (El-Hasan El-Muäddib, TA.) As cites this verse:

* نَضَّرَ اللّٰهُ أَعْظُمًا دَفَنُوهَا *
* بِسِجِسْتَانَ طَلْحَةَ الطَّلَحَاتِ *

[*May God grant enjoyment to bones which they have buried in Sijistán:* (I mean) *Talhat-et-Talahát*]. (TA.) And it is said in a trad., نَضَّرَ اللّٰهُ عَبْدًا سَمِعَ مَقَالَتِي فَوَعَاهَا ثُمَّ أَدَّاهَا إِلَى مَنْ يَسْمَعْهَا, (Sh, S,* A,* Mgh,* TA,) or ▾ نَضَّرَ, (Sh, S, in which latter we read امرأ in the place of عبدا, and A, in which we find مَنْ in the place of عبدا, and Mgh; the reading ▾ نضّر alone being given in the copies which I have of the S and A;) *May God cause to have enjoyment,* or *a plentiful and pleasant and easy life,* [*the servant,* or *man, who hears what I say, and keeps it in mind, then conveys it to him who hears it:*] (S, Mgh, in explanation of the latter reading, and TA, in explanation of both readings:) or † *may God make to have a good rank* or *station* &c. (Mgh, in explanation of the former reading.)

2. نَضَّرَهُ اللّٰهُ: see نَضَرَهُ, throughout.

4. انضر: see نَضَرَ, in two places. — انضرهُ اللّٰهُ: see نَضَرَهُ, throughout.

نَضْرٌ (S, A, Msb, K) and ▾ نُضَارٌ (S, A, K, [in the CK نَضار] and TA) and ▾ نَضِيرٌ (S, Msb, K) and ▾ أَنْضَرُ (K [without tenween, though this is not shown in the K, as it is originally an epithet, though it may be obsolete as an epithet,]) *Gold;* (S, A, Msb, K;) as also ▾ نِضَارٌ: (Es-Sukkaree:) or *silver;* (K;) as also ▾ نِضَارٌ: (Es-Sukkaree:) or *generally the former:* (TA:) pl. [of pauc.] (of the first, S.) أَنْضُرٌ, (S, K,) and [of mult.] نِضَارٌ: (K:) or (so accord. to the S and A, but in the K, and) ▾ نُضَارٌ signifies *what is pure,* (S, A, K,) of gold &c., (A,) or of native or unwrought gold or silver, (Lth, K,) and of wood, (Lth,) or of anything: (S:) and is used as an epithet, applied to gold: (TA:) and ▾ نَضْرَةٌ [n. un. of نَضْرٌ] signifies *a molten piece of gold.* (TA.)

نَضِرٌ: see نَاضِرٌ.

نَضْرَةٌ *Beauty* (S, Msb, K,) *and brightness:* (S, TA:) so in the Kur, lxxvi. 11. (Jel.) [The above explanation in the Msb and K, "beauty," is evidently imperfect. Accord. to the Msb, the word is a simple subst., not an inf. n.] † *Pleasantness* of countenance. — نَضْرَةُ النَّعِيمِ † *The beauty and brightness of aspect characteristic of enjoyment, or of a plentiful and pleasant and easy state of existence:* so in the Kur, lxxxiii. 24: (Bd, Jel:) or *the brightness, or glistening, and moisture* (نَدًا) [*upon the skin*] *characteristic thereof.* (Fr.) — *Enjoyment;* or *a plentiful and pleasant and easy life;* syn. نَعْمَةٌ [in the CK نِعْمَة]. (A, K.) — *Richness;* or *competence* or *sufficiency.* (A, K.) — *Life.* (A, K.) — See also نَضْرٌ.

نُضَارٌ: } see نَضْرٌ; each in two places. See also غَرَبٌ.
نِضَارٌ: }

نَضِيرٌ: see نَاضِرٌ, in two places: — and see نَضْرٌ.

نَاضِرٌ (A, L, K) and ▾ نَضِيرٌ (A, L, Msb, K) and ▾ نَضِرٌ, (A, L,) [being epithets from نَضَرَ and نَضُرَ and نَضِرَ, respectively,] and ▾ أَنْضَرُ, accord. to the K, but in the place of this we find in the corresponding passage in the L the verb أَنْضَرَ, with the addition "is like نَضَرَ," (TA,) *Beautiful*

(Mṣb, Ḳ) *and bright.* (TA.) So in the Ḳur, lxxv. 22, وُجُوهٌ يَوْمَئِذٍ نَاضِرَةٌ † *Faces on that day shall be beautiful and bright:* (Bḍ, Jel:) or *shining by reason of enjoyment,* or *of a beautiful and pleasant and easy state of existence.* (Fr.) [These epithets have also other, similar, significations, shown by explanations of نَضْرٌ and its variations.] نَاضِرٌ is coupled with غَضٌّ, as an epithet applied to a boy, (A,) and so ▼ نَضِيرٌ; (TA,) and نَاضِرَةٌ with غَضَّةٌ, applied to a girl, (A,) and so نَضِيرَةٌ; (TA;) and thus used are tropical. (A.) — نَاضِرٌ also signifies *Intense in greenness:* (Ḳ:) you say أَخْضَرُ نَاضِرٌ [*intense,* or *bright, green*], (Ṣ, Ḳ,) like as you say أَصْفَرُ فَاقِعٌ and أَبْيَضُ نَاصِعٌ: (Ṣ:) and in like manner it is used as an intensive epithet applied to any colour: you say أَحْمَرُ نَاضِرٌ [*intense,* or *bright, red*], and أَصْفَرُ نَاضِرٌ [*intense,* or *bright, yellow*]: (Ḳ:) so says IAạr: (TA:) or أَخْضَرُ نَاضِرٌ signifies *smooth green,* accord. to A'Obeyd, and Az adds, *glistening in its clearness.* (TA.)

أَنْضَرُ : see نَضْرٌ : — and see نَاضِرٌ.

[نضف, &c.
See Supplement.]

نطأ

[1. نَطَأَ بِسَلْحِهِ : see نطأ.]

نطب

1. نَطَبَهُ (aor. ـِ, inf. n. نَطْبٌ, TA,) *He struck* [or *fillipped*] *his ear with his finger.* (Ḳ.) ▼ انطب أُذُنَهُ, and أَنْقَرَ, and بَلَّطَ, signify *the same.* (AA.)

3. نَاطَبَهُمْ, (inf. n. مُنَاطَبَةٌ, TA,) *He incited them against each other,* (Ḳ,) *and acted in an evil* or *mischievous manner towards them.* (TA.)

4: see 1.

نَطْبَةٌ i. q. نَطْبَةٌ, i. e., *A single act of piercing,* or *pecking, with the beak,* of a cock, &c. (Az.)

نِطَابٌ The *head.* (Th, Ḳ.) Respecting the saying of El-Jo'eyd El-Murádee,

نَحْنُ ضَرَبْنَاهُ على نِطَابِهِ *

ISk says, No one has explained it, and the reading better known is على تِطْيَابِهِ, meaning "notwithstanding the sweetness (طيب) that was in him:" for the man spoken of was going in to a bride of the tribe of Murád: but accord. to some, نطاب here signifies The *tendon of the neck;* syn. حَبْلُ العُنُقِ; so in the Ḳ, on the authority of Aboo-'Adnán alone; or حبل العَاتِقِ, accord. to IAạr, who cites this verse:

* نَحْنُ ضَرَبْنَاهُ عَلَى نِطَابِهِ *
* قُلْنَا بِهِ قُلْنَا بِهِ قُلْنَا بِهِ *

[*We smote him on the tendon of the upper part of his shoulders: we slew him: we slew him: we slew him*]. قلنا به signifies قَتَلْنَاهُ. (TA.)

نَاطِبَةٌ, and نَاطِبٌ, sing. of نَوَاطِبُ in the following sense: (TA:) The *holes that are made in a thing with which one clears,* or *clarifies,* [i. e. *strains,* or *filters*], *and through which what is cleared* [or *strained*] *passes forth:* (Ḳ:) the *holes of a strainer for wine, &c.* (TA.) — See مِنْطَبٌ.

مِنْطَبٌ and مِنْطَبَةٌ and ▼ نَاطِبٌ *A strainer; a colander.* (Ḳ.)

مَنْطَبَةٌ *Stupid; foolish; of little sense:* (Ḳ:) an epithet applied to a man. (TA.)

نطح

1. نَطَحَهُ, aor. ـَ and ـِ, (Ṣ, Ḳ,) inf. n. نَطْحٌ, (Ṣ,) *He* (a ram, Ṣ, L, and the like, L) *smote him with his horn.* (Ḳ.) — مَا نَطَحَتْ فِيهِ جَمَّآءُ ذَاتَ قَرْنٍ [*A horned animal did not smite with its horn for him a hornless ewe*]: a proverb, said of him who has perished unavenged. (L.) [See also Freytag's Arab. Prov., ii. 507.] — نَطَحَهُ عَنْهُ ‡ *He pushed him,* or *thrust him, away from him, and removed him.* (A.)

3. نَاطَحَا, inf. n. نِطَاحٌ (L, Mṣb) and مُنَاطَحَةٌ, (Mṣb,) *They two* (rams or he-goats) *smote each other with their horns.* (L.) — بَيْنَهُمَا نِطَاحٌ ‡ [*Between them two is a contention like that of two rams*]; said of two learned men, and of two merchants. (A.) — جَرَى لَنَا فِي السُّوقِ نِطَاحٌ ‡ [*There happened to us in the market a contention like that of two rams*]. (A.) — نَاطَحَهُ ‡ [*He,* or *it, faced,* or *was* or *came opposite to him,* or *it*]: نِطَاحٌ is syn. with مُقَابَلَةٌ in the dial. of El-Ḥijáz. (TA.)

6: see 8. — تَنَاطَحَتِ الأَمْوَاجُ, and السُّيُولُ, ‡ [*The waves, and the torrents, conflicted,* or *dashed together.*] (A.)

8. انتطحت الكِبَاشُ, and ▼ تناطحت, (Ṣ, Ḳ,) *The rams smote one another with their horns.* (Ḳ.) — لَا يَنْتَطِحُ فِيهَا عَنْزَانِ [*Two she-goats will not, in it, smite each other with their horns*]: i. e., two weak persons will not encounter each other in it: alluding to a case in which there will not happen any discord or contention. (L, from a trad.)

نَطَّاحٌ : see نَطُوحٌ.

نَطِيحٌ *Smitten with the horn and so killed:* fem. with ة: (L, Ḳ:) pl. نَطْحَى (L) and نَطَائِحُ: (Lḥ, L:) you say also نَعْجَةٌ نَطِيحٌ, as well as نطيحة. (L.) — Also نَطِيحَةٌ *A sheep* or *goat* (Az) *smitten with the horn and so killed,* (Az, Ṣ,) and of which the flesh is therefore unlawful to be eaten: (Az:) the ة is added because it is made a subst., not an epithet: (Az:) or because the quality of a subst. predominates in it, as in the case of فَرِيسَةٌ and أَكِيلَةٌ and رَمِيَّةٌ. (Ṣ.) — نَطِيحٌ and ▼ نَاطِحٌ ‡ *What comes to thee from before thee,* (or *faces thee,* L,) *of birds and wild animals* (Ṣ, L, Ḳ) *&c., which one rouses by throwing a stone* or *by crying out, and from the course of which one augurs evil or good:* (L:) contr. of قَعِيدٌ. (Ṣ.) [The نطيح or ▼ ناطح is of evil omen.] — Hence, (TA,) نَطِيحٌ ‡ An *unfortunate,* or *unlucky,* man. (Ḳ.) — نَطِيحٌ A horse *having a blaze,* or *white mark on his face, extending to one of his ears,* which is deemed unlucky: (L:) or a horse *having on his forehead two circular* or *spiral curls of hair* (دَائِرَتَانِ), which are disliked: (Ṣ, L, Ḳ:) if there be but one, it is called دَائِرَةُ اللَّطَاةِ; and this is not disliked; (Ṣ;) or it is called لَطْمَةٌ; and the horse, لَطِيمٌ. (L.)

كَبْشٌ نَطَّاحٌ [*A ram that smites much with his horn*]: (Ṣ:) and ▼ نَطُوحٌ [signifies the same: and] is applied to a man [app. as meaning *who pushes, thrusts,* or *repels, much,* or *vehemently*]. (IAạr, TA in art. ردس.)

دَائِرَةُ النَّاطِحِ *A certain circular* or *spiral curl of hair on a horse,* which is deemed unlucky. (L.) [See نَطِيحٌ.] — نَاطِحٌ ‡ *A difficulty; a distressing event; an affliction; a calamity:* pl. نَوَاطِحُ. (Ṣ, Ḳ.) Ex. أَصَابَهُ نَاطِحٌ *A difficulty,* or *distressing event, befell him.* (Ṣ.) نَوَاطِحُ الدَّهْرِ *The difficulties, &c., of fortune.* (Ṣ.) — النَّطْحُ ‡ وَالنَّاطِحُ [*The two stars called*] الشَّرَطَانِ, [q. v.,] *which are* [*the two stars in*] *the two horns of Aries:* (Ṣ, Ḳ:) [*the first of the Mansions of the Moon:* the latter is β, and the former α:] ISd says, that ▼ النَّطْحُ is *a star which is one of the Mansions of the Moon, and from* [*the auroral rising of*] *which one augurs evil:* and IAạr says, that one says, نَطْحٌ and النَّطْحُ, without and with ال; and the like in the case of the name of any of the Mansions of the Moon. (TA.) The Arabs said إِذَا طَلَعَ النَّطْحُ طَابَ السَّطْحُ ‡ [*When En-Naṭ-ḥ rises aurorally, the house-top becomes pleasant* as a place on which to sit in the evening, or on which to sleep]. (A.) — مَا لَهُ نَاطِحٌ وَلَا خَابِطٌ *He has neither sheep, or goat, nor camel.* (Ṣ, Ḳ.)

نطر

1. نَطَرَ, (IḲṭṭ, Mṣb,) aor. ـُ, (TA,) inf. n. نَطْرٌ

(IKṭṭ, Mṣb, Ḳ) and نِطَارَةٌ, (Ṣgh, Ḳ,) *He kept,* or *watched, vines,* (IKṭṭ, Mṣb, Ḳ,) and *palm-trees,* (Ḳ,) and *seed-produce.* (TA.) See نَطْرَةٌ and نَاطُورٌ.

نَطْرَةٌ, with the unpointed ط, signifies The *act of guarding,* or *watching with the eyes:* and hence the word ▼نَاطُورٌ. (IAạr, Mṣb, TA.)

نَطْرُونٌ, with fet-h, [*Natron;*] the *Armenian* بُورَق, or بُوْرَق; (thus differently written here in different copies of the Ḳ;) or [rather] the *Egyptian* بُورَق: (Ḳ, art. برق:) the best kind [of بورق] is the Armenian, which is soft, or fragile, light, and white: then the rose-coloured: and the strongest is the Ifreekee: there is a kind found in Egypt, in two places: one of these is in the western part of the country, in the neighbourhood of a district called Eṭ-Ṭarráneh; and it is transparent, green and red; the green being the more in request; the other is in [the district called] El-Fákooseeyeh; and this is not so good as the former. (TA.) [See also بُورَق.]

نُطَارٌ *A scarecrow* (خَيَالٌ) *set up in the midst of seed-produce.* (Ṣgh, Ḳ.)

نَاطِرٌ: see نَاطُورٌ.

نَاطُورٌ *A keeper,* or *watcher,* (Ṣ, Mṣb, Ḳ, &c.,) *of vines,* (Ṣ, Ḳ,) and *of palm-trees,* (Ḳ,) and *of seed-produce:* (Mṣb, TA:) as also ▼نَاطُورَةٌ (El-Bári', Mṣb) and ▼نَاطِرٌ: (Ṣ, Ḳ:) pl. (of the first, TA) نَوَاطِيرُ (Az, Ṣ, A, Mṣb, Ḳ) and (of the last, TA) نُطَّارٌ and نُطَرَآءُ and نَطَرَةٌ: (Ḳ:) it is a foreign word, (أَعْجَمِىٌّ, Ḳ,) not pure Arabic, (TA,) of the dial. of the people of Es-Sawád: (Lth, Mṣb, TA:) Az says, I know not whether it be taken from the language of the people of Es-Sawád or be Arabic: (TA:) accord. to AḤn, it is Arabic: (TA:) and IAạr says, that it is from نَطْرَةٌ, meaning as explained above: (Mṣb, TA:) IDrd says, that it is with ظ, (A, Mṣb,) from النَّظَرُ; (A;) but in the language of the Nabatheans with ط; (Mṣb;) that the Nabatheans change the former letter into ط. (A.)

نَاطُورَةٌ: see نَاطُورٌ.

نطس

1. نَطِسَ, aor. ـَ, (Ṣ, Ḳ,) inf. n. نَطَسٌ, (Ṣ,) *He was,* or *became, learned,* or *knowing,* (Ḳ,) *in affairs, and skilful therein:* (TA:) or *he examined things minutely, and attained the utmost knowledge of them.* (Ṣ.)

4. مَا أَنْطَسَهُ *How intelligent and knowing is he in affairs!* (TA.)

5. تنطّس *He took extraordinary pains,* or *exceeded the usual bounds, in cleansing or purifying himself,* or *in removing himself far from unclean things or impurities:* (Aṣ, Ṣ:) or *he shunned,* or *removed himself far from, unclean things:* (M, A, Ḳ:) and *he was dainty, nice, exquisite, refined,* or *scrupulously nice, and exact,* syn. تَأَنَّقَ, (Aṣ, M, A, Ḳ,) in cleanliness; (Ḳ;) and in speech, (A, Ḳ,) *so as never to speak otherwise than chastely;* (TA;) and in diet and apparel, (A, Ḳ,) *so as never to eat or wear anything but what was clean,* (A,) or *so as never to eat anything but what was clean nor wear anything but what was good;* (TA;) and in all affairs. (Ḳ.) It is said in a trad. of 'Omar, لَوْ لَا التَّنَطُّسُ مَا بَالَيْتُ أَلَّا أَغْسِلَ يَدِى, (Ṣ, M,) i. e., *Were it not for the being scrupulously nice and exact, I had not cared for my not washing my hand.* (M.) —— تنطّس فيه *He examined it* (anything) *minutely.* (A.) —— تنطّس الأَخْبَارَ, (Ṣ,) or عَنِ الأَخْبَارِ, (M, A,) *He searched,* or *sought, for,* or *after, news,* or *tidings; searched* or *inquired into, investigated, scrutinized,* or *examined, news,* or *tidings.* (Ṣ, M, A.)

نَطْسٌ : } see نَطِسٌ; the former, in two places;
نُطُسٌ : } and the latter, in four.

نَطِسٌ *Learned,* or *knowing,* (A, Ḳ;) as also ▼نَطُسٌ (Ḳ) and ▼نَطْسٌ (A, Ḳ) and نِطَاسِىٌّ and ▼نَطَاسِىٌّ: (Ḳ:) or *learned,* or *knowing, in affairs, and skilful therein:* as also ▼نَطْسٌ and ▼نَطُسٌ: (ISk, TA:) *intelligent,* or *skilful, and scrupulously nice and exact* (مُتَنَوِّق), *in affairs:* (A:) or one *who examines things minutely, and attains the utmost knowledge of them:* as also ▼نَطُسٌ and ▼مُتَنَطِّسٌ: (Ṣ:) or *learned,* or *knowing, in affairs:* نِطِّيسٌ ▼ *skilful in physic &c.;* as also ▼نَطُسٌ and ▼نِطَاسِىٌّ: (M:) or ▼نِطِّيسٌ (Ṣ, A, Ḳ, TA) and ▼نَطَاسِىٌّ and ▼نِطَاسِىٌّ (Ṣ, TA) and ▼نَطَاسِىٌّ, (A'Obeyd, Ṣ,) *a student of physic,* (Ṣ, Ḳ, TA,) *who examines it minutely;* (TA;) or *learned,* or *knowing, in physic;* in Greek نُسْطَاس [γνώστης]: (A, TA:*) and ▼مُتَنَطِّسٌ one *who is dainty, nice, exquisite, refined,* or *scrupulously nice and exact* (مُتَنَوِّق), *and who chooses* or *selects* [*what is best*]; (IAạr;) or any one *who takes extraordinary pains,* or *exceeds the usual bounds,* in a thing: (M:) also ▼نَطِيسٌ, [without teshdeed,] a *skilful* man: (TA:) and ▼نُطُسٌ, [pl. of نَطِسٌ or نَطُسٌ or نَطِيسٌ,] *skilful physicians.* (A, Ḳ.) —— Also, One *who shuns, or removes himself far from, unclean things;* (Ḳ, TA;) *who is scrupulously nice and exact* (مُتَأَنِّق) *in affairs:* (TA:) and نَطِسَةٌ a woman *who shuns, or removes herself far from, foul, evil,* or *unseemly, things:* (AA, TA:) and نُطُسٌ, [pl. of نَطِسٌ,] men *who do thus:* (Ḳ, TA:) and ▼نُطَسَةٌ a man *who shuns much, or removes himself very far from, unclean things, and is very dainty, nice, exquisite, refined,* or *scrupulously nice and exact* (كَثِيرُ التَّأَنُّقِ) in cleanliness, and in speech, and in diet and apparel, and in all affairs. (Ḳ,* TA.) See 5.

نُطُسٌ :
نُطَسَةٌ :
نَطِيسٌ : } see نَطِسٌ, throughout.
نِطَاسِىٌّ :
نِطِّيسٌ :

نَاطِسٌ, (accord. to one copy of the Ṣ, and the L, and the CḲ, and a MS. copy of the Ḳ,) or ▼نَاطُوسٌ, (accord. to the TA, as from the Ḳ,) or both, (accord. to one copy of the Ṣ,) *A spy, who searches for news,* or *tidings, and then brings them.* (Ṣ, L, Ḳ, TA.)

نَاطُوسٌ: see نَاطِسٌ.

مُتَنَطِّسٌ: see نَطِسٌ, in two places.

نطش

نَطْشَانُ an imitative sequent to عَطْشَانُ; (Ṣ, Ḳ;) not used alone. (Ṣ, art. عطش.)

[نطع, &c.

See Supplement.]

نظر

1. نَظَرَ إِلَيْهِ, (Ṣ, M, A, Mṣb, Ḳ,) and نَظَرَهُ, (M, A, Mṣb, Ḳ,) aor. ـُ, (M, A, &c.,) and أَنْظُورُ is substituted for أَنْظُرُ in the dial. of certain Arabs, (IDrd, TṢ, Ḳ,) or, accord. to Lb. in the Bughyet-el-Ámál, the و is here added only [by poetic license,] to make the sound of the ḍammeh full, agreeably with other instances; (TA;) and نَظِرَ إِلَيْهِ, and نَظِرَهُ, aor. ـَ, (A, Ḳ,) the verb being like سَمِعَ accord. to the correct copies of the Ḳ, [and so in the A,] but in one copy of the Ḳ, like ضَرَبَ; (TA;) inf. n. نَظَرٌ, (Ṣ, M, A, Mṣb, Ḳ,) and نَظْرٌ is allowable, as a contraction of the former, (Lth,) and نَظَرَانٌ (Ṣ, Ḳ,) and مَنْظَرٌ (M, A, Ḳ) and مَنْظَرَةٌ and تَنْظَارٌ, (M, Ḳ,) [which last is an intensive form; *He looked at,* or *towards, in order to see, him,* or *it;*] *he considered,* or *viewed, him or it with his eye;* (Ṣ, A, Ḳ;) *with the sight of the eye;* (Mṣb;) [i. e. *looked at him* or *it;*] as also ▼تنظّرهُ: (Ḳ:) and ▼انتظرهُ signifies the same as تنظّرهُ and نَظَرَهُ [but app. in another sense, to be mentioned below, and not in the sense explained above, though the latter is implied in the TA; and the same may be meant when it is said that ▼تنظّر is syn. with نَظَرَ, if this assertion, which I find in the M, have been copied

without consideration, and be not confirmed by an example]: (TA:) or نَظَرَ إِلَيْهِ signifies *he extended*, or *stretched*, or *raised*, [or *directed*,] *his sight towards him* or *it*, *whether he saw him* or *did not see him*. (TA.) The usage of النَّظَرُ as relating to the sight is most common with the vulgar, but not with persons of distinction, who use it more in another sense, to be explained below. (TA.) You say, نَظَرَ إِلَيْهِ نَظْرَةً حُلْوَةً [*He looked at him*, or *towards him*, *with one sweet look*.] (A.) And نَظَرَ فِى المِنْظَارِ [*He looked in the mirror*]. (A.) And نَظَرَ فِى الكِتَابِ [*He looked into*, or *inspected*, *the writing* or *book*], (A, Mṣb,) which is for نَظَرَ المَكْتُوبَ فِى الكِتَابِ [*he looked at what was written in the writing* or *book*], or has a different meaning to be explained below. (Mṣb.) And هُوَ يَنْظُرُ حَوْلَهُ [lit., *He looks around him*; meaning,] *he looks much*. (A.) [See also نَظْرٌ below.] — نَظَرَتِ الأَرْضُ, (Ṣgh, Ḳ,) and نَظَرَتِ الأَرْضُ بِعَيْنٍ, and بِعَيْنَيْنِ, (A,) ‡ *The earth*, or *land*, *showed* (A, Ṣgh, Ḳ) *to the eye* (Ṣgh, Ḳ) *its plants* or *herbage*. (A, Ṣgh, Ḳ.) — نَظَرَ إِلَيْهِ ‡ *It looked towards*, meaning *faced*, *him* or *it*. So in the Ḳur, [vii. 197,] وَتَرَاهُمْ يَنْظُرُونَ إِلَيْكَ وَهُمْ لَا يُبْصِرُونَ ‡ *Thou seest them look towards thee*, i.e., *face thee*, *but they see not*; referring to idols, accord. to A'Obeyd. (TA.) And you say, دَارِى تَنْظُرُ إِلَى دَارِ فُلَانٍ ‡ *My house faces the house of such a one*. (Ṣ.) And نَظَرَ إِلَيْكَ الجَبَلُ ‡ *The mountain faced thee*: (A:) as in the following ex.: إِذَا أَخَذْتَ فِى طَرِيقِ كَذَا فَنَظَرَ إِلَيْكَ الجَبَلُ فَخُذْ عَنْ يَمِينِهِ أَوْ يَسَارِهِ ‡ [*When thou takest such a road, and the mountain faces thee, then take thou the way by the right of it* or *the left of it*.] (Ṣ.) — [Hence, perhaps,] نَظَرَ الدَّهْرُ إِلَى بَنِى فُلَانٍ فَأَهْلَكَهُمْ [app. meaning, † *Fortune opposed the sons of such a one and destroyed them*]: (Ṣ [immediately following there the ex. which immediately precedes it here:]) or نَظَرَ إِلَيْهِمِ الدَّهْرُ signifies ‡ *Fortune destroyed them*: (M, A:) but (says ISd) I am not certain of this. (M.) — النَّظَرُ also signifies † *The turning the mind in various directions in order to perceive* a thing [mentally], and *the seeing* a thing: and sometimes it means † *the considering and investigating*: [and as a subst., *speculation*, or *intellectual examination*:] and sometimes, † *the knowledge that results from* [*speculation* or] *investigation*. (El-Baṣáïr.) It is mostly used as relating to the intellect by persons of distinction; and as relating to the sight, most commonly by the vulgar. (TA.) [It is said that] when you say نَظَرْتُ إِلَيْهِ, it means only [*I looked at*, or *towards*, *him* or *it*] *with the eye*: but when you say نَظَرْتُ فِى الأَمْرِ, it may mean [† *I looked into*, *inspected*, *examined*, or *investigated*, *the thing* or *affair*] *by thought and consideration*, *intellectually*, or *with the mind*: (TA:) [this remark, however, is not altogether correct, as may be seen from what follows: the truth seems to be, that نَظَرَهُ and نَظَرَ إِلَيْهِ may be used in the latter of these two senses, though نَظَرَ فِيهِ is most common in this sense.] It is said in the Ḳur, [x. 101,] قُلِ ٱنْظُرُوا مَا ذَا فِى السَّمٰوَاتِ † *Say*, *Consider ye what is in the heavens*. (TA.) And you say, نَظَرَ إِلَيْهِ *He saw it*, *and* † *thought upon it*, *and endeavoured to understand it*, or *to know its result*. (TA.) [And *He looked to it*, or *at it*, or *examined it*, *intellectually*; *regarded it*; *had a view to it*.] And نَظَرَ فِيهِ † *He considered it*: (TA:) or *thought upon it*; namely a writing or book; or when such is the object it may have another meaning, explained before; and an affair: and with this is held to accord the saying وَفِيهِ نَظَرٌ, q. v. infrà, voce نَظَرٌ: (Mṣb:) and ‡ *he thought upon it*, *measuring it*, or *comparing it*. (M, Ḳ, TḲ. In the M and Ḳ, only the inf. n., نَظَرٌ, of the verb in this sense is mentioned.) And نَظَرَ فِى أَمْوَالِ الأَيْتَامِ † *He considered*, or *examined*, [or *estimated*,] *the possessions of the orphans*, *in order to know them*. (Mṣb.) And similar to this is the phrase [in the Ḳur, xxxvii. 86,] فَنَظَرَ نَظْرَةً فِى النُّجُومِ, meaning, † *And he examined the science of the stars*: (Mṣb:) [or *he took a mental view of the stars*, *as if to divine from them*.] النَّظَرُ when used unrestrictedly by those who treat of scholastic theology means الاِعْتِبَارُ [† *The thinking upon a thing*, *and endeavouring to understand it*, or *to know its result*; or *judging of what is hidden from what is apparent*; or *reasoning from analogy*]. (MF.) — نَظَرَ بَيْنَهُمْ, inf. n. نَظَرٌ, [app. for نَظَرَ فِى مَا بَيْنَهُمْ,] † *He judged between them*. (Ḳ.) — نَظَرَتْ, (TA,) inf. n. نَظَرٌ, † *She practised divination*; (Ḳ,* TA;) which is a kind of examination with insight and skill. (TA, from a trad.) — أُنْظُرْ لِى فُلَانًا ‡ [*Look thou out for such a one for me*;] *seek thou for me such a one*. (A, TA.) — أُنْظُرْنِى † *Listen thou to me*. (M, Ḳ, TA [in the CḲ, erroneously, أَنْظِرْنِى.]) The verb [says ISd] has this meaning in the Ḳur, ii. 98. (M.) — أَنَا أَنْظُرُ إِلَى ٱللّٰهِ ثُمَّ إِلَيْكَ [lit., *I look to God*, *then to thee*; meaning,] ‡ *I look for the bounty of God*, *then for thy bounty*. (A.) — نَظَرَ ٱللّٰهُ إِلَيْهِ ‡ *God chose him*, *and compassionated him*, *pitied him*, or *regarded him with mercy*; because looking at another is indicative of love, and not doing so is indicative of hatred: (IAth:) or † *God bestowed benefits upon him*; *poured blessings*, or *favours*, *upon him*: (El-Baṣáïr:) and نَظَرَ لَهُمْ ‡ *he compassionated them*, *and aided them*; (Ṣgh, Ḳ;) and simply, *he aided them*: (Ḳ,* TA:) and نَظَرَ لَهُ † *he accomplished his want*, or *that which he* (another) *wanted*. (Mṣb.) — نَظَرَهُ is also syn. with ↓ إِنْتَظَرَهُ, q. v. — Also syn. with أَنْظَرَهُ, q. v. — Also نَظَرَهُ, (Ḳ, TA,) inf. n. نَظْرٌ; (TA;) or ↓ نَظَّرَهُ; (so in a copy of the M, and in the CḲ; but from the mention of the inf. n. in the TA, the former seems to be the right reading;) *He sold it* (a thing, M) *with postponement of the payment*; *he sold it upon credit*. (M,* Ḳ,* TA.) See also 4. — [In these last three acceptations, accord. to the A, the verb is used properly, not tropically.]

= نُظِرَ *He was*, or *became*, *affected by what is termed a* نَظْرَة; (Ḳ, TA;) i.e., *a stroke of an* [*evil*] *eye*; (TA;) [or *of an evil eye cast by a jinnee*;] or *a touch*, or *slight taint of insanity*, *from the jinn*; (Ḳ;) or *a swoon*. (Ḳ, TA.)

2: see 1, last signification but one. — نظّر فيه [*He said of it* فِيهِ نَظَرٌ, q. v.]. (TA passim.)

3. نَاظَرَهُ فِى أَمْرٍ, inf. n. مُنَاظَرَةٌ, (T, Ṣ,*) ‡ *He considered*, or *examined*, or *investigated*, *with him a thing or an affair*, *to see how they should do it*: (T, TA:) *he investigated*, or *examined*, *with him a thing*, *and emulated him*, or *vied with him*, *in doing so*, *each of them adducing his opinion*: (TA:) [*he held a discussion with him respecting a thing*:] or نَاظَرَهُ is syn. with جَادَلَهُ: (Mṣb:) or مناظرة signifies the *examining mentally*, or *investigating*, *by two parties*, *the relation between two things*, *in order to evince the truth*; (KT; and Kull, p. 342;) and sometimes *with one's self*; but مجادلة signifies the disputing respecting a question of science for the purpose of convincing the opponent, whether what he says be wrong in itself or not. (Kull.) — Also ناظره [‡ *He*, or *it*, *looked towards*, or *faced*, *him* or *it*; *was opposite*, or *corresponded*, *to him* or *it*. (See نَظِيرٌ.)] — ‡ *He was*, or *became*, *like him*: (A, Ḳ:) or *like him in discourse* or *dialogue*. (TA.) — جَيْشٌ يُنَاظِرُ الأَلْفَ ‡ *An army that is nearly equal to a thousand*. (A.) — نَاظَرَ فُلَانًا بِفُلَانٍ ‡ *He made*, or *called*, *such a one like such a one*. (Ḳ.) Hence the saying of Ez-Zuhree, (Ḳ,) Moḥammad Ibn-Shiháb, (TA,) لَا تُنَاظِرْ بِكِتَابِ ٱللّٰهِ وَلَا بِكَلَامِ رَسُولِ ٱللّٰهِ, i.e., *Thou shalt not call anything like the book of God*, *nor like the words of the apostle of God*: (A'Obeyd, T, Ḳ:) or *thou shalt not compare anything*, *nor call anything like*, *to the book of God*, &c.: (A,) or *thou shalt not apply* [*aught of*] *the book of God*, *nor the words of the apostle of God*, *as a proverb to a thing that happens*: (A'Obeyd, T, Ḳ; in which last, we read لِشَىْءٍ لِغَرَضٍ, in the place of the right reading, لِشَىْءٍ يَعْرِضُ: TA:) for, as Ibráheem En-Nakha'ee says, they used to dislike the mentioning a verse of the Ḳur-án on the occasion of anything happening, of worldly events; (T;) as a person's saying to one who has come at a time desired by the former, (TA,) or to one named Moosà, who

has come at a time desired, (Ḳ,) جِئْتَ عَلَى قَدَرٍ يَا مُوسَى [Thou hast come at a time appointed, O Moosà: (Ḳur, xx. 42:)] (T, Ḳ:) and the like: (T:) but the first explanation is the most probable. (TA, as from Az; but I do not find it in the T.)

4. أُنْظِرَ بِهِ ‡ [He, or it, was made like]. You say, مَا كَانَ هٰذَا نَظِيرًا لِهٰذَا وَلَقَدْ أُنْظِرَ بِهِ ‡ [This was not like this, but has been made like]: (T, Ḳ:) like as you say, مَا كَانَ خَطِيرًا لَهُ وَلَقَدْ أُخْطِرَ بِهِ. (T.) ═ انظره He postponed him; delayed him: (M, A, Mṣb, Ḳ:) he granted him a delay or respite; let him alone, or left him, for a while: (T, TA:) as, for instance, a debtor, (T, Mṣb, TA,) and a man in difficult circumstances: (TA:) and † نَظَرَهُ signifies the same. (Mṣb.) You say, بِعْتُهُ شَيْئًا فَأَنْظَرْتُهُ I sold to him a thing, and granted him a delay. (T.) And a person speaking says to him who hurries him, أَنْظِرْنِى أَبْتَلِعْ رِيقِى Grant me time to swallow my spittle. (T.) And it is said in the Ḳur, [xv. 36 and xxxviii. 80,] فَأَنْظِرْنِى إِلَى يَوْمِ يُبْعَثُونَ Then delay me until the day when they shall be raised from the dead. (TA.) See also 8. — He sold to him a thing with postponement of the payment; he sold to him a thing upon credit. (M.) See also 1, last signification but one.

5: see 1, first signification. ═ See also 8.

6. تناظرا ‡ They faced each other. (Ḳ.) You say, تناظرت الدَّارَانِ ‡ The two houses faced each other. (M.) And دُورُنَا تَنَاظَرُ, (Ṣ,) or تَتَنَاظَرُ, [which is the original form,] (A,) ‡ Our houses faced one another. (Ṣ, A.) — See also تَرَاوَضَا.

8. انتظره: see 1, first sentence. ═ He looked for him; expected him; awaited him; waited for him; watched for his presence; syn. اِرْتَقَبَ حُضُورَهُ; (TA;) and تَأَنَّى عَلَيْهِ; (M, Ḳ;) and † نَظَرَهُ (aor. ـُ, T &c., inf. n. نَظَرٌ Ṣ, Ḳ) signifies the same; (T, M, A, Mṣb, Ḳ;) and so † تَنَظَّرَهُ, (M, A, Ḳ,) and † أَنْظَرَهُ; (Zj, TA;) [but respecting the last two, see what is said below:] but when you say انتظر without any objective complement, the meaning is, [he waited; or] he paused, and acted or behaved with deliberation, or in a patient, or leisurely, manner. (Lth, T.) It is said in the Ḳur, [lvii. 13,] أُنْظُرُونَا نَقْتَبِسْ مِنْ نُورِكُمْ Wait for us (اِنْتَظِرُونَا) that we may take of your light: and accord. to Zj, أَنْظِرُونَا [which is another reading] is said to mean the same: or the latter means delay us: accord. to Fr, however, the Arabs say أَنْظِرْنِى meaning Wait thou for me (اِنْتَظِرْنِى) a little. (T.) † التَّنَظُّرُ also signifies The expecting, or waiting for, a thing: (TA:) or the expecting, or waiting for, a thing expected: (M, Ḳ, TA:) or † تنظّرهُ signifies he expected, or waited for, (انتظر,) him, or it, leisurely; and so † استنظره. (Ṣ.) You say also, انتظر بِهِ خَيْرًا أَوْ شَرًّا (M, A, Ḳ, in art. ربص, in the last of which is added يَحُلُّ بِهِ) [He looked for, expected, awaited, or waited for, something good or evil to befall him, or betide him].

10. استنظرهُ: see 8, last signification but one. — He asked of him, or desired of him, a postponement, or delay. (M, A, Ḳ.)

نَظْرٌ: see نَظِيرٌ. ═ A man says to another, بَيْعٌ, [or perhaps بِيعْ, like the word used in reply to it, here following, and like خِطْبٌ and نِكْحٌ meaning, I sell,] and the other says, نِظْرٌ, meaning, Grant me a delay (أَنْظِرْنِى) that I may buy (أَشْتَرِى) of thee. (M, TA.)

نَظَرٌ: see 1. [Used as a subst., as well as when used as an inf. n.,] it has no pl. (Sb, in TA, voce فِكْرٌ.) — مِنْ نَظَرٍ, and ضَرَبْنَاهُمْ بِنَظَرٍ ‡ We saw them. (A, TA.) — بَيْنَنَا نَظَرٌ ‡ Between us is the extent of a look in respect of nearness. (A, TA.) — حَيٌّ نَظَرٌ, (Ḳ,* TA,) and حَيٌّ حِلَالٌ وَرِئَآءٌ وَنَظَرٌ, (Ṣ,) and حِلَالٌ وَنَظَرٌ, (A,) ‡ A tribe near together, (Ṣ, A, Ḳ,*) of which the several portions see one another. (Ṣ, A.) — وَفِيهِ نَظَرٌ † But it requires consideration, by reason of its want of clearness, or perspicuity: (Mṣb:) [a phrase used to imply doubt, and also to insinuate politely that the words to which it relates are false, or wrong:] like فِيهِ تَأَمُّلٌ. (MF, art. صفح.) — هُوَ بِخَيْرِ النَّظَرَيْنِ, said in a trad., of one who has purchased a ewe or she-goat that has been kept from being milked for some days; meaning, † He has the option of adopting the better of the two things; he may either retain it or return it. (TA.)

نَظْرَةٌ A look: a quick look or glance: (T:) pl. نَظَرَاتٌ. (A.) Hence the trad., لَا تُتْبِعِ النَّظْرَةَ النَّظْرَةَ فَإِنَّ لَكَ الأُولَى وَلَيْسَتْ لَكَ الآخِرَةُ [Thou shalt not make a look to follow a look; for the former is thine of right, but the latter is not thine: i. e., when thou hast once looked at anything forbidden, unintentionally, thou shalt not look at it a second time]. (T, TA.) And the saying of a certain wise man, مَنْ لَمْ تَعْمَلْ نَظْرَتُهُ لَمْ يَعْمَلْ لِسَانُهُ [He whose look does not produce an effect, his tongue does not produce an effect]; (T;) meaning, that he who is not restrained from a fault or offence by being looked at is not restrained by speech. (TA.) — A stroke of an [evil] eye: (TA:) a stroke of an [evil] eye by which one is affected from the jinn's looking at him; (T, Ṣ;*) as also سَفْعَةٌ: (T:) or a touch, or a slight taint or infection of insanity, (طَائِفٌ,) from the jinn: or a swoon. (M, Ḳ.) — An alteration of the body or complexion by emaciation or hunger or travel &c. (Ṣ, M, Ḳ.) — Foulness; ugliness: (AA, TA:) evilness; or badness, of form or appearance: a fault; a defect; an imperfection. (M, Ḳ.) — † Reverence, veneration, awe, or fear. (IAạr, T, Ḳ.) — ‡ Compassion; pity; mercy. (IAạr, T, Ḳ.)

نَظِرَةٌ A postponement; a delay. (T, Ṣ, M, Mṣb, Ḳ.) It is said in the Ḳur, [ii. 280,] فَنَظِرَةٌ إِلَى مَيْسَرَةٍ [Then let there be a postponement, or delay, until he shall be in an easy state of circumstances]; (T, M, Mṣb;) i. e., فَإِنْظَارٌ, (T,) or فَتَأْخِيرٌ: (Mṣb:) and accord. to another reading, † فَنَاظِرَةٌ; like كَاذِبَةٌ, in the Ḳur, lvi. 2. (M.) You say also, بَاعَ مِنْهُ الشَّىْءَ بِنَظِرَةٍ He sold to him the thing with postponement of the payment; he sold to him the thing upon credit. (M.) And اِشْتَرَيْتُهُ مِنْهُ بِنَظِرَةٍ, and بِإِنْظَارٍ, I bought it of him with postponement of the payment; I bought it of him upon credit. (T.)

نَظَرِىٌّ † [Speculative knowledge or science; such as is acquired by study;] that of which the origination rests upon speculation, and acquisition by study; as the conception of the intellect or mind, and the assent of the mind to the position, that the world has had a beginning. (Ḳ, T.) [It is opposed to بَدِيهِىٌّ and to ضَرُورِىٌّ.]

سَمْعَةٌ نَظْرَةٌ, and vars. thereof, see in art. سمع.

نَظَارِ, like قَطَامِ, (Ṣ, Ḳ,) an imp. n., (T,) meaning, Wait thou: syn. اِنْتَظِرْ. (T, Ṣ, Ḳ.)

نَظُورٌ and † نَظُورَةٌ and † نَاظُورَةٌ and † نَظِيرَةٌ A chief person, whether male or female, to whom one looks. (M, Ḳ.) You say, فُلَانٌ نَظِيرَةُ † قَوْمِهِ, and † نَظُورَةُ قَوْمِهِ, Such a one is the person to whom his people look, (Fr, T, Ṣ,) and whom they imitate, or to whose example they conform. (Fr, T.) All these words are also used in a pl. sense: (M, Ḳ:) or [so in some copies of the Ḳ; but in others, and,] نظورة and نظيرة have نَظَائِرُ for their pl., (Ṣ, Ḳ,) sometimes. (Ḳ.) — Also, نَظُورٌ A man who neglects not to look at, (M, L, Ḳ,) or to consider, (A,) that which, (M, A, L,) or him who, (Ḳ,) disquiets him, or renders him solicitous. (M, A, L, Ḳ.)

نَظِيرٌ ‡ *Looking to,* or *facing,* another person or thing; *opposite* or *corresponding to* another person or thing; as also ↓ مُنَاظِرٌ; syn. مُقَابِلٌ. (A.) [Hence, النَّظِيرُ, and نَظِيرُ السَّمْتِ, ‡ *The nadir; the point opposite to the zenith.*] نَظِيرُكَ signifies الَّذِى يُنَاظِرُكَ, (M,) or الذى تُنَاظِرُهُ, وَيُنَاظِرُكَ, (T,) [which I suppose to mean ‡ *He who looks towards,* or *faces, thee; who is opposite,* or *corresponds, to thee;* or *he towards whom thou lookest, &c., and who looks towards thee, &c.:* though susceptible of other interpretations: see 3.] — ‡ *Like; a like; a similar person or thing:* (AO, T, Ṣ, M, A, Ḳ;) *equal; an equal:* (Mṣb:) applied to anything: (TA:) as also ↓ نِظْرٌ; (AO, Ṣ, Ḳ;) like نِدٌّ and نَدِيدٌ; (AO, Ṣ;) and ↓ مُنَاظِرٌ: (Ḳ:) fem. نَظِيرَةٌ: (T, M, A:) pl. masc., نُظَرَآءُ: (M, A, Mṣb, Ḳ:) and pl. fem. نَظَائِرُ, (T, A,) applied to words and to all things. (T.) You say, فُلَانٌ نَظِيرُكَ ‡ *Such a one is thy like.* (T.) And هٰذَا نَظِيرُ لِهٰذَا, (T,) or نَظِيرُ هٰذَا, (Mṣb,) ‡ *This is the like of this,* (T,) or *the equal of this.* (Mṣb.) And عَدَدْتُ إِبِلَ فُلَانٍ نَظَائِرَ ‡ *I counted,* or *numbered, the camels of such a one in pairs,* or *two by two;* (Aṣ, T, Ḳ;*) if by looking at their aggregate, you say, عَدَدْتُهَا جِمَارًا. (Aṣ, T.)

نَظُورَةٌ: see نَظُورٌ, in two places. — See also نَظِيرَةٌ.

نَظِيرَةٌ: see نَظُورٌ, in two places. — Also, *A scout,* or *scouts;* (T, Ṣgh, Ḳ;) and so ↓ نَظُورَةٌ: (Ṣgh, Ḳ:) pl. of both, نَظَائِرُ. (TA.) — Fem. of نَظِيرٌ, q. v. (T, &c.). [And hence,] النَّظَائِرُ [the pl.] *The more excellent of men:* (Ḳ,* TA:) because they resemble one another in dispositions and actions and sayings. (TA.)

نَظَّارٌ ‡ A horse (A, Ḳ) *that raises his eye by reason of his sharpness of spirit:* (A:) or *sharp-spirited, and raising his eye.* (T, Ḳ.)

نَظَّارَةٌ *A people looking at a thing;* (Ṣ, Ḳ;) as also ↓ مَنْظَرَةٌ. (Ḳ.) — See also مِنْظَارٌ.

نَاظِرٌ act. part. n. of نَظَرَ; *Looking;* &c.: pl. نُظَّارٌ. (Mṣb.) — النَّاظِرُ [*The pupil,* or *apple, of the eye,*] the *smallest black of the eye,* (Ṣ, Mṣb,) *in which is* [seen] *what is termed* إِنْسَانُ العَيْنِ, (Ṣ,) [and] *with which the man sees;* (Mṣb;) *the black spot in the eye;* (M, Ḳ;) *the clear black spot that is in the middle of the* [main] *black of the eye, with which the looker sees what he sees:* or *that part of the eye which resembles a mirror, in which, when one faces it, he sees his person:* (TA:) or *a duct* (عِرْق) *in the nose, wherein is the water of sight:* (M, Ḳ:) [app. a loose description of *the optic nerve:*] or *the sight itself:* (M, Ḳ:) or *the eye:* (Ḳ:) or the eye is called ↓ النَّاظِرَةُ; (Ṣ, A;*) the pl. of which is نَوَاظِرُ. (A.) — شَدِيدُ النَّاظِرِ, (so in a copy of the M and of the A and in some copies of the Ḳ,) or سَدِيدُ النَّاظِرِ, (so in some copies of the Ḳ and in the TA,) A man *clear of suspicion, who looks with a full gaze:* (M, Ḳ:) or *clear of that with which he is upbraided.* (A.) — النَّاظِرَانِ *Two veins at the two edges of the nose, commencing from the inner angles of the eyes, towards the face.* (Zj, in his Khalḳ el-Insán.) — Also, نَاظِرٌ † *A guardian; a keeper; a watcher:* (Ṣ, Mṣb:) and, as also ↓ نَاظُورٌ, *i. q.* نَاطُورٌ, (Ḳ, TA,) [which last is] a word of the Nabathean dialect. (TA.) — [The dim. is نُوَيْظِرٌ.] You say, عُيَيْنَتِى نُوَيْظِرَةٌ إِلَى ٱللّٰهِ ثُمَّ إِلَيْكُمْ ‡ *My eye* (lit. *my little eye*) *is looking to God for His bounty, then to you* for your bounty. (A.) — In the Ḳur, [lxxv. 23,] the words إِلَى رَبِّهَا نَاظِرَةٌ have been explained as signifying *Waiting for* (مُنْتَظِرَةٌ) *their Lord:* but this is a mistake; for the Arabs do not say نَظَرْتُ إِلَى الشَّىْءِ in the sense of إِنْتَظَرْتُهُ, but they say نَظَرْتُ فُلَانًا in that sense. (T.)

نَاظِرَةٌ: see نَاظِرٌ. — See also نَظْرَةٌ.

نَاظُورٌ: see نَاظِرٌ.

نَاظُورَةٌ: see نَظُورٌ.

أَنْظُورٌ for أَنْظُرُ: see 1.

مَنْظَرٌ [*A place in which a thing is looked at*]: *a place, or state, in which one likes to be looked at.* (T, A, TA.) You say, فُلَانٌ فِى مَنْظَرٍ وَمَسْمَعٍ وَفِى رِيٍّ وَمَشْبَعٍ ‡ *Such a one is in a state in which he likes to be looked at and listened to* [*and in a state in which he is satisfied with drink and food*]. (T, A, TA.) And لَقَدْ كُنْتَ عَنْ هٰذَا المَقَامِ بِمَنْظَرٍ ‡ *Thou wast in a state* [*in*] *which thou likedst* [*to be looked at*], *away from this place of abode.* (T, TA.) — The *aspect,* or *outward appearance,* of a thing; *opposite of* مَخْبَرٌ: (Ṣ, art. خبر:) [when used absolutely, *a pleasing,* or *goodly, aspect;* or *beauty of aspect;* as also ↓ مَنْظَرَةٌ: this is implied by the usage of مَنْظَرَانِىٌّ, q. v., and is well known:] or *what one looks at and is pleased by* or *displeased by;* as also ↓ مَنْظَرَةٌ: (M, Ḳ:) or the former, *a thing that pleases and rejoices the beholder when he looks at it:* (T:) and the ↓ latter, the *aspect* (مَنْظَر) *of a man when one looks at it and is pleased by it or displeased by it.* (T, TA.*) You say, لَهُ مَنْظَرٌ حَسَنٌ [*He has a goodly aspect*]. (A.) And ٱمْرَأَةٌ حَسَنَةُ المَنْظَرِ, and ↓ المَنْظَرَةِ, [*A woman goodly of aspect.*] (Ṣ.) And مَنْظَرُهُ خَيْرٌ مِنْ مَخْبَرِهِ [*His aspect is better than his internal state*]. (Ṣ.) And إِنَّهُ لَذُو مَنْظَرٍ بِلَا مَخْبَرٍ, (T,) and ذُو مَنْظَرَةٍ ↓ بِلَا مَخْبَرَةٍ, (A,) [*Verily he has a pleasing aspect without a pleasing internal state.*]

مَنْظَرَةٌ *A high place on which a person is stationed to watch;* (Ṣ;) *a place on the top of a mountain, where a person observes and watches the enemy:* (T:) and مَنَاظِرُ [the pl.] *eminences; or elevated parts of the earth;* or *high grounds:* (M, Ḳ:) because one looks from them. (M.) — Its application to *A certain separate place of a house,* [generally *an apartment on the ground-floor overlooking the court,* and also *a turret,* or rather *a belvedere,* and *any building,* or *apartment, commanding a view,*] is vulgar. (TA.) — See also نَظَّارَةٌ. — And see مَنْظَرٌ, in five places.

مَنْظَرِىٌّ: see what next follows.

مَنْظَرَانِىٌّ (Ṣ, M, A, Ḳ) and ↓ مَنْظَرِىٌّ, (M, Ḳ,) the latter contr. to analogy, (M,) A man (M,) *of goodly aspect.* (M, Ḳ.) You say, رَجُلٌ مَنْظَرَانِىٌّ مَخْبَرَانِىٌّ [*A man of goodly aspect* and *of pleasing internal,* or *intrinsic, qualities*]; (Ṣ, A;) i. e., ذُو مَنْظَرٍ and ذُو مَخْبَرٍ. (TA, art. خبر.)

مِنْظَارٌ *A mirror* (A, Ḳ) *in which the face is seen.* (TA.) — Also, *A telescope; a thing in which what is distant is seen* [*as though it were*] *near:* vulgarly, ↓ نَظَّارَةٌ. (TA.)

مَنْظُورٌ A man *looked at with an evil eye:* (A, TA;) *affected by what is termed a* نَظْرَة; (T, TA;) i. e., *a stroke of an* [*evil*] *eye;* [or *of an evil eye cast by a jinnee;* or *a touch,* or *slight taint of insanity, from the jinn;*] or *a swoon.* (TA.) — A person, (T,) or chief person, (A,) *whose bounty is hoped for,* (T, A,) *and at whom eyes glance.* (A.) — مَنْظُورَةٌ A woman *in whom is a* نَظْرَة, meaning, *a fault, defect,* or *imperfection.* (Ḳ,* TA.)

مُنَاظِرٌ: see نَظِيرٌ.

[نظف, &c.
See Supplement.]

نعب

1. نَعَبَ, aor. ـَ and ـِ, inf. n. نَعْبٌ and نَعِيبٌ (Ṣ, Ḳ) and نُعَابٌ (Ḳ) and نَعَبَانٌ and تَنْعَابٌ (Ṣ, Ḳ) *He* (a raven, or crow, غُرَاب,) *uttered a cry, cried out,* or *croaked:* (Ṣ:) or *uttered the cry,* or *croak, that is asserted to be ominous of separation:* [but see below:] or *moved about his head without crying:* (Mṣb:) *he* (a raven, or crow, or other animal,) *cried out:* or *stretched out his neck, and moved about his head, in crying out.* (Ḳ.) The نَعِيب of the raven, or crow, is said to be ominous of good; and its نَعِيق, of evil. (Kifáyet el-Mutahaffidh.) — نَعِيبٌ also signifies † The *neighing* of a horse. (TA.) — نَعَبَ الدِّيكُ ‡ [*The cock crowed*] is sometimes said, metaphorically. (Ṣ.) — نَعَبَ المُؤَذِّنُ ‡ *The chanter of the call to prayer* —

stretched out his neck, and moved about his head, in his cry. (A, L, Ḳ.) — نَعَبَ, aor. ـِ, inf. n. نَعْبٌ, *He* (a camel, Ḳ) *went with a quick pace:* (Ṣ, Ḳ:) or, *with a certain kind of pace:* (Ḳ:) or *he* (a camel) *moved about his head, in proceeding at a quick rate; like a* بُخْتِىّ *camel, raising his head:* (TA:) or, inf. n. نَعَبَانٌ, *he stretched out his neck.* (A.) Accord. to some, نَعْبٌ signifies The *moving* of a she-camel's head *forwards in her march,* or *pace.* [Ṣ, accord. to an excellent copy, in which the original words are thus given: يُقَالُ إِنَّ النَّعْبَ تَحَرُّكُ رَأْسِهَا الخ: in another copy, تُحَرِّكُ رَأْسَهَا; making نَعْب an epithet of a she-camel that so moves her head.]

4. انعب † *He* (a man) *cried out,* or *stretched out his neck and moved about his head, in disturbances, broils,* or *the like:* syn. نَعَبَ فِى الفِتَنِ. (TA.)

رِيحٌ نَعْبٌ *A rapid wind.* (Ḳ.)

نَعُوبٌ: see نَاعِبَةٌ.

نُعَابٌ The *young one of a raven,* or *crow:* syn. فَرْخُ غُرَابٍ: or *a raven,* or *crow,* [absolutely]; syn. غُرَابٌ. In a prayer of David occur the words يَا رَازِقَ النُّعَابِ فِى عُشِّهِ [*O Sustainer of the young raven* (or *young crow*) *in his nest!*]. It is said that the young raven (or young crow), when it comes forth from its egg, is white, like a lump of fat, and that the old bird, on seeing it, dislikes and abandons it; that thereupon God sends to it gnats, which light upon it on account of its foul greasy smell, and that it lives upon them until it is fledged and becomes black, when its parents return to it. (L.)

نَعَّابَةٌ: see نَاعِبَةٌ.

نَاعِبَةٌ (Ḳ) and ↓ نَعُوبٌ and ↓ نَعَّابَةٌ (Ṣ, Ḳ) and ↓ مِنْعَبٌ (so in the correct copies of the Ḳ: in the L, مِنْعَبَةٌ: accord. to MF, مُنْعِبٌ: TA) *A swift she-camel:* (Ṣ, Ḳ:) pl. of the first, and of [the masc. epithet] نَاعِبٌ, نَوَاعِبُ and نُعُبٌ: and of نعوب, نُعُبٌ. (TA.) [The last pl. is the only one mentioned in the Ṣ, Ḳ, which do not point out its proper sing.] See also نَعْبٌ in 1.

مِنْعَبٌ An *excellent, fleet* horse, (Ṣ, Ḳ,) *that stretches out his neck like the raven,* or *crow:* and (or accord. to some, TA) one *that follows his own way, heedless of the bridle,* [app., *lowering his head, and stretching out his neck,*] syn. الذى يَسْطُو بِرَأْسِهِ, (Ḳ,) *without any increase in the rate of his run.* (TA.) — See نَاعِبَةٌ. — *A stupid,* or *foolish, and clamourous* man. (Ḳ.)

نعت

1. نَعَتَ, aor. ـَ, inf. n. نَعْتٌ; and ↓ انتعت; *He described,* or *characterized,* or *designated,* (Ṣ, Ḳ,) a thing; (Ṣ;) syn. وَصَفَ: (Ṣ, Ḳ:) or *he described* a thing *by mentioning what was in it,* or *what it possessed;* whereas, in the وَصْف of a thing one may exaggerate: (L:) [*he distinguished* a person or a thing *by an epithet:* and hence, *he qualified* a substantive *by an epithet:* and *he used* a word *as an epithet:*] or *he described* a thing *by mentioning what was in it that was good,* or *goodly;* not with reference to what was bad, or foul, or ugly; unless by a straining of the meaning one say نَعْتُ سَوْءٍ; whereas وَصْف is said with respect to what is good, or goodly, and what is bad, or foul, or ugly: (IAth:) or نَعَتَ signifies *he described by mentioning the make,* or *form,* or *other outward characteristic,* as tallness and shortness; and وَصَفَ respects action, as beating: or, accord. to Th, نَعَتَ signifies *he described by mentioning something in some particular place in the body,* such as lameness; whereas وَصَفَ is used with respect to what is common to the whole, as greatness, and generosity; therefore God is an object of وَصْف, but not of نَعْت. (TA.) — نَعَتَ نَفْسَهُ بِالْخَيْرِ [*He described himself as possessing,* or *characterized by,* or *distinguished by, goodness.*] (Mṣb.) — نَعُتَ, aor. ـُ, inf. n. نَعَاتَةٌ, *He* (a man) *was naturally endowed with powers of description, and skilful in the use of those powers.* (TA.) — نَعُتَ, aor. ـُ, inf. n. نَعَاتَةٌ, *He* (a horse) *was,* or *became, what is termed* نَعْتٌ, i.e., *generous,* or *fleet, &c.* (L, Ḳ.) — نَعَتَ, (L,) or نَعِتَ, of the same measure as فَرِحَ, (Ḳ,) *He* (a horse) *affected,* or *endeavoured,* or *constrained himself, to be,* or *become, what is termed* نَعْتٌ, i.e., *generous,* or *fleet, &c.* (L, Ḳ.) MF remarks that نَعِتَ, in this sense, is strange, as فَعِلَ is not a measure denoting تَكَلُّف. (TA.)

4. انعت *His face became beautiful,* or *goodly, so that he was described* (Ḳ) *as characterized by beauty,* (TA,) [or, *so that he became distinguished by an epithet*].

8. انتعت *He,* or *it, was,* or *became, described:* (TA:) [*he,* or *it, was,* or *became, distinguished by an epithet: he,* or *it, was,* or *became, characterized,* or *distinguished, by that which made him to excel others of his kind:* see نَعْتٌ]. See 1.

10. استنعتهُ *He asked him to describe him,* or *it.* (T, Ḳ.)

نَعْتٌ *An epithet;* or *that whereby a person* or *thing is described:* [hence, *an epithet whereby a substantive is qualified:*] (TA:) pl. نُعُوتٌ: it has no other pl. than this. (ISd.) [Respecting distinctions said to exist between نَعْتٌ and وَصْفٌ or صِفَةٌ, see 1.] [You say,] لَهُ نُعُوتٌ وَمَنَاعِتُ جَمِيلَةٌ [*He has goodly epithets applied to him, and goodly qualities,* or *properties, which are causes,* or *occasions, of epithets*]. (A.) — كَمَثَلِ كَذَا [, a phrase similar to كَنَعْتِ كَذَا, meaning *Like such a thing.* See an ex. voce سَبْعٌ.] — نَعْتٌ Anything *excellent.* (TA.) — [Hence,] فَرَسٌ نَعْتٌ, and ↓ مُنْتَعِتٌ, and ↓ نَعْتَةٌ, [in the CḲ, نَعْتَت,] and ↓ نَعِيتٌ, and ↓ نَعِيتَةٌ, *A generous,* or *a fleet,* or *swift, horse, that excels in running, and outstrips others.* (Ḳ.) [And so] ↓ مُنْتَعِتٌ A beast of carriage, or a man, *characterized,* or *distinguished, by that which makes him to excel others of his kind:* a horse *described as distinguished by generousness,* or *by fleetness,* or *swiftness, and by outstripping others.* (TA.)

نَعْتَةٌ: see نَعْتٌ.

عَبْدُكَ نَعْتَةٌ, or أَمَتُكَ نَعْتَةٌ, *Thy male slave,* or *thy female slave, is of the highest quality.* (Ḳ.) But in the A it is said, عَبْدُكَ نَعْتٌ, and أَمَتُكَ نَعْتَةٌ. (TA.)

نَعِيتٌ A *generous, excellent, surpassing,* man. (TA.) See also نَعْتٌ.

نَعِيتَةٌ: see نَعْتٌ.

نَاعِتٌ *Describing; a describer:* pl. نُعَّاتٌ. (TA.)

مَنْعُوتٌ [A person or thing *described; distinguished by an epithet:* and hence, a substantive *qualified by an epithet*]. — مَنْعُوتٌ بِالْكَرَمِ [*Described as possessing,* or *characterized by,* or *distinguished by, generosity; distinguished by the epithet of generous*]. (A.)

مُنْتَعِتٌ: see نَعْتٌ.

نعث

1. نَعَثَهُ, aor. ـَ; and ↓ انتعثهُ; *He took it.* (Ḳ.)

4. انعث فِى مَالِهِ *He was prodigal of his wealth:* (Ḳ:) or *he scattered it:* or it signifies قَدَّمَ فِيهِ. (L.) = انعث *He set about,* or *commenced fitting himself out,* or *equipping himself for journeying.* (Ḳ.) — هُمْ فِى إِنْعَاثٍ (in the CḲ, and in a MS. copy of the Ḳ, أَنْعَاثٍ,) *They have striven, laboured,* or *exerted themselves, in their affair.* (Ḳ.)

8: see 1.

نعج

1. نَعَجَ, aor. ـَ, inf. n. نَعْجٌ (Ṣ, Ḳ) and نُعُوجٌ, (Ḳ,) a verb similar to طَلَبَ, (Ṣ, Ḳ,) aor. ـُ, inf. n. طَلَبٌ; (Ṣ;) so in the handwriting of J; (IB;) or, with reference to a colour, نَعِجَ, aor. ـَ, inf. n. نَعَجٌ, a verb like صَخِبَ, aor. ـَ, inf. n. صَخَبٌ; (accord. to an insertion in a copy of the Ṣ read

to IB, TA, [and so in one of M. Fresnel's copies of the Ṣ, and in a copy in my possession, and so in the L, in which both forms of the verb are given,]) *He, or it,* [a colour,] *was of a clear,* or *pure white.* (Ṣ, L, Ḳ.) ═ نَعِجَ, aor. ـَ, inf. n. نَعَجٌ, *He* (a man, Az, or a camel, Ṣ) *became fat:* (T, Ṣ, Ḳ:) said by AA to occur in a poem of Dhu-r-Rummeh, but not found in his poetry by Sh, who deems it strange: Az, however, confirms it by the authority of an Arab of the desert; and adds, that it signifies *he* (a man) *became fat and in good condition: and he increased, and became swollen,* or *inflated: and* نَبِجَ is said to signify the same. (TA.) — نَعِجَ, aor. ـَ, inf. n. نَعَجٌ, *He* (a man, Ṣ) *became heavy in the stomach* (القَلْب) *from eating mutton.* (Ṣ, Ḳ.) ═ نَعَجَتْ فِى سَيْرِهَا, (inf. n. نَعْجٌ, L.) *She* (a camel) *was quick,* or *swift, in her pace:* (Ṣ, L:) she went with a certain pace: (L:) a dial. form of مَعَجَتْ. (Ṣ.)

4. أَنْعَجَ القَوْمُ *The people's camels became fat.* (Ṣ, Ḳ.)

نَعِجٌ [and ↑ أَنْعَجُ] *Of a pure white colour:* (L:) [pl. of the latter نُعْجٌ]. — نِسَآءٌ نُعْجُ المَحَاجِرِ دُعْجُ النَّوَاظِرِ [*Women of a clear white colour in the parts around the eyes; intensely black and wide, in the eyes*]. (A.) ═ نَعِجٌ A man *heavy in the stomach* (القَلْب) *from eating mutton:* pl. نَعِجُونَ. (Ṣ, TA.)

نَعْجَةٌ, (Ṣ, Ḳ,) and ↑ نِعْجَةٌ, accord. to a reading of El-Ḥasan, وَلِىَ نِعْجَةٌ وَاحِدَةٌ, [Ḳur, xxxviii. 22,] (TA,) *A ewe*; the *female of the sheep:* (L, Ḳ:) also, the *female of the wild bull:* and, *of the gazelle:* and, *of the wild sheep:* (TA:) [but see below:] pl. نِعَاجٌ and نَعَجَاتٌ. (Ṣ, Ḳ.) — نَعْجَةُ الرَّمْلِ *The* [*wild*] *cow:* pl. نِعَاجُ الرَّمْلِ: no other wild animal but the cow (accord. to A'Obeyd, Ṣ,) is thus called: (Ṣ, Ḳ:) [but see above]. The Arabs speak of gazelles as though they were goats, terming the male تَيْسٌ; and of wild bulls or cows as though they were sheep, terming the female نَعْجَةٌ. (AAF.) — Also نَعْجَةٌ ‡ *A woman;* as likewise شَاةٌ. (TA.)

نِعْجَةٌ: see نَعْجَةٌ.

نَاعِجٌ A camel *of beautiful colour, and highly esteemed.* (TA.) نَاعِجَةٌ A she-camel *of beautiful colour:* (TA:) or a *white* she-camel, (Ṣ, Ḳ,) *of generous race:* (TA:) a *swift* she-camel: a she-camel *upon which one hunts wild cows:* (Ṣ, Ḳ:) such is *of the kind called* مَهْرِيَّة: (IJ:) or one that is *light,* or *active:* (TA:) pl. نَوَاعِجُ. (Ṣ.) — also A woman *of beautiful complexion,* or *colour.* (TA.) ═ أَرْضٌ نَاعِجَةٌ *Plain,* or *even, land,* (Ṣ, Ḳ,) *fertile, and producing the kind of tree called* رِمْث. (Aboo-Kheyreh.)

أَنْعَجُ: see نَعِجٌ.

نعر

1. نَعَرَ, (Ṣ, A, Mṣb, Ḳ,) aor. ـِ (Ṣ, Ḳ) and ـَ, (Ḳ,) [in the Mṣb, ـُ, but this I suppose to be an error in transcription,] the first of which is the most common, (Ḳ,) or the most common when the verb relates to a vein, accord. to Fr, as cited by Ṣgh, (TA,) inf. n. نَعِيرٌ (Ṣ, A, Mṣb, Ḳ) and نُعَارٌ, (A, Ḳ,) or this latter is a simple subst., (Mṣb,) and نَعْرَةٌ, (A,) [or this also is a simple subst.,] *He* (a man, Ḳ, or a beast of carriage, Mṣb,) *uttered a sound, or noise,* (Ṣ, A, Mṣb, Ḳ,) *with,* (A, Ḳ,) or *in,* (Ṣ,) *his* خَيْشُوم [or *the innermost part of his nose*]: (Ṣ, A, Ḳ:) but Az, says, I have not heard this explanation from any of the leading authorities. (TA.) — Also, (TA,) inf. n. نَعِيرٌ, (Ḳ,) *He called out,* or *cried out vehemently,* in war, or in some evil case. (Ḳ,* TA.) And نَعَرَتْ, inf. n. نَعِيرٌ, *She* (a woman) *clamoured, and acted in a foul* or *immodest manner.* (TA.) — نَعَرَ العِرْقُ, (Ṣ, Ḳ,) or نَعَرَ العِرْقُ بِالدَّمِ, (A,) aor. ـَ, (Fr, Ṣgh, Ḳ,) and ـِ, (Ṣ, Ḳ,) the former of which is the more common, (Fr, Ṣgh,) inf. n. نَعْرٌ, (Ṣ, TA,) or نَعِيرٌ and نُعَارٌ, (as app. implied in the Ḳ, but perhaps not intended to be so,) ‡ *The vein gushed with blood:* (Ṣ, Ḳ:) or, (aor. ـُ, inf. n. نُعُورٌ and نَعِيرٌ, TA,) *made a sound by reason of the blood coming forth:* (Ḳ:) or *gushed with blood, and made a sound at the coming forth of the blood.* (A.)

نَعْرَةٌ *A sound, or noise, in the* خَيْشُوم [or *innermost part of the nose*]; (Ṣ, Ḳ:) [as also ↑ نُعَارٌ. (See 1.)] — نَعَرَاتٌ [the pl.] is also applied to The *call of the* مُؤَذِّن. (Ṣ.)

نَعْرَى: see نَاعِرٌ.

نُعَارٌ: see نَعْرَةٌ.

نَعُورٌ:
نَعَّارٌ and نَعَّارَةٌ: } see نَاعِرٌ.

نَاعِرٌ *Uttering a sound* or *noise* [*with,* or *in, the* خَيْشُوم, or *innermost part of the nose*]. (Sh.) And ↑ نَعَّارٌ *Clamorous:* (Ḳ, TA:) ↑ fem. with ة, applied to a woman, and signifying the same: (A:) or, so applied, it signifies *clamorous and foul,* or *immodest:* (Ḳ:) and ↑ إِمْرَأَةٌ غَيْرَى نَعْرَى *a* [*very jealous*] *clamorous woman;* (Ḳ;) in which phrase, نعرى may not be regarded as fem. of نَعْرَانُ, because [epithets of the measures] فَعْلَى and فَعْلَانُ come from verbs of the class of فَرِحَ; not from those of the class of مَنَعَ [or that of ضَرَبَ]. (Az, Ḳ.) — [And so] ↑ نَعَّارٌ *One who drives away the beasts and cries out after them.* (TA, art. زغق.) — You say also, أَطَرْتُ بِهٰذَا صَوْتًا نَعَّارًا ↑ [lit., *I made a clamorous voice to fly with this;* meaning,] ‡ *I published this.* (A.) — Also نَاعِرٌ ‡ A vein *flowing with blood:* (Sh:) [or *gushing with blood;* &c. (See its verb, above.)] And ↑ نَعَّارٌ ‡ A vein *gushing with blood;* and so ↑ نَعُورٌ: (Ṣ:) *that does not cease to flow with blood;* as also ↑ نُعُورٌ (TA) and ↑ نَاعُورٌ: (Ḳ, TA:) and ↑ نَعَّارٌ applied to a wound signifies the same; as also تَعَّارٌ, with ت and ع, and ↑ تَغَّارٌ, with ت and غ: (IAạr, Az:) and ↑ نَعُورٌ applied to a wound signifies ‡ *making a sound by reason of the vehemence with which the blood comes forth.* (TA.)

نَاعُورٌ, (Ṣ, A, Mgh, Mṣb,) or ↑ نَاعُورَةٌ, (Ḳ,) *A* [*machine of the kind called*] دُولَاب [q. v.], (A, Ḳ,) or مَنْجَنُون [q. v.], (Mgh, Mṣb,) *with which water is drawn* [*for irrigation*], (Ṣ,) *and which is turned by water,* (Ṣ, Mgh, Mṣb,) *and makes a noise,* or [*creaking*] *sound by* [*its revolving*]: (Ṣ:) so called because of its نَعِير [or *sound*]: (A, Mgh, Mṣb:) [app. also *any rotary machine for raising water to irrigate land:* see Niebuhr's 'Voyage en Arabie,' tome i., p. 220 et seq.:] it is used on the banks of the Euphrates (A, TA) and the 'Áṣee: (TA:) pl. نَوَاعِيرُ. (Ṣ, A, Mṣb.) — And the former, The *wing* (جَنَاح) *of a mill* or *mill-stone.* (Ḳ.) — Also ↑ نَاعُورَةٌ *A bucket with which water is raised.* (Ḳ.) — See also نَاعِرٌ.

نَاعُورَةٌ: see نَاعُورٌ.

نعس

1. نَعَسَ, (Ṣ, A, Mṣb, Ḳ,) aor. ـُ, (Ṣ, M, and so in a copy of the B by the author of the Ḳ,) or ـَ, (A, Ḳ,) [the latter being agreeable with analogy,] inf. n. نُعَاسٌ, (Ṣ, A, Ḳ,* TA,) or this is a simple subst., (Mṣb,) [*He drowsed; he was,* or *became, drowsy,* or *heavy with sleepiness:* or *he slumbered,* or *dozed:*] the inf. n. is *syn.* with وَسَنٌ: (Ṣ, A, Ḳ:) or ↑ نُعَاسٌ signifies *languor in the senses,* (Ḳ, TA,) *arising from the heaviness* [*which is the prevenient sign*] *of sleep:* (TA:) or the *beginning of sleep:* (M, art. وسن:) or its proper signification is, accord. to Az, (Mṣb, TA,) وَسَنٌ (Mṣb) or سِنَةٌ (TA) *without sleep:* (Mṣb, TA,) or سِنَةٌ is in the head, and نُعَاسٌ is in the eye: or سنة is the vapour (ريح) of sleep which begins in the face, then is transmitted to the heart, and you say, of a man, يَنْعَسُ, and then, يَنَامُ. (Mṣb, art. نوم.) It is said in a proverb,

مَطْلٌ كَنُعَاسِ الكَلْبِ [*A delaying of the payment, of a debt,* or *the like, like the drowsing,* or *slumbering, of the dog:*] i. e. continual: (Ṣ, TA:) for the dog is characterized by much نعاس, and, as is said in the B, is accustomed to open his eyes [only] sufficiently for the purpose of guarding, and this he does time after time. (TA.) —— نَعَسَ, (TḲ,) inf. n. نَعْسٌ, (IAạr, Ḳ,) † *It* (a man's judgment, and his body,) *was soft,* and *weak.* (IAạr, Ḳ, TḲ.) —— † *It* (a market) *was,* or *became, stagnant,* or *dull, with respect to traffic.* (Ḳ, TA.)

4. انعس † *He begat heavy, sluggish, lazy, indolent,* or *torpid, sons.* (AA, Ḳ.)

6. تناعس *He feigned himself* [*drowsing,* or *slumbering,* or] *sleeping.* (Ḳ,* TA.) —— ‡ *It* (lightning) *became faint.* (A, TA.)

نَعْسَةٌ [*A single fit of drowsiness:* or *of slumber:*] *a single movement of the head in drowsing* or *slumbering.* (TA.) You say, رَكِبَتْهُ نَعْسَةٌ شَدِيدَةٌ [*A vehement fit of drowsiness,* or *of slumber, came upon him*]. (A.) And نَعَسْتُ نَعْسَةً وَاحِدَةً [*I drowsed,* or *slumbered, once*]. (Ṣ.)

نَعْسَانٌ: see نَاعِسٌ.

نُعَاسٌ: see 1.

نَعُوسٌ A she-camel *bountiful in yielding milk;* (Ṣ, A, Ḳ;) *that drowses,* or *slumbers, in yielding milk;* (A;) or because, in yielding milk, she drowses, or slumbers: (Ṣ:) or *having much milk, that drowses,* or *slumbers, when milked:* (M:) or *that closes her eyelid on being milked.* (Az, TA.)

نَعَّاسَةٌ: see نَاعِسٌ.

نَاعِسٌ, part. n. of نَعَسَ, [*Drowsing, drowsy,* or *heavy with sleep:* or *slumbering,* or *dozing:*] (Ṣ, Mṣb, Ḳ:) as also ▼ نَعْسَانٌ; (Lth, Fr, Th, Mṣb, Ḳ;) but this latter is rare; (Fr, Th, Mṣb, Ḳ;) and by some disallowed: (TA:) fem. of the former with ة: (Mṣb, TA:) and of the latter نَعْسَى, made to accord. with وَسْنَى, fem. of وَسْنَانٌ; and this is best in poetry: (Lth, Mṣb, TA:) and ▼ نَعَّاسَةٌ is also used as an epithet [in an intensive sense] applied to a female: (TA:) the pl. of نَاعِسٌ is نُعَّسٌ; like رُكَّعٌ, pl. of رَاكِعٌ: and that of نَاعِسَةٌ is نَوَاعِسُ. (Mṣb.) —— جَدُّهُ نَاعِسٌ ‡ [*His good fortune is slumbering*]. (A, TA.)

نعش

1. نَعَشَهُ, aor. َ, (Ṣ, Ḳ,) inf. n. نَعْشٌ, (Ṣ,) *He* (God) *raised him; lifted him up;* (Ṣ, Ḳ;) as also ▼ انعشهُ; (Lth, Ks, Ḳ;) which is disallowed by ISk, who says that it is a vulgar word, and by J after him, but is correct; (TA;) and ▼ نَعَّشَهُ, (AA, Ḳ,) inf. n. تَنْعِيشٌ: (AA, TA:) or *He* (God) *set him up,* or *upright;* as also ▼ انعشهُ: (Mṣb:) [see an ex. in a verse cited voce شَمَلٌ:] or *he* [app. a man] *raised him,* or *lifted him up, after a stumble,* or *trip.* (Sh.) You say also, نَعَشْتُ الشَّجَرَةَ *I set the tree upright,* when it was leaning. (TA.) And نَعَشَ طَرْفَهُ *He raised his eye,* or *eyes.* (Ṣ,* Ḳ.) —— [Hence,] aor. and inf. n. as above, (TA,) ‡ *He recovered him from his embarrassment,* or *difficulty:* (A:) ‡ *he restored him from a state of poverty to wealth,* or *competence,* or *sufficiency;* (Ḳ, TA;) as also ▼ انعشهُ: (TA:) and ‡ *he recovered him from a state of perdition* or *destruction.* (TA.) And نَعَشَكَ ٱللّٰهُ ‡ *May God restore thee from poverty to wealth,* or *competence,* or *sufficiency:* or *make thee to continue in life; preserve thee alive.* (A.) And ▼ انعشهُ † *He set him up, and strengthened his heart.* (TA.) And الرَّبِيعُ يَنْعَشُ النَّاسَ ‡ (A, TA,) [*The spring,* or *spring-herbage,* or *the season,* or *rain, called* الربيع,] *makes men to live and enjoy plenty of herbage* or *the like.* (TA.) —— [Hence also,] نَعَشَ المَيِّتَ, (Sh, Ḳ,) aor. as above, (Sh,) and so the inf. n. (TA) ‡ *He eulogized,* or *praised, the dead man,* (Sh, Ḳ,) *and exalted his praise,* or *fame,* or *honour.* (Sh.) —— نَعَشُوا المَيِّتَ also signifies *They carried the dead man upon the* نَعْش, q. v. (A [where this signification is indicated, but not expressed: it is shown, however, by an explanation of pass. part. n. (q. v. infra) in the TA.]) —— نُعِشَ عَلَى جِنَازَتِهَا *A* نعش [q. v.] *was made for her bier.* (Mgh, from a trad. of, or relating to, Fátimeh.)

2. نَعَّشَهُ: see 1. ═ Also, (Ḳ,) or نَعَّشَ لَهُ, (Ṣ,) inf. n. تَنْعِيشٌ, (Ḳ,) *He said to him* نَعَشَكَ ٱللّٰهُ [which see above, in 1, and also below, in 8]: (Ṣ, Ḳ:) in [some copies of] the Ṣ, نَعَّشَكَ الله. (TA.)

4: see 1, in four places.

8. انتعش *He rose;* or *became raised,* or *lifted up:* (TA:) *he rose after his stumble,* or *trip:* (Ṣ, A, Mṣb, Ḳ:) and in like manner you say of a bird, (A, TA,) meaning *it rose* [*after falling* or *alighting*], (TA,) and *he raised his head.* (TA.) Hence the saying, تَعِسَ فَلَا ٱنْتَعَشَ *May he fall, having stumbled,* or *stumble and fall, and not rise* [*again*]: a form of imprecation. (TA.) And hence the saying of 'Omar, اِنْتَعِشْ نَعَشَكَ ٱللّٰهُ *Rise thou: may God raise thee:* or نعشك الله has here one of the two meanings assigned to it before, in 1. (TA.) —— [And hence,] ‡ *He recovered,* or *became recovered, from his embarrassment,* or *difficulty.* (A, TA.)

نَعْشٌ *A state of elevation,* or *exaltation.* (Sh.) See 1. —— *A state of remaining; lastingness; endurance; permanence;* or *continuance;* syn. بَقَآءٌ. (Sh, Ḳ.) ═ [*A kind of litter,* or] *a thing resembling a* مِحَفَّة, upon which the *king used to be carried, when sick:* (IDrd, Mṣb, Ḳ:) not the نَعْش of a corpse. (IDrd, Mṣb.) This is said to be the primary application. (TA.) —— And hence, (TA,) *A bier,* (Ṣ, A, Mṣb, Ḳ,) *when the corpse is upon it,* for otherwise it is called سَرِيرٌ: (Ṣ, IAth, Mṣb:) it is called by the former name because of its height, or its being raised: (Ṣ, TA:) pl. نُعُوشٌ: (Mṣb:) also, *a reticulated thing,* (Az, Mgh, TA,) *resembling a* مِحَفَّة, (Mgh,) *which is put as a cover over a* [*dead*] *woman when she is placed upon the bier;* (Az, Mgh, TA;) but this is properly called حَرَجٌ, though people called it نَعْش, which is properly only the bier itself. (Az, TA.) —— [And hence,] بَنَاتُ نَعْشٍ الكُبْرَى [or بَنَاتُ نَعْشٍ, together with نَعْش or نَعْشَ الكُبْرَى, constitute † *The constellation of Ursa Major:* or *the principal stars thereof:*] *seven stars; whereof four* [*which are in the body*] *are called* نَعْش [or نَعْشٌ], *and three* [*which are in the tail*] *are called* بَنَات, (Ṣ, Ḳ,) i. e., بنات نعش: (TA:) and in like manner بنات نعش الصُّغْرَى, (Ḳ,) or الصُّغْرَى, [together with نعش الصُّغْرَى constitute † *the constellation of Ursa Minor:* or *the principal stars thereof; seven in number; whereof the four in the body are called* نعش, *and the three in the tail are called* بنات]: (Ṣ:) [the former four] said to be likened to the bearers of a bier, because they form a square: (IDrd, TA:) [the بنات being so called as being likened to damsels or to men (for بنات is pl. of اِبْنٌ applied to an irrational thing as well as pl. of بِنْتٌ) following a bier:] Sb and Fr agree that نعش is imperfectly decl. because determinate and of the fem. gender: (Ṣ:) or it is perfectly decl. when indeterminate, but not when determinate [by having the epithet الكُبْرَى or الصُّغْرَى added to it]: (Aboo-'Amr Ez-Záhid, Ḳ:) بَنُو نَعْشٍ also occurs, in poetry; (Sb, Ṣ, Ḳ;) because a single one [of the stars thereof] is called اِبْنُ نَعْشٍ, (Lth, Ḳ,) being made to accord. in gender with كَوْكَبٌ; but when they say أَرْبَع or ثَلَاث, they say بَنَات: (Lth, TA:) [this is agreeable with a general rule; accord. to which, بَنَاتٌ is the pl. of اِبْنٌ applied to anything but a human being:] the pl. of بنات نعش is النَّوَاعِشُ; like as أَبَارِصُ is pl. of سَامُّ أَبْرَصَ. (L, TA.) See also نُعَيْشٌ. —— Also نَعْشٌ *A piece of wood,* (Ḳ, TA,) *of the length of twice the stature of a man,* (TA,) *upon the head of which is a piece of rag,* (Ḳ, TA,) *called* حَرَجٌ, (TA,) *with which young ostriches are hunted* or *captured.* (Ḳ, TA.)

نُعَيْشٌ [or نَعْشٌ † *The small star called*] السُّهَى, *which is* [*by the star* ζ] *in the middle of* بَنَات نَعْش. So in the saying, هُوَ أَخْفَى مِنْ نُعَيْشٍ فِي بَنَاتِ نَعْشٍ [*He, or it, is more obscure than No'eysh among the Benát Naash*]. (A, TA.)

النَّوَاعِش : see نَعْش, near the end.

مَنْعُوش A corpse *carried upon a* نَعْش, or bier. (Ṣ, A,* Mṣb.)

[نعظ, &c.

See Supplement.]

نغب

1. نَغَبَ, aor. ـُ and ـِ, (inf. n. نَغْبٌ, TA,) *He* (a man, TA) *swallowed* saliva. (Ḳ.) — نَغَبَ, (inf. n. نَغْبٌ, TA,) *It* (a bird) *sipped* water: you do not say of a bird شَرِبَ. (Ḳ.) — نَغَبَ *He* (a man) *took in gulps,* or *gulped,* in drinking: (Ḳ:) and likewise an ass. (TA.) — نَغِبْتُ مِنَ الإِنَاءِ نُغَبًا, with kesr, *I drank in gulps from the vessel.* (ISk, Ṣ.)

نَغْبَةٌ *A hungering.* (Ḳ.) A tribe's *wanting food,* or *hungering:* syn. إِقْفَارُ الحَيِّ. (Ḳ, as in some copies: [app. the right reading:] in other copies, أَقْفَار, which is pl. of قَفْرٌ. TA.) — See نُغْبَةٌ.

نُغْبَةٌ and ♦ نَغْبَةٌ *A gulp;* or *as much as is swallowed at once;* of water &c.: (Ṣ, Ḳ:) or the ♦ latter signifies *a single act of gulping:* (Ḳ:) differing from the former like as [its syn.] جَرْعَةٌ does from جُرْعَةٌ: (TA:) pl. of the former نُغَبٌ: (Ṣ:) for which نُغَمٌ occurs in a verse. (TA.) — Ex. وَاهًا مَا أَبْرَدَهَا مِنْ نُغْبَةٍ مَا أَبْرَدَهَا عَلَى الفُؤَادِ تَعْسًا لِلْيَدَيْنِ وَالفَمِ ‡ [*Excellent! How cool a gulp is it! How cool is it to the heart! May the hands and mouth perish!*] said on hearing of the death of an enemy, or of any trial or affliction that has befallen him. (A.) — نَغْبَةٌ *A foul action.* (Ṣ, Ḳ.) So in the following saying, مَا جُرِّبَتْ عَلَيْهِ نَغْبَةٌ قَطُّ [*A foul action was never found to be chargeable upon him.*] (Ṣ.)

نغت

1. نَغَتَ, aor. ـِ, inf. n. نَغْتٌ, He *pulled* hair; syn. جَذَبَ. (Ḳ.)

نغث

نَغْثٌ *Lasting and vehement evil.* (IAạr, Ḳ.) — وَقَعْنَا فِى نَغْثٍ *We fell into lasting and vehement evil.* (L.)

نغر

1. نَغَرَتِ القِدْرُ, (Ṣ, Ḳ, TA,) aor. ـَ; and نَغِرَت (Ḳ, and so in a copy of the A,) aor. ـَ; and نَغُرَت, aor. ـُ; (Ḳ;) inf. n. نَغْرٌ (IḲṭṭ, Ḳ) [of the first] and نَغَرٌ (IḲṭṭ, TA) and نَغَرَانٌ (Ḳ, TA) and نَغِيرٌ, (TA,) *The cooking-pot boiled; estuated; became in a state of violent commotion;* syn. غَلَتْ, (Aṣ, Ṣ, IḲṭṭ, A, L,) and فَارَتْ. (Aṣ, Ḳ.) — Hence, (TA,) نَغِرَ الرَّجُلُ, (Ṣ,) or نَغَرَ, (so in a copy of the A,) ‡ *The man became angry,* or *vehemently* or *most vehemently angry,* or *affected with latent anger without power to exercise it:* (Ṣ, A:) or *his inside boiled by reason of such anger:* (Aṣ, Ṣ:) and نَغِرَ عَلَيْهِ, aor. ـَ; and نَغَرَ, aor. ـِ; and نَغُرَ, aor. ـُ; (Ḳ;) the first of which is the most common; (TA;) inf. n. نَغَرٌ [of the first] and نَغَرَانٌ; and ♦ تَنَغَّرَ; (Ḳ;) [after which last, in the CḲ, the word غَلَى, commencing the explanation, is omitted;] *his inside boiled against him by reason of anger:* (Ḳ:) or *by reason of vehement* or *most vehement anger,* or *latent anger without power to exercise it:* (TA:) or (so accord. to the TA; but in the Ḳ, and) ♦ تَنَغَّرَ عَلَيْهِ *he became changed,* or *altered, to him, and threatened him with evil:* (ISk, Ṣ, Ḳ, TA:) and نَغَرَ, aor. ـِ, inf. n. نَغْرٌ, also signifies *he held enmity in his heart, watching for an opportunity to indulge it; or he hid enmity and violent hatred in his heart; or he bore rancour, malevolence, malice,* or *spite.* (TA.)

5: see 1, in two places.

6. تَنَاغَرَ *i. q.* تَنَاكَرَ [app. meaning, ‡ The *behaving with mutual enmity* or *hostility*]. (Ḳ.)

نَغِرٌ ‡ [*Angry* or *vehemently* or *most vehemently angry,* or *affected with latent anger without power to exercise it:* as is implied in the Ṣ: or] *having his inside boiling by reason of anger:* (Ṣ,* Ḳ:) and [it is said that] إِمْرَأَةٌ نَغِرَةٌ signifies *a woman very jealous;* syn. غَيْرَى: (Ḳ:) [but] it is related in a trad. of 'Alee, that a woman came to him and told him that her husband had illicit intercourse with her female slave; whereupon he said, "If thou be speaker of truth, we stone him; and if thou be a speaker of falsehood, we whip thee:" and she said, رُدُّونِى إِلَى أَهْلِى غَيْرَى نَغِرَةً, (Ṣ, TA,) meaning, [*Restore ye me to my family, very jealous,*] *with my inside boiling by reason of anger,* or *vehement* or *most vehement anger,* or *latent anger without power to exercise it:* this is the explanation given by Aṣ: and ISd says, that he holds نغرة to signify here *angry,* not *very jealous;* since it is related that an Arab said to a woman, أَغَيْرَى أَنْتِ أَمْ نَغِرَةٌ [*Art thou very jealous* or *angry?*] (TA.)

نُغَرٌ *Certain birds like sparrows,* (Ṣ,) or *a species of sparrows,* (Mṣb,) *with red beaks:* (Ṣ, Mṣb:) n. un. with ة: (Ṣ:) or the *young ones of sparrows:* (Ḳ:) n. un. as above: (TA:) or the *young ones of the sparrows;* (Sh, Mṣb;) *which you always see in a lean state:* (Sh:) or [*a species*] *of young sparrows:* (TA:) or the *bird called* بُلْبُل: (Mṣb, Ḳ:) it is said that the people of El-Medeeneh call the بُلْبُل by the names of نُغَرٌ and حُمَّرَةٌ; and it is *said to resemble the sparrow;* and the fem. is with ة: (Mṣb:) or (TA; in the Ḳ, and) *a species of the* حُمَّر, (Ḳ, TA; in the CḲ, erroneously, حُمُر;) *red in the beaks and in the lower parts of the* أَحْنَاك [or *portions beneath the beaks*]: (TA:) or the *males thereof:* (Ḳ:) pl. نِغْرَانٌ, (Ṣ, Mṣb, Ḳ,) like as صِرْدَانٌ is pl. of صُرَدٌ. (Ṣ, Mṣb.) Its dim. is نُغَيْرٌ (Ṣ, Mṣb, Ḳ) occurring in a trad.; يَا أَبَا عُمَيْرٍ مَا فَعَلَ النُّغَيْرُ [*O Aboo-'Omeyr, what did the little nughar?*]; (Ṣ, Ḳ;) said by Mohammad to a little child of Aboo-Talhah El-Anṣáree, who had a bird, or birds, of this name, which died. (TA.)

نغروق

See art. غرنق.

نغص

1. نَغِصَ, aor. ـَ, (Ṣ, Ḳ,) inf. n. نَغَصٌ, (Ṣ,) *He* (a man, Ṣ,) *failed of having his desire fully accomplished:* (Ṣ, Ḳ:) but Lth says, that it is more commonly with teshdeed, i. e. ♦ نَغَّصَ, [unless this be a mistake for نُغِّصَ,] inf. n. تَنْغِيصٌ. (TA.) — And in like manner, (Ṣ,) *He* (a camel) *failed of having his full,* or *complete, draught,* or *drink.* (Ṣ, Ḳ.) — And *It* (beverage) *was imperfect,* or *defective.* (Ḳ.) — See also 5. — نَغْصٌ (L, Ḳ) and نَغَصٌ (L, TA) [both inf. ns., the verb of the former being app. نَغَصَ, used intransitively, and that of the latter نَغَصَ, used transitively, followed by إِبِلَهُ,] also signify The *bringing one's camels to the drinking-trough, and, when they have drunk, turning them back, and bringing others;* (Ḳ;) *taking forth, from every two camels, a strong camel, and putting in its place a weak camel; and thus as it were, making their drinking troublesome.* (TA.) — You say also, نَغَصَ الرَّجُلُ الرَّجُلَ *The man prevented the man from obtaining his share of water by interposing to hinder his camels from drinking:* and in like manner, ♦ أَنْغَصَهُ رَعْيَهُ [*He prevented him from obtaining his share of pasturage for his camels*]: the verb in the latter instance being with أ. (TA.) — See also 2.

2. نغّص عَلَيْنَا *He cut short a thing of which we loved to have much,* or *abundance.* (IAạr, TA.) — نغّص عَلَيْهِ; and ♦ نَغِصَ عليه, inf. n. نَغَصٌ; but the former is the more common; *He rendered* [an affair, or circumstances, or a state,] *troublesome,* or *perturbed, to him;* syn. كَدَّرَ. (IḲṭṭ, TA.) You say, نغّص اللّٰهُ عَلَيْهِ العَيْشَ, (Ṣ, Ḳ,) inf. n. تَنْغِيصٌ; (Ṣ;) and نغّصه (Ṣ, Ḳ) and ♦ انغص عليه العيش; (Ḳ;) *God rendered life troublesome,* or *perturbed, to him;* syn. كَدَّرَهُ: (Ṣ, Ḳ:) the first of these is the most common:

(TA:) the second occurs in poetry; the pronoun in this relating to a man. (Akh, Ṣ, TA.) ═ See also نَغِضَ.

4: see 1, last sentence: — and see also 2.

5. تنغّصت عيشته, (Ṣ,) or مَعِيشَتُهُ, (Ḳ,) *His state of life,* (Ṣ,) or *his means of subsistence,* (Ḳ,) *became troublesome,* or *perturbed,* or *attended with trouble*; syn. تَكَدَّرَتْ. (Ṣ, Ḳ.) You say also, نَغِصَ أَمْرُهُ, inf. n. نَغَصٌ, [*His affair,* or *case, became troublesome, &c.*;] (A;) [for] ▾ نَغَصَ is syn. with تَنَغَّصَ as signifying تَكَدَّرَ. (Ḥar, p. ٢٧٣).

6. تناغصت الإِبِلُ عَلَى الحَوْضِ *The camels crowded,* or *pressed, together to the drinking-trough.* (Ks, Ḳ.*)

نُغُصٌ is said to signify *Things that prevent one from attaining an object of desire.* (Ḥar, p. ٢٧٣.)

مُنَغِّصٌ Any one *who cuts short a thing of which one loves to have more.* (IAạr, TA.)

نغض

1. نَغَضَ, aor. ـِ, (Ks, Ṣ, A, Mṣb, Ḳ,) and ـُ, (Ṣ, A, Ḳ,) inf. n. نَغْضٌ (Ṣ, Mṣb, Ḳ) and نُغُوضٌ (Ṣ, Ḳ,) and نَغَضَانٌ and نَغَضٌ, (Ḳ,) *It was* or *became, in a state of motion, commotion, agitation, or convulsion; it shook; shook about; wabbled; tottered; wagged; nodded;* syn. تَحَرَّكَ, (Ṣ, A, Mṣb, Ḳ,) and اِضْطَرَبَ, (A, Ḳ,) فِى اِرْتِجَافٍ; (TA;) as also ▾ انغض (Mṣb, Ḳ) and ▾ تنغّض: (Ḳ:) it is said of a man's head; (Ṣ, TA;) and also, (Ṣ, A,) with نَغَضَانٌ and نَغْضٌ for its inf. ns., (Ṣ,) of a camel's saddle, (Ṣ, A,) and of the central incisor (Ṣ, TA) of a child, (Ṣ,) or of any tooth, as also ▾ the last of the verbs above mentioned; (A;) and of other things; (Mṣb, TA;) نَغْضٌ signifying any *moving in a shaking* or *tremulous* or *convulsive manner* (فِى اِرْتِجَافٍ); (Ṣ, TA;) and نَغَضَتْ and ▾ تَنَغَّضَتْ, said of a tooth, being *syn. with* رَجَفَتْ. (A.) — Also, inf. n. نَغَضَانٌ, *He,* or *it, was,* or *became, disquieted, agitated,* or *violently agitated.* (TA.) — نَغَضُوا إِلَى العَدُوِّ ‡ *They rose and hastened and went forth to,* or *towards, the enemy.* (A, TA.) — نَغَضَ also signifies † *It* (a thing, TA) *was,* or *became, dense:* (so in some copies of the Ḳ) or *much in quantity:* (so in other copies of the Ḳ:) or *much in quantity, and dense.* (TA.) And ‡ *It* (a cloud) *was,* or *became, dense, and then became ready to rain, and was seen to move about, one part into another, without its going along:* (Ṣ:) or *was seen to become ready to rain, without motion, not travelling along:* (A:) or *it travelled along.* (IF.) [See نَاغِضٌ, below.] — نَغَضَ أَمْرُهُ † *His affair,* or *case, was,* or *became, in a weak,* or *unsound, state;* syn. وَهَى. (TA.) ═ See also 4, in two places.

4. انغض: see 1. ═ انغضهُ *He put it in a state of motion, commotion, agitation,* or *convulsion; shook it; shook it about; made it to wabble,* or *totter; wagged it; nodded it;* as also ▾ نَغَّضَهُ; (Ṣ, Mṣb, Ḳ, TA;) and ▾ نَغَضَ بِهِ: (A:) namely a thing: (Mṣb:) or his head; (Ṣ, A, TA;) *in wonder;* (A;) or *as one in wonder at a thing;* (Ṣ, TA;) or *in disapproval* of a thing told him; (AHeyth, TA;) or *in derision;* or *as though asking the meaning of what was said, inclining to the speaker.* (TA.) Hence, in the Ḳur, [xvii. 53,] فَسَيُنْغِضُونَ إِلَيْكَ رُؤُوسَهُمْ (Ṣ, TA) *And they will shake,* or *wag, their heads at thee, in derision.* (TA.)

5: see 1, in three places.

نَغْضٌ One *who shakes his head, and trembles in his gait:* (Ḳ:) an inf. n. used as an epithet. (TA.) — *A male ostrich that shakes his head:* (Ṣ:) or نَغْضٌ, as also ▾ نُغْضٌ, is a name of *the male ostrich;* determinate; (Ḳ;) being a name of the species; like أُسَامَةُ: (TA:) so called because, when he hastens his gait, he moves up and down: (Lth:) or a name of *the male ostrich that has a habit of going round about:* (AHeyth, Ḳ:) and ▾ نَغْضَةٌ [is the n. un., signifying] *an ostrich.* (TA.) — See also نَاغِضٌ.

نُغْضٌ: see نَاغِضٌ, in three places.

نَغِضٌ: see نَغْضٌ.

نَغْضَةٌ *A tree.* (IḲt.) — See also نَغْضٌ.

نَغُوضٌ A she-camel *having a large hump:* because, when it is large, it shakes, or quakes. (IF, Ḳ.)

نَغَّاضٌ [*In a state of much motion, commotion, agitation, or convulsion; shaking, shaking about, wabbling, tottering, wagging, or nodding, much*]. You say, إِبِلٌ نَغَّاضَةٌ بِرِحَالِهَا [*Camels jogging much with their saddles;* or *jogging much their saddles*]. (A, TA.) — See also نَاغِضٌ. — نَغَّاضُ البَطْنِ *Wrinkled in the belly:* an expression applied to Mohammad, (Ḳ,) by 'Alee, who thus explained it: because of the elevation of the wrinkled parts above the even surface of the belly: or it may be derived from غُضُونٌ, meaning "wrinkles" in the belly, by transposition of letters. (TA.)

نَاغِضٌ [*In a state of motion, commotion,* or *agitation,* or *convulsion; shaking; shaking about; wabbling; tottering; wagging; nodding:* pl. نُغَّضٌ]. You say, مَحَالٌ نُغَّضٌ [*Great pully-sheaves in a state of motion, &c.*]. (Ṣ, TA.) And غَيْمٌ نَاغِضٌ (Ḳ) and ▾ نَغَّاضٌ (Ṣ, Ḳ) ‡ *A cloud,* or *clouds, becoming dense, and then ready to rain, and seen to move about, one part into another, without going along:* (Ṣ:) or *in a state of motion,* or *commotion, one part after another,* (Ḳ, TA,) *not travelling along:* (TA:) or *seen to move about, one part into another, without going along.* (L.) — Also, (Ṣ, Ḳ,) or ▾ نَاغِضَةٌ, (so in a copy of the A,) and ▾ نُغْضٌ and ▾ نَغْضٌ, (A, Ḳ,) but this is rare, (TA,) *A cartilage:* (Ṣ:) or the *cartilage* of the shoulder-blade: (A, Ḳ:) or the *part thereof where it moves to and fro:* (Ḳ:) or the *upper part of the end of the cartilage* of the shoulder-blade: (TA:) or the ▾ نُغْضٌ of the shoulder-blade is the *thin bone at the extremity* thereof: (Sh:) or the ▾ نُغْضَانِ are the *parts of the root* of the shoulder-blade *that move about in walking:* (L:) and the نَاغِضٌ of a man is the *base of the neck, where he moves about his head,* (Sh.)

نَاغِضَةٌ: see نَاغِضٌ.

[نغف, &c.

See Supplement.]

نغا

نُغَاةٌ *One of several parts,* or *portions, of scattered herbage:* or *one of several adjacent meadows* (رِيَاض), *separated from, and rising above, the greater part of the pasture:* pl. نُغًا. (Ḳ.)

نفت

1. نَفَتَتِ القِدْرُ, (Ṣ, Ḳ,) aor. ـِ, inf. n. نَفِيتٌ (Ṣ) and نَفْتٌ and نَفَتَانٌ, (L,) *The cooking-pot boiled:* (Ḳ:) or *threw forth what resembled arrows, by reason of* [*its vehement*] *boiling:* (Ṣ, L:) [see also نَفَثَتْ, and نَفَطَتْ:] or [*boiled so that*] *the broth,* or *gravy, stuck to its sides:* (Ḳ:) or *the broth boiled in the cooking pot, and what dried thereof stuck to the sides of the pot:* (L:) you say [also] ▾ تَنَافَتْ القِدْرُ, and تَنَافَطُ, [for تَتَنَافَتُ and تَتَنَافَطُ]. (Ṣ, L [but in the latter, these two verbs are written without the syll. points].) — يَنْفِتُ غَضَبًا, as also يَنْفِطُ, † *He boils with anger.* (Ṣ:) — يَنْفِتُ عَلَيْهِ غَضَبًا, as also ينفط, † *He boils against him with anger.* (TA.) — صَدْرُهُ يَنْفِتُ بِالعَدَاوَةِ ‡ [*His breast boils with enmity*]. (A.) [See also نَفَثَ.] — نَفَتَ, aor. ـِ, inf. n. نَفْتٌ and نَفَتَانٌ (L, Ḳ) and نَفِيتٌ and نُفَاتٌ, (L,) † *He* (a man, L) *was angry:* (Ḳ, L:) or نَفَتَانٌ resembles coughing: [so that the verb seems to signify *he made a noise like coughing, by reason of anger:*] (L:) or *he blew in anger:* (L:) or *he blew,* (نَفَخَ, as in the copies of the Ḳ in my hands,) or *swelled,* or *became inflated,* (انتفخ,

as in the TA,) by reason of anger. (Ḳ.) — نَفَتَ, (aor. ـِ , L,) inf. n. نَفْتٌ, *It* (flour or the like) *had water poured upon it, and swelled,* or *became inflated,* (تَنَفَّخَ,) *in consequence.* (L, Ḳ.)

6 : see 1.

مِرْجَلٌ نَفُوتٌ *A cooking-pot throwing forth what resembles arrows, by reason of [its vehement] boiling: &c.* (Ṣ, L.)

نَفِيتَةٌ *A certain kind of food, thicker than what is called* سَخِينَةٌ; (Ḳ;) *i.q.* حَرِيقَةٌ; *made by sprinkling flour upon water or milk,* (*fresh milk,* L,) *until it becomes swollen or inflated,* (يَنْفِت,) (Ṣ, L,) *when it is supped,* or *sipped* (يتحسّى); (L;) it is thicker than سَخِينَة; the master of a family uses it plentifully for his household in times of scarcity: (Ṣ, L:) they only eat نفيتة and سخينة in a time of straitness, and dearness, and leanness of the cattle: Az says, in art. حذرق, سخينة is flour thrown upon water or milk, and cooked, and then eaten with dates or [here a word in the L is illegible; after which we read] and it is [what is called] حَسَاء; and it is also called سَخُونَةٌ: and نَفِيتَةٌ and حَرِيقَةٌ and حَرِيرَةٌ and نَفِيثَةٌ are *a kind of* حسا, *between thick and thin.* (L.) [See also خَزِيرٌ, and حَرِيقَةٌ.]

نفث

1. نَفَثَ, aor. ـِ and ـُ, inf. n. نَفْثٌ (Ṣ, Ḳ) and نَفَثَانٌ, (TA,) [*He puffed;* or *blew, without spitting:* or *he sputtered,* or *blew forth a little spittle in minute scattered particles:* or] *he spat:* or *he* [*did as though he*] *spat without ejecting spittle:* and نَفَثَ فِى العُقْدَةِ signifies *he spat, ejecting a little spittle, upon the knot,* in enchantment: (Mṣb:) or النَّفْثُ is *like* النَّفْخُ, or *blowing, and less than* التَّفْلُ, or *spitting,* or *ejecting spittle from the mouth:* (Ṣ, Ḳ:) or *like blowing, with* [*the emission of*] *spittle:* (Keshsháf;) or *like blowing,* as done in enchantment, *without spittle:* the action, if accompanied by spittle, being termed التفل: this is the most correct explanation: ('Ináyeh:) or *gentle blowing without spittle:* (الاذكار:) or *more than blowing;* or *like blowing; but less than spitting: sometimes without spittle,* thus differing from التفل; *and sometimes with a little spittle,* thus differing from النفخ: or *the emitting wind from the mouth, together with a little spittle.* (MF.) — لَا بُدَّ لِلْمَصْدُورِ أَنْ يَنْفِثَ [*He who has a disease in his chest must spit*]. A proverb. (Ṣ.) — نَفَثَهُ مِنْ فِيهِ, aor. ـِ, inf. n. نَفْثٌ, *He ejected it from his mouth.* (Mṣb.) — [Hence,] نَفَثَ اللّٰهُ الشَّىْءَ فِى القَلْبِ ‡ *God cast,* or *put, the thing into the heart.* (Mṣb) — نُفِثَ فِى رُوعِى كَذَا ‡ *Such a thing was inspired,* or *put, into my mind.* (A.) — نَفَثَ فِى رُوعِى ‡ *He* (the Holy Spirit [Gabriel]) *inspired,* or *cast,* or *put, into my mind,* or *heart.* (Nh, from a trad.) — [You say,] لَوْ نَفَثَ عَلَيْكَ فُلَانٌ قَطَّرَكَ [*If such a one blew,* or *spat, upon thee, he would throw thee down upon thy side.*]. Said to one who tries his strength with one superior to him. (A.) — نَفَثَ عَلَىَّ غَضَبًا as though meaning *He blew at me by reason of the violence of his anger.* (L.) [See also نَفَتَ.] — الحَيَّةُ تَنْفِثُ السَّمَّ إِذَا نَكَزَتْ [*The serpent ejects venom from its mouth when it inflicts a wound with its nose*]. (Ṣ.) — نَفَثَ *It* (a wound) *emitted* blood. (TA.) — [From the blowing or spitting upon the knots:] نَفَثَهُ, inf. n. نَفْثٌ, *He enchanted him.* (Mṣb.) — نَفَثَتِ القِدْرُ, aor. ـِ, inf. n. نَفِيثٌ and نَفْثٌ, *The cooking-pot boiled:* or, *boiled, and threw forth what resembled arrows, by reason of the vehemence of its boiling.* (Mṣb.) [See also نَفَتَت.] It is when it begins to boil. (TA.)

نَفْثُ الشَّيْطَانِ *Poetry:* (Ḳ, from a trad.:) called نفث because it is like a thing which a man spits, or blows, (يَنْفِثُ,) from his mouth, like incantation. (A'Obeyd.) — ذَا مِنْ نَفَثَاتِ فُلَانٍ *This is of the poetry of such a one.* (TA.)

دَمٌ نَفِيثٌ *Blood emitted by a wound* (Ṣ, Ḳ) or *vein.* (TA.)

مِتْنَاثٌ كَأَنَّهَا نُفَاثٌ [*A plain land that produces many plants,* or *herbs,* or *much herbage,*] *as though blowing forth,* or *spitting forth, the plants,* or *herbs.* (L, from a trad.) [The correctness of نُفَاثٌ is questioned by El-Khaṭṭábee. May it not be a mistake for نَفَّاثٌ?]

نُفَاثَةٌ *What one blows,* or *spits,* (يَنْفِثُ,) *from his mouth.* (Ṣ.) — *What a person having a disease in his chest blows forth or spits out,* يَنْفِثُ. (Ḳ.) — *What remains in one's mouth, of a* سِوَاك, *or tooth-stick, and is spit out:* (Ṣ:) *a particle broken off* (شَظِيَّةٌ: so in the L &c.: in the Ḳ, شَطِيبَةٌ:) *from a* سواك, *or tooth-stick, remaining in the mouth, and spit out.* (L, Ḳ.) One says, لَوْ سَأَلَنِى نُفَاثَةَ سِوَاكٍ مَا أَعْطَيْتُهُ *If he asked me for a particle of a tooth-stick, remaining in my mouth, I would not give him (it).* (Ṣ.)

نَفِيثَةٌ *A certain kind of food.* (See نَفِيتَةٌ and وَطِيئَةٌ.)

نَفَّاثٌ *An enchanter; one who is in the habit of enchanting:* fem. with ة. (Mṣb.) — النَّفَّاثَاتُ فِى العُقَدِ [Ḳur, cxiii. 4,] *The women who blow, without spitting,* saying something at the same time, *upon the knots* which they tie in a thread, or string: (Jel:) meaning *the enchantresses.* (Ṣ, Ḳ, Jel.) [See a verse cited voce عَاضِهَةٌ.]

نَافِثٌ *Enchanting.* (Mṣb.)

مَنْفُوثٌ A man *enchanted.* (A.)

نفج

1. نَفَجَ, (Ṣ, Ḳ,) aor. ـُ, inf. n. نُفُوجٌ; (Mṣb;) and ▼ انتفج; (TA;) *It* (a hare, Ṣ, Ḳ, or other animal, Mṣb) *sprang up* (Ṣ, Ḳ) from its hole; or *leaped.* (TA.) — نَفَجَ; (TA;) and ▼ انفج, (Ṣ,) inf. n. إِنْفَاجٌ; (Mṣb;) and ▼ انتفج; (TA;) *He made* a hare *to spring up* (Ṣ, &c.) from its hole; or *to leap.* (TA.) — نَفَجَ, aor. ـِ and ـُ, inf. n. نَفْجٌ; and ▼ انتفج; *It* (a jerboa) *ran:* (M:) or *slackened his run.* (A.) — نَفَجَ, and ▼ انتفج, and ▼ تنفّج, *It* (anything) *rose;* or *became elevated,* or *exalted.* (TA.) — نَفَجَ, aor. ـُ, inf. n. نَفْجٌ, *He made* anything *to rise;* or *to become elevated,* or *exalted.* (TA.) — نَفَجَتِ الفَرُّوجَةُ *The chicken came forth* from its egg. (Ṣ, Ḳ.) — نَفَجَ, (aor. ـُ, inf. n. نَفْجٌ, Ṣ,) *It* (a woman's breast) *heaved up* her shift. (Ṣ, Ḳ.) — نَفَجَتِ الرِّيحُ ‡ *The wind came with force:* (Ṣ, Ḳ:) or, *suddenly.* (TA.) — نَفَجَ, inf. n. نَفْجٌ, *He magnified,* or *made great,* him, or it. (Mṣb, TA.) [And so,] ▼ انتفج *It became great.* (TA.) — نَفَجَ, aor. ـُ, inf. n. نَفْجٌ; (Mṣb;) and ▼ انتفج, (TA,) and ▼ تنفّج; (Ḳ;) *He boasted of that which he did not possess,* (Mṣb,) *and which was not in him:* (TA:) or, *of more than he possessed.* (Ḳ.)

4: see 1, and 10.

5: see 1, in two places.

8. إِنْتَفَجَا جَنْبَا البَعِيرِ *The sides of the camel became elevated,* (Ṣ, Ḳ,) [or *bulging,*] *and great, naturally.* (TA.) — Hence the expression إِنْتِفَاجُ الأَهِلَّةِ † [*The swelling out of the new moons*], in a trad. respecting the signs [of the last day]. (TA.) — See 1 throughout.

10. استنفج (IAạr, M) and ▼ انفج, (M,) *He* (a sportsman) *drew forth* a jerboa [&c. from its hole]. (M.) — Hence, (TA,) † *He drew forth, and caused to appear,* the anger of a person. (Ḳ.)

نَفْجٌ and ▼ نَفَاجَةٌ ‡ [*A boasting of that which one does not possess,* or *the like:* see 1, and نَفَّاجٌ]. (A.) [See also نَفْخ.]

نُفُجُ الحَقِيبَةِ A woman, (Ḳ,) and a man, (TA,) *large in the buttocks:* (Ḳ, TA:) or *prominent therein.* (TA in art. حقب.)

نَفْجَةٌ *A single leap* of a hare from the place where it has been lying. In a trad., a sedition, or disturbance, is likened to this in regard of the shortness of its duration. (TA.)

نَفَاجَةٌ : see نَفْجٌ and نَفَّاجٌ.

نَفِيجَةٌ *A bow* (Ṣ, Ḳ) *made of a piece of wood of the kind of tree called* نَبْع ; not known by Aboo-Sa'eed with ج [in the place of ح]. (Ṣ [so in the copies of that work which I am using, three in number: but in one copy, "except with ح"].)

نَفَّاجٌ ‡ A *proud* man; as also ▼ مُنْتَفِجٌ : (Ḳ:) a *boastful and proud man*: (ISk, Ṣ:) a man *who praises himself for that which is not in him*: one *who says that which he does not, and who boasts of that which does not belong to him and which is not in him*; as also ▼ ذُو نَفْجٍ (and ▼ ذُو نَفَاجَةٍ, A): or one *who boasts of that which he does not possess*: and said to be not of high repute. (TA.) [See also نَقَّاشٌ.]

نَافِجٌ : see نَافِجَةٌ.

نَافِجَةٌ The *commencement of anything*, (so in two copies of the Ṣ, and so in the Mṣb,) or *of any wind*, (so in one copy of the Ṣ,) *that begins with vehemence*, or *violence*: (Ṣ, Mṣb:) or *a wind that begins with vehemence*: (Ḳ:) or, *that comes with vehemence*: (A:) Aṣ thinks it to be *attended by cold*: AḤn says, that sometimes the north wind rises upon people when they have been sleeping, and almost destroys them with cold at the close of the night, when the former part of the night has been warm: (TA:) or *a wind that rises upon one suddenly and vehemently, when he is not aware*: (Sh:) pl. نَوَافِجُ. (A.) — نَافِجَةٌ ‡ *A cloud abounding with rain*: (Ṣ, Ḳ:) so called from the same word as signifying "a wind that comes with vehemence:" (TA:) thus called by the name of the thing which is its cause. (Ṣ.) = نَافِجَةٌ The *hinder part of a rib*: (Ṣ:) or, *of the ribs*: (Ḳ:) as also ▼ نَافِجٌ: (TA:) pl. نَوَافِجُ. (Ṣ.) = نَافِجَةٌ † *Camels which a man inherits, and whereby his camels are increased in number.* (TA.) — نَافِجَةٌ ‡ *A daughter*: so called because she increases the property of her father by her dowry: (Ḳ:) or, *that increases the property of her father*; for he takes her dowry (consisting of camels, TA) and adds it to his property, (or camels, TA,) so that the amount becomes raised. (Ṣ.) The Arabs used to say, in the time of paganism, when a daughter was born to one of them, هَنِيْئًا لَكَ النَّافِجَةُ *May she who is to increase thy property by her dowry be productive of enjoyment to thee!* (Ṣ.) = نَافِجَةٌ *A bag, follicle, or vesicle, of musk*: (Ḳ:) pl. نَوَافِجُ: (Ṣ:) an arabicized word, (Ṣ, Ḳ,) from [the Persian] نَافَهْ; and therefore some say that it is properly written نَافَجَةٌ: or, accord. to the Mṣb, it is Arabic, and a bag of musk is so called because of its high value, from نَفَّجَهُ "he magnified him, or it:" but this requires consideration. (TA.) See فَارَةُ المِسْكِ, voce فَارٌ.

أَنْفُجَانِىٌّ One *who exaggerates, or exceeds the due bounds, in speech*; (Ḳ;) and *who boasts of that which he does not possess.* (TA.)

مَنَافِجُ *Pieces of stuff with which women make their buttocks to appear large*; syn. عُظَّامَاتٌ. (Ḳ.)

مُنْتَفِجُ الجَنْبَيْنِ A man *having elevated*, [or *bulging*,] *sides.* (A.) — مُنْتَفِجٌ A camel *having prominent flanks.* (TA.) See نَفَّاجٌ.

نفح

1. نَفَحَ, aor. َ, (Ṣ, L, Ḳ,) inf. n. نَفْحٌ (L, Ḳ) and نُفُوحٌ (L) and نُفَاحٌ and نَفَحَانٌ, (Ḳ,) *It* (perfume) *diffused its odour.* (Ṣ, L, Ḳ.) — نَفَحَتِ الرِّيحُ, (Ṣ, Mṣb, Ḳ,) aor. َ, inf. n. نَفْحٌ, (Mṣb,) ‡ *The wind blew*: (Ṣ, Mṣb, Ḳ:) or *blew gently*; *began to be in a state of commotion*: (A:) نَفَحَتْ and نَفَخَتْ are syn., except that the effect of النَّفْخ is greater than that of النَّفْح: (Zj:) or, accord. to Aṣ, (Ṣ,) or IAạr, (TA,) نَفْحٌ relates to a cold, or cool, wind; and نَفْخٌ, to a hot wind: (Ṣ, TA:) [but see نَفْحَةٌ]. — نَفَحَتْهُ الجنوب بِبَرْدِهَا ‡ *The south wind blew upon it with its cold, or coolness.* (IB.) — نَفَحَ العِرْقُ, (aor. َ, inf. n. نَفْحٌ, Ṣ,) ‡ *The vein ejected, or spirted forth, blood.* (Ṣ, Ḳ.) And in like manner, نَفَحَتِ الطَّعْنَةُ بِالدَّمِ ‡ *The stab ejected, or spirted forth, blood.* (TA.) — نَفَحَ اللَّبَنَ نَفْحَةً ‡ *He churned the milk once.* (A.) = نَفَحَهُ بِالسَّيْفِ ‡ *He struck him, or it, lightly, or slightly, with the sword*: (A:) *he reached, or hit, him, or it,* (تَنَاوَلَهُ,) *with the sword* (Ṣ, L, Ḳ) *from a distance,* (Ṣ, L,) *by a side-blow,* شَزْرًا. (L.) — نَفَحَ, inf. n. نَفْحٌ, *He struck, smote,* or *beat.* (L.) See 3. — نَفَحَ, inf. n. نَفْحٌ, *He threw,* or *cast.* (L.) — نَفَحَ شَيْئًا † *He thrust, or pushed, or repelled, a thing from him.* (L.) — نَفَحَتِ الدَّابَّةُ, aor. َ, inf. n. نَفْحٌ, *The horse, or the like, kicked, or struck, with its hind leg*: (L:) or, *with its hoof*: (Mṣb:) or, *with the extremity of its hoof*: النَّفْحُ is said to be with one hind leg; and الرَّمْحُ, with both hind legs together. (L.) نَفَحَتِ النَّاقَةُ *The she-camel struck, or kicked, with her hind leg.* (Ṣ.) أَبْطَلَ نَفْحَ الدَّابَّةِ *He made the kicking of the horse, or the like, with its hind leg, to be of no account*; not to require anything to be paid by its owner. (L.) [See 3 in art. عقب.] = نَفَحَهُ بِشَىْءٍ, (inf. n. نَفْحٌ, Mṣb,) ‡ *He gave him a thing.* (Ṣ, Ḳ.) — نَفَحَهُ نَفْحَةً ‡ *He gave him a gift*; or *conferred upon him a favour*]. (Ṣ.) [See an ex. voce عَرَبَةٌ.]

3. نَافَحُوهُمْ (inf. n. مُنَافَحَةٌ, TA) ‡ *They contended with them with swords face to face*; or *encountered them in war face to face, having before their faces neither shields nor anything else*; syn. كَافَحُوهُمْ: (Ṣ, Ḳ:) originally signifying *they approached them in fight so near that the breath of each party reached the other.* (TA.) — نَافَحَهُ ‡ *He contended with him.* (Ḳ.) — نَافَحَ عَنْهُ; (Ṣ, A;) and ▼ نَفَحَ عَنْهُ, (A,) inf. n. نَفْحٌ; (IAạr;) ‡ *He contended for him, or in defence of him*; (Ṣ;) *repelled from him, and defended him*: (IAạr, A:) as also نَاضَحَ. (TA.)

نَفْحَةٌ *An odour,* whether good or bad: or *a plenteous odour*; differing from نَفْخَةٌ, which is a slight odour: (AḤn, in L, art. نفخ:) pl. نَفَحَاتٌ. (L.) You say لَهُ نَفْحَةٌ طَيِّبَةٌ, (Ṣ, L,) and خَبِيثَةٌ, (L,) *It has a good, or sweet, and a bad, or foul, odour.* (L.) — نَفْحَةٌ ‡ *A blast, or breath, of wind.* (Ḳ.) — نَفْحَةٌ مِنَ الصَّبَا ‡ *A pleasant and fragrant blast of the east wind.* And نفحةٌ مِنْ سَمُومٍ ‡ *A grievous blast of hot wind.* (AHeyth.) — نَفْحَةٌ مِنَ العَذَابِ † *A part, or portion, of punishment*: (Ṣ, Ḳ:) or *a grievous blast of punishment*: (AHeyth:) or *a most violent infliction of punishment.* (L.) — نَفْحَةُ الدَّمِ ‡ *The first gush of blood from a wound.* (Khálid Ibn-Jembeh, L.) — نَفْحَةٌ ‡ *A single churning* (مَخْضَةٌ: so in the A and TA: in the CḲ and a MS. copy of the Ḳ, مَحْضَةٌ, with ح unpointed:) of milk. (A, Ḳ.) — [See 1.] — نَفْحَةٌ ‡ *A gift*: (Mṣb:) [pl. نَفَحَاتٌ.] — لَا تَزَالُ لِفُلَانٍ نَفَحَاتٌ مِنَ المَعْرُوفِ (Ṣ, L) *There cease not to be attributable to such a one acts of kindness, or favours.* (L.) — تَعَرَّضُوا لِنَفَحَاتِ رَحْمَةِ اللّٰهِ ‡: (TA:) see art. عرض, voce تَعَرُّضٌ.

رِيحٌ نَفُوحٌ ‡ *A wind that blows violently, and raises the dust.* (L.) — يَمَانِيَةٌ نَفُوحٌ ‡ *A south wind* (Ṣ, IB) *that blows coldly, or coolly.* (IB.) — دَابَّةٌ نَفُوحٌ *A horse, or the like, that kicks with its hind leg*: or, *with the extremity of its hoof.* (L.) [See 1.] — نَفُوحٌ ‡ *A she-camel whose milk comes forth without its being drawn from the teat*: (Ṣ, Ḳ:) and an udder *that does not retain its milk.* (AZ.) See نَفَّاحٌ. = قَوْسٌ نَفُوحٌ ‡ *A bow that sends the arrow far*; or *that impels the arrow with force*: (Ṣ, A, Ḳ:) as also ▼ نَفِيحَةٌ (Ḳ) and ▼ مِنْفَحَةٌ: (TA:) each of which two words is a name for *a bow*: (Ṣ, with respect to the former, and TA, with respect to the latter:) pl. of the former نَفَائِحُ: (Ṣ:) and ▼ نَفِيحَةٌ signifies *a branch of the tree called* نَبْع, *of which a bow is made.* (ISk, Ṣ, Ḳ.) [See also نَفِيجَةٌ, with ج.]

نَفِيحَةٌ : see نَفُوحٌ.

مِسْكٌ نَفَّاحٌ [*Musk that diffuses much odour* or *fragrance*]. (A, art. خطر.) = طَعْنَةٌ نَفَّاحَةٌ ‡ *A stab that ejects, or spirts forth, blood, much, or vehemently.* (TA.) † طَعْنَةٌ نَفُوحٌ ‡ *A stab that ejects its blood quickly.* (T.) — نَفَّاحٌ ‡ *One who gives many gifts.* (TA.) — النَّفَّاحُ, (Ḳ,) or النَّفَّاحُ بِالخَيْرِ, (TA,) *The Bestower of* [*many*] *benefits* upon mankind, or the creation: (Ḳ:) an epithet applied to God; but disapproved by some, because not so applied in the Ḳur-án or the traditions.

نَافِحٌ *Diffusing odour; fragrant.* Ex. نَافِجَةٌ نَافِحَةٌ *A bag, or vesicle, of musk diffusing odour, or fragrant:* pl. نَوَافِحُ. (A.)

إِنْفَحَةٌ (Ṣ, Ḳ, &c.) said to be the most common form of the word, (TA,) for which one should not say أَنْفَحَةٌ, (ISk,) but this is mentioned by Ibn-Et-Teiyánee and the author of the 'Eyn, (MF,) and sometimes it is written and pronounced إِنْفَحَّةٌ, (Ḳ,) or this is the most common form, (Mṣb,) and most approved, (ISk,) and sometimes إِنْفِحَةٌ, (Ḳ,) and † مِنْفَحَةٌ, (IAạr, Ṣ, Ḳ,) and بِنْفَحَةٌ, (IAạr, Ḳ,) with ب in the place of the م, (TA,) [*The rennet,* or *rennet-bag, of a kid* or *lamb;* i.e.] *A substance that comes forth from the belly of a kid, containing coagulated milk which is termed* لِبَأٌ*, used as a means of converting fresh milk into cheese:* (IDrst:) or *a thing that is taken forth from the belly of a sucking-pig,* (or *lamb,* Mṣb,) *of a yellow colour, and squeezed in some cotton,* (*which is soaked, into milk,* L, Mṣb,) *whereupon it* (i.e. *the milk,* MF) *becomes thick, like cheese:* (L, Mṣb, Ḳ:) or *the stomach* (كَرِش) *of a lamb* or *kid before it eats:* (AZ, Ṣ, Mṣb:) when it eats, it is called كَرِش. (AZ, Ṣ.) F imputes inadvertence to J in his explaining انفحة by the term كَرِش; but he does not explain it by this term absolutely; and F adds to his own explanation what makes it exactly the same as that of J, [except that he makes it relate to a kid only,] saying "when the kid eats, it," that is the انفحة, "is called كَرِش." (MF.) None but a ruminating animal has an انفحة. (Lth.) The pl. is أَنَافِحُ. (Ṣ, Ḳ.) Any انفحة, especially [that of] the hare, if hung upon the thumb of a person suffering from a fever, cures him. (Ḳ.) — إِنْفَحَةٌ also signifies *A kind of tree* (شَجَر) *resembling the* بَاذِنْجَان. (Ḳ.)

مِنْفَحَةٌ: see نَفُوحٌ and إِنْفَحَةٌ.

نفخ

1. نَفَخَ بِفَمِهِ, (Ḳ,) aor. ُ, [accord. to Golius and Freytag, incorrectly, ِ; see Ḳur, iii. 43, &c.] inf. n. نَفْخٌ; (Mṣb;) and † نَفَّخَ, (Ḳ,) inf. n. تَنْفِيخٌ; (TA;) *He blew with his mouth; sent forth wind from his mouth;* (Ḳ;) this is done in taking rest, and in labour or exertion, and the like. (L.) نَفَخَ is mostly used as a neut. v.; but sometimes it is trans., as many have asserted: you say نَفَخَ الصُّورَ, as well as نَفَخَ فِيهِ, *He blew the trumpet,* or *blew into the trumpet:* (MF, TA:) نَفَخَهُ is a dial. form of نَفَخَ فِيهِ: (Ṣ:) also, نَفَخَ فِى النَّارِ [*he blew the fire;* or *blew into the fire*]: [see 8 (last sentence) in art. قوت:] and نَفَخَ فِى الزِّقِّ [*he blew into,* or *inflated, the skin*]: and sometimes one says نَفَخَهُ. (Mṣb.) نُفِخُوا occurs in a verse of El-Ḳaṭámee for نُفِخُوا. (Ṣ.) — نَفَخَ الشَّيْطَانُ فِى أَنْفِهِ † ‡ [*The devil blew into his nose*]: said of him who aspires to that which is not for him. (TA.) — نَفَخَ شِدْقَيْهِ ‡ [*He inflated,* or *puffed out, the sides of his mouth;* meaning] *he was proud,* or *affected pride.* (A.) — نَفَخَهُ, aor. ُ, inf. n. نَفْخٌ, *It* (food) *inflated him,* or *filled him.* (L.) — نَفِخَ, aor. َ, inf. n. نَفَخٌ, (Ṣ, L,) *He* (a man, Ṣ, and a horse, L) *had inflated testicles.* (Ṣ, L.) — Also, *He* (a beast of carriage) *had his pasterns inflated with wind.* When a beast thus affected walks, the humour subsides. (L.) — نَفَخَ بِهَا *Pepedit; crepitum ventris emisit.* (Ṣ, Ḳ.) — نَفَخَتِ الرِّيحُ *The wind came suddenly.* (L.) — نَفَخَتْ بِهِمِ الطَّرِيقُ ‡ *The road cast* [or *brought*] *them suddenly* [to a place]: from نفخت الريح. (L.) — نَفَخَتِ الضُّحَى, inf. n. نَفْخٌ, ‡ *The morning became advanced, and the sun high.* (L, Ḳ.) You say also † انتفخ النَّهَارُ ‡ *The day became advanced, the sun being high,* (Ṣ, L,) *an hour before noon.* (L.)

2: see 1.

5: see 8.

8. انتفخ *It* (a thing, Ṣ, as a skin, Mṣb,) *became inflated,* or *puffy;* (Ṣ, A, Mṣb;) as also † تنفّخ: (A:) also, *it became swollen;* i. q. وَرِمَ. (Ḳ, art. ورم.) — انتفخ *He became inflated,* or *filled,* by food. (L.) See 1. — إِنْتِفَاخُ الأَهِلَّةِ ‡ *The bigness* [or *swelling*] *of the new moons.* Occurring in a trad. respecting the signs of the last day. (L.) [See انتفخ.] — انتفخ عَلَىَّ † ‡ [*He became inflated against me;* i.e.] *he was angry with me.* (TA.) And انتفخ لَهُ † [*He behaved angrily to him*]. (TA in art. زحو.)

نَفْخٌ [*Flatulence.* — And hence,] ‡ *Boastfulness; arrogance; pride;* (Ṣ, Ḳ;) [*inflation with pride*]: pride was termed by Mohammad نَفْخُ الشَّيْطَانِ. (TA, art. همز.) — رَجُلٌ ذُو نَفْخٍ, as also ذو نَفَخٍ, ‡ *A boastful, arrogant, proud man;* (Ṣ;) [*a man inflated with pride*].

نَفْخٌ † A young man (TA) *full of youthfulness* [or *youthful plumpness* or *vigour*]; (Ḳ;) and so, without ة, a damsel. (TA.)

نَفْخَةٌ and نُفْخَةٌ and نِفْخَةٌ *Inflation of the belly* (Ṣ, Ḳ) by food &c. (TA.) You say بِهِ نفخة *He has an inflation of the body:* (Ḳ:) and أَجِدُ نفخة *I experience an inflation of the body.* (Ṣ.) — [And *A flatulent humour* of any kind: a meaning well known.] — النَّفْخَةُ *The blast* [*of the horn*] *of the day of resurrection.* (L.) — نَفْخَةٌ *A slight odour:* differing from نَفْحَةٌ, which is a plenteous odour. (L.) — نَفْخَةُ الشَّبَابِ ‡ *The chief part of youth.* (L.) نَفْخَةُ الرَّبِيعِ ‡ *The time of the season called* الربيع *when the earth produces herbs,* or *herbage:* (A:) or نُفْخَةُ الربيع, and نِفْخَتُهُ, *the time of that season when vegetation has ended.* (AZ:) — نَفْخَةٌ *A disease that attacks a horse, and makes his testicles to swell.* (L.) — See نُفَّاخٌ.

نَفْخَاءُ (applied to land, or ground, Ṣ) i. q. نَبْخَاءُ: (Ṣ, L, Ḳ:) or *elevated and good* or *fertile ground, in which is no sand nor stones, producing a few trees;* and so نَبْهَاءُ, except that this latter is more flat and extensive: or *soft land, in which is elevation:* (L:) or *tumid earth, that breaks in pieces when trodden upon:* (TA, voce رَخَّاءُ:) pl. نَفَاخِىُّ: it has a form of pl. proper to substs. because it is an epithet in which the quality of a subst. predominates. (L.) — نَفْخَاءُ *The upper part of the bone of the* سَاق [or *shank,* or *tibia*]. (Ḳ.)

نَفِيخٌ *One who is employed to blow a fire.* (Ḳ.)

نُفَّاخٌ *An inflation of a humour occasioned by disease,* (T, Ḳ,) *arising in any part:* (T:) *a humour;* as also † نُفْخَةٌ. (L.) — See نُفَّاخَةٌ.

نُفَّاخَةٌ *A bubble* upon water. (L, Ḳ [but in some copies of the Ḳ, for الحِجَارَة is erroneously put الحجارة.]) — [The *air-bladder of a fish;*] *an inflated thing in the belly of a fish, which is* (*as they assert,* L,) *its* نِصَاب [app. meaning its *most essential part,* or *element,*] *by means of which it rises in the water, and moves to and fro* (L, Ḳ.) — *A bladder of a plant* (Ṣ, O, L, voce قَثَاذ, &c.) N. un. of نُفَّاخٌ (AḤn, in TA, voce عُشَر.) [And in anatomy, *A cell.*]

مَا بِالدَّارِ نَافِخُ ضَرَمَةٍ [*There is not in the house a blower of a fire;* i. e.,] *there is not in the house any one.* (Ṣ.) — نَافِخٌ حِضْنَيْهِ [A man *inflating,* or *puffing out, his sides;*] *inflated, and ready to do mischief,* or *evil.* (L, from a trad.)

أَنْفَخُ A man, (Ṣ, L, Ḳ,) and a horse, (L,) *having inflated testicles:* (Ṣ, L, Ḳ:) *syn. of* آدَرُ. (Mgh, in art. ادر.) — Also, A beast of carriage *having his pasterns inflated with wind:* see نَفِخَ. (L.)

رَجُلٌ أُنْفُخَانٌ, and إِنْفِخَانٌ, and أُنْفُخَانِىٌّ, and إِنْفِخَانِىٌّ, fem. with ة, † *A man full of fat;* (Ḳ;) *inflated with flaccid fat,* and so ▼ رجل مَنْفُوخٌ; pl. مَنْفُوخُونَ. (TA.)

مِنْفَخٌ: see what follows.

مِنْفَاخٌ (Ṣ, L, Mṣb, Ḳ) and ▼ مِنْفَخٌ (Mṣb) *The instrument with which a fire is blown:* (Mṣb, Ḳ:) *a blacksmith's bellows:* the *thing with which a fire* or *other thing is blown:* (L:) the *thing into which one blows.* (Ṣ.) See also كِيرٌ. — مِنْفَاخُ الرَّاعِى *The instrument* [i. e. *reed-pipe*] *of the pastor, with which he calls together the camels.* (A, TA, voce شَبَّاعٌ.)

مَنَافِخُ الشَّيْطَانِ † *The suggestions of the devil.* (TA.)

مَنْفُوخٌ † *Big-bellied;* (Ḳ, TA;) [*inflated in the belly*]. — Also, (Ḳ,) ▼ مُنْتَفِخٌ, (TA,) ‡ *Fat;* as an epithet; (A, Ḳ;) [*inflated,* or *swollen, with fat*]. See أُنْفُخَانٌ. — مَنْفُوخٌ ‡ *A coward:* so called because he swells out his lungs. (L.)

مُنْتَفِخٌ: A man *inflated,* or *puffed,* or *filled, with pride,* and *with anger.* (L.) See مَنْفُوخٌ.

نفد

1. نَفِدَ, aor. ـَ, inf. n. نَفَادٌ (Ṣ, A, L, Mṣb, Ḳ) and نَفَدٌ, (L, Ḳ,) *It* (a thing, Ṣ, &c.) *passed away and came to an end; became spent, exhausted,* or *consumed; failed entirely; ceased;* syn. فَنِىَ (Ṣ, A, L, Mṣb, Ḳ) and ذَهَبَ (Ṣ, L, Ḳ) and اِنْقَطَعَ. (L, Mṣb.)

4. انفدهُ (Ṣ, A, L, Mṣb, Ḳ) and ▼ استنفدهُ (A, L, Ḳ) and ▼ انتفدهُ (Ḳ) *He caused it to pass away or come to an end; spent, exhausted,* or *consumed, it; caused it to fail entirely; caused it to cease; made an end of it.* (Ṣ, A, L, Mṣb, Ḳ.) — انفدوا مَا عِنْدَهُمْ, and ▼ استنفدوهُ, *They spent, exhausted,* or *consumed, what they had.* (A, L.) — استنفد ▼ وُسْعَهُ *He spent, exhausted,* or *exerted, to the utmost his ability* or *power.* (Ṣ, L, Mṣb.) — انفد القَوْمُ *The people came to that state that their travelling-provisions were exhausted,* or *had come to an end:* (Ṣ, A, L, Ḳ:) or, (in the Ḳ, and,) *their property had passed away and come to an end.* (Ṣ, L, Ḳ.) — انفدت الرَّكِيَّةُ *The well lost its water.* (L, Ḳ.)

3. نافدهُ, (inf. n. مُنَافَدَةٌ, L,) [*He exerted his whole power, or ability, in contention, dispute,* or *litigation, with him:* see مُنَافِدٌ:] *he contended with him in arguments, pleas,* or *allegations, so as to put an end to his argument, and overcome him:* (L:) or *he contended with him before a judge;* (IAth, L, Ḳ;) *contended, disputed,* or *litigated with him.* (Ḳ.) It is said in a trad., إِنْ نَافَدْتَهُمْ نَافَدُوكَ (Ṣ, L) *If thou contend with them before a judge, they will so contend with thee:* or *if thou allege to them, they will allege to thee:* (IAth, L;) but accord. to one relation, the verb is with ق: (Ṣ, L:) and accord. to another, the latter verb is with ذ, نافذوك. (L.)

6. تنافدوا *They contended, disputed,* or *litigated, together.* (A.) See 3, and see also تنافذوا, with ذ.]

8. انتفدهُ: see 4. — *He exacted, took,* or *received, it fully,* or *wholly.* (Ḳ.) — انتفد مِنْ عَدْوِهِ *He exacted the full,* or *utmost, rate of his running.* Said with reference to a horse. (M, L.) — انتفد اللَّبَنَ *He drew forth the milk.* (Ḳ.)

10: see 4.

مُنَافِدٌ A man *who exerts his whole power,* or *ability, in contention, dispute,* or *litigation,* (Ṣ, L,) *and who does so well, so as to put an end to the arguments, pleas,* or *allegations, of his adversary, and overcome him:* (L:) *who contends with his adversary in arguments, pleas,* or *allegations, so as to put an end to his argument.* (A, L.) One says, لَيْسَ لَهُ رَافِدٌ وَلَا مُنَافِدٌ *He has not an aider,* or *assistant, nor one who contends &c.* (A, TA.)

فِيهِ مُنْتَفَدٌ عَنْ غَيْرِهِ *In him is that which renders thee in no need of any other.* (Aboo-Sa'eed, T, L, Ḳ.*) — إِنَّ فِى مَالِهِ لَمُنْتَفَدًا *Verily in his wealth is ample provision.* (AZ, T, L, Ḳ.*) — تَجِدُ فِى البِلَادِ مُنْتَفَدًا (in the TḲ مُتَنَفَّدًا) *Thou wilt find in the countries,* or *towns, a place to which to flee and in which to seek gain;* syn. مُرَاغَمًا وَمُضْطَرَبًا. (Ḳ.) See also مُنْتَفَذٌ.

قَعَدَ مُنْتَفَدًا *He sat aside,* or *apart.* (IAạr, L, Ḳ.)

نفذ

1. نَفَذَ, aor. ـُ, (M, L,) inf. n. نَفَاذٌ and نُفُوذٌ, (M, L, Ḳ,) *It went,* or *passed, through:* (L:) or *it went,* or *passed, through* a thing, *and became clear of it.* (M, L, Ḳ.) — نَفَذْتُ *I went,* or *passed, through.* (L.) — نَفَذَ السَّهْمُ, aor. ـُ, inf. n. نُفُوذٌ and نَفَاذٌ, *The arrow perforated, transpierced,* or *pierced through,* the animal at which it was shot, *and went forth from it:* (Mṣb:) or نَفَذَ السَّهْمُ الرَّمِيَّةَ, (M, L,) and نَفَذَ مِنْهَا, (Ṣ, L,) and فِيهَا, (M, A, L,) aor. ـُ, (M, L,) inf. n. نَفَاذٌ (M, A, L, Ḳ) and نُفُوذٌ (A) and نَفَذٌ, (M, L, Ḳ,) *the arrow penetrated into the inside of the animal at which it was shot, and its extremity went forth from the other side,* or *protruded from it, the rest remaining therein; the extremity of the arrow passed through the animal at which it was shot, the rest remaining therein;* (M, L, Ḳ:) *a part of the arrow passed through,* or *went forth* or *protruded from, the animal at which it was shot.* (A, art. صرد.) See سَهْمٌ نَافِذٌ. — نَفَذَتِ الطَّعْنَةُ *The wound made by a spear* or *the like passed through,* or *beyond, the other side.* (T L.) — أَنْفُذْ عَنْكَ *Go thou from thy place; pass thou from it.* (L.) [See also عَنْ.] — نَفَذَ لِوَجْهِهِ *He went his way.* (TA.) — نَفَذَ الطَّرِيقُ ‡ *The road was* [*a thoroughfare* (see نَافِذٌ)] *pervious,* or *passable, to every one in common.* (Mṣb.) — هٰذَا الطَّرِيقُ يَنْفُذُ إِلَى مَكَانِ كَذَا [*This road is a thoroughfare, along which every one may pass, to such a place*]. (T, M,* L.) — نَفَذَ المَنْزِلُ إِلَى الطَّرِيقِ ‡ *The house,* or *abode,* [*was a thoroughfare, and*] *communicated with the road.* (Mṣb.) — نَفَذَ القَوْمَ *He passed through the people, and left them behind him;* (T, M, L, Ḳ;) as also ▼ أَنْفَذَهُمْ; (L, Ḳ;) or only the former is used in this sense. (L.) See also the latter. — نَفَذَهُمُ البَصَرُ ‡ *The sight reached them, and extended beyond them:* (Ks, L:) or, *extended over them all:* (A'Obeyd, L:) you say also, ▼ أَنْفَذَهُمُ البَصَرُ in the former sense: (L:) [or *The sight penetrated into the midst of them:* see أَنْفَذَ القَوْمَ.] — نَفَذَ رَأْيُهُ † *His judgment was penetrating;* syn. ثَقَبَ. (Ḳ in art. ثقب.) — نَفَذَ فِى الأَمْرِ ‡ *He acted,* or *went on, with penetrative energy,* or *with sharpness, vigorousness, and effectiveness, in the affair;* syn. مَضَى. (Ṣ, Ḳ, art. مضى.) — نَفَذَ الكِتَابُ إِلَى فُلَانٍ, inf. n. نَفَاذٌ and نُفُوذٌ, ‡ [*The letter passed to, came to,* or *reached, such a one*]: (Ṣ, L:) [and in like manner, الرَّسُولُ *the messenger:* see 4.] — نَفَذَ الأَمْرُ, and القَوْلُ, † *The command,* or *order,* and *the saying, was effectual; had effect; was,* or *became, executed,* or *performed;* syn. مَضَى. (Mṣb.) — نَفَذَ العِتْقُ † [*The act of emancipation had,* or *took effect; was,* or *became, executed,* or *performed:* and in like manner, a covenant, contract, sale, &c.: see 4]. App. a met. expression, from نُفُوذُ السَّهْمِ; because there is no retracting it. (Mṣb.) — يَنْفُذُ بَيْنَنَا ‡ *He shall judge between us, and make his command* or *order to have effect,* or *execute* or *perform it.* (L.) — لَهُ نَفَاذٌ فِى الأُمُورِ ‡ [*He has ability in affairs, to execute,* or *perform*]. (A.)

2: see 4.

3. نافذهُ † *He cited him before a judge.* It is said in a trad., ان نَافَذْتَهُمْ نَافَذُوكَ *If thou cite them before a judge, they will do the same to thee;* meaning, *If thou say to them, they will*

say to thee. Accord. to one relation, the verb is with ق and د. (L.) [Accord. to another, it is with ف and ذ.]

4. انفذ السَّهْمَ, (A, Mṣb,) and ↓ نفّذهُ, (Mṣb,) *He made the arrow to pierce, and go forth from, or to pass through,* the animal at which it was shot: (Mṣb:) [or, *to penetrate within* the animal at which it was shot, *and to protrude its extremity from the other side, the rest remaining within*; accord. to the explanation of نَفَذَ السَّهْمُ in the M, L, Ḳ: or *to penetrate* the animal at which it was shot, *and to protrude a part of it from the other side*; accord. to the explanation of سَهْمٌ نَافِذٌ in the A, art. صرد.] You say also, أَنْفَذْتُ فِيهِ السَّهْمَ [*I made the arrow to pierce, or penetrate, him, &c.*] (A.) — رَمَيْتُهُ فَأَنْفَذْتُهُ *I shot, or cast, at him, and pierced, or made a hole, through him.* (Mgh.) — See 1. — انفذ الأَمْرَ † [*He brought to pass the command, or order; made it effectual; made it to have effect; executed or performed it:* and in like manner, the saying: see 1]. — † *He executed, performed, or accomplished, the affair.* (M, L, Ḳ.) — انفذ القَوْمَ *He became [or entered] among the people:* (M, L:) in the copies of the Ḳ, explained by صَارَ مِنْهُمْ; but the correct reading is بَيْنَهُمْ [as in the M and L]: (TA:) or *he penetrated into them, and went, or walked, in the midst of them.* (T, L, Ḳ.) See also نَفَذَ القَوْمَ. — انفذ كِتَابًا إِلَى فُلَانٍ; (Ṣ, L;) and ↓ نفّذهُ, (A,) inf. n. تَنْفِيذٌ; (Ṣ, L;) ‡ [*He sent, or transmitted, a letter to such a one; caused it to pass to or to reach him*]: and in like manner, رَسُولًا *a messenger.* (A.) — انفذ عَهْدَهُ, inf. n. إِنْفَاذٌ, † *He made his covenant, or contract, or the like, to take effect; executed or performed it:* [and in like manner, an act of emancipation: see 1.] (L, TA.)

6. تَنَافَذُوا إِلَيْهِ † *They came to him,* (namely, a judge,) *and referred to him their cause, or suit, for judgment.* When each party adduces his plea, or allegation, one says تنافدوا, with د, unpointed. (Aboo-Sa'eed, T, L, Ḳ.*)

طَعْنَةٌ نَافِذَةٌ i.q. طَعْنَةٌ لَهَا نَفَذٌ; (Ṣ;) *A wound having a passage through the other side;* by نَفَذٌ being meant مَنْفَذٌ, or نُفُوذٌ: (T, L:) pl. أَنْفَاذٌ. (A.) Ḳeys Ibn-El-Khaṭeem says (see Ḥam. p. 85),

* طَعَنْتُ ٱبْنَ عَبْدِ القَيْسِ طَعْنَةَ ثَائِرٍ *
* لَهَا نَفَذٌ لَوْلَا الشُّعَاعُ أَضَاءَهَا *

(T, Ṣ, L) *I pierced the son of 'Abd-El-Keys with the wound of one making an angry assault, that had a passage through, which, but for the spirtling blood, would have made it show the light through him.* (T, L [See also شُعَاعٌ.])

See also مَنْفَذٌ. — نَفَذٌ ‡ *A place, or way, or means, of exit, escape, or safety;* syn. مَخْرَجٌ (T, Ṣ, A, L, Ḳ.) So in the saying أَتَى بِنَفَذِ مَا قَالَ ‡ *He effected a means of escape from [the natural consequences of] what he had said;* i.e., بِالمَخْرَجِ مِنْهُ. (T, Ṣ, A, L, Ḳ.) It occurs in a trad., where it is said, that unless a man who has published against a Muslim a charge of which he is clear do this, he is to be punished. (T, L.) — نَفَذٌ a subst., (M, L,) used in the sense of إِنْفَاذٌ: (T, M, L, Ḳ:*) نَفَذُ أَمْرٍ signifying † [*The making a command, or order, effectual; making it to have effect; to be executed or performed;*] i.q. إِنْفَاذُهُ: (T, L:) you say, أَمَرَ بِنَفَذِهِ † *He commanded that it should have effect, or be executed or performed;*] i.e., بِإِنْفَاذِهِ: (M, L:) and قَامَ المُسْلِمُونَ بِنَفَذِ الكِتَابِ † [*The Muslims accomplished the execution, or performance, of what was in the Scripture:*] i.e. بِإِنْفَاذِ مَا فِيهِ. (T, A, L.)

نُفُوذٌ: see نَافِذٌ.

أَمْرٌ نَفِيذٌ † *An affair arranged, or made easy.* (L.) See also نَافِذٌ.

نَفَّاذٌ: see نَافِذٌ.

سَهْمٌ نَافِذٌ [*An arrow that perforates, transpierces, or pierces through, and goes forth from, or passes through, the animal at which it is shot;* accord. to the explanation of the verb in the Mṣb: or, *that penetrates into the inside of the animal at which it is shot, and of which the extremity goes forth from the other side,* or *protrudes from it, the rest remaining therein;* accord. to the explanation of the verb in the M, L, Ḳ: or,] *of which a part has passed through the animal at which it is shot:* when the extremity only has passed through, it is termed صَارِدٌ; and when the whole of it has passed through, مَارِقٌ. (A, art. صرد.) — طَعْنَةٌ نَافِذَةٌ *A wound made by a spear or the like passing through both sides:* (M, L:) pl. طَعَنَاتٌ نَوَافِذُ. (A.) See also نَفَذٌ. — طَرِيقٌ نَافِذٌ ‡ *A road which is a thoroughfare;* (T, M, L, Ḳ;) [*pervious;*] *not stopped up;* (T, L;) *along which every one may pass.* (T, A, L, Mṣb.) See also مَنْفَذٌ. — نَافِذٌ sing. of نَوَافِذُ, (Mṣb,) which signifies All the *holes, or perforations, by which joy or grief is conveyed to the mind (of a man,* Mṣb); *as the two ear-holes,* (IAar, on the authority of Abu-l-Mekárim, T, L, Mṣb, Ḳ,) *and the two nostrils, and the mouth, and the anus:* (IAạr, T, L, Ḳ:*) called by the doctors of practical law مَنَافِذُ, which is contr. to analogy: see مَنْفَذٌ. (Mṣb.) — نَافِذٌ and ↓ نُفُوذٌ and ↓ نَفَّاذٌ [but the second and third are intensive epithets] ‡ A man (M, L) *penetrating,* or *acting with a penetrative energy,* or *sharp, energetic, vigorous, and effective,* (مَاضٍ,) *in all his affairs.* (M, L, Ḳ.) — رَجُلٌ نَافِذٌ فِى أَمْرِهِ ‡ *A man penetrating,* or *acting with a penetrative energy,* or *sharp, vigorous, and effective, in his affair;* (Ṣ, L;) and فِى الأُمُورِ *in affairs.* (A.) — أَمْرُهُ نَافِذٌ † *His command,* or *order, is effectual; has effect; is executed,* or *performed;* syn. مَاضٍ (Ḳ;) *and obeyed;* (Ṣ, L, Mṣb, Ḳ;*) as also ↓ نَفِيذٌ. (Ḳ.) — دَائِرَةٌ نَافِذَةٌ *A feather,* or *curl of hair in a horse's coat, of the kind which, when it is only on one side, is called هَقْعَة, but which is on both sides.* (AO, T, L.)

هٰذَا مَنْفَذُ القَوْمِ, and ↓ نَفَذُهُمْ; and هٰذِهِ مَنَافِذُهُمْ, and أَنْفَاذُهُمْ, [*This is the place of passage of the people, and these are their places of passage*]. (A.) — هٰذَا الطَّرِيقُ مَنْفَذٌ لِمَحَلِّ كَذَا ‡ *This road is a way along which every one may pass to such a place.* (A.) — فِيهِ مَنْفَذٌ لِلقَوْمِ ‡ *In it* (the road) *is a [free, or an open,] passage to, or for, the people.* (T, L.) See also نَافِذٌ.

مَنْفِذٌ, in measure like مَسْجِدٌ, [or مَنْفَذٌ, agreeably with analogy, as it is written in copies of the T, A, L,] *A place by which a thing passes through;* [*a thoroughfare; an outlet; a place of egress:*] pl. مَنَافِذُ. (Mṣb.) See also نَافِذٌ.

مُتَنَفَّذٌ † *Ample room, space, or scope, or liberty to act &c.:* (syn. سَعَةٌ, (M, L, Ḳ, TA,) and مَنْدُوحَةٌ: (TA:) [*ample means of escape:* see also نَفَذٌ:] you say, إِنَّ فِى ذٰلِكَ لَمُتَنَفَّذًا *Verily in that there is ample room, scope, or means [for action, or for escape].* (TA.) See also مُتَنَفَّذٌ.

نفر

1. نَفَرَ, (T, M, L, Mṣb, Ḳ,) aor. ـِ, (T, M, Ḳ,) and ـُ, (M, Ḳ,) inf. n. نَفْرٌ and نَفَرَانٌ (M, Ḳ) or نُفُورٌ, (Mṣb,) said of a wild animal, (T, Mṣb,) a gazelle, (M, Ḳ,) or other beast, (M,) *He took fright, and fled, or ran away at random;* or *became refractory, and went away at random;* or *ran away,* or *broke loose, and went hither and thither by reason of his sprightliness;* syn. شَرَدَ; (M, Ḳ;) as also ↓ استنفر; (T, Mṣb, Ḳ;) and so the former verb *in* speaking of a camel, or a beast: (L, art. شرد:) you say, نَفَرَتِ الدَّابَّةُ, (T, Ṣ, M, A, Ḳ,) aor. ـِ and ـُ, (T, Ṣ, M, Ḳ,) inf. n. نُفُورٌ and نِفَارٌ (T, Ṣ, M, A, Ḳ) and نَفْرٌ: (A:) or this signifies *the beast was, or became, impatient* (A, Ḳ, TA) *of* or *at a thing,* (TA,) [or *shied at it,*] *and retired to a distance;* (A, Ḳ, TA;) and ↓ إِسْتَنْفَرَ signifies the same as نُفُورٌ: (Ṣ:) or نَفَرَ, inf. n.

نِفَارٌ [and نُفُورٌ], signifies *he fled, and went away or aside or apart or to a distance.* (M.) — [Hence, نَفَرَ, aor. ـِ and ـُ, inf. n. نُفُورٌ and نِفَارٌ and نَفْرٌ and نَفِيرٌ, as used in the following phrases.] نَفَرْتُ مِنْ هٰذَا الأَمْرِ ‡ *I shrank from this thing* or *affair; was averse from it; did not like* or *approve it.* And نَفَرَ فُلَانٌ مِنْ صُحْبَةِ فُلَانٍ ‡ [*Such a one shrank,* or *was averse, from the companionship of,* or *the associating with, such a one*]. And نَفَرَتِ المَرْأَةُ مِنْ زَوْجِهَا ‡ [*The woman was averse from her husband; or shunned* or *avoided him*]. (All from the A.) And you say of a man's disposition, تَنَفَّرَ ♦ عَنِ الحَقِّ ‡ [*It shunned,* or *was averse from, the truth*]. (Bd, lxvii. 21.) — إِلَّا نُفُورًا, in the Ḳur, [xvii. 43, and xxxv. 40,] means ‡ *Save in aversion:* and نَفِيرٌ is like نُفُورٌ: and the subst. is نَفَرٌ, with two fet-ḥahs. (Mṣb) — نَفَرَ الشَّىْءُ مِنَ الشَّىْءِ, inf. n. [نُفُورٌ and] نِفَارٌ, *The thing receded, withdrew, removed,* or *became remote* or *aloof, from the thing.* (A'Obeyd, T, Ṣ.) [See also 3.] — Hence it is, I think, that نَفَرَ is used as signifying ‡ *It became swollen,* in the following words of a trad. of 'Omar: تَخَلَّلَ رَجُلٌ فِى زَمَانِهِ بِالقَصَبِ فَنَفَرَ فُوهُ ‡ *A man, in his time, picked his teeth with reeds, and in consequence his mouth became swollen:* as though the flesh, disliking the disease, receded from it, and so became swollen. (A'Obeyd, T, Ṣ.*) You say also, نَفَرَتِ العَيْنُ, aor. ـِ and ـُ, inf. n. نُفُورٌ, ‡ *His eye became inflamed and swollen:* and so you say of other parts of the person. (M, Ḳ.*) And نَفَرَ الجُرْحُ, inf. n. as above, ‡ *The wound became swollen:* (T, Mṣb:) or *it became so after healing.* (W, i. 42.) And نَفَرَ الجِلْدُ ‡ *The skin became swollen,* (Ṣ, A,) *and the flesh receded from it.* (A.) [All these significations seem to be derived from the first in this art.: and so several others which follow.] — نَفَرْتُ إِلَى اللّٰهِ, inf. n. نِفَارٌ, *I betook myself to God by reason of fear, seeking protection.* (IKṭṭ.) — نَفَرُوا, (Mṣb,) inf. n. نَفْرٌ, (M, Mṣb, Ḳ,) *They became separated,* or *dispersed:* (M,* Mṣb, Ḳ:*) and so نَفَرَتْ, said of camels. (TA.) Hence, (M,) the saying, لَقِيتُهُ قَبْلَ كُلِّ صَيْحٍ وَنَفْرٍ, (Ṣ, M, A,) a proverb, in which the last word is used tropically; (A;) explained in art. صيح, q.v. (Ṣ.) [And غَضِبَ مِنْ غَيْرِ صَيْحٍ وَلَا نَفْرٍ, explained in the same art.] — نَفَرَ الحَاجُّ مِنْ مِنًى, (M, Mṣb, Ḳ,) aor. ـِ, (Ṣ, M, Ḳ,) inf. n. نَفْرٌ (M, Mṣb, Ḳ) and نَفَرٌ (M) and نُفُورٌ (Ḳ) [and نَفِيرٌ], *The pilgrims removed from Minè.* (Mṣb.) Hence, النَّفِيرُ, and النُّفُورُ, and النَّفْرُ, and يَوْمُ النَّفْرِ, (Ṣ, M, Ḳ,) and لَيْلَةُ النَّفْرِ, (Ṣ, TA,) and النَّفَرُ, (TA,) [*The day of,* and *the night immediately preceding, the removing from Minè*]; *after the day called* يَوْمُ القَرِّ; (Ṣ;) [therefore, *the twelfth of Dhu-l-Ḥijjeh:*] or there are two days thus called: (Mṣb:) يَوْمُ النَّفْرِ الأَوَّلُ is [the day above mentioned,] *the second of the days called* أَيَّامُ التَّشْرِيقِ; (IAth, Mṣb;) and يَوْمُ النَّفْرِ الآخِرُ, (IAth,) or الثَّانِى, (Mṣb,) is *the third thereof:* (IAth, Mṣb:) the order is this; يَوْمُ النَّحْرِ, then يَوْمُ القَرِّ, then يَوْمُ النَّفْرِ الأَوَّلُ, then يَوْمُ النَّفْرِ الآخِرُ. (T, L.) — نَفَرُوا فِى الأَمْرِ, (Ṣ, M,) or لِلْأَمْرِ, (Ḳ,) aor. ـِ, (M, Ḳ,) inf. n. نُفُورٌ (Ṣ, M, Ḳ) and نِفَارٌ (M, Ḳ) and نَفِيرٌ; (Zj, M, Ḳ;) and تنافروا ♦; (M, Ḳ;) *They went,* or *went away, to execute the affair:* (M, Ḳ:) and in like manner, فِى القِتَالِ *to fight.* (M.) And نَفَرُوا, alone, *They went forth to war against unbelievers* or *the like.* So in the Ḳur, ix. 82, وَقَالُوا لَا تَنْفِرُوا فِى الحَرِّ قُلْ نَارُ جَهَنَّمَ أَشَدُّ حَرًّا [*And they said, Go not ye forth to war against the unbelievers in the heat: say, The fire of hell is hotter*]: and so in the same chap., v. 39: (Jel:) and in the same book, iv. 73. (Bd.) You say also, نَفَرُوا لَهُمْ *They went forth to fight them.* (TA, from a trad.) And نَفَرُوا إِلَى الحَرْبِ *They hastened to the war,* or *to war.* (Mṣb.) — [Hence,] نَفَرُوا مَعَهُ; and أَنْفَرُوهُ ♦, (M, Ḳ,) inf. n. إِنْفَارٌ; (TA;) *They aided and succoured them:* (M, Ḳ:) or the former verb, alone, *they,* being asked to do so, *complied, and went forth to aid.* (TA.) — نُفِرَ بِنَا: see 2.

2. نفّر, (T, M, A, Mṣb,) inf. n. تَنْفِيرٌ; (Mṣb;) and انفر ♦; (T, Ḳ;) and استنفر ♦; (T, M, A, Mṣb;) *He made* (wild animals, T, Mṣb, or an antelope, Ḳ, or a beast of carriage, M,) *to take fright, and flee,* or *run away at random:* (Ḳ, TA:) or *he made* a beast of carriage *to become impatient, and to retire to a distance:* (A:) or *he scared away; or made to flee, and go away,* or *aside,* or *apart,* or *to a distance:* (so accord. to an explanation of the intrans. v. from which it is derived, in the M:) you say نَفَّرْتُهُ and اِسْتَنْفَرْتُهُ ♦ and أَنْفَرْتُهُ ♦: and in like manner, نَفَّرَ عَنْهُ, and أَنْفَرَ عَنْهُ, [meaning, *he scared away,* or *made to take fright and flee, &c., from him* or *it:*] (TA:) and التَّنْفِيرُ عَنْهُ, and الإِنْفَارُ عَنِ الشَّىْءِ, and الاِسْتِنْفَارُ, all signify the same, [i. e., *the scaring away, &c., from a thing.*] (Ṣ.) It is said in a trad. of Zeyneb, the daughter of Moḥammad, فَأَنْفَرَ بِهَا المُشْرِكُونَ بَعِيرَهَا حَتَّى سَقَطَتْ *And the polytheists made her camel to take fright and run away at random with her, so that she fell.* And in like manner you say, نُفِرَ بِنَا, and أُنْفِرَ بِنَا, [or نُفِّرَ بِنَا? *Our camels were scared away with us;* or *made to take fright and run away at random with us:* or] *we were made to be persons having camels taking fright and running away at random.* And تَنْفِيرٌ signifies The *chiding* camels or sheep or goats, *and driving them from the pasturage.* (TA.) — [Hence] بَشِّرُوا وَلَا تُنَفِّرُوا † [*Rejoice people by what ye say, and*] do not *encounter them with* [*roughness and violence and*] *that which will incite them to* نُفُور [i. e. *flight* or *aversion*]. (TA.) See the act. part. n., below. — [Hence also,] نَفِّرْ عَنْهُ, (Ṣ, Ḳ,) inf. n. تَنْفِيرٌ, (TA,) † *Give thou to him a* لَقَب [meaning a *nickname* or *name of reproach*], (Ṣ,) or *a* لَقَب *that is disliked:* (Ḳ:) as though they held such to be تَنْفِيرٌ لِلْجِنِّ وَالعَيْنِ عَنْهُ [*a means of scaring away the jinn,* or *genii, and the evil eye, from him*]. (Ṣ, Ḳ.) An Arab of the desert said, When I was born, it was said to my father, نَفِّرْ عَنْهُ: so he named me قُنْفُذ [hedge-hog], and surnamed me أَبُو العَدَّاءِ [father of the quick runner]. (Ṣ.)

3. [نَافَرَا, inf. n. مُنَافَرَةٌ, ‡ *They shunned* or *avoided each other; regarded each other with aversion.* But perhaps this signification is only post-classical. — And hence, ‡ *They* (two things) *were incongruous,* or *discordant, each with the other.* But perhaps this signification, also, is only post-classical. See also 6.]

4: see 2, in several places. — أَنْفَرُوا *Their camels took fright and ran away at random,* (نَفَرَتْ, Ḳ, TA,) *and became separated* or *dispersed.* (TA.) — See also 1, last signification.

5. تنفّر عَنِ الحَقِّ: see 1.

6. [تنافروا ‡ *They shunned* or *avoided one another; regarded one another with aversion.* But perhaps this signification is only post-classical. — And hence, تنافرت الأَشْيَآءُ ‡ *The things were incongruous,* or *discordant, one with another.* But perhaps this signification, also, is only post-classical. See also 3.] — تنافروا فِى الأَمْرِ, or تنافرا لِلْأَمْرِ: see 1, towards the end. See also in the Ḳ: and compare 6 in arts. نفد and نفذ.

10. إِسْتَنْفَرَهُمْ *He* (the Imám) *incited,* and *summoned* or *invited them to go forth,* لِجِهَادِ العَدُوِّ *to war against the enemy:* (T, Mgh:) or *imposed upon them the task of going forth to war, light and heavy:* [see Ḳur, ix. 41:] (A:) or *he demanded, sought,* or *desired, of them aid.* (M,* Ḳ, TA.) — See also 2, in three places. — And see 1, in two places, near the beginning.

نَفْرٌ: see نَافِرٌ, of which it is a quasi-pl.: — and نَفِيرٌ: — and نَفَرٌ.

نَفْرٌ an imitative sequent to عَفْرٌ, (T, M, Ḳ,) and so is ▾ نَفِرٌ to عَفِرٌ, (Ṣgh, Ḳ, but omitted in some copies of the Ḳ,) and ▾ نِفْرِيَةٌ to عِفْرِيَةٌ, (T, M, Ḳ,) and ▾ نِفْرِيتٌ to عِفْرِيتٌ, (T, Ṣ, M, Ḳ,) and ▾ نُفَارِيَةٌ to عُفَارِيَةٌ, (T, M, Ḳ,) and ▾ نِفْرِيتَةٌ to عِفْرِيتَةٌ; (Ḳ;) denoting corroboration. (Ṣ.)

نَفَرٌ *A number of men, from three to ten;* (Ṣ, Mṣb;) as also ▾ نَفْرٌ and ▾ نَفَرَةٌ and ▾ نَفِيرٌ: (Ṣ:) or *to seven:* (so in a copy of the Mṣb, [but probably سبعة is a mistake for تسعة *nine:* this appears likely from what here follows:]) or *a number of men less then ten;* (AZ, T, M, Ḳ;) as also ▾ نَفِيرٌ; (Ḳ;) and so رَهْطٌ; (AZ, T;) and some add, *excluding women:* (TA:) accord. to Fr, (Ṣ,) a man's *people* or *tribe consisting of* his *nearer relations;* as also ▾ نَفْرَةٌ; syn. رَهْطٌ, (Ṣ, IAth,) and عَشِيرَةٌ: (IAth:) [see also نَفْرَةٌ:] accord. to Kr, (M,) *all the men* or *people:* (M, Ḳ:) accord. to Lth, you say, هٰؤُلَآءِ عَشَرَةُ نَفَرٍ, i. e. *these are ten men:* but one does not say, عِشْرُونَ نَفَرًا, nor more than عَشَرَةٌ: and Abu-l-'Abbás says, that نَفَرٌ, like قَوْمٌ and رَهْطٌ, has a pl. signification, without any proper sing.; and is applied to men, exclusively of women: (T:) it is a quasi-pl. n.: (TA:) and its pl. is أَنْفَارٌ; (M, Ḳ;) occurring in a trad., in the phrase أَحَدُ مِنْ أَنْفَارِنَا, which IAth explains as meaning *any one of our people;* syn. قَوْمِنَا: (TA:) and ▾ نَفِيرًا, occurring, in the accus. case, in the Ḳur, xvii. 6, is, accord. to Zj, a pl. [or rather quasi-pl. n.] of نَفَرٌ, like عَبِيدٌ and كَلِيبٌ. (M.) [See also نَفِيرٌ, below.] Imra-el-Ḳeys says, describing a man as an excellent archer,

فَهْوَ لَا تَنْمِى رَمِيَّتُهُ •
مَا لَهُ لَا عُدَّ مِنْ نَفَرِهْ •

(Ṣ,) *And he is such that the animal shot by him does not go away after it has been shot and then die. What aileth him? May he* be killed, so as *not to be numbered among his people.* The latter hemistich is a proverb. (Meyd.) The poet here utters an imprecation against the man, but in so doing praises him; as when you say, of a man whose action pleases you, مَا لَهُ قَاتَلَهُ ٱللّٰهُ and أَخْزَاهُ ٱللّٰهُ [q. v.]. (Ṣ.) The rel. n. is ▾ نَفَرِىٌّ. (Sb, M.) ═ [Accord. to the Mṣb, it is also a simple subst. from نَفَرَ: and app. as signifying especially *Aversion.*]

نِفْرٌ: see نَفْرٌ.

نَفْرَةٌ: see نَفِيرٌ. — A man's *near kinsmen;* syn. أُسْرَةٌ (T, Ḳ) and فَصِيلَةٌ; (Ḳ;) *who are angry on account of his anger;* (Ḳ;) as also ▾ نُفْرَةٌ, mentioned by Ṣgh and others, (TA,) and ▾ نُفُورَةٌ (T, Ḳ) and ▾ نَافِرَةٌ (A,* Ḳ) and ▾ نَفَرٌ: (T:) and نُفُورَةٌ signifies a man's *near kinsmen* (أُسْرَة) *who go forth with him to war when an event befalls him* or *oppresses him severely* or *suddenly.* (TA.) You say, جَآءَنَا فِى نَفْرَتِهِ and ▾ نَفَرِهِ, (T, TA,) &c., (TA,) *He came to us among his near kinsmen,* (T, TA,) *&c.* (TA.) And, غَلَبَتْ نُفُورَتُنَا نُفُورَتَهُمْ *Our near kinsmen overcame their near kinsmen.* (T, TA.) See also نَفَرٌ, in two places: and see نَفِيرٌ.

نُفْرَةٌ (Ṣgh, Ḳ) and ▾ نُفَرَةٌ (Ḳ) *A thing that is hung upon a child for fear of,* (Ḳ,) or *to repel,* (Ṣgh,) *the evil eye.* (Ṣgh, Ḳ.) ═ See also نَفْرَةٌ.

نَفَرِىٌّ: see نَفَرٌ, last sentence but one.

نِفْرِيَةٌ and نِفْرِيتٌ and نِفْرِيتَةٌ: see نَفْرٌ.

نِفَارٌ a subst. from نَفَرَتِ الدَّابَّةُ. Ex. فِى الدَّابَّةِ نِفَارٌ [*In the beast of carriage is a disposition to take fright and run away at random*]. (Ṣ.) And in like manner, from نَفَرَ said of a wild animal. (Mṣb.)

نُفُورٌ: see نَافِرٌ.

نَفِيرٌ *A people hastening to war,* or *to some other undertaking:* an inf. n. used as a subst.: (Mṣb:) or *a people going to execute an affair:* (Ṣ:) or *a people going with one to fight;* as also ▾ نَفْرَةٌ [q. v.] and ▾ نَفَرٌ: (M, Ḳ:) each is a noun having a pl. signification: (M:) or the first and last signify *a company of men:* and the pl. of each is أَنْفَارٌ: (M:) or the first, (Ṣ,) or all, (Ḳ,) *a people,* (Ṣ,) or *company,* (Ḳ,) *preceding in an affair:* (Ṣ, Ḳ:) or the first, *those of a man's people who go forth with him to war:* or it is a pl. [or quasi-pl.] of نَفَرٌ, signifying *men assembled to go to the enemy:* (Bḍ, xvii. 6:) or *aiders,* or *assistants.* (M.) [See نَفَرٌ, in two places.] You say, جَآءَتْ نَفْرَةُ بَنِى فُلَانٍ, and نَفِيرُهُمْ, *The company of the sons of such a one, that came forth to execute an affair, arrived.* (Ṣ, TA.) نَفِيرُ قُرَيْشٍ means *Those of Ḳureysh who went forth to Bedr* to defend the caravan of Aboo-Sufyán, (M,) which was coming from Syria. (T.) Hence the proverb, فُلَانٌ لَا فِى العِيرِ وَلَا فِى النَّفِيرِ [*Such a one is neither in the caravan nor in the company going forth to fight*]: applied to him who is not regarded as fit for a difficult undertaking: because none held back from the caravan and the fight except him who was crippled by disease and him in whom was no good: (TA:) or the original words of the proverb are لَا فِى العِيرِ وَلَا فِى النَّفِيرِ: and these words were first said by Aboo-Sufyán, with reference to the Benoo-Zuhrah, when he found them turning back towards Mekkeh; and, accord. to Aṣ, are applied to a man who is held in low and little repute. (Mgh.) [See also Freytag's Arab. Prov., ii. 500.]

نُفُورَةٌ: see نَفْرَةٌ, in three places.

نُفَارِيَةٌ: see نَفْرٌ.

نَافِرٌ [and نَفُورٌ] and ▾ مُسْتَنْفِرٌ signify the same; [i.e., *Taking fright, and fleeing,* or *running away at random:* or *being,* or *becoming, impatient, of* or *at a thing, and retiring to a distance:* or *fleeing, and going away* or *aside* or *apart* or *to a distance:* or the second, being of an intensive form, signifies, as also ▾ يَنْفُورٌ, *that does so much* or *often;* or *wont* or *apt to do so:*] (TA:) and نَفْرٌ is a pl. of نَافِرٌ, (Ḳ,) or [rather] a quasi-pl., like as صَحْبٌ is of صَاحِبٌ, and زَوْرٌ of زَائِرٌ. (M.) You say, دَابَّةٌ نَافِرٌ, and ▾ نَفُورٌ, [*A beast that takes fright and runs away at random:* &c.:] (M, Ḳ:) accord. to IAạr, one should not say نَافِرَةٌ (M) [unless using it as an epithet applied to a broken pl. of a subst., as will be seen below]. It is said in a proverb, كُلُّ أَزَبَّ نَفُورٌ ▾ [*Every one,* of camels, *that is hairy on the face is wont to take fright and run away at random:* see art. زب]. (M.) You say also ظَبْىٌ يَنْفُورٌ ▾, (M, Ḳ,*) in some copies of the Ḳ, نيفور, (TA,) *A gazelle that takes fright and flees much* or *often;* or *that is wont to do so.* (M, Ḳ.*) And it is said in the Ḳur, [lxxiv. 51,] كَأَنَّهُمْ حُمُرٌ مُسْتَنْفِرَةٌ ▾ فَرَّتْ مِنْ قَسْوَرَةٍ, i.e., نَافِرَةٌ, [*As though they were asses taking fright and running away at random, that have fled from a lion:*] and (accord. to one reading, T) ▾ مُسْتَنْفَرَةٌ, (T, Ṣ,) meaning, *made to take fright and run away at random;* (T;) or *frightened,* or *scared.* (Ṣ.) — أَنَا نَافِرٌ مِنْ هٰذَا الامر ‡ *I shrink from this thing or affair; am averse from it; do not like or approve it.* And هِىَ نَافِرَةٌ مِنْ زَوْجِهَا ‡ [*She is averse from her husband; she shuns* or *avoids him*]. (A.)

نَوْفَرٌ: see art. نيلوفر.

نَافِرَةٌ: see نَفْرَةٌ.

مُنَفِّرٌ act. part. n. of 2, q.v. — † One *who encounters people with roughness and violence* [*and that which incites them to flight* or *aversion:* see 2]. (TA, from a trad.)

مُسْتَنْفِرٌ:
مُسْتَنْفَرٌ:
يَنْفُورٌ:
} see نَافِرٌ; the first and third in two places.

نفز

1. نَفَزَ, (Ṣ, A, Mṣb, Ḳ,) aor. ـِ, (Ṣ, Mṣb, Ḳ,) inf. n. نَفَزَانٌ (Ṣ, Ḳ) and نَفْزٌ (Mṣb, TA) and نُفُوزٌ, (TA,) *He* (an antelope) *leaped, jumped, sprang,* or *bounded;* (Ṣ, A, Ḳ;) as also ▾ نفّز: (A:) or *did so in his running:* (Aṣ, TA:) or *did so and alighted with his legs spread:* when he alights with his legs together, the action is termed قَفَزَ: (TA:) or *did so after putting his legs together:* (AZ, TA:) or *leaped upwards with all his legs at once and put them down without separating them:* (Mṣb:) or *raised his legs together and put them down together:* or *ran at the utmost vehement rate of the running termed* إِحْضَار. (TA.)

2: see 1. — نَفَّزَهُ, (Ḳ,) or نَفَّزَتْهُ, (Ṣ, A,) *He,* or *she, danced,* or *dandled, him,* (Ṣ, A, Ḳ,) namely, a child; (Ṣ, A;) as also نقّزته. (TA, art. نقز.)

6. تنافزوا *They* (children) *contended together in leaping, jumping, springing,* or *bounding,* in play. (A, Ḳ.)

نَفْزَةٌ An antelope's *running by reason of fright.* (AA, TA.)

نَفُوزٌ (Ṣ) and ▾ يَنْفُوزٌ (Ḳ) An antelope *that leaps, jumps, springs,* or *bounds,* (Ṣ, Ḳ,) [*in one or other of the manners described above,*] *much,* or *vehemently.* (TA.)

نَافِزَةٌ, sing. of نَوَافِزُ, (TA,) which signifies The *legs* of a beast of carriage: (Ḳ, TA:) but the word commonly known is نَوَاقِزُ, with ق. (TA.)

يَنْفُوزٌ: see نفوز.

نفس

1. نَفُسَ, aor. ـُ, inf. n. نَفَاسَةٌ (Ṣ, M, A, Mṣb, Ḳ) and نِفَاسٌ and نَفَسٌ (Ḳ) and نُفُوسٌ; (TA;) and ▾ أَنْفَسَ, (M, A, Mṣb,) inf. n. إِنْفَاسٌ; (A, Mṣb;) *It was,* or *became, high in estimation, of high account,* or *excellent;* (M, Mṣb, TA;) [*highly prized; precious,* or *valuable;*] *and therefore,* (TA,) *was desired with emulation,* or *in much request:* (Ṣ, Ḳ, TA:) and the ▾ latter verb, said of property, *it was,* or *became, loved, and highly esteemed.* (TA.) — نَفِسَ بِهِ, (Ṣ, M, Mṣb, Ḳ,) aor. ـَ, (Ḳ,) inf. n. نَفَسٌ (M) [and app. نَفْسٌ as will be shown below] and نَفَاسَةٌ and نَفَاسِيَةٌ, which last is extr., (M, TA,) *He was,* or *became, avaricious, tenacious,* or *niggardly, of it,* (Ṣ, M, Mṣb, Ḳ,) *because of its being in high estimation,* or *excellent.* (Mṣb.) Hence the saying in the Ḳur, [xlvii. 40,] فَإِنَّمَا يَبْخَلُ عَنْ نَفْسِهِ [app. meaning *He is only avaricious from his avarice.*] (TA.) You say, نَفِسَ عَلَيْهِ بِالشَّىْءِ, (M,) or عَنْهُ [in the place of عليه], (TA,) *He was,* or *became, avaricious,* &c., *of the thing, towards him,* or *withholding it from him.* (M, TA.) And نَفِسَ عَلَيْهِ الشَّىْءَ, (Ṣ, M, Ḳ, TA,) and بِالشَّىْءِ, (M,) inf. n. نَفَاسَةٌ, (Ṣ, Ḳ, TA,) *He was,* or *became, avaricious,* &c., *of the thing, towards him, and thought him not worthy of it, and was not pleased at its coming to him:* (TA:) or [simply] *he thought him not worthy of it;* (Ṣ, M, Ḳ;) as also ▾ نافسهُ فيه; of which last verb we have an ex. in the phrase تُنَافِسُ دُنْيَا, used by a poet in speaking of the tribe of Ḳureysh, meaning either تُنَافِسُ فِى دُنْيَا [*they think* others *not worthy of worldly good*], or تُنَافِسُ أَهْلَ دُنْيَا [*they think the possessors of worldly good unworthy* thereof]. (M.) [See also 3, below.] You say also, نَفِسْتَ عَلَيَّ بِخَيْرٍ قَلِيلٍ, (A, Ḳ,) or بِخَيْرٍ, (Ṣ,) and نَفِسْتَ عَلَيَّ خَيْرًا كَثِيرًا, (A,) inf. n. نَفَسٌ and نَفَاسَةٌ, (A,) *Thou enviedst me* (Ṣ, A, Ḳ) *good,* (A, Ḳ,) or *a little good,* (Ṣ,) and *much good,* (A,) *and didst not consider me worthy of it.* (A.) And فُلَانٌ مَا يَتَنَفَّسُ عَلَيْنَا الغَنِيمَةَ وَالظَّفَرَ [app. meaning *Such a one does not envy us the spoil and the victory.*] (A, in continuation of what here immediately precedes.) And مَا هٰذَا النَّفَسُ *What is this envying?* (A, TA.) — نُفِسَتْ; (Ṣ, M, A, Mṣb, Ḳ;) and نَفِسَتْ, (Ṣ, M, Mṣb, Ḳ,) as some of the Arabs say, (Mṣb,) aor. ـَ; (Mṣb, Ḳ;) inf. n. نِفَاسٌ and نَفَاسَةٌ (Ṣ, M) and نَفْسٌ, (M, TA,) or the first of these ns. is a simple subst.; (Mṣb;) ‡ *She* (a woman) *brought forth;* (Ṣ, M, Ḳ;) and نُفِسَتْ وَلَدًا [*she brought forth a child*]: (Th, M:) and نُفِسَتْ بِوَلَدِهَا [*she brought forth her child*]. (A.) You say also, وَرِثَ فُلَانٌ هٰذَا قَبْلَ أَنْ يُنْفَسَ فُلَانٌ, meaning, *Such a one inherited this before such a one was born.* (Ṣ.) — Also, both these verbs, (Mṣb, Ḳ,) or the latter, نَفِسَتْ, only, (Az, Mgh, TA,) or the latter is the more common, (Ḳ,) the former, which is related on the authority of Aṣ, not being well known, (Mṣb,) ‡ *She* (a woman) *menstruated.* (Az, Mgh, Mṣb, Ḳ.) [In the CḲ, a confusion is made by the omission of a و before the verb which explains this last signification.] This signification and that next preceding it are from نَفْسٌ meaning "blood." (Mgh.) — نَفَسْتُهُ بِنَفْسٍ ‡ *I smote him with an* [*evil* or *envious*] *eye.* (Ṣ, Ḳ, TA.)

2. نفّسهُ فيه, or بِهِ: see 4. — نفّس كُرْبَتَهُ, (A, Mgh, Mṣb, Ḳ,*) and نفّس عَنْهُ كُرْبَتَهُ, (Ṣ,) inf. n. تَنْفِيسٌ (Ṣ, Mṣb, Ḳ) and [quasi-inf. n.] نَفَسٌ, (Ḳ,) ‡ *He* (God) *removed,* or *cleared away, his grief,* or *sorrow,* or *anxiety:* (Ṣ, A, Mgh, Mṣb, Ḳ*:) and نفّس عَنْهُ signifies the same; (M, Mgh;) and *He made his circumstances ample and easy;* (M, TA;) and *he* (a man) *eased him,* or *relieved him,* syn. رَفَّهَ: (Ṣ, TA:) and also, this last phrase, *he granted him a delay:* the objective compliment being omitted: and نَفِّسْنِى is used as meaning *grant thou to me a delay:* or, elliptically, نَفِّسْ كُرْبِى or غَمِّى [*remove thou my grief,* &c.]. (Mgh.) — [Hence] حَرْفُ تَنْفِيسٍ, applied to the prefix سَ [and its variants سَوْفَ &c.], meaning *A particle of amplification;* because changing the aor. from the strait time, which is the present, to the ample time, which is the future. (Mughnee, in art. س.) — نفّس القَوْسَ ‡ *He cracked the bow:* (Kr, M:) [see 5:] accord. to ISh, *he put* (حَطَّ) *its string* [*upon the bow*]. (TA.)

3. نافس فِى الشَّىْءِ, (Ṣ, Ḳ,*) inf. n. مُنَافَسَةٌ and نِفَاسٌ, (Ṣ,) *He desired the thing,* [or *aspired to it,*] *with generous emulation;* (Ṣ, Ḳ;) as also ▾ تنافس: (Ḳ:) and نافس صَاحِبَهُ فِيهِ [*he vied with his companion in desire for it*]: (A:) or تنافسوا ▾ فيه signifies *they desired it* [or *aspired to it*]: (Ṣ:) or *they vied, one with another, in desiring it;* or *they desired it with emulation;* syn. تَرَاغَبُوا: (A, TA:) [and يُتَنَافَسُ فيه *it is emulously desired;* or *in request;* or *in great request:*] or مُنَافَسَةٌ and ▾ تَنَافُسٌ signify the *desiring to have a thing, and to have it for himself exclusively of any other person;* from نَفِيسٌ, signifying a thing "good, or goodly, or excellent, in its kind:" (TA:) and تنافسنا فيه and تَنَافَسْنَا ذٰلِكَ الأَمْرَ *we envied one another for that thing, and strove for priority in attaining it.* (M.) See also نَفِسَ عَلَيْهِ الشَّىْءَ, with which نَافَسَهُ فِيهِ is syn. (M.)

4. انفس: see نَفُسَ, in two places. — انفسهُ *It* (a thing, TA) *pleased him,* (Ḳ, TA,) *and made him desirous of it:* (TA:) or *became highly esteemed by him.* (IḲṭṭ.) — أَنْفَسَنِى فِيهِ *He made me desirous of it;* (Ṣ, M, A, Ḳ;) as also نَفَّسَنِى فيه, (IAạr, M, TA,) or بِهِ. (So in my copy of the A.) — مَا أَنْفَسَهُ *How powerful is his evil, or envious, eye!* (Lḥ, M.)

5. تنفّس [*He breathed*] is said of a man and of every animal having lungs: (Ṣ:) [or it signifies] *he drew* (اِسْتَمَدَّ) *breath:* (M:) or [*he respired,* i.e.] *he drew breath with the air-passages in his nose; to his inside, and emitted it.* (Mṣb.) You say also, تنفّس الصُّعَدَاءَ [*He sighed:* see also art. صعد]. (Ṣ.) — ‡ *He* (a man) *emitted wind from beneath him.* (TA.) — Also, (TA,) or تنفّس فِى الإِنَآءِ, (Ḳ,) ‡ *He drank* (Ḳ, TA) *from the vessel* (TA) *with three restings between draughts, and separated the vessel from his mouth at every such resting:* (Ḳ, TA:) and, contr., the latter phrase, † *he drank* [*from the vessel*] *without separating it from his mouth:* (Ḳ, TA:) which latter mode of drinking is disapproved. (TA.) — Also تنفّس † *He lengthened in speech; he spoke long;* for when a speaker takes breath, it is easy

to him to lengthen his speech; and تنفس فى الكلام signifies the same. (TA.) — ‡ *It* (said of the day, M, A, and of the dawn, A, and of other things, M) *became extended;* (M;) *it became long;* (M, A;) or, said of the day, accord. to Lḥ, *it advanced so that it became noon:* (M:) or *it increased:* (Ṣ:) and *it extended far:* and hence it is said of life, meaning either *it became protracted, and extended far,* or *it became ample:* (M:) and, said of the dawn, *it shone forth,* (Akh, Ṣ, Ḳ, TA,) *and extended so that it became clear day:* (Fr, TA:) or *it broke, so that things became plain in consequence of it:* (TA:) or *it rose:* (Mujáhid:) or *its dusty hue shone at the approach of a gentle wind.* (Bḍ, lxxxi. 18.) You say also, تنفّس بِهِ العُمْرُ ‡ [*Life became long,* or *protracted,* &c., *with him*]. (A.) And تنفّست دِجْلَةُ † *The water of the Tigris increased.* (TA.) — تنفّس المَوْجُ ‡ *The waves sprinkled the water.* (Ṣ, Ḳ.) — تنفّست القَوْسُ ‡ *The bow cracked.* (Ṣ, M, Ḳ.) It is only the stick that is not split in twain that does so; and this is the best of bows. And تنفّس in the same sense is said of an arrow. (M.) — [تنفّس عَلَيْهِ الشَّىْءَ app. signifies the same as نَفِسَ عليه الشىء, q. v.]

6: see 3, throughout.

نَفْسٌ The *soul;* the *spirit;* the *vital principle;* syn. رُوحٌ: (Ṣ, M, A, Mṣb, Ḳ:) but between these two words is a difference [which must be fully explained hereafter, though IṢd says, that it is not of the purpose of his book, the M, to explain it]: (M:) in this sense it is fem.: (Mṣb:) pl. [of pauc.] أَنْفُسٌ and [of mult.] نُفُوسٌ. (M, Mṣb.) You say, خَرَجَتْ نَفْسُهُ [*His soul,* or *spirit, went forth*]; (Aboo-Is-ḥáḳ, Ṣ, M, Mṣb, Ḳ;) and so جَادَتْ نَفْسُهُ. (Mṣb.) And a poet says, not Aboo-Khirásh as in the Ṣ, but Ḥudheyfeh Ibn-Anas, (IB,)

* نَجَا سَالِمٌ وَالنَّفْسُ مِنْهُ بِشِدْقِهِ *

* وَلَمْ يَنْجُ إِلَّا جَفْنَ سَيْفٍ وَمِئْزَرَا *

i. e., [*Sálim escaped when the soul was in the side of his mouth; but he escaped not save*] *with the scabbard of a sword and with a waist-wrapper.* (Ṣ.) In the same sense the word is used in the saying, فِى نَفْسِ فُلَانٍ أَنْ يَفْعَلَ كَذَا وَكَذَا [but this seems rather to mean, *It is in the mind of such a one to do so and so*]. (Aboo-Is-ḥáḳ, M.) Some of the lexicologists assert the نَفْس and the رُوح to be one and the same, except that the former is fem., and the latter [generally or often] masc.: others say, that the latter is that whereby is life; and the former, *that whereby is intellect,* or *reason;* so that when one sleeps, God takes away his نفس, but not his روح, which is not taken save at death: and the نَفْس is thus called because of its connexion with the نَفَس [or breath]. (IAmb.) Or every man has نَفْسَانِ [*two souls*]: (I'Ab, Zj:) نَفْسُ العَقْلِ [*the soul of intellect,* or *reason,* also called النَّفْسُ النَّاطِقَةُ (see رُوحٌ)], *whereby one discriminates,* [i. e., *the mind,*] (I'Ab,) or نَفْسُ التَّمْيِيزِ [*the soul of discrimination*], which quits him when he sleeps, so that he does not understand thereby, God taking it away: (Zj:) and نَفْسُ الرُّوحِ [*the soul of the breath*], *whereby one lives,* (I'Ab,) or نَفْسُ الحَيَاةِ [*the soul of life*], and when this quits him, the breath quits with it; whereas the sleeper breathes: and this is the difference between the taking away of the نفس of the sleeper in sleep and the taking away of the نفس of the living [at death.] (Zj.) Much has been said respecting the نَفْس and the رُوح; whether they be one, or different: but the truth is, that there is a difference between them, since they are not always interchangeable: for it is said in the Ḳur, [xv. 29 and xxxviii. 72,] وَنَفَخْتُ فِيهِ مِنْ رُوحِى [And I have blown into him of my spirit.]; not مِنْ نَفْسِى: and [v. 116,] تَعْلَمُ مَا فِى نَفْسِى [to be explained hereafter]; not فِى رُوحِى, nor would this expression be well except from Jesus: and [lviii. 9,] وَيَقُولُونَ فِى أَنْفُسِهِمْ [*And they say in their souls,* or *within themselves*]: for which it would not be well to say فِى أَرْوَاحِهِمْ: and [xxxix. 57,] أَنْ تَقُولَ نَفْسٌ [*That a soul shall say*]; for which no Arab would say أَنْ تَقُولَ رُوحٌ: hence, the difference between them depends upon the considerations of relation: and this is indicated by a trad., in which it is said that God created Adam, and put into him a نَفْس and a رُوح; and that from the latter was his quality of abstaining from unlawful and indecorous things, and his understanding, and his clemency, or forbearance, and his liberality, and his fidelity; and from the former, [which is also called النَّفْسُ الأَمَّارَةُ, q. v., in art. أمر,] his appetence, and his unsteadiness, and his hastiness of disposition, and his anger: therefore one should not say that نَفْسٌ is the same as رُوحٌ absolutely, without restriction, nor رُوحٌ the same as نَفْس. (R.) The Arabs also make the discriminative نَفْس to be two; because it sometimes commands the man to do a thing or forbids him to do it; and this is on the occasion of setting about an affair that is disliked: therefore they make that which commands him to be a نفس, and that which forbids him to be as though it were another نفس: and hence the saying, mentioned by Z, فُلَانٌ يُؤَامِرُ نَفْسَيْهِ ‡ [*Such a one consults his two souls,* or *minds*]; said of a man when two opinions occur to him. (TA.) [بِنَفْسِى فُلَانٌ is an elliptical phrase sometimes used, for بِنَفْسِى فُلَانٌ مَفْدِىٌّ, which see in art. فدى.] — † *A thing's self;* (Ṣ, M, A, Ḳ, TA;) used as a corroborative; (Ṣ, TA;) its *whole,* (Aboo-Is-ḥáḳ, M, TA,) and *essential constituent:* (Aboo-Is-ḥáḳ, M, A, Ḳ, TA:) pl. as above, أَنْفُس and نُفُوس. (M.) You say, رَأَيْتُ فُلَانًا نَفْسَهُ † *I saw such a one himself,* (Ṣ,) and جَآءَنِى بِنَفْسِهِ [or, more properly, جَآءَنِى هُوَ بِنَفْسِهِ (see, under the head of بِ, a remark on that preposition when used in a case of this kind, redundantly,)] *He came to me himself.* (Ṣ, Ḳ.) And وَلِىَ الأَمْرَ بِنَفْسِهِ [*He superintended, managed,* or *conducted, the affair in his own person*]. (Ḳ, in art. بشر, &c.) And حَدَّثَ نَفْسَهُ [*He talked to himself; soliloquized*]. (Mṣb, in art. بلو; &c.) And قَتَلَ فُلَانٌ نَفْسَهُ † [*Such a one killed himself*]: and أَهْلَكَ نَفْسَهُ † *made his whole self to fall into destruction.* (Aboo-Is-ḥáḳ, M.) And hence, (TA,) from نَفْسُ الشَّىْءِ signifying ذَاتُهُ, (M,) the sayings mentioned by Ṣb, نَزَلْتُ بِنَفْسِ الجَبَلِ † [*I alighted in the mountain itself*]: and نَفْسُ الجَبَلِ مُقَابِلِى † [*The mountain itself is facing me*]. (M, TA.) [Hence also the phrase] فِى نَفْسِ الأَمْرِ [meaning † *in reality; in the thing itself*]: as in the saying, قَلَّلَهُ فِى نَفْسِهِ وَإِنْ لَمْ يَكُنْ قَلِيلًا فِى نَفْسِ الأَمْرِ † [*He held it to be little in his mind though it was not little in reality*]. (Mṣb, art. قل.) The words of the Ḳur, [v. 116,] تَعْلَمُ مَا فِى نَفْسِى وَلَا أَعْلَمُ مَا فِى نَفْسِكَ mean † *Thou knowest what is in myself,* or *in my essence, and I know not what is in thyself,* or *in thine essence:* (Bḍ, Ḳ:) or *Thou knowest what I conceal* (M, Bḍ, Jel) *in my* نفس [or *mind*], (Bḍ, Jel,) *and I know not what is in thyself,* or *in thine essence, nor that whereof Thou hast the knowledge,* (M,) or *what Thou concealest of the things which Thou knowest;* (Bḍ, Jel;) so that the interpretation is, *Thou knowest what I know, and I know not what Thou knowest:* (M:) or نفس is here syn. with عِنْد; and the meaning is, تَعْلَمُ مَا عِنْدِى وَلَا أَعْلَمُ مَا عِنْدَكَ; (Ḳ,* TA;) [i. e., *Thou knowest what is in my particular place of being, and I know not what is in thy particular place of being;* for] the adverbiality in this instance is that of مَكَانَة, not of مَكَان: (TA:) but the best explanation is that of IAmb, who says that نفس is here syn. with غَيْب; so that the meaning is, *Thou knowest* غَيْبِى [*my hidden things,* or *what is hidden from me, and I know not thy hidden things,* or *what Thou hidest*]; and the correctness of this is testified by the concluding words of the verse, إِنَّكَ أَنْتَ عَلَّامُ الغُيُوبِ [for Thou art he who well knoweth the hidden things]: (TA:) [and here it must be remarked that] العَيْبُ, which occurs afterwards in the Ḳ as one of the significations of النَّفْسُ, is a mistake for الغَيْبُ, the word used by IAmb in explaining the above verse. (TA.) — † *A person; a being; an individual;* syn.

شَخْص; (Mṣb;) *a man,* (Sb, Ṣ, M, TA,) *altogether, his soul and his body;* (TA;) *a living being, altogether.* (Mgh, Mṣb.) In this sense of شخص it is masc.: (Mṣb:) or, accord to Lḥ, the Arabs said, رَأَيْتُ نَفْسًا وَاحِدَةً † [*I saw one person*], making it fem.; and in like manner, رَأَيْتُ نَفْسَيْنِ ٱثْنَتَيْنِ † [*I saw two persons*]; but they said, رَأَيْتُ ثَلَاثَةَ أَنْفُسٍ † [*I saw three persons*], and so all the succeeding numbers, making it masc.: but, he says, it is allowable to make it masc. in the sing. and dual., and fem. in the pl.: and all this, he says, is related on the authority of Ks: (M:) Sb says, (M,) they said ثَلَاثَةُ أَنْفُسٍ, (Ṣ, M,) making it masc., (Ṣ,) because they mean by نفس "a man," (Ṣ, M,) as is shown also by their saying نَفْسٌ وَاحِدٌ: (M:) but Yoo asserts of Ru-beh, that he said ثَلَاثُ أَنْفُسٍ, making نفس fem., like as you say ثَلَاثُ أَعْيُنٍ, meaning, of men; and ثَلَاثَةُ أَشْخُصٍ, meaning, of women: and it is said in the Ḳur, [iv. 1, &c.,] ٱلَّذِى خَلَقَكُمْ مِنْ نَفْسٍ وَاحِدَةٍ † [*who created you from one man*], meaning, Adam. (M.) You also say, مَا رَأَيْتُ ثَمَّ نَفْسًا † *I saw not there any one.* (TA.) —— † *A brother:* (IKh, IB:) *a copartner in religion and relationship:* (Bḍ, xxiv. 61:) *a copartner in faith and religion.* (Ibn-'Arafeh.) † It is said in the Ḳur, [xxiv. 61,] فَإِذَا دَخَلْتُمْ بُيُوتًا فَسَلِّمُوا عَلَى أَنْفُسِكُمْ *And when ye enter houses, salute ye your brethren:* (IB:) or *your copartners in religion and relationship.* (Bḍ.) And in verse 12 of the same chapter, بِأَنْفُسِهِمْ means † *Of their copartners in faith and religion.* (Ibn-'Arafeh.) —— ‡ *Blood:* (Ṣ, M, A, Mgh, Mṣb, Ḳ:) [or the *life-blood:* in this sense, fem.:] pl. [of pauc. أَنْفُسٌ and of mult.] نُفُوسٌ: (IB:) so called [because the animal soul was believed by the Arabs, as it was by many others in ancient times, (see Gen. ix. 4, and Aristotle, De Anim. i. 2, and Virgil's Æn. ix. 349,) to diffuse itself throughout the body by means of the arteries: or] because the نفس [in its proper sense, i. e. the soul,] goes forth with it: (TA:) or because it sustains the whole animal. (Mgh, Mṣb.) You say, سَالَتْ نَفْسُهُ ‡ [*His blood flowed*]. (Ṣ.) And نَفْسٌ سَائِلَةٌ ‡ [*Flowing blood*]. (Ṣ, A, Mgh.) And دَفَقَ نَفْسَهُ ‡ *He shed his blood.* (A, TA.) —— ‡ The *body.* (Ṣ, A, Ḳ.) —— † [Sometimes it seems to signify The *stomach.* So in the present day. You say, لَعِبَتْ نَفْسُهُ, meaning *He was sick in the stomach.* See غَثَتْ نَفْسُهُ, in art. غثى; and مَذِرَتْ مَعِدَتُهُ and نَفْسُهُ, in art. مذر.] —— † [The *pudendum:* so in the present day: in the Ḳ, art. حشو, applied to a woman's *vulva.*] —— [From the primary signification are derived several others, of attributes of the rational and animal souls; and such are most of the significations here following.] —— † *Knowledge.* (A.) [See, above, an explanation of the words cited from ch. v. verse 116 of the Ḳur-án.] —— † *Pride:* (A, Ḳ, TA:) *and self-magnification;* syn. عِزَّةٌ. (A, Ḳ.) —— † *Disdain,* or *scorn.* (A, Ḳ.) —— † *Purpose,* or *intention:* or *strong determination:* syn. هِمَّةٌ. (A, Ḳ.) —— † *Will, wish,* or *desire.* (A, Ḳ.) —— [*Copulation:* see 3, art. رود.] —— [† *Stomach,* or *appetite.*] —— ‡ *An* [*evil* or *envious*] *eye,* (Ṣ, M, A, Ḳ, TA,) *that smites the person* or *thing at which it is cast:* pl. أَنْفُسٌ. (TA.) [See 1, last signification.] So in a trad., in which it is said, that the نَمْلَة and the حُمَة and the نَفْس are the only things for which a charm is allowable. (TA.) You say, أَصَابَتْ فُلَانًا نَفْسٌ ‡ [*An evil* or *envious eye smote such a one*]. (Ṣ.) And Moḥammad said, of a piece of green fat that he threw away, كَانَ فِيهَا سَبْعَةُ أَنْفُسٍ, meaning, ‡ *There were upon it seven* [*evil* or *envious*] *eyes.* (TA.) —— † *Strength of make, and hardiness,* of a man: and † *closeness of texture, and strength,* of a garment or piece of cloth. (M.) ═ *Punishment.* (A, Ḳ.) Ex. وَيُحَذِّرُكُمُ ٱللّٰهُ نَفْسَهُ, (Ḳ,) in the Ḳur, [iii. 27 and 28, meaning, *And God maketh you to fear his punishment*]; accord. to F; but others say that the meaning is, *Himself.* (TA.) ═ *A quantity* (Ṣ, M, Ḳ,) *of* قَرَظ, and *of other things, with which hides are tanned,* (Ṣ, Ḳ,) *sufficient for one tanning:* (Ṣ, M, Ḳ:) or *enough for two tannings:* (TA:) or *a handful thereof:* (M:) pl. أَنْفُسٌ. (M.) You say, هَبْ لِى نَفْسًا مِنْ دِبَاغٍ [*Give thou to me a quantity of material for tanning sufficient for one tanning,* or *for two tannings, &c.*]. (Ṣ.)

نَفَسٌ [*Breath;*] *what is drawn in by the air-passages in the nose,* [or *by the mouth,*] *to the inside, and emitted;* (Mṣb;) *what comes forth from a living being in the act of* تَنَفُّس. (Mgh:) or the *exit of wind from the nose and the mouth:* (M:) pl. أَنْفَاسٌ. (Ṣ, M, A, Mgh, Mṣb, Ḳ.) —— *A gentle air:* pl. as above. (M, Mṣb.) You say also, نَفَسُ الرِّيحِ [*The breath of the wind*]: and نَفَسُ الرَّوْضَةِ *the sweet* [*breath* or] *odour* [*of the meadow,* or *of the garden,* &c.]. (TA.) —— [Hence, app., its application in the phrase] نَفَسُ السَّاعَةِ [*The blast of the last hour;* meaning,] *the end of time.* (Kr, M.) —— [Hence also, † *Speech:* and *kind speech:* (see an ex. voce أَمْلَحُ:) so in the present day.] —— [And † *Voice,* or *a sweet voice, in singing:* so in the present day.] —— *A gulp,* or *as much as is swallowed at once in drinking:* (Ṣ, L, Ḳ:) but this requires consideration; for in one نَفَس a man takes a number of gulps, more or less according to the length or shortness of his breath, so that we [sometimes] see a man drink [the contents of] a large vessel in one نَفَس, at a number of gulps: (L:) [therefore it signifies sometimes, if not always, *a draught,* or *as much as is swallowed without taking breath:*] pl. as above. (Ṣ.) You say, إِكْرَعْ فِى ٱلْإِنَآءِ نَفَسًا أَوْ نَفَسَيْنِ ‡ [*Put thou thy mouth into the vessel and drink*] *a gulp,* or *two gulps:* [or *a draught,* or *two draughts:*] and exceed not that. (Ṣ.) And شَرِبْتُ نَفَسًا وَأَنْفَاسًا ‡ [*I drank a gulp, and gulps:* or *a draught, and draughts*]. (A.) And فُلَانٌ شَرِبَ ٱلْإِنَآءَ كُلَّهُ عَلَى نَفَسٍ وَاحِدٍ ‡ [*Such a one drank the whole contents of the vessel at one gulp:* or *at one draught*]. (L.) —— ‡ Every *resting between two draughts:* (M, TA:) [pl. as above.] You say, شَرِبَ بِنَفَسٍ وَاحِدٍ ‡ [*He drank with one resting between draughts*]. (A.) And شَرِبَ بِثَلَاثَةِ أَنْفَاسٍ ‡ [*He drank with three restings between draughts*]. (A, Ḳ.) [And hence,] شَرَابٌ ذُو نَفَسٍ ‡ *Beverage in which is ampleness,* [*so that one pauses while drinking it, to take breath,*] *and which satisfies thirst.* (IAạr, Ḳ.) And شَرَابٌ غَيْرُ ذِى نَفَسٍ ‡ *Beverage of disagreeable taste,* (A, Ḳ,*) *changed in taste and odour,* (Ḳ,) *in drinking which one does not take breath* (A, Ḳ) *when he has tasted it;* (Ḳ;) *taking a first draught, as much as will keep in the remains of life, and not returning to it.* (TA.) —— [And hence it is said that] نَفَس signifies † *Satisfaction,* or the *state of being satisfied, with drink;* syn. رِىّ. (IAạr, Ḳ.) —— [Hence also,] ‡ *Plenty, and redundance.* So in the saying إِنَّ فِى ٱلْمَآءِ نَفَسًا لِى وَلَكَ [*Verily in the water is plenty, and redundance, for me and for thee*]. (Lḥ, M.) —— ‡ *A wide space:* (TA:) ‡ *a distance.* (A.) You say, بَيْنَ ٱلْفَرِيقَيْنِ نَفَسٌ ‡ *Between the two parties is a wide space.* (TA.) And بَيْنِى وَبَيْنَهُ نَفَسٌ ‡ *Between me and him is a distance.* (A.) —— ‡ *Ample scope for action &c.:* and *a state in which is ample scope for action &c.:* syn. سَعَةٌ, (Ṣ, M, A, Mgh, Ḳ,) and فُسْحَةٌ, (A, Ḳ,) in an affair. (Ṣ, M, A, Ḳ.) You say, لَكَ فِى هٰذَا نَفَسٌ [*There is ample scope for action &c. for thee in this.* (Mgh.) And أَنْتَ فِى نَفَسٍ مِنْ أَمْرِكَ ‡ [*Thou art in a state in which is ample scope for action &c. with respect to thine affair.* (Ṣ, M.) And إِعْمَلْ وَأَنْتَ فِى نَفَسٍ مِنْ أَمْرِكَ ‡ *Work thou while thou art in a state in which is ample scope for action &c.* (فِى فُسْحَةٍ وَسَعَةٍ) *with respect to thine affair,* before extreme old age, and diseases, and calamities. (TA.) See also نُفْسَةٌ. —— ‡ *Length.* (M.) So in the saying زِدْنِى نَفَسًا فِى أَجَلِى ‡ [*Add thou to me length in my term* *of life*]: (M:) or *lengthen thou my term of life.* (TA.) You say also, فِى عُمْرِهِ ▾ مُتَنَفَّسٌ ‡ [*In his life is length*: see 5]. (A, TA.) — The pl., in the accus. case, also signifies † *Time after time.* So in the saying of the poet,

عَيْنَىَّ جُودَا عَبْرَةً أَنْفَاسَا

[*O my two eyes, pour forth a flow of tears time after time*]. (Ṣ.) ═ نَفَسٌ is also a subst. put in the place of the proper inf. n. of نَفَّسَ; and is so used in the two following sayings, (Ḳ, TA,) of Moḥammad. (TA.) لَا تَسُبُّوا الرِّيحَ فَإِنَّهَا مِنْ نَفَسِ الرَّحْمٰنِ, i. e. ‡ [*Revile not ye the wind, for*] *it is a means whereby the Compassionate removes grief*, or *sorrow*, or *anxiety*, (Ḳ, TA,) *and raises the clouds*, (TA,) *and scatters the rain, and dispels dearth*, or *drought.* (Ḳ, TA.) And أَجِدُ نَفَسَ رَبِّكُمْ مِنْ قِبَلِ الْيَمَنِ ‡ *I perceive your Lord's removal of grief*, &c., *from the direction of El-Yemen*: meaning, through the aid and hospitality of the people of El-Medeeneh, who were of El-Yemen; (Ḳ, TA;) i. e., of the Anṣár, who were of [the tribe of] El-Azd, from El-Yemen. (TA.) It is [said by some to be] a metaphor, from نَفَسُ الهَوَآءِ, which the act of breathing draws back into the inside, so that its heat becomes cooled and moderated: or from نَفَسُ الرِّيحِ, which one scents, so that thereby he refreshes himself: or from نَفَسُ الرَّوْضَةِ. (TA.) You also say, مَا لِى نَفَسٌ, meaning, ‡ *There is not for me any removal*, or *clearing away, of grief.* (A.) ═ It is also used as an epithet, signifying † *Long*; (AZ, Ḳ;) applied to speech, (Ḳ,) and to writing, or book, or letter. (AZ, Ḳ.)

نُفْسَةٌ, (Ṣ, Mgh, Ḳ,) with ḍamm, (Ḳ,) [in a copy of the Ṣ, نَفْسَةٌ,] † *Delay*; syn. مُهْلَةٌ; (Ṣ, Mgh, Ḳ;) and *ample space*, syn. مُتَّسَعٌ. (TA.) Ex. لَكَ فِى هٰذَا الأَمْرِ نُفْسَةٌ † [*Thou shalt have, in this affair, a delay, and ample space*]. (Ṣ, Mgh,* TA.) See also نَفَسٌ.

[نَفْسِىٌّ *Relating to the* نَفْس, or *soul*, &c.: *vital*: and *sensual*; as also ▾ نَفْسَانِىٌّ.]

نُفَسَآءُ (Th, Ṣ, M, Mgh, Mṣb, Ḳ, &c.) and نَفَسَآءُ and نَفْسَآءُ (M, Ḳ) ‡ *A woman in the state following childbirth*: (Ṣ, M,* Mgh,* Mṣb,* Ḳ:) or *bringing forth*: and *pregnant*: and *menstruating*: (Th, M:) and نَافِسٌ signifies the same; (Mṣb;) and so ▾ مَنْفُوسَةٌ: (A:) [see نُفِسَتْ:] dual نُفَسَاوَانِ; the fem. ء being changed into و as in عُشَرَاوَانِ: (Ṣ:) pl. نِفَاسٌ, (Ṣ, M, Mgh, Mṣb, Ḳ,) like as عِشَارٌ is pl. of عُشَرَآءُ, (Ṣ, Mṣb, Ḳ,) the only other instance of the kind, (Ṣ, Ḳ,) and نُفَاسٌ, (M, Ḳ,) which is also the only instance of the kind except عُشَارٌ, (Ḳ,) and نُفَّسٌ, and نُفْسٌ (M) and نُفُسٌ (M, Ḳ) and نُفَسٌ (Ḳ) and نُفَسَاوَاتٌ (Ṣ, M, Ḳ) and [accord. to analogy, of نَافِسٌ,] نَوَافِسُ. (Ḳ.)

نَفَسَانٌ, or نَفْسَانِىٌّ: see نَفُوسٌ.

نَفْسَانِىٌّ: see نَفْسِىٌّ: — and نَفُوسٌ.

نِفَاسٌ ‡ *Childbirth* (Ṣ, Ḳ) from نَفْسٌ signifying "blood." (Mṣb, TA.) See نُفِسَتْ. — [And The *state of impurity consequent upon childbirth.* See 5, in art. علّ.] — Also, ‡ The *blood that comes forth immediately after the child*: an inf. n. used as a subst. (Mgh.) — A poet says, (namely, Ows Ibn-Ḥajar, O, in art. طرق,)

لَنَا صَرْخَةٌ ثُمَّ إِسْكَاتَةٌ
كَمَا طَرَّقَتْ بِنِفَاسٍ بِكْرٌ

[*We utter a cry; then keep a short silence; like as when one that has never yet brought forth experiences resistance and difficulty in giving birth to a child, or young one*]; meaning, بِوَلَدٍ. (Ṣ.)

نَفُوسٌ *An envious man*: (M, TA:) ‡ one *who looks with an evil eye, with injurious intent, at the property of others*: (M, A,* TA:) as also ▾ نَفَسَانٌ, (TA,) or ▾ نَفْسَانِىٌّ. (A.)

نَفِيسٌ A thing *high in estimation*; *of high account*; *excellent*; (Lḥ, M, Mṣb, TA;) [*highly prized*; *precious*; *valuable*; *and therefore* (TA) *desired with emulation*, or *in much request*; (Ṣ, Ḳ, TA;) *good, goodly*, or *excellent, in its kind*; (TA;) and ▾ نَافِسٌ signifies the same, (M,) and so does ▾ مُنْفِسٌ, (Lḥ, M, A, Mṣb, Ḳ,) and ▾ مَنْفُوسٌ: (Ḳ:) it signifies thus when applied to property, as well as other things; as also ▾ مُنْفِسٌ: (Lḥ, M:) and, when so applied, *of which one is avaricious*, or *tenacious*: (M:) or ▾ مُنْفِسٌ, so applied, *abundant*; *much*; (Ḳ;) as also ▾ مُنْفَسٌ: (Fr, Ḳ:) and ▾ نَافِسٌ, a thing *of high account* or *estimation, and an object of desire*: (TA:) this last is also applied, in like manner, to a man; as also نَفِيسٌ: and the pl. [of either] is نِفَاسٌ (M, TA) You also say, ▾ أَمْرٌ مَنْفُوسٌ فِيهِ, meaning, *A thing that is desired.* (M.) And ▾ شَىْءٌ مُتَنَافَسٌ فِيهِ *A thing emulously desired*, or *in much request.* (A.) — Also, [as an epithet in which the quality of a subst. predominates,] *Much property*; (Ṣ, A, Ḳ;) and so ▾ مُنْفِسٌ. (Ṣ.) You say, لِفُلَانٍ مُنْفِسٌ and نَفِيسٌ *Such a one has much property.* (Ṣ.) And مَا يَسُرُّنِى بِهٰذَا الأَمْرِ مُنْفِسٌ and نَفِيسٌ [*Much property does not rejoice me with this affair*]. (Ṣ.)

نَافِسٌ: see نَفِيسٌ, in three places. ═ See also نُفَسَآءُ. ═ ‡ *Smiting with an evil*, or *envious, eye.* (Ṣ, M, Ḳ.) ═ The *fifth of the arrows used in the game called* المَيْسِر; (Ṣ, M, Ḳ;) *which has five notches; and for which one wins five portions if it be successful, and loses five portions if it be unsuccessful*: (Lḥ, M:) or, as some say, the *fourth.* (Ṣ.)

هٰذَا أَنْفَسُ مَالِى *This is the most loved and highly esteemed of my property.* (Ṣ, TA.) ═ بَلَّغَكَ اللّٰهُ أَنْفَسَ الأَعْمَارِ ‡ [*May God cause thee to attain to the most protracted*, or *most ample, of lives*: see 5]. (A, TA.) And دَارُكَ أَنْفَسُ مِنْ دَارِى ‡ *Thy house is more ample*, or *spacious, than my house*: (M:) and the like is said of two places: (M:) and of two lands. (A.) And هٰذَا الثَّوْبُ أَنْفَسُ مِنْ هٰذَا ‡ *This garment*, or *piece of cloth, is wider and longer and more excellent than this.* (M.) And ثَوْبٌ أَنْفَسُ الثَّوْبَيْنِ ‡ *A garment*, or *piece of cloth, the longer and wider of the two garments*, or *pieces of cloth.* (A.)

مُنْفَسٌ: }
مُنْفِسٌ: } see نَفِيسٌ; for the latter, throughout.

مَنْفُوسٌ: see نَفِيسٌ, in two places. ═ ‡ *Brought forth; born.* (Ṣ, M, A, Mṣb, Ḳ.) It is said in a trad., مَا مِنْ نَفْسٍ مَنْفُوسَةٍ إِلَّا وَقَدْ كُتِبَ مَكَانُهَا مِنَ الجَنَّةِ أَوِ النَّارِ ‡ [*There is not any soul born but its place in Paradise* or *Hell has been written*]. (Ṣ.) — مَنْفُوسَةٌ applied to a woman: see نُفَسَآءُ. ═ ‡ *Smitten with an evil*, or *envious, eye.* (M.)

[مُتَنَفَّسٌ *A place of passage of the breath.*] — سَحَرٌ مُتَنَفَّسٌ: see نَفَسٌ. — See also فِى عُمْرِهِ مُتَنَفَّسٌ.

مُتَنَفِّسٌ [*Breathing*;] *having breath*: (TA:) or *having a soul*: (so in a copy of the M:) an epithet applied to everything *having lungs.* (Ṣ, TA.) — غَائِطٌ مُتَنَفِّسٌ ‡ *A depressed expanse of land extending far.* (A, TA.) — أَنْفٌ مُتَنَفِّسٌ ‡ *A nose of which the bone is wide and depressed*; or *depressed and expanded*; or *a nose spreading upon the face*: syn. أَفْطَسُ. (A, TA.)

شَىْءٌ مُتَنَافَسٌ فِيهِ: see نَفِيسٌ.

نفش

1. نَفَشَ, (Ṣ, A,) aor. ـُ, (Ṣ,) inf. n. نَفْشٌ, (Ṣ, A, Ḳ,) *He separated*, or *plucked asunder*, or *loosened*, a thing, *with his fingers, so that it became spread*, or *sparse*, or *dispersed*; (A, Ḳ;) as also ▾ نَفَّشَ, inf. n. تَنْفِيشٌ: (Ṣ, Ḳ:) or the latter has an intensive signification: and accord. to some, the former signifies *he separated* a thing not difficult to separate, such as cotton and wool: or *he pulled*

wool *until its parts became separated*, or *plucked asunder*, or *loosened*: (TA:) or *he spread*, or *dispersed*, a thing. (MF.) You say, نَفَشْتُ القُطْنَ and الصُّوفَ [*I separated*, or *plucked asunder*, or *loosened, with my fingers*, &c., *the cotton* and *the wool*]. (Ṣ, A.) نَفْش is likewise *syn. with* نَدْف [the *separating and loosening* cotton *by means of a bow and a wooden mallet*]. (TA.) You also say, نَفَشَ الرُّطْبَةَ, inf. n. as above, meaning, *He separated what was collected together*, or *compacted, in the* [*kind of trefoil called*] رطبة. (TA.) And, of a cock, (T, Ṣ, in art. بول,) or of a حُبَارَى, (Ḳ, in that art.,) when about to fight, (T, Ḳ, ibid.,) نَفَشَ بُرَائِلَهُ [*He ruffled the feathers around his neck*]. (T, Ṣ, Ḳ, ibid.) ═ It is also intrans., *syn. with* انتفش, q. v. (TA.) — [And hence,] نَفَشَتِ الغَنَمُ, (Ṣ, A, Ḳ,) and الإِبِلُ, (Ṣ, Mṣb, Ḳ,) accord. to IDrd the former only, but accord. to others the latter also, and in like manner one says of all beasts, though mostly of غَنَم, (TA,) aor. ـُ (Ṣ, Mṣb, Ḳ) and ـِ, (Ṣ, Ḳ,) inf. n. نَفْشٌ, (Mṣb, Ḳ,) or نُفُوشٌ, (Ṣ,) or both; (TA;) and نَفِشَت, aor. ـَ; (IAạr, Ṣgh, Ḳ;) *The sheep or goats*, and *the camels, pastured by night without a pastor*: (Ṣ, Mṣb, Ḳ:) or *without the knowledge of a pastor*: (TA:) or *dispersed themselves* by night: (A:) or *dispersed themselves and pastured by night without knowledge* [*of the pastor*]: or *the sheep or goats entered among seed-produce*: (TA:) occurring in the Ḳur, xxi. 78: (Ṣ, TA:) the subst. is نَفَش, signifying their *dispersion of themselves and pasturing by night without a pastor*. (Mṣb.)

2: see 1, first signification.

4. انفش الغَنَمَ, (Ṣ, A, Ḳ.) and الإِبِلَ, (Ṣ, Ḳ,) *He* (the pastor) *sent the sheep or goats*, and *the camels*, (Ḳ,* TA,) or *left them*, (Ṣ, TA,) *to pasture by night without a pastor*; (Ṣ, Ḳ, TA;) *neglecting them*: (TA:) or *to disperse themselves* by night. (A.)

5. تنفّشت الهِرَّةُ, (Ṣ, A, Ḳ,) and ↓ انتفشت, (Ṣ, A,) *The cat bristled up her hair*. (Ṣ, A, Ḳ.) And in like manner you say of a hyena. (A, TA.*) And تنفّش الدِّيكُ, (A,) or الطَّائِرُ, (Ḳ,) and ↓ انتفش, (A, TA,) *The cock*, (A,) or *bird*, (Ḳ,) *ruffled*, (A,) or *shook*, (Ḳ,) *his feathers, as though he feared*, (A, Ḳ,) or *threatened*, (A,) or *trembled*. (Ḳ.)

8. انتفش *i. q.* نَفَشَ used intransitively, [signifying *It* (a thing, or cotton, and wool, and the like,) *became separated*, or *plucked asunder*, or *loosened, with the fingers, so that it became spread*, or *sparse*, or *dispersed*; &c., being] quasi-pass. of نَفَشَ used transitively. (TA.) See also مُنْتَفِش. And see 5, in two places.

نَفْش *Wool*. (IAạr, Ḳ.) — [Hence, app., the saying,] إِنْ لَمْ يَكُنْ شَحْمٌ فَنَفَشٌ, [lit., *If there be not fat, then* let there be *wool*;] meaning, † *If there be not action, then* [let there be] *a show of action*: (IAạr, Az, L:) or the last word signifies *a little milk*: (Meyd, cited by Freytag: see his Arab. Prov., i. 70:) it also signifies, [and perhaps in the above saying,] ‡ *abundance of speech* or *talk, and of pretensions*. (MF.) ═ See also 1, at the end. ═ And see نَافِش.

نَفَّاش † *Proud and boastful*; or one *who praises himself for that which is not in him*; or *who says that which he does not*. (TA.) ═ *A kind of* لَيْمُون [or *citron*; the *limon sponginus rugosus* Ferrari; (Delile, Floræ Aegypt. Illustr., no. 749)] *of the largest size*. (TA.)

نَافِش, applied to a camel [and to a sheep or goat]; fem. نَافِشَةٌ; (Mṣb;) part. n. of 1. (Mṣb, TA.) You say, إِبِلٌ نَافِشَةٌ (Mṣb) and نَفْشٌ [quasi-pl. n. of نَافِش] (Ṣ, Ḳ) and نِفَاشٌ (Mṣb) and نُفَّاشٌ (Ṣ, Ḳ) and نُفَّشٌ [pls. of نَافِش] (TA) and نَوَافِشُ [pl. of نَافِشَةٌ], (Ṣ, Ḳ,) [and in like manner غَنَمٌ,] *Camels* [and *goats*] *pasturing by night without a pastor*: (Ṣ, Mṣb, Ḳ:) or *dispersing themselves and pasturing by night without knowledge* [*of the pastor*]. (TA.) نَفَشٌ are only by night; but هَمَلٌ, by night and by day. (Ṣ.)

عِهْنٌ مَنْفُوشٌ (Ṣ) *Wool of various colours separated and loosened by means of the bow and wooden mallet*: (Bḍ, Jel, ci. 4:) and in like manner, ↓ قُطْنٌ مُنْتَفِشٌ [*cotton that is separated*, or *plucked asunder*, or *loosened, with the fingers, so that it becomes spread*, or *dispersed*; &c.: see 1 and 8]. (TA, voce هَيَّانٌ.) See also مُتَنَفِّش, below.

مَنْفُوش — أَمَةٌ مُنْتَفِشَةُ الشَّعَرِ : see مُنْتَفِش *A female slave having shaggy* or *dishevelled hair*; (A;) *i. q.* شَعْثَاءُ. (Ḳ.) — مُنْتَفِش is likewise applied to anything *Swollen*, or *humid, and loose* or *flaccid* or *soft within*; as also ↓ مُتَنَفِّش. (Az, Ḳ.) — You say also, أَنْفٌ مُنْتَفِشٌ ‡ *A nose short in the* مَارِن [or *soft part*], *and spreading upon the face, like the nose of the* زِنْجِىّ: (A:) and أَرْنَبَةٌ مُنْتَفِشَةٌ has the like signification; as also ↓ مُتَنَفِّشَةٌ; (TA;) or it means *an end of a nose spreading upon the face*: (Ḳ:) and ↓ مُتَنَفِّشُ المَنْخِرَيْنِ, in like manner, *wide in the two nostrils*. (TA.) See also مُتَنَفِّش.

مُتَنَفِّش: see مُنْتَفِش, in three places.

نفض

1. نَفَضَ, (Ṣ, A, Mgh, Mṣb, Ḳ,) aor. ـُ, (Ṣ, Mṣb,) inf. n. نَفْضٌ, (Ṣ, Mgh, Mṣb,) *He shook* (Ṣ, A, Mgh, Mṣb, Ḳ) a thing, (Mgh, Mṣb,) or a garment, or piece of cloth, (Ṣ, A, Ḳ,) *in order that what was upon it, of dust &c., might fall off* (Ṣ,* A,* Mgh, Ḳ,*) or *to remove from it dust and the like*; (Mṣb;) *he took* a thing *with his hand, and shook* it, or *shook* it *violently, to remove the dust from it*: (TA:) and in like manner, a tree, *in order that what was upon it* [*of fruit* or *of leaves*] *might fall off*; (Ṣ, A;) [as, for instance,] a tree of the kind called عِضَاه, *to shake off its leaves*. (TA.) You say also, نَفَضَ عَنْهُ التُّرَابَ and الغُبَارَ [*He shook off from it the dust*]. (A.) And نَفَضْتُ الوَرَقَ مِنَ الشَّجَرَةِ, inf. n. as above, [*He shook off the leaves from the tree*;] *he made the leaves to fall from the tree*. (Mṣb.) And نَفْض also signifies The *sprinkling* or *scattering in drops*, (syn. رَشّ,) water, and blood, (A, Ḳ, in art. رش,) and tears, (Ḳ, ibid.) &c. (A, ibid.) — [Hence,] نَفَضَتْهُ الحُمَّى (Ṣ, A, Ḳ) ‡ *The fever made him to shiver*, or *tremble*. (Aṣ, TA.) — And نَفَضَتِ المَرْأَةُ كَرِشَهَا, (Ḳ,) or نَفَضَتْ كَرِشَهَا, (Ṣ,) or نَفَضَتْ وَلَدَهَا مِنْ بَطْنِهَا, (A,) ‡ *The woman bore many children*; *was prolific*. (Ṣ, Ḳ, TA.) And نَفَضَتِ الإِبِلُ † *The she-camels brought forth*, (Ṣ, L, Ḳ,) *all of them*; (L;) and ↓ انفضت signifies the same. (IDrd, Ṣ, Ḳ.) And نَفَضَتِ الدَّجَاجَةُ بَيْضَهَا ‡ [*The hen laid her eggs*; or *all her eggs*]. (A, TA.) — [Hence also,] قَامَ يَنْفُضُ الكَرَى ‡ [*He arose, shaking off drowsiness*]. (A, TA.) And نَفَضَ الأَسْقَامَ عَنْهُ وَٱسْتَصَحَّ ‡ [*He shook off maladies from him, and recovered from his sickness*]; i. e. *his health became in a sound state*. (A, TA.) And نَفَضَ مِنْ مَرَضِهِ, (A,) inf. n. نُفُوضٌ, (A, Ḳ,) ‡ *He recovered*, or *became free, from his disease*. (A, Ḳ,* TA.) — And نَفَضْتُ لَهُ مَا فِى جِرَابِى † *I showed him what was in my heart*. (Er-Rághib, TA, in art. شكو and شكى.) — And نَفَضَ الطَّرِيقَ ‡ *He cleared the road of robbers, and intercepters of travellers*: ‡ *he guarded the road*. (A, TA. [The latter signification is shown by an explanation of the act. part. n.]) It is said in the trad. of Aboo-Bekr and the cave [in which Moḥammad was hiding himself], أَنَا أَنْفُضُ مَا حَوْلَكَ ‡ *I will guard what is around thee, and go round about to try if I can see a pursuer*. (TA.) You say also, نَفَضَ المَكَانَ, (Ṣ, Ḳ,) aor. as above, (TA,) inf. n. نَفْضٌ; (Ṣ, TA;) and ↓ استنفضهُ, and ↓ تنفّضهُ; (Ṣ, Ḳ;) ‡ *He looked trying to see all that was in the place*; (Ṣ;) or *he looked at all that was in the place so as to know it*. (Ḳ.) And hence نَفَضَ signifies † *He searched to the utmost*. (L.) And إِذَا تَكَلَّمْتَ نَهَارًا فَٱنْفُضْ وَإِذَا تَكَلَّمْتَ لَيْلًا فَٱخْفِضْ (Ṣ, Ḳ,* TA) ‡ *When thou speakest by day, look aside, or about, to try if thou see any one whom thou dislikest*; (Ṣ, Ḳ, TA;) *and when thou speakest by night, lower thy voice*. (TA.) And ↓ استنفض القَوْمَ ‡ *He looked at the people*, or *company of men, endeavouring to obtain a clear*

knowledge of them; or considered, or examined, them repeatedly, in order to know them. (TA.) The saying of El-'Ojeyr Es-Saloolee,

• إِلَى مَلِكٍ يَسْتَنْفِضُ ♦ القَوْمَ طَرْفُهُ •

means ‡ [*To a king whose eye*] *looks at the people, or company of men, and knows who among them has the right on his side: or looks to see in whom among them is mental perception, sagacity, intelligence, forecast, or skill in affairs, and which of them is of the contrary description*: (TA:) [or] فُلَانٌ يَسْتَنْفِضُ ♦ طَرْفُهُ القَوْمَ means ‡ [*The eye of*] *such a one makes the people, or company of men, to tremble, by reason of his awfulness.* (A, TA.) — You also say, الإِبِلُ تَنْفُضُ الأَرْضَ † *The camels traverse the land.* (IAar.) — And نَفَضَ القُرْآنَ, (IAar,) or السُّوَرَ, (Ḳ,) aor. ـُ, inf. n. نَفْضٌ, (IAar,) ‡ *He read, or recited,* (IAar, Ḳ,) *the Ḳur-án,* (IAar,) or *the chapters thereof.* (Ḳ.) — And نَفَضْنَا حَلَائِبَنَا, inf. n. نَفْضٌ; and ♦ اِسْتَنْفَضْنَاهَا; ‡ *We milked our milch beasts to the uttermost, not leaving any milk in their udders*: (TA:) and انتفض ♦ الفَصِيلُ مَا فِى الضَّرْعِ ‡ *the young camel sucked out all that was in the udder.* (A, TA.) ═ [It is also used intransitively in the following exs., as well as in some instances given above. Thus نَفَضَ الشَّجَرُ app. signifies *The trees shook off, or dropped, their leaves or fruit.* (See an ex. voce عَتِيقٌ, last sentence but one.) — And hence] one says, نَفَضَ مَا فِى الجُلَّةِ [app. meaning *What was in the palm-leaf basket became exhausted*; like نَفِدَ; or it may be syn. with انتفض]; (A, Ḳ;) or جَمِيعُ مَا فِيهَا [*all that was in it*; which shows that ما in the former instance is virtually in the nom. case]. (TA.) See also 4, in two places. — And نَفَضَ الصِّبْغُ, (ISh, Mgh, Ḳ,) inf. n. نَفْضٌ, (ISh, TA,) or نُفُوضٌ, (TA,) ‡ *The dye* (ISh, Ḳ, TA,) of a red or yellow garment, or piece of cloth, (ISh, TA,) *lost somewhat of its colour.* (ISh, Ḳ, TA.) And hence, (Mgh,) نَفَضَ الثَّوْبُ, (A, Mgh,) aor. ـُ, (A,) inf. n. نُفُوضٌ, (A, Mgh,) ‡ *The garment, or piece of cloth, lost its dye*: (A:) or *lost somewhat of its colour, of redness, or yellowness*: (Mgh:) or *the colour of its dye faded away so that there remained nothing but the trace.* (TA.) نُفُوضٌ, accord. to the lawyers, signifies † The *being scattered, strewn, strewed,* or *dispersed*: and accord. to [the Ḥanafee Imám] Mohammad, the *non-transition of the trace of the dye to another thing*: or *its exhaling a sweet odour.* (Mgh [but it seems that the particle لا, which I have rendered "non," is inserted by mistake in my copy of the Mgh.]) — نَفَضَ الزَّرْعُ, (Ḳ,) or نَفَضَ الزَّرْعُ سَبَلًا, (TA,) † *The seed-produce put forth the last of its ears.* (Ḳ, TA.) And نَفَضَ الكَرْمُ † *The grape-vine opened its bunches, or racemes.* (Ḳ.) [See also 8.]

2. نَفَّضَ, (Ṣ, TA,) inf. n. تَنْفِيضٌ, (TA,) *He shook* a garment, or piece of cloth, and a tree, *much, or vehemently, in order that what was upon it might fall off.* (Ṣ, TA.*) — Said of a horse, i.q. رَفَّضَ, q.v. (TA in art. رفض.)

4. نَفَضَ ♦ مَا فِى الجُلَّةِ i.q. أَنْفَضَتِ الجُلَّةُ, (A, Ḳ,) or جَمِيعُ مَا فِيهَا: (TA:) see 1. — انفضوا originally signifies *They shook their provision-bags, in order that the dust or the like might fall from them.* (A.) And hence, (A,) ‡ *Their travelling-provisions became consumed,* (Ṣ, M, A, Ḳ, TA,) *and their wheat,* or *food*; (M, TA;) like أَرْمَلُوا; (Ṣ, M, Ḳ,* TA;) as though they shook their provision-bags in order that the dust or the like might fall from them, because of their being empty; (TA;) as also ♦ نَفَضُوا: (Ḳ:) or انفضوا, (Ḳ,) or, as IDrd says, انفضوا زَادَهُمْ, making the verb trans., (TA,) *They consumed their travelling-provisions.* (IDrd, Ḳ.) And ‡ Their camels, or the like, (أَمْوَالُهُمْ,) *died,* or *perished.* (Ṣ, Ḳ.) إِنْفَاضٌ [the inf. n.] also signifies † The *suffering hunger,* or *famine*: and *want.* (TA.) — انفضت الإِبِلُ: see نفضت.

5. تنفّض المَكَانَ: see 1.

8. انتفض *It* (a thing, Mgh, Mṣb, or a garment, or piece of cloth, Ṣ, A, Ḳ, and a tree, Ṣ, A) *shook,* or *became shaken,* (Ṣ, A, Mgh, Mṣb, Ḳ,) *so that what was upon it, of dust &c., fell off,* (Mgh,) or *so that the dust and the like became removed from it.* (Mṣb.) Hence the saying in a trad., يَنْتَفِضُ بِهِ الصِّرَاطُ, i.e. [*The bridge extending over hell will shake with him so that he will fall from it*: or] *will shake him,* or *shake him violently,* or [app. a mistake for *and*] *make him to fall.* (Mgh.) — ‡ *He trembled, quaked,* or *shivered*: said of a man, and of a horse. (A, TA.) — † *It* (a grape-vine) *became beautiful and bright in its leaves*: (Ḳ:) [as though its dust became shaken off.] ═ It is also used transitively: see 1, latter half: and see 10, in three places.

10. استنفض القَوْمُ ‡ *The people,* or *company of men, sent forth a* نَفِيضَة, (Ṣ, Ḳ,* TA,) or *party of scouts*: (TA:) or *sent forth* نَفَضَة, or *persons to clear the roads of robbers and of intercepters of travellers, or to guard the roads.* (A, L, TA.) — استنفض المَكَانَ: and القَوْمَ: see 1, in four places. — استنفضهُ also signifies ‡ *He extracted, educed,* or *elicited, it.* (A, Mgh,* Ḳ.) You say, اِسْتَنْفَضْتُ مَا عِنْدَهُ ‡ *I extracted, educed,* or *elicited, what he had.* (A, TA.*) — And hence, (Mgh,) استنفض ‡ *He performed the act of cleansing termed* اِسْتِنْجَآء, (Mgh, Ḳ,) with three stones, (Mgh,) or with the stone: (Ḳ:) or this is from نَفَضَ الثَّوْبَ; because the person who performs this act shakes off from himself what is annoying, with the stone; i.e., removes it. (TA.) You say also, استنفض الذَّكَرَ ‡ *He took extraordinary pains in cleansing,* or *he cleansed entirely,* (اِسْتَبْرَأَ,) *the penis from the remains of the urine*; as also ♦ انتفضهُ; (Ḳ;) and ♦ انتفض [alone]: (TA:) and ♦ this last, *he sprinkled some water upon his pudendum after the ablution termed* وُضُوْء. (TA in art. نصح.) — [Hence also,] استنفضنا حَلَائِبَنَا: see 1.

نَفَضٌ *What has fallen, of the produce of a tree*; (TA;) *what has fallen, of leaves,* and *of fruit*: (Ṣ, Mṣb, Ḳ:) or *a thing that one shakes* [or *has shaken*] *off*: (T in art. ذرى:) of the measure فَعَلٌ in the sense of the measure مَفْعُولٌ, (Ṣ, Mṣb, TA,) like قَبَضٌ in the sense of مَقْبُوضٌ, (Ṣ, TA,) and هَدَمٌ in the sense of مَهْدُومٌ: (TA:) and (Ḳ, TA) *what has fallen,* (TA,) *of grapes,* [in the CḲ we find حَبُّ العِنَبِ for حَبُّ العِنَبِ, the reading in other copies of the Ḳ,] *when they are found* (يُوجَدُ) [in the CḲ يُؤْخَذُ, thus, with خ, and with the unpointed د,]) *one with another,* (Ḳ, TA,) or *cleaving one to another*: (L, TA:) or *what has fallen, of dates, at the feet of the palm-trees*: (M, TA:) or *what has fallen, of fruit, at the feet of trees*; as also ♦ أَنَافِيضُ: (A:) or ♦ this last signifies *leaves that are shaken off upon the* نِفَاض, q.v.; as also ♦ نِفَاضٌ [which is app. pl. of نَفَضٌ, like as جِبَالٌ is pl. of جَبَلٌ]: (Ṣgh, Ḳ:) the sing. of انافيض is ♦ أُنْفُوضَةٌ. (TA.) [See also نُفَاضَةٌ.] ═ قَوْمٌ نَفَضٌ [app. quasi-pl. of ♦ نَافِضٌ, like as خَدَمٌ is of خَادِمٌ,] ‡ *A people, or company of men, whose travelling-provisions have become consumed.* (ISh.)

نَفْضَةٌ ‡ The *shivering,* or *trembling, attending a fever termed* النَّافِض; (Ṣ, Ḳ;) as also ♦ نُفَضَةٌ (Ṣgh, Ḳ) and ♦ نُفَضَآءُ. (Ṣ, Ḳ.) [See also نَفِيضَى.] The subst. [from these words, which seems to indicate that they are inf. ns. or from نَفَضَتْهُ الحُمَّى, which precedes them in the Ḳ,] is ♦ نُفَاضٌ [app. signifying ‡ *A shivering,* or *tremour, attending that fever*]. (Ḳ.) ═ † *A rain which falls upon a piece of land and misses another piece.* (Ṣ.) [In the O and Ḳ in art. عهد, written نَفْضَة.]

نَفَضَةٌ: see نَفِيضَةٌ, in two places.

نُفَضَةٌ: see نَفْضَةٌ.

نَفِيضَى: see نَفْضٌ.

نُفَضَآءُ: see نَفْضَةٌ.

نُفَاضٌ: see نَفْضَةٌ: ═ and see نِفَاضٌ.

نُفَاضٌ: see نُفَاضَةٌ. ═ Also, and ♦ نِفَاضٌ, ‡ The

failure of travelling-provisions; i. e. *their being consumed*: or *dearth*, or *drought*: (Ṣ, Ḳ:) the latter of the words, and of the explanations, on the authority of Th. (Ṣ.) Hence, النفاض يُقَطِّرُ الجَلَبَ, (Ṣ, Ḳ,) a proverb, meaning, ‡ *The failure of provisions*, (TA,) or *dearth*, or *drought*, (Ṣ, Ḳ, TA,) *causes the camels, driven* or *brought from one place to another, to be disposed in files for sale*, (Ṣ, Ḳ, TA,) in order that their owners may buy provisions with their price. (TA.)

نِفَاضٌ: see نُفَاضَةٌ: and نَفَضٌ. — *A piece of cloth upon which the leaves of the* سَمُر *and the like fall, it being spread*, (Ḳ, TA,) *and the tree being beaten with a staff*, or *stick*: (TA:) pl. نُفُضٌ: (Ḳ:) and [in like manner] ▼ مِنْفَضٌ and ▼ مِنْفَاضٌ signify *a garment of the kind called* كِسَآء, *upon which the* نَفَض [or *leaves* or *fruit of a tree*] *fall*: (A, TA:) or ▼ مِنْفَضٌ signifies *i. q.* مِنْسَفٌ, (Ṣ, Ḳ,) i. e. *a vessel* (وِعَآء) *in which dates* [*and grain*] *are shaken to remove the dust &c.* (TA.) — *A garment of the kind called* إِزَار *worn by boys*: (Ṣ, Ḳ:) pl. as above. (TA.) You say also, مَا عَلَيْهِ نِفَاضٌ, (Ṣ, Ḳ,) meaning *He has not upon him any clothing*. (Ibn-'Abbád, Ḳ.)

نَفُوضٌ ‡ A woman *having many children*; *prolific*. (Ṣ, A, Ḳ.) — رَجُلٌ نَفُوضٌ لِلْكَلَامِ ‡ *A man who considers, examines*, or *studies, speech*, or *language*, or *does so repeatedly, in order to obtain a clear knowledge of it*. (TA.)

نُفَاضَةٌ *What has fallen in consequence of shaking to cause something upon it to fall*; (Ṣ;) *what has fallen from a thing so shaken*; (IDrd, Ḳ;) *whatever it be*; *as, for instance, of leaves*; and mostly, *of leaves of the* سَمُر *in particular, when collected and beaten off* [or rather *beaten off and collected*] *in a garment*, or *piece of cloth*; (IDrd, L, TA;) [like نَفَضٌ, q. v.;] and ▼ نُفَاضٌ signifies the same; (Ṣ, Ḳ;) and ▼ نِفَاضٌ also. (Ḳ.) And *What remains in one's mouth, of a* سِوَاك [or *tooth-stick*], *and is spit out*; or *a particle broken off therefrom, remaining in the mouth, and spit out*; *i. q.* نُفَاثَةُ سِوَاكٍ, (IAạr, Ḳ,) and ضُوَازَةُ. (IAạr.)

نَفِيضَةٌ ‡ *A company sent forth into the land to see whether there be in it an enemy*, (Ṣ, Ḳ,) or *not*, (Ḳ,) or *any* [*cause of*] *fear*; (Ṣ;) like طَلِيعَةٌ; (Ṣ, TA;) as also ▼ نَفَضَةٌ; [pl. of ▼ نَافِضٌ, like as طَلَبَةٌ is of طَالِبٌ:] (Ṣ, Ḳ:) or the former signifies men *going before an army*, *as scouts*, or *explorers*: (Aṣ, in TA, voce حَضِيرَةٌ:) or men *who explore a place thoroughly*: and also, *a single person*: (A'Obeyd, in TA, ibid.:) or *a scout*, or *scouts, stationed on a mountain* or *other elevated place*: (TA:) or *one who guards the road*: (A, TA:) or *a company* [*of men*]: (TA:) and ▼ the latter, *persons who clear the roads of robbers and of intercepters of travellers*; or *who guard the roads*: (A, TA:) the pl. of the former is نَفَائِضُ; (Ṣ;) which also signifies *persons who throw pebbles in order to know if there be behind them anything that they dislike*, or *an enemy*. (Ḳ.) — Also, the pl., † *Lean*, or *emaciated*, camels; (Ṣ, Ḳ;) accord. to AA, as occurring in a verse of Aboo-Dhu-eyb, in which he says,

* تُلْقِى النَّفَائِضُ فِيهِ السَّرِيحَا *

(Ṣ, TA,) *In which the lean*, or *emaciated, camels cast the shoes*; meaning that these have become dissundered; or, as Akh says, *the thongs so called* [*by which their shoes are fastened*], these being dissundered; فيه referring to the road; but some read, فِيهَا, referring to the roads, mentioned before: (TA:) Aṣ reads نفائض, as well as AA: (Ṣ, TA:) but others read the word with ق, as pl. of نِقْضٌ, and signifying "jaded" camels: (so in a copy of the Ṣ:) or نفائض signifies camels *which traverse the land*. (IAạr, Ḳ.) — The sing. is also said to signify *Waters where there is not any one*. (IAạr, Sh; both in the TA, voce حَضِيرَةٌ, q. v., and the former also in this art.)

نِفِّيضَى *Motion*: and *tremour*, or *shivering*; as also ▼ نِفِّضَّى and ▼ نَفَضَى. (O, Ḳ.) [See also نُفْضَةٌ.]

نَافِضٌ ‡ *A fever attended with shivering*, or *trembling*: (Ṣ, A,* Ḳ:) of the masc. gender: (ISd, Ḳ:) but applied as an epithet to حُمَّى [which is fem.]. (TA.) Contr. of صَالِبٌ. (Ṣ, in art. صلب.) You say, أَخَذَتْهُ حُمَّى نَافِضٍ, (Ṣ, Ḳ,) and حُمَّى بِنَافِضٍ, (Ḳ,) which is the more approved form, (TA,) and حُمَّى نَافِضٌ, (Ḳ,) the latter word being sometimes thus used as an epithet; the second meaning ‡ *Fever took him*, or *affected him, with* [*a shivering*, or *trembling*, or] *violent shivering* or *trembling*; (TA;) [and the first and third, *fever attended with shivering*, or *trembling, took him*, or *affected him*.] — See also نَفِيضَةٌ. — and نَفَضٌ. — ثَوْبٌ نَافِضٌ ‡ *A* garment, or piece of cloth, which has lost its dye: (A:) or *which has lost somewhat of its colour, of redness*, or *yellowness*. (Mgh.)

أُنْفُوضَةٌ: pl. أَنَافِيضُ: see نَفَضٌ, in three places.

دَجَاجَةٌ مُنْفِضٌ, (A,) or منفضة [i. e. مُنْفِضَةٌ], (TA,) ‡ *A hen that has laid her eggs*, or *all her eggs*, (نَفَضَتْ بَيْضَهَا, A, TA,) *and desisted*, (A,) or *become weary*. (TA.)

مِنْفَضٌ: } see نِفَاضٌ; for the former, in two
مِنْفَاضٌ: } places.

مَنْفُوضٌ ‡ *Made to shiver*, or *tremble, by fever*. (Ṣ, Ḳ.)

نفط

1. نَفِطَتْ يَدُهُ, (Ṣ, Mṣb,) or كَفُّهُ, (Ḳ,) aor. ـَ, (Mṣb, Ḳ,) inf. n. نَفَطٌ and نَفِيطٌ (Ṣ, Mṣb, Ḳ,) and نَفْطٌ; (Ḳ;) or, accord. to AZ, نَفَطَتْ, aor. ـِ, inf. n. نَفْطٌ and نَفِيطٌ; (TA;) *His hand became blistered*, or *vesicated*; *it had water*, or *fluid, between the skin and the flesh*; (AZ, Mṣb;) *i. q.* مَجِلَتْ; (Ṣ, Ḳ;) as also ▼ تَنَفَّطَتْ: (Ṣ:) or *it became ulcerated by work*. (Ḳ.) — نَفَطَتْ, aor. ـِ, inf. n. نَفِيطٌ (ADḳ, Ṣ, Ḳ) and نَفْطٌ, (TA,) *She* (a goat) *did what was like sneezing* (نَثَرَتْ) [app. meaning *scattered forth moisture* or *the like*]) *with her nose*: (ADḳ, Ṣ, Ḳ:) or *sneezed*. (Ḳ.) It is said in a proverb, لَا تَنْفِطُ فِيهِ عَنَاقٌ, meaning † *Blood-revenge will not be taken for him*; i. e. for this slain person. (TA.) — Also, (Ṣ, Ḳ,) aor. ـِ, inf. n. نَفِيطٌ, (Ṣ,) *It* (a cooking-pot, قِدْرٌ,) *boiled*, (Ṣ, Ḳ,) *and poured forth* [*some of its contents*], (Ṣ,) or *so that it threw forth what resembled arrows*; (TA;) a dial. var. of نَفَثَتْ. (Ṣ.) — نَفَطَ, aor. ـِ, ‡ *He was angry*: or *he burned with anger*: as also ▼ تنفّط. (Ḳ, TA.) You say, إِنَّ فُلَانًا لَيَنْفِطُ غَضَبًا, (Ṣ, TA,) ‡ *Verily such a one burns with anger*: (TA:) or it is like يَنْفِثُ [meaning *boils with anger*: or *makes a noise like coughing, in anger*: or *blows, in anger*]: (Ṣ:) [for the inf. n.] نَفَطَانٌ signifies the *doing what resembles coughing*: and *blowing, on an occasion of anger*: and so نَفَثَانٌ. (TA.) — Also, (Ḳ,) aor. ـِ, inf. n. نَفِيطٌ, said of an antelope, الضَّبِى in the Ḳ, being a mistake for الظَّبْى, as in the TṢ and L, (TA,) † *He uttered a sound*, or *cry*. (TṢ, L, Ḳ.) — † *He* (a man) *spoke*, or *talked, unintelligibly*; (Ḳ, TA;) *as though by reason of his anger*. (TA.) — نَفَطَتْ أَسْتُهُ † *His anus emitted wind with a sound*. (Ibn-'Abbád, Ḳ.)

3: see 6.

4. انفط *It* (work) *caused* the hand *to become blistered*, or *vesicated*: or *caused it to become ulcerated*. (Ḳ.) [See 1, first sentence.]

5: see 1, in two places.

6. تَنَافَطَ القِدْرُ [for تَتَنَافَطُ, in the CḲ ▼ تُنافِطُ,] *The cooking-pot throws forth foam*; (Ḳ;) a dial. var. of تَنَافَثَ [q.v.] (TA.)

نَفْطٌ, accord. to the T, *Pustules which come forth upon the hand, in consequence of work, full of water,* or *fluid;* (Mgh;) *blisters,* or *vesicles, upon the hand;* a contraction of ▼ نَفِطٌ; which is pl. [or rather coll. gen. n.] of ▼ نَفِطَةٌ, sometimes contracted into ▼ نَفْطَةٌ; and sometimes نَفِطَاتٌ is used as pl. of ▼ نَفِطَةٌ: (Mṣb:) or ▼ نَفِطَةٌ signifies [simply] *a pustule;* as also ▼ نَفْطَةٌ and ▼ نِفْطَةٌ; (Ḳ;) and the lawyers call it ▼ نَفَّاطَةٌ, from this word as signifying "a place whence نفط issues," or it may be [originally] an intensive act. part. n. (Mṣb.) — Also, and ▼ نَفِطٌ, (Mṣb,) or ▼ نَفِطَةٌ and ▼ نَفْطَةٌ and ▼ نِفْطَةٌ, (Mgh, Ṣgh, Ḳ,) The *small-pox:* (Mgh, Ṣgh, Mṣb, Ḳ:) accord. to Z, ▼ نفط [so in the TA, without any syll. signs,] signifies, in the dial. of Hudheyl, the *small-pox in children* and *in sheep* or *goats.* (TA.) ═ See also what next follows.

نِفْطٌ and ▼ نَفْطٌ, (Ṣ, Mṣb, Ḳ,) the former of which is the more chaste, (ISk, Ṣ, Mṣb, Ḳ,*) or, as some say, the latter, (Mṣb,) or the latter is a mistake, (Aṣ, Ḳ,) [*Naphtha:* and *petroleum:* both so called in the present day:] *a certain oil,* (Ṣ,) *well known,* (Ḳ,) *with which camels are smeared for the mange,* or *scab, and galls on the back, and tikes; it does not include what is termed* كُحَيْل: (ISd, TA:) or, accord. to AḤn, *i.q.* كُحَيْل: accord. to A'Obeyd, *i.q.* قَطِرَان; but AḤn denies this; and says that it is *an exuding fluid* (حُلَابَة) *of a mountain,* [*found*] *in the bottom of a well, with which fire is kindled:* (TA:) *the best is the white: it is a dissolvent; and opens obstructions; removes the colic; and kills worms that are in the vulva, when used in the manner of a suppository.* (Ḳ.)

نَفِطٌ:
نَفْطَةٌ:
نِفْطَةٌ:
نَفِطَةٌ:
} see نَفْطٌ, throughout: — and for the last, see also نَفِيطَةٌ.

نُفَاطَةٌ [accord. to the CḲ, but erroneously, نُفَاطٌ]: see نَفَّاطَةٌ, in two places.

كَفٌّ نَفِيطَةٌ *A hand ulcerated by work:* or *blistered,* or *vesicated; having water* or *fluid, between the skin and the flesh:* and ▼ نَافِطَةٌ signifies the same; and so ▼ مَنْفُوطَةٌ; (Ḳ;) of which last, however, ISd says, it is thus related by the lexicologists; but there is no way of accounting for it in my opinion; for it is from أَنْفَطَ. (TA.) [Golius also mentions ▼ نَفِطَةٌ as signifying A hand *affected with pustules;* on the authority of Meyd; and it is agreeable with analogy.]

نَفَّاطٌ *A thrower of* نِفْط [or *naphtha*]: pl. ▼ نَفَّاطَةٌ, [or rather this is a coll. gen. n.,] (Mṣb,) and نَفَّاطُونَ. (Mgh.)

نَفَّاطَةٌ *A place whence* نفط [or *naphtha*] *is extracted;* (El-Fárábee, Mṣb, Ḳ;) as also ▼ نُفَاطَةٌ; (Ḳ;) but the former is the more known; (TA;) *a place where it is generated; a mine,* or *source, thereof;* a word similar to مَلَّاحَةٌ (Mgh, Mṣb) and قَيَّارَةٌ: (Mgh:) pl. نَفَّاطَاتٌ. (Mṣb.) — *A kind of lamp made to give light by means thereof;* as also ▼ نُفَاطَةٌ; (Ḳ;) but the former is the more known. (TA.) — *An instrument with which* نفط *is thrown;* (Mgh;) *an instrument of copper,* or *brass, in which* نفط *is thrown,* (Ḳ, TA,) and fire; (TA;) *a* قَارُورَة *of* نفط, *which is thrown:* (Mṣb:) pl. as above. (Mgh.) You say, خَرَجَ النَّفَّاطُونَ بِأَيْدِيهِمُ النَّفَّاطَاتُ [*The throwers of naphtha went forth, having in their hands the instruments with which to throw it*]. (Mgh.) — See also نَفَّاطٌ. — And see نَفْطٌ.

كَفٌّ نَافِطَةٌ: see نَفِيطَةٌ. — رَغْوَةٌ نَافِطَةٌ *Froth,* or *foam, having bubbles:* (Az, Mṣb:) pl. نَوَافِطُ. (TA.)

كَفٌّ مَنْفُوطَةٌ: see نَفِيطَةٌ.

[نفع, &c.

See Supplement.]

نقب

1. نَقَبَ, aor. ـُ, inf. n. نَقْبٌ, *He perforated, pierced, bored,* or *made a hole through,* or *in,* or *into,* anything: like ثَقَبَ. (TA.) *He made a hole through* a wall. (Ṣ.) — نَقَبَ سُرَّةَ الدَّابَّةِ, aor. ـُ, *He* (a farrier) *perforated the navel of the beast in order that a yellow fluid might issue forth.* (Ṣ.) See مِنْقَبٌ. — نَقَبَ العَيْنَ, aor. ـُ, inf. n. نَقْبٌ, *He performed, upon the eye, what is called* القَدْحُ in the language of the physicians; i.e., *a remedial operation for the black fluid that arises in the eye:* from the phrase next following: (IAth:) [but this is not a good explanation: the meaning is *he performed upon the eye the operation of couching, for the cataract:* so in many Arabic works, ancient and modern: (IbrD:) the couching-needle is called مِقْدَحٌ, and إِبْرَةُ القَدْحِ, in the present day]. — نَقَبَ حَافِرَ الدَّابَّةِ *He* (a farrier) *pierced a hole in the hoof of the beast,* in order to extract what had entered into it. (IAth.) — نَقَبَتْهُ نَكْبَةٌ, (aor. ـُ, inf. n. نَقْبٌ, TA,) *A misfortune, an evil accident,* or *a calamity befell him,* (Ḳ,) *and overcame him,* or *afflicted him;* like نَكَبَتْهُ. (TA.) [In the CḲ, for أَصَابَتْهُ, is put اثابته.] — نَقَبَ فِى الأَرْضِ, aor. ـُ, and ▼ نقّب and ▼ انقب, *He went,* or *went away, through the land,* or *country:* (Ḳ:) [in the CḲ and some MS. copies of the Ḳ, we afterwards find نَقِبَ فِى البِلَادِ with kesr to the ق, explained as signifying *he proceeded,* or *journeyed, through the lands:*] ▼ انقب *he proceeded,* or *journeyed,* through the country: (IAar:) فَنَقَّبُوا فِى البِلَادِ [Ḳur, l. 35,] *they proceeded,* or *journeyed, through the lands,* seeking for a place of refuge: (Ṣ:) or *they traversed the lands, and journeyed through them, much, &c.:* (Fr.:) or *they went about and about, and searched, &c.* (Zj.) نَقَّبْتُ ▼ فِى الآفَاقِ, in a verse of Imra-el-Ḳeys, *I journeyed through the tracts of the earth, and came and went.* (TA.) — نَقِبَ خُفُّ البَعِيرِ, aor. ـَ, or نَقِبَ البَعِيرُ, (L, TA,) and ▼ انقب, (L,) *The camel walked barefooted,* syn. حَفِىَ, (L, Ḳ,) *until his feet became worn in holes:* (TA:) or نَقِبَ البَعِيرُ, (Ṣ, Ḳ,) and ▼ انقب, (Ḳ,) *the camel's feet became thin,* [or *were worn thin;* which is also a signification of حَفِىَ]. (Ṣ, Ḳ.) — نَقِبَتْ أَقْدَامُنَا *Our feet became thin in the skin, and blistered, by reason of walking.* (L.) — نَقَبَ الخُفَّ, aor. ـُ, *He patched the boot; repaired it by patching.* (Ḳ.) Also, *He made the boot thin: he made* [or *wore*] *holes in it.* (Mṣb.) — نَقِبَ الخُفُّ, aor. ـَ, (inf. n. نَقَبٌ, TA,) *The boot became lacerated,* or *worn through, in holes.* (Ṣ, Ḳ, TA.) [And in like manner *The sole of the foot* of a camel or of a man: see below: and see an ex. voce أَظَلُّ.] — نَقَبَ, aor. ـُ, inf. n. نَقْبٌ, *He* (a horse) *put his feet together in his running* (فِى حُضْرِهِ), [for which Golius and Freytag appear to have read فِى خُضْرِهِ,] Ḳ,) *not spreading his fore feet, his running being* [*a kind of*] *leaping.* (TA.) ═ نَقَبَ عَنِ الأَخْبَارِ, aor. ـُ, *He scrutinized, investigated, searched into, examined into,* or *inquired into, the news;* (Ḳ;) and, in like manner, anything else: (MF:) [as also ▼ نقّب: see the phrase نقّبوا فى البلاد, explained above:] or *he told, announced,* or *related, the news.* (Ḳ.) — إِنِّى لَمْ أُومَرْ أَنْ أَنْقُبَ عَنْ قُلُوبِ النَّاسِ *Verily I have not been commanded to scrutinize and reveal what is in the hearts of men.* (TA, from a trad.) — نَقَبَ عَلَى قَوْمِهِ, aor. ـُ, inf. n. نِقَابَةٌ, *He acted as the* نَقِيب *over his people; was their* نقيب: (Ṣ, Ḳ:) but of a man who was not نقيب, and has become so, you say نَقُبَ, with ḍamm, aor. ـُ, inf. n. نَقَابَةٌ, with fet-ḥ, *He became* نقيب; (Fr., Ṣ, Ḳ;) as also نَقِبَ, aor. ـَ: (IKṭṭ, Ḳ:) or نقابة with kesr is a subst.; and with fet-ḥ, an inf. n.; (Ṣ, Ḳ;) like وِلَايَةٌ and وَلَايَةٌ: so says Sb. (Ṣ.) ═ نَقَبَ الثَّوْبَ, aor. ـُ, inf. n. نَقْبٌ, *He made the piece of cloth into a* نُقْبَة. (Ṣ.)

2: see 1.

3. نَاقَبْتُهُ, inf. n. نِقَابٌ; as also لَقِيتُهُ نِقَابًا; *I met him face to face*: or *without appointment*, (Ḳ,) *and unintentionally*: (TA:) or *unexpectedly*. (Ṣ.) نِقَابًا is in the accus. case as an inf. n.; or as a word descriptive of state. (TA.) — وَرَدْتُ المَاءَ نِقَابًا, (Ṣ,) or نَقِيتُ الماء نقابا, (Ḳ,) *I came upon the water unexpectedly, without seeking for it.* (Ṣ, Ḳ.)

4: see 1. — انقب *His camel's feet became thin*; [or *were worn thin*;] (Ṣ, Ḳ;) or *were worn in holes by walking*. (TA.) = *He became a door-keeper*, or *chamberlain*; Arab. حَاجِب: (Ḳ:) or *he became a* نَقِيب. (L, Ḳ, &c.)

5: see 8.

8. انتقبت (Ṣ, Ḳ, Mṣb) and ♦ تنقّبت (Mṣb) *She* (a woman) *veiled her face with a* نِقَاب. (Ṣ, Ḳ, Mṣb.) — تنقب ♦ بِعِمَامَتِهِ: see تَخَتَّمَ.

نَقْبٌ (Ṣ, Ḳ) and ♦ نُقْبَةٌ (Ṣ) *A hole, perforation*, or *bore*, (Ḳ,) in, or through, a wall, (Ṣ,) or anything whatever: (TA:) or *a large hole, perforation*, or *bore, passing through a thing*; such as is small being termed ثَقْبٌ, with ث: (Mgh, in art. ثقب:) pl. of the former نُقُوبٌ (Mṣb) and أَنْقَابٌ and نِقَابٌ. (TA, and some copies of the Ḳ.) — نَقْبٌ (Ḳ) and ♦ نَاقِبَةٌ (Ṣ) *An ulcer that arises in the side*, (Ṣ, ISd, Ḳ,) *attacking the inside of the body*, (Ṣ, ISd,) *and having its head inwards*; (ISd;) [as also ♦ نَقَّابَةٌ, for] نَقَّابَاتٌ signifies *ulcers that come forth in the side and penetrate into the inside.* (TA voce ذُبَالٌ.) See نُقْبٌ. — نَقْبٌ (Ṣ, Ḳ) and ♦ نُقْبٌ (Ḳ) and ♦ مَنْقَبٌ and ♦ مَنْقَبَةٌ (Ṣ, Ḳ) *A road* (or *narrow road*, TA,) *in a mountain*: (ISk, Ṣ, Ḳ:) *a road between two mountains*: (IAth:) pl. (of the first and second, TA,) أَنْقَابٌ (a pl. of pauc., TA,) and نِقَابٌ; (Ḳ;) and of the third and fourth, مَنَاقِبُ. (TA.) See also مَنْقَبَةٌ.

نُقْبٌ (Ṣ, Ḳ,) and ♦ نُقَبٌ (Ḳ: but the former is the more common: TA) and ♦ نُقُبٌ (Ḳ) [the first is a coll. gen. n., of which the n. un. is نُقْبَةٌ [q.v.], of which it is called in the Ṣ the pl.: but نُقَبٌ is the pl. of نُقْبَةٌ:] *Scab*, [or *scabs*,] (Ḳ,) absolutely: (TA:) or *scattered scabs* (Ṣ, Ḳ,) *when they first appear*: (Ṣ:) النُّقْبَةُ is *the first that appears of the scab*; and is so called because the scabs perforate the skin: you say, of a camel, بِهِ نُقْبَةٌ: (Aṣ:) *the first that appears of the scab, in a patch like the palm of the hand, in the side of a camel*, or *on his haunch*, or *his lip*: *then it spreads over him until it covers him entirely.* (ISh.) Moḥammad, denying that any disease was transmitted from one thing to another, and being asked how it was that a نُقْبَة spread in camels, asked what transmitted the disease to the first camel. (TA.) — فُلَانٌ يَضَعُ الهِنَآءَ مَوَاضِعَ النُّقْبِ ‡ [*Such a one puts the tar upon the places of the scabs*]: said of one who is clever, or skilful, and who does or says what is right. (A.) [See also ثَاَبٌ.]

نَقِبٌ, and, as a fem. epithet, ♦ نَقْبَاءُ, *A camel whose feet have become worn in holes*, [or *worn thin*,] *by walking*. (TA.) See the verb. — The former may also signify *Having the scab*, or *what first appears thereof*. (TA.) See نُقْبٌ.

نُقَبٌ: see نُقْبٌ.

نُقْبَةٌ *A mark, trace*, or *vestige*: ex. عَلَيْهِ نُقْبَةٌ *Upon him*, or *it, is a mark, &c.* (T.) — See نُقْبٌ. — نُقْبَةٌ † *Rust*, (Ḳ,) upon a sword or the head of an arrow or a spear: (M:) or نقب [i.e. ♦ نُقْبٌ, q.v., a coll. gen. n., of which نُقْبَةٌ is the n. un.; or نُقَبٌ, pl. of نُقْبَةٌ;] signifies ‡ *traces of rust* upon a sword or an arrow-head or a spear-head, likened to the first appearances of the scab. (A.) = نُقْبَةٌ The *face*: (Ṣ, Ḳ:) or the *parts surrounding the face*: (L:) pl. نُقَبٌ. (TA.) — نُقْبَةٌ *A garment resembling an* إِزَار, *having a sewed waistband* or *string*, (حُجْزَةٌ مَخِيطَةٌ: so in the Ṣ, M, L: whence it appears that the reading in the Ḳ, حجزة مُطيقة, is erroneous: TA: [F having, it seems, found مُحِيطَة written in the place of مَخِيطَة:]) *without a* نَيْفَق [which is the *part turned down at the top, and sewed, through which the waistband passes*], (Ṣ, Ḳ,) *tied as trousers*, or *drawers, are tied*: (Ṣ:) or *a pair of trousers*, or *drawers, having a waistband, but without a part turned down at the top, and sewed, for the waistband to pass through*: if it have this, (i.e., a نيفق,) it is called سَرَاوِيلُ: (TA:) or a piece of rag of which the upper part is made like drawers, or trousers: (L:) or *a pair of drawers*, or *trousers, without legs*. (M, voce إِتْبٌ, TA.) = نُقْبَةٌ The *state*, or *condition*; *quality, mode*, or *manner*; *state with regard to apparel &c.*; *external form, figure, feature*, or *appearance*; of any thing: syn. هَيْئَةٌ. (T.) = نُقْبَةٌ *Colour*. (Ṣ, Ḳ.) — فَرَسٌ حَسَنُ النُّقْبَةِ *A horse of beautiful colour*. (TA.) — See also نَقِيبَةٌ.

نِقْبَةٌ *A mode of veiling the face with the* نِقَاب: (Ḳ:) pl. نِقَبٌ. (TA.) — إِنَّهَا لَحَسَنَةُ النِّقْبَةِ (Ṣ) *Verily she has a comely mode of veiling her face with the* نقاب. (TA.)

نِقَابٌ [*A woman's face-veil*;] (Ṣ, Ḳ;) *a veil that is upon* [or *covers*] *the soft*, or *pliable, part of the nose*; (AZ;) [*not extending higher*:] *a woman's veil that extends as high as the circuit of the eye*: (Mṣb:) it is of different modes: Fr says, When a woman lowers her نقاب to her eye, it [the action] is termed وَصْوَصَةٌ; and when she lowers it further, to [the lower part of] the circuit of the eye, it [the veil] is called نقاب; and if it is on the extremity of the nose, it is [properly] called لِفَامٌ: (T:) the نقاب, with the Arabs, is *that* [*kind of veil*] *from out of which appears the circuit of the eye*: and the meaning of the saying in a trad., النِّقَابُ مُحْدَثٌ is, that women's shewing the circuits of the eyes is an innovation; not that they used not to veil their faces: the [kind of] نقاب which they used reached close to the eye, and they showed one eye while the other was concealed; whereas the [kind of] نقاب, which only shows both the eyes [without their circuits], was called by them وَصْوَصَةٌ [a mistake for وَصْوَاصٌ] and بُرْقُعٌ: [in the original, والنقاب لا يبدو منه الّا العينان وكان اسمه الخ: but the و before كان is erroneously introduced, and perverts the sense, which is otherwise plain, and agreeable with what is said before:] then they innovated the [veil properly called] نقاب: (A'Obeyd:) pl. نُقُبٌ. (Mṣb.) = نِقَابٌ and ♦ مِنْقَبٌ *A road through a rugged tract of ground*: (Ḳ:) the former word used both as a sing. and a pl. (TA.) = نِقَابٌ (a strange form of epithet, MF,) ‡ A man *of great knowledge*; *very knowing*: (Ṣ, Ḳ:) or *possessing a knowledge of things*, or *affairs*: or, as also ♦ مِنْقَبٌ, mentioned by IAth and Z, a man *possessing a knowledge of things, who scrutinizes* or *investigates them much*; *who is intelligent*, and *enters deeply into things*. (TA.) = نِقَابٌ The *belly*. Hence the proverb, فَرْخَانِ فِى نِقَابٍ [*Two young birds in one belly*]: applied to two things that resemble one another. (Ḳ.) In like manner one says كَانَا فِى نِقَابٍ وَاحِدٍ [*They were in one belly*]; meaning *they were like each other*. (A.)

نَقِيبٌ i.q. مَنْقُوبٌ, A thing *perforated, pierced, bored*, or *having a hole made through*, or *in*, or *into it*. (TA.) — نَقِيبٌ *A musical reed*, or *pipe*. (Ḳ.) — The *tongue of a pair of scales*, or *balance*. (Ḳ.) — A dog *having the upper part of his windpipe* (غَلْصَمَتُهُ: so in the Ṣ, Ḳ: or *having his windpipe*, حَنْجَرَتُهُ: so in the A) *perforated*, (Ṣ, Ḳ,) *in order that his cry may be weak*: a base man performs this operation on his dog, in order that guests may not hear its cry. (Ṣ: and the like is said in the L.) = نَقِيبُ قَوْمٍ *The intendant, superintendent, overseer*, or *inspector, of a people*; *he who takes notice*, or *cognisance, of their actions, and is responsible for them*; i.q. عَرِيفُهُمْ and شَاهِدُهُمْ and ضَمِينُهُمْ: (Ṣ, Ḳ:) *like* أَمِينٌ and كَفِيلٌ: (Zj:) *their head*, or *chief*: (TA:) *like* عَرِيفٌ [q.v.]; i.e., *one who is set over a people, and investigates their affairs*: (L:) or, as some say, *the greatest*, or *supreme, chief of a people*: so called [from نَقَبَ "he scrutinized, or investigated,"] because he is acquainted with the secret affairs of the people, and knows their virtues, or generous actions, and is the way by which one obtains knowledge of their affairs: (TA:) pl. نُقَبَاءُ. (Ṣ.)

نِقَابَةٌ The *office of* نَقِيب. (Sb: see 1.)

نَقِيبَةٌ *Mind:* syn. نَفْسٌ. (Ṣ, Ḳ.) You say فُلَانٌ مَيْمُونُ النقيبة *Such a one is of a fortunate mind,* (A'Obeyd, Ṣ,) when the person referred to is *fortunate in his affairs, succeeding in what he seeks after,* or *strives to accomplish:* (ISk, Ṣ:) or when he is *fortunate in his counsel,* or *advice:* (Th, Ṣ:) or the phrase signifies *such a one is fortunate in his actions, and in gaining what he seeks.* (TA.) See also what follows. نَقِيبَةٌ is also said, in the Ḳ, to signify the same as عَقْلٌ (*understanding, intellect,* or *intelligence*); but, says SM, I have not found this in any other lexicon: only I have found the word explained in the L as signifying يُمْنُ الفِعْلِ (*good fortune attending,* or *resulting from, an action*): so probably عَقْلٌ is a mistake for فِعْلٌ. (TA.) — Also, *Counsel,* or *advice.* (Ḳ.) See above. — Also, *Penetration of judgment; acuteness; sagacity.* (Ibn-Buzurj, Ḳ.) — Also, *Nature;* or *natural,* or *native, disposition, temper,* or *other quality:* (Ḳ:) *i. q.* نَقِيمَةٌ and عَرِيكَةٌ and طَبِيعَةٌ. (T, art. عرك.) Agreeably with this explanation, the phrase above mentioned is rendered in the T, in art. عرك, *Such a one is of a fortunate nature,* or *natural disposition:* (TA:) or it signifies, in this phrase, as also ▼ نقيمة, *i. q.* لَوْنٌ, *Colour, complexion, species, &c.* (IAạr.) Also هُوَ حَسَنُ النَّقِيبَةِ *He is of a good nature,* or *natural disposition:* and in like manner, فُلَانٌ فِى مَنَاقِبَ ▼ جَمِيلَةٍ *Such a one is a person of good dispositions,* or *natural qualities.* (L.) ═ نَقِيبَةٌ A she-camel *having a large udder:* (ISd, Ḳ:) *having her udder bound up with a cloth* or *the like, on account of its greatness and excellence:* but AM says this is a corruption, and that the correct word is ثَقِيبة, with ث, meaning a she-camel "abounding with milk." (TA.)

نُقَابَةٌ: see نُقْبٌ.

نَاقِبٌ and نَاقِبَةٌ [the former omitted in some copies of the Ḳ] *A disease that befalls a man in consequence of long sluggishness,* or *indolence:* (Ḳ:) or, as some say, the *ulcer that arises in the side.* (TA.) See نُقْبٌ.

أَنْقَابٌ, a pl. without a sing., The *ears:* (M, Ḳ,) or, accord. to some, its sing. is نُقْبٌ. (TA.) El-Kaṭámee says,

• كَانَتْ خُدُودُ هِجَانِهِنَّ مُمَالَةً •
• أَنْقَابُهُنَّ إِلَى حُدَاءِ السُّوقِ •

[*The cheeks of their white camels were with their ears inclined to the singing of the drivers*]. But أَنْقَا بِهِنَّ, "by reason of their pleasure," is also read, for أَنْقَابُهُنَّ: (TA:) [so that the meaning is *The cheeks of their white camels were inclined, by reason of their pleasure, to the singing of the drivers*].

مَنْقَبٌ The *navel:* or [*a place*] *before it:* (Ḳ:) *where the farrier makes a perforation in order that a yellow fluid may issue forth:* (Ṣ:) so in a horse. (TA.) — See نَقْبٌ.

مِنْقَبٌ *An iron instrument with which a farrier perforates the navel of a beast of carriage* (Ṣ, Ḳ) *in order that a yellow fluid may issue forth.* (Ṣ.) See مَنْقَبٌ, and نِقَابٌ.

مَنْقَبَةٌ: see نَقْبٌ. — *A narrow way between two houses,* (L, Ḳ,) *along which one cannot pass.* (L.) It is said in a trad., that one does not possess the right of pre-emption (الشُّفْعَة) with respect to a منقبة; and this word is explained as signifying *a wall:* syn. حَائِطٌ: [and so in the Ḳ:] or *a way between two houses, as though it were perforated from one to the other:* or *a road,* or *way, over an elevated piece of ground.* (L.) ═ مَنْقَبَةٌ *A virtue; an excellence; contr. of* مَثْلَبَةٌ: (Ṣ:) *a cause of glorying:* (Ḳ:) *generosity of action,* or *conduct:* (L:) *a* [*good disposition,* or *natural quality:* [see نَقِيبَةٌ:] (TA:) *a memorable,* or *generous action, and* [*good*] *internal quality:* (A:) pl. مَنَاقِبُ: (TA:) رَجُلٌ ذُو مَنَاقِبَ *A man of memorable,* or *generous, actions, and* [*good*] *internal qualities.* (A.)

نقت

1. نَقَتَ, [aor. ـُ,] inf. n. نَقْتٌ, *He took out,* or *extracted, marrow* [from a bone]. (Ḳ.) Az, quotes, from Aboo-Turáb, on the authority of Aboo-'Ameythel, نُقِتَ العَظْمُ, and نُكِتَ, *The marrow of the bone was taken out,* or *extracted.* (L.) And J says, نَقَتُّ المُخَّ aor. ـُ, inf. n. نَقْتٌ, is a dial. form of نَقَوْتُهُ, meaning, *I took out,* or *extracted the marrow* [from a bone]: as though they had changed the و into ت. (L.) But it is said in a marginal note in the Ṣ, Aboo-Sahl El-Harawee says, What I remember to have heard is نَقَثْتُ العَظْمَ, aor. ـُ, inf. n. نَقْثٌ, I took out, or extracted, the marrow from the bone; and so إِنْتَقَثْتُهُ, with the three-pointed ث; and نَقَوْتُهُ, and إِنْتَقَيْتُهُ, and نَقَيْتُهُ. (TA.)

نقث

1. نَقَثَ, aor. ـُ; and ▼ نَقَّثَ, (inf. n. تَنْقِيثٌ, Ṣ,) and ▼ انتقث; *He hastened, was quick.* (Ṣ, Ḳ.) — خَرَجْتُ أَنْقُثُ *I went forth hastening.* (Ṣ.) — خَرَجَ يَنْقُثُ السَّيْرَ, and ▼ يَنْتَقِثُ, *He went forth hastening in his pace.* (TA.) — نَقَثَ حَدِيثَهُ [aor. ـُ,] *He mixed,* or *confounded, his discourse, like as one mixes food.* (Ḳ.) ═ نَقَثَهُ بِالكَلَامِ, [aor. ـُ,] (and ▼ انتقثه, TA,) *He hurt him by words.* (Ḳ.) ═ نَقَثَ الأَرْضَ, aor. ـُ, inf. n. نَقْثٌ, *He dug up the earth* with a hoe or shovel. (AZ.) — نَقَثَ شَيْئًا; (or, accord. to the TA, عَنْ شَىْءٍ,) and ▼ انتقث, *He dug up the earth from a thing.* (Ḳ.) — نَقَثَ العَظْمَ (aor. ـُ, inf. n. نَقْثٌ, TA;) and ▼ انتقثه; and ▼ تنقّثه; (TA;) *He took out,* or *extracted, the marrow from the bone.* (Ḳ.) See also نَقَتَ. (TA.) — نَقَثَ, inf. n. نَقْثٌ; and ▼ نَقَّثَ, inf. n. تَنْقِيثٌ; *He removed* a thing. Ex. لَا تُنَقِّثُ مِيرَتَنَا *She used not to remove our wheat,* or *provision, nor to take it forth, nor scatter it;* but kept it faithfully. (TA, from a trad.)

2: see 1.

5. تنقّث *He endeavoured to make* a woman *incline to him, and to render* her *affectionate to him:* (Ḳ:) as though he drew forth her love, like as one draws forth the marrow from a bone. (TA.) — تنقّث ضَيْعَتَهُ *i. q.* تَعَهَّدَهَا. (TA.) — See 1.

8: see 1.

نَقْثٌ *Malicious,* or *mischievous, misrepresentation; calumny; slander.* (IAạr.)

نُقَاثٌ (in measure like قُطَامٌ) *The hyena.* (Ḳ.)

نَبِيثَتُهَا *i. q.* نَقِيثَةُ البِئْرِ. (TA voce قَاحَةٌ, in art. قوح.)

نقح

1. نَقَحَ شَيْئًا, aor. ـَ, (inf. n. نَقْحٌ, TA,) *He peeled,* or *barked, a thing; peeled off, stripped off,* or *removed, its outer covering.* (Ḳ, TA.) نَقَحَ العُودَ, (Mṣb,) or العَصَا, (T,) aor. ـَ, inf. n. نَقْحٌ, (Mṣb,) *He pared,* or *trimmed, the stick,* or *staff, by cutting off its knots:* (T, Mṣb:) and in like manner you say of anything from which you pare off somewhat. (T.) — نَقَحَ الجِذْعَ, inf. n. نَقْحٌ; (Ḳ;) and ▼ نقّحه, (Ḳ,) inf. n. تَنْقِيحٌ; (Ṣ;) *He pared off the knots of the palm-trunk:* (Ḳ:) or *he pruned,* or *trimmed, the trunk of the palm-tree, by cutting off the stumps of the branches,* or *by cutting off the superfluous branches.* (Ṣ.) — نَقَحَ, (TA,) and ▼ انقح, (Ḳ,) *He stripped off the ornaments of his sword* [*to sell them*] *in a time of dearth and poverty.* (Ḳ, TA.) — نَقَحَ العَظْمَ, aor. ـَ, (Ḳ,) inf. n. نَقْحٌ; (TA;) and ▼ نقّحه, (inf. n. تَنْقِيحٌ, Ṣ;) and ▼ انتقحه; (Ṣ, Ḳ;) *He extracted the marrow from the bone:* (Ṣ, Ḳ:) or

نقحه has an intensive signification. (Mṣb.) — نَقَّحَ شَيْئًا *He separated what was good from what was bad of the thing.* (Mṣb.)

2. نقّح الشِّعْرَ, inf. n. تَنْقِيحٌ; (Ṣ, Ḳ;) and انقحهُ ▼, inf. n. إِنْقَاحٌ; (Ḳ;) ‡ *He trimmed, pruned, or put into a right or proper state, poetry, or verses.* (Ṣ, Ḳ.) — نقّح الكَلَامَ ‡ *He scrutinized the language, and examined it well: or he put it to rights, or trimmed it, and removed its faults, or defects.* (TA.) — See 1.

4: see 1 and 2.

5. تنقّح شَحْمُهُ, (Ḳ,) or شَحْمُ النَّاقَةِ, (Ṣ,) or شَحْمُ نَاقَتِهِ, (TA, &c.,) ‡ *His fat,* (Ḳ,) or *the fat of the she-camel,* (Ṣ,) or *the fat of his she-camel,* (TA, &c.,) *became little in quantity, or diminished,* (Ṣ, Ḳ, &c.,) or *partially went away.* (A.)

8: see 1.

خَيْرُ الشِّعْرِ الحَوْلِىُّ المُنَقَّحُ ‡ [*The best of poetry is that which is a year old, and trimmed, or pruned*]. (Ṣ.)

نقخ

1. نَقَخَ, aor. ـَ, (Ṣ, L, Ḳ,) inf. n. نَقْخٌ (Ṣ, L) and نُقَاخٌ, (L,) *He struck, smote, or beat.* (Ḳ.) نَقَخَ رَأْسَهُ *He struck his head* with a staff, or sword, or some other hard thing: or *he struck his head so that the brain came forth:* (L:) or *he broke his head so as to disclose the brain;* as also نقف. (Ṣ, L.) نَقَخَ دِمَاغَهُ *He broke his brain.* (Ḳ.) — Also, نَقَخَ (L) and انتقخ ▼ (L, Ḳ) *He extracted* marrow (L, Ḳ) from a bone. (L.) — نَقَخَ العَطَشَ بِبَرْدِهِ † *It* (sweet water) *broke,* [or *abated,* or *allayed,*] *thirst, by its coolness,* or *coldness.* (L, from a trad.)

8: see 1.

نُقَاخٌ *Sweet water; that has no saltness;* (AO, Th, Ṣ;) *that strikes* (يَنْقَخُ) *the heart* (or *almost does so,* L) *by its coldness:* (Ṣ:) or *cold,* or *cool, and sweet, and clear, water:* (Ḳ:) or *sweet water, that breaks* [or *abates* or *allays*] (يَنْقَخُ, i. e. يَكْسِرُ,) *thirst by its coolness,* or *coldness:* (L, from a trad.:) or *abundant water which a man makes to well forth in a place where was no water.* (ISh.) — Also, *Pure, mere, unadulterated,* or *genuine.* (T, Ḳ.) — هٰذَا نُقَاخُ العَرَبِيَّةِ (Fr) ‡ *This is pure Arabic;* or *the purest, choicest, best,* or *most excellent, of Arabic.* (Fr, A.) — Also نُقَاخٌ *Sleep in health and safety.* (Abu-l-'Abbás, Ḳ.)

نقد

1. نَقَدَ الدَّرَاهِمَ, (Ṣ, A, L, Mṣb) aor. ـُ, (L, Mṣb,) inf. n. نَقْدٌ (L, Mṣb, Ḳ) and تَنْقَادٌ; (L, Ḳ;) and انتقدها ▼ (Ṣ, L, Mṣb, Ḳ) and تنقّدها ▼; (L, Ḳ;) *He picked,* or *separated, the money,* or *pieces of money,* (Lth, L, Ḳ,) *and put forth the bad;* (Ṣ, L, Ḳ;) *he picked,* or *separated, the good money from the bad:* (A:) *he examined the money,* or *pieces of money, to pick, or separate, the good from the bad:* (Mṣb:) and the verbs are used in the same sense with respect to other things than pieces of money. (Ḳ.) — [نَقَدَ, aor. ـُ, inf. n. نَقْدٌ, q. v. infra, *He gave cash,* or *ready money; paid in cash,* or *ready money.* Often used in this sense.] — نَقَدَهُ الثَّمَنَ, aor. ـُ, inf. n. نَقْدٌ; *He gave him the price in cash,* or *ready money:* (L:) or simply *he gave him the price;* as also نَقَدَ لَهُ الثَّمَنَ: (A:) and نَقَدَهُ الدَّرَاهِمَ, and نَقَدَ لَهُ الدَّرَاهِمَ, *he gave him the money,* or *pieces of money.* (Ṣ, L, Mṣb.) — [Hence, from the first meaning,] نَقَدَ الكَلَامَ, [and الشِّعْرَ,] and so *He picked out the faults of the language,* [and *of the poetry;*] syn. نَاقَشَهُ. (TA.) — ▼ اِنْتَقَدَ الشِّعْرَ عَلَى قَائِلِهِ ‡ [*He picked out the faults of the poetry and urged them against its author.*] (A.) — نَقَدَهُ بِنَظَرِهِ, and نَقَدَ إِلَيْهِ, aor. ـُ, (L,) inf. n. نَقْدٌ (L, Ḳ) ‡ *He looked furtively at,* or *towards it:* (L, Ḳ:*) and so نقده بِعَيْنِهِ: (L:) and نقد بِعَيْنِهِ اليه *he continued looking furtively at,* or *towards, it:* you say also, مَا زَالَ بَصَرُهُ يَنْقُدُ إِلَى ذٰلِكَ [*his gaze ceased not to be furtively directed at,* or *towards, that*]: as though likened to the look of a man picking, or separating, what is good from what is bad: (A:) and مَا زَالَ يَنْقُدُ بَصَرَهُ إِلَى الشَّىْءِ *he ceased not to look at,* or *towards, the thing.* (Ṣ, L.) ═ نَقِدَ, (Ṣ, L,) [aor. ـَ,] inf. n. نَقَدٌ; (Ṣ, L, Ḳ;) and, as some say, نَقَدَ; (Ṣ, L;) *It* (a tooth, Ṣ, L, Ḳ, and a horn, T, L, and a hoof of a horse or the like, L,) *became eroded,* (T, Ṣ, L, Ḳ,) *and much broken:* (L, Ḳ:) and *it* (the hoof of a horse or the like) *scaled off, part after part:* (Ṣ, L:) *it* (the trunk of a tree) *became worm-eaten.* (L.)

3. ناقده ‡ *He reckoned with him to the utmost,* syn. نَاقَشَهُ, (Ṣ, A, L, Ḳ,) فِى أَمْرٍ *in,* or *respecting, an affair,* (Ṣ, L,) [*picking out his faults*].

4. انقد *It* (a tree) *put forth its leaves.* (L, Ḳ.)

5: see 1.

8. انتقد الدَّرَاهِمَ *He received the money,* or *pieces of money;* (Lth, Ṣ, L, Mṣb, Ḳ;) and الثَّمَنَ *the price.* (A.) — See 1. ═ انتقد *It* (a worm) *ate the trunk of a tree, and rendered it hollow.* (L.) ═ *He* (a boy) *grew up into manhood.* (Ḳ.)

نَقْدٌ [properly an inf. n. used in the sense of a pass. part. n., and thus signifying "paid," *Cash,* or *ready money:* or simply *money*]. You say نَقْدٌ جَيِّدٌ [*Good cash,* or *ready money:* or *good money*]: pl. نُقُودٌ جِيَادٌ. (A.) النَّقْدَانِ signifies *Silver and gold money; dirhems and deenárs.* (TA in art. عرض.) — نَقْدٌ *Payment in cash,* or *ready money; contr. of* نَسِيْئَةٌ: (L, Ḳ:) the *giving of* نَقْد [i. e., *cash,* or *ready money*]: (Ḳ:) [an inf. n.: see 1]. — الدِّرْهَمُ نَقْدٌ *The piece of money is of full weight,* (Ṣ, L, Ḳ,*) *and good.* (Ṣ, L.) — هٰذِهِ مِائَةٌ نَقْدُ النَّاسِ [*This is a hundred, ready money of the people*] is a phrase used by the Arabs, in which ل is meant to be understood [before النَّاس: i. e. النَّاس is for لِلنَّاسِ; and نَقْدُ for نَقْدٌ, as an epithet of مائة: you may also say نَقْدَ النَّاسِ, making نقد a denotative of state; but] the epithetic mode of construction is that which prevails in this case. (Sb, L.) — نَقْدٌ. — The saying of the poet,

• تَنْتَجُنَّ وَلَدًا أَوْ نَقْدًا •

means *She will certainly bring forth a she-camel, which shall be a permanent acquisition for breeding, or a male, which shall be sold:* for they seldom kept the male camels. (Th, L.)

نُقْدٌ (Lḥ, L, Ḳ,) and نُقُدٌ ▼ (Ḳ) and نَقْدٌ ▼, (Lḥ, Az, L,) the form most frequently heard by Az from the Arabs, (L,) or نَقَدٌ ▼, (Ḳ,) [coll. gen. n.] *A certain kind of tree,* (Lḥ, L, Ḳ,) accord. to AA, *of the description termed* حُوصَة, *having a blossom resembling the* بَهْرَمَان, i. e., the عُصْفُر [or bastard-saffron]; (AḤn, L;) *its blossom is yellow,* and it grows in plain, or soft, grounds: (Az, L:) n. un. with ة; (Ḳ;) نُقْدَةٌ (Lḥ, Ṣ, L) and نُقُدَةٌ (TA) and نَقْدَةٌ (Lḥ, L) and نَقَدَةٌ. (TA.) — Also نُقْدَةٌ ▼, (L,) or نُقَدَةٌ ▼, (IAạr, L, Ḳ,) The كَرَوْيَاء [or *caraway*]. (IAạr, L, Ḳ.) — See نَقَدٌ.

نُقَدٌ: see نَقَدٌ.

نَقَدٌ [a coll. gen. n.] *A kind of sheep, of ugly form;* (Ḳ;) *a kind of sheep of El-Baḥreyn, having short legs and ugly faces:* (Ṣ, L:) or *a kind of small sheep of El-Ḥijáz:* (L:) or, simply, *lambs:* (A, L:) [see an ex. in a prov. cited voce شَامِر in art. شمر:] n. un. with ة: (Ṣ, L:) applied alike to the male and female: (L:) pl. نِقَادٌ, and [quasi-pl. n.] نِقَادَةٌ. (L, Ḳ.) Aṣ says, that the best of wool is that of نَقَد. And one says, أَذَلُّ مِنَ النَّقَدِ [*More abject,* or *vile, than the sheep called* نقد]. (Ṣ, L.) —— Also, † The *lower sort of people.* (L.) —— See نُقْدٌ and نَقِدٌ.

نَقْدٌ, (L,) or ▼ نِقْدٌ, (Ḳ,) *Slow in growing up into manhood, and having little flesh:* (L, Ḳ:) [and so ▼ نُقْدٌ, accord. to the CḲ: but ويُضمّ is there put by mistake for وبِضَمٍّ: and the former, (Ṣ, L,) or ▼ نَقَدٌ, (Ḳ,) a boy *despised and little in the eyes of others, that scarcely grows up into manhood;* (Ṣ, L, Ḳ;) sometimes thus applied. (Ṣ, L.) —— نَقْدٌ A horn *eaten,* or *eroded, at the root.* (L.) See also نَقِدٌ.

نُقُدٌ and نُقَدٌ and نُقْدَةٌ and نِقْدَةٌ: see نُقْدٌ.

نُقَادَةٌ The *choice part* of a thing. (JK.) —— هُوَ مِنْ نُقَادَةِ قَوْمِهِ ‡ *He is of the best of his people.* (A.)

نَقَّادٌ *A shepherd who tends the kind of sheep called* نَقَد: (L, Ḳ:) or *a possessor of skins of that kind of sheep.* (Th, L.) —— See نَاقِدٌ.

نَاقِدٌ [*One who picks,* or *separates, money, and puts forth the bad; who picks,* or *separates, good money from bad:*] *who examines money, to pick,* or *separate the good from the bad:* [as also ▼ نَقَّادٌ:] pl. نُقَّادٌ (Mṣb) [and نَقَدَةٌ]. —— نَاقِدُ شِعْرٍ, and ▼ نَقَّادُهُ ‡ *One who picks out the faults of poetry;* and, the ▼ latter, *one who is accustomed to do so.*] مِنْ نُقَّادِهِ and هُوَ مِنْ نَقَدَةِ الشِّعْرِ ‡ [*He is one of those who pick out the faults of poetry*]. (A.)

أَنْقَدُ *The hedge-hog;* القُنْفُذُ; (Ṣ, L, Ḳ;) a proper name, like أُسَامَةُ applied to the lion: (Ṣ:) as also الأَنْقَدُ; (Ḳ;) but some disallow the prefixing of the art.; (TA;) and الأُنْقُدُ. (L.) Hence the saying, بَاتَ بِلَيْلِ أَنْقَدَ, (Ṣ, L,) or بِلَيْلَةِ أَنْقَدَ, (A, L,) *He passed the night of the hedge-hog;* i. e. *sleepless:* (L:) because the hedge-hog remains sleepless (and sees, L) all night: (Ṣ, L, Ḳ:) and أَسْرَى مِنْ أَنْقَدَ [*A greater journeyer by night than the hedge-hog*]. (A, L.) —— أَنْقَدُ لَيْلٍ *A calumniator; a slanderer;* as also قُنْفُذُ لَيْلٍ. (L, art. قنفذ.) —— Also, الأَنْقَدُ [L, Ḳ,) and ▼ الإِنْقِدَانُ (Ḳ) *The tortoise:* (L, Ḳ:) or the latter, *the male tortoise:* (Lth:) as also with ذ. (TA.)

الإِنْقِدَانُ: see preceding sentence.

نقذ

1. نَقِذَ, aor. ـَ, inf. n. نَقَذٌ; (Mṣb, Ḳ;) or نَقَذَ, (A, L,) aor. ـُ, (L,) inf. n. نُقُوذٌ; (A, L;) *He became safe, in safety, saved,* or *liberated; he escaped.* (A, L, Mṣb, Ḳ.) —— نَقَذًا لَكَ *Safety to thee!* Said to a man stumbling. (A, Ḳ.) —— See also 4.

2: see 4.

4. انقذه, (Ṣ, A, L, Mṣb, Ḳ,) inf. n. إِنْقَاذٌ; (Ḳ;) and ▼ استنقذه; and ▼ تنقّذه; (Ṣ, A, L, Ḳ;) and ▼ نقّذه, inf. n. تَنْقِيذٌ; and ▼ نَقَذَهُ, [aor. ـُ,] inf. n. نَقْذٌ; (Ḳ;) *He saved, rescued,* or *liberated, him* or *it,* (Ṣ, A, L, Mṣb, Ḳ,) from such a one, (Ṣ, L,) and from evil. (Mṣb.)

5: see 4.

10: see 4.

نَقَذٌ A thing *that one has saved, rescued,* or *liberated;* (Ṣ, L, Mṣb, Ḳ;) of the measure فَعَلٌ in the sense of the measure مَفْعُولٌ, like نَفَضٌ and قَبَضٌ; (Ṣ, L;) as also ▼ نَقِيذٌ and نَقِيذَةٌ: (L:) a man *saved,* or *rescued,* or *liberated:* (L:) also, a horse *taken from another people:* (L:) or a camel &c. *taken by, and then recovered from, the enemy;* as also نَقِيذٌ and نَقِيذَةٌ; pl. نَقَائِذُ: (A:) or ▼ نَقِيذَةٌ signifies a horse *saved,* or *rescued,* or *liberated,* (Ṣ, L, Ḳ,) *and taken,* (Ṣ, L,) *from the enemy;* (Ṣ, L, Ḳ;) pl. نَقَائِذُ: (Ṣ, L;) or the sing. of نقائذ, signifying horses *saved,* or *rescued,* or *liberated, from the hands of men,* or *of the enemy,* is ▼ نَقِيذٌ, without ة: (IAạr, L:) and, accord. to El-Mufaddal, (L,) ▼ نَقِيذَةٌ signifies *a coat of mail,* دِرْعٌ; (L, Ḳ;) because it saves the person wearing it from the sword: (L:) and Az says, I have read in the handwriting of Shemir, that it signifies *a coat of mail saved,* or *rescued, from the enemy.* (L.) You say also, هُوَ نَقِيذَةُ بُوسٍ, and هُمْ نَقَائِذُ بُوسٍ, *He is saved,* or *rescued, from distress,* or *adversity;* and *they are &c.* (A.) —— مَا لَهُ نَقَذٌ وَلَا شَقَذٌ *He possesses not anything.* (Ḳ.)

نَقِيذٌ and نَقِيذَةٌ: see نَقَذٌ. —— Also the latter, A woman *having had a husband.* (Ḳ.)

الأَنْقَذُ [or أَنْقَذُ, without the art.,] *The hedge-hog;* القُنْفُذُ: (Ḳ;) as also with د. (TA.)

نقر

1. نَقَرَ, (Ṣ, A, Mṣb, Ḳ,) aor. ـُ, inf. n. نَقْرٌ, (Ṣ, Mṣb,) *He* (a bird) *pecked,* or *picked up,* (Ṣ, A, Mṣb, Ḳ,) a grain, (Ṣ,) or grains, (A, Mṣb,) *from this place and that,* (A, Ḳ,) بِمِنْقَارِهِ *with his beak.* (A.) [Accord. to the TA, the addition "from this place and that," which is found in the Ḳ and A, and in one place in the Ṣ, seems to be unnecessary. And ▼ انتقر signifies the same: see 8, in art. قب.] —— [Hence, because of the sure aim with which a bird pecks a thing,] the same verb, having the same [aor. and] inf. n. signifies, ‡ *It* (an arrow) *hit* the butt. (Mṣb.) And *He* (an archer) *hit* the butt, *without making his arrow to pass through, partly* or *wholly.* (TA.) —— [Hence also,] † *He took* [or *picked*] a thing, as, for instance, food, *with the finger.* (TA.) —— Also, (M, Ḳ,) aor. and inf. n. as above, (M, TA,) *He struck* a thing (IḲṭṭ, Ḳ,* TA,) with a thing: (IḲṭṭ, TA:) [generally, *he struck, knocked,* or *pecked,* a thing *with a pointed instrument,* like as a bird strikes a thing with its beak:] *he struck* [or *pecked*] a mill-stone, or a stone, &c., with a مِنْقَار [which is a *pick,* or a *kind of pickaxe;* i. e., *he wrought it into shape, and roughened it in its surface, with a pick*]. (M, TA.) —— [Hence,] ‡ *He wrote* [or *engraved writing*] فِى حَجَرٍ *upon a stone.* (A, Ḳ.) Whence the saying, التَّعْلِيمُ فِى الصِّغَرِ كَالنَّقْرِ عَلَى الحَجَرِ [or, as in a verse of Niftaweyh, فِى الحَجَرِ, i. e., *Teaching in infancy is like engraving writing upon stone*]. (TA.) —— *He struck* [or *fillipped*] a man's head, and in like manner a lute, and a tambourine, with his finger. (TA.) You say also ▼ أَنْقَرَ أُذُنَهُ, meaning, *He struck* [or *fillipped*] *his ear with his finger.* (AA, in TA, art. نطب.) —— [Hence,] نَقَرَ, [aor. ـُ, inf. n. نَقْرٌ, as appears from what follows;] and ▼ أَنْقَرَ; ‡ [*He made a snapping with his thumb and middle finger;*] *he struck his thumb against the end of the middle finger and made a sound with them.* (A.) [And in like manner the former verb used transitively; as in the following instance:] وَضَعَ طَرَفَ إِبْهَامِهِ عَلَى بَاطِنِ سَبَّابَتِهِ ثُمَّ نَقَرَهَا ‡ *He put the end of his thumb against the inner side of his first finger, then made a snapping with it*]. (TA.) See also نَقْرٌ, below. —— [Hence also,] نَقَرَ بِالدَّابَّةِ, (T, A, TṢ,) or بِالفَرَسِ, (Ṣ,) aor. ـُ, (TA,) inf. n. نَقْرٌ; (T, Ṣ, TṢ;) and ▼ أَنْقَرَ, (A, TṢ,) inf. n. إِنْقَارٌ; (TṢ;) ‡ *He made a* [*smacking* or] *slight sound, to put in motion the* [*beast* or] *horse, by making his tongue adhere to his palate and then opening* [or *suddenly drawing it away*]: (Ṣ:) or *he struck with his tongue the place of utterance of the letter* ن *and made a* [*smacking*] *sound* [*by suddenly withdrawing his tongue*]: (A:) نَقْرٌ signifies the *making the end of the tongue to adhere to the palate, then making a sound* [*by suddenly withdrawing it*]: (M, Ḳ:) or one's *putting his tongue above his central incisors, at the part next the palate, then making a smacking sound* [so I render ثُمَّ يَنْقُرُ]: (TA:) [the sounds thus described, which are nearly the same, are commonly made by the Arabs in the present day, in urging beasts of carriage:] or *an agitation of the tongue* (Ḳ, TA) *in the mouth, upwards and downwards:* (TA:) or *a sound,* (so in some copies of the Ḳ and in the TA,) or *slight sound,* (so in the TṢ [as mentioned in the TA] and in some copies of the Ḳ) *by which a horse is put in motion:* (TṢ, Ḳ:) or نَقَرَ بِلِسَانِهِ, accord. to IḲṭṭ, signifies *he struck his palate with his tongue* to quiet the horse: but this is at variance with what is said by Az, J, and ISd, and requires consideration. (TA.) A poet, (Ṣ,) Fedekee El-Minḳaree, (Ḳ,) i. e., 'Obeyd

Ibn-Máweeyeh, of the tribe of Ṭeiyi, (TA,) uses النَّقُرْ for النَّقْرُ, meaning النَّقْرُ بِالْخَيْلِ [*The smacking with the tongue to urge the horses*]: pausing after the word, at the end of a hemistich, he transfers the vowel of the ر to the ق, (Ṣ, Ḳ,) agreeably with the dial. of certain of the Arabs, (TA,) that the hearer may know it to be the vowel of the [final] letter when there is no pause; (Ṣ;) like as you say, هٰذَا بَكُرْ and مَرَرْتُ بِبَكِرْ: but this is not done when the word is in the accus. case: (Ṣ, Ḳ:) and if you choose, you may make the final letter quiescent in pausing, though it is preceded by a quiescent letter. (Ṣ.) — Hence also, فَإِذَا نُقِرَ فِى النَّاقُورِ [Ḳur, lxxiv. 8,] ‡ *For when the horn shall be blown*: (Ṣ,* A,* Bḍ, Ḳ:) from نَقْرٌ signifying ‡ the *making a sound*: originally, *striking*, which is the cause of sound. (Bḍ.) See also نَاقُورٌ, below. — Also, نَقَرَ *He bored, perforated*, or *made a hole through* or *in* or *into*, a thing: (TA:) or *he did so with a* مِنْقَار: (Ṣ:) and, inf. n. نَقْرٌ, *he hollowed out*, or *excavated*, a piece of wood. (Mgh, Mṣb.) نُقِرَ and ♦ اِنْتَقَرَ, (so in some copies of the Ḳ,) or ♦ أُنْتُقِرَ, (so in other copies of the Ḳ and in the TA,) both in the pass. form, (TA,) said of stone and of wood and the like, signify alike, (Ḳ,) *It was bored*, or *perforated*, or *it had a hole made through* or *in* or *into it*: (TA:) [and *it was hollowed out*.] You say, نَقَرَ البَيْضَةَ عَنِ الفَرْخِ, (Ḳ,) aor. ـُ, inf. n. نَقْرٌ, (TA,) *He made a hole in the egg* [*so as to disclose the young bird*]. (Ḳ.) And نَقَرَتِ الخَيْلُ بِحَوَافِرِهَا, (A,) and انتقرت ♦ بحوافرها نُقَرًا, (Lth, Ḳ,) *The horses made hollows in the ground with their hoofs*. (Lth, A, Ḳ.) And in like manner, ♦ انتقرت السُّيُولُ نُقَرًا *The torrents left hollows in the ground, in which water was retained*. (TA.) — Hence, نَقَرَ عَنِ الأَمْرِ; (Mṣb;) and ♦ نَقَّرَ عَنْهُ, (Ṣ, Ḳ,) inf. n. تَنْقِيرٌ; (Ṣ;) and ♦ نقّرهُ; and ♦ تنقّرهُ; and ♦ انتقرهُ; (Ḳ;) ‡ *He searched* or *inquired into the thing; investigated, scrutinized*, or *examined, it*; (Ṣ, Mṣb, Ḳ, TA;) *and endeavoured to know it*: (TA;) and so نَقَرَ عَنِ الخَبَرِ ‡ *he investigated the news, and endeavoured to know it*. (A.) [And hence,] نقّر ♦ السَّهْمَ بَيْنَ إِصْبَعَيْهِ, (Ḳ, in art. حن,) or عَلَى الإِبْهَامِ, inf. n. تَنْقِيرٌ, (Ḳ, in art. دوم,) [*He tried the sonorific quality of the arrow by turning it round between his fingers, or upon his thumb*: see حَنَّانٌ, and دَوَّمَ السَّهْمَ, and see also 4, in art. دوم: or] نقّر السَّهْمَ signifies *he made the arrow to produce a sharp sound* [by turning it round between his fingers, or] upon his thumb. (TḲ, in art. دوم.)

2: see 1, last two sentences.

4: see 1, in three places, in the first half. — انقر عَنْهُ, (Ṣ, Ḳ,) inf. n. إِنْقَارٌ, (TA,) *He refrained, forbore, abstained*, or *desisted, from it* or *him*; *he left*, or *relinquished, it* or *him*. (Ṣ,* Ḳ.) Hence the saying, ضَرَبَهُ فَمَا أَنْقَرَ عَنْهُ حَتَّى قَتَلَهُ *He beat him and left him not until he killed him*. (TA.) And hence the saying of I'Ab, مَا كَانَ ٱللّٰهُ لِيُنْقِرَ عَنْ قَاتِلِ ٱلْمُؤْمِنِ, i.e., *God will not leave the slayer of the believer* until He destroy him. (Ṣ, TA.)

5: see 1, last signification.

8: see 1, latter part, in four places.

نَقْرٌ ‡ *A slight sound that is heard in consequence of striking the thumb against the middle finger* [*and then letting them fly apart in opposite directions, passing each other*]: (Ṣ, Ḳ:) [or the *snapping with the fingers*, or *with the thumb and middle finger*, or *with the thumb and first finger*; as also ♦ نَقِيرٌ: n. un. of the former with ة.] One says, مَا أَثَابَهُ نَقْرَةً ‡ [*He did not reward him with* even *a snap of the fingers*;] meaning, *with anything*: (Ṣ, Ḳ [in the former of which it is implied that نقرة thus used is from نَقْرٌ in the first of the senses explained above:]) not used thus save in a negative phrase. (Ṣ.) A poet says,

• وَهُنَّ حَرًى أَلَّا يُثِبْنَكَ نَقْرَةً •
• وَأَنْتَ حَرًى بِالنَّارِ حِينَ تُثِيبُ •

‡ [*And they are fit*, or *worthy, not to reward thee with anything, and thou art fit for*, or *worthy of, the fire of hell when thou rewardest*]. (Ṣ.) Or the right reading in both these instances is ♦ نُقْرَةً, with ḍamm. (TA.) [See نُقْرَةٌ.] One says also, لَمْ يَكْتَرِثْ لِى بِقَدْرِ نَقْرَةِ إِصْبَعٍ ‡ [*He did not care for me so much as a snap of a finger*]. (A.) [See also an ex. in a verse cited in the first paragraph of art. شأو.] I'Ab, in explanation of the words of the Ḳur, [iv. 123,] وَلَا يُظْلَمُونَ نَقِيرًا, put the end of his thumb against the inner side of his first finger, then made a snapping with it (ثُمَّ نَقَرَهَا), and said, This is what is termed ♦ نَقِيرٌ; [denoting the lit. meaning to be ‡ *And they shall not be wronged a snap of the fingers*.] (TA.) But see نُقْرَةٌ, below. — Also, *A sound*, or *slight sound, by which a horse is put in motion*: (TṢ, Ḳ:) as also ♦ نَقِيرٌ: (TA:) or the former has one or other of the different significations assigned to it above, in the explanations under the head of نَقْرٌ بِالدَّابَّةِ. (Ḳ, &c.)

نَقْرَةٌ: see نَقْرٌ.

نَقَرَةٌ: see نَقْرٌ, in four places.

نُقْرَةٌ *A small hollow* or *cavity in the ground*: (Ṣ:) or *a hollow* or *cavity in the ground, not large*: (Mṣb:) or *a hollow* or *cavity in the ground in which water stagnates*: (TA:) or *a round* وَهْدَة [or *hollow*] *in the ground*, (Ḳ, TA,) *not large, in which water stagnates*: (TA:) pl. نُقَرٌ (A, Ḳ) and نِقَارٌ: (Ḳ:) ♦ نَقِيرٌ also signifies *a hollow*, or *cavity, in the ground*; and its pl. is أَنْقِرَةٌ. (Ṣ.) — Hence, (Ṣ,) The *place where the* قَمَحْدُوَة [or *occiput*] *ends, in the back part of the neck*; (Ḳ;) i.e., the *hollow in the back of the neck*; (TA;) what is called نُقْرَةُ القَفَا; (Ṣ, A, Mṣb;) i.e., the *hollow where the brain ends*; the cupping in that part occasions forgetfulness: (Mṣb:) [and *any similar hollow*; as the *pit* of the stomach: and *a dimple*: accord. to present usage; and in this sense it is used in the A, Ḳ, and TA, voce فَحْصَة.] — The *cavity*, or *socket*, of the eye. (Ḳ.) — *Foramen ani*; syn. ثُقْبُ الإِسْتِ: (Ḳ:) but in the L it is said that نُقْرَةُ الوَرِكِ signifies *the hole*, or *perforation, that is in the middle of the haunch*; [app. meaning *the sacro-ischiatic foramen*: see الفَائِلُ, in art. فيل: but perhaps it may sometimes mean *the socket of the thigh-bone*; for نُقْرَةٌ signifies *any socket of a bone*.] (TA.) — The *little spot* [or *embryo*] *upon the back of a date-stone*, (AḤeyth, Ḳ,) *which is as though it were hollowed*, (TA,) *and from which the palm-tree grows forth*; (AḤeyth;) as also ♦ نَقِيرٌ (Ṣ, A, Mṣb, Ḳ) and ♦ نَقْرٌ (Ḳ) and ♦ أُنْقُورٌ. (Ṣgh, Ḳ.) You say, مَا أَثَابَهُ نُقْرَةً, (El-Baṣáïr, TA,) and ♦ نَقِيرًا, (A,) lit., [*He did not reward him*] *with* even *a little spot on the back of a date-stone*; (A, El-Baṣáïr;) meaning, ‡ *with the meanest thing*. (El-Baṣáïr.) In the Ṣ and Ḳ, ما اثابه نَقْرَةً: see نَقْرٌ.] And مَا أَغْنَى عَنِّى نُقْرَةً ‡ *He did not stand me in stead of the meanest thing*. (A.) Lebeed says, bewailing the death of his brother Arbad,

• وَلَيْسَ النَّاسُ بَعْدَكَ فِى نَقِيرٍ ♦ •

lit., [*And the people, after thee, are not worth*] *a little spot on the back of a date-stone*; meaning, لَيْسُوا بَعْدَكَ فِى شَىْءٍ ‡ [*after thee they are not worth anything*]. (Ṣ.) And hence, accord. to ISk [and the Jel], the saying in the Ḳur, [iv. 123,] وَلَا يُظْلَمُونَ نَقِيرًا [*And they shall not be wronged even as to a little spot on the back of a date-stone*.] (TA.) Hence also, [in verse 56 of the same chap.,] لَا يُؤْتُونَ النَّاسَ نَقِيرًا ‡ *They would not give men a thing as inconsiderable as the little hollow in the back of a date-stone*. (Jel.) See also نَقْرٌ. — The *place in which a bird lays its eggs*: (Ḳ:) pl. نُقَرٌ. (TA.)

نَقِيرٌ: see نَقْرٌ, in three places. — What is *bored*, or *perforated*; and what is *hollowed out*, or *excavated*; (مَا نُقِبَ, TA, and مَا نُقِرَ, Ḳ, TA;) of stone, and of wood, and the like. (Ḳ, TA.) — *A piece of wood*, (Mṣb,) or *a block of wood*, (أَصْلُ خَشَبَةٍ, Ṣ, Ḳ,) or *a stump*, or the *lower part*, (أَصْل,) *of a palm-tree*, (T,) *which is hollowed out, and in which the beverage called* نَبِيذ *is made;* (T, Ṣ, Mṣb, Ḳ;) *the* نبيذ *whereof becomes strong:* (Ṣ, Ḳ:) or *a stump,* or the *lower part,* (اصل,) *of a palm-tree, which it was a custom of the people of El-Yemámeh to hollow out, then they crushed in it ripe dates and unripe dates, which* [*with water poured upon them*] *they left until fermentation had taken place therein and subsided:* (A'Obeyd:) or *a stump,* or the *lower part,* (اصل,) *of a palm-tree, whereof the middle was hollowed out, then dates were put in them, with water, which became intoxicating* نبيذ: (IAth:) the word is of the measure فَعِيلٌ in the sense of the measure مَفْعُولٌ. (Mṣb.) It is said in a trad., that Moḥammad forbade النَّقِير, (Ṣ,* Mṣb,* TA,) meaning, the نبيذ thereof. (TA.) —— *A trunk of a palm-tree, hollowed out, and having the like of steps made in it, by which one ascends to* غُرَف [*or upper chambers*]. (Ḳ. [See also عَجَلَةٌ.]) —— See also نُقْرَةٌ, throughout.

نُقَارَةٌ The *quantity* [of grain] *which a bird pecks,* or *picks up.* (Ḳ.) See 8, in art. قب. —— *What remains from the boring,* or *excavating,* (نَقْر,) *of stones:* like نُجَارَةٌ and نُحَاتَةٌ. (TA.)

نَقَّارٌ *An engraver:* or, accord. to Az, *one who engraves stirrups and bits and the like:* and *one who bores* (يَنْقُرُ) *mill-stones.* (TA.) —— ‡ *One who investigates, scrutinizes,* or *examines, and endeavours to know, affairs,* and *news.* (TA.)

نَاقِرٌ act. part. n. of نَقَرَ. —— ‡ *An arrow that hits,* (Mṣb,) or *has hit,* (Ṣ, A, Ḳ,) *the butt,* (Ṣ, Ḳ,) or *the eye of the target:* (A:) if it do not hit the butt it is not so called: (Ṣ, TA:) [but see a phrase following:] pl. نَوَاقِرُ. (A, Mṣb.) —— [Hence,] أَخْطَأَتْ نَوَاقِرُهُ ‡ [lit., *His arrows that were wont to hit the butt missed*]; meaning, *he did not continue in the right course.* (TA.) [And hence,] نَاقِرَةٌ ‡ *A calamity;* (Ḳ, TA;) pl. نَوَاقِرُ. (TA.) One says, رَمَاهُ الدَّهْرُ بِنَاقِرَةٍ, and بِنَوَاقِرَ, ‡ *Fortune smote him with a calamity,* and *with calamities.* (TA.) —— Also, نَاقِرَةٌ ‡ *A right argument, allegation, evidence,* or *the like;* syn. حُجَّةٌ مُصِيبَةٌ: in the Ḳ, a و is incorrectly inserted between these two words: but the pl., نَوَاقِرُ, is afterwards correctly rendered in the Ḳ. (TA.) One says, أَتَتْنِى عَنْهُ نَوَاقِرُ ‡ *There came to me, from him, speech which displeased me,* or *grieved me:* or *right arguments,* or *the like,* (Ḳ, TA,) *like arrows hitting the mark.* (TA.) In the L, رَمَاهُ بِنَوَاقِرَ ‡ *He cast at him words that hit the mark.* (TA.)

نَاقُورٌ ‡ *A horn in which one blows;* syn. صُورٌ: (Ṣ, Ḳ:) in the Ḳur, lxxiv. 8, the *horn in which the angel shall blow for the congregating at the resurrection:* the blast there mentioned is said to be the second blast: Fr. says that it is the first of the two blasts. (TA.)

أُنْقُورٌ: see نُقْرَةٌ.

مِنْقَرٌ: see مِنْقَارٌ.

مُنْقَرُ العَيْنِ, (Ḳ,) and ▼ مُنْتَقِرُهَا, (Ṣgh, Ḳ,) or ▼ مُنْتَقَرُهَا, (CḲ,) *Having the eye sunken.* (Ḳ.)

مِنْقَارٌ The *beak of a bird; that which is to a bird as the mouth to a man;* (Mṣb;) because it pecks, or picks up, with it: (TA:) or of a bird which is not one of prey; that of a bird of prey being called مِنْسَرٌ: (Fs, and Ṣ in art. نسر, and MF:) therefore the explanation in the Ḳ, which is, the مِنْسَر of a bird, is incorrect: (MF:) [and the dual signifies the *two mandibles* of a bird; used in this sense in the TA, art. صغو:] pl. مَنَاقِيرُ. (Ṣ.) —— Hence, (TA,) The *fore part* of the خُفّ [app. meaning the foot of a camel, not a boot]. (Ḳ.) —— [*A kind of pick-axe;* or *a pick, by which a mill-stone, or the like, is pecked,* or *wrought into shape, and roughened in its surface;* (see 1;)] *an iron instrument like the* فَأْس, (A, Ḳ,) *slender, round, and having a* خُلْف [or *pointed head*], (TA,) *with which one pecks,* (يُنْقَرُ بِهَا, A, Ḳ, TA,) *and cuts stones, and hard earth;* (TA;) *used* [*also*] *by a carpenter:* (Ṣ:) and ▼ مِنْقَرٌ signifies [app. the same, or nearly the same,] *i. q.* مِعْوَلٌ: (Ṣ, Ḳ:) [the former is applied in the present day to *a chisel:*] pl. of the former, مَنَاقِيرُ; (Ṣ;) and of the latter, مَنَاقِرُ. (TA.) Dhu-r-Rummeh says,

* كَأَرْحَآءِ رَقْدٍ زَلَّمَتْهَا المَنَاقِرُ *

[*Like mill-stones of Rakd* (a mountain so called) *which the minkars have rounded*]. (TA.) See زَلَّمَ.

مُنْتَقِرُ العَيْنِ, or مُنْتَقَرُهَا: see مُنْقَر.

نقرس

نِقْرِسٌ [*Arthritis,* or *gout:* or, specially, *podagra,* or *gout in the foot* or *feet:*] *a certain disease, well known;* (Ṣ, Mṣb;) *a swelling and pain in the joints:* (Az, TA:) or *in the leg* or *foot:* (TA:) or *in the joints of the ankles and the toes:* (Ḳ:) or *a swelling in the joints of the foot, and mostly in the great toe, a property of which is that it does not collect thick purulent matter, nor exude moisture, because it is in a member not fleshy:* and of the same kind are arthritis, or pain of the joints, (وَجَعُ المَفَاصِلِ,) and sciatica, or hip-gout, (عِرْقُ النَّسَا,) but differing in name because differing in state. (Mṣb.)

نقز

1. نَقَزَ, (Ṣ, A,) aor. ـُ, (Ṣ, TA,) and ـِ, (TA,) inf. n. نَقْزٌ and نَقَزَانٌ (Ṣ, Ḳ,) and نُقَازٌ, (TA,) *He* (an antelope, Ṣ and A) *leaped, jumped, sprang,* or *bounded,* (Ṣ, A, Ḳ,) as also ▼ نقّز, (M, TA,) in his running, (Ṣ,) or *on his* نَوَاقِز, i. e., his *legs:* (A:) or *he* (generally referring to a raven or crow, or a sparrow, or locust, or the like,) *leaped, jumped, sprang,* or *bounded, upwards; he hopped:* (TA:) or *he put his legs together in leaping, jumping, springing,* or *bounding:* when the legs are spread, the action is termed نَقْز. (IDrd, TA.)

2: see 1. —— Also, inf. n. تَنْقِيزٌ, *He made to leap, jump, spring,* or *bound:* (Ṣ:) and نقّزت *she* (a woman) *danced,* or *dandled,* her child; (Ḳ,* TA;) as also نفّزت. (Ṣ, &c., art. نفز.)

نَوَاقِزُ, [pl. of نَاقِزَةٌ,] The *legs* of an antelope, (A,) or of a beast of carriage. (Ḳ.) See also نَافِزَةٌ.

نقس

1. نَقَسَ *It* (a نَاقُوس) *sounded.* (TA.) === نَقَسَ, (Ṣ, A, Mṣb,) or نَقَسَ النَّاقُوسَ, (Mgh, Ḳ,) aor. ـُ, inf. n. نَقْسٌ, (Ṣ, Mgh, Mṣb,) *He struck,* or *beat, the* ناقوس, (Ṣ, Mgh, Mṣb, Ḳ,) بِالوَبِيلِ *with the* وبيل. (Mgh, Ḳ.) You say, نَقَسَتِ النَّصَارَى and ▼ انتقست *The Christians struck,* or *beat the* ناقوس. (A.) It is said in a trad., that the Muslims were near to doing so, (كَادُوا يَنْقُسُونَ, Ṣ, TA,) or used to do so, (كَانُوا يَنْقُسُونَ, Mgh,) until 'Abd-Allah Ibn-Zeyd dreamed of the [mode of calling to prayer termed] أَذَان. (Ṣ, Mgh, TA.)

2. نَقَّسَ دَوَاتَهُ, inf. n. تَنْقِيسٌ, *He put ink* (نِقْس) *into his receptacle for ink.* (Ṣ,* Ḳ.)

8: see 1.

نِقْسٌ *Ink;* syn. مِدَادٌ [which is a more common term]; (A, Ḳ;) *that with which one writes:* (Ṣ, TA:) pl. أَنْقُسٌ (Ṣ, Ḳ) and أَنْقَاسٌ. (Ṣ, A, Ḳ.)

نَاقُوسٌ The *thing which the Christians strike,* or *beat,* (Ṣ, A, Mgh, Mṣb, Ḳ,) *to notify the times of prayer,* (Ṣ, A, Mgh, Ḳ,) *as a sign for commencing their prayer;* (Mṣb;) being *a piece of wood, long,* (A, Mgh, Ḳ,) *and large* (Ḳ,) [*suspended to two cords,* (Golius,)] *with another which is short,* [*with which the former is struck,* or *beaten,*] *and which is called* وَبِيلٌ: (A, Ḳ:) pl. نَوَاقِيسُ (Ṣ, TA) and نُقُسٌ, as though the ا in the sing. were imagined to be suppressed in forming the latter pl. (TA.) —— [Hence, in the present day, applied to *A bell:* and particularly to the *bell of a church* or *convent.*]

نقش

1. نَقَشَ, (Ṣ, M, Mṣb,) aor. ـُ, (M, Mṣb,) inf. n. نَقْشٌ, (Ṣ, M, A, Mṣb, Ḳ,) *He variegated* a thing; or *decorated* or *embellished* it; syn. نَمْنَمَ; as also ▼ انتقش: (M:) [*he charactered* in any manner a coin &c.:] and *he engraved*, agreeably with modern usage: *he coloured* a thing *with two colours*, (Ḳ,) or *with colours*; (A, Ḳ;) and ▼ نَقَّشَ, (Ṣ,) inf. n. تَنْقِيشٌ, (Ṣ, Ḳ,) signifies the same. (Ṣ, Ḳ.) — نَقَشَ فى خَاتَمِهِ كَذَا, and عَلَى فَصِّ خَاتَمِهِ, (A,) inf. n. as above, (Ḳ,) [*He engraved upon his signet-ring such a thing*, and *upon the stone of his signet-ring*: and نَقَشَ also signifies *he marked with a cutting* or *a pointed instrument*: *he sculptured* a thing in any manner.] — نَقَشَ الرَّحَا ‡ *He pecked the mill-stone with a* مِنْقَار; syn. نَقَرَهَا. (A, TA.) — نَقَشَ, inf. n. as above, also signifies *He*, or *it, scratched, lacerated*, or *wounded in the outer skin*. (TA.) They said, كَأَنَّ وَجْهَهُ نُقِشَ بِقَتَادَةٍ [*As though his face were scratched*, or *lacerated, by a tragacanth-bush*]; syn. خُدِشَ: relating to hatefulness, and austerity or moroseness of countenance, (M, TA,) and anger. (M.) — نَقْشُ العِذْقِ signifies *The striking the raceme of dates with thorns, in order that the dates may ripen*: (Ṣ, Ḳ:) or *and their consequently ripening*. (AA.) And one says, نُقِشَ العِذْقُ, meaning, *The raceme of dates had specks apparent in it, in consequence of ripening*. (Ṣ.) — And [hence, perhaps,] نَقَشَ is used as ‡ *syn. with* جِمَاعٌ (Ṣ, A, Ṣgh, Ḳ,) accord. to AA, (Ṣ,) or IAạr; (Ṣgh;) نَقَشَ signifying ‡ *Inivit* puellam. (T, Ḳ.) [This signification is mentioned in the A among those which are proper; but in the TA it is said, to be tropical.] — Also نَقَشَ, (Ṣ, M, A, Mṣb,) aor. as above, (M, TA,) and so the inf. n., (Ṣ, M, Mṣb, Ḳ,) *He extracted*, or *drew*, or *pulled, out*, or *forth*, a thorn (Ṣ, M, A, Mṣb, Ḳ) from his foot, (Ṣ, M,) *with the* مِنْقَش or مِنْقَاش; (Mṣb, Ḳ;*) as also ▼ انتقش: (Ṣ, M, A, Ḳ:) thought by A'Obeyd to be from المُنَاقَشَةُ; but others say the reverse: (TA:) and in like manner, bones from a wound in the head: (Ṣ, Ḳ:) and *he plucked out* (Ṣ, A,) hair, (A,) *with the* مِنْقَاش; (Ṣ, A;) as also ▼ انتقش. (A.) A certain poet says, (namely, Yezeed Ibn-Maḳsam [?] Eth-Thaḳafee, O in art. شوك,)

لَا تَنْقُشَنَّ بِرِجْلِ غَيْرِكَ شَوْكَةً

فَتَقِى بِرِجْلِكَ رِجْلَ مَنْ قَدْ شَاكَهَا

[*Do not thou by any means extract from the foot of another a thorn, and so preserve, by* (risking) *thy foot, the foot of him who has pierced himself therewith*]: the [former] بِ is put in the place of عَنْ: he says, do not thou extract from the foot of another a thorn and put it in thy foot: (TA:) or مَنْ شَاكَهَا means *who has entered among the thorns*. (Ṣ and O, in art. شوك.) And it is said in a trad. of Aboo-Hureyreh, عَثَرَ فَلَا ٱنْتَعَشَ وَشِيكَ فَلَا ٱنْتَقَشَ [*May he stumble, and not rise again; and may he be pierced with a thorn, and not extract the thorn*]: (M, TA:*) the words meaning an imprecation. (TA.) See also 8, below. — [Hence,] نَقَشَ, aor. as above, (TA,) and so the inf. n., (Ḳ,) *He cleared* the nightly resting-place of sheep or goats *from thorns and the like*, (Ḳ,) or *from what might hurt them, of stones and thorns and the like*. (TA.) — Hence also, نَقَشَ عَنِ الشَّىْءِ, (TḲ,) inf. n. as above, (IDrd, Ḳ,) *He explored the thing to the utmost*. (IDrd, Ḳ, TḲ.) — [Hence also,] مَا نَقَشَ مِنْهُ شَيْئًا † *He did not obtain from him anything*: but the word commonly known is نَتَشَ. (M, TA.) See also 8.

2: see 1, first sentence.

3. ناقشهُ, (Mṣb,) or ناقشهُ الحِسَابَ, (Ṣ,* M, A,) and فِى الحِسَابِ, (A,) inf. n. مُنَاقَشَةٌ (Ṣ, M, Mṣb, Ḳ) and نِقَاشٌ, (M, TA,) *He did the utmost with him, or went to the utmost length with him, in reckoning*, (Ṣ, M, Mṣb, Ḳ,) *so as to omit nothing therein*: (A'Obeyd:) A'Obeyd thinks that نَقْشٌ signifying the "extracting" a thorn from the foot is from this; but others say the reverse; that the primary signification of مُنَاقَشَةٌ is *the extracting a thorn from the body with difficulty*; and that it then became [conventionally regarded as] a proper term in the sense of doing the utmost, or going to the utmost length, in reckoning; as observed by MF. (TA.) It is said in a trad., مَنْ نُوقِشَ الحِسَابَ عُذِّبَ, (Ṣ,) or هَلَكَ, (M,) *He with whom the utmost is done in reckoning* (Ṣ, M,) *is punished*, (Ṣ,) or *perishes*. (M.) See also 4. — [Hence,] ناقش الكَلَامَ † *He picked out the faults of the language*; syn. نَقَدَهُ. (TA, art. نقد.)

4. انقش على غَرِيمِهِ *He went to the utmost length against his debtor*. (IAạr, Ḳ.) See also 3.

5: see 8, last signification.

8. انتقش: see 1, first signification. — Also, (Ḳ,) or انتقش عَلَى فَصِّهِ, (Lth, A,) *He ordered* (Lth, A, Ḳ) the نَقَّاش [or engraver], (Lth, Ḳ,) *to engrave upon the stone of his signet-ring*. (Lth, A, Ḳ.) — *He extracted*, or *drew*, or *pulled, out*, or *forth*, a thing; (Ḳ;) such as a thorn and the like: (TA:) *syn. with* نَقَشَ, as shewn above; see 1, in three places. (Ṣ, M, A, Ḳ.) — [Hence,] *He* (a camel) *struck the ground* (Ṣ, Ḳ) *with his fore leg*, (Ṣ,) or *with his foot*, (Ḳ,) *on account of something entering into it*; (Ṣ, Ḳ;) [i.e., *to beat out a thorn or the like*.] — [Hence also,] ‡ *He chose*, or *selected*, a thing. (M, A, Ḳ.) You say, of a man who has chosen (A, L) a man, (A,) or a thing, (L,) for himself, جَادَ مَا ٱنْتَقَشَهُ لِنَفْسِهِ ‡ *Good*, or *excellent, be that which he has chosen for himself*: (A, L:) or, accord. to the O, when a man has chosen for himself a servant (خَادِمًا) [which suggests that this may be a mistranscription for جَادَ مَا] إِنْتَقَشْتَ هٰذَا لِنَفْسِكَ [*thou hast chosen this for thyself*]. (TA.) [Hence also,] انتقش مِنْهُ حَقَّهُ ‡ [*He took from him his right*, or *due*]. (A.) And انتقش جَمِيعَ حَقِّهِ, and ▼ تَنَقَّشَهُ, ‡ *He took from him the whole of his right*, or *due, not leaving thereof anything*. (M, TA.) See also 1, last signification.

نَقْشٌ [an inf. n. (see 1) used as a simple subst.; or in the sense of a pass. part. n. in which the quality of a subst. is predominant: *Variegation*; or *variegated work*: *decoration, embellishment, a picture*; or *decorated*, or *embellished*, or *pictured, work*: *broidery*: *tracery*: (significations well known: see نَقَّاش:)] *engraved work* upon a signet: [and *any sculptured work*:] pl. نُقُوشٌ. (A.) Also The *impress* of a signet. (Mgh, in art. ختم.) And *A mark*, or *trace, upon the ground*; as, for instance, of ashes. (AHeyth.) — See also مَنْقُوشٌ.

مَنْقُوشٌ: see نَقْشٌ.

نِقَاشَةٌ The *art*, or *occupation, of the* نَقَّاش, (M, Ḳ, TA,) *who does variegated*, or *decorated* or *embellished, work*; (M;) *of him who does what is termed* نَقْش: (TA:) [and *of him who engraves upon signet-rings*: and *of him who does any sculptured work*.]

نَقَّاشٌ *One who does variegated*, or *decorated* or *embellished, work*; (M;) *who does what is termed* نَقْش: (TA:) and *one who engraves upon the stones of signet-rings*: (Lth, Ḳ:) [and *one who does any sculptured work*.]

مِنْقَاشٌ: see مِنْقَشٌ.

مُنَقَّشٌ: see مَنْقُوشٌ, first sentence.

شَجَّةٌ مُنَقِّشَةٌ: see مَنْقُوشٌ, last signification.

مِنْقَاشٌ *An instrument with which variegated*, or *decorated* or *embellished, work is done*: pl. مَنَاقِيشُ: (M:) [and *an instrument with which engraving*, or *any sculptured work, is done*: so in the present day.] — Also, [*A kind of tweezers*;] *an instrument with which one extracts*, or *draws* or *pulls out* or *forth, thorns*; as also ▼ مِنْقَشٌ, (Mṣb, Ḳ;) [of which latter the pl. is مَنَاقِشُ, occurring below:] and *with which one plucks out* (Ṣ, A) *hair*. (A.) [Hence the saying,] إِسْتَخْرَجْتُ حَقِّى مِنْهُ بِالمَنَاقِشِ ‡ *I wearied myself in extorting my right, or due, from him*. (A.)

مَنْقُوشٌ A garment, or piece of cloth, (A,) or other thing, (TA,) [*variegated*; or *decorated*, or *embellished*: *charactered* in any manner, as a coin &c.: (see 1:)] *coloured* (A, TA) *with two colours*, (TA,) or *with colours*; (A, TA;) as also ▼ مُنْتَقَشٌ. (A, TA.) — [A signet-ring *engraved*: and anything *sculptured*. (See 1.)] — عِذْقٌ مَنْقُوشٌ *A raceme of dates struck with thorns, and consequently ripened*: (AA:) [or *having specks apparent in it, in consequence of ripening*: (see نُقْشُ العِذْقِ:)] and بُسْرٌ مَنْقُوشٌ *full-grown unripe dates pricked with thorns in order that they may ripen*: (M, TA:) and رُطَبٌ مَنْقُوشٌ *fresh ripe dates soaked with water*; syn. رَبِيطٌ: (Ṣgh, TA:) called by the vulgar معذب [app. مُعَذَّبٌ]; (TA;) as also نَقْشٌ. (Ḳ [accord. to some copies; and in the TA: accord. to other copies of the Ḳ, نَقْشٌ; but expressly said in the TA to be with fet-ḥ.]) — شَجَّةٌ مَنْقُوشَةٌ *A wound in the head from which bones are extracted*: (Ṣ, Ḳ:) and شَجَّةٌ ▼ مُنَقِّشَةٌ *a wound in the head from which bones are removed*; (AA, El-Ghanawee, Aboo-Turáb;) i. q. مُنَقِّلَةٌ. (Ḳ.)

لَطَمَهُ لَطْمَ المُنْتَقِشِ, (Ṣ,) or لَطْمَةَ المُنْتَقِشِ, (Ḳ,) [*He gave him a* violent *slap*, like *the slap of the camel striking the ground with his fore-leg*, or *with his foot, on account of something entering into it*:] from إِنْتَقَشَ, said of a camel, as explained above. (Ṣ, Ḳ.)

نقص

1. نَقَصَ, (Ṣ, M, Mgh, Mṣb, Ḳ,) aor. ـُ, (M, Mṣb,) inf. n. نُقْصَانٌ (Ṣ, M, A, Mgh, Mṣb, Ḳ) and نَقْصٌ, (Ṣ, M, A, Mṣb, Ḳ,) or the former of these two only, the latter being the inf. n. of the trans. verb, (MṢ,) and نَقِيصَةٌ (M) and تَنْقَاصٌ, (Ḳ,) [which last is an intensive form,] said of a thing, (Ṣ, M,) intrans., (Ṣ, M, Mgh, Mṣb, Ḳ,) *It lost somewhat, decreased, diminished, lessened, wasted, waned*, or *became defective* or *deficient* or *incomplete* or *imperfect, after having been whole* or *complete* or *perfect*: (IḲṭṭ, Mṣb, TA:) or *he*, or *it, lost*, or *suffered loss* or *diminution*, (A, Ḳ,) *with respect to lot or portion*: (Ḳ:) and ▼ انتقص signifies the same; (Ṣ, A, Mgh, Mṣb, Ḳ;) and so does ▼ تنقّص; (TḲ, [probably from the TA,] art. أفن;) and so does ▼ تناقص: (TA:) [or this last signifies *it lost somewhat, decreased*, &c., *gradually*; contr. of تزايد.] It is said in a trad., (Mgh,) شَهْرَا عِيدٍ لَا يَنْقُصَانِ, (Mgh, Ḳ,) i. e. Ramaḍán and Dhu-l-Ḥijjeh, (Mgh,) meaning, *Two months of festival are not defective* virtually (فِى الحُكْمِ) though they be defective in number [of days]; (Ḳ;) i. e. let no doubt occur in your hearts when ye fast nine and twenty days [instead of thirty]; nor if there happen a mistake respecting the day of the pilgrimage, will there be any deficiency in your performance of the rites thereof: (TA:) or, as some say, *two months of festival will not be defective* in one and the same year; but Eṭ-Ṭaḥáwee disapproves of this explanation: some say that the meaning is, that though they be defective, or one of them be so, yet their recompense will be complete. (Mgh.) It is also said in a trad., إِنَّ العَمَلَ فِى عَشْرِ ذِى الحِجَّةِ لَا يَنْقُصُ ثَوَابُهُ عَمَّا فِى شَهْرِ رَمَضَانَ [*Verily the deed* that is done *on the tenth of Dhu-l-Ḥijjeh, the recompense thereof will not fall short of that which is in the month of Ramaḍán*: for نَقَصَ عَنْ كَذَا means *It fell short of such a thing*.] (Mgh.) [On the expression فِى النُّقْصَانِ, as used in grammar, see غُفَيْرٌ.] — نَقَصَهُ, (Ṣ, M, Mgh, Mṣb, Ḳ,) aor. ـُ, (Mṣb,) inf. n. نَقْصٌ, (MṢ,) [and accord. to the TḲ تَنْقَاصٌ and نُقْصَانٌ also, which last, however, is said in the MṢ to be an inf. n. of the intrans. verb only,] *He made it to lose somewhat, decreased it, diminished it, curtailed it, lessened it, wasted it, impaired it, took from it*, or *made it defective* or *deficient* or *incomplete* or *imperfect, after it had been whole* or *complete* or *perfect*; (Mṣb;) *he made it* (i. e. a share, or portion) *defective* or *deficient*: (Ḳ:) [the pronoun often relates to a man: see an ex. in art. ضوز, and another in art. وكس:] this is the [most] chaste form of the verb, and is that which occurs in the Ḳur.: (Mṣb:) ▼ انقصهُ also signifies the same; (M, Mṣb, Ḳ;) and so does ▼ نقّصهُ, (Mṣb, Ḳ,) inf. n. تَنْقِيصٌ: (TA:) but these two are of weak authority, and do not occur in chaste language: (Mṣb:) and ▼ انتقصهُ signifies the same: (Ṣ, Mgh, Mṣb, Ḳ:) or this last signifies *he took from it by little and little*; as also ▼ تنقّصهُ. (M,* TA [in the latter of which this is plainly said of both of the last two verbs; but in the M, it seems rather to be said of تنقّصه only.]) [See an ex. of the verb followed by من voce طَرَفٌ. You say also, نَقَصَ مِنْهُ كَذَا *He cut off from it such a thing*.] — نَقَصَهُ is doubly trans.: (Mṣb:) you say نَقَصَهُ حَقَّهُ, (A, Mgh, Mṣb, TA,) inf. n. نَقْصٌ; (A, Mgh;) and in like manner, ▼ انتقصهُ حَقَّهُ; (M, A,* Mgh,* TA;*) *He diminished*, or *impaired, to him his right*, or *due*; *endamaged him*; or *made him to suffer loss*, or *damage*, or *detriment, in respect of it*; *curtailed him, abridged him, deprived him*, or *defrauded him, of a portion of it*; (Mṣb,* TA;) contr. of أَوْفَاهُ: (TA:) [and *he abridged him, deprived him*, or *defrauded him, of it altogether*; for نَقَصَهُ أَهْلَهُ وَمَالَهُ signifies sometimes *He deprived him of his family and his property altogether*: as appears from the following ex.:] نُقِصَ أَهْلَهُ وَمَالَهُ وَبَقِىَ فَرْدًا [*He was deprived of his family and his property, and remained alone*]. (T, art. وتر.) ▼ إِنْتِقَاصُ الحَقِّ also signifies *The denying*, or *disacknowledging, the right*, or *due*. (TA.) — See also 5.

2:
4: } see نَقَصَهُ.

5. تنقّصهُ: see نَقَصَهُ: — تنقّص: see نَقَصَ. — *He attributed to him defect*, or *imperfection*; i. e. to a man; (M;) as also ▼ انتقصهُ, and ▼ استنقصهُ: (M, TA:) *he attributed* or *imputed to him, charged him with*, or *accused him of, a vice, fault*, or *the like*; *detracted from his reputation*; *censured him*; *reproached him*; *spoke against him*; *impugned his character*; (Ṣ, A, Ḳ;) as also ▼ انتقصهُ: (A:) [and نَقَصَهُ signifies the same; for] IḲṭṭ says, that ▼ نقص [app. نُقِصَ], inf. n. نَقِيصَةٌ, signifies طعن عليه [app. طُعِنَ عَلَيْهِ]. (TA.)

6: see نَقَصَ, where two meanings are assigned to it.

8. انتقص: see نَقَصَ. — انتقصهُ: see نَقَصَهُ, in four places. — See also 5, in two places.

10. استنقص الثَّمَنَ *He* (the buyer, Ṣ) *asked, demanded*, or *desired, a diminution, a lessening, a lowering*, or *an abatement, of the price*. (Ṣ, A, Ḳ.) — See also 5.

نَقْصٌ: see 1. — [Used as a subst., *Loss*, or *loss of somewhat, decrease, a state of diminution* or *lessening* or *washing* or *waning, defect, defectiveness, deficiency, incompleteness*, or *imperfection, after wholeness* or *completeness*, or *perfectness*; as also ▼ نُقْصَانٌ; and ▼ مَنْقَصَةٌ signifies the same as نَقْصٌ] as here rendered, agreeably with the explanation (i. e. of منقصة) in the PṢ., which is كَمِىٌ: or, accord. to the A, مَنْقَصَةٌ seems to be syn. with نَقِيصَةٌ in the sense assigned to this last in the Ṣ, or in certain senses assigned to it in the Ḳ, which see below; and thus to be more restricted in application than نَقْصٌ]. (Ṣ, TA.) — *Weakness of intellect*: (M, TA:) and *weakness* with respect to religion and intellect. (TA.) You say, دَخَلَ عَلَيْهِ نَقْصٌ فِى دِينِهِ وَعَقْلِهِ [*There came upon him a weakness in his religion and his intellect*]: but one should not say ▼ نُقْصَانٌ [in this case]: (Ḳ:) app. because النَّقْصُ is "weakness;" whereas النُّقْصَانُ is only "a going away [of part of a thing] after [its having been in] a state of completeness." (TA.)

نُقْصَانٌ: see 1: — see also نَقْصٌ, in two places. — It also signifies *The quantity that is gone*, or *lost, of a thing that is decreased* or *diminished* or *lessened*. (Lth, A, Ḳ.) You say, نُقْصَانُهُ كَذَا وَكَذَا *The quantity that is gone*, or *lost, of it is such and such*. (TḲ.)

نَقِيصَةٌ: see 1. — *A defect, an imperfection, a fault, a vice*, or *the like*; syn. عَيْبٌ: (Ṣ, TA:)

or *a low,* or *base, quality, property, natural disposition, practice, habit,* or *action;* (Ḳ, TA;) of a man: (TA:) or *a weak quality, &c.:* (IDrd, Ḳ, TA:) but the attribution of weakness to a quality, &c., requires consideration: and it seems that what is meant by lowness, or baseness, is what leads to نَقْص: (TA:) [مَنْقَصَةٌ ♦, also, accord. to the A, seems to be syn. with نَقِيصَةٌ in one or another of the senses explained above; but its primary signification is probably *a cause of* نَقْص, like as that of مَبْخَلَةٌ is a cause of بُخْل, and that of مَجْبَنَةٌ a cause of جُبْن: the pl. of نَقِيصَةٌ is نَقَائِصُ: and that of مَنْقَصَةٌ is مَنَاقِصُ.] You say, مَا فِيهِ نَقِيصَةٌ and ♦ مَنْقَصَةٌ [*There is not in him any defect, imperfection, fault,* or *vice, &c.*]: and فُلَانٌ ذُو نَقَائِصَ and مَنَاقِصَ [*Such a one has defects, &c.*]. (A, TA.) — As a subst. from تَنَقَّصَهُ and اِنْتَقَصَهُ and اِسْتَنْقَصَهُ, [or, accord. to IḲṭṭ, as an inf. n. from نَقِصَ, and therefore from نَقَصَهُ also, (see 5,)] it signifies The *attributing* to a man *defect,* or *imperfection:* (M:) the *attributing* or *imputing* to men, *charging* them *with,* or *accusing* them *of, vices, faults,* or *the like; censuring* them; *reproaching* them; *speaking against* them; *impugning* their *characters.* (Ḳ.) A poet says,

* فَلَوْ غَيْرُ أَخْوَالِى أَرَادُوا نَقِيصَتِى *
* جَعَلْتُ لَهُمْ فَوْقَ العَرَانِينِ مِيسَمَا *

[*But if others than my maternal uncles had desired to attribute to me defect, &c., I had set a brand upon them above the noses*]. (M, TA.)

نَاقِصٌ act. part. n. of 1. — دِرْهَمٌ نَاقِصٌ signifies *A dirhem deficient in weight;* (Mṣb;) *light and deficient:* and نُقَّصٌ occurs as pl. of ناقص thus applied, agreeably with analogy. (Mgh.) — [Hence, فِعْلٌ نَاقِصٌ meaning *An incomplete,* i. e. *a non-attributive, verb:* opposed to فِعْلٌ تَامٌّ.]

مَنْقَصَةٌ: pl. مَنَاقِصُ: see نَقِيصَةٌ, in four places: — and see also نَقْصٌ.

مَنْقُوصٌ pass. part. n. of نَقَصَهُ. (A, Ḳ.)

نقض

1. نَقَضَهُ, (M, Mgh, Mṣb,) aor. ـُ, (M, Mṣb, TA,) inf. n. نَقْضٌ, (Ṣ, M, A, Mgh, Mṣb, Ḳ,) *He undid it; took it;* or *pulled it, to pieces: untwisted it: unravelled it: unwove it: dissolved it: broke it:* or *rendered it uncompact, unsound,* or *unfirm,: after having made it compact, sound,* or *firm:* (JK, M, A, Mṣb, Ḳ, TA:) namely a building, or structure: and a rope, or cord: (Ṣ, A, Mgh, Mṣb, Ḳ, TA:) and silk, or flax: (TA:) and cloth: (L:) and ‡ a compact, contract, or covenant; (Ṣ, A, Mṣb, Ḳ, TA;) and † a sale: (Mgh:) and † other things; (A, Ḳ, TA;) such as † an affair, or a case; and † the state of a place through which the invasion of an enemy is feared: (TA:) *contr. of* أَبْرَمَهُ, (M, A, Ḳ, TA,) as relating to a building or structure, and to a rope or cord, (A, Ḳ, TA,) and to a compact or contract or covenant, &c.: (Ḳ, TA:) or *i. q.* حَلَّ بَرْمَهُ, as relating to a rope or cord, and to a compact or contract or covenant: (Mṣb:) or *i. q.* هَدَمَهُ, as relating to a building or structure: (TA:) or the inf. n. signifies إِفْسَادُ مَا أَبْرَمْتَ, as relating to a building or structure, (JK, TA,) and to a rope or cord, (JK,) and to a compact or contract or covenant. (TA.) [It is said in the Ḳ, that النَّقْضُ is the contr. of الإِبْرَامُ, like الاِنْتِقَاضُ and التَّنَاقُضُ: but this is a glaring mistake; and seems to be a corruption of the following passage in the M: النَّقْضُ ضِدُّ الإِبْرَامِ نَقَضَهُ يَنْقُضُهُ نَقْضًا وَٱنْتَقَضَ وَتَنَاقَضَ, which is meant to indicate that انتقض and تناقض are quasi-passives of نَقَضَهُ: and in like manner, the passage in the A, النَّقْضُ فِى البِنَآءِ وَالحَبْلِ وَغَيْرِهِ ضِدُّ الإِبْرَامِ وَٱنْتَقَضَ وَتَنَقَّضَ, indicates that انتقض and تنقّض are quasi-passives of نَقَضَهُ. Further, it should be observed that نَقَضَهُ, as relating to a building, is not well explained by هَدَمَهُ; for you say, نَقَضَ البِنَآءَ مِنْ غَيْرِ هَدْمٍ, (mentioned in the Ṣ and A, &c., in art. قوض,) meaning *He took to pieces the building without demolishing,* or *destroying.*] — [Hence,] نَقَضَ فُلَانٌ وَتْرَهُ [lit. *Such a one undid,* or *untwisted, his bow-string*]; meaning ‡ *such a one took,* or *had taken, his blood-revenge.* (A, TA.) And الدَّهْرُ ذُو نَقْضٍ وَإِمْرَارٍ [lit. *Time,* or *fortune, has a property of untwisting and twisting tightly*]; meaning ‡ *that which time,* or *fortune,* [as it were] *twists tightly,* [or *makes firm,*] *it,* at another time, [as it were] *untwists,* or *undoes.* (TA.) And نَقَضْتُ مَا أَبْرَمَهُ ‡ *I annulled* [*what he confirmed,* or *made firm*]. (Mṣb.) And يَنْقُضُ عَلَيْهِ ‡ [*He undoes,* or *annuls,* or *contradicts, what he* (another) *has said*]; said of a poet replying to another poet. (Lth, A, Ḳ.) — نقض السقف, [i. e., app., نَقَضَ السَّقْفِ,] also signifies تحريك خشبه [i. e. تَحْرِيكُ خَشَبِهِ, The *moving,* or *shaking, of the pieces of wood,* or *rafters, of the roof*]. (TA. [But perhaps the phrase to be explained is ♦ نَقَّضَ السَّقْفُ, and the explanation, correctly, تَحَرَّكَ خَشَبُهُ, i. e. *The pieces of wood,* or *rafters, of the roof moved,* or *shook,* (for this, I am informed, is agreeable with modern usage,) app. *so as to produce a sound:* see also 5.]) — See also 4.

2: see 4, in two places: — and 5; and see 1, next before the last break.

3. المُنَاقَضَةُ فِى القَوْلِ is ‡ The *saying that which is contradictory in its meaning* [or *meanings;* as though one of its meanings undid, or annulled, the other]: (Ṣ,* Ḳ, TA:) from نَقْضُ البِنَآءِ: and meaning ‡ the *contending with another in words,* [or *in contradiction,*] *each rebutting what the other said.* (TA.) You say, نَاقَضَهُ فِى الشَّىْءِ, inf. n. مُنَاقَضَةٌ and نِقَاضٌ, ‡ *He contradicted him in,* or *respecting, the thing.* (M, TA.*) And قُلْتُ لَهُ نِقَاضًا ‡ *I contradicted him with respect to his saying, and his satirizing of me.* (M, TA.) And ناقض أَحَدُ الشَّاعِرَيْنِ الآخَرَ ‡ [*One of the two poets contradicted the other*]. (A.) And ناقض قَوْلُهُ الثَّانِى الأَوَّلَ ‡ [*His second saying contradicted the first*]. (A, TA.) And ناقض آخِرُ قَوْلِهِ الأَوَّلَ ‡ [*The last part of his saying contradicted the first*]. (Mgh.) [See also 6.]

4. انقض الكَمْأَةَ, (M, Ḳ, TA,) and انقض عَنْهَا, (M, TA,) *He removed the crust of earth from over the truffles:* (M:) or *he extracted,* or *took forth, the truffles from the earth.* (Ḳ, TA.) — انقض الكَمْءُ *The crusts of earth broke up* (تَقَلْفَعَتْ) *from over the truffle;* as also ♦ نَقَّضَ. (M, TA.) [See also 5.] — انقضت الأَرْضُ *The earth showed* [or *put forth*] *its plants,* or *herbage.* (M, TA.) — انقض also signifies *It produced, made, gave, emitted,* or *uttered, a sound, noise, voice,* or *cry:* (Ṣ, M, Ḳ, TA:) and [particularly] *a slight sound like what is termed* نَقْرٌ: (Ṣ, TA:) said of a joint of a man, (M, Ḳ,) and of the fingers [when their joints are made to crack], and of the ribs, (A,) [see also 5,] and of a camel's saddle, (A, TA,) and of a cupping-instrument when the cupper sucks it, (TA,) [&c., (see نَقِيضٌ,)] and of an eagle, (Ṣ, M, Ḳ,) and of a hen (Ṣ, A) on the occasion of her laying eggs, (A,) and of a chicken, (M, A, Ḳ,) and of an ostrich, and of a quail, and of a hawk, and of a scorpion, and of a frog, and of the [kind of lizard called] وَزَغ, and of the وَبْر [or Syrian hyrax], (M, Ḳ,) and of a young camel, the sounds of which are denoted by إِنْقَاضٌ and كَتِيتٌ, as those of a camel advanced in age are by قَرْقَرَةٌ and هَدِيرٌ: (Ṣ:) or إِنْقَاضٌ relates to animate things; and ♦ نَقْضٌ, inf. n. of نَقَضَ, aor. ـُ and ـِ, to inanimate things. (M, Ḳ.) [Accord. to the A, whether said of animate things or of inanimate, it is proper, not tropical; but accord. to what is said in the TA voce نَقِيضٌ, it is properly said of animate things, and tropically of inanimate; though, if any such distinction exist, the reverse seems to me to be more probable.] — You say also, انقض بِالدَّابَّةِ, (Ḳ,) or بِالحِمَارِ, (Lth,) or, as Aṣ says, (M, TA,) بِالعَيْرِ, (M,) or بِالبَعِيرِ, (TA,) and بِالفَرَسِ, (M, TA,) *He made a sound to the beast of carriage,* (M, Ḳ,) or *to the ass,* (Lth, Aṣ, M,) or *to the camel,* (Aṣ, TA.) and *to*

the horse, (Aṣ, M, TA,) *at the two sides of his tongue, after making it cleave to the roof of his mouth,* (Lth, M, Ḳ, TA,) *without removing its extremity from its place,* (Lth, TA,) *in order to chide the beast:* (L:) or انقض بِهِ signifies *i. q.* نَقَّرَ بِهِ [q. v.]; (Aṣ, M, A, TA;) the object being a [camel such as is called] قَعُود; (A;) or whatever be the object. (Aṣ, M, TA.) And انقض بِالْمَعْزِ, (Ṣ, Ṣgh, Ḳ,) or بِالعَنْزِ, (M, A,) *He called the goats,* (Ṣ, Ṣgh, Ḳ,) or *the she-goat;* (M, A;) accord. to AZ, (Ṣ, Ṣgh,) or Ks. (M, L.) And انقض بِهِ *He made a sound to him like as when thou makest a smacking with the tongue to a sheep* or *goat,* [in the TA, كما تنقر الشاة, for which I read كَمَا تَنْقُرُ بِالشَّاةِ,] *deeming him ignorant.* (TA.) And *He made a clapping to him with one of his hands upon the other, so as to cause a* [*sound such as is termed*] نَقِيض *to be heard.* (El-Khaṭṭábee.) — انقض أَصَابِعَهُ (M, A, Ḳ) *He made a sound, or sounds,* [app. *a cracking of the joints,*] *with his fingers:* (M:) [and so ↓ نَقَّضَهَا, inf. n. تَنْقِيض: (see فَرْقَعَ:)] or *he struck with his fingers in order that they might make a sound,* or *sounds:* (Ḳ:) if it mean cracking of the joints (فَرْقَعَة), it is disapproved; but if clapping, it is not. (TA.) And انقض العِلْكَ *He caused the* [*kind of gum called*] علك *to make a sound,* or *sounds;* [i. e., in chewing it, as many women do;] the doing of which is disapproved. (Ṣ, L, Ḳ. [But in the Ṣ and L, it said that إِنْقَاضُ العِلْكِ signifies تَصْوِيتُهُ, which does not necessarily indicate that the former verb is transitive.]) — Hence, (Ṣ, M, TA,) انقض الحِمْلُ ظَهْرَهُ (Ṣ, M, A, Mṣb, Ḳ*) *The load made his back to sound by reason of its weight:* (M:) or *pressed heavily upon him,* (Ṣ, M, Mṣb, Ḳ,) *so that his back was heard to make a sound such as is termed* نَقِيض; (M, Ḳ;* i. e. *the sound of the camel's saddle when it becomes infirm by reason of the weight of the load;* (Bḍ, xciv. 3;) or *a slight sound, as when a man makes a smacking with his tongue* (يُنْقِضُ) *to his ass, in driving him:* (TA:) or *oppressed his back by its weight:* (Mṣb:) or *rendered him lean, or emaciated;* جَعَلَهُ نِقْضًا, i. e. مَهْزُولًا. (Ibn-'Arafeh, Ḳ.) Thus in the phrase اَلَّذِى أَنْقَضَ ظَهْرَكَ, (Ṣ, M, Ḳ,) in [xciv. 3, of] the Ḳur. (Ṣ, M.)

5. تنقّض: see 8. — تنقّضت الأَرْضُ عَنِ الكَمْأَةِ *The earth clave, or cracked, or burst, from over the truffles;* (Ṣ, A,* TA;) syn. تَفَطَّرَتْ. (Ṣ, TA.) In all the copies of the Ḳ, we find تنقّض الدَّمُ, explained by تَقَطَّرَ; [as though meaning *The blood was made to drop, drip,* or *fall in drops;*] but how likely is this to be a mistranscription. (TA.) [The right reading of the phrase is probably تنقّض الكَرْمُ; and of the explanation, تَفَطَّرَ; and if so, the phrase is like أَنْقَضَ الكَرْمُ, and نَقَّضَ, explained above: see 4, second sentence.] — تنقّض البَيْتُ *The house,* or *chamber, became cleft,* or *cracked, in several places, so as to cause a sound to be heard.* (Ḳ, TA.) And تنقّض is also said of a building, [app. in the same sense,] like ↓ نَقَّضَ. (TA.) [See نَقَّضَ السَّقْفُ, in 1, next before the last break.] You say also, تنقّضت عِظَامُهُ ‡ *His bones made a sound* [app. *in being broken*]. (IF, Ḳ, TA.) [See also 4.]

6. تناقض: see 8. — تَنَاقُضٌ also signifies ‡ *Mutual contradiction,* or *repugnancy;* contr. of تَوَافُقٌ. (O, TA.) You say, فِى كَلَامِهِ تَنَاقُضٌ (A, Mgh, Mṣb, TA,) ‡ [*In his speech is contradiction,* or *repugnancy, between different parts;*] *one part of his speech necessarily implies the annulment of another part;* (Mṣb;) *his second saying contradicted* (نَاقَضَ) *his first.* (TA.) And تَنَاقَضَ القَوْلَانِ, (A, Mgh,) or الكَلَامَانِ, (Mṣb,) ‡ *The two sayings,* or *sentences, contradicted each other;* or *were mutually repugnant;* as though each undid the other; (Mṣb;) [*they annulled each other.*] And تناقض الشَّاعِرَانِ ‡ [*The two poets contradicted each other.*] (A, TA.) And تناقض مَعْنَاهُ ‡ *Its meaning was contradictory.* (Ṣ,* Ḳ, TA.) — [It is also used transitively:] you say, تَنَاقَضَا البَيْعَ † *They two mutually dissolved the sale:* as though compared with the saying تَرَاءَوُا الهِلَالَ, meaning "they [together] saw the new moon;" and تَدَاعَوُا القَوْمَ, meaning "they [together] called the people;" and تَسَاءَلُوهُمْ, meaning "they [together] asked them;" notwithstanding that تناقض is [properly] intransitive. (Mgh.) And تَنَاقَضُوا عُهُودَهُمْ † [*They mutually dissolved,* or *broke, their compacts, contracts,* or *covenants*]. (T, voce تناكثوا.)

8. انتقض quasi-pass. of نَقَضَهُ [*It became undone; taken,* or *pulled to pieces: untwisted: unravelled: unwoven: dissolved; broken:* or *rendered uncompact, unsound,* or *infirm, after it had been made compact, sound,* or *firm*]: (M, A, Mgh, Mṣb, TA:) as also ↓ تنقّض, (A,) and ↓ تناقض: (M, TA:) [respecting the first and last, see a remark upon a mistake in the Ḳ, following the first sentence in 1: but انتقض afterwards occurs in the Ḳ used properly in the phrase مَا ٱنْتَقَضَ مِنَ البُنْيَانِ *i. q.* اِنْتَكَثَ: (Ṣ:)] said of a building, or structure: and of a rope, or cord: (A, Mgh, Mṣb, TA:) [and of silk, or flax: and of cloth: (see 1:)] and ‡ of a compact, contract, or covenant: (TA:) [and of a sale: (see 1:)] and ‡ of other things. (A, TA.) — [Hence,] انتقضت القَرْحَةُ ‡ *The wound,* or *ulcer, became recrudescent.* (IF,* A.) And انتقض الجُرْحُ بَعْدَ بُرْئِهِ † *The wound became in a bad,* or *corrupt, state, after its healing.* (Mṣb.) And انتقض الأَمْرُ بَعْدَ ٱلْتِئَامِهِ (A,* Mṣb, TA) ‡ *The affair,* or *case, became in a bad,* or *unsound state, after it had been in a sound state.* (Mṣb.) And انتقض أَمْرُ الثَّغْرِ بَعْدَ سَدِّهِ † [*The state of the place through which the invasion of an enemy was feared became unfortified, after its being fortified,* or *closed*]. (TA.) And انتقضت الطَّهَارَةُ † *The state of purity became annulled.* (Mṣb.) And انتقض عَلَيْهِ الشِّعْرُ ‡ [*The poetry became undone, annulled,* or *contradicted, by a reply against him:* see يَنْقُضُ عَلَيْهِ]. (A, TA.)

11. انقاضّ *It* (a wall) *cracked, without falling down;* like إِنْقَضَّ. (Ḳ in art. قض.) See also إِنْقَاضَ, in art. قيض.]

نُقْض: see نِقْض, in two places.

نِقْض *i. q.* ↓ مَنْقُوض [*Undone; taken,* or *pulled, to pieces: untwisted: unravelled: unwoven: dissolved; broken:* &c. (see 1:)] (Ṣ, Mgh, Mṣb, Ḳ:) like نِكْثٌ (Ṣ, TA) in the sense of مَنْكُوثٌ: (TA:) as also ↓ نُقْض; (Mgh, Mṣb;) and ↓ نَقْض: (Ṣgh:) but El-Ghooree allows only the first: (Mgh:) Az, however, mentions only the second; (Mṣb;) which signifies as above, applied to a building, or structure; (M, Mgh;) or *what has become taken, or pulled, to pieces,* (مَا ٱنْتَقَضَ,) *of a building,* or *structure;* (Ḳ;) as also the first: (TA:) or نِقْض signifies مَا نَقَضْتَ *what thou hast undone; taken,* or *pulled, to pieces; untwisted;* &c.]: (M:) and *what is undone, of* [*the stuff of the tents called*] أَخْبِيَة, *and of* [*the garments called*] أَكْسِيَة, *and twisted a second time;* (M, Ḳ;) as also ↓ نُقْض; (Ḳ;) and ↓ نُقَاضَةٌ: (L:) or this last signifies *what is undone of a hair-rope:* (Ṣ, O, Ḳ:) the pl. of نِقْض is أَنْقَاضٌ [a pl. of pauc.], (M,) and of the same, (Mṣb,) or of ↓ نُقْض, (Mgh, Mṣb,) نُقُوضٌ. (Mgh, Mṣb.) — ‡ *Emaciated,* or *rendered lean,* (Ṣ, M, Ḳ,) *by travel;* (Ṣ, Ḳ;) *upon which one has journeyed time after time:* (O:) Seer says, *as though travel had unknit its frame;* (M, TA;) thus indicating it to be tropical: (TA:) applied to a male camel, (Ṣ, M, Ḳ,) and to a horse, (M.) and to a female camel, (Ṣ, Ḳ,) or the female is termed نِقْضَةٌ: (M, Ḳ:) pl. أَنْقَاضٌ, (Sb, Ṣ, Ḳ,) only, (Sb, M,) both of the masc. and fem.; in the latter, the ة being imagined to be elided; (M;) and نَقَائِضُ is [also said to be] a pl. of نِقْض signifying *jaded,* applied to a she-camel. (So in a copy of the Ṣ in art. نقس.) — [See an ex. in a verse cited voce سَدٌّ.] — The *place,* (Ṣ,) or *crust of earth,* (M, Ḳ,) that becomes broken from over truffles; (Ṣ, M, Ḳ;) for when they are about to come forth, they break asunder the surface of the earth: (O:) pl. [of pauc.] أَنْقَاض and [of mult.] نُقُوض. (M, Ḳ.) — Accord. to the Ḳ, *i. q.* نَقْض; but the latter is a mistranscription; (TA;) *Honey that has in it* [*worms of the kind called*] سُوس; *wherefore it is taken,* (M, Ḳ in art. نقض,) *and pounded,* (Ḳ, ubi supra,) *and the place of the bees is smeared* (يُلْطَخُ [in a copy of the M يُطْبَخُ, which is doubtless a mistranscription,]) *therewith, together with myrtle* (آس), *and the bees then come to it, and deposit their honey in it;* (M, Ḳ, ubi supra;) on the authority of El-Hejeree: (M:) or the *dung of bees in the place where they deposit their honey:* (IAạr, AḤn, Ḳ, ubi supra:) or the *bees that have died therein.* (Ṣgh, Ḳ, ubi supra.) ═ See also نَقِيض.

نَقَض: see نِقْض, in two places.

نَقِيض ‡ *A contradictor:* applied to a man: fem. with ة. (M, TA.) You say [also], ذَا نَقِيضُ ذَاكَ ‡ *This is a contradictor* [i. e. *the contrary*] *of that:* (A, TA:) [or *this is inconsistent with that:* for] النَّقِيضَانِ لَا يَجْتَمِعَانِ وَلَا يَرْتَفِعَانِ [*what are termed* نقيضان *cannot be coëxistent in the same thing, nor simultaneously nonexistent in the same thing*]; as existence itself and non-existence, and motion and rest. (Kull, pp. 231, 232.) You say also, هٰذِهِ قَصِيدَةٌ نَقِيضُ قَصِيدَةِ فُلَانٍ ‡ [*This poem is a contradictor of the poem of such a one*]. (A.) And النَّقِيضَةُ in poetry is ‡ *That by which one undoes or annuls or contradicts* [*what another poet has said*]: (Ṣ:) or نَقِيضَةُ الشِّعْرِ *consists in a poet's putting forth poetry, and another poet's undoing* or *annulling* or *contradicting it, by putting forth what is different therefrom:* (Lth, Ḳ,* TA:) the subst. is نَقِيض: [or rather this seems to be an epithet in which the quality of a subst. is predominant, and syn. with نَقِيضَة:] and the act of the two is termed مُنَاقَضَة ▼: the pl. of نَقِيضَة is نَقَائِض: (TA:) you speak of the نَقَائِض of Jereer and El-Farezdaḳ. (A, TA.) ═ *A sound, noise, voice,* or *cry;* (Lth, Ṣ, M, O, Ḳ;) as also نَقْض ▼ accord to the Ḳ; but this is an enormous error: (TA:) the former, of the joints (Lth, M, Ḳ) of a man, (M,) [a meaning also assigned to نقض in the Ḳ,] and of the fingers, and of the ribs, (Lth, M, A,) and of camels' saddles, (Ṣ, Ḳ,) or of a camel's saddle, (M, O, Ḳ, [but in CḲ, for الرَّحْل, we find الرِّجْل, the foot,]) and of camels' litters, (Ṣ, Ḳ,) and of tanned skins, (Ḳ,) or of a tanned skin, (M,) and of a bow-string, (M, Ḳ,) and of نِسْع [q. v.] (O, Ḳ,) when new, (O,) and of the sucking of a cupping-instrument; (Ḳ;) [in all these senses said in the TA to be tropical; but see 4;] and also the former, (Ṣ, M, TA,) in the Ḳ, erroneously, the latter word, (TA,) of an eagle, (Ṣ, M, Ḳ,) and of chickens, and of an ostrich, and of a quail, and of a hawk, and of a scorpion, and of a frog, and of the [kind of lizard called] وَزَغ, and of the وَبْر [or Syrian hyrax; &c., see 4.] (M.)

نُقَاضَة: see نِقْض.

نَقِيضَة: see نَقِيض.

مَنْقُوض: see نِقْض.

مُنَاقَضَة: see نَقِيض.

مُنْتَقِض *i. q.* مُتَرَيِّع, [*Refraining,*] see art. ريع.

نقط

1. نَقَطَ الكِتَابَ, (Ṣ, Mṣb,) or الحَرْفَ, (Ḳ,) aor. ـُ, inf. n. نَقْط, (Ṣ, Mṣb,) *He pointed,* or *dotted,* [*the book,* or *writing,* or] *the letter,* or *word, with the diacritical points* or *point;* and *with the syllabical points* or *point, by which are shown the pronunciation and division of syllables and the desinential syntax;* syn. أَعْجَمَهُ; as also نَقَّطَهُ ▼, inf. n. تَنْقِيط: (Ḳ:) and نقّط ▼ المَصَاحِفَ, [*he so pointed the copies of the Ḳur-án.*] (Ṣ.)

2: see 1, in two places. — نقّط ثَوْبَهُ بِالزَّعْفَرَانِ وَالمِدَادِ, inf. n. تَنْقِيط, [*He made specks,* or *small spots, upon his garment, with saffron, and ink;*] (Lth;) and نقط عَلَى ثَوْبِهِ [signifies the same]. (A, TA, in art. رقط.) And نَقَّطَتِ المَرْأَةُ وَجْهَهَا وَخَدَّهَا بِالسَّوَادِ تَتَحَسَّنُ بِذٰلِكَ [*The woman made specks,* or *small spots, upon her face, with black, beautifying herself thereby*]. (TA.)

5. تنقّط [quasi-pass. of 2; *It became pointed,* &c. — And hence,] ‡ *It* (a place) *became scattered with spots,* or *portions, of herbage.* (Ḳ, TA.)

نَقْطَة inf. n. un. of 1, [*A single act of pointing,* &c.] (Mṣb.)

نُقْطَة *A diacritical point* of a letter or word: *a syllabical point* thereof: see 1:] (Ḳ:) [*a point, dot, speck, speckle,* or *small spot: a mathematical point;* i. e.] the *extremity of a line:* (TA:) pl. نُقَط (Ṣ Mṣb, Ḳ,) and نِقَاط. (AZ, Ṣ, Ḳ.) Hence, one says, مَا ٱخْتَلَفَا فِى نُقْطَةٍ *They two did not differ respecting* so small a thing as *a point* of a letter or word. (TA.) And [hence] the vulgar say, when they admire one, هُوَ نُقْطَةٌ فِى مُصْحَفٍ † [*He is like a point,* or *stop, in a copy of the Ḳur-án;* because the stops in the Ḳur-án are generally ornamented, and often very beautifully, with gold and colours]. (TA.) — † [*Any very small thing, that may be likened to a point, dot,* or *speck.* Hence,] 'Alee is related to have said, العِلْمُ نُقْطَةٌ إِنَّمَا كَثَّرَهَا الجَاهِلُونَ † [*Science,* or *knowledge, is a very small thing: only the ignorant have made it to be much*]. (TA.) And you say, أَعْطَاهُ نُقْطَةً مِنْ عَسَلٍ ‡ [*He gave him a drop,* or *very small quantity, of honey*]. (TA.) — ‡ [*A portion* of a thing, or *some* of a number of things, *in a separate,* or *scattered, state, here and there.*] You say, مَا بَقِىَ مِنْ أَمْوَالِهِمْ إِلَّا نُقْطَةٌ ‡ *There remained not of their possessions* [aught] *save some palm-trees and a portion of seed-produce here and there.* (IAạr, TA.) And نُقَطٌ مِنْهُ, and فِى الأَرْضِ نِقَاطٌ مِنَ الكَلَإِ, ‡ *In the land are scattered spots,* or *portions, of herbage.* (Ḳ,* TA.) — † *A thing; an affair; a matter; a case; an event; an action.* (TA.)

نُقَيْطَة dim. of نُقْطَة. (TA.)

نَقَّاط *One who points copies of the Ḳur-án &c.;* i. e. *adds the diacritical and other points.* (Ṣ,* TA.)

كِتَابٌ مَنْقُوطٌ (Mṣb, TA) *A book,* or *writing, pointed with the diacritical,* or *other, points.* (TA.)

[نقع, &c.

See Supplement.]

نكأ

1. نَكَأَ القَرْحَةَ, (Ṣ, Ḳ,) inf. n. نَكْءٌ, (Ṣ,) *He peeled off the scab from the sore* (Ṣ, Ḳ,) *before it was healed, and it became moist in consequence.* (Ḳ.) [See also نَكَى.] ═ نَكَأَ العَدُوَّ, and فِى العَدُوِّ, dial. form of نَكَى [q. v.]. (Ḳ.) By some rejected. (TA.) ═ نَكَأَهُ حَقَّهُ (like زَكَأَهُ, TA), inf. n. نَكْءٌ, *He paid him his due.* (Ḳ.) — هُنِّئْتَ وَلَا تُنْكَأْ, (Ṣ,) and تُنْكَ, (TA,) and تُنْكَهْ (Ṣ, for تُنْكَ or تُنْكَأْ, TA), *Mayest thou be made to have enjoyment in that which thou hast received, and not experience pain!* (Ṣ.) *Mayest thou gain what is good, and may harm not befall thee!* (T:) or, with the latter of the two verbs without ء (تنك), *may God not make thee discomfited!* (AHeyth, L.) [Accord. to AHeyth, as mentioned in the TA, the latter verb in this proverb is written تُنْكَهْ and تَنْكَهْ; but the right reading is doubtless تُنْكَ and تُنْكَهْ: this is shown by the explanation there following.]

8. انتكأت القَرْحَةُ *The scab peeled off from the sore before it was healed, and it became moist in consequence.* (A, TA.) ═ انتكأ مِنْهُ حَقَّهُ (like ازدكأ, TA) *He received from him his due.* (Ḳ, TA.)

نُكَأَةٌ and زُكَأَةٌ *One who pays his debts, and does not put off.* (Ḳ.) ═ نُكَأَةُ الطُّرْثُوثِ, and نُكَأَةٌ, dial. form of نُكَعَة [q. v.]. (Ḳ.)

نكب

1. نَكَبَ عَنْهُ, aor. ـُ, inf. n. نُكُوبٌ (Ṣ, Ḳ) and نَكْبٌ; and نَكِبَ, aor. ـَ, inf. n. نَكَبٌ; (M, L, Ḳ;)

and ▼ تنكّب, (inf. n. تَنْكِيبٌ, TA;) and ▼ تنكّب; (Ḳ;) *He deviated, or turned aside, or away, from it,* (Ḳ,) from the road, (Ṣ,) or from another thing. (TA.) [You say] ▼ نكّبهُ الطَّرِيقَ, (الطريق being put in the accus. case, inf. n. تَنْكِيبٌ, TA,) and نكّب بِهِ [عَنِ الطريقِ], *He deviated, or turned aside, or away, with him from the road; led him, or caused him to turn, aside, or away, from the road.* (Ḳ.) — [So] ▼ نكّبه, inf. n. تَنْكِيبٌ, *He turned aside, or away, from him, and separated himself from him.* (Ṣ.) — ▼ تنكّبه *He went, or turned, aside, or away, or apart, from him; avoided him; went, or removed, to a distance, from him.* (Ṣ.) — ▼ تنكّب عَنَّا *He turned aside, or away, from us.* (TA.) — نَكَبَ عَنْ طَرِيقٍ, and ▼ نكّب عَنِ الصَّوَابِ, aor. ـُ, inf. n. نُكُوبٌ; and ▼ نكّب عن الصواب; † *He deviated from the right course of action &c.* (Az.) — نَكَبَتِ الرِّيحُ, aor. ـُ, inf. n. نُكُوبٌ, *The wind blew obliquely, in a direction between [the directions of] two [cardinal] winds.* (Ḳ.) See نَكْبَاءُ. ═ نَكَبَ, aor. ـُ, inf. n. نَكْبٌ, *He threw, cast, or flung.* (Ḳ, TA.) — نَكَبَ بِهِ *He threw him down* (Ḳ) عَلَى الأَرْضِ *upon the ground.* (TA.) — نَكَبَهُ الدَّهْرُ, aor. ـُ, inf. n. نَكْبٌ and نَكْبٌ, † *Fortune overcame him, or afflicted him: or smote him with an evil accident, a disaster, an affliction, or a calamity.* (Ḳ.) — نُكِبَ † *He was overcome, or afflicted, by fortune: or was smitten by fortune with an evil accident, a disaster, or the like.* (Ṣ, TA.) See نَكْبَةٌ. — نَكَبَ الإِنَاءَ, (aor. ـُ, inf. n. نَكْبٌ, TA,) *He [threw down, i.e.] poured out the contents of the vessel:* (Ḳ:) but only said of what is not fluid; as dust and the like. (TA.) — نَكَبَ كِنَانَتَهُ, inf. n. as above, *He inverted, or inclined, his quiver,* (Ṣ,) *so as to pour out the arrows contained in it:* (TA:) or *he scattered the contents of his quiver.* (Ḳ.) [See also نَكَتَ.] — نَكَبَتْهُ الحِجَارَةُ, aor. ـُ, inf. n. نَكْبٌ, *The stones wounded him, and made him bleed, [in the foot].* (Ṣ.) نكبت الحجارة رِجْلَهُ *The stones wounded his foot, and made it bleed: or hit, or struck, or hurt, it.* (Ḳ.) النَّكْبُ is when a stone wounds, &c., a nail, a hoof, or a camel's foot. (TA.) — نُكِبَتْ إِصْبَعُهُ *His toe was hit, or hurt, by the stones.* (TA.) ═ نَكِبَ, aor. ـَ, inf. n. نَكَبٌ, *He (a camel) had a disease in the shoulder-joint, or in the shoulder-blade, and in consequence halted.* (Ṣ.) See نَكَبٌ. — نَكِبَ, aor. ـَ, inf. n. نَكَبٌ, *He (a man) had a pain in his shoulder-joint.* (TA.) ═ نَكَبَ عَلَى قَوْمِهِ, aor. ـُ, inf. n. نِكَابَةٌ (Ṣ) and نُكُوبٌ, (Lḥ, Ḳ,) ‡ *He was, or acted as,* مَنْكِبٌ *over his people:* (Ṣ, Ḳ:) or *was* عَرِيف *over them.* (M.)

2. نكّبه, inf. n. تَنْكِيبٌ, *He removed, or put aside, or away, or out of the way, him, or it.* Thus it is both trans. and intrans. (Ḳ.) See 1. — نَكِّبْهُ عَنَّا *Put him away from us; put him out of our way.* (TA.)

5. تنكّب (Ṣ, Ḳ) and ▼ انتكب (Ḳ) *He threw* his bow, (Ṣ, Ḳ,) or his quiver, (Ḳ,) *upon his shoulder; he shouldered it.* (Ṣ, Ḳ.) — تنكّب عَلَى قَوْسٍ *He leaned upon a bow:* and, in like manner, upon a staff. (TA, from a trad.) ═ See 1.

8: see 5.

نَكْبٌ *i. q.* نَكْبَاءُ, q. v. — See also نَكْبَةٌ.

نَكَبٌ *An inclining* in a thing: (Ṣ:) or *what resembles an inclining* in a thing. (M, Ḳ.) — *A halting* in a camel (ISd, Ḳ) *by reason of a pain in his shoulder-joint:* (ISd:) or *a disease which attacks camels in the shoulder-joints, in consequence of which they halt:* (Ṣ, Ḳ:) or only *in the shoulder-joint.* (El-Ádebbes, Ṣ, Ḳ.)

نَكْبَةٌ *A hurt [of the foot] by a stone, causing a bleeding: or a hit by a stone [upon the foot].* Ex. لَيْسَ دُونَ هٰذَا الأَمْرِ نَكْبَةٌ وَلَا ذُبَاحٌ *There is not in the way of the attainment of this thing a hurt [of the foot] by a stone, &c., nor a crack in the inside of the foot.* (IAạr, ISd.) [See also ذُبَاحٌ.] Hence نَكْبَةٌ in the sense immediately following. (TA.) — ‡ *A misfortune; an evil accident; a disaster; an affliction; a calamity:* (Ṣ, Ḳ, TA:) as also ▼ نَكْبٌ: (Ḳ:) pl. of the former نَكَبَاتٌ; (Ṣ;) and of the latter, نُكُوبٌ. (Ḳ.)

نُكْبَةٌ *A heap of corn, not measured nor weighed:* syn. صُبْرَةٌ. (Ḳ.)

نَكِيبٌ The *circuit* (دَائِرَة: in some copies of the Ṣ, دابرة: but this, as IḲṭṭ says, is a mistake; and the former is the correct word: TA) *of a hoof,* (Ṣ, Ḳ,) *and of a camel's foot.* (Ṣ.) See مَنْكُوبٌ.

أَنْكَبُ: see النَّكْبَاءُ.

نَاكِبٌ, and ▼ عَنْهُ, أَنْكَبُ عَنِ الحَقِّ, ‡ A man *deviating from the right course of action &c.* (A.) — نَكْبَاءُ [fem. of أَنْكَبُ] an epithet applied to *Any wind that blows obliquely, taking a direction between [the directions of] two [cardinal] winds:* (TA:) *a wind that blows obliquely, deviating from the direction whence blow the right* (القُوَّمُ) [or the cardinal]) *winds:* (Ṣ:) or *a [particular] wind that blows obliquely, and takes a direction between [the directions of] two [cardinal] winds;* (Ḳ;) which destroys the camels and sheep &c., and restrains the rain: (TA:) or *a wind that blows in a direction between that of the east, or easterly, wind,* (الصَّبَا,) *and that of the north, or northerly, wind,* (الشَّمَال): (AZ, Ḳ:) that between the south, or southerly, and east, or easterly, winds, being called جِرْبِيَاءُ: (AZ:) [but see this word, and see below:] or what are termed نُكْبُ الرِّيَاحِ [نُكْبٌ being pl. of نكباء] are four: (IAạr, Th, Ṣ, Ḳ:) namely, first, the نكباء الصَّبَا وَالجَنُوبِ *the wind that blows in a direction between that of the east, or easterly, and that of the south, or southerly, wind;* also called الأَزْيَبُ; (Ṣ, Ḳ;) which is a very thirsty wind, that dries up much the leguminous plants; but Eṭ-Ṭarábulusee, in the Kf, and Mbr and IF, assert that the ازيب is the جنوب; not its نكباء: (TA:) second, the نكباء الصَّبَا وَالشَّمَالِ *the wind that blows in a direction between that of the east, or easterly, and that of the north, or northerly, wind;* also called الصَّابِيَةُ, and called also ▼ النُّكَيْبَاءُ, (Ṣ, Ḳ,) a diminutive meant to convey the opposite of a diminutive sense; for they find this wind to be very cold; (Ṣ;) it is very boisterous and very cold; unattended by rain or by any good: (TA:) third, the نكباء الشَّمَالِ وَالدَّبُورِ *the wind that blows in a direction between that of the north, or northerly, and that of the west, or westerly, wind;* also called الجِرْبِيَاءُ; and termed نَيِّحَةُ الأَزْيَبِ *the opposite wind to the* ازيب; (Ṣ, Ḳ;) a cold wind; (Ṣ;) and sometimes attended by a little rain; but Ibn-El-Ajdábee asserts that the جربياء is the شمال: (TA:) fourth, the نكباء الجَنُوبِ وَالدَّبُورِ *the wind that blows in a direction between that of the south, or southerly, and that of the west, or westerly, wind;* also called الهَيْفُ; (in the CḲ, الهَيْفُ;) and termed نَيِّحَةُ النُّكَيْبَاءِ *the opposite wind to the* نكباء; (Ṣ, Ḳ;) a hot wind (Ṣ) and very thirsty. (TA.) Accord. to Ibn-Kubás, *the tract whence blows the* نكباء [by which he means only the wind that blows from the north-east or thereabout] *is that extending between the point where rises the* ذِرَاع [or the asterism composed of the stars α and β of Gemini, *E. 33° N., in central Arabia; or* α and β of Canis Minor, *E. 7° N., in the same latitude*] *and the pole-star:* and the tract between the pole-star and the point where sets the ذراع is the tract whence blows the شمال. Sh says, Each of the four [cardinal] winds has its نكباء, which is called in relation to it: that of the صبا is *that which is between it and the* شمال; [*blowing from the north-east, or thereabout;*] and it resembles it in gentleness; sometimes having sharpness, or vehemence; but this is seldom; only once in a long space of time: that of the شمال is *that which is between it and the* دبور; [*blowing from the north-west, or thereabout;*] and it resembles it in coldness: it is called الشَّمَالُ الشَّامِيَّةُ: each of them is called by the Arabs شَامِيَّةٌ: that of the دبور is *that which is between it and the* جنوب; *blowing from the point where sets* سُهَيْل [or *Canopus; i. e., S. 29° W., in the latitude of central Arabia*]; and it resembles it in its violence and boisterousness: and that of the جنوب

is that which is between it and the صبا; [blowing from the south-east, or thereabout;] and it is the wind most resembling it in its softness and in its gentleness in winter. (L.) The pl. of نكباء is نُكْبٌ, as shown above. (Ṣ, Ḳ &c.) [See also دَبُورٌ نكب — [.تبع in art. تَبُوعُ الشَّمْسِ [app. ♦ نَكْبٌ, originally an inf. n., used as an epithet, and therefore applicable without ة to a fem. noun] i.q. نَكْبَآءُ; [app., The نكباء of the دبور; a south-westerly wind]. (TA.) — أَنْكَبُ A camel having a disease in the shoulder-joint, or in the shoulder-blade, and in consequence halting: (Ṣ:) a camel that walks on one side, or inclining, or as though he walked on one side. (L.) — قَامَةٌ نَكْبَآءُ An inclining pulley: and قِيَمٌ نُكْبٌ inclining pulleys. (TA.) — أَنْكَبُ † Overpowering, or oppressive; unjust, or tyrannical. (Ṣ, TA.) — الدَّهْرُ أَنْكَبُ لَا يَلْبَثُ † Fortune abounds with evil accidents, or disasters, or afflictions, or calamities; i.e. it deviates much, or often, from the right course: it will not remain in one state: or, accord. to one relation, الدهر انكث الخ. A proverb. (TA.) — أَنْكَبُ A man not having with him a bow. (Ṣ, Ḳ.)

مَنْكِبٌ (masc., Lḥ, Ḳ) The shoulder; i.e. the place of junction of the os humeri and the scapula, (Ṣ, Ḳ,) in a man &c.; (ISd;) the place of junction of the os humeri and the scapula and the [tendon called] حَبْلُ العَاتِقِ, in a man and a bird and any other thing. (TA.) [It seems to be regarded by some as originally signifying "a place of deflection:" but] Sb denies its being a noun of place, because, were it so, it would be مَنْكَبٌ: he does not allow it to be included in the class of مَطْلِعٌ, because this is extr. Pl. مَنَاكِبُ. رَجُلٌ شَدِيدُ المَنَاكِبِ signifies A man having a strong shoulder: as though the sing. were applied to denote each part of the joint, and the pl. to denote the whole. (TA.) — هَزُّوا مَنَاكِبَهُمْ ‡ [They shook their shoulder-joints;] i.e., they rejoiced, or were joyful, or happy. (TA.) — خِيَارُكُمْ أَلْيَنُكُمْ مَنَاكِبَ فِى الصَّلَاةِ † [The best of you are the most easy of you in the shoulder-joints in prayer:] meaning, those of you who keep [most] still therein: or, as some say, those who [most readily] give room to such as enter the rank in prayer. (TA, from a trad.) — مَنْكِبُ الفَرَسِ The star β in Pegasus. (El-Ḳazweenee &c.) — مَنْكِبُ الجَوْزَآءِ The bright, and very great star, α, in the right shoulder-joint, of Orion. (El-Ḳazweenee &c.) — مَنْكِبٌ ‡ The side of anything; or a lateral, or an adjacent, part, quarter, or tract, thereof: (Ḳ:) pl. مَنَاكِبُ: ex. سِرْنَا فِى مَنْكِبٍ مِنَ الأَرْضِ We proceeded, or journeyed, along a side, or lateral part, of the land: and, in like manner, مِنَ الجَبَلِ of the mountain: (TA:) so in the Kur, lxvii. 15, the pl. signifies the sides, &c., of the earth: (Fr:) or its roads, accord. to some: (TA:) or its mountains: (Zj:) which last signification in this case is preferred by Az: (TA:) or the sing. signifies an elevated place, or part, of the earth, or land. (Ṣ.) — المَنَاكِبُ ‡ The feathers next after the قَوَادِم; [which latter are the anterior, or primary, feathers of a bird's wing;] (Ḳ;) the feathers of the wing of a vulture or an eagle that are next after the قوادم, which are the strongest and most excellent of the feathers; (TA;) four [feathers] in the wing of a bird, next after the قوادم: (Ṣ:) [the four secondary feathers of the wing:] in the wing of a bird are twenty feathers: the first of them are those called القوادم; the next, المناكب; the next, الخَوَافِى; the next, الأَبَاهِر; the next, الكُلَى. (L.) It is a word without a sing. (Ḳ.) ISd says, I know not a sing. to it; but by analogy it should be مَنْكَبٌ. (TA.) — رَاشَ سَهْمَهُ بِمَنَاكِبَ ‡ He feathered his arrow with feathers such as are described above. (TA.) — مَنْكِبٌ ‡ i.q. عَرِيفٌ, i.e. The intendant, superintendent, &c., of a people: or an aider, helper, or assistant, of a people: (Ḳ:) or the assistant of an عريف: (Mṣb:) one below an عريف: (IAth:) or the chief of the عُرَفَآء [pl. of عريف]; (Lth, Ṣ;) there being over so many عرفاء a منكب: (Lth [see عَرِيفٌ:]) pl. مَنَاكِبُ. (TA.)

مِنْكَابٌ عَنِ الحَقِّ [† One who deviates much from the right course of action &c.] (TA.)

مَنْكُوبٌ and نَكِبٌ, accord. to the copies of the Ḳ, but the latter word is a mistake for ♦ نَكِيبٌ, Having the foot wounded, and made to bleed, by stones: or hit, or struck, or hurt, by stones. (Ḳ.) See 1. — مَنْكُوبٌ † Overcome or afflicted, by fortune: or smitten with an evil accident, or the like. (Ṣ, TA.) See نُكِبَ.

يَنْكُوبٌ [like يَحْمُورٌ in measure: in the CḲ, مَنْكُوبٌ:] A road deviating from the right course or direction. (Ḳ.)

نكت

1. نَكَتَ, aor. ـُ, inf. n. نَكْتٌ, (or نَكَتَ الأَرْضَ بِقَضِيبٍ, [&c.,] TA.) He struck the ground with a stick, (Ṣ, M, Ḳ,) or with his finger, (M,) so that it made a mark, or marks, upon it, (Ṣ, Ḳ,) with its extremity; an action of one reflecting, or meditating, and anxious. (TA.) [Thus our Saviour seems to have done in the case of the woman taken in adultery: see S. John viii. 6 and 8.] — Also, He struck the ground with pebbles. (TA.) — Hence, ‡ He reflected, or meditated, and talked to himself (TA, from a trad.) — نَكَتَ, aor. ـُ, (Ṣ, Ḳ,) inf. n. نَكْتٌ, (Ḳ,) He (a horse) bounded (نَبَا, Ṣ, Ḳ) from the ground, (Ṣ,) in running. (TA.) — نَكَتَهُ He threw it down upon the ground. (TA.) — نَكَتَ كِنَانَتَهُ He scattered the contents of his quiver. (TA.) See نكب. — طَعَنَهُ فَنَكَتَهُ He thrust him, or pierced him, and threw him down upon his head. (Aṣ, Ṣ, Ḳ.*) — نُكِتَ It (a cooked bone, containing marrow,) was struck with the edge of a cake of bread, or with some other thing, to cause the marrow to fall out. (TA.) نُكِتَ العَظْمُ The marrow of the bone was taken out, or extracted. (Aboo-'Ameythel.) Mentioned in art. نقت, q. v. (TA.) — نَكَتَ فِى كَلَامِهِ, and فِى قَوْلِهِ, [aor. ـُ, inf. n. نَكْتٌ ? (in the TA, the verb is written without the syll. points, but the form commonly known in the present day, and occurring in many late works, is ♦ نَكَّتَ, inf. n. تَنْكِيتٌ;) ‡ He made use of nice, or subtile, sayings, expressions, or allusions, such as are termed نُكَت, pl. of نُكْتَةٌ)]. (A.) — نَكَتَ فِى العِلْمِ بِمُوَافَقَةِ فُلَانٍ أَوْ مُخَالَفَةِ فُلَانٍ He alluded (أَشَارَ) [with respect to science, to the agreement of such a one, or the disagreement of such a one]. (L.)

2. نَكَّتَ الرُّطَبُ, inf. n. تَنْكِيتٌ, The dates began to ripen [and to become speckled]. (Mṣb.) — See 1.

8. انتكت He was thrown down upon his head; or fell down upon his head, having been thrust, or pierced. (Ṣ, Ḳ.*)

نَكْتٌ: see نُكْتَةٌ.

نُكْتَةٌ A point; a dot; a speck; a minute spot; i.q. نُقْطَةٌ: (Ṣ, Ḳ:) pl. نُكَتٌ, (Mṣb, &c.) agreeably with analogy, (TA,) and نِكَاتٌ, (Ḳ,) deviating from analogy, and, accord. to some, نُكَاتٌ, in which the ا is said to be added لِلْإِشْبَاعِ, or to render the sound of the fet-ḥah full, like رُخَالٌ: (TA:) the last of these pls. has been heard [from the classical Arabs]; (Esh-Shiháb, in the Expos. of the Shifá;) or it is vulgar. (Mṣb.) — نُكْتَةٌ [A small spot, or mark,] resembling dirt upon a mirror: (Ḳ:) نُكْتَةٌ سَوْدَآءُ A small [black] mark, like a spot, or dot, resembling dirt upon a mirror or a sword or the like. (L, from a trad.) — نُكْتَةٌ [A spot in the eye;] what resembles a وَقْرَة in the eye. (L.) — [♦ نُكَتٌ seems to be a quasi-pl. of نُكْتَةٌ, like as نُقَطٌ is said to be (by some persons in the present day) of نُقْطَةٌ, and to signify Any small spots, or specks, in a thing, differing therefrom in colour. Such I suppose to be meant by the words in the L, كل نقط فى شىء خالف لونه نكت.] — نُكْتَةٌ ‡ A nice, subtile, subtilely excogitated, quaint, *facetious, or witty, saying, expression, or allusion,* (لَطِيفَة) *that makes an impression upon the heart;* from النَّكْتُ [the striking the ground with a stick &c., so as to make a mark, or marks, upon it with its extremity]: also, *a question educed by reflection,* [بِالتَّفَكُّرِ, as the passage here translated is given in the Kull, p. 362, but in the TA بالنقل, which is an evident mistake, as might be shown by many authorities,] *which makes an impression upon the heart, on hearing or considering which one generally makes marks upon the ground with the finger or the like:* (El-Fenáree's Expos. of the Telweeḥ:) *a nice, or subtile, saying, expression, or allusion, that requires one to reflect, and* [*induces one*] *to make marks upon the ground with a stick or the like:* (from a scholium quoted by De Sacy, Anthol. Gr. Ar., 303:) [*a nice, subtile, abstruse,* or *mystical, point,* or *allusion:* the *point of a saying* or *sentence, especially one that is difficult to be understood: a conceit expressed in words difficult to be understood: a quaint conceit: a point of wit: a facetious saying* or *allusion:*] pl., generally, نُكَتٌ. — جَآءَ بِنُكْتَةٍ ‡ [*He uttered a nice, or subtile, saying, expression, or allusion, &c.*]. (A.)

نَكِيتٌ *Spoken against; having his reputation wounded.* (TA.)

نَكَّاتٌ (and ♦ مُنْكِتٌ TA) ‡ One *who speaks much,* or *frequently, against others; who wounds the reputations of others, much,* or *frequently.* (K.) — زَيْدٌ نَكَّاتٌ فِي الأَعْرَاضِ *Zeyd is one who wounds the reputations* of others *much,* or *frequently.* (TA.)

نَاكِتٌ *A distortion in a camel's elbow, so that it lacerates his side:* (El-'Adebbes El-Kinánee, Ṣ, K:) or the *cutting of a camel's side by his elbow:* (L:) or [*that fault in a camel*] *when his elbow makes a mark,* or *marks, upon his side:* in this case you say, بِهِ نَاكِتٌ: but when it makes an incision, or incisions, in his side, you say بِهِ حَازٌّ: (IAạr) or نَاكِتٌ is similar to نَاحِزٌ, i. e. *the elbow's striking, and making a mark,* or *marks, upon the edge of the callous lump beneath his breast;* in the case of which you say بِهِ نَاكِتٌ: (Lth:) and nearly the same is said in the A. (TA.)

مَنْكُوتٌ A cooked bone, containing marrow, *that is struck with the edge of a cake of bread,* or *with some other thing, to cause the marrow to fall out.* (TA.)

مُنْكِتٌ: see نَكَّاتٌ. — رُطَبَةٌ مُنْكِتَةٌ *A date beginning to ripen* [*and to become speckled*]. (Ṣ, K.)

ظَلِفَةٌ مُنْكِتَةٌ The *extremity of the curved piece of wood termed* حِنْو *in the kind of saddle called* قَتَب, *and in that called* إِكَاف, *when it is short, and wounds the side of the camel.* (TA.)

نكث

1. نَكَثَ, (Ṣ, K,) aor. ـُ, (K, Mṣb,) and ـِ, (K,) inf. n. نَكْثٌ, (TA,) *He undid* [*the threads of*] a garment of the kind called كِسَآء, &c.: (Mṣb:) *he undid,* or *untwisted,* a rope. (Ṣ, K.) — نَكَثَ السِّوَاكَ, aor. ـُ, inf. n. نَكْثٌ; *He,* or *it, made the head of the tooth-stick to be uncompacted, disintegrated, disunited,* or *seperated, in its fibres:* and so the verb signifies with respect to other things. (TA.) [See also 8.] — نَكَثَ, (aor. ـُ, and ـِ, K, inf. n. نَكْثٌ, TA,) ‡ *He dissolved, violated,* or *broke,* a covenant, or compact, (Ṣ, K,) or an act of inauguration, &c. (TA.) — نَكَثَ عَنِ الأَمْرِ i. q. نَكَصَ (Aboo-Turáb, in TA, art. نكص.)

5: see 8.

6. تَنَاكَثُوا عُهُودَهُمْ ‡ *They mutually dissolved,* or *broke, their covenants,* or *compacts;* syn. تَنَاقَضُوهَا. (K.)

8. انتكث *It* (a garment of the kind called كِسَآء, &c., Mṣb, or a rope, Ṣ, K) *was undone,* or *untwisted.* (Ṣ, K, &c.) — انتكث السِّوَاكُ [so accord. to the TA: in the K, ♦ نَكَثَ:] (TA:) and ♦ تنكّث, (TA, in art. شعث,) *The head of the tooth-stick became uncompacted, disunited,* or *separated, in its fibres.* (TA.) — انتكث [*He was,* or *became, emaciated,* or *lean; he* (a camel) *became lean after having been fat.* See 4, in art. رأى.] — انتكث ‡ *It* (a covenant, or compact, Ṣ and K, or an act of inauguration, &c., TA,) *was dissolved, violated,* or *broken.* (Ṣ, K, &c.) — انتكث مِنْ حَاجَةٍ إِلَى أُخْرَى, (K,) or لِأُخْرَى, (Ṣ,) ‡ *He turned from a thing that he wanted to another thing,* (Ṣ, K,) having desired, or sought, the former. (TA.)

نِكْثٌ *What is undone, to be spun again,* (A, Mṣb,) *of the garments called* أَكْسِيَة, *and of the stuff of the tents called* أَخْبِيَة: (A:) pl. أَنْكَاثٌ: (Mṣb:) or *threads of an old and worn-out stuff, of wool or hair, untwisted, and mixed with new wool* [*or hair*], *and beaten with* مَطَارِق, *and spun a second time:* or *old and worn-out thread of wool or common hair or the soft hair called* وَبَر; so called because it is untwisted, and twisted again: (TA:) it is when the old and worn-out materials of the garments called اكسية (and of the tents called اخبية, Ṣ) are undone, to be spun again. (Ṣ, K.) [SM seems to have understood, from the expl. in the Ṣ and K, that نِكْثٌ is an inf. n.; for he adds,] the subst. is ♦ نَكِيثَةٌ: (TA:) [i. e., this last word has the signification assigned above to نِكْثٌ, from the A and Mṣb]. — هِيَ تَغْزِلُ النِّكْثَ, and الأَنْكَاثَ, *She spins what has been undone, to be spun again, &c.* (A.) — حَبْلٌ نِكْثٌ, and ♦ نَكِيثٌ, (TA,) and أَنْكَاثٌ, and ♦ مَنْكُوثٌ, (K,) *A rope undone,* or *untwisted,* (K, TA,) *at its end.* (TA.)

نُكَاثٌ *Pustules which come forth in the mouths of camels:* (K:) as also نُكَاتٌ. (TA.) — *A disease in the* نُكْفَتَانِ *of a camel, which are two prominent bones by the fat parts of the two ears:* it is also called نُكَافٌ. (TA.)

نَكِيثٌ: see نِكْثٌ.

نُكَاثَةٌ The *broken particles of the end of a* سِوَاك [or *tooth-stick*], *remaining in the mouth.* (K.) — Also, *What is undone,* or *untwisted, of the end of a rope,* (K,) *&c.* (TA.)

نَكِيثَةٌ: see نِكْثٌ. — Subst. from انتكث الحَبْلُ [*What is undone, or untwisted, of a rope*]. (TA.) — ‡ *Breach of promise;* syn. خُلْفٌ. (Ṣ, K.) Ex. قَالَ فُلَانٌ قَوْلًا لَا نَكِيثَةَ فِيهِ *Such a one said a saying in which was* [*intended*] *no breach of promise.* (Ṣ.) — ‡ *A difficult,* or *an arduous, affair,* or *case, in which a people dissolves,* or *breaks,* (تَنْكُثُ) [*its covenants,* or *compacts*]. (Ṣ, K.) — *A great affair.* (TA.) — *The utmost of* one's *endeavour,* or *effort:* (Ṣ, K:) *power,* or *strength:* (K:) pl. نَكَائِثُ. (TA.) Ex. بَلَغَ فُلَانٌ نَكِيثَةَ بَعِيرِهِ *Such a one exerted the utmost endeavour,* or *effort,* [or *power,* or *strength,*] *of his camel,* in journeying. (Ṣ.) [See also نَجِيثَةٌ.] — نَكِيثَةٌ *Nature; natural,* or *native, disposition, temper,* or *other property.* (K.) — النَّكِيثَةُ † *The mind; the soul;* syn. النَّفْسُ: (Ṣ, K:) so called because the vexation of those things of which it is in need dissolve (تَنْكُثُ) its powers, and old age destroys it: the ة is added because it is a subst. (TA.) Ex. فُلَانٌ شَدِيدُ النَّكِيثَةِ *Such a one is strong in mind.* (Ṣ.) Pl. نَكَائِثُ. (TA.)

نَكَّاثٌ *One who undoes,* or *untwists, thread, and twists it again,* or, *to twist it again.* (TA.) [See نِكْثٌ.] — نَكَّاثٌ لِلْعَهْدِ ‡ *One who is wont to dissolve, violate,* or *break, his covenant,* or *compact.* (TA.)

مَنْكُوثٌ: see نِكْثٌ.

مُنْتَكِثٌ *Emaciated; lean:* (K:) a camel *that has been fat, and has become lean.* (TA.)

نكح

1. نَكَحَ, (Ṣ, K, &c.,) aor. ـِ, (Mṣb, K,) and ـَ, (K,) the latter agreeable with analogy, but by some rejected, and the former contr. to analogy, but more common, and the form used

in the Kur, (TA,) the only instance of an aor. of this form from a verb having ح for its last radical letter, except ينطح and يمنح and ينضح and ينبح and يرجح and يأنح and يأزح and يملح, (ISd,) [and يضح] inf. n. نِكَاحٌ (Ṣ, Ḳ, &c.) and نَكْحٌ; (ISd, Ḳ;) *Inivit feminam*: and (sometimes, Ṣ) *he married, took in marriage*, or *contracted a marriage with*, a woman: as also ▾ استنكح (Ṣ, Ḳ, &c.) [and ▾ ناكح, inf. n. مُنَاكَحَةٌ:] used only with reference to a man: (ISd:) but Th uses it with reference to flies: (TA:) J says, that it is sometimes used in the latter sense; but accord. to the Mṣb it is more commonly so used; (MF;) and it is used only in this sense in the Ḳur: (TA:) IF and others say, that it signifies coitus; and coitus without marriage; and marriage without coitus: (Mṣb:) [but] in the Time of Ignorance, when a man demanded a woman in marriage he said, إِنْكِحِينِى; and when he desired fornication, he said, سَافِحِينِى. (TA, in art سفح.) It is disputed whether it be proper or tropical in these two senses; or proper in one, and tropical in one: (MF:) it is said to be from نَكَحَهُ الدَّوَى, or from نَكَحَ المَطَرُ الأَرْضَ, or from تَنَاكَحَتِ الأَشْجَارُ; and if so, it is tropical in both the above senses; and the opinion that it is so is confirmed by this, that the signification of marriage is not understood unless by a word or phrase in connexion with it, as when you say نَكَحَ فِى بَنِى فُلَانٍ [*he took a wife from among the sons of such a one*]; nor is that of coitus unless by the same means, as when you say نَكَحَ زَوْجَتَهُ [*inivit conjugem suam*]; and this is one of the signs of a tropical expression. (Mṣb.) — نَكَحَتْ *She married*, or *took a husband*. (Ṣ, Ḳ.) — نَكَحَ المَطَرُ الأَرْضَ *The rain became commingled with the soil:* (Mṣb:) or, *rested upon the ground so as to soak it;* syn. إِعْتَمَدَ عَلَيْهَا: (Ḳ:) as also ▾ نَاكَهَا. (L.) — نَكَحَهُ الدَّوَى *The disease infected him* (خَامَرَهُ), *and overcame him.* (Mṣb.) — نَكَحَ النُّعَاسُ عَيْنَهُ ‡ *Drowsiness overcame his eye;* (Ḳ;) as also نَاكَهَا: and in like manner ▾ استنكح النَّوْمُ عَيْنَهُ *sleep overcame his eye.* (TA.)

3: see 1.

4. انكحهُ المَرْأَةَ *He married the woman to him.* (TA.) — أَنْكَحَهَا *He married the woman;* i. e. *gave her in marriage.* (Ṣ, Ḳ.) — أَنْكِحُوا الحَصَى أَخْفَافَ الإِبِلِ ‡ [*Accustom ye the feet of the camels to pebbles*]. (A.)

6. تناكحوا *They intermarried; contracted marriages together.* (Commencing a trad. in the Jámi' eṣ-Ṣagheer.) [And تَنَاكَحَا *Se invicem futuerunt:* see 6, in art. ردف.] — تَنَاكَحَتِ الأَشْجَارُ *The trees became drawn*, or *connected, together.* (Mṣb.)

10: see 1.

نَكْحٌ and ▾ نُكَحٌ substs. from أَنْكَحَهَا, [The *act of giving a woman in marriage*]. (Ḳ.) — [These two words are properly quasi-inf. ns. of أَنْكَحَ, signifying as explained above; and, like inf. ns., may be used as epithets, meaning *A giver of a woman in marriage*, correlative to خِطْبٌ.] It was a custom, in the time of paganism, for a man to come to a tribe asking for a woman in marriage; and he would stand up in their assembly, and say خِطْبٌ, i.e., I have come as an asker of a woman in marriage; whereupon it would be said to him نِكْحٌ, meaning *We marry her to thee*, or *give her to thee in marriage*, [or, more lit., *we are givers of her in marriage:* for an inf. n. or quasi-inf. n. used as an epithet is used without variation as sing., dual., and pl.; and masc. and fem.]. ▾ نُكَحٌ was also said: but نِكْحٌ is here said for the sake of resemblance to خِطْبٌ. (L.) You say هُوَ نِكْحُهَا *He is the person who gives her in marriage:* and هِىَ نِكْحَتُهُ *She is the person whom he gives in marriage.* (Lḥ, L.) — نِكْحٌ and ▾ نُكَحٌ, [and, accord. to Lth and ISh, نِكْحٌ: see إِبْدٌ:] are also two words by which the [Pagan] Arabs used to take women in marriage: (Ṣ:) [meaning *A giver of a woman in marriage*]. (MF, in art. خطب.) A man used to say to Umm-Khárijeh, in asking her in marriage, خِطْبٌ, and she used to reply نِكْحٌ: hence the saying أَسْرَعُ مِنْ نِكَاحِ أُمِّ خَارِجَةَ [*Quicker than the marriage of Umm-Khárijeh*]. (Ṣ, Ḳ.) [See خِطْبٌ].

نِكْحٌ: see نَكْحٌ.

نُكَحٌ: see نُكَحَةٌ.

رَجُلٌ نُكَحَةٌ, (Ṣ, Ḳ,) and ▾ نُكَحٌ (Ḳ) *A man who marries much*, or *often:* (Ṣ, Ḳ, TA:) AZ explains the former by شَدِيدُ النِّكَاحِ, [app. meaning *vehement in coitus*,] and mentions as its pl. نُكَحَاتٌ: (TA:) [and ▾ نَكَّاحٌ (A, TA, art. تيس, &c.) signifies the same.]

نَكَّاحٌ: see نُكَحَةٌ.

نَاكِحٌ (Ṣ, Ḳ) and نَاكِحَةٌ, (Ḳ,) the latter occurring in poetry, (TA,) *A woman married;* (TA;) *having a husband.* (Ṣ, Ḳ, TA.) Ex. هِىَ نَاكِحٌ فِى بَنِى فُلَانٍ *She has a husband among the sons of such a one.* (Ṣ.)

مَنْكَحٌ and مَنْكُوحَةٌ: see مَنَاكِحُ.

مَنَاكِحُ *Women*, or *wives;* syn. نِسَآءٌ: (Ḳ:) a pl. having no sing.; or its sing. is ▾ مَنْكَحٌ; [or ▾ مَنْكَحٌ, which occurs in the Ṣ and Ḳ, art. علث, evidently as signifying a wife; as though being a place of نِكَاح;] or ▾ مَنْكُوحَةٌ. (TA.) إِنَّ المَنَاكِحَ خَيْرُهَا الأَبْكَارُ [*Verily the best of women to take in marriage are virgins*]. A proverb. (TA.)

نكد

1. نَكِدَ, aor. ـَ, (Ṣ, Ḳ, &c.,) inf. n. نَكَدٌ, (Ṣ, L, Mṣb,) *It* (a man's life) *was*, or *became, hard*, or *strait, and difficult.* (Ṣ, L, Mṣb, Ḳ.) — نَكِدَ *It* (a she-camel's milk) *became deficient.* (R.) — نَكِدَتْ *It* (water) *became exhausted.* (A.) — نَكِدَتِ الرَّكِيَّةُ *The well came to have little water.* (Ṣ, L, Ḳ.) — نَكِدَ, aor. ـَ, inf. n. نَكَدٌ, *He was*, or *became, unpropitious, and mean:* (L:) *he became hard*, or *difficult:* (Mṣb:) *he gave little:* or *gave not at all:* you say also نَكِدَ بِحَاجَتِنَا *he was niggardly of that which we wanted.* (L.) — نَكَدَهُ حَاجَتَهُ, نَكَدَ حَاجَتَهُ, aor. ـُ; (Ḳ;) or (L,) *He withheld from him*, or *refused him, his want.* (L, Ḳ.) — نَكَدَهُ, aor. ـُ, *He withheld from him*, or *refused him, what he asked:* or [in the CḲ, and] the same, (Ḳ,) or نَكَدَهُ مَا سَأَلَهُ, aor. ـُ, inf. n. نَكْدٌ, (L,) *he gave him not save the least of what he asked.* (L, Ḳ.) — نُكِدَ, [in measure] like عُنِىَ, *He had many askers and gave little.* (Ḳ.) — نَكَدَ, aor. ـُ, *He* (a raven or crow) *croaked with his utmost force;* (A, Ḳ;) *as though vomiting;* as also ▾ تنكّد. (A.)

2. نَكَّدَ عَطَآءَهُ بِالْمَنِّ *He impaired his gift by reproach.* (A.) — نكّد وَسَقُهُ *He spent*, or *exhausted, what he possessed, in consequence of frequent petitions.* (A.) — نكّدهُ *He vexed, distressed*, or *troubled, him;* (Gol, from Meyd;) [as also نكّد عَلَيْهِ].

3. ناكدهُ *He treated him*, or *behaved towards him, with hardness, harshness*, or *ill-nature.* (Ṣ, L, Ḳ.)

4. سَأَلَهُ فَأَنْكَدَهُ *He asked of him, and found him hard*, or *difficult*, (A, L,) *and mean*, or *niggardly:* (L:) or *found him to have only what was scanty*, or *little.* (L.) طَلَبَ مِنْهُ حَاجَةً فَأَنْكَدَ — *He sought*, or *desired, of him a thing that he wanted, and he was niggardly.* (A.)

5. تنكّد [*He became vexed, distressed*, or *troubled*]. (A.) See Bḍ, in lxviii. 25: and see 1.

6. تناكدا *They treated each other with hardness, harshness*, or *ill-nature.* (Ṣ, L, Ḳ.)

نَكْدٌ: see نَكَدٌ, and نَكِدٌ.

نَكَدٌ and ▾ نُكْدٌ *Scantiness of a gift;* (L, Ḳ;) *and its not being enjoyed*, or *found pleasant, by the receiver.* (L.) — See what follows.

نَكْدًا لَهُ وَجَحْدًا, نَكَدًا لَهُ وَجَحَدًا, and ▾, [*May God decree straitness*, or *difficulty, to him, and poverty*]: forms of imprecation. (L.) — نَكْدٌ *Anything that brings evil upon the person whom it affects.* (L.) See نَكِدٌ.

نَكِدٌ [*Hard, strait, or difficult*; applied to a man's life; (see 1;) and to fortune, as in an ex. voce إِيدٌ.] — Water *little in quantity.* (L.) — لَا يَخْرُجُ إِلَّا نَكِدًا, in the Ḳur, [vii. 56,] accord. to the common reading, or ♦ نَكَدًا, accord. to the reading of the people of El-Medeeneh, or, as it may be read, accord. to Zj, ♦ نَكْدًا and ♦ نُكْدًا, means, accord. to Fr, *It* [the herbage] *will not come forth save with difficulty*: (L:) or, *scantily and unprofitably.* (Beyḍ.) — نَكِدٌ (Ṣ, A, L, Mṣb, Ḳ,) and ♦ نَكْدٌ and ♦ نَكَدٌ and ♦ أَنْكَدُ (L, Ḳ) A man who is *unpropitious,* (L, Ḳ,) *and mean,* (L,) *and hard,* or *difficult*: (Ṣ, A, L, Mṣb, Ḳ:) and a people you term أَنْكَادٌ and مَنَاكِيدُ (Ṣ, L, Ḳ) and نَكْدٌ and نُكْدٌ. (A.) — نَكِدٌ and ♦ أَنْكَدُ A man *that brings evil upon others.* (L.)

نَكَادٌ *Hardness,* or *difficulty,* in a man. (A.) See نَكِدَ.

أَرَضُونَ نِكَادٌ *Lands possessing little goods.* (L.)

نَاكِدٌ : see أَنْكَدُ.

أَنْكَدُ — نَكْدَآءُ A she-camel *abounding with milk*; (IF, L, Ḳ;) as also ♦ نَاكِدٌ: (L:) a she-camel *that has no young one living, and therefore abounding with milk, because she does not suckle*; (L; Ḳ;) so نَكْدَآءُ مِقْلَاتٌ, of which the pls. occur in a verse of El-Kumeyt cited voce شَخَبَ: (Ṣ:) also, contr., a she-camel *having no milk*: (IF, A, Ḳ:) or *having little milk*; as also ♦ نَاكِدٌ: and both words, a she-camel *whose young one has died*: (L:) pl. (of both words, L) نُكْدٌ (Ṣ, L, Ḳ.) See also مَنْكُودٌ. — أَنْكَدُ *Unfortunate; unlucky.* (Ṣ.) See نَكِدٌ.

مَنْكُودٌ : see مُنْكَدٌ.

مَنْكُودٌ *A small, or scanty, gift*; (A, L, Ḳ;) as also ♦ مُنْكَدٌ. (A.) — مَنْكُودٌ A man *having many askers and giving little*: (TA:) or a man *pressed with petitions*; as also مَعْرُوكٌ and مَشْفُوهٌ and مَعْجُوزٌ. (IAạr, L.)

جَآءَهُ مُنْكِدًا *He came to him unwelcomely*: or, *empty*: or, as Th says, it is correctly مُنْكِزًا, from نَكَزَتِ البِئْرُ, though أَنْكَزَ as meaning "his wells became exhausted," has not been heard. (L.)

نكر

1. نَكِرَهُ: see 4, in several places. — نَكِرَ, inf. n. نَكَارَةٌ, [*He was,* or *became, ignorant*: or perhaps only the inf. n. of the verb in this sense is used: see نَكَارَةٌ, below. — And, contr., *He possessed cunning*; meaning both *intelligence with craft and forecast*; and simply *intelligence,* or *skill and knowledge*: or perhaps only the inf. n. of the verb in this sense is used: see نُكْرٌ.] — *It* (a thing, or an affair,) *was,* or *became,* مُنْكَر [app. here meaning *disapproved*; or *bad, evil, abominable,* or *foul*; or *disallowed*]. (A.) — Also, (Ṣ, Ḳ,) inf. n. نَكَارَةٌ, (TḲ,) or نُكْرٌ, (TA,) *It* (a thing, or an affair,) *was,* or *became, difficult, hard, arduous,* or *severe.* (Ṣ, Ḳ.*)

2. نَكَّرَهُ, (inf. n. تَنْكِيرٌ, Mṣb,) *He changed,* or *altered, him* or *it,* (Ṣ, A, Mṣb, TA,) *to an unknown state,* (Ṣ, TA,) *so as not to be known*; (TA;) [*he disguised him* or *it.*] It is said in the Ḳur, [xxvii. 41,] نَكِّرُوا لَهَا عَرْشَهَا *Alter ye her throne so that it may not be known to her.* (TA.) See also 4, last signification but one. — [In grammar, *He made it* (a noun) *indeterminate.*]

3. نَاكَرَهُ, (Ṣ, TA,) inf. n. مُنَاكَرَةٌ, (A, Ḳ,) *He strove,* or *endeavoured, to outwit, deceive, beguile,* or *circumvent, him*; or *he practised with him mutual deceit, guile,* or *circumvention*; syn. خَادَعَهُ and دَاهَاهُ: the inf. n. is also explained by مُرَاوَغَةٌ as well as مُخَادَعَةٌ [both of which signify the same]. (TA.) — Hence, (TA,) *He contended with him in fight*; (Ṣ, Ḳ;) and *in war,* or *hostility.* (A, Ḳ.) It is said of Moḥammad, by Aboo-Sufyán (Ṣ, TA) Ibn-Ḥarb, (TA.) لَمْ يُنَاكِرْ أَحَدًا إِلَّا كَانَتْ مَعَهُ الأَهْوَالُ, (Ṣ, TA,) meaning, *He did not war with any one without being aided by terror* [cast into the hearts of his opponents]. (TA.) And one says, بَيْنَهُمَا مُنَاكَرَةٌ *Between them two is war,* or *hostility,* (A, TA,*) *and fighting.* (TA.)

4. أَنْكَرَهُ, (Ṣ, A, Mṣb, Ḳ, &c.,) inf. n. إِنْكَارٌ; (Mṣb, &c.;) and ♦ نَكِرَهُ, (Ṣ, A, Mṣb, Ḳ, &c.,) aor. ـَ, (L,) or it does not admit the variations of tense like other verbs, (IḲṭṭ, Mṣb,) it is not used in the future tense, nor in commanding nor in forbidding, (Lth,) inf. n. نَكَرٌ (Ḳ) and نُكْرٌ and نُكُورٌ (Ṣ, Ḳ) and نَكِيرٌ; (Ḳ;) and ♦ اِسْتَنْكَرَهُ; (Ṣ, M, A, Ḳ;) and ♦ تَنَاكَرَهُ; (M, Ḳ;) signify the same; (Ṣ, A, Mṣb, Ḳ, &c.;) i. e., *He ignored, was ignorant of, did not know, failed to know,* or [rather] *was unacquainted with, it* (i. e. a thing, or an affair, IḲṭṭ, Ḳ) or *him* (a man, Ṣ); syn. جَهِلَهُ; (Kr, Ḳ;) or *contr. of* عَرَفَهُ: (Ṣ,* IḲṭṭ, Mṣb:) [see also نَكَارَةٌ:] some, however, say, the نَكِرَ has a more intensive signification than أَنْكَرَ: and some, that نَكِرَ has for its objective complement an object of the mind; and أَنْكَرَ, an object of the sight: (A, TA:) or [the converse is the case;] نَكِرَ has for its objective complement an object of the sight; and أَنْكَرَ, an object of the mind: (Kull, p. 81:) [but both forms seem to have been generally used indiscriminately.] El-Aạshà says,

• وَأَنْكَرَتْنِي وَمَا كَانَ الَّذِي نَكِرَتْ •
• مِنَ الحَوَادِثِ إِلَّا الشَّيْبَ وَالصَّلَعَا •

[*And she did not know me; and the accidents which she did not know were none others than hoariness, and baldness of the fore part of the head*]. (Ṣ, TA.) And it is said in the Ḳur, [xi. 73,] نَكِرَهُمْ ♦ وَأَوْجَسَ مِنْهُمْ خِيفَةً [*He knew not what they were, and conceived a fear,* or *a kind of fear, of them*]: (TA:) نَكِرَهُمْ here signifies أَنْكَرَهُمْ: (Jel:) or it means أَنْكَرَ ذٰلِكَ مِنْهُمْ [q. v. infra]. (Bḍ.) — أَنْكَرَهُ also signifies *He denied,* or *disacknowledged, it*; (L, art. جحد; [and this signification, as well as the first, may be meant to be indicated by those who say that أَنْكَرَهُ signifies the contr. of عَرَفَهُ;]) [and so ♦ نَكِرَهُ; for] إِنْكَارٌ signifies *i. q.* جُحُودٌ, (Ṣ, TA,) and so نُكْرَانٌ [which is an inf. n. of نَكِرَهُ]. (TA.) [In this sense it is doubly trans.:] you say, أَنْكَرْتُهُ حَقَّهُ, meaning, *I denied,* or *disacknowledged, to him his right.* (Mṣb.) The cause of إِنْكَار with the tongue is إِنْكَار with the mind, but sometimes the tongue denies, or disacknowledges, (يُنْكِرُ,) a thing when the image thereof is present in the mind; and this is lying; as is the case in the following passage of the Ḳur, [xvi. 85,] يَعْرِفُونَ نِعْمَةَ ٱللّٰهِ ثُمَّ يُنْكِرُونَهَا [*They confess,* or *acknowledge, the favour of God; then they deny,* or *disacknowledge, it*]. (B.) See also نَكِيرٌ. — Also, *He deemed it strange, extraordinary,* or *improbable.* (MF, voce عَجِبَ.) — [Also *He denied,* or *negatived, it.* — *He disbelieved it.* — And *He disapproved it; he disliked it; he deemed it,* or *declared it to be, bad, evil, abominable,* or *foul; he disallowed it*: so accord. to explanations of the pass. part. n., q. v. infra; and accord. to common usage of classical and of modern times.] It is said of Abraham, when the angels came to him, and he saw that their hands did not touch the meat which he had brought to them, نَكِرَهُمْ, meaning, أَنْكَرَ ذٰلِكَ مِنْهُمْ [*He deemed that conduct of their's evil,* or *disapproved it*: or, perhaps, *he did not know what that conduct of their's was,* or *what it indicated*]: ♦ نَكِرَ and أَنْكَرَ and ♦ اِسْتَنْكَرَ [of which last see an ex. voce تَبِرَ] signify the same. (Bḍ, xi. 73.) And you say, أَنْكَرْتُ عَلَيْهِ فِعْلَهُ, meaning, *I blamed,* or *found fault with, his deed, and forbade it; I disapproved and disallowed his deed*: (Mṣb:) [and *I manifested,* or *showed,* or *declared, disapproval,* or *disallowance, of his* deed: and in like manner, أَنْكَرْتُ عَلَيْهِ, elliptically; فِعْلَهُ, (his deed,) or قَوْلَهُ, (his saying,) or the like, being understood; like عَيَّرَ عَلَيْهِ for عَيَّرَ عَلَيْهِ فِعْلَهُ or the like: see نَكِيرٌ.] — إِنْكَارٌ also signifies The *changing* [a thing; like تَنْكِيرٌ]: (T, Mṣb, TA:) or the *changing what is* مُنْكَر [here app. meaning *disapproved*: see نَكِيرٌ, which is syn. with it, but is a simple subst.]. (Ṣ, TA.) — مَا أَنْكَرَهُ *How great is his cunning!* meaning both *his intelligence and craft, and forecast*; and simply, *his intelligence*, or *skill and knowledge*. (TA.) And مَا كَانَ أَنْكَرَهُ *How great was his cunning*, &c. (TA.)

5. تنكّر *He*, or *it*, *changed*, or *altered*, *himself*, or *itself*; or *became changed*, or *altered*; (Ṣ, A, Mṣb, TA;) *to an unknown state*: (Ṣ, TA:) [*he assumed an unknown appearance: he disguised himself*; or *became disguised*:] *he became changed or altered in countenance by anger so that he who saw him did not know him*: (Ḥar, p. 144:) or تَنَكُّرٌ signifies the *changing*, or *altering oneself*, or *itself*; or *becoming changed*, or *altered*; *from a state which pleases one to a state which one dislikes*. (T, Ḳ.) — إِيَّاكَ وَالتَّنَكُّرَ *Avoid thou evil disposition*. (Mgh.) — تَنَكَّرَ لِى فُلَانٌ *Such a one* [*became changed*, or *altered*, *in countenance to me by anger so that I did not know him*; or] *met me in a morose manner*. (A, TA.) [In art. شنف in the Ḳ, تَنَكُّرَهُ occurs.]

6. تناكرهُ: see 4, first signification. — تناكر *He feigned ignorance*. (Ṣ, A, Ḳ.) — تناكروا *They acted with mutual hostility*. (TṢ, A, Ḳ.)

10. اِسْتَنْكَرَهُ: see 4, first signification, and also in the latter part. — اِسْتِنْكَارٌ also signifies The *inquiring respecting*, or *seeking to understand*, *a thing*, or *an affair*, *which one disapproves*; (Ḳ, TA;) *when one disapproves confirming*, or *establishing*, *the opinion expressed by an inquirer*, or *disapproves that his opinion should be contrary to what he has expressed*. (TA.)

نَكْرٌ: see نُكْرٌ. = See also نَكِرٌ.

نُكْرٌ (Ṣ, Ḳ) and ↓ نَكْرٌ [but the former is the more common] and ↓ نَكَارَةٌ (Ṣ, A, Ḳ) and ↓ نَكْرَآءُ (A, Ḳ) *Cunning*; meaning both *intelligence mixed with craft and forecast*; and [simply] *intelligence*, or *sagacity*, or *skill and knowledge*; syn. دَهَآءٌ; (Ṣ, A, Ḳ;) and فِطْنَةٌ. (A, Ḳ.) See also نَكُرَ. You say of a man who is intelligent and evil, or cunning, مَا أَشَدَّ نُكْرَهُ, and ↓ نَكْرَهُ [*How great is his cunning*, &c.!] (Ṣ.) And فَعَلَهُ مِنْ نُكْرِهِ, and ↓ نَكَارَتِهِ, *He did it of his cunning*, &c. (TA.) And it is said in a trad. of Mo'áwiyeh, إِنِّى لَأَكْرَهُ النَّكَارَةَ فِى الرَّجُلِ *Verily I hate cunning* (الدَّهَآء) *in the man*. (TA.) = نُكْرٌ, as an epithet, applied to a thing, or an affair, *Difficult, hard, arduous*, or *severe*; as also ↓ نُكُرٌ (M, A, Ḳ) and ↓ نَكِيرٌ: (TA:) and *i.q.* مُنْكَرٌ, q.v. (Ṣ, A, Ḳ.)

نُكْرٌ [app. *Difficulty, hardness, arduousness*, or *severity*;] a subst. from نَكُرَ, in the sense of صَعُبَ [It was difficult, &c.]. (IḲṭṭ, TA.)

نُكُرٌ: see نُكْرٌ, in two places.

نَكِرٌ and ↓ نَكُرٌ (Ṣ, Ḳ) and ↓ نُكُرٌ and ↓ مُنْكَرٌ, (Ḳ,) epithets applied to a man, *Possessing cunning*; or *intelligence mixed with cunning and forecast*; (Ṣ, Ḳ;) and [simply] *intelligent*, or *skilful and knowing*: (Ḳ:) and so, applied to a woman, ↓ نَكِرٌ (Ḳ) and ↓ نَكُرٌ (L, TA [but this is probably a mistake for ↓ نُكُرٌ]) and ↓ نَكْرَآءُ, but أَنْكَرُ is not applied to a man in this sense, (Az, TA,) nor is مُنْكَرَةٌ to a woman: (TA:) pl. of the first and second (Ṣ, Ḳ,) and third, (Ḳ,) أَنْكَارٌ: (Ṣ, Ḳ:) and of the last, مَنَاكِيرُ; (Sb, Ṣ, Ḳ;) or, applied to men, مُنْكَرُونَ; and to other things, مَنَاكِيرُ [which is irreg.]. (Az, TA.) — Also, نَكِرٌ and ↓ نَكُرٌ One *who disapproves what is bad, evil, abominable*, or *foul*; expl. by اَلَّذِى يُنْكِرُ الْمُنْكَرَ: pl. as above. (Ṣ.)

نَكُرٌ: see نَكِرٌ: and مُنْكَرٌ. = See also نَكِرٌ, in two places.

نَكِرَةٌ a subst. from إِنْكَارٌ, (Ḳ,) with which it is syn., [app. signifying (like نَكَرَةٌ) *Ignorance*: or *denial*: or *disapproval*, or *the like*], (TḲ,) like نَفَقَةٌ from إِنْفَاقٌ. (Ḳ.) It is said, in a certain trad., كُنْتَ لِى أَشَدَّ نَكِرَةً, (TA,) i.e. إِنْكَارًا, (TḲ,) [*Thou wast to me most ignorant*, &c.]

نَكَرَةٌ *Ignorance*, &c., (إِنْكَار,) of a thing; (TA;) *contr. of* مَعْرِفَةٌ; (Ṣ, Ḳ;) and so ↓ نَكَارَةٌ; syn. جَهَالَةٌ; as in the phrase فِيهِ نَكَارَةٌ [*In him is ignorance*]. (A.) See also نَكِرَةٌ. — [As *contr.* of مَعْرِفَةٌ, it is also, in grammar, an epithet applied to a noun, signifying *Indeterminate*, or *indefinite*.]

نَكْرَآءُ: see مُنْكَرٌ. — *A calamity*: (Ḳ:) *rigour*, or *severity*, of fortune; (A, TA;) as also [its dim.] نُكَيْرَآءُ. (TA.) = See also نُكْرٌ. = And see نَكِرٌ.

نَكِيرٌ *i.q.* إِنْكَارٌ [in the sense of *Denial*]. (Ḳ.) It is said in the Ḳur, xlii. 46, فَمَا لَكُمْ مِنْ نَكِيرٍ, *And there shall be for you no* [power of] *denial* of your sins. (Bḍ, Jel.) And one says, شُتِمَ فُلَانٌ فَمَا كَانَ عِنْدَهُ نَكِيرٌ [*Such a one was reviled and he had no denial* to make]. (A.) — [Also, *i.q.* إِنْكَارٌ in the sense of *Disapproval*, or *the like*: and *manifestation thereof*. See what here follows.] — Also, *i.q.* إِنْكَارٌ in the sense of The *changing* [a thing]: (T, Mṣb, TA:) or the *changing what is* مُنْكَر [here app. meaning *disapproved*]: (Ṣ, TA:) a simple subst. (T, TA.) The words of the Ḳur, [xxii. 43 and lxvii. 18,] فَكَيْفَ كَانَ نَكِيرِ are explained as signifying *And how was my changing* [of their condition]! (TA:) or the meaning is, *and how was my manifestation of disapproval of their conduct*, (إِنْكَارِى عَلَيْهِمْ,) by changing favour into trial, and life into destruction, and a flourishing condition into a state of ruin! (Bḍ, xxii. 43.) In [some of] the copies of the Ḳ, it is said that نَكِيرَةٌ [but in a MS. copy I find نَكِيرٌ and so in the CḲ] is a subst. from تَنَكَّرَ as signifying the *changing*, or *altering*, *oneself*, or *itself*; or *becoming changed*, or *altered*; *from a state which pleases one to a state which one dislikes*: but a different statement is found in the T: [see above:] and نكيرة is not mentioned by any authority. (TA.) = *A strong* fortress. (Ṣgh, Ḳ.) See نُكْرٌ. = See also مُنْكَرٌ.

نَكَارَةٌ: see نَكَرَةٌ. = See also نُكْرٌ.

أَنْكَرُ *Worse*, and *worst*; *more*, and *most*, *evil*, *abominable*, or *foul*. So it is explained as occurring in the Ḳur. [xxxi. 18,] إِنَّ أَنْكَرَ الْأَصْوَاتِ لَصَوْتُ الْحَمِيرِ [*Verily the most abominable of voices is the voice of asses*]. (TA.) — See also نَكِرٌ: and the fem., نَكْرَآءُ, see above.

مُنْكَرٌ contr. of مَعْرُوفٌ. (Ḳ:) [an explanation including several significations, here following.] — [*Ignored*, or *unknown*; as also ↓ مَنْكُورٌ, for] مَنْكُورٌ is *syn. with* مَجْهُولٌ [the pass. part. n. of the verb by which أَنْكَرَهُ is explained by Kr and in the Ḳ]; (TA;) and ↓ مُسْتَنْكَرٌ signifies the same. (L.) For the pls. of مُنْكَرٌ, see نَكِرٌ. — [*Denied*, or *disacknowledged*. (See the verb.) — *Deemed strange, extraordinary*, or *improbable*. (See again the verb.)] — Any action *disapproved*, or *disallowed*, *by sound intellects*; or *deemed*, or *declared*, *thereby*, *to be bad, evil, hateful, abominable, foul, unseemly, ugly*, or *hideous*; or *pronounced to be so by the law because the mind deliberates respecting the regarding it as such*: and thus it is used in the Ḳur, ix. 113 [and other places]: (B, TA:) or anything *pronounced to be bad, evil, hateful, abominable*, or *foul, and forbidden, and disapproved, disliked*, or *hated*, *by the law*: (TA:) a saying, or an action, *unapproved, not approved, unaccepted*, or *not accepted*, by God: (KT:) *unbecoming, indecent*, or *indecorous*. (KL.) See مَعْرُوفٌ, voce عَرَفَ. = مُنْكَرٌ and ↓ نُكُرٌ and ↓ نُكْرٌ (Ṣ, A, Mṣb, Ḳ) and ↓ نَكْرَآءُ (Ṣ, Mṣb Ḳ) are all syn., (Ṣ, A, Mṣb, Ḳ.) [and are used as epithets in which the quality of a subst. predominates,] signifying *a bad, an evil, a hateful, an abominable, a foul, an unseemly, an ugly*, or *a hideous*, [and *a formidable*,] *thing* or *affair* [or *action* or *saying* or *quality*, &c.]: (Mṣb:) [in this sense, its pl. is مُنْكَرَاتٌ and مَنَاكِيرُ; as will be seen below:] ↑ نُكْرٌ is *contr. of* عُرْفٌ [which is syn. with مَعْرُوفٌ]. (TA.) You say فِيهِمِ العُرْفُ والنُّكْرُ, and اَلْمَعْرُوفُ وَالْمُنْكَرُ, [*In them are good and evil qualities.*] And هُمْ يَرْكَبُونَ الْمُنْكَرَاتِ, and المَنَاكِيرَ, [*They commit bad, evil, abominable, or foul, actions.*] (A.) And it is said in the Ḳur, [xviii. 73,] لَقَدْ جِئْتَ شَيْئًا نُكْرًا [*Verily thou hast done a bad, an evil, an abominable, or a foul, thing*]. (Ṣ.) — *The name of one of two angels, the other of whom is named* نَكِيرٌ; (Ṣ;) who are the two triers of [the dead in] the graves. (ISd, Ḳ.) — See also نَكِرٌ.

مَنْكُورٌ: see مُنْكَرٌ, first signification. The pl. is مَنَاكِيرُ, [which is also a pl. of مُنْكَرٌ,] accord. to Sb, who mentions it because, accord. to rule, the pl. of a sing. of this class is formed by the addition of و and ن for the masc., and ا and ت for the fem. (Abu-l-Ḥasan, TA.)

خَرَجَ مُتَنَكِّرًا *He went forth disguised; or changed in outward appearance, or state of apparel.* (TA.)

مُسْتَنْكَرٌ: see مُنْكَرٌ, first signification.

طَرِيقٌ يَنْكُورٌ *A road, or way, in a wrong direction.* (Ṣ, Ḳ.)

[نكز,
See Supplement.]

نكس

1. نَكَسَهُ, (Ṣ, A, Mṣb, Ḳ,) aor. ـُ, inf. n. نَكْسٌ, (Ṣ, Mṣb,) *He turned it over, or upside down; inverted it; reversed it; changed its manner of being, or state:* (Sh, Mṣb:*) *he turned it over upon its head:* (Ṣ, A, Ḳ:) and *he turned it fore part behind; made the first part of it to be last; or put the first part of it last:* (Sh:) and ↑ نَكَّسَهُ, (Ṣ, A, Ḳ) inf. n. تَنْكِيسٌ, (Ṣ,) signifies the same; (Ṣ,* A, Ḳ;) or has an intensive sense. (TA.) You say, نُكِسَ السَّهْمُ فِي الكِنَانَةِ *The arrow was turned, or put, upside down in the quiver.* (TA.) And it is said in the Ḳur, [xxxvi. 68,] وَمَنْ نُعَمِّرْهُ نَنْكُسْهُ فِي الخَلْقِ, or, accord. to the reading of 'Ásim and Ḥamzeh, ↑ نُنَكِّسْهُ; meaning, *And him whom We cause to live long, We cause him to become in a state the reverse of that in which he was, in constitution; so that after strength, he becomes reduced to weakness; and after youthfulness, to extreme old age.* (TA.) — نَكَسْتُ فُلَانًا فِي ذٰلِكَ الأَمْرِ † *I made such a one to enter again into that affair, or state, after he had got out of it.* (ISh.) [Hence the saying in the Ḳur, xxi. 66,] ثُمَّ نُكِسُوا عَلَى رُؤُوسِهِمْ † *Then they were made to return to their disbelief:* (Jel:) or ‡ *then they reverted to disputation, after they had taken the right course by means of consulting together;* their return to falsity being likened to a thing's becoming upside down: and there are two other readings; ↑ نُكِّسُوا, and نَكَسُوا; the latter meaning نَكَسُوا أَنْفُسَهُمْ: (Bḍ;) or † *then they reverted from what they knew,* of the evidence in favour of Abraham. (Fr.) — [And hence,] نَكَسَهُ, and نَكَسَهُ إِلَى مَرَضِهِ, ‡ *It made him to fall back into his disease.*] (TA, in art. هيض.) And نُكِسَ, (Ṣ, Mṣb, Ḳ,) or نُكِسَ فِي مَرَضِهِ, (A, TA,) inf. n. نُكْسٌ (Ṣ, Mṣb, Ḳ) and نَكْسٌ (TA, [but see what is said of this below]) and نُكَاسٌ, (Sh, Ḳ,) ‡ *He relapsed into his disease, after convalescence, or after recovery, but not complete, of health and strength:* (Ṣ, A, Ḳ:) or *the disease returned to him;* [*he relapsed into the disease;*] as though he were made to turn back to it. (Mṣb.) You say, أَكَلَ كَذَا فَنُكِسَ ‡ [*He ate such a thing, and relapsed into his disease*]. (A, TA.) And تَعْسًا لَهُ وَنُكْسًا, and sometimes one says, نَكْسًا, (Ṣ, Ḳ,) in this case, (Ṣ,) for the sake of mutual resemblance, (Ṣ, Ḳ,) or because نَكْسًا is a dial form [of نُكْسًا], (Ṣ,) [meaning, † *May he fall upon his face,* or the like, (see art. تعس,) *and relapse into disease:* or] *may he fall upon his face, and not rise after his fall until he fall a second time:* and in like manner you say, ↑ تَعَسَ وَٱنْتَكَسَ. (Mṣb, art. تعس.) [See also 8.] You say also, نُكِسَ الجُرْحُ † [*The wound broke open again; or became recrudescent*]. (Ṣ, in arts. عرب and حبط, &c.) — And نَكَسَ الطَّعَامُ وَغَيْرُهُ دَآءَ المَرِيضِ ‡ *The food, &c., made the disease of the sick man to return.* (Ḳ.) And نَكَسَ الخِضَابَ عَلَى رَأْسِهِ ‡ *He put the dye upon his head repeatedly, or several times.* (A, TA.*) — Also نَكَسَ [or more probably نُكِسَ] † *He* (a man) *became weak and impotent.* (Sh, in TA.) And نُكِسَ عَنْ نُظَرَائِهِ, like عُنِىَ, † *He fell short of his fellows; was unable to attain to them.* (TA.) — نَكَسَ رَأْسَهُ, and ↑ نَكَّسَهُ, (TA,) [and نَكَسَ alone, (see نَاكِسٌ,)] and ↑ نَكَّسَ, (L, TA, art. بقو,) and ↑ انتكس, (TA,) [and in like manner ↑ تنكّس, said of a flower-stalk in the M and Ḳ, voce قِشْبٌ,] *He bent, or inclined, his head;* (TA;) *he lowered, or stooped, his head; bent, or hung, it down towards the ground;* absolutely; or *by reason of abasement.* (So accord. to explanations of the act. part. n., below.)

2: see 1, throughout.

5: see 1, last sentence.

8. انتكس quasi-pass. of نَكَسَهُ; (Ṣ, A, TA;) [and therefore signifying *It became turned over, or upside down; became turned over upon its head; became inverted; became reversed; became changed in its manner of being, or state; it became turned fore part behind; its first part was made to be last, or was put last:*] *he fell upon his head.* (Ḳ.) This last signification [understood figuratively] it is said to have in the phrase تَعَسَ وَٱنْتَكَسَ, a form of imprecation, meaning, † *May he be disappointed,* or *fail, of attaining his desire:* for he who is overthrown in his affair (مَنِ ٱنْتَكَسَ فِي أَمْرِهِ) is disappointed of attaining his desire, and suffers loss. (TA.) [See also 1, where this form of imprecation is differently explained.] — Also, i. q. نَكَسَ رَأْسَهُ. (TA.) [See 1, last signification.]

نِكْسٌ An arrow *having its notch broken, and its top therefore made its bottom:* (Ṣ, A, Ḳ:) pl. [of pauc.] أَنْكَاسٌ (A, TA) and [of mult.] نُكُسٌ. (A.) — A head, or blade, of an arrow &c., *having its tongue* (سِنْخ) *broken, and its point therefore made its tongue:* (Ḳ:) pl. أَنْكَاسٌ. (TA.) — A bow *of which the foot is made* [*of*] *the head of the branch;* as also ↑ مَنْكُوسَةٌ. This peculiarity is a fault. (Ḳ.) — A child *such as is termed* يَتْنٌ [*born preposterously, feet foremost;* but يَتْنٌ is an inf. n., and I have not found it used as an epithet anywhere but in this instance]; (Ḳ;) i. q. مَنْكُوسٌ; and mentioned by IDrd; but he says that it is not of established authority. (TA.) — ‡ *Low,* or *ignoble; base; vile; mean,* or *sordid:* See a verse cited voce أَشْعَلُ: (A:) ‡ one *who falls short of the utmost point of generosity;* (Ḳ;) or *of courage and generosity:* (TA:) † *weak;* (Ṣ, Ḳ;) applied to a man: (Ṣ:) † *short:* (AHn:) pl. أَنْكَاسٌ. (A, Ḳ.) — See also مُنْكَسٌ: — and نُكُسٌ.

نُكُسٌ, [app. pl. of نِكْسٌ,] † Old men *tottering by reason of age* (مُدْرَهِمُّونَ) *after attaining to extreme old age.* (Ḳ.)

نَاكِسٌ *Lowering his head; bending,* or *hanging, down his head towards the ground;* [absolutely;] (Ṣ, Ḳ;) [or] *by reason of abasement:* (TA:) pl. [properly نَاكِسُونَ; (see Ḳur, xxxii. 12;) and sometimes] نَوَاكِسُ, (Ṣ, Ḳ,) used [only] in poetry, (Ṣ, TA,) by reason of necessity, (TA,) and anomalous, (Ṣ, Ḳ,) like فَوَارِسُ. (Ṣ.) El-Farezdaḳ says,

* وَإِذَا ٱلرِّجَالُ رَأَوْا يَزِيدَ رَأَيْتَهُمْ *
* خُضُعَ الرِّقَابِ نَوَاكِسَ الأَبْصَارِ *

[*And when the men see Yezeed, thou seest them depressed in the necks, lowering the eyes*]: (Ṣ:) thus the verse is related by Fr and Ks: Akh says, that it is allowable to say نَوَاكِسِ الأَبْصَارِ, after the manner of the phrase جُحْرُ ضَبٍّ خَرِبٍ; [see art. خرب;] and Aḥmad Ibn-Yaḥyà adds

ى in relating it; saying نَوَاكِسِى الأَبْصَارِ. (TA.) [See the remarks on فَوَارِسُ, pl. of فَارِسٌ.]

مِنْكَسٌ A horse *that does not raise*, or *elevate, his head*, (Ṣ, IF, Ḳ,) *nor his neck, when running, by reason of weakness:* (IF, Ḳ:) or *that has not reached the other horses* (Lth, Ḳ) *in their heat,* or *single run to a goal;* (Lth;) i. e., *by reason of his weakness and impotence;* as also ▼ نِكْسٌ. (TA.)

وَلَدٌ مَنْكُوسٌ *A child* [*preposterously brought forth; whose feet come forth before his head.* (A, Mṣb, and so in a copy of the Ṣ.) See also نِكْسٌ. — وِلَادٌ مَنْكُوسٌ [*Preposterous childbirth*] is *when the feet come forth before the head;* (Ḳ, and so in a copy of the Ṣ, [and that this is what was meant by the author of the Ṣ seems to be indicated by what immediately follows]) *i. q.* يَتْنٌ. (Ṣ.) — طَوَافٌ مَنْكُوسٌ *A circuiting of the Kaabeh performed in a way contrary to the prescribed custom, by saluting the black stone and then going towards the left.* (Mgh.) — قَرَأَ القُرْآنَ مَنْكُوسًا *He read or recited, the Ḳur-án, beginning from the last part thereof,* (Ḳ,) i. e. *from* [*the commencement of the latter of*] *the* مُعَوِّذَتَانِ [or *last two chapters*], (TA,) *and ending with the* فَاتِحَة [or *first chapter*]; *contrary to the prescribed mode:* (TA:) or *beginning from the end of the chapter, and reading it,* or *reciting it, to its beginning, invertedly;* (Ḳ;) a mode which A'Obeyd thinks impossible; and therefore he holds the former explanation to be the right: (TA:) each of these practices is disapproved, excepting the former in teaching children, [in which case it is generally adopted in the present day,] (Ḳ,) and [in teaching] the foreigner the [portion of the Ḳur-án called the] مُفَصَّل; an indulgence being granted to these two only because the long chapters are difficult to them: but if any one knows the Ḳur-án by heart, and intentionally recite it from the last part thereof to the first, this is forbidden: and if we disapprove this, still more is the reciting from the end of the chapter to the beginning disapproved, if the doing this be possible. (TA.) — مَنْكُوسٌ also signifies ‡ *Suffering a relapse into disease, after convalescence;* or *after recovery, but not complete, of health and strength.* (Ḳ.) — مَنْكُوسَةٌ applied to a bow: see نِكْسٌ.

نكش

1. نَكَشَ البِئْرَ, (Ṣ, A,) or الرَّكِيَّةَ, (Ḳ,) aor. ـُ (Az, Ṣ, ISd, Ḳ) and ـِ, (IDrd, Ḳ,) inf. n. نَكْشٌ, (A,) *He entirely exhausted the water of the well:* (Az, Ṣ, A:) and (A) *he extracted what was in the well, of black fetid mud* (حَمْأَة [in some of the copies of the Ḳ, خَبِيئَة, which is a mistranscription,]) *and of clay;* (A, Ḳ;) as also ▼ اِنْتَكَشَهَا. (Ṣgh, Ḳ.) Hence the saying, فُلَانٌ بَحْرٌ لَا يُنْكَشُ † [*Such a one is*] *a sea,* or *great river, which will not be entirely exhausted, nor will diminish.* (Ḳ.) And عِنْدَهُ شَجَاعَةٌ لَا تُنْكَشُ (Ṣ, TA) ‡ *He has courage which will not be exhausted:* said of 'Alee, by a man of Ḳureysh. (TA.) — And نَكَشَ الشَّىْءَ *He consumed the thing; made it come to an end, fail, cease, perish,* or *come to nought:* (A, Ḳ:) and the same, (ISd, A,) aor. and inf. n. as above, (M,) or نَكَشَ مِنْهُ, (Lth, Ḳ,) *he made an end of the thing;* or *ceased from it, having finished it.* (Lth, ISd, A, Ḳ; but in [some of] the copies of the Ḳ, فَزِعَ is put by mistake for فَرَغَ, in this explanation. TA.) One says, اِنْتَهَوْا إِلَى عُشْبٍ فَنَكَشُوهُ *They came at last to herbage, and consumed it.* (Ṣ,* TA.) And لُمْعَةٌ مَا تُنْكَشُ [*A piece of herbage beginning to dry up*] *that is not extirpated,* or *cut off entirely with its roots.* (Ḳ.) — نَكْشٌ also signifies † The *scrutinizing* or *investigating,* or *searching* or *examining* or *inquiring into, affairs.* (TA.) [You say, app., نَكَشَ عَنِ الأُمُورِ, meaning, *He scrutinized,* &c., *affairs.*] — And نَكْشَانٌ is like نَكْشٌ [but in what sense is not said]. (TA.)

8: see 1, first sentence.

نَكَّاشٌ † A man *who scrutinizes* or *investigates,* or *searches* or *examines* or *inquires into, affairs;* (TA;) as also ▼ مِنْكَشٌ. (IDrd, Ḳ.)

مِنْكَشٌ: see نَكَّاشٌ.

مِنْكَاشٌ *a dial. form of* مِنْقَاشٌ, but of weak authority. (TA.)

مَنْكُوشٌ A receptacle of the kind called سَفَط *of which the contents have been taken out.* (TA.) — هُوَ مَنْكُوشٌ مِنَ المَنَاكِيشِ † [*He is one of those who are empty,* or *devoid of good*]: a phrase denoting vituperation. (TA.)

نكص

1. نَكَصَ عَنِ الأَمْرِ, (A, Ḳ,) [aor. ـُ, and sometimes ـِ, as will be shown below,] inf. n. نُكُوصٌ (Ṣ, IF, A, Mṣb, Ḳ) and نَكْصٌ (A, Ḳ) and مَنْكَصٌ (Ḳ) and نَكْصَانٌ, (MA,) *He receded, retired,* or *drew back from the thing,* or *affair; refrained, forbore, abstained,* or *desisted, from it; recoiled from it, shrank from it,* or *drew back from it in awe* or *fear;* (Ṣ, IF, A, Mṣb, Ḳ;) as also نَكَتَ عَنْهُ. (Aboo-Turáb, TA.) You say also, نَكَصَ عَلَى عَقِبَيْهِ, (Ṣ, Mṣb, Ḳ,) or على عَقِبِهِ, (A,) aor. ـِ (Ṣ, Mṣb) and ـُ, (Ṣ,) or the latter only, (Ṣgh, TA,) or the former is allowable, (Zj, TA,) *He turned back from a thing to which he had applied himself;* (IDrd, Ṣ,* A,* Mṣb,* Ḳ, TA;) meaning a good thing; and sometimes an evil thing; (IDrd, TA;) or meaning particularly a good thing; or extr. with respect to an evil thing. (Ḳ.) [See the Ḳur, xxiii. 68.] Hence ▼ انتكص [as syn. with نكص], though we have not heard it. (Mgh.)

8: see above.

حَظُّهُ نَاقِصٌ وَجَدُّهُ نَاكِصٌ ‡ [*His lot,* or *portion, is decreasing,* or *deficient, and his good fortune is receding*]. (A, TA.)

مَنْكَصٌ, (O, B, Ḳ,) like مَقْعَدٌ, (TA,) [in the CḲ, erroneously, مُنْكَص,] *A place to which one removes, withdraws,* or *retires afar off;* syn. مُتَنَحًّى. (O, B, Ḳ.) El-Aạshà says, praising 'Alḳamah Ibn-'Olátheh,

• أَعَلْقَمُ قَدْ جَبَّرَتْنِى الأُمُورُ •
• إِلَيْكَ وَمَا كَانَ لِى مَنْكَصُ •

[*O 'Alḳamah, affairs have compelled me to have recourse to thee, and there was not for me any place to which to retire.* (TA.)

[نكظ, &c.
See Supplement.]

نمأ

نَمْأٌ and نَمْءٌ *Little lice.* (Kr, Ḳ.) [See also نِمْئَةٌ.]

نمت

نَمْتٌ *A certain plant, having a fruit that is eaten.* (L, Ḳ.) The only explanation given by several lexicographers. (TA.)

نمذج

نَمُوذَجٌ (Ḳ, Mṣb &c.) and أُنْمُوذَجٌ; which latter is said to be a corruption in the TṢ and the Ḳ; but this is denied by El-Khafájee and by Mṭr; and learned men, in early and in late times, have constantly used the word انموذج without any expression of disapproval; Z and El-Ḥasan Ibn-Rasheeḳ El-Ḳeyrawánee, two leading lexicologists, having even named thereby books written by them; (MF;) vulgo نَمُونَه [which is a Persian word]; (TA;) *A model, an exemplar, a pattern,* or *a likeness of a thing, after the similitude of which a thing is made:* (Mṣb:) *a model,* or *likeness, of a thing;* (Ḳ;) i.e., *a thing that is made in the form,* or *after the fashion, of another thing, that the mode of the latter may be known thereby:* (TA:) a *thing which shows the mode,* or *quality,* or *qualities, of another thing:* (Mṣb:) an arabicized word, (Ḳ,) from [the Persian] نَمُودَه.

نمر

1. نَمِرَ, aor. ـَ, (Ṣ, Ḳ,) inf. n. نَمَرٌ, (Ṣ,) [*It was,*

or *became, spotted like a leopard* or *panther:* see also 5:] *it* (a cloud, or collection of clouds,) *became of the colour of the* نَمِر [*leopard* or *panther*], (Ṣ, Ḳ,) *spots being seen in their interstices.* (Ṣ.) ═ See also 5, in three places.

2. نَمَّرَ, inf. n. تَنْمِيرٌ, † *He, or it, changed,* or *altered, and rendered morose,* his face. (T.) ═ See also 5, in two places.

5. تَنَمَّرَ [*He made himself like a leopard* or *panther, in diversity of colours:* see also 1]. 'Amr Ibn-Maạdee-Kerib says,

* قَوْمٌ إِذَا لَبِسُوا الحَدِيـ *
* ـدَ تَنَمَّرُوا حَلَقًا وَقِدَّا *

[*A people* who, *when they put on* armour of *iron* mail,] *make themselves like the leopard* or *panther* (نمر) *in the diversity of colours of the iron* [*rings*] *and the thongs.* (Ṣ.) —— † *He made himself like the leopard* or *panther* (نمر, Ḳ, TA) *in ill-nature:* (TA:) ‡ *he became angry;* as also ↓ نَمِرَ, (M,) aor. ـَ, inf. n. ↓ نَمَرٌ; (TA;) and ↓ نَمَّرَ: (M:) ‡ *he became evil in disposition;* as also ↓ نَمِرَ: (T:) ‡ *he became angry and evil in disposition;* as also ↓ نَمِرَ and ↓ نَمَّرَ; (IḲṭṭ, Ṣgh, Ḳ;) *like the* نمر: (TA:) ‡ *he strained the voice in threatening:* (Ṣgh, Ḳ:) and تَنَمَّرَ لَهُ † *he became ill-natured and altered to him, and threatened him;* because the نَمِر is never met otherwise than angry and ill-natured. (Aṣ, Ṣ, Ḳ.)

نَمْرٌ: see نَمِرٌ.

نَمِرٌ: see أَنْمَرُ, throughout. —— نَمِرٌ (Ṣ, A, Mṣb, Ḳ, &c.) and نِمْرٌ, (M, A, Mṣb, Ḳ,) which is a contraction of the former, (Mṣb,) or a dial. form, (TA,) [The *leopard;*] *a certain wild beast,* (Ṣ, A, Mṣb, Ḳ, &c.) *well known,* (A, Ḳ,) *more malignant than the lion,* (T, M, Mgh, Mṣb,) *and bolder,* (Mṣb,) *so called because of his* نُمَر [or *spots*], (M, Ḳ,) *being of divers colours,* (M,) *called in Persian* پَلَنْك: (Mgh:) fem. with ة: (Ṣ, Mṣb:) pl. [of pauc.] أَنْمُرٌ (M, Ḳ) and أَنْمَارٌ, (M, Mṣb, Ḳ,) and [of mult.] نُمُورٌ, (Ṣ, M, Mṣb, Ḳ,) held by Th to be pl. of نِمْرٌ, (M,) and نُمُورَةٌ (Mṣb, and so in some copies of the Ḳ) and نُمُرٌ, (Ṣ, M, Ḳ,) which occurs in poetry, and is anomalous, perhaps a contraction of نُمُورٌ, (Ṣ,) and not mentioned by Sb, (M,) and نُمْرٌ, (M, Ḳ,) which is the most common in occurrence, but, accord. to Th, he who uses it makes the sing. أَنْمَرُ, (M,) and نِمَارٌ, (M, Ḳ,) held by Th to be pl. of نِمْرٌ, (M,) and نِمَارَةٌ. (Ḳ.) As the نَمِر is one of the most abominable and malignant of wild beasts, one says, لَبِسَ فُلَانٌ لِفُلَانٍ جِلْدَ النَّمِرِ, meaning, ‡ *Such a one became changed,* or *altered, to such a one;* or *met him in a morose manner:* (IB:) or *became very rancourous,* or *malicious, towards him.* (TA.) The kings of the Arabs, when they sat [in judgment] to slay a man, used to attire themselves in skins of the نَمِر, and then give orders for the slaying of him whom they desired to slay. (IB.) ═ See also نَمِرٌ, throughout.

نُمْرَةٌ *A spot,* or *speck, of any colour whatever:* pl. نُمَرٌ. (M, Ḳ.)

نَمِرَةٌ *A garment of the kind called* بُرْدَةٌ, *of wool,* (Ṣ, Ḳ, TA,) *striped,* (TA,) *worn by the Arabs of the desert:* (Ṣ, Ḳ, TA:) or *a garment of the kind called* شَمْلَةٌ, (M, Ḳ,) or كِسَآء, (A, Mgh, Mṣb,) *having white and black stripes,* or *lines,* (M, Mgh, Mṣb, Ḳ,) *worn by the Arabs of the desert:* (A, Mṣb:) and *a garment of the kind called* حِبَرَةٌ; (M, Ḳ;) so called because of the diversity of the colours of its stripes: (M:) or *any* مِئْزَر, *of those worn by the Arabs of the desert, that is a striped* شَمْلَة: (IAth:) or *a striped* إِزَار *of wool;* (TA;) pl. نِمَارٌ: (IAth, Mṣb:) it is an epithet in which the quality of a subst. predominates. (TA.) It is said in a trad. of Saạd, نَبَطِىٌّ فِى حُبْوَتِهِ أَعْرَابِىٌّ فِى نَمِرَتِهِ أَسَدٌ فِى تَامُورَتِهِ [*A Nabathean in his ḥubweh* (a long piece of cloth, or the like, wound round the back and legs of a person sitting with his thighs against his belly); *an Arab of the desert in his nemireh; a lion in his den*]. (Ṣ.) —— See also أَنْمَرُ.

مَآءٌ نَمِيرٌ (T, Ṣ, M, A, Ḳ) and ↓ نَمِرٌ, (M, Ḳ,) *Wholesome water, whether sweet or not sweet:* (Ṣ, Ḳ:) or *sweet and wholesome water:* (T, A:) or *wholesome in satiety:* (TA:) or *copious:* (Ibn-Keyrán, M, Ḳ:) or *increasing in quantity,* syn. نَامٍ, (Aṣ, T, TA,) or زَاكٍ, (Ḳ,) *whether sweet or not sweet:* (T, TA:) or *increasing in quantity in the beasts* [app. meaning while they drink], زَاكٍ فِى المَاشِيَةِ نَامٍ, T, M,) *whether sweet or not sweet.* (M.) [As زَاكٍ is coupled with نَامٍ, app. as an explicative adjunct, in the T and M, I think that I have here rendered it correctly: otherwise I should have supposed it to mean, perhaps, *pure.*] —— حَسَبٌ نَمِيرٌ, (Ṣ, M, A, Ḳ,) and ↓ نَمِرٌ, (M, Ḳ,) ‡ *i. q.* زَاكٍ [see above]: (Ṣ, M, A, Ḳ:) pl. أَنْمَارٌ. (M.)

أَنْمَرُ *Spotted white and black:* (M, Ḳ:) or *in which is black and white;* applied to a wild beast; as also ↓ نَمِرٌ: (A:) fem. نَمْرَآءُ; (M, A, Ḳ;) applied to a ewe or she-goat: (A:) pl. نُمْرٌ: (A:) also أَنْمَرُ a horse, (Ṣ, Ḳ,) and an ostrich, (Ḳ,) *variegated like the* نَمِر, (Ṣ, Ḳ, TA,) *having one spot white and another of any colour:* (Ṣ, TA:) pl. as above: (TA:) or, applied to an ostrich, *in which is blackness and whiteness:* pl. as above: (Ṣ:) and a lion in which is dust-colour and blackness: and ↓ مُنَمَّرٌ a bird *having black spots;* also sometimes applied as an epithet to a horse such as is termed بِرْذَوْن. (TA.) Also, A collection of clouds *of the colour of the* نَمِر, *spots being seen in their interstices:* (Ṣ:) or *having black and white spots:* (TA:) and ↓ نَمِرٌ signifies a collection of clouds *having marks like those of the* نَمِر: or *small portions near together:* n. un. with ة: (M:) or ↓ نَمِرَةٌ signifies *a small portion of a cloud:* and its pl. [or rather the coll. gen. n.] is نَمِرٌ. (Ḳ.) It is said in a proverb, أَرِنِيهَا نَمِرَةً أُرِكْهَا مَطِرَةً [*Show thou it to me spotted like the leopard, I will show it to thee raining*]: (Ṣ, Ḳ:) alluding to an event which one certainly knows will happen when the symptoms thereof appear: (Meyd, Ḳ, TA:) originally said by Aboo-Dhu-eyb El-Hudhalee: (TA:) نَمِرَة is here like خَضِرًا in the Ḳur, vi. 99, for أَخْضَرَ: (Akh, Ṣ:) by rule, it should be نَمْرَآءَ, (Ḳ, TA,) fem. of أَنْمَرُ. (TA.) —— See also نَمِر.

مُنَمَّرٌ: see أَنْمَرُ. [In the TA, voce حِبَرَةٌ, it is applied as an epithet to a garment of the kind called بُرْد: and in the Ḳ, voce حَبِير, to a cloud, or collection of clouds: in the former case, it app. signifies *striped,* (see نَمِرَةٌ,) or, as in the latter case, *spotted.*]

نمس

1. نَمَسَهُ, aor. ـِ, inf. n. نَمْسٌ, *He concealed it;* namely, a secret. (Ṣ.) See also 2. —— *He spoke,* or *discoursed, secretly to him,* or *with him; he acquainted him with a secret;* (Ṣ;) as also ↓ نَامَسَهُ, (Ṣ, M, A, Ḳ,) inf. n. مُنَامَسَةٌ (M, A) and نِمَاسٌ. (M.) You say, مَا أَشْوَقَنِى إِلَى مُنَامَسَتِكَ [*How great is my desire, or longing, for thy secret discourse!*] (A, TA.) ═ [And it seems to be indicated in the M, that نَمَسَ, aor. and inf. n. as above, signifies *He became a confidant,* or *acquainted with another's secrets.*] ═ [Hence, perhaps,] نَمَسَ بَيْنَهُمْ, inf. n. as above; (IAạr;) and ↓ أَنْمَسَ بَيْنَهُمْ, (IAạr, Ḳ,) inf. n. إِنْمَاسٌ; (IAạr;) *He created discord,* or *dissension, among them,* (IAạr, Ḳ,) *and incited them one against another,* or *went about among them with calumnies.* (IAạr.) See also 2. ═ نَمِسَ, aor. ـَ, inf. n. نَمَسٌ, *It* (clarified butter, Ṣ, A, Ḳ, or oil, M, and perfume, and the like, A, and anything sweet or good, M) *became bad,* or *corrupt,* (Ṣ, A, Ḳ,) *so as to be slimy, ropy,* or *viscous;* (TA;) *became altered* (M, TA) *and bad, in the manner described above:* (TA:) and ↓ نَمَّسَ, said of [the preparation made of churned milk called] أَقِط, *it became stinking,* or *fetid.* (TA.) See also 2, below.

2. نَمَّسَ عَلَيْهِ الأَمْرَ, (A,* TA,) inf. n. تَنْمِيسٌ,

(A, K,) *He concealed from him the thing*, or *affair*; or *made it dubious*, or *confused, to him*; syn. لَبَّسَهُ. (A, K,* TA.) See also 1, first signification. ═ نمّس بصاحبه *He calumniated his companion*; syn. نمّ به. (A.) See also 1. ═ نمّس شعره *His hair became befouled by oil*. (M.) See also 1, last sentence.

3. نامس *He* (a hunter) *entered a* نَامُوس, i. e., *lurking-place*, or *covert*. (K.) See also 7. ═ نَمَّسَهُ : see نامسهُ.

4. نَمَّس بِنهرِ : see انمس بنهر.

5. تنمّس *He* (a hunter) *made for himself a* نَامُوس, i. e., *lurking-place*, or *covert*. (A.) — تَنَمَّسَ بِهِ : see نَامُوسٌ.

7. اِنْمَسَ, of the measure اِنْفَعَلَ, (S, CK [in some copies of the K, افتعل, which is a mistake,]) *He concealed himself*: (S, K:) or انمس فِى الشَّىْءِ signifies *he entered into the thing* (M, IKtt) *and concealed himself*. (IKtt.) See also one of the explanations of نَامُوسٌ, in which this verb occurs: and see 3.

نِمْسٌ [The *ichneumon*; so called in the present day;] *a certain small beast*, (IKt, El-Fárábee, S, M, Msb, K,) *broad, as though it were a piece of* قَدِيد [or *salted* or *sun-dried flesh-meat*], (S,) *found in the land of Egypt*, (S, K,*) *one of the most malignant of wild animals*, (M,) *that kills the* [*kind of serpent called*] ثُعْبَان: (IKt, El-Fárábee, S, M, Msb, K:) *the keeper of vines* or *palm-trees* or *seed-produce* (النَّاطُورُ) *takes it for his use, when he is in vehement fear of serpents of the kind above mentioned: for it attacks them, making itself thin and slender as though it were a piece of rope; and when it winds itself upon them, they draw back their breath vehemently, and it takes their breath; thus the serpent becomes inflated in its inside, and is cut asunder*: (TA:) or *i. q.* اِبْنُ عِرْسٍ [*the weasel*]: (IKt, TA:) or *a certain small beast, resembling the cat, generally frequenting gardens*; accord. to IF, *also called* دَلَق [q. v.]; (Msb;) the *beast called* دَلَهْ [the Persian original of دَلَق]; [see اِبْنُ مِقْرَضٍ, in art. قرض;] called نمس from نَمَسَ in the first of the senses explained above: (A;) or *i. q.* ظَرِبَانٌ: (El-Mufaddal Ibn-Selemeh, TA:) from these various sayings, it appears that several species are called by this name: (TA:) pl. [of pauc.] أَنْمَاسٌ (TA) and [of mult.] نُمُوسٌ. (Msb.) You say, فِى النَّاسِ أَنْمَاسٌ [app. meaning, *Among men are some that are malignant as the animals called* انماس]. (A, TA.)

نَمَسٌ The *odour of milk*, and *of grease* or *gravy*; as also نَسَمٌ. (M.)

نَمِسٌ, applied to clarified butter, (A,) or oil, (M,) and perfume, and the like, (A,) and anything sweet or good, (M,) *Bad*, or *corrupt*, (A, TA,) *so as to be slimy, ropy*, or *viscous*; (TA;) *altered*, (M, TA,) *and bad, in the manner described above*: (TA:) and ♦ مُنْمِسٌ, applied to أَقِط, [see 1, last signification,] *stinking*, or *fetid*. (TA.)

نَمَّاسٌ : see نَامُوسٌ.

نَامُوسٌ *A secret*: (Seer, M:) [pl. نَوَامِيسُ.] — [Hence, app., rather than from the Greek νόμος as some have supposed,] *Revelation*. So in a trad. respecting fines for bloodshed; in which it is said, قَضَيْتَ فِينَا بِالنَّامُوسِ [*Thou hast pronounced judgment respecting us according to revelation*]. (Mgh.) [But see a remark on this signification in what follows.] — [And hence,] The *law of God*. (KT.) — [And from the first,] *An evasion, artifice*, or *expedient, by which a man conceals himself*; expl. by مَا يَنْمَسُ بِهِ الرَّجُلُ مِنَ الاِحْتِيَالِ; (S;) or مَا تُنْمَسُ بِهِ مِنَ الاِحْتِيَالِ: (K [but here, app., تُنْمَسُ is a mistake for تَنَمَّسُ:]) *deceit; guile; circumvention*. (A, TA.) You say, فُلَانٌ صَاحِبُ نَامُوسٍ, and نَوَامِيسَ, *Such a one is a person of deceit*, &c., and *of deceits*, &c. (A, TA.) And hence the phrase نَوَامِيسُ الحُكَمَآءِ [app. meaning *The artifices of the wise men*]. (TA.) — [Also, in post-classical writings, A man's *honour*, or *reputation, which should be preserved inviolate*; syn. عِرْض.] — [The remaining significations I regard as being derived from those above mentioned; supposing a prefixed noun to be understood; in some instances, صَاحِب, or ذُو; in others, مَحَلّ, or مَكَان.] — *A confidant; one who possesses*, or *is acquainted with, secrets*, or *private affairs*; (S, M, A, Mgh, Msb, K;) of a king, (Mgh, TA,) or governor, or prince, (A,) or other man; (A'Obeyd, S, M, Msb, TA;) *whom one acquaints with his private affairs, and distinguishes by revealing to him what he conceals from others*: (A'Obeyd, S:) or *one who possesses*, or *is acquainted with, secrets*, or *private affairs, of a good nature*: (K, TA:) and جَاسُوسٌ signifies one who possesses, or is acquainted with, secrets, or private affairs of an evil nature. (TA.) [The author of the Mgh thinks that the second of the significations mentioned above, i. e. "revelation," is derived from this; a prefixed noun [such as كِتَاب, perhaps,] being understood.] Hence, (Mgh,) النَّامُوسُ, (A'Obeyd, S, M, Msb, K,) or النَّامُوسُ الأَكْبَرُ, (A, TA,) is applied to [*The angel*] *Gabriel*; (A'Obeyd, S, M, A, &c.) by the people of the scriptures; [meaning, the Christians, and perhaps, the Jews also;] (S, Mgh;) because God has distinguished him by communicating to him revelations and hidden things with which no other is acquainted. (TA.) — *A repository* (وِعَآء) *of knowledge*. (M.) — *Skilful; intelligent*. (K,* TA.) — *One who enters into affairs with subtle artifice*. (As, K.*) — *A calumniator*; syn. نَمَّامٌ; (K;) as also ♦ نَمَّاسٌ. (A, K.) — *A liar*. (M.) — The *lurking-place*, or *covert*, (قُتْرَة, q. v.,) *of a hunter*, (S, M, A, K,) *in which he lies in wait for the game*: (TA:) sometimes written with ء [نَأْمُوسٌ]; but for what reason [says ISd] I know not. (M.) — *A snare*; syn. شَرَك: (K:) because it is concealed beneath the ground. (TA.) — The *covert*, or *retreat, of a lion*; as also ♦ نَامُوسَةٌ. (K.) — The *chamber*, or *cell, of a monk*. (TA, K,* voce نَأْمُور.)

نَامُوسَةٌ : see نَامُوسٌ, last signification but one.

أَنْمَسُ *Of a dusky*, or *dingy, colour*, (K,) [*like the* نِمْس, or *ichneumon*.] — Hence, [its pl.] نُمْسٌ is applied to [*A certain species* (*namely the* كُدْرِىّ) *of*] *the kind of birds called* قَطًا. (K.)

نَمِسٌ : see مُنْمِسٌ.

مُنَامِسٌ *Entering a* نَامُوس [or *hunter's lurking-place*]. (S.)

نمش

1. نَمِشَ, aor. ـَ, (K,) inf. n. نَمَشٌ, (TA,) *He*, or *it, was*, or *became, speckled with white and black*: or *marked with spots upon the skin differing from it in colour*. (K.) See نَمَشٌ below. ═ نَمَشَهُ, inf. n. نَمْشٌ, *He variegated it*; or *decorated*, or *embellished, it*; (TA;) [as also ♦ نَمَّشَهُ, but app. in an intensive sense, for its inf. n.] تَنْمِيشٌ is *syn. with* تَدْبِيجٌ. (TA.) — [And hence, app.,] † *He mixed*, or *confounded, it*; e. g., good speech with bad; as also the ♦ latter of these two words. (TA.)

2 : see 1, in two places.

نَمْشٌ *A mark, trace, vestige*, or *relic*. (TA.)

نَمَشٌ *White and black specks* (S, A, Mgh, K) in a colour: (TA:) or *spots in the skin differing from it in colour*; (IDrd, A, K;) sometimes in horses, and mostly in such as are of a sorrel colour. (TA.) — *Lines*, or *streaks, of variegations* or *decorations* in variegated or figured cloth, &c. (K.) — *Whiteness in the roots*, or *lower parts, of the nails, which goes away and returns*. (TA.)

نَمِشٌ *Speckled with white and black*; applied to a bull; (TA:) and so ♦ أَنْمَشُ; (Mgh, TA;) applied to a man. (Mgh.) You say, ثَوْرٌ نَمِشٌ, meaning, *A wild bull, which has specks* (S, TA) *and lines*, or *streaks*. (TA.) And ثَوْرٌ نَمِشٌ

القَوَائِمِ *A bull having black lines, or streaks, in the legs.* (A.) And ♦ عَنْزٌ نَمْشَآءُ *A she-goat that is black speckled with white, or white speckled with black.* (TA.) —— ‡ سَيْفٌ نَمِشٌ *A sword in which are diversified wavy streaks.* (A, K,* TA.) —— بَعِيرٌ نَمِشٌ *A camel having in his foot a mark that becomes distinctly shown upon the ground, without any mark thereon made artificially;* (Ibn-'Abbád, K;) and so بعير نَمِشٌ. (Ibn-'Abbád, TA.)

أَنْمَشُ : fem. نَمْشَآءُ : see نَمِشٌ, in two places.

نمط

2. تَنْمِيطٌ signifies The *directing,* or *guiding,* to a thing. (K.) You say, مَنْ نَمَّطَكَ عَلَى هٰذَا الشَّىْءِ *Who directed thee,* or *guided thee, to this thing?* syn. دَلَّكَ عَلَيْهِ. (Ibn-'Abbád.)

نَمَطٌ The *facing,* or *outer covering,* (ظِهَارَة,) *of a bed* (T, Mgh, K) *upon which one sleeps,* (Mgh,) or *of a thing that is spread upon the ground to sit or lie upon,* (T, K,) *whatever it be:* (K:) or *a sort of carpet* or *other thing that is spread upon the ground:* (S, K:) and *a woollen cloth* (Mgh, Msb, K) *which is thrown over the* [*kind of vehicle called*] هَوْدَج, (Mgh, K,) *having a fine nap, or pile,* (TA,) *of some colour; what is white being seldom or never so called:* (Msb:) or *a sort of dyed cloth, like* زَوْج, *these names being seldom or never applied but to what is coloured red or green or yellow; what is white not being called* نَمَط: (Az, L:) and *a cloth that is spread beneath a horse's saddle:* (Meyd, as cited by Golius:) some say, that it is *a receptacle like the* سَفَط: (Har, p. ٢٧٣ [but this I think doubtful:]) pl. أَنْمَاطٌ [properly a pl. of pauc. but used also as one of mult.] (S, Mgh, Msb, K) and نِمَاطٌ. (IB, K.) == *A body of men* (S, Mgh, Msb, K) *whose case is one;* i. e. *a class of men.* (S, K.) It is said in a trad., (S, Mgh,) of 'Alee, (Mgh,) خَيْرُ هٰذِهِ الأُمَّةِ النَّمَطُ الأَوْسَطُ *The best of this people is the middle body thereof* (S, Mgh) *whose case is one;* i. e. *the middle class thereof:* (S, in which is added, يَلْحَقُ بِهِمُ التَّالِى وَيَرْجِعُ إِلَيْهِمُ الغَالِى [*he who falls short shall be made to reach them, and he who exceeds the due bounds shall be brought back to them:*]) A'Obeyd says, (Mgh, TA,) the meaning of this saying of 'Alee is, (TA,) that he disliked the exceeding of the due bounds and the falling short (Mgh, TA) in religion. (TA.) == *A way:* (Msb, TA:) *a way, course, mode,* or *manner, of acting, conduct,* or *the like;* (Mgh, K;) as also ♦ انمط: (TA [so there written, without any syll. points:]) *a tenet,* or *body of tenets, belief, creed, opinion,* or *persuasion, which one takes to,* or *holds:* (Mgh, TA:) *a kind,* or *way, of speech.* (TA.) You say, اِلْزَمْ هٰذَا النَّمَطَ *keep thou to this way.* (TA.) And تَكَلَّمُوا عَلَى نَمَطٍ وَاحِدٍ *They spoke according to one way, course, mode, or manner, &c.* (Mgh.) —— ‡ *A sort,* or *species,* (Mgh, Msb, K,) of a thing, (K,) of goods or commodities, of learning or science, &c. (TA.) You say, عِنْدِى مَتَاعٌ مِنْ هٰذَا النَّمَطِ ‡ *I have goods of this sort,* or *species.* (Mgh.) And هٰذَا مِنْ نَمَطِ هٰذَا ‡ *This is of the sort,* or *species, of this.* (Msb.)

أَنْمَاطِىٌّ : see نَمَطِىٌّ.

انمط : see نَمَطٌ.

أَنْمَاطِىٌّ [*A maker,* or *seller, of* أَنْمَاط, pl. of نَمَط:] a rel. n. from نَمَطٌ ; as also ♦ نَمَطِىٌّ : (K, TA:) the former [from the pl.,] like أَنْصَارِىٌّ : the latter from the sing., agreeably with analogy. (TA.)

[نمق, &c.

See Supplement.]

نهأ

1. نَهِئَ, aor. ـَ ; and نَهُؤَ, aor. ـُ ; (S, K;) and نَهُؤَ ; (as in one copy of the S;) inf. n. نَهْءٌ (S, K) and نَهَأٌ (S) and نَهَآءَةٌ (S, K) and نُهُوءٌ (K) and نُهُوءٌ (S, K) and نَهَاوَةٌ, (the last dev. from rule); (K;) *It* (flesh-meat) *was not,* or *did not become, thoroughly cooked.* (S, K.) —— مَا أُبَالِى مَا نَهِئَ مِنْ ضَبِّكَ وَلَا مَا نَضِجَ [*I care not what is insufficiently cooked, of thy* ضَبّ, *nor what is thoroughly cooked:* i. e. I care not whether evil or good befall thee]. (S,* TA,) A proverb. (TA.) == شَرِبَ حَتَّى نَهَأَ, aor. ـَ , *He drank till he was full.* (K,* TA.)

4. انهأ (S, K) inf. n. إِنْهَآءٌ, (S,) *He insufficiently cooked* flesh-meat. (S, K.) —— *He did a thing not firmly, not soundly, not thoroughly.* (K.)

نُهُوءٌ The *state of being not thoroughly cooked.* (TA.)

نَهِىءٌ (S, K) and ♦ مُنْهَأٌ (S) *Insufficiently cooked* flesh-meat. (S, K.)

نَاهِئٌ *Satiated with food and with drink.* (IAar.)

مُنْهَأٌ : see نَهِىءٌ.

نهب

1. نَهَبَ النَّهْبَ aor. ـَ , and ـُ ; and نَهِبَهُ, aor. ـَ ; (inf. n. نَهْبٌ ; TA ;) and ♦ انتهبه ; [and ♦ ناهبه ;] *He took the spoil, plunder,* or *booty.* (K.) ♦ الإِنْتِهَابُ is *The taking of spoil, plunder,* or *booty, by whomsoever will:* you say ♦ أَنْهَبَ الرَّجُلُ مَالَهُ [*the man allowed,* or *gave, his property to be taken as spoil*], ♦ فَٱنْتَهَبُوهُ, and نَهَبُوهُ, and ♦ نَاهَبُوهُ, which all signify the same, [*and they took it as spoil*]. (S.) —— نَهَبَهُ الكَلْبُ, aor. ـَ , *The dog seized him* (a man) *by the tendon of his heel.* (S, K.) —— نَهَبُوهُ ; (S, K;) and ♦ ناهبوه, (K,) inf. n. مُنَاهَبَةٌ ; (TA;) ‡ *They carped at him in their speech,* (S, K,) or, *with their tongues, and spoke roughly, harshly,* or *coarsely, to him:* [as though they plundered him of his good name]. (A.)

3 : see 1. —— ناهب الفَرَسُ الفَرَسَ, inf. n. مُنَاهَبَةٌ, ‡ *The* [*one*] *horse emulated,* or *contended with, the* [*other*] *horse in running.* (TA: and agreeably with this the inf. n. is explained in the S and K.) —— Used not only with reference to a horse. The Rájiz says,

* نَاهَبْتُهُمْ بِنَيْطَلٍ جَرُوفِ *

[*I emulated them, or contended with them, with a bucket that took up much water*]. (S.) See also 6.

4. انهب الرَّجُلُ مَالَهُ (S) *The man allowed, or gave, his property to be taken as spoil, plunder, or booty.* (TA.) It is doubly trans.: you say أَنْهَبْتُ زَيْدًا المَالَ [*I allowed Zeyd to take the property as spoil*]. (Msb.) See 1. انهبهُ فُلَانًا *He offered it,* or *exposed it, to such a one,* [to be taken as spoil]. (TA.)

6. تناهب الفَرَسَانِ ‡ *The two horses emulated,* or *contended with, each other.* (TA.) See also 3. —— تَنَاهَبَا المَآءَ *i. q.* تَجَاشَعَاهُ, q. v. (TA, in art. جشع.) —— تَنَاهَبَتِ الإِبِلُ الأَرْضَ ‡ *The camels took much of the ground with their legs:* (K:) [app. meaning, *took wide strides over it:* not, as rendered by Golius, "multum pulveris pedibus suis rapuerunt;" nor, as rendered by Freytag, "multum terræ pedibus abstulerunt."]. —— الإِبِلُ يَتَنَاهَبْنَهُ يَنْهَبْنَ السُّرَى, and يَتَنَاهَبْنَهُ, [*The camels perform the night-journey with large strides*]: and [in like manner] تناهبت الأَرْضَ. Camels that do so are termed إِبِلٌ نَوَاهِبُ. (A.)

8 : see 1. —— انتهب الفَرَسُ الشَّوْطَ ‡ *The horse gained the winning-post;* or *won the race.* (K, TA.)

نَهْبٌ *Spoil; plunder; booty;* (S, K;) as also ♦ نُهْبَةٌ : (TA, art. خلس :) ex. أَتَى لَهُ بِنَهْبٍ *he came to him with,* or *brought to him, spoil:*

(TA:) pl. نِهَابٌ (Ṣ, Ḳ) and نُهُوبٌ: (Nh, &c.:) ▼ نُهْبَى also signifies *the same;* and thus is similar to نُحْلَى, meaning عَطِيَّةٌ: and also signifies *what is allowed, or given, to be taken as spoil, plunder, or booty;* and thus is similar to رُقْبَى and عُمْرَى; (IAth;) and so ▼ نُهْبَةٌ (Mṣb) [and ▼ نُهَّبَى and ▼ نُهَيْبَى:] a man, named Fizr, said of some goats which he drove forth, هِىَ النُّهَيْبَى, or النُّهْبَى, accord. to different readings; meaning that it was not allowable to any one person to take of them more than one: (TA:) or نَهْبٌ signifies *what is taken as spoil, plunder, or booty; or so taken by whomsoever will, of what is allowed to be so taken:* syn. مَا ٱنْتُهِبَ: (Lḥ, Ḳ:) and ▼ نُهْبَى, *what is allowed to be so taken;* syn. إِسْمُ مَا أُنْهِبَ: (Ṣ:) or *what is taken as spoil, plunder, or booty;* syn. إِسْمُ مَا نُهِبَ. (So in one copy of the Ṣ.) — [Hence] نَهْبٌ *An incursion made into an enemy's territory for the sake of acquiring spoil, plunder, or booty; and a spoiling, or plundering.* (TA.) — أَحْرَزْتُ نَهْبِى وَأَبْتَغِى النَّوَافِلَ, in a trad. of Aboo-Beker, means *I have accomplished what I had to perform of the prayers termed* الوِتْر *before my sleeping, lest the occasion for my doing so should slip from me; and when I awake, I perform the prayers termed* النوافل. (TA.) [He termed the وتر prayers نَهْب because he performed them before the right time.] — نَهْبٌ ‡ *A kind of* رَكْض [i. e., app., of *running,* with reference to a horse]. (Lḥ, Ḳ.)

نُهْبَةٌ and ▼ نُهْبَى (Lḥ, Mgh, Mṣb, Ḳ) and ▼ نُهَّبَى and نُهَيْبَى (Ḳ) *Spoil, plunder, or booty; a thing taken as spoil:* (Mgh, Mṣb:) and also *Spoliation; a taking of spoil, plunder, or booty:* (Mgh:) substs. from نَهَبَ: (Ḳ:) and substs. in the sense of إِنْتِهَابٌ: (Lḥ, Mgh:) ▼ نُهْبَى is explained in the Towsheeḥ as signifying *the taking of a Muslim's property by force:* it is said, [of Moḥammad,] in a trad., that he scattered some articles of property, and the people did not take them; so he asked them why they did not take; and they replied أَوَلَيْسَ قَدْ نَهَيْتَ عَنِ النُّهْبَى [*Hast thou not forbidden spoliation?*]; but he said إِنَّمَا نَهَيْتُ عَنْ نُهْبَى العَسَاكِرِ [*I have only forbidden soldiers' spoliation*]. (TA.) See نَهْبٌ.

نُهْبَى / نُهَّبَى / نُهَيْبَى } : see نَهْبٌ and نُهْبَةٌ.

إِبِلٌ نَوَاهِبُ [pl. of نَاهِبٌ and نَاهِبَةٌ]: see 6.

مِنْهَبٌ *A horse that excels in running:* (Ḳ:) and in like manner an ass. (TA.)

مَنْهُوبٌ *What is sought, or sought after, quickly:* syn. مَطْلُوبٌ مُعَجَّلٌ. (Ḳ.)

نهت

1. نَهَتَ, aor. ـِ, [contr. to analogy,] inf. n. نَهِيتٌ (Ṣ, Ḳ) and نُهَاتٌ (Ḳ) *He cried out,* or *uttered a cry:* (TA:) [see إِنْهَتَى عَلَيْهَا voce نَهِيتٌ:] *he uttered the kind of sound termed* زَئِير; [i. e., *he* (a lion, TA) *uttered a sound from his chest; or roared:*] (Ḳ:) or *he uttered a sound lower than that which is termed* زئير: (Ṣ:) or *he breathed hard; or emitted the voice,* or *the breath, with a moaning;* i. q. زَحَرَ, (Ḳ,) and طَحَرَ: (TA:) or *he uttered a sound from his chest on an occasion of distress.* (TA.)

النَّهَّاتُ and ▼ المِنْهَتُ and ▼ المُنْهِتُ (thus the last is written accord. to the Ḳ, but it occurs in a verse written ▼ المُنْهَتُ, TA, and in this latter manner it is written in the L,) *The lion.* (Ḳ.) — أَسَدٌ نَهَّاتٌ, (Ṣ, L,) and ▼ مُنْهِتٌ, (L,) [*A lion uttering frequently a low growl*]. (Ṣ, L.) — حِمَارٌ نَهَّاتٌ ‡ *An ass that brays much, or frequently.* (Ṣ, Ḳ.) — رَجُلٌ نَهَّاتٌ ‡ *A man that breathes hard; or emits the voice,* or *the breath, with a moaning.* (Ṣ, Ḳ.*) See مُطْلَخِمّ.

النَّاهِتُ *The throat; the guttur:* (Ḳ:) so called because the sound termed نَهِيت proceeds from it. (TA.)

المِنْهَتُ, and المُنْهَتُ, and المُنْهِتُ: see النَّهَّاتُ.

نهج

1. نَهَجَ, (Ḳ, Mṣb,) aor. ـَ, inf. n. نُهُوجٌ; (Mṣb;) and ▼ انهج; (Ṣ, Ḳ;) *It* (a road, or way, Ṣ and Mṣb, and an affair, TA,) *became manifest, plainly apparent,* or *open;* (Ṣ, Ḳ, Mṣb,) and so, with respect to a road, ▼ استنهج. (Ḳ.) — نَهَجَ, (Ṣ, Ḳ, Mṣb,) and ▼ انهج, (Ḳ, Mṣb,) *He,* or *it, rendered* (a road, Ṣ and Mṣb, and an affair, TA,) *manifest, plainly apparent,* or *open:* (Ṣ, Ḳ, Mṣb:) — إِعْمَلْ عَلَى مَا نَهَجْتُهُ لَكَ *Do according to that which I have made manifest to thee.* (Ṣ.) — نَهَجَ, aor. ـَ, (inf. n. نَهْجٌ; TA,) and ▼ انهج; *It* (attrition, TA) *wore out,* or *rendered worn out, a garment.* (Ḳ.) — نَهِجَ, aor. ـَ; (A'Obeyd, Ṣ, Ḳ;) and نَهَجَ, (Ḳ,) but this is disallowed by A'Obeyd, (Ṣ,) and نَهُجَ, and ▼ انهج; (Ḳ;) *It* (a garment) *became old and worn out:* (Ḳ:) or ▼ انهج signifies *it began to become worn out:* (Ṣ:) and *it became old and worn out, but without being rent in several parts.* (TA.) انهج فِيهِ البِلَى [*The effect of*] *attrition spread through it.* (IAṭr.) — نَهَجَ الطَّرِيقَ *He went along the road.* (Ṣ, Ḳ.) — نَهِجَ, aor. ـَ, inf. n. نَهَجٌ; (Ṣ, Ḳ;) and نُهِجَ, inf. n. نَهْجَةٌ; (ISh;) this inf. n. also mentioned by Lth, who knew no verb belonging to it; (L;) and نَهَجَ, aor. ـِ, (Ḳ,) inf. n. نَهِيجٌ; (L, in art. أنح;) and ▼ انهج, inf. n. إِنْهَاجٌ; (L;) *He was out of breath; breathed short,* or *unintermittedly; panted;* (Ṣ, L, Ḳ;) by reason of violent motion: said of a man, and of a beast of carriage, (L,) and of a dog. (T.) One says, فُلَانٌ يَنْهَجُ فِى النَّفَسِ ▼ فَمَا أَدْرِى مَا أَنْهَجَهُ *Such a one is out of breath,* or *breathes short,* or *unintermittedly,* or *pants for breath, and I know not what hath caused him to be so,* or *to do so.* And it is said in a trad., رَأَى رَجُلًا يَنْهَجُ *He saw a man breathing short,* or *unintermittedly,* or *panting for breath, by reason of fatness, and putting forth his tongue,* from fatigue or the like. (Ṣ.)

4. ضَرَبَهُ حَتَّى انهج *He beat him until he became stretched along:* or, *until he wept:* (TA:) [but probably بكى "he wept" is a mistake for بَلِىَ *he became worn* with the beating]. — انهج *He,* or *it, caused him* (a man, Ṣ, and a beast of carriage, TA) *to be out of breath,* or *to breath short,* or *unintermittedly,* or *to pant for breath.* (Ṣ, TA.) [See an ex. voce نَهِجَ.] *He rode a beast of carriage so as to cause it,* or *until he caused it, to be out of breath, &c.,* (Ṣ, Ḳ,) *and to become fatigued,* or *jaded.* (TA.) — See 1, throughout.

10: see 1. — فُلَانٌ يَسْتَنْهِجُ سَبِيلَ فُلَانٍ, (Ṣ,) or طَرِيقَ فُلَانٍ, (Ḳ,) *Such a one follows the way of such a one.* (Ṣ, Ḳ.)

نَهْجٌ (Ṣ, Ḳ,) and ▼ نَهَجٌ (L) and ▼ مَنْهَجٌ and ▼ مِنْهَاجٌ (Ṣ, Ḳ) *A manifest, plainly apparent,* or *open, road,* or *way:* (Ṣ, L, Ḳ:) and so طَرِيقٌ ▼ نَاهِجَةٌ: (TA, from a trad.:) pl. of the first نَهَجَاتٌ and نُهُجٌ and نُهُوجٌ: (L:) [and of the third مَنَاهِجُ.] — طُرُقٌ نَهْجَةٌ *Manifest roads,* or *ways.* (L.) — And نَهْجُ الطَّرِيقِ [*The plain,* or *open, track of the road*]. (M, Ḳ, in art. سن.)

نَهَجٌ: see نَهْجٌ.

نَاهِجَةٌ: see طَرِيقٌ نَهْجٌ.

مَنْهَجٌ and مِنْهَاجٌ: see نَهْجٌ.

نهد

1. نَهَدَ, aor. ـُ, (Ṣ, L, Mṣb, Ḳ,) and ـَ, (Mṣb, Ḳ,) inf. n. نُهُودٌ, (Ṣ, L, &c.,) *It* (a girl's or woman's breast) *was,* or *became, swelling, prominent,* or *protuberant:* (Ṣ, L, Mṣb, Ḳ:) or *became full.* (Munjid of Kr.) [See also كَعَبَ, and فَلَكَ;

and see also نَاهِدٌ.] — نَهَدَتْ, aor. ـُ, and ـَ; and ▾ نَهَّدَتْ, (inf. n. تَنْهِيدٌ, TA,) *She* (a woman [or girl]) *came to have swelling, prominent,* or *protuberant, breasts.* (L, Ḳ.) — نَهَدَتِ القِرْبَةُ *The skin became nearly full.* (A.) — نَهَدَتِ الدَّلْوُ إِلى المِلْءِ, inf. n. نَهْدٌ, *The bucket became nearly full.* (A'Obeyd, L, TA.) — نَهَدَ, (M, L, Ḳ,) aor. ـَ, (L,) inf. n. نُهُودٌ, (M, L,) and نَهْدٌ, (L,) *He* (a man) *rose;* (M, L;) *i. q.* نَهَضَ; (Ḳ;) or the latter signifies "he rose from sitting;" whereas the former signifies "he rose under any circumstances." (M, L.) — نَهَدَ لَهُ, (L,) and إِلَيْهِ, (Th, L,) *He rose to him.* (Th, L.) — نَهَدَ لِلْعَدُوِّ, (A'Obeyd, L, Ḳ,) and إِلَى العَدُوِّ, (Ṣ, L, Mṣb,) aor. ـَ, (Ṣ, L, Mṣb,) and ـُ, (Mṣb,) inf. n. نَهْدٌ (Mṣb, Ḳ) and نُهُودٌ, (Ḳ,) *He attacked,* or *assaulted;* or *rose and hastened and went forth to,* or *towards, the enemy;* (Ṣ,* L, Mṣb;) *i. q.* نَهَضَ: (Ṣ, L:) *he directed his course towards the enemy, and commenced fighting with them.* (A'Obeyd, L, Ḳ.) — نَهَدَ, (IḲṭṭ,) inf. n. نُهُودٌ, (Ḳ,) *It* (a thing, IḲṭṭ) *went,* or *went away,* (مَضَى,) in any case. (IḲṭṭ, Ḳ.) ═ نُهُودٌ also signifies The *being strong.* (TA.) — نَهُدَ, aor. ـُ, inf. n. نُهُودَةٌ, *He* (a horse) *was,* or *became, large and tall:* (Ṣ, L:) or *bulky and strong:* or *goodly in body and limbs, and tall:* (L:) or *goodly, large in body and limbs, fleshy and tall.* (Ḳ.) ═ نَهَدَ, and ▾ انهد, *He honoured* (عَظَّمَ) a gift. (IḲṭṭ, Ḳ.)

2: see 1, near the beginning.

3. ناهدهُ, inf. n. مُنَاهَدَةٌ, *i. q.* نَاهَضَهُ; (Ṣ, A, L, Mṣb, Ḳ;) *He attacked* or *assaulted him,* or *rose and hastened and went forth to* or *towards him,* in war; *he directed his course towards him, and commenced fighting with him.* (M, L.) — ناهدهُ, inf. n. مُنَاهَدَةٌ, *He contended* or *disputed with him,* in an absolute sense. (TA.) ═ نَاهَدَهُمْ, [inf. n. مُنَاهَدَةٌ,] *He contributed with them to the expenses of a journey* or *an expedition, clubbing with them,* i. e. *sharing equally with each of them.* (L.) See also 6. ═ ناهدهُ, inf. n. مُنَاهَدَةٌ, *He played with him at the game in which one puts forth as many of his fingers as he pleases, and the other does the like; he played with him at the game of morra;* the inf. n. expl. by مُسَاهَمَةٌ بِالأَصَابِعِ, (Ṣ, L, Ḳ,) and مُخَارَجَةٌ, q. v. (TA.)

4. انهد *He filled* a tank or cistern, (Ṣ, L,) and a drinking-bowl, (A,) and a vessel, (L, Ḳ,) *so that it overflowed:* (L:) or *nearly filled* it. (A, L, Ḳ.) — نَاقَةٌ تُنْهِدُ الإِنَآءَ *A she-camel that fills the vessel* [with her milk]. (IAạr, L.) — انهدهُ *He made him,* or *it, to rise.* (L.) ═ See 1.

5. تنهّدت *He sighed; breathed with an expression of pain, grief,* or *sorrow;* or *uttered a prolonged breathing.* (TA.)

6. تناهدوا *They attacked* or *assaulted one another,* or *rose and hastened and went forth to* or *towards one another,* in war; *they directed their courses one towards another, and commenced fighting.* (A, Mṣb.) ═ تناهدوا; (Ṣ, Mgh, L, Ḳ;) and ▾ ناهدوا, (L, Mṣb,) inf. n. مُنَاهَدَةٌ; (Mṣb;) *They clubbed,* i.e. *contributed equally to, the expenses which they had to incur,* (Ṣ, Mgh, L, Ḳ,) *on the occasion of a journey,* (Ḳ,) or *an expedition against an enemy;* (L;) or *contributed equal shares of food and drink:* (ISd, L:) the first who instituted this practice is said to have been Ḥudeyn Er-Raḳáshee: (TA:) or *they contributed, each giving his share, for the purchase of wheat,* or *food, for their eating in common.* (Mṣb.) — تناهدوا الشَّىْءَ *They took the thing and shared it between them.* (L.) ═ تناهدوا *They played together the game of morra,* described in one of the explanations of نَاهَدَهُ. (Ṣ, TA, art. خرج.)

نَهْدٌ *A high,* or *elevated,* thing: (L, Ḳ:) as a shoulder-joint, (L,) and a horse. (TA.) — *A girl's* or *woman's breast:* so called because of its prominence, or protuberance: (Mṣb:) [pl. نُهُودٌ]. — كَعْثَبٌ نَهْدٌ *A pubes swelling forth,* or *prominent:* opposed to هَيْدَبٌ. (L.) — شَابٌّ نَهْدٌ *A strong, bulky, youth,* or *young man.* (L, from a trad.) — نَهْدٌ *A generous man,* (Ṣ, Ḳ,) *who aims at means of acquiring eminence,* or *nobility.* (Ṣ.) — نَهْدٌ *A horse large and tall:* (Lth, Ṣ, L:) or *bulky and strong:* or *goodly in body and limbs, and tall:* (L:) or *goodly, large in body and limbs, fleshy, and tall:* (Ḳ:) fem. with ة. (L.) — نَهْدُ القَذَالِ, and القُصَيْرَى, *A horse large and prominent in the back of the head,* and, *in the short ribs.* (Lth, L.) — النَّهْدُ and ▾ النَّاهِدُ *The lion:* (Ḳ:) from نُهُوضٌ in the sense of نُهُودٌ and قُوَّةٌ. (TA.) ═ نَهْدٌ *Aid; assistance.* (L.) See نِهْدٌ. — طَرَحَ نَهْدَهُ مَعَ القَوْمِ *He aided,* or *assisted, the people.* (L.) — Also, *He contributed with the people to the expenses of a journey* or *expedition, sharing equally with each of them.* (L.) See also 3. ═ And see نَهِيدٌ.

نِهْدٌ (L, Ḳ) and sometimes ▾ نَهْدٌ, (Ḳ,) or the latter signifies the action described in the following explanation, (L,) *A contribution,* or *that which is contributed, to the expenses of a journey, equally shared by each member of the party:* (L, Ḳ:) or *a contribution that is made for an expedition against an enemy, by a clubbing,* i. e. *an equal sharing of the expenses, so that there shall be no defrauding of one by another, and no obligation of one to another.* (IAth, L.) See 3 and 6. You say, هَاتِ نِهْدَكَ *Give thou thy contribution to the expenses of the journey,* or *expedition, equally with thy companions.* (L.)

نَهْدَانُ or نَهْدَانٌ, (Ṣ, L, Ḳ,) fem. نَهْدَى and نَهْدَانَةٌ, (L,) *A tank* or *cistern,* (Ṣ, L, Ḳ,) and bowl, (Ṣ, A, L,) or vessel, (L, Ḳ,) *full, but not yet overflowing:* (Ṣ, L, Ḳ:) or *full so as to overflow:* (L:) or *nearly full:* (A, L:) or *filled high:* (L:) or *two-thirds full.* (Ḳ.)

نِهَادُ مِائَةٍ *The amount,* or *number, of a hundred.* (Ḳ.)

نَهِيدٌ Fresh butter that is *not thin:* (Ṣ, L:) or *thin* butter: (Ḳ:) or fresh butter *of which the milk has not been quite thick and fit for churning:* or *a large lump of fresh butter;* as also ▾ نَهِيدَةٌ and ▾ نَهْدٌ: (L:) or ▾ نَهِيدَةٌ signifies *fresh butter made of milk that has not become thick and fit for churning, and which is therefore little in quantity, and sweet:* (AḤát, L:) or زُبْدَةٌ نَهِيدَةٌ *fresh butter expressed from a skin by squeezing it.* (L, art. زغد.)

نَهِيدَةٌ: see نَهِيدٌ. — The *hearts of the grains of colocynths, boiled until thoroughly cooked and thick, and then having a little flour sprinkled upon them, after which they are eaten.* (Ṣ, L, Ḳ.*)

نَاهِدٌ A girl's breast that is *swelling, prominent,* or *protuberant:* pl. نَوَاهِدُ; which denotes more than فَوَالِكُ. (A'Obeyd, L.) — Also, and ▾ نَاهِدَةٌ (Ṣ, L, Mṣb, Ḳ) and ▾ مُنْهِدٌ, (L, Ḳ,) or مُنَهِّدَةٌ, (as in the TA,) A girl, or woman, *having swelling, prominent,* or *protuberant, breasts:* (Ṣ, L, Mṣb, Ḳ:) or a woman *whose breasts have become full:* (Munjid of Kr:) pl. نَوَاهِدُ. (Mṣb.) — نَاهِدٌ A boy *nearly come to the age of puberty.* (A.) — نَاهِدٌ *Attacking* or *assaulting,* or *rising and hastening and going forth to* or *towards an enemy:* pl. نُهَّادٌ. (Mṣb.) — See نَهْدٌ.

نَاهِدَةٌ: see نَاهِدٌ.

نَهْدَآءُ [fem. of أَنْهَدُ] *An elevated sand,* (Ṣ, L, Ḳ,) *like a compact hill, fertile, producing trees:* (L:) or *a tract of ground such as is called* نَفْخَآءُ, *but more flat and extensive:* (L, art. نفخ:) it is used as an epithet; but not the masc. أَنْهَدُ. (L.) — هُوَ أَنْهَدُ القَوْمِ *He is the strongest and hardiest of the people.* (R.)

مُنْهِدٌ: see نَاهِدٌ.

نهر

1. نَهَرَ, (Ṣ, Mṣb,) aor. ـَ, (Mṣb,) *It* (water) *ran upon,* or *along, the ground,* (Ṣ, TA,) *and made for itself a* نَهْر [*or channel like that of a river*]. (Ṣ.) See also 10. — *It* (anything, as in one copy of the Ṣ, or anything copious, as in another copy of the Ṣ and in the TA) *ran,* or *flowed;* (Ṣ, TA;) as also ▾ استنهر, (Ṣ,) or ▾ انتهر. (TA.) — *It* (blood) *flowed with force:* (Mṣb:)

and ▼أَنْهَرَ *it* (blood) *flowed* (Ḳ, TA) *like a river:* (TA:) and the latter also, *it* (a vein) *flowed and would not stop;* (Ḳ, TA;) meaning, *it flowed like a river;* (TA;) as also ▼انتهر: (Ṣgh, Ḳ, TA:) and ▼انهر also signifies the same said of the belly; (TA;) or *it* (the belly) *became loose,* or *relaxed;* or *it discharged itself;* (JK;) as also ▼انتهر. (JK, Ḳ.) ═ نَهَرَ, (Ṣ, Ḳ,) aor. ـَ, (Ḳ,) inf. n. نَهْرٌ, (TA,) *He* (a man, Ṣ) *dug a* نَهْر [or channel for a river]: (Ṣ, TA:) *he made a* نَهْر [or river] *to run,* or *flow.* (K, TA.) ═ نَهَرَ, inf. n. نَهْرٌ, *He made an inroad* or *incursion,* or *inroads* or *incursions, into the territory* or *territories of enemies, in the day-time.* (TA.) ═ نَهَرَهُ, (Ṣ, Mgh, Mṣb, Ḳ, &c.,) aor. ـَ, inf. n. نَهْرٌ; (TA;) and ▼انتهرهُ; (Ṣ, Mgh, Mṣb, Ḳ, &c.;) *He chid him; he checked him, restrained him,* or *forbade him, with rough speech;* syn. زَجَرَهُ, (Mgh, Mṣb, Ḳ, and so in a copy of the Ṣ,) or زَبَرَهُ, (as in another copy of the Ṣ,) بِكَلَامٍ غَلِيظٍ: (Mgh:) *he addressed him with chiding speech,* (JK, A,) *forbidding him from doing evil.* (JK. [in the TA, citing the last explanation from the T, عَنْ خَيْرٍ is erroneously put for عَنْ شَرٍّ.]) It is said in the Ḳur, [xciii. 10,] وَأَمَّا ٱلسَّائِلَ فَلَا تَنْهَرْ [*And as for the beggar, thou shalt not chide* him, or *address* him *with rough speech*]. And in a trad., مَنِ ٱنْتَهَرَ صَاحِبَ بِدْعَةٍ مَلَأَ ٱللّٰهُ قَلْبَهُ أَمْنًا وَإِيمَانًا وَآمَنَهُ ٱللّٰهُ مِنَ ٱلْفَزَعِ ٱلْأَكْبَرِ [*Whoso chideth,* or *checketh with rough speech, the author of an innovation in religion, God will fill his heart with security and faith, and God will preserve him from the greatest terror*]. (TA.)

4. انهر: see 1, in three places. ═ ‡ *He made* blood *to flow:* (Ṣ:) or *to appear and flow:* (Ḳ:) or *to flow amply and copiously:* (Mgh:) or *to flow with force:* (Mṣb:) or *he poured it forth copiously.* (TA.) It is said in a trad., أَنْهِرِ الدَّمَ بِمَا شِئْتَ إِلَّا مَا كَانَ مِنْ سِنٍّ أَوْ ظُفُرٍ [*Make thou the blood to flow, &c., with what thou pleasest, except with what is* made *of a tooth* or *a talon.*] (Mgh, Mṣb.) The issuing forth of the blood from the place of slaughter is likened to the flowing of water in a river. (TA.) —— † *He made it wide;* (Ṣ, Ḳ;) namely, a spear-wound or the like, (Ṣ, TA,) or a نَهْر [or channel of a river], as is implied in the Ḳ, but in other lexicons as in the Ṣ. (TA.) ═ *He was,* or *became, in day-time:* (Ṣ,* Ḳ,* TA:) *he entered upon day-time:* (MṢ:) from النَّهَارُ. (Ṣ.)

8: see 1, in five places.

10: see 1. —— *It* (a river [in the CḲ النَّهَرَ is put by mistake for النَّهْرُ]) *took a place,* (JK,) or *a settled place,* (Ḳ,) *for its channel.* (JK, Ḳ.) —— *It* (a thing) *became wide.* (Ṣ.)

نَهْرٌ and ▼نَهَرٌ (Ṣ, A, Mgh, Mṣb, Ḳ) *A channel in which water runs:* (A, Ḳ:) so most say: or the *water itself* [*that runs therein;* i.e., *a river; a rivulet; a brook; a canal of running water*]: (TA:) or *a wide channel in which water runs:* originally, the *water* [*that runs therein*]: (Mgh:) or properly, *wide running water:* and by a secondary application, which is tropical, ‡ the *trench* or *channel* [*in which it runs*]: (Mṣb, TA*:) pl. [of pauc.] أَنْهُرٌ, (Mṣb, Ḳ,) a pl. of the former, (Mṣb,) and أَنْهَارٌ, (Ṣ, Mṣb, Ḳ,) a pl. of the latter, (Mṣb,) [but used as a pl. of either, both of pauc. and of mult., and the most common of all the pls.,] and نُهُرٌ, (Mṣb, and so in some copies of the Ḳ,) with two ḍammehs, a pl. of the former, (Mṣb,) or نُهْرٌ (as in some copies of the Ḳ and in the TA,) and نُهُورٌ. (IAạr, Ḳ.) You say, جَرَى النَّهْرُ [*The river ran,* or *flowed*]; like as you say, جَرَى الْمِيزَابُ. (Mṣb.) And نَهْرٌ كَثِيرُ الْمَآءِ [*A channel of running water having much water*]. (A.) And ▼نَهَرٌ is also used in a pl. sense; as in the Ḳur, [liv. 54], فِي جَنَّاتٍ وَنَهَرٍ [*In gardens and among rivers*], i.e., أَنْهَارٍ; like the phrase in the Ḳur, [same chap. verse 45,] وَيُوَلُّونَ الدُّبُرَ, (Fr, Ṣ,) meaning الْأَدْبَارَ: (Fr, TA:) but it is otherwise explained. (Ṣ.) See نَهْرٌ below.

نَهَرٌ: see نَهْرٌ, in two places. ═ *Amplitude:* (Ḳ:) or *light and amplitude:* so, accord. to some, in the Ḳur, liv. 54, differently explained above: see نَهْرٌ: (Ṣ, TA:) or, accord. to Th, نَهَر is a pl. [or rather quasi-pl.] of نُهُرٌ, which is a pl. of نَهَارٌ. (TA.)

نَهِرٌ *Much;* (TA;) as also ▼نَهِيرٌ; (Ḳ, TA;) both applied to water. (TA.) —— A *wide* نَهْر [or river, or channel in which water runs]. (Ḳ.) ═ رَجُلٌ نَهِرٌ *A man of day-time;* syn. صَاحِبُ نَهَارٍ; (Ṣ, Ḳ;) *who makes inroads* or *incursions into the territories of enemies therein:* (Ṣ:) or *who works therein:* (A:) a kind of rel. n.; as is shown by the ex.

لَسْتُ بِلَيْلِيٍّ وَلٰكِنِّي نَهِرْ •
لَا أُدْلِجُ اللَّيْلَ وَلٰكِنْ أَبْتَكِرْ •

[*I am not one of the night-time, but I am one of the day-time: I do not journey in the night, but I go forth early in the morning*]: as though he said ▼نَهَارِىٌّ. (Sb.) The verse is correctly related as above; not as it is given in the Ṣ. (IB.) —— See also أَنْهَرُ.

نَهَارٌ *Day;* or *day-time; contr. of* لَيْلٌ: (Ṣ, TA:) or *broad daylight,* (Mgh,) *from sunrise to sunset:* (Mgh, Mṣb, Ḳ:) this is the original signification: (TA:) or this is the signification in the vulgar conventional language: but in the classical language it signifies the *time from the rising of the dawn to sunset:* (Mṣb:) or the *light between the rising of the dawn and sunset:* (Ḳ:) and so accord. to the lawyers: (TA:) in the trads., it is the whiteness of the نهار, and the blackness of the ليل; and there is nothing intervening between the ليل and the نهار: but sometimes the Arabs amplified, and applied نهار to the *time from the clear shining of the dawn to the setting* [*of the sun*]: (Mṣb:) or (so accord. to the TA, but in some copies of the Ḳ, and) the *spreading of the light* [*which is a cause*] *of sight,* and *its dispersion:* (Ḳ:) in this explanation in the L, in the place of وَٱفْتِرَاقُهُ we find وَٱجْتِمَاعُهُ [and *its collecting together*]: (TA:) it is also syn. with يَوْمٌ; and is so when used without restriction in the non-fundamental sciences of religion, (الفُرُوع,) as in the phrases صُمْ نَهَارًا [*fast thou a day*] and إِعْمَلْ نَهَارًا [*work thou a day*]: and it may be so used, or in its proper classical sense, when prefixed to يَوْمٌ, governing the latter in the gen. case: (Mṣb:) it has no proper dual, (Mgh, Mṣb,) and no proper pl., (Ṣ, Mgh, Mṣb, Ḳ,) like عَذَابٌ and سَرَابٌ; (Ṣ, Ḳ;) the former of which, however, has a pl. assigned to it [by Zj and] in the Ḳ, namely, أَعْذِبَةٌ; (MF:) [and respecting the latter see شَرَابٌ, with ش;] [for] نهار is a name applied to *every* يَوْم [or *day*]; and لَيْلٌ, to every لَيْلَة [or night]: one does not say نَهَارٌ وَنَهَارَانِ, nor لَيْلٌ وَلَيْلَانِ: but the sing. of نهار is يَوْمٌ: (TA:) and the dual, يَوْمَانِ: (Mṣb, TA:) and the pl., أَيَّامٌ: (Mṣb:) and the contr. of يَوْمٌ is لَيْلَةٌ: so says Az, on the authority of AHeyth: (TA:) or it has pls.; namely, أَنْهُرٌ, (IAạr, Ṣ, Ḳ,) a pl. of pauc., (Ṣ,) in some lexicons أَنْهِرَةٌ, (TA,) [also a pl. of pauc.,] and نُهُرٌ, (Ṣ, Mgh, Mṣb, Ḳ,) a pl. of mult. (Ṣ.) [See also نَهَرٌ.] Ibn-Keysán cites the following ex.,

لَوْلَا الثَّرِيدَانِ لَمُتْنَا بِالضُّمُرْ •
ثَرِيدُ لَيْلٍ وَثَرِيدٌ بِالنُّهُرْ •

[*Were it not for the two thereeds* (or *messes of crumbled bread moistened with broth*), *we had died of leanness: the thereed of night, and thereed in the day-times*]. (Ṣ.)

نَهِيرٌ: see نَهِرٌ.

نَهَارِىٌّ: see نَهِرٌ. —— *Food that is eaten in the beginning of the day.* (TA.)

نَهَارٌ أَنْهَرُ, and ▼نَهِرٌ, [*A bright day:*] in each of these phrases the epithet has an intensive effect, (Ḳ,* TA,) as the epithet in لَيْلٌ أَلْيَلُ. (TA.)

مَنْهَرٌ *The place of a river.* (T, TA.) —— *A place which the water hollows out in a* نَهْر [or *channel of a river*]. (Ḳ.) —— *A cleft,* (Ḳ, TA,) or *hole,* (TA,) *in a fortress, passing through* [*the wall*], *whence water runs,* (Ḳ, TA,) or *by which water enters:* (TA:) pl. مَنَاهِرُ. (TA.)

نهز

1. نَهَزَ, aor. ـَ, (Mṣb,) inf. n. نَهْزٌ, (Mṣb, TA,) *He rose to take a thing with his extended hand.* (Mṣb, JK, TA.) He took a thing with his extended hand. (JK, TA.) See also 3 and 8. — نَهَزَ الشَّىْءُ *The thing became near.* (Ḳ.) See also 3, in two places.

3. ناهزهُ, inf. n. مُنَاهَزَةٌ, *He strove with him,* or *made haste, to outstrip him; to be,* or *get, before him; to precede him.* (TA.) You say, ناهز الصَّيْدَ *He made haste to get before the game,* or *object of the chase,* (Ḳ, TA,) *and seized it before its escape.* (TA.) And نَاهَزْتُهُمُ الفُرَصَ [*I strove with them,* or *made haste, to be before them in taking,* or *seizing, the opportunities,* or *the turns for drawing water* or *the like*]. (Ṣ, A.) A poet says,

* نَاهَزْتُهُمْ بِنَيْطَلٍ جَرُوفِ *

[*I strove with them,* or *made haste, to be before them* in drawing water *with a capacious bucket*]. (Ṣ.) — Also, (Ḳ,) inf. n. as above, (TA,) *He approached it; drew near to it; nearly attained to it;* (Ḳ, TA;) as also ↓ نَهَزَهُ. (TA.) You say, ناهز البُلُوغَ, (Ṣ, Mṣb,) and الحُلُمَ, (A, TA,) *He* (a boy, S, Mṣb) *approached, drew near to,* or *nearly attained to, puberty.* (Ṣ, A, Mṣb.) And ناهز الخَمْسِينَ [*He approached,* or *nearly attained to,* the age of *fifty*]. (A, TA.) And ناهز لِلْفِطَامِ, (A, Mṣb,) inf. n. as above, (Mṣb,) *He* (a child) *approached,* or *drew near to, the* [time of] *weaning;* (A, Mṣb;) as also ↓ نَهَزَ لَهُ, (Mṣb, TA,) aor. ـَ. (Mṣb.) — See also 8.

6. تناهزا *They strove together,* or *made haste, each to be,* or *get, before the other.* (Ḳ.) You say, هُمَا يَتَنَاهَزَانِ إِمَارَةَ بَلَدِ كَذَا *They strive together,* or *make haste, each to be before the other in obtaining the government of such a town,* or *country.* (Ṣ,* TA.) And تَنَاهَزُوا الفُرَصَ [*They strove together,* or *made haste, to be before one another in taking,* or *seizing, the opportunities,* or *the turns for drawing water* or *the like:* see 3.] (A.)

8. انتهز الفُرْصَةَ *He took,* or *seized,* [or *availed himself of,*] *the opportunity;* syn. اِغْتَنَمَهَا: (Ṣ, A, Ḳ:) or *he arose and hastened to be before another,* or *others, in taking,* or *seizing, the opportunity;* or simply *he hastened to take it.* (Mṣb.) You say, انْتَهِزْهَا قَدْ أَمْكَنَتْكَ قَبْلَ الفَوْتِ [*Take thou,* or *seize thou, it;* (meaning the opportunity;) for *it hath become within thy power; before the escape* thereof]. (TA.) And اِنْتَهِزْ فَقَدْ أَعْرَضَ لَكَ [*Take thou,* or *seize thou, the opportunity; for it hath offered itself to thee*]. (A, TA.) Also, انْتَهَزَهَا *He took it,* or *them,* [but to what the pronoun refers is not shown,] *with his extended hand, from a near spot;* and so ↓ نَاهَزَهَا. (TA.) And انتهز الشَّىْءَ *He accepted the thing, and hastened to take it with his extended hand.* (TA.)

نُهْزَةٌ *An opportunity; a time at which,* or *during which, a thing may be done* or *had;* syn. فُرْصَةٌ. (Ṣ, Ḳ.) — *A thing that offers itself to one as a prey,* or *spoil.* (JK, L.*) You say, فُلَانٌ نُهْزَةُ المُخْتَلِسِ [*Such a one is the prey of the snatcher*]; meaning, *such a one is the prey of every one.* (L.) And هٰذِهِ نُهْزَةٌ فَٱخْتَلِسْهَا [*This is a thing that offers itself as a prey, therefore snatch thou it.*] (A.)

نَاهِزٌ *Approaching,* or *near, to the time of weaning;* applied to a boy; (JK, Mṣb, TA;) and to a girl; (TA;) or the epithet applied to the latter is with ة. (JK, Mṣb.)

نهس

1. نَهَسَهُ, (Ṣ, A, Mṣb, Ḳ,) aor. ـَ (Mṣb, Ḳ, MṢ) and ـِ; (Mṣb;) and نَهِسَهُ, aor. ـَ; (Fr, Ḳ;) inf. n. نَهْسٌ (Ṣ, Mṣb, TA) and نَهَسٌ; (TA;) *He* (a man, Ṣ, Mṣb) *took it* (namely flesh or flesh-meat) *with his fore teeth,* (Ṣ, A, Mṣb, Ḳ,) *to eat it,* (Mṣb,) and *plucked it off;* (A, Ḳ;) as also ↓ انتهسهُ: (Ṣ:) *and he ate it off from a bone* (تَعَرَّقَهُ) *with his fore teeth:* (Lḥ, TA:) or *he pulled it off with the central incisors, to eat it:* (TA:) and *he took it with the fore part of his mouth;* as also ↓ انتهسهُ: (A:) or *he took it with his mouth:* (IAth, TA:) or *he took it with his mouth to bite it and make a mark upon it without wounding it:* (TA, art. نهش:) and *he* (a dog, and any animal having a canine tooth,) *bit it:* or *seized it, and then pulled it,* or *pulled it vehemently,* or *rent it with his teeth:* but there is a difference of opinion respecting this verb in all its significations: some say that it is with the unpointed س; and thus, only, it is mentioned by ISk, who says, I heard El-Kilábee say, of a dog and of a wolf and of a serpent, ↓ انتهسهُ and نَهَسَهُ; (Mṣb;) [and J says, the نَهْسُ of the serpent is the same as its نَهْشُ; (Ṣ;) you say نَهَسَتْهُ الحَيَّةُ in the sense of نَهَشَتْهُ [*the serpent bit him*]: (Z, Ṣgh:) others say that the verbs are with س and ش throughout; and thus says IF on the authority of Aṣ: Az cites Lth as saying that نَهْشٌ, with the pointed ش, signifies taking, or reaching, from a distance, like the نهش of the serpent; and نَهْسٌ, with the unpointed letter, the *seizing upon* flesh, or flesh-meat, *and pulling* it, or *pulling* it *vehemently,* or *rending* it *with the teeth:* Th says that the latter is *with the extremities of the teeth;* and the former, with the teeth [absolutely], and with [those that are termed] the أَضْرَاس: IḲoot says, like Lth, that one says of the serpent (الحَيَّة), نَهَشَتْهُ, with the pointed ش; and of the dog and wolf and hyena, نَهَسَهُ, with the unpointed letter. (Mṣb.)

8: see 1, in three places.

نَهُوسٌ: see نَهَّاسٌ, in two places.

نَهِيسٌ: see مَنْهُوسٌ, in two places.

نَهَّاسٌ A dog *that is wont to bite;* (Mṣb;) and ↓ نَهُوسٌ, applied to a she-camel, signifies the same; (TA;) and the latter, a lion *that bites a thing when able to do so:* (IKh:) or the former, a dog *that is wont to seize, and then pull,* or *pull vehemently,* or *rend with his teeth.* (Mṣb.) — *A lion;* as also ↓ نَهُوسٌ and ↓ مِنْهَسٌ. (Ḳ.) — *A wolf.* (TA.)

مَنْهَسٌ *A place from which a thing* [such as herbage &c.] *is taken with the mouth and eaten:* (Ḳ,* TA:) pl. مَنَاهِسُ. (TA.) You say, أَرْضٌ كَثِيرَةُ المَنَاهِسِ *Land abounding in such places.* (TA.)

نَهَّاسٌ: see مِنْهَسٌ.

مَنْهُوسٌ A man *having little flesh;* (Ṣ, A, Ḳ;) [*as though it were partly eaten off the bones;*] as also ↓ نَهِيسٌ. (TA.) You say also, مَنْهُوسُ القَدَمَيْنِ, (A, Ḳ,) or الكَعْبَيْنِ, (TA,) A man (TA) *having little flesh upon the feet,* (A,* Ḳ,* TA,) or *upon the ankles.* (TA.) And وَظِيفٌ نَهِيسٌ ↓ [*A shank* of a quadruped] *light of flesh.* (TA.) See also مَنْهُوشٌ.

نهش

1. نَهَشَهُ, (Ṣ, Ḳ,) aor. ـَ, (Ḳ,) inf. n. نَهْشٌ, (Ṣ,) i. q. نَهَسَهُ; (Ṣ, Ḳ;) i. e. *He took it with his mouth to bite it and make a mark upon it without wounding it:* [&c.:] (TA:) or *he took it* (namely flesh or flesh-meat) *with his fore teeth:* (Ṣ:) and so accord. to some, ↓ انتهشهُ. (Ṣ.) And *It* [a serpent or scorpion] *bit him;* or *stung him;* syn. لَسَعَهُ: (Ḳ:) you say, نَهَشَتْهُ الحَيَّةُ *the serpent bit him.* (Ṣ.) And *He* (a dog, TA) *bit him, or it;* (Ḳ;) as also نَهَسَهُ. (TA.) Or *He took it with his* [*teeth that are called*] أَضْرَاس: whereas نَهَسَهُ signifies he took it with the extremities of the teeth: (Ḳ:) or نَهْشٌ is less then نَهْسٌ; the latter signifying the taking, or reaching, with the mouth; but the former, the *taking,* or *reaching, from a distance, like the* نهش *of the serpent.* (Lth, TA.) [For other observations on these two verbs, see art. نهس.] — نَهَشَهُ الدَّهْرُ فَٱحْتَاجَ (IAạr, Ṣ, Ḳ) ‡ *Time,* or *fortune, bit him, so that he became in want.* (TA.) — نَهَشَتْ وَجْهَهَا *She* (a woman) *seized the flesh of her face with her nails.* (TA.) — نَهَشَهُ

also signifies † *He, or it, harassed, distressed, fatigued,* or *wearied him.* (IAth.) — نُهِشَ, inf. n. as above, † *He became emaciated,* or *lean:* and أُنْتُهِشَتْ ♦ أَعْضَادُنَا † *our arms from the elbow upwards became emaciated:* (TA:) and نُهِشَتْ عَضُدَاهُ † *his arms from the elbow upwards became slender,* (ISh, Ḳ, [but in the CḲ دَقَّتَا is put by mistake for دَقَّتَا]) *and their flesh became little.* (ISh.)

8: see 1, in the first and last sentences.

نَهْشٌ: see مَنْهُوشٌ.

نَهِشٌ: see مَنْهُوشٌ, in five places. — As an epithet applied to a camel, *i. q.* نَمِشٌ, (Ibn-'Abbád, Ḳ,) as explained in art. نمش. (Ibn-'Abbád, TA.)

مَنْهُوشٌ: see نَهِيشٌ.

مَنْهُوشٌ † A man *harassed, distressed, fatigued,* or *wearied:* (Ṣ, IAth, Ḳ:) ‡ *bitten by time,* or *fortune, so as to be in want,* (IAạr, Ṣ, Ḳ, TA,) † and *emaciated,* or *lean:* or *having little flesh, even if fat:* or *light;* as also ♦ نَهِشٌ and ♦ نَهْشٌ and ♦ نَهِيشٌ. (TA.) Applied to the pudendum muliebre, † *Having little flesh;* as also ♦ نَهِشٌ. (TA.) And in like manner, مَنْهُوشُ الفَخِذَيْنِ † *Emaciated,* or *lean, in the thighs.* (TA.) And مَنْهُوشُ القَدَمَيْنِ † A man *having little flesh upon the feet.* (IAạr, K.) And ♦ نَهِشُ اليَدَيْنِ ‡ A man, (TA,) or a beast of carriage, (Ṣ,) *light in the arms,* or *fore legs;* (Ṣ, Ḳ, TA;) as though from ♦ نَهْشُ الحَيَّةِ: (Ṣ:) and so ♦ نَهِشُ القَوَائِمِ, ‡ *light in the legs,* (Ḳ, TA,) *in passing along, and having little flesh upon them;* (TA;) as also ♦ نَهِشُ المُشَاشِ. (Ṣ,* TA.) [But see also مُشَاشٌ.]

مُنْتَهِشَةٌ A woman *scratching her face in affliction* or *misfortune.* (Ḳ, TA.) Such Moḥammad cursed. (TA.)

نهض

1. نَهَضَ, aor. ـَ, inf. n. نُهُوضٌ (Ṣ, A, Mgh, Mṣb, Ḳ) and نَهْضٌ, (Ṣ, A, Ḳ,) *He rose, or stood up,* syn. اِرْتَفَعَ, (Mṣb,) or قَامَ, (Ṣ, Mgh, O, Ḳ,) عَنْ مَكَانِهِ *from his place;* (Mṣb;) as also ♦ انتهض, syn. قَامَ: (IAạr:) or the former, *he quitted a place:* and *he rose from it:* (M, TA:) or *he rose from sitting;* thus differing from نَهَدَ, which signifies "he rose" under any circumstances: (M, L, in art. نهد:) [and *he rose and went:* or *he rose and hastened,* as shown below:] and ♦ انتهض, *he was,* or *became, made,* or *excited, to rise,* or *stand up;* quasi-pass. of أَنْهَضَهُ. (Ṣ.) You say, نَهَضَ إِلَيْهِ *He rose,* or *stood up, to him:* (Mgh:) and لِلْأَمْرِ [*to do, or perform, an affair*]. (Ṣ, Ḳ.*) And نَهَضَ إِلَى العَدُوِّ *He* [*rose and*] *sped, or hastened, to,* or *towards, the enemy.* (Mṣb.) [See also نَهَدَ.] And نَغَضْنَا إِلَيْهِمْ and نَهَضْنَا إِلَى القَوْمِ [*We rose and sped, or hastened, to,* or *towards, the people,* or *company of men:*] both signify the same. (Abu-l-Jahm El-Jaafaree.) And ♦ انتهضوا نَهَضُوا لِلْقِتَالِ and ♦ تناهضوا signify the same as [*They rose and sped, or hastened, to fight,* or *to the fight*]. (TA.) — ‡ *It* (a plant) *stood erect;* or *became strong and erect.* (Ṣ, A, Ḳ.) — ‡ *It* (a bird) *spread,* or *expanded, its wings to fly.* (Ṣ, A, Mgh, Ḳ.) You say, فَرْخٌ عَاجِزُ النَّهْضِ [*A young bird lacking the power of spreading its wings to fly*]. (A, TA.) [See an ex. in a verse of El-Ḥoṭeiah cited in the first paragraph of art. خلف.] — نَهَضَتْ نَفْسُهُ (Ḳ in art. جشأ, &c.) and نَهَضَتْ نَفْسُهُ إِلَيْهِ (Ṣ in the same art., and A in art. جهش, &c.) signify [the same, i. e.] ♦ جَشَأَتْ † [*His soul,* or *stomach, heaved,* &c.] (Ṣ, A, Ḳ, in the arts. above mentioned.) — نَهَضَ الشَّيْبُ فِى الشَّبَابِ ‡ [*Hoariness arose in youth*]. (A, TA.) Aṣ cites the following verse from an anonymous poet:

* تَنْتَهِضُ ♦ الرِّعْدَةُ فِى ظُهَيْرِى *
* مِنْ لَدُنِ الظُّهْرِ إِلَى العُصَيْرِ *

† [*Tremor arises in my little back from the time of noon to the little evening*]. (TA.)

3. ناهضهُ, (Ṣ, A, &c.,) inf. n. مُنَاهَضَةٌ, (TA,) *He rose with him,* or *against him, and withstood him,* or *opposed him, in contention;* syn. قَاوَمَهُ; (Ṣ, Mgh, Ḳ;) namely his adversary. (A, Mgh.)

4. انهضهُ *He made him,* or *excited him, to rise,* or *stand up:* (Ṣ, A,* Ḳ, TA:) or *he roused him,* or *put him in motion to rise.* (TA.) You say also, ♦ إِنْتَهَضْتُهُ لِلْأَمْرِ, [if this be not a mistranscription for أَنْهَضْتُهُ,] *I made him to rise to* [*do, or perform,*] *the affair.* (Mṣb.) And انهضهُ عَلَى الشَّىْءِ † *He strengthened him to rise, and do,* or *perform, the thing.* (TA.) — انهض القِرْبَةَ ‡ *He nearly filled the water-skin* [*so as to make it rise*]. (Ḳ, TA.) — أَنْهَضَتِ الرِّيحُ السَّحَابَ ‡ *The wind bore and drove along the cloud,* or *clouds.* (TA.)

6. تناهضوا فِى الحَرْبِ (Ṣ, A, Mgh, Ḳ) *They rose, one with another,* or *one against another, and withstood,* or *opposed, one another, in war,* or *battle:* (Mgh:) or *each party of them rose and hastened* (نَهَضَ) *to,* or *towards, the other, in war,* or *battle.* (Ṣ, Ḳ.*) See also 1.

8: see 1, in four places: — and see 4.

10. استنهضهُ لِأَمْرِ كَذَا *He ordered him,* or *commanded him, to rise to* [*do, or perform,*] *such an affair.* (Ṣ, Ḳ.*) [And استنهضهُ فِى أَمْرٍ *He sent him on an affair, to perform it.*]

نَهْضَةٌ [inf. n. of un. of 1; *A single act of rising,* &c.: and] *a motion,* or *movement:* pl. نَهَضَاتٌ. (Mṣb.) You say, جَاءَتْ مِنْهُ نَهْضَةٌ, (A, TA,) or كَانَتْ مِنْهُ نَهْضَةٌ, *There was* [*a rising,* or] *a motion,* or *movement, on his part,* (Mṣb,) لِمَحَلِّ كَذَا [*to such a place*], (A, TA,) or إِلَى كَذَا [*to,* or *towards, such a thing*]. (Mṣb.) And هُوَ كَثِيرُ النَّهَضَاتِ [*He is a person of frequent risings,* or *motions* or *movements*]. (A, TA.) — Also, † *Power,* or *ability;* and *strength.* (TA.)

نُهْضَةٌ [The *act of rising,* or *standing up:* or the *state of being made,* or *excited, to rise,* or *stand up:*] a subst. from الإِنْتِهَاضُ. (TA.)

نَهَّاضٌ [One *who frequently rises;* or *who frequently rises from,* or *quits, his place:*] *quick in motion.* (Expos. of the Mo'allaḳát, printed at Calcutta, p. ٧٠.) — هُوَ نَهَّاضٌ بِهٰؤُلَاءِ ‡ [app. *He is wont to rise with these, for their assistance:* see ♦ نَاهِضَةٌ]. (A, TA.) — هُوَ نَهَّاضٌ بِبَزْلَاءَ: see art. بزل.

نَاهِضٌ [act. part. n. of 1, *Rising,* or *standing up:* &c.]. — † *Energetic, sharp, vigorous,* or *effective, in his agency,* or *work.* (TA.) — ‡ A young bird *whose wings have become complete,* (Ṣ, A, Mgh,) or *whose wing has become complete,* (Ḳ,) *and which has risen,* (Ṣ,) or *is able,* (A, Mgh,) or *ready,* (Ḳ,) *to fly:* (Ṣ, A, Mgh, Ḳ:) or *that has spread its wings to fly;* or *that has raised itself to quit its place:* applied by some particularly to the young of the eagle: (TA:) pl. نَوَاهِضُ. (A, Mgh.) [See also عَاتِقٌ.]

نَاهِضَةُ رَجُلٍ ‡ *A man's people,* (L,) or *the sons of his father or ancestor,* (Ṣ, O, Ḳ,) *who rise for him,* (O,) or *with him,* (Ḳ,) or *with whom he rises, in a case that grieves him,* (L,) or *who are angry for him,* (Ṣ,) or *who are angry by reason of his anger, and rise to aid him:* (TA:) and *his people,* (A,) or *servants,* (Ḳ,) or *those,* (Ṣ,) *who undertake,* or *manage, his affairs:* (Ṣ, A, Ḳ:) or *his aiders,* or *assistants.* (A, in art. ظهر.) You say, مَا لِفُلَانٍ نَاهِضَةٌ ‡ *Such a one has not any* (Ṣ, A) *people,* (A,) or *servants,* (TA,) *who undertake,* or *manage, his affairs.* (Ṣ, A, TA.)

[نهل, &c.
See Supplement.]

نوأ

1. نَآءَ, aor. يَنُوءُ, inf. n. نَوْءٌ (Ṣ, Ḳ) and تَنْوَآءٌ, (Ḳ,) *He rose,* or *arose, with effort and difficulty.* (Ṣ, Ḳ.) — نَآءَ بِحِمْلِهِ *He rose with his burden with effort and difficulty:* (TA:) *he rose with his burden oppressed by its weight.* (Ṣ, Ḳ.) —

تَنُوْءُ بِعَجِيزَتِهَا *She rises with her buttocks oppressed by their weight:* said of a woman. (Ṣ.) — نَآءَ بِصَدْرِهِ *He arose.* [App. said originally, if not only, of a camel.] (TA.) — نَآءَ بِهِ and ↑ انَاءهُ, *It* (a burden) *oppressed him by its weight, and bent him,* or *weighed him down.* (Ṣ, Ḳ.) — تَنُوْءُ بِهَا عَجِيزَتُهَا *Her buttocks oppress her by their weight:* said of a woman. (Ṣ.) — نَآءَ *He was oppressed by weight,* (Ḳ,) *and fell down:* (Ṣ, Ḳ:) thus the verb bears two [partially] opposite significations. (Ḳ.) — نَآءَ بِجَانِبِهِ † *He behaved proudly.* (TA, art. مط.) — نَآءَ النَّجْمُ, aor. يَنُوْءُ, inf. n. نَوْءٌ; and ↑ استناء and إِسْتَنَآءَ (Ḳ; the latter being formed by transposition, TA) *The star,* or *asterism,* [generally said of one of those composing the Mansions of the Moon,] *set* (accord. to some), or *rose* (accord. to others), *aurorally,* i. e. *at dawn of morning.* (TA.) See نَوْءٌ. [It seems that ناء is used in both these senses because the star or asterism appears as though it were nearly overcome by the glimmer of the dawn.] = نَآءَ, (Ḳ,) formed by transposition from نَأَى, (TA,) or a dial. form of this latter, (Ṣ, TA,) *He,* or *it, was,* or *became, distant; removed to a distance; went far away.* (Ṣ, Ḳ.) — ناء به [*It rendered him distant,* or *removed him to a distance*]. (TA.) = مَا سَآءَكَ وَنَآءَكَ (Ṣ) [see explained in art. سوأ]: ناءك is here used for أَنَآءَكَ, in order to assimilate it to ساءك; (Ṣ;) like as they say هَنَأَنِى وَمَرَأَنِى, for أَمْرَأَنِى. (TA.)

3. نَاوَأَهُ, inf. n. مُنَاوَأَةٌ and نِوَآءٌ, *He contended with him for glory; vied with him.* (Ḳ.) — *He acted hostilely towards him.* (Ṣ, Ḳ.) Sometimes without ء; but originally with ء; being derived from نَآءَ إِلَيْكَ and نُؤْتُ إِلَيْهِ. (Ṣ.)

4: see 1.

10. استناء بِنَجْمٍ [*He prognosticated rain &c. by reason of the rising* or *setting of a star* or *an asterism aurorally,* i. e., *at dawn of morning:* or *he regarded a star* or *an asterism as a* نَوْء]. (L.) It is said, لَا تَسْتَنِىْءُ العَرَبُ بِالنُّجُومِ كُلِّهَا [*The Arabs do not prognosticate rain &c. by reason of the auroral rising* or *setting of all the stars,* or *asterisms:* or *do not regard all the stars* or *asterisms as* أَنْوَآء]. (Sh, L.) إِسْتَنَآؤُوا الوَسْمِىَّ, the ء being transposed, *They expected,* or *looked for, the rain called* الوسمى, [*from the auroral rising* or *setting of a star* or *an asterism*]. (AḤn.) = إِسْتَنَآءَهُ † *He sought,* or *asked a gift,* or *present of him.* (Ḳ.)

نَوْءٌ, pl. أَنْوَآءٌ and نُوْآنٌ, (Ṣ, Ḳ,) *A star,* or *an asterism, verging to setting:* or *the setting of the star,* or *asterism, in the west, aurorally,* i. e., *at dawn of morning,* and *the rising of another, opposite to it, at the same time, in the east:* (Ḳ:) or *the setting of one of the stars,* or *asterisms, which compose the Mansions* [*of the Moon* (see مَنَازِلُ القَمَرِ)], *in the west, aurorally,* i. e., *at dawn of morning,* and the *rising of its* رَقِيب, *which is another star,* or *asterism, opposite to it, at the same time, in the east, each night for a period of thirteen days:* thus does each star, or asterism, of those Mansions, [one after another,] to the end of the year, except الجَبْهَة, the period of which is fourteen days: (Ṣ:) [or it signifies the *auroral rising,* and sometimes the *auroral setting, of one of those stars,* or *asterisms;* as will be shown below: I do not say "heliacal" rising because the rising here meant continues for a period of thirteen days]. Accord. to the T, نوء signifies the *setting* of one of the stars, or asterisms, above mentioned: and AḤn says, that it signifies its *first setting in the morning, when the stars are about to disappear; which is when the whiteness of dawn diffuses itself.* (TA.) A'Obeyd says, I have not heard نوء used in the sense of "setting," or "falling," except in this instance. (Ṣ.) It is added, [whether on his or another's authority is doubtful,] that the [pagan] Arabs used to attribute the rains and winds and heat and cold to such of the stars, or asterisms, above mentioned as was *setting* at the time [*aurorally*]; or, accord. to Aṣ, to that which was *rising in its ascendency* [*aurorally*]; and used to say, مُطِرْنَا بِنَوْءِ كَذَا [*We have been given rain by such a* نوء]; (Ṣ;) or they attributed heat [and cold] to the *rising* of the star or asterism, and rain [and wind], to its نَوْء [meaning its *setting*]. (AḤn, Har, p. 216.) This the Muslim is forbidden to say, unless he mean thereby, "We have been given rain at the period of such a نوء;" God having made it usual for rain to come at [certain of] the periods called انواء. Again, A'Obeyd says, The انواء are *twenty-eight stars,* or *asterisms;* sing. نوء: the *rising* of any one of them in the east [*aurorally*] is called نوء; and the *star,* or *asterism,* itself is hence thus called: but sometimes نوء signifies the *setting.* Also, in the L it is said, that each of the above-mentioned stars, or asterisms, is called thus because, when that in the west sets, the opposite one rises; and this *rising* is called النوء; but some make نوء to signify the *setting;* as if it bore contr. senses. (TA.) [El-Ḳazweenee mentions certain physical occurrences on the occasions of the انواء of the Mansions of the Moon; and in each of these cases, except three, the نوء is the *rising,* not the setting. Two of the excepted cases are doubtful: the passage relating to the third plainly expresses an event which happens at the period of the *auroral setting* of الصَّرْفَة; namely the commencement of the days called أَيَّامُ العَجُوز; corresponding, accord. to El-Maḳreezee, with the rising of الفَرْغُ المُقَدَّمُ, the رقيب of الصرفة: and it is said in the Ṣ, art. عجز, on the authority of Ibn-Kunáseh, that the ايام العجوز fall at the period of the نوء of الصرفة. (The auroral setting of الصرفة, at the commencement of the era of the Flight, in central Arabia, happened about the 9th of March O. S.; and this is the day of the N. S., the 26th of February O. S., on which commence the ايام العجوز accord. to the modern Egyptian almanacs.) Hence it appears, that *sometimes the setting,* but *generally the rising,* was called the نوء. Moreover, the ancient Arabs had twenty-eight proverbial sayings (which are quoted in the Mir-át ez-Zemán, and in the work of El-Ḳazweenee) relating to the *risings* of the twenty-eight Mansions of the Moon: such as this: إِذَا طَلَعَ الشَّرَطَانْ إِسْتَوَى الزَّمَانْ "When Esh-Sharaṭán rises, the season becomes temperate:" or, perhaps, "— the night and day, become equal." (If this latter meaning could be proved to be the right one, we might infer that the Calendar of the Mansions of the Moon was in use more than twelve centuries B.C.; and that for this reason الشرطان was called the first of the Mansions; though it may have been first so called at a later period as being the first Mansion in the first Sign of the Zodiac. But I return to the more immediate object which I had in view in mentioning the foregoing sayings.) I do not find any of these sayings (though others, I believe, do) relating to the settings. Hence, again, it appears most probable, that the *rising,* not the setting, was generally called نوء.] — [In many instances,] الأَنْوَآء signifies *The Mansions of the Moon* [themselves]; and نَوْءٌ, any *one of those Mansions:* and they are also called نُجُومُ المَطَرِ [*the stars,* or *asterisms, of rain*]. (Mgh, in art. خطأ.) IAṣr says that the term نوء was not applied except in the case of a star, or asterism, accompanied by rain: (TA:) [see exs. under خَطَّ and خَطَأٌ: but most authors, it seems, apply this term without such restriction: it is sometimes given to *certain stars* or *asterisms, which do not belong to the Mansions of the Moon;* as will be seen below: and it is applied, with the article, especially to الثُّرَيَّا]. — Accord. to AZ, as cited by AM, the first rain is that called الوَسْمِىّ: the انواء of which are those called العَرْقُوَتَانِ المُؤَخَّرَتَانِ, the same, says AM, as الفَرْغُ المُؤَخَّر, [the 27th Mansion of the Moon, which, about the period of the commencement of the era of the Flight, (to which period, or thereabout, the calculation of AZ, here given, most probably relates,) set aurorally, (for by the term نوء AZ means a star or asterism, at the *setting* of which rain usually falls,) in central Arabia, on the 21st of Sept. O.S, as shewn in the observations on the منازل القمر in this lexicon]: then, الشَّرَطُ, [one of the شَرَطَانِ, the 1st Mansion, which, about the period above mentioned, set aurorally on the 17th of Oct.]: then, الثُّرَيَّا, [the 3rd Mansion, which, about that period, set on the 12th of Nov.]. Then comes the rain called الشَّتَوِىُّ: the انواء of which are الجَوْزَاء [meaning الهَقْعَةُ, the 5th Mansion, which, about the period above mentioned, set aurorally on the 8th of Dec.]: then, الذِّرَاعَانِ, [i. e. الذِّرَاعُ المَقْبُوضَةُ and الذِّرَاعُ المَبْسُوطَةُ; the former of which, about the same period, set anti-heliacally on the 3rd of January, the proper relative time of the setting of the 7th Mansion; and the latter, on the 16th of January, the proper relative time of the setting of the 8th Mansion;] and their نَثْرَة, [the 8th Mansion, which, about that period, set aurorally on the 16th of Jan.]: then, الجَبْهَةُ, [the 10th Mansion, which set aurorally, about that period, on the 11th of Feb.] In this period, the شتوى rain ends; and that called الدَّفَئِىُّ (q. v.) begins, and [after this] الصَّيْفُ. All the rains from the وسمى to the دفئى are called رَبِيع. Then, [after the دفئى,] comes the صَيْف: the انواء of which are السِّمَاكَانِ (الرَّقِيبُ and الأَعْزَلُ); [the former of which is, accord. to El-Ḳazweenee, the 14th Mansion, which, about the period above mentioned, set aurorally on the 4th of April: the latter seems to be the رقيب of الثريّا (see رقيب); i. e. الإِكْلِيلُ, the 17th Mansion, which, about the same period, set aurorally on the 13th of May]; a period of about forty days. Then comes الحَمِيمُ, [see this word, said by some to be] a period of about twenty nights, commencing at the [auroral] rising of الدَّبَرَانُ, [at the epoch of the Flight, about the 26th of May, O.S.,] which has [little rain, or none, and is therefore said to have] no نوء. Then comes الخَرِيفُ [a period of little rain]: the انواء of which are النَّسْرَانِ [or the two vultures, النَّسْرُ الطَّائِرُ and النَّسْرُ الوَاقِعُ, which, in central Arabia, about the period above mentioned, set aurorally on the 24th of July, O.S., both together]: then, الاخضر, [which I have not been able to identify with any known star or asterism, in the TT with صح written above it, to denote its being correctly transcribed]: then, العَرْقُوَتَانِ الأُولَيَانِ, the same says AM, as الفَرْغُ المُقَدَّمُ, [the 26th Mansion, which, about the same period, set on the 8th of Sept.]. (T, TT, TA.*) — [Hence,] نَوْءٌ [also means † The *supposed effect* of a star or asterism so termed *in bringing rain &c.*: whence the phrase لَا نَوْءَ لَهُ *It has no effect upon the weather*; said of a particular star or asterism: see البُطَيْنُ. — Also, *Rain consequent upon the annual setting* or *rising* of a star so termed: so in many instances in Ḳzw's account of the Mansions of the Moon.] And ‡ *Herbs*, or *herbage*: so called because regarded as the consequence of what is [more properly] termed نوء: [i. e., the auroral setting or rising of a star or asterism, or the rain supposed to be produced thereby.] Ex. جَفَّ النَّوْءُ *The herbage dried up.* (IKṭ.) Also, ‡ *A gift*, or *present*. (Ḳ.)

أَنْوَأُ *More*, or *most*, *acquainted with the* أَنْوَاء. (Ḳ, and some copies of the Ṣ.) [See نَوْءٌ.] It is an anomalous word, though of a kind of which there are some other examples; for it has no verb; and, by rule, a noun of this class is not formed but from a verb. (TA.)

مُسْتَنَآءٌ † *One of whom a gift*, or *present*, *is sought*, or *asked*. (Ḳ.)

نوب

1. نُبْتُهُ, aor. يَنُوبُ, inf. n. نَوْبٌ; and ▼ إِنْتَبْتُهُ; *I came to him by turns.* (TA.) — ▼ إِنْتَابَهُمْ, inf. n. إِنْتِيَابٌ, *He came to them time after time.* (Ṣ, Ḳ.) The Hudhalee (Aboo-Sahm Usámeh, TA,) says,

* أَقَبُّ طَرِيدٌ بِنُزْهِ الفَلَا *
* ةِ لَا يَرِدُ المَاءَ إِلَّا ٱنْتِيَابَا *

(Ṣ) *Slender in the belly, an object of the chase, in a part of the desert far from water and pasture; he will not come to the water otherwise than time after time.* The poet is describing a wild ass. (IB.) Accord. to one relation, the last word is ٱئْتِيَابَا, meaning "coming by night." (Ṣ.) — [Also, ▼ انتاب, app., *He did a thing time after time: did a thing by turns.* (See مُنْتَابٌ.)] — نَابَ, aor. يَنُوبُ, inf. n. نَوْبٌ, *He drove camels early in the morning to the water, and was* [*again*] *at the water in the evening, going to it* [*thus*] *time after time.* (IAar.) — نَابَ إِلَى ٱللّٰهِ; (Ḳ;) and ▼ اناب إِلَيْهِ, (Ṣ, Ḳ,) inf. n. إِنَابَةٌ; (TA;) *He returned from disobedience to obedience to God; he returned unto God* [*repenting*]; *he repented:* (Ṣ, Ḳ:) or the latter, *he returned unto God;* syn. رَجَعَ: (Mṣb:) or ناب signifies *he kept to obedience unto God:* [this is given in the Ḳ as another and distinct signification of ناب:] and اناب signifies as before explained: or *he returned to the performance of God's commands, not departing from anything thereof:* or *he returned time after time:* the lit. signification, accord. to the Keshsháf and AHei, is *he entered upon the good turn.* (TA, where for الخيل read الخير.) — نَابَ عَنِّى, aor. يَنُوبُ, inf. n. نَوْبٌ and مَنَابٌ (Ṣ, Ḳ: but the former inf. n., which is mentioned by Th, is omitted in some copies of the Ṣ) and نِيَابَةٌ (Mṣb: [the only inf. n. there mentioned:] but this last, though also mentioned in the L, is rejected by Th and the other early authorities as not belonging to the classical language of the Arabs: TA:) *He supplied my place; served for me; acted in my place* or *stead*, or *as my substitute, lieutenant, deputy, factor*, or *agent*; (Ṣ, Ḳ, &c.;) نَابَ عَنْهُ — فِى كَذَا *in such an affair.* (Mṣb.) — [and نَابَ مَنَابَهُ *It* (a thing) *supplied its* (another thing's) *place.* (TA.) — نَابَهُ أَمْرٌ, aor. يَنُوبُ, (Ṣ,) inf. n. نَوْبٌ and نَوْبَةٌ; (Ḳ, TA;) and ▼ إِنْتَابَهُ; (Ṣ;) *a thing*, or *an event*, [generally a misfortune, or an evil accident,] *befell him; betided him; happened to him.* (Ṣ, Ḳ.)

3. نَاوَبَهُ, (inf. n. مُنَاوَبَةٌ, TA,) *He did* [or *took*] *a thing with him, each taking his turn:* syn. سَاهَمَهُ. (Ḳ.) — نَاوَبْتُهُ, inf. n. مُنَاوَبَةٌ, i. q. عاقبه [q.v., here signifying *I shared with him:* see 6]. (Mṣb.)

4. أَنَبْتُهُ عَنْهُ, (Ḳ,) and ▼ اِسْتَنَبْتُهُ, (TA,) *I made him to supply his* [another's] *place; to act in his place* or *stead*, or *as his substitute, lieutenant, deputy, factor*, or *agent;* (Ḳ, Mṣb;) فِى كَذَا *in such an affair.* (Mṣb.) — See 1. — أَتَانِى فُلَانٌ فَمَا أَنَبْتُ لَهُ *Such a one came to me, and I cared not for him*, or *paid any regard to him.* (A.)

6. تَنَاوَبْنَا الخَطْبَ, and الأَمْرَ, *We performed the affair*, or *business*, *by turns;* or *turn after turn.* (T.) هُمْ يَتَنَاوَبُونَ النَّوْبَةَ فِيمَا بَيْنَهُمْ فِى المَاءِ وَغَيْرِهِ [*They took turns in the case of a thing that was between them; in the case of water &c.*] (Ṣ.) — تَنَاوَبُوا عَلَيْهِ *They did it by turns; this person doing it one time; and that, another.* (Mṣb.) — تَنَاوَبُوا, as also تنازلوا and تطاعموا, *They* (a people on a journey) *ate with*, or *at the tent of*, [*meaning, of the food of*,] *this man on one occasion of alighting, and another man on another occasion of alighting; each one of them having his turn to supply the food of one day.* (ISh.) — تَنَاوَبُوا عَلَى المَاءِ, (Ḳ,) or تناوبوا الماء, (L,) *They shared the water among themselves* [*by turns*] *by means of the* حَصَاةُ القَسْمِ, (Ḳ,) or المَقْلَةُ; (L;) *which is a pebble that is put into a vessel; then as much water as will cover the pebble is poured into the vessel:* this is done by persons on a journey when they have little water; and thus they divide it into shares. (Ḳ, arts. قسم and مقل.) — المَنَايَا تَتَنَاوَبُنَا *Deaths come to us by turns; to each of us in his turn.* (TA.)

8: see 1.

10: see 4.

النَّوْبُ *What is a day's and a night's journey distant from one:* (Ṣ, Ḳ:) what is a night's journey distant is called القَرَبُ: originally in the case of going to water: (Ṣ:) or *what is three days' journey distant*: or *what is two leagues* (فَرْسَخَانِ) *distant*; or *three*. (TA.) Lebeed says,

* إِحْدَى بَنِى جَعْفَرٍ كَلِفْتُ بِهَا *
* لَمْ تُمْسِ مِنِّى نَوْبًا وَلَا قَرَبَا *

[*I have become enamoured of one of the descendants of Jaafar: she has not become a day's and a night's journey* (or *three days' journey* or *two leagues*,) *distant from me, nor a night's journey distant*]. (Ṣ.) Or نوب signifies [in these words of the poet] *near*, so that he might visit her repeatedly; and قرب and نوب are synonymous: (IAar:) or قرب [is used by him to signify that at such a distance] he might come to her once in three days. (AA.) —— نَوْبٌ *Strength*: (Ḳ:) as also ▼ نُوبَةٌ: ex. أَصْبَحْتَ لَا نُوبَةَ لَكَ *Thou hast become without strength*: and تَرَكْتُهُ لَا نَوْبَ لَهُ *I left him without strength*. (TA.) —— نَوْبٌ *Nearness*. (ISk, Ṣ, Ḳ.) —— نَوْبٌ a pl. (or rather a quasi. pl. n., TA) of نَائِبٌ: (RA, Ḳ:) [but in what sense I do not find: app., as the act. part. n. of نَابَ "it befell, &c."]

نُوبٌ *Bees*: pl. of نَائِبٌ: (Ṣ, Ḳ:) from نَوْبَةٌ "a turn that falls to a man at a certain time," accord. to Aṣ: or so called because they feed and return to their place: (Ṣ:) and if so, the sing. is نائب: (TA:) or so called because they are of a colour inclining to black; (Ṣ, from A'Obeyd; or, as in some copies of the Ṣ, A'Obeydeh;) or as likened to the nation of negroes called النُّوبَةُ: and if so, the word has no sing. (TA.) See also نُوبٌ. —— النُّوبُ (Ṣ, Ḳ) and ▼ النُّوبَةُ (Ṣ) [*The Nubians*;] *a nation of the Negroes* [or rather *Ethiopians*]: (Ṣ, Ḳ:) or the latter is the name of *their country*; *an extensive country south of Upper Egypt*. (Ḳ, TA.) —— ▼ نُوبِىٌّ [*A Nubian*;] *an individual of the nation above mentioned*. (Ṣ.) See نُوبَةٌ. —— ▼ أَسْوَدُ نُوبِىٌّ: see نُوبِىٌّ.

نَوْبَةٌ *A turn which comes to one*, or *which one takes*; the *time at which*, or *during which*, *anything is*, or *is to be, done*, or *had*, *in succession*; *an opportunity*: (Ṣ,* Ḳ, MF:) pl. نُوَبٌ, (Ṣ,) which is extr. [with respect to analogy.] (TA.) See نَوْبٌ. —— نَوْبَةٌ and ▼ نِيَابَةٌ *A coming to water*, *&c., one time*, or *turn*, *after a former time*, or *turn*. This is the meaning of the words in the following phrases, mentioned [but not explained] in the Ṣ and Ḳ: جَاءَتْ نَوْبَتُكَ and جاءت نِيَابَتُكَ, *Thy time*, or *turn*, *to come to water*, *&c.*, *in succession*, *has arrived*: (TA:) pl. of the former word نُوَبٌ. (Ṣ, Ḳ.) —— نَوْبَةٌ *An assembly*, *a company*, *troop*, or *congregated body*, *of men*. (Ḳ.)

نُوبَةٌ: see نُوبٌ and نَائِبَةٌ.

نِيَابَةٌ: see نَوْبَةٌ.

نَائِبٌ خَيْرٌ *Abundant* good, (Ḳ,) *that comes again and again* [*by turns*]. (A.) —— حُمَّى نَائِبَةٌ *A quotidian fever*. (Ṣ.) —— نَائِبَةٌ *Guests coming time after time*. (TA, from a trad.) —— See نُوبٌ. —— نَائِبٌ *One who supplies the place of another*; *who acts in his place* or *stead*, or *as his substitute*, *lieutenant*, *deputy*, *factor*, or *agent*: pl. نُوَّابٌ. (Mṣb.) —— نَائِبَةٌ *What befalls*, *betides*, or *happens*, *that is afflictive*, *distressing*, *difficult*, or *unfortunate*: pl. نَوَائِبُ and نُوَبٌ; the latter of which is extr.: (TA:) or rather this latter is pl. of نُوبَةٌ, which is syn. with نائبة, (MF,) a subst. from نَابَهُ أَمْرٌ, (Ṣ,) [and therefore signifying *an accident*, or *a casualty*, *&c.*; and as such this pl. is not extr., but analogous:] *an evil accident*; *a misfortune*; *a disaster*; *a calamity*; *an affliction*: pl. نَوَائِبُ: (Ṣ:) only signifying what is evil: (Mṣb:) or, accord. to some, *an accident*, *whether good or evil*: ex. Lebeed says,

* نَوَائِبُ مِنْ خَيْرٍ وَشَرٍّ كِلَاهُمَا *
* فَلَا الْخَيْرُ مَمْدُودٌ وَلَا الشَّرُّ لَازِبُ *

[*Accidents of a good nature*, *and of an evil*, *both of them*; *and neither is the good prolonged*, *nor the evil constant*]: or *what befalls*, *betides*, or *happens*, *to a man*, *of difficult*, *arduous*, *distressing*, or *afflictive*, *events*, or *affairs*, *and accidents*: [*a difficulty*, or *difficult affair*] in a trad. respecting Kheyber it is said, قَسَمَهَا نِصْفَيْنِ نِصْفًا لِنَوَائِبِهِ وَحَاجَاتِهِ وَنِصْفًا بَيْنَ الْمُسْلِمِينَ [*He divided it into two halves*; *half for his own difficulties*, or *difficult affairs*, *and wants*, *and half among the Muslims*]. (TA.)

مَنَابٌ *A road to water*. (Ḳ.) —— مَنَابٌ ‡ *i.q.* مَرْجِعٌ: ex. إِلَيْهِ مَنَابِى ‡ [*To him is my recourse*]. (A.)

مُنَابٌ pass. part. n. of 4, A person *made to supply another's place*; *&c.* (Mṣb.) —— أَمْرٌ مُنَابٌ فِيهِ *An affair in which a person is made to supply another's place*; *in which a person is made to act in the place* or *stead of another person*; or *as another's substitute*. (Mṣb.) See the verb.

مَنُوبٌ عَنْهُ A person *whose place is supplied by another*; *in whose place* or *stead*, or *as whose substitute*, *another person acts*. (Mṣb.) —— أَمْرٌ مَنُوبٌ فِيهِ *An affair in which a person supplies the place of another*; *in which a person acts in the place* or *stead of another*, or *as another's substitute*. (Mṣb.) See the verb.

مُنِيبٌ, from اناب الى الله, *Repenting*, &c. (TA.) —— مُنِيبٌ act. part. n. of 4, A person *making* another *to supply his* or *another's place*; *&c.* (Mṣb.) —— See the verb. —— مُنِيبٌ *Copious* rain: and *good* rain, *of the* [*rain termed*] رَبِيعٌ: (Ḳ:) or, accord. to En-Naḍr Ibn-Shumeyl, copious rain (مَطَرٌ جَوْدٌ) is termed منيب: and you say, أَصَابَنَا رَبِيعٌ صِدْقٍ منيب [*There fell upon us an excellent*, *copious rain*, *of such as is termed* ربيع; meaning] *good* rain, *but inferior to what is termed* جود; but this is an excellent rain if followed by other rain. (TA.)

مُنْتَابٌ act. part. n. of 8. —— [*Coming by turns*: *&c.*] —— *Visiting*. (RA.) —— *Doing a thing time after time*: *doing a thing by turns*. (TA.)

نوت

1. نَاتَ, aor. يَنُوتُ, inf. n. نَوْتٌ, *He* (a man) *moved from side to side in walking*; as also نَاتَ, aor. يَنِيتُ: (L:) or *he so moved by reason of weakness*, or *infirmity*: (Ḳ:) or, *by reason of drowsiness*, like as the sailor turns the vessel from side to side. (L.)

نَاتٌ *i.q.* نَاسٌ *Mankind*; or *men*: (Ṣ, Ḳ:) like أَكْيَاتٌ for أَكْيَاسٌ; the س being changed into ت [see art. س], accord. to the dial. of certain of the Arabs; as related by Az. (Ṣ.)

نُوتِىٌّ [and ▼ نُوَّاتٌ] *A sailor upon the sea*, (Ṣ, Ḳ,) *who turns about the ship in the sea*: (TA:) pl. of the former نَوَاتِىُّ, (Ṣ, Ḳ,) [and of the latter] نُوَّاتُونَ. (TA.) Accord. to J, from the language of the people of Syria: accord. to others, an arabicized word [from the Greek ναύτης]. (TA.)

نُوَّاتٌ: see نُوتِىٌّ.

نوث

نَوْثَةٌ *i.q.* حَمْقَةٌ. (L.)

نوح

1. نَاحَتِ الْمَرْأَةُ, aor. تَنُوحُ, inf. n. نَوْحٌ and نِيَاحٌ (Ṣ, Ḳ) and نُوَاحٌ, (L, Ḳ,) or this is a simple subst., (Mṣb,) and نِيَاحَةٌ, (A, L, Ḳ,) or this also is a simple subst., (Ṣ, Mṣb, [and as such it is also mentioned in the Ḳ,]) and مَنَاحٌ (Ḳ) and مَنَاحَةٌ, (L,) [*The woman wailed*]. You say نَاحَتْ عَلَى الْمَيِّتِ, (Mṣb,) and عَلَى زَوْجِهَا, and نَاحَتْهُ, (L, Ḳ,) but ناحت عليه is preferred, (TA,) [*She wailed for*, or *bewailed*, *the dead*, and, *her husband*]. Also, نَاحَ على الميّت. (A.) نَاحَ and ▼ استناح are syn. (L, Ḳ.) [In the Ṣ it is implied that it is tropical: see نَائِحَةٌ: but in the A it is said to be proper.] —— نَاحَتِ الْحَمَامَةُ, (L,) inf. n. نَوْحٌ, (L, Ḳ,) *The pigeon cooed* (L, Ḳ) *in a plaintive* or *wailing manner*. (L.) Some say that this is tropical; but most, that it is proper. (MF.) —— الطَّيْرُ تَنُوحُ [*The birds warble plaintively*.] (A.)

3. ناوح بَعْضُهَا بَعْضًا *One of them was opposite*

to, or *faced, another*. Said of mountains, and in like manner of winds. (Ṣ, L.)

5. تنوّح *It* (a thing) *moved about, hanging down; it dangled.* (Ṣ, Ḳ.)

6. الطُّيُورُ تَتَنَاوَحُ [*The birds warble plaintively, one to another*]. (A.) See an ex. in art. فوح, conj. 6. — تناوحت الرِّيَاحُ *The winds blew violently* [as is generally the case when they blow from opposite directions]. (TA.) See an ex. voce سهو. — تناوحا *They two were opposite, one to the other; they faced each other.* (Ṣ, Ḳ.) You say so of two mountains, and of two winds. (Ṣ, L.)

10: see 1. — استناح *He* (a wolf) *howled,* (L, Ḳ,) *and was listened to and followed by other wolves.* (L.) — *He* (a man) *wept and induced another, or others, to weep:* (Ḳ:) or *he wept so as to induce another, or others, to weep.* (L.)

نَائِحَةٌ: see نَوْحٌ.

نَوْحَةٌ and ▼ نَيْحَةٌ *Strength; force.* (L.)

نَيْحَةٌ: see نَوْحَةٌ.

نُوَاحٌ: see نِيَاحَةٌ.

نِيَاحَةٌ (Ṣ, Mṣb, Ḳ) and ▼ نُوَاحٌ (Mṣb) substs. from نَاحَتِ المَرْأَةُ, q. v. [*A wailing,* or *bewailing a dead person*].

نَائِحَةٌ: see نَوْحٌ.

نَيِّحَةُ رِيحٍ أُخْرَى *A counterwind,* or *wind which is the opposite, of another wind.* (Ṣ, A, L.) One that blows transversely with respect to another is called the نَيِّحَة of the latter. (Ṣ, L.)

نَائِحَةٌ: see نَوَّاحَةٌ.

نَائِحَةٌ: see النَّوَاحِي.

نَائِحَةٌ [*A wailing woman*]: (Mṣb:) pl. نَوَائِحُ and نَائِحَاتٌ: and you also say ▼ نِسَآءٌ نَوْحٌ, and ▼ نَوْحٌ, and أَنْوَاحٌ: (Ṣ, Ḳ:) نَوَائِحُ is an epithet applied to *women who assemble in a* مَنَاحَة: and ▼ مَنَاحَةٌ (also) and ▼ نَوْحٌ signify *women who assemble together for the purpose of mourning.* (L.) نَوَائِحُ are so called from التَّنَاوُحُ, signifying "the being opposite, one to another:" (Ṣ:) [if so, it is app. a tropical term: but accord. to the A, التناوح, as above explained, is tropical]. Also ▼ نَوَّاحَةٌ [*A woman who wails much,* or *frequently; who is in the habit of wailing; a professional wailing woman*]. Ex. هِيَ نَوَّاحَةُ بَنِى فُلَانٍ [*She is the professional wailing woman of the sons of such a one*]. (A.) — حَمَامَةٌ نَائِحَةٌ, and ▼ نَوَّاحَةٌ, *A pigeon that coos in a plaintive or wailing manner.* (L.) — نَوَائِحُ also signifies *Standards,* or *ensigns, opposite one to another, in battle.* (L.) — Also, *Swords.* In this sense, it occurs written ▼ النَّوَاحِي, by transposition. (Ks, L.)

مَنَاحَةٌ *A place of* نَوْح [or *wailing for a dead person*]: (Mṣb:) pl. مَنَاحَاتٌ and مَنَاوِحُ. (A, L.) Ex. كُنَّا فِى مَنَاحَةِ فُلَانٍ [*We were in the place of wailing of,* or *for, such a one*]. (Ṣ, Ḳ.) — See نَائِحَةٌ.

الرِّيَاحُ المُتَنَاوِحَةُ *The winds called* النُّكْبُ: [see نَكْبَآءُ:] so called because they are opposite, one to another: they blow in times of drought, when rains are scanty, and when the air is dry, and the cold severe. (L.)

نوخ

1. نَاخَ: see 10.

2. نَوَّخَ ٱللّٰهُ ٱلْأَرْضَ طَرُوقَةً لِلْمَآءِ † *God made,* or *may God make, the land capable of receiving the water* [of the rain *so as to be impregnated,* or *fertilized,* or *soaked, thereby*]: expl. by جَعَلَهَا مِمَّا تُطِيقُهُ. (Ṣ.) — See 4.

4. اناخ (Ṣ, L, Mṣb) and ▼ نوّخ (L, Mṣb) *He* (a man) *made a camel to lie down upon his breast* [*with his legs folded,* as is done on the occasions of mounting and dismounting, &c.]. (Ṣ, L, Mṣb.) Also, ▼ تنوّخ (Ṣ, L, Ḳ) and اناخ (Ḳ) and ▼ استناخ (L) *He* (a stallion-camel) *made a she-camel to do so in order that he might cover her:* (Ṣ, Ḳ:) or *made her do so and then covered her.* (L.) — اناخ بِهِ البَلَآءُ والذُّلُّ ‡ [*Trial,* or *affliction, and abasement, befell him*]. (A.)

5: see 4. — and 10.

10: see 4. — Also, استناخ (Ṣ, L, Mṣb) and ▼ تنوّخ (L, Mṣb) *He* (a camel) *lay down upon his breast* [*with his legs folded*]. (Ṣ, L, Mṣb.) Also, استناخت and ▼ تنوّخت *She* (a camel) *did so in order to be covered by the stallion.* (Ḳ.) It is said that one should not use, in the sense of the quasi-pass. of the trans. v. اناخ, the form ▼ نَاخَ, nor ▼ اناخ: (Mṣb:) but the authors on verbs mention اناخ in a neuter sense; and IAạr says, that one says اناخ, but not ناخ: (MF:) or IAạr says, ▼ تنوّخ البَعِيرُ, but not ناخ nor اناخ: (L:) [and F says, that] one should not say, in the sense of استناخت and ▼ تنوّخت as explained above, either ناخت or اناخت. (Ḳ.)

نَوْخَةٌ *A remaining, staying, abiding,* or *dwelling,* in a place. (L, Ḳ.)

نَائِخَةٌ A *distant* land: (Ḳ:) or it is [correctly] نَابِخَةٌ, with ب. (TA.)

مُنَاخٌ: see مُنَاخٌ.

مُنَاخٌ *A place in which camels are made to lie down upon their breasts,* [*with their legs folded*]; (Mṣb;) *a place where they so lie;* (Ḳ;) *a nightly resting-place of camels.* (Mṣb, voce مُرَاحٌ.) In a trad. in which it occurs, accord. to one relation it is ▼ مَنَاخٌ. (TA.) — Also, *A time at which camels so lie.* (MF.) — Also, pass. part. n. of اناخ; and used as an inf. n. of that verb, like إِنَاخَةٌ. (MF.) — هٰذَا مُنَاخُ سَوْءٍ ‡ *This is a disagreeable place.* (A.)

المُنِيخُ *The lion.* (Ḳ)

نور

1. نَارَ intrans., in the sense of أَنَارَ: see the latter, in two places. — نَارُوا النَّارَ: see 5. — نُرْتُ البَعِيرَ ‡ *I made a mark upon the camel with a hot iron.* (M, Ḳ.) See نَارٌ.

2. نوّر, intrans., in the sense of أَنَارَ, from النُّورُ: see 4, in two places. — نوّر بِالفَجْرِ, (Mgh, Mṣb,) inf. n. تَنْوِيرٌ, (Mṣb,) *He performed the prayer of daybreak when the dawn had become light:* (Mgh, Mṣb:) ‡or *when the horizon had become bright:* (TA:) تَنْوِيرُ الفَجْرِ, without ب, is an amplification. (Mgh.) تَنْوِيرٌ as a subst. from this verb, see below. — نوّر, trans., in the sense of أَنَارَ, from النُّورُ: see 4, in three places. — نوّر, (Ṣ, A, Mṣb, Ḳ,) inf. n. تَنْوِيرٌ, (Ṣ, Ḳ,) *It* (a tree, Ṣ, A, Mṣb, Ḳ, and a plant, Mṣb) *blossomed,* or *flowered; it put forth its* نَوْر; (Ṣ, A, Mṣb, Ḳ;) as also ▼ أَنَارَ, (Ṣ, Mṣb, Ḳ,) originally أَنْوَرَ. (TA.) See also 4. — *It* (seed-produce) *attained to maturity:* (Ḳ:) [see an ex. in a verse cited in art. سمو, conj. 3:] تَنْوِيرٌ, the inf. n. of the verb in this sense, has a pl. تَنَاوِيرُ. (TA.) — نوّره *He smeared him* or *it with* نُورَة. (Mgh, Mṣb.) — نوّر ذِرَاعَهُ, (Ṣ, Ḳ,) inf. n. تَنْوِيرٌ, (TA,) *He pricked his fore-arm with a needle, and then sprinkled* نَؤُور, [q. v.] *upon it.* (Ṣ, Ḳ.)

4. انار, (inf. n. إِنَارَةٌ, Mṣb,) *It* (a thing) (Ṣ, Mṣb) *gave light;* or *shone;* or *shone brightly;* (Ṣ, A,* Mṣb, Ḳ;*) as also ▼ نوّر, (Lḥ, Ṣ,* A, Mṣb, Ḳ,) inf. n. تَنْوِيرٌ; (Ṣ, Mṣb;) and ▼ استنار; (Ṣ, A, Mṣb, Ḳ;) and ▼ نَارَ, (A, Mṣb, Ḳ,) aor. يَنُورُ, (Mṣb,) inf. n. نَوْرٌ, (Ḳ, TA,) or نُورٌ, (as in a copy of the A,) or نِيَارٌ; (Mṣb;) and ▼ تنوّر: (Ḳ:) نوّر (Ṣ,* Mgh, Mṣb, Ḳ) and انار (Mgh, Mṣb) and استنار, (Mṣb,) said of the dawn, signify as above; (Mgh, Mṣb;) or *its light appeared.* (Ṣ,* Ḳ.) — [Hence,] ▼ نَارَتِ الفِتْنَةُ, aor. تَنُورُ, *Sedition,* or *discord,* or *the like, happened and spread.* (Mṣb.) — [Hence also,] انار and أَنْوَرَ, (Ḳ,) the latter being the original form;

said of a plant; (TA;) *It became beautiful*: and *it became apparent*. (Ḳ, TA.) And أَنْوَرَتِ الشَّجَرَةُ *The tree became beautiful in its verdure*: or, as some say, *put forth its blossoms* or *flowers*. (TA.) See also 2. — انار and ▾ نوّر *He made to give light; to shine*; or *to shine brightly*. (Mṣb.) ▾ التَّنْوِيرُ and الإِنَارَةُ signify the same. (Ṣ.) You say, انار السِّرَاجَ, and ▾ نوّرهُ, (A,) and ▾ نوّر المِصْبَاحَ, (Mṣb,) *He made the lamp to give light*; or *to become bright*. (Mṣb.) — انار المَكَانَ *He illumined*, or *lighted, the place*; (Ḳ;) i. e., *put light* [or *a light*] *in it*. (TA.) — [Hence,] اناره ‡ *He elucidated it; rendered it apparent* or *plainly apparent, conspicuous, manifest*, or *evident*; (TA;) as also ▾ نوّرهُ. (A, TA.*) — And hence, انار ٱللّٰهُ بُرْهَانَهُ ‡ *God taught him*, or *dictated to him, his proof*. (TA.)

5: see 4, first signification. — تنوّروا النَّارَ مِنْ بَعِيدٍ, (Ṣ, Ḳ,) and ▾ نَارُوهَا, (Ḳ,) *They looked at the fire*, or *endeavoured to see it* (تَبَصَّرُوهَا,) *from afar*: (Ṣ, Ḳ:) or تنوّر النَّارَ *he looked at the fire*, or *endeavoured to see it*, (تَبَصَّرَهَا,) *and repaired towards it*: (A:) or *he came to the fire*: it has this signification as well as the first. (TA.) — تنوّر الرَّجُلَ, and المَرْأَةَ, *He looked at the man*, and *the woman, at or by a fire, from a place where the latter did not see him; he stood in the dark to see the man, and the woman, by the light of the latter's fire, without the latter's seeing him*: تَنَوُّرٌ being like تَضَوُّؤٌ. (TA.) — See also 8.

8. انتار, (Th, T, Ṣ, M, Ḳ,) imp. إِنْتَرْ; (T;) and إِنْتَوَرَ, (T, Ḳ,) imp. إِنْتَوِرْ; (T;) and ▾ تنوّر; (Ṣ, M, A, Mgh, Mṣb, Ḳ;) or only انتار and انتور; not تنوّر; (T;) or some say انتار; [implying that most say تنوّر;] (Ṣ;) *He smeared himself with* نُورَة [which is differently explained in the lexicons, so that these verbs are made to bear different meanings by different lexicons]. (Th, T, Ṣ, M, A, Mgh, Mṣb, Ḳ.)

10: see 4, first signification. — استنار بِهِ *He sought the aid of its light*: (TA:) or *of its rays*. (M, Ḳ.)

نَارٌ a word of which the meaning is well known; (M, Ḳ;) [*Fire*; not well explained as signifying] the *flaming*, or *blazing*, (لَهِيب,) *that is apparent to the sense*: (TA:) its ا is originally و: (Ṣ, TA:) it is fem.; (Ṣ, M, Mṣb:) and sometimes masc.: (AḤn, M, Ḳ:) and the dim. is نُوَيْرَةٌ, with و because it is the original medial radical, (Ṣ,) and with ة because نار is fem.: (Mṣb:) pl. [of pauc.] أَنْوُرٌ, (Ṣ, M, L,) in the Ḳ أَنْوَارٌ, [which is a mistake, though this is also said to be a pl. of نار,] (TA,) and [of mult.] نِيرَانٌ [which is the most common form] (Ṣ, M, Ḳ) and نُورٌ (AAF, Ṣ, M, Mṣb, Ḳ) and نِيَارٌ, (M, Ḳ,) and نِيَرَةٌ and أَنْيَارٌ also occurs, in the phrase نَارُ الأَنْيَارِ, in a trad. respecting the prison of hell; this phrase, if correctly related, perhaps meaning نَارُ النِّيرَانِ, and انيار being originally أَنْوار. (IAth.) النَّارُ is also applied to *The fire of hell*. (TA.) The Arabs say, in cursing their enemies, أَبْعَدَ ٱللّٰهُ دَارَهُمْ وَأَوْقَدَ نَارًا أَثَرَهُمْ [*May God make their abode distant, and kindle a fire after them!*] And it was a custom of Arab women, as related by IAạr, on the authority of El-'Okeyleeyeh, when they feared evil from a man, and he removed from them, to kindle a fire behind him, with the view of causing his evil to depart with him. (T.) — نَارُ ٱلْمُهَوِّلِ *A fire which the Arabs used to kindle, in the time of ignorance, on the occasion of entering into a confederacy: they threw into it some salt, which crackled* (يُفَقِّعُ) *when the fire burned it: with this they frightened* [*one another*] *in confirmation of the swearing*. (T.) — نَارُ الحُبَاحِبِ has been explained in art. حب. — نَارٌ also signifies simply *Heat*. (TA.) — Also, ‡ [The *fire*, meaning] the *evil, and excitement*, or *rage*, of *war*; as also ▾ نَائِرَةٌ. (TA.) You say, أَوْقَدَ نَارَ الحَرْبِ ‡ [*He kindled the fire of war*]. (A.) — Also, ‡ *Opinion; counsel; advice*. (IAạr, T, Ḳ.) So in the trad., لَا تَسْتَضِيئُوا بِنَارِ المُشْرِكِينَ, (T,) or بِنَارِ أَهْلِ الشِّرْكِ, (Ḳ,) ‡ [*Seek ye not to enlighten yourselves by the counsel of the polytheists*; i.e.,] *seek ye not counsel of the polytheists*. (IAạr, T, A.*) — Also, ‡ *Any brand*, or *mark, made with a hot iron, upon a camel*; (Aṣ, T, Ṣ, M, A, Ḳ;) as also ▾ نُورَةٌ (M, Ḳ) and ▾ نُورٌ: (TA:) pl. as above: (M:) or the pl. is نِيَارٌ, and the pl. of نار that burns is نِيرَانٌ. (IAạr, Th, T.) The Arabs say, مَا نَارُ هٰذِهِ النَّاقَةِ ‡ *What is the brand, or mark, of this she-camel, with which she is burned?* (T, Ṣ, A.*) And they say, in a proverb, نِجَارُهَا نَارُهَا (T, Ṣ) *Their origin is indicated by their mark with which they are burned*. (T.) The Rájiz says,

حَتَّى سَقَوْا آبَالَهُمْ بِالنَّارِ
وَالنَّارُ قَدْ تَشْفِى مِنَ الأُوَارِ

[*Until*, or *so that, they watered their camels because of the brand that they bore: for the fire*, or *the brand, sometimes cures of the heat of thirst*]: (T, Ṣ:*) he means, that, when they saw their marks with which they were burned, they left the water to them. (Ṣ. For another reading of this verse, see بِ.) See also نَجْرٌ.

نَوْرٌ *Blossoms*, or *flowers*, (M, Mṣb, Ḳ,) of a tree, and of a plant: (Mṣb:) or *white blossoms* or *flowers*; the yellow being called زَهْرٌ; (M, Ḳ;) for they become white, and then become yellow: (M:) and ▾ نُوَّارٌ and ▾ نَوْرَةٌ signify the same as نَوْرٌ: (M, Ḳ:) or [rather] نَوْرٌ and نُوَّارٌ signify the same; (Ṣ, Mṣb;) [but the former is often used as a generic n., signifying *a kind of blossom* or *flower*: though both are coll. gen. ns.;] and نَوْرَةٌ is the n. un. of نَوْرٌ, like as تَمْرَةٌ is of تَمْرٌ; (Mṣb;) and نُوَّارَةٌ is the n. un. of نُوَّارٌ: (Ṣ, M, L:) and the pl. of نَوْرٌ is أَنْوَارٌ. (M, Mṣb, Ḳ.)

نُورٌ *Light*; syn. ضِيَآءٌ, (Ṣ,) or ضَوْءٌ; (M, A, Mṣb, Ḳ;) *whatever it be*; (M, A, Ḳ;) *contr. of* ظُلْمَةٌ: (Mṣb:) or the *rays thereof*: (M, A, Ḳ:) accord to Z, ضِيَآءٌ [with which ضَوْءٌ is syn.] is more intense than نُورٌ: in the Ḳur, x. 5, the sun is termed ضياء, and the moon نور: and it is said that ضياء is essential, but نور is *accidental* [*light*]: (TA:) it is of two kinds, the light of the present world and that of the world to come; and the former is either perceived sensibly, by the eye, and this is what diffuses itself from luminous bodies, as the sun and moon and stars, and is mentioned in the Ḳur, x. 5, referred to above; or perceived by the eye of the intellect, and this is what diffuses itself of the divine lights, as the light of reason and the light of the Ḳur-án; of which divine light mention is made in the Ḳur, v., former part of verse 18, and xxiv., latter part of verse 35; and both of these in common are spoken of in the Ḳur, vi. 1 and xxxix. 69: that of the world to come is mentioned in the Ḳur in lvii. 12 [and lxvi. 8]: (B:) the pl. is أَنْوَارٌ (Ṣ, M, Mṣb, Ḳ) and نِيرَانٌ; (M, Ḳ;) the latter mentioned by Th: (M:) and ▾ نُورَانِيَّةٌ signifies the same as نُورٌ. (TA.) As نور is a convenience of the pious in the present world and the world to come, it is said in the Ḳur, [lvii. 13,] ٱنْظُرُونَا نَقْتَبِسْ مِنْ نُورِكُمْ [*Wait ye for us that we may take of your light*]. (B.) [See also ظُلْمَةٌ.] — It is also applied to *Mohammad*: (T, M, Ḳ:) it is said by Aboo-Is-ḥaḳ to be so applied in the Ḳur, v. 18. (T.) — And *That which manifests things*, (Ḳ, TA,) *and shows to the eyes their true* or *real state*: and therefore النُّورُ is applied in the Ḳur, vii. 156, to ‡ *that* [*revelation*] *which the Prophet brought*. (TA.) — النُّورُ is also one of the names of God; meaning, accord. to IAth, *He by whose light the obscure in perception sees, and by whose guidance the erring is directed aright*: or *the Manifest, by whom is every manifestation*. And ٱللّٰهُ نُورُ السَّمٰوَاتِ وَالأَرْضِ [in the Ḳur, xxiv. 35,] means *God is the enlightener of the heavens and of the earth*: like as فُلَانٌ غِيَاثُنَا means مُغِيثُنَا: (TA:) or, as some say, *the right director of the inhabitants of the heavens and of the inhabitants of the earth*. (T.) — See also نَارٌ, last signification.

نُورَةٌ : see نَوْرٌ.

نُورَةٌ : see نَارٌ, last signification. — I. q. هِنَآءٌ [a word well known to mean *Tar*, or *liquid pitch*, or *a kind thereof*; but I do not know this signification as applying to نُورَةٌ, nor, app., did ṢM, for he has made it to be the same with that which here next follows, from the T]: (M, Ḳ:) or *a kind of stone burned and made into* كِلْس [or *quick-lime*] *and used as a depilatory for the pubes*: (T:) or *lime-stone*; syn. حَجَرُ الكِلْسِ: and by a secondary and predominant application, *a mixture of quick lime* (كلس) *with arsenic*, or *orpiment*, (زِرْنِيخ,) *and other things, used for removing hair*: (Mṣb:) [*a depilatory composed of quick lime with a small proportion* (*about an eighth part*) *of orpiment*: it is made into a paste with water, before application; and loosens the hair in about two minutes; after which it is immediately washed off: thus made in the present day:] some say that it is an Arabic word; and others, that it is arabicised. (Mṣb) See 8.

نُورَانِيَّةٌ : see نُورٌ.

نَيِّرٌ *Giving light, shining, bright*, or *shining brightly*; (A, Mṣb;) as also ↓ مُنِيرٌ and ↓ مُسْتَنِيرٌ (A) [and ↓ نَائِرٌ.] — *Beautiful in colour, and bright*; as also ↓ مُنِيرٌ and ↓ أَنْوَرُ: (TA:) or the last signifies [simply] *beautiful*; (Ḳ;) or *conspicuous and beautiful*. (TA.) It is said of Mohammad, كَانَ أَنْوَرَ المُتَجَرَّدِ: *He was beautiful and bright in the colour* [*of what was unclad*] *of his body*. (TA.)

نُؤُورٌ, (Ṣ, Mṣb, and so in some copies of the Ḳ,) or نَؤُورٌ, (T, M, and so in some copies of the Ḳ,) or both, the former being the original form, (Ṣ, TA,) i. q. نِيلَنْجٌ [i. e. *Indigo-pigment*]; (Ṣ, Ḳ;) or نِيلَنْجٌ; [which appears from what follows to be the right reading, though both نيلج and نيلنج are used in the present day for the purpose described in explanations of نوور, to give a greenish colour to the marks made in tatooing;] (Mṣb;) i. e., (so accord. to the Ṣ and Mṣb; but in the Ḳ, and) the *smoke* [meaning the *smoke-black*] *of fat*, (IAṣr, T, Ṣ, M, Mṣb, Ḳ,) *that adheres to the* طَسْت, (IAṣr, T,) *with which the punctures made in tatooing are dressed*, (Ṣ, Mṣb,) or *filled in*, (M,) *that they may become green*; (Ṣ, Mṣb;) or *with which the women of the Arabs of the time of ignorance tattooed themselves*: (T:) i. q. غُنْج [q. v.]; (IAṣr, T:) or, accord. to Lth, the *smoke* [or *smoke-black*] *of the wick, used as a collyrium* or *for tatooing*; but, [says Az,] I have not heard that the women of the Arabs used this as a collyrium in the time of ignorance nor in the time of El-Islám; their using it for tatooing, however, is mentioned in their poems: (T:) or *lamp-black*; the *black pigment* (نقس) *prepared from the smoke of the lamp; used for tattooing*. (Comm. on the Mo'allakát, printed at Calcutta, p. 143.) — Also, *A kind of small stone, resembling* إِثْمِد, *which is bruised*, or *brayed, and then taken up, like as medicine is by the lip*. (M.) [The same is found in the Ḳ, excepting that, in this latter lexicon, the explanation is less full, and اللِّثَةَ is substituted for الشَّفَةَ, the reading in the M.]

نَوَّارٌ and نُوَّارَةٌ : see نَوْرٌ.

نَائِرٌ : see نَيِّرٌ. — ‡ *Apparent* or *plainly apparent, conspicuous, manifest*, or *evident*; as also ↓ مُنِيرٌ. (Thus the pl. fem. of each of these is explained in the TA.) — فِتْنَةٌ نَائِرَةٌ *Sedition*, or *discord*, or *the like, happening and spreading*. (Mṣb.) — And نَائِرَةٌ alone, *Sedition*, or *discord*, or *the like*: (Mṣb:) or *sedition*, or *discord*, or *the like, happening*: (TA:) and *rancour, malevolence*, or *spite*: (T:) *enmity*, or *hostility*, (T, Ṣ, A, Mṣb,) *and violent hatred*. (Ṣ, A, Mṣb.) See also نَارٌ. You say, سَعَيْتُ فِى إِطْفَآءِ النَّائِرَةِ *I laboured in stilling the sedition*, or *discord*, or *the like*. (Mṣb.) And بَيْنَهُمْ نَائِرَةٌ *Between them is enmity*, or *hatred, and violent hatred*. (A, Mṣb.) — One *who occasions evils among men*. (T.)

أَنْوَرُ : see نَيِّرٌ, in two places. — ذَا أَنْوَرُ مِنْ ذَاكَ [*This is lighter*, or *brighter, than that*]. (TA.)

تَنْوِيرٌ The *time when the dawn shines*, or *becomes light*. (T, Mgh.) You say, صَلَّى الفَجْرَ فِى التَّنْوِيرِ *He performed the prayer of daybreak when the dawn shone*, or *became light*. (Mgh.) See also 2.

مَنَارٌ [originally مَنْوَرٌ] *A place of light*; as also ↓ مَنَارَةٌ. (M, Ḳ.) — *A sign*, or *mark, set up to show the way*: (Aṣ, T, Ṣ, M, Ḳ:) and *a thing that is put as a limit* or *boundary between two things*; (M, Ḳ;) or *between two lands*, (Aṣ, T,) *made of mud* or *clay* or *of earth*: (Aṣ, TA:) pl. مَنَائِرُ [respecting which see مَنَارَةٌ]. (A.) It is [also used as a coll. gen. n.; as, for instance, where it is] said, in a trad., لَعَنَ ٱللّٰهُ مَنْ غَيَّرَ مَنَارَ الأَرْضِ *May God curse him who alters the marks of the limit between two lands*: (T, TA:) or it may mean مَنَارَ الحَرَمِ *the boundary-marks of the Haram* [or *sacred territory* of Mekkeh], which [it is said] were set up by Abraham. (T, TA.*) And it is said in another trad., إِنَّ لِلْإِسْلَامِ صُوًى وَمَنَارًا ‡ *Verily there are to El-Islám signs and ordinances whereby it is known*. (TA.) — See also صُوَّمَعَةٌ. — The *middle*, or *main part and middle*, or *part along which one travels*, (مَحَجَّة,) *of a road*. (M, Ḳ.)

مُنِيرٌ : see نَيِّرٌ, in two places. — See also نَائِرٌ.

مَنَارَةٌ, originally مَنْوَرَةٌ; (A, Ḳ;) see مَنَارٌ. — *A stand for a lamp; a thing upon which a lamp is put*: (T, Ṣ, M, A, Ḳ:) of the measure مَفْعَلَةٌ, with fet-h (Ṣ, Mṣb) to the م; (Ṣ;) but by rule it should be with kesr, because it is an instrument. (Mṣb.) Aboo-Dhu-eyb uses it, for the sake of metre, in the place of مِصْبَاح, in likening a bright spear-head, without rust, to a lamp. (M.) — Also, *A candle having a* سِرَاج [or *lighted wick*]. (T.) — [*A pharos*, or *lighthouse*.] — The *menáreh* [or *turret of a mosque*, whence the English term "minaret," so written in imitation of the Turkish pronunciation,] *upon which the time of prayer is proclaimed*; (Ṣ, Mṣb;) syn. مِئْذَنَةٌ, (Ḳ, TA,) vulgarly مَأْذَنَةٌ [which is the form given in the CḲ]. (TA.) — [*Any pillar-like structure*. (See زُوْنُوقٌ.)] — The *perch* of a hawk, or falcon. (See مَرْبًا.)] — The pl. is مَنَاوِرُ and مَنَائِرُ: he who uses the latter likens the radical letter to the augmentative; (Ṣ, Mṣb, Ḳ;) like as they say مَصَائِبُ, which is originally مَصَاوِبُ. (Ṣ, Mṣb.)

مُسْتَنِيرٌ : see نَيِّرٌ.

نوس

1. نَاسَ, aor. يَنُوسُ, (Ṣ, M, A, Mṣb,) inf. n. نَوْسٌ (Ṣ, M, A, Ḳ) and نَوَسَانٌ, (M, A, Ḳ,) *It* (a thing, Ṣ, M, as a lock of hair, and an ear-ring, A) *moved to and fro*; (Ṣ, A, Ḳ;) *it was in a state of commotion, and moved to and fro*, (M, TA,) *hanging down*; (TA;) *it dangled*, or *hung down and was in a state of commotion* or *agitation*. (M, Mṣb [but in the M, the verb in this last sense has only the former of the two inf. ns. assigned to it, though the other equally belongs to it.]) You say also, نَاسَ لُعَابُهُ *His slaver flowed and was in a state of commotion*. (M.) [See also 5.]

4. انَاسَهُ *He made it to move to and fro*; (Ṣ, A;) *he made it to be in a state of commotion*, (M, Ḳ, TA,) *and to move to and fro*, (M,) *and to hang down*; (TA;) *he made it to dangle*, or *to hang down and be in a state of commotion* or *agitation*. (M.) It is said in a trad. (Ṣ, M, TA) of Umm-Zarạ, (Ṣ, TA,) أَنَاسَ مِنْ حُلِيٍّ أُذُنَىَّ [*He made my two ears to move to and fro, &c., with ornaments*]; (Ṣ, M, TA;) meaning, that he ornamented her two ears with [ear-rings of the kinds called] قُرْطَة and شُنُوف, which moved to and fro, &c., in them. (TA.)

5. تنوّس *It*, (a branch of a tree,) *being blown by the wind, became shaken thereby, so that it moved much to and fro*; as also تنوّع. (TA.) [See also 1.]

نَاسٌ is applied to *Men*, and to *jinn*, or *genii*;

(Ṣ, Mṣb, Ḳ;) but its predominant application is to the former: (Mṣb:) it is said by some to be applied to both in the former of the last two verses of the Ḳur, ٱلَّذِى يُوَسْوِسُ فِى صُدُورِ ٱلنَّاسِ مِنَ ٱلْجِنَّةِ وَٱلنَّاسِ [*who suggesteth what is vain in the breasts of people of the jinn and mankind*]; unless by it be meant النَّاسِى [the forgetting]; or من الجنّة والناس is added in explanation of a preceding word, الوَسْوَاس, or of الذى, or it is in dependence upon يوسوس; (Bḍ;) [but what corroborates the first explanation is the fact that] men and jinn are both termed رِجَال in the Ḳur, lxxii. 6; and the Arabs used to say, رَأَيْتُ نَاسًا مِنَ الجِنّ [*I saw people of the jinn*]: (Mṣb:) it is a pl. of إِنْسٌ, (Ḳ,) originally أُنَاسٌ, (Ṣ, Ḳ,) a pl. which is rare [as to form]; (Ḳ;) or أُنَاسٌ is pl. of إِنْسَانٌ; (M, art. أنس;) and ناس has the article ال prefixed to it, (Ṣ, M,) but not as a substitute for the suppressed ء, because, were it so, it would not be found prefixed to the original, أُنَاسٌ, whereas it is found prefixed to this latter: (Ṣ:) this derivation, however, from أُنَاسٌ, contradicts its belonging to art. نوس: (MF;) [but some hold that it does belong to this art.; and the form of its dim., to be mentioned below, favours their opinion: Fei says,] it is a noun applied to denote a pl., like قَوْمٌ and رَهْطٌ; and its sing. is إِنْسَانٌ, from a different root: it is derived from نَاسَ, aor. يَنُوسُ, signifying "it hung down and was in a state of commotion:" and [agreeably with this derivation it is said that] its dim. is نُوَيْسٌ: (Mṣb:) some, again, said that النَّاس is originally النَّاسِى. (L, TA, voce إِنْسٌ.) See also إِنْسٌ, throughout. — See also نَوَّاسٌ.

[نَاسُوتٌ *Human nature; humanity;* as also إِنْسَانِيَّةٌ: probably post-classical: opposed to لَاهُوتٌ, q. v., in art. لـه.]

نَوَسَاتٌ: see نَوَّاسٌ.

نَوَّاسٌ A [*lock of hair such as is called*] ذُؤَابَةٌ, *that moves to and fro*: (Ḳ, in explanation of ذُو نُوَاسٍ the name of a king of El-Yemen:) or ▼ نُوَاسَةٌ has this signification: (A:) [the former, therefore, is a coll. gen. n., and this is indicated in the Ṣ; and the latter is its n. un.:] and ▼ نَوَسَاتٌ signifies *i. q.* ذَوَائِبُ, [pl. of ذُؤَابَةٌ,] because they move about much. (TA.) — *What hangs to the roof,* (M, A, &c. [a signification assigned in the Ḳ to نَاسٌ, probably through the careless omission of the word النُّوَاس by an early transcriber,] *consisting of smoke,* (A, TA,) [or *soot,*] *&c.* (TA,) The word in the T and O, as well as in the A [and M], is نُوَاسٌ. (TA.) — *The web of a spider*: because of its fluttering. (M.)

نُوَاسَةٌ: see نُوَاسٌ.

نَوَّاسٌ, applied to man, (Ṣ,) *Quivering* (مُضْطَرِبٌ), *and flaccid,* or *flabby*. (Ṣ, Ḳ.)

نَائِسٌ act. part. n. of 1. Ex. خُيُوطٌ نَائِسَةٌ *Threads dangling* or *hanging down and moving about*. (TA.)

نَاوُوسٌ, (M, Mṣb,) or نَاؤُوسٌ, (Mgh,) *Burial-places of Christians*: (M:) or *a burial-place of Christians*: (Mgh, Mṣb:) [De Sacy observes, that En-Nuweyree and El-Maḳreezee constantly use this word in speaking of the burial-places of the ancient kings of Egypt, and that it is from the Greek ναος: ("Relation de l'Égypte par Abd-allatif;" p. 508:) Freytag, on the authority of Meyd., explains it as signifying *a coffin in which a corpse is enclosed*: and 'Abd-el-Laṭeef applies the expression نَاوُوسٌ مِنْ حَجَرٍ to the *sarcophagus* in the Great Pyramid: (see "Abd-ollatiphi Hist. Æg. Comp.;" p. 96:)] if Arabic, (M,) of the measure فَاعُولٌ: (M, Mgh, Mṣb:) pl. نَوَاوِيسُ. (Mgh, TA.)

نوش

1. نَاشَهُ, aor. يَنُوشُ, (Ṣ, A, Mṣb,) inf. n. نَوْشٌ, (Ṣ, A, Mṣb, Ḳ,) *He took it,* or *reached it, absolutely,* or *with the hand,* or *with the extended hand*; (Ṣ, A, Mṣb, Ḳ;) as also ▼ تناوشهُ, (A, TA,) inf. n. تَنَاوُشٌ; (Ṣ, Mgh, Mṣb, Ḳ;) and ▼ انتاشهُ, (A, TA,) inf. n. إِنْتِيَاشٌ: (Ṣ, Ḳ:) it is also written with ء; (A, Ḳ, TA, in art. نأش;) and so is تَنَاوُشٌ. (Mṣb, and Ḳ in art. نأش.) And *He took him,* or *reached him, to seize his beard,* or *his head*. (ISk, Ṣ.) You say, نَاشَهُ نَوْشَةً خَفِيفَةً [*He reached him with a feeble,* or *slight reach,* with his spear or the like]. (A.) And الرِّمَاحُ تَنُوشُهُ *The spears reach him*: occurring in a poem of Dureyd Ibn-Eṣ-Ṣimmeh. (TA.) And الظِّبَآءُ تَنُوشُ الأَرَاكَ [*The antelopes reach and take* with their mouths *of the trees called* اراك]; as also ▼ تَنْتَاشُهُ. (A.) And النَّاقَةُ تَنُوشُ بِفِيهَا الحَوْضَ [*The she-camel reaches and takes with her mouth of the water of the drinking-trough*]. (TA.) A poet says, (ISk, Ṣ,) namely, Gheylán Ibn-Ḥoreyth Er-Raba'ee, (TA,)

* فَهْىَ تَنُوشُ الحَوْضَ نَوْشًا مِنْ عَلَا *
* نَوْشًا بِهِ تَقْطَعُ أَجْوَازَ الفَلَا *

And she reaches and takes of the drinking-trough, from above it, a copious draught by means of which she traverses [*the middles of the*] *waterless deserts* without needing other water. (Ṣ.) You say also, نُشْتُ مِنَ الطَّعَامِ شَيْئًا *I obtained somewhat of the food*. (TA.) And الوَصِيَّةُ نَوْشٌ مِنَ المَعْرُوفِ [*The testament is* a means of *an attaining of benefit*]: i. e., the testator gives [for يَتَنَاوَلُ in my original I read يُنَاوِلُ] to the legatee without diminishing his property [during his own life]. (TA.) And it is said in the Ḳur, [xxxiv. 51,] وَأَنَّى لَهُمُ ▼ ٱلتَّنَاوُشُ مِنْ مَكَانٍ بَعِيدٍ meaning, [*But how shall*] *the attaining* of belief [*be possible to them from a distant place,* i. e.,] in the world to come, when they have disbelieved in him [namely Moḥammad] in the present world? in which passage some read [ٱلتَّنَاؤُشُ,] with ء. (Ṣ.) [See art. نأش.] Accord. to Ibn-'Abbád, in this instance, ▼ التناوش signifies *Returning*. (Ḳ,* TA.) And 'Áïsheh said of her father, فَٱنْتَاشَ ▼ الدِّينَ بِنَعْشِهِ إِيَّاهُ *And he restored the religion, and laid hold upon it and took it from the abyss into which it had fallen;* [*by his exalting it;*] in which instance, also, the verb is sometimes pronounced with ء. (TA.) — نَاشَ بِهِ, aor. as above, *He clung,* or *clave, to him,* or *it*. (TA.) — نُشْتُهُ خَيْرًا, (Lth, Ṣ,) inf. n. نَوْشٌ, (Lth,) *I made him to attain good;* (Lth, Ṣ;) and شَرًّا *evil*. (Lth.)

3. نَاوَشُوهُمْ بِالرِّمَاحِ, [inf. n. مُنَاوَشَةٌ, *They reached,* or *thrust, them with the spears, in near, but not close, conflict, being in like manner reached,* or *thrust, by them,*] (A, Mgh,) is from تَنَاوُشٌ in the first of the senses assigned to it above: (Mgh:) مُنَاوَشَةٌ, in conflict, is the *reaching one another* [with spears or other weapons] (ISk, Ṣ, Ḳ) *when the two parties are near* [*but not close*]: (ISk, Ṣ, TA) and is like مُهَاوَشَةٌ, i. e., *conflicting*. (TA.) See also 6. — ناوش الشَّىْءَ *He mixed with* [or *engaged in*] *the thing*. (IAạr.)

6: see 1, in three places. — تَنَاوَشُوهُمْ بِالرِّمَاحِ *They* [*reached* or] *thrust them with the spears,* [*in near, but not close, conflict,*] *being in like manner* [*reached* or] *thrust by them*: (Mṣb:) تَنَاوُشٌ is the *reaching one another* with the spears [or other weapons] *when the two parties are not close together*. (TA.) See also 3.

8: see 1, in three places. — انتاشهُ also signifies *He caused him to come,* or *go, forth* (Ḳ, TA) from a place of destruction: or *he took, led,* or *drew, him forth* therefrom: (TA:) and *he saved him,* or *rescued him,* from destruction. (A,* TA.)

نَوُوشٌ *Strong*: (Ḳ:) a man *possessing might,* or *strength, courage, valour,* or *prowess*: (Ṣ, TA:) as also نَؤُوشٌ, q. v. (TA.) [In two copies of the Ṣ, I find the latter only, with ء].

نوص

1. نَاصَ, (M, Ḳ,) aor. يَنُوصُ, (M,) inf. n. نَوْصٌ

and مَنَاصٌ (M, Ḳ) and مَنِيصٌ (M) and نَوِيصٌ (Ḳ) and نِيَاصٌ, (Ḳ, accord. to the TA,) or نِيَاصَةٌ, (accord. to a MS. copy of the Ḳ, and accord. to to the CḲ,) and نَوَصَانٌ, (Ḳ,) *He put himself in motion:* (Ḳ:) or *he put himself in motion and went away.* (M, TA.) You say, مَا يَنُوصُ فُلَانٌ لِحَاجَتِى *Such a one does not put himself in motion for* [the accomplishment of] *my want.* (TA.) And مَا بِهِ نَوِيصٌ *There is not in him strength* (Ṣ, M) *and motion* [or *activity*]. (Ṣ, TA.) — نَاصَ لِلْحَرَكَةِ, inf. n. نَوْصٌ and مَنَاصٌ, *He prepared himself for motion.* (M, TA.) — نَاصَ الفَرَسُ, (Lth, M,) inf. n. نَوْصٌ, (Lth, TA,) *The horse,* having his bridle pulled in, and being put in motion, *raised his head;* as also ↓ استناص: (Lth, M:) or ↓ إِسْتِنَاصَةٌ signifies a horse's *putting himself in motion to run.* (Ḳ.) — نَاصَ إِلَيْهِ, (Ḳ,) inf. n. نَوْصٌ, (TA,) *He rose to him.* (Ḳ.) — نَاصَ, aor. يَنُوصُ, inf. n. نَوْصٌ, *He turned aside,* or *away:* (M, TA:) *he drew back, receded, retreated,* or *retired;* (Ṣ, Ḳ*;) as also ↓ استناص: (Ṣ:) *he fled;* or *turned away and fled:* (TA:) *he escaped, and outwent:* (Mṣb:) and, inf. n. مَنِيصٌ and مَنَاصٌ, *he escaped;* or *became safe,* or *secure:* (M:) and accord. to IB, نُوصٌ, with ḍamm, [app. as an inf. n.,] also signifies the act of *fleeing.* (TA.) You say, نَاصَ عَنِ الأَمْرِ *He turned aside,* or *away, from the thing,* or *affair; he declined from it; he avoided it;* as also لَاصَ. (Aboo-Turáb, TA.) And نَاصَ عَنْهُ, inf. n. نَوْصٌ, *He removed, withdrew,* or *retired to a distance, and separated himself, from him,* or *it.* (Ibn-'Abbád, Ḳ.) And نَاصَ عَنْ قِرْنِهِ, (Ṣ, A,) aor. يَنُوصُ, inf. n. نَوْصٌ and مَنَاصٌ, (Ṣ,) *He fled,* or *turned away and fled, from his opponent,* or *adversary,* (Ṣ, A,) *and eluded him,* (Ṣ,) or *removed, withdrew,* or *retired to a distance, from him.* (A.) And it is said in the Ḳur, [xxxviii. 2,] وَلَاتَ حِينَ مَنَاصٍ, meaning, *When it was not a time of fleeing:* (Az, TA:) or *when it was not a time of drawing back and fleeing:* (Ṣ, TA:) or *when it was not a time of seeking,* or *petitioning, and of being aided,* or *succoured.* (M, TA.)

3: see جُرَّةٌ.

10: see 1, in three places.

نَوْصٌ *A wild ass;* (Ṣ, M, Ḳ;) because he ceases not to raise his head, going to and fro, like one running away at random. (Lth, Ḳ.*)

نَائِصٌ *Raising his head, and running away at random:* (M:) or a wild ass *raising his head, and going to and fro, like one running away at random:* (Lth, Ḳ*:) and ↓ مَنِيصٌ a horse *raising his head.* (TA.)

مَنَاصٌ *A place to which one has recourse for refuge, protection, preservation,* or *concealment; a place of refuge;* (Ṣ, Mṣb, Ḳ;) *a place to which one flees;* (Ṣ;) *a place of safety,* or *security.* (A.) = See also 1, throughout.

مَنِيصٌ: see نَائِصٌ.

نوط

1. نَاطَهُ, aor. يَنُوطُ, inf. n. نَوْطٌ, *He suspended it; hung it.* (Ṣ, Mṣb, Ḳ.) You say, نُطْتُ القِرْبَةَ بِنِيَاطِهَا [*I suspended the water-skin by its* نياط, q.v.]. (TA.) And نِيطَ عَلَيْهِ الشَّىْءُ *The thing was suspended to him,* or *it:* and نُوِّطَ عليه: (TA:) or ↓ نُوِّطَ عَلَيْهِ. (Ṣ; accord. to two copies: the pronoun relating to a camel when loaded.) And نِيطَ بِهِ الشَّىْءُ *The thing was attached to,* or *connected with, him,* or *it.* (TA.) It is said in a trad., مَا أَخَذْنَاهُ إِلَّا عَفْوًا بِلَا سَوْطٍ وَلَا نَوْطٍ i.e. [*We took him not save with ease;*] *with neither beating,* [lit. *with neither whip,*] *nor hanging* [or *clinging*]. (TA.) And in a proverb, كُلُّ شَاةٍ بِرِجْلِهَا سَتُنَاطُ [*Every sheep,* or *goat, shall be hung by its hind leg*]: i.e. every one who commits a crime shall be punished for it: or, accord. to Aṣ, one ought not to punish for a crime, or an offence, any but the committer thereof. (TA.) And Ḥassán Ibn-Thábit says,

• وَأَنْتَ دَعِىٌّ نِيطَ فِى آلِ هَاشِمٍ •
• كَمَا نِيطَ خَلْفَ الرَّاكِبِ القَدَحُ الفَرْدُ •

[*And thou art an adopted person, who is connected with the family of Háshim, like as the single drinking-cup is connected behind the rider*]. (TA.) See also شَاقَ, in art. شوق.

2: see 1.

8. انتاط *It was,* or *became, suspended,* or *hung; it hung;* (Ḳ, TA;) بِهِ *to him,* or *it.* (TA.) — [And hence,] ‡ *It was,* or *became, distant,* or *remote,* or *far-extending.* (Ṣ, TA.) You say, انتاطت المَفَازَةُ, and, by transposition, إِنْتَطَتْ, ‡ *The desert extended far;* [*as though it were connected with a desert like it;* (see نِيَاطٌ;)] *it was far-extending.* (TA.) And انتاطت المَغَازِى ‡ *The places of war were distant,* or *far-extending:* from نِيَاطُ المَفَازَةِ, meaning "the far extent of the desert:" or from النَّوْطُ. (TA.) And انتاطت الدَّارُ ‡ *The house,* or *place of abode,* &c., *was distant.* (IAạr, Ḳ, TA.)

نَوْطٌ *A thing,* (Ṣ, Ḳ,) *whatever it be,* (Ṣ,) *that is suspended,* or *hung, from another thing;* (Ṣ, Ḳ;) an inf. n. used as a subst.: (Ḳ:) and particularly *a thing that is put,* or *hung, upon a camel,* (عِلَاوَةٌ,) *between two halves of a load,* بَيْنَ العُودَيْنِ, (Ḳ,) or, as A'Obeyd says, بين عِدْلَيْنِ, [which, if not a mistranscription, app. means *between the two staves of the saddle*]; (TA;) the علاوة being thus called because it is suspended (تُنَاطُ) to the load: (Z, TA:) and *a small* [*receptacle of palm-leaves, of the kind called*] جُلَّة, (Az, Ṣ, Ḳ,) *containing dates* (Ṣ, Ḳ) *and the like,* (Ḳ,) *which is suspended from a camel,* (Ṣ,) *being hung, by its handles, from the saddle of the camel of burden;* (Az, TA;) such, says Az, I have heard thus called by the people of El-Baḥreyn: (TA:) pl. [of pauc.] أَنْوَاطٌ (Ṣ, Ḳ) and [of mult.] نِيَاطٌ: (Az, Ḳ:) the former is pl. of نَوْطٌ in the general sense first mentioned above; and also signifies *what is suspended* (نُوِّطَ, as in two copies of the Ṣ, or نُوطَ, as in the TA) *upon the camel when he is loaded:* (Ṣ, TA:) and i.q. مَعَالِيقُ [*things suspended to a beast of burden; such as the* قُمْقُمَة *and the* مِطْهَرَة *and the* قِرْبَة]. (Ṣ, Ḳ.) It is said in a proverb عَاطٍ بِغَيْرِ أَنْوَاطٍ *Taking* [or *reaching to take*] *without* there being there *anything suspended;* which is like the saying "Driving by singing without having a camel." (Ṣ, L, [See also art. عطو.]) And in another proverb, إِنْ أَعْيَا البَعِيرُ فَزِدْهُ نَوْطًا [*If the camel be fatigued, add thou to him an appendage to his full load*]: meaning, if he be slow and inobsequious in his pace, do not thou lighten his burden: (Ḳ:) accord. to Aṣ, إِنْ أَعْيَا فَزِدْهُ نَوْطًا is a proverb relating to the pressing a niggardly man. (TA.) — ذَاتُ أَنْوَاطٍ the name of *A particular tree,* (Ṣ, TA,) *of great size,* (Ṣ,) *which was worshipped in the time of ignorance,* said by IAth to be the name of *a particular gum-acacia-tree* (سَمُرَة) *to which the believers in a plurality of gods used to suspend their weapons, and around which they used to circuit.* (TA.) — النَّوْطُ المُذَبْذَبُ occurs in a trad. as meaning *The leg of a rider,* from fatigue or some other cause, *ever dangling,* or *moving to and fro.* (TA.)

نَيْطٌ: see نِيَاطٌ, in two places: and see art. نيط.

نِيَاطٌ The *loop-shaped handle* (عُرْوَة) of a قِرْبَة [or water-skin]: (Mṣb:) the [*appendage called*] مُعَلَّق [q.v.] of a bow; (Ṣ, Ḳ;) by which it is suspended: (Ḳ, voce خُطْمَر:) and of a قِرْبَة; [by which it is suspended; (see 1, second sentence;)] and of anything. (Ḳ.) — See also شِنَاق. — Also (Ṣ, Mṣb [in the Ḳ, "or," which is evidently a mistake,]) النِّيَاطُ [i.e. نِيَاطُ القَلْبِ *The suspensory of the heart;*] *a vein,* (Ṣ, Mṣb,) or *a thick vein,* (Ḳ,) [app. *the ascending aorta,*] *by which the heart is suspended* (Ṣ, Mṣb, Ḳ) *from,* (مِنْ, Ṣ, Mṣb [or possibly this may mean forming a part of,]) or *to,* (إِلَى, Ḳ,) *the* وَتِين, [which seems here to signify the *descending aorta,* or, accord.

to the second rendering of من, suggested above, the *aorta altogether*,] (Ṣ, Mṣb, Ḳ,) *the cutting,* or *severing, of which causes death*; (Ṣ, Mṣb;) as also † نَيْطٌ: (Ṣ:) pl. [of pauc.] أَنْوِطَةٌ and [of mult.] نُوطٌ, with ḍamm, (Az, Ḳ,) because the ى in نِيَاطٌ is originally و: the latter is allowable when the number is not meant [to be limited to a few]: or, accord. to some, there are two things thus called: the upper being that of the heart: and the lower, *the* فَرْج. (Az, L.) [Hence,] المُقَطَّعَةُ النِّيَاطِ (Ḳ, and so in a copy of the Ṣ, excepting that the former word is there without the article,) is applied to ‡ *The* أَرْنَب [or *female hare*], (Ṣ, Ḳ,) like مُقَطَّعَةُ الأَسْحَارِ, (Ṣ,) as an appellation of good omen, i.e. as meaning that her نياط will be severed: or, as some say, المُقَطِّعَةُ النِّيَاطِ, (Ḳ, and so in some copies of the Ṣ, excepting that the former word is there without the article,) as meaning that, by reason of her swiftness, her نياط, or [as in the A,] the نياط of [every one of] the dogs [that pursue her], will be severed. (Ḳ.) Hence also the saying, رَمَاهُ ٱللّٰهُ بِالنَّيْطِ †, meaning [*God smote him,* or *may God smite him,*] *with death.* (Ṣ.) [See also art. نيط.] [Hence likewise,] النِّيَاطُ is applied to ‡ *Two stars* [app. σ and τ of Scorpio] *between which is* قَلْبُ العَقْرَبِ [which is *the star* and *of that constellation*]. (Ṣgh, Ḳ, TA.) — Also, *i.q.* الفُؤَادُ [which generally means *The heart*; but is probably here used in one of its other senses, namely, *the appendages of the œsophagus, consisting of the liver and lungs and heart*]. (Ḳ.) — Also, *A certain vein lying within the* صُلْب [i.e. *backbone,* or *back*], *beneath the* [*portion of flesh and sinew called the*] مَتْن; and so † النَّائِطُ: (Ḳ:) or the latter is *a vein extending in,* or *along, the* صُلْب, [in some copies of the Ḳ, قَلْب, which, as is said in the TA, is a mistake,] *by the cutting of which the* مَصْفُور [or *person in whose belly is yellow water,* as explained in the TA,] *is treated for the purpose of cure.* (Ṣ, Ḳ.) — نِيَاطُ المَفَازَةِ ‡ *The far extent of the desert*: (TA:) or *of the way thereof; as though it were connected with another desert,* (Ṣ, Ḳ,) *hardly coming to an end.* (Ṣ, TA.) [Thus,] البَعِيدُ نِيَاطُهُ, applied to the Ḥijáz, means † مُعَلَّقُهُ [i.e. *Whereof every connected part,* or *appendant tract, is far-extending*]. (Ḥam, p. ١٥١). The Rájiz, El-'Ajjáj, says,

• وَبَلْدَةٍ بَعِيدَةِ ٱلنِّيَاطِ •
• مَجْهُولَةٍ تَغْتَالُ خَطْوَ ٱلخَاطِى •

† [*Many a region far extending, unknown, rendering unapparent* the trace of *the stepping of the stepper*]. (Ṣ and O in the present art. and in art. غول.)

النَّائِطُ: see نِيَاطٌ.

تَنَوُّطٌ, (Ṣ, Ḳ,) like تَكَرُّمٌ, (Ḳ,) and تُنُوِّطٌ, (Ṣ, Ḳ,) with ḍamm to the ت (Ḳ) and fet-ḥ to the ن (TA) and kesr to the و, (Ḳ,) or تَنْوِطٌ, (as in some copies of the Ṣ,) and تُنَوِّطٌ, (TA, voce تُبَشِّرٌ,) *A certain bird, that lets down strings from a tree,* (Aṣ, Ṣ, Ḳ,) *and weaves its nest like an oil-flask, suspended to those strings,* (Ḳ,) *then produces her young therein;* and hence its appellation: (Aṣ, Ṣ:) *a certain bird, like the* قَارِيَة *in blackness,* [or rather *in dinginess,*] *that constructs its nest between two twigs,* or *branches,* or *upon one twig,* or *branch, making its nest long, so that a man cannot reach its eggs until he introduces his arm to the shoulder-joint*: or, accord. to Aboo-Alee, *a certain bird, that suspends pieces of the bark of trees* [*formed into strings*], *and makes its nest at their extremities, to protect itself from serpents and men and* ذَرّ [or *young ants,* or small red ants]: (TA [see also صَافِر:]) *called in Persian* كِيبُو: (Ḳzw:) n. un. with ة. (Ṣ, Ḳ.) [See De Sacy's Chrest. Arabe, 2nd ed., vol. iii., p. 499.] Hence the proverb, أَصْنَعُ مِنْ تَنَوُّطٍ [*More skilled in fabricating than a* تنوّط]. (Meyd.)

تَنْوَاطٌ *What is hung* (Ṣ, Ḳ) *from,* (Ṣ,) or *upon,* (Ḳ,) *the* [*kind of vehicle called*] هَوْدَج, *for ornament*: (Ṣ, Ḳ:) or the *implements,* or *apparatus, &c., that are hung upon a horse.* (Ḥam, p. ٣٢١) — And hence, ‡ *Adventives;* or *persons who introduce themselves among a people, and live among them, not being of their race;* and *persons whose fathers are free men,* or *Arabs, and whose mothers are slaves, and who have become conjoined with the genuine and pure Arabs, not being of them*: for ذُو التَّنْوَاطِ; [or ذَوُو التَّنْوَاطِ;] the latter of these two words being originally an inf. n.: or it may be an inf. n. used as an epithet. (Ḥam, ibid.) [See also مَنُوطٌ.]

مَنَاطٌ *A place of suspension,* or *hanging.* (Mṣb.) — [Hence the saying,] فُلَانٌ مِنِّى مَنَاطَ الثُّرَيَّا ‡ [*Such a one is with respect to me* as though he were *in the place of suspension of the Pleiades*]; i.e., in distance: (Sb, Ṣ, Ḳ* [in the Ḳ, هذا is put for فُلَانٌ; and in the CḲ, مَنَاطُ is erroneously put for مناط]:) or the meaning is, in such a station: the prep. being understood, as in دَخَلْتُ البَيْتَ and ذَهَبْتُ الشَّأْمَ: Z says, هُمْ مِنِّى مَنَاطَ الثُّرَيَّا ‡ [*they are &c.*] by reason of their elevated state. (TA.)

مَنُوطٌ *Suspended; hung.* (Ḳ.) You say, هٰذَا مَنُوطٌ بِهِ *This is suspended,* or *hung, to him,* or *it.* (Ḳ.) — [Hence the saying,] هٰذَا رَجُلٌ مَنُوطٌ بِالقَوْمِ † *This is a man adventive to the people; one who has introduced himself among them, and lives among them, not being of their race*: (Ḳ,* TA:) or *i.q.* دَعِىٌّ [*one whose origin,* or *lineage, is suspected; &c.*]: (Ḳ:) and مَنُوطٌ مُذَبْذَبٌ is also applied to *a person of this latter description who betakes himself to a people;* the latter epithet being added to denote that he knows not to whom to assert himself related, like the wind wavering to the right and left. (TA.) See also تَنْوَاطٌ.]

مُنْتَاطٌ ‡ *Distant,* or *remote;* and *far extending.* (TA.) You say, مُنْتَاطُ المَحَلِّ ‡ *Whose place of abode is distant.* (TA.) And غَايَةٌ مُنْتَاطَةٌ ‡ *A distant goal,* or *scope;* or *a far-extending space.* (TA.)

[نوع, &c.
See Supplement.]

نيأ

1. نَآءَ, aor. يَنْىءُ, (so in the Ṣ, Nh, L, Mṣb; but in some copies of the Ḳ, ينأ, [which appears to be put by mistake for the inf. n. in the acc. case];) inf. n. نَيْءٌ, (Ṣ,) and نِىٌّ, without ء, and نُيُوءٌ, (Sh,) *It* (flesh meat, &c.) *was not,* or *did not become, sufficiently cooked; it was insufficiently cooked*: (Ṣ, Ḳ:) (like نَهِئَ:) or *it was untouched by fire;* [i.e., *raw*]. (L.) — *It* (a thing) *was not firmly, not soundly, not thoroughly, done.* [See 4.] (TA.)

2: see 4.

4. اناء الأَمْرَ *He did the thing not firmly, not soundly, not thoroughly.* † نَيَّأَ الامر, accord. to the Ḳ, signifies *the same*: but this is unknown, and not authorized by transmission [from the Arabs of the classical ages], and therefore not mentioned by IM nor by other leading lexicographers: the correct phrases are [when the verb is intrans.] ناء الامرُ [and اللحمُ], and [when it is trans.] اناء اللحمَ [and الامرَ]: the forms of the verb being like بَانَ and أَبَانَ. (TA.) — اناء, (Ṣ, incorrectly written in the Ḳ أَنْبَأَ, TA,) inf. n. إِنَاءَةٌ, *He insufficiently cooked* flesh-meat [&c.]. (Ṣ, Ḳ.)

نِىْءٌ Flesh meat &c. *insufficiently cooked*: (Ṣ, Ḳ:) or *untouched by fire;* [i.e., *raw*]. (L.) It was also pronounced by the Arabs نِىٌّ; but the original word is with ء. (TA.) — Wine *untouched by the fire*: cooked [or mulled] wine being called نَضِيجٌ, (TA [written نِىّ, without ء]). — *Pure* [*and sweet*] milk: sour milk being called نضيج: or milk *just drawn from the udder, before it is put into the skin.* (TA [written نِىّ, without ء.])

نَىٌّ [for نَىْءٌ] *Fat,* as contradistinguished from flesh, [which is app. called نَضِيجٌ]. (TA.)

نُيُوءَةٌ and نُيُوءٌ The *state of being insufficiently cooked*: (Ṣ, Ḳ:) or *of being untouched by fire;* [i.e., *rawness*]. (L.)

نيب

1. نَابَهُ, aor. يَنِيبُ, *He hit him on his* ناب, i.e., his *canine tooth*. (Ṣ, Ḳ.)

2. نَيَّبَ السَّهْمَ *He bit the wood of the arrow, to know whether it were strong or weak, and made an impression upon it with his canine tooth.* (Ṣ, Ḳ.) — نَيَّبَ فِيهِ *He* (a beast of prey) *made an impression upon him with his canine tooth: he fixed his canine teeth in him.* (TA.) — نيّبت *She* (a camel) *became extremely old:* (Lḥ, Ṣ, Ḳ:) *became what is termed a* ناب. (A.) — نيّب and ▼ تنيّب † *It* (a plant) *put forth its root.* (Ḳ.) Also signifying the same with reference to white, or hoary hair. The root is thought by ISd to be thus likened to a canine tooth. (TA.) — ظَفَّرَ فُلَانٌ فِى كَذَا وَنَيَّبَ ‡ *Such a one clung to, caught to, or took fast hold upon, such a thing:* [lit., *stuck his nails and dog-teeth into it*]. (A.) See also ظَفَّرَ.

5: see 2.

نَابٌ [originally نَيَبٌ, The *canine tooth*, or *dog-tooth*; or *eye-tooth*; the *tusk*, or *tush*; or the *fang*; of certain animals:] *one of the teeth;* (Ṣ;) the *tooth that is* [*next*] *behind the* رَبَاعِيَة, [or *next but one to the central pair of incisors*:]. (M, Ḳ.) [In this sense, the word is masc.:] the tooth thus called is masc., when thus called: [though if you call it سِنّ, it is fem.:] but ناب when fem. signifies "an old she-camel": (Mṣb:) or, accord. to the M and Ḳ, it is fem. only in each of the above senses, without distinction. (TA.) Sb says, that the Arabs observed the pronunciation termed imáleh (إِمَالَة) in the case of ناب in the nom., [as well as in the acc. and gen., in which latter case this pronunciation is agreeable with analogy on account of the final kesreh,] likening its ا to that in رَمَى, [in which it is expressed in writing by ى,] because it is changed from ى: but this is extr. That is, this pronunciation of ا changed from و or ى is only observed [regularly] when the said ا is a final radical letter; and specially in verbs: the instances of this kind that occur in nouns are extr.; and more so are those in which the ا changed from ى is a medial radical letter. (TA.) [But the restriction to the case of verbs is inconsistent with what is said by Ibn-Málik and other high authorities: and so, too, is the restriction to the case of a final radical letter.] Pl. أَنْيُبٌ (Lḥ, Ḳ) and أَنْيَابٌ [both pls. of pauc.: but the latter is used as a pl. of mult.:] and نُيُوبٌ; (Ṣ, Ḳ;) the latter contr. to analogy, (Ṣ,) because [نَابٌ is originally نَيَبٌ, and] a word of the measure فَعَلٌ does not [regularly] assume the measure فُعُولٌ in the pl.; (TA;) to which should be added نِيُوبٌ, a dial. var., as in the case of every pl. of the measure فُعُولٌ of which the medial radical letter is ى: (M, F:) and pl. pl. أَنَايِيبُ. (Ḳ, TA.) Ibn-Seenà says that no animal has both a ناب and a horn. (Mṣb.) — نَابٌ *An aged she-camel:* (Ṣ, Ḳ:) not applied to a male camel: (Ṣ:) so called because of the length of her tush; (Ṣ;) by synedoche; the whole being called by the name of a part: (TA:) as also ▼ نَيُوبٌ; (Ḳ;) accord. to some copies of the Ḳ, نَيُّوبٌ; but this is a mistake: (TA:) pl. of the former أَنْيَابٌ and نُيُوبٌ (Ḳ) and نِيبٌ: (Ṣ, Ḳ:) or these are pls. of both the forms of sing. (Ḳ, accord. to some copies; and TA.) Sb is of opinion that نِيبٌ is pl. of ناب, and says that the Arabs have made it of the measure فُعْلٌ [as it is said to be in the Ṣ, for it is originally نُيْبٌ,] like as they have the pl. of دَارٌ, disliking the sound of نُيُوبٌ, because the ى is with ḍammeh, and preceded by ḍammeh, and followed by و. It is also said to be pl. of ▼ نَيُوبٌ; as it is related, on the authority of Yoo, that certain of the Arabs say صِيدٌ and بِيضٌ, as pls. of صَيُودٌ and بَيُوضٌ, agreeably with the dial. of those who say رُسْلٌ [instead of رُسُلٌ]; namely, the tribe of Temeem: but their not saying نُيُبٌ, like as they say صُيُدٌ and بُيُضٌ, is an argument in favour of the opinion of Sb. — لَا أَفْعَلُ ذٰلِكَ مَا حَنَّتِ النِّيبُ [*I will not do that as long as aged she-camels yearn towards their young ones:* i.e., I will never do it]. A proverb. (Ṣ.) — The dim. of نَابٌ is نُيَيْبٌ, without ة, because ناب, as applied to an aged she-camel, is like an epithet: (Ṣ:) or rather this formation of the dim. without ة is a dev. from constant rule. (MF.) Sb says, that some of the Arabs make the dim. of ناب to be نُوَيْبٌ, because many an ا such as that in ناب is changed from و: [or rather, this is generally the case:] but this, says Ibn-Es-Sarráj, is an error on his part [who does so]. (Ṣ.) This apparently means, that Ibn-Es-Sarráj accuses Sb of an error; but such is not the case: for Sb himself says "but this is an error on their part;" i.e., on the part of the Arabs who say نويب for نييب. (IB.) — نَابُ قَوْمٍ ‡ *The lord, master, or chief, of a people:* (Ṣ, Ḳ:) pl. أَنْيَابٌ. (TA.) — عَضَّتْهُ أَنْيَابُ الدَّهْرِ, and نُيُوبُهُ, [‡ *The dog-teeth of fortune bit him*]. (A.) — انياب are likewise met. assigned to evil, or mischief. (TA.)

نَيُوبٌ: see ناب.

نُيَّبٌ [as though pl. of نَائِبٌ or نَائِبَةٌ] an epithet added to نُيُوبٌ as signifying "canine teeth," to render the signification intensive, or energetic. (TA.)

أَنْيَبُ *Having a large, or thick, canine tooth,* (Ḳ,) *that does not bite a thing without breaking it.* (Th.)

نيت

1. نَاتَ, aor. يَنِيتُ, inf. n. نَيْتٌ; as also نَاتَ, aor. يَنُوتُ, inf. n. نَوْتٌ; (L, Ḳ;) *He* (a man) *moved from side to side in walking:* (L, art. نوت:) or *he so moved by reason of weakness,* or *infirmity:* (Ḳ:) or, *by reason of drowsiness.* (L, art. نوت, q. v.)

نير

1. نَارَ الثَّوْبَ, aor. يَنِيرُهُ, (T, Ṣ, M, A, Ḳ,) inf. n. نَيْرٌ; (T, M, Ḳ;) and ▼ نَيَّرَهُ, (T, M, A, Mgh, Ḳ,) inf. n. تَنْيِيرٌ; (T;) and ▼ انارهُ, (T, Ṣ, M, A, Mgh, K,) and هَنَارَهُ, (Ṣ, M, TA,) like أَرَاقَ and هَرَاقَ, (Ṣ,) aor. of the latter يُهْنِيرُهُ, (M, TA,) inf. n. إِهْنَارَةٌ, (M,) or هِنَارَةٌ; (TA;) *He made, or put, to the piece of cloth, a* نِير; (T, Ṣ, M, Ḳ;) i. e., *an* عَلَم [or *ornamental border*]; (T, Ṣ,* M,* A, Mgh, Ḳ,* TA;) syn. أَعْلَمَهُ: (A:) and *a woof;* (Ṣ,* A, Mgh, TA;*) syn. أَلْحَمَهُ; (A;) contr. of أَسْدَاهُ and سَدَّاهُ. (Mgh.) — هُوَ يُسَدِّى الأُمُورَ وَيُنِيرُهَا (A) or يُسْدِى (TA) ‡ [*He commences things, or affairs, and completes them*].

2: see 1.

4. انارهُ and هَنَارَهُ: see 1, throughout.

نِيرٌ: see نِير.

نِيرٌ The عَلَم [or *ornamental border*] of a piece of cloth: (T, Ṣ, M, A, Ḳ:) pl. أَنْيَارٌ. (M, Ḳ.) It is related that 'Omar disliked it, (TA,) and that he forbade it. (T, TA.) — Hence, ‡ The *side* (طُرَّة) of a road: (T:) or the *side* (جَانِب), *and wide* or *widening part* (صَدْر), of a road: (so in some copies of the Ḳ, and in the TA; but in some copies of the former, "or" is put in the place of "and:") or the *conspicuous part* of a road: (Ṣ:) or the *conspicuous furrowed part* of a road. (M, A, Ḳ.) — The *unwoven end* (هُدْب) of a piece of cloth. (Ibn-Keysán, M, Ḳ.) — The *woof* of a piece of cloth. (T, Ṣ, A, Mgh, Ḳ.) When cloth is woven with a double woof, (عَلَى نِيرَيْنِ,) it is more close in texture and more lasting. (Ṣ.) ثَوْبٌ ذُو نِيرَيْنِ signifies *A piece of cloth strongly woven, with a double woof:* (A:) or *a piece of cloth woven with double thread:* (T:) and [in like manner] ▼ ثَوْبٌ مُنَيَّرٌ *a piece of cloth woven with a double woof;* (Lḥ, M, Ḳ;) i. e., *with a double thread:* (TA:) also called دَيَابُوذ, (T, TA,) an arabicized word; (TA;) in Persian دُو بُود, or دُو پُود, (as in different copies of the Ḳ,) or دُو بَاف. (T.) This mode of weaving is termed مُنَامَّة, which is the making the woof of a double thread, and putting two threads together upon the حَفَّة [which here means the yarn-beam, on which the warp is rolled]. (T.) — Hence, نَاقَةٌ ذَاتُ نِيرَيْنِ ‡ *A she-camel having an accession of fat upon former fat:* (T:) or *having, upon her, layers* (صَحَائِف) *of fat;* as also ذَاتُ أَنْيَارٍ: (A:) or *advanced in years, yet having some remains of strength;* (M, K;) and sometimes the epithet is applied in like manner to a woman: (M:) and نَاقَةٌ ذَاتُ أَنْيَارٍ *a she-camel having thick flesh.* (TS.) Also, رَجُلٌ ذُو نِيرَيْنِ ‡ *A man whose strength is double the strength of his companion:* (S:) or *strong and firm.* (A.) And رَأْىٌ ذُو نِيرَيْنِ ‡ *Right opinion* or *counsel.* (A.) And حَرْبٌ ذَاتُ نِيرَيْنِ ‡ *Violent war.* (T, A.) = The *canes* (قَصَب) *and threads* (خُيُوطَة) [*in a loom*], *when they are put together:* (M, K:) [it is a coll. gen. n., of which the n. un. is with ة, as appears from what here follows:] ♦ نِيرَةٌ is a subst., signifying the *threads and canes,* (خُيُوطَة and قَصَبَة, [or *warp and,* app., *cane-roll, on which the warp is rolled when put into the loom, and from which it is gradually unrolled as the work proceeds,*] *when they are put together:* when they are separate, the threads are called خُيُوطَةٌ; and the cane, قَصَبَةٌ, or, if a staff, عَصًا: (AZ, Sh, T:) نِيرَةٌ is also explained as signifying *one of the implements of the weaver, with which he weaves;* namely, the *transverse piece of wood* [*in the loom;* the same as is described above]. (T.) In the following verse of an unknown poet,

• تَقْسِمُ أَسْتِيًّا لَهَا بِنَيْرِ ♦ •
• وَتَضْرِبُ النَّاقُوسَ وَسْطَ الدَّيْرِ •

[*She divides warp that she has with cane-rolls, and beats the nákoos in the midst of the convent*], the author may mean بِنِيرٍ, and may have altered the word by necessity; or ♦ نَيْرٌ may be a dial. form of نِيرٌ. (M.) One says of a man who neither harms nor profits, مَا أَنْتَ بِسَتَاةٍ وَلَا لُحْمَةٍ وَلَا نِيرَةٍ ‡ [lit. *Thou art not a warp nor a woof nor a cane-roll*]. (T.) [See also a similar saying voce حَفَّة.] = [The *yoke of a bull;* the *piece of wood that is upon the neck of the bull, together with its apparatus:* (M, K:) or the *piece of wood that is placed transversely upon the necks of the two bulls* (T, S) *yoked together for ploughing:* (T:) called نِيرُ الفَدَّانِ: (S:) pl. [of pauc.] أَنْيَارٌ and [of mult.] نِيرَانٌ: (S, M, K:) of the dial. of Syria. (M.)

نِيرَةٌ: see نِيرٌ.

مُنِيرٌ act. part. n. of 4: see 1. — [Hence the saying,] أَنْتَ فِى هٰذَا الأَمْرِ بِمُنِيرٍ وَلَا مُلْحِمٍ ‡ [*Thou art not in this affair a commencer nor a finisher:* or *a person who will do harm nor one who will profit*]. (TA.)

مُنَيَّرٌ: see نِيرٌ. — ‡ A skin that is *thick* (A, K, TA) *and strong,* (TA,) *like a piece of cloth with a double woof.* (A, TA.)

مُنْيَارٌ, for مُنَارٌ, pass. part. n. of 4. (Ks, Lh, M.)

نيس

نَيْسَانُ [vulg. نِيسَان] *The seventh of the Greek* [or *Syrian*] *months;* (K;) [*corresponding to April, O. S.*] It is [said to be] a property of the water of its rain, that dough kneaded with it ferments without other treatment. (TA.)

نيط

1. نَاطَ, aor. يَنِيطُ, inf. n. نَيْطٌ, *It was,* or *became, distant,* or *remote,* or *far-extending;* as also ♦ انتاط. (K.) [See the latter in art. نوط.]

8: see 1.

نَيْطٌ: see نِيَاطٌ, in art. نوط, in two places. — *Death:* or *a bier:* or the *term of existence:* (K:) or the *death which God connects* (يَنُوطُهُ) [*with one*]: (IAar:) and if so, the ى is interchangeable with و, (IAth, TA,) the word being originally نَيْوِطٌ, then نَيِّطٌ, and then نَيْطٌ: (TA:) if a contraction, it is like هَيْنٌ and هَيِّنٌ, and لَيْنٌ and لَيِّنٌ. (Az, TA.) You say, رَمَاهُ ٱللّٰهُ بِالنَّيْطِ meaning [*God smote him,* or *may God smite him,*] *with death:* (S, in art. نوط, and TA:) or [*may God smite him*] *with the death which He connects* [*with him*]; as also رَمَاهُ ٱللّٰهُ بِنَيْطِهِ. (IAar.) And أَتَاهُ نَيْطُهُ *His term of existence came to him.* (TA.) And رُمِىَ فُلَانٌ فِى نَيْطِهِ *Such a one was cast into his bier;* meaning, when he died. (TA.) See طِنْ ‡.

نِيَاطٌ : } see art. نوط.
نَائِطٌ : }

[نيف, &c.
See Supplement.]

نيلوفر

نِيلُوفَرُ, (Msb,) and نَيْلُوفَرُ, (Msb, and so in the CK,) or نَيْلُوفَرٌ, (so in copies of the K, and so accord. to the TA,) or, as some say, نَيْنُوفَرٌ, or نِينُوفَرٌ, (accord. to different copies of the K,) [The *nymphæa,* or *lotus of Egypt* and *of Syria;*] *a certain well-known plant;* (Msb;) *a kind of sweet-smelling plant, which grows in stagnant waters,* (K, TA,) *called by the people of Egypt* بشنين, [i.e. بَشْنِين,] *and by the vulgar* نُوفَر; (TA;) [both of which last names are now given in Egypt to the *nymphæa lotus,* or *white lotus,* found in the neighbourhoods of Rosetta and Damietta; and the former, also, or perhaps both, to the *nymphæa cærulea,* or *blue lotus,* found in the same parts, and, until within a few years, in a lake on the north of Cairo, called Birket er-Ratlee, whence I have twice procured roots of this plant:] نيلوفر [written in Persian نِيلُوفَرْ and نِيلُوپَرْ and نِيلُوبَرْكْ &c.] is a Persian word (أَعْجَمِيَّة), and is said to be composed of نِيل, [or indigo,] with which one dyes, and the name for a wing, [i.e., پَرْ;] as though "winged with نيل [or indigo];" because the leaf is as though its two wings were dyed [with indigo]: (Msb:) the plant so called is cold in the third degree, moist in the second degree, emollient, good for cough and for pains of the side and lungs and chest; when its root, or lower part, (أَصْل,) is kneaded with water, and used as a liniment, several times, it removes the disease called البَهَق; and when kneaded with زِفْت, it removes the disease called دَآءُ الثَّعْلَبِ: (K, TA:) an excellent beverage is also prepared from it. (TA.) The imám Bedr-ed-Deen Mudhaffar, son of the Kádee of Baalabekk, says, in his book entitled Suroor en-Nefs, that it is of many species; whereof [one or more] in Syria, used in perfume; and a species in Egypt, blue; and that its temperament is cold and moist in the second degree; that the smelling it is useful against hot diseases, and anxiety; and its juice in like manner; and that the beverage prepared from it is useful as a remedy for cough and roughness [of the throat] and pain of the side and chest, and is a laxative. The author of the Irshád and that of the Moojiz also mention, that the beverage prepared from it is an exception from other sweet beverages inasmuch as it does not become converted into yellow bile, which is wonderful; and its oil is more cold and moist than that of violets; and there is no flower more cold and moist than it. Er-Rázee, too, says that the smelling it is one of the causes of weakening the generative faculty, and that the beverage is one of the causes of stopping it; [for which purpose, or as an antiaphrodisiac, it is used in the present day by some of the women of Cairo;] notwithstanding which, it rejoices the heart, and is useful for palpitation of the heart. This art. is omitted by J and Sgh and the author of the L. (TA.)

نينوفر

نَيْنُوفَرٌ, or نِينُوفَرٌ: see art. نيلوفر.

ه

[*The twenty-sixth letter of the alphabet*; called هَآءٌ: it is one of the class termed حَلْقِيَّةٌ [or *guttural*], and is a radical letter, except when written with two dots, ة; for which, and for the pronominal values of ه, &c., see the Supplement. — As a numeral it denotes *five.*]

ها

R. Q. 1. هَأْهَأَ بِالإِبِلِ, (El-Umawee, Ṣ, Ḳ,) inf. n. هِيهَآءٌ and هَأْهَآءٌ, (Ḳ,) the latter extr., (TA,) [see قَأْقَأَ,] *He called the camels to food, or provender, by the cry* هِئْ هِئْ: (Ṣ, Ḳ:) or he *chid* them, (زَجَرَهَا), by the cry هَأْهَأْ. (Ḳ.) [See also arts. جا and جيا.] — هَأْهَأَ, inf. n. هَأْهَأَةٌ, *He chid* a dog. (TA.) — *He called* a dog. (TA.) — هَأْهَأَ, inf. n. هَأْهَآءٌ, *He laughed loud and long:* [a word imitative of the sound]. (Ḳ, TA.)

هِئْ, subst. from هَأْهَأَ, [*A call to camels to food, or provender*]. (Ṣ, Ḳ.) هِئْ and جِئْ are said to be thus written by Az's own hand, with kesr: and are thus written in the Jáme' [of Kz]. (L.) [See arts. جا and جيا.]

هَأْهَأٌ and هَأْهَآءٌ One *who laughs loud and long.* (Ḳ, TA.) — جَارِيَةٌ هَأْهَآءٌ *A damsel who laughs loud and long.* (Lḥ, TA.)

هب

1. هَبَّتِ الرِّيحُ, (Ṣ, &c.,) aor. تَهُبُّ, (M, &c.,) contr. to analogy; for all reduplicate triliteral verbs that are intrans. have kesr in the aor., except twenty-eight, of which this is one; (Lb;) inf. n. هُبُوبٌ and هَبِيبٌ (Ṣ, Ḳ) and هَبٌّ; (Ḳ;) but this last is not of high repute; (IDrd;) *The wind blew; rose; was in a state of commotion.* (Ṣ, Ḳ, &c.) — It is also said of a foul, or stinking, odour. (Mṣb, in art. فوح.) — يَوْمٌ تَهُبُّهُ النَّكْبَآءُ is for تَهُبُّ فِيهِ [*A day in which the wind called* النكباء *blows*]. (TA, art. حص.) — هَبَّ † *It* (a star) *rose:* (TA:) [and in like manner, the dawn: see عُطَاسٌ.] — هَبَّ إِلَى الصَّلَاةِ *He arose,* or *went,* or *betook himself, to prayer.* (ISh, from a trad.) — هَبَّ, inf. n. هَبٌّ, ‡ *He was brisk; lively; sprightly.* (TA.) — هَبَّ, inf. n. هَبٌّ and هُبُوبٌ and هِبَابٌ, *He* (any person or animal marching or journeying) *was brisk, lively,* or *sprightly, and quick:* (Ḳ:) or هَبَّ, aor. يَهِبُّ, with kesr, inf. n. هَبٌّ and هُبُوبٌ, *he* (any such person or animal) *was brisk, lively,* or *sprightly:* and هَبَّ, [aor. يَهُبُّ,] inf. n. هُبُوبٌ and هِبَابٌ, *he* (the same) *was quick, and brisk, &c.*: ex. هَبَّتِ النَّاقَةُ, aor. تَهُبُّ, with ḍamm, inf. n. هِبَابٌ, *The she-camel was quick in her march, or pace:* (TA:) and هَبَّ البَعِيرُ, inf. n. هِبَابٌ, *The camel was brisk, lively,* or *sprightly,* in his march, or pace. (Lḥ, Ṣ, TA.) See also R. Q. 1. = هَبَّ, aor. يَهُبُّ, (Ṣ,) inf. n. هَبٌّ and هُبُوبٌ (Ḳ) and هَبِيبٌ; (TA;) and ▼هَبْهَبَ, inf. n. هَبْهَبَةٌ; (Ḳ;) † *He awoke,* or *became roused,* from his sleep. (Ṣ, Ḳ.) — هَبَّ يَفْعَلُ كَذَا ‡ *He began to do so; set about doing so; i.q.* طَفِقَ. (Ṣ, Ḳ.) — [You say] مِنْ أَيْنَ هَبَبْتَ † *Whence hast thou come?* (Ḳ;) as though you said مِن اين جِئْتَ; i.e., من اين ٱنْتَبَهْتَ لَنَا *Whence hast thou been roused* [to come] to us. (Ṣ.) [And] أَيْنَ هَبِبْتَ عَنَّا, with kesr, (in some copies of the Ḳ, حَنَّا is put for عَنَّا; but this is a mistake; TA;) *Where hast thou absented,* or *hidden, thyself, from us?* or, rather, *where hast thou been absent,* or *hidden, from us?* (Yoo, Ḳ.) — هَبَّ ‡ *He was absent a long time.* (Yoo, Ḳ.) = هَبَّ, (Ṣ, Ḳ,) aor. يَهِبُّ, (Mṣb,) or يَهُبُّ, (Az, TA,) inf. n. هَبَّةٌ (Ṣ) [and, app., هِبَّةٌ,] and هَبٌّ, (TA,) *It* (a sword, Ṣ, Ḳ, and a spear, Ṣ,) *shook,* or *quivered,* (Ṣ, Ḳ,) *and penetrated* into the thing struck with it. (Ṣ, Mṣb.) — هَبَّهُ, (aor. يَهُبُّ, TA,) inf. n. هَبٌّ and هَبَّةٌ and هِبَّةٌ; and ▼اهتبّه; (Sh,* Ḳ;) *It* (a sword, Sh,) *cut him,* or *it;* or *cut it off.* (Sh, Ḳ.) — هُبَّ *He was routed,* or *put to flight,* in battle. (IAar, Ḳ.) — هَبَّ, aor. يَهِبُّ (Ṣ, Ḳ) and يَهُبُّ, (Ḳ,) the latter dev. from rule, and not found in other lexicons, but see what is cited above from Lb, that هَبَّ is one of the twenty-eight verbs which thus deviate from rule, (TA,) inf. n. هَبِيبٌ and هِبَابٌ and هِبَّةٌ; and ▼اهتبّ; (Ṣ, Ḳ;) and ▼هَبْهَبَ, (Ḳ,) inf. n. هَبْهَبَةٌ; (TA;) ‡ *He* (a goat) *was excited with lust:* (TA;) or *uttered a sound,* or *cry,* [or *rattled,*] *and was excited by desire of the female;* or *uttered a sound,* or *cry,* [or *rattled,*] *when so excited,* or *at rutting-time:* (Ṣ, Ḳ:) or هَبْهَبَ signifies *he uttered a sound,* or *cry,* [or *rattled,*] *at rutting-time:* (TA:) or هَبَّ, inf. n. هِبَابٌ and هَبِيبٌ; and ▼اهتبّ; *He* (a stallion-camel, &c.) *desired copulation.* (M.) — هَبَبْتُ بِهِ *I called him* (a goat, TA) *ad initum; ut femellam conscenderet.* (Ḳ.) [F observes, that J's giving هَبْهَبْتُهُ in this sense is a mistake: but MF remarks, that what J says is ▼هَبْهَبْتُهُ, he (MF) having examined many copies of the Ṣ and found them all alike in this case, and that this is correct; and this is the reading that I find in both of M. Fresnel's copies of the Ṣ: see also تَهَبْهَبَ, given in the Ṣ as quasi-passive of هَبْهَبْتُهُ: SM, however, states in the TA, that the reading found by him in a copy of the Ṣ in the handwriting of Yáḳoot, the author of the Moạjam, collated with the copy of Aboo-Zekereeya Et-Tebreezee and that of Aboo-Sahl El-Harawee, is هببت به, as in the Ḳ; and this, he says, is the genuine reading.]

2. هَبَّبَهُ *He tore it, or rent it, much.* (Ḳ.)

4. اهبّ الرِّيحَ, and ▼استهبّها, [*He* (God) *caused the wind to blow; to rise; to be in a state of commotion*]. (A.) = اهبّه † *He awoke him,* or *roused him,* from his sleep. (Ṣ.) ▼هَبَّهُ is said to signify the same; and in proof thereof is adduced a reading in the Ḳur, deviating from that which is universally received as correct; مَنْ هَبَّنَا مِن مَرْقَدِنَا, instead of مَنْ بَعَثَنَا, *Who hath roused us from our sleeping-place?* [ch. xxxvi., v. 52;] but IJ rejects this reading, unless it be elliptical, for هَبَّ بِنَا. (TA.) = اهبّ السَّيْفَ *He shook the sword; or made it to quiver.* (Lḥ, Sh.)

5. تَهَيَّبَ ‡ *It* (a garment) *became worn out*, or *ragged*. (Ṣ, Ḳ, TA.)

8: see 1.

10: see 4.

R. Q. 1. هَبْهَبَهُ: see هَبَبْتُ بِهِ. — هَبْهَبَ, inf. n. هَبْهَبَةٌ, *He was quick*, or *swift*. (Ḳ.) See also 1. — هَبْهَبَ, inf. n. هَبْهَبَةٌ, *It* (the سَرَاب, or mirage,) *glistened*, or *shone*; syn. تَرَقْرَقَ; (Ḳ;) i.e., لَمَعَ. (TA.) — هَبْهَبَ, inf. n. هَبْهَبَةٌ, *He urged*, or *checked*, [app. the former,] *with his voice*; syn. زَجَرَ; (Ḳ;) by saying هَبْ, (R, as cited by MF,) or هَبْ هَبْ: [so I understand from the TA, where it is said والفعل منه هَبْ هَ بْ; for which it is evident that we should read وَٱسْمُ الفِعْلِ منه الخ; meaning "its" (imperative) verbal n. &c.:] accord. to some, used specially with reference to a horse: see هاب [in art. هيب]. (TA.) You also say هَبْهَبَ بِهِ. (TA.) — هَبْهَبَ, inf. n. هَبْهَبَةٌ, *He slaughtered* [a beast]. (Ḳ.)

R. Q. 2. تَهَبْهَبَ *He* (a goat, TA, called ad initum, Ṣ) *shook himself*; syn. تَزَعْزَعَ. (Ṣ, Ḳ.) See هَبَبْتُ بِهِ. — جَيْشٌ يَتَهَبْهَبُ *An army of which one part presses upon another*. (TA, art. جعب.)

هِبَبٌ, pl. of هِبَّةٌ: see ثَوْبٌ هَبَائِبُ.

الهَبَّةُ *The wind*. (TA, voce كُبَّةٌ.)

هَبَّةٌ (Ṣ) and ▼ هِبَّةٌ, (Ḳ,) both of which forms are correct, (TA,) ‡ The *penetration* of a sword, (Ṣ, Ḳ,) or spear, into the thing that is struck with it, *and its shaking*, or *quivering*. (Ṣ.) — ذُو هَبَّةٍ A sword *that shakes*, or *quivers, and penetrates into the thing struck with it*: (Ṣ:) and, *that falls with vehemence*. (TA.) — هَبَّةٌ (Ṣ, Ḳ) and ▼ هِبَّةٌ, (Ḳ,) or the latter only, (TA,) † *An hour*, or *a short time*, (ساعة,) *remaining before dawn*. (Aṣ, Ṣ, Ḳ.) — هَبَّةٌ (Ṣ, Ḳ) and ▼ هِبَّةٌ, (Ḳ,) or the latter only, (TA,) ‡ *An indefinite period* of time; syn. حِقْبَةٌ: (Ṣ, Ḳ:) *a long time*; syn. دَهْرٌ. (Az.) Ex. عِشْنَا بِذٰلِكَ هَبَّةً مِنَ الدَّهْرِ *We lived therein*, or *in that* [*state*], *some time*, [or *a long time*]: like the saying سَبَّةً. (AZ, Ṣ.) — [You say] رَأَيْتُهُ هَبَّةً *I saw him once* (Ḳ) *in life*. (TA.) — قَدْ جَاءَنِي هَبَّةً *He has come* [*in*] *to me once*. Occurring in a trad.; said by a woman in allusion to her husband's having once come in to her: (TA:) *i.q.* وَقْعَةٌ. (Mṣb.) See art. عسل in the Mgh.

هِبَّةٌ: see هَبَّةٌ throughout. — *A state*, or *condition*: [or perhaps the meaning intended is the *state of being brisk, lively*, or *sprightly, and quick*]. (Ḳ.) Ex. إِنَّهُ لَحَسَنُ الهِبَّةِ *Verily he is in a good state*, or *condition*, *&c.* (TA.) — هِبَّةٌ The *state* of a stallion *when excited by desire of the female*. (Ṣ.) See 1. — هِبَّةٌ *A piece of a garment*, or *the like*: (Ḳ:) pl. هِبَبٌ: (Ṣ, Ḳ:) *a piece of rag*. (TA.) — See ثَوْبٌ هَبَائِبُ.

هَبِّى mentioned in the Nawádir of Th, and said to be from هُبُوبُ الرِّيحِ, but not of established authority: [unexplained]. (TA.)

هَبْهَبٌ A wolf that is *light*, or *active, and quick*, or *swift, of pace*. (Ḳ.) See هَبْهَبِىٌّ. — *A certain valley of hell, the place of abode of tyrants, oppressors, and the like*. (TA, from a trad.)

هَبْهَبِىٌّ *Quick*, or *swift*: as also ▼ هَبْهَبٌ and ▼ هَبْهَابٌ. (Ḳ.) — A *light*, or *active*, camel: fem. with ة. (Ḳ.) — هَبْهَبِىٌّ *One who serves well*; *a good servant*. (Ḳ.) — *Any one who does well a small thing*: accord. to some, specially, *a cook*, and *a roaster of meat*. (TA.) — *A butcher*; syn. قَصَّابٌ: [from هَبْهَبَ "he slaughtered"]. (IAạr, Ḳ.) — هَبْهَبِىٌّ *One who sings well to camels, to urge*, or *excite, them*. (Ḳ.) — هَبْهَبِىٌّ *A pastor*: (Ṣ:) or *a pastor of sheep* or *goats*: or the *he-goat of a flock*. (Ḳ.)

هَبَابٌ i. q. هَبَآءٌ [*Dust, &c.*: see هَبُوبٌ]. (Ḳ.)

هَبُوبٌ and ▼ هَبُوبَةٌ and ▼ هَبِيبٌ A wind *that* [*blows violently, and*] *raises the dust*. (Ṣ, Ḳ.)

هَبُوبَةٌ: } see هَبُوبٌ.
هَبِيبٌ: }

هَبْهَابٌ: see هَبْهَبِىٌّ. — *Clamorous*; *a bawler*. (Ḳ.) — هَبْهَابٌ The سَرَاب, or *mirage*. (M, Ḳ.) — هَبْهَابٌ *A certain game of children*, (Ḳ,) *of the children of El-'Irák*, (TA,) or *of the children of the Arabs of the desert*. (T.)

ثَوْبٌ هَبَائِبُ, (Aṣ, Ṣ, Ḳ,) as also خَبَائِبُ, (Aṣ, Ṣ,) and ▼ أَهْبَابٌ, and ▼ هِبَبٌ, (Ḳ,) ‡ *A garment rent in pieces, ragged*, or *tattered*. (Aṣ, Ṣ, Ḳ.)

رِيحٌ هَابَّةٌ [*A wind blowing*; *rising*; *in a state of commotion*.] (A.)

ثَوْبٌ أَهْبَابٌ: see ثَوْبٌ هَبَائِبُ.

[مَهَبٌّ *A place of blowing of the wind*.]

مِهْبَابٌ (Ṣ, L, Ḳ) and ▼ مُهْتَبٌّ (Ṣ) and ▼ مِهَبٌّ, of the same measure as مُعْطَشٌ, (L,) ‡ A he-goat *that is much excited with lust*: or *that rattles much, and is much excited by desire of the female*: or *that rattles much when so excited*: see 1. (Ṣ, Ḳ.)

مُهْتَبٌّ and مِهَبٌّ: see مِهْبَابٌ.

هبت

1. هَبَتَهُ, aor. ـِ, (inf. n. هَبْتٌ, TA,) *He beat, struck*, or *smote, him* (A, 'Obeyd, Ṣ, Ḳ) with a sword. (Sh.) Ex. هَبَتُوهُمَا حَتَّى قَرِعُوا مِنْهُمَا *They smote them both with swords until they slew them*. (TA, from trad.) — هَبَتَهُ, aor. ـِ, *He*, or *it, lowered him*, syn. هَبَطَهُ and طَأْطَأَهُ and حَطَّهُ, (Ḳ,) with respect to station, rank, or dignity: (TA:) and *abased him*; *debased him*; *rendered him abject, vile, despicable*, or *ignominious*. (L.) Ex. هَبَتَهُ المَوْتُ عِنْدِى مَنْزِلَةً *Death lowered him in my estimation with respect to rank*, or *dignity*, because he died upon his bed, and did not die a martyr. From a trad. (Fr.) — هُبِتَ *He was lowered* with respect to rank, station, or dignity. (Fr.) — هُبِتَ (like عُنِىَ, [i.e. pass. in form, but neut. in signification,] (Ḳ,) *He* (a man) *was cowardly, and his intellect quitted him*: (Ṣ, Ḳ:) *he was without intellect*. (TA.) — هَبَتَ, aor. ـِ: see هَبِيتٌ.

هَبْتٌ *Softness*; *laxity*. (L.) — *Stupidity, foolishness, stupefaction*. (TA.)

هَبْتَةٌ *Weakness* (Ṣ, Ḳ) in intellect. (Ṣ.) Ex. فِى عَقْلِهِ هبتة *There is a weakness in his intellect*. (Ṣ.) فيه هبتة *There is a stroke of stupidity in him*: or *there is in him what resembles heedlessness, and unsoundness of intellect*: (TA:) or هَبْتَةٌ signifies *loss of reason*. (TA in art. خلع.) مَا تَسْأَلُ عَنْ شَيْخٍ نَوْمُهُ سُبَاتٌ وَلَيْلُهُ هُبَاتٌ *Dost thou not inquire respecting an old man, whose sleep is that of a sick person*, or *of one far advanced in years*, or *whose sleep is light*, (TA, art. سبت,) [*and whose night is one of languor*]. From a trad. هبات, here, is from هَبْتٌ, as signifying "softness, and laxity." (TA.)

هَبِيتٌ One *in whom is sudden fright*, or *terror, and a shrinking* (تَلَبُّدٌ) [*by reason of fear*]. (L.) — هَبِيتٌ and ▼ مَهْبُوتٌ A *cowardly* man, *whose intellect is quitting him*: (Ṣ, Ḳ:) a man *without intellect*. (TA.) — In the saying of a poet, نَشْوَتُهَا هَبِيتٌ, quoted, but not expl., by Th, هبيت is thought by ISd to be of the measure فَعِيلٌ in the sense of the measure فَاعِلٌ, and to signify, شَىْءٌ يَهْبِتُ, i.e. A thing *that stupefies*, or *renders foolish, and confounds, perplexes*, or *amazes, and thus stills*, or *quiets and causes to sleep*. The poet says,

• تُرِيكَ قَذَى بِهَا إِنْ كَانَ فِيهَا •
• بُعَيْدَ النَّوْمِ نَشْوَتُهَا هَبِيتُ •

[he is app. describing clear and strong wine, and says, *It will show thee a mote in it, if it be therein: a little after sleep*, (even,) *the intoxication* (which is the result) *thereof is a thing that stupefies, &c.*]. (TA.)

مَهْبُوتٌ *Confounded; perplexed; amazed; i. q.* مَهْفُوتٌ. (TA, art. هفت.) مَهْبُوتُ الفُؤَادِ A man *of a cowardly heart, without intellect.* (Ṣ.) See هَبِيتٌ —— مَهْبُوتٌ *Lowered* with respect to rank, station, or dignity. (Fr.) —— مَهْبُوتُ التَّرَاقِى *Having depressed, deficient, collar-bones,* or *clavicles.* (Fr.) = مَهْبُوتٌ A bird *that is sent forth at random; without being rightly directed;* [*without being let fly at some other particular bird*]. Thought by IDrd to be a post-classical word in this sense. (TA.)

هبث

1. هبث مَالَهُ, aor. ِ, inf. n. هَبْثٌ, *He scattered,* or *squandered, his property.* (L.)

Q. Q. 1. هَنْبَثَ: see هَنْبَثَةٌ.

هَنْبَثَةٌ *A severe, difficult,* or *afflictive, affair:* (Ṣ, Ḳ:) pl. هَنَابِثُ: the ن is an augmentative letter. (TA.) The pl. also signifies *calamities:* and *confused affairs and news.* (TA.) —— Also, *Confusion in speech,* or, *in what is said:* (Ṣ, Ḳ:) [probably an inf. n., of which the verb is هَنْبَثَ].

هبج

1. هَبِجَ, aor. َ, inf. n. هَبَجٌ; (L;) and ↓ تهبّج *He,* or *it* [a camel's udder], *became swollen;* or *had a tumour* [or هَبَج]. (Ṣ, L, Ḳ.) —— هَبِجَ *It* (a man's face) *became swollen, and contracted:* (L:) [and so ↓ تهبّج, in the Ḳ, art. رهل: see its part. n.] —— هَبَجَهُ, (Ṣ, Ḳ,) aor. ِ, (Ḳ,) or ُ, [which is more probably right,] (L,) inf. n. هَبْجٌ, (Ṣ, L,) *He beat him,* or *struck him,* (Ṣ, Ḳ,) with a staff, or stick: like خَبَجَهُ (Ṣ) [and خَبَجَهُ]: or, *with uninterrupted blows, but not violently:* or, *with a piece of wood, like as one beats a dog in killing him:* or *he beat him in any part of him that he saw.* (TA.)

2. هبّجهُ, inf. n. تَهْبِيجٌ, *It caused him,* or *it,* [a camel's udder], *to become swollen;* or *to have a tumour* [or هَبَج]. (Ṣ, Ḳ.) —— هبّج وَجْهَهُ [*It rendered his face swollen:* see هَبِجَ:] said of much sleep. (TA, in art. رهل.) —— هبّج *He killed a dog,* [app. by beating]. (L.)

5: see 1.

هَبَجٌ *A thing like a tumour, in a she-camel's udder:* (Ṣ, Ḳ:) it is *a tumour,* or *swelling, of the slightest kind.* (TA.)

هَبِجٌ: see what follows.

مُهَبَّجٌ A man *swollen;* or *affected with a tumour.* (TA.) A *swollen* face of a man; (A;) as also ↓ هَبِجٌ, (L,) and ↓ مُتَهَبِّجٌ (A.) —— A man *heavy,* or *dull, in spirit;* syn. ثَقِيلُ النَّفْسِ. (Ṣ, Ḳ.)

مُتَهَبِّجٌ: see مُهَبَّجٌ.

هبد

1. هَبَدَ الهَبِيدَ, aor. ِ, (L, Ḳ,) inf. n. هَبْدٌ, (L,) *He broke* هَبِيد, (Lth, L, Ḳ,) i. e. *colocynths:* (Lth, L:) or (in the Ḳ, and) *he cooked* هَبِيد [i. e., *colocynths or their seeds*]: (L, Ḳ:) or (in the Ḳ, and) *he gathered* هَبِيد [i. e. *colocynths*]; (L, Ḳ;) as also ↓ تهبّدهُ and ↓ اهتبدهُ; (Ḳ;) or ↓ تهبّد and ↓ اهتبد; which are said of an ostrich and of a man: and these two verbs signify *he* (an ostrich or a man) *extracted* هَبِيد [or *colocynth-seeds*] *to eat:* (L:) you say of an ostrich ↓ هُوَ يَتَهَبَّدُ *he extracts the seeds of the colocynth to eat them:* and ↓ تهبّد signifies *he took a colocynth,* or *colocynths, and broke it,* or *them:* (Ṣ, L:) or *he* (an ostrich) *broke a colocynth,* or *colocynths, and ate its,* or *their seeds:* (A:) and *he gathered colocynths and macerated them in water:* (L:) and ↓ اهتبد *he* [an ostrich] *pierced colocynths with his beak, and ate their seeds:* (T, L:) and *he took the seeds of dry colocynths, and put them in a place, and poured upon them water, and rubbed and pressed them with the hand, then poured off from them the water, and did this for some days, until their bitterness was gone; after which they are bruised,* or *brayed, and cooked:* (Ṣ, L:) or *he prepared for food* (عَالَجَ) *the pulp of colocynths.* (AHeyth, L. [See an ex. in a verse cited voce راجلة.]) —— Also هَبَدَهُ, (aor. as above, L,) *He fed him* (namely a man, Ḳ) with هَبِيد. (L, Ḳ.)

5 and 8: see 1.

هَبْدٌ: see هَبِيدٌ.

هَبِيدٌ The *colocynth;* as also ↓ هَبْدٌ: (L, Ḳ:) or the *seeds of the colocynth;* (Ṣ, A, L, Ḳ;) as also هَبْدٌ: (L, Ḳ:) n. un. of the former, [which is a coll. gen. n.,] with ة: (L:) or the *pulp* of the colocynth. (AHeyth, L.) —— [See بَرُوقٌ.] —— Also, *A certain food, which is eaten in cases of necessity, made by breaking colocynths, and taking forth their seeds, and macerating these in water, that their bitterness may go, and then cooking them:* (Nh, L:) or *colocynths macerated for some days in water, then washed, and, after their upper rind has been thrown away, cooked; to which is added some flour; and sometimes* عَصِيدَة *is made of it:* (AA, L:) or *a food made by macerating in water the seeds of dried colocynths, and heating this water until its bitterness has gone, then pouring upon it some grease, and sprinkling upon it a little flour, after which it is supped.* (L.)

رَجُلٌ هَابِدٌ *A man who gathers colocynths:* (TA:) and هَوَابِدُ [pl. of هَابِدَةٌ] *women who gather colocynths.* (Ḳ.)

[هذب: see هبذ.]

هبر

[1. هَبَرَ, &c.: see Supplement.]

ضَرْبٌ هَبْرٌ: see سَعْرٌ.

هِبْرِيَةٌ (Ṣ, Ḳ) and ↓ هُبَارِيَةٌ (TA) [*Scurf on the head;*] *what is in the hair of the head, resembling bran;* (Ṣ;) the *dirt of the head, that clings to the lower part of the hair, resembling bran;* (Ḳ;) as also إِبْرِيَةٌ (TA) and تِبْرِيَةٌ. (AO, Ṣ, Ḳ, in art. تبر.) —— Also, [both ↓ words,] *What flies about, of,* or *from, feathers,* (Ḳ, TA,) and *the like:* (TA:) and the former, *what flies about, of,* or *from, the down of cotton:* (Ḳ:) or the *fine down that flies about from cotton:* (L:) and *what becomes scattered about, and compacted, of,* or *from, canes,* or *reeds, and the* بَرْدِىّ [or *papyrus*]: (Yaḳoob:) pl. of the former, هِبْرِيَاتٌ. (TA.)

هُبَارِيَةٌ: see above, in two places.

هُبُورٌ *Barley growing,* or *growing forth;* in the Nabuthaean language. (Sa'eed ibn Jubeyr, TA, art. عصف.)

هبش

1. هَبَشَ, aor. ِ, (Ṣ, TA,) inf. n. هَبْشٌ, (Ṣ, A, Ḳ,) *He collected* a thing; (TA;) as also هَبِشَ, aor. َ: (ISk, ISd:) *he collected;* and *gained* or *earned,* or *sought sustenance;* (Ṣ, A, Ḳ;) as also ↓ تهبّش: (Ṣ, A:) or *he practised some art* or *trade, to procure sustenance;* and *he exercised art, craft, cunning,* or *skill, in the management of his affairs:* (TA:) and ↓ اهتبش and ↓ تهبّش *he gained* or *earned,* or *sought sustenance;* and *collected;* and *exercised art, craft, cunning,* or *skill, in the management of his affairs:* (ISd, TA:) and ↓ هبّش, inf. n. تَهْبِيشٌ, *he collected much;* syn. جمّع. (Ḳ.) You say, هُوَ يَهْبِشُ لِعِيَالِهِ *He collects; and gains* or *earns,* or *seeks sustenance; for his family,* or *household;* (Ṣ;) as also ↓ يَتَهَبَّشُ: (Ṣ, A:) or *practises some art or trade, to procure sustenance for them; exercises art, craft, cunning,* or *skill, in the management of his affairs, for them.* (TA.) [See also حَبَشَ.] —— هَبَشْتُهُ, (Ḳ,) inf. n. as above, (TA,) *I obtained it,* (Ḳ, TA,) *by collecting and gaining* or *earning.* (TA.) And ↓ اهتبش مِنْهُ عَطِيَّةً *He obtained from him a gift.* (Ḳ.) —— هَبَشَ الغَنَمَ, inf. n. as above, [app. meaning *He roused and scared the sheep* or *goats, and drove and collected them* to some

person or place,] is like نَجْشُ الصَّيْدِ. (Ibn-'Abbád.)

2: see 1.

5. تَهَبَّشَ: see 1, in three places. ═ Also, and ↓ اهتبش, *It became collected; or it collected itself:* or the former, *it became collected, or it collected itself, from several places:* syns. تَجَمَّعَ and اِجْتَمَعَ. (Ḳ.) And تَهَبَّشَ القَوْمُ *The company of men became collected as an army, or a military force; or collected itself into an army, or a military force.* (TA.)

8: see 1, in two places: ═ and see 5.

هُبَاشَةٌ i.q. حُبَاشَةٌ; (Ṣ, Ḳ;) i.e., *What is collected,* of men, and of property: (Ṣ, TA:) *a company, or body, of men, not of one tribe:* (TA, in art. حبش:) and *what one gains or earns, and collects,* of property: pl. هُبَاشَاتٌ. (TA.)

هَبَّاشٌ *One who collects;* and *who gains, or earns, or seeks sustenance:* (Ṣ:) or *who does so much;* (Lth, Ḳ, TA;) and *who exercises art, craft, cunning, or skill, in the management of his affairs, for his family, or household.* (Lth, TA.)

مَهْبُوشٌ *Collected;* and *gained* or *earned.* (Ṣ,* TA.)

هبط

1. هَبَطَ, (Ṣ, Mṣb, Ḳ,) aor. ـِ and ـُ, (Mṣb, Ḳ,) but the latter is of rare occurrence, (Mṣb,) inf. n. هُبُوطٌ, (Ṣ, Ḳ,) of that whereof the aor. is ـِ, and of that whereof the aor. is ـُ; (TA;) or of the latter only, that of the former being هَبْطٌ; (Mṣb;) *He,* or *it,* (said of water &c., Mṣb,) *descended:* (Ṣ, Mṣb, Ḳ:) and ↓ تهبّط *he descended,* or *went down,* or *went down a declivity;* and *it sloped down;* syn. اِنْحَدَرَ; (TA;) and ↓ انهبط signifies the same as this last; or † *he became lowered,* or *degraded;* syn. اِنْحَطَّ; (Ḳ;) being quasi-pass. of ↓ أَهْبَطَهُ, (Ṣ, TA,) and it may be also of هَبَطَهُ, as is said in the M. (TA.) You say, هَبَطْنَا فِى حَدُورٍ صَعْبَةٍ [*We descended a difficult declivity*]. (A, in art. حدر.) And هَبَطَ الوَادِىَ, (Bḍ, ii. 58, and Mṣb,) [as though it were trans., for فِى الوَادِى,] inf. n. هُبُوطٌ, (Mṣb,) *We descended into the valley.* (Bḍ, Mṣb.) And هَبَطَ مِنْهُ *He came forth from it.* (Bḍ, ubi supra.) It is said in the Ḳur, ii. 58, اِهْبِطُوا مِصْرًا *Descend ye into Misr:* (Bḍ:) accord. to one reading, اُهْبُطُوا. (Bḍ, TA.) You say also هَبَطَ بَلَدَ كَذَا *He entered such a town or country.* (Ḳ.) And هَبَطْتُ مِنْ مَوْضِعٍ إِلَى مَوْضِعٍ *I removed him from a place to a place.* (Mṣb.) — هَبْطٌ also signifies ‡ The *falling into evil:* (Ḳ, TA:) and ‡ the *being, or becoming, low, abject, mean, or vile:* (TA:) and ‡ the *suffering loss,* or *diminution.* (Ḳ, TA.)

You say, هَبَطَ مِنْ مَنْزِلَتِهِ ‡ *He fell from his honourable station.* (TA.) [See also 7, mentioned above.] And هَبَطَ فُلَانٌ ‡ *Such a one became low, abject, mean,* or *vile.* (TA.) And هَبَطَ مِنَ الخَشْيَةِ ‡ *He became mean,* or *abject, and lowly,* or *submissive, from fear.* (TA.) [See Ḳur, ii. 69.] And هَبَطَ القَوْمُ, aor. ـِ, ‡ *The people, or company of men, became in a state of abasement and diminution.* (TA.) Whence the trad., (TA,) اَللّٰهُمَّ غَبْطًا لَا هَبْطًا, (Ṣ, TA,) i. e. نَسْأَلُكَ الغِبْطَةَ وَنَعُوذُ بِكَ مِنْ أَنْ نَهْبِطَ عَنْ حَالِنَا [‡ *O God,* we ask of Thee *a good state,* or *condition,* and we put our trust in Thee for preservation *that we may not become brought down from our state*]: (Ṣ:) mentioned [and explained] before, in art. غبط, q. v. (TA.) [But in this instance, هَبْطًا may be regarded as the inf. n. of the trans. v. to be mentioned below.] You say also, هَبَطَتْ إِبِلِى وَغَنَمِى, aor. ـِ, inf. n. هُبُوطٌ, † *My camels, and my sheep, or goats, suffered loss,* or *diminution:* and in the same sense هَبَطَ is said of flesh, and of fat, and of fatness. (TA.) And هَبَطَ ثَمَنُ السِّلْعَةِ ‡ *The price of the commodity,* or *article of merchandise, became diminished,* or *lessened,* (Ṣ, Mṣb, Ḳ, TA,) *below its former full rate;* (Mṣb;) *became lowered,* or *abated.* (TA.) And هَبَطَ العِدْلُ † *The counterpoising portion of the load became adjusted* or *arranged, made even,* or *made easy,* upon the camel. (TA.) ═ هَبَطَهُ, (Ṣ, Mṣb, Ḳ,) aor. ـِ, (Ḳ,) inf. n. هَبْطٌ, (Ṣ,) *He made him,* or *it,* (namely water, &c., Mṣb,) *to descend;* (Ṣ, Mṣb, Ḳ;) [*he sent, or cast, him, or it, down;*] as also ↓ اهبطهُ. (Ḳ.) You say, أَهْبَطَتْهُمُ ↓ السَّنَةُ إِلَى الأَمْصَارِ [*The year of dearth, or drought, caused them to go down to the cities, or great towns*]. (A, in art. حسر.) And هَبَطَهُ بَلَدَ كَذَا *He,* or *it, caused him to enter such a town or country.* (Ḳ.) [And هَبَطَ بِهِ عَلَى مَكَانٍ *He, or it, made him to alight upon a place:* see an ex. voce زَخَّ.] — ‡ *He lowered him,* or *degraded him, from his state,* or *condition;* (Fr;) as also ↓ اهبطهُ; (Fr, Ṣ;) i.e., God did so; (Fr;) or a man: (Ṣ:) *it* (time, or fortune,) *caused his wealth, and his goodness* or *beneficence, to go away, after he had abounded therein.* (TA.) — هَبَطَ المَرَضُ لَحْمَهُ ‡ *The disease rendered him lean; emaciated him:* (Ṣ, Ḳ:) or *diminished his flesh.* (TA.) — هَبَطَ ثَمَنَ السِّلْعَةِ, (Ṣ, Ḳ,) inf. n. هَبْطٌ, (Ḳ,) ‡ *He* (God, Ḳ, or a man, Ṣ) *diminished,* or *lessened, the price of the commodity,* or *article of merchandise;* (Ṣ, Ḳ;) *he lowered,* or *abated, it;* (TA;) as also ↓ اهبطهُ, said of a man: (A'Obeyd, Ṣ, M:) or هَبَطَ مِنَ الثَّمَنِ † *he diminished somewhat from the price;* and sometimes ↓ اهبطهُ is used in this sense. (Mṣb.) — هَبَطَ العِدْلَ † *He adjusted* or *arranged, made even,* or *made easy, the counterpoising portion of the load* upon the camel. (TA.) — هَبَطَ فُلَانًا *He beat,* or *struck, such a one.* (Ḳ.)

4: see هَبَطَهُ, in five places.

5: } 7: } see هَبَطَ, first sentence.

هَبْطَةٌ *A low,* or *depressed, piece of land* or *ground;* (Mgh, Ḳ;) *contr. of* صَعْدَةٌ. (Mgh.)

هَبُوطٌ *A declivity,* or *declinal place: a place of descent,* or *by which one descends;* (Ṣ, Mṣb, Ḳ;) *a place which brings one down from a higher to a lower place.* (Az, TA.)

هَبِيطٌ ‡ *Lean,* or *emaciated,* by reason of disease; as also ↓ مَهْبُوطٌ: (Ḳ:) both are applied to a camel, signifying *whose fatness has become diminished;* as also ↓ هَابِطٌ: (TA:) and the first, to a she-camel, signifying *lean, and lank in the belly;* (AO, Ṣ;) or to a wild bull, to which a she-camel is likened in respect of her swiftness, and her briskness, liveliness, or sprightliness: (IB:) and ↓ the second signifies *rendered lean, or emaciated, by disease, so that his flesh quivers.* (TA.)

هَابِطٌ [act. part. n. of 1, both intrans. and trans.] The rájiz says,

• مَا رَاعَنِى إِلَّا جَنَاحٌ هَابِطَا •
• عَلَى البُيُوتِ قَوْطَهُ العُلَابِطَا •

[*Nothing surprised me but the wolf sending down upon the tents his flock of sheep, or goats, fifty or more in number*]: he means مُهْبِطًا قَوْطَهُ: so says ISd: or he may mean هَابِطًا عَلَى قَوْطِهِ [*descending upon his flock, &c.*]; making هابطا trans. by ellipsis: (TA:) جناح, in this verse, is the name of a wolf. (TA, in art. جنح.) — See also هَبِيطٌ.

مَهْبِطُ الوَحْىِ [*The place of descent of revelation;*] *a name of Mekkah.* (Mṣb, TA.)

مَهْبُوطٌ ‡ A man *whose state, or condition has become unsound.* (TA.) — See also هَبِيطٌ, in two places.

[هبع, &c.
See Supplement.]

هت

1. هَتَّ, aor. ـِ, inf. n. هَتِيتٌ, *He* (a بَكْر, or young camel,) *uttered a sound resembling a squeezing of the voice* (شبه العصر للصوت): you say, of a بكر, observes Az, يَهِتُّ, inf. n. as above; then, يَكِشُّ, inf. n. كَشِيشٌ; then يَهْدِرُ, inf. n. هَدِيرٌ. (L.) — هَتَّ الهَمْزَةَ, aor. ـُ, inf. n. هَتٌّ, *He uttered the letter hemzeh.* (L.) [See مَهْتُوتٌ.] —

هتّ, aor. ـُ, inf. n. هَتٌّ, *He uttered, recited,* or *repeated,* a speech or the like, *with uninterrupted fluency;* syn. سَرَدَ (Ṣ, L, Ḳ) and تَابَعَ. (L.) — [Hence] هَتَّتْ غَزْلَهَا, aor. ـُ, inf. n. هَتٌّ, *She spun her thread one part immediately after another:* (TA:) *she spun her thread continuously:* (Az:) هَتٌّ signifies a woman's *spinning* thread *continuously.* (Ḳ.) = هَتٌّ, aor. ـُ, inf. n. هَتٌّ; and ▼ هَتْهَتَ, inf. n. هَتْهَتَةٌ; *He broke* a thing, (Ḳ,) *so that it became reduced to small fragments,* or *particles:* (TA:) *he stamped upon a thing vehemently, so that he broke it.* (TA.) — هَتٌّ, aor. ـُ, inf. n. هَتٌّ, *He rent* clothes. (IAạr, Ḳ.) — Also, † *He rent* the reputation of another. (IAạr, Ḳ.) = هَتٌّ, aor. ـُ, inf. n. هَتٌّ, *He removed* the leaves of a tree [*by rubbing* or *scraping the branches*]; syn. حَتٌّ; (Ḳ [in the CḲ, هَتّ, is put for حتّ;]) i. e. *he took* them. (TA.) = هَتٌّ, aor. ـُ, inf. n. هَتٌّ, *He poured out,* or *forth,* [water, &c.] (Ḳ.) — هَتَّ المَزَادَةَ *He poured out,* or *forth,* [*the contents of*] *the* مزادة. (TA.) — هَتَّ شَيْئًا *He poured out,* or *forth, one part* or *portion of a thing immediately after another.* (TA.) — السَّحَابَةُ تَهُتُّ المَطَرَ *The cloud pours forth the rain continuously.* (TA.) = هَتٌّ, aor. ـُ, inf. n. هَتٌّ, *he lowered* (حَطَّ) a person *with respect to rank,* or *dignity, in* [*the manner of*] *paying honour* [*to him*]. (IAạr, Ḳ.) [Comp. هبت.]

R. Q. 1. هَتْهَتَ *He urged* a camel (زَجَرَهُ) *on the occasion of drinking, by the cry* هَتْ هَتْ. (AHeyth, Ḳ.) See هَتْ, below. — هَتْهَتَ, inf. n. هَتْهَتَةٌ; as also تَهْتَهَ; *He twisted,* or *distorted, his tongue in speaking.* (Az.) — Also هتهت; (and ▼ هَتَّ, TA, [aor. ـِ ?] ;) *He was quick,* or *rapid,* in his speech. (Ḳ.) — See هَتٌّ.

هَتْ, (TA,) or هَتْ هَتْ, (Ḳ,) *A cry by which a camel is urged* (يُزْجَرُ) *on the occasion of drinking.* (Ḳ.) — إِذَا وَقَفْتَ البَعِيرَ عَلَى الرَّدْهَةِ فَلَا تَقُلْ لَهُ هَتْ; or, as some say, فَلَا تُهَتْهِتْ بِهِ [*When thou hast made the camel to stand over the hollow in the rock in which the rain-water has collected, say not to him* هَتْ]. A proverb; meaning, accord. to AHeyth, when thou hast shewn a man his right course of conduct, do not urge him. (TA.) — هَتُّ قَوَائِمِ البَعِيرِ *The sound of the falling of the camel's feet* [*upon the ground*]. (L.) = تَرَكَهُمْ هَتًّا بَتًّا [*He left them routed,* or *broken asunder, and cut off;*] *he broke them asunder:* or *he cut them in pieces.* (L.)

هَتِيتٌ *A sound.* Occurring in a trad. as signifying a sound made by wine poured out upon the ground. (L.) = هَتِيتٌ and ▼ مَهْتُوتٌ *A thing broken so as to be reduced to small fragments,* or *particles: stamped upon vehemently, so as to be broken.* (TA.)

هَتَّاتٌ: see مِهَتٌّ.

رَجُلٌ مِهَتٌّ, and ▼ هَتَّاتٌ, *A man quick and voluble in speech;* (Ṣ, Ḳ;) *incorrectly, and vainly,* or *frivolously, loquacious; a great babbler.* (TA.)

مَهْتُوتٌ: see هَتِيتٌ. — الهَمْزَةُ صَوْتٌ مَهْتُوتٌ فِى أَقْصَى الحَلْقِ [*Hemzeh is a sound uttered* (after a suppression of the breath) *in the most remote part of the throat*]. (Kh, L.) Sb applied the term المَهْتُوتُ to the letter ه, because of its weakness and lowness. (L.) — أَسْرَعُ مِنَ المُهْتَهِتَةِ *Quicker than the quick-speaking woman.* (IAạr.)

هتأ

1. هَتَأَ, aor. ـَ, (Ḳ,) inf. n. هَتْءٌ, (TA,) *He beat* a person (Ḳ) with a staff or stick. (TA.) — هَتِئَ, aor. ـَ, *He was bent,* or *crooked.* (Ḳ.)

5. تهتّأ *It* (a garment) *became ragged, and worn out.* (Ṣ, Ḳ.)

مَضَى مِنَ اللَّيْلِ هَتْءٌ, and ▼ هِتْءٌ, (ISk, Ḳ,) and ▼ هَتِىْءٌ, (Lḥ, Ḳ,) and ▼ هَتِىٌّ, (Lḥ,) and ▼ هِتَاءٌ, and ▼ هِيتِئٌ (same measure as زِبْرِجٌ, as in the TA), or ▼ هِتْيَأٌ, (as in the CḲ and a MS. copy) and ▼ هِيتَاءٌ, (Ḳ,) and ▼ هَتَأَةٌ, (AHeyth, Ḳ,) *A portion of the night elapsed* (Ḳ, &c.) — مَا بَقِىَ مِنْ غَنَمِهِمْ إِلَّا هِتْءٌ *There remained not, of their sheep,* or *goats, save a part, less than the part that had gone away.* (TA.)

هِتْءٌ: see هَتْءٌ.

هَتْأَةٌ and ▼ هُتْوَةٌ *A rent.* (Ḳ.) — *A swelling:* syn. نُتُوٌّ. (TA.)

هَتْأَةٌ: }
هِتَاءٌ: } see هَتْءٌ.
هَتِىْءٌ: }
هَتِىٌّ: }

هُتْوَةٌ: see هَتْأَةٌ.

هِتْيَأٌ: }
هِيتَاءٌ: } see هَتْءٌ.
هِيتِئٌ: }

أَهْتَأُ *Humpbacked.* (Ḳ.)

هتر

1. هَتَرَهُ, aor. ـِ, (Ḳ, TA,) like يَضْرِبُ, (TA [in the CḲ, ـُ, but this is evidently a mistake,]) *It* (old age, Ḳ, TA, and disease and grief, TA), *made him to be such as is called* مُهْتَرٌ; [i.e., *made him to lose his reason,* or *intellect:* or *to be addicted to,* or *fond of, speaking of a thing:* which latter signification seems to be particularly indicated in the lexicon from which this is taken; but the former seems the more appropriate.] (Ḳ.)

3. هاتره, [inf. n. مُهَاتَرَةٌ and هِتَارٌ,] *He encountered him with mutual reviling, saying what was false:* (Ḳ,* TA:) so says IAmb, on the authority of AZ; but, says Th, accord. to others, المُهَاتَرَةُ signifies *the saying* [*that*] *whereof one part contradicts,* or *annuls, another:* and hence one says, دَعِ الهِتَارَ [*leave the saying that whereof one part contradicts another*]. (TA.)

4. أُهْتِرَ *He became disordered in his intellect:* (A, TA:) or *he became so by reason of old age:* (Ṣ:) or *he lost his reason from old age,* (AZ, A'Obeyd, Ḳ,) as also ▼ إِسْتُهْتِرَ, (AZ, TA,) or *from disease,* or *grief;* as also أَهْتَرَ. (Ḳ.) See also 10, in two places.

5. تهتّر *He was,* or *became, stupid, and ignorant.* (Ḳ: but only the inf. n. is there mentioned.)

6. تهاتروا *They accused each other falsely.* (Ṣ, A, Mgh, Mṣb, Ḳ.) — And hence, تهاترت الشَّهَادَاتُ, (A, Mgh,) البَيِّنَاتُ, (Mṣb,) and *The testimonies,* or *evidences, became null:* (Mgh, Mṣb:) or *belied one another.* (A.)

10. إِسْتَهْتَرَ: see 4. — *He was,* or *became, much given to false,* or *vain, sayings,* or *actions.* (TA [but this seems rather to be أُسْتُهْتِرَ: see its part. n., below.]) — † *He followed his own natural desire, not caring what he did.* (Mṣb [but this also seems to be in the pass. form.]) — أُسْتُهْتِرَ بِكَذَا ‡ *He became addicted to,* or *fond of, such a thing,* (Ḳ, TA,) *not talking of any other thing,* (TA,) *nor caring what was done to him,* (Ḳ, TA,) *nor how he was reviled:* (Ḳ:) *he became addicted to,* or *fond of, such a thing, not talking of, nor doing, any other thing:* and *he became fascinated by such a thing, and lost his reason on account of it, and his strong determination became turned towards it, so that he talked much and vainly respecting it.* (TA.) — إِسْتُهْتِرَ بِفُلَانَةَ, [or أُسْتُهْتِرَ,] and ▼ أُهْتِرَ بِهَا, [or أَهْتَرَ,] ‡ *He* [*became attached,* or *devoted, to such a woman so that he*] *cared not what was said of him on her account, nor how he was reviled:* (A, TA:) and ▼ أُهْتِرَ also signifies † *he became addicted* or *given to,* or *fond of, speaking of a thing.* (Ḳ.)

هَتْرٌ The *loss of reason from old age or disease or grief.* (Ḳ.)

هِتْرٌ *An error in speech.* (Ṣ, A, Mgh, Mṣb, Ḳ.) You say, جَآءَ بِهِتْرٍ مِنَ القَوْلِ *He uttered* *an error of speech.* (A.) And ▼ هِتْرٌ هَاتِرٌ *A great error of speech.* (Ṣ, Ḳ.*) — *A falsehood; a lie.* (Ḳ.) You say, قَوْلٌ هِتْرٌ *A false saying.* (TA.)

هَاتِرٌ: see هِتْرٌ.

تَهَاتِرُ *Testimonies, or evidences, that belie one another:* as though pl. of تَهْتَرٌ: (Ḳ:) or *any evidences, or testimonies, that are not legal proofs.* (Mgh [but in my copy of that work written تَهَاتُر.])

مُهْتَرٌ *Disordered in his intellect,* (Ṣ,) or *having lost his reason,* (AZ, A'Obeyd, Ḳ,) *from old age,* (AZ, A'Obeyd, Ṣ, Ḳ,) or *from disease,* or *grief:* (Ḳ:) if from أُهْتِرَ, it is anomalous, (Ḳ, TA,) like مُحْصَنٌ, &c. (TA.) — † *Addicted or given to, or fond of, speaking of a thing.* (Ḳ.) See also مُسْتَهْتَرٌ.

مُهْتِرٌ *Erring in his speech.* (TA.)

مُسْتَهْتِرٌ *Much given to false, or vain, sayings, or actions:* (Ḳ:) or one *who says what is false, or erroneous:* or one *who cares not what is said of him, nor how he is reviled:* or † *attached,* or *devoted,* (مُسْتَهْتَرٌ,) *to the world.* (IAth, TA.) — مُسْتَهْتَرٌ بِشَىْءٍ ‡ *Addicted to, or fond of, a thing,* (Ḳ, TA,) or *fascinated by it,* (A,) *not talking of any other thing,* (TA,) *nor caring what is done to him,* (A, Ḳ, TA,) *nor how he is reviled,* (Ḳ,) *having lost his reason;* (A;) as also ▼ مُهْتَرٌ. (A.) You say, فُلَانٌ مُسْتَهْتَرٌ بِالشَّرَابِ ‡ *Such a one is addicted to, or fond of, drink, not caring what is said of him.* (Ṣ.)

[هتش, &c.

See Supplement.]

هث

1. هَثَّ, aor. ـُ, inf. n. هَثٌّ, *He mixed a thing, one part with another.* (M.) — هَثَّ, [aor. ـِ,] inf. n. هَثٌّ, *He lied.* (IAạr, Ḳ.)

R. Q. 1. هَثْهَثَ, inf. n. هَثْهَثَةٌ, *He mixed,* or *confounded;* like مَثْمَثَ. (TA.) هثهث أَمْرَهُ *He confounded his affair.* (TA.) — هَثْهَثَ, inf. n. هَثْهَثَةٌ, *It was mixed,* or *confounded.* (Ṣ, Ḳ.) — هَثْهَثَ, (inf. n. هَثْهَثَةٌ, Ḳ,) *He* (a magistrate, Ṣ) *acted unjustly, injuriously,* or *tyrannically.* (Ṣ, Ḳ.) — هثهث النَّاسَ *He* (a magistrate) *acted unjustly, injuriously, or tyrannically, towards the people.* (TA.) ═ هَثْهَثَ, inf. n. هَثْهَثَةٌ, *It sent forth quickly:* (Ḳ:) [ex.] هَثْهَثَتِ السَّحَابَةُ بِقَطْرِهَا وَثَلْجِهَا *The cloud sent forth quickly its rain and its snow.* (Ṣ.) ═ هَثْهَثَ, inf. n. هَثْهَثَةٌ (and هثهات, TA) *He trod, or trampled, vehemently.* (Ḳ.) — *It* (a pasturing herd or flock) *trod* the fresh green pasture *until it was destroyed,* حتى يوتى [So in the L: app. حَتَّى يُؤْتَى.]

هَثٌّ and ▼ هَثْهَثَةٌ and ▼ هثهات *A confusion of sounds, noises, or voices, in war:* or *a raising of a loud cry,* or *clamour,* or *confused noise.* (M.) [App. inf. n., of which the verbs are هَثَّ and هَثْهَثَ.]

هَثْهَثَةٌ and ▼ هُثَاهِثٌ *A word imitative of somewhat of the speech of him who has the vitious kind of pronunciation termed لُثْغَة.* (TA.) See هَثٌّ.

هُثَاهِثٌ *Quick* (Ḳ) rain. (TA.) — هُثَاهِثٌ *Confused; confounded:* (Ḳ:) an epithet applied to a man. (TA.) — See هَثٌّ. — And see هَثَّاثٌ and هَثْهَثَةٌ. — هُثَاهِثٌ A town, or district, *abounding with dust.* (Ḳ.)

هُثَاهِثٌ: see هَثٌّ.

هَثَّاثٌ and ▼ هُثَاهِثٌ *A liar.* (Ḳ.) — Also, the latter, A man *who tells unmixed lies.* (TA.)

[هثم, &c.

See Supplement.]

هج

1. هَجَّتِ النَّارُ, aor. ـِ, inf. n. هَجِيجٌ and هَجٌّ; (L;) *The fire burned fiercely,* or *intensely;* or *flamed,* or *blazed,* or *burned without smoke, fiercely,* or *intensely:* or, *made a noise,* or *sound:* هَجِيجُ النَّارِ being the same as أَجِيجُهَا, (Ṣ, L, Ḳ,) like as هَرَاقَ is the same as أَرَاقَ: (Ṣ, L:) or, *burned, and caused a sound,* or *noise, to be heard by its burning.* (L.) ═ See art. عج, last para.

2. هجّج النَّارَ *He made the fire to burn fiercely,* or *intensely;* or *to flame,* or *blaze,* or *burn without smoke, fiercely,* or *intensely:* or, *to make a noise,* or *sound,* or *to burn so as to cause a sound, or noise, to be heard by its burning.* (L.) — هجّج *He* (a camel) *had his eyes sunk in his head by reason of hunger or thirst or fatigue;* not by their natural formation. (Lth, Aṣ.) — هَجَّجَتْ عَيْنُهُ [so in three copies of the Ṣ, and in the L; not هَجَّتْ, as Golius seems to have found it written in a copy of the Ṣ;] *His eye became sunk in its socket.* (Aṣ, Ṣ.) In the saying of the daughter of El-Khuss, when she was asked how she knew a she-camel to be pregnant, أَرَى العَيْنَ هَاجٌّ وَالسَّنَامَ رَاجٌّ وَتَمْشِى فَتَفَاجُّ [*I see the eye to have become sunk, and the hump to have shaken, or moved to and fro, and she walks, and straddles in doing so*], هاجّ may be [an act. part. n.] formed from هَجَّجَتْ, although this form of the verb be not used; and she makes العين masc., meaning thereby العُضْو or الطَّرْف; for properly she should have said هَاجَّةٌ: or هاجّ is used [instead of هَجَّجَتْ] in imitation of راجّ [and تفاجّ]. (L.)

3. هاجّ فِى هَدِيرِهِ *He* (a camel) *made his braying to reciprocate.* (L.)

4: see عجّ, last paragraph.

8. اهتجّ فِيهِ *He persevered* (تَمَادَى) *in it,* (Ḳ,) i.e., in his judgment, *not listening to the counsel of any one.* (TA.)

10. استهجّ *He followed his own judgment,* (Ḳ,) *whether erring* or *taking a right course, without consulting any one.* (TA.)

R. Q. 1. هَجْهَجَ بِالسَّبُعِ, (Ṣ, Ḳ,) and السَّبُعَ, (L,) *He cried out to the lion* or *other beast of prey,* (Ṣ, Ḳ,) *and chid him, in order that he might refrain, forbear,* or *abstain.* (Ṣ.) [See هَجْ.] — هَجْهَجَ بِالجَمَلِ *He chid the camel, saying to him* هِيجْ; (Ḳ; [in the CḲ هَيجْ: see art. هيج:]) or هِيجِ; (accord. to the TA;) [but it occurs in a verse written هِيجِ:] and in like manner بِالنَّاقَةِ, *the she-camel.* (L.) — هَجْهَجَ فِى هَدِيرِهِ, said of a stallion-camel, (Ṣ,) *He made a vehement noise in his braying.* (L.)

هَجْ and هَجَ, (Ṣ, Ḳ,) like as one says بَخْ and بَخٍ, (Ṣ,) or هِجِى, as related by Lḥ, (L,) and هَجٍ, (Ḳ,) or هَجٍ هَجٍ and هَجْ هَجْ and هَجَا هَجَا, (Az,) *Cries by which one chides a dog,* (Ṣ, Ḳ,) *and a lion, and a wolf, &c., to quiet him:* (Az:) and sometimes one says هَجَا هَجَا, (ISd,) and, if he please, هَجَا, once, (Az,) *to chide camels:* (ISd, Az:) and هَجٍ, or هَجْ at the end of a verse, is *a cry by which a she-camel is chidden.* (L.) For هَجْ هَجْ, one also says جَهْ جَهْ, by transposition. (L.)

هَجْهَجْ, (Ḳ,) and هَجْهَجِ, (Ṣ,) but the latter is only used by poetic licence, (Ḳ,) *A cry by which sheep or goats (and a dog,* Az,) *are chidden,* or *checked,* or *urged,* (Ṣ, Ḳ.)

هَجْهَجَةٌ *A word imitative of the cry of a man when he cries out to a lion.* (Lth.) [See هَجْ.]

هَجَاجٌ *One in whom is no good.* (L, art. عَجَاج.)

هَجَاجَيْكَ, (Aṣ, Ṣ, Ḳ,) as also هَذَاذَيْكَ, (Aṣ, Ṣ,) in the dual number, like حَوَالَيْكَ and دَوَالَيْكَ, (TA,) supposing [it to be addressed to] two [persons], (Aṣ, Ṣ, Ḳ,) or هجاجيك هُنَا وَهُنَا, i.e., *Refrain thou! or forbear thou! or abstain thou!* (TA;) said to people when one desires their refraining, or forbearing, or abstaining, from a thing: (Aṣ, Ṣ, Ḳ:) and to a lion, and a wolf, &c., to quiet him. (Lḥ.)

رَكِبَ هَجَاجِ, (indecl., Ṣ,) and هَجَاجٍ, [in form], like قَطَامِ, (Ṣ, Ḳ,) or ركب مِنْ أَمْرِهِ هجاج, and ركب هَجَاجَيْهِ, in the dual. form, (TA,) *He went at random*, or *heedlessly, without any certain aim*, or *object; or went his own way, without consideration, not obeying a guide to the right course;* or *pursued a headlong*, or *rash, course*. (Ṣ, Ḳ.)

هَجِيجٌ (Ṣ, Ḳ) and ▼ إِهْجِيجٌ (Ḳ) *A deep valley:* (Ṣ, Ḳ:) or *deep*, as an epithet, applied to a valley: of the dial. of El-Yemen: pl. [of the former] هُجَّانٌ. (TA.)

هَجَاجَةٌ, (Ḳ,) without the art. ال, (TA,) or رَجُلٌ هَجَاجَةٌ, (Ṣ,) and ▼ هَجْهَاجٌ and ▼ هَجْهَاجَةٌ, (Ḳ,) *A stupid*, or *foolish, man; one of little sense:* (Ṣ, Ḳ:) and the first, *one who consults not any one, but follows his own judgment whether he err* or *take a right course:* (Sh:) or *without heart and without intellect* or *intelligence:* (AA in TA, art. رع:) and the second, *a rude, coarse*, or *churlish, and stupid*, or *foolish, man:* (Ḳ:) and the third, *a man of much evil*, or *mischief, and of little understanding:* or, accord. to AZ, *of no understanding, and of no judgment*. (TA.)

هَجْهَاجٌ A camel *that brays vehemently*. (Ḳ.) A word imitative of the sound which a stallion-camel makes in his braying. (TA.) — هَجْهَاجٌ *Wont to take fright, and to run away*. (Ṣ, Ḳ.) — See هَجَاجَةٌ.

هَجْهَاجَةٌ: see هَجَاجَةٌ.

عَيْنٌ هَاجَّةٌ, (Ṣ, L,) and ▼ مُهَجَّجَةٌ, (L,) *An eye sunk in its socket*. (Ṣ, L.) [See 2.]

مُهَجْهِجٌ and مُهَجْهِجَةٌ *A person chiding a lion by a cry*. (L.) [See هَجِ.]

مُهَجَّجَةٌ: see هَاجَّةٌ.

هجأ

1. هَجَأَ, (Ṣ, Ḳ,) aor. ـَ, inf. n. هَجْءٌ and هُجُوءٌ, (Ḳ,) *It* (his hunger) *became appeased*, (Ṣ, Ḳ,) *and departed*, or *ceased*. (Ḳ.) — هَجَأَ *He ate food*. (Ḳ.) — هَجَأَ, (Ḳ,) inf. n. هَجْءٌ, (TA,) *He filled his belly*. (Ḳ.) — هَجَأَ and ▼ اهجأ *He stayed*, or *restrained*, camels (Ḳ) or sheep or goats, (TA,) *that they might pasture*. (Ḳ, TA.) هَجِئَ, aor. ـَ, *He had raging hunger*. (Ḳ.)

4: see 1. — اهجأ جُوعَهُ, inf. n. إِهْجَآءٌ, *It* (food) *appeased his hunger; or caused it to depart*, or *cease*. (Ṣ, Ḳ.) — اهجأ حَقَّهُ, (Ḳ,) and اهجى, (TA,) *He paid him his due*. (Ḳ.) — اهجأهُ شَيْئًا *He gave him a thing to eat*. (Ḳ.)

5. تهجّأ الحَرْفَ i.q. تهجّى. (Ḳ.)

هَجَأٌ *Any state, or case, in which one has been, and which has ceased*. (Ḳ.) It also occurs without ء, هَجًا. (TA.)

هُجَأَةٌ *Foolish; stupid*. (Ḳ.)

هجب

1. هَجَبَ, aor. ـُ, inf. n. هَجْبٌ, *He drove*, or *urged along*. (Ḳ.) — Also, *He beat with a stick*, or *staff*. (Ḳ.) — Also, هَجَبَ, inf. n. as above, *He was quick*, or *swift*, (Ḳ,) *in his pace &c*. (TA.) — This art. is omitted by most of the lexicographers, because not regarded by them as of established authority. (TA.)

هجد

1. هَجَدَ, (Ṣ, A, L, Mṣb,) aor. ـُ, (L, Mṣb,) inf. n. هُجُودٌ; (L, Mṣb, Ḳ;) and ▼ تهجّد, (Ṣ, A, L, Mṣb, Ḳ,) and ▼ اهجد, (L, Ḳ,) and ▼ هجّد; (IAạr, L;) *He* (a man, L) *slept:* (L, Mṣb, Ḳ:) or *slept in the night:* (IAạr, Ṣ, A, L:) or, *in the latter part of the night*. (L.) — Also هَجَدَ and ▼ تهجّد (Ṣ, A, L, Mṣb, Ḳ [in some copies, of the last of which the former verb is written ▼ هجّد and so in the TA) *He remained awake*, or *was sleepless* or *wakeful in the night:* (Ṣ, A, L:) and hence the *praying in the night* is called تَهَجُّدٌ: (Ṣ, L:) or *he awoke from sleep* (Ḳ) *to pray*, or *for some other purpose:* (TA:) or *he prayed in the night;* (Mṣb;) as also ▼ هجّد: (IAạr, L:) thus these verbs bear two contr. significations: (Ṣ, A, L, Mṣb, Ḳ:) and ▼ تهجّد *he relinquished sleep for prayer:* (A:) so in the Ḳur, xvii., 81. (Beyḍ.)

2: see 1, in three places. — Also هجّدهُ, inf. n. تَهْجِيدٌ, *He made him*, or *caused him, to sleep;* (Ṣ, L, Ḳ;) as also ▼ اهجدهُ. (Ibn-Buzurj, L, Ḳ.) — Also, *He awoke him from sleep*. (Ibn-Buzurj, L, Ḳ.) Thus it bears two contr. significations. (Ḳ.) — See also 4.

4: see 1: and 2. — Also اهجدهُ *He found him* (namely a man, Ḳ) *sleeping*. (L, Ḳ.) — And اهجد *He* (a camel) *laid the fore-part of his neck* (the part called جِرَان) *upon the ground;* (ISk, Ṣ, L, Ḳ;) as also ▼ هجّد, (IḲṭṭ, El-Baṣáïr, Ḳ, TA, [in the CḲ هَجَدَ]) inf. n. تَهْجِيدٌ. (IḲṭṭ, El-Baṣáïr, TA.)

5: see 1, in three places.

هَجِدْ, (as in some copies of the Ḳ,) or هِجِدْ, (accord. to others and the TA,) *A cry by which a horse is chidden*. (Ḳ.)

هُجُودٌ: see هَاجِدٌ.

هَاجِدٌ *Sleeping:* (T, L, Mṣb:) pl. هُجُودٌ and هُجَّدٌ. (Mṣb.) [See an ex. in a verse cited voce مُرِمٌ, in art. رم.] — Also, (L,) and ▼ هَجُودٌ (L, Ḳ) and ▼ مُتَهَجِّدٌ (T, L) *Praying in the night:* (T, L, Ḳ:) pl. of the first, (L,) or second, (L, Ḳ,) هُجُودٌ and هُجَّدٌ. (L, Ḳ.) هُجَّدٌ and هُجُدٌ are also fem. pls. [app. in both of the above senses]. (A.)

مُتَهَجِّدٌ: see هَاجِدٌ.

هجر

1. هَجَرَهُ, (Ṣ, A, &c.,) aor. ـُ, (Mṣb,) inf. n. هَجْرٌ (Ṣ, A, Mgh, Mṣb, Ḳ) and هِجْرَانٌ, (Ṣ, A, Mgh, Ḳ,) or the latter is a simple subst., (Mṣb,) *He cut him off from friendly* or *loving, communion* or *intercourse; contr. of* وَصَلَهُ: (Ṣ, Mgh:) *he forsook*, or *abandoned, him;* syn. قَطَعَهُ: (Mṣb, TA:) *he cut him;* meaning, *he ceased to speak to him, or to associate with him;* syn. صَرَمَهُ, (A, Mgh, Ḳ,) and قَطَعَ كَلَامَهُ. (Mgh.) It is said in the Ḳur, [iv. 38,] وَٱهْجُرُوهُنَّ فِى ٱلْمَضَاجِعِ, i.e., [*And cut ye them off from loving intercourse*] *in the sleeping-places*, in order to obtain their obedience. (Mṣb.) See also 3. — *He left it; forsook it; relinquished it; abandoned it; deserted it; quitted it: abstained from it: neglected it: shunned* or *avoided it; was averse from it:* syn. تَرَكَهُ; (A, Mṣb, Ḳ, TA;) and رَفَضَهُ; (Mṣb;) and فَارَقَهُ: (B:) and أَغْفَلَهُ: and أَعْرَضَ عَنْهُ: (TA:) namely, a thing to which it was necessary for him to pay frequent attention: (Lth, TA:) as also ▼ أَهْجَرَهُ; (Ḳ;) which latter is of the dial. of Hudheyl: (TA:) and هُجِرَ *he, or it, was left;* &c. (IḲṭṭ.) هِجْرَانٌ may be with the body and with the tongue and with the heart or mind: it is with the first in the passage of the Ḳur cited above: it may be with any of the three in the Ḳur, [lxxiii. 10,] where it is said, وَٱهْجُرْهُمْ هَجْرًا جَمِيلًا [*And avoid thou them*, i.e., avoid the associating with them in person, or speaking to them, or entertaining friendship for them in thy heart, *with an avoiding of a becoming kind*]: and it is with all the three in the following ex. in the Ḳur, [lxxiv. 5,] وَٱلرُّجْزَ فَٱهْجُرْ [*And idolatry avoid thou*]. (B.) You say also, هَجَرَ الشِّرْكَ, inf. n. هَجْرٌ and هِجْرَانٌ, [*He abstained from*, or *avoided, polytheism*, or *the associating of others with God*,] هِجْرَةً حَسَنَةً [*with a good manner of abstaining*, or *avoiding*]. (Lḥ, Ḳ.) And it is said in a trad., وَلَا يَسْمَعُونَ القُرْآنَ إِلَّا هَجْرًا, meaning, [*And they hear not the Ḳur-án save*] *with neglect of it, and aversion from it:* the reading الَّا هُجْرًا, mentioned by IḲt, and his explanation of it, *save with foul speech*, are both said by El-Khaṭṭábee to be erroneous. (TA.) — هَجَرَ, [aor. ـُ,] inf. n. هَجْرٌ, *He* (a man) *went, removed, retired*, or *withdrew himself, to a distance, far away*, or *far off*. (TA.) —

هَجَرَ فِى الصَّوْمِ, (Ḳ,) aor. ـُ , inf. n. هِجْرَانٌ, (TA,) *He abstained from sexual intercourse in fasting.* (Ḳ.) ═ هَجَرَ, (Lth, Fr, Ṣ, A, Ḳ, &c.,) or هَجَرَ فِى كَلَامِهِ, (Mṣb,) aor. ـُ , (Lth, Fr, Ṣ, &c.,) inf. n. هَجْرٌ, (Lth, Ṣ, A, Mgh, Mṣb,) with fet-ḥ, (Mgh,) or هُجْرٌ, with ḍamm, (Ḳ,) and هِجِّيرَى, (A, Ḳ,) or this is a simple subst., (Lth,) and إِهْجِيرَى, (Ḳ,) [or this and that which immediately precedes it are intensive inf. ns.,] *He* (a sick man, Lth, Ṣ, Mṣb, Ḳ, or one having the disease termed بِرْسَام, A'Obeyd, A, or having a fever, A'Obeyd, and one sleeping, Fr, Ḳ) *talked nonsense; talked irrationally* or *foolishly* or *deliriously,* (Lth, Fr, Ṣ, A, Mgh, Mṣb, Ḳ,) *and confusedly:* (Mṣb:) or هِجِّيرَى signifies the *talking much, and saying what is evil.* (Sb.) In the Ḳur, [xxiii. 69,] instead of تَهْجُرُونَ, in the phrase سَامِرًا تَهْجُرُونَ, [*Holding discourse by night, talking irrationally* or *foolishly,*] I'Ab reads تُهْجِرُونَ from ▼ أَهْجَرَ, [q.v.,] from الهُجْرُ. (TA.) — See also 4. — هَجَرَ بِهِ, aor. ـُ , inf. n. هَجْرٌ, *He dreamed of him* or *it;* or *saw him* or *it in sleep:* or *he did so and talked foolishly* or *deliriously.* (TA.)

2. هجّر, (Lth, A, Ḳ, &c.,) inf. n. تَهْجِيرٌ, (Ṣ, Mṣb, Ḳ,) *He journeyed in the time called the* هَاجِرَة; (Lth, Ṣ, A, Mgh, Ḳ;) as also ▼ تَهَجَّرَ; (IAar, Ṣ, A, Ḳ;) and ▼ اهجر: (Ḳ:) or *he went forth in that time:* (Az, TA:) or *he was* (صَارَ) *in that time:* (Mṣb: [but in my copy of that work, صار is perhaps a mistake for سَارَ:]) or ▼ اهجر has this last signification; (Lth, TA;) or signifies *he entered upon that time;* like اظهر. (A.) — *It* (the day) *attained to the time called the* هَاجِرَة. (Ṣ, TA.)

3. هاجرهُ, (A,) inf. n. مُهَاجَرَةٌ; (B;) and ▼ اهتجرهُ; (A;) *He cut him off from friendly,* or *loving, communion* or *intercourse, being so cut off by him;* or *he cut him,* or *ceased to speak to him, being in like manner cut by him:* and *he forsook,* or *abandoned, him, being forsaken,* or *abandoned, by him:* (A,* B:) this is the primary signification of the former. (B.) — هاجر, (T, A, Mṣb, Ḳ,) inf. n. مُهَاجَرَةٌ (T, Ṣ, A, Mṣb) and هِجْرَةٌ, (A,) or the latter is a simple subst., (Mgh, Mṣb,) *He* (an inhabitant of the desert) *went forth from his desert to the cities* or *towns:* this is the primary acceptation, with the Arabs, of the verb [when intrans.]: also, *he* (any one) *left his place of abode, emigrating to another people:* (Az:) *he departed,* or *went forth, from one land to another,* (Ṣ, Ḳ,) or *from one country,* or *district,* or *town, to another:* (Mṣb:) and, as used in the Ḳur, ii. 215, [and in many other instances in the same and other books,] *he went forth* [or *emigrated*] *from the territory of the unbelievers to the territory of the believers* [or *to any place of safety* or *refuge on account of religious persecution, &c.*] (B.) See an ex. voce تَهَجَّرَ; and see هِجْرَة.

4. اهجرهُ: see هَجَرَهُ ═ اهجر فِى مَنْطِقِهِ, (Ṣ,* Mgh, Mṣb, Ḳ,) or simply اهجر, (A,) inf. n. إِهْجَارٌ (Ṣ, Ḳ) and هُجْرٌ, (Lḥ, Kr, Ḳ,) or the latter is, correctly speaking, a simple subst., (TA,) *He spoke,* or *uttered, foul, evil, bad, abominable,* or *unseemly, language:* (Ṣ, A, Mgh, Ḳ:) or *he did so much; beyond what he used to do before;* as also ▼ هَجَرَ, aor. ـُ , (Mṣb,) inf. n. هُجْرٌ: (L, TA:) and in like manner, *he talked much of that which was not fit, suitable, meet,* or *proper.* (Ṣ.) — اهجر بِهِ *He mocked,* or *scoffed,* or *laughed at him, derided him,* or *ridiculed him, and said respecting him what was foul, evil, bad, abominable,* or *unseemly.* (Mṣb, Ḳ.) ═ See also 2, in two places.

5. تهجّر *He affected to be like the* مُهَاجِرُون [or *emigrants from the territory of the unbelievers to that of the believers*]. (A'Obeyd, Ṣ, A, Ḳ.) Hence the trad., هَاجِرُوا ▼ وَلَا تَهَجَّرُوا, (A'Obeyd, Ṣ, A,) i.e., *Perform ye the* هِجْرَة with sincerity towards God, *and affect not to be like those who do so without your being really such as do so:* said by 'Omar. (A'Obeyd, TA.) ═ See also 2.

6. تهاجروا [*They cut one another off from friendly* or *loving communion* or *intercourse;* or *they cut,* or *ceased to speak to, one another:* *they forsook,* or *abandoned, one another:* as also ▼ اهتجروا]. (A.) You say also هُمَا يَتَهَاجَرَانِ, and ▼ يَهْتَجِرَانِ, i.e., يَتَقَاطَعَانِ [*They two cut each other off &c.*]: (Ḳ:) تَهَاجُرٌ is *syn. with* تَقَاطُعٌ. (Ṣ.)

8: see 3 and 6; the latter in two places. — [*He journeyed in the time of the* هَاجِرَة: see 8 in art. عشو.]

هَجْرٌ: see هُجْرٌ: ═ and see also هَاجِرَةٌ.

هُجْرٌ, a subst. from أَهْجَرَ; (Ṣ, Mgh;) or from its syn. هَجَرَ; (Mṣb;) *Foul, evil, bad, abominable,* or *unseemly, language,* or *talk;* (Aṣ, Ks, T, Ṣ, A, Mgh, Mṣb, Ḳ;) as also ▼ هُجْرَآءُ; (Ṣgh, Ḳ;) and ▼ هَاجِرَةٌ; of which last the pl. is هَوَاجِرُ, incorrectly said by IJ to be an irreg. pl. of هُجْرٌ; or ▼ هَاجِرَةٌ may be an inf. n., like كَاذِبَةٌ &c. (IB.) You say, قَالَ هُجْرًا وَبُجْرًا, and ▼ هَجْرًا وَبَجْرًا, [*He said*] *a foul* [*and a wonderful*] *thing:* ▼ هَجْرٌ is an inf. n., and هُجْرٌ is a simple subst. (L, TA.) And ▼ رَمَاهُ بِالْهَاجِرَاتِ *He assailed him with foul words:* هاجرات being a word of the same class as لَابِنٌ and تَامِرٌ. (A, Mṣb.) And ▼ رَمَاهُ بِهَاجِرَاتٍ, (Ṣ, Ḳ,) or بِالْهَاجِرَاتِ, and ▼ بِمُهْجِرَاتٍ, (A,) and بِالْمُهْجِرَاتِ, (A, Mṣb,) *He accused him of evil things that exposed him to disgrace:* (Ṣ, Ḳ:) or *of foul,* or *evil, actions.* (A, Mṣb.) And ▼ تَكَلَّمَ بِالْمَهَاجِرِ (in the CḲ بالمُهاجِر) *He spoke foul,* or *evil, language.* (L, Ḳ.)

هِجْرٌ : } see هِجْرَةٌ.
هُجْرَةٌ : }

هِجْرَةٌ, a subst. from هَجَرَهُ, (Ṣ, Ḳ,) as also ▼ هِجْرَانٌ, (Mṣb,) signifying The *cutting another off from friendly* or *loving communion* or *intercourse:* (Ṣ:) *cutting one;* or *ceasing to speak to him:* (Ḳ:) *forsaking, abandoning, deserting,* or *shunning* or *avoiding, one.* (Mṣb.) It is said in a trad., لَا هِجْرَةَ بَعْدَ ثَلَاثٍ [*There shall be no cutting off from friendly communion after three* nights with their days,]: the meaning is, هَجْر as contr. of وَصْل; i.e., such anger as exists between Muslims, or a failing, or falling short, with respect to the duties of society, exclusively of what relates to religion: but the هِجْرَة of those who follow their own natural desires [in matters of religion], and of innovators [in religion], should continue even as long as they do not repent, and return to the truth. (TA.) — [Also, *A mode,* or *manner, of cutting another off from friendly* or *loving communion* or *intercourse:* &c. See 1, where an ex. occurs.] — Also, *A removal from the desert to the towns* or *villages:* this was its [primary] acceptation with the Arabs: and the *forsaking of his country,* or *district,* or *the like, by an inhabitant of the desert,* or *by an inhabitant of a town,* or *village,* or *cultivated district, and taking up his abode in another country* or *district,* or *the like,* an *emigration;* (TA;) the *forsaking of one's home and removing to another place;* (Mgh;) the *forsaking of a country,* or *district,* or *the like, and removing to another;* (Mṣb;) the *going forth from one land to another;* as also ▼ هُجْرَةٌ: (Ḳ:) [and *an emigration from the territory of the unbelievers to the territory of the believers,* or *to any place of safety* or *refuge on account of religious persecution &c.:* see 3, last signification:] a subst. from هَاجَرَ. (Mṣb, TA.) — [الهِجْرَةُ, peculiarly, *The emigration,* or *flight,* (for it was really a flight,) of Moḥammad, from Mekkeh to Yethrib, which latter was afterwards called El-Medeeneh. Hence, تَأْرِيخُ الهِجْرَةِ *The era of the Hijreh,* or *Flight.* The epoch of this era is not the date of the Flight itself, as some have imagined, (for this took place on an uncertain day, most probably the first or second, of the third lunar month of the Arabian year,) but is the first day of the Arabian year in which the Flight happened: and as I believe that all European writers who have attempted to fix it, prior to M. Caussin de Perceval, have erred respecting it, the true date, as shown by him, (see his "Essai sur l'Histoire des Arabes," &c., in the places referred to in the index to that work,) I think it important here to mention. The first year of the Flight was the two hundred and eleventh year of a period during which the Arabs made use of a defective luni-solar reckoning, making every third year to consist of thirteen lunar months; the others consisting of twelve such months. This mode of reckoning was abolished by Moḥammad in the twelfth month of the tenth year of the Flight, at the time of the pilgrimage; whence it appears that the first year of the Flight commenced, most probably, on Monday, the nineteenth of April, A.D. 622; or perhaps on the eighteenth; for the actual appearance of the new moon properly marked its commencement, and, as the new moon happened about sunset on the sixteenth, it may perhaps have been seen on the eve of the eighteenth. According to M. Caussin de Perceval, the first ten years of the Flight commenced at the following periods.

1st.	[Mon.]	Apr. 19, 622
2nd.	[Sat.]	May 7, 623
3rd.	[Th.]	Apr. 26, 624
4th.	[Mon.]	Apr. 15, 625
5th.	[Sat.]	May 3, 626
6th.	[Th.]	Apr. 23, 627
7th.	[Tu.]	Apr. 12, 628
8th.	[Mon.]	May 1, 629
9th.	[Fri.]	Apr. 20, 630
10th.	[Tu.]	Apr. 9, 631

Thus it appears that the first and fourth and seventh years were of thirteen lunar months each; and the seventh was the last year that was thus augmented: therefore, with the eighth year commenced the reckoning by common lunar years; and from this point we may use the tables which have often been published for finding the periods of commencement of years of the Flight. We must not, however, rely upon the exact accuracy of these tables: for the commencement of the month was generally determined by actual observation of the new moon; not by calculation; and we often find that a year was commenced, according as the place of observation was low or high, or to the east or west of the place to which the calculation is adapted, or according as the sky was obscure or clear, a day later or earlier than that which is indicated in the tables; and in some cases, even two days later. The twelfth day of the third month of the first year of the Flight, the day of Moḥammad's arrival at Ḳubà, was Monday: therefore the first day of the year was most probably the nineteenth of April, as two months of thirty days each, or twenty-nine days each, seldom occur together. But the tenth day of the first month of the sixty-first year, the day on which El-Ḥoseyn was slain at Kerbelà, was Friday: therefore the first day of that year, at that place, must have been Wednesday, the third of October, A.D. 680; not the first of October, as in most of the published tables above mentioned. (For the principal divisions of the Arabian year when the luni-solar reckoning was instituted, see زَمَنٌ).] الهِجْرَتَانِ means [*The two emigrations*, or *flights*; namely,] *the* هِجْرَة *to Abyssinia and the* هِجْرَة *to El-Medeeneh*. (Ṣ, Ḳ.) And ذُو الهِجْرَتَيْنِ *He* (of the صَحَابَة [or Companions of Moḥammad] TA) *who emigrated*, or *who has emigrated, to Abyssinia and to El-Medeeneh*. (Ḳ.)

هُجْرَآءُ : see هُجْرٌ.

هِجْرَانٌ : see هِجْرَةٌ.

هِجْرِيًّا : see هِجِّيرٌ.

هَجِيرٌ *Left; forsaken; relinquished; abandoned; deserted; quitted: abstained from: neglected: shunned* or *avoided*. (TA.) ═ See also هَاجِرَةٌ, in three places.

هَجِيرَةٌ : see هَاجِرَةٌ.

هِجِّيرٌ *Custom; manner; habit; wont: state; condition; case*; syn. دَأْبٌ, (T, Ṣ, A, Ḳ,) and عَادَةٌ, (Ṣ, TA,) and دَيْدَنٌ, (TA,) and شَأْنٌ: (T, A, Ḳ:) and the *speech*, or *language*, of a man; [or *what one is accustomed to say*;] syn. كَلَامٌ: (T, TA:) as also ↓ هِجِّيرَى, (T, Ṣ, A, Ḳ,) and ↓ إِهْجِيرَى, (Ṣ, Ḳ,) and ↓ إِهْجِيرَآءُ, and ↓ أُهْجُورَةٌ, and ↓ هِجْرِيًّا, (Ḳ,) and إِجْرِيًّا, and إِجْرِيَّآءُ. (Ṣ.) You say, مَا زَالَ ذٰلِكَ هِجِّيرَهُ, (A, Ḳ,* TA [in the CḲ, هٰذَا هِجِّيرَتُهُ,]) and هِجِّيرَاهُ, (Ṣ, A, Ḳ,) and إِهْجِيرَاهُ, &c., (Ḳ,) *That ceased not to be his custom*, &c. (Ṣ, A, Ḳ.*) And ↓ مَا لَهُ هِجِّيرَى غَيْرُهَا *He has no custom, &c., other than it*. (TA, from a trad.)

هِجِّيرَى : see هِجِّيرٌ.

هَاجِرٌ, act. part. n. of 1, q. v. — *Talking nonsense; talking foolishly* or *deliriously*. (Ṣ, TA.) See 1, last signification but one.

هَاجِرَةٌ : see هُجْرٌ, in four places. ═ الهَاجِرَةُ, (Ṣ, A, Mgh, Mṣb, Ḳ,) and ↓ الهَجِيرُ, (Ṣ, Mṣb, Ḳ,) and ↓ الهَجِيرَةُ, (A, Ḳ,) and ↓ الهَجْرُ, (Ṣ, Ḳ,) *Midday when the heat is vehement*: (Ṣ:) or *midday in summer*, or *in the hot season*: (Mgh, Mṣb:) or the *period from a little before noon to a little after noon in summer*, or *in the hot season, only*: (En-Naḍr, ISk:) or *from the time when the sun declines from the meridian*: (Aboo-Sa'eed:) or *midday, when the sun declines from the meridian, at the* ظُهْر: or *from its declining until the* عَصْر: because people [then] shelter themselves in their tents or houses; as though they forsook one another (تَهَاجَرُوا): (Ḳ:) or *the vehemence of the heat* (Ḳ, TA) *therein*: (TA:) and الهُوَيْجِرَةُ [dim. of الهَاجِرَةُ] *the period a little after the* هَاجِرَة: (Es-Sukkaree:) [pl. of the first, هَوَاجِرُ.] You say, طَبَخَتْهُ الهَوَاجِرُ [*The vehement midday heats affected him with a hot*, or *burning, fever*]. (A.) And ↓ صَلَاةُ الهَجِيرِ *The prayer of noon*; as also الهَجِيرُ, elliptically. (TA.) See also ظَهِيرَةٌ.

أُهْجُورَةٌ : }
إِهْجِيرَى : } see هِجِّيرٌ.
إِهْجِيرَآءُ : }

أَتَيْنَا أَهْلَنَا مُهْجِرِينَ *We came to our family in the time of the* هَاجِرَة. (Ṣ.) — مُهْجِرَاتٌ and مُهَاجِرٌ: see هُجْرٌ.

هَلْ مُهْجِرٌ كَمَنْ قَالَ *Is one who journeys in the* هَاجِرَة *like him who stays during the time of midday?* (TA, from a trad.)

مَهْجُورٌ *Cut off from friendly* or *loving communion* or *intercourse; forsaken*, or *abandoned: cut*, or *not spoken to*. (Mgh, Mṣb.) In like manner مَهْجُورًا is used in the Ḳur, [xxv. 32,] signifying *avoided*, or *forsaken, with the tongue*, or *with the heart* or *mind*. (B.) [But see what here follows.] ═ Talk, or language, *uttered irrationally* or *foolishly* or *deliriously*. It is related by Aboo-'Obeyd, on the authority of Ibráheem, that the words of the Ḳur, إِنَّ قَوْمِى ٱتَّخَذُوا هٰذَا ٱلْقُرْآنَ مَهْجُورًا, [xxv. 32,] mean, *Verily my people have made this Ḳur-án a thing of which they have said what is not true*: because the sick man, when he talks irrationally or foolishly or deliriously, says what is not true: and the like is related on the authority of Mujáhid. (Ṣ.)

مُهَاجَرٌ *A place to which one emigrates*. (Mṣb.)

مُهَاجِرٌ Any one, whether an inhabitant of the desert [as in the primary acceptation of the epithet] or an inhabitant of a town or village or cultivated district, *who emigrates*; or *who forsakes his country* or *district* or *the like, and takes up his abode in another country* or *district* or *the like*. Hence المُهَاجِرُونَ applied to *The emigrants* to El-Medeeneh: because they forsook their places of abode in which they were reared, for the sake of God, and attached themselves to an abode in which they had neither family nor property, when they emigrated to El-Medeeneh. (TA.)

هجس

1. هَجَسَ الشَّىْءُ فِى قَلْبِهِ, (A,) or فِى صَدْرِهِ, (Ḳ,) or بِالقَلْبِ, (Mṣb,) aor. ـِ, (Ṣ, Ḳ, MṢ, TA,) or ـُ, (Mṣb,) inf. n. هَجْسٌ, (Mṣb, TA,) *The thing fell into*, or *occurred to*, or *bestirred itself in, his mind*, or *the mind*; or *occurred to his mind*, or *the mind, after having been for-*

gotten; syn. وَقَعَ and خَطَرَ; (Mṣb;) or, of the phrase in the A and that in the Ḳ, خَطَرَ بِبَالِهِ, (A, Ḳ,) and وَقَعَ فِى خَلَدِهِ: (TA:) or هَجْسٌ signifies [the thing's] *talking, or suggesting something, to the person's mind,* in his bosom; expl. by the words أَنْ يُحَدِّثَ نَفْسَهُ فِى صَدْرِهِ; like وِسْوَاسٌ: (Ḳ,* TA:) and hence the phrase in a trad., وَمَا يَهْجِسُ فِى الضَّمَائِرِ, meaning, *and what falls into, or occurs in, and bestirs itself in, the minds,* (يَخْطُرُ بِهَا,) *and revolves therein,* of matters of discourse, and of thoughts: (TA:) or هَجَسَ فِى صَدْرِى شَىْءٌ signifies *i.q.* حَدَسَ [app. meaning *a thing came at random into my mind*]: (Ṣ, L:) and you say also, هَجَسَ فِى نَفْسِى [*it fell into, or occurred to, my mind;* &c.]. (TA.)

5. تَهَجَّسَ *I.q.* أَقَامَ. (T, art. عرص.)

هَجْسٌ *A low voice, or sound,* (نَبْأَةٌ,) *which one hears but does not understand.* (Ṣ.) — See also هَاجِسٌ.

هَاجِسٌ *A thing, or an idea, or object of thought, or an opinion, coming at random into, falling into, occurring to, or bestirring itself in, the mind;* (Ṣ, A,* Mṣb;) syn. خَاطِرٌ: (Ṣ, TA:) an epithet in which the quality of a subst. predominates: (TA:) and ▼هَجْسٌ also signifies *anything falling into, or occurring to, the mind:* (Lth, Ḳ:) pl. of the former, هَوَاجِسُ. (A, TA.)

[هجع, &c.

See Supplement.]

هد

1. هَدَّ, aor. ـُ, (Ṣ, L, Mṣb,) inf. n. هَدٌّ (Ṣ, L, Mṣb, Ḳ) and هُدُودٌ, (L, Ḳ,) *He demolished a* a building; (Aṣ, Ṣ, A, L, Ḳ:*) *threw it down;* (TA;) *pulled it down to the ground:* (Aṣ, Ṣ, A, L:) *demolished it with violence:* (L, Ḳ:*) *demolished it at once, with a vehement noise.* (Mṣb.) — [Hence you say,] مَا هَدَّهُ كَذَا † *Such a thing did not break him,* or *it.* (Ṣ, L.) — هَدَّ رُكْنِى, and هَدَّنِى الأَمْرُ, † *The thing distressed, and broke,* or *crushed, me.* And [in like manner] مَا هَدَّنِى مَوْتُ أَحَدٍ † [*The death of any one has not distressed, nor broken,* or *crushed, me*]. (L.) And هَدَّتْهُ المُصِيبَةُ *The* ‡ *calamity debilitated,* or *enervated, him.* (Ṣ, A, L.) — هَدَّ, aor. ـِ, and ـَ, inf. n. هَدٌّ, *He* (a man) *was, or became, weak,* (L, Ḳ,) *in body;* (L;) *became extremely aged,* or *decrepit.* (TḲ.) — See 7. — هَدَّ, aor. ـِ, inf. n. هَدِيدٌ, *It* (a wall or the like, Ṣ, L, or a part of a mountain, L, by its falling, Ṣ, L) *made a noise;* (Ṣ;) or, *a violent noise.* (L.) — هَدَّتْ *It* (the sky) *sent forth a noise,* or *sound, occasioned by the falling of rain.* (L.) — هَدَّ, aor. ـِ, (L,) inf. n. هَدِيدٌ, (Ṣ, L,) *It* (the sound called هَادٌّ, from the sea,) *made a murmuring.* (Ṣ,* L.) — هَدَّ, aor. ـِ, inf. n. هَدٌّ, *He* (a camel) *brayed.* (TḲ.) See also R. Q. 1. — مَرَرْتُ بِرَجُلٍ هَدِّكَ مِنْ رَجُلٍ *I passed by a man who is sufficient for thee as a man;* (L, Ḳ;) as also هَدَّكَ: (Ḳ:) an expression of praise: (L:) or it means, *the description of whose good qualities would be burdensome to thee:* there are two dial. forms used in this case: some use هَدّ as an inf. n., [in the sense of an epithet, (marginal note in a copy of the Ṣ,) saying, in such a phrase as the above, هَدِّكَ,] in which case, it has no fem. nor dual. nor pl. form; (Ṣ, L;) the sing. and dual and pl. are the same: (Ḳ:) and some make it a verb, and give it [a fem. and] a dual and a pl., and say, مررت برجل هَدَّكَ من رجل, as above, (Ṣ, L,) and بِٱمْرَأَةٍ هَدَّتْكَ مِنِ ٱمْرَأَةٍ, (Ṣ, L, Ḳ,) like as you say كَفَاكَ and كَفَتْكَ, (L,) and بِرَجُلَيْنِ هَدَّاكَ, and بِٱمْرَأَتَيْنِ هَدَّتَاكَ, and بِرِجَالٍ هَدُّوكَ, and بِنِسْوَةٍ هَدَدْنَكَ. (Ṣ, L, Ḳ.) — IAạr also cites the following ex. [by El-Ḳattál El-Kilábee, (marginal note in a copy of the Ṣ.)]

* وَلِى صَاحِبٌ فِى الغَارِ هَدَّكَ صَاحِبًا *

as meaning, [*And I have a companion in the cave;*] *of how great estimation, and how ingenious, and how knowing, is he* [*as a companion*]! describing a wolf: (L:) in which he who reads هَدَّكَ makes هَدَّ a verb; and as such it has a dual and pl. and fem.: but some read هَدِّكَ, making it an inf. n. used as an epithet; and as such it has no dual nor pl. nor fem. (Marginal note in a copy of the Ṣ.) — هَدَّ الرَّجُلُ also signifies *Excellent is the man:* (ISd, L:) and إِنَّهُ لَهَدَّ الرَّجُلُ *Verily, excellent is the man* (L, Ḳ) *in hardiness and strength:* (L:) and لَهَدَّ الرَّجُلُ *How hardy is the man!* (L.) — In a trad., Aboo-Lahab is related to have said, لَهَدَّ مَا سَحَرَكُمْ صَاحِبُكُمْ, [meaning *How greatly hath your companion enchanted you!*]: لَهَدَّ is an expression of wonder. (L.) — فُلَانٌ يُهَدُّ *Such a one is praiseworthy for hardiness* (Ṣ, L, Ḳ) *and strength.* (Ṣ, L.)

2. هَدَّدَهُ, (Mṣb, Ḳ,) inf. n. تَهْدِيدٌ (Ṣ, L) and تَهْدَادٌ; (L:) and ▼تَهَدَّدَهُ; (Ṣ, L, Mṣb;) *He threatened him;* (L;) *threatened him with punishment;* (Mṣb;) *frightened,* or *terrified, him.* (Ṣ, L, Ḳ.)

5: see 2.

7. انهدّ *It* (a building) [*fell down:* or] *became demolished at once, with a vehement noise:* (Mṣb:) and ▼هَدَّ, aor. ـِ, *it* (a wall) *fell down;* mentioned by AHei; and also by Es-Semeen, who concedes it; (MF;) but this form of the verb is commonly known only as transitive. (TA.) — *It* (a mountain) *broke down.* (Ṣ, L.)

10. استهدّهُ *He regarded him as weak.* (L.)

R.Q. 1. هَدْهَدَ, (Ṣ, L, Ḳ,) inf. n. هَدْهَدَةٌ, (Ṣ, L,) *He* (a bird) *cooed;* syn. قَرْقَرَ: (L, Ḳ, TA [in the CḲ, قَرْقَرَ]:) *he* (a pigeon) *cooed;* syn. هَدَرَ, and هَدَلَ: (TA:) or *made a murmuring* or *confused noise* in cooing: (Ṣ, L, accord. to the explanation of هَدْهَدَةٌ:) and *he* (a camel, Ṣ, L) *brayed;* syn. هَدَرَ: (Ḳ:) or *made a murmuring* or *confused noise* in braying. (Ṣ, L.) See also 1. — هَدْهَدَتْ, (inf. n. هَدْهَدَةٌ, L,) *She* (a woman, Ṣ, L) *shook,* or *rocked,* a child (Ṣ, L, Ḳ) in its cradle, (L,) *in order that it might sleep.* (Ṣ, L, Ḳ.) — هَدْهَدَ *He sent,* or *threw,* a thing *down,* from a high place to a low one. (L, Ḳ.)

هَدٌّ *A weak man;* (Aṣ, Ṣ, L, Ḳ;) i.e., *weak in body;* (L;) as also ▼هِدٌّ: (Ḳ:) or, accord. to IAạr, the latter only, meaning *cowardly and weak:* (Ṣ, L:) or هَدٌّ (Sh, L) and ▼أَهَدُّ (L, Ḳ) and ▼هَدَادَةٌ (Sh, L, Ḳ) signify a *cowardly* (*and weak,* TA) man: (Sh, L, Ḳ:) and ▼قَوْمٌ هَدَادٌ *a cowardly people:* (Sh, L:) pl. of هَدٌّ, هَدُّونَ: (L, Ḳ:) it has no broken pl.: (L:) and of هِدٌّ, هِدُّونَ. (Ḳ.) A man says to another, in threatening him, إِنِّى لَغَيْرُ هَدٍّ *Verily I am not weak.* (Ṣ, L.) — هَدٌّ *Extreme old age; decrepitude.* (Ḳ, TA.) See 1. — هَدٌّ *A rough,* or *harsh, sound;* as also ▼هَدَدٌ. (L, Ḳ.) — هَدٌّ *The braying of a camel.* (Lḥ, L, Ḳ.) See 1. — هَدٌّ *A generous, liberal, bountiful man.* (IAạr, Ṣ, L, Ḳ.*) — *A strong man.* (IAạr, L.) — مَرَرْتُ بِرَجُلٍ هَدِّكَ مِنْ رَجُلٍ and لِى صَاحِبٌ هَدَّكَ صَاحِبًا: see 1.

هِدٌّ and هَدَدٌ: see هَدٌّ.

هَدَّةٌ *The sound of the fall of a wall or the like:* (Ṣ:) or *a violent sound occasioned thereby,* or *by the fall of a part of a mountain.* (L.) — *The sound of rain falling from the sky.* (L.) — *A sinking, and falling in, of the ground.* (L.)

هَدْهَدٌ *The voices,* or *cries, of jinn,* or *genii:* without a singular. (L, Ḳ.)

هُدْهُدٌ *A certain bird,* (Ṣ, L, Mṣb, Ḳ,) *well known;* (L, Mṣb, Ḳ;) [namely, the *hoopoe,* or *upupa* of Linnæus; so this bird is called in the present day; and this, accord. to a common tradition, is the bird mentioned in the Ḳur, xxvii. 20;] as also هُدَهِدٌ (Ḳ) and ▼هُدَاهِدٌ: (Ṣ, L, Ḳ:) or the last, *a certain bird resembling the pigeon:* (Lth, Az, L:) or (in the Ḳ, and) هُدْهُدٌ signifies *a pigeon that cooes much;* (IDrd in explanation of v. 20 of ch. xxvii. of the Ḳur., and AḤn, L, Ḳ;) as also ▾ هُدَاهِدٌ: (IDrd, AḤn, L:) and *any bird that coos; that utters the cry called* قُرْقُرَة; (L, Ḳ, TA [in the CḲ, يُقَرْقِرُ is put for يُقَرْقِرُ]) as also ▾ هُدَاهِدٌ: (Aṣ, L:) pl. (of all, Ḳ) هَدَاهِدُ (Ṣ, L, Ḳ) and هَدَاهِيدُ: (Kr, L, Ḳ:) but ISd says of the latter, I know not how this is, unless the sing. be هُدْهَادٌ. (L.) Er-Rá'ee says,

• كَهُدَاهِدٍ كَسَرَ الرُّمَاةُ جَنَاحَهُ •

[*Like a* هداهد *whose wing the shooters have broken*]: (Ṣ, L:) Aṣ says, he means the فَاخِتَة, or the دُبْسِىّ, or the وَرَشَان, or the هُدْهُد, or a man, or camels: and Lḥ says, that Ks asserts him to mean, by هداهد, the dim. of هُدْهُد: but Aṣ disapproves of this; and so does ISd; but the latter adds, that it may perhaps be for هُدَيْهِد; as some of the Arabs say دَوَابَّة and شَوَابَّة for دُوَيْبَّة and شُوَيْبَّة; though they are only known to change the ى into ا before a double consonant. (L.)

هَدْهَدَةٌ [an inf. n. used as a simple subst.] The *murmuring* or *confused sound of* the *cooing* of pigeons, and *of* the *braying* of a camel [and of thunder (see زَمْزَمَة)]: pl. هَدَاهِدُ. (Ṣ, L.)

هَدَادٌ and هَدَادَةٌ: see هَدٌّ.

هُدَاهِدٌ A stallion-camel *that brays much among the she-camels but does not cover them.* (L.) — See هُدْهُد.

هَدِيدٌ *A voice, cry, sound, or noise.* (L.) See also 1. — *A threatening from behind one.* (Aṣ, L.)

هَادٌّ *A certain murmuring sound from the sea;* (Ḳ;) *a sound which is heard by people inhabiting the sea-shore, coming to them from the direction of the sea, murmuring over the land, and sometimes followed by an earthquake.* (Ṣ, L.)

هَادَّةٌ *Thunder.* (L, Ḳ.) Ex. مَا سَمِعْنَا العَامَ هَادَّةً *We have not heard this year thunder.* (L.)

أَهَدُّ: see هَدٌّ.

هدأ

1. هَدَأَ, aor. ـَ, inf. n. هَدْءٌ and هُدُوْءٌ, *He, or it, was quiet, or still, calm, or unruffled;* (Ṣ, Ḳ;) *was motionless; was silent:* (TA:) [and so, app., ▾ اهدأ: see مُهْدِئٌ:] — تَهَدَّى and هَادٍ occur for هَادِئٌ and تَهَدَّأَ. (TA.) — هَدَأَ عَنْهُ *It* [pain or the like] *became appeased, and quitted him.* (TA.) — See 4. — أَتَانَا وَقَدْ هَدَأَتِ الرِّجْلُ ‡ *He came to us when the foot (of the passenger by night) had become still.* (Ṣ.) — أَتَانَا بَعْدَ مَا هَدَأَتِ الرِّجْلُ وَالعَيْنُ ‡ *He came to us after the foot (of the passenger by night), and the eye, were at rest.* (Ṣ, TA.) — هَدَأَ بِالمَكَانِ ‡ *He stayed, abode, or dwelt, in the place.* (Ḳ.) — هَدَأَ, (inf. n. هُدُوْءٌ, TA,) ‡ *He died.* (Ḳ.) = هَدِئَ, aor. ـَ, (Ḳ,) inf. n. هَدَأٌ, (TA,) i. q. جَنِئَ, *He had a curving back, &c.:* (Ḳ:) or *he had depressed and even shoulders, inclining towards the breast; not erect, or elevated:* (Lth, and others:) or *he was humpbacked.* (Ṣ, TA.) — هَدِئَ *It* (a camel's hump) *was bent by much lading,* (Ḳ,) *and had its soft hair* (وَبَر) *sticking upon it, without its being wounded.* (TA.)

4. اهدأ *He rendered quiet, still, motionless, silent.* (Ḳ, TA.) — لَا أَهْدَأَهُ اللّٰهُ *May God not give him rest from his labour, or fatigue!* (Ḳ.) — هَدَأَ ▾ الصَّبِىَّ, and اهدأه, [the latter only I find mentioned in one copy of the Ṣ: but both are mentioned in another, as well as in the TA:] *He patted the child with his hand, and quieted him, that he might sleep:* (Ṣ, TA:) or, accord. to Az, اهدأت صَبِيَّهَا signifies *She spoke soothingly to her child, and quieted him, that he might sleep:* and مُهْدَأٌ is a child *thus soothed.* (T.) — Accord. to IAạr, مهدأ in the following verse of 'Adee Ibn-Zeyd, [quoted in the Ṣ,]

• شَئِزٌ جَنْبِى كَأَنِّى مُهْدَأٌ •
• جَعَلَ القَيْنُ عَلَى الدَّفِّ إِبَرْ •

signifies a child *soothed in order that he may go to sleep.* Others read it as an inf. n. (TA.) = اهدأ ‡ *He wore out* a garment. (A.) — اهدأه اللّٰه *God made it* (a shoulder) *to be in the state described in the explanation of the word* أَهْدَأُ. (Ḳ.) — اهدأه *It* (old age, Ḳ, or beating, TA) *rendered him what is termed* أَهْدَأُ. (Ḳ.)

هَدْءٌ: see 1. — أَتَانَا بَعْدَ هَدْءٍ مِنَ اللَّيْلِ, (Ṣ, Ḳ,) and ▾ هُدُوْءٍ, (Ḳ,) and ▾ هَدْأَةٍ, (Ṣ, Ḳ,) and ▾ مَهْدَإٍ, and ▾ هَدِىٍّ, and ▾ هُدُوْءٍ, (Ḳ; the last is also an inf. n. and a pl.; TA,) ‡ *He came to us after a period, or portion, of the night;* (Ṣ, TA;) or *after about a third or fourth part of the night had elapsed,* (Ṣ, TA,) *when men were asleep,* (Ṣ,) or *at rest, and the night, and the foot of the passenger, were still:* (Sb, Ḳ:) or هَدْءٌ is the *first third part* of the night; *from the commencement to the third,* (Ḳ,) *when it begins to be still.* (TA.) = هَدْءٌ and هَدْىٌ (in which the ى is said to be substituted for ء, TA) *Way, or manner, of life.* (AHeyth, Ḳ.) = مَرَرْتُ بِرَجُلٍ هَدْئِكَ مِنْ رَجُلٍ i. q. هَدْكَ: (see art. هد:) the latter is that which is commonly known and approved. (Ez-Zejjájee.)

هُدُوْءٌ: see هَدْءٌ.

هَدَأٌ *Smallness of a camel's hump, occasioned by his being much laden.* (Ḳ.) It is less than what is termed حنب [a word app. incorrectly written, but which I am unable to correct]. (TA.)

هَدْأَةٌ *Quiet; stillness; rest from motion; silence.* (Lḥ.) = See هَدْءٌ, and أَهْدَأُ.

مَا لَهُ هَدْأَةُ لَيْلَةٍ, (Ḳ,) mentioned by Lḥ, but not explained by him: thought by ISd to mean *He has not a night's food:* (and so accord. to the Ḳ:) i.e., what may quiet his hunger or sleeplessness or anxiety. (TA.)

هُدَأَةٌ *A kind of run.* (Ḳ.)

أَتَانَا هُدُوْءًا ‡ *He came to us after a sleep:* (Ṣ:) *after men were at rest, and sleeping.* (TA.) = See هَدْءٌ.

هَدِىٌّ: see هَدْءٌ.

هُدَأَةٌ *A slender* horse: (Ḳ:) generally said to be a term peculiarly applied to the male only: but said by some to be common to the male and the female. (MF.)

هُوَ أَهْدَأُ مِمَّا كَانَ ‡ *He is more quiet,* or *more at rest, than he was:* i. e., *he is dead.* From a trad. Said by Umm-Suleym to Aboo-Ṭalḥah, respecting her son, to comfort the heart of his father. (TA.) = أَهْدَأُ i. q. أَجْنَأُ, *Having a curving back, &c.:* (Ḳ:) *humpbacked:* (Ṣ:) or a person *having the shoulders depressed, and even, and inclining towards the breast; not erect* or *elevated:* fem. هَدْآءُ: you also say مَنْكِبٌ أَهْدَأُ *a shoulder such as is described immediately above:* and أَهْدَأُ a *crooked* man: (Lth, and others:) also a shoulder *of which the upper part is swollen,* or *filled with fat and flesh, and its strength relaxed.* (Ḳ: in some copies of which we read استرخى: in others, حمله: [the former is the reading that I adopt].) — هَدْآءُ (so in the CḲ and a MS. copy: in the TA, ▾ هَدْأَةٌ, [which seems to be an error];) A she-camel *having her hump bent by much lading,* (Ḳ,) *and the soft hair* (وَبَر) *sticking upon it, without its being wounded.* (TA.)

مَهْدَأٌ: see هَدْءٌ.

مُهْدَأٌ: see 4.

مُهْدِئٌ *Still; motionless.* (TA, in art. خمد.)

مُهْدَأَةٌ *State, or condition.* (Ṣ.)

تَرَكْتُهُ عَلَى مُهَيْدِئَتِهِ *I left him in the state,* or *condition, wherein he was:* (Aṣ, Ṣ, Ḳ:) dim. of مَهْدَأَةٌ. (Ṣ.)

هدب

1. هَدَبَهُ, aor. ـِ, *He cut it; or cut it off.* (Ḳ, TA.) See also هَدَّبَ. — هَدَبَ, (aor. ـِ, inf. n. هَدْبٌ, Ṣ,) *He milked* a camel: (ISk, Ṣ, Ḳ:) or *he milked* any animal *with the ends of his fingers.*

(IKtt.) — هَدَبَ (Ṣ, Ḳ,) aor. ـِ ; or ▼ هدّب, inf. n. تَهْدِيبٌ ; and ▼ اهتدب ; (TA ;) *He plucked*, or *gathered*, fruit; (Ṣ, Ḳ,) or [the kind of leaves called] هَدَبٌ. (TA.) = هَدِبَ, (inf. n. هَدَبٌ, TA ;) and ▼ اهدب ; *It* (a tree) *had long and pendulous branches*, or *twigs*. (Ḳ.) The latter verb is explained by IKtt as signifying *It* (a tree) *had numerous branches*. (TA.) This is not derived from the هَدَب of the أَرْطَى and the like. (AḤn.) — هَدِبَتِ العَيْنُ, aor. ـَ, (inf. n. هَدَبٌ, TA,) *The eye had long lashes*. (Ḳ.)

2 : see 1. = هدّب السَّوْطَ [?] *i.q.* عَذَّبَ, q.v. (A, in TA, voce عذّب. q.v.)

4 : see 1. — اهدب *It* (a tree) *produced*, or *put forth, its* هَدَب. (TA.)

5. تهدّب [*It* (a part of a cloud) *hung down like the unwoven end, or extremity, of a garment*]. (Ṣ.) See هَيْدَبٌ.

8 : see 1.

هُدْبٌ and ▼ هُدُبٌ, (Ḳ,) the latter a dial. form of the former, (TA,) coll. gen. ns., and ▼ هَيْدَبٌ, (Ḳ,) also a coll. gen. n., (TA,) and ▼ هُدَّابٌ, [likewise a coll. gen. n.,] and ▼ هُدْبَةٌ, [which is rather the n. un. of هُدْبٌ,] (TA,) of a garment, or piece of cloth, *i.q.* خَمْلٌ : (Ḳ : in like manner, ▼ هُدْبَةٌ and ▼ هُدُبَةٌ are explained in the Ṣ by خَمْلَةٌ :) or rather, The [*fringe*, or] *unwoven end*, or *extremity*, of a garment, or of a piece of cloth ; its *end*, or *extremity, that has not been woven* : or *an end*, or *extremity, consisting of warp without woof* : sometimes it is twisted, and [as it forms *a fringe*,] it preserves the edge [of the woven part] of the the garment, &c. : (whereas خمل signifies the "nap, or villous substance," of a garment, &c. : [such is the meaning of the words ما يتخلّل الثوب كله كالزِّئْبِرِ : this is what is generally meant by خمل :] and this is mostly in what are called قَطَائِفُ : MF :) or the *extremity* of a garment, &c. *next* [*the part called*] *the* طُرَّة : (TA :) or the هدبة of a garment, &c., is the *same as the* طُرَّة : (Mṣb :) n. un. of the first word, (هُدْبٌ or هُدُبٌ,) with ة : (Ḳ :) so too of هيدب, (TA,) [and of هدّاب]. The pl. of هُدْبَةٌ is هُدَبٌ. (Mṣb.) — هُدْبٌ, (Ḳ,) or هُدْبُ العَيْنِ, (Ṣ,) and ▼ هُدُبٌ, (Ḳ,) which is a dial. form of هدب, (TA,) coll. gen. ns., The *eye-lashes* ; the *hairs that grow upon the edges of the eyelids* : (Ṣ, Ḳ :) n. un. with ة : (Ḳ :) pl. أَهْدَابٌ. (Mṣb.)

هَدَبٌ [generally signifies *slender sprigs, like strings, garnished with minute, amplexicaul, appressed, acute leaves, overlying one another like the scales of a fish* : see عَبَلٌ :] the *branches*, or *twigs*, of the أَرْطَى and similar trees (Ḳ) that have no leaves : a coll. gen. n., of which the n. un. is with ة ; and the pl., أَهْدَابٌ. (TA.) [The *foliage of the cypress and tamarisk*, and *the like* :] *leaves of a tree that are permanent*, (*and that have not a projecting nerve along the middle*, TA,) *as those of the cypress* (Ḳ) *and tamarisk and* سَمُر. (TA.) *Those parts of a plant that are not* وَرَق, *but that have the place of* وَرَق : (AḤn, Ḳ :) or *any* وَرَق *that have not width* ; (Ṣ, Ḳ ;) *as those of the* أَثْل *and* سَرْو *and* أَرْطَى *and* طَرْفَآء : (Ṣ :) as also ▼ هُدَّابٌ, (Ṣ, Ḳ,) both of which are coll. gen. ns., of which the ns. un. are with ة : pl. أَهْدَابٌ, (Ḳ,) which is a regular pl. of هَدَبٌ ; (TA ;) and ▼ هُدَّابٌ : (Ḳ, accord. to the TA : but in a MS. copy, هُدَّابَةٌ ; and in the CḲ, هَدَّابَةٌ :) but in the M, هُدَّابٌ is said to be a noun signifying the هُدْب of a garment, &c., and the هَدَب of the أَرْطَى. (TA.) Az says, that عَبَلٌ is precisely the same as هَدَبٌ. (TA.) — ▼ هُدَّابٌ is also said to signify *Inclining branches, or twigs*. (TA.) — Also, ▼ هُدَّابُ النَّخْلِ *Palm-branches* ; syn. سَعَفُهُ. (Ṣ.) = أَهْدَابٌ is said to be used by Aboo-Dhu-eyb, in the phrase سَبِطُ الاهداب, as signifying The *shoulder-blades* : but IṢd, who mentions this, denies its correctness. (TA.)

هَدِبٌ A horse *having a long forelock*. The هُدْبَانٌ or هِدْبَانٌ [pl. of هَدِبٌ, but whether هدبان is not shown,] are among those horses that are held in high estimation among the Arabs, and are distinguished as belonging to different tents, or houses. (TA.) — الهَدِبُ † *The lion*. (Ḳ.) But accord. to Lth, ▼ أَهْدَبُ, as an epithet applied to felt and the like, signifies † *Having long nap*, or *villous substance* : (TA :) and as an epithet applied to a lion, accord. to the A, it signifies ‡ *Having long shag* [or *shaggy hair*] : (TA :) whence it is seen that the correct word [applied to the lion] is أَهْدَبُ, [q.v.] not هَدِبٌ. (TA.)

هُدُبٌ and هُدُبَةٌ : see هُدْبٌ.

هُدْبَةٌ (TA) and ▼ هُدَبَةٌ (Kr, Ḳ) *A certain bird* : (Ḳ :) or *a small dust-coloured bird, resembling the* هَامَة, *except in being smaller than this latter*. (L.) El-Jáhidh says, The Arabs have not a name for that [kind of bird] which sees not in the night : it is that which is called شبكور [a Persian word, written شَبْكُور], more frequently than هدبة. (A.) = N. un. of هُدْبٌ, q.v.

هدبة [written without the syll. points ; probably هُدْبَةٌ ;] *A piece, part*, or *portion*. (TA.)

هُدَبَةٌ : see هُدْبَةٌ.

هُدُبٌ : see هَيْدَبٌ.

هُدَّابٌ : see هُدْبٌ and هَدَبٌ and هَيْدَبٌ.

هِنْدَبٌ (Ṣ, Ḳ, a word of a rare measure, TA,) and ▼ هِنْدَبَآءُ (Ḳ : [but it is not there said whether it be imperfectly or perfectly declinable : accord. to Ibn-Buzurj, as mentioned in the TA, it is fem., and therefore imperfectly decl. : but from the ns. un. given below, it appears to be masc., and perfectly decl. : probably, therefore, all the forms of the word ending with long or short alif may be correctly pronounced without, and with, tenween :]) and ▼ هِنْدَبَى (ISk, Ṣ, Mṣb) and هِنْدِبَآءُ and هِنْدِبَى ; (Az, Ṣ, Ḳ, Mṣb ;) but the word which is used by most of the Arabs of the desert is the first : (Az :) IKt only mentions the third form : (Mṣb :) also ▼ هِنْدَبَاةٌ ; (Ṣ ;) or [هندبى and هندبا are coll. gen. ns., and] هِنْدَبَاةٌ is a n. un., (AḤn, Ḳ,) as also هندباءة : (AḤn, TA :) *A certain leguminous plant*, (Ṣ, Ḳ,) *well known*, (Ḳ,) *of the description termed* أَحْرَار ; [i.e., *of a slender and soft nature, and eaten crude* ;] (TA ;) [*lichorium, intybus and endivia* ; *wild and garden-succory, and endive* : also called in the present day شِكُّورِيَة :] *a plant of middling temperament*, (مُعْتَدِلَة,) *useful for the stomach and the liver and the spleen, when eaten* ; *and for the sting of a scorpion, when applied externally, with its roots* : he who cooks it errs more than he who washes it [and so uses it]. (Ḳ.) F mentions the names of this plant in art. هندب, as though the ن were a radical letter, which no one asserts it to be : J [and others], in art. هدب. (TA.)

هِنْدَبَاةٌ and هِنْدِبَآءُ, هِنْدَبَى, see هِنْدَبٌ.

هَيْدَبٌ : see هُدْبٌ. — [Its pl., هَيَادِبُ, is also applied to *Filaments, capillaments*, or *fringe-like appertenances*, of a flower.] — هَيْدَبٌ ‡ *A cloud*, or *clouds, hanging down*, (Ḳ,) *approaching* [*the earth*], *like the* هُدْب [or *unwoven end* or *extremity*,] *of a* (قَطِيفَة) : (TA :) or the هيدب of a cloud is its ذَيْل [or *skirt*] : (Ḳ :) or *what hangs down*, of it, *like the unwoven end*, or *extremity, of a garment*, (مَا تَهَدَّبَ مِنْهُ,) *when it is about to rain, resembling strings*. (Ṣ.) — هَيْدَبٌ ‡ *A pendulous* (or *flabby*, TA,) *pubes* of a woman : (Ḳ :) likened to the هيدب of a cloud. (TA.) — هَيْدَبٌ ‡ *Tears flowing in a continued succession*. (Ḳ.) On the authority of Lth, who cites the following verse :

* بِدَمْعٍ ذِى حَزَازَاتٍ *
* عَلَى الخَدَّيْنِ ذِى هَيْدَبْ *

[*With hot tears upon the cheeks, flowing in a continued succession*]. But it is said in the L, I have not heard هيدب used as an epithet applied to rain falling continuously, nor as an epithet applied to tears ; and the verse which Lth adduces as an authority is forged. (TA.) —

هَيْدَبٌ (Ṣ, Ḳ) and ↓ هُدُبٌ and ↓ هُدَّابٌ (Ḳ) *Impotent in speech or actions*; syn. عَيِىٌّ; (in one copy of the Ḳ غَبِىٌّ, or *unintelligent*; TA;) *and heavy, or dull*: (Ṣ, Ḳ:) or هيدب signifies *impotent in speech or actions; dull of speech and understanding; heavy*: and *hard*, or *churlish; heavy, or dull; having much hair*: (Az:) or, as some say, one *who has upon him dangling strings, or the like, hanging from the suspensory of a sword, or other thing, and resembling the* هيدب *of a cloud*: or, as some say, this word signifies *stupid; foolish; of little sense*: and ↓ هدبٌ, *weak*. (TA.)

هَيْذَبَى *A kind of pace of a horse, in which exertion, or energy, is employed; a certain hard pace of a horse*. (Ḳ.) See also هَيْذَبَى.

رَجُلٌ هَيْدَبِىُّ الكَلَامِ † *A man of much speech, or talk; of many words*. (Ḳ.) App. from the هَيْدَب of a cloud. (TA.)

أَهْدَبُ A man *having long*, or *large, eyelashes*. (Ḳ.) Lth explains it by the words طَوِيلُ أَشْفَارِ العَيْنِ كَثِيرُهَا; [and J in a similar manner;] but Az disapproves of this expression, because اشفار العين signifies "the edges of the eyelids," whence the eyelashes grow: (TA:) أَهْدَبُ الأَشْفَارِ, and ↓ هَدِبُ الاشفار, [the same;] *having long eyelashes*. (TA.) عَيْنٌ هَدْبَآءُ *An eye having long lashes*. (TA.) — شَجَرَةٌ هَدْبَآءُ *A tree having long and pendulous branches*. (Ḳ.) — أُذُنٌ هَدْبَآءُ ‡ *A pendulous, flabby, ear*. (TA, from a trad.) — لِحْيَةٌ هَدْبَآءُ ‡ *A lank, not crisp, beard*: and so ↓ عُثْنُونٌ هَدِبٌ. (TA.) — نَسْرٌ أَهْدَبُ ‡ *A vulture having long feathers which reach to the ground*. (TA.) See هَدِبٌ.

مُهَدَّبٌ *Having an unwoven end, or extremity*; syn. ذُو هُدَّابٍ: occurring as an epithet applied to the kind of stuff called دِمَقْس. (TA.)

هدبد

هُدَبِدٌ and ↓ هُدَابِدٌ *Very thick* milk: (Ṣ, L, Ḳ:) *sour and thick* milk. (L.) The former word is a contraction of the latter. (Ṣ.) — Also the former, *Smallness of the eyes, and weakness of the sight*; or *nyctalopia*, or *the seeing better by night than in the day, and in a cloudy day than in a clear one*; syn. خَفَشٌ: (L, Ḳ:) or (so in the L, in the Ḳ, and) *weakness of the eye*, (Ḳ,) or, *of the sight*: (L:) or (so in the L; in the Ḳ, and) [*that weakness of the sight which is termed*] عَشًا, [which is *a badness of sight by night and day*; or *the quality of seeing by day but not by night*,] (El-Mufaddal, L, Ḳ,) also termed شُبْكَرَةٌ: (El-Mufaddal, L:) or *weakness of the sight, with a flowing of the tears at most times*; syn. عَمَشٌ: (Ṣ, L:) or this is a mistake: (Ḳ:) or *any injurious affection of the eye*. (M, F.) — Also, *Weak-sighted*: (L, Ḳ:) an epithet applied to a man. (L.) — Also, *Black gum* (L, Ḳ) *which flows from trees*. (L.)

هُدَابِدٌ: see هُدَبِدٌ.

هدج

1. هَدَجَ, aor. ـِ, inf. n. هَدَجَانٌ (Ṣ, Ḳ) and هَدَاجٌ (Ḳ) and هَدْجٌ, (TA,) ‡ *He walked gently, in a weak manner*: (TA:) or *he walked in the manner of an old man*; (Ṣ, Ḳ;) *and the like*: (TA:) or *he* (an old man) *walked with short steps*: or *walked hastily, without desiring to do so*: (TA:) or *he walked with unintermitting steps*: (Aṣ:) or *he walked in a shaking manner, by reason of old age*. (IAạr.) — هَدَجَ, (Ṣ,) aor. ـِ, inf. n. هَدَجَانٌ; and ↓ استهدج; (TA;) *He* (an ostrich) *walked, or went*, (or *ran*, TA,) *in a tremulous manner*. (Ṣ, TA.) — هَدَجَتِ القِدْرُ ‡ *The cooking-pot boiled vehemently*. (TA.) — هَدَجَتْ, (Ṣ,) inf. n. هَدْجٌ, (L,) *She* (a camel) *yearned towards her young one*; حَنَّتْ عَلَى وَلَدِهَا; (Ṣ, L;) as also ↓ تهدّجت; (L;) [*and, app., uttered the cry produced by yearning towards her young one*: see below:] or the latter signifies *she was affectionate to her young one*. (Ṣ, Ḳ.) — Also, inf. n. as above, † *It* (the wind) *made a sound*; syn. حَنَّتْ and صَوَّتَتْ; from هدجت النّاقة. (L.)

2. هدّجت ‡ *She* (a camel) *became high and big in the hump, so that it bore a resemblance to a* هَوْدَج. (TA.)

5. تهدّج *It* (the voice, or a sound) *became much intercepted, or interrupted*, (تَقَطَّعَ) *with a tremulous manner*. (Ṣ, Ḳ.) See 1. — تهدّجوا عَلَيْهِ *They made apparent, or manifest, his gracious actions, or qualities, or his favours, or kindnesses*. (TA.)

10: see 1.

هَدَجَةٌ, (a subst., L,) The *yearning*, or the *cry produced by yearning towards her young one, of a camel*; حَنِينُ النَّاقَةِ: (Ḳ:) or the *yearning of a she-camel towards her young one*; حَنِينُ النَّاقَةِ عَلَى وَلَدِهَا. (Ṣ, L.)

هَدَجْدَجٌ: see هَدَّاجٌ.

هَدُوجٌ: see مِهْدَاجٌ — قِدْرٌ هَدُوجٌ ‡ *A cooking-pot that boils vehemently*: (TA:) or, *quickly*. (Ḳ.)

هَدَّاجٌ and ↓ هَدَجْدَجٌ One *who walks in the manner termed* هَدَجَان: see 1. (Ḳ.) — An ostrich *that so walks, or runs*. (Ṣ, TA.) One says ظَلِيمٌ هَدَّاجٌ, and نَعَامٌ هَدَّاجٌ and هَوَادِجُ: (TA:) [the last is pl. of ↓ هَادِجَةٌ, fem. act. part. n. of هَدَجَ]. — Also, the ↓ latter, *An ostrich*: so called because it so walks, or runs: (TA:) [and so ↓ هَادِجَةٌ, pl. هَوَادِجُ, as in the following example.] نَظَرْتُ إِلَى الهَوَادِجِ عَلَى الهَوَادِجِ [*I looked at the women's camel-litters upon the* camels like *ostriches*]. (A.)

هَدَّاجٌ: see هَادِجَةٌ.

هَوْدَجٌ [*A kind of camel-vehicle for women*;] the *vehicle of the Arab women of the desert*: (JK:) *a kind of vehicle for women*, (Ṣ, Ḳ,) *having a dome-like top* (مُقَبَّب); *and one not having such a top*: (Ṣ:) or [*a camel-vehicle for women*] *made with staves, over which are put pieces of wood, and covered with a dome-like top*: (M:) or *a camel-vehicle* (مَحْمِل) *having a dome-like top* (قُبَّة), *covered with pieces of cloth, in which women ride*: (Et-Towsheeḥ:) pl. هَوَادِجُ. (TA.) [See مَحَارَةٌ and مَحْمِلٌ.]

مِهْدَاجٌ A she-camel *that yearns*, or *that utters the cry produced by yearning towards her young one*: (Ḳ:) or *that yearns towards her young one*: (Ṣ, L:) as also ↓ هَدُوجٌ. (TA.) — Also, † A wind *that has a sound*; لَهَا حَنِينٌ: (Ṣ, L:) from حَنَّتِ النَّاقَةُ. (L.)

مُسْتَهْدِجٌ *Haste*. (Ḳ.)

مُسْتَهْدِجٌ *Hasty*. (Ḳ.)

هدر

1. هَدَرَ, aor. ـِ (Ṣ, A, Mṣb, Ḳ) and ـُ, (Mṣb, Ḳ,) inf. n. هَدْرٌ (Ṣ, Mṣb, Ḳ) and هَدَرٌ, (Ḳ,) or the latter is a simple subst., (Mṣb,) *It* (a man's blood, Ṣ, A, Mṣb, Ḳ, or another thing, Ḳ) *went for nothing*; [meaning, in the case of blood, *unretaliated, and uncompensated by a mulct*; as shown below, voce هَدَرٌ;] *it was*, or *became, of no account, null*, or *void*; (Ṣ, A, Mṣb, Ḳ;) as also ↓ اهدر. (Mṣb.) = هَدَرَهُ, (A, Mṣb, Ḳ,) aor. ـُ, (Mṣb,) *He* (a man, Mṣb, Ḳ, or the Sultán, Ṣ, A,) *made it* (a man's blood) *to go for nothing*; [meaning, *unretaliated, and uncompensated by a mulct*;] *he made it to be of no account*; (A, Mṣb, Ḳ;) as also ↓ اهدره; (Ṣ, A, Mṣb, Ḳ;) which means *he made it* (a man's blood) *allowable to be taken, or shed*. (Ṣ, TA.) Thus these two verbs are trans. as well as intrans. (Mṣb.) It is said in a trad., مَنِ اطَّلَعَ فِى دَارٍ بِغَيْرِ إِذْنٍ فَقَدْ هُدِرَتْ عَيْنُهُ [*Whoso looketh into a house without permission, his eye shall be allowed to be put out*; or] *the putting out of his eye shall go for nothing, unretaliated, and uncompensated by a mulct*. (TA.) One says also, هَدَرْتَنِى بِإِسْقَاطِ الحَدِّ عَنِّى [*Thou hast made me* (meaning my offence) *to pass unnoticed*, or *hast taken no account of*

me, by annulling in respect of me the prescribed castigation]. (Ḳ, art. تبرج.) And El-'Ajjáj says,

• وَهَدَرَ الجِدُّ مِنَ النَّاسِ الهَدَرْ •

which El-Báhilee explains as meaning, *And the worthless people have made good fortune to become of no account.* (TA.) ═ هَدَرَ, (Ṣ, Ḳ,) aor. ـِ (Ḳ) [and app. ـُ also], inf. n. هَدِيرٌ (Ṣ, Ḳ) and هَدْرٌ (Ḳ) and هُدُورٌ, (TA,) said of a camel, (Ṣ, Ḳ,) that is advanced in age, (Ṣ, in art. نقض,) [*He brayed*; i. e.,] *he reiterated his voice in his* حَنْجَرَة [or *windpipe*, or *the head of his windpipe*]: (Ṣ:) or *he uttered his voice, not in a* شِقْشِقَة [q. v.]: (Ḳ:) and † هدّر, (Ṣ, Ḳ,) inf. n. تَهْدِيرٌ, (Ṣ,) signifies the same: (Ṣ, Ḳ:) Z mentions also تَهْدَارٌ as an inf. n. of هَدَرَ said of a stallion, [meaning a stallion-camel.] (TA.) — Hence the saying, (TA,) هُوَ يَهْدِرُ فِى مَنْطِقِهِ, and فِى خُطْبَتِهِ, ‡ [*He is sonorous and fluent in his speech*, and *in his oration*:] and هَدَرَتْ شِقْشِقَتُهُ ‡ [*His utterance was sonorous and fluent.*] (A, TA.) — هَدَرَ is also said of a calf, [signifying, † *He lowed.*] (TA, art. كت, from the Nh.) — Also, of a lion, [signifying, † *He roared.*] (Ṣ, TA, voce قَبْقَبَ.) — Also هَدَرَ, (Ṣ, A, Mṣb, Ḳ,) aor. ـِ (Mṣb, Ḳ) and ـُ, (Mṣb,) inf. n. هَدِيرٌ (Ṣ, IḲṭṭ, Mṣb, TA) and هَدْرٌ and تَهْدَارٌ, (Ḳ,) said of a pigeon, ‡ *It uttered a cry*: (Ṣ, Ḳ:) or *cooed*, syn. قَرْقَرَ, (A,) or سَجَعَ, (Mṣb,) *and reiterated its voice*, or *cry, in its* حَنْجَرَة [or *windpipe*, or *the head of its windpipe*]: (A:) its cry being apparently likened to the هَدِير of the camel: and هَدَلَ signifies the same. (TA.) — Also هَدَرَ said of a boy, (Aṣ,) when he desires to speak, being young, or little, (Abu-s-Semeyda',) † *He uttered a sound*, or *cry*: as also هَدَلَ. (Aṣ, TA.) — It is also said of thunder; inf. n. هَدِيرٌ; signifying, ‡ *It made a* [*loud*, or *rumbling*,] *sound*, or *noise*. (A.) — You say also, of شَرَاب [or wine], هَدَرَ, (Ṣ, Ḳ,) aor. ـِ, inf. n. هَدْرٌ and تَهْدَارٌ, (Ṣ, TA,) meaning, † *It fermented*; syn. غَلَى. (Ṣ, Ḳ.) And هَدَرَتْ جَرَّةُ النَّبِيذِ, (TA,) aor. ـِ, (A, TA,) inf. n. هَدِيرٌ and تَهْدَارٌ, (TA,) ‡ [*The jar of* نبيذ *fermented.*] El-Akhṭal says, describing wine,

• كُمَّتْ ثَلَاثَةَ أَحْوَالٍ بِطِينَتِهَا •

• حَتَّى إِذَا صَرَّحَتْ مِنْ بَعْدِ تَهْدَارِ •

[*It was stopped three years with its lump of clay, until, when it became free from froth, after fermenting*]. (Ṣ, TA.)

2. هدّر, said of a camel: see 1.

4. اهدر: see هَدَرَ ═ اهدرهُ: see هَدَرَهُ.

6. تهادروا *They made one another's blood to go for nothing*; [meaning, *unretaliated, and uncompensated by a mulct*;] *they made it to be of no account.* (Ḳ, TA.)

هَدْرٌ: see هَدَرٌ: ═ and see also هَادِرٌ.

هُدَرٌ: see هَادِرٌ.

هَدَرٌ, a subst. from هَدَرَ in the first of the senses explained above. (Mṣb.) You say, ذَهَبَ دَمُهُ هَدَرًا, (Ṣ, A, Mṣb,) and † هَدْرًا, (Ṣ, Mṣb,) *His blood went for nothing*, or *as a thing of no account*, (Ṣ, A, Mṣb,) *unretaliated*, (Ṣ, Mṣb,) *and uncompensated by a mulct.* (Ṣ, TA.) — Also, applied to blood, &c., *A thing that goes for nothing*; [meaning, in the case of blood, *unretaliated, and uncompensated by a mulct*;] *what is of no account, ineffectual, null*, or *void*; (A, Ḳ;) [as also جُبَارٌ.] You say, دِمَاؤُهُمْ هَدَرٌ بَيْنَهُمْ *Their blood* (lit. bloods) *is made to go for nothing*, or *to be of no account, among them*: (Ḳ,* TA:) *is allowed to be taken*, or *shed*. (TA.) — See also هَادِرٌ.

هُدَرَةٌ: } see هَادِرٌ; the former, in two places.
هُدَرَةٌ: }

جَرَّةٌ هَدُورٌ ‡ [*A jar of wine or* نَبِيذ *fermenting much*]. (TA.)

فَحْلٌ هَدَّارٌ [*A stallion-camel that brays much*]. (TA.) See also هَادِرٌ. — رَعْدٌ هَدَّارٌ ‡ [*Loud*, or *rumbling, thunder*]. (A.)

هَادِرٌ, applied to a man, ‡ *Low; ignoble; mean; of no account; worthless*; (Ḳ;) as also † هَدْرٌ, (Kr, Ḳ,) and † هُدَرَةٌ; (Ṣ, Ḳ;) which last is also applied to a woman: (Ḳ, TA: [in the former of which it seems to be implied that هُدَرَةٌ and † هِدَرَةٌ are also applied, each, to a man and to a woman; but it appears from what is said in the TA that this is not the case:]) pl. هَدَرَةٌ and هُدَرَةٌ and هِدَرَةٌ; the first of which is the most agreeable with analogy, like كَفَرَةٌ, pl. of كَافِرٌ; the second being of a measure exclusively belonging to words which are unsound [in the last radical letter], as in the instances of غُزَاةٌ and قُضَاةٌ, [originally غُزَوَةٌ and قُضَيَةٌ, pls. of غَازٍ and قَاضٍ,] unless, indeed, it be a quasi-pl. n.; and some disapprove it, finding fault with IAạr who relates it: the third, moreover, is not a pl. of a form, [regularly] belonging to a sing. of the measure فَاعِلٌ, whether sound or unsound: (ISd, TA:) [or, accord. to Sb, it is a quasi-pl. n.:] or it is pl. of † هِدْرٌ, (TA,) which signifies a *heavy* man, (Ḳ, TA,) *in whom is no good*; analogous with قِرَدَةٌ, pl. of قِرْدٌ: (TA:) and † هَدَرٌ [a quasi-pl. n. of هَادِرٌ, like as خَدَمٌ is of خَادِمٌ,] signifies *low, ignoble*, or *mean*, people, *in whom is no good.* (TA.) You say, هُمْ هَدَرَةٌ, (Ṣ, A, Ḳ,) and هُدَرَةٌ, (IAạr, TṢ, Ḳ,) and هِدَرَةٌ, (IAạr, ISd, Ḳ,) ‡ *They are low, ignoble*, or *mean, people; of no account*, or *worthless.* (IAạr, Ṣ, A,* Ḳ, &c.) ═ [*A braying* camel: fem. with ة: pl. of the latter, هَوَادِرُ. You say,] إِبِلٌ هَوَادِرُ [*Braying camels*;] *camels reiterating their voices in their* حَنَاجِر. (Ṣ.) See also مُهْدِرٌ, and مُبَحْثِرٌ, and هَدَّارٌ. — [Hence the saying,] فُلَانٌ فَحْلٌ هَادِرٌ ‡ [app. *Such a one is a vigorous orator of sonorous and fluent speech*]. (A.)

كَالْمُهْدِرِ فِى الْعُنَّةِ [*Like the brayer in the enclosure of wood*, or *canes*, or *trees*]: a proverb: applied to a man who raises a cry and clamour which is followed by nothing, (Ṣ, A,*) or who raises a cry and clamour and does not make his saying or action to have effect: (A, Ḳ:) like the camel that is confined in the enclosure of wood or canes or trees, prevented from covering, and brays. (Ṣ, Ḳ.)

[هدف, &c.

See Supplement.]

هذ

1. هَذَّ, aor. ـُ, (Ṣ, L,) inf. n. هَذٌّ (Ṣ, L, Ḳ) and هَذَذٌ (L, Ḳ) and هُذَاذٌ, (Ḳ, TA,) or هَذَاذٌ, (CḲ, [which latter is the correct reading, (see هَذَاذَيْكَ,) and, accord. to the JK, is a quasi-inf. n.],) *He cut quickly*, or *cut off quickly*; as also † اهتذّ: (Ṣ, L, Ḳ:) or *he cut* anything. (Ḳ.) — هَذَّهُ بِالسَّيْفِ, inf. n. هَذٌّ, *He cut him*, or *it, in pieces with the sword.* (L.) — هَذَّ, aor. ـُ, (Ṣ, L,) inf. n. هَذٌّ (Ṣ, L, Ḳ) and هَذَذٌ (L, Ḳ) and هُذَاذٌ, (Ḳ, TA,) or هَذَاذٌ; (CḲ [see above];) and † اهتذّ; (Ḳ;) ‡ *He read*, or *recited, quickly.* (Ṣ, L, Ḳ.) You say, هَذَّ قِرَاءَتَهُ, aor. ـُ, inf. n. هَذٌّ, ‡ *He performed his reading*, or *recitation, quickly.* (Mṣb.) And هُوَ يَهُذُّ القُرْآنَ ‡ *He reads*, or *recites, the Ḳur-án rapidly and uninterruptedly*: (Ṣ, A, L:) and in like manner, الحَدِيثَ *the narrative*; (Ṣ, L;) and الشِّعْرَ *the poetry.* (L.)

8: see 1.

هَذٌّ, or هُذٌّ: see هَذُوذٌ.

هَذُوذٌ (Ṣ, L, Ḳ) and هَذَّاذٌ (Ḳ) and † هَذٌّ, (L, CḲ,) or † هُذٌّ, (as in some copies of the Ḳ, and in the TA,) and † هَذْهَاذٌ and هُذَاهِذٌ, (L, Ḳ [the last in the CḲ هَذَاهِذٌ,]) *Sharp; quickly cutting*: (Ṣ, L, Ḳ:) the first, which is masc. and fem., and the second, applied to a knife; (Ṣ,* L;) and the last two, to a sword. (L.)

هَذَاذَيْكَ, (as Aṣ says, Ṣ) is said to people when you desire them to refrain, or forbear, or abstain, from a thing; as also هَجَاجَيْكَ; supposing [it to be addressed to] two [persons]; (Ṣ, L;) [but it is addressed to one;] meaning *Refrain thou! or forbear thou! or abstain thou!* (TA, art. هج.) 'Abd-Beni-l-Ḥas-ḥás says,

• إِذَا شُقَّ بُرْدٌ شُقَّ بِٱلْبُرْدِ مِثْلُهُ •
• هَذَاذَيْكَ حَتَّى لَيْسَ لِلْبُرْدِ لَابِسُ •

[*When a burd* (a kind of garment) *is rent, the like thereof is rent with the burd—refrain thou—so that there is no wearer of the burd,* it having been rent so as to fall off: but it seems more proper to render it here, *with rending after rending,* which is nearly the original signification, as will be presently shown; and, thus rendered, it does not interrupt the sentence]: the women assert that, when, in the act of concubitus, [app., for the first time,] somewhat of the garment of the man is rent, love continues between the pair; but otherwise, that they desert each other. (Ṣ, L. [This verse is related with several variations: see another reading of it voce دَوَالَيْكَ, in art. دول.]) — ضَرْبًا هَذَاذَيْكَ *With a beating, or striking, with cutting after cutting;* (L, Ḳ;) ♦ هَذًّا بَعْدَ هَذٍّ, (L,) i.e., قَطْعًا بَعْدَ قَطْعٍ: (L, Ḳ:) or *with a beating,* or *striking, successively; uninterruptedly;* وِلَآءً تِبَاعًا. (JK.) — In the saying of the poet,

• فَبَاكَرَ مَخْتُومًا عَلَيْهِ سَيَاعُهُ •
• هَذَاذَيْكَ حَتَّى أَنْفَدَ الدَّنَّ أَجْمَعَا •

[in which, for انفد, in the L and TA, I substitute انفذ,] AḤn says, that it signifies هَذٌّ i.e., شُرْبًا بَعْدَ شُرْبٍ ,بَعْدَ هَذٍّ; the poet meaning *And he applied himself early to a jar full of wine, [with its mud-plaster sealed upon it, with drinking after drinking, until he exhausted all that was in the jar,]* and emptied it. (L.)

قَرَبٌ هَذْهَاذٌ † *A long and difficult night journey to water:* (L, Ḳ:) or *quick.* (JK, Ḳ.) — See هذوذ.

هَذَاذٌ: see هَذُوذٌ. — Also, † *A camel that outstrips others.* (Ḳ.)

هذأ

1. هَذَأَ, aor. ـَ, inf. n. هَذْءٌ, *He cut* a thing (Aṣ, Ṣ, Ḳ) [*quickly*], with a sword, &c. (TA.) It signifies a quicker act than does هَذَّ. (Ḳ.) — هَذَأَ *He destroyed* the enemy. (Ḳ, TA.) — هَذَأَهُ بِلِسَانِهِ, (Ḳ,* TA,) inf. n. هَذْءٌ, (TA,) *He hurt,* or *offended,* [or *cut,*] *him with his tongue;* (TA;) *made him to hear what he disliked.* (Ḳ.) — هَذَأَتِ الإِبِلُ *The camels fell down,* [and, app., *died,*] *one after another:* syn. تَسَاقَطَتْ. (Ḳ.) — هَذِئَ مِنَ البَرْدِ, [aor. ـَ,] *He perished of cold.* (Ḳ.) — هَذَأَ الكَلَامَ *He was loquacious, with error.* (TA.)

5. تهذّأ *It* (a wound, or an ulcer.) *became putrid,* or *rotten, and dissundered,* or *ragged.* (Ṣ, Ḳ.)

هَذَأَةٌ i.q. مِسْحَاةٌ [q.v., in arts. سحى and سحو.] (Ḳ.)

هَذَأٌ and ♦ هَذَّآءٌ *A sharp* sword, (TA [but the orthography is not quite clear].) [See also art. هذى.]

هَذَّآءٌ: see هَذَأٌ.

هَذَا: see art. ذا.

هذب

1. هَذَبَهُ, aor. ـِ, inf. n. هَذْبٌ, *He cut it;* or *cut it off:* (A, Ḳ:) like هَدَبَهُ. (TA.) — هَذَبَهُ, aor. ـُ, inf. n. هَذْبٌ; (Ḳ;) and ♦ هذّبه, inf. n. تَهْذِيبٌ; (Ṣ;) *He cleansed it; purified it; cleared it.* (Ṣ, Ḳ.) — هَذُبَ, aor. ـُ, inf. n. هَذْبٌ, *It was pure, clear.* (Ḳ: but only the inf. n. is there mentioned.) — مَا فِى مَوَدَّتِهِ هَذْبٌ *There is no purity in his love.* (TA.) — هَذَبَهُ, aor. ـِ, inf. n. هَذْبٌ; and ♦ هذّبه, (inf. n. تَهْذِيبٌ, TA); *He put it into a right, or proper, state; put it to rights; trimmed, adjusted, repaired, mended, amended, reformed,* or *improved, it.* (Ḳ.) — هَذَبَ النَّخْلَةَ *He trimmed the palm-tree by clearing it of the fibrous substance called* لِيف. (Ḳ.) — MF says, on the authority of the etymologists, that the original signification of ♦ تَهْذِيبٌ and هَذْبٌ is The *clearing,* or *trimming,* of trees, *by cutting off the extremities of the branches, in order that they may increase in growth and beauty;* that they were then used to signify the *cleansing,* or *purifying,* of anything; *and putting it into a right, or proper, state; trimming it;* or *adjusting it; and clearing it of any dirty* or *filthy things,* or *the like, mixed with it;* so that these became their proper meanings by general acceptation: and that they were then used to signify the *trimming and embellishing* of verse, *and clearing it of whatever might vitiate it in the opinion of the chaste in language, and the philologists:* but the truth is what is said in the L; that the original signification of تهذيب is the *clearing* the colocynth *of its pulp, and preparing its seeds so that they may lose their bitterness, and become sweet.* (TA.) = هَذَبَ, (aor. ـِ, inf. n. هَذْبٌ, TA,) *It* (a thing) *flowed.* (Ḳ.) — هَذَبَ, (aor. ـِ, TA,) inf. n. هَذْبٌ and هَذَابَةٌ; (Ḳ;) and ♦ اهذب, (Ḳ,) inf. n. إِهْذَابٌ; (Ṣ;) and ♦ هذّب, (Ḳ,) inf. n. تَهْذِيبٌ; (Ṣ;) and ♦ هَاذَبَ; (Ḳ;) *He* (a man, &c., Ḳ, as a horse in his running, and a bird in his flying, TA,) *was quick,* or *swift,* (Ḳ,) *in his pace* or *course:* (TA:) *he was quick in flying, in running, and in speech.* (Ṣ.) — هَذَبَ *He ran vehemently.* (Aṣ.) — يهذب الرُّكُوعَ [app. يُهَذِّبُ] *He makes the inclinations of his head and body* [in prayer] *in quick succession.* (TA, from a trad.) — See also art. هبد. — هَذَبَ القَوْمُ *The people were very noisy,* or *clamourous,* (Ḳ,) *and loquacious.* (TA.)

2: see 1. — هذّب, inf. n. تَهْذِيبٌ, *He trimmed* an arrow; or *shaped it with nicety, by the second operation:* the first operation is called تَشْذِيبٌ. (AḤn.) — هَذَّبَ عَنْهَا i.q. فَرَّقَ, accord. to Es-Sukkaree, who cites the following verse of one of the Hudhalees: (namely Aboo-Khirásh, L, art. طرد:)

• فَهَذَّبَ عَنْهَا مَا يَلِى البَطْنَ وَٱنْتَحَى •
• طَرِيدَةَ مَتْنٍ بَيْنَ عَجْبٍ وَكَاهِلِ •

[app., *He removed from her what was next the belly, and directed himself to a line of the back, between the rump-bone and withers*]. (TA.)

3: see 1.

4. اهذبت السَّحَابَةُ *The cloud poured forth* its water *quickly.* (Ḳ.) See 1.

5. تهذّب [*It became nicely, neatly,* or *properly, trimmed*]: said of a thing from which one has cut off whatever required to be cut off, so that it has become free from everything unseemly. (A, TA, art. حذف.) — تَهَذَّبْتُ عَلَى يَدِكَ [*I was,* or *have been, amended,* or *improved, by thy agency,* or *means*]. (A, TA, art. ثقف.)

حَمِيمٌ هَذَبٌ, after the manner of a rel. n., *A rain following vehement heat, that pours down quickly:* see 4: syn. ذُو إِهْذَابٍ. (TA.)

هَيْذَبَى *A kind of pace of a horse;* (Ṣ;) *like* هَيْدَبَى: (Ḳ:) a subst. from هَذَبَ "he was quick, or swift, in his pace." (TA.) The former is also mentioned by Az, in the T; IDrd only mentions the latter word. (TA.) — *A running with a leaning on one side.* Ex. مَشَى الهَيْذَبَى [*He went leaning on one side*]. (IAmb.) But for this some read مشى الهَوْبَذَى, which is equivalent to هيذبى. (TA.)

رَجُلٌ مُهَذَّبٌ ‡ *A man of purified natural dispositions,* or *manners,* or *morals;* (Ṣ, Ḳ;) *a man of integrity; free from vices,* or *faults.* (L.)

مُهَذِّبٌ *Quick,* or *swift,* [*in pace, &c.*]. (TA.) — المُهَذِّبُ is also a name of *The Devil;* who is also called المُذْهِبُ, meaning "he who embellishes, or gives a goodly appearance to, acts of disobedience [to God]." (Fr.)

إِبِلٌ مَهَاذِيبُ *Quick*, or *swift, camels.* (Ḳ.)

هذر

1. هَذَرَ كَلَامَهُ, aor. ـِ, (A, Ḳ,) inf. n. هَذْرٌ, (TA,) *His speech*, or *talk, was much*, or *abundant, and erroneous and false* or *vain* or *frivolous.* (A, Ḳ.) — هَذَرَ, aor. ـُ and ـِ, *He talked much; babbled; was loquacious*, or *garrulous:* (JK:) [or *he talked irrationally:*] or هَذَرَ فِى مَنْطِقِهِ, aor. ـُ and ـِ, inf. n. هَذْرٌ (Ṣ, Mṣb, Ḳ) and تَهْذَارٌ, (Ḳ,) which latter has an intensive signification, (TA,) *he confounded in his speech, and talked what was not fit* or *meet* or *proper:* (Mṣb:) or *he talked much and badly:* or *erroneously:* (Ḳ:) or *he talked nonsense; he talked irrationally, foolishly*, or *deliriously:* (Ṣ;) as also ▾ اهذر: (Ḳ:) and ▾ اهذر فى كَلَامِهِ *he talked much; babbled; was loquacious*, or *garrulous.* (Ṣ, TA.)

4: see 1, in two places.

لَا نَزْرٌ وَلَا هَذْرٌ *Not little nor much:* (TA:) or *not scanty*, so as to indicate impotence, *nor much and corrupt:* said of the speech of Moḥammad. (Ḳ, art. نزر.) [See هَذَرٌ, from which it is altered to assimilate it in form to نَزْرٌ.]

هَذَرٌ, a subst. from هَذَرَ فِى مَنْطِقِهِ, (Ṣ, Mṣb,) *Much talk; babble:* (JK:) or *nonsense;* or *irrational, foolish*, or *delirious, talk:* (Ṣ:) or *confused and improper speech:* (Mṣb:) or *speech*, or *talk, that is much and bad:* or *erroneous:* (A, Ḳ:) or *that is not regarded as of any weight or worth.* (TA.) See also هَذْرٌ.

هَذِرٌ: see هَذِرٌ.

هَذِرٌ, an epithet from هَذَرَ, applied to a man, [signifying, *Loquacious; garrulous; babbling; a great talker; a babbler:* or *nonsensical, irrational, foolish*, or *delirious, in his talk:* or one *who speaks confusedly and improperly:* or *who speaks, or talks, much and badly:* or *erroneously:*] (JK, Ṣ, Ḳ:) as also, [but in an intensive sense,] ▾ هَذُرٌ (Ḳ) and ▾ هُذَرَةٌ (Ṣ, Ḳ) and ▾ هُذُرَّةٌ (Ḳ) and ▾ هَذَّارٌ (Ṣ, Ḳ) and ▾ هِذْرِيَانٌ (Ḳ) and ▾ هَيْذَارٌ (JK, A, Ḳ) and ▾ مِهْذَرٌ (Ḳ) and ▾ مِهْذَارٌ, (JK, Ṣ, A, Mṣb, Ḳ,) [signifying, *very loquacious*, &c.:] and, [but in a doubly intensive sense,] ▾ هَيْذَارَةٌ (JK, Ḳ) and ▾ مِهْذَارَةٌ, (JK, A, Ḳ,) [signifying *very very loquacious*, &c.:] fem. هَذِرَةٌ (Ḳ) and ▾ هَيْذَرَةٌ (TA) and ▾ مِهْذَارٌ [without ة]: (Ḳ:) or ▾ هِذْرِيَانٌ signifies one *who talks badly*, or *corruptly, and much:* (TA:) or *light in speech and in service:* (Ṣ, TA:) the pl. of ▾ مِهْذَارٌ is مَهَاذِيرُ, not مِهْذَارُونَ. (ISd, TA.)

هُذَرَةٌ:
هُذُرَّةٌ:
هِذْرِيَانٌ:
هَذَّارٌ:
هَيْذَرَةٌ:
هَيْذَارٌ:
هَيْذَارَةٌ:
مِهْذَرٌ:
مِهْذَارٌ:
مِهْذَارَةٌ:

} see هَذِرٌ; the third, in two places.

هذرب

Q. 1. هَذْرَبَ, inf. n. هَذْرَبَةٌ, *He talked much and quickly:* (Ḳ:) a dial. form of هَذْرَمَ, or mispronounced for the latter word. (TA.) See also هَذْرَبَ.

هُذَيْرَبَى (accord. to the TA, هُذَيْرِبَى, and so in Golius's Lex.,) *Custom; habit.* Ex. هٰذِهِ هذيرباه *This is his custom;* or *habit.* (Ḳ.)

هُذْرُبَانٌ *Light*, or *active*, (and *quick*, TA,) *in his speech and in his service.* (Ḳ.) See also هِذْرِيَانٌ, in art. هذر.

[هذف, &c.

See Supplement.]

هذلم

Q. 1. هَذْلَمَ, inf. n. هَذْلَمَةٌ, *He was light*, or *active, and quick.* (Ḳ.) But IDrd and others assert it to be a word mispronounced for هَذْرَمَ. (MF.)

هر

1. هَرَّ, (Ṣ, A, Mṣb, Ḳ,) aor. يَهِرُّ, (Ṣ, Mṣb, Ḳ,) inf. n. هَرِيرٌ, (Ṣ, A, &c.,) said of a dog, [*He snarled*, or *howled*, or *whined;*] *he uttered a cry less vehement than barking* (Ṣ, A, Mṣb, Ḳ,) *by reason of his little patience of cold;* (Ṣ, Ḳ;) إِلَيْهِ *at him:* (Ḳ:) or *barked and grinned, displaying his fangs.* (L, TA.) It is said in a trad., إِنَّ الكَلْبَ يَهِرُّ مِنْ وَرَآءِ أَهْلِهِ *Verily the dog* [*snarls*, or] *barks and grins, displaying his fangs, behind his master:* meaning, that courage is a quality implanted by nature in a man, so that he engages in wars naturally, and from care to defend what should be inviolable, not reckoning upon a reward, like as the dog naturally barks and grins, displaying his fangs, to defend his masters. (L, TA.) — هَرِيرٌ is also applied to other sounds than the cry of the dog; as in the instance of هَرِيرُ الرَّحَى † *The sound of the turning of the mill-stone.* (TA.) You say also هَرَّتِ القَوْسُ † *The bow made a sound.* (AḤn, Ḳ.) And the looking of courageous men, one at another, is likened to هَرِير. (ISd, Mṣb.) — هَرَّ فِى وَجْهِ السَّائِلِ ‡ *He grinned in the face of the beggar, showing his teeth, and looking sternly, austerely*, or *morosely.* (A, TA.) — [Hence, perhaps,] هَرَّهُ, (Ṣ, Ḳ,) aor. يَهُرُّ and يَهِرُّ, (Ḳ,) [the latter irreg., like يَرُمُّ as aor. of the trans. v. رَمَّ,] inf. n. هَرٌّ (Ṣ, Ḳ) and هَرِيرٌ, (Ḳ,) ‡ *He disliked, disapproved of*, or *hated, him* or *it.* (Ṣ, Ḳ.) You say, هَرَّهُ النَّاسُ ‡ *The people disliked*, &c., *his vicinity.* (A.) And هَرَّ الكَاسَ, and الحَرْبَ, (Ṣ, A,) inf. n. هَرِيرٌ, (Ṣ,) ‡ *He disliked*, &c., *the cup of wine*, and *war.* (Ṣ, A.) ═ هَرَّهُ البَرْدُ, (Ḳ,) aor. يَهُرُّهُ, inf. n. هَرٌّ, (TA,) *The cold made him* (a dog) [*to snarl*, or *howl*, or *whine;* or] *to cry* [*in the manner described above*]; as also ▾ أَهَرَّهُ, (Ḳ,) inf. n. إِهْرَارٌ. (TA.) It is said in a proverb, (TA,) شَرٌّ أَهَرَّ ▾ ذَا نَابٍ [*It is*, or *was, an evil thing that made the fanged animal to snarl*, &c.]: alluding to the appearance of the signs and symptoms of evil: the sayer thereof, hearing the cry (هَرِير) of a dog, feared the assault of evil, and therefore said this to denote the magnitude of the case in his mind; meaning, nought but an evil thing made the fanged animal to cry: and for this reason, the use of an indeterminate word as an inchoative is well. (Ḳ.)

3. هَارَّهُ i.q. هَرَّ فِى وَجْهِهِ, (Ṣ, Ḳ,) i.e., ‡ *He grinned in his face, showing his teeth, and looking sternly, austerely*, or *morosely*, (A,) *like a dog.* (TA.)

4: see 1, last signification, in two places.

هِرٌّ *A male cat;* syn. سِنَّوْرٌ; (Ṣ, A, Ḳ;) which latter is uncommon in the language of the Arabs; (IAmb, in Mṣb, art. سنر;) fem. هِرَّةٌ; (Ṣ, A, Mṣb, Ḳ:) or هِرٌّ is applied to the *male* and the *female;* and the latter is sometimes called هِرَّةٌ: (IAmb, Mṣb:) the pl. of هِرٌّ is هِرَرَةٌ; and that of هِرَّةٌ is هِرَرٌ; and the dim. of هِرَّةٌ is هُرَيْرَةٌ. (Mṣb.) ═ Also, a subst. from هَرَّهُ meaning "he disliked, disapproved of, or hated, him or it." (Ṣ) It is said in a proverb, (Ṣ,) لَا يَعْرِفُ هِرًّا مِنْ بِرٍّ, (Ṣ, A, Ḳ,) meaning *He knows not him who dislikes* or *hates him from him who behaves towards him with goodness and affection and gentleness, and regard for his circumstances:* (Ṣ, TA:) this is the best explanation of it: (TA:) or *the action of him who grins in his face, showing his teeth, and looking sternly, austerely*, or *morosely, from the action of him who holds loving communion with him:* (A:) or *the calling of sheep* or *goats*, (Ṣ,) or *the calling of them to water*, (Ḳ,) *from the driving of them:* (Ṣ:) or *the calling of sheep* or *goats to provender from the calling of them to water:* (IAạr:) or *the driving of sheep* or *goats* (Yoo, Ḳ) *from the calling of them.* (Yoo, TA.) It has been explained [more fully] in art. بر. (Ḳ.)

هُرَارٌ : see هَارٌّ.

هَارٌّ A dog [*that snarls,* or *howls,* or *whines, by reason of his little patience of cold:* or] *that barks and grins, displaying his fangs:* and هَرَّارٌ ♦ signifies the same [but in an intensive manner; *that snarls, &c., much:*] or the latter signifies a dog *that grins* [*much*], *displaying his fangs:* or *that barks much:* or *that barks* [*much*] *and grins, displaying his fangs.* It is said in a trad., لَا أَعْقِلُ الكَلْبَ الهَرَّارَ ♦ [properly signifying, *I will not pay a fine for killing the dog that barks much,* is expl. as] meaning, I will not impose anything [as a fine] for the killing of a dog that barks much; because such a dog annoys by his barking. (TA, [see art. عقل.]) — عَادَ لَنَا المَطِىُّ هَارًّا *The riding-camels returned to her,* or *it, one grinning* (تَهِرُّ) *in the face of another, showing its teeth,* in consequence of fatigue. (TA.)

هرا

1. هَرَاهُ البَرْدُ *The cold destroyed him,* or, perhaps, *debilitated him;* i.e., a beast; lit., *broke him:* syn. كَسَرَهُ. (TA.) [See also هَزَأَ.] — هُرِىَ, like عُنِىَ, [i.e., pass. in form, but neut. in signification,] (incorrectly written in the Ṣ هَرِىَ, Ḳ,) *It* (a camel or sheep &c., or a man,) *perished of cold,* or *heat.* (Ks, Ḳ.) — هَرَاهُ البَرْدُ, inf. n. هَرْوٌ, (Aṣ, Ṣ, Ḳ,) and هَرَاوَةٌ ♦; (Ḳ;) and اهراهُ ♦; (Fr, Ṣ, Ḳ;) *The cold affected him so severely as nearly to kill him:* (Aṣ, Ṣ, Ḳ:) or *so severely as to kill him.* (Ḳ.) — هَرَأَتِ الرِّيحُ *The wind was,* or *became, intensely cold.* (Ḳ.) — هَرَأَ, (Ḳ,) inf. n. هَرْءٌ; (TA:) and هَرَّأَ ♦; (Ḳ;) and اهرأ ♦, (Fr, Ḳ,) inf. n. إِهْرَآءٌ; (TA;) *He cooked* flesh-meat *thoroughly:* (Ḳ:) or *so that it fell off from the bone.* (Ṣ, Ḳ.) — هَرِىَ, aor. َ, inf. n. هَرْءٌ and هُرُوٌّ; (Ḳ;) and تهرّأ ♦; (Ṣ, Ḳ;) *It* (flesh-meat) *was thoroughly cooked:* (Ḳ:) or *was cooked so as to fall off from the bone.* (Ṣ,* TA.) — هَرَأَ فِى مَنْطِقِهِ, (Ṣ, Ḳ,) aor. َ, (Ḳ,) inf. n. هَرْءٌ, (TA,) *He was loquacious:* or *he was loquacious, with incorrectness;* (TA;) as also هَرَأَ الكَلَامَ: (ISk, Ṣ:) or *he was very foul in his speech:* or *was very incorrect,* or *faulty, therein:* (Ḳ:) or, simply, *he was foul,* (Ṣ,) or *incorrect,* or *faulty,* (TA,) *in his speech:* (Ṣ, TA:) also اهرأ ♦ الكَلَامَ *he multiplied his words but spake not to the point,* or *correctly.* (Ḳ.) — إِنَّ مَنْطِقَهُ نَهْرًا, inf. n. هَرْءٌ, [*Verily his speech is prolix:* or *is vitious, and disorderly*]. (TA.)

2: see 1.

4: see 1. — اهرأ فِى الرَّوَاحِ *He entered upon the cool time of the evening:* (Ṣ, Ḳ:*) or properly said only of the evening of the hot season. (Ḳ.) [See also اهزأ.] — أَهْرِئْ عَنْكَ مِنَ الظَّهِيرَةِ *Stay thou until the mid-day heat shall have become assuaged, and the air be cool.* (TA, in this art.; and IAạr, in TA, art. فيح.) — اهرأ *He slew a person.* (Ḳ.) — See 1, last sentence but one.

5. تهرّأ *He* (a beast) *was destroyed,* or, perhaps, *debilitated,* by the cold; lit., *was broken:* syn. تكسّر. (TA.) — See 1.

هَرِئٌ (so in the TA: in one copy of the Ṣ, هَرِىٌ: in another, هُرِىٌ:) and مُهَرَّأٌ ♦ (TA) Meat *thoroughly cooked:* (TA:) or *cooked so as to fall off from the bone.* (Ṣ,* TA.)

هُرَأٌ : see هُرَآءٌ.

هُرَآءٌ, or مَنْطِقٌ هُرَآءٌ, (Ṣ, Ḳ,) *Loquacity:* or *vitious, disorderly, speech:* (Ḳ:) or *loquacity with incorrectness.* (Ṣ.) — هُرَّآءٌ, (Ḳ,) fem. with ة, pl. with ون; (TA;) and هُرَأٌ ♦; (Ḳ;) *A great talker of nonsense.* (Ḳ.)

هِرَآءٌ *A young shoot of a palm-tree,* (AḤn, Ḳ,) *when first plucked from the mother-tree.* (Aṣ.) — الهِرَآءُ *A certain devil whose office it is to suggest foul dreams.* (Ḳ.)

قِرَّةٌ لَهَا هَرِيئَةٌ *Cold that occasions injury and death to men and to cattle &c.* (El-Fezáree, ISk, Ṣ.) — Also, هَرِيئَةٌ The *time in which cold thus affects them.* (TA.)

مَهْرُوٌّ, from هُرِىَ, pl. with ون, [in the CḲ, for مَهْرُوُّونَ is put مَهْرُوونَ,] *Perishing of cold,* or *heat.* (Ks, Ḳ.) — Explained by AḤn [in his book on plants] by the words الَّذِى قَدْ أَنْضَجَهُ البَرْدُ [meaning, What is *nipped, shrunk, shrivelled,* or *blasted, by the cold:* see art. نضج]. (TA.)

مُهَرَّأٌ : see هَرِئٌ.

هرب

1. هَرَبَ, (Ṣ, Ḳ,) aor. ُ; not ِ, as some have imagined on account of the measure of the first of the following inf. ns., imagining thence also that the pret. is هَرِبَ; nor َ with the pret. هَرَبَ, as some have supposed because of the guttural letter; for a guttural letter, when it is the first, is not reckoned as having any influence on the form of the aor.; nor ُ, as some have thought; (TA;) inf. n. هَرَبٌ (Ṣ, Ḳ) and مَهْرَبٌ and هَرَبَانٌ; (Ḳ;) *He* (a man, or any animal, TA) *fled; ran away.* (Ṣ, Ḳ.) — إِلَيْكَ مِنْكَ المَهْرَبُ [*To Thee I flee for refuge from Thee;* i.e., from thy punishment: addressed to God]. (TA.) — هَرَبَ مِنَ الوَتِدِ نِصْفُهُ *Half of the wooden pin, peg,* or *stake, disappeared* [*in the ground*]. (Ḳ.) — هَرِبَ, aor. َ, *He became extremely aged, old and weak,* or *decrepit;* i.q. هَرِمَ; (Ḳ;) of which it is a dial. form. (TA.)

2. هرّبه, inf. n. تَهْرِيبٌ, *He made,* or *caused, him to flee,* or *run away.* (Ṣ, Ḳ.) See also 4.

4. اهربه *He forced,* or *compelled, him to flee,* or *run away.* (Ḳ.) See also 2. — اهربتِ الرِّيحُ *The wind raised and carried away the dust,* (Ḳ,) *causing dust and dry herbage &c. to accumulate on the ground.* (TA.) — اهرب *He* (a horse, or other animal that runs, Lḥ) *strove,* or *exerted himself, in going away,* or *in flight, being frightened,* (ISk, Ṣ, Ḳ,) or *not being frightened.* (TA.) See جَاءَ مُهْرِبًا. — اهرب *He went,* or *travelled, far into,* or *through, the land.* (TA.) [هَرَّبَ ♦ فِى الأَرْضِ, mentioned also in the TA, seems to signify the same.] — اهرب فِى الأَمْرِ *He immersed himself in the affair; took extraordinary pains in it.* (Ḳ.) See جَاءَ مُهْرِبًا.

6. تهاربوا (Ṣ, O, Ḳ, art. فر,) *They fled, one from another.* (TḲ.)

هُرْبٌ The *thin integument of fat that covers the stomach and intestines:* or the *fat* [or *caul*] *that is spread over the intestines:* i.q. ثَرْبُ البَطْنِ: (Ḳ:) a word of the dial. of El-Yemen. (TA.)

مَا لَهُ هَارِبٌ وَلَا قَارِبٌ *He has not* [of camels &c.] *any that returns from water, nor any that comes to it;* i.e., *he has not anything;* (Kh, Ṣ, Ḳ;) or, *he has not anything, nor has he any people;* an expression similar to مَا لَهُ سَعْنَةٌ وَلَا مَعْنَةٌ: (Lḥ:) accord. to IAạr, هَارِبٌ signifies *one who returns from water;* and قَارِبٌ, *one who seeks,* or *journeys to, water:* (TA:) or the meaning is *no one flees from him, nor does any one approach him;* i.e., *he is a person of no account.* (Aṣ, Ḳ.) [In the TA a trad. is quoted which confirms the former signification.] See also art. قرب.

مَهْرَبٌ *A place to which one flees; a place of refuge.* (Mṣb.) — فُلَانٌ لَنَا مَهْرَبٌ † *Such a one is a refuge to us.* (TA.)

جَاءَ مُهْرِبًا *He came striving,* or *exerting himself, in the affair:* (Lḥ:) or, as some say, *he came fleeing and in fright.* (TA.)

مِهْرَبٌ *A piece of wood,* or *wooden implement, which the sower,* or *ploughman, draws forward and backward* [*over the ground*]. (Ḳ.) [A piece of the trunk of a tree, or of a thick branch, is thus drawn over the soil after sowing.]

هربذ

هِرْبِذٌ sing. of هَرَابِذَةٌ, which signifies The *servants,* or *ministers of the fire* (Ṣ, Ḳ) *of the Magians;* (Ḳ;) the *servants,* or *ministers,* (قَوَمَة,

L, Ḳ, by which is meant خَدَم, TA,) *of the fire-temple of the Indians:* (L, Ḳ:) or the *judges of the Magians:* (L:) or the *great men of the Indians: or their learned men:* (L, Ḳ:) a Persian word, [originally هِرْبِذ,] arabicized. (Ṣ, L.)

هَرْبَذَةٌ *A pace less quick than that termed* خَبَبٌ. (Ṣ, L, Ḳ.)

هِرْبِذَى *A proud and self-conceited manner of walking, or going;* (L, Ḳ;) which is (L) *a manner of waking or going like that of the* هَرَابِذَة [pl. of هِرْبِذ]. (A'Obeyd, L.) A'Obeyd mentions it in speaking of the paces of camels; and says that it is without a parallel in form. (L.) — عَدَا الجَمَلُ الهِرْبِذَى *The camel ran inclining towards one side.* (Ṣ, L, Ḳ.)

هرت

1. هَرَتَ شَيْئًا, [aor. ِ and ُ,] inf. n. هَرْتٌ; *He rent, or slit, a thing, to widen it.* (TA.) — هَرَتَ شِدْقَهُ, [aor. ِ and ُ,] inf. n. هَرْتٌ, *He drew the side of his mouth towards the ear.* (TA.) — هَرِتَ, aor. َ, (inf. n. هَرَتٌ, Ṣ,) *He was wide, or ample, in the sides of the mouth: he had a wide mouth.* (Ṣ, Ḳ, TA.) — هَرَتَ الثَّوْبَ, (Ṣ,) aor. ِ and ُ, inf. n. هَرْتٌ, (ISd, Ḳ,) *He rent the garment.* (Az, Ṣ, ISd, Ḳ.) — هَرَتَ عِرْضَهُ (Ṣ) aor. ِ and ُ, inf. n. هَرْتٌ, (Ḳ,) *He wounded his reputation;* syn. طَعَنَ فِيهِ; (Ṣ;) as also هَرَدَ and هَرَطَ. (TA.) [Accord. to the Ḳ, هَرَتَ seems to signify the same as طَعَنَ absolutely; but in the TA, the signification is restricted as above.] — هَرَتَ اللَّحْمَ, (Ṣ, Ḳ,) aor. ِ and ُ, inf. n. هَرْتٌ; (Ḳ;) [and ↑ هَرَّتَهُ; see مُهَرَّتٌ;] *He cooked the flesh-meat thoroughly:* (Ḳ:) *cooked it so that it fell off from the bones.* (Ṣ.)

2: see 1, last sentence.

الهَرْتُ and الهُرُوتُ: see الهَرِيتُ.

هَرِيتٌ *Wide, or ample.* (Ḳ.) — *Wide, or ample, in the sides of the mouth:* (Ṣ:) as also ↑ أَهْرَتُ, and هَرِيتُ الشِّدْقِ, and ↑ مَهْرُوتُهُ, and ↑ مُنْهَرِتٌ. (TA.) *A wide-mouthed horse;* as also ↑ أَهْرَتُ; and camel. (TA.) [See an ex. in a verse cited voce رَسَنٌ.] — حَيَّةٌ هَرِيتُ الشِّدْقِ, and ↑ مَهْرُوتَتُهُ, *A serpent having a wide mouth.* (TA.) — ↑ أَسَدٌ أَهْرَتُ *A lion wide in the sides of the mouth.* (Ṣ.) — ↑ رَجُلٌ أَهْرَتُ *A man having a wide mouth.* (TA.) — ↑ مَهْرُوتُ الفَمِ *Having a mouth wide in the sides.* (Ṣ.) — ↑ كِلَابٌ مُهَرَّتَةُ الأَشْدَاقِ *Dogs wide in the sides of the mouth.* (Ṣ.) [See an ex., voce عَذَبٌ.] — الهَرِيتُ and ↑ الهَرْتُ and ↑ الهُرُوتُ and ↑ الهَرَّاتُ (Ḳ) and ↑ المَهْرُوتُ (L) *The lion.* (Ḳ.) — Also هَرِيتٌ *A woman in whom the division between the vagina and the rectum has been broken through.* (Ṣ, Ḳ.) Sometimes employed in this sense. (Ṣ.) — هَرِيتٌ *A rent garment.* (ISd.) — هَرِيتٌ *A wounded reputation.* (ISd.) = رَجُلٌ هَرِيتٌ *A man who does not keep a secret, and who talks foully.* (Ḳ.)

الهَرَّاتُ: see الهَرِيتُ.

هَارُوتُ [*A certain fallen angel, the companion of* مَارُوتُ]; *the name of an angel, or of a king;* but the former accord. to the more common opinion: generally and most correctly held to be a foreign name. (TA.)

أَهْرَتُ: see هَرِيتٌ throughout. — أَهْرَتُ الشِّقْشِقَةِ † an epithetic appellation given to a خَطِيب; pl. هُرْتٌ; (TA;) [like ذُو شِقْشِقَةٍ, q. v.]

مَهْرُوتٌ: see هَرِيتٌ.

مُهَرَّتٌ: see هَرِيتٌ. = Flesh-meat *thoroughly cooked, so that it has fallen in pieces;* as also مُهَرَّدٌ; or this latter [only] is the correct word. (TA, from a trad.)

مُتَهَارِتٌ *Twisting about the sides of the mouth, and drawing them often, or much, towards the ears.* (TA, from a trad.)

مُنْهَرِتٌ: see هَرِيتٌ.

هرث

هِرْثٌ An *old, worn-out,* garment. (Ḳ.) [See also هَرِيتٌ.]

هرج

1. هَرَجَ, aor. ِ, inf. n. هَرْجٌ, *He did, acted, or occupied himself, much in a thing;* (Ṣ, L;) *expatiated, or took a wide range, in it.* (L.) This is the original signification. (Ṣ.) — هَرَجَ فِي الحَدِيثِ, (aor. ِ, inf. n. هَرْجٌ, Mṣb.) *He launched into, and expatiated in, or was diffuse in, discourse, talk, or narration:* (Ḳ:) this is the signification in most frequent use: (TA:) or *he made a confusion, or confounded, therein.* (Ḳ, Mṣb.) — هَرَجَ, aor. ُ and ِ, inf. n. هَرْجٌ, *Multum inivit:* (Ṣ, L:) or [simply] *inivit ancillam suam.* (Ḳ.) — هَرَجَ, aor. ِ, (inf. n. هَرْجٌ, Ṣ, TA,) *He* (a horse) *ran much:* (Ṣ, L:) or *ran quickly, or swiftly:* (Mṣb:) or [simply] *ran.* (Ḳ.) — هَرَجَ النَّاسُ, aor. ِ, (inf. n. هَرْجٌ, Ṣ,) *The people fell into a state of trial, or civil war or conflict and faction, or discord, or discussion,* (فِتْنَة,) *and confusion, or disorder,* (Ṣ, Ḳ,) *and slaughter.* (Ḳ.) — هَرِجَ, aor. َ, (inf. n. هَرَجٌ, Ṣ,) *He* (a camel) *became perplexed in his sight, by reason of the vehemence of heat, and his being much smeared with pitch,* (Ṣ, Ḳ,) *and being heavily laden.* (TA.)

2. هَرَّجَ البَعِيرَ, inf. n. تَهْرِيجٌ, and ↑ اهرجهُ, inf. n. إِهْرَاجٌ; *He incited, or urged, the camel to journey on (during the hottest time of the day,* Ṣ) *until he* [the camel] *became perplexed in his sight by reason of the vehemence of the heat.* (Ṣ, Ḳ.) — هَرَّجَ بِالسَّبُعِ, inf. n. تَهْرِيجٌ, *He cried out to the lion or other beast of prey, and chid him.* (Ṣ, Ḳ.) = هَرَّجَ, inf. n. تَهْرِيجٌ, *It* (beverage of the kind called نَبِيذ) *affected, or took effect upon, a person.* (Ṣ, Ḳ.)

4: see 2. — أَهْرَجَ *The heat reached his* (a camel's) *inside.* (L.)

6. تهارجوا *Iniverunt, alii alias.* (TA.)

7. انهرج *He was, or became, affected* by beverage of the kind called نَبِيذ. (Ṣ, CḲ.)

هَرْجٌ *Trial, or civil war, or conflict and faction, or discord, or dissension,* (فِتْنَة,) *and confusion,* or *disorder:* (Ṣ:) *vehement and much slaughter:* (TA:) in a trad. respecting the signs of the last day, *conflict, and confusion, or disorder:* (TA:) or *slaughter;* as explained by Moḥammad himself: (Ṣ:) and so, accord. to Aboo-Moosà, it signifies in the language of Abyssinia. (TA.) Ibn Ḳeys Er-Ruḳeiyát said, in the days of the faction of Ibn-Ez-Zubeyr,

* لَيْتَ شِعْرِى أَأَوَّلُ الهَرْجِ هٰذَا *

* أَمْ زَمَانٌ مِنْ فِتْنَةٍ غَيْرِ هَرْجِ *

Would that I knew whether this be the first of the slaughter predicted as a sign of the last day, or whether it be a time of trial, or civil war, &c., other than the slaughter so predicted. (Ṣ.)

هَرَّاجٌ: see مِهْرَجٌ.

هَرَاجَةٌ *An assembly, or a company, of men who launch into, and expatiate in, or are diffuse in, discourse, talk, or narration.* (Ḳ.)

مُهْرِجٌ A man *whose camels are affected with the scab, and have therefore been smeared with pitch, and to whose insides the heat has penetrated.* (TA.)

مِهْرَجٌ and ↑ هَرَّاجٌ A horse *that runs much:* (Ṣ, Ḳ:) and ↑ مِهْرَاجٌ a horse *that runs vehemently.* (TA.)

مِهْرَاجٌ: see مِهْرَجٌ.

هرجب

Q. 1. هَرْجَبَ, inf. n. هَرْجَبَةٌ, *He was quick, or swift.* (IḲṭṭ.)

هِرْجَابٌ and هِرْجَبٌّ *Tall*, or *long*, as an epithet of a man &c. (Ḳ.) —— هِرْجَابٌ *A tall*, or *long-bodied*, (طَوِيلَةٌ) *and bulky*, she-camel: (Ṣ:) as also هِرْجَالٌ: pl. هَرَاجِيبُ. —— هِرْجَابٌ Anything *great, large*, or *bulky*: so in the Moạjam: or *extending long, horizontally*. (TA.) —— نَخْلَةٌ هِرْجَابٌ *A tall palm-tree*. (TA.)

هرد

1. هَرَدَ, (Ṣ, L, Ḳ,) aor. ـِ, (Ḳ,) inf. n. هَرْدٌ, (L,) *He rent*, or *tore*, (Ṣ, L, Ḳ,) a garment, or piece of cloth; (Ṣ, L;) as also هَرَتَ: (Az, L:) *he rent*, or *tore, to injure*, or *spoil*, (L, Ḳ,) not to amend: (L:) *he* (a puller) *rent*, or *tore, and beat*, a garment, or piece of cloth: (L:) and ♦ هرّد *he rent*, or *tore, much*. (L.) —— هَرَدَ عِرْضَهُ, aor. ـِ, (L,) inf. n. هَرْدٌ, (Ṣ, L, Ḳ,) *He wounded his reputation*. (Ṣ, L, Ḳ.) —— هَرَدَ, aor. ـِ, (Ṣ, L, Ḳ,) inf. n. هَرْدٌ, (L,) *He cooked* flesh-meat *so that it fell off from the bones*: (Ṣ, L, Ḳ:) or *cooked* it *much*: (Aṣ, L:) or *cooked* it *thoroughly and well*: (ISd, L, Ḳ:) and ♦ هرّد, (Ḳ,) inf. n. تَهْرِيدٌ, (Ṣ, L,) signifies the same, (Ṣ, L, Ḳ,) but with an intensiveness: (Ṣ, L:) or *he put* flesh-meat *into the fire, and cooked* it *thoroughly*. (AZ, L.) —— هَرِدَ, (L, Ḳ, TA,) or هَرَدَ, (AZ, L, CḲ,) and ♦ تهرّد, (TA,) *It* (flesh-meat) *became cooked so that it fell off from the bones*: or, *cooked much*: or, *cooked thoroughly and well*: (L, Ḳ:*) or *it, being put into the fire, became thoroughly cooked*. (AZ, L.)

Irreg. verb. هَرَدْتُ الشَّىْءَ, aor. أُهَرِيدُهُ, [in the CḲ, أُهْرِيدُهُ,] (Lḥ, M, art. رود; and Ḳ,) inf. n. هِرَادَةٌ, (Lḥ, M in art. رود,) *i.q.* أَرَدْتُهُ [q.v., in art. رود, *I willed, wished*, or *desired, the thing*]. (Lḥ, M, art. رود; and Ḳ.)

2: see 1. —— هرّد, inf. n. تَهْرِيدٌ, *He wore a* مُهَرَّد, (Ḳ,) i.e., a *yellow garment, dyed with* هُرْد. (TA.)

5: see 1.

هُرْدٌ *Certain roots with which one dyes*, (L, Ḳ,) *of a yellow colour*: (TA:) or (so accord. to the L; but in the Ḳ, and) *i.q.* كُرْكُمٌ: (L, Ḳ:) or the *yellow* كُرْكُم: correctly, the *roots of the* كُرْكُم, or وَرْس: (TA:) and *a certain red earth* (Ḳ) with which one dyes. (TA.)

هُرْدِىٌّ, (Aṣ, Ṣ, L, Ḳ, [but in the last it is not shown whether it be with or without tenween]) of the measure فُعْلِى, (Ṣ, L,) of the fem. gen., (IAmb,) but AḤn says, I know not whether it be masc. [and therefore with tenween] or fem. [and therefore without tenween], (L.) [in one instance in the L, and in a copy of the Ḳ, written هردا, which is evidently wrong,] and هُرْدَاءُ, [i. e. هُرْدَآءُ or هُرْدَآءٌ,] (L, Ḳ,) and ♦ هُرْدَانٌ, (L,) *A certain plant*; (Aṣ, Ṣ, L, Ḳ;) *a certain herb, of which AḤn says, that he had not met with a description of it*: (L:) and ♦ هَيْرُدَانٌ is also the name of *a certain plant*, (Ḳ,) *like* هُرْدِى, (L,) or *i.q.* هُرْدَانٌ. (TA.)

هُرْدِىٌّ: see مُهَرَّدٌ.

هُرْدَانٌ: see هُرْدِى.

هَيْرُدَانٌ: see هُرْدِى.

هَرِيدٌ and ♦ مَهْرُودٌ A garment, or piece of cloth, *rent*, or *torn*; (L;) as also هَرِيتٌ. (AZ.)

مَهْرُودٌ: see هَرِيدٌ. —— Also, (Ṣ, L, Ḳ,) A garment, or piece of cloth, *dyed yellow* (Ṣ, L) *with* هُرْد; (L;) and so ♦ مُهَرَّدٌ (L) and ♦ هُرْدِىٌّ: (Ḳ,* TA,) or, as Sh says, accord. to information given to Aboo-'Adnán by an intelligent Arab of the desert, of the people called Báhileh, *dyed with* وَرْس, *and then with saffron, so as to become of a colour like that of the flower of the* حَوْذَانَة: (Az, L:) or *of a light yellow colour*. (IAmb, L.)

مُهَرَّدٌ: see مَهْرُودٌ.

هردب

Q. 1. هَرْدَبَ, inf. n. هَرْدَبَةٌ, (and هردب, TA, [a strange form: perhaps a mistake for هَرْدَابٌ or هِرْدَابٌ:]) *He ran heavily*. (IḲṭṭ &c., and Ḳ.)

هِرْدَبَّةٌ (and هِرْدَبٌّ, TA) *An old woman*. (Ṣ, Ḳ.) —— Also, (as some say, TA,) *Having a swollen belly, and cowardly*: (Ṣ, Ḳ:) or *cowardly, bulky, of little sense, swollen in the belly, and having no heart*. (TA.) —— Accord. to Az, in the T, A *large, long-bodied* man is called هِرْدَبَّةٌ. (TA.)

هرس

1. هَرَسَهُ, aor. ـُ, (IF, A, Mṣb,) inf. n. هَرْسٌ, (IF, Ṣ, A, Mṣb, Ḳ,) *He bruised, brayed*, or *pounded, it; crushed it so as to break it; broke it*, or *broke it in pieces, by beating*; (Ṣ, IF, Mṣb, TA;) namely, grain, (Mṣb,) or some other thing: (IF, Mṣb:) or *he did so vehemently*, or *violently*: (A, Ḳ:) or *with something broad*: or *with some preservative between it and the ground*. (TA.)

هَرِيسٌ *Grain*, (Mṣb,) or *wheat*, (A,) *bruised, brayed*, or *pounded*, (A, Mṣb,) *vehemently*, or *violently*, (A,) *with the* مِهْرَاس, *before it is cooked*; for when it is cooked, it is termed هَرِيسَةٌ: (Mṣb:) [of the measure فَعِيلٌ in the sense of the measure مَفْعُولٌ:] from the verb above-mentioned. (Ḳ.) You say, عِنْدِى هَرِيسٌ لِلْهَرِيسَةِ *I have wheat bruised, &c., for the* هَرِيسَة. (A.)

هَرِيسَةٌ *Grain*, (Mṣb,) or *wheat*, (TA,) *bruised, brayed*, or *pounded*, [*vehemently*, or *violently*, (see هَرِيس,)] *and then cooked*: (Mṣb, TA:) [or *a kind of thick pottage, prepared of cooked wheat and cooked flesh-meats much pounded together*: (Golius; app. on the authority of Ibn-Maạroof:) but this is probably one of the kinds of هريسة peculiar to post-classical times; which kinds are many: see De Sacy's Relation de l'Égypte par Abd-Allatif, pp. 307 and 312:] of the measure فَعِيلَةٌ in the sense of the measure مَفْعُولَةٌ: (Mṣb:) from the verb above-mentioned: (Ṣ, Ḳ:) pl. هَرَائِسُ. (A.)

هَرَّاسٌ *A maker*, or *preparer, of* هَرِيسَة: (Mgh, Mṣb, Ḳ:) and *a seller thereof*. (Mgh.)

مِهْرَاسٌ [in the M, voce جُرْنٌ, q.v., accord. to the TA, مهرس, i.e., app. مِهْرَسٌ,] *A stone hollowed out*, (Ṣ, Mgh, Mṣb,) *oblong*, (Mgh, Mṣb,) *and heavy, resembling a* [*vessel of the kind called*] تَوْر, q.v., (Mgh,) *in which one bruises, brays*, or *pounds, and from which one performs the ablution termed* وُضُوء; (Ṣ, Mgh, Mṣb;) and it is *also made of brass*; *and grain and other things are bruised in it*: (Mṣb:) and sometimes, by a tropical application, ‡ *one of wood*, (Mgh, Mṣb,) *used for the same purpose*: (Mṣb:) or a *mortar*; syn. هَاوُونٌ: (Ḳ;) or *thing in which grain is bruised*: (A, TA,) and also, (A, Ḳ,) tropically, (A,) ‡ *a hollowed stone*, (A, Ḳ,) *of oblong shape*, (A,) *from which one performs the ablution above mentioned*; (A, Ḳ;) *consisting of a bulky stone, which several men cannot lift nor move because of its weight, capable of holding much water*. (TA.)

هرش

1. هَرِشَ, aor. ـَ, (Ṣgh, Ḳ,) inf. n. هَرَشٌ, (TḲ,) † *He* (a man, TA) *was*, or *became, evil*, or *bad, in disposition*. (Ṣgh, Ḳ.) —— هَرِشَ الدَّهْرُ, (Ibn-'Abbád, A, Ḳ,) and الزَّمَانُ, (A,) aor. ـَ and ـِ, (A, Ḳ,) inf. n. هَرْشٌ, (TḲ,) ‡ *Time*, or *fortune, was*, or *became, distressful*, or *calamitous*. (I'Abbád, A, Ḳ.) [In the A, app. by inadvertence, هرش الدهر is mentioned as proper; and هرش الزمان, as tropical.]

2. هَرَّشَ بَيْنَ الكِلَابِ, (A,* Ḳ,* TḲ,) inf. n. تَهْرِيشٌ, (Ṣ, A, Ḳ,) *He excited strife*, or *quarrelling, between*, or *among, the dogs*; syn. حَرَّشَ: (Ṣ,* A, Ḳ, TḲ:) and ♦ هارش بَيْنَ الكِلَابِ, (A, Mgh, TA,) or بِالكِلَابِ, (Ṣ,) or بَعْضَ الكِلَابِ عَلَى بَعْضٍ, (Ḳ,* TḲ,) inf. n. مُهَارَشَةٌ, (Ṣ, A, Mgh, Ḳ) and هِرَاشٌ, (Ṣ, Mgh,) *he incited the dogs to attack one another*. (Ṣ, Mgh, Ḳ.) —— [Hence,] هَرَّشَ بَيْنَ القَوْمِ, (A,) or بَيْنَ النَّاسِ, (Ḳ,) inf. n. as above, (Ṣ, Ḳ,) ‡ *He excited discord, dissension,*

disorder, strife, quarrelling, or *animosity, between,* or *among, the people.* (Ṣ,* A, Ḳ.)

3. هَارَشَا [*They fought and assailed each other*]: said of two dogs. (A.) See also 6. — [Hence,] كَلْبٌ هِرَاشٌ [*An irritable,* or *a quarrelsome, dog*]; like كَلْبٌ حِرَاشٌ. (TA.) — See also 2. — هِرَاشٌ is also used to signify The *fighting against each other* of men. (Mgh.)

6. تَهَارَشَتِ الكِلَابُ, and ↓ اهترشت, (A, Ḳ, TA,) and ↓ هَارَشَ بَعْضُهَا بَعْضًا, (A,) *The dogs fought and assailed one another.* (TA.)

8: see 6.

هرشب

هِرْشَبَّةٌ *An old woman far advanced in years:* (Ḳ:) *a worn-out old woman;* as also هِرْشَفَّةٌ. (T.)

هرمت

هَرَامِيتُ *Wells:* (Ḳ;) a pl. that has no sing.; or its sing. is هُرْمُوتٌ or هِرْمِيتٌ; or perhaps the ت is an augmentative letter: (MF:) or, accord. to the L, it is a name of a certain group of wells in the tract of Ed-Dahma, said to have been dug by Luḳmán the son of 'Ád: or, accord. to Aṣ, certain wells on the left of Ḍareeyeh: if so, F has erred in prefixing to it the art. ال. (TA.)

هز

1. هَزَّهُ, (Ṣ, A, Mṣb, Ḳ,) and هَزَّ بِهِ, [respecting which see what is said on an ex. below,] (A, Ḳ,) aor. ـُ, (A, Mṣb,) inf. n. هَزٌّ, (Ṣ, A, Mṣb,) [*He shook it;*] *he put it in motion,* or *into a state of commotion;* (Ṣ, A, Mṣb, Ḳ;) as also ↓ هزّزه, (Ṣ, Ḳ,) and هزّز بِهِ, (TA,) inf. n. تَهْزِيزٌ; (Ḳ;) and ↓ هَزْهَزَهُ, (Ṣ, Ḳ,) inf. n. هَزْهَزَةٌ; (TA;) meaning, *he made it move by pulling and pushing;* or *he made it move to the right and left:* or, accord. to Er-Rághib, *he did so with violence,* or *vehemence.* (TA.) It is said that هَزَّ is trans. by itself, and by means of ب, like أَخَذَ and تَعَلَّقَ: it is trans. in the latter manner in the Ḳur., [xix. 25,] where it is said, وَهُزِّى إِلَيْكِ بِجِذْعِ النَّخْلَةِ [*And shake thou towards thee the trunk of the palm-tree*], i.e. حَرِّكِى: but ISd says, that the verb is here made trans. by means of ب because it is used in the sense of جُرِّى: and MF says, that, properly, it is not trans. by means of ب. (TA.) You say, هَزَّ السَّيْفَ وَغَيْرَهُ [*He shook the sword, &c.*] (A.) And هَزَّتِ الرِّيحُ الأَغْصَانَ, (A,) and الشَّجَرَ, and ↓ هَزْهَزَتْهَا, (Ṣ,) [*The wind shook the branches,* and *the trees,*] and هَزَّتِ النَّبَاتَ *it shook* (حَرَّكَتْ) *the plants:* but this has also a tropical signification, which see below. (TA.) — You say also, أَهُزُّ عِطْفَىَّ, and مَنْكِبَىَّ, ‡ [lit., *I shake my shoulder-blade,* and *my shoulder-joint;*] meaning, *I walk with an elegant and a proud and self-conceited gait; I behave with pride and self-conceitedness.* (Mgh.) And هَزَّ عِطْفَيْهِ لِكَذَا ‡ [lit., *He shook his sides at such a thing;* app. meaning, *he was active,* or *prompt, and brisk,* or *was moved with alacrity, to do such a thing,* or *he was rejoiced at such a thing:* like ↓ اِهْتَزَّ لَهُ, q. v.]: and in like manner, هَزَّ مَنْكِبَيْهِ. (A.) [In like manner also you say,] هَزَّ مَا رَأَيْتُ مِنْ عِطْفِى [app. meaning, accord. to a gloss cited by De Sacy in his Anthol. Gr. Ar., p. 309, ‡ *What I saw rejoiced me:* or, as rendered by him, p. 286, *ce dont j'étois temoin, réveilla en moi le courage.*] (Z, in his preface to the Keshsháf.) And هَزَّ الإِبِلَ, (Ṣ, A, Ḳ,) aor. ـُ, inf. n. هَزٌّ (TA) and هَزِيزٌ, (Ṣ, Ḳ, TA,) ‡ *He* (a man urging his beasts by singing) *made the camels to be brisk,* or *sprightly,* by his singing to urge them. (Ṣ,* A, Ḳ.) And هَزَّهَا السَّيْرُ ‡ [*The journeying made them to be brisk,* or *sprightly*]. (TA.) And هَزَّ بِهِ السَّيْرُ † *The pace brought him on quickly.* (TA.) And هَزَزْتُ فُلَانًا لِخَيْرٍ † *I made such a one to rejoice* [or *to be prompt and brisk* (see the quasi-pass., 8,) *to do good*]: said of a generous man: (En-Naḍr, TA:) and ↓ هَزْهَزْتُهُ and هَزْهَزْتُ مِنْهُ [app. signify the same]. (A.) And جَآءَ فُلَانٌ يَهُزُّ المَشْىَ, and يَهُضُّهُ, † *Such a one came walking impulsively:* (JK in art. هض:) or *with a graceful gait, impulsively.* (Ibn-El-Faraj, TA, in art. هض.) — You also say, of a plant, or herbage, هَزَّتْهُ ↓ الرِّيَاحُ وَالأَمْطَارُ ‡ *The winds and the rains made it to become tall.* (A, TA.*) — هَزَّ الكَوْكَبُ: see 8. — [مَهَزَّةٌ seems to be an inf. n. of هَزَّهُ.] You say رُمْحٌ لَدْنُ المَهَزَّةِ (Ṣ, TA, art. عرص,) [app. for عِنْدَ المَهَزَّةِ,] *A spear that vibrates,* or *quivers, when shaken.* (TA, ibid.)

2: see 1, in two places.

5: see 8.

8. اهتزّ, (inf. n. اِهْتِزَازٌ,) quasi-pass. of هَزَّهُ, (TA,) [*It shook;* or *quivered;*] *it became in motion,* or *in a state of commotion;* (Ṣ, Mṣb, Ḳ;) as also ↓ تهزّز, (Ṣ, Ḳ,) quasi-pass. of هزّزه; (TA;) and ↓ تَهَزْهَزَ, (Ṣ, A, Ḳ,) [quasi-pass. of هَزْهَزَهُ; meaning, accord. to explanations of هَزَّهُ in the TA, *it became moved by being pulled and pushed;* or *it became moved to the right and left:* or *it became so moved with violence,* or *vehemence.*] — اهتزّ المَآءُ فِى جَرْيِهِ ‡ [app. *the water quivered in its running*]: and اِهْتَزَّ الكَوْكَبُ فِى ٱنْقِضَاضِهِ ‡ [*the star in its shooting,* or *darting, down*]: (Ṣ, A, TA:) and اهتزّ الكَوْكَبُ ‡ *the star shot,* or *darted, down* [app. *with a quivering motion*]; (O, L, TA;) as also هَزَّ. (A, Ḳ.) — اهتزّ المَوْكِبُ ‡ *The procession,* or *cavalcade, went quickly:* (En-Naḍr, TA:) or *made a noise and clamour.* (Ṣ.) — اهتزّت الإِبِلُ ‡ *The camels,* being urged on by the singing of their driver, *became brisk,* or *sprightly.* (Ṣ,* A, TA.) You say also, اهتزّ لِلْأَمْرِ ‡ *He was,* or *became, active,* or *prompt, and brisk,* or *cheerfully excited, at a thing,* or *to do a thing.* (TA.) [Ex.] اهتزّ لِخَيْرٍ ‡ *He rejoiced* [or *was active* or *prompt, &c., to do good*]: said of a generous man. (En-Naḍr, TA.) And هُوَ يَهْتَزُّ لِلْمَعْرُوفِ ‡ [*He rejoices,* or is *active,* or *prompt, &c., to do what is beneficent,* or *kind*]. (A.) [Hence the saying,] فُلَانٌ لَا يَهْتَزُّ وَلٰكِنَّهُ يَكِزُّ ‡ [*Such a one does not rejoice, &c., to give, but he shrinks from giving*]. (A, TA, art. كز.) [Hence also,] اِهْتَزَّ عَرْشُ الرَّحْمٰنِ لِمَوْتِ سَعْدٍ ‡ *The empyrean of the Compassionate rejoiced at the death of Saad;* (En-Naḍr, IAth, Ḳ, TA;) meaning Saad Ibn-Mo'ádh; (TA;) i. e., when he [meaning his soul] was taken up; (IAth, TA;) because of the honour in which he was held by his Lord; (Ḳ;) or *the inhabitants of the empyrean rejoiced at his death:* these words occur in a trad., of which there is another relation, اهتزّ العَرْشُ: and some say, that by العرش is meant the bier upon which Saad was removed to his grave. (TA.) You also say, تَهَزْهَزَ ↓ إِلَيْهِ قَلْبِى ‡ *My heart became moved by a cheerful,* or *joyful, affection towards him.* (Ḳ, TA.) — اهتزّ النَّبَاتُ ‡ *The plant,* or *herbage, became tall.* (A, TA.) — اهتزّت الأَرْضُ ‡ *The land produced plants,* or *herbage:* (A:) or *became put in motion, and produced plants,* or *herbage.* (TA.)

R. Q. 1. هَزْهَزَهُ, and هَزْهَزْتُهُ, and هَزْهَزْتُ مِنْهُ: see 1. — Also, the first, (inf. n. هَزْهَزَةٌ, TA,) ‡ *He subdued him,* or *rendered him submissive;* syn. ذَلَّلَهُ. (Ḳ,* TA.)

R. Q. 2. تَهَزْهَزَ: see 8, in two places. — Also, ‡ *He became subdued,* or *submissive;* quasi-pass. of هَزْهَزَهُ. (TA.)

هَزَّةٌ ‡ *Brisk and rejoicing to do evil* or *mischief;* applied to a woman: pl. هَزَّاتٌ. (A, TA.)

هِزَّةٌ ‡ *Briskness,* or *sprightliness:* (Ṣ, Ḳ:) and ‡ *briskness, sprightliness, alacrity,* or *cheerfulness, disposing one to promptness in acts of liberality, kindness, and beneficence;* or *liberality of disposition;* syn. أَرْيَحِيَّةٌ; (Ḳ;) and [in like manner] ↓ هَزِيزٌ ‡ *briskness,* or *sprightliness, of camels when urged on by the singing of their driver.* (A, TA.) — ‡ *A kind of pace,* or *manner of going, of camels;* (Aṣ, Ḳ;) *when the train goes quickly:* (Aṣ,* En-Naḍr, TA:) or *a state of commotion of a train* or *procession* or *cavalcade:* (ISd, TA:) or the *confused sound thereof.* (IDrd, TA.) — ‡ The *sound of the boiling of a cooking-pot:* (Ṣ, Ḳ:) † the *reiterating sound of thunder;* as also ↓ هَزِيزٌ:

(Ḳ:) which latter has likewise the following similar significations: † *a sound*, or *noise*; (Ḳ;) as, for instance, *a sound*, or *noise*, *of turning* of a mill; as also أَزِيزٌ [inf. n. of أَزَّ]: (TA:) and ‡ the *murmuring of the wind* (Ṣ, Ḳ) *when it shakes the trees*: (Ṣ:) or *the sound of the blowing of the wind*: (TA:) or the *lightness of the wind*, and the *quickness of its blowing*. (A, TA.)

هَزِيزٌ: see هِزَّةٌ.

هَزَائِزُ † *Difficulties*, *afflictions*, or *calamities*: [a pl.] having no singular. (Th, TA.)

كَوْكَبٌ هَازٌّ ‡ [*A star shooting*, or *darting*, *down*; or *quivering in doing so*: see 8]. (Ṣ, TA.)

هَزْهَزَةٌ: see R. Q. 1, of which it is the inf. n.: and see هَزَاهِزُ.

هَزَاهِزُ [app. pl. of هَزْهَزَةٌ] *Seditions*, or *discords*, or *dissensions*, (فِتَنٌ,) *in which people are in a state of commotion*: (Ṣ, Mṣb:) or *wars and difficulties* or *afflictions* or *calamities that put into a state of commotion*: (A:) or the *excitement of commotion in men*, *by trials*, or *trying events*, *and by wars*; (Ḳ,* TA;) as also ▼ هَزْهَزَةٌ. (Ḳ.)

هزأ

1. هَزَأَ مِنْهُ, (Ḳ,) and بِهِ; (Ṣ, Ḳ;) and هَزِئَ (Ṣ, Ḳ) followed by منه and به; (Akh, Ṣ;) but accord. to Yoo, we should say هزئ به only; not منه; (TA;) aor. ـَ, inf. n. هُزْءٌ and هُزُؤٌ (Ṣ, Ḳ) and هُزُوءٌ (TA) and مَهْزَأَةٌ; (Ṣ, Ḳ;) and ▼ تهزّأ به, (AZ, Ṣ, Ḳ,) and ▼ استهزأ به; (Ṣ, Ḳ;) *He mocked at*, *scoffed at*, *laughed at*, *derided*, or *ridiculed*, *him*. (Ṣ, Ḳ.) —— The most approved reading of ▼ مُسْتَهْزِئُونَ in the Ḳur, ii. 13, is with the ء fully pronounced: some alleviate it: and some read مُسْتَهْزِيُونَ: and some مُسْتَهْزُونَ; (but this pronunciation is of weak authority;) and say إِسْتَهْزَيْتُ for إِسْتَهْزَأْتُ. (Zj.) —— السَّرَابُ يَهْزَأُ بِالرَّكْبِ ‡ [*The mirage mocks the company of riders*]. (A.) ═ هَزَأَ, (Ḳ,) inf. n. هَزْءٌ, (TA,) *He*, or *it*, *broke* a thing. (Ḳ.) —— A poet says, describing a coat of mail,

* لَهَا عُكَنٌ تَرُدُّ النَّبْلَ خُنْسًا *
* وَتَهْزَأُ بِالْمَعَابِلِ وَالْقِطَاعِ *

[*It has creases that repel the arrows, making them to recede, and break the broad and long arrow-heads, and those which are small and broad*]. The ب in بالمعابل is redundant. This is the opinion of the lexicologists, except ISd, who thinks that this is an error, and that تهزأ here means "mocks." (TA.) ═ هَزَأَ إِبِلَهُ, (Ḳ; but it is thought that this may be a mistake for هَزَّأَ, TA,) inf. n. هَزْءٌ; (TA;) and ▼ اهزأ ها; (Ḳ;) *He killed his camels with cold*. IAạr says, that اهرأه and اهزأه البَرْدُ both signify *The cold killed him*. (TA.) ═ هَزَأَ *He put in motion*, [or *excited*,] the beast on which he rode. (Aṣ, Ḳ.) ═ هَزَأَ and هَزِئَ *He died* (Ḳ) *in his place*, or *on the spot*; i. e. *unexpectedly*, or *suddenly*: (Z:) improperly objected against by Ibn-Eṣ-Ṣáïgh. ('Ináyeh, MF.)

4. اهزأ *He entered upon the time of severe cold*. (Ḳ.) See also اهرأ, which is the word commonly known. (TA.) —— See 1. ═ اهزأتْ بِهِ نَاقَتُهُ *His she-camel hastened with him*. (Ḳ.)

5: } see 1.
10: }

هُزْأَةٌ One *who is mocked at*, *scoffed at*, *laughed at*, *derided*; a *ridiculous* person. (Ṣ, Ḳ.)

هُزَأَةٌ One *who mocks at*, *scoffs at*, *laughs at*, *derides*, or *ridicules*, *others*. (Ṣ, Ḳ.)

غَدَاةٌ هَازِئَةٌ ‡ *A morning intensely cold*: as though mocking men when they shrug and shiver. (A.)

مَفَازَةٌ هَازِئَةٌ بِالرَّكْبِ, and with هُزَأَةٌ for هازئة, ‡[*A desert that mocks the company of riders*]. (A.)

هزب

هَوْزَبٌ A camel *strong in running*; syn. قَوِىُّ الجَرْىِ: (Ḳ, and so in a copy of the Ṣ:) or a *strong and bold* camel; syn. قَوِىٌّ جَرِىءٌ: (so in the Ṣ, in several copies): a *strong* camel: (El-Jarmee:) a camel *advanced in age*, *and bold*. (Aṣ.) —— هَوْزَبٌ *A vulture*, (Ḳ,) *advanced in age*. (TA.)

هَيْزَبٌ *Sharp*; *fierce*; syn. حَدِيدٌ. —— لَيْثٌ هَيْزَبٌ *A sharp*, or *fierce*, *lion*: (Ḳ, accord. to the TA:) or *a strong lion*. (CḲ.)

هَازِبَا and هَازِبَى *A kind of fish*. (Ḳ.)

هزبر

هِزَبْرٌ and هِزْبِرٌ and هُزَابِرٌ, (Ḳ,) or the first [only], (TA,) *Thick and bulky*: and *strong and hard* or *hardy*: pl. هَزَابِرُ. (Ḳ.) You say, نَاقَةٌ هِزَبْرَةٌ *A hard*, or *hardy*, *she-camel*. (IAạr.) —— Also, the first, (Ṣ, Ḳ,) and the second and third, (Ṣgh, Ḳ,) The *lion*: (Ṣ, Ṣgh, Ḳ,) accord. to some, because of his thickness and bulkiness. (TA.) Some say that the ه is a radical letter: others, that it is augmentative, and that the word is from زَبْرٌ, signifying the "act of repelling with strength." (MF, TA.)

هزج

1. هَزِجَ, aor. ـَ, (Ṣ, Ḳ,) inf. n. هَزَجٌ; (L;) *He sang in a certain manner*, *with trilling*, or *quavering*; as also ▼ تهزّج; (Ṣ, Ḳ;) and ▼ هزّج: (Ḳ:) or ▼ تهزّج signifies *he reiterated*, or *made to reciprocate*, *the graceful modulations of his voice*: or *prolonged his voice*, *without elevating it*: (Aboo-Is-ḥáḳ, L:) or هَزَجٌ does not at all signify trilling, or quavering; and therefore IAạr has applied هَزِجٌ as an epithet to a dog that barks much. (L.) —— *He read*, or *recited*, *with a prolonging and trilling of the voice*, *making the sounds to follow closely*, *one upon another*; as also ▼ تهزّج. (TA.)

2. هزّج الصَّوْتَ, inf. n. تَهْزِيجٌ, *He* (a singer [or a reader or reciter]), *made the sounds of the voice to be closely consecutive*, *and uttered in a light and quick manner*. (L.) —— هزّج صَوْتَهُ, and ▼ تهزّجهُ, [the latter app. a mistake for تهزّج فِيهِ,] *He made the sounds of his voice to be closely consecutive*, or *near together*. (TA.) —— See 1.

4. اهزج *He* (a poet) *composed*, or *uttered*, *verses of the metre termed* الهَزَج. (Ḳ.)

5. تهزّجت القَوْسُ ‡ *The bow twanged*, on the archer's loosing the string after drawing it. (Ṣ, Ḳ, TA.) —— See 1, and 2.

هَزَجٌ ‡ The *twanging* of a bow, on the archer's loosing the string after drawing it; and of a lute-string: in the TA, i.q. رَنَّةٌ: pl. أَهْزَاجٌ and pl. pl. أَهَازِيجُ: or perhaps this latter is a pl. of which the sing. is ▼ أُهْزُوجَةٌ, like أَرَاجِيزُ as is pl of أُرْجُوزَةٌ: and the twanging of a bow-string or lute-string may be likened to *an ode* or *a song of the metre termed* الهَزَج, which is perhaps, judging from analogy, the proper signification of اهزوجة.]

لِلْعُودِ وَالقَوْسِ أَهَازِيجُ ‡ [*To the lute and the bow there are twangings*]. (A.) El-Kumeyt says, [speaking of a bow,]

* لَمْ يَعِبْ رَبُّهَا وَلَا النَّاسُ مِنْهَا *
* غَيْرَ إِنْذَارِهَا عَلَيْهِ الحَمِيرَا *
* بِأَهَازِيجَ مِنْ أَغَانِيِّهَا الجُشِّ *
* وَإِتْبَاعِهَا النَّحِيبَ الزَّفِيرَا *

[*Neither its owner nor the people imputed a fault to any of its properties, except its warning the* (wild) *asses of his presence by the twangings of its harsh singings, and its causing a groaning sound to follow the loud*, or *prolonged*, *wailing*]. (Ṣ.) —— هَزَجٌ *One of the modes of singing* (الأَغَانِىّ), *in which is a trilling*, or *quavering*: (Ṣ, Ḳ:) pl. أَهْزَاجٌ. (L.) [But see 1.] —— *A voice that excites lively emotions of joy or grief*. (Ḳ.) —— *A fine*, or *delicate*, *and elevated*, *voice*. (TA.) —— *A voice in which is hoarseness*, or *harshness*. (Ḳ.) —— *Any speech of which the component parts are closely consecutive*, or *near together*, (Ḳ,) *uttered in a light*, or *quick*, *manner*: pl. as above. (L.) ——

الهَزَج *The name of a certain kind of metre of verse;* (Ṣ, Ḳ;) *consisting of four feet, each of the measure* مَفَاعِيلُنْ: *originally of six feet,* like the رَجَز and the رَمَل, in each of which, [as in the هَزَج,] each foot consists of one element of the kind termed وَتِدٌ مَجْمُوعٌ, and of two elements of the kind termed سَبَبٌ خَفِيفٌ: so called because of the mutual nearness of its component parts. (TA.) —— هَزَجٌ *Lightness,* or *agility.* (TA.) —— *Quickness in the falling, and putting down, of the legs* [*upon the ground*]. (TA.) —— ‡ The *sound* of thunder. (S.) —— † The *buzzing* of flies. (L.)

هَزِجٌ A singer [or reader or reciter] *who prolongs his voice, with trilling,* or *quavering, making the sounds to follow close, one upon another.* (A.) —— هَزِجُ العَشِيِّ, occurring in a verse of 'Antarah, cited voce دقّ, The cat *that cries* for food *at supper-time:* (EM, p. 233:) or the dog *that barks much in the evening;* meaning, in* the night: or *buzzing* flies *in the evening.* (L.) —— هَزِجٌ A child, and a horse, *whose legs fall,* or *are put down, quickly* [*upon the ground*]. (TA.) —— ‡ *Sounding* thunder, as also ▾ مُتَهَزِّجٌ. (L.) —— ‡ A *twanging* lute [and bow]. (A.) —— ‡ A cloud *sounding* with thunder. (A.) —— هَزِجُ الصَّوْتِ, and ▾ هُزَامِجُهُ, One *who makes the sounds of his voice to follow close, one upon another.* (L.)

هَزْمَجَةٌ *Uninterrupted speech* or *language.* (Ḳ.) —— *Confusion of voice* or *sound beyond measure;* (Ḳ;) as also هَزْلَجَةٌ. (Ḳ, TA, art. هزلج.) —— [The م is an augmentative letter: see هُزَامِجٌ.]

هُزَامِجٌ A voice, or the like, *of which the sounds are closely consecutive.* The م is an augmentative letter. (Ṣ, Ḳ.) —— صَوْتٌ هُزَامِجٌ *A confused voice* or *sound.* The sound so called is less than what is termed رُغَاءٌ. (L.) —— [See also هَزِجٌ.]

أُهْزُوجَةٌ: see هَزَجٌ.

مُتَهَزِّجٌ: see هَزِجٌ.

هزر [See Supplement.]

هَزَارٌ [The *nightingale;*] *a certain bird,* (Ḳ, TA,) *the same that is called* عَنْدَلِيبٌ, (Ṣ, Ḳ, art. عندلب,) *of sweet voice;* improperly said in the Ḳ to be what is called in Persian هَزَارْ دَسْتَانْ; for هزار itself is Persian, and signifies "a thousand," and دَاسْتَانْ means [as also دَسْتَانْ in that language] "a tale;" as though this bird, in the sweetness of its warbling and the pleasantness of its melody, told a thousand tales; being thus called by way of hyperbole and excessive praise: then they contented themselves by employing the word هزار alone; and the Arabs used it, and prefixed to it the article ال: (TA:) the pl. is هَزَارَاتٌ. (Mṣb.)

هزرب

Q. 1. هَزْرَبَ, inf. n. هَزْرَبَةٌ, *He was light,* or *active, and quick,* or *swift.* (IḲṭṭ, Ḳ.) A dial. form. of هَذْرَبَ. (TA.)

[هزع &c.
See Supplement.]

هزلج

Q. 1. هَزْلَجَ, inf. n. هَزْلَجَةٌ, *He* (an ostrich, or anything,) *was quick,* or *swift.* (TA.)

هَزْلَجَةٌ: see 1; and art. هزج.

هَزْلَجٌ A *quick,* or *swift,* he-ostrich. (Ḳ.)

هِزْلَاجٌ *Quick,* or *swift:* (TA:) a *light,* or an *agile, (and swift,* or *quick,* TA,) wolf: (Ṣ, Ḳ:) pl. هَزَالِيجُ and هَزَالِجُ. (TA.) Accord. to Kr, it is derived from الهَزَجُ. (TA.) [See هَزْمَجَةٌ in art. هزج.]

[هزم
See Supplement.]

هزمج

هَزْمَجَةٌ and هُزَامِجٌ: see art. هزج.

[هس
See Supplement.]

هسب

هَسْبٌ *Sufficiency;* like حَسْبٌ. (Ḳ.)

[هسد &c.
See Supplement.]

هش

1. هَشَّ, aor. يَهِشُّ; (JK, TA;) or هَشَّ, sec. pers. هَشِشْتَ, aor. يَهَشُّ; (Mṣb;) inf. n. هَشَاشَةٌ (JK, A, Mṣb, TA) [and هُشُوشٌ and هُشُوشَةٌ and هَشٌّ, as appears from what follows]; *It,* (a thing) *was,* or *became, soft, yielding, flaccid, flabby, lax, slack, uncompact, crummy, fragile, frangible, brittle, friable, easily* or *quickly broken;* (JK, A, Mṣb, TA;) syn. كَانَ فِيهِ رَخَاوَةٌ, (JK,) or لَانَ وَٱسْتَرْخَى, (A,* TA,) or كَانَ رِخْوًا لَيِّنًا, (Mṣb.) You say, هَشَّ الخُبْزُ, aor. ـَ, (Ṣ, Ḳ,) inf. n. هُشُوشَةٌ (Ḳ) and هَشٌّ, (TA,) meaning, صار هَشًّا; (Ṣ, Ḳ;) i. e., *The bread became* [*soft,* &c., or] *easy to break.* (TA.) And هَشَّ العُودُ, (IAạr, Mṣb,) aor. [ـَ, or] ـِ, (Mṣb,) inf. n. هُشُوشٌ, (IAạr, Mṣb,) *The wood, or stick, broke in pieces:* (IAạr:) or *became easily* or *quickly broken.* (Mṣb.) And هَشَّتِ الشَّجَرَةُ, inf. n. هَشٌّ, *The tree dropped its leaves, one after another.* (Mṣb [in which it seems to be indicated that the aor. of the verb in this sense is ـُ; but this is contr. to rule in an intrans. verb of this class; and I think it improbable.]) —— هَشَّ, inf. n. هُشُوشَةٌ, † *He* (a man) *became weak; unable to endure difficulty* or *distress.* (TA.) And هَشَّ, aor. ـَ, † *He affected languor,* or *languidness;* syn. تَكَسَّرَ: and *he became old,* or *aged.* (TA.) ═ هَشَّ, (Mṣb, Ḳ,) first pers. هَشِشْتُ, (Ṣ, Mṣb, Ḳ,) aor. يَهَشُّ; (Mṣb, Ḳ,) and هَشَّ, first pers. هَشَشْتُ, aor. يَهِشُّ; (Mṣb, Ḳ;) inf. n. هَشَاشَةٌ (Ṣ, Mṣb, Ḳ) and هَشَاشٌ; (A, Ḳ;) ‡ *He was,* or *became, cheerful, brisk, lively,* or *sprightly:* (Ṣ, Ḳ:) or *he smiled, and was,* or *became cheerful, brisk, lively,* or *sprightly.* (Mṣb.) You say, هَشِشْتُ بِفُلَانٍ, (Ṣ, TA,) and هَشِشْتُ بِهِ, (TA,) ‡ *I was,* or *became, cheerful,* &c., *in behaviour towards such a one:* (Ṣ:) or *I was,* or *became cheerful in countenance,* or *joyful,* or *pleased, at meeting with such a one.* (TA.) And هُوَ يَهَشُّ إِلَى إِخْوَانِهِ, ‡ *He is cheerful,* &c., *towards his brethren*]. (A.) And دَخَلْتُ عَلَيْهِ فَٱهْتَشَّ ▾ بِى ‡ [*I went in to him, and he was cheerful,* &c., *in his behaviour towards me*]; like إِهْتَزَّ لِى. (A,* TA.) And هَشِشْتُ لِلْمَعْرُوفِ, (JK, TA,*) and هَشَشْتُ, (TA,) inf. n. هَشَاشَةٌ (Ṣ) and هَشَاشٌ, (A,) ‡ *I was,* or *became, cheerful, brisk,* &c., *to do what was kind,* or *beneficent:* (Ṣ,* TA:) or *I desired to do it:* (JK:) and ▾ إِهْتَشَشْتُ للمعروف *I was,* or *became, cheerful,* &c., *and desirous, to do what was kind,* or *beneficent.* (TA.) And هُوَ ذُو هَشَاشٍ إِلَى الخَيْرِ ‡ [*He possesses cheerfulness, briskness, liveliness,* or *sprightliness, of disposition to do good*]. (A.) Accord. to Sh, هَشِشْتُ signifies † *He rejoiced, and desired;* or *was,* or *became, joyful, and desirous.* (TA.) And the phrase هَشِشْتُ إِلَى ٱمْرَأَتِى, if correct, means either † *I inclined towards my wife,* or *I was,* or *became, brisk,* or *sprightly, in disposition towards her.* (Mgh.) And accord to ISd, هَشَاشُ القَوْمِ [so in the TA, but accord. to the JK هَشَاهِشُ,] † *The people's being in a state of commotion,* or *agitation.* (TA.) ═ هَشَّ الوَرَقَ, aor. ـُ, (Ṣ, A, Ḳ,) and ـِ, (Ṣgh, Ḳ,) inf. n. هَشٌّ, (Ṣ,) *He beat the leaves* with a staff, or stick, *in order that they might fall;* (Ṣ, A, Ḳ;) as also ▾ هَشْهَشَهُ. (Z, TA.) It is said in the Ḳur, [xx. 19,] (Ṣ,) وَأَهُشُّ بِهَا عَلَى غَنَمِى [*And I beat the leaves with it in order that they may fall upon my sheep,* or *goats*]: (Ṣ, A:) or, accord. to Fr, *and I beat the dry trees with it in order that their leaves may fall so that my sheep,* or *goats, may feed upon them;* and so says Aṣ: (TA:) Lth says, that الهَشّ signifies thy *drawing towards thee a branch of a tree:* and also, thy *scattering its leaves towards thee with a staff,* or *stick:* (JK,* TA:) but Az says, that the correct ex-

planation is that given by Fr and Aṣ; not the former of the two explanations given by Lth. (TA.) [The verb also seems to have a similar application in a more extended sense; for it is said that] هَشَّ, aor. ـُ, inf. n. هَشٌّ, signifies He (a man) assaulted (صَالَ) with his staff, or stick. (Mṣb.) You say also, هَشَّ الهَشِيمَ *He broke in pieces the dry herbage* or *the like*. (TA.)

2. هَشَّشَهُ, (JK, Ḳ,) inf. n. تَهْشِيشٌ, (TA,) † *He deemed him*, or *reckoned him*, *weak*, or *feeble*, (JK, Ḳ,*) *and soft*, or *gentle*. (TA.) ═ ‡ *He*, or *it*, *rendered him brisk*, *lively*, or *sprightly*; *and joyful*, *glad*, or *happy*: (Ḳ:) and ▼ استهشّهُ ‡ *it* (a thing, JK, TA) *incited him*, or *excited him*, *to briskness*, *liveliness* or *sprightliness*; syn. إِسْتَخَفَّهُ. (JK, Ḳ, TA.) You say, ▼ فُلَانٌ مَا يَسْتَهِشُّهُ النَّعِيمُ ‡ [*Such a one*, *weal*, or *welfare*, *does not excite him to briskness*, &c.] (A, TA.)

8. اهتشّ *He was*, or *became*, *cheerful*, &c.: see 1, in two places.

10: see 2, in two places.

R. Q. 1. هَشْهَشَهُ: see 1, latter part. — *He moved*, or *put in motion*, or *into a state of commotion*, *him*, or *it*. (IDrd, Ḳ.)

هَشٌّ A thing, (Ṣ, Mṣb,) or anything, (JK,) *soft*, *yielding*, *flaccid*, *flabby*, *lax*, *slack*, *uncompact*, *crummy*, *fragile*, *frangible*, *brittle*, *friable*, *easily* or *quickly broken*; (JK,* Ṣ,* A,* Mṣb, Ḳ,* TA;) syn. رِخْوٌ لَيِّنٌ; (Ṣ, A, Ḳ;) as also ▼ هَشِيشٌ. (JK, Ṣ, Ḳ.) You say, خُبْزٌ هَشٌّ, (Ṣ, Ḳ,) and ▼ هَشَاشٌ, (Ḳ,) *Bread that is* [*soft*, &c., or] *easy to break*. (TA.) And خُبْزَةٌ هَشَّةٌ *A lump of dough*, *baked in a fire in the ground*, *that is dry*, or *hard*: asserted by IḲṭṭ to have two contr. significations. (TA.) [But to this assertion it may be replied, that dry bread is easy to break.] And in like manner, أُتْرُجَّةٌ هَشَّةٌ *A citron easy to break*: or *dry*, or *hard*. (TA.) And عُودٌ هَشٌّ *Wood*, or *a stick*, *that is easily*, or *quickly broken*. (Mṣb.) — [Hence,] هُوَ هَشُّ الْمَكْسِرِ, (JK, Ṣ, A, Ḳ,) or الْمَكْسَرِ, (TA, [but this is contr. to all the other authorities that I know,]) and الْمَكَسَّرِ, (TA,) ‡ *He is easy*, or *compliant*, *when asked*: (A:) or *he is of easy nature*, or *disposition*, (JK, Ṣ, Ḳ,) *with respect to what is sought*, or *demanded*, *of him*, *of things needed*: (Ṣ:) said in praise of a man (Ṣ, TA) when it means [lit.] that he is not one whose wood gives only a sound when one endeavours to produce fire from it; but said in dispraise of a man when it means [lit.] that he is one whose wood is weak. (TA.) [And in like manner] ▼ هَشِيشٌ (Ḳ) and ▼ هَاشٌّ (TA) signify ‡ One *who rejoices*, or *is glad*, *when asked*. (Ḳ, TA.) You say, ▼ هُوَ هَاشٌّ عِنْدَ السُّؤَالِ, and ▼ هَشِيشٌ, ‡ *He is one who rejoices*, or *is glad*, *at being asked*. (TA.) — [Hence also,] رَجُلٌ هَشٌّ إِلَى إِخْوَانِهِ, (TA,) or and ▼ هَاشٌّ, (JK,) ‡ *A man who is cheerful*, *brisk*, *lively*, or *sprightly*, *in his behaviour towards his brethren*. (JK, TA.) And رَجُلٌ هَشٌّ بَشٌّ ‡ *A man who is cheerful*, *brisk*, *lively*, or *sprightly*: (Ṣ:) or *cheerful in countenance*; *pleasant* [*therein*]. (Ṣ, TA in art. بش.) And أَنَا بِهِ هَشٌّ بَشٌّ ‡ *I am cheerful*, *brisk*, *lively*, or *sprightly*, *in behaviour towards him*; (Ḳ;) *joyful*; *happy*. (TA.) And رَجُلٌ هَشٌّ فُؤَادُهُ ‡ *A man quick*, or *prompt*, *to do good*. (Aṣ.) And فَرَسٌ هَشُّ العِنَانِ † [*A horse that is brisk*, *lively*, or *sprightly*; lit.,] *light of rein*. (TA.) And فَرَسٌ هَشٌّ ‡ *A horse that sweats much*; (JK, IF, Ḳ;) *contr. of* صَلُودٌ; (Ṣ;) or *not* صلود. (A.)

هَشَاشٌ: see هَشٌّ, second sentence.

هَشُوشٌ † A ewe, or she-goat, *abounding with milk*. (Ṣ, Ḳ.)

هَشِيشٌ *Dry herbage*, syn. هَشِيمٌ, (Ḳ, TA,) *for the horses of the people of* الأَسْيَافِ [app. meaning *the shores of 'Omán*] *in particular*. (TA.) ═ See also هَشٌّ, in three places. — Also, † A man *who is niggardly towards his family*, or *others*, *with respect to food*; syn. مُقَتِّرٌ. (TA.) [Thus it bears two contr. significations.]

هَشِيشَةٌ is thought by ISd to signify *Leaves* [app. *beaten from a tree*]. (TA.)

قِرْبَةٌ هَشَاشَةٌ *A water-skin from which the water flows by reason of its thinness*. (Ḳ.)

هَشْهَشَةٌ † *Motion*; or *commotion*. (JK.) [هَشَاهِشُ is app. its pl.: see 1, next before هَشَّ الوَرَقَ.]

هَشْهَاشٌ ‡ *Good in disposition*; *liberal*, or *bountiful*. (IAạr, Ḳ.)

هَاشٌّ: see هَشٌّ, in three places.

مُهَشْهِشَةٌ, in the copies of the Ḳ erroneously written مُتَهَشْهِشَةٌ, (TA,) † A woman *who manifests love to her husband*, *and rejoices in him*. (Ḳ,* TA.)

[هشر &c.

See Supplement.]

هصب

1. هَصَبَ, aor. ـِ, inf. n. هَصْبٌ, *He fled*; *ran away*. (Ḳ.)

هصر

1. هَصَرَهُ, (Ṣ, A, Ḳ,) and هَصَرَ بِهِ, (Ṣ, Ḳ,) aor. ـِ, (Ḳ,) inf. n. هَصْرٌ, (A, Ḳ,) *He pulled it*: and *he inclined it*: or *he pulled and inclined it*: (A, Ḳ, TA [but in the last of these, only هَصَرَهُ is given in this sense, agreeably with the A:]) *he brought it near*; (Ḳ;) which is near in meaning to "he inclined it:" (TA:) *he took hold of its* (a branch's) *head and inclined it towards him*: (Ṣ:) or *he inclined it* (a branch) *towards him*: (A:) or *he bent it* (a branch) *and drew it towards him*: (Mgh:) *he bent it*; namely, a pliant thing, such as a branch and the like: (A, Ḳ:) and *he broke it without separating*: (Ḳ:) or *he bent it*, namely, anything: (A,* Ḳ:) as also ▼ اهتصرهُ. (Ḳ.) Imra-el-Ḳeys says, (Ṣ, TA,) using the verb tropically, (TA,)

* فَلَمَّا تَنَازَعْنَا الحَدِيثَ وَأَسْمَحَتْ *

* هَصَرْتُ بِغُصْنٍ ذِي شَمَارِيخَ مَيَّالِ *

And when we discoursed together, *and she became compliant*, *I pulled*, (TA,) or, *laying hold of its head*, *inclined towards me*, (Ṣ,) *a branch with fruit-stalks*, *waving from side to side*: the poet meaning, by the branch, her body, because bending, and soft or supple, like a branch, and likening her hair to the fruit-stalks of the raceme of a palm-tree, in respect of its abundance and luxuriance. (TA.) And it is said in a trad., respecting the building of the mosque of Ḳubà, رَفَعَ حَجَرًا ثَقِيلًا فَهَصَرَهُ إِلَى بَطْنِهِ *He raised a heavy stone*, *and inclined it towards his belly*. (TA.) And in another trad., كَانَ إِذَا رَكَعَ هَصَرَ ظَهْرَهُ *He used*, *when he bowed himself* [*in prayer*], *to bend down his back towards the ground*: (TA:) or هَصَرَ ظَهْرَهُ signifies *he bent his back much*, *making it even with his neck*. (Mgh.) — ‡ *He pushed him* or *it*; so accord. to all the copies of the Ḳ; but accord. to other authorities, ‡ *he pressed* or *squeezed*, *him* or *it*: and *he pressed*, or *squeezed*, *him* or *it vehemently*. (TA.) You say, هَصَرَ قِرْنَهُ, aor. and inf. n. as above, ‡ *He pressed*, or *squeezed*, *his adversary*. (TA.) — Also, (Ḳ,) or هَصَرَهُ [alone], (Ṣ,) † *He broke it*; (Ṣ, Ḳ;) as also ▼ اهتصرهُ. (Ṣ.) You say of a lion, هَصَرَ الفَرِيسَةَ, (A, TA,) aor. and inf. n. as above, ‡ *He broke* [*the neck of*] *the prey*, *and inclined it towards him*. (TA.) And هَصَرَ رَأْسَ الفَرِيسَةِ, and بِرَأْسِهَا, (A, TA,) ‡ *He* [*broke the head of*, or] *slew the prey*. (TA.) ═ هَصَرَ جَدُّهُ, aor. ـُ, [inf. n. هَصْرٌ,] ‡ *His good fortune declined*. (TA.)

5: see 7.

7. انهصر and ▼ اهتصر *It became pulled*: and *it became inclined*: or *it became pulled and inclined*: *it was brought near*: *it* (a pliant thing, such as a branch and the like,) *bent*: *it broke*, *without separating*: or *it* (anything) *bent*: (Ḳ:) or *it* (a branch) *inclined and bent*: (TA:) or *fell upon the ground*: (AḤn, TA:) and ▼ تهصّر *it* (a branch)

hung down, or was pendent. (TA.) [It seems to be implied in the Ḳ that انهصر and ▾ اهتصر are quasi-passives of هَصَرَهُ in all its senses.]

8. اهتصر : see 7. — اهتصرهُ : see 1, in two places. — اهتصر النَّخْلَةَ He placed the racemes of the palm-tree upon the branches, and put them straight or even. (T, Ḳ.)

هَصِرٌ ‡ A man who presses, or squeezes, vehemently; as also ▾ هُصَرٌ. (TA.) — ‡ The lion; as also ▾ هَصَرٌ and ▾ هُصَرَةٌ (Ḳ) and ▾ هَصُورٌ (Ṣ, Ḳ) and ▾ هَصَوَرٌ and ▾ هَصَوْرَةٌ (Ḳ) and ▾ هَصَّارٌ (Ṣ, Ḳ) and ▾ هَاصِرٌ (Ḳ) and ▾ هَيْصَرٌ (Ṣ, Ḳ [in the CḲ (هَيْصُورٌ)]) and ▾ هَيْصَارٌ and ▾ مِهْصَرٌ and ▾ مِهْصَارٌ and ▾ مِهْصِيرٌ and ▾ مُهْتَصِرٌ: (Ḳ:) or هَصُورٌ is an epithet applied to a lion, (A, TA,) as also ▾ هَصَّارٌ and ▾ هَيْصَرٌ [&c.], (A,) signifying, that slays and breaks: (TA:) pl. [of هَاصِرٌ] هَوَاصِرُ and [poeticè] هَوَاصِيرُ. (TA.) — جَدٌّ هَصِرٌ ‡ Declining good fortune. (TA.)

هُصَرٌ:
هُصَرَةٌ:
هَصُورٌ:
هَصَوَرٌ:
هَصَوْرَةٌ:
هَصَّارٌ:
هَاصِرٌ:
هَيْصَرٌ: } see هَصِرٌ.
هَيْصَارٌ:
هَيْصُورٌ:
مِهْصَرٌ:
مِهْصَارٌ:
مِهْصِيرٌ:
مُهْتَصِرٌ:

[هصم, &c.
See Supplement.]

هض

1. هَضَّهُ, (Ṣ, A, Ḳ,) aor. ـُ, (Ṣ,) inf. n. هَضٌّ, (TA,) He broke it; as also ▾ اهتضّهُ; (Ṣ, Ḳ;) and ▾ هَضْهَضَهُ; (Ḳ;) inf. n. هَضْهَضَةٌ: (TA:) and the first, (Ṣ, A,) or ▾ all, (Ḳ,) he bruised, brayed, pounded, or crushed, it; (Ṣ, Ḳ;) i. q. رَضَّهُ; i. e. a stone, &c.: (A:) or he broke it in a manner falling short of what is termed هَدّ, [in the CḲ, incorrectly حَدّ,] but exceeding what is termed رَضّ: (Lth, Ḳ:) or, accord. to some, the first, he broke it leisurely, or gently: and the ▾ last, he broke it hastily. (TA.) You say, الفَحْلُ يَهُضُّ أَعْنَاقَ الفُحُولِ (Ṣ, A) The stallion breaks, or crushes, the necks of the [other] stallions; as also ▾ يُهَضْهِضُهَا. (TA.) And الإِبِلُ تَهُضُّ الأَرْضَ The camels bruise the ground. (L.) — Also, هَضَّتِ الإِبِلُ † The camels hastened, or went quickly. (Ḳ.) And جَآءَتِ الإِبِلُ تَهُضُّ السَّيْرَ, inf. n. as above, † The camels came hastening, or quickly. (TA.) And جَآءَ فُلَانٌ يَهُضُّ المَشْىَ, (Ibn-El-Faraj, JK, Ḳ,*) and يَبُزُّهُ, (Ibn-El-Faraj, JK,) † Such a one came walking impulsively: (JK:) or with a graceful gait, (Ibn-El-Faraj, Ḳ,) impulsively. (Ibn-El Faraj.) — هَضّ is also syn. with حَضّ. (Ibn-'Abbád, Ḳ.)

2. هضّض He bruised the ground vehemently with his feet. (TA.)

7. انهضّ It broke, or became broken: (Ṣ, Ḳ:) it became bruised, brayed, pounded, or crushed: (Ṣ:) quasi-pass. of هَضَّهُ and اهتضّهُ. (TA.)

8: see 1, in two places. — اهْتَضَضْتُ نَفْسِى لِفُلَانٍ † I held myself to have fallen short of my duty to such a one; syn. إِسْتَزَدْتُهَا. (JK, Ṣ, Ḳ [in one copy of the Ṣ, إِسْتَزَلْتُهَا].) — اِهْتَضَضْتُ مِنْ فُلَانٍ شَيْئًا † I took from such a one a thing. (JK.)

R. Q. 1. هَضْهَضَهُ: see 1, in three places.

هَضَّآءُ A company (Ṣ, Ḳ) of men; of the measure فَعْلَآءُ, like صَحْرَآءُ; mentioned by Th; (Ṣ;) and by Aṣ; (TA;) or a company of horses, or horsemen: (A, TA:) and a [troop of horse such as is termed] كَتِيبَة: because they break things. (TA.)

هَضِيضٌ A thing (Ṣ) broken: bruised, brayed, pounded, or crushed: as also ▾ مَهْضُوضٌ, (Ṣ, Ḳ,) and ▾ مُنْهَضٌّ. (Ṣ.)

هُضَاضَةٌ, like سُحَابَةٌ, (Ḳ,) or هَضَاضَةٌ, (so in the JK,) † What is taken (مَا يُهْتَضُّ [in the CḲ, erroneously, يُنْهَضُّ,]) from any one. (JK [where it immediately follows the phrase اِهْتَضَضْتُ مِنْ فُلَانٍ شَيْئًا explained as above], Sgh, Ḳ.)

فَحْلٌ هُضَاضٌ A stallion that breaks, or crushes, the necks of the [other] stallions; (Ṣ, A, Ḳ;) as also ▾ هُضَاهِضٌ: (JK, Ḳ:) or a stallion that throws down a man, and a camel, then leans, bears, or presses, upon him with his breast. (IDrd.)

هُضَاهِضٌ: see what next precedes.

مَهْضُوضٌ: } see هَضِيضٌ.
مُنْهَضٌّ:

مُهَضْهِضَةٌ ‡ A woman (TA) who annoys, or molests, her fellow-wife or female neighbour, or her fellow-wives or female neighbours: (so accord. to different copies of the Ḳ:) transmitted by Sgh. (TA.)

هضب

1. هَضَبَتِ السَّمَآءُ, aor. ـِ, The sky rained: (Ḳ:) or rained for some days incessantly. (TA.) See هَضْبَةٌ. — هَضَبَتْهُمُ السَّمَآءُ The sky rained upon them: (Ṣ:) it wetted them much. (TA.) — يَهْضِبُ بِالشِّعْرِ وَبِالخُطَبِ ‡ He pours forth verses, and discourses in rhyming prose, or the like. (A.) — هَضَبَ فِى الحَدِيثِ and ▾ اهتضب, (Ṣ, Ḳ,) and ▾ اهضب (Ḳ, but omitted in the TA,) † He launched into discourse, (Ṣ, Ḳ,) and talked much, or launched into discourse time after time, (TA,) and raised his voice. (Ṣ, TA.) — اِهْضِبُوا يَا قَوْمِ Talk, or speak, O people. (Ṣ.) — هَضَبَ and ▾ اهضب He talked loud. (AA.) — هَضَبَ He (a man) walked in the manner of a stupid, dull, unexcitable person. (Ḳ.) — هَضَبَ القَوْمَ: see ضَبَبَ, and هَاضِبٌ.

4: see 1.

8: see 1. — اهتضب It (the vibrating of a bow-string) produced a twanging. (TA.)

10. استهضب It became what is termed هَضْبٌ, (Ḳ,) or هَضْبَةٌ; (A;) i. e. a mountain of the kind so termed. (A.)

هَضْبٌ A kind, mode, or way. A. Heyth quotes the following verse of El-Kumeyt, describing a horse:

* مُخْتَلِفٌ بَعْضُهُ وَرْدٌ وَسَائِرُهُ *
* جَوْنُ أَفَانِينَ إِجْرِيَّاهُ لَا هَضْبُ *

The poet means, that his running, or usual running, was of different, or various, kinds; not of one هضب, or kind. (L.) — See هَضْبَةٌ.

هَضْبَةٌ : see هَضْبٌ.

هَضْبَةٌ A rain: (Ṣ, Ḳ:) or a rain consisting of many drops: (IAth:) or a lasting rain, consisting of great drops: or a single fall thereof: (TA:) or hard rain: (Mṣb:) pl. هِضَبٌ, (Ṣ, Ḳ,) like بِدَرٌ pl. of بَدْرَةٌ, (Ṣ,) extr. [with respect to rule], (TA,) and هِضَابٌ, (Ḳ,) or this is pl. of هَضْبٌ accord. to the Ṣ; (TA;) and pl. pl. أَهَاضِيبُ; (Ḳ;) or this is pl. of هِضَابٌ, which is pl. of ▾ هَضْبٌ, signifying fine showers of rain after other rain; syn. حَلَبَاتُ قَطْرٍ بَعْدَ قَطْرٍ; (AZ, Ṣ;) and this is what is correct: (TA:) or ▾ هَضْبٌ signifies a fine rain; or a fine shower of rain; syn. حَلْبَةُ قَطْرٍ: it is also said, in the L, that ▾ أُهْضُوبَةٌ is syn. with هَضْبٌ, [either in one of the last two senses, or as a coll. gen. n. of which هَضْبَةٌ is the n. un., which it is said to be below,] and that اهاضيب is its pl.: ▾ هُضُوبَةٌ also is the same as اهضوبة: so in the phrase أَصَابَتْهُمُ الهُضُوبَةُ مِنَ المَطَرِ [The fine shower, or showers, of rain (or *the shower of rain*, or *of copious rain*, or *of lasting rain consisting of large drops*, or *hard rain*,) *fell upon them*]; mentioned in the Ḳ: it is also said in the L, that هَضْبٌ forms in the pl. أَهْضَابٌ, and then أَهَاضِيبُ; like as قَوْلٌ forms أَقْوَالٌ, and then أَقَاوِيلُ. (TA.) ▼ هَضَبٌ is also said to be a pl. of هَضْبَةٌ; but it is rather a coll. gen. n., [of which هَضْبَةٌ is the n. un.]: and هُضُبٌ is also added to the list of the pls. of the same word; but this, accord. to the Ṣ, on the authority of AA, is pl. [or rather a quasi-pl. n.] of هَاضِبٌ, [act. part. n. of 1,] like as تُبَعٌ is of تَابِعٌ, and بُعُدٌ of بَاعِدٌ. (TA.) —— هَضْبَةٌ *A hill*; (IAth:) or *a mountain spreading over the surface of the ground*: (Ṣ, Mṣb, Ḳ:) or *a mountain composed of one mass of rock*: (Ḳ:) or *any firm, hard, large mass of rock*: (TA:) or *a long inaccessible mountain, separate from others; but only of red mountains*: (Ḳ:) or *a hill, such as is termed* أَكَمَةٌ, *with few plants*, or *little herbage*: (Mṣb:) pl. هِضَبٌ and هِضَابٌ; (Ṣ, Ḳ;) and pl. pl. أَهَاضِيبُ. (Ḳ, TA.) أَهَاضِبُ is used, by poetical licence, for اهاضيب, in a poem of one of the Hudhalees: (TA:) [or it is pl. of أَهْضُبٌ, which is pl. of pauc. of هَضْبٌ]. هَضْبٌ is also said, in the Ṣ, and L, to be a pl. of هَضْبَةٌ; but it is rather a coll. gen. n. (TA.) — *An elevated*, or *overlooking, tract of sand*. (TA, art. طود.) —— † *A run*; *a single run*. (AHeyth.)

هِضَبٌّ ‡ A horse *sweating much*; or *that sweats much*. (Ṣ, Ḳ.) — *Hard*, or *firm, and strong*, or *robust*. (Ḳ.) — *Large*, or *bulky*; as an epithet applied to the kind of lizard called ضَبّ, and to other things. (TA.)

غَنَمٌ هَضِيبٌ *Sheep or goats having little milk*: (Ḳ:) app. from الهَضْبُ, signifying حَلْبَةُ القَطْرِ. (TA.)

هُضُوبَةٌ: see هَضْبَةٌ.

هَاضِبٌ, used after the manner of a rel. n., signifying ذُو هَضْبٍ: so in the following expression in a verse of Aboo-Ṣakhr El-Hudhalee; فِى يَوْمٍ مِنَ اللَّهْوِ هَاضِبِ; which means *In a day when the people had played much, and quickly*: explained by the words كَانُوا قَدْ هَضَبُوا فِى اللَّهْوِ. (TA.)

أُهْضُوبَةٌ: see هَضْبَةٌ.

رَوْضَةٌ مَهْضُوبَةٌ [*A meadow, or the like, rained upon*: or *much wetted by rain*]. (TA.)

[هضل &c.
See Supplement.]

هفت

1. هَفَتَ, aor. ـِ, inf. n. هَفْتٌ; (TA;) and ▼ تهافت; (Ṣ, Ḳ;) *It fell continuously*, or *successively*, (Ṣ, Ḳ,) *part by part*, (Ṣ,) or *part after part, like as snow*, or *fine rain, falls*. (TA.) ▼ تهافت is mostly used with reference to something evil; (TA;) [as] يَتَهَافَتُونَ فِى النَّارِ [*They shall fall successively into the fire of hell*]; (TA, from a trad.;) [and] تَهَافَتَ الفَرَاشُ فِى النَّارِ *The moths fell successively into the fire*; (Ṣ;) [and] تَهَافَتَ القَوْمُ *The people fell down successively dead*; (TA;) [and] تَهَافَتُوا عَلَيْهِ *They fell upon him successively*. (TA.) — هَفَتَ and ▼ تَهَافَتَ *It* (snow, and fine rain,) *fell quickly*. (TA.) — هَفَتَ, [aor. ـِ,] inf. n. هَفْتٌ, *He*, or *it, fell*; *fell down*. (TA.) — هَفَتَ, aor. ـِ, (Ṣ, Ḳ,) inf. n. هَفْتٌ and هُفَاتٌ; (TA;) and ▼ انهفت; (Ṣ;) *It was*, or *became, depressed*, or *lowered*; syn. إِنْخَفَضَ and إِتَّضَعَ. (Ṣ, Ḳ.) — هَفَتَ and ▼ انهفت *It was*, or *became, lessened*, or *diminished*. (IḲṭṭ.) — هَفَتَ, (aor. ـِ, inf. n. هَفْتٌ, TA,) *It became minute, fine*, or *slender*; syn. دَقَّ. (Ḳ.) — هَفَتَ, (aor. ـِ, Ḳ,) inf. n. هَفْتٌ and هُفَاتٌ, *It flew about*, or *became dispersed, by reason of its lightness*. (Ṣ, Ḳ.) — هَفَتَ, aor. ـِ, *He talked much, without consideration*. (Ḳ, TA.)

6. تهافت *It* (a garment) *fell in pieces, piece after piece falling off, and became worn out*. (TA.) — تهافت *It was continuous*, or *successive*; syn. تَتَابَعَ. (Ḳ.) — See also 1. — تهافت النَّاسُ عَلَى المَآءِ *The people pressed*, or *crowded, to the water*, [*one after another*, or *party after party*]. (Mṣb.)

7: see 1.

هَفْتٌ Rain *falling quickly*. (Ḳ.) — *A depressed*, or *low, piece of ground*: (Ḳ:) like هَجْلٌ. (Az.) —— كَلَامٌ هَفْتٌ *Inconsiderate loquacity*. (TA.) — هَفْتٌ *Abundant stupidity*: (Ḳ:) *surpassing stupidity*. (IAạr.)

هُفَاتٌ *Stupid*; *foolish*; *of little sense*. (Ṣ, Ḳ.) [But see its syn. لَفَاتٌ, voce أَلْفَتُ.] Authorities differ respecting this word and لَفَاتٌ, whether they should be written with ت or with ة or with both. (TA.)

حَبٌّ هَفُوتٌ *Grain that falls to the bottom of the cooking-pot, and swells out quickly*. (Lth.)

وَرَدَتْ هَفِيتَةٌ مِنَ النَّاسِ *There came a party of men whom a year of drought had compelled to emigrate*. (Ṣ.)

مَهْفُوتٌ *Confounded*; *perplexed*; *amazed*: (Ḳ:) like مَبْهُوتٌ. (TA.)

[هفو &c.
See Supplement.]

هقب

هَقْبٌ *Width*; *amplitude*; *largeness*. (Ḳ.)

هِقَبٌ *A word by which a horse is checked*, or *urged*. (Ḳ.)

هِقَبٌّ *Having a large*, or *ample, throat*, (Ḳ,) *swallowing everything*. (TA.) — *Large, big*, or *bulky, and tall*, or *long*; an epithet applied to an ostrich, (Lth, Ḳ,) and to other things: (Ḳ:) or *long*, or *tall*, as an epithet applied to other things than the ostrich. (TA.)

هَقَبْقَبٌ *Hard*, or *firm, and strong*, or *robust*. (Ḳ.)

[هقع &c.
See Supplement.]

هلب

1. هَلِبَ, aor. ـَ, inf. n. هَلَبٌ, *He had much hair* [of the kind termed هُلْب]; *was very hairy*. (Ḳ.) — هَلَبَ الفَرَسَ, and هَلَبَ ذَنَبَ الفَرَسِ, aor. ـُ, inf. n. هَلْبٌ, *He shore the tail of the horse*: (Mṣb:) *shore it*, or *cut it off, utterly*. (TA.) هَلَبَهُ; (Ṣ, Ḳ;) and ▼ هلّبه, (Ḳ,) inf. n. تَهْلِيبٌ; (TA;) *He plucked from him* (i. e. a horse, Ṣ,) *his* هُلْب [or *coarse hair, of the tail &c.*]. (Ṣ, Ḳ.) — هُلِبَ *It* (a tail) *was entirely cut off*. (TA.) —— هَلَبَهُمْ بِلِسَانِهِ, aor. ـُ; and ▼ هلّبهم, (inf. n. تَهْلِيبٌ, TA;) ‡ *He satirized and reviled them*: (Ḳ:) *he carped at them severely with his tongue*. (TA.) —— هَلَبَ, aor. ـُ; and ▼ اهلب, (inf. n. إِهْلَابٌ, TA;) *He* (a horse) *prosecuted*, or *continued, his course*, or *run, uninterruptedly*; syn. تَابَعَ الجَرْىَ: (Ḳ:) and, the latter verb, *he* (a horse,) *was ardent*, or *impetuous, in his course*, or *running*; as also أَلْهَبَ. (Aṣ, in TA, art. لهب.) [See also ضِهَبٌ.] —— هَلَبَتِ السَّمَآءُ القَوْمَ [القَوْمَ] *The sky wetted the people with dew* (نَدًى): or, *with continual rain*. (Ḳ.) هَلَبَتْنَا السَّمَآءُ *The sky wetted us with dew* (ندى) or *the like*; (TA;) as also ▼ أَهْلَبَتْنَا: (T:) *the sky rained upon us a copious*, or *an excellent, rain*. (TA.)

2: } see 1.
4: }

5. تهلّب and ▼ انهلب [*He, a horse, had his tail shorn*: see 1:] *he had his* هُلْب [or *coarse hair, of the tail &c.*,] *plucked out*. (Ḳ.)

7: see 5.

8. اهتلب *He drew* a sword from its scabbard. (TA.)

هُلْبٌ, [a coll. gen. n.,] *Hair, absolutely*: or *coarse hair*; (Ḳ;) as the *hair of the tail of a she-camel*: (Az:) or *hair of the tail*: or *pigs' bristles, with which skins and the like are sewed*: (Ḳ:) J gives this last signification to ▼ هُلْبَةٌ: and also, *coarse hair of the tail &c.*: (so in the Ṣ:) but هُلْبَةٌ is the n. un. (TA.) — هُلْبٌ, The *eyelashes*. (TA.) — هُلْبٌ, coll. gen. n., *Hair that one plucks from the tail*: n. un. with ة. (TA.) — هُلْبٌ [pl. of هُلْبَةٌ] *Tails and manes plucked out.* (TA.) = هُلْبٌ *Continuance*, or *constant succession, of rain.* (TA.)

رَجُلٌ هَلِبٌ [*A man having much hair; of the kind called* هُلْب; *very hairy*: see هَلِبَ:] *a man whose* هُلْب *is growing forth.* (TA.)

هُلْبَةٌ The *hair that is above the pubes, extending near to the navel.* (TA.) See هُلْبٌ. = هُلْبَةٌ *Severity*, or *pressure*, of fortune: like كُلْبَةٌ and جُلْبَةٌ. (Ṣ.) — Also, and ♦ هُلُبَةٌ, *Severity*, or *intenseness*, of winter. (Ḳ.) أَتَيْتُهُ فِى هلبةِ الشِّتَاءِ *I came to him during the severe*, or *intense, cold of winter.* (El-Umawee.)

هُلُبَةٌ: see هُلْبَةٌ.

هَلُوبٌ A woman *who draws near to her husband*, or *ingratiates herself with him*; syn. مُتَقَرِّبَةٌ مِنْ زَوْجِهَا; (Ḳ, TA;) *and is loving*, or *affectionate, to him; and distant with respect to others.* (TA.) — Also, contr., A woman *who is distant*, or *shy, with respect to her husband*, or *who alienates herself from him*, or *avoids* or *shuns him*, (Ḳ,) *and draws near to*, or *ingratiates herself with, her special friend.* (TA.) — From هَلَبَهُ بِلِسَانِهِ "he carped at him severely with his tongue;" because a wife carps either at her husband or at her friend: or, accord. to IAạr, in the former sense, from ♦ يَوْمٌ هَلَّابٌ "a day of gentle, constant, innocuous rain;" and in the latter sense from the same phrase as signifying "a day of rain attended by thunder and lightning and terrors, and destructive to dwellings." (TA.)

هَلِيبٌ and هُلَيْبٌ: see هَلَّابٌ.

هُلَابَةٌ The *filth that is washed away from the membrane which encloses the fœtus*: (Ḳ:) i. q. حُوَلَاءُ: [a word which has two applications, which see:] also called هُلَابَةُ السقاء: (TA:) [but السقاء is written by mistake for السَّقْىِ]. [See also هُلَاتَةٌ.]

هَلَّابٌ (Ḳ) and هَلَّابَةٌ (Ṣ, Ḳ) *A cold wind, with rain.* (Ṣ, ISd, Ḳ.) — يَوْمٌ هَلَّابٌ *A day in which is wind and rain*: (Ṣ:) *a day of rain attended by thunder and lightning and terrors, and destructive to dwellings.* (IAạr.) — Also, *A day of gentle, constant, innocuous rain.* (IAạr.) — Also, *A day of dry cold; or dry by reason of cold.* (Az, in the T, art. حلب.) — عَامٌ هَلَّابٌ, and ♦ أَهْلَبُ, *A year of much rain.* (Ḳ.) — ♦ عَامٌ أَهْلَبُ ‡ *A plentiful*, or *fruitful, year; a year of abundant herbage*, or *vegetation*: like أَزَبُّ. (Ṣ.) — هَلَّابٌ and ♦ مُهَلِّبٌ and ♦ هَلِيبٌ, (Ḳ,) or as in one copy of the Ḳ, that of Eṭ-Ṭabláwee, the last is ♦ هُلَيْبٌ, (TA,) and this is the more correct reading, (MF,) [*Three*] *very cold days, in Kánoon el-'Owwal* [or *January O.S.*]: or *in the severe*, or *intense, cold of winter*: (Ḳ:) or *in the severe*, or *intense, cold of the month* [*above mentioned*], *in the latter part of it.* (L.) = هَلَّابٌ ‡ *One who satirizes* [*and reviles*] *much*: (ISh:) [*who carps much and severely at others with his tongue*: see 1].

مُدَحْرِجُ البَعْرِ and هَالِبُ الشَّعْرِ [*Two*] *days of winter.* (Ḳ.) — See art. دحرج. — لَيْلَةٌ هَالِبَةٌ *A rainy night.* (Ḳ.)

أَهْلَبُ *Having much hair* [of the kind called هُلْب]; *very hairy*: (Ḳ:) fem. هَلْبَاءُ. (CḲ.) A horse *having much hair of the kind called* هلب: (Ṣ:) a *coarse-haired* man: (TA:) a man *having coarse hair upon the part where are the two veins called* الأَخْدَعَانِ, *and upon his body*: (TA:) *having much hair upon the head and body.* (TA.) — أَهْلَبُ A tail *cut off.* (Ḳ.) — Also, [accord. to the CḲ, *or*,] *Having no hair upon it*: and, contr., *Having much hair*: (Ḳ:) [in each sense, as seems to be implied in the Ḳ, an epithet applied to a tail: but, app., accord. to the TA, applied to a horse]. — هَلْبَاءُ, fem., A beast of carriage (TA) *having much hair.* (Ḳ, TA.) — هَلْبَاءُ The *podex*; syn. إِسْتٌ: (Ḳ:) used as a subst.; originally an epithet. (TA.) — إِيَّاكَ وَأَهْلَبَ العَضْرَطِ *Beware of him who has a hairy podex.* Originally said by a woman to her son, who was boasting that he found no one whom he did not overcome, and who was afterwards thrown down by a man answering to this description. A proverb used in cautioning the self-conceited. (Meyd, TA.) — أَرْضٌ هَلْبَاءُ ‡ *Land abounding with plants, or herbage.* (TA.) — Also, [contr.,] ‡ *Land of which the herbage has been eaten.* (TA.) — هُلْبَةٌ هَلْبَاءُ (in the CḲ, هَلْبَةٌ هُلْبَاءُ) *A severe calamity.* (Ḳ.) — See هَلَّابٌ.

لَهُ أُهْلُوبٌ *He* [a horse] *has ardour*, or *impetuosity, in his running &c.*: formed by transposition from, or a dial. form of, أُلْهُوبٌ. (M.) عَدْوُهُ ذُو أَهَالِيبَ [*His* (a horse's) *running is of ardent*, or *impetuous, modes*, or *manners*]. (TA.) — أُهْلُوبٌ *A kind*, or *way* [of speech]: syn. فَنٌّ (Ḳ) and أُسْلُوبٌ: (AO:) pl. أَهَالِيبُ. (AO, Ḳ.) — اهلوبٌ من الثَّنَاءِ *A kind*, or *way, of praising*, or *eulogizing.* (TA.)

مَهْلُوبٌ (Ṣ, A, L, Mṣb) and ♦ مُهَلَّبٌ (TA) A horse *having his tail shorn*: (Mṣb:) *having the hair of his tail utterly removed*: (L:) *having his* هُلْب [or *coarse hair, of the tail &c.*,] *shorn*: (A:) *having his* هلب *plucked out.* (Ṣ, TA.)

مُهَلَّبٌ: see مَهْلُوبٌ.

مُهَلِّبٌ: see هَلَّابٌ.

هلبث

هِلْبَاثٌ *A kind of dates.* Said to be the only kind brought from El-Baṣrah to the Sultán. (AḤn.)

هِلْبَوْثٌ *Stupid; foolish; of little sense*: or *dull of speech and understanding; doltish; heavy*; syn. فَدْمٌ. (Ṣ, and some copies of the Ḳ.)

هلبج

هِلْبَاجَةٌ *Stupid; foolish; of little sense*: (Ṣ:) or *one unsurpassed in stupidity, foolishness*, or *paucity of sense*: or *heavy, dull, stupid, and of little use*: (TA:) or a *heavy*, or *dull, man*: (T:) as also هِلْبَاجٌ: (L:) Khalaf El-Aḥmar says, I asked an Arab of the desert respecting the meaning of هلباجة, and he said, It means a *stupid*, or *foolish*, man, or *one of little sense, bulky*, or *corpulent, impotent in speech or actions, and heavy*, or *dull*, or *doltish, a great eater*, who — who — who —, and he continued to add to his interpretation something each time; after which he said to me, desiring to depart, he is *one who comprises every evil quality.* (Ṣ, Ḳ.*)

هلت

1. هَلَتَ, [aor. ـُ and ـِ ?] inf. n. هَلْتٌ, *He peeled* a thing; or *deprived* it *of its outer covering*, or *crust*; syn. قَشَرَ. (Ḳ.) — هَلَتَ الدَّمَ, as also سَلَتَ, *He peeled off*, or *scraped off*, (قشر,) *the* [*dried*] *blood* with a knife. (Lḥ, L.) — هَلَتَ دَمَ البَدَنَةِ, [as also سَلَتَ,] *He scratched the skin of the* بدنة [or *beast brought to Mekkeh for sacrifice*, or *there sacrificed*, or the right reading is النَّدَبَةَ, i. e. *the scar.* (see سَلَتَ,)] *with a knife, so that he made the blood to appear.* (Lḥ, L, TA.)

7. انهلت يَعْدُو i. q. انسلت, (in the CḲ, انهلت يَعْدُو وانسلت,) *He withdrew himself privately*, or *stole away, without being known to do so, running.* (Ibn-El-Faraj, Ḳ.)

هَلَتَى *A certain plant*; (Ṣ, Ḳ;) *when it dries, it becomes red; and when it is eaten, and grows, it is called* جُمَيْز: or, accord. to Az, *a certain tree, growing like the* صِلِّيَان, *except that its colour inclines to red*: or, accord. to Aboo-Ziyád, as AḤn says, *a plant of the kind called* طَرِيفَة, *growing like the* صِلِّيَان *and the* نَصِىّ, *red when fresh and moist, and more red when it has dried; it is watery; and the camels and sheep &c. scarcely ever eat it when they find any other herbage to serve them in its stead.* (TA.)

هُلَاتَةٌ The *black filth that is washed away from the membrane which encloses a young lamb or kid in its mother's womb.* (Ḳ, TA.) [For غُسَالَةُ الشُّخْلَةِ السَّوْدَاءِ, as in the copies of the Ḳ in my hands, I read السوداء. — See also هُلَابَةٌ.]

هَلَتَاتٌ [accord. to the TA and a MS. copy of the Ḳ: in the CḲ هُلَتَاتٌ:] *A company of people staying,* or *abiding, in a place; and of people journeying.* (Ḳ.) So accord. to AZ; but accord. to ISk, with ث. (L.)

هلث

هَلْثَى *An assembly, a company,* or *congregated body, of men.* (IAạr.) [Or perhaps it is هَلْثَى.] — Also, and ↓هَلْثَاة [or perhaps ↓هَلْثَآءٌ] and ↓هِلْثَآءٌ and ↓هَلْثَاةٌ and ↓هِلْثَاةٌ and ↓هُلْثَةٌ *An assembly, a company,* or *a congregated body,* (*composed of a great number of men,* TA,) *whose voices are raised high.* (Ḳ.) [That هِلْثَآء is with tenween is expressly shown by Fr.: but whether هَلْثَآء is so is doubtful.] — Also ↓هِلْثَاةٌ, with the second syll. short, *An assembly,* or *a company, more in number than what is called* وَضْمَة. (Th.) — جَآءَتْ هِلْثَاةٌ ↓ مِنْ كُلِّ وَجْهٍ *There came parties from every direction.* (Th.)

هَلْثَةٌ: }
هِلْثَآءٌ: } see هَلْثَى.

هِلْثَآءٌ [app. هَلْثَآءٌ], coll. gen. n., n. un. with ة, *A kind of palm-tree, slender below, and thick at the head; the unripe dates of which are of a reddening yellow, disagreeable in taste; and its fresh ripe dates of the best,* or *sweetest, kind.* (Aboo-Ḥátim, in Mṣb.) — See هَلْثَى.

هَلْثَاةٌ: see هَلْثَى and هُلَاثٌ.

هُلَاثٌ and ↓هَلْثَاةٌ and ↓هِلْثَاةٌ *Flaccidness,* or *languor,* (إِسْتِرْخَآء,) *that comes upon a man.* (Ḳ.)

هَلَائِثُ *People of the lower,* or *lowest, class.* (TA.) — هُوَ مِنْ هَلَائِثِهِمْ, mentioned, but not explained, by IAạr: thought by ISd to signify *He is of the dregs of them:* or, *of their assembly,* or *company.* (TA.)

هلج

إِهْلِيلَجٌ (IAạr, Ṣ, Ḳ) and إِهْلِيلِجٌ, (Fr, Sh, Ḳ,) but this is disapproved by IAạr, who observes that there are no words in Arabic of the measure إِفْعِيلِل, but there are of the measure إِفْعِيلَل, as إِهْلِيلَجٌ and إِبْرِيسَمٌ and إِطْرِيفَلٌ, (Ṣ,) and هَلِيلَجٌ, (L,) but this is disallowed by ISk, (Ṣ,) [a coll. gen. n.,] n. un. with ة, (Ḳ,) an arabicized word, (Ṣ,) from اهليله, (TA,) [or rather هَلِيلَه, a Persian word,] *A well-known fruit,* [the *fruit of the myrobalan,* as well as the *myrobalan-tree,*] *one kind of which is yellow,* (Ḳ,) *and another kind black, the latter being in the highest state of ripeness, and another kind called* كَابُلِى: *it is useful as a remedy for quinseys, and preserves the intellect, and removes the head-ache,* (*when used made into a conserve,* TA,) *and is, in the stomach, like an intelligent housewife, who is a good manager, in the house:* (Ḳ, TA; but omitted in some copies of the Ḳ:) *so is this medicine to the brain and stomach.* (TA.) [See also بِلِيلَجٌ, in art. بلج.]

هلجب

هِلْجَابٌ *A large cooking-pot.* (Ḳ.)

[هلد &c.
See Supplement.]

هلقب

جُوعٌ هِلْقَبٌ *Vehement hunger.* (AA, T, L.) See also هِلْقِتٌ.

هلقت

جُوعٌ هِلْقِتٌ *Vehement hunger.* (Ḳ.) [See also هِلْقِسٌ.]

هماً

1. هَمَأَ, aor. ـَ, (Ḳ,) inf. n. هَمْءٌ; (TA;) and ↓اهمأ; (Ḳ;) *He rent,* (Ḳ,) i. e., *pulled so that it tore,* (TA,) a garment: (Ḳ:) *he wore out,* or *rendered threadbare,* [*and ragged*]. (Ḳ.)

4: see 1.

5: see 7.

7. انهمأ (Ḳ) and ↓تهمّأ (Ṣ, Ḳ) *It* (a garment) *became rent:* (TA:) *became worn-out,* or *threadbare,* (Ṣ, Ḳ,) *and ragged.* (Ṣ.)

هِمْءٌ *A worn-out, threadbare,* or *ragged, garment:* pl. أَهْمَآءٌ. (Ḳ.)

همت

1. هَمَتَ, [aor. ـِ,] *It* (ثَرِيد) *became hidden in the grease;* (Ḳ;) *became overspread by the grease.* (TA.)

4. اهمت الكَلَامَ, and الضَّحِكَ, *He made speech, and laughter, low; he spoke, and laughed, low.* (Ḳ.) It is said to be from الهَمْسُ; the س being changed into ت. (MF.)

همج

1. همج, [app. هَمِجَ, aor. ـَ,] inf. n. هَمَجٌ, *He hungered; was hungry.* (L.) — هَمَجَتِ الإِبِلُ مِنَ المَآءِ, (Ṣ, Ḳ,) aor. ـُ, inf. n. هَمْجٌ, (Ṣ,) *The camels drank of the water at one draught,* (Ṣ, Ḳ,) *until they satisfied their thirst.* (Ṣ.)

4. اهمج, (inf. n. إِهْمَاجٌ, TA,) *He* (a horse, Ṣ, Ḳ, or other animal that runs, Lḥ,) *strove* or *exerted himself, in his running,* (Ṣ, Ḳ,) *and then ran impetuously, so as to raise the dust.* (TA.)

هَمَجٌ *Hunger:* or (in the Ḳ, and) *bad management of the means of subsistence.* (Ṣ, Ḳ.) هَمَجٌ هَامِجٌ ↓ [*Severe hunger:* or *very bad management of the means of subsistence:*] (Ṣ, Ḳ:) the latter word is added to give intensiveness to the signification; (TA;) or to corroborate; (Ṣ, Ḳ;) as in the case of لَيْلٌ لَائِلٌ. (Ṣ.) — هَمَجٌ *Small flies, like gnats, that fall upon the faces of sheep* or *goats, and asses,* (Ṣ, Ḳ,) *and into their eyes:* (Ṣ:) or *gnats;* so called from هَمَجٌ signifying "hunger;" because when they are hungry they live, but when they become satiated they die: or صِغَارُ الدَّوَابِّ: (L:) [but this is evidently a mistake for صِغَارُ الذُّبَابِ the *young ones,* or *little ones, of flies:*]) or *any grubs that burst forth from flies* or *from gnats:* (Lth, A:) pl. of هَمَجَةٌ, (Ṣ,) [or rather this is the n. un. of هَمَجٌ, which is a coll. gen. n.]. — هَمَجٌ *Lean sheep* or *goats:* (Ḳ:) [a coll. gen. n.,] n. un. with ة. (Ṣ, Ḳ.) — هَمَجٌ ‡ *Stupid,* or *foolish, men;* or *men of little sense:* (Ḳ:) or *stupid,* or *foolish, young men of the meaner sort:* (Ṣ:) or simply *young men of the meaner sort:* or *a mixed and low set of men:* or *disorderly vagabonds:* (TA:) you say also رَجُلٌ هَمَجٌ and هَمَجَةٌ *a stupid,* or *foolish, man;* and رِجَالٌ هَمَجٌ, and أَهْمَاجٌ: (TA:) or هَمَجَةٌ signifies a *stupid,* or *foolish,* man, *who has not firm command of himself.* (Aboo-Sa'eed.) — هَمَجٌ *Old and weak ewes:* (Ḳ:) [a coll. gen. n.,] n. un. with ة: which also signifies simply *a ewe.* (TA.) — قَوْمٌ هَمَجٌ *A people in whom is no good.* (TA.) — هَمَجٌ هَامِجٌ ↓ *Young men of the meaner sort;* like هَمَجٌ alone: and *a mixed set of men who have no intelligence nor manliness.* (TA.)

هَمِيجٌ A doe-antelope *scared,* or *frightened, by* [*the small flies called*] هَمَج: (Ṣ:) a *young* doe-antelope, (Ḳ,) *of beautiful body:* (L:) one *lank in the belly:* or one *that has two streaks of a colour different from that of the rest of the body in* [*the two parts called*] *the* طُرَّتَانِ: (Ḳ:) or one *that has two such streaks on her back;* which is only the case in such as are white; and also applied to the male: (TA:) or one *that has been attacked by a pain in consequence of which her face has become flabby.* (Ḳ.)

هَامِجٌ: see هَمَجٌ. — ‡ [A people] *left to mix tumultuously, one part with another.* (Ḳ.) [The explanation seems to be borrowed from the Ḳur, xviii. 99.]

همد

1. هَمَدَتِ النَّارُ, aor. ـُ, (Ṣ, A, L,) inf. n. هُمُودٌ, (Ṣ, A, L, Ḳ,) *The fire became extinguished* (Aṣ, Ṣ, A, L, Ḳ) *entirely; went out entirely,* (Aṣ, Ṣ, A, L,) *none of it remaining:* (L:) or *lost its heat:* (L, Ḳ:) when [only] its flame has ceased, you say of it خَمَدَتْ. (Aṣ, L.) — هَمَدَ, (M, A, L,) aor. ـُ, (M, L,) inf. n. هُمُودٌ, (M, L, Ḳ,) ‡ *He died;*

[became extinct;] (M, A, L, Ḳ;) perished; (TA;) like as did Thamood; (Lth, A, L;) as also خَمَدَ. (A.) — كَادَ يَهْمُدُ مِنَ الجُوعِ ‡ He nearly perished of hunger. (L.) — هَمَدَ, aor. ـُ, (Ṣ, A, L,) inf. n. هُمُودٌ (Ṣ, L, Ḳ) and هَمْدٌ, (L, Ḳ,) ‡ It (a garment, or piece of cloth,) became dissundered (L, Ḳ) and worn-out, (Ṣ, A, L, Mṣb,) by being long folded, (A, L, Mṣb, Ḳ,) so that a person looking at it would imagine it sound, but, when he touched it, would find it fall to pieces. (A,* L, Mṣb.*) — هَمَدَتِ الرِّيحُ † The wind became still. (Mṣb.) — هَمَدَتِ الأَرْضُ, inf. n. هُمُودٌ, ‡ The land became lifeless, without herbage, without wood, and without rain. (L, Ḳ.) — هَمَدَ شَجَرُ الأَرْضِ ‡ The trees of the land became worn-out, or wasted; and perished. (L.) — هَمَدَتْ أَصْوَاتُهُمْ † Their voices became silent. (L.)

4. اهمد, inf. n. إِهْمَادٌ, † He stilled, or quieted. (Ḳ.) — He (God, and a man,) killed, or destroyed, a man, or men. (A.) — اهمد الأَمْرَ ‡ He put an end to the affair. (A.) — اهمد القَحْطُ الأَرْضَ ‡ Drought rendered the land sterile, so that it contained no herbage but such as was dried up and broken. (L.) — اهمد, (inf. n. إِهْمَادٌ, Ḳ.) † He kept silence in an unpleasant case. (L, Ḳ.) — اهمد, (Ṣ, L,) inf. n. إِهْمَادٌ, (L, Ḳ,) He remained, continued, stayed, abode, or dwelt, (Ṣ, L, Ḳ,) in a place: (Ṣ, L:) he was still; (Ḳ;) i. e., did not move. (TA.) = اهمد, (Ṣ, L) inf. n. إِهْمَادٌ, (L, Ḳ,) He hastened, or was quick, (Ṣ, L, Ḳ,) in going along: (Ṣ, L:) thus it bears two contr. significations: (Ṣ, L, Ḳ:) he (a dog) ran; syn. أَحْضَرَ. (L.) = اهمدوا فِى الطَّعَامِ, (inf. n. إِهْمَادٌ, Ḳ,) They fell to eating of the food. (Ibn-Buzurj, L, Ḳ.*)

هَمْدٌ: see هَامِدٌ.

هَمْدَةٌ † Apoplexy: carus: syn. سَكْتَةٌ. (Ṣ, L.) — [A trance. (See رَقْدَةٌ.)]

هَمِيدٌ ‡ Sheep or goats that have died: (L:) or the beasts or the like (مال) that are registered in the government-accounts as due from a man. (ISh, L, Ḳ.) You say, أَخَذَنَا بِالهَمِيدِ He (the collector) exacted from us taking for the sheep or goats that had died: (L:) or, taking what was registered as due from us in the government-accounts. (ISh, L.) — See هَامِدٌ.

هَامِدٌ and ♦ هَمْدٌ and ♦ هَمِيدٌ ‡ In a state of death, or extinction]. (M, L.) — هَامِدٌ ‡ A garment, or piece of cloth, [dissundered and] worn-out by being long folded, so as, when touched, to fall to pieces: (A:) or anything old and worn-out: (L, Mṣb:) pl. هُمَّدٌ. (A.) See 1. — أَرْضٌ هَامِدَةٌ ‡ Land in which is no herbage: (Ṣ:) and in the same sense هَامِدٌ is applied to a place: (Ḳ:) or sterile land, (A, L,) the herbage of which is dried up and broken, (A,) or containing no herbage except what is dried up and broken: (L:) dry and dusty: pl. هَوَامِدُ. (L.) — هَامِدٌ ‡ Old and worn-out or wasted, blackened, and changed, [for the worse]. (Ḳ.) — ‡ A tree black and wasted: (L:) or dried up; (A;) as also herbage. (Ṣ, L, Ḳ.) — ‡ Fruit black and stinking. (A, L.) — ‡ A date just ripe, thick-skinned and yellow. (TA.) رَمَادٌ هَامِدٌ Ashes [in a state of extinction or] wasted, (L,) and compacted together, and changed in appearance. (A, L.)

همذ

هُمَاذِىٌّ, (Ṣ, L,) or هُمَاذِىٌّ, (L, in all its senses,) Quickness (L, Ḳ) in running: (L:) or exertion, or haste, in pace, or in going. (Sh, L.) — Violence, of rain: (A'Obeyd, Ṣ, L, Ḳ:) and [so in the L: in the TA, as some say,] violent occasions of rain, and of mutual reviling, and of running; which are sometimes violent, and at other times remit: (L:) and violence of heat; (IAạr, L, Ḳ;) as also حُمَاذِىٌّ. (IAạr, L.) You say, يَوْمٌ ذُو هُمَاذِىٍّ, and حُمَاذِىٍّ, A day of violent heat. (IAạr, L.) — Quick, or swift; (A'Obeyd, Ṣ, L, Ḳ;) applied to a she-camel, (A'Obeyd, Ṣ, L, Ḳ,) and to a he-camel. (A'Obeyd, Ṣ, L.)

همر

1. هَمَرَهُ, (Ṣ, A, Ḳ,) aor. ـُ (Ṣ, Ḳ) and ـِ, (Ḳ,) inf. n. هَمْرٌ, (Ṣ,) He, or it, poured it; poured it out or forth; (Ṣ, A, Ḳ;) namely, water, (Ṣ, TA,) and tears, and rain, and the like. (TA.) هَمَرَ مَا فِى الضَّرْعِ — He drew forth all the milk that was in the udder. (Ṣ, Ḳ.) — هَمَرَ لَهُ مِنْ مَالِهِ † He gave to him of his property. (Ṣ, Ḳ.) — هَمَرَ الكَلَامَ, (Ḳ,) or فِى كَلَامِهِ, (A,) aor. ـُ, inf. n. هَمْرٌ; (TA;) and ♦ إِنْهَمَرَ بِالكَلَامِ (Ṣ;) ‡ He talked much. (Ḳ.) = هَمَرَ, intrans.: see 7, in two places.

7. انهمر It poured; poured out or forth; (Ḳ;) said of rain, and of tears; (TA;) as also ♦ هَمَرَ, (Ḳ,) aor. ـِ, inf. n. هُمُورٌ; (TA;) [and so, app., ♦ اهتمر, q. v.;] it flowed; said of water, (Ṣ, Ḳ,) of rain, and of tears; like انهمل: (TA:) and in like manner, هَمَرَتْ ♦ عَيْنُهُ بِالدَّمْعِ His eye flowed with tears; as also هَمَلَتْ. (A.) — انهمر بالكلام: see 1.

8. اهتمر: see 7. — ‡ He (a horse) ran (Ṣ, Ḳ, TA) like a torrent. (TA.)

هَمْرٌ Much sand; as also ♦ يَهْمُورٌ. (Ḳ.)

هَمْرَةٌ A fall of rain. (Ḳ.) — ‡ Angry speech. (Ṣgh, L, Ḳ.)

هَمَرَى: see هَمَّارٌ.

هَمَّارٌ A cloud pouring forth much rain; as also ♦ هَامِرٌ. (Ḳ.) — Applied to a man, (Ṣ,) ‡ Loquacious, garrulous; babbling; a great talker; a babbler; or nonsensical, irrational, foolish, or delirious, in his talk; as also ♦ مِهْمَرٌ and ♦ مِهْمَارٌ (Ṣ, Ḳ) and ♦ يَهْمُورٌ. (Ṣgh, Ḳ.) And ♦ مِهْمَرٌ ♦ خَطِيبٌ ‡ An orator copious in speech. (A, TA.) And ♦ هَمَرَى, applied to a woman, ‡ Clamorous; (Ḳ, TA;) abounding in talk or speech, like a pouring torrent. (TA.)

هَامِرٌ Pouring rain, and tears; as also ♦ مُنْهَمِرٌ. (TA.) See also هَمَّارٌ.

مِهْمَرٌ: } see هَمَّارٌ; the former, in two places.
مِهْمَارٌ: }

مُنْهَمِرٌ: see هَامِرٌ.

يَهْمُورٌ: see هَمْرٌ: = and see also هَمَّارٌ.

همرج

Q. 1. هَمْرَجَ عَلَيْهِ الخَبَرَ, (inf. n. هَمْرَجَةٌ, L, Ḳ,) He rendered the news, tidings, or information, confused to him. (Ṣ, L, Ḳ.*)

هَمْرَجَةٌ Confusion; (Ḳ, L;) as also هَمْرَجٌ, and ♦ هَمْرَجٌ, and هَمَرَّجَةٌ: ex. of the last وَقَعَ القَوْمُ فِى هَمَرَّجَةٍ The people fell into a state of confusion: (L:) and the third (L) and fourth (TA) signify also civil war, or conflict and faction, or discord, or dissension; syn. فِتْنَةٌ. (L, TA.) — A confused manner, or state, in walking. (Ṣ.) — A confused noise, or mixture of voices, or unintelligible sounds, of men; as also ♦ هَمْرَجَانٌ. (Ḳ.) — Lightness, or agility, and quickness. (Ḳ.) — What is vain, or false; syn. بَاطِلٌ. (Ḳ.) — الغُولُ هَمْرَجَةٌ مِنَ الجِنِّ The Ghool are a mixture of the Jinn. (L.)

هَمْرَجٌ: see هَمْرَجَةٌ. — Penetrating (مَاضٍ) in affairs. (Ḳ.)

هَمْرَجَانٌ: see هَمْرَجَةٌ.

همز

1. هَمَزَهُ, (Ṣ, A, Mṣb, Ḳ,) aor. ـِ (Ṣ, Mṣb, Ḳ) and ـُ, (Ḳ,) inf. n. هَمْزٌ, (Ṣ, Mṣb, Ḳ,) He pressed it; squeezed it; pinched it; (Ṣ, A, Mṣb, Ḳ,) as, for instance, a walnut, (A, TA,) or other thing, (Ṣ, TA,) in the hand; (Ṣ, A, TA,) and a man's head; (Ṣ, A, TA;) and a spear-shaft, with the مِهْمَاز, to straighten it. (TA.) — He pushed, impelled, or repelled, him or it, (Ṣ, Ḳ, TA,) meaning anything; as also لَمَزَهُ &c.

(TA.) You say, هَمَزَتْهُ إِلَيْهِ الحَاجَةُ *Want impelled, or drove, him to him or it.* (TA.) — *He struck, or beat, him;* (Ṣ, Ḳ, TA;) as also لَمَزَهُ &c. (TA.) — *He goaded, or spurred, him;* (Ḳ, TA;) *he urged him on* (namely a horse) *with the* مِهْمَاز, *to make him run.* (Mṣb.) — *He bit him.* (IAạr, Ḳ.) — *He broke it.* (Ḳ.) = ‡ *He* (the devil) *suggested evil to his mind.* (JK, A, TA.) You say, أَعُوذُ بِاللّٰهِ مِنْ هَمْزِهِ; and مِنْ هَمَزَاتِ الشَّيَاطِينِ; ‡ *I seek refuge in God from his* [the devil's] *evil suggestion; and from the evil suggestions of the devils.* (A.) = ‡ *He blamed, upbraided, or reproached, him; he found fault with him;* syn. of the inf. n. عَيْبٌ, (Fr, in TA, art. لمز; and IAạr, in TA, in the present art.) as also لَمَزَهُ: (Fr, in TA, art. لمز; and Ṣ,) or *he spoke evil of him, or spoke of him in a manner that he disliked, mentioning vices or faults as chargeable to him, behind his back, though it might be with truth;* syn. إِغْتَابَهُ فِى غَيْبَتِهِ: (Mṣb:) and [so] هَمَزَهُ فِى قَفَاهُ *he backbit him.* (JK, A.) = هَمَزَ الحَرْفَ, (Ṣ, O,) or الكَلِمَةَ, aor. ـِ, inf. n. هَمْزٌ, (Mṣb,) [*He pronounced the word with the sound termed* هَمْز, or هَمْزَة, *of which the sign is* ء,] is from هَمَزَهُ in the first of the senses explained above; (Ṣ, Mṣb,) because what is termed هَمْز in speech, (Ṣ,) or هَمْزَة, (Kh, TA,) [i. e. the sound so called,] is [as it were] pressed, or squeezed, (Kh, Ṣ, TA,) from its place of utterance [by a sudden emission of the voice forced out after a compression of the passage whereby it has been stopped]. (Kh, TA.) It was said to an Arab of the desert, أَتَهْمِزُ الفَأْرَةَ, [meaning *Dost thou pronounce* الفأرة *with hemz, or hemzeh?*] and he said, [understanding the words to mean *dost thou squeeze the rat, or mouse?*] السِّنَّوْرُ يَهْمِزُهَا [*The cat squeezes it*]. (Ṣ.) See هَمْز, below. [And see also نَبْر.]

7. انهمز [quasi-pass. of هَمَزَهُ; *It was pressed, squeezed, or pinched: he was pushed,* &c. The first of these significations is indicated, or implied, in the JK and the TA.] — انهمز الحَرْفُ [*The word was pronounced with the sound termed* هَمْزَة, or هَمْز]. (Ṣ.)

هَمْزُ الشَّيْطَانِ was explained by Moḥammad as meaning ‡ *Madness, or insanity;* syn. مُوتَةٌ, i. e. جُنُونٌ; because it arises from the goading and pressing or pinching of the devil. (A'Obeyd, Ḳ.) See 1; and see also هَمَزَات, voce هَمْزَةٌ. = هَمْز, (Ṣ,) and هَمْزَة, (Kh, TA,) [the former a gen. n., and the latter the n. un.,] The *sister of alif; one of the letters of the alphabet;* [*written thus* ء;] a genuine word, old, heard [from the Arabs of classical times], and well known; so called for a reason mentioned above: see 1, last signification: so says Kh; therefore no regard is due to what is said in certain of the expositions of the Keshsháf, that the term همزة thus used has not been heard [from any of the Arabs of classical times], and that its name is أَلِفٌ: (TA:) several persons say, that the term همزة is mostly applied to the movent [alif], and الف to the quiescent letter. (MF, TA.) See the letter ا.

هَمْزَةٌ n. un. of هَمْزٌ, q. v. — هَمَزَاتُ الشَّيَاطِينِ ‡ *The vain suggestions of the devils, which they inspire into the mind of a man.* (Ṣ, TA.) See also 1; and see هَمْز.

هُمَزَةٌ *i. q.* غَمَّازٌ; (Ḳ;) i. e., (TA,) One *who blames, upbraids, reproaches, or finds fault with, others, much, or habitually;* (Ṣ, TA;) as also ↓ هَمَّازٌ (Ṣ, TA) and ↓ هَامِزٌ; (Ṣ, Ḳ;) and so لُمَزَةٌ: (Ṣ, Ḳ, art. لمز:) [or rather] the first and second are intensive epithets (TA) [but the third is not intensive]: or one *who backbites his brother;* as also ↓ هَمَّازٌ: (Lth, A, TA:) or one *who defames men* (يَخْلُفُهُمْ مِنْ وَرَائِهِمْ وَيَأْكُلُ لُحُومَهُمْ); and the action thus signified is like غِيبَة, and may be [*by making signs*] *with the side of the mouth, and with the eye, and with the head;* as also ↓ هَمَّازٌ: (TA:) or, conjointly with لُمَزَةٌ, one *who speaks evil of men, or backbites them, and defames them:* (Aboo-Is-hák, TA:) or both together, one *who goes about much, or habitually, with calumny, or slander, separating companions and exciting enmity between friends:* (Abu-l-'Abbás, TA:) هُمَزَةٌ is applied to a man and to a woman; (Ṣ, TA;) [like لُمَزَةٌ;] for its ة is to denote intensiveness, and not the fem. gender: (TA:) ↓ هُمَّازٌ [which is the pl. of هَامِز] signifies persons *who blame, upbraid, reproach, or find fault with, others behind their backs, much, or habitually:* (IAạr, TA:) [or, more correctly, it has not an intensive signification.] See also لُمَزَةٌ.

هَمَّازٌ: } see هُمَزَةٌ, throughout.
هَامِزٌ: }

مِهْمَزٌ: see مِهْمَاز.

مِهْمَزَةٌ *An instrument for beating,* (مِقْرَعَةٌ, AHeyth, Ḳ, TA,) *of copper or brass,* [app. meaning *a kind of spur, or a goad,*] *with which beasts of carriage are urged on:* pl. مَهَامِزُ: (AHeyth, TA:) or *a staff* or *stick:* (Ḳ:) or *a staff, or stick, with an iron in its head, with which the ass is goaded, or urged on.* (Sh, Ḳ.) See also مِهْمَاز. — [The pl., مَهَامِز, of this word or of مِهْمَز, is also applied to *An instrument, or instruments, with which spear-shafts are pinched and straightened:* see 1, first signification.]

مِهْمَازٌ and ↓ مِهْمَزٌ (Ṣ, Mṣb, Ḳ) *A well-known thing;* (Mṣb;) [namely, *a spur;*] *an iron which is* [*attached* or *fixed*] *in the hinder part of the boot of him who breaks, or trains, beasts of carriage:* (Ṣ, Ḳ:) pl. [of the former] مَهَامِيزُ (Ḳ) and [of the latter] مَهَامِزُ. (Ṣ, Ḳ.) See also مِهْمَزَة.

همس

1. هَمَسَ, aor. ـِ, (A, TA,) inf. n. هَمْسٌ (AHeyth, L, TA) and هَمِيسٌ and هُمُوسٌ, (L, TA,) *He spoke inaudibly:* (AHeyth, TA:) or *in a low, faint, gentle, or soft, manner,* (AHeyth, TA,) *so as to be hardly intelligible.* (TA.) It is said in a trad. فَجَعَلَ بَعْضُنَا يَهْمِسُ إِلَى بَعْضٍ *And some of us began to speak to others in a low, faint, gentle, or soft, manner, so as to be hardly intelligible.* (TA.) And in another trad., كَانَ إِذَا صَلَّى العَصْرَ هَمَسَ بِشَىْءٍ لَا نَفْهَمُهُ *He used, when he performed the afternoon-prayer, to utter something in a low, faint, gentle, or soft manner, we not understanding it.* (TA.) You say also, هَمَسَ إِلَىَّ بِحَدِيثِهِ [*He uttered his discourse to me inaudibly: or in a low, faint, gentle, or soft, manner.*] (A.) And الشَّيْطَانُ يَهْمِسُ بِوَسْوَسَتِهِ صَدْرَ الإِنْسَانِ [*The devil speaks inaudibly in his suggesting vain or unprofitable things into the bosom of man*]. (A.) And هَمَسَ الشَّيْطَانُ فِى الصَّدْرِ *The devil suggested vain, or unprofitable things in the bosom;* syn. وَسْوَسَ. (TA.) See also هَمْس below. — Also, aor. and inf. n. as above, *He made the faintest, or slightest, sound in treading.* So in the saying, هَمْسًا وَصَهْ and إِهْمِسْ وَصَهْ *Make thou the faintest, or slightest, sound in treading, and be thou silent:* addressed by a thief to his companion. (TA.) And hence the saying of the Rájiz,

فَهُنَّ يَمْشِينَ بِهِ هَمِيسَا *

And they walk with him making the faintest, or slightest, sound in treading. (Ṣ.) هَمِيس also signifies The *walking softly; with a soft-sounding tread:* (TA:) [and so هَمْس; as in the saying,] سَمِعْتُ هَمْسَ الأَخْفَافِ وَالأَقْدَامِ [*I heard the soft-sounding treading of the feet of camels and of the feet of men*]. (A.) See also هَمْس below. = هَمَسَ الصَّوْتَ, aor. ـِ, inf. n. هَمْسٌ, *He made the sound, or voice to be low, faint, gentle, or soft.* (Mṣb.) And هَمَسَ الكَلَامَ, [aor. and] inf. n. as above, [*He spoke in a low, faint, gentle, or soft manner;* like همس alone; lit.,] *he made speech, or the speech to be low, faint, gentle, or soft.* (A, TA.) = هَمَسَ الطَّعَامَ, (TḲ), [aor. and] inf. n. as above, (AZ, Ḳ,) *He chewed the food with the mouth closed:* (AZ, Ḳ, TA:) or *without opening the mouth.* (TA.) You say, هُوَ يَأْكُلُ هَمْسًا *He eats without opening his mouth.* (A.) Hence, a toothless old woman's eating is termed هَمْس. (AHeyth.) هَمَسَهُ also signifies [simply] *He chewed it.* (TA.)

3. هامسهُ, inf. n. مُهَامَسَةٌ, *He spoke, or discoursed secretly to him, or with him.* (A.) You say also, هَامَسُوا, (TḲ,) inf. n. as above, (Ḳ,) *They spoke, or discoursed, secretly together;* as also ↓ تهامسوا. (Ḳ,* TḲ.)

6: see 3.

هَمْسٌ *A low, faint, gentle, or soft, sound.* (Ṣ, A, Mṣb, Ḳ.) So it has been explained as occurring in the words of the Ḳur, [xx. 107,] فَلَا تَسْمَعُ إِلَّا هَمْسًا [*So that thou shalt not hear aught save*] *a low, faint, gentle, or soft, sound,* arising from the shifting of the feet from place to place towards the scene of congregation [for the general judgment]: or, as Az thinks, the meaning here is, *the sound of the patting, or pattering, of the feet* (خَفْقُ الأَقْدَامِ) *upon the ground.* (TA.) — The *faint,* or *gentle, sound of the voice in the mouth, of such kind as has no mixture of the voice of the chest, nor loudness of utterance.* (Lth, Ḳ.) See also مَهْمُوسٌ. — And *Anything low, faint, gentle,* or *soft,* (كُلُّ خَفِيٍّ, Ḳ, TA,) *of speech* and *the like:* (TA:) [see again, مَهْمُوسٌ:] or the *faintest,* or *slightest, sound of the feet;* (Ṣ, K;) i. e., *of their tread upon the ground:* (TA:) so [accord. to J] in the instance in the Ḳur, [xx. 107,] mentioned above: (Ṣ:) and [in like manner] ↓ هَمِيسٌ signifies the *sound of the shifting from place to place of the feet of camels.* (Ḳ.) See also 1.

هَمِيسٌ: see 1: and see هَمْسٌ.

كَلَامٌ مَهْمُوسٌ [*Speech spoken inaudibly:* or *in a low, faint, gentle, or soft manner, so as to be hardly intelligible:* see 1: or] *speech not spoken out or openly.* (A,* Mṣb.) — حَرْفٌ مَهْمُوسٌ, (Mṣb,) or حَرْفُ الهَمْسِ, (IJ,) [*A letter which is pronounced with the breath only, without the voice; a non-vocal letter; a sound with which the breath passes forth, not from the voice of the chest, but passing forth gently;* (IJ;) *contr. of* مَجْهُورٌ: (Mṣb:)] الحُرُوفُ المَهْمُوسَةُ are *the letters* (*ten in number,* Ṣ,) *which are comprised in the saying* حَثَّهُ شَخْصٌ فَسَكَتَ: (Ṣ, Ḳ:*) so called [accord. to some] because the stress is made weak in the place where any one of them occurs until the breath has passed forth with it. (Sb, Ṣ.)

[همش &c.

See Supplement.]

هملج

Q. 1. هَمْلَجَ, (L, Mṣb,) inf. n. هَمْلَجَةٌ, (Ṣ, L, Ḳ, &c.,) *He* (a hackney, or pacing horse, بِرْذَوْن, Ṣ, L, &c., i. e. a رَهْوَان, TA,) *went an easy and quick pace;* (Mṣb;) *he* (a hackney, or pacing horse, or a beast,) *went a good and quick pace; he went at a good and quick and graceful pace;* (L;) *he* (a beast of carriage) *went a good pace.* (Abridgment of the 'Eyn.) See نَصَبَ السَّيْرَ.

هَمْلَجَةٌ, as a simple subst., (*An easy and quick,* or *good and quick,* or *good and quick and graceful,* or *good, pace* of a hackney, or pacing horse, or beast of carriage:] pl. هَمَالِجُ. (L.)

هِمْلَاجٌ, (Ṣ, Ḳ, &c.,) used as the act. part. n. of هَمْلَجَ, (Abridgment of the 'Eyn,) whence it would seem that the regular form of the act. part. n., مُهَمْلِجٌ, has not been used, (Mṣb,) an epithet applied to a hackney, or pacing horse, بِرْذَوْن, (Ṣ, Ḳ, &c.,) or a beast of carriage, (L,) both to the male and female, (L, Mṣb,) *Going,* or *that goes, an easy and quick pace;* (Mṣb;) *a good and quick pace; a good and quick and graceful pace;* (L;) *a good pace:* (Abridgment of the 'Eyn:) syn. مُهَمْلَجٌ: (Ḳ: in the CḲ مُهَمْلِجٌ:) *a man's beast for riding:* (L:) pl. هَمَالِيجُ: (Ṣ:) a Persian word, arabicized: (Ṣ, L, Ḳ:) [but I have not found its original in a Persian lexicon]. — شَاةٌ هِمْلَاجٌ *A sheep in which is no marrow, by reason of its leanness.* (Ḳ.)

أَمْرٌ مُهَمْلَجٌ *An affair rendered manageable,* or *easy.* (L, Ḳ.) — *An affair proved by experience.* (L.)

[همى &c.

See Supplement.]

هنأ

1. هَنُوَ, aor. ـُ, inf. n. هَنَاءَةٌ; and هَنِئَ, aor. ـَ; *It came, or happened, without inconvenience,* or *trouble:* (Ḳ:) [*it was pleasant,* or *productive of enjoyment:* see what immediately follows]. — هَنُوَ الطَّعَامُ (Ṣ, Ḳ*) aor. ـُ, inf. n. هَنَاءَةٌ (Ṣ, Ḳ) and هَنَاءٌ and هَنْءٌ, (Ḳ,) or هِنْءٌ (as in some copies of the Ḳ, and in the L); epithet هَنِىْءٌ; (Ṣ;) and هَنِئَ, (Akh, Ṣ, Ḳ,) aor. ـَ, inf. n. هَنْءٌ; (TA;) and هَنَأَ, aor. ـِ, (Lth,) *The food was,* or *became, pleasant,* or *productive of enjoyment, to the eater:* or *easy to swallow; not attended by trouble:* [*agreeable:*] or *not succeeded by harm, even after digestion.* (Z, cited voce مَرُؤَ.) — هَنَأَنِى الطَّعَامُ, (Akh, Ṣ, Ḳ), and هَنَأَ لِى, aor. ـِ and ـَ (Ṣ, Ḳ) and ـُ, (Ḳ,) unexampled, says Akh, in the class termed mahmooz, (Ṣ,) [though بَرَأَ and قَرَأَ are similar with respect to their having ḍamm to the aor.,] inf. n. هَنْءٌ and هِنْءٌ, (Ṣ, Ḳ,) [*The food was pleasant,* or *productive of enjoyment, to me:* or *easy to swallow; &c.:* see هَنُوَ]. هَنَأَهُ — مرأ: see art. هَنَأَنِى الطَّعَامُ وَمَرَأَنِى — هنأ لَهُ ذٰلِكَ, and ذٰلِكَ *That* (thing) *was pleasant,* or *productive of enjoyment, to him; &c.* (TA.) [See هَنُوَ.] — هَنَأَنِى خَبَرُ فُلَانٍ *The news of such a one was pleasant to me to hear.* (TA.) — هَنِئَ الطَّعَامَ, aor. ـَ; and تهنّأ ↓ بالطَّعامِ, (Ṣ, Ḳ,) and تهنّأ الطَّعامَ, and استهنأهُ, (TA,) [*He enjoyed the food; found it pleasant,* or *productive of enjoyment; &c.:* see هَنُوَ:] *he found the food to be productive of no evil result, and not attended by inconvenience.* (TA.) — هَنِئَ, (AZ, Ṣ, Ḳ,) aor. ـَ, inf. n. هَنْأٌ and هَنْءٌ, (Ḳ,) *He* (a beast) *lighted upon a good piece of herbage, but did not satiate himself therewith.* (AZ, Ṣ, Ḳ.) — أَكَلْنَا هٰذَا الطَّعَامَ حَتَّى هَنِئْنَا مِنْهُ *We ate this food until we were satiated with it.* (TA.) — هَنِئَتِ الإِبِلُ *The camels were satiated* with herbage. (TA.) — هَنِئَ بِهِ *He rejoiced in him,* or *it.* (Ḳ.) — هَنَأَنَا اللّٰهُ الطَّعَامَ [*God made the food pleasant, or productive of enjoyment, to us: &c.: made us to enjoy it:* see هَنُوَ]. (TA.) — هَنَأَتْنِيهِ العَافِيَةُ [*Health made it pleasant,* or *productive of enjoyment, to me: &c.*]. (Ḳ.) — لِيَهْنِئْكَ الفَارِسُ [*May the horseman give thee joy:* a form of congratulation on the exploits of a horseman; i. e., I congratulate thee on the exploits of the horseman]: also written and pronounced لِيَهْنِيكَ: لِيهنك, though it occurs in a trad., pronounced لِيَهْنِكَ or لِيَهْنَكَ, (but which pronunciation is to be preferred is disputed,) is said to be a vulgarism, and not allowable. (TA.) — هَنَأَهُ, aor. ـِ (Ḳ) [and app., ـُ (see هَانِئٌ)], inf. n. هَنْءٌ, (TA,) *He fed him; or gave him to eat.* (Ḳ.) — هَنَأَهُ, aor. ـِ and ـُ, (Ṣ, Ḳ,) inf. n. هَنْءٌ; (Ṣ;) and ↓ اهنأهُ; (IAạr, Ḳ;) *He gave him, or bestowed upon him:* (Ṣ, Ḳ:) *gave him plentifully.* (TA.) — هَنَأَ الطَّعَامَ, inf. n. هَنْءٌ and هِنْءٌ (Ḳ) and هَنَاءَةٌ (as in some copies of the Ḳ) or هَنَاءٌ (as in others) or هِنَاءٌ (as in others) or هَنَاةٌ (as in the CḲ), *He made the food good; qualified it properly; seasoned it:* syn. أَصْلَحَهُ. (Ḳ.) — هَنَأَ مَالَهُ, (TA,) and ↓ اهتنأ ماله, (Ḳ,) *He put his property in a right, or good, state.* (Ḳ.) — هَنَأَ القَوْمَ, aor. ـِ, *He nourished, or maintained, the people;* (Ṣ;) *satisfied their wants; bestowed upon them.* (TA.) Ex. هَنَأَهُمْ شَهْرَيْنِ [*He maintained them two months*]. Hence the proverb quoted in illustration of the word هَانِئٌ, accord. to the second reading. (TA) — هَنَأَهُ *He aided, succoured, or defended, him.* (Ḳ.) — هَنَأَ الإِبِلَ, aor. ـِ (Ṣ, Ḳ,) and ـُ and ـَ (Ḳ: dev. from constant rule as shown above: TA), inf. n. هَنْأٌ and هِنَاءٌ, (TA,) *He smeared the camels with* هِنَاء, which is *tar,* or *liquid pitch,* syn. قَطِرَان, (AZ, Ṣ, Ḳ,) or *a kind thereof,* (TA,) [as a

remedy for, or preservative against, the mange, or scab]. — لَيْسَ الهَنْءُ بِالدَّسِّ *The smearing of a camel* [*all over*] *with* هِنَآء *is not* [*merely*] *smearing the cavities under the shoulders, and the like,* which the mange, or scab, more quickly attacks. A proverb, applied to him who does not a thing thoroughly. (TA.) — See 2.

2. هَنَّاهُ وَمَنَّاهُ (in a trad. respecting the prostration for inattention) *He* (the devil) *made him to think of pleasant things,* or *things productive of enjoyment, and of things wished for,* or *objects of desire,* in his prayer. The former verb is pronounced thus to assimilate it to the latter. (TA.) — هَنَّأَهُ بِالأَمْرِ, inf. n. تَهْنِئَةٌ and تَهْنِىْءٌ; (Ṣ, Ḳ;) and ♦ هَنَأَهُ, (Ḳ,) inf. n. هَنْءٌ; (TA;) *He congratulated him on the thing,* (Ṣ, Ḳ,) such as the possession of a government, &c.: (Ṣ:) *he said to him* لِيَهْنِئْكَ [*May it give thee joy*]. (Ḳ.) — [When the agent of the verb is God, the meaning necessarily is, *He granted him enjoyment in the thing; made him to have enjoyment in it.*] — هُنِّئْتَ وَلَا تُنْكَهْ: see art. نكأ.

4: see 1.

5. تهنّأ *He gave many gifts.* (IAạr.) — تهنّأ بِكَذَا [unless it be a mistake for تهيّأ, as IbrD suggests, which I think not improbable, though mentioned in this art. in the TA] *He prided himself in such a thing:* syn. تمرّأ and تغبّط and تسمّن and تخيّل and تزيّن. (TA.) — See 1.

8: see 1.

10. استهنأهُ *He asked him for aid, succour,* or *defence.* (Ḳ.) — *He asked him for a gift.* (Ḳ, TA.) — *He conceded to him,* or *gave him, a part of his dues,* or *rights.* (TA.) — See 1.

هِنْءٌ *A gift.* (Ṣ, Ḳ.) ═ *A part of the night.* (Ḳ.) ═ هِنْءٌ subst. from هَنَأَ الإِبِلَ; (Ḳ;) i. e., The *smearing with* هِنَآء. (MF.)

إِبِلٌ هَنَائِى *Camels which have lighted upon a good piece of herbage, but are not satiated therewith.* (Ḳ.)

هِنَآءٌ *Tar,* or *liquid pitch;* syn. قَطِرَانٌ: (Ṣ, Ḳ:) or *a kind thereof.* (TA.) See also نُورَةٌ; and قَالِبٌ. ═ هِنَآءٌ dial. var. of إِهَانٌ, (Ḳ,) or formed from the latter by transposition, (TA,) *A raceme of a palm-tree.* (AḤn, Ḳ.) [See إِهَانٌ.]

هَنِىْءٌ *What comes or happens to one without inconvenience,* or *trouble:* (Ṣ, Ḳ:) [*what is pleasant,* or *productive of enjoyment; an unalloyed gratification,* i. e., *a thing that gives unalloyed enjoyment;* see what follows:] as also ♦ مَهْنَأٌ, (Ḳ,) a subst., sometimes written and pronounced مَهْنًا; pl. مَهَانِئُ, sometimes written and pronounced مَهَانٍ. (TA.) [See مهنأ also below.] — *Pleasant,* or *productive of enjoyment, to the eater:* or *easy to swallow; not attended by trouble:* or *not succeeded by harm, even after its digestion.* (Z, cited voce مَرُؤَ.) — هَنِيْئًا مَرِيْئًا [May it be, or Eat it, or Drink it, *with enjoyment, and with wholesome result:* or *with ease in the swallowing, and with quickness in digesting: &c.*: see مَرُؤَ]. (Ṣ.) — هَنِيْئًا لَهُ ذٰلِكَ [*May that be productive of enjoyment to him!*]. (TA.) — هَنِيْئًا and مَرِيْئًا are of the number of epithets which are employed after the manner of inf. ns. significant of a prayer or good wish, governed in the acc. case by a verb understood. (Sb.)

هُنَيْئَةٌ (Ḳ) and هُنَيَّةٌ and هُنَيْهَةٌ (the second is the most usual; and the third is said to be formed by substituting ه for ء; but accord. to some, the word is incorrectly written with ء, [so says F,] and is a dim. formed from هَنْوَةٌ, which becomes first هُنَيْوَةٌ, and then هُنَيَّةٌ: see art. هنو:) (TA:) *A little; a little while.* (Ḳ.)

هَانِئٌ *A servant.* (Ḳ.) — هَانِئًا occurs in this sense in a trad.; but the reading commonly known is مَاهِنًا. If right, it is an act. part. n. from هنأ "he gave." (TA.) — إِنَّمَا سُمِّيتَ هَانِئًا لِتَهْنَأَ, or لِتَهْنِئَ; the former is the reading of El-Umawee; the latter, of Ks; *Thou art only named Hánì* (Giver, or Nourisher,) *that thou mayest give,* accord. to both readings; or *that thou mayest nourish,* or *maintain, and supply people's wants;* لتعول وتكفى: (TA:) [such is said to be the meaning of لتهنأ here:] and accord. to El-Umawee, لتهنئ signifies لِتَمْرِىَ, (Ṣ,) [which is app. the same as لتعول]. A proverb: said to him who is known for his beneficence, in order that he may continue to do as he has been wont. (TA.)

مَهْنَأٌ: see هَنِىْءٌ. — لَكَ المَهْنَأُ, (Ṣ,) and المَهْنَا, (TA,) [*Unalloyed gratification to thee!*] — لَكَ المَهْنَأُ وَعَلَيْهِ الوِزْرُ [*To thee be unalloyed gratification, and on him be the burden,* or *sin*]: said, accord. to a trad., to one who asked whether he should accept an invitation to eat the food of one who received unlawful interest or profit; and also said with respect to eating the food of a tyrannical intendant. (TA.)

مَهْنُوْءٌ A camel *smeared with* هِنَآء. (Ṣ.)

هنب

هَنَبٌ [probably an inf. n., of which the verb is هَنِبَ, aor. َ,] *Weakness of understanding; want of discrimination; stupidity; foolishness; littleness of sense.* (Ṣ.)

هَنْبَى &c.: see هُنَبَاءُ.

هُنَبَاءُ (incorrectly written by J, in a verse which he quotes, هَنَبَاءُ, Ḳ, TA; but in an old and excellent copy of the Ṣ, I find the word written هُنَبَاءُ;]) and هُنْبَى (Ḳ) and هَنْبَاءُ and ♦ هَنْبَى (IDrd, Ḳ) A woman *of weak understanding; without discrimination; stupid; foolish; of little sense:* (Ṣ, Ḳ:) accord. to some, as mentioned in a note by Aboo-Zekereeya, in the Ṣ, in this art., هُنْبَى signifies an *insane* woman; or one *possessed by a jinnee.* (TA.) هُنَبَاءُ is the only word of the measure فُعَلَاءُ known to Aṣ. (TA.) Accord. to the Ḳ, IDrd writes اِمْرَأَةٌ هَنْبَاءُ and هَنْبَى: but this is [thought to be] a mistake: he gives the two forms هُنَبَاءُ and هُنْبَى, as stated by IM and others; and, app., هَنْبَى. (TA.) — The first and second of these three words also signify A man who is *stupid, foolish,* or *of little sense.* (Ḳ.)

مِهْنَبٌ *Exceedingly stupid,* or *foolish.* (IAạr, Az, Ḳ.)

هنبت

Q. 1. هَنْبَتَ, inf. n. هَنْبَتَةٌ, *He was languid and sluggish.* (IḲṭṭ, Ḳ.) It may be said that the ن is augmentative, and that the word is derived from هَبْتَةٌ, signifying "weakness." (TA.)

هنتب

Q. 1. هَنْتَبَ فِى أَمْرِهِ *He was remiss in his affair.* (Ḳ.) See also هَنْبَتَ.

هند

2. هَنَّدَتْهُ, inf. n. تَهْنِيدٌ, *She* (a woman) *behaved towards him in a blandishing manner:* (IDrd, L:) *she enamoured him by blandishment,* (L, Ḳ,) *and by amatory conversation* or *conduct:* (L:) *she enslaved him by amatory conversation,* or *conduct.* (Ṣ, L.) [Thought by Golius to be derived from هِنْد, a proper name of a woman.] — هَنَّدَتْ بِقَلْبِهِ *She deprived him of his heart.* (Ibn-El-Mustaneer, L.) ═ هنّد, inf. n. تَهْنِيدٌ, *He made* a sword *of Indian iron.* This is the original signification. (T, L.) — *He sharpened* a sword. (L, Ḳ.)

هِنْدٌ a name for *A hundred camels;* (M, L, Ḳ;) as also ♦ هُنَيْدَةُ; (T, Ṣ, M, A, L, Ḳ;) which latter is a determinate noun, imperfectly decl., not admitting the art. ال, [though it is written with it in the Ṣ, and in a verse cited in the Ṣ and L,] nor having a pl., nor a proper sing.: (T, L:) [see an ex. in a verse cited voce سَوْف:] or the former is a name for *more than a hundred camels and less:* (Ḳ:) or *a little more and a little less:* (M, L:) or *two hundred camels:* (M,

A, L, Ḳ:) so accord. to Ez-Ziyádee, as mentioned by ISd, who adds that he had not heard it from any other than IJ: (L:) and the latter, *a hundred of other things:* (Ṣ, L:) or *any hundred:* (AO, Ṣ, L:) also the former, *two hundred years:* and the latter, [written with the art. ال,] *a hundred years.* (Th, ISd, L.) ═ الهِنْدُ *The name of a well-known nation;* (M, L, Ḳ;) or *of a country:* (Ṣ, L:) [*the Indians:* and *India:*] rel. n. ↓ هِنْدِىٌّ: pl. هُنُودٌ: (Ṣ, L, Ḳ:) and الأَهَانِدُ signifies *the men of* الهِنْد [or *India*]; as also الهَنَادِكُ, (L, Ḳ,) pl. of هِنْدِكِىٌّ [q. v. in art. هندك]. (L.) — See also أَحْمَسُ.

هِنْدِىٌّ: see هِنْدٌ. — Also, *Indian aloes-wood.* (L.) — سَيْفٌ هِنْدِىٌّ, (L,) and ↓ هُنْدُوَانِىٌّ, [in the CḲ هِنْدُوَانِىٌّ,] and هِنْدُوَانِىٌّ, (Ṣ, A, L, Ḳ,) *A sword made in the country of* الهِنْد, [or *India,*] *and well fabricated:* (L:) or, *made of the iron of that country:* (A:) as also ↓ مُهَنَّدٌ, in the latter sense, (Ṣ, A, L,) and in the former: (L:) so termed in relation to the people called الهِنْد: (Ḳ:) and ↓ سَيْفٌ مُهَنَّدٌ *a sharpened,* or *sharp, sword.* (L.)

هُنْدُوَانِىٌّ: see هِنْدِىٌّ.

هُنَيْدَةُ: see هِنْدٌ.

مُهَنَّدٌ: see هِنْدِىٌّ.

هندب

هِنْدَبٌ and هِنْدَبَآءٌ &c.: see art. هدب.

هندز

هِنْدَازٌ, (Ṣ, Ḳ,) with kesr, (Ḳ,) found in the work of Az, in several places, written with fet-ḥ, [هَنْدَازٌ,] (TA,) *A limit;* syn. حَدٌّ: (Ḳ:) [or rather *a measure:*] an arabicized word, from أَنْدَازَه, (Ṣ, Ḳ,) with fet-ḥ, (Ḳ,) which is Persian: (Ṣ:) the arabicized word is with kesr to the first letter because of the rareness of the measure فَعْلَالٌ in the cases of words not reduplicative. (Ḳ.) You say, أَعْطَاهُ بِلَا حِسَابٍ وَلَا هِنْدَازٍ [*He gave to him without calculation and without measure*]. (Ṣ.)

هِنْدَازَةٌ The *cubit with which* [*certain*] *cloths and the like are measured;* [*about twenty-five inches in length:*] also a Persian word arabicized. (TA.)

مُهَنْدِزٌ *One who determines the measures and proportions of subterranean channels for water, and of buildings:* [*an architect:* and also *a geometrician:*] from هِنْدَازٌ: but they change the ز into س, (Ṣ, Ḳ,) and say مُهَنْدِسٌ, (Ṣ,) because there is not in the [genuine] language of the Arabs a ز with a د before it. (Ṣ, Ḳ.)

هندس

هَنْدَسَةٌ [The *art of determining the measures and proportions of subterranean channels for water:* and hence, the *art of architecture:* and the *practice,* and *science, of geometry:*] a subst. from مُهَنْدِسٌ, q. v. (Ṣ, Ḳ.)

مُهَنْدِسٌ *One who determines the measures and proportions of subterranean channels for water:* [and hence, *an architect:* and *a geometrician:*] derived from هِنْدَازٌ, (Ṣ, Ḳ,) which is Persian [in origin], (Ṣ,) arabicized from آبْ أَنْدَازْ; (Ḳ;) انداز signifying "the act of measuring," and آب signifying "water;" (TA;) the ز being changed into س because there is not in the [genuine] language of the Arabs a ز after د. (Ṣ, Ḳ.)

هنر

4. هَنَارَ الثَّوْبَ, aor. يُهْنِيرُهُ, inf. n. اهْنَارَةٌ, or هِنَارَةٌ; for أَنَارَهُ: see art. نير.

[هنع &c.
See Supplement.]

هنقب

هَنْقَبٌ, (Ḳ) by some written هِنْقَبٌ, (TA,) *Short:* (Ḳ:) but it is not a word of established authority. (IDrd.)

[هنم &c.
See Supplement.]

هوأ

1. هَآءَ بِنَفْسِهِ إِلَى المَعَالِى, (Ṣ, Ḳ,) aor. يَهُوْءُ, (Ṣ,) inf. n. هَوْءٌ, (TA,) *He raised his mind to high things, or objects; purposed,* or *aspired to, high things.* (Ṣ, Ḳ, TA.) The vulgar say, يَهْوِى بِنَفْسِهِ. (Ṣ.) — مَا هُؤْتُ هَوْءَهُ *I did not know it, nor desire,* or *mean,* [*to do it;* i. e., *I did it not knowingly, nor intentionally*]. (TA.) — هُؤْتُ بِهِ خَيْرًا, (Az, Ṣ, Ḳ) and شَرًّا, (Ḳ,) and هُؤْتُهُ بِخَيْرٍ and بِشَرٍّ, (Lḥ,) inf. n. هَوْءٌ, (TA,) *I thought him to be possessed of good,* (Az, Ṣ, Ḳ,) and, *of evil.* (Ḳ, TA.) — هُؤْتُهُ بِمَالٍ كَثِيرٍ *I thought him to be possessed of much wealth.* (TA.) — إِنِّى لَأَهُوءُ بِكَ عَنْ هٰذَا الأَمْرِ *Verily I exalt thee above this thing; I hold thee above it*]. (Lḥ.) — هُؤْتُ بِهِ *I rejoiced in him, or it.* (AA, Ḳ.) — هُوءَ إِلَيْهِ, aor. يَهُوءُ, *He purposed,* or *intended, it.* (Ḳ.) ═ هَآءَ and هَآءِ and هَأْ, in imperative senses, and the forms into which they are inflected, see below.

3. هَاوَأَهُ *He contended with him for superior glory:* like هَاوَاهُ. (IAạr.) [See also art. هوى.]

هَآءِ, هَأْ, هَآءَ, &c. — هَآءِ, with kesr, is syn. with هَاتِ, *Give;* [or changed from this verb;] and is thus inflected: sing. masc. هَآءِ, fem. هَائِى; dual. masc. and fem. هَائِيَا; pl. masc. هَاؤُوا, fem. هَائِينَ: (Ṣ, Ḳ: like هَاتِ, هَاتِى; هَاتِيَا; هَاتُوا, هَاتِينَ: ء holding the place of ت: Ṣ.) — But هَآءَ, with fet-ḥ, is syn. with هَاكَ, *Take;* [or changed from this word;] and is thus inflected: sing. masc. هَآءَ, fem. هَآءِ, without ى; dual masc. and fem. هَاؤُمَا; pl. masc. هَاؤُمْ, [so in the Ḳ, and so I find it in one copy of the Ṣ: in another copy of the latter, هَاؤُمُ, as it is pronounced before a conjunctive ا; for instance, in the Ḳur, lxix, 19:] fem. هَاؤُنَّ, (Ṣ, Ḳ:) or هَاؤُمْنَ: (L:) [which last does not exactly correspond with the model هَاكُنَّ: but I think it most probable that هَاكُنَّ is changed by idghám from هَاكُمْنَ; and in like manner, that هَاؤُنَّ is changed from هَاؤُمْنَ:] (like هَاكَ, هَاكِ; هَاكُمَا; هَاكُمْ, هَاكُنَّ: ء holding the place of ك: Ṣ:) also, sing. masc. هَأْ (originally هَآءَ, Ṣ), fem. هَائِى; dual masc. (Ṣ) and fem. (Ṣ, Ḳ) هَاءَا; (Ṣ, Ḳ;) pl. masc. هَاؤُوا, (Ṣ,) fem. هَأْنَ: (Ṣ, Ḳ:) also, sing. masc. and fem. هَأْ; dual. masc. هَآءَا, fem. هَائِيَا; pl. masc. هَاؤُوا, fem. هَاؤُنَّ. (TA.) — [See a saying of 'Omar cited voce رَمَآءٌ, in art. رمى.] — When it is said to thee هَآءَ *Take,* thou sayest مَا أَهَآءُ *What shall I take?* syn. مَا آخُذُ; and مَا أُهَآءُ, in the pass. form, *What shall I receive,* or *be given?* syn. مَا أُعْطَى. (Ṣ.) [Also, in the TA, it seems to be said that أَهَآءَ signifies أَعْطَى *He gave,* or *made to take:* but this is uncertain; as the former verb is there written اهاء, and the latter is without the syll. points]. — هَآءَ is also syn. with لَبَّيْكَ *At thy service!* &c.. (Ḳ, TA.) ═ لَا هَا ٱللّٰهِ ذَا, or, more chastely, لَا هَآءَ ٱللّٰهِ ذَا, or the former is a barbarism; originally لَا وَٱللّٰهِ هٰذَا: ها and ذا are separated, and the name of God is introduced between them; (Ḳ;) and the meaning is *No, by God,* (*I did not*) *this!* (Ṣ, art. ها, q. v.) or *No, by God, this* (*is what I swear by*)! (Ḳ.)

هَوْءٌ *Mind; purpose; aspiration; desire; ambition.* (Ṣ, Ḳ, TA.) Ex. بَعِيدُ الهَوْءِ *A person of far-reaching aspiration,* or *ambition.* (Ṣ, TA.) — هَوْءٌ *Penetrating judgment.* (Ḳ.) — وَقَعَ فِى هَوْئِى, and ↓ هُوئِى, *It occurred to my mind,* or *imagination.* (Ḳ.)

هُوْءٌ: See preceding sentence.

مُهْوَانٌّ (Ṣ, Ḳ) and ▼ مُهْوَئِنٌّ (Ḳ) *A wide desert, or wide tract of the kind called* صَحْرَآء. (Ṣ, Ḳ.) —— *Custom*: syn. عَادَةٌ. (Ḳ.) —— *A part of the night.* (Ḳ.) —— The mention of مهوانّ in this art., by J, says IB, and F after him, is wrong; for its measure is مفوعلّ; the و being an augmentative letter. [But if so, F has himself done wrong, in mentioning it, not only here, but also in art. هون, (where, if the و be augmentative, it is equally inappropriate,) as though it were a quasi-quadriliteral-radical word, of the measure مفعالّ.] ISd gives it as formed by transposition from the root هنأ, and explains it as signifying *a wide place.* (TA.)

مُهْوَئِنٌّ : see مُهْوَانٌّ.

هوب

1. هُوبَ : see art. هيب.

هَوْبٌ *Distance; remoteness.* (Ṣ, Ḳ.) —— تَرَكْتُهُ فِى هَوْبٍ دَابِرٍ, and ▼ هُوبِ دَابِرٍ, (Ṣ, Ḳ,) or, accord. to some, as stated in a marginal note in a copy of the Ṣ, in the handwriting of Aboo-Zekereeya, فى هوب دابر, with هوب as a prefixed n., (TA,) *I left him in such a place that it was not known where he was*: (Ṣ, Ḳ:) هوب دابر being the name of a land over which the Jinn, or genii, have obtained ascendancy: (TA:) or the correct reading is [هوت] with ت. (Ḳ.) ═ هَوْبٌ *A stupid, or foolish, and loquacious,* man: (A'Obeyd, Ṣ, Ḳ:) pl. أَهْوَابٌ. (TA.) ═ هَوْبٌ The *heat,* or *burning, of fire*; (Ṣ, Ḳ;) *and its flaming,* or *blazing*; of the dial. of El-Yemen: also, the *heat,* or *burning of the sun*: also of the dial. of El-Yemen. (TA.)

هُوبٌ : see هَوْبٌ.

مَهُوبٌ : see art. هيب.

هوت

2. هَوَّتَ بِهِ, inf. n. تَهْوِيتٌ, *He called out to him*; (Ḳ;) saying حَوْتَ حَوْتَ: (TA, art. حيت:) *he cried out to him, and called him.* (Ṣ.) A dial. form of هَيَّتَ. (TA.) [See هَيَّتَ.]

هُوتَةٌ : see what follows.

هُوتَةٌ (Ḳ) and ▼ هَوْتَةٌ (Ṣ, Ḳ) *A low, or depressed, tract, or piece, of land*: (Ṣ, Ḳ:) or *a deep place*: (IAth:) or the *space between two mountains*: (IAạr:) pl. هُوَتٌ (as in the CḲ) or هُوت (as in the TA.) It may be said that هُوتٌ and هَوْتٌ are coll. gen. ns. [of each of which the n. un. is with ة]. (TA.) —— Also هُوتَةٌ *A road, or way, descending to water.* (IAạr.) —— صَبَّ ٱللّٰهُ عَلَيْهِ هُوتَةً ▼ وَمُوتَةً an imprecation, respecting which ISd says, I know not what is هوتة here. [It probably signifies *A cry*, such as destroyed the tribe of Thamood: see هَوَّتَ.] (TA.)

مَضَى هِيتَآءٌ مِنَ ٱللَّيْلِ *A certain time, or portion, of the night passed.* Accord. to Aboo-'Alee, هيتاء is of the measure فِعْلَآء, and quasi-coordinate to سِرْدَاحٌ, and belonging to this art. (TA.)

هِيتَاهْ هِيتَاهْ *A cry by which the Arabs urge on a dog against the game which they are pursuing.* (TA.) [In the L written هَيْتَاهْ, and mentioned in art. هيت.]

هوث

تَرَكْتُهُمْ هَوْثًا بَوْثًا *He made a great slaughter among them.* (TA.) [See art. بوث.]

هَوْثَةٌ *A thirst.* (Ḳ.)

هوج

1. هَوِجَ, aor. ـَ, inf. n. هَوَجٌ; (L;) and ▼ تَهَوَّجَ; (A, TA;) *He* (a man) *was characterized by what is termed* هَوَجٌ, (L, A,) which is similar to هَوَكٌ; (L;) i.e., *stupidity, foolishness,* or *paucity of sense*: (JK, L:) *tallness, combined with hastiness, and stupidity* or *foolishness* or *paucity of sense*: (Ṣ:) or *tallness, with stupidity* or *foolishness* or *paucity of sense and levity* or *fickleness* or *unsteadiness, and hastiness*: (Ḳ:) or *tallness, with levity* or *fickleness* or *unsteadiness, and hastiness*: (TA:) or *tallness,* (A,) or *excessive tallness,* (L,) *with stupidity* or *foolishness* or *paucity of sense.* (L.)

4. اهوجهُ *He found him to be such a man as is termed* أَهْوَجُ. (L.)

5: see 1.

هَوَجٌ : see 1. —— فِى فُلَانٍ عَوَجٌ, and هَوَجٌ, are syn., [meaning *In such a one is a deviation from rectitude*]. (AA, L.)

هَاجَةٌ a dial. form of حَاجَةٌ; but of weak authority. (L, from a trad.)

أَهْوَجُ A man *characterized by what is termed* هَوَجٌ; (Ṣ, L, &c.;) *stupid, foolish,* or *having little sense*: (JK, L:) or *tall, with hastiness, and stupidity* or *foolishness* or *paucity of sense, &c.*: (Ṣ, &c.:) fem. هَوْجَآءُ: (A:) [pl. هُوجٌ.] —— أَهْوَجُ ٱلطُّولِ ‡ A man *exceedingly,* or *excessively, tall.* (A.) —— Also أَهْوَجُ ‡ *A courageous man, who throws himself into a scene of war.* (A.) —— أَهْوَجُ ‡ A he-camel *that goes quickly, as though characterized by what is termed* هَوَجٌ: fem. هَوْجَآءُ: [pl. هُوجٌ:] or the fem. epithet only is used, applied to a camel; and you say نَاقَةٌ هَوْجَآءُ; (TA;) i.e., *a she-camel that goes quickly, &c.*, as explained above; (Ṣ, Ḳ;) *and that does not always care where she puts her feet on the ground.* (A.) —— رِيحٌ هَوْجَآءُ ‡ *Any wind that blows violently*: (IAạr:) or *a wind of which the blasts are closely consecutive, as though characterized by what is termed* هَوَجٌ: or *a wind that carries away the dust, and makes a trace upon the ground like that made by dragging the skirt*: (TA:) or *a wind that tears up the tents*: (Ṣ, Ḳ:) pl. هُوجٌ. (Ṣ.)

هود

1. هَادَ, aor. يَهُودُ, (Ṣ, L, &c.,) inf. n. هَوْدٌ, (Ṣ, L, Ḳ, &c.,) *He returned* (IAạr, A, L, Mṣb) *from evil to good or from good to evil*: (IAạr, L:) *he repented,* (Ṣ, A, L, Ḳ,) *and returned to the truth*; (Ṣ, L, Ḳ;) as also ▼ تهوّد: (L:) and the latter, *he repented and did righteously.* (AO, Ṣ, A, L.) —— هُدْنَا إِلَيْكَ *We have turned unto Thee with repentance.* [Ḳur, vii, 155.] So accord. to Mujáhid and Sa'eed Ibn-Jubeyr and Ibráheem. (L.) It is made trans. by means of الى because implying the meaning of رَجَعْنَا. (ISd, L.) —— هَادَ, (Ṣ, A, L,) aor. يَهُودُ, inf. n. هَوْدٌ; (L;) and ▼ تهوّد; (Ṣ, A, L, Mṣb, Ḳ;) *He became a Jew*; (Ṣ, A, L, Ḳ;) *he became of the Jewish religion.* (L, Mṣb.)

2. هوّدهُ, (L, Mṣb, Ḳ,) inf. n. تَهْوِيدٌ, (Ṣ,) *He made him* (his son [for instance] Mṣb) *a Jew*; (Ṣ, L, Mṣb;) *he turned him to the religion of the Jews*; (L, Ḳ;) *taught him that religion, and initiated him in it.* (L.) ═ تَهْوِيدٌ The *talking together of jinn, or genii*: (L, Ḳ:) so termed because of the gentleness and weakness of their voices. (L.) —— هوّد, inf. n. تَهْوِيدٌ, *He reiterated his voice, or quavered, or trilled, gently.* (Ibn-Jebeleh, L, Ḳ.) —— هوّد, (L,) inf. n. تَهْوِيدٌ, (Ḳ,) *He sang*; syn. غَنَّى: (Aboo-Málik, L:) *he sang, or gladdened, and diverted*; syn. طَرَّبَ وَأَلْهَى. (Ḳ.) See also مُهَوِّدٌ. ═ هوّد, inf. n. تَهْوِيدٌ, *He went, or proceeded, gently, or in a leisurely manner,* (Ṣ, L, Ḳ,) like the manner termed دَبِيبٌ: from ٱلْهَوَادَةُ. (Ṣ, L, Ḳ.) It is said in a trad., أَسْرِعُوا ٱلْمَشْىَ فِى ٱلْجَنَازَةِ وَلَا تُهَوِّدُوا كَمَا تُهَوِّدُ ٱلْيَهُودُ وَٱلنَّصَارَى [*Make ye your pace to be quick at a funeral, and go ye not in a gentle or leisurely manner like as go the Jews and the Christians*]. (Ṣ.) See also 5. —— هوّد, (L,) inf. n. تَهْوِيدٌ, (Ṣ, L, Ḳ,) *It* (beverage, or wine,) *intoxicated* (Ṣ, L, Ḳ) a person: and *rendered* him *languid, and caused him to sleep.* (L.) —— هوّد, inf. n. تَهْوِيدٌ and تَهْوَادٌ; (L, Ḳ;) and ▼ تهوّد; (TA;) *He uttered a weak, gentle,* (L, Ḳ,) *and languid,* (L,) *voice.* (L, Ḳ.) —— هوّد, inf. n. تَهْوِيدٌ (Ṣ, L, Ḳ) and تَهْوَادٌ; and ▼ تهوّد; (Ḳ;) *He was low, not loud,* in speech, or utterance. (Ṣ, L, Ḳ) —— هوّد, inf. n. تَهْوِيدٌ (L, Ḳ) and تَهْوَادٌ; and

† تَهَوَّدَ; (L;) *He was slow, or tardy, in his pace,* (L, Ḳ,) *and gentle.* (L.) — هَوَّدَ *He* (a man) *rested; or was still, quiet, or at rest.* (Aboo-Málik, L.) — هَوَّدَ, inf. n. تَهْوِيدٌ, *He slept.* (Ṣ, L.) — هَوَّدَ, inf. n. تَهْوِيدٌ and تَهْوَادٌ; and † تَهَوَّدَ; *He was gentle; he acted, or behaved, in a gentle manner.* (L.) — Also, The *murmuring and gentle sounding of the wind over sand.* (L.) — هَوَّدَ, inf. n. تَهْوِيدٌ, *He ate of a camel's hump;* (Ḳ;) or *what is termed* هُودَةٌ. (TA.)

3. هَاوَدَهُ, (A,) inf. n. مُهَاوَدَةٌ, (Ṣ, A, L, Ḳ,) *He made peace with him; reconciled himself with him;* (A;) syn. of the inf. n. مُوَادَعَةٌ; (A, L;) in the Ḳ, مُوَاعَدَةٌ, which is a mistake; (TA;) and مُصَالَحَةٌ, (Ṣ, L,) and مُهَاوَنَةٌ: (TA:) and also مُرَاجَعَةٌ [app. signifying the *restoring* a person, or *taking* him *back, into one's favour*]. (TA.) — *He inclined towards him reciprocally;* syn. مَايَلَهُ: and هَاوَدَا *They two inclined each towards the other;* syn. مَايَلَا: (TḲ:) syn. of the inf. n. مُمَايَلَةٌ. (Ṣ, L.) — *He returned to him, or it, time after time;* syn. عَاوَدَهُ: (TḲ:) syn. of the inf. n. مُعَاوَدَةٌ. (Ḳ.)

5: see 1 and 2. — تَهَوَّدَ فِى مَشْيِهِ *He walked gently, imitating the motions of the Jews in their reciting* or *reading.* (El-Baṣáir.) See also 2. — تَهَوَّدَ *He became allied,* or *allied himself,* or *sought to ally himself,* (تَوَصَّلَ, Ḳ, and تَقَرَّبَ, El-Baṣáir,) *by a bond of relationship;* or *by some other sacred* or *inviolable bond* or *tie,* or *a quality &c. to be regarded as sacred* or *inviolable* or *rendering him entitled to respect* or *reverence.* (Ḳ, El-Baṣáir.) See also مُتَهَوِّدٌ.

يَهُودُ: see الْهُودُ.

هُوَدَةٌ: see هُودَةٌ.

هُودَةٌ *A camel's hump:* (Ṣ, Ḳ:) or the *base of the hump:* (Sh, L:) as also † هُوَدَةٌ: (L:) pl. هُوَدٌ: (Ṣ, L, Ḳ:) [or rather, this is a coll. gen. n., and هُودَةٌ is the n. un.].

هَوَادَةٌ *Gentleness; lenity;* (A, L, Ḳ;) *and that kind of conduct whereby one hopes to effect the adjustment of an affair between a people:* (L, Ḳ:) *quietness:* (L:) *peace,* or *reconciliation: inclination,* or *affection:* (Ṣ, L:) *favour,* or *partiality:* (L:) *facilitation, whereby a person is indulged in an affair.* (L, Ḳ.) Ex. لَا تَأْخُذُهُ فِى ٱللّٰهِ هَوَادَةٌ *Quietness with respect to* a restrictive ordinance of *God, with favour* or *partiality* towards any one, *will not affect him,* or *influence him.* And لَا تَأْخُذُهُ فِيكَ هَوَادَةٌ *Favour* or *partiality with respect to thee will not affect him,* or *influence him.* (L, each from a trad.) — هَوَادَةٌ also signifies *A sacred* or *inviolable bond* or *tie;* or *a quality &c. to be regarded as sacred* or *inviolable,* or *rendering one entitled to respect* or *reverence:* and *a bond of relationship.* (L.)

هَائِدٌ *Returning* (Mṣb) [*from evil to good* or *from good to evil:* see 1:] *repenting and returning to the truth:* (Ṣ, L:) pl. هُودٌ, (Ṣ, A, L, Mṣb,) like as بُزْلٌ is pl. of بَازِلٌ. (Ṣ, L, Mṣb.)

يَهُودُ and الْيَهُودُ and † الْهُودُ [the second of which is the most common,] signify the same, (Ṣ, A, L, Mṣb, Ḳ,) *A certain tribe;* [namely, *the Jews:*] (L:) يَهُودُ is said by some to be originally يَهُوذُ, and arabicized by the change of ذ into د; but ISd disapproves of this assertion: others say, that it is from هَادَ "he repented:" (L:) it is imperfectly decl., because it is a proper name and of the measure of a verb; and [of the fem. gen., as it is said to be in the Ṣ and L,] because it means a قَبِيلَة: but it is allowable to prefix to it the art. ال, and to say الْيَهُودُ: (Mṣb:) this, however, is allowable only on the ground of its being, with the art. prefixed, for الْيَهُودِيُّونَ; for it is of itself determinate: (Ṣ, L:) [thus] يَهُودُ is [as it were] pl. of † يَهُودِيٌّ; (L;) which is the rel. n. of يَهُود, or, accord. to Ṣgh, of يَهُوذَا [or Judah], thus written by him with the unpointed د in this instance, the son of يَعْقُوب [or Jacob]: (Mṣb:) يَهُودُ (sometimes, TA) has يَهْدَانُ as a pl.: (Ḳ:) this pl. occurs in a poem of Ḥassán: (TA:) Fr, says, of هُودًا, in the Ḳur, ii, 105, that it is for يَهُودًا [app. a mistake for يَهُودَ]; or that it may be pl. of هَائِدٌ. (L.)

يَهُودِيٌّ: see يَهُودُ.

الْيَهُودِيَّةُ *The Jewish religion.* (L.)

غِنَآءٌ مُهَوِّدٌ [in some copies of the Ṣ, مُهَوَّدٌ,] *A low, not loud, singing.* (Ṣ, L.) — مُهَوِّدٌ also signifies *Gladdening, and diverting;* syn. مُطْرِبٌ and مُلْهٍ. (IAạr, L.)

مُتَهَوِّدٌ *Allied,* or *allying himself,* or *seeking to ally himself,* (مُتَوَصِّلٌ, IAạr, Sh,) *by what is termed* هَوَادَةٌ. (IAạr, Sh, L.) See 5.

هوذ

الْهُوذَةُ, (L, Ḳ,) or هُوذَةُ, [without the art. ال, as a proper name,] (Ṣ, L,) written by Ed-Demeeree with ḍamm, but fault has been found with him for this, (MF,) [*The bird called*] *the* قَطَاة: (Ṣ, L, Ḳ:) or, as some say, *the female* قَطَاة: (L:) or هُوذَةٌ, (as a determinate noun) is *the name of a certain bird,* (L, Ḳ,) *different from the above:* (L:) pl. هُوَذٌ, (as in the CḲ and a MS copy of the Ḳ) or هُوذٌ, formed by eliding the augmentative letter: (TA:) [and this seems to be the correct reading; for it occurs in a verse, cited in the TA, in which the measure required it to be of one syllable: it therefore appears that هُوذٌ is a coll. gen. n., of which the n. un. is with ة.]

هور

1. هَارَهُ, (Ḳ,) [aor. يَهُورُهُ,] inf. n. هَوْرٌ, (TA,) *He threw it down; pulled it down; pulled it to pieces;* or *demolished it;* namely, a building; (Ḳ;) and in like manner, a جُرْف [i. e. an abrupt, water-worn, bank, rising by the bed of a torrent or stream]; (TA [in which هُؤُورٌ is given as an inf. n. of this verb; but it is more probably an inf. n. of the intrans. verb only, agreeably with analogy;]) as also † هَوَّرَهُ, (Ṣ, A,) the pronoun relating to a building, (A,) and to a جُرْف; (Ṣ;) and هَيَّرَهُ [in illustration of which see what is said of تَهَيَّرَ, below]; (Ṣ, art. هير;) and † تَهَوَّرَهُ, in which the pronoun relates to the upper part of a جُرْف, or to the brink of a well. (TA.) — هَارَ الْقَوْمَ, (Ḳ,) aor. يَهُورُهُمْ, inf. n. هَوْرٌ, (TA,) ‡ *He slew the people, and threw them down prostrate, one upon another,* (Ḳ,) *like as when a* جُرْف *falls down.* (TA.) And [in like manner you say,] ضَرَبَ فُلَانًا فَهَارَهُ † *He smote such a one and prostrated him;* as also † هَوَّرَهُ. (Ḳ,* TA.) — هَارَ, (Ṣ, A, Mṣb, Ḳ,) aor. يَهُورُ, inf. n. هَوْرٌ (Ṣ, Mṣb) and هُؤُورٌ, (Ṣ,) *It became thrown down, pulled down, pulled to pieces, or demolished;* or *it fell in ruins,* or *to pieces;* (Ṣ, A, Ḳ;) said of a building, (Ḳ,) and of a جُرْف [explained above]; (Ṣ, A;) as also † انهار and † تهوّر (Ṣ, A, Ḳ) and تَهَيَّرَ, (Ḳ,) which last has ى as being interchangeable with و, or it may be of the measure تَفَيْعَلَ [originally تَهَيْوَرَ]: (TA:) or *it fell; it fell,* or *tumbled, down; it collapsed; broke down;* said of a building; (TA;) as also † انهار and † تهوّر; (Mṣb, TA;) said of a building, (TA,) and of a جُرْف, (Mṣb,) or of the upper part of the latter, and of the brink of a well; (TA;) [and † اِهْتَوَرَ, q. v., probably signifies the same:] or *it cracked, without falling;* said of a جُرْف: (Mṣb:) or *it cracked in its hinder part, remaining yet in its place;* said of a building. (TA.)

2. هَوَّرَهُ: see هَارَهُ, in two places.

5. تَهَوَّرَ: see هَارَ, in two places; in the former of which, تَهَيَّرَ is also mentioned as syn. with تَهَوَّرَ. — ‡ *He plunged,* or *fell, into an affair with little care* [*for the consequence thereof*]: (Ṣ, Ḳ:) or تَهَوَّرَ فِى الْأُمُورِ *he plunged,* or *fell, into affairs without thought,* or *reflection,* or *consideration:* (A:) or تَهَوُّرٌ is *a state,* or *condition, adventitious to the irascible faculty, by reason of which one ventures upon affairs not fit,* or *meet, to be ventured upon; as the fighting with unbelievers*

when they are more than double the number of the Muslims. (KT.) — تَهْوُرَهٌ : see هَارَةٌ.

7 : see هَارَ, in two places.

8. اِهْتَوَرَ : see هَارَ, last signification. — *It* (a thing, Ṣ) *perished.* (Ṣ, Ḳ.)

هَائِرٌ and هَارٍ, (Ṣ, A, Mṣb, Ḳ,) the latter formed by transposition from the former, [first into هَارِىٌ, and then into هَارٍ,] (Ṣ, TA,) like as شَائِكُ السِّلَاحِ is changed into شَاكِى السِّلَاحِ, (Ṣ,) applied to a building, (Ḳ,) and to a جُرُف, [explained above, (see هَارَةٌ,)] (Ṣ, A, Mṣb,) *Becoming thrown down, pulled down, pulled to pieces,* or *demolished:* (Ṣ, A, Ḳ:) or *falling; falling,* or *tumbling, down:* (IAạr:) or *cracking, without falling:* (Mṣb:) or *cracking in its hinder part, remaining yet in its place.* (TA.) See an ex. of the latter voce جُرُف: and another in the Ḳur, ix. 110.]

مُتَهَوِّرٌ A man *plunging,* or *falling,* or *who plunges,* or *falls, into an affair with little care [for the consequences thereof].* (Ṣ.) See 5.

هوس

هَوَسٌ *Somewhat of madness,* or *insanity,* or *diabolical possession,* (Ṣ, A, Ḳ,) *in the head:* (A:) or *a vertigo,* or *giddiness, and confused noise, in the head.* (A, TA.) — Hence used by the vulgar to signify *Hope.* (TA.)

مُهَوَّسٌ *Affected with somewhat of madness,* or *insanity,* or *diabolical possession.* (Ibn-'Abbád, Ḳ.) — A man *who talks to himself.* (A.) — Sometimes, One *who is affected with melancholy, and with vain,* or *unprofitable, suggestions.* (TA.) — And One *who occupies himself with the science of alchemy.* (TA.)

هوش

1. هَاشَ, aor. يَهُوشُ, inf. n. هَوْشٌ, (Ṣ, A, Mṣb,) *It* (a company of men) *was,* or *became, in a state of conflict and faction, sedition, discord,* or *dissension:* (Mṣb:) *he,* or *it,* (a number of people,) *fell into a bad state,* or *state of disorder* or *disturbance;* as also هَوِشَ, like سَمِعَ; [indicating that its aor. is ـَ, and its inf. n. as above;] and ▼ تَهَوَّشَ: (TA:) *it* (a company of men, Ṣ, A) *was,* or *became, roused,* or *excited;* (A, TA;) *in a state of commotion, agitation, convulsion, tumult,* or *disturbance;* (Ṣ, A, TA;) and in like manner, ▼ هَوَّشَ, said of the belly, *it was,* or *became, in a state of commotion, agitation, &c., by reason of leanness:* (Ṣ:) or هَوِشَ, like سَمِعَ, [see above,] (Ḳ,) aor. ـَ, inf. n. هَوْشٌ, (TḲ,) *he* (a man, TḲ) *was,* or *became in a state of commotion, agitation, &c.;* or *his belly became small,* syn. صَغُرَ, (Ḳ, TA, [or *empty,* (صَغُرَ being perhaps a mistranscription for صَفِرَ, for it is said in another part of this art. in the TA that الهَوْشُ signifies "the belly's being empty,")] *by reason of leanness;* from IF: (TA:) or it (the belly) became so. (IF, TA.) — هَاشَتِ الإِبِلُ, (JḲ, TA,) or الخَيْلُ, (A,) فِى الغَارَةِ, (JK, A,) aor. تَهُوشُ, (JK,) inf. n. هَوْشٌ, (JK, TA,) *The camels,* (JK, TA,) or *the horses,* (A,) *took fright, and ran away at random,* (JK, A, TA,) *and became dispersed,* (TA,) or *separated themselves,* (JK,) *and went to and fro,* (JK, A,) *in the hostile sudden attack made by a party of armed horsemen.* (JK, A, TA.) — هُشْتُ إِلَى فُلَانٍ *I became agile* or *brisk, and advanced towards such a one.* (TA.) And هَاشَ أَهْلُ الحَرْبِ بَعْضُهُمْ لِبَعْضٍ *The warriors became agile* or *brisk, and hastened, one to another;* [in like manner] ▼ تَهَاوَشُوا. (A.) — Also, [aor. and] inf. n. as above, *He collected:* and *mixed,* or *confused,* or *confounded.* (TA.) You say, هُشْتُ مَالًا حَرَامًا *I collected unlawful wealth.* (Ṣgh, TA.) And هَاشَهُمْ and ▼ هَوَّشَهُمْ *He mixed,* or *confused,* or *confounded, them; and collected them hence and thence.* (A.) See also 2.

2. هَوَّشَ: see 1, first sentence: — and see 5. — Also, هَوَّشْتُهُمْ *I occasioned variance between them,* or *among them.* (Mṣb.) And هَوَّشَ بَيْنَهُمْ *He created,* or *excited, disorder, disturbance, discord,* or *dissension, between them,* or *among them.* (TA.) — And hence, (Mṣb,) هَوَّشَ, (Ṣ, Mṣb, Ḳ,) inf. n. تَهْوِيشٌ, (Ḳ,) *He mixed, confused,* or *confounded,* (Ṣ, Mṣb, Ḳ, TA,) a company of men, (Ṣ, TA,) *one with another;* (TA;) and general rules; (Mṣb;) and anything. (Ṣ.) See also 1, last sentence: and see شَوَّشَ. [Hence also,] هَوَّشَتِ الرِّيحُ بِالتُّرَابِ *The wind brought the dust of various sorts [mixed together].* (Ṣ,* IF, Ḳ.)

3. هَاوَشَهُمْ *He mixed, mingled,* or *consorted, with them:* (Ḳ:) or *did so to create,* or *excite, disorder, disturbance, discord,* or *dissension;* or *to make mischief:* (TA:) and مُهَاوَشَةٌ signifies *conflicting;* like مُنَاوَشَةٌ. (TA, art. نوش.)

5. تَهَوَّشَ: see 1, first sentence. — Also تَهَوَّشُوا *They mixed,* or *mingled, together;* or *became mixed, confused,* or *confounded, together;* as also ▼ تَهَاوَشُوا; (Ḳ;) and ▼ هَوَّشُوا. (JK, TA.) — And تَهَوَّشُوا عَلَيْهِ *They collected themselves together against him.* (IF, Mṣb, Ḳ.)

6. تَهَاوَشُوا: see 1, near the end: — and see 5.

هَوْشٌ *A large number:* (Ṣ, Ḳ:) or, as the women of Temeem say, *a multitude of men;* and *of beasts of carriage;* as also بَوْشٌ: (Aboo-'Admán:) and *men collected together in war.* (TA.) You say, ▼ جَآءَ بِالهَوْشِ الهَائِشِ *He came with multitude,* or *the multitude;* (Ḳ;) like as you say, جَآءَ بِالبَوْشِ البَائِشِ. (TA.)

هَوْشَةٌ *Conflict and faction, sedition, discord,* or *dissension:* (A'Obeyd, Ṣ, A, Mṣb, Ḳ:) *excitement: commotion, agitation, convulsion, tumult,* or *disturbance:* (Ṣ, A, Ḳ:) and *confusion:* (A, Mṣb, Ḳ:) and ▼ هُوَاشَةٌ is like هَوْشَةٌ; (TA;) or signifies *war.* (JK.) You say, وَقَعَتْ هَوْشَةٌ فِى السُّوقِ [*Conflict and faction, &c., happened in the market*]. (A.) And it is said in a trad., إِيَّاكُمْ وَهَوْشَاتِ اللَّيْلِ وَهَوْشَاتِ الأَسْوَاقِ (Ṣ, TA) *Beware ye of the misfortunes, calamities,* or *evil accidents, of night; and of the wrong courses, and trickery and robbery, of the markets.* (TA.) هَوْشَاتُ السُّوقِ, thus related by Th, but not explained by him, is thought by ISd to mean *The confusion of the market, and the defrauding there practised in buying and selling.* (TA.) See also هَيْشَةٌ in two places.

هُوَاشَةٌ *A mixed,* or *confused, assembly, company,* or *assemblage,* of men; ('Arrám;) as also ▼ هُوَيْشَةٌ: (Ḳ,* TA:) and هُوَاشَاتٌ, [the pl. of the former,] *collections of men,* and *of camels,* (Ṣ, Ḳ,) *mixed,* or *confounded, together:* (Ṣ:) and *what is collected of unlawful wealth* or *property;* (Ḳ,* TA;) and *of lawful.* (TA.) See also مَهَاوِشُ. — See also هَوْشَةٌ.

هُوَيْشَةٌ : see هُوَاشَةٌ.

هَوَّاشٌ and هَوَّاشَةٌ Camels *unlawfully collected:* (JK:) or the latter, camels *taken from this and that place:* (TA:) and the latter also, camels *taking fright and running away at random.* (JK.) See also هَائِشٌ.

هَائِشٌ : see هَوْشٌ. — إِبِلٌ هَوَائِشُ, [pl. of هَائِشَةٌ,] *Camels taking fright and running away at random, in a state of confusion, attacked by a party of armed horsemen:* (Lth:) or *taking fright and running away at random,* (JK, A,) *separating themselves,* (JK,) *and going to and fro.* (JK, A.) See also هَوَّاشٌ. — هَائِشَةٌ *A great viper.* (TA.)

تَهْوَاشٌ :
تَهْوِيشٌ :
تَهَاوُشٌ and تَهَاوِشُ : } see مَهَاوِشُ.
مَهْوَشٌ :

مَهَاوِشُ *What is gotten by force or theft:* (Ḳ:) or *any wealth,* or *property,* (Ṣ,) *that is gotten by unlawful means,* (JK, Ṣ,) *such as force and theft and the like:* (Ṣ:) pl. of ▼ مَهْوَشٌ: (A:) or as though pl. of this latter word, as signifying *collected;* and *mixed, confused,* or *confounded.* (TA.) It is said in a trad., مَنْ أَصَابَ مَالًا مِنْ

مَهَاوِش أَذْهَبَهُ ٱللّٰهُ فِى نَهَابِرَ [*Whoso getteth wealth, or property, of such as is unlawfully acquired, God will make it to pass away in places of destruction*]: (Ṣ:) but this is variously related; some saying ▾ تَهَاوُش; and some, تَهَاوِش; and some, نَهَاوِش, with ن, which is explained in the Ḳ as signifying مَظَالِم: the relation given in the Ṣ is that which is commonly known by the lexicologists; but all are correct, excepting that تَهَاوِش, with ت, and with a kesreh to the و, is disapproved by some of the lexicologists: (TA:) this last word is a contraction of تَهَاوِيش, pl. of ▾ تَهْوَاش, of the measure تَفْعَال from الهَوْش, (Ḳ, TA,) meaning "the collecting"; and "mixing," "confusing," or "confounding": (TA:) or from هُشْتُ مَالًا حَرَامًا. (Ṣgh, TA.) A poet says,

تَأْكُلُ مَاجَمَعْتَ مِنْ تَهْوَاشِ

[*Thou eatest what thou hast collected of things unlawfully acquired*]. (Ṣgh, TA.)

[هوع &c.
See Supplement.]

هيا

1. هَآءَ, aor. يَهَآءُ and يَهِىْءُ, (Ḳ; the latter not of respectable authority, Lḥ;) inf. n. هَيْئَةٌ, *He was, or became, of good, or goodly, form or appearance, or other properties denoted by the term* هَيْئَةٌ, q.v. (Ḳ.) — [هَيُؤَ, accord. to the Ḳ, signifies *the same:* but see below.] — هَيُؤَ, accord. to IHsh and others, the only verb of this form whose medial radical letter is ى: (MF:) accord. to the Ḳ, syn. with هَآءَ, in a sense indicated above: but IJ states that it has a superlative sense; that it is to be classed with قَضُوَ "excellent [or how excellent (see بَطُؤَ voce بُطْآنَ)] is he in his judging!" and رَمُوَ "excellent [or how excellent] is he in his throwing, or shooting!" [wherefore it signifies *Excellent, or how excellent, is he in his form or appearance!* &c.;] and that it is, like قَضُوَ [and رَمُوَ], invariable [as to person, tense, and mood]. He observes that, as a verb of the measure فَعُلَ is formed from one whose final radical letter is ى, [as قَضُوَ and رَمُوَ from قَضَى and رَمَى,] so is this formed on the same measure from a verb whose medial radical letter is ى: and that it is invariable [as to person, tense, and mood,] because of its resemblance, in its superlative sense, to the class of verbs of wonder, and to نِعْمَ and بِئْسَ. He further remarks, that they [the Arabs] have abstained from forming a verb on the measure فَعُلَ [variable as to person, tense, and mood,] from one whose medial radical letter is ى, fearing to make what is difficult to pronounce still more so; for in that case they would be obliged to say بُعْتُ, أَبُوعُ, and بُوعًا; and, as would also happen if a variable verb of the same measure were formed from one whose final radical letter is ى, the change of ى into و, which is more difficult to pronounce, would thus become frequent. (TA.) — هَآءَ إِلَيْهِ, aor. يَهَآءُ, inf. n. هِيئَةٌ, *He desired, longed for, longed to see, him or it.* (Ḳ.)

2. هَيَّأَ, inf. n. تَهْيِئَةٌ and تَهْيِىْءٌ, [primarily signifies *He invested him with, or made him to have,* هَيْئَةٌ, as meaning *garb, guise,* &c. See Bḍ xviii. 9. — And hence,] *He prepared, provided, disposed, arranged,* or *put into a right,* or *good state,* &c. (Ṣ, Ḳ.) [And hence, *He rendered* an affair *feasible,* or *practicable; he facilitated it.*]

5. تَهَيَّأَ [*He,* or *it, was,* or *became, prepared, provided, disposed, arranged,* or *put into a right* or *good state,* &c. And hence, *It* (an affair) *was,* or *became, feasible,* or *practicable:* and *it* (a thing) *was,* or *became, attainable,* or *within power or reach.*] — تَهَيَّأَ لِلْأَمْرِ; and هَآءَ لَهُ, (Ṣ, Ḳ,) aor. يَهَآءُ (Ḳ) and يَهِىْءُ, (Ṣ, Ḳ,) inf. n. هَيْئَةٌ; (Ṣ;) *He prepared himself for the thing.* (Ḳ.) Ex. وَقَالَتْ هِئْتُ لَكَ *And she said, I have prepared myself for thee:* accord. to one reading [for هَيْتَ, in the Ḳur, xii. 23]. (Akh, Ṣ.) — [See also تَهَيَّأَ]. — تَهَيَّأَ لَهُ الأَمْرُ, (Mṣb, Ḳ, art. اتى, &c.,) or الشَّىْءُ, (Ṣ, art. اتى, &c.,) *The thing,* or *affair, was,* or *became, feasible,* or *practicable, to him;* and *the thing was attainable.*] — تَهَيَّأَ لِلْبُكَآءِ [*He was ready,* or *about, to weep:* a phrase of frequent occurrence; like أَرَادَ البُكَآءَ, and هَمَّ بِالْبُكَآءِ.] (Ṣ, art. جهش, &c.)

6. تَهَايَؤُوا عَلَى ذٰلِكَ *They agreed together upon that,* or *to do that.* (Ḳ,* TA.)

هَىْءَ هَىْءَ and هِىْءَ هِىْءَ The *calling,* or *a call, to food and beverage.* (Ḳ.) — The *calling,* or *a call, to camels to drink:* (Ḳ:) or, [rather,] *a call to camels to food,* or *provender.* (TA.) — [See arts. جيا and ها.]

يَا هَىْءَ مَا لِى [but see شَىْءٌ] [*Oh! what has happened to me?*] an expression of regret; هَىْءَ being a word signifying *regret* for a thing that passes away from one, or escapes him: (Ṣ, TA:) or, (as some say, TA,) an expression of wonder: (Ḳ:) see also يَا فَىْءَ and يَا شَىْءَ, which are syn. with يَا هَىْءَ: (TA:) or هَىْءَ, (accord. to certain of the lexicologists, as related by IB, TA,) is an imperative verbal noun, signifying *Attend!* (تَنَبَّهْ); like صَهْ, which signifies "Be silent!" (Ḳ;) the interjection يا being put before it in like manner as it is in the saying of Esh-Shemmákh,

أَلَا يَا ٱسْقِيَانِى قَبْلَ غَارَةِ سِنْجَالِ

[*Come now! O, give me to drink, before the expedition of Sinjál!*]; (TA;) and هَىْءَ being indeclinable, with a vowel for its termination to obviate the occurrence of two quiescent letters, and with fet-hah as the final vowel because it is more easy of pronunciation than the others in this case. (Ḳ, TA.) — [See also art. شيا.]

هَيْئَةٌ and ▾ هِيئَةٌ *Form, fashion, shape, aspect,* or *appearance; figure, person, mien, feature,* or *lineaments;* (Ṣ, TA;) *guise;* or *external state* or *condition;* (Mṣb;) *state with regard to apparel and the like;* or *garb;* (Lth;) *state, condition,* or *case; quality, mode* or *manner of being:* (Ḳ:) pl. هَيْئَاتٌ and هَيَآتٌ. (TA.) — حَسَنُ الهَيْئَةِ [*of goodly form, aspect,* or *appearance, guise, state of apparel, garb,* &c.]. (Ṣ.) — [Also, *goodliness of form* &c.: see 1. See also سَمْتٌ, for an addition.] — [هَيْئَةٌ عَارِضَةٌ, in Logic, *An accidental mode.*] — أَقِيلُوا ذَوِى الهَيْآتِ عَثَرَاتِهِمْ, in a trad., signifies, *Forgive ye the people of good qualities &c., who keep to one state and way, their slips.* It alludes to those who make a slip unwittingly. (TA.)

هِيئَةٌ: see هَيْئَةٌ.

هَيِىْءٌ: see what next follows.

هَيِّئٌ and ▾ هَيِىْءٌ A person *of good,* or *goodly, form* or *appearance,* or *other properties denoted by the term* هَيْئَةٌ. (Ḳ.)

مُهَيَّأٌ [*Prepared,* &c.] — Also i.q. زُمَّاوَرْدٌ, q.v. (MF, art. ورد.)

مُهَايَأَةٌ *A thing respecting which persons have agreed together.* (Ḳ, TA.)

مُتَهَيِّئَةٌ A camel *that seldom fails of becoming pregnant when she has been covered.* (Ḳ.)

هيب

1. هَابَهُ, (Ṣ, Ḳ, &c.,) first pers. هِبْتُ, originally هَيِبْتُ, (Ṣ,) aor. يَهَابُ, (Ṣ, Ḳ,) [originally يَهْيَبُ,] and يَهِيبُ, (IKtt, cited by MF,) imp. هَبْ, originally هَابْ, (Ṣ,) inf. n. هَيْبَةٌ (Ṣ, Ḳ, Mṣb) and مَهَابَةٌ (Ṣ, Ḳ) and هَيْبٌ; (Ḳ;) and ▾ اهتابه and ▾ تهيّبه; (Ḳ;) [*He revered, venerated, respected, honoured, dreaded,* or *feared, him* or *it;*] *he regarded him* or *it,* i.e., anything, TA,) *with reverence, veneration, respect, honour, dread,* or *awe;* (Ṣ, Ḳ,* Mṣb, TA;) *and fear;* (Ṣ, Ḳ;) *cautious fear,* or *caution.* (Ḳ, Mṣb.) — هَبِ النَّاسَ يَهَابُوكَ *Reverence men,* [and] *they will reverence thee.* (TA.) — هُوبَ, in which the original ى is changed into و, [*He* (a man) *was regarded with reverence, veneration,* or *awe; with fear;* or *with cautious fear,* or *caution*]. (Ṣ, Ḳ.)

2. هَيَّبْتُهُ إِلَيْهِ *I made it to be regarded by him with reverence, veneration, or awe; with fear; or with cautious fear, or caution.* (Ṣ, Ḳ.)

4. اهاب بِصَاحِبِهِ ‡ *He called his companion.* And in like manner, أَهَبْتُ بِهِ إِلَى الخَيْرِ ‡ *I called him, or invited him, to what was good.* (MF.) — اهاب بالإِبِلِ *He called to the camels, in driving them or urging them, by the cry* هَابْ هَابْ. (Ḳ.) — اهاب بِغَنَمِهِ *He* (a pastor) *cried out to his sheep, or goats, in order that they might stop, or return:* and اهاب بالبَعِيرِ [*He cried out to the camel, for the same purpose*]. (Ṣ.) الإِهَابَةُ is *The crying out* to camels, *and calling* them. (Aṣ and others.) — اهاب بالخَيْلِ *He called the horses, or called out to them by the cry* هَابِ, (so in the Ṣ and in a MS. copy of the Ḳ: in the CḲ, هَابْ,) *or by the cry of* هَبْ *and* هَبِى, meaning *Come! Approach!* or *Advance boldly!* (Ḳ.) Az remarks his having heard هاب used [as a cry] only to horses; not to camels. (TA.) See هَبْهَبْ, in art. هب.

5: see 1. — تَهَيَّبَنِى *It filled me with awe,* or *fear:* (El Jarmee:) *it made me to fear:* (Ṣ, ISd, Mṣb:) *I regarded it with awe,* or *fear;* i.q. تَهَيَّبْتُهُ: (Th:) *I feared it;* i.q. خِفْتُهُ. (Ṣ, ISd, Ḳ.) Ibn-Muḳbil says,

• وَمَا تَهَيَّبُنِى المَوْمَاةُ أَرْكَبُهَا •
• إِذَا تَجَاوَبَتِ الأَصْدَاءُ بِالسَّحَرِ •

[*And the waterless desert fills me not with awe,* or *fear;* (or *makes me not to fear, &c.;*) *I ride over it when the male owls* (?) *answer one another at early dawn:* تهيّبنى being for تَتَهَيَّبُنِى]. (Ṣ, &c.)

8: see 1.

هَبْ (Ḳ) and ▾ هَابِ and ▾ هَبِى, (Ṣ, Ḳ,) [but respecting the second of these words see 4,] *Cries to horses, meaning, Come! Approach!* (Ṣ, Ḳ,) or *Advance boldly!* (Ḳ.)

هَابِ and هَبِى: see هَبْ.

هَابْ † *A serpent.* (Ḳ.) — هَابْ *A calling to camels, in driving,* or *urging, them, by the cry* هَابْ هَابْ. (Ḳ.) — See 4.

هَيَّبَانٌ : } see هَائِبٌ, and مَهِيبٌ.
هَيُوبٌ : }

هَيْبَةٌ and ▾ مَهَابَةٌ: see 1. — [As substs., *Reverence, veneration, respect, honour, dread,* or *awe; fear; cautious fear,* or *caution.*] — Also, *great, reverend,* or *venerable, dignity; a quality inspiring reverence* or *veneration* or *respect* or *honour; venerableness; awfulness; a quality inspiring dread* or *awe.* (MF.)

هَيِّبٌ: see هَائِبٌ.

هَيَّبَانٌ: see هَائِبٌ. — هَيْبَانٌ (Ḳ) or [rather] ▾ هَيَّبَانٌ, (TA, [see هَائِبٌ,]) *A he-goat:* (Ḳ:) explained by the word تَيْسٌ; but this is a signification not found [by SM] elsewhere, and appears to be a mistake for مُنْتَفِشٌ; for in the L and other lexicons we find the word explained by مُنْتَفِشٌ خَفِيفٌ, *Scattered, and light;* with a citation of the following verse of Dhu-r-Rummeh:

• تَمُجُّ اللُّغَامَ الهَيَّبَانَ كَأَنَّهُ •
• جَنَى عُشَرٍ تَنْفِيهِ أَشْدَاقُهَا الهُدْلُ •

[*She ejects from her mouth the scattered and light froth, as though it were plucked fruit of the 'oshar which the flabby sides of her mouth cast forth:*] and we also find, in the R, قُطْنٌ هَيَّبَانٌ explained as signifying *cotton that is plucked,* or *teased with the fingers, so as to become scattered;* syn. منتفش: or هيّبان signifies, in the above-cited verse, accord. to some, *Light,* [which signification is also given in the Ḳ, but in the CḲ displaced; following, instead of preceding, the word الرَّاعِى, and without و before it;] *and separated into small particles:* (TA:) [or] the *froth of the mouth of camels;* (Az, Ḳ;) i.q. لُغَامٌ: (Mj, Sifr es-Sa'ádeh:) Az cites the above verse; and says, that the fruit of the عُشَر [or asclepias gigantea] comes forth like a small pomegranate, and, when burst open, discloses what resembles [white] raw silk; to which the poet likens the froth of the camel's mouth. (TA.) — هَيْبَانٌ (or هَيَّبَانٌ, TA,) *A pastor.* (Ḳ, from Es-Seeráfee.) [Accord. to the CḲ, *a light,* or *an active pastor:* but see above.] — هَيَّبَانٌ (or ▾ هَيْبَانٌ, TA,) *Dust,* or *earth:* syn. تُرَابٌ. (Ḳ.) — See هَائِبٌ.

هَيْبَانٌ: see هَيَّبَانٌ.

هَيَّابٌ : } see هَائِبٌ.
هَيَّابَةٌ : }

هَائِبٌ [act. part. n. of هَابَ, *Regarding with reverence, veneration, dread,* or *awe; with fear; with cautious fear,* or *caution;*] *fearing men.* (Ḳ.) This is the original [simple] epithet. (TA.) — The following, which are explained in the Ḳ in the same manner as the above, are intensive epithets: (TA:) namely ▾ هَيُوبٌ (Ṣ, Ḳ) and هَيُوبَةٌ, (Ṣ, L,) [in which the ة is added to strengthen the intensiveness,] and ▾ هَيَّابٌ and هَيَّابَةٌ, (Ṣ, Ḳ,) in which ة is added for the purpose above mentioned, (TA,) and ▾ هَيِّبٌ, (Ḳ,) which may be contracted into هَيْبٌ, (TA,) and ▾ هَيَّبَانٌ (Ḳ) and ▾ هَيْبَانٌ (Ṣ, Ḳ) and ▾ هَيِّبَانٌ; (Ḳ;) of which last two forms, the latter only is admitted by some of the learned; but MF admits only the former of them; asserting فَيْعَلَانٌ to be unknown as the measure of an unsound word, like as فَيْعِلَان is unknown as that of a sound word except in extr. instances; (TA;) [*Having much reverence, veneration, dread,* or *awe; much fear; much cautious fear,* or *caution:*] *fearing men* [much]: (Ḳ:) *a coward, who regards men with awe,* or *fear, &c.:* (Ṣ:) [The last of these epithets is also explained in the CḲ as signifying *having much fear,* or *very fearful;* (كَثِيرُ الخَوْفِ;) and *a coward:* but in the TA and in a MS copy of the Ḳ, الخوف is omitted; and in the TA is added by the author, after كثير, the words من كلّ شىء; as though the meaning of the word were "much, or many, of any thing:" the correct reading seems to be the former, and the meaning intended by SM, *having much fear,* or *very fearful, of everything:* in like manner] ▾ هَيُوبٌ signifies a man *who fears everything.* (TA.) — ▾ الإِيمَانُ هَيُوبٌ [*Faith is fearful,* or *very fearful;* i. e.,] *he who possesses faith fears acts of disobedience:* occurring in a trad.: (Ṣ:) in this case, هيوب is used in the sense of an act. part. n.: or it signifies [*faith is feared;* or *regarded with reverence, &c.;* i. e.,] *he who possesses faith is feared,* or *regarded with reverence, &c.:* in which case هيوب is used in the sense of a pass. part. n. (TA.)

هٰذَا الشَّىْءُ مَهْيَبَةٌ لَكَ [*This thing is a cause of awe,* or *fear, to thee*]. (Ṣ.)

مَهِيبٌ: see مَهَابٌ.

مَهَابَةٌ: see هَيْبَةٌ.

مَهُوبٌ: see مَهِيبٌ.

مَهِيبٌ and ▾ مَهُوبٌ, (Ṣ, Ḳ,) the former agreeable with rule, (TA,) and ▾ هَيُوبٌ, (Ḳ) [respecting which see also هَائِبٌ,] and ▾ هَيَّبَانٌ, (Th, IM, Ḳ,) [*Regarded with reverence, veneration, respect, honour, dread,* or *awe; with fear; with cautious fear,* or *caution;*] a man *whom others regard with reverence, &c.;* (Ṣ;) a man *whom others fear.* (Ḳ.) — مَكَانٌ مَهُوبٌ, formed from the verb هُوبَ, the original ى being changed into و, (Ṣ, Ḳ,) *A place regarded with awe,* or *fear;* (Ṣ;) *a place in which one is impressed with awe,* or *fear:* as also ▾ مَكَانٌ مَهَابٌ: (Ṣ, Ḳ:) مَهَابٌ signifies *a place of awe,* or *fear.* (IB.) — المَهِيبُ and المَهُوبُ and ▾ المُتَهَيِّبُ † *The lion:* (Ḳ:) because regarded with awe, or fear, by men. (TA.)

المُتَهَيِّبُ: see المَهِيبُ.

هيت

2. هَيَّتَ بِهِ, (Ṣ, Ḳ,) inf. n. تَهْيِيتٌ, (TA,) as also هَوَّتَ, (Ṣ,) *He cried out to him, and called*

him, (Ṣ, Ḳ,) *saying*, هَيْتَ هَيْتَ; or saying يَاهْ يَاهْ, which is a cry by which a pastor calls his companion from afar; or, accord. to AZ, saying يَا هَيَا [or rather يَا هَيَاهْ: see art. يه]. (TA.)

3. هَاتِ *Give me*: (Ḳ:) هَاتِ يَا رَجُلُ *Give me, O man*: (T, Ṣ, M:) *i. q.* أَعْطِنِى: (T, Ṣ, M, Ḳ:) to two men, هَاتِيَا: to a plurality of men, هَاتُوا: to a woman, هَاتِى: to two women, هَاتِيَا: to a plurality of women, هَاتِينَ: you say هَاتِ لَا هَاتَيْتَ [*Give me: mayest thou not give* (hereafter)! an imprecation, of the like of which there are many examples]; and هَاتِ إِنْ كَانَتْ بِكَ مُهَاتَاةٌ [*Give me, if there be in thee* (*a disposition for*) *giving*]; and مَا أُهَاتِيكَ [*I do not give thee*], like as you say, مَا أُعَاطِيكَ; but you do not say هَاتَيْتُ; nor do you use this verb in a prohibitive manner: [it is used neither affirmatively nor prohibitively:] accord. to Kh, هَاتِ is from آتَى, aor. يُوتِى; the ا being changed into ه. (Ṣ.) [But آتَى is of the measure أَفْعَلَ; and هَاتِ is the imp. from the measure فَاعَلَ. See also art. هتى, where it is mentioned again in the Ṣ and Ḳ.]

هَيْتَ an exclamation denoting wonder: the Arabs say, هَيْتَ لِلْحِلْمِ [*What forbearing mildness, or clemency!*]. (L.) — هَيْتَ لَكَ, (Akh, Ṣ, Ḳ, &c.,) and هَيْتُ لك, (Akh, Ḳ,) and هَيْتُ لك, (Akh, IB, Ḳ,) and the first letter is sometimes with kesreh; (Ḳ;) as is related on the authority of 'Alee, (TA,) [so that you say هِيتَ and هِيتِ and هِيتُ, the first of which three forms is mentioned by Fr, Akh, IB, and the third by Fr, IB; but for the second I find no other authority than that implied above;] of all which, the most common is هَيْتَ لك, with fet-hah to the ه and ت: (Zj:) هَيْتَ is of the dial. of Ḥowrán, whence it became introduced into Mekkeh; and هِيتَ, of the dial. of El-Medeeneh: (Fr:) [imper. verbal ns.] *i. q.* هَلُمَّ, *Come!* (Akh, Ṣ, L, Ḳ,) or تَعَالَ the same, (Fr, Ks,) or أَقْبِلْ, the same, or *Come forward!* (L.) It occurs in the Ḳur, xii. 23; where it is commonly read هَيْتَ لَكَ; (Zj;) but 'Alee and Ibn-'Abbás are said to have read هِئْتُ لَكَ, with hemzeh. [See art. هيأ.] (TA.) هَيْتَ is itself invariable whether used to denote the sing. or pl. or fem. or masc.; but the difference of number is observed in what follows it; for you say هَيْتَ لَكُمَا [*Come ye two!*] and هَيْتَ لَكُنَّ [*Come ye* women! &c.]: (Ṣ:) you also say simply هَيْتَ [*Come!*] and this is also said to signify *Hasten!* and *Set forth journeying* through the land, or earth. (TA.) Authorities differ respecting this word; whether it be Arabic or arabicised; and whether it be a noun or a verb; &c. Accord. to AZ, as related by Az, هيت لك is arabicized in the Ḳur, from the Hebrew هيتا كخ [app. a mistake for هيتا لخ, which I suppose to be meant for עַתָּה לְכָה "Now, come!" occurring in Gen. xxxi. 44]. (TA.)

هَيْتَ هَيْتَ: see 2.

هَيْتٌ *A low*, or *depressed, piece of ground*: (Ḳ:) *a piece of ground having a low*, or *depressed, bottom*: (TA:) *i. q.* هُوَّةٌ and هُوتَةٌ. (IAṣr.)

هَيْتَآءٌ, and هَيْتَاهٌ: see art. هوت.

هَيَّاتٌ [*Clamorous; calling out often*, or *much*]. (Ṣ.)

هيث

1. هَاثَ لَهُ, aor. يَهِيثُ, inf. n. هَيْثٌ and هَيَثَانٌ, *He gave him a little*, or *something little in quantity*. (AZ, Ṣ, Ḳ.) [See also حَثَا, in art. حثو.] — هَاثَ فِى كَيْلِهِ, inf. n. هَيْثٌ, *He gave little in his measure*, or *in his measuring*; *i. q.* حَثَا, inf. n. حَثْوٌ: it is like what is termed جِزَافٌ. (TA.) = هَاثَ, aor. يَهِيثُ, inf. n. هَيْثٌ, *It was in a state of motion*, or *commotion*; (Ṣ, Ḳ;) like هَاشَ, aor. يَهِيشُ, inf. n. هَيْشٌ. (Ṣ.) — هَاثَ القَوْمُ, inf. n. هَيْثٌ; and ↑ تَهَايَثَ; *The party became intermixed* in altercation. (TA.) — هَاثَ بِرِجْلِهِ التُّرَابَ, aor. يَهِيثُ, *He dug up the dust*, or *earth, with his foot*. (TA.) — هَاثَ, aor. يَهِيثُ, inf. n. هَيْثٌ: (TA;) and ↑ اِسْتَهَاثَ; (Ḳ;) *He corrupted*, or *marred; acted corruptly; did mischief*; syn. أَفْسَدَ. (Ḳ, TA.) — هَاثَ فِى مَالِهِ, aor. يَهِيثُ, inf. n. هَيْثٌ, *He acted corruptly* (أَفْسَدَ) *with his property*; (Ḳ;) as also عَاثَ; (TA;) [*he scattered and marred his property; squandered it; expended it quickly*: see art. عيث]. — Also, [contr.,] *He acted rightly with his property*. (TA.) — هَاثَ فِى شَىْءٍ *He acted corruptly with a thing; and took it without gentleness*; (TA;) [as also عَاثَ]. — هَاثَ الذِّئْبُ فِى الغَنَمِ *The wolf did mischief among* [or *worried*] *the sheep*, or *goats*; (TA;) [as also عَاثَ]. = هَاثَ مِنَ المَالِ, aor. يَهِيثُ, inf. n. هَيْثٌ, *He obtained what he wanted of the property*. (Ḳ.)

3. هَايَثَهُ, inf. n. مُهَايَثَةٌ, *He contended*, or *disputed, with him for superiority in abundance*, or *multitude*; as, for instance, of wealth, or of dependants or followers. (TḲ.) مُهَايَثَةٌ is syn. with مُكَاثَرَةٌ. (Ḳ.) — See 10.

5. تَهَيَّثَ *He gave*. (Ḳ.) تَهَيَّثَ لَهُ شَيْئًا *He gave him a thing*. (TḲ.)

6: see 1.

10. اِسْتَهَاثَ (and ↑ هَايَثَ, TA,) *He deemed* [a thing] *much*; syn. اِسْتَكْثَرَ. (Ḳ.) اِسْتَهَاثَ مَا أَعْطَاهُ [*He deemed what he gave him much*]. (TḲ.) — See 1.

هَيْثَةٌ *An assembly, a company, a congregated body*, (Aṣ, Ṣ, Ḳ,) *of men*, or *people*; like هَيْشَةٌ. (Aṣ, Ṣ.)

هَائِثَةٌ The *clamour*, or *confused noise*, (جَلَبَة,) of a people. (L.)

مُهَايِثٌ *Taking much; one who takes much*. (Ḳ.)

هيج

1. هَاجَ, aor. يَهِيجُ, inf. n. هَيْجٌ and هَيَجَانٌ [the most common form]; and هِيَاجٌ; and ↑ اِهْتَاجَ, and ↑ تَهَيَّجَ; *It* (a thing, Ṣ) *became raised, roused, excited, stirred up*, or *provoked*; syn. ثَارَ: (Ṣ, L, Ḳ:) it became so by reason of distress, or difficulty; or of harm, or injury: you say هَاجَ بِهِ الدَّمُ, inf. n. هَيْجٌ and هَيَجَانٌ, *The blood became roused*, or *stirred up, in him*: (A, L:) and in like manner, المِرَّةُ *the gall*, or *bile*: and الغُبَارُ *the dust*. (A.) See also هَائِجٌ. — هَاجَ, inf. n. هِيَاجٌ and هُيُوجٌ and هَيَجَانٌ; and ↑ اِهْتَاجَ; ‡ *He* (a stallion-camel) *became excited by lust; initum appetivit; brayed, and became excited by lust*. When this is the case, he becomes lean, and his price is lessened. (L.) — هَاجَتْ عَيْنُهُ, (Ṣ, art. مرح; and L, art. رمد; &c.) inf. n. هَيَجَانٌ, (Ḳ, art. رمد; &c.) *His eye became inflamed; painful and swollen; affected with ophthalmia*; (L, art. رمد;) *i. q.* رَمِدَ. (Ṣ, art. رمد; and L, Ḳ,* in the same art.) — هَاجَ بِهِ فَهَجَاهُ ‡ [*He became excited against him*, or *attacked him, and satirized him*]. (A.) — هَاجَ الهِجَآءُ بَيْنَهُمَا ‡ [*Satire was excited between them two*. (A.) — هَاجَتِ الحَرْبُ (inf. n. هَيْجٌ, Mṣb) ‡ *War became excited*, or *raised*. (A, Mṣb.) — هَاجَ الشَّرُّ بَيْنَهُمْ ‡ *Evil became excited among them*. (A.) — هَاجَ, inf. n. هَيْجٌ, *He*, or *it, was in a state of commotion*. (L.) — هَاجَتِ السَّمَآءُ فَمُطِرْنَا *The sky became cloudy and windy, and we were rained upon*. (TA.) — هَاجَ; (Ṣ, Ḳ;) [followed by an accus., and also by بِ;] and ↑ هَيَّجَ, inf. n. تَهْيِيجٌ, the most common form;] and ↑ هَايَجَ; (Ṣ;) *He*, or *it, raised, roused, excited, stirred up*, or *provoked*, (Ṣ, Ḳ,) a thing; (Ṣ;) syn. أَثَارَ. (Ḳ.) Thus the first of these verbs is trans. as well as intrans. (Ṣ.) All have the same meaning: (Ṣ:) or the second has an intensive signification. (Mṣb.) — هَاجَ الغُبَارَ, and ↑ هَيَّجَهُ, [which is more common,] *He raised the dust*. (TA.) — هَيَّجَ ↑ الشَّرَّ ‡ *He excited evil*

among a people. (A) — هَيَّجْتُ ♦ النَّاقَةَ فَانْبَعَثَتْ I roused the she-camel, and she became roused. (A.) — هَيَّجْتُهُ فَهَاجَ I roused him, and he became roused. (TA.) — هَاجَتْ لَهُ الدَّارُ الشَّوْقَ The dwelling excited his longing desire. (A.) — هَاجَ He, or it, disquieted, and scared, a person. (L.) — هَاجَ الإِبِلَ, inf. n. هَيْجٌ, He put the camels in motion, by night, towards the watering-place and pasture. (L.) — هَاجَتِ الإِبِلُ The camels thirsted. (Ḳ.) — هَاجَ, (inf. n. هِيَاجٌ, Ṣ, and هَيْجٌ, TA,) ‡ It (a plant, or herbage,) dried up: (Ṣ, Ḳ:) [it withered:] it (a leguminous plant) became yellow: (Mṣb:) or dried up and became yellow: and became tall. (L.) — هَاجَتِ الأَرْضُ, inf. n. هِيَاجٌ and هَيْجٌ and هَيَجَانٌ, ‡ The plants, or herbage, or leguminous plants, of the land dried up. (L.)

2: see 1 and 4.

3. هَايَجَهُ, (TḲ,) inf. n. هِيَاجٌ, (Ṣ, Ḳ,) He fought with him; engaged in a conflict, or combat, with him. (TḲ.) — يَوْمُ الهِيَاجِ The day of fight, conflict or combat. (Ṣ, Ḳ.*) — See 1.

4. أَهَاجَتِ الرِّيحُ النَّبْتَ ‡ The wind dried up, or caused to dry up, the plants, or herbage: (Ṣ, Ḳ*:) and [so] ♦ هَيَّجَتْهُ. (O, Ḳ in art. صوع.) — أَهْيَجْنَا الأَرْضَ ‡ We found the land to have its plants or herbage, dried up. (Ṣ, Ḳ.)

5: see 1.

6. تَهَايَجُوا † They leaped, or sprung up, together, to fight, one against another. (Ṣ, Ḳ.)

8: see 1.

هِيجِ : see هِيجْ.

هَيْجٌ Civil war; or conflict and faction; or discord, or dissension; syn. فِتْنَةٌ. (L.) See هَيْجَآءُ. — Excitement of the blood: or, of coitus: or, of longing desire. (L.) — يَوْمُ هَيْجٍ A day of wind: or, of clouds, or mist, and rain. (Ḳ, TA: [but accord. to some copies of the Ḳ, instead of "and rain," "or, of rain."]) — هَاجَ لَهُ هَيْجٌ حَسَنٌ, said with respect to a cloud, or body of clouds, when first rising; (Aṣ;) [meaning, It hath had a good rising, or hath risen well, so as to present, at its first rising, a good, or promising, appearance: an expression like نَشَأَ لَهُ نَشْءٌ حَسَنٌ, q. v., art. نشأ]. — هَيْجٌ, † Yellowness: [app. in a plant]: (L:) or a state of drying up. (IAạr, L.) See هَائِجٌ.

هِيجِ, indecl., with kesreh for its termination, and ♦ هِيجْ, Cries by which a she-camel is chidden. (Ḳ.) [See also هَجْهَجَ, in art. هج.]

هَاجَةٌ A ewe that does not desire the ram: as though deprived of excitement. (M.) — هَاجَةٌ A female frog. (L, Ḳ.) See an ex. in a verse cited voce صُبَارَةٌ. — An ostrich. (L.) Pl. of both, هَاجَاتٌ. (L, Ḳ.) Dim. هُوَيْجَةٌ and هُيَيْجَةٌ. (L.)

هَيْجَى : see هَيْجَآءُ.

هَيْجَآءُ and ♦ هَيْجَى (Ṣ, L, Ḳ) and ♦ هَيْجٌ and ♦ هِيَاجٌ (L) the third [as also the fourth] originally an inf. n., (Mṣb,) War. (Ṣ, L, Ḳ.)

هَيِّجٌ : see هَائِجٌ.

هِيَاجٌ : see 1 and 3; and هَيْجَآءُ.

شَىْءٌ هَيُوجٌ, and ♦ مِهْيَاجٌ, A thing, or person, that raises, rouses, excites, stirs up, or provokes, much: each of these epithets having a trans. signification. The former is also used as a fem. epithet. (L.)

هَائِجٌ ‡ Anger; an ebullition of anger, rage, or passion; syn. فَوْرَةٌ. (Ṣ, Ḳ.) Ex. هَاجَ هَائِجُهُ ‡ His anger became roused, or excited; (Ṣ;) became violent; (TA;) he became inflamed with anger. (A.) And هَدَأَ هَائِجُهُ ‡ The ebullition of his anger, rage, or passion, became appeased. (Ṣ.) — هَائِجٌ (Ṣ, Ḳ) and ♦ هَيِّجٌ (TA) ‡ A stallion excited by lust; initum appetens. (Ṣ, Ḳ.) — أَرْضٌ هَائِجَةٌ ‡ Land of which the leguminous plants have dried up, or become yellow: (Ṣ, Ḳ:) or, as in some lexicons, [and as in one copy of the Ṣ in my hands,] and become yellow: (TA:) or, of which the leguminous plants have dried up. (TA.) بَقْلٌ هَائِجٌ, and ♦ هَيْجٌ, ‡ Leguminous plants dried up, or drying up, [and yellow]. (L.)

مِهْيَاجٌ A she-camel that is excited by desire for its accustomed place, and hastens thither. (Ṣ, Ḳ.) — See هَيُوجٌ. — مِهْيَاجٌ A camel that thirsts before [other] camels. (Ḳ.)

هيد

1. هَادَ, aor. يَهِيدُ, inf. n. هَيْدٌ; (Ṣ, L, Ḳ;) and ♦ هَيَّدَ, (L, Ḳ,) inf. n. تَهْيِيدٌ; (TA;) He moved, or put in motion, (Ṣ, L, Ḳ,) a thing, (Ṣ,) or anything: this is the original signification. (L.) — هَادَ, aor. يَهِيدُ, inf. n. هَيْدٌ and هَادٌ; (L, Ḳ;) and ♦ هَيَّدَ; (Ḳ;) It frightened, or terrified, and afflicted, distressed, or oppressed, a person. (L, Ḳ.) — هَادَ, aor. يَهِيدُ, inf. n. هَيْدٌ; (L, Ḳ;) and ♦ هَيَّدَ; (Ḳ;) He repaired; put into a right or proper state. (L, Ḳ.) It is said in a trad., with reference to the Mosque (of Moḥammad, L), هِدْهُ, (Ṣ, L,) meaning Repair it: (L:) or pull it down, and then repair it: (Ṣ, L:) or pull it down, and recommence the building of it, and repair it, and put it into a right or proper state. (L.) — هَادَ, (Yaạḳoob, Ṣ, L, Ḳ,) aor. يَهِيدُ, inf. n. هَيْدٌ, and هَادٌ; (L;) and ♦ هَيَّدَ; (Yaạḳoob, Ṣ, L:) He chid a man; and turned him away, or back, from a thing: (Ṣ,* L, Ḳ:) or يَهِيدُ is only used with a negative in this sense. (Yaạḳoob, Ḳ.) — هَادَ He removed a person or thing from his or its place. (L, Ḳ.*) — هَادَ He or it disquieted, disturbed, or unsettled, a person. (Ḳ.) — مَا يَهِيدُنِى كَذَا Such a thing does not move me; (L;) it does not disquiet, disturb, or unsettle, me; I am not moved by it; do not care for it, or regard it. (Ṣ, L.) Accord. to Yaạḳoob, يهيد is only thus used with a negative. (Ṣ, L.) One says, لَا يَهِيدَنَّكَ هٰذَا عَنْ رَأْيِكَ Let not this move thee at all from thine opinion. (TA.)

2: see 1.

هَادْ : see هَيْدْ.

هَيْدْ and ♦ هِيدْ and هَادْ (Ṣ, L, Ḳ) and هَيْدِ and هِيدِ and هَادِ (IB, L) and هِيدُ (L) Cries by which camels are chidden (Ṣ, L, Ḳ) and urged. (L.) — Also هَيْدْ A mode of singing to camels, to urge or excite them: (L:) or the commencement of such singing: (TA:) when a man is about to sing to camels for this purpose, he says هِيدْ هِيدْ, and then sings, or prolongs and modulates his voice. (L, TA.) — هَيْدَ مَا لَكَ, (T, L, Ḳ,) and هِيدَ ما لك, (Sh, L,) and هِيدُ ما لك, (L,) [What is thy state, or condition, or thy affair, or business?] forms of speech used in inquiring of a man respecting his state, or condition, or his affair, or business; (T, L, Ḳ;) like as you say يَا هٰذَا مَا لَكَ. (T, L.) One says, لَقِيَهُ فَقَالَ لَهُ هَيْدَ مَا لَكَ [He met him, and said to him, What is thy state, &c.?] and لَقِيتُهُ فَمَا قَالَ لِى هَيْدَ مَا لَكَ [I met him, and he said not to me, What is thy state, &c.?] (Lḥ, L,) and يَا هَيْدَ مَا أَصْحَابُكَ, and يَا هَيْدَ مَا لِأَصْحَابِكَ, [What is the state, &c., of thy companions?] (Ks, L,) and one says, لَوْ شَتَمْتَنِى مَا قُلْتُ هَيْدَ مَا لَكَ, meaning, [Hadst thou reviled me, or shouldst thou revile me, I had not said, or would not say,] What is thine affair? (Aṣ, on the authority of 'Eesà Ibn-'Omar.) When a stray-camel passes by a man, and he does not turn him aside, nor does he regard it, you say, مَرَّ بَعِيرٌ فَمَا قَالَ لَهُ هَيْدَ مَا لَكَ, and, as related by an Arab of the desert, هِيدِ ما لك, with kesr to the د, [A camel passed by, and he said not to him, What is thy state, &c.?] (AZ, L.) — مَا لَهُ هَيْدٌ وَلَا ♦ هَادٌ He has no motion: (L, Ḳ:) or neither هيد nor هاد is to be said to him; meaning, he is not to be moved, nor withheld *from a thing, nor chidden away from it.* (Ṣ, L.) —— هَيْدٌ *i. q.* هَيْدَبٌ *A flabby pubes.* (Fr, in TA, voce كَعْثَبٌ.)

هَيْدٌ : see هَيْدٌ.

هَيْدَان [whether with or without tenween is not shown] *Cowardly*; or *a coward*: (Ṣ, L;) a *heavy, cowardly* man; like هِدَانٌ. (L.)

هير

2. هَيَّرَهُ : see هَوَّرَهُ.

5. تَهَيَّرَ : see تَهَوَّرَ.

هيش

1. هَاشَ القَوْمُ, aor. يَهِيشُ, (Ṣ,) inf. n. هَيْشٌ, (Ṣ, Ḳ,) *The people,* or *company of men, were,* or *became, in a state of commotion and excitement,* (Ṣ, Ḳ,*) عَلَيْنَا *against us.* (Ṣ.) —— هَاشَ القَوْمُ بَعْضُهُمْ إِلَى بَعْضٍ *The people,* or *company of men, leaped,* or *sprang, one,* or *one portion, towards another, for fight,* or *conflict*: (TA:) and ▼ تَهَيَّشَ النَّاسُ بَعْضُهُمْ إِلَى بَعْضٍ *The men,* or *people, leaped,* or *sprang, one,* or *one portion, towards another,* (JK,) *in the slightest kind of conflict.* (TA.) —— هَاشَ فِى النَّاسِ, (JK, TA,) inf. n. هَيْشٌ, (JK, Ḳ,) *He created,* or *excited, disorder, disturbance, discord,* or *dissension, between,* or *among, the people; made mischief among them.* (JK, Ḳ,* TA.) —— هَاشَ الرَّجُلُ, (JK,) inf. n. هَيْشٌ, (JK, Ḳ,) *The man used,* or *uttered much foul speech* or *language.* (JK. Ṣgh, Ḳ.*) —— هَاشَ, aor. as above, (TA,) and so the inf. n., (Fr, Ḳ,) *He collected.* (Fr, Ḳ, TA.) [In this sense, as well as the first, it is like هاش having هَوْشٌ for its inf. n.]

5 : see 1.

هَيْشَةٌ *i. q.* هَوْشَةٌ ; (Ṣ, Ḳ;) *Conflict and faction, sedition, discord,* or *dissension.* (JK, Ḳ.) It is said in a trad., (TA,) لَيْسَ فِى الهَيْشَاتِ قَوَدٌ, (Ḳ, TA,) or, accord. to one relation, فِى الهَوْشَاتِ, (TA,) *There is no retaliation for one slain in cases of conflict and faction,* &c., when the slayer is unknown. (Ḳ, TA.) And هَيْشَات in the phrases هَيْشَاتُ الأَسْوَاقِ and هَيْشَاتُ اللَّيْلِ is like هَوْشَات. (TA.) —— *A company of men*: (JK, Ṣ:) or *a mixed,* or *confused, company.* (Ḳ.)

هيض

1. هَاضَهُ, aor. يَهِيضُ, (Ṣ, Ḳ,) inf. n. هَيْضٌ, (Ṣ,) *He broke it,* namely, a bone, *after it had become set*; as also ▼ اهتاضهُ: (Ṣ, Ḳ:) and in like manner, a wing. (TA.) —— ‡ *It* (a thing) *made him to fall back into his disease*; (Ṣ, A, TA;) and so هَاضَهُ إِلَى مَا بِهِ. (TA.) You say also, هَاضَ الحُزْنُ القَلْبَ † *Grief affected the heart time after time.* (TA.) And ▼ تَهَيَّضَهُ الغَرَامُ [*Vehemence of desire*] *returned to him a second time.* (A,* TA.) —— † *It softened him,* or *it.* (TA.) And so IAạr explains the verb as occurring in the saying of 'Áisheh, لَوْنَزَلَ بِالجِبَالِ الرَّاسِيَاتِ مَانَزَلَ بِأَبِى لَهَاضَهَا † [*Had that befallen the firm mountains which befell my father,*] *it had softened them.* (TA.) [See also an ex. of a similar meaning voce ظلع.] —— ‡ *It* (drowsiness) *made him languid.* (A, TA.) —— ‡ *He broke him,* or *defeated him*: as in the imprecation uttered by 'Omar the son of 'Abd-el-'Azeez against Yezeed the son of El-Mohelleb, when he broke his prison, and escaped, اَللّٰهُمَّ إِنَّهُ قَدْ هَاضَنِى فَهِضْهُ ‡ *O God, verily he hath broken me,* or *defeated me, and encroached on me* (ادَّخَلَ عَلَىَّ), *then do Thou break him,* or *defeat him, and requite him for that which he hath done.* (TA.)

2. هَيَّضَهُ † *He roused, excited,* or *provoked, him*; and *it,* namely the heart. (IB.)

5 : see 7 : —— and see also 1.

7. انهاض *It* [a bone] *broke,* or *became broken,* (JK, Ḳ,) *after having been set*; (JK;) and ▼ تهيّض signifies the same. (Ḳ.)

8 : see 1.

هَيْضٌ † *Any pain following upon pain.* (Ṣ, TA.) See also هَيْضَةٌ. —— † *Softness.* (TA.)

هَيْضَةٌ, (Lth, Ḳ,) or ▼ هَيْضٌ, (JK,) † *A disease after a disease*: *a return of anxiety,* or *disquietude of mind*; and *of grief.* (Lth, JK, Ḳ.) —— بِهِ هَيْضَةٌ † *He has a purging and vomiting together*; [i.e. *the cholera*: used in this sense in the present day:] (Ṣ, Ḳ:) or *a discharge of the belly alone.* (TA.) You say also, أَصَابَتْ فُلَانًا هَيْضَةٌ, meaning † *A change of his temperament, such as often occasions laxness of the bowels, causing a frequent going to and from the privy, affected such a one, from the disagreement with him of something which he had eaten.* (TA.) —— بِهِ هَيْضَةُ الكَرَى ‡ *In him is the languor produced by drowsiness.* (A, TA.)

مَهِيضٌ A bone *broken after having become set*; (Ṣ, A, Ḳ;) as also ▼ مُهْتَاضٌ (Ṣ) and ▼ مُنْهَاضٌ. (Ṣ, A.)

مُهْتَاضٌ : } see مَهِيضٌ.
مُنْهَاضٌ : }

مُسْتَهَاضٌ [A beast] *that has had a leg broken, and has recovered, and has been hastily laden and driven, and whose bone has consequently broken a second time, after it had become set and nearly well*: or, accord. to ISh, one *that has been diseased, and recovers, and is hastily put to work, so that he is distressed thereby*; or *that eats food,* or *drinks beverage, and in consequence relapses into disease.* (TA.)

هيط

1. مَا زَالَ يَهِيطُ, inf. n. هَيْطٌ ; and مَا زَالَ فِى هَيْطٍ وَمَيْطٍ ; *He ceased not to be engaged in crying out,* or *vociferating,* or *calling for aid* or *succour*; *and in evil,* or *mischief*; *and raising a clamour,* or *confused noise.* (Ḳ.) IḲṭṭ says, that يهيط has no pret. (TA.) [See also 3.]

3. هِيَاطٌ [in the senses assigned to it in what here follows] is an inf. n. of which the verb [هَايَطَ] is obsolete. (L.) You say, مَا زَالَ فِى هِيَاطٍ وَمِيَاطٍ *He ceased not to be in a state of approaching,* or *drawing near, and retiring to a distance*: (Ḳ:) or هِيَاطٌ signifies the act of *advancing*: (Lḥ:) or هِيَاطٌ and مِيَاطٌ respectively signify the *most vehement driving in coming to water,* and the *most vehement driving in returning from water*; and the meaning is, *going and coming*: (Aboo-Ṭálib:) or both signify the *being in a state of commotion, tumult,* or *disturbance*; as some say, *arising from their saying "No, by God," and "Yes, by God:"* (TA:) [it is also said that] مُهَايَطَةٌ [which is likewise an inf. n. of هَايَطَ] signifies the act of *crying out,* or *vociferating*; *and raising a clamour,* or *confused noise*; [(see also 1;) and so, app., هِيَاطٌ; for it is immediately added,] one says, وَقَعَ القَوْمُ فِى هِيَاطٍ وَمِيَاطٍ [as though meaning *the people,* or *company of men, fell into vociferating,* &c.]. (Ṣ.) بَيْنَهُمَا مُهَايَطَةٌ is also said to signify *Between them two is low, faint,* or *gentle, speaking.* (TA.) [See مِيَاطٌ.] —— Accord. to IAạr, هايطه signifies *He esteemed him weak.* (TA.)

6. تهايطوا *They came together,* or *coalesced, and arranged,* or *adjusted, their affairs*; (Fr., Ṣ, Ḳ;) contr. of تمايطوا. (Fr, Ṣ.)

هَائِطٌ and مَائِطٌ are explained by IAạr as signifying *Going and coming.* (TA.)

[هيع &c.
See Supplement.]

و

The twenty-seventh letter of the alphabet; called وَاوٌ: it is one of the class termed شَفَهِيَّةٌ [or labials], and is a letter of augmentation. — For the uses of و as a particle see Supplement; for و in the sense of بل see a verse in art. قصد; و giving fulness of sound to ـُ, see نظر; و used in the sense of ب, see a verse in art. غسل. — As a numeral it denotes *Six*.

وا

R. Q. 1. وَأْوَأَ, inf. n. وَأْوَأَةٌ, *He* (a dog) *barked.* (A.) — Also inf. n. وَأْوَاءٌ ([respecting the form of which see ظَأْظَأَ] in the CK and a MS. copy, وَأْوَأ) *He* (a jackal, اِبْنُ آوَى,) *cried,* or *barked.* (K.) — [See also وَعْوَعَ.]

وأب

1. وَأَبَ, aor. يَئِبُ, inf. n. وَأْبَةٌ [app. a mistake for وَأْبٌ and إِبَةٌ], *It* (a hoof) *was contracted in its edges,* or *in its fore edges.* (Az.) See وَأْبٌ. — وَأَبَ, aor. يَئِبُ, (S, K,) inf. n. وَأْبٌ (S) and إِبَةٌ (S, K) *He contracted himself,* or *drew himself together,* or *shrank; and was ashamed.* (S, K.) — وَأَبَ (TA) and ↑ اِتَّأَبَ (S, K) *He was ashamed,* (S, K,) مِنْ شَىْءٍ *of a thing.* (TA.) — وَأَبَ, aor. يَئِبُ, *i.q.* انف [app. meaning *He was disdainful*]. (TA.) — وَئِبَ, [aor. يَوْأَبُ: see وَطِئَ:] *He was angry.* (K.)

4. أَوْأَبَهُ *He did to him an action of which one should be ashamed:* (S, K:) or *he made him angry:* [mentioned twice in the K: once as though there were no difference of opinion respecting it:] or *he turned him,* or *drove him, back with ignominy, from his affair,* or *from the object of his want:* (so in the copies of the K; but in an old copy, relied upon as correct, of the Tahdheeb el-Af'ál, *from his companion,* عن صاحبه: TA:) as also ↑ اِتَّأَبَهُ; (K;) meaning *he turned him,* or *drove him, back with ignominy:* (TA:) or اوءبه also signifies *he turned him,* or *drove him, back from his affair,* or *from the object of his want.* (S.)

8. اِتَّأَبَ: see 1 and 4.

وَأْبٌ, as an epithet applied to a solid hoof, *Strong, contracted in the edges,* or *in the fore edges, and light:* (K:) or simply *strong:* (L, art. وضح:) or *round like a cup* (*such as is called* قَعْبٌ); *cup-shaped;* (S, K;) *and that takes* [app. meaning *occupies*] *much of the ground:* [(see also تَنَاهَبَ:) accord. to Freytag, *hollowed within, so that it takes up* (tollat) *much earth:*] (K:) or *i.q.* حفيظ: (Az, as cited in the TA:) [but this I incline to think a mistake for خَفِيفٌ *light:*] or *of excellent size:* (K:) or *of moderate size; not wide, nor contracted.* (T.) — وَأْبٌ الحَوَافِرِ *Having hoofs contracted in the edges,* or *in the fore edges.* (Az.) See also وَأْبٌ above. — وَأْبٌ *A large,* or *big, and wide,* arrow: (K:) [but I think that, for مِنَ القِدَاحِ, in the K, we should read مِنَ الأَقْدَاحِ; and that وأب is therefore an epithet applied to a cup, such as is called قَدَحٌ; as Golius and Freytag have understood it; and not to a قِدْحٌ: see what follows]. إِنَآءٌ وَأْبٌ *A large,* or *big, and wide, vessel: a wide vessel:* pl. أُوْآبٌ. قَدَحٌ وَأْبٌ *A large,* or *big, deep, and wide,* [*cup*]. (TA.) — قِدْرٌ وَأْبَةٌ *A wide,* or *ample, cooking-pot.* (TA.) — See also وَئِيبٌ. — وَأْبٌ *A great* camel: (S, K:) accord. to some. (S.) — وَأْبَةٌ A *short and broad* she-camel, or woman. (TA.) — A female *of middling make, between good and bad,* or *handsome and ugly.* (TA.) — *A small hollow,* or *cavity, in a rock, that retains water.* (S, K.) — بِئْرٌ وَأْبَةٌ *A wide and deep well:* (K:) or *a deep well.* (L, K.)

وَئِيبٌ *Wide,* or *ample:* syn. رَغِيبٌ. (TA.) — قِدْرٌ وَئِيبَةٌ *A deep cooking-pot.* (T, K.)

إِبَةٌ, (S, K,) in which the ة is a substitute for the [incipient radical] و, (S,) and ↑ تُوْبَةٌ, (S, K,) in which the ت is originally و, (S,) and ↑ مُوْئِبَةٌ, (K,) *A disgrace; a shame; a thing of which one should be ashamed: disgrace,* or *ignominy:* (S, K:) *shame;* (K;) *and a contracting of one's self,* or *shrugging:* (TA:) *a vice; fault;* or *the like.* (Aboo-'Amr Esh-Sheybánee.) — Ex. نَكَحَ فُلَانٌ فِى إِبَةٍ [*Such a one married in a manner that was disgraceful;* or, *of which one should be ashamed:* i.e., *married a woman of low origin,* or *the like*]. (S.) — Dhu-r-Rummeh says,

> إِذَا المَرَئِىُّ شَبَّ لَهُ بَنَاتٌ
> عَصَبْنَ بِرَأْسِهِ إِبَةً وَعَارَا

[*When the Maraee has daughters that have attained to puberty, they bind upon his head disgrace and ignominy*]. (S.) — طَعَامٌ ↑ تُوْبَةٌ (or طَعَامٌ ذُو تُوْبَةٍ, as in the TA,) *Food of which one should be ashamed to eat.* Mentioned by AA on the authority of an eloquent Arab of the desert. (S.)

تُوْبَةٌ and مُوْئِبَةٌ: see إِبَةٌ.

مُوْئِبَاتٌ *Foul,* or *disgraceful, qualities,* or *dispositions.* (S, K.)

وأد

1. وَأَدَ, aor. يَئِدُ, (inf. n. وَأْدٌ, S, L, &c.) *He buried* his daughter *alive* (S, L, Msb, K) *in the grave,* (S, L,) *and put a load of earth upon* her. (A.) It was customary for a man in the time of paganism, when a daughter was born to him, to bury her alive when her mother brought her forth, from fear of reproach and want: but this is forbidden in the Kur. xvii. 33: and some of them used to bury their children alive in times of famine: (L:) the tribe of Kindeh used to bury their daughters alive. (S, L.) — الوَأْدُ الخَفِىُّ a term used in a trad. as meaning *Extractio penis tempore concubitus, ne conciperet femina:* as also ↑ المَوْؤُودَةُ الصُّغْرَى because this act resembles that of burying a child alive, and is done with the same motive. (L.)

5. توادت عَلَيْهِ الأَرْضُ *The earth, or the land, hid, or concealed him, and [as it were] removed him*: (T, :) formed by transposition from تَوَدَّأَت, [q.v. in art. ودأ]. (T.) See 8.

8. اِتَّأَدَ (originally اِوْتَأَدَ, Ṣ,) and ♦ تَوَأَّدَ *He acted, or behaved, with moderation, gentleness, or deliberation, moderately, gently, deliberately, or contr. of hastily: with gravity, staidness, sedateness, or calmness*: (T, Ṣ, M, A, L, Mṣb, Ḳ:) from تُؤَدَةٌ [q.v.]: (Ṣ:) or from وَأْدٌ: or, as some say, formed by transposition, and from تَأَوَّدَتْ فِي قِيَامِهَا, meaning "she (a woman) bent in her rising, by reason of her heaviness." (T, L.) Ex. اِتَّأَدَ فِي أَمْرِهِ, and ♦ تَوَأَّدَ فِيهِ, *He acted with moderation, gentleness, &c., in his affair*: (Ṣ,* A, L,* Mṣb:) and فِي مَشْيِهِ *in his walk, or pace, or gait.* (Ṣ, L.)

وَأْدٌ and ♦ وَئِيدٌ *A sound, or noise*; (Ḳ;) absolutely: (TA:) or *a loud sound or noise*; (Ṣ, L, Ḳ;) as that of a wall falling, and the like. (L.) — The *sound occasioned by vehement or heavy treading of the ground*: the *heavy sound* of the feet of camels. (L.) — Also the former, (L,) or both, (Ḳ,) The *braying* (هَدِير) of a camel. (L, Ḳ.)

وَئِيدٌ and وَئِيدَةٌ (L, Ḳ) and ♦ مَوْؤُودَةٌ, (Ṣ, L, Ḳ,) and, by abbreviation, مَوْدَةٌ, (Abu-l-'Abbás, T,) A daughter *buried alive.* (Ṣ, L, Ḳ.) — ♦ المَوْؤُودَةُ الصُّغْرَى: see الوَأْدُ الخَفِىُّ, voce وَأْدٌ. (L.) — See also تُؤَدَةٌ. — See وَأْدٌ.

وَائِدٌ A man *burying, or who buries, his daughter, or daughters alive.* (L.)

تُؤَدٌ: see تُؤَدَةٌ.

تُؤَدَةٌ (T, Ṣ, M, L, Mṣb, Ḳ) and تُؤْدَةٌ (M, L, Ḳ) and تودة, without ء, [i.e., تُودَةٌ or تُوَدَةٌ,] (TA,) and ♦ تُؤَدٌ (M, L, Ḳ) and ♦ وَئِيدٌ: (Ḳ;) the first originally وُؤَدَةٌ; like as تُكَأَةٌ is originally وُكَأَةٌ; (T, L;) *Moderation; gentleness; deliberateness; a leisurely manner of proceeding, or of deportment, &c.; contr. of hastiness*: and *gravity; staidness; sedateness; calmness*: syn. تَأَنٍّ, (T, M, L, Ḳ,) and تَمَهُّلٌ, (T, L,) and رَزَانَةٌ, (M, L, Ḳ,) and سَكِينَةٌ. (Mṣb.) Ex. فَعَلَهُ فِي تُؤَدَةٍ *He did it in a moderate manner; with gentleness; &c.*] (A.) And مَشَى عَلَى تُؤَدَةٍ (Ṣ, Mṣb) [*He walked moderately; gently; &c.;*] *calmly*; or *quietly.* (Mṣb.) ♦ مَشَى مَشْيًا وَئِيدًا i.q. عَلَى تُؤَدَةٍ [*He walked moderately; gently; &c.*]; (Ṣ;) *calmly, or quietly.* (Mṣb.)

مَوْؤُودَةٌ and مَوْدَةٌ: see وَئِيدٌ and وَأْدٌ.

مَوَائِدُ *Calamities*, : (IAạr, T, Ḳ:) formed by transposition from مَآوِدُ. (IAạr, T.) See art. اود.

[وَرَأَ: see وَرَأَ.

وَاصِ &c., See Supplement.]

وب

1. وَبَّ (originally أَبَّ, the ا being changed into و, Az,) inf. n. وَبٌّ; and ♦ وَبْوَبَ, inf. n. وَبْوَبَةٌ; *He prepared to charge, or make an assault, in battle.* (Ḳ.) See art. أب.

R. Q. 1. وَبْوَبَ: see 1.

وبأ

1. وَبِئَتِ الأَرْضُ, (Ṣ, Ḳ,) aor. تِيبَأُ, (Ḳ, TA,) or تَيْبَأُ, (CḲ,) and تَوْبَأُ, (accord. to the Ḳ: in the (Ṣ and) L and other lexicons, only this last aor. is mentioned; but it is asserted on the authority of AZ, who says that this form of the pret. is of the dial. of the Ḳusheyrees, that the aor. is تِيبَأُ, with kesr to the ت,[contr. to analogy,] TA,) inf. n. وَبَأٌ; (Ḳ;) or وَبَاءَةٌ; (Ṣ;) and وَبِئَت, aor. تَيْبَأُ and تَوْبَأُ; (Moo'ab and Jámi') and وَبُؤَتْ, inf. n. وَبَاءٌ and وَبَاءَةٌ and أَبَاءٌ and أَبَاءَةٌ (Ḳ, the و being changed into ا in the latter two); and with و without ء, [i.e., وَبُوَتْ]; (Moo'ab and Jámi'] and وُبِئَتْ, (Ṣ, Ḳ,) like عُنِىَ, [i.e., pass. in form, but neut. in signification,] (Ḳ,) aor. تِيبَأُ, (L and other lexicons,) in which, the و being changed into ى, the vowel of the first letter necessarily becomes kesr, (TA,) or تُوبَأُ, (Ṣ,) inf. n. وَبْءٌ, (Ḳ, TA: in the CḲ وَبَأٌ,) or وَبَاءَةٌ; (Ṣ, L, &c.;) and ♦ أَوْبَأَتْ, (Ṣ, Ḳ,) inf. n. إِيبَاءٌ; (TA;) *The land was, or became, afflicted with* وَبَأ: (Ḳ:) or, *much afflicted with disease.* (Ṣ.) — وَبَأَ, aor. يَوْبَأُ; (Ḳ; contr. to rule, which requires that the aor. should be يَبَأُ; MF;) and ♦ وَبَّأَ; *He put* the utensils, or goods, *one upon another*; or *packed* them *up*: or *he prepared, set in order,* or *arranged,* them; syn. عَبَّأَ. (Ḳ.) — وَبَأَ إِلَيْهِ; (Ṣ, Ḳ: Ibn-El-Mukarram says, I think that Th has mentioned وَبَّأَتْ, without teshdeed; but I am not confident of it; TA;) and ♦ اوبأ, inf. n. إِيبَاءٌ; (Ṣ, Ḳ;) dial. vars. of وَمَأَ and أَوْمَأَ; (Ṣ;) *He made a sign to him*: (Ṣ, Ḳ:) or اوبأ اليه signifies *he made a sign to him with his fingers, forwards, that he should approach*; and اومأ اليه "he made a sign to him with his fingers, backwards, that he should retire, or remain behind." So accord. to the Ḳ; but this is at variance with what the leading lexicographers have transmitted. In the L it is said, اومأ and اوبأ are dial. syns. of ومأ and وبأ اليه he made a sign to him: or, accord. to some, اومأ اليه signifies "he made a sign with his hand to him, (i.e., to a person before him,) turning his fingers towards the palm of his hand, in order that he should approach him;" [in doing which, the palm of the hand is held towards the person beckoned;] and ♦ اوبأ إِلَيْهِ *he made a sign to him*; (i.e., to a person behind him,) *opening his fingers* [*from the palm*] *towards the back of the hand, in order that he should retire, or remain behind*; [in doing which, the palm of his hand is towards himself]. El-Ferezdaḳ says,

* تَرَى النَّاسَ إِنْ سِرْنَا يَسِيرُونَ خَلْفَنَا *

* وَإِنْ نَحْنُ وَبَأْنَا إِلَى ♦ النَّاسِ وَقَّفُوا *

[*If we journey on, thou seest the people journey on behind us; and if we make a sign to the people to remain behind, they stop, one after another*]. ♦ أَوْبَأْنَا is also read in this verse for وَبَأْنَا. Ibn-Buzruj says, that اومأ signifies "he made a sign with the eyebrows, and the eyes;" and ♦ وَبَّأَ, *he made a sign with the hands, and a garment, and the head.* (TA.) — وَبَأَتْ إِلَيْهِ, aor. تَبَأُ, *She* (a camel) *yearned towards it* [i.e., towards her young one]; or *uttered to it the cry produced by yearning*: syn. حَنَّتْ. (Ḳ.)

2: see 1.

4. اوبأ *It became unwholesome*: syn. صَارَ وَبِيئًا. (TA.) — See 1. — أُوبِىَ *He* (a young weaned camel) *suffered in the stomach from indigestion, in consequence of repletion.* (Ḳ, TA.) — مَآءٌ لَا يُوبِى, like لا يُوبِى, *Water that does not fail,* or *stop.* The like is said of pasture. (TA.)

5: see 10.

10. استوبأ (Ṣ, Ḳ,) and ♦ توبّأ (TA) *He found,* or *deemed,* a country, (Ṣ, Ḳ,) or water, (TA,) *unhealthy,* or *unwholesome*: (Ḳ, TA:) [see وَبَأ:] or, *much afflicted with disease.* (Ṣ.)

وَبَأٌ and ♦ وَبَاءٌ, (Ṣ, Ḳ,) and also without ء, [وَبًا,] (TA,) *Plague,* or *pestilence*; syn. طَاعُونٌ: (Ḳ:) or *a common,* or *general,* [or *an epidemic,*] *disease*: (Ṣ:) or *any such disease*: (Ḳ:) or *a quickness, and commonness, of death among men.* (TA.) Accord. to Ibn-En-Nefees, it is *a corruption happening to the substance of the air, by reason of causes in the heavens* or *the earth*; *as stinking water, and carcases, such as are the result of bloody battles.* Accord. to the ḥakeem Dá-ood, it is *a change effected in the air by events in the higher regions, as the conjunction of beaming stars; and by events in the lower regions, as bloody battles, and the opening of graves, and the ascending of putrid exhalations; with which causes conspire the changes of the seasons and elements, and the revolutions of the universe.* They mention also its signs; among which are fever, small-pox, defluxions, itch or scab, tumours, &c. What is said in the Nuzheh necessarily implies that the طاعون is one of the different kinds of وبا; as the physicians hold to be the case: but the opinion which the critics among the professors of practical law and the relaters of traditions hold is, that these two diseases are distinct, the one from the other; the وبا being *an unwholesomeness in the air, in consequence of which diseases become common among men*; and the طاعون being that kind [of disease] with which men are smitten by the jinn, or genii: an opinion which they corroborate by the words in a trad. إِنَّهُ وَخْزُ أَعْدَائِكُمْ مِنَ الجِنِّ [Verily it is the unpenetrating thrusting of your enemies among the jinn]. (TA.) The pl. of وَبَأٌ is أَوْبَآءٌ; and of ♦ وَبَآءٌ, أَوْبِئَةٌ, (Ṣ, Ḳ, TA) or أَوْبِيَةٌ. (CḲ.)

وَبِئَةٌ The *state of* a land *being afflicted with* وَبَأٌ. (Ḳ.)

أَرْضٌ وَبِئَةٌ, and ♦ وَبِيئَةٌ, (Ṣ, Ḳ,) and ♦ مَوْبُوءَةٌ, (Ṣ, L,) and مُوبِئَةٌ, (Ṣ, Ḳ,) *a land much, or often, afflicted with* وَبَأٌ: (Ḳ:) or, *much afflicted with disease*. (Ṣ.)

وَبَآءٌ: see وَبَأٌ.

وَبِىْءٌ *Sick; unwell*; (IAạr:) See أَرْضٌ وَبِئَةٌ. — وَبِىْءٌ *Unwholesome* water. (TA.)

مُوبِئٌ *Engendering* وَبَأٌ. (TA.) — جُرْعَةُ شَرُوبٍ أَنْفَعُ مِنْ عَذْبٍ مُوبٍ *A draught of brackish water is more profitable than sweet water that engenders* وَبَأٌ. (A trad.) Here the ء is omitted in the last word to assimilate it to شروب. It is a proverb, applied to two men; one, superior in station, and more slim; the other, inferior in station, but more useful. (TA.) — See أَرْضٌ وَبِئَةٌ. — مُوبِئٌ Water *that is little in quantity; and failing*, or *stopping*. (Ḳ.)

مَوْبُوءَةٌ: see أَرْضٌ وَبِئَةٌ.

وبت

1. وَبَتَ بِالمَكَانِ, aor. يَبِتُ, (inf. n. وَبْتٌ, L,) *He remained, stayed, abode*, or *dwelt, in the place*. (Ḳ.)

وبخ

2. وَبَّخَهُ, inf. n. تَوْبِيخٌ, *He reproved him*, or *blamed him*, (L, Mṣb, Ḳ,) بِسُوءِ فِعْلِهِ *for his evil action* or *conduct*: (L:) *reproved* or *blamed him*, or *did so severely*, or *with the utmost severity; and threatened him*: (Ṣ, L, Ḳ:) *reproached* or *upbraided him*. (El-Fárábee, Mṣb.) أَبَّخَهُ is a dial. form of the same: (IAạr:) or its hemzeh is a substitute for the و. (ISd.)

وَبْخَةٌ *A burning reproof*: (L:) as also وَمْخَةٌ; (IAạr;) in which the ب is changed into م because of the nearness of their places of utterance. (AM.)

وبد

1. وَبِدَ, (Ḳ,) aor. يَوْبَدُ, (TA,) inf. n. وَبَدٌ, (Ṣ, M, L, Ḳ,) *It* (life, or manner of living,) *was*, or *became, hard, strait*, or *difficult*: (Ṣ, M, L, Ḳ:) *it* (a man's state, or condition,) *was*, or *became, evil*, (Ṣ, M, L, Ḳ,) *by reason of the largeness of his family, and the littleness of his property*: (M, L:) you say وَبِدَتْ حَالُهُ. (M, L.) See also وَبَدٌ below. — وَبِدَ عَلَيْهِ, (Ṣ, M, L,) aor. ـَ, (Ḳ,) inf. n. وَبَدٌ, (M, L, Ḳ,) *He was angry with him*: (Ṣ, M, L, Ḳ:) like وَمِدَ. (Ṣ, L.) — وَبِدَ, aor. ـَ, inf. n. وَبَدٌ, *It* [a day, &c.] *was*, or *became, hot, and without wind*: (M, L:) like وَمِدَ. (M, L.) — وَبِدَ, aor. ـَ, inf. n. وَبَدٌ, *It* (a garment) *became old and worn-out*. (M, L, Ḳ.)

وَبْدٌ: see وَبَدٌ.

وَبَدٌ *Hardness, straitness*, or *difficulty, of life*, or *manner of living: evilness of one's state*, or *condition*, (Ṣ, M, L, Ḳ,) *by reason of the largeness of his family, and the littleness of his property*: (M, L:) *indigence*; (M;) *poverty, adversity*; (T, L;) *largeness of family, and littleness of property*: (Ḳ:) pl. أَوْبَادٌ. See 1. — وَبَدٌ, an inf. n. used as an epithet, and [therefore] sing. and pl., A man, and men, *in an evil state*, or *condition*: and sometimes أَوْبَادٌ is used as its pl.; (Ṣ, L, Ḳ;) as though it were imagined to be a proper epithet: (Ṣ, L:) or this is for ذَوُوا أَوْبَادٍ: (M, L:) also ♦ مُسْتَوْبِدٌ signifies the same [applied to a single person]: (Ṣ, L, Ḳ:) and وَبْدٌ, (TA,) or ♦ وَبِدٌ, (L,) a *poor* man: pl. أَوْبَادٌ. (L, TA.) — وَبَدٌ *A vice, fault*, or *defect*. (M, L, Ḳ.)

مُسْتَوْبِدٌ: see وَبَدٌ.

وبر

1. وَبِرَ, (Ṣ, Mṣb,) aor. ـَ, inf. n. وَبَرٌ, (Mṣb,) *He* (a camel) *had much* وَبَر [i. e. *fur*, or *soft hair*]. (Ṣ, Mṣb.)

وَبْرٌ, a pl. [or rather a coll. gen. n.] of which the sing. [or n. un.] is with ة; (Ṣ, Mgh;) or a masc. n., of which the fem. is with ة, (Lth, T, M, Mṣb, Ḳ,) and also a pl. [or coll. gen. n.], (M,) [The *hyrax Syriacus*; believed to be the animal called in Hebr. שָׁפָן;] *a certain small beast*, (Lth, T, Ṣ, Mgh, Mṣb, Ḳ,) *like the cat*, (Mṣb, Ḳ,) or *of the size of the cat*, (Lth, T, M, Mgh,) or *smaller than the cat*, (Ṣ,) *of the beasts of the desert*, (M,) *of a dust-colour*, (Lth, T, Mgh, Mṣb,) or *of a hue between dust-colour and white*, (طَحْلَآءُ, this epithet being applied to وَبْرَةٌ, Ṣ,) or *white*, (TA,) *having beautiful eyes*, (Lth, T, Mgh,) or *having eyes bordered with black*, or *very black eyes*, (كَحْلَآءُ, Mṣb,) *having no tail*, (Ṣ, Mṣb,) or *having a small tail*, (Mgh,) [Golius says, on the authority of Dmr., "longiore caudâ," which is a mistake, for it has no tail,] *said to be of the weasel-kind*, (Mṣb,) *very shy*, (Lth, T, Mgh,) *living in low grounds*, (Lth, T,) *and dwelling in houses* [*of its own* or *of men*], (Ṣ,) or *it is confined in houses, and is taught; and it is eaten, because it feeds upon leguminous plants*: (Mgh:) *it is* [*said to be*] *a ruminant*; [*but this is not the case*;] and therefore it is said in a trad., that when a man in a state of إِحْرَام kills it, he must sacrifice a sheep or goat: (TA:) [a full and correct description of this animal is given in art. "Shaphan" of Dr. Kitto's "Cyclopædia of Biblical Literature:"] pl. وِبَارٌ (Ṣ, M, Mṣb, Ḳ) and وُبُورٌ and وِبَارَةٌ (M, Ḳ) and إِبَارَةٌ, (M, TA,) with hemzeh in the place of the و. (TA.) One says, فُلَانٌ أَسْمَحُ مِنْ مُخِّ الوَبْرِ [*Such a one is more liberal than the marrow of the webr*]: because the marrow of the webr comes forth easily. (IAạr, T.) And فُلَانٌ أَذَمُّ مِنَ الوِبَارَةِ [*Such a one is more dispraised than the webrs*]. (Fr, T.) — أَيَّامُ العَجُوزِ, الوَبْرُ *One of the days called*, (Ṣ, M, Ḳ,) *which are seven, falling at the end of winter*: or it is called وَبْرٌ, without the article: for the Arabs say, صِنٌّ وَصِنَّبْرٌ وَأُخَيُّهُمَا وَبْرٌ [*Ṣinn and Ṣinnabr and their little brother Webr*]: but this may be for the sake of the rhyme. (M.)

وَبَرٌ The صُوف, [here meaning the *fur*, or *soft hair*,] of the camel, (Lth, T, Ṣ,* M, A, Ḳ,) and of the hare or rabbit, and the like; (Lth, T, M, A, Ḳ;) and in like manner, that of the سَمُّور [or sable], and of the fox, and of the فَنَك [or marten]: (T:) or it is to the camel *like wool* (صوف) *to the sheep*; and so to the hare or rabbit, and the like: (Mṣb:) originally an inf. n.: (Mṣb:) n. un. with ة: (Ṣ:) pl. أَوْبَارٌ. (M, Mṣb, Ḳ.) — أَهْلُ الوَبَرِ ‡ *The people of the deserts*; [or rather *the people of the tents*;] because they make their tents of the وَبَر of camels [as well as of goat's hair, which is not included in the term وَبَر, but is called شَعَر]: opposed to أَهْلُ المَدَرِ, the people of the cities and of the towns and villages. (TA.) See also مَدَرٌ. — أَخَذَ الشَّىْءَ بِوَبَرِهِ ‡ *He took the thing altogether; he took the whole of the thing*: as also أَخَذَهُ بِزَوْبَرِهِ. (A.)

وَبِرٌ A camel *having much* وَبَر [i. e. *fur*, or *soft hair*]; (Ṣ, M,* A,* Mṣb, Ḳ;) and in like manner, a hare or rabbit, and the like; (Ḳ;) as also ♦ أَوْبَرُ: (Ṣ, M, A, Ḳ:) fem. of the former, وَبِرَةٌ; (M, A, Mṣb, Ḳ;) and of the latter, وَبْرَآءُ. (M, A, Ḳ.)

أَوْبَرُ: see وَبِرٌ. — بَنَاتُ أَوْبَرَ, (Aṣ, A'Obeyd, AHn, T, Ṣ, M, Ḳ,) and بَنَاتُ الأَوْبَرِ, (AZ, T, Ṣ, M,) the art. being added by poetic license, (M,) *A species of* كَمْأَة [or *truffles*], *downy*, (AZ, Aṣ, A'Obeyd, T, Ṣ, M, [the epithet thus rendered is written in copies of the Ḳ مُزَغَّبَة, and in the T, Ṣ, M, مُزْغِبَة, but in art. زغب in the TA it seems to be indicated that it is probably مُزَغِّبَة,]) *small, and of the colour of earth*: (AZ, Ṣ, Ḳ:) or, accord. to AḤn, *truffles* (كَمْأَة) *like pebbles, small, found in places where they have broken through the crust of the soil, in number from one to ten; they are bad in flavour; and are the first of* كَمْأَة: or, as he says in another place, *they are like* كَمْأَة, *but are not* كَمْأَة; *and they are small:* (M: see also جَبْءٌ:]) n. un. إِبْنُ أَوْبَرَ. (Aṣ, A'Obeyd, T.) You say, إِنَّ بَنِى فُلَانٍ مِثْلُ بَنَاتِ أَوْبَرَ [*Verily the sons of such a one are like benát-owbar*]: one imagines that there is good in them [when there is none]. (M.) And لَقِيتُ مِنْهُ بَنَاتِ أَوْبَرَ *I experienced from him* [*a disappointment,* or] *a calamity,* or *misfortune.* (Ṣgh, Ḳ.) — دَاهِيَةٌ وَبْرَآءُ, (Ṣ, A, art. شعر), † *An evil, a foul,* or *an abominable, calamity,* or *misfortune.* (TA, voce أَشْعَرُ, q. v.)

وبش

2. وبّش (TA,) or وبّش أَوْبَاشًا, (Ṣ, L,) inf. n. تَوْبِيشٌ, (TA,) *He collected companies, bodies,* or *forces, of various tribes,* for war. (Ṣ,* L, TA.)

وَبْشٌ (ISd, TA,) and ▼ وَبَشٌ (ISd, Ḳ,) sings. of أَوْبَاشٌ (ISd, Ḳ, TA) which signifies *A medley,* or *mixed multitude;* (Ṣ, A, Ḳ;) and the *lowest* or *basest* or *meanest sort,* or *refuse,* or *riffraff;* (A, Ḳ;) of men, or people; (Ṣ, TA;) or of troops, or soldiers; (A;) like أَوْشَابٌ; [and similar to أَشْوَابٌ, but more particular;] and said to be a pl., formed by transposition, of بَوْشٌ [q. v.]: (Ṣ) or *sundry,* or *separate, sorts,* of men, or people: (Aṣ, ISd, TA:) and of trees and plants: (ISd, TA:) or *a small number, and those separate,* of trees and plants. (A, TA.) — [Hence, app.,] وَبْشُ الكَلَامِ † *What is bad of speech,* or *language.* (TA.)

وَبَشٌ: see وَبْشٌ.

وبص

1. وَبَصَ, (Ṣ, M, A, Mṣb, Ḳ,) aor. يَبِصُ, (Ṣ, Ḳ,) inf. n. وَبِيصٌ (Ṣ, M, A, Mṣb, Ḳ) and وَبْصٌ (M, Ḳ) and بِصَةٌ, (M, TA,) said of lightning, (Ṣ, A, Ḳ,) and of other things, (Ṣ, M,) *It shone, gleamed,* or *glistened.* (Ṣ, M, A, Mṣb, Ḳ.) You say, [also,] وَبَصَتِ النَّارُ, inf. n. وَبِيصٌ, *The light shone,* or *shone brightly;* accord. to AḤn; and ▼ أَوْبَصَتْ نَارِى, signifies *my light shone,* or *shone brightly:* (M:) or the latter signifies *my light showed its flame:* (Ḳ:) or *my light began to show its flame:* (ISk, Ṣ:) or ▼ اوبصت النَّارُ signifies *the fire appeared* on being struck. (TA.) And وَبِيصُ الطِّيبِ signifies *The shining of perfume.* (Mgh, TA.)

4: see 1. — [Hence,] اوبصت الأَرْضُ † *The land began to show its plants,* or *herbage.* (ISk, Ṣ.) — أَوْبَصْتُ نَارِى *I made my fire to burn,* or *blaze, intensely.* (A.)

وَبْصَةٌ: see وَابِصٌ.

وَبْصَانُ (Fr, M, Ḳ) and وُبْصَانُ, (IDrd, Ḳ,) [or وَبَصَانُ and وُبَصَانُ, (see art. بصن,)] in some copies of the Jm., بُصَّانُ, [which see in art. بص,] (TA,) *The month of* رَبِيعٌ الآخِرُ: (M, Ḳ:) i. e. the name of that month in the Time of Ignorance: pl. وَبْصَانَاتٌ. (TA.)

وَبِيصَةٌ: see وَابِصٌ.

وَبَّاصٌ: see what follows, in four places.

وَابِصٌ *Shining, gleaming,* or *glistening:* (Mṣb:) and ▼ وَبَّاصٌ, (as in some copies of the Ḳ,) or both, (M,) *shining, gleaming,* or *glistening, much:* (M, and some copies of the Ḳ:) or the latter, *shining, gleaming,* or *glistening much in colour;* (so in other copies of the Ḳ;) in which last sense, both are added to the epithet أَبْيَضُ: (TA:) and ▼ وَبَّاصٌ, applied to a cloud, signifies also *intensely shining,* or *gleaming, with lightning.* (M.) You say ▼ قَمَرٌ وَبَّاصٌ [*A moon shining brightly*]. (A.) And ▼ الوَبَّاصُ signifies *The moon.* (IAạr, Ḳ.) — وَابِصَةٌ signifies i. q. بَرْقَةٌ [app. *A flash of lightning*]: (M:) and *fire;* as also ▼ وَبِيصَةٌ: (IAạr, Ḳ:) and *a live coal;* as also ▼ وَبْصَةٌ. (M.) — رَجُلٌ وَابِصَةُ السَّمْعِ, (M,) or وَابِصَةٌ سَمْعٍ, (Ṣ, A, Ḳ,) means *A man who relies upon what is said to him:* such a man is called أُذُنٌ: and the epithet is made fem. because أُذُنٌ is meant: or the ة may be added to render it intensive: (M:) or the meaning is, *who trusts in all that he hears:* (Ṣ, Ḳ:) or *who hears speech and trusts in it:* (A:) or *who hears what is said and relies upon it, and thinks it true, but is not yet sure.* (TA.) You say also, وَابِصَةُ سَمْعٍ بِفُلَانٍ [*One who relies upon what he hears of,* or *from, such a one*]: and وَابِصَةُ سَمْعٍ بِهٰذَا الأَمْرِ [*One who relies upon what he hears of this affair*]. (TA.)

[وبط &c.
See Supplement.]

وت

وَتٌّ (L, Ḳ) and وَتٌّ and وَتَّةٌ (Ḳ) or وَتَّةٌ (L) The *cry of the bird called* وَرَشَان. (AA, L, Ḳ.) أَوَتَّ signifies He cried as cries the ورشان. (IAạr, L.)

وَتَاوِتُ i. q. وَسَاوِسُ *Evil suggestions, &c.* (Ḳ.) The س is thus changed, in poetry, into ت, as in نَاتٌ and أَكْيَاتٌ. (MF.)

وتا

1. وَتَا, aor. يَتَأُ, (Ḳ,) inf. n. وَتْءٌ, (TA,) *He was heavy and slow* in his gait, *by reason of age,* or *by nature.* (Ḳ.) Not mentioned by J. because esteemed by him not chaste. (TA.)

تَيْتَأٌ: see art. تأ.

وتب

1. وَتَبَ, aor. يَتِبُ, inf. n. وَتْبٌ, *He remained fixed in the place, and did not move.* (Ḳ.) Omitted by most of the lexicographers; and said by some to be a word mispronounced [app. for وَثَبَ]. (TA.)

وتح

1. وَتُحَ, aor. يَوْتُحُ, inf. n. وَتَاحَةٌ (Ṣ, Ḳ) and وُتُوحَةٌ (Ḳ) and وَتْحَةٌ, (L,) *It* (a thing, Ṣ, or a gift, Ḳ) *was little,* or *small, and paltry, mean,* or *contemptible.* (Ṣ, L, Ḳ.) — وَتَحَ عَطَآءَهُ, aor. يَتِحُ; (Ḳ;) and ▼ اوتحهُ; (Ṣ, Ḳ;) and ▼ وتّحهُ, inf. n. تَوْتِيحٌ; (Ṣ;) *He made his gift little,* or *small,* (Ṣ, Ḳ,) *and paltry, mean,* or *contemptible.* (Ḳ.) — ▼ اوتح لَهُ الشَّىْءَ *He made the thing little to him.* (L.) — ▼ اوتح *He became a person of little property.* (Ḳ)

2: see 1 and 4.

4: see 1. — اوتح فُلَانًا *He harassed and distressed him;* syn. جَهَدَهُ وَبَلَغَ مِنْهُ; (L, Ḳ;) and in like manner, اوتح جَهْدَهُ, and اوتح مِنْهُ, and ▼ وتّح. (L.) — اوتح, in this sense, occurs in a verse as related by Th: as related by IAạr it is اوتغ. (TA.)

5. توتّح مِنَ الشَّرَابِ *He drank a little of the beverage:* (Ṣ, L:) or, as also توتّح الشَّرَابَ, *he drank the beverage by little and little.* (TA.)

شَىْءٌ وَتْحٌ, and ▼ وَتَحٌ, (Ṣ, Ḳ,) and ▼ وَتِحٌ, and ▼ وَتِيحٌ, (Ḳ,) *A little,* or *small, and paltry, mean,* or *contemptible, thing.* (Ṣ, Ḳ.) One says also شَىْءٌ وَتْحٌ وَعْرٌ *A small,* or *little,* or *scanty, thing:* the latter of the two epithets being an imitative sequent; (Ṣ;) or, correctly, a corroborative. (Marg. note in a copy of the Ṣ.) ما اغنى, a phrase like مَا أَغْنَى عَنِّى وَتْحَةً ▼ — عَنِّى عَبْكَةً, (L,) or *He,* or *it, was of no profit,* or *advantage, to me.* (L, Ḳ.) — طَعَامٌ وَتْحٌ *Food in which is no good;* like وَخْتٌ. (L.) — ▼ رَجُلٌ وَتْحٌ *A vile, mean,* or *contemptible, man.* (Ṣ.)

وَتَحٌ, وَتِحٌ, وَتْحَةٌ, وَتِيحٌ } see وَتْحٌ.

وتد

1. وَتَدَ, aor. يَتِدُ, imp. تِدْ, inf. n. وَتْدٌ (Ṣ, L, Ḳ, &c.) and تِدَةٌ; (M, L, Ḳ, &c.;) and ▼ اوتد; (A, Mṣb, Ḳ;) and ▼ وتّد, (M, Mgh,) inf. n. تَوْتِيدٌ;

(TA;) *He knocked with a mallet,* (Mgh,) *and fixed,* or *made firm* or *fast,* a wooden pin, peg, or *stake,* (Ṣ,* M, A,* L, Mṣb, Ḳ,) in the ground or in a wall. (Mṣb.) —— وَتَدَ, (M, L, Ḳ,) [aor. يَتِدُ,] inf. n. وَتْدٌ and تِدَةٌ; (M, L;) and ♦ وتّد; (M, L, Ḳ;) *It* (a wooden pin, peg, or stake,) *was,* or *became, fixed, firm,* or *fast.* (M, L, Ḳ.) —— وَتَدَ ٱللّٰهُ الأَرْضَ بِالجِبَالِ, and ♦ أَوْتَدَهَا; ‡ [*God made the earth firm,* or *fast by means of the mountains.* (A.) —— وتّد رِجْلَهُ فِي الأَرْضِ † *He fixed his foot firmly upon the ground.* (L.) —— وتّد ♦ فِي بَيْتِهِ ‡ *He remained fixed in his house.* (L.) —— وتّد ♦ *It* (growing corn) *put forth its stalks, and became firm and strong.* (L.) —— وتّد ♦, (Ṣ, L,) inf. n. تَوْتِيدٌ, (Ḳ,) ‡ *Libidine venereâ exarsit vir:* (Ṣ, L:) *erexit penem.* (Ḳ.) —— It was said to an Arab of the desert, What is نَطْشَان? and he answered, العَطْشَانَ ♦ يُوَتِّدُ ‡ [*It corroborates the word* عطشان]: or, as some relate it, شَىْءٌ نَتِدُ بِهِ كَلَامَنَا [*A thing,* meaning a word, *by which we corroborate our speech*]. (A.)

2 and 4: see 1.

وَتْدٌ and وُدٌّ and وَتِدٌ: see وَتَدٌ.

وَتِدٌ, (Ṣ, M, Ḳ, &c.,) of the dial. of El-Ḥijáz, and the most chaste form, (Mṣb,) and ♦ وَتَدٌ, (Ṣ, M, Mṣb, Ḳ,) and ♦ وَتْدٌ, (L, Ḳ,) and ♦ وَدٌّ, (Ṣ, M, Mṣb,) of the dial. of Nejd, (Mṣb,) the ت being made quiescent, and then changed into د, and incorporated into the final د, (Ṣ,* Mṣb,) and ♦ وَتِيدٌ, (L, art. ودّ,) *A wooden pin, peg,* or *stake, which is fixed in the ground* or *in a wall:* (M, L, Ḳ:) pl. أَوْتَادٌ. (Ṣ, M, L, Ḳ.) [You say,] أَذَلُّ مِنْ وَتِدٍ بِقَاعٍ [*More vile than a wooden peg in a plain*]: because it is always knocked. A proverb. (TA.) —— وَتِدٌ وَاتِدٌ, an expression like شُغْلٌ شَاغِلٌ, (Aṣ, Ṣ,) the latter word a corroborative; (Ḳ;) or *A wooden pin, peg,* or *stake, firm,* or *fast,* (A, L,) *and erect.* (L.) —— أَوْتَادُ الأَرْضِ ‡ [lit. *The pegs,* or *stakes, of the earth;* i. e.] *the mountains:* (A, L, Ḳ:) so called because they make the earth firm, or fast. (L.) —— أَوْتَادُ البِلَادِ † *The chiefs of the towns, provinces,* or *countries.* (L, Ḳ.) —— أَوْتَادُ الفَمِ ‡ *The teeth.* (L, Ḳ, TA.) —— وَتِدٌ, of a sandal, † The *part that projects from the ear* [or *loop*]. (L.) —— وَتِدٌ † [*A peg of a* بَيْت, q.v.;] *a portion,* or *division, of a foot of a verse, consisting of three letters:* (L, Ḳ*:) it is *of two kinds: one consisting of two movent letters followed by a quiescent letter;* as لَهُو and عَلَنْ; which kind is called وَتِدٌ مَقْرُونٌ, *a conjoined peg;* because each two letters are conjoined by a vowel: *the other consisting of three letters; one movent, then one quiescent, then one movent;* as لَاتُ in مَفْعُولَاتُ; which kind is called وَتِدٌ مَفْرُوقٌ, *a disjoined peg;* because the quiescent letter disjoins the two movent letters: pl. أَوْتَادٌ. زِحَاف does not take place in the اوتاد, because the foot depends upon them; but it does in the أَسْبَاب. (L.) —— وَتِدٌ (A, L, Ḳ) and وَتِدَةٌ (L) of the ear, ‡ [The *tragus;*] the *small prominent thing in the anterior part,* (A, L, Ḳ,) *like a teat,* (A, L,) *next the uppermost part of the side of the beard:* (L:) or the *prominent part next the temple:* (L:) or the وَتِدَانِ of the two ears are the *two parts in the interior thereof resembling a* وَتِد, *also called the* عَيْرَانِ. (Ṣ.)

وَتِيدٌ: see وَتِدٌ.

وَاتِدٌ ‡ A man *standing fixed,* or *firm,* or *motionless.* (A, L.) —— ‡ An *erect* horn. (A.) —— *Fixing,* or *making firm* or *fast,* a wooden pin, peg, or stake. (L.)

مَوْتُودٌ A wooden pin, peg, or stake, *fixed,* or *made firm* or *fast.* (L.)

مِيتَدَةٌ (Ṣ, L, Ḳ,) and مِيتَدٌ (L, Ḳ) *A mallet* (مِرْزَبَّة, L, Ḳ,) *with which wooden pins, pegs,* or *stakes are knocked* [*into the ground* or *a wall*]. (Ṣ, L, Ḳ.)

وتر

1. وَتَرَهُ, aor. يَتِرُهُ, inf. n. وَتْرٌ; (Mṣb;) and ♦ اوترهُ; (Ṣ, Mṣb, Ḳ;) *He made it,* (a number, Mṣb,) *sole;* or *one, and no more:* syn. أَفَذَّهُ, (Ṣ, Ḳ,) or أَفْرَدَهُ. (Mṣb.) It is said that the latter verb only is used in relation to a number; but both are said to be thus used in the M [as well as in the Mṣb.] (TA.) —— [And *He made it to be an odd number.*] You say, وَتَرَ القَوْمَ, (M, Ḳ,) aor. ـِ, inf. n. وَتْرٌ; (M;) and ♦ أَوْتَرَهُمْ; (M, Ḳ;) *He made the people, they being an even number, to be an odd number.* (M, Ḳ, TA.) 'Aṭà says, كَانَ القَوْمُ وِتْرًا فَشَفَعْتُهُمْ وَكَانُوا شَفْعًا فَوَتَرْتُهُمْ [*The people were an odd number and I made them an even number, and they were an even number and I made them an odd number*]. (TA.) You say also, وَتَرَ الصَّلَاةَ, (Mṣb, Ḳ,) and ♦ أَوْتَرَهَا, (T, Ṣ, Mṣb, Ḳ,) and ♦ وتّرها, (Ḳ,) and أَوْتَرَ فِي الصَّلَاةِ, (Lḥ, M,) *He made the prayer to be such as is termed* وِتْر [i. e., *to consist of an odd number of rek'as;* as is done in the case of a prayer which is performed in the night, consisting of three rek'ahs, and particularly called صَلَاةُ الوِتْرِ]; (Ṣ,* Mṣb, Ḳ;*) *he performed prayers of double rek'ahs, two and two together, and then performed the prayer of one rek'ah at the end, making what he performed an odd number:* (T:) and ♦ أَوْتَرَ, alone, signifies *he performed the prayer called* الوِتْر [explained above]; (T, M, A, Mgh, Ḳ;) or *he performed prayers of* [*an odd number of rek'ahs,*] *two and two together, and then a single rek'ah at the end.* (TA.) It is said in a trad. إِنَّ ٱللّٰهَ وِتْرٌ يُحِبُّ الوِتْرَ فَأَوْتِرُوا يَا أَهْلَ القُرْآنِ [*Verily God is one only: He loveth the odd number: therefore perform ye the prayer of an odd number of rek'ahs, O people of the Kur-án*]. (T.) And in another trad., إِذَا ٱسْتَجْمَرْتَ فَأَوْتِرْ *When thou employest stones in the purification termed* إِسْتِنْجَآء, *use an odd number;* (TA;) i. e. use three stones for that purpose, or five, or seven, and not an even number. (T.) —— وَتَرَهُ, (T, Ṣ, A, Mgh,) aor. يَتِرُهُ, inf. n. وَتْرٌ (Ṣ,) and وِتْرٌ and تِرَةٌ, (T, Ṣ,) *He slew his relation, and so separated him from him, and rendered him solitary:* (A, Mgh:) or *he slew a person belonging to him, or related to him, without the latter's obtaining revenge,* or *retaliation, for the blood of the slain:* (Ṣ:) or *he slew a person belonging to him, or related to him;* or *took property belonging to him.* (T.) It is also doubly trans.: you say, وَتَرَ فُلَانٌ فُلَانًا أَهْلَهُ *Such a one committed a crime against such a one by slaying his family;* or *by taking them away:* (T:) and وَتَرَهُ مَالَهُ (T, M, Ḳ) † *he committed a crime against him by taking away his property:* (T:) or † *he made him to suffer loss* or *detriment in respect of his property;* or *he deprived him of it in part,* or *altogether;* syn. نَقَصَهُ إِيَّاهُ: (T,* M, Ḳ:) and وَتَرَهُ حَقَّهُ, (Ṣ, A, Mgh, Mṣb,) aor. as above, (Mṣb,) ‡ *he made him to suffer loss* or *detriment in respect of his right or due;* or *he abridged him,* or *deprived him,* or *defrauded him, of it partially,* or *wholly;* syn. نَقَصَهُ. (Ṣ, Mgh, Mṣb.) It is said in a trad., مَنْ فَاتَتْهُ صَلَاةُ العَصْرِ فَكَأَنَّمَا وُتِرَ أَهْلَهُ وَمَالَهُ (T, M,* Mṣb,* TA) *By whomsoever the prayer of the afternoon passeth unobserved, he is as though he had his family slain and his property taken away:* or *as though he had his family and his property taken away:* (T:) or *as though he were deprived* (نُقِصَ) *of his family and his property,* (T, M, Mṣb, TA,) *and remained alone:* (T, TA:) the loss of the family and property is thus likened to the loss of the recompense: اهله and ماله being in the accus. case as objective complements: (Mṣb:) اهله is a second objective complement: for the first is understood, as implied in the verb: but if we read أَهْلُهُ وَمَالُهُ, accord. to another relation, اهله supplies the place of the agent, nothing being understood, and the family and property are the objects to which the loss is made to relate. (TA.) And it is said in another trad., مَنْ جَلَسَ مَجْلِسًا لَمْ يَذْكُرِ ٱللّٰهَ فِيهِ كَانَ عَلَيْهِ تِرَةٌ † *He who sitteth in an assembly in which God is not mentioned is obnoxious to detriment,* or *loss:* or, as some say, *to a claim of reparation for wrongful conduct.* (TA.) And it is said in the Ḳur, [xlvii. 37,] وَلَنْ يَتِرَكُمْ أَعْمَالَكُمْ † *And He will not deprive you of aught* of the recompence *of your deeds:* (Zj, T:) or *will not make you to suffer loss in respect of your deeds;* like

as you say دَخَلْتُ البَيْتَ, meaning دَخَلْتُ فِى البَيْتِ. (Ṣ.) — [Also,] وَتَرَهُ, (M, Ḳ,) aor. يَتِرُهُ, (Ḳ,) inf. n. وَتْرٌ (M, Ḳ) and وِتْرٌ (TA) and تِرَةٌ, (M, Ḳ,) *He executed blood-revenge upon him:* or *did so wrongfully:* (M,* Ḳ,* TḲ:) expl. by أَصَابَهُ بِذَحْلٍ. (TḲ.) — *He overtook him* (أَدْرَكَهُ) *with some displeasing,* or *abominable,* or *evil, action.* (M, Ḳ.) — *He frightened him; terrified him.* (Fr, Ḳ.) ═ وَتَرَ القَوْسَ: see 2, in two places.

2. وتّر الصَّلَاةَ: see 1, near the beginning. ═ وتّر القَوْسَ *He fastened, bound, firmly,* or *braced, the string of the bow;* expl. by شَدَّ وَتَرَهَا; (Lḥ, M, Ḳ;) as also ▾ أَوْتَرَهَا; (Lḥ, M, Mṣb;) both these signify the same; (Ṣ, in which the meaning is not explained;) and ▾ وَتَرَهَا, (M, TA,) inf. n. وَتْرٌ: (TA:) or ▾ اوترها signifies *he put to it a string:* (M, Ḳ:) and ▾ وَتَرَهَا, (M, Ḳ,) aor. يَتِرُهَا, (Ḳ,) inf. n. تِرَةٌ, (TA,) *he attached to it its string:* (M, Ḳ:) this, accord. to some, is the proper signification of the last. (M.) It is said in a proverb, إِنْبَاضٌ بِغَيْرِ تَوْتِيرٍ [*Twanging* the bow *without bracing the string*]: (Ṣ:) or لَا تُعْجِلِ الإِنْبَاضَ قَبْلَ التَّوْتِيرِ [*Hasten not the twanging* of the bow *before the bracing of the string*]: alluding to the hastening a thing before its proper time. (M.) [See also art. نبض. And see 2 in arts. جنب and حنب.]

3. واتر بَيْنَ أَخْبَارِهِ, (A, and so in some copies of the Ḳ,) or ▾ أَوْتَرَ, (M, and so in some copies of the Ḳ,) and واتر أَخْبَارَهُ, (M,) and بين كُتُبِهِ, (M, Ḳ; in the latter of which وَاتَرَهُ is put by mistake for وَاتَرَهَا, as is observed in the TA,) and كُتُبَهُ, (M, A, Ḳ,) inf. n. مُوَاتَرَةٌ (Ṣ, M, Ḳ,) and وِتَارٌ, (M, Ḳ,) *He made his tidings,* or *narrations,* and *his writings,* or *letters, to follow one another:* (M, A, Ḳ:) or *with some intervals between them;* for مواترة between things is only when there is some interval between them; otherwise it is مُوَاصَلَةٌ and مُدَارَكَةٌ: (Ṣ, Ḳ:) or واتر الكُتُبَ signifies *he made the writings,* or *letters, to follow one another nearly, one by one, without ceasing:* (Ṣ:) or *he made them to follow one another with a small interval between every two:* (T:) and واتر الخَبَرَ *he made the tidings,* or *narration, to follow one part after another:* or, accord. to Aṣ, *with a small space between every two portions thereof:* from وِتْرٌ in the sense of فَرْدٌ. (T.) You say also واتر بَيْنَ مِيرِهِمْ *He made their supplies of wheat to come to them without stopping; time after time.* (TA, from a trad.) And it is said in a trad., لَا بَأْسَ أَنْ يُوَاتِرَ قَضَآءَ رَمَضَانَ *There will be no harm in his performing the fast of Ramaḍán at intervals, fasting one day and breaking fast one day:* (TA:) مُوَاتَرَةُ الصَّوْمِ is *the fasting one day and breaking fast one day,* or *two; performing it separately:* it does not mean المُوَاصَلَة, because it is from الوِتْرُ, (Ṣ, Ḳ, TA,) i. e., الفَرْدُ. (TA.)

4: see 1, in seven places, first part. — اوتر بَيْنَ أَخْبَارِهِ: see 3. ═ اوترهُ *He made him to attain,* or *obtain, his blood-revenge.* (Az, TA; and L in art. ثأر.) See an ex., voce ثَأْرٌ. ═ اوتر القَوْسَ: see 2, in two places.

5. توتّر ‡ *It* (a sinew, or nerve, T, M, A, Ḳ, and a vein, M, TA, not the neck, for العُنُق in the Ḳ is a mistake for العِرْق, TA) *became tense,* (M, Ḳ, TA,) *like a bow-string.* (M, TA.)

6. تواتر *It was consecutive:* or *was so with intervals:* (M, A, Ḳ:) or *was so with separation,* or *interruption.* (Mṣb.) You say, تواترت الإِبِلُ, and القَطَا, and so of any other things, *The camels,* and *the birds of the kind called* القطا, &c., *came one near after another, not in a rank.* (Lḥ, M.) And تواترت الخَيْلُ *The horses came following one another.* (Mṣb.) And تواترت الكُتُبُ *The writings,* or *letters, came one near after another, separately.* (Ṣ.)

وَتْرٌ: see وِتْرٌ, throughout.

وِتْرٌ and ▾ وَتْرٌ, (T, Ṣ, M, A, Mṣb, Ḳ, &c.,) the former, [which is the more common,] in the dial. of Nejd, (Lḥ, M,) and of the tribe of Temeem, (T, Ṣ, M, Mṣb,) and of the people of El-'Áliyeh, (ISk, as on the authority of Yoo, and Ṣ) or the latter in the dial. of the people of El-'Áliyeh, (T, as on the authority of Yoo,) or of the people of El-Ḥijáz, (Lḥ, Ṣ, M,) *Single; sole; only; one, and no more:* syn. فَرْدٌ: (T, Ṣ, M, A, Mṣb, Ḳ:) or مَا لَمْ يُشْفَعْ مِنَ العَدَدِ: (M, A, Ḳ; except that in the Ḳ, instead of يُشْفَعْ, we find يَتَشَفَّعْ:) or *contr. of* شَفْعٌ: (Mgh:) [and *an odd number*:] all [even and odd] numbers are termed [respectively] شَفْعٌ and وِتْرٌ, whether many or few. (T.) — وِتْرًا وِتْرًا [*Singly; separately; one by one*]. (Ṣ, Ḳ.) [See شَفْعٌ.] — الوِتْرُ, one of the names of God, *The Single; the Sole; the One; He who has no equal, or like; the Unequalled;* syn. الفَرْدُ and النِّدُّ. (TA.) — صَلَاةُ الوِتْرِ, and الوِتْرُ alone: see 1, first part: it was sometimes said by Moḥammad to be *a single* رَكْعَة. (T.) — In the words of the Ḳur, [lxxxix. 2,] وَالشَّفْعِ وَالوَتْرِ by the former is meant all creatures which are created in pairs; and by the latter, *God:* (T:) or [by the former, Adam and his wife; and] by the latter, *Adam,* who was made a pair with his wife: (I'Ab, T:) or by the former, the day of the sacrifice; (T;) and by the latter, *the day of 'Arafeh.* (T, Ḳ.) (See more voce شَفْعٌ.] ═ Also وِتْرٌ and ▾ وَتْرٌ, (T, Ṣ, M, A, Mṣb, Ḳ,) the former, [which is the more common,] in the dial. of Nejd, (Lḥ, M,) and of the tribe of Temeem, (Lḥ, T, Ṣ, M, Mṣb,) and of the people of El-'Áliyeh, (T, as on the authority of Yoo,) and El-Ḥijáz, (Ṣ,) or the latter in the dial. of the people of El-'Áliyeh, (ISk, as on the authority of Yoo, and Ṣ,) and El-Ḥijáz, (Lḥ, M,) *Blood-revenge;* or *retaliation of murder* or *homicide:* or *a seeking to revenge,* or *retaliate, blood:* or *a desire,* or *seeking, for retaliation of a crime* or *of enmity:* syn. ذَحْلٌ: (T, Ṣ, M, Mṣb, Ḳ:) or *wrongful conduct therein:* as also ▾ تِرَةٌ and ▾ وَتِيرَةٌ, in either sense: (M, Ḳ:) or *a crime which a man commits against another by slaughter* or *by plundering* or *by capture:* (TA:) pl. [of وِتْرٌ] أَوْتَارٌ and [of تِرَةٌ] تِرَاتٌ. (A.)

وَتَرٌ The *string,* and the *suspensory,* syn. شِرْعَةٌ and مُعَلَّقٌ [the latter signifying properly the *appendage,* (see نِيَاطٌ, and see خُطْمِ القَوْسِ بِالوَتَرِ)] (M, Ḳ,) of a bow: (Ṣ, M, Mṣb, Ḳ:) [and in like manner, *a chord* of a lute and the like:] pl. أَوْتَارٌ (Ṣ, M, Mṣb, Ḳ) and وِتَارٌ. (Fr, Sgh, TA.) — Also pl. [or rather coll. gen. n.] of وَتَرَةٌ [q. v.] in all the senses of the latter. (Ḳ.)

وَتَرَةٌ, of the nose, The *partition between the two nostrils* [*consisting of the septum and subseptum narium,* or the *subseptum* alone]; (Ṣ, A, Mṣb;) as also ▾ وَتِيرَةٌ: (Ṣ, A, Mṣb, Ḳ:) or the former signifies *what is between the two nostrils:* (M:) or the *junction that is between the two nostrils:* (T:) or the *edge of the nostril:* (M, Ḳ:) accord. to Lḥ, (M,) *what is between the tip of the nose and the* سَبَلَة [or *middle of the mustache;* app. meaning, the *subseptum narium*]: (M, Ḳ:) and the latter, the *partition between the two nostrils, of the fore part of the nose, exclusive of the cartilage;* [i. e., app. the *subseptum narium:* (AZ, T:) and the former, in a horse, *what is between the tip of the nose and the upper part of the lip:* (M:) pl. [or rather coll. gen. n.] of the former, in all its senses, وَتَرٌ. (Ḳ.) In a trad. in which it is said that the fine for destroying the وَتَرَة is a third of the fine for homicide, by this word is meant the وَتَرَة of the nose. (TA.) — The *sinew,* or *nerve,* (عَقَبَة,) of the back (مَتْن). (M.)

وَتِيرٌ: see وَتِيرَةٌ, near the end.

وَتِيرَةٌ: see وِتْرٌ. ═ *A way, course, mode,* or *manner of acting,* or *conduct,* or *the like:* (Ṣ, M, A, Mgh, Mṣb, Ḳ:) and *nature,* or *disposition:* (A, Mgh:) from تَوَاتَرَ: (Th, M, A, Mgh:) or *a road keeping close to a mountain,* (Ḳ, TA,) *and pursuing a regular, uniform course:* (TA:) or *constancy,* or *perseverence, in a thing,* (AO, T, Mṣb, TA,) or *in a work.* (TA.) You say, مَا زَالَ عَلَى وَتِيرَةٍ وَاحِدَةٍ *He ceased not to follow,* or *continue in, one way,* (&c.,) *of acting* or *the like:* (T, Ṣ, M, A:) or *one disposition.* (A.) And هُمْ عَلَى وَتِيرَةٍ وَاحِدَةٍ *They follow,* or *con-*

tinue in, one way, &c. (A, Mgh, Mṣb.) —— *Remissness,* or *languor,* syn. فَتْرَةٌ, (Ṣ, M, Mṣb, Ḳ,) in an affair: (M, Ḳ:) and syn تَوَانٍ [which signifies the same]: and *faultiness;* syn. غَمِيزَةٌ, (M, Ḳ,) [in some copies of the latter, غَمِيرَةٌ, with the unpointed ر.]) You say, مَا فِى عَمَلِهِ وَتِيرَةٌ *There is no remissness,* or *languor, in his work.* (Ṣ, A, Mṣb.) And سَيْرٌ لَيْسَ فِيهِ وَتِيرَةٌ *A journeying,* or *pace, in which is no remissness,* or *languor.* (Ṣ.) —— *Delay.* (M, Ḳ.) —— *Confinement; restriction; restraint.* (M, Ḳ.) —— *I. q.* وَتْرَةٌ, as explained above. —— *A ring* (Ṣ, M, Ḳ) *of* عَقَب [or *sinew*], (Ṣ,) *by aiming at which one learns the art of piercing with the spear;* (Ṣ, M, Ḳ;) also called دَرِيَّةٌ: (Ṣ:) or *a ring that is made at the end of a spear* or *spear-shaft, by aiming at which one learns the art of shooting,* or *casting* [*the lance*]; *made of bow-string* or *of other string* or *thread.* (M.) —— *A white rose:* (Ṣ, M, A, Ḳ:) or *red rose:* (Kr, M, Ḳ:) or *a rose-flower; a rose-blossom:* (AḤn, M, Ḳ:*) n. un. of ↓ وَتِيرٌ (AḤn. M.) —— *A star,* or *blaze,* or *white mark, on the forehead* or *face of a horse, when round,* (T, M, A, Ḳ,) *and small:* (A:) when long, it is called شَادِخَةٌ: (AO, T:) likened to the ring above mentioned, thus called; (T;) or to a white rose, which is also thus called. (A.) See غُرَّةٌ.

تِرَةٌ: see وِتْرٌ. The ت is substituted for the elided و. (TA.)

جَاؤُوا تَتْرَى, and تَتْرًى, with and without tenween, and with ت substituted for the original incipient و, (T,* Ṣ,* M, A,* Mṣb,* Ḳ,) in the former whereof, (Ṣ, M,) which is the better, (Ṣ,) and the more common, (Fr,) pronounced by Ḥamzeh and Ibn-'Ámir and Ks with imáleh, [i. e. tetrè,] (Bḍ, xxiii. 46,) the ا [which is written ى] is a sign of the fem. gender, and in the latter whereof it is an ا of quasi-coördination, (Ṣ, M,) from وِتْرٌ in the sense of فَرْدٌ, (Ṣ,) *They came following one another; one after another;* (A, Mṣb;) syn. مُتَوَاتِرِينَ: (M, Ḳ:) or *interruptedly.* (Yoo, T.) It is said in the Ḳur, [xxiii. 46,] ثُمَّ أَرْسَلْنَا رُسُلَنَا تَتْرَى, or تَتْرًى, *Then we sent our apostles one after another:* (Ṣ:) or *interruptedly; at intervals:* (Yoo, T, M:) or *making a long time to intervene between every two.* (T.)

فَرَسٌ مُوَتَّرُ الأَنْسَاءِ ‡ *A horse contracted in the* [*veins called*] أَنْسَاء, [pl. of نَسًا,] as though they were braced, or made tense. (A,* TA.) See شَنِجٌ.

مَوْتُورٌ *One who has his relation slain, and so is separated from him, and rendered solitary:* (TA:) and *one who has a person belonging to him, or related to him, slain, and has not obtained revenge,* or *retaliation, for his blood:* (Ṣ, Ḳ, TA:) *a seeker of blood-revenge,* or *retaliation;* one *to whom belongs the revenging of blood,* or *retaliation.* (TA.) [See an ex. voce ثَأْرٌ.]

مُتَوَاتِرٌ *Consecutive, but with small intervals:* thus differing from مُتَدَارِكٌ and مُتَتَابِعٌ. (Lḥ, M. [But see تَتَابَعَ.]) You say, جَاؤُوا مُتَوَاتِرِينَ: explained above, voce تَتْرَى. (M, Ḳ.) خَبَرٌ مُتَوَاتِرٌ *Tidings,* or *a narration, told,* or *related, by one from another:* (T:) or *by one after another.* (TA.)

[وتغ &c.

See Supplement.]

وث

وُثُوثَةٌ *Weakness; impotence.* (L.)

وَثْوَاثٌ *A weak, impotent,* man. (L.)

وثا

1. وَثَأَتْ يَدُهُ, aor. تَثَأُ, inf. n. وَثْءٌ; (AZ;) and وَثِئَتْ, (a form disapproved by some, TA,) aor. the same, inf. n. the same and وَثَأٌ, (Ḳ, TA,) or وَثَأٌ; (CḲ and a MS. copy) and وُثُوءٌ; and وُثِئَتْ, (Ṣ, Ḳ,) like عُنِىَ, [i.e., pass. in form, but neut. in signification,] (Ḳ,) which is the chaste form of the verb; and to the inf. ns. are added, on the authority of the Wá'ee, وُثُوءٌ and وَثَاءَةٌ; (TA;) [but it is not said to which form or forms of the verb these belong;] *His hand became affected by what is termed* وَثْءٌ. (Ḳ.) —— وَثَأَ يَدَهُ, (Ṣ, Ḳ) and ↓ أَوْثَأَ, (Ḳ,) *He caused his hand to be affected by what is termed* وَثْءٌ. (Ṣ, Ḳ.) —— اللّٰهُمَّ ثَأْ يَدَهُ [*O God, bruise his hand! &c.*] is a form of curse used by the Arabs. (IAạr.) —— وَثَأَ اللَّحْمَ *He,* or *it,* (i.e. a blow,) *deadened the flesh.* (Ḳ.) [—— وَثَأَ الوَتِدَ ‡ i.q. شَعَثَ, q.v. (A.)

4: see 1.

وَثْءٌ and وَثَاءَةٌ *A breaking of the flesh without separation of the parts,* (وَصْمٌ,) *not reaching to the bone,* (Ḳ,) *producing a swelling:* (TA:) or *a pain in the bone, without fracture:* (IḲoot, Ḳ:) or *a dislocation* (Ḳ, TA) and *concussion of the joints, which affects the hand, without fracture:* (TA:) or [*an injury*] *resembling dislocation; in the flesh as a fracture in a bone:* (AM:) or *a bruising* or *breaking of the flesh without breaking the bone:* (IAạr.:) or *a bruising of the skin and flesh, reaching to the bone, without its breaking:* (TA:) or *a bruising of the bone, without breaking:* (Lth, Ṣ:) in which last sense, Lth uses also the word وَثَأٌ. (TA.) The ء in وَثْءٌ is sometimes omitted, and the word is written وَثْىٌ, like يَدٌ and دَمٌ. وَثْىٌ is condemned as vulgar. وَثْىٌ is authorized by Aṣ; but وَثْىٌ (which is said by the vulgar, Ṣ, [and is disallowed in the Ḳ,]) and وَثْوٌ are disallowed by him. (TA.)

وَثِىءٌ *Having a broken hand:* (TA: [but see وَثْءٌ:]). —— يَدٌ وَثِيئَةٌ, and ↓ وَثِيئَةٌ, (Ḳ,) and ↓ مَوْثُوءَةٌ, (Ṣ, Ḳ,) *A hand affected by what is termed* وَثْءٌ. (Ḳ.)

وَثِيئَةٌ and مَوْثُوءَةٌ: see وَثِىءٌ.

مِيثَأَةٌ *A mallet with which pegs,* or *stakes,* or *tent-pins, are driven.* (TA.)

وثب

1. وَثَبَ, aor. يَثِبُ, inf. n. وَثْبٌ and وُثُوبٌ (the latter agreeable with analogy, TA,) and وَثَبَانٌ and وَثِيبٌ (Ṣ, Ḳ) and وِثَابٌ (Ḳ; but this is generally affirmed to be an inf. n. of وَاثَبَ, TA;) and ثِبَةٌ, (Ibn-Málik and others) *He leaped; jumped; sprang; bounded:* (Ṣ, Ḳ:) or *he leaped down,* or *downwards.* (Mgh, Mṣb, art. طفر.) —— وَثَبَ المَوْضِعَ [*He leaped,* or *jumped, upon,* or *over the place*]. (TA.) —— وَثَبَ إِلَى الشَّرَفِ وَثْبَةً ‡ [*He made a single leap to eminence,* or *nobility*]. (TA.) —— وَثَبَ إِلَيْهِ [app., *He leaped,* or *sprang up,* or *he hastened, to him*]. (TA.) —— الوُثُوبُ, except in the dial. of Ḥimyer, signifies *The act of rising,* or *standing up.* (TA.) —— It is also much used by the vulgar as signifying *The act of hastening to a thing;* as observed by MF, who is wrong in saying that there is nothing in the lexicons that favours its being so used. (TA.) —— وَثَبَ, [aor. يَثِبُ,] inf. n. وَثْبٌ, in the dial. of Ḥimyer signifies *He sat; sat down.* (Ḳ, TA, from a trad.) ثِبْ in that dial. signifies *Sit; sit down.* (Ṣ.) It is related that Zeyd Ibn-Abd-Allah Ibn-Dárim came as an envoy to one of the kings of Ḥimyer, and found him at a hunting-place belonging to him, on a high mountain, and he saluted him, and mentioned to him his lineage, or relationship; whereupon the king said to him ثِبْ, meaning اِجْلِسْ, *Sit;* but the man thought that he commanded him to leap from the mountain; and he said, "Thou shalt find me, O king, very obedient:" then he leaped from the mountain, and perished. So the king said, "What ailed him?" And they explained to him his case, and his mistake respecting the word: upon which he said لَيْسَتْ عِنْدَنَا عَرَبِيَّتْ مَنْ دَخَلَ ظَفَارِ حَمَّرَ i.e., [" Arabic is not current with us:" (for, probably, in the time of this king, the term عَرَبِيَّة was only applied to the general language of Arabia:) "whoso entereth Ḍhafári,] let him learn [or, rather, speak, as MF says,] the Ḥimyeree language." (Mz., 16th نوع.) [The principal facts of this anecdote are also mentioned in the Ṣ, on the authority of Aṣ.] By the king's saying عَرَبِيَّتْ was meant العَرَبِيَّةُ: the ة is pronounced ت in the case of a pause (which is the case here) in their dialect. (Ṣ.) Or, accord. to another relation of the above anecdote, the king said لَيْسَ عِنْدَنَا عَرَبِيَّتْ كَعَرَبِيَّتِكُمْ [" Arabic like

your Arabic is not current with us:"] and this, says ISd, is the right reading in my opinion: for the king did not mean to exclude himself from the Arabs. (MF.)

2. وثّبه, inf. n. تَوْثِيبٌ, *He seated him upon a cushion:* (Ṣ, Ḳ:) asserted to be of the dial. of Ḥimyer. (MF.) — وثّبه وِسَادَةً, (Ṣ, Ḳ,) in some copies of the Ḳ وِثَبَةً, (TA,) *He threw to him a cushion* (Ṣ, L, Ḳ) *that he might sit upon it:* (Ṣ:) [app. in the dial. of Ḥimyer]. — وَثَّبْتُهُ وِثَابًا *I spread for him a bed, or the like.* (TA.)

3. واثبه *He leaped, or sprang, upon him, or at him; he assaulted or assailed him;* syn. سَاوَرَهُ (Ṣ, Ḳ) and ثَاوَرَهُ (Ḳ, art. ثور) and صَاوَلَهُ. (Ḳ, art. صول.) — [Also, perhaps, *He contended with him in leaping, jumping, springing, or bounding.*] — [واثبه] is also mentioned in the TA as having a signification not explained in the Ḳ: app., *He contended with him in hastening to a thing.*]

4. اوثبه *He made him to leap, jump, spring, or bound.* (Ṣ, Mṣb.) — اوثبه المَوْضِعَ [*He made him to leap, or jump, upon, or over, the place*]. (TA.)

5. تَوَثَّبَ فُلَانٌ فِى ضَيْعَةٍ لِى ‡ *Such a one took possession unjustly of an estate belonging to me; he seized upon it unjustly.* (Ṣ, Ḳ.) — تَوَثَّبَ فِى أَرْضِهِ عَلَى أَخِيهِ ‡ *He took possession of his land with injustice towards his brother.* (A.) — تَوَثَّبَ عَلَى مَنْزِلَتِهِ ‡ *He took possession unjustly of the place occupied by him.* (A.)

6. هُمْ يَتَوَاثَبُونَ عَلَى كَذَا *They leap, or rush, together upon such a thing* [*in an evil, or injurious, or a contentious manner*]. (Ṣ, art. كلب.) — التَّوَاثُبُ is syn. with التَّكَالُبُ. (Ṣ, Ḳ, art. كلب.)

وَثْبَةٌ *A single leap, jump, spring, a bound:* (TA:) or *a leap down, or downwards.* (Mgh, Mṣb, art. طفر.)

ثُبَةٌ *An assembly; a company; a troop; a congregated body.* (Ḳ.) [But it seems rather to belong to the root ثبى, as remarked by Freytag; or, accord. to some, to art. ثوب. See arts. ثبى and ثوب.]

وَثَبَى : see وَثَّابٌ.

وِثَابٌ *A throne, or couch;* syn. سَرِيرٌ: (Ḳ;) accord. to some, *that is always occupied by the king; or that the king does not cease to occupy:* (TA:) [app. of the dial. of Ḥimyer]. — *A bed; or what is spread to lie or recline upon:* (Ḳ:) ex. وَثَّبْتُهُ وِثَابًا *I spread for him a bed, or the like:* (TA:) or *places where persons sit;* syn. مَقَاعِدُ: (Ṣ, Ḳ:) in which case it is a pl., as some have expressly affirmed it to be: (TA:) accord. to IF and others, of the dial. of Ḥimyer. (MF.) Applied to heaven (السَّمَآء) as being the sitting-places of the angels. (Ṣ.)

ظَبْىٌ وَثَّابٌ *An antelope that leaps, jumps, springs, or bounds, quickly.* فَرَسٌ وَثَّابَةٌ *A mare that leaps, &c., quickly.* (TA.) — وَثَبَى ▼ i. q. وَثَّابَةٌ; (Ḳ;) i. e., *That leaps, &c., quickly.* (TA.)

مُوثَبَانٌ *A king who sits still, and does not undertake military expeditions:* (Ṣ, Ḳ:) asserted to be of the dial. of Ḥimyer. (MF.)

مِيثَبٌ *A plain, or level, land, or tract of land.* (Ḳ.) — *A leaper, or jumper.* (IAạr, Ḳ.) — Also, [contr.,] *A sitter:* (IAạr, Ḳ:) [app. in the dial. of Ḥimyer]. — *What is elevated, of land.* (Ḳ.) — *A rivulet, stream, or streamlet:* syn. جَدْوَلٌ. (Ḳ.)

وثج

1. وَثُجَ, aor. يَوْثُجُ, inf. n. وَثَاجَةٌ; (Ṣ, Ḳ;) and ▼ اوثج, and ▼ استوثج; (TA;) *It* (anything, Ṣ,) *became dense; thick; compact.* (Ṣ, Ḳ.) — وَثُجَ, aor. يَوْثُجُ, inf. n. وَثَاجَةٌ, *He became abundant in flesh;* or very fleshy: وَثُرَ, inf. n. وَثَارَةٌ, signifying he became abundant in fat; or very fat: and both signify *he became bulky, or big; or large in body, corpulent and fleshy.* (AZ, Ṣ.) — وَثُجَ النَّبْتُ *The herbage, or plants, became dense, thick, or compact, and tall.*

4. أَوْثِجْ لَنَا مِنْ هٰذَا الطَّعَامِ *Give us much of this food.* (TA.) See 1.

10. استوثج *It became in a complete, or perfect, state:* (TA:) or *it became so in a certain way:* (Ṣ:) one says استوثج النَّبْتُ ‡ *the plants, herbs, or herbage, clung together, one part to another, and became in a complete, or perfect, state.* (Ṣ, Ḳ.) — See 1. — استوثج المَالُ *The property* [app. meaning camels or the like] *became much, or abundant.* (Ṣ, Ḳ.) — استوثج مِنَ المَالِ *He desired, wished for, or longed for, much of property* [app. meaning camels or the like]; syn. اِسْتَكْثَرَ: (Aṣ, Th, Ṣ, Ḳ*:) as also استوثق. (TA.) — استوثجت *She* (a woman) *became large in body, or corpulent and fleshy, and perfect in make.* (T.)

وَثِيجٌ Anything (Ṣ) *dense; thick; compact.* (Ṣ, Ḳ.) — A horse, (Ṣ,) and a camel, (TA,) *compact in flesh:* (Ṣ:) or *strong.* (TA.) — *Dense, thick, or compact,* herbage. (TA.) [See also ارض موثنجة.] — ثَوْبٌ وَثِيجٌ ‡ *A garment, or piece of cloth, of firm texture.* (A.) [See also ثياب موثوجة.]

وَاثِجٌ, applied to herbage, *Dense, thick, or compact, and tall.* (TA.)

أَرْضٌ مُوثَنْجَةٌ (in the CḲ مُؤْتَنْجَةٌ [which is evidently a mistake]) *Land abounding with herbage, or pasture,* (Ṣ, Ḳ,) *and with tangled trees;* as also وَثِيجَةٌ: (ISh:) *land of which the herbage is dense, thick, or compact.* (TA.) [See also وَثِيجٌ.]

ثِيَابٌ مُوثُوجَةٌ *Garments, or pieces of cloth, of which the threads and texture are slack, or loose.* (Ḳ, from Sh, on the authority of a man of Báhileh: but see وَثِيجٌ. TA.)

وثر

1. وَثُرَ, aor. ـُ, inf. n. وَثَارَةٌ; [and app., وَثْرٌ; (see the second signification;)] *It* (a thing, Ṣ, M, Mṣb, or a bed, A) *was, or became, plain, level, smooth, soft, or easy to lie or ride or walk upon.* (Ṣ, M, A, Mṣb, Ḳ.) — وَثُرَتِ العَجُزُ; and وَثَرَت, inf. n. as above, ‡ *The buttocks became fat.* (A.) See also وَثَارَةٌ, below. ═ وَثَرَهُ, (M, A, Ḳ,) aor. يَثِرُهُ, (Ḳ,) inf. n. وَثْرٌ (M, TA) and ثِرَةٌ; (TA;) and ▼ وثّره, inf. n. تَوْثِيرٌ; (M, A, Ḳ;) *He made it plain, level, smooth, soft, or easy to lie or ride or walk upon.* (M, A, Ḳ.) And وثّر مَرْكَبَهُ *He made the thing on which he rode smooth, soft, or easy to ride upon.* (A, Mṣb.)

2: see 1, in two places.

4. مَا أَوْثَرَ فِرَاشَكَ *How smooth, soft, or easy to lie upon, is thy bed!* (A, TA.)

10. استوثر الفِرَاشَ *He found, or deemed, the bed smooth, soft, or easy to lie upon.* (A,* TA.) — إِذَا تَزَوَّجْتَ آمْرَأَةً فَاسْتَوْثِرْهَا ‡ [*When thou takest a woman as thy wife, choose her fat, suitable for a bedfellow:* see وَثِيرٌ]. (A, TA.)

وَثْرٌ : see وَثِيرٌ.

وِثْرٌ : see وَثِيرٌ, in three places. — See also مِيثَرَةٌ, throughout.

وُثْرٌ : see وَثِيرٌ.

وُثَارٌ : see وِثَارٌ.

وِثَارٌ, a subst., *Plainness, levelness, smoothness, softness, or state of being easy to lie or ride or walk upon;* as also ▼ وُثَارٌ. (M, Ḳ.) ═ See also وَثِيرٌ, in two places.

وَثِيرٌ *Plain, level, smooth, soft, or easy to lie or ride or walk upon;* (T, Ṣ, M, A, Ḳ;) as also ▼ وِثْرٌ (T, Ṣ, Ḳ) and ▼ وَثْرٌ and ▼ وُثْرٌ; (M, Ḳ;) applied to a bed, (T, Ṣ, A, Ḳ,) and anything upon which one sleeps, (T, TA,) or sits, (TA,) and finds it to be thus, (T, TA,) and to other things: (M, Ḳ;) and *thick and soft;* applied to a bed: (Mṣb:) [and ▼ وِثَارٌ seems to signify the same; or this and ↑ وِثْرٌ are epithets in which the quality of a subst. predominates:] fem. وَثِيرَةٌ. (M Ḳ.) You say, مَا تَحْتَهُ وِثْرٌ, and وِثَارٌ, (Ṣ, TA,) *There is not beneath him a smooth*, or *soft*, *bed.* (TA.) — وَثِيرَةٌ ‡ A woman *having much flesh:* (IDrd, Ṣ, Mṣb, Ḳ:) or *fat;* (T, A, Ḳ;) *suitable for a bedfellow:* (T, Ḳ:) and وَثِيرَةُ العَجُزِ ‡ *large,* (T,) or *fat,* (A,) or *soft,* (M,) *in the buttocks:* (T, M, A:) pl. وِثَارٌ and وَثَائِرُ. (M, Ḳ.) — See also مِيثَرَةٌ, throughout.

وَثَارَةٌ: see 1. — ‡ *Abundance of fat:* (AZ, Ṣ:) or *of flesh:* (Ḳ:) or the latter is termed وَثَاجَةٌ. (AZ, Ṣ.)

أَوْثَرُ *More* [and *most*] *smooth,* or *soft;* applied to a bed. (TA, from a trad.)

مِيثَرَةٌ, (T, Ṣ, M, A, Mgh, Mṣb, Ḳ,) of the measure مِفْعَلَةٌ, from الوَثَارَةُ, (TA,) without hemz, (Ṣ, TA,) originally مِوْثَرَةٌ, (Mṣb,* TA,) the و being changed into ى because of the kesreh before it, (TA,) and ↑ وَثِيرٌ and ↑ وِثْرٌ, (Ḳ,) or [only] مِيثَرَةٌ, (TA, &c.,) of a horse's saddle, (T, M, A, Mgh, Mṣb, Ḳ,) and of a camel's saddle, (T,) *A thing in the form of a pillow, made for the saddle, like the* صُفَّة [q. v.], (M, Mgh, Ḳ,) *to render it soft,* or *easy to ride upon:* (T:) or the *saddle-cloth* or *housing* (لِبْدَة) of a horse: (Ṣ:) pl. مَوَاثِرُ and مَيَاثِرُ, (Ṣ, M, A, Mgh, Mṣb, Ḳ,) the latter agreeing with the sing., (Mṣb,) retaining the permuted letter, as is the case in أَعْيَادٌ, pl. of عِيدٌ. (IJ, M.) — Also, accord. to the Ḳ, [referring to the three words above,] or [correctly] the red مَيَاثِرُ, (المَيَاثِرُ الحُمْرُ,) which are forbidden to be used, (Ṣ, IAth, TA,) *Certain things to ride upon,* (مَرَاكِب, Ṣ, IAth, Ḳ, TA,) *used by the* أَعَاجِم, (Ṣ,) or عَجَم, (IAth, TA,) [meaning *Persians* or *other foreigners,*] *made of* دِيبَاج or حَرِير [*silk brocade* or *other silk*]: (Ṣ, IAth, Ḳ, TA:) or the red مِيثَرَة, (مِيثَرَةُ الأُرْجُوَانِ,) forbidden, in a trad., to be used, is *a stuffed thing to ride upon, which is put upon a camel's saddle:* (TA:) and the red مِيثَرة which is put upon a horse's saddle is included in the prohibition. (IAth, TA.) — Also, the first of the above three words, (M,) or all of them (Ḳ) *A garment* or *piece of cloth which is put as a covering over other garments* or *pieces of cloth.* (M, Ḳ.) — Also, (accord. to the Ḳ [referring to the three words above,] or [correctly] مَيَاثِرُ, (TA,) The *skins of beasts of prey.* (Ḳ, TA.)

[وثق &c.

See Supplement.]

وج

وَجٌّ *A kind of medicine;* (Ṣ, Ḳ;) *certain twigs,* or *rods, with which one fumigates;* (TA;) or *which are used medicinally* or *remedially;* (T;) [*acorum,* (Golius,) or *acorus; sweet-cane,* or, as some say, *galangal:* see Diosc., l. i., c. 2., referred to by Golius:] thought by El-Jawáleeḳee to be not pure Arabic; i. e., an arabicized word, from the Persian [وَج]: (TA:) so says J. (Ṣ.)

وجأ

1. وَجَأَ, (Ṣ, Mṣb, Ḳ,) aor. يَوْجَأُ, and sometimes يَجَأُ, (Mṣb,) inf. n. وَجْءٌ; (TA;) and ↑ توجّأ; (Ḳ;) *He beat,* or *struck,* or *smote,* a person with his hand, (Ṣ*, Ḳ,) or with a knife, (Ṣ, Mṣb, Ḳ,) or the like, on any part. (Mṣb.) — وَجَأَ عُنُقَهُ, inf. n. وَجْءٌ, *He beheaded him:* syn. ضَرَبَ عُنُقَهُ. (Ṣ.) — وَجَأَ ‡ Inivit feminam. (Ḳ.) — وَجَأَ التَّيْسَ, inf. n. وَجْءٌ and وِجَآءٌ, (or the latter is a simple subst., TA,) *He beat the veins of the testicles of the goat between two stones, without extracting the testicles themselves:* or *he bruised* or *beat the goat's testicles until they broke,* (Ḳ,) *and he became like one gelded.* (TA.) You say also وَجَأَ الكَبْشَ. (Ṣ.) [See وِجَآء.] وُجِئَ *He* (a goat) *had the operation termed* وَجْء *performed upon him.* (Ḳ.) — *He was struck* with a knife. (Ṣ.) — وَجَأَ ‡ *He bruised,* or *pounded,* dates *until they cohered.* Hence وَجِيئَةٌ, q. v. (TA.)

2: see 1. — وَجَّأَ الرَّكِيَّةَ, inf. n. تَوْجِئَةٌ, *He found the well to be what is termed* وَجْآءُ, [fem. of أَوْجَأُ, q. v.: app. signifying *without water*]. (Ḳ.)

4. اوجأ عَنْهُ *He repelled from him; removed,* or *put away, from him.* (Ḳ*, TA.) — اوجأ *He came in search of a thing that he wanted,* or *in pursuit of game, and did not attain it.* (Ḳ.) — *It* (a well) *failed;* i. e., *its water ceased:* or *it contained no water.* (TA.) [See also أَوْجَى.]

8. اِتَّجَأَ التَّمْرُ ‡ *The dates became closely packed,* or *pressed together:* (Ḳ:) *they were bruised,* or *pounded, until they cohered.* (TA.)

مَآءٌ وَجْءٌ, and ↑ وَجَأٌ, and ↑ وَجَآءٌ, *A water where there is no good:* (Ḳ:) [app., *a source of water where there is no herbage,* or *pasture;* or, more probably, *a source without water;* or *a water that has failed:* see 2 and 4.]

وَجَأٌ and وَجَآءٌ: see مَآءٌ وَجْءٌ.

وِجَآءٌ, a subst., *A striking* with a knife or the like, on any part. (Mṣb.) [See also 1.] — وِجَآءٌ The *bruising of the veins of the testicles until they break, so that it is like gelding.* (Ṣ.) [See also 1.]

وَجِيءٌ and ↑ مَوْجُوءٌ A goat *on which has been performed the operation called* وَجْء. (Ḳ.) [See 1.] — The latter is said to be used in a trad. as signifying *Gelded.* — Also the latter, *Struck* with a knife. (Ṣ.)

وَجِيئَةٌ † *Dates,* (Ḳ,) or *locusts,* (ISk, Ṣ, Ḳ,) *bruised,* or *pounded, and then stirred up with clarified butter* (سَمْن), *or with oil, and so eaten:* (Ṣ, Ḳ:) or *dates moistened with milk* or *with clarified butter, and then bruised,* or *pounded, until they are consolidated:* (TA:) or *dates bruised,* or *pounded, until the stones come forth, and then moistened with milk* or *with clarified butter so that they become macerated and cohering, in which state they are eaten.* (ISk, Ṣ.) — Also, *A cow.* (IAạr., Ḳ.)

مَوْجُوءٌ: see وَجِيءٌ.

وجب

1. وَجَبَ, aor. يَجِبُ, inf. n. وَجْبَةٌ (Lḥ, Ḳ) and وَجْبٌ (Lḥ) *It* (a wall, or the like, Mṣb, or a house, or anything, Lḥ,) *fell down.* (Lḥ, Ḳ, Mṣb.) See وَجْبَةٌ. — وَجَبَ, inf. n. وَجْبَةٌ, *It fell to the ground.* (TA.) — وَجْبَةٌ does not signify a single act; but is an inf. n. in an absolute sense, unrestricted to the signification of a single act: ex. وَجْبَةُ الشَّمْسِ *The falling of the sun, in setting.* (TA.) — فَإِذَا وَجَبَتْ جُنُوبُهَا [Ḳur. xxii. 37,] is said to signify *And when their sides fall down upon the ground:* or *and when their souls depart, and they fall down.* (TA.) — وَجَبَتِ الشَّمْسُ, (Ṣ, Ḳ,) inf. n. وَجْبٌ and وُجُوبٌ (Ḳ) and وَجْبَةٌ (see above), *The sun set.* (Ṣ, Ḳ.) — وَجَبَتِ العَيْنُ ‡ *The eye was,* or *became, sunk in the head.* (Ḳ.) — وَجَبَ, (Ṣ, Ḳ,) aor. يَجِبُ, inf. n. وُجُوبٌ and مَوْجِبٌ, (TA,) *He fell down and died:* (Ṣ:) *he died.* (Ḳ.) — Hudbeh Ibn-Khashram says,

* فَقُلْتُ لَهُ لَا تَبْكِ عَيْنُكَ إِنَّهُ *
* بِكَفَّيَّ مَا لَاقَيْتُ إِذْ حَانَ مَوْجِبِي *

[*And I said to him, Let not thine eye weep; for by my own hands is occasioned what I experience, now that my death has come to pass*]. By موجب he means مَوْتٌ. (TA.) — [See also وَجْبَةٌ, which seems to be a third inf. n. of the verb in this sense.] — وَجَبَ, (aor. يَجِبُ, TA,) inf. n. وَجِيبٌ (Th, Ṣ,) and وَجْبٌ and وَجَبَانٌ (Ḳ) and وُجُوبٌ and وَجْبَةٌ, (TA,) *It* (the heart) *palpitated, beat, throbbed;* (Ḳ;) *was agitated,* or *in a state of commotion.* (Ṣ.) — وَجَبَتِ الإِبِلُ, and ↑ وَجَّبَت, *The camels could scarcely arise from the places where they lay down.* (TA.) — وَجُبَ, [aor. يَوْجُبُ,] inf. n. وُجُوبَةٌ, *He was cowardly,* or *pusillanimous.* (Ṣ, Ḳ.) — وَجَبَهُ عَنْهُ *He drove him back,* or *turned him back, from it,* (Ḳ,) *when he had long kept to it.* (Nawádir el-Aạráb.)

—— وَجَبَ and ▾ اوجب and ▾ وجّب ‡ He (a man, TA,) ate once a day. (Th, Ḳ.) See وَجْبَةٌ. ═ وَجَبَ, aor. يَجِبُ, inf. n. وُجُوبٌ (Ṣ, Ḳ,) and جِبَةٌ, (Ḳ,) It (a thing) was, or became, necessitated, necessary, requisite, or unavoidable: it was binding, obligatory, incumbent, or due: syn. لَزِمَ; (Ṣ, Ḳ, Mṣb;) [lit. accord. to some, it fell on a person: see 4;] and ثَبَتَ, (Telweeḥ,) which means nearly the same as لَزِمَ. (TA.) —— For a fuller explanation, see its syn. حَقَّ. [In the science of the fundamentals of religion, It necessarily was or existed; was a thing of which the nonexistence could not be mentally conceived: as is the essence of God. (Ibr.D.)] —— وَجَبَ عَلَيْهِ كَذَا, or أَنْ يَفْعَلَ كَذَا, Such a thing, or the doing of such a thing, was binding, incumbent, or obligatory upon him; was unavoidable to him; lay on him; was his necessary, or indispensable duty: or was binding, incumbent, or obligatory upon him, by God's express appointment, so that he would be punished for neglecting it: and it was that which should be preferred and approved. See وَاجِبٌ.] —— See also another explanation, afterwards. —— وَجَبَ البَيْعُ, aor. يَجِبُ, inf. n. جِبَةٌ (Lḥ, Ṣ, Mṣb) and وُجُوبٌ (Lḥ, Mṣb) The sale was, or became, binding, or obligatory; (Mṣb, TA;) ratified, fixed, settled, decided, or determined; (Mṣb;) completed, accomplished, or concluded; it had, or took, effect; it was extended, or performed; or it was, or became, effectual: (TA:) and وَجَبَتْ بَيْعَتُهُ, i. q. بَتَّتْ, q. v. (M, in art. بت.) —— It is said in a trad., إِذَا كَانَ البَيْعُ عَنْ خِيَارٍ فَقَدْ وَجَبَ [When the sale is optional, it is binding, or obligatory]: i. e., when one says, after the contract, "Take thy choice to reject the sale, or to make it effectual," and the person so addressed chooses to do the latter, the sale is binding, even if the two parties have not yet separated. (TA.) —— In like manner, وَجَبَ الحَقُّ, inf. ns. as above, The right, due, or claim, was, or became, binding, or obligatory; or fixed, settled, decided, or determined. (Mṣb.) —— وجب الوجب, inf. n. وجب: (TA: [unexplained; but following وَجْبٌ as signifying "a bet, &c.:" app. meaning The bet, wager, or stake, became due, or incumbent]. —— [وَجَبَ عَلَيْهِ It was, or became, necessitated, necessary, requisite, or unavoidable, for him to do, or suffer, such a thing; and hence, sometimes, it was, or became, binding, obligatory, or incumbent, on him.] —— وَجَبَ عَلَيْهِ القَوْلُ [The saying or sentence became necessitated to take effect upon him; or it became requisite that the saying or sentence should take effect upon him.] Jel, in xxxvi. 6, &c. —— [وَجَبَ لَهُ كَذَا Such a thing was, or became, due to him; as, for instance, a reward, or a punishment.] —— وَجَبَ عَلَيْهِ القَتْلُ [Slaughter was, or became, his due.] (TA, in art. بقى, &c.)

2. وَجَّبَ بِهِ الأَرْضَ, inf. n. تَوْجِيبٌ, He threw him down upon the ground. (Ṣ.) —— وجّب, inf. n. تَوْجِيبٌ, The camel lay upon his breast with folded legs, falling down upon the ground. (TA.) —— وجّبت, inf. n. تَوْجِيبٌ, She (a camel) became milkless: (TA:) or [her biestings coagulated in her udder: see وَجْبٌ]. —— وجّب, (inf. n. تَوْجِيبٌ, Ḳ,) He was fatigued, tired, or weary: (Ṣ, Ḳ:) said of a camel. (Ṣ.) —— وجّب اللِّبَأُ, inf. n. تَوْجِيبٌ, The biestings coagulated in the udder. (Ḳ.) ═ وجّب, (inf. n. تَوْجِيبٌ, TA,) He milked (a camel, Ḳ,) but once in the course of each day and night. (Ṣ, Ḳ.) —— وجّب, inf. n. تَوْجِيبٌ, He accustomed himself, (Lḥ, Ṣ,) in which case you also say وجّب لِنَفْسِهِ, (Lḥ,) and his family, or household, and his horse, (Lḥ, Ḳ,) to eat but one meal (Ḳ) in the course of each day and night. (Lḥ, Ṣ.) —— See 1. ═ وجّب He took, got, or won, a bet, wager, or stake, at a shooting-match or race. (L, in TA, voce نَدَبٌ.) —— See 4.

3: see 4.

4. اوجبهُ, (Ṣ, Ḳ,) and ▾ وجّبهُ (Ḳ) but this latter is by some rejected, (TA,) He (God, Ṣ) made it, or rendered it necessary, requisite, or unavoidable; necessitated it; made it, or declared it to be, binding, incumbent, or obligatory: (Ṣ, Ḳ:) [lit. accord. to some, he made it to fall on a person: see فَرَضَ.] —— اوجب البَيْعَ, (Lḥ, Ṣ,) inf. n. إِيجَابٌ, (Lḥ,) He made, or rendered, or declared, the sale binding, or obligatory; (Mṣb, TA;) ratified it; made, or rendered, it fixed, settled, decided, or determined; (Mṣb;) completed, accomplished, or concluded; effectual. (TA.) —— اوجب لَكَ البَيْعَ He made the sale to thee to be binding, or obligatory; &c. (Lḥ, Ḳ.) —— In like manner, ▾ وَاجَبَهُ البَيْعَ, inf. n. مُوَاجَبَةٌ and وِجَابٌ; (Lḥ; in quoting whose words, the author of the Ḳ has made an omission, so as to cause it to appear that these two words are inf. ns. of اوجب; TA;) He, with his (another's) concurrence, made the sale to him to be binding, or obligatory; &c. (TA.) —— اوجب عَلَيْهِ شَيْئًا [He made a thing, or declared it to be, binding, obligatory, or incumbent, upon him; or unavoidable to him]. (TA.) —— اوجب عَلَيْهِ القَضَآءَ He necessitated the sentence to take effect upon him; syn. حَقَّقَهُ and أَحَقَّهُ. (TA, in art. حق.) —— اوجب He did a great sin, or an act of great goodness, making [the punishment of] hell, or [the reward of] paradise, the consequence thereof [unless followed by different conduct &c.]: (Ṣ, Ḳ:) he committed sins for which he who should punish him would be excusable, because he deserved punishment. (IAạr, in TA, art. لوط.) —— It is said, in a trad., that some persons came to Mohammad, saying, إِنَّ صَاحِبًا لَنَا أَوْجَبَ, i. e., Verily a companion of our's hath committed a sin for which he has become deserving of hell: to which he replied, Command him to emancipate a slave [as an expiation]. (TA.) —— In another trad. it is said, أَوْجَبَ ذُو الثَّلَاثَةِ وَالإِثْنَيْنِ, meaning, He of whom three children, or two, have gone before him [to paradise] hath become entitled to paradise. (TA.) —— أَوْجَبَ لَهُ الجَنَّةَ أَوِ النَّارَ It (an action) procured for him as a necessary consequence thereof [the reward of] paradise, or [the punishment of] hell; or made such to be to him a necessary consequence thereof; [unless followed by repentance &c.:] (Ṣ, Ḳ*:) [it required for him paradise or hell.] —— [يُوجِبُ كَذَا It necessitates, or renders necessary, such a thing. —— It requires such a thing, as a necessary consequence. —— It necessarily implies the coexistence of such a thing therewith. Used in physics &c., and perhaps in classical writings.] —— أَوْجَبْتُ لِفُلَانٍ حَقَّهُ means I regarded such a one's right or due: and you say فَعَلْتُ ذٰلِكَ إِيجَابًا لِحَقِّهِ [I did that from regard to his right or due] (Ḥar. p. 490); [and اوجبهُ لَهُ He made it, or declared it to be due to him]. —— [اوجبهُ also signifies He affirmed it, he averred it; i. q. أَثْبَتَهُ as contr. of نَفَاهُ. —— And It necessarily occasioned it.] ═ اوجب عَلَيْهِ He beat him, overcame him, in a case of laying a bet, wager, or stake, at a shooting-match or race. (TA.) ═ اوجب اللّٰهُ قَلْبَهُ God made his heart to palpitate, beat, or throb; [to be agitated, or in a state of commotion]. (Lḥ, Ḳ.) ═ See 1.

6. تَوَاجَبُوا They laid a bet, wager, or stake, one with another, at a shooting-match or race: as though one party of them made a thing binding, or obligatory, on another party of them. (TA.)

10. استوجبهُ He had a right or just title or claim, to it; deserved it; merited it: syn. اِسْتَحَقَّهُ [q. v.] (Ṣ, Ḳ.) See the act. part. n. below. —— استوجب إِثْمًا i. q. اِسْتَحَقَّهُ; (TA, in art. حق;) which means He did what necessitated sin; (Ksh, Bḍ, Jel, in v. 106;) [was guilty of a sin;] and deserved its being said of him that he was a sinner. (Ksh.) —— رَكِبَ خَطِيئَةً اسْتَوْجَبَ بِهَا النَّارَ [He committed a sin for which he became deserving of hell]. (TA.)

وَجْبٌ and ▾ مُوَجِّبٌ A she-camel whose biestings coagulate in her udder. (Ḳ.) —— وِجَابٌ Places in which water stagnates: (Ḳ:) pl. of وَجْبٌ. (TA.) —— وَجْبٌ A large skin of the kind called سِقَآء, made of the (complete, TA,) hide of a he-goat: pl. وِجَابٌ. (AḤn, Ḳ.) —— وَجْبٌ Stupid; foolish; of little sense. (Ḳ.) —— وَجْبٌ (Ṣ, Ḳ) and ▾ وَجَّابٌ (Ḳ) and ▾ وَجَّابَةٌ (IAạr, Ḳ) and ▾ مُوَجَّبٌ (IAạr) A coward; cowardly; pusillanimous. (Ṣ, Ḳ, &c.) [The second and third, and more especially the latter, are probably intensive epithets.] — وَجْبٌ *A bet, wager,* or *stake, at a shooting-match* (Lḥ, Ḳ) or *a race.* (IAạr; and L in TA, voce نَدَبٌ.)

وَجْبَةٌ inf. n. of وَجَبَ "it fell down, &c.," q. v. — بِجَنْبِهِ فَلْتَكُنِ الوَجْبَةُ, a proverb, (Ṣ,) [(*May a disease be*) *in his side,* or (*may God afflict him,* or *smite him, with a disease*) *in his side, and may falling down upon the ground, and dying, happen* (or *be the result thereof*)! i.e. رَمَاهُ ٱللّٰهُ بِجنبه داءٌ فلتكن الوجبة به or بِدَاءٍ بجنبه الخ. (Freytag, Arab. Prov. i. 156)]. — وَجْبَةٌ *A falling with a sound,* or *noise, such as that produced by the fall of a wall* or *the like:* (Ṣ, Ḳ:) [see 1, where it is given as an inf. n. unrestricted to the signification of a single act:] or the *sound of a thing falling* (Ḳ) *and producing a sound such as above mentioned.* (TA.) — وَجْبَةٌ *An eating but once in the course of a day and night:* (Ṣ, Ḳ:) or *an eating but once in a day until the like eating in the following day:* (Ḳ:) an inf. n. (Lḥ) [restricted to the signification of a single act]: you say, فُلَانٌ يَأْكُلُ وَجْبَةً *Such a one eats but once* (T) *in the course of the day and night.* (AZ, Ṣ.) [See also صَيْرَمٌ.] — In a trad. respecting the expiation of an oath, it is said, يُطْعِمُ عَشَرَةَ مَسَاكِينَ وَجْبَةً وَاحِدَةً [*He shall feed ten poor men with a meal sufficient for a day and a night*]. (TA.)

وُجَابٌ: see وُجُوبٌ.

وَجِيبَةٌ *A daily allowance of food:* or *daily maintenance:* syn. وَظِيفَةٌ: (Ḳ:) i. e., *what a man is accustomed to allow himself* [*each day*] *as that which is necessary, and fixed:* but the word in the A is وَجْبَةٌ, q. v. (TA.) — وَجِيبَةٌ [*A term employed in the case of*] *one's concluding a sale, and then taking it* [*meaning what is sold to him*] *by regular successive portions, one after another,* (AA, Ṣ, Ḳ,) or, as some say, *on the condition of his taking a portion of it every day,* (TA,) *until he has taken the whole of his* وَجِيبَة: (Ḳ:) [which hence appears to signify both the act above described and also *what is due to one of a thing purchased and taken in this manner;* but more probably the latter is the only meaning intended]. When a person has finished doing this, one says to him قَدِ ٱسْتَوْفَيْتَ وَجِيبَتَكَ [*Thou hast taken the whole of what was due to thee of the thing purchased and taken by thee in the manner above described*]. (Ṣ.)

[وُجُوبِىٌّ *Obligatory,* or *incumbent:* opposed to ٱمْتِنَاعِىٌّ.]

وَجَّابٌ and وَجَّابَةٌ: see وَجْبٌ.

وَاجِبٌ *Slain:* (Ṣ:) *dying;* or *dead.* (TA.) So in the following verse of Ḳeys Ibn-El-Khaṭeem:

* أَطَاعَتْ بَنُو عَوْفٍ أَمِيرًا نَهَاهُمُ *
* عَنِ السِّلْمِ حَتَّى كَانَ أَوَّلَ وَاجِبِ *

[*The sons of 'Owf obeyed a commander who forbade them to make peace until he was the first who was slain,* or *who died*]. (Ṣ, TA.) — وَاجِبٌ [act. part. n. of وَجَبَ; *Necessary; requisite; unavoidable: binding, incumbent,* or *obligatory.* In the science of the fundamentals of religion, *Necessarily being* or *existing; of which the nonexistence cannot be mentally conceived:* as the essence of God. (IbrD.)] — Accord. to [the Imám] Aboo-Ḥaneefeh, وَاجِبٌ [in matters of religion] is not so strong a term as فَرْضٌ: [and so may be rendered *incumbent,* or *obligatory;* or *that which is a necessary,* or *indispensable, duty; yet not so decisively* or *manifestly shown to be such as that which is termed* فرض:] or, accord. to Esh-Sháfi'ee, these two terms are syn., signifying [*binding, incumbent,* or *obligatory, by God's express appointment, as*] *a thing for neglecting which one will be punished:* and واجب signifies *that which should be preferred and approved;* thus explained by El-Khaṭṭábee as occurring in the following trad.: غُسْلُ ٱلْجُمُعَةِ وَاجِبٌ عَلَى كُلِّ مُحْتَلِمٍ *The ablution prescribed to be performed on Friday is an act which every one who has experienced a nocturnal pollution should prefer and approve.* (TA.) — فِعْلٌ وَاجِبٌ [*A verb expressing an event as a positive fact*] is such, for instance, as in the phrase بَيْنَمَا أَنَا كَذَا إِذْ جَآءَ زَيْدٌ [while I was thus, or in this state, lo, or behold, Zeyd came]. (Ṣ, L, art. اذ.)

مُوجَبٌ *An effect; that which is produced by an operating cause; a result; a consequence.* (Mṣb.) — [كَلَامٌ مُوجَبٌ, lit. *An affirmed sentence;* i. q. مُثْبَتٌ as contr. of مَنْفِىٌّ; virtually *the same as* ▼ كَلَامٌ مُوجِبٌ, *an affirmative sentence.*]

[مُوجِبٌ *A place where one falls down and dies; where one dies*]. — خَرَجَ ٱلْقَوْمُ إِلَى مَوَاجِبِهِمْ, i. e. إِلى مَصَارِعِهِمْ; *The people went forth to the places where they should be prostrated;* or, *as implied in the Ṣ, where they should fall down and die;* or *where they should die*]. (Ṣ.) — مُوجِبٌ [and ▼ مُوجِبَةٌ] *A cause; an efficient; that which produces,* or *effects, anything.* (Mṣb.) — See كَلَامٌ مُوجَبٌ. — مُوجِبٌ *A name of the month* ٱلْمُحَرَّمُ (Ḳ) *in ancient times.* (TA.)

مُوجِبَةٌ *A great sin for which one deserves punishment* [*in the world to come*]: (TA:) or *a great sin, and also an act of great goodness, which makes* [*the punishment of*] *hell,* or [*the reward of*] *paradise, the consequence thereof unless followed by repentance &c.*] (Ḳ.) — اللّٰهُمَّ إِنِّى أَسْأَلُكَ مُوجِبَاتِ رَحْمَتِكَ [*O God, I ask of thee those things which will procure thy mercy!*]. (TA, from a trad.) — See مُوجِبٌ.

مُوَجِّبٌ One *who eats but once in the course of a day and a night.* (AZ, Ṣ.) — مُوَجِّبٌ A beast of carriage *that is frightened at everything.* (ISd.) Not known to AM. (TA.) — See وَجْبٌ in two places.

ٱللّٰهُ مُسْتَوْجِبُ ٱلْحَمْدِ *God is worthy,* or *deserving, of praise; has a right,* or *just title* or *claim, to it; deserves it; merits it:* syn. هُوَ وَلِيُّهُ, and مُسْتَحِقُّهُ. (TA.)

وجع

1. وَجَعَ, aor. يَوْجَعُ, inf. n. وَجْعٌ, *He had recourse,* or *betook himself,* to a thing or place, *for protection* or *concealment.* (L.) [As also ▼ وَجَّعَ.] See 4.

2: see 4.

4. اوجعه إِلَيْهِ *He compelled* or *constrained* or *necessitated him to have recourse to,* or *to betake himself to, him* or *it for protection* or *concealment* or *the like.* (Ḳ.) — اوجع ٱلْبَيْتَ *He curtained the house,* or *chamber,* or *tent;* (Ḳ, TA;) *hung a curtain upon it.* (TA.) — اوجع *He held fast, and defended,* a thing. (L.) — اوجع, (L, Ḳ,) and ▼ وَجَّعَ, (Ḳ, TA,) or ▼ وَجَعَ, (as in the L and CḲ,) *It* (a thing) *appeared; became apparent.* (L, Ḳ.) — اوجع لَنَا ٱلطَّرِيقُ *The road became apparent* or *conspicuous to us.* (Ṣ.) — اوجعتِ ٱلنَّارُ *The fire became apparent* or *conspicuous.* (Ṣ.) — اوجع *He reached,* in digging, *smooth rock,* (Ṣ, Ḳ,) which is called وَجَاحٌ. (Ḳ.) — اوجعهُ ٱلْبَوْلُ *The urine oppressed him by his wanting to void it.* (Ṣ, L, Ḳ.)

وَجْعٌ *A place to which one has recourse for protection* or *concealment; a place of refuge; an asylum:* (L:) [as also ▼ وَجَعٌ:] *a place resembling a* غار [or *cave in a mountain*]. (L, K.)

وِجَاحٌ and وُجَاحٌ and وَجَاحٌ, (Ṣ, L, Ḳ,) of which three forms IAạr prefers the first, (L,) and sometimes the و is changed into ا, and one says إِجَاحٌ and أُجَاحٌ and أَجَاحٌ, (Ṣ,) and in one dial. وجاحِ, indecl., with kesreh for its termination, (L,) and جَاحٌ, (Ḳ, in art. جوح,) *A thing by which a person* or *thing is veiled, concealed,* or *hidden; a veil; a covering; a curtain.* (Ṣ, L, Ḳ.) — جَآءَ فُلَانٌ وَمَا عَلَيْهِ وِجَاحٌ *Such a one came having upon him nothing to veil*, or *conceal, him*. (L.) — لَيْسَ دُونَهُ وَجَاحٌ *There is nothing that veils*, or *conceals, before*, or *in the way to, him*, or *it*. (L.) — لَيْسَ بَيْنِى وَبَيْنَهُ وَجَاحٌ *There is nothing that veils*, or *conceals, between me and him*, or *it*. (L.) — وَجَاحٌ *Water in a tank* or *cistern sufficient to cover its bottom*. (Ṣ.) — وَجَاحٌ The *remains* of a thing, such as property, &c. (Az.) — لَقِيتُهُ أَدْنَى وَجَاحٍ *I met him, he being the first object that I saw*. (Ṣ, Ḳ.) = *Smooth rock*. (Ḳ.)

وُجَاحٌ: وِجَاحٌ: أُجَاحٌ: أَجَاحٌ: إِجَاحٌ: وِجاحٌ: جَاحٌ: see وَجَاحٌ.

وَجِحٌ: see مُوجَحٌ.

مُوجَحٌ A garment *closely woven*, (Ṣ, Ḳ,) *and firm*: (Ṣ:) or *of close texture, and thick*: or *strong*: or *narrow and firm*: (TA:) as also ▼ وَجِحٌ: (Ṣ, Ḳ, TA:) from أَوْجَحَهُ البَوْلُ. (Ṣ.) — مُوجَحٌ *A smooth skin*. (Ḳ.) = مُوجَحٌ *Constrained, compelled*, or *necessitated, to have recourse to*, or *to betake himself to, a thing* or *place, for protection* or *concealment* or *the like*; syn. مُلْجَأٌ. (L, Ḳ, TA [in the CḲ مُلْجَأً, which is the signification of وَجَحٌ]) Az says, that the word which he retains in his memory is مُنْحَجٌ, with the ح before the ج; and that the two words may be two dial. forms. = مُوجَحٌ, or ▼ مُوجِحٌ, accord. to two different relations of a trad. in which it occurs, *Oppressed by the want to void his urine*. (L.)

مُوجِحٌ One *who veils*, or *conceals*, or *hides*, a *thing*. (L.) = See مُوجَحٌ.

بَابٌ مُوجَوجٌ *A closed door*: (Ṣ, Ḳ:) or *a door before which is a curtain*. (TA.)

طَرِيقٌ مُوجِحٌ *A conspicuous, open, wide road*. (L.)

وجد

1. وَجَدَهُ, aor. يَجِدُ and يَجُدُ, (Ṣ, L, Mṣb, Ḳ,) the latter of the dial. of the tribe of 'Ámir (Ṣ, L, Mṣb) Ibn-Ṣaṣa'ah, (MF,) and without a parallel (Ṣ, L, Mṣb, Ḳ) in verbs of this class, (Ṣ, L, Mṣb,) the و in it being dropped because it falls out in the original form of the aor., (Mṣb,) both of which forms are said by several authors to apply to the verb in all its significations, though F seems to restrict the latter to two significations, (TA,) inf. n. وُجُودٌ (Ṣ, L, Mṣb, Ḳ) and وِجْدَانٌ (L, Mṣb, Ḳ,) and إِجْدَانٌ, (IAạr, L, Ḳ,) in which the و is changed into ء, (L,) and وَجْدٌ and وُجْدٌ and جِدَةٌ; (L, K;) and وَجِدَهُ, aor. يَجِدُ; (Ḳ;) but this form of the verb is not found in the lexicons, [the Ḳ only accepted,] (MF,) in the sense here assigned to it; (TA;) *He found it; lighted on it; attained it; obtained it by searching* or *seeking; discovered it; perceived it; saw it; experienced it*, or *became sensible of it*; (F, in the Ḳ and in the Baṣáïr, on the authority of Abu-l-Ḳásim El-Iṣbahánee;) namely, a thing sought, sought for or after, or desired; (Ṣ, L, Ḳ;) and simply a thing. (L.) وُجُود is of several kinds. It is The *finding, &c., by means of any one of the five senses*: as when one says وَجَدْتُ زَيْدًا [*I found, &c., Zeyd*]: and وَجَدْتُ طَعْمَهُ, and رَائِحَتَهُ, and صَوْتَهُ, and خُشُونَتَهُ, [*I found*, or *perceived, &c., its taste*, and *its odour*, and *its sound*, and *its roughness*]. Also, The *finding, &c., by means of the faculty of appetite*, [*or rather of sensation*, which is the cause of appetite:] as when one says وَجَدْتُ الشِّبَعَ [*I found, experienced*, or *became sensible of, satiety*]. Also, The *finding, &c., by the intellect*, or *by means of the intellect*: of which kind is one's knowing God: and here it should be observed, that وجود attributed to God is simple knowledge: (Abu-l-Ḳásim El-Iṣbahánee, cited in the Baṣáïr:) وَجَدَ اللّٰهُ, wherever it occurs, means *God knew*. (Er-Rághib, Z, &c.) i.e., in the Ḳur-án. (TA.) — وَجَدَ [*He found, in the sense of*] *he knew* [*by experience*]. (A, TA, &c.) [In this sense, it is a verb of the kind called أَفْعَالُ القُلُوبِ; having two objective complements; the first of which is called its noun, and the second its predicate.] Ex. وَجَدْتُ زَيْدًا ذَا الحِفَاظِ *I* [*found*, or] *knew Zeyd to possess the quality of defending those things which should be sacred*, or *inviolable*. (A.) Used in this sense, as doubly trans., its inf. n. is وِجْدَانٌ (Akh) and وُجُودٌ. (Seer.) It is also used as singly trans., as syn. with عَلِمَ. (TA.) — When وَجَدَ signifies *he found*, or *lighted on*, a thing after it had gone away, its inf. n. is وِجْدَانٌ. (IḲṭṭ.) — وَجَدَ الضَّالَّةَ, (Ṣ, A, Mṣb,) aor. يَجِدُ (Mṣb) and يَجُدُ, (MF,) inf. n. وِجْدَانٌ (Ṣ, Mṣb) and وُجْدٌ (Mṣb) [*He found the stray beast*]. — لَمْ أَجِدْ مِنْ ذٰلِكَ بُدًّا, for which one also says لَمْ أَجِدْ, *I found no means of avoiding*, or *escaping, that*. (Ḳz, TA.) — وَجَدَ, (L,) and وَجَدَ فِى المَالِ, (Fs, T, Ṣ, L, Mṣb,) and وَجَدَ المَالَ وَغَيْرَهُ, (Lḥ, M, Ḳ,) aor. يَجِدُ, (Lḥ, M, L, Ḳ,) inf. n. وُجْدٌ and وَجْد and وِجْدٌ and جِدَةٌ (Lḥ, T, Ṣ, M, Ḳ) and وِجْدَانٌ (T, L) and وُجُود, (Yz,) *He became possessed of wealth*, or *property*: (T:) or *he was*, or *became, rich; possessed of competence*, or *sufficiency; in no need; without wants*, or *with few wants*; (Ṣ, M, L, Ḳ;) *so as not to be poor afterwards*: (L:) and *he gained, acquired*, or *earned wealth*. (Exps. of the Fs.) Hence the saying of the Arabs, وُجْدَانُ الرِّقِينِ يُغَطِّى أَفَنَ الأَفِينِ [*The possession of money hides the weakness of judgment of the weak in judgment*]. (T, L.) = وَجَدَ عَلَيْهِ, (Ṣ, L, Ḳ, &c.) aor. يَجِدُ (Fs, M, L, Ḳ) and يَجُدُ; (M, L, Ḳ;) and وَجِدَ, as heard by Fr from certain of the Arabs; (Ḳzz;) inf. n. مَوْجِدَةٌ, (Fs, Ṣ, A, L, Mṣb, Ḳ,) by some pronounced مُوجِدَةٌ, (Fr,) and وَجْدٌ and جِدَةٌ (L, Ḳ) and وِجْدَانٌ (Lḥ, Ṣ, M, L) and وُجُودٌ (Fr, Ḳzz) *He was angry with him*: (Fs, Ṣ, A, L, Mṣb, Ḳ) or *he was angry with him with the anger that proceeds from a friend*. (TA, voce عَتْبٌ.) = وَجَدَ بِهِ, (aor. يَجِدُ, L,) inf. n. وَجْدٌ, *He loved him*. (L, Ḳ.) وَجَدَ بِهَا, (A, L,) and ▼ تَوَجَّدَ, (A,) *He loved her*; (A, L;) *he loved her passionately* or *fondly*. (L.) لَهُ بِهَا وَجْدٌ *He has a love* [or *passionate* or *fond love*] *for her*. (A.) = وَجَدَ, [aor. يَجِدُ,] ('Eyn, Fs, Ṣ, L, Mṣb, &c.,) and وَجَدَ, [aor. يَوْجَدُ,] (El-Hejeree, M, Ḳ,) the latter the only form mentioned in the Ḳ, but the former is the only form generally known, (MF, TA,) and وَجِدَ, (Lḥ, M, L,) inf. n. وَجْدٌ, (Ṣ, L, Mṣb, Ḳ, &c.,) *He grieved; mourned; sorrowed*. (Ṣ, L, Mṣb, Ḳ, &c.) You say, وَجَدْتُ بِهِ, (Mṣb,) and ▼ تَوَجَّدتُ لَهُ, (Ṣ, L,) *I grieved, mourned*, or *sorrowed, for such a one*. (Ṣ, L, Mṣb.) Ibn-Hishám El-Lakhmee says, that in this sense وجد is not transitive: (MF:) [i. e., without a prep.]. = وُجِدَ, (inf. n. وُجُودٌ, A, Mṣb,) *It existed; it became existent* (A, Mṣb) from a state of nonexistence. (Ṣ, L, Ḳ.)

4. اوجدهُ إِيَّاهُ *He* (God, Ṣ, A, L) *made him to find, attain*, or *obtain, it*; (Lḥ, Ṣ, A, L, Ḳ;) namely, the thing that he sought, sought for or after, or desired; (Ṣ, L, Ḳ;) or a stray beast. (A.) — اوجدهُ *He* (God, Ṣ, &c.) *enriched him; made him to be possessed of wealth* or *property; to be possessed of competence* or *sufficiency; to be in no need*, or *without wants*, or *with few wants*. (Ṣ, A, L, Ḳ.) Ex. الحَمْدُ لِلّٰهِ الَّذِى أَوْجَدَنِى بَعْدَ فَقْرٍ وَآجَدَنِى بَعْدَ ضَعْفٍ *Praise be to God who enriched me after poverty and strengthened me after weakness*. (Ṣ, L.) — *He strengthened him after weakness*; like آجَدَهُ. (Ḳ.) [But see what immediately precedes.] = اوجدهُ, (inf. n. إِيجَادٌ, TA,) *He* (God) *made it*; meaning, *created it; originated it; caused it to*

be or exist, or to come to pass; brought it into existence (Ṣ, L, Mṣb, Ḳ) from a state of non-existence, (Mṣb,) not after the similitude of anything preëxisting. (TA.) وَجَدَهُ in this sense is not allowable. (Ṣ, L, Ḳ.)

5. تَوَجَّدَهُ *He complained of it;* namely, sleeplessness by night, (L, Ḳ,) &c., (Ḳ,) or a particular affair. (L.) ═ See 1, in two places.

6. تواجد *He feigned,* or *made a show of, love* [or *passionate love*]. (A.)

وَجْدٌ and جِدَةٌ: see وُجْدٌ; and see 1.

وُجْدٌ and ▼ وِجْدٌ and ▼ وَجْدٌ [and ▼ جِدَةٌ &c., see 1,] (the first of which is the most chaste, IKh, MF) *Richness,* or *competence,* or *sufficiency; state of being in no need,* or *of having no wants,* or *few wants:* (M, L, Ḳ:) *ability; capacity; power.* (M, L.) — هٰذَا مِنْ وُجْدِى *This is a result of my power,* or *ability.* (L.)

وَاجِدٌ, act. part. n of 1, *Finding;* or *a finder; &c.* (L.) — *Rich; possessing competence,* or *sufficiency; in no need; without wants,* or *with few wants;* (L;) *solvent; one who finds that wherewith to pay what he owes.* (A'Obeyd, L.) Ex. لَىُّ الوَاجِدِ يُحِلُّ عُقُوبَتَهُ *The solvent man's putting off the payment of his debt with promises repeated time after time makes his punishment allowable.* (L, from a trad. See Mgh art. لوى.) الوَاجِدُ, as an epithet applied to God, *He who has no wants.* (IAth, L.) ═ هُوَ وَاجِدٌ عَلَى صَاحِبِهِ *He is angry with his companion.* (A.) ═ أَنَا وَاجِدٌ لِلشَّىْءِ *I am able to do the thing.* (Mṣb.) ═ هُوَ وَاجِدٌ بِفُلَانَةَ, and عَلَيْهَا, and ▼ مُتَوَجِّدٌ, *He is in love* [or *passionately in love*] *with such a female.* (A.) — وُجْدٌ is mentioned in the Towsheeḥ as a pl. of وَاجِدٌ; but this is strange. (TA.)

مَوْجُودٌ, part. n. of وُجِدَ, *Being,* or *existing; come to pass:* (Ṣ, L, Ḳ:) or, as an irreg. pass. part. n. of أَوْجَدَهُ, *caused to be,* or *exist;* or *to come to pass; brought into existence:* (MF:) pl. مَوْجُودَاتٌ: which is a term applied to three kinds of things: namely, that which exists and has neither beginning nor end; and such is only God: that which exists and has a beginning and an end; as the substances of the present world: and that which exists and has a beginning but no end; as men in the world to come. (TA.) — [*Present.*] — مَوْجُودٌ A thing *within one's power; over which one has power.* (Mṣb.)

مُتَوَجِّدٌ: see وَاجِدٌ.

وجذ

وَجْذٌ *A small,* or *round, hollow,* or *cavity, in a mountain,* (Ṣ, L, Ḳ,) *in which water collects,* (Ṣ,) or *which retains water,* (L, Ḳ,) *and in which it stagnates:* (L:) or *a pool:* (L:) and (some say, TA) *a tank,* or *cistern:* (Ḳ:) pl. وِجَاذٌ (Ṣ, L, Ḳ) and وِجْذَانٌ. (L, Ḳ.)

مَكَانٌ وَجِذٌ *A place abounding with* وِجَاذ, pl. of وَجْذٌ. (Ḳ.)

وجر

1. وَجَرَهُ, (Ṣ, Mgh, Mṣb, Ḳ,) and وَجَرَهُ دَوَآءً, (AZ, A,) [or وُجُورًا,] aor. يَجِرُهُ, (Mṣb,) inf. n. وَجْرٌ; (AZ, Ḳ;) and ▼ أَوْجَرَهُ, [which is the more common,] (Ṣ, A, Mgh, Mṣb, TA,) and اوجره دَوَآءً, or وُجُورًا, (TA,) inf. n. إِيجَارٌ; (Mṣb;) *He put,* or *poured, medicine into his* (a child's, Ṣ, or sick person's, Mṣb) *mouth;* (AZ, Ḳ;) *into any part of his mouth:* (ISk, ISd:) or *into the middle of his mouth:* (Ṣ, Mgh:) or *into his fauces:* (Mṣb:) *with a* مِيجَرَة: (A:) and اوجره المَآءَ [*he poured the water into his mouth:* or *into the middle of his mouth:* or *into his fauces*]. (A'Obeyd.) — وَجَرَهُ الرُّمْحَ; (IKṭṭ;) or ▼ أَوْجَرَهُ الرُّمْحَ, (A'Obeyd, Ṣ, A, Ḳ,) which latter only is allowable; (A'Obeyd, Ṣ;) or the latter is what is commonly known, but the former may be a dial. form thereof; (IAth;) and أَوْجَرَهُ بِالرُّمْحِ; (Lth;) ‡ *He pierced him in his mouth with the spear:* (A, Ḳ:) or *in his breast,* or *chest:* (Lth, Ṣ, IKṭṭ;) and وَجَرَهُ بِالسَّيْفِ, inf. n. وَجْرٌ, occurs in a trad., signifying, ‡ *he pierced him with the sword.* (IAth, TA.) — And in like manner you say, ▼ أَوْجَرَهُ الغَيْظَ ‡ [app. *He infused into him wrath,* or *rage*]. (A'Obeyd, TA.) — Also, وَجَرَهُ, aor. يَجِرُهُ, inf. n. وَجْرٌ, ‡ *He made him to hear what he disliked,* or *hated:* (Ḳ, TA:) but the form commonly known is ▼ أَوْجَرَهُ, as A'Obeyd says. (TA.)

4: see 1, throughout.

5. تَوَجَّرَ *He swallowed* a medicine (Ḳ, TA) *by little and little,* or *by degrees.* (TA.) — *He drank* water *against his will.* (Aboo-Kheyreh, Ḳ.)

8. إِتَّجَرَ, (Ṣ, Ḳ,) originally إِوْتَجَرَ, (Ṣ,) *He physicked himself with the medicine termed* وَجُور. (Ṣ, TA.)

وَجْرٌ and وِجَارٌ and وَجَارٌ The *hole,* or *den,* (جُحْر, A, Ḳ,) or *subterranean habitation,* (سَرَب, T, Ṣ,) of the hyena, (T, Ṣ, A, Ḳ,) &c., (A, Ḳ,) or, and the like, (T,) such as the lion, and the wolf, and the fox, and the like: (M, TA:) pl. [of pauc.] أَوْجِرَةٌ and [of mult.] وُجُرٌ. (Ḳ.) A poet uses the expression كِلَابُ وِجَارٍ, applying وجار metaphorically to the place of the dog: but it is not improbable that the correct relation may be ضِبَاعُ وِجَارٍ: though it may be allowable to call hyenas كِلَاب, as her young ones are called جِرَآء. (M.)

وَجُورٌ (Ṣ, A, Mgh, Mṣb, Ḳ) and وُجُورٌ (Ḳ) *Medicine which is put,* or *poured, into the mouth;* (Ḳ;) *into any part of the mouth:* (ISk, ISd:) or *into the middle of the mouth:* (Ṣ, Mgh:) or *into the fauces:* (Mṣb:) or *into the middle of the fauces:* (TA:) of a child, Ṣ, TA, or sick person; (Mṣb;) with a مِيجَرَة. (A.) — Also the former, ‡ [*A thing which one is made to hear and which he dislikes,* or *hates:*] a subst. from وَجَرَهُ in the last of the senses explained above. (Ḳ.)

مِيجَرٌ (Ṣ, Ḳ) and مِيجَرَةٌ (A, Ḳ) *A thing like the* مُسْعُط, *with which medicine is put,* or *poured,* (Ṣ, Ḳ,) *into the mouth,* (Ḳ,) or *into the middle of the mouth,* (Ṣ,) [or *into the fauces.*]

وجز

1. وَجُزَ, ـُ, inf. n. وَجَازَةٌ (A, Mṣb, TA) and وَجْزٌ, (M, TA,) [*It* (an expression, or speech, or language,) *was brief,* or *concise:* or] *it* (an expression) *was brief, and quickly intelligible:* (Mṣb:) or *it* (a man's speech) *was of few words;* (A;) as also ▼ أَوْجَزَ, said of language: (A, Ḳ:) or both signify *it* (language) *was of few words, with eloquence.* (M, TA.) — وَجُزَ فِى مَنْطِقِهِ, aor. ـُ; (A, Ḳ;) or فِى كَلَامِهِ; (Mṣb;) and وَجَزَ فِيهِ, aor. يَجِزُ; inf. n. وَجَازَةٌ; (A, Ḳ;) of the former verb; (TA;) and [of the latter] وَجْزٌ and وُجُوزٌ; (A, Ḳ;) and ▼ اوجز فيه; (Mṣb;) [*He was brief,* or *concise, in his speech,* or *language; contr. of* أَطْنَبَ: or] *he was of few words in his speech:* (A, Ḳ:*) or *he was brief, and quickly intelligible, in his language:* (Mṣb:) or ▼ اوجز signifies *he was quick and brief* in speaking. (Nh, TA.) See this latter verb below. ═ وَجَزَ اللَّفْظَ: see 4.

4: see 1, in four places. ═ اوجز اللفظ [*He made the expression brief,* or *concise;* and in like manner, the speech, or language: or] *he made the expression brief, and quickly intelligible;* as also ▼ وَجَزَهُ, aor. يَجِزُهُ: (Mṣb:) or اوجز كَلَامَهُ, (A, Ḳ,) inf. n. إِيجَازٌ, (A,) *he made his language to be of few words:* (A, Ḳ:) or اوجز الكَلَامَ *he abridged the language;* (Ṣ;) *i. q.* اِخْتَصَرَهُ; though there is a logical distinction between the two, for the mention of which this is not the place: (M, TA:) the difference is said to be this; that the former signifies *he expressed the correct meaning concisely, without regard to the original words;* and the latter, "he curtailed the words, preserving the meaning." (MF, in art. خصر.) — اوجز العَطِيَّةَ *He made the gift prompt,* or *speedy:* (A, Ḳ:) or *he made the gift little,* or *small.* (L, TA.) ═ اوجز عَلَى القَتِيلِ *He hastened and completed,* or *made certain, the slaughter of the slain man; i. q.* أَجْهَزَ عَلَيْهِ. (Abu-l-Miḳdám Es-Sulamee, in TA, art. نجز.)

5. توجّز الشىءَ *He sought, asked, or demanded, the accomplishment of the thing*; syn. تَنَجَّزَهُ: (Ṣ, Ḳ:) *he sought, asked, or demanded, it*; syn. اِلْتَمَسَهُ; (Ḳ;) *and asked for its accomplishment*; تنجّزه meaning اِلْتَمَسَهُ وَسَأَلَ نَجَازَهُ. (TA.)

وَجْزٌ *Quickness; speed; haste.* (TA.) As an epithet, applied to a man, (TA,) *Quick of motion* (Ḳ, TA) *in that which he begins*: (TA:) fem. with ة: (Ḳ:) and *quick*, applied to a camel. (TA.) — Also, applied to a man, (TA,) *Prompt, or quick, in giving.* (Ḳ.) — Also, وَجْزٌ (Ṣ, Ḳ) and ↓ وَجِيزٌ (Ṣ, A, Mṣb) and ↓ وَاجِزٌ (TA) and ↓ مُوجَزٌ (Ṣ, Ḳ) and ↓ مُوجِزٌ, (Ṣ,) applied to an expression, (Mṣb,) or language, (Ṣ, A, Ḳ, TA,) [*Brief, or concise*:] or *brief, or quickly intelligible*: (Mṣb:) or *consisting of few words*: (A, TA:) or *abridged*: (Ṣ:) or *light, or easy*, (خَفِيفٌ, Ḳ, TA,) *and keeping within just, or moderate, bounds*: (TA:) and all these epithets (all but the last accord. to the Ḳ, and the last also accord. to the TA,) are likewise applied to the thing, or an affair, [app. meaning, *small, or slight, or the like*:] (Ḳ, TA:) and the first is also applied to a gift, and to beneficence, meaning, *little*, or *small*. (TA.)

وَجِيزٌ: }
وَاجِزٌ: } see وَجْزٌ, in two places.

مُوجَزٌ and مُوجِزٌ: see وَجْزٌ, in two places. — موجز: [so in the L and TA: it may be either مُوجَزٌ or مُوجِزٌ:] *One of the names of* [*the month of*] صَفَر: [app. for one or other of the reasons mentioned voce صَفَرٌ:] thought by ISd, to be an appellation used in the time of the tribe of 'Ád [who are also said to have called this month نَاجِرٌ]. (L, TA.)

مِيجَازٌ [*Brief, or concise, in speech*;] a man *who uses few words in speech and in reply*, &c. (IDrd, Ḳ,* TA.)

وجس

1. وَجَسَ, aor. يَجِسُ, inf. n. وَجْسٌ and وَجَسَانٌ, *He was frightened at some sound, or other thing, that fell into his mind, or ear.* (TḲ.) [See also وَجْسٌ, below; and see 4, and 5.] This combination of letters generally denotes the perception of a thing of which one bears not any sound. (Ṣgh.) — وَجَسَ الشَّىْءُ, [aor. app. as above,] inf. n. وَجْسٌ, *i. q.* خَفِىَ [app. meaning *The thing was unperceived*, or *hardly perceived, by the eye*, or *ear*, or *mind*; *was hidden*, or *concealed*; *was low, faint, gentle*, or *soft, to the ear*; or *was obscure to the mind*]. (IḲṭṭ.)

2: see 5, last signification but one.

4. اوجس *He conceived a thing in his mind*; syn. أَضْمَرَ. (A.) So in the Ḳur, [xx. 70,] فَأَوْجَسَ فِى نَفْسِهِ خِيفَةً *And he conceived in his mind a fear*: (Aboo-Is-ḥáḳ, Ṣ:) and ↓ تَوَجَّسَ signifies the same: (Ṣ:) or the above words of the Ḳur. signify *he perceived*, or *felt, and conceived, in his mind a fear*; (Ḳ;) and in like manner in the same book, [xi. 73, and] li. 28: or, as Aboo-Is-ḥáḳ says, in one place, اوجس signifies *fear fell into his mind.* (TA.) See also 1, and 5.

5. توجّس *He listened to* (Ṣ, A, Ḳ) a sound, (A,) or a low, faint, gentle, or soft, sound. (Ṣ, Ḳ.) Ex. توجّس رِكْزًا [*He listened to a low, sound*], occurring in a poem of Dhu-r-Rummeh: or, as some say, it means *he perceived a low sound, and listened to it, being in fear.* (TA.) [See also 4, where another signification of the same verb is mentioned; and see 1.] And ↓ اِسْتَوْجَسَتْ آذَانُهَا *Their ears* (referring to camels) *listened*, or *endeavoured to hear.* (IB, [in a marg. note in my copy of the TA, art. أنس.]) — [Hence,] توجّس عَنِ الأَخْبَارِ *He sought to learn the news, or tidings, without others' knowing of him.* (AZ, in TA, voce تَحَدَّسَ.) — Also, توجّست الأُذُنُ *The ear heard a low, faint, gentle, or soft sound*; as also ↓ وَجَّسَتْ. (TA.) — Also, توجّس *He tasted* food, and beverage, *time after time, little and little at a time.* (Ḳ.)

10: see 5.

وَجْسٌ *A fright of the heart*: (Ṣ:) or *fright that falls into the heart, or into the ear, from a sound or some other thing*; (Lth, A, K;) as also ↓ وَجَسَانٌ. (K.) [See 1, of which each is an inf. n.] — *A low, faint, gentle, or soft, sound.* (A'Obeyd, Ṣ, K.) [And particularly The *sound denoted in the words here following, and explained in a former art., voce* قَهَرَ.] It is said in a trad., نَهَى عَنِ الوَجْسِ, meaning, *He forbade a man's being with his slave-girl, or his wife, when another female would hear their low sound.* (K,* TA.) And in another it is said, respecting the same case, that they used to dislike [what is termed] الوَجْسُ. (Ṣ.) = See also أَوْجَسُ.

وَجَسَانٌ: see 1, and وَجْسٌ.

وَجَّاسٌ is syn. with عَالِمٌ [*Knowing*, &c.]; and therefore made trans. by means of بِ in the saying of Aboo-Dhu-eyb,

* ذُو مِرَّةٍ بِدِوَارِ الصَّيْدِ وَجَّاسُ *

[*An intelligent person, acquainted with the circumvention of game*: see دَاوَرَهُ]: (M, art. دور:) (ISd holds it to be a possessive epithet, since it has no known verb [of a suitable meaning that is unaugmented]: or [the meaning of these words is, *a person possessing skill in circumventing game, a listener*, or *attentive*, to their sounds and motions; for], accord. to Es-Sukkaree, وجّاس means يَتَوَجَّسُ. (TA.)

وَاجِسٌ *An opinion, idea, or object of thought, bestirring itself, or occurring, in the mind*; syn. هَاجِسٌ, (Ṣ, Ḳ,) i. e., خَاطِرٌ. (TA.)

أَوْجَسُ *A little* of food, and of beverage. (Ḳ.) One says, مَا ذُقْتُ عِنْدَهُ أَوْجَسَ *I tasted not, at his abode, any food*; (El-Umawee, Ṣ;) and [in like manner] ↓ وَجْسًا. (TA.) And مَا فِى سِقَائِهِ أَوْجَسُ *There is not in his skin a drop*: thus the phrase is given, without the mention of beverage: or *a drop of water.* (TA.) It is said that the word is not used except in negative phrases. (TA.) — Also, الأَوْجُسُ and الأَوْجَسُ (Ṣ, Ḳ) the latter on the authority of Yaḳoob, (Ṣ, TA,) but the former is the more chaste, (TA,) *Time*; syn. الدَّهْرُ. (Ṣ, Ḳ.) Hence the saying, (TA,) لَا أَفْعَلُهُ سَجِيسَ الأَوْجَسِ, (Ṣ, Ḳ,) and الأَوْجُسِ, (Ṣ,) *I will not do it ever.* (ISk, Ṣ, Ḳ.) And لَا أَفْعَلُهُ سَجِيسَ عُجَيْسِ الأَوْجَسِ *I will not do it while time lasts.* (El-Fárisee.)

[وجع, &c.

See Supplement.]

وح

R. Q. 1. وَحْوَحَ, inf. n. وَحْوَحَةٌ, *He uttered a sound accompanied by a hoarseness, roughness, harshness, or gruffness, of the voice*: (Ṣ, Ḳ:) *he made his breath to reciprocate in his throat, so as to be audible, by reason of cold*; (TA:) *he blew upon his hand by reason of intense cold.* (Ṣ, Ḳ.)

وَحْوَحٌ A *strong* man, (L, Ḳ,) *who breathes hard at his work by reason of his briskness and vigour*; (L;) as also ↓ وَحْوَاحٌ. (Ḳ.) — Also the former, (L, Ḳ,) and the latter, (L,) A *quick, or prompt, and sharp-spirited*, man. (L, Ḳ.) — Also the former, (Ṣ, Ḳ,) and the latter, (Ṣ,) A *light*, or an *active*, or *agile*, man. (Aṣ, Ṣ, Ḳ.) — Also both words, *A lord*, or *chief*: pl. وَحَاوِحَةٌ and وَحَاوِحُ. (L.) — Also both words, A *barking*, or *howling*, dog. (L, Ḳ.)

وَحْوَاحٌ: see what precedes.

وحب

وُحَابٌ *A disease that attacks camels.* (Ḳ, TA.) By some written وُجَابٌ; [and so in the CḲ;] but the correctness of this is improbable. (TA.)

وحت

طَعَامٌ وَحْتٌ *Food in which is no good.* (L.)

وحد

1. وَحَدَ, aor. يَحِدُ; (T, L, Mṣb;) and وَحِدَ, (Lḥ, M, L, Ḳ,) aor. يَوْحَدُ (Lḥ) and يَحِدُ; (Ḳ;)

with the latter aor., like وَرِثَ, aor. يَرِثُ; but وَحَدَ with this aor. is not mentioned by the lexicologists or grammarians [except F]; (MF;) [and its aor. is therefore probably يَوْحَدُ, only, agreeably with analogy, for which reason it seems to be omitted in the M;] and وَحُدَ, (Lḥ, M, L, Mṣb, Ḳ,) aor. also يَحِدُ; (Ḳ;) but this is without a parallel, and without any authority [except F]; (MF;) or يَوْحُدُ; (L;) [but this is also extr., and is probably a mistake for يَوْحَدُ, which is the form agreeable with analogy;] inf. n. حِدَةٌ (T, M, L, Mṣb, Ḳ) and وَحْدٌ (M, L, Ḳ) and وَحَدٌ (L) and وَحْدَةٌ, (L, Ḳ,) or وُحْدَةٌ, (as in some copies of the Ḳ and in the TA) and وُحُودٌ (Ḳ) and وَحَادَةٌ (M, L, Mṣb, Ḳ) and وُحُودَةٌ; (Ḳ;) *He, or it, was, or became, alone, by himself* or *itself, apart from others;* (T, L, Mṣb;) as also [↓ اِتَّحَدَ; and ↓ تَوَحَّدَ; and] ↓ استوحد; (A:) *he was, or became, alone, without anyone to cheer him by his society, company,* or *conversation:* (L:) *he remained alone, by himself, apart from others;* (Lḥ, M, L, Ḳ;) as also ↓ تَوَحَّدَ. (M, L, Ḳ.) See also 5, below.

2. وَحَّدَهُ, (inf. n. تَوْحِيدٌ, Ḳ,) *He made it one;* or *called it one:* (Ḳ:) like as one says ثَنَّاهُ, and ثَلَّثَهُ: (Ṣ, L:) as also أَحَّدَهُ. (TA.) Similar verbs are formed from the other nouns significant of numbers, to عَشَرَةٌ. (Esh-Sheybánee, Ḳ.) — وَحَّدَ لِٱمْرَأَتِهِ, or عِنْدَهَا, *He remained one night with his wife:* and in like manner the verb is used in relation to any saying or action. (TA, voce سَبَّعَ.) — وَحَّدَ ٱللّٰهَ, inf. n. تَوْحِيدٌ, *He asserted,* or *declared, God to be one; he asserted, declared,* or *preferred belief in, the unity of God:* as also أَحَّدَهُ. (T, L.) — اَلتَّوْحِيدُ *The belief in God alone;* (L, Ḳ;) *in his unity.* (L.)

4. اوحد ٱللّٰهُ جَانِبَهُ [*God rendered him solitary*]; i.e., *he remained alone;* (Ḳ;) or *was made to remain alone.* (L.) — اوحدهُ لِلْأَعْدَآءِ *He left him* [*alone*] *to the enemies.* (L, Ḳ.) — اوحدهُ *He* (God) *made him the unequalled one of his time:* (Ṣ, L, Ḳ:) *made him to have no equal.* (A.) — اوحدهُ ٱلنَّاسُ *The people left him alone,* or *by himself.* (L.) — أَوْحَدْتُهُ بِرُؤْيَتِى, inf. n. إِيحَادٌ, [*I singled him by my sight;*] *I saw none save him.* (Ṣ, L.) — اوحدت *She* (a ewe) *brought forth one only:* (Ṣ, Ḳ:) like أَفْذَتْ. (Ṣ.) — اوحدت بِهِ *She* (a woman) *brought him forth an unequalled one.* (L, from a trad.)

5. تَوَحَّدَهُ ٱللّٰهُ بِعِصْمَتِهِ, (Ṣ,) or توحّدهُ بعصمته, (L, Ḳ,) *God protected him himself, not committing him to the care of another.* (Ṣ, L, Ḳ.) — توحّد بِالأَمْرِ *He was,* or *became, alone, without any to share* or *participate with him, in the affair.* (L.) — توحّد بِرَأْيِهِ *He was,* or *became, alone, without any to share,* or *participate with him, in his opinion.* (Ṣ, L.) — See 1.

8. [اِتَّحَدَ *It was,* or *became, one.* And hence, اِتَّحَدَ مَعَهُ *He was,* or *became, one with him* in interests &c.] — اتّحد *It* (a number of things, or substances, two and more, KT,) *became one.* (KT, KL.) See 1.

10: see 1.

حِدَةٌ: see وَحْدٌ. — فَعَلَهُ مِنْ ذَاتِ حِدَتِهِ, and من ذى حدته, and على ذات حدته, and من ذات رَأْيِهِ, and ذات نَفْسِهِ, *He did it of himself; of his own accord; of his own judgment.* (AZ, L, Ḳ.)

وَحْدٌ: see 1, and وَحِيدٌ. — رَأَيْتُهُ وَحْدَهُ (Ṣ, L, Ḳ) *I saw him alone.* (Ṣ, L.) وحد is here an inf. n., having no dual nor pl. (Ḳ.) The Koofees hold it to be in the acc. case as an adv. n. of place: the Baṣrees, as an inf. n., in every instance; as though thou saidst أَوْحَدْتُهُ بِرُؤْيَتِى إِيحَادًا, meaning "I saw none save him," and then substituted وحده: or, as Abu-l-'Abbás says, it may mean the man's being himself alone; as though thou saidst رَأَيْتُ رَجُلًا مُنْفَرِدًا ٱنْفِرَادًا, and then substituted وحده. (Ṣ.) Or it is in the acc. case as a denotative of state accord. to the Baṣrees [and the grammarians in general]; not as an inf. n., J being in error in what he says on this matter: (IB, Ḳ:) the Baṣrees hold it to be a noun occupying the place of an inf. n. in the acc. case as a denotative of state; like جَآءَ زَيْدٌ رَكْضًا, meaning رَاكِضًا: (IB:) excepting some of them, as Yoo, who holds it to be in the acc. case as an adv. n. of place, for عَلَى وَحْدِهِ, (IB, Ḳ,) like عِنْدَهُ: (TA:) and there is a third opinion, that of Hishám; that it is in the acc. case as an inf. n. (L.) Or, (accord. to IAạr, L,) it is a noun used as a noun absolutely: (L, Ḳ:) so in the dial. of the Benoo-Temeem: (Mṣb:) you say جَلَسَ وَحْدَهُ, and عَلَى وَحْدِهِ, and جَلَسَا عَلَى وَحْدِهِمَا, and وَحْدَيْهِمَا, and جَلَسُوا عَلَى وَحْدِهِمْ, [*He sat alone,* and *they two sat alone,* and *they sat alone*]. (L, Ḳ.) When not preceded by a prefixed n. [or a prep.], it is always in the acc. case: (Lth, L:) you say, لَا إِلٰهَ إِلَّا ٱللّٰهُ وَحْدَهُ [*There is no deity but God alone*]: and مَرَرْتُ بِزَيْدٍ وَحْدَهُ [*I passed by Zeyd alone*]: (L:) [excepting in a few cases, such as the phrases] قُلْنَا هٰذَا ٱلْأَمْرَ وَحْدَيْنَا [*We two alone said this thing*], and قَالَتَاهُ وَحْدَيْهِمَا [*They two women alone said it*]; mentioned by AZ. (L.) You say also, هٰذَا عَلَى وَحْدِهِ, and ↓ عَلَى حِدَتِهِ, *This is by itself;* (L, Ḳ;) and هُمَا عَلَى حِدَتِهِمَا *They two are by themselves:* and هُمْ عَلَى حِدَتِهِمْ *They are by themselves:* (L:) and أَعْطِ كُلَّ وَاحِدٍ مِنْهُمْ عَلَى حِدَتِهِ *Give thou to every one of them by himself;* syn. على حِيَالِهِ. (Ṣ.) The ة in حِدَةٌ is a substitute for the و (Ṣ, L) which is cut off from the beginning. (L.) — وَحْدٌ, (Ḳ,) or ↓ وَحَدٌ, (L,) A wild animal *alone, by itself,* or *apart from others.* (L, Ḳ.) — وَحْدٌ, (Ḳ,) or ↓ وَحَدٌ, (L,) A man *whose lineage and origin are unknown.* (Lth, L, Ḳ.) — وَحْد is used as the complement of a prefixed n. only in the following phrases: (A'Obeyd, Ṣ, L:) هُوَ نَسِيجُ وَحْدِهِ, which is an expression of praise; (Ṣ, L, Ḳ;) meaning, ‡ *He is one unequalled; one who has no second:* (L:) or *he is a man of right judgment:* you say also هُمَا نَسِيجَا وَحْدِهِمَا, and هِىَ نَسِيجَةُ وَحْدِهَا, and هُمْ نُسَجَآءُ وَحْدِهِمْ, and هُنَّ نَسَائِجُ وَحْدِهِنَّ: (Lth, L:) [see art. نسج:] it is as though you said نَسِيجُ إِفْرَادٍ: you put وحده in the place of an inf. n. in the gen. case: (Ṣ:) and رَجُلُ وَحْدِهِ, (IAạr, L,) and رُجَيْلُ وَحْدِهِ, (Ṣ, L,) [*A man unequalled; who has no second,* and *a little man* (probably meaning the contr.) &c.]: and قَرِيعُ وَحْدِهِ *A man with whom no one contends in excellence:* (Lth, L:) and عُيَيْرُ وَحْدِهِ, and جُحَيْشُ وَحْدِهِ, which are expressions of dispraise; (Ṣ, L, Ḳ;) meaning, ‡ *One who does not consult, nor mix with, any one, and who is contemptible and weak:* (Sh, L:) وَحْد being used in the manner of an inf. n., not being an epithet nor an enunciative so as to be in concordance with the preceding noun, would be more properly in the acc. case; but the Arabs use it in these instances as the complement of a prefixed n.: (Lth, L:) these expressions are indeterminate: for the Arabs say, رُبَّ نَسِيجِ وَحْدِهِ قَدْ رَأَيْتُ ‡ [*Few unequalled men have I seen*]. (Hishám, Fr., L.)

وَحَدٌ: see وَحْدٌ and وَحِيدٌ.

وَحِدٌ: see وَحِيدٌ.

وَحْدَةٌ *The state of being alone,* or *apart from others; solitariness; solitude.* (Sb, Ṣ.) See 1. — وَحْدَةُ ٱلْقَبْرِ [*The solitude of the grave*]. (A.) — [لَيْلَةُ ٱلْوَحْدَةِ *The night of solitude;* the first night after burial: so called because the soul is believed to remain in the grave during this night, and then to depart to the place appointed for the residence of good souls until the last day, or to the appointed prison in which wicked souls await their final doom. See also لَيْلَةُ ٱلْوَحْشَةِ.]

وَحْدَانِيَّةٌ The *unity* of God: (L, Ḳ:*) as also أَحَدِيَّةٌ. (Mṣb.)

وَحْدَانِىٌّ One *who is singular in his religious opinions; who separates himself from the general body of believers:* a rel. n. from ٱلْوَحْدَةُ; the ا and ن being added to give intensiveness to the signification. (L.)

مَوْحَد : see وُحَادَ.

وَحِيدٌ (Ṣ, L, Mṣb, Ḳ) and ▾ مُتَوَحِّدٌ (L, Ḳ) and ▾ وَحْدٌ and ▾ وَحِدٌ (Ṣ, L, Mṣb, Ḳ) and ▾ وَحُدٌ (M, L) and ▾ وَاحِدٌ (L) A man *alone; by himself; apart from others; solitary; lonely:* (Ṣ, M, L, Mṣb, Ḳ;) as also أَحَدٌ: (M, L, Ḳ:) or, accord. to Az, one should not say رَجُلٌ أَحَدٌ, nor دِرْهَمٌ أَحَدٌ, nor شَىْءٌ أَحَدٌ, though some of the lexicologists assert that أَحَدٌ is originally وَحَدٌ: for أَحَدٌ is an epithet applied to God alone: (L:) the fem. epithet used in this sense is وَحِدَةٌ: (Ḳ:) and ▾ وَاحِدٌ in this sense receives the dual form: and the pl. is وُحْدَانٌ and أُحْدَانٌ and وِحَادٌ. (L.) رَجُلٌ وَحِيدٌ *A man who has no one to cheer him by his society, conversation, or company.* And ▾ رَجُلٌ مُتَوَحِّدٌ *A man who remains alone, by himself, apart from others, or solitary, not mixing with other people, not sitting with them.* (L.) See also وَحْدٌ.

وَاحِدٌ *One;* the *first of the numbers:* (Ṣ, L, Mṣb, Ḳ:) syn. [in many cases, which will be shown below,] with أَحَدٌ: (Ḳ:) [and *one alone:* a *single* person or thing:] fem. وَاحِدَةٌ: (L, Mṣb:) it sometimes receives the dual form; (L, Ḳ;) as in the expression ٱلْتَقَيْنَا وَاحِدَيْنِ [*We met, we being each of us one alone*]; cited from a poet by IAạr: or the dual form pertains to it in another sense, explained below, namely "alone:" (L:) pl. وَاحِدُونَ (Ṣ, L, Ḳ) and وُحْدَانٌ and أُحْدَانٌ; (Ṣ, L;) in the last of which, ا is substituted for و because of the ḍammeh: (L:) one says, أَنْتُمْ حَىٌّ وَاحِدٌ, and حَىٌّ وَاحِدُونَ, (Ye are one tribe, L) like as one says شِرْذِمَةٌ قَلِيلُونَ: (Fr, Ṣ, L:) آحَادٌ may also be a pl. of وَاحِدٌ [and therefore originally أَوْحَادٌ,] like as أَشْهَادٌ is pl. of شَاهِدٌ. (Th, Mṣb.) Its proper signification is A thing *having no subdivision:* and it is secondarily applied to any existing thing; so that there is no number to which it may not be applied as an epithet; wherefore one says, عَشَرَةٌ وَاحِدَةٌ [*One ten*], and مِائَةٌ وَاحِدَةٌ [*One hundred*]. (Er-Rághib.) It is interchangeable for أَحَدٌ when used as an epithet applied to God; and in certain nouns of number. [See art. أحد.] In most cases differing from these two, there is a difference in usage. The latter is used in affirmative phrases as a prefixed noun only, governing the noun which follows it in the gen. case; and is used absolutely in negative phrases: whereas the former is used in affirmative phrases as a prefixed n. and otherwise. (Mṣb.) [See, again, art. أحد.] — لَسْتُ فِى هٰذَا ٱلْأَمْرِ بِأَوْحَدَ ▾ *I am not alone, without a parallel,* or *match, in this affair:* (Ṣ,* L, Ḳ:*) or simply, *I am not alone in it.* (T, L.) The fem. وَحْدَآءُ is not used. (Ṣ, L.) — أُحْدَانٌ, the pl. of ▾ اوحد, is applied by a poet to dogs *having no equals* or *matches.* (Ṣ, L.) — فُلَانٌ لَا وَاحِدَ لَهُ *Such a one has no equal, like, parallel,* or *match.* (Ṣ, M, L.) — Also, *One that has no equal; one unequalled.* (L.) — فُلَانٌ وَاحِدُ دَهْرِهِ *Such a person is the unequalled one of his age.* (Ṣ, L.) And in like manner, (TA,) فُلَانٌ أَوْحَدُ ▾ أَهْلِ زَمَانِهِ (Ṣ, L) *Such a person is the unequalled one of the people of his time.* (TA.) The pl. of ▾ اوحد [as well as of واحد in the same sense] is أُحْدَانٌ, (originally وُحْدَانٌ, Ṣ) like as سُودَانٌ is pl. أَسْوَدُ. (Ṣ, L.) — وَاحِدُ أُمِّهِ [*An unequalled son of his mother*], is an indeterminate expression, like نَسِيجُ وَحْدِهِ, q. v. (Hishám, Fr. L.) — Also, A man *pre-eminent in knowledge* or *science,* or *in valour in war,* (L, Ḳ [in the CḲ, for بَأْس is put ناس]) or *in other qualities;* as though having no equal, and thus being alone: (L:) pl. أُحْدَانٌ and وُحْدَانٌ. (L, Ḳ.) — ٱلْوَاحِدُ and ▾ ٱلْمُتَوَحِّدُ, (M, L, Ḳ,) and ▾ ٱلْأَوْحَدُ and ٱلْأَحَدُ (T, L) epithets applied to God, *The One, the Sole; He whose attribute is unity:* (M, L, Ḳ:) or the first signifies *the One in essence, who has no like nor equal;* and the second, *the One in attributes, beside whom there is no other:* or the first, *the One who is not susceptible of division into parts* or *portions, nor of duplication, and who has no equal nor like:* (TL:) or *the One who has ever been alone, without companion:* (IAth, L:) and there is no being but God to whom the first and second of these epithets are applicable together, or to whom the second is applicable alone. (T, L.) See also أَحَدٌ, in art. أحد. — ٱلْإِنْسَانُ وَٱلْفَرَسُ وَاحِدٌ فِى ٱلْجِنْسِ *The human being and the horse are one in genus.* And زَيْدٌ وَعَمْرٌو وَاحِدٌ فِى ٱلنَّوْعِ *Zeyd and 'Amr are one in species.* (Er-Rághib.) — وَاحِدٌ *Singular, as opposed to plural:* pl. وُحْدَانٌ. (The lexicons, passim.) — أَصْحَابِى وَأَصْحَابُكَ وَاحِدٌ [*Thy companions and my companions are one and the same*]. And ٱلْجُلُوسُ وَٱلْقُعُودُ وَاحِدٌ [الجلوس and القعود *are one and the same*]. (L.) — See وَحِيدٌ. — حَادِىَ عَشَرَ, masc., and حَادِيَةَ عَشْرَةَ, fem., *Eleventh.* In this case, [and in similar instances, as حَادِى وَعِشْرُونَ *Twenty-first,* &c.,] حادى and حادية are formed by transposition from وَاحِدٌ and وَاحِدَةٌ, by putting the first radical letter after the second. [When without the article, it is indecl.: but when rendered determinate by the article, the first word is decl.] You say, هُوَ حَادِىَ عَشَرَهُمْ [*He is the eleventh of them*]: and ٱلْيَوْمُ ٱلْحَادِى عَشَرَ [*The eleventh day*]: and ٱللَّيْلَةُ ٱلْحَادِيَةُ عَشْرَةَ [*The eleventh night*]. (ISd, L.) [The rules respecting حَادِىَ عَشَرَ and its fem. are the same as those respecting ثَالِثَ عَشَرَ and its fem., explained in art. ثلث, q.v.] — بِوَاحِدَةٍ signifies *i.q.* فَقَطْ: and is often used in the sense of ٱلْبَتَّةَ. (MF, voce ذُرُوحٌ.)

إِحْدَى : see art. أحد.

أُحَادَ : see مَوْحَدَ.

أَوْحَدُ : see وَاحِدٌ.

مُوحِدٌ A ewe *bringing forth,* or *that brings forth, one ewe only.* (Ṣ, Ḳ.) [See مُفْرِدٌ.]

مَوْحَدَ and ▾ وُحَادَ and أُحَادَ [used adverbially] are imperfectly decl. because of their having the quality of an epithet and deviating from their original form, (Ṣ, L,) which is وَاحِدًا: (L, Ḳ:) or because they differ from their original both as to the letter and the meaning; the original word being changed as above stated, and the meaning being changed to وَاحِدًا وَاحِدًا: (Ṣ, L:) you say دَخَلُوا مَوْحَدَ مَوْحَدَ, (Ṣ, L, Ḳ,) [and وُحَادَ وُحَادَ,] and أُحَادَ أُحَادَ, (L, Ḳ,) *They entered one* [and] *one,* [*one and one*]; or *one* [*by*] *one,* [*one by one*]; (Ḳ;) or *one at a time; one after another.* (Ṣ, L.)

[مُوَحَّدَةٌ, (not مُوحَدَةٌ,) conv. term in lexicology, *Having one diacritical point; one-pointed:* an epithet added to باء to prevent its being mistaken for تاء, ثاء, or ياء. (The lexicons, passim.)]

مِيحَادٌ *One of several hills, such as are called* أَكَمَات, *separate* or *remote, one from another:* pl. مَوَاحِيدُ. (L, Ḳ.) F remarks, that J is in error in saying, ٱلْمِيحَادُ مِنَ ٱلْوَاحِدِ كَٱلْمِعْشَارِ مِنَ ٱلْعَشَرَةِ: (TA:) but the meaning of this is, that it denotes *one part* or *portion;* like as مِعْشَارٌ signifies one of ten: (L:) [i.e., the former signifies *one of several things whereof each is alone,* or *by itself:*] and the same explanation is given by [several] old authors. (TA.) [In one copy of the Ṣ, instead of ٱلْعَشَرَةِ, I find ٱلْعُشْرِ; which affords a good sense, i.e., that ميحاد, is syn. with وَاحِدٌ; and may be the true reading.]

مُتَوَحِّدٌ : see وَحِيدٌ and وَاحِدٌ.

وحش

1. وَحَشَ, aor. ـِ, [inf. n., probably, وُحُوشَةٌ or وَحَاشَةٌ or both,] *It* (a place) *abounded with wild animals.* (IḲṭṭ.) [The meaning assigned to this verb in Freytag's Lex. belongs not to it, but to

وَحَشَ بِهِ .[= وَحَشَ بِهِ, or بِهَا,] aor. يَحِشُ, (IAạr, Ḳ,) inf. n. وَحْشٌ; (TḲ;) and ↓ وحّش بِهِ, (Ṣ, Ḳ,) or بِهَا, (Ṣ, A,) which latter form of the verb is disapproved by IAạr, but both are correct; (TA;) and ↓ توحّش [app. used alone, the objective complement being understood]; (TA;) *He threw it*, or *them*, *away*, (Ṣ, Ḳ,) or *to a distance*, (A,) namely, his garment, (Ṣ, Ḳ,) or his garments, (A,) and his sword, (TA,) and his spear, (Ṣ, TA,) and his weapon, or weapons, (Ṣ, A,) or anything, (TA,) *to lighten himself*, (A,) or *his beast of carriage*, (TA,) *in fear of his being overtaken*: (Ṣ, Ḳ:) [or *in any case*; for] it is said in a trad. of El-Ows and El-Khazraj, فَوَحَشُوا بِأَسْلِحَتِهِمْ وَاعْتَنَقَ بَعْضُهُمْ بَعْضًا [*Then they threw away their weapons, and embraced one another*]. (TA.)

2: see 1.

4. اوحش *It* (a place, A, Mṣb, or a place of alighting or abode, Ṣ, Ḳ) *was*, or *became, desolate, deserted*, or *destitute of human beings*; (Ṣ, A, Mṣb, Ḳ,) *the people having gone from it*; (Ṣ, Ḳ;) as also ↓ توحّش. (A, Mṣb, Ḳ.) And [in like manner you say of a land,] ↓ توحّشت الأَرْضُ, [and ↓ استوحشت, (see أَرْضٌ وَحْشَةٌ, voce وَحْشٌ,)] *The land was*, or *became* وَحْشَة (Ṣ, TA) [i. e. *desolate, deserted*, &c.] — *He* (a man) *was*, or *became, hungry*; (Ṣ, A, Ḳ, TA;) *not having eaten anything, so that his inside was empty*; (TA;) as also ↓ توحّش: (A:) or the latter signifies *his belly became empty by reason of hunger*. (Ṣ, Ḳ.) Also the former, *His provisions became spent*, or *exhausted*. (Ṣ, Ḳ.) You say, قَدْ أَوْحَشْنَا مُنْذُ لَيْلَتَيْنِ *Our provisions have been spent for two nights*. (Ṣ.) You say also, ↓ توحّش لِلدَّوَآءِ (Ṣ, A, Ḳ*) *He made himself hungry*; (A;) or *made his inside*, (Ṣ,) or *his stomach*, (Ḳ,) *empty of food* (Ṣ, Ḳ) and *beverage*; (Ḳ;) *for the purpose of drinking medicine*. (Ṣ,* A,* Ḳ.) = اوحش الأَرْضَ *He found the land to be* وَحْشَة (Aṣ, Ṣ, Ḳ) [i. e. *desolate, deserted*, or *destitute of human beings* — اوحش الرَّجُلَ (Ṣ, A) *He made the man lonely*, or *solitary*; and *sad, sorrowful*, or *disquieted* or *troubled in mind*; [by his absence, or withdrawal of himself; and *afraid*;] or *he made him to feel*, or *experience*, وَحْشَة [i. e. *loneliness*, or *solitude*, &c.]; (Ṣ;) *contr. of* آنَسَهُ, (Ṣ, Ḳ, in art. أنس,) inf. n. إِيحَاشٌ. (Ṣ, in that art.) Hence the saying of the people of Mekkeh, [and of Egypt,] أَوْحَشْتَنَا [*Thou hast made us lonely*, &c., by thine absence]. (TA.) [See also an ex. from a poet, voce أُنْسٌ: And see its quasi-pass., 10.]

5. توحّش *He* (a beast) *became wild*, or *shy*; syn. تأبّد, (Ṣ, A, Ḳ, &c., in art. أبد,) and تَأَبَّدَ. (A, L, in that art.) And *He* (a man) *became unsocial, unsociable, unfamiliar*, or *shy*; *like a wild animal*; syn. أَبِدَ, (Ṣ, Ḳ, ubi supra,) and تَأَبَّدَ: (A, Ḳ, ubi supra;) and ↓ استوحش signifies the same; (see this verb below;) or *he became*, or *made himself, as though on a par with the wild animals*; expl. by لَحِقَ بِالْوَحْشِ. (TA.) [See exs. of both voce أُنْسٌ.] — See also 4, in five places. — And see 1.

10. استوحش: see 5. — It is also quasi-pass. of أَوْحَشَ الرَّجُلَ, (Ṣ, TA,) and [thus] signifies *He felt*, or *experienced*, وَحْشَة [i. e. *loneliness*, or *solitude*, &c.; and *sadness, grief, sorrow*, or *disquietude* or *trouble of mind*, &c.; and *fear*, &c.]. (Ṣ,* Ḳ, TA.) And استوحش إِلَى الشَّىْءِ [*He felt a want of the thing*]. (Ḳ, voce عُرِىَ, q. v.) You say also استوحش مِنْهُ, (A, TA,) or عَنْهُ, (Mṣb,) [meaning *He was afraid of*, or *feared, him*, or *it*; agreeably with an explanation of the inf. n. in Ḥar, p. 331: see also an instance below, voce وَحْشٌ: or] meaning *he was shy of him*; *averse from him*; *unsocial, unsociable*, or *unfamiliar, with him*; *and like a wild animal*. (TA.) — استوحشت الأَرْضُ: see 4. = [*He deemed* a word, or sound, &c., *strange*, or *uncouth*.]

حِشَةٌ: pl. حِشُونَ: see وَحْشٌ.

وَحْشٌ, applied to a country, or region, (Ṣ, Ḳ,) and a place, (TA,) and a house (دَارٌ), (A,) and [its fem.] وَحْشَةٌ, applied to a land (أَرْضٌ), (Ṣ, TA,) to a house (دار); (A;) *Desolate, deserted*, or *destitute of human beings* or *inhabitants*; (Ṣ, Ḳ, TA;) as also ↓ مُوحِشٌ and ↓ مُتَوَحِّشٌ: (A:) and أَرْضٌ وَحْشَةٌ and ↓ مُسْتَوْحِشَةٌ signify the same. (Ḳ, TA.) You say also, بِلَادٌ حِشُونَ *Countries*, or *regions, desolate, deserted*, &c.; after the manner of سِنُونَ; and in the accus. and gen., حِشِينَ: pl., as Az says, of ↓ حِشَةٌ, originally وَحْشٌ, [So I read instead of وَحْشَةٌ, which is evidently a mistranscription,] the و being wanting, as it is in زِنَةٌ and صِلَةٌ and عِدَةٌ. (TA.) You also say, لَقِيتُهُ بِوَحْشِ إِصْمِتَ, (Ṣ, Ḳ,) and إِصْمِتَةَ, (TA,) i. e., *I found him*, or *met him*, *in a desolate*, or *deserted, country*, or *region*. (Ṣ, Ḳ.) [See remarks on the last word in the former phrase in art. صمت.] And in like manner, تَرَكْتُهُ بِوَحْشِ المَتْنِ *I left him in the desert part of the elevated plain, where one could not reach him*. (L, TA.*) And [hence] حِمَارُ وَحْشٍ *An ass of a desert*; [i. e. *a wild ass*;] as also حِمَارٌ وَحْشِىٌّ. (Ṣ, Ḳ.) [And بَقَرُ الوَحْشِ *The bull and cow*, or *bulls and cows*, collectively, *of the desert*; i. e., *the wild bull and cow*, or *bulls and cows*.] — [Hence also] *Animals* (حَيَوَانٌ) [which is used as a sing. and a pl., but is here meant to be understood collectively, as appears from what follows,]) *of the desert*, (Ṣ, A, Ḳ, TA,) *such as are not tame*; (TA;) [i. e. *wild animals*;] of the fem. gender; (TA;) as also وُحُوشٌ (Ṣ) and ↓ وَحِيشٌ: (Ḳ:) these three words are all used in a collective sense: (ISh:) and ↓ وَحْشِىٌّ signifies *a single one of such animals*; (Ṣ, Ḳ;) like زَنْجِىٌّ in relation to زَنْجٌ, and رُومِىٌّ to رُومٌ: (TA:) or وَحْشٌ signifies *such as is not tame, of beasts of the desert*; and *everything that is afraid of human beings* (كُلُّ شَىْءٍ يَسْتَوْحِشُ عَنِ النَّاسِ); as also ↓ وَحْشِىٌّ, as though the ى were a corroborative, as in دَوَّارِىٌّ: or, accord. to El-Fárábee, وَحْشٌ in the pl. [lexicologically, but not in the language of the grammarians] of ↓ وَحْشِىٌّ, like as رُومٌ is of رُومِىٌّ: (Mṣb:) or it is used as a sing., as well as collectively; for you say, هٰذَا وَحْشٌ ضَخْمٌ [*this is a bulky wild animal*], and هٰذِهِ شَاةٌ وَحْشٌ [*this is a wild sheep or goat*, &c.]: (ISh:) وُحُوشٌ is a pl. of وَحْشٌ, (Mṣb, Ḳ,) and so is وُحْشَانٌ, (Sgh, Ḳ,) and so is وَحِيشٌ, [lexicologically, but grammarians term it a quasi-pl. n.,] like as ضَئِينٌ is of ضَأْنٌ: (Sgh, TA:) or وُحُوشٌ is its only broken pl. (TA.) — [Hence also, *Wild*, or *shy*; applied to girls or women: see an ex. of the word in this sense voce تَوٌّ, where it has a redundant ن affixed to it.] — [Hence also] *Lone*; *solitary*; *without company*. You say, مَشَى فِى الأَرْضِ وَحْشًا *He walked*, or *went*, *in the land alone, having no other with him*. (TA.) — [Hence also] *Hungry*; (Ṣ, A, Ḳ;) as also ↓ مُوحِشٌ, (AZ, A,) and ↓ مُتَوَحِّشٌ, (A,) and ↓ وَحِشٌ: (TA:) pl. of the first, أَوْحَاشٌ (Ṣ, A, Ḳ) [and وَحْشُونَ]. You say, بَاتَ فُلَانٌ وَحْشًا, (Ṣ, A,* Ḳ,*) and مُوحِشًا, and مُتَوَحِّشًا, (A,) *Such a one passed the night hungry*, (Ṣ, A, Ḳ,) *not having eaten anything, so that his inside was empty*. (TA.) And بِتْنَا وَحْشِينَ *We passed the night without food*. (TA.) [In another place in the TA, we find لَقَدْ بِتْنَا لَيْلَتَنَا هٰذِهِ وَحْشِى, and so in the L; the last word being evidently a mistranscription, for وَحْشِينَ: and it is added, as though the speaker meant, جَمَاعَةَ وَحْشِى; doubtless a mistake for جَمَاعَةَ وَحْشٍ so that the saying seems to mean, *We have passed this our night* like *a company of wild animals*.]

وَحِشٌ: see وَحْشٌ, last signification.

وَحْشَةٌ *Loneliness*; *solitude*; *lonesomeness*; *solitariness*; *desolateness*; syn. خَلْوَةٌ: (Ṣ, Ḳ:) *sadness*; *grief*; *sorrow*; *disquietude*, or *trouble, of mind*: (Ṣ, Ḳ, TA:) or *sadness*, &c., *arising from loneliness* or *solitude*: (TA:) *fear*: (Ḳ, TA:) or *fear*, or *fright, arising from loneliness* or *solitude*: (TA:) *a state of disunion* between men, *and remoteness of hearts from feelings of love* or *affection*; from وَحْشٌ signifying "a wild beast," or "wild beasts, of the desert:" (Mṣb:) *unsociableness; unfriendliness; unsocialness; unfamiliarity; shyness; wildness:* [in all the above senses] *contr. of* أُنْسٌ. (T, Ṣ, A, Ḳ, in art. أنس.) [Hence, لَيْلَةُ الوَحْشَةِ *The night of loneliness*, &c.; the first night after burial: also called لَيْلَةُ الوَحْدَةِ, q. v.] You say, تَرَكْتُهُ فِى وَحْشَةٍ *I left him in loneliness*, or *solitude*. (TḲ.) And أَخَذَتْهُ الوَحْشَةُ *Sadness, grief, sorrow*, or *disquietude* or *trouble of mind*, or *sadness*, &c., *arising from loneliness* or *solitude, laid hold upon him*. (TA.)

وَحْشِىٌّ [*Of*, or *belonging to*, or *relating to, the desert:* and hence, *wild; untamed; undomesticated; uncivilized; unfamiliar:* and often used as an epithet in which the quality of a subst. is predominant]: see وَحْشٌ, in three places: *i. q.* حُوشِىٌّ; (Ṣ, Mṣb, art. حوش;) *contr. of* أَهْلِىٌّ. (TA, in art. اهل.) — كَلَامٌ وَحْشِىٌّ *i. q.* حُوشِىٌّ, q. v. (Ṣ, A, art. حوش:) and in like manner, لَفْظَةٌ وَحْشِيَّةٌ *i. q.* حُوشِيَّةٌ. (Mz, 13th نوع.) — The *right* side of anything: (AZ, AA, Ṣ, Ḳ, &c.:) or the left side (Aṣ, Ṣ, A, Ḳ,) of anything. (Aṣ, Ṣ.) [For more full explanations of this term, and its contr. إِنْسِىٌّ, in relation to a beast and to a man, see the latter term: of a beast, accord. to most authorities, it is The *right, far* or *off*, side. See an ex. in a verse cited voce دَفٌّ.] Of the arm or hand, and of the leg or foot, The *back*; إِنْسِىٌّ signifying the side that is towards the man: (Ṣ:) or of the foot, the former means [the *outer side*, or] the side *that is the more remote from the other foot*; the latter being the contr., or that which is towards the other foot. (TA.) Of a bow, (Ṣ, Ḳ,) or of a Persian bow, (TA,) The *back*; and إِنْسِىٌّ, the side that is towards thee: (Ṣ, Ḳ:) or of a bow, whether Persian or not is not said, the former means the side *against which the arrow does not lie*. (TA.) And الجَانِبُ الوَحِيشُ signifies the same as الوَحْشِىُّ. (IAạr.) — *A sort of fig, that grows in the mountains and in the remote parts of valleys, of every colour, black and red and white; it is the smallest of figs*, [in the TA, smaller than the تين,] *and when eaten newly plucked it burns the mouth; but it is dried.* (AḤn, L.) — رِيحٌ وَحْشِيَّةٌ [or وَحْشِيَّةٌ] *A wind that enters one's clothes, by reason of its vehemence.* (Ḳ.)

وَحْشَانُ, applied to a man, *Sad; sorrowful:* pl. وَحَاشَى. (Ḳ.)

وَحِيشٌ: see وَحْشٌ, (of which it is a quasi-pl. n.,) in two places: — and see وَحْشِىٌّ.

مُوحِشٌ: see وَحْشٌ, first sentence, and near the end.

أَرْضٌ مَوْحُوشَةٌ *A land having*, (Fr, Ṣ, A,) or *abounding with*, (Ḳ,) *wild animals*, or *animals of the desert*. (Fr, Ṣ, A, Ḳ.) [See أَرْضٌ مَجْرُودَةٌ, in art. جرد.] In [some of] the copies of the Ḳ, مُوحِشَةٌ, which is a mistake. (TA.)

مُتَوَحِّشٌ: see وَحْشٌ, first sentence, and near the end.

أَرْضٌ مُسْتَوْحِشَةٌ: see وَحْشٌ, first sentence.

[وحف &c.

See Supplement.]

وخ

R. Q. 1. وَخْوَخَ *His belly was*, or *became, flabby*. (TA, voce خَبْخَبَ.)

وَخْوَاخٌ A *fat and fleshy* man, *whose flesh shakes:* (L:) *having a flaccid belly, and dilated skin;* (L, Ḳ;) as also بَخْبَاخٌ: (L:) *lazy;* (L, Ḳ;) *unwilling to work:* (L:) *lazy* or *heavy:* (L:) *weak:* (Ṣ, Ḳ:) *a weak coward:* (L:) *ad venerum impotens;* (L, Ḳ;) as also بَخْبَاخٌ and ذَوْذَخٌ: (L:) *qui se polluit, aut concacat, tempore coitus;* as also نخباخ and ذوذخ. (IAạr.) — Anything *flaccid:* (L:) and particularly a *flaccid* date: (Ḳ:) or a date *having a flaccid skin:* (L:) or a date *having no sweetness nor taste.* (IAạr.)

وخد

1. وَخَدَ, aor. يَخِدُ, inf. n. وَخْدٌ and وَخَدَانٌ (Ṣ, A, L, Ḳ) and وَخِيدٌ, (Ḳ,) *He* (a camel) *went along throwing out his legs like the ostrich:* (Ṣ, L, Ḳ:) or *went quickly:* or *went with wide steps:* (L, Ḳ:) as also خَدَى: (L:) also said of a horse, (Kr, L,) and of an ostrich. (TA.) See نَصَّ السَّيْرَ.

وَخُودٌ:
وَخَّادٌ: } see وَاخِدٌ.

وَاخِدٌ and وَخَّادٌ (Ṣ, L, Ḳ,) and وَخُودٌ (L, Ḳ) A camel *going along*, or *that goes along, throwing out his legs like the ostrich:* (Ṣ, L, Ḳ:) or, *quickly:* or, *with wide steps.* (L, Ḳ.) The second [which is an intensive or frequentative epithet] is also applied to an ostrich: and the third [which is intensive] to a she-camel. (L.)

وخذ

1. وَخَذَ &c.: see art. أخذ.

وخز

1. وَخَزَهُ, (Ṣ, A, Mṣb,) aor. يَخِزُهُ, (Mṣb,) inf. n. وَخْزٌ (Ṣ, A, Mṣb, Ḳ) *He pierced, stabbed*, or *pricked him*, with a spear, (Ṣ, A, Mṣb, Ḳ,) or other thing, (Ḳ,) or with the like of a spear, as a dagger, (Ṣ,) and a needle, (A, Mṣb,) &c., (Mṣb,) *not making the instrument to pass through:* (Ṣ, A, Mṣb, Ḳ:) or, as some say, *he did so making the instrument to pass through:* in a trad., the plague (الطَّاعُون) is said to be a وَخْز inflicted by jinn, or genii; and the word in this instance is explained by some agreeably with the former rendering, and by some agreeably with the latter: or وَخْز signifies *a slight piercing*, and is *like a goading:* so accord. to Khálid Ibn-Jembeh, who uses the expression وَخَزَ فِى سَنَامِهَا بِمِبْضَعِهِ [*He made a slight stab in her hump with his scarifier*]. (TA.) وَخْزٌ also signifies The *act of scarifying;* syn. تَبْزِيغٌ. (Ḳ. [So in a MS copy of the Ḳ, and this is the right reading: in the TA, تَبْزِيع, written with ع unpointed: in the CḲ, تَنْزِيع, with ن and ع instead of ب and غ.]) You say of a farrier, وَخَزَهُ بِمِبْضَعٍ وَخْزًا خَفِيفًا لَا يَبْلُغُ العَصَبَ [*He scarified it with a scarifier slightly, not penetrating to the sinews*]; the pronoun referring to the hoof of a horse or the like, and the place of the operation being the part called the أَشَاعِر. (Aboo-'Adnán, TA.)

وَخْزٌ The *plague;* syn. طَاعُونٌ. (TA.) See above. — *Pain:* [or, app., *a piercing*, or *pricking, pain:*] as in the following ex.: إِنِّى لَأَجِدُ فِى يَدِى وَخْزًا [*Verily I feel, in my arm*, or *hand, a pain*, or *a piercing*, or *pricking, pain*]. (IAạr, TA.)

وخش

1. وَخُشَ, aor. ـُ, inf. n. وَخَاشَةٌ and وُخُوشَةٌ (Ṣ, Ḳ) and وُخُوشٌ, (TA,) *It* (a thing, Ṣ, TA,) *became bad, vile*, or *base*. (Ṣ, Ḳ, TA.)

وَخْشٌ *Bad, vile*, or *base;* applied to anything: (Ḳ:) *low, ignoble, vile, base*, or *mean;* the *refuse*, or *lowest* or *basest* or *meanest sort*, of mankind; (Lth, Az, Ṣ, Mṣb, Ḳ;) the *abject, contemptible*, or *despicable*, thereof; (Lth, Az, Mṣb;) used as a pl., (Ṣ, Mṣb, Ḳ,) and dual, (Mṣb,) and sing., and masc. and fem., without variation: (Mṣb, Ḳ:) but sometimes it is made fem. by the addition of ة: (IAạr, ISd:) and has the dual form: (Ṣ, Ḳ:) and has for its pl. أَوْخَاشٌ (Ṣ, Ḳ) and وِخَاشٌ; (Ḳ;) or the latter is pl. of وَخْشَةٌ. (TA.) You say, رَجُلٌ وَخْشٌ and اِمْرَأَةٌ وَخْشٌ and قَوْمٌ وَخْشٌ [*A man*, and *a woman*, and *a company of men, low, ignoble*, &c.]. (TA.) And ذٰلِكَ رَجُلٌ مِنْ وَخْشِ النَّاسِ *That is a man of the low, ignoble, vile, base*, or *mean, of mankind.* (Ṣ.) And جَآءَنِى أَوْخَاشٌ مِنَ النَّاسِ *Some of the refuse*, or *lowest* or *basest* or *meanest sort, of mankind came to me.* (Ṣ.) And وَخْشَنٌ is the *same as* وَخْشٌ: (TA:) the rájiz (Dahlab, TA) says,

جَارِيَةٌ لَيْسَتْ مِنَ الوَخْشَنِّ •

[*A girl who is not of the low, or ignoble, &c.*]; meaning الوَخْشُ; adding a double ن. (Ṣ, TA.)

وَخْشَنٌ : see وَخْشٌ.

وخض

See وخط in two places.

وخط

1. وَخَطَهُ, aor. يَخِطُ, (TA,) inf. n. وَخْطٌ, (Aṣ, Ṣ, Ḳ,) *He pierced him through:* (Ṣ, Ḳ, TA:) or *he pierced him slightly;* (Ḳ, TA;) *not through:* (TA:) or *he pierced him so as to penetrate into his inside; not piercing him through;* (Aṣ, TA;) بِالرُّمْحِ *with the spear;* as also وَخَضَهُ. (TA.) [See also وَخَزَهُ.] — [And hence,] وَخَطَهُ الشَّيْبُ, (Ṣ, Ḳ,) aor. as above, (Ḳ,) and so the inf. n., (TA,) ‡ *Hoariness, or whiteness, became intermixed in his hair;* (Ṣ, Ḳ, TA;) as also وَخَضَهُ: (TA:) or *appeared* or *spread upon him:* or *his blackness and whiteness* [*of hair*] *became equal:* (Ḳ:) and you say of the man, وُخِطَ: (Ḳ,* TA:) or this signifies *his head became hoary,* or *white.* (TA.)

5. تَوَخَّطَ : see 2, in art. خيط.

وَخْطٌ [originally an inf. n. (see above)] is said to signify ‡ *A little, somewhat,* or *a small degree,* of hoariness, or whiteness of the hair. (TA.) — You say also, بِهَا وَخْطٌ مِنْ وَحْشٍ ‡ *In it* [meaning a land (أَرْض)] *is a small number of wild animals.* (TA.)

طَعْنٌ وَخَّاطٌ [*A piercing, of one or another of the kinds described above, that is much,* or *frequent*]: and in like manner رُمْحٌ وَخَّاطٌ [*a spear so piercing, much,* or *frequently*]. (TA.)

مَوْخُوطٌ A man (TA) *having hoariness,* or *whiteness, intermixed in his hair:* or *upon whom hoariness,* or *whiteness, has appeared and spread:* or *whose blackness and whiteness* [*of hair*] *have become equal:* (Ḳ:) or *whose head has become hoary,* or *white.* (TA.)

[وَخَفَ &c.

See Supplement.]

ود

1. وَدَّهُ, first pers. وَدِدْتُ, (Ṣ, M, L, Mṣb, Ḳ, &c.) and وَدَدْتُ, (Ks, Z, Ḳ,) [but most disallow this] aor. يَوَدُّ, inf. n. وُدٌّ and وِدٌّ and وَدٌّ, (Ṣ, M, L, Ḳ,) of which three forms the first is the most common, (MF,) and مَوَدَّةٌ, (Ṣ, M, L, Ḳ,) or this last is a simple subst., (Mṣb,) and مَوْدَّةٌ (CḲ and some MS. copies of the Ḳ) and مِوَدَّةٌ, (accord. to some other copies of the Ḳ, this and the next preceding deviating from the common forms of inf. ns., TA,) and مَوْدِدَةٌ (M, Ks, Ḳ) and مَوْدُودَةٌ, (TA,) but these last two are allowable only in poetry, and deviate from constant rule, the former doubly, (Kz, MF, TA,) and وَدَادٌ and وِدَادٌ and وُدَادٌ, (M, L, Ḳ,) the first of which last three forms is the most common, (MF,) and وَدَادَةٌ (M, L, Ḳ) and, accord. to some, وِدَادَةٌ and وُدَادَةٌ, (MF, TA,) and, as in a copy of the Ḳ esteemed of good authority, مَوْدُودَةٌ, (TA,) *He loved,* or *affected, him,* or *it,* (Ṣ, M, L, Mṣb, Ḳ,) i. e. any means of attaining or doing good. (AZ, M, L.) The form وَدَدْتُ is disallowed by the Baṣrees who hold it to be erroneous: and Zj says, We know that Ks did not mention وَدَدْتُ without having heard it; but he heard it from him who was no authority. (T, L.) — أُوْدُدْهُ, an imp. form [of ↑ أَوَدَّهُ], without idghám, accord. to the dial. of El-Ḥijáz, occurs in a trad., meaning *Love thou it,* or *affect it.* (L.) — وَدِدْتُ لَوْ أَنَّكَ تَفْعَلُ ذٰلِكَ and وَدِدْتُ لَوْ تَفْعَلُ ذٰلِكَ, (Ṣ, L,) aor. as above, inf. n. وُدٌّ and وَدٌّ and وَدَادَةٌ (Ṣ, L, Mṣb) and وَدَادٌ (Ṣ, L) or وِدَادٌ, (T, in TT,) *I wished that thou wouldest do that.* (Ṣ, L.) — وَدِدْتُ لَوْ كَانَ كَذَا *I wished that it had been so.* (Mṣb.) — وَدِدْتُ الشَّىْءَ *I wished for the thing.* Fr says, This is the more approved form; but some say وَدَدْتُ: in both cases the aor. is يَوَدُّ only. (L.) [Respecting the latter form of the pret., see above.] This is a secondary signification of the verb. (TA.)

3. وَادَّهُ, inf. n. مُوَادَّةٌ and وِدَادٌ, *He loved,* or *affected him, being loved,* or *affected, by him.* (Mṣb.)

4: see 1.

5. تَوَدَّدَهُ *He attracted to himself his love,* or *affection.* (IAạr, L, Ḳ.) — تَوَدَّدَ إِلَيْهِ *He manifested,* or *showed, love,* or *affection, to him.* (L, Mṣb, Ḳ.)

6. هُمَا يَتَوَادَّانِ, (Ṣ, L,) inf. n. تَوَادٌّ, (Ḳ,) *They two love,* or *affect, each other.* (Ṣ, L, Ḳ.)

وُدٌّ (Ṣ, L, Ḳ) and ↑ وِدٌّ (L, Ḳ) and ↑ وَدٌّ (IJ, L, Ḳ) and ↑ وَدِيدٌ (Ṣ, L, Ḳ) A person *loved,* or *beloved; an object of love; a friend;* syn. مُحِبٌّ and حَبِيبٌ and صَدِيقٌ (L) and مُحَبٌّ. (Ḳ: in the CḲ مُحِبٌّ.) — Also, ↑ وُدٌّ (TA) and ↑ وَدُودٌ (Ṣ, L, Mṣb) and ↑ وَدِيدٌ (TA) and ↑ وَادٌّ (Kz) A person *who loves; loving; affectionate:* (Ṣ, L, Mṣb, TA:) the first also used in a pl. sense, (L, Ḳ,) being [originally] an inf. n. (TA) and the second used alike as masc. and fem. (Ṣ, L, Mṣb.) — Also, ↑ وِدٌّ and ↑ وَدُودٌ and ↑ مَوَدٌّ, (Ḳ,) also written ↑ مِوَدٌّ, (MF,) A man (TA) *loving much; having much love* or *affection; very loving* or *affectionate.* (Ḳ, MF.) — Pl. أَوْدَادٌ, (L, Ḳ,) pl. of وُدٌّ, (TA,) and also a pl. [of وِدٌّ] in the second of the above senses; (Ḳ;) and وِدَادٌ, [pl. of وُدٌّ or وَدِيدٌ] in the first of the above senses; (L;) and أَوُدٌّ, (Ṣ, L, Ḳ,) pl. of وُدٌّ (TA) in the second of the above senses; (Ḳ;) or of وِدٌّ; (Ṣ, TA;) and أَوِدٌّ, (L, Ḳ,) [an irreg. pl., or quasi-pl. n., upon which I find no remark,] in the first of the above senses, (L,) or the second; (Ḳ;) and وُدَّادٌ, pl. of وَادٌّ; (Kz;) and أَوِدَّآءُ, (Ṣ, L, Ḳ,) pl. of وَدِيدٌ (TA) in the first of the above senses, (L,) or in the second; (L;) and أَوِدَّةٌ, (Ḳ,) also pl. of وَدِيدٌ (TA) in the second of the above senses; (Ḳ;) and وُدَدَآءُ, pl. of وَدُودٌ (Ṣ) in the second of the above senses, (Ṣ, Ḳ,) [and the third]; and وَدِيدٌ is also mentioned as a pl. in the second of the above senses in the Ḳ; but this is probably a mistake for وِدَادٌ. (TA.) — IAth says, that ↑ وُدٌّ, used as an epithet, is for ذُو وُدٍّ; but وُدٌّ does not require ذو to be understood, being syn. with صَدِيقٌ. (L.)

وَدٌّ : see 1, and وُدٌّ. — وَدٌّ and ↑ وُدٌّ (the former is the more common, L) *A certain idol* (Ṣ, L, Ḳ) *which pertained to the people of Noah, and then to Kelb, and was at Doomet-el-Jendel:* (Ṣ, L:) or *a certain good man, who lived between Adam and Noah, and of whom, after his death, was made an image, which, after a long time, became an object of worship;* like سُوَاعٌ and يَغُوثُ and يَعُوقُ and نَسْرٌ, mentioned therewith in the Ḳur, lxxi. 22 and 23: (Bḍ:) and the former, *a certain idol belonging to Ḳureysh,* also called أُدّ. (L.) — بِوَدِّكَ *By thy Wedd!* meaning the idol so named. (L.) — وَدٌّ *A wooden pin, peg,* or *stake; i. q.* وَتِدٌ: (Ṣ, Ḳ:) of the dial. of Temeem; (IDrd;) or of Nejd: as though they made the ت quiescent and incorporated it into the د. (Ṣ.)

وِدٌّ : see 1, and وُدٌّ, and وَدٌّ. — بِوُدِّى أَنْ يَكُونَ كَذَا *I wish that such a thing may be.* In the following saying of the poet,

• أَيُّهَا العَائِدُ المُسَائِلُ عَنَّا •
• وَبِوِدِّيكَ لَوْ تَرَى أَكْفَانِى •

[*O thou visitor of the sick, inquiring respecting us, wishing that thou mayest see my grave-clothes*], the kesreh of the د is lengthened for sake of the measure. (Ṣ, L.)

وَدُودٌ : see وُدٌّ. — الوَدُودُ, as an epithet applied to God, *The loving towards his servants,* (IAmb, L,) or, *towards those who obey:* (Beyḍ, lxxxv. 14:) or *He who regards with approbation his righteous servants:* or *He who is beloved in the hearts of his saints.* (IAth, L.)

وَدُودٌ also, A mare *that puts forth all her power of running.* (ISd, L.)

وَدِيدٌ : see وُدٌّ.

وَادٌّ : see وُدٌّ.

أَوَدُّ *More* or *most, loving* or *affectionate.* Said to be also used as a pl., for أَوَدُّونَ. (L.)

مَوَدٌّ and مُوَدٌّ: see وِدٌّ.

مَوَدَّةٌ *Love; affection.* (Msb.) See also 1. — Also, *A letter; an epistle:* and *letters,* or *epistles:* syn. كِتَابٌ and كُتُبٌ. (IAạr, L, Ḳ.) Said to have the latter meaning in the Ḳur, lx. 1, in the first of the instances of its occurrence there: (L, Ḳ:) but this is a strange interpretation. (TA.)

ودأ

1. وَدَأَهُ, aor. يَدَأُ, *He made it even or plain.* (Ḳ.) ═ See 5. ═ وَدَأَ (aor. يَدَأُ, T) *Veretrum exseruit* equus: (T, Ḳ:) but AHeyth says that this is an error, and that the correct word is without ء: [i.e., وَدَى, q.v.]. (TA.) ═ دَأْنِى [imp.], *i.q.* دَعْنِى, *Let me* &c. (Ḳ.) Said by some to be of weak authority. (TA.)

2. وَدَّأَ عليه الأَرْضَ, inf. n. تَوْدِئَةٌ, *He made the earth even,* or *plain, over him.* (AZ, Ṣ, Ḳ.) — وَدَّأَتْهُ الأَرْضُ *The earth,* or *the land, hid,* or *concealed, him.* (TA.) [See also 5.] — وَدَّأَ, *He,* or *it, buried.* (IAạr.) — وَدَّأَ بِهِمْ, inf. n. تَوْدِئَةٌ; (Ṣ, L;) accord. to the Ḳ, وَدَأَ; but this is incorrect; (TA;) *He covered,* or *overwhelmed, them with evil,* or *with ill treatment.* (L, Ḳ.)

5. تودّأت عَلَيْهِ الأَرْضُ *The earth became even,* or *plain, over him,* (Ḳ,) as over a dead body in the grave: (TA:) or *enclosed him:* or *was overturned over him:* or *was broken in pieces over him.* (Ḳ.) — *The earth,* or *the land, hid,* or *concealed, him.* (TA.) [See also 2.] This phrase is used when a person has gone away to the more distant parts of the earth, or land, so that it is not known what he has done: also, when a man has died; even if among his family. (ISh.) — تودّأت عَنْهُ الأَخْبَارُ *News,* or *tidings, of him were cut off,* or *ceased to come;* like ↓ وُدِئَتْ, *and were hid.* (Ḳ.) [In the Ḳ we read, و[تودّأت] عليه و[تودّأت] عنه الاخبارُ انقطعت: whence it seems that تودّأت عليه الاخبار الخ also has the above signification. But in the TA, after عليه, in the passage above quoted from the Ḳ, is inserted الارض. This word, however, has, I think, been inserted through inadvertence: if not, تودّأت عليه الارض signifies *The land was interrupted to him, and hid:* as also ↓ وُدِئَت.] — تودّأ عَلَى مَالِهِ *He took his property* or *wealth, and kept it carefully.* (Ḳ.) ═ تودّأ عَلَيْهِ *He,* or *it, destroyed him.* (Ṣ, Ḳ.)

وَدْءٌ *Perdition; destruction.* (Ḳ.)

مُوَدَّأٌ [Earth *made even,* or *plain,* over a person: or earth *hiding,* or *concealing,* him;] like مُمَحَّصٌ for مُمَحَّصٌ, &c. (TA.) — *A grave.* (See below.) — Zuheyr Ibn-Mes-ood Ed-Ḍabbee says, in an elegy on his brother Ubei,

أُبَىُّ إِنْ تُصْبِحْ رَهِينَ مُوَدَّإٍ ✱ زَلْجِ الجَوَانِبِ قَعْرُهُ مَلْحُودُ

[*O Ubei! if thou become a deposit in a place over which the earth is made even,* or *plain,* (or *in a place that hideth thee,* or *in a grave,*) *with smooth,* or *slippery, sides, and having its bottom hollowed out laterally,* —] (Ṣ, TA. See Ḥam, p. 466.) — مُوَدَّاةٌ *A place of destruction,* or *perdition;* or *a desert in which is no water.* (AA, Ṣ, Ḳ.) — Also, accord. to IAạr, or without ة, as in an example which he quotes, *A grave.* (TA.)

ودب

وَدْبٌ *An evil state,* or *condition.* (L, Ḳ.)

ودج

1. وَدَجَ, (Ṣ, Ḳ,) aor. ـِ, (Ṣ,) inf. n. وَدْجٌ (L, Ḳ) and وِدَاجٌ; (L;) and ↓ ودّج, inf. n. تَوْدِيجٌ; (Ḳ;) but the latter has an intensive signification; (Msb;) *He cut the vein called* الوَدَج: (Ḳ:) *he bled a beast by cutting the vein so called;* ودج with reference to a beast, as the object of the act, being the same as فَصَدَ with reference to a man. (Ṣ.) — وَدَجَ, inf. n. وَدْجٌ, ‡ *He put to rights; put into a right* or *proper state; adjusted.* (Ṣ, Ḳ.) وَدَجَ المَالَ *He put the property into a right* or *proper state.* (Msb.) وَدَجَ بَيْنَ القَوْمِ *He adjusted differences between the people,* (Ṣ, Msb,) *and put an end to evil.* (TA.)

2: see 1.

3. وادجهُ, inf. n. مُوَادَجَةٌ, ‡ *He acted towards him with gentleness and good nature.* (ISh, A.)

وَدَجٌ, (Ṣ, Ḳ,) also written with kesreh, [app. وِدَجٌ, but perhaps وَدِجٌ,] (Msb,) and وِدَاجٌ, (Ṣ, Ḳ,) [A name given to *each of the external jugular veins;*] *a certain vein in the neck;* (Ṣ, Ḳ;) *one of two veins, which are called the* وَدَجَانِ: (T, Ṣ, &c.:) these are *two veins extending from the head to the lungs;* and the pl. is أَوْدَاجٌ: (M:) or *two great veins on the right and left of the pit between the clavicles:* (Msb, TA:) they are *by the side of the* وَرِيدَانِ, [here app. meaning the *two carotid arteries,*] *and are of the number of the veins in which the blood* [*merely*] *runs,* whereas the وريدان are for pulsation and for [the diffusion of] the soul, النفس [i.e النَّفَس, not النَّفْس; for, accord. to the Arabs, the animal soul (الرُّوحُ الحَيَوَانِىُّ), as is said in the KT,) diffuses itself throughout the body, from the heart, by means of the pulsing veins, or arteries]: (T, Msb, TA:) accord. to some, the ودج and وريد are the same; [meaning, that each of these names is applied to the external jugular vein:] (Msb:) or the اوداج are the *veins which surround the windpipe:* (TA:) or the ودج is the *vein called the* أَخْدَع, [elsewhere said to be a branch from the وريد, in the place where one is cupped,] *which the slaughterer* [*of an animal*] *cuts through, thereby putting an end to life.* (Msb.) — وَدَجَانِ ‡ *Two brothers:* (Ṣ, Ḳ:) *two persons mutually attached;* likened to the two veins so called. (A.) بِئْسَ وَدَجَا حَرْبٍ هُمَا *Two evil brothers of war are they two.* (Ṣ.) ═ وَدَجٌ ‡ *A cause; a means whereby one attains to a thing;* syn. سَبَبٌ and وَسِيلَةٌ; (Ḳ;) or, as in some lexicons, وُصْلَةٌ. (TA.) Ex. كَانَ فُلَانٌ وَدَجِى إِلَى كَذَا *Such a one was my means of attaining to such a thing.* (TA.)

ودح

4. اودح *He confessed;* syn. أَقَرَّ: (L, Ḳ:) or *he confessed a falsehood,* or *what was false:* (ISk, T, Ḳ:) or *he confessed himself submissive to him who would lead, guide,* or *govern, him:* (AZ, T, Ḳ:) *he was submissive,* or *prompt in obedience, and humble.* (Ṣ, Ḳ.) — *He* (a ram) *held back, and would not mount the female.* (Ṣ, Ḳ.) — اودحت الإِبِلُ *The camels became fat and in good condition.* (Ṣ, Ḳ.)

[ودر, &c.

See Supplement.]

وذأ

1. وَذَأَهُ, (Ṣ, Ḳ,) aor. يَذَأُ, (TA,) inf. n. وَذْءٌ, (Ṣ,) *He imputed to him a vice, fault,* or *the like; despised him;* (Ṣ, Ḳ;) *chid him;* (Ṣ, Ḳ;) *and blamed,* or *reproached him.* (A'Obeyd.) ═ وَذَأَتْ عَنْهُ عَيْنُهُ *His eye recoiled from him,* or *it:* syn. نَبَتْ عنه. (Ḳ.)

8. إِتَّذَأَ, quasi-pass. of وَذَأَ, *He was charged with a vice, fault, or the like;* &c. (Ṣ, Ḳ.)

وَذْءٌ *Disapproved,* or *hateful, language;* (Ḳ;) whether it be reviling or of another description.

مَا بِهِ وَذْأَةٌ (like وَذْيَةٌ) *There is no fault,* or *defect,* (عِلَّة,) *in him or it.* (Aboo-Málik, Ḳ.*)

وذب

وِذَابٌ The *stomach of a ruminant beast,* (or, as in some lexicons, the *stomachs of such beasts,* TA,) *with the intestines,* or *guts, into which milk is put, and which are then cut in pieces,* [*and eaten*]: a pl. which has no sing. (ISd, Ḳ.) — Also The *perforations,* or *punctures, made in sewing,* or the *loops,* (the word in the original is

خُرُوب, pl. of خُرْبَة: in some of the lexicons, خُرَز: but both these words relate to the same things: TA: [whence it appears that, accord. to the author of the TA, &c., the former of the above two meanings is the one intended:]) *of a* مَزَادَة. (Ḳ.)

وذح

1. وَذِحَتِ الشَّاةُ, aor. تَوْذَحُ and تَيْذَحُ (Ṣ, Ḳ) or تِيذَحُ, (TA,) inf. n. وَذَحٌ, (Ṣ,) *The sheep was,* or *became, foul with* وَذَح [q.v. infrà]. (Ṣ, Ḳ.) — وَذِحَ, inf. n. as above, *He suffered from an inflammation and excoriation of the inner sides of his thighs;* (En-Naḍr, L, Ḳ;*) as also مَذِحَ (En-Naḍr, L.)

وَذَحٌ The *dung and urine that have clung to the wool of sheep,* (Ḳ,) or *to their tails and the inner sides of the roots of their thighs* (أَرْفَاغِهَا), *and dry* [*thereon*]: (Ṣ:) or the *filth that clings to the rump,* or *buttocks, of the ram:* (Th:) n. un. with ة: pl. وُذْحٌ; like بُدْنٌ, (Ṣ, Ḳ,) pl. of بَدَنَةٌ. (Ṣ.)

وذر

1. وَذِرَهُ, of the same measure as وَسِعَهُ, (Ṣ, Ḳ, TA,) or وَذَرَهُ, (Lth, ISk, T, TA,) is the original pret. of which the aor. is يَذَرُهُ (Lth, ISk, T, Ṣ, Ḳ, TA) signifying, *He leaves, lets alone,* or *ceases* or *desists from, it,* or *him; he leaves it undone;* syn. يَدَعُهُ, (ISk, T, Ṣ, Ḳ, TA,) and يَتْرُكُهُ; (Mṣb;) imp. ذَرْهُ, syn. دَعْهُ: (ISk, T, Ṣ, Ḳ, TA:) but the pret. is not used, (Lth, Sb, ISk, T, Ṣ, M, Mṣb, Ḳ,) تَرَكَهُ being used in its stead; (Lth, T, Ṣ, TA;) and because its pret. is not used, the aor. is of the measure يَفْعَلُ; for if there were a pret., [it would most probably be of the measure فَعَلَ, as this is the regular measure of trans. unaugmented triliteral verbs, and] the aor. would be of the measure يَفْعُلُ or يَفْعِلُ: (Sb, M, TA:) nor is the inf. n. used, (Lth, T, M, Mṣb, Ḳ, TA,) تَرْكٌ being used in its stead, (Lth, T, M, TA,) i. e., instead of وَذْرٌ: (Ḳ:) nor is the act. part. n., (ISk, T, Ṣ, Mṣb, Ḳ,) namely وَاذِرٌ, instead of which تَارِكٌ is used: (ISk, T, Ṣ:) or the pret. is sometimes used, (Mṣb, Ḳ,) though rarely, (Mṣb,) or by the deviation from the constant course of speech: (Ḳ:) so in the Ḳ; but in the M it is said, that the phrase لَمْ أَذِرْ وَرَائِى شَيْئًا [*I left not behind me anything,* with kesr to the ذ, and so in the original copy of the TT,] is related on the authority of some of the Arabs. (TA.) You say, دَعْ ذَا and ذَرْ ذَا [*Leave thou,* or *let alone,* or *cease* or *desist from, this*]. (ISk, T.) It is said in the Ḳur, [lxxiii. 11,] وَذَرْنِى وَٱلْمُكَذِّبِينَ *And leave me,* or *let me alone, with the beliers,* or *descrediters;* (Bḍ;) *commit their case to me,* (Bḍ, TA,) *and busy not thy heart respecting them;* (TA;) for I will stand thee in stead to recompense them. (Bḍ.)

[وذف, &c.

See Supplement.]

ورأ

1. وَرَأَ, aor. يَرَأُ, *He repelled, pushed,* or *thrust.* (Ḳ.) = وَرِئَ مِنَ الطَّعَامِ *He was,* or *became, filled with food.* (Ḳ.) = مَا وَرِئْتُ, and مَا وُرِئْتُ †, *I knew not.* (Ḳ.) مَا أُورِئْتُ † بِالشَّىْءِ *I knew not the thing,* or *of the thing.* (L.)

2 and 4: see 1.

5. تَوَرَّأَتْ عَلَيْهِ ٱلْأَرْضُ i. q. تَوَدَّأَتْ, *The earth became even,* or *plain, over him:* or *enclosed him:* &c. (IJ, Ḳ.)

10. اِسْتَوْرَأَتِ ٱلْإِبِلُ *The camels took fright and ran away, in a body, one after another:* (Aṣ:) accord. to AZ, this is said when they have taken fright and ascended a mountain; but if they have taken fright and run away in a plain, one says اِسْتَأْوَرَتْ: so in the dial. of the tribe of 'Okeyl. [Thus in the TA in this art.: but see اِسْتَوْرَتْ.]

وَرَآءُ and وَرَآءَ and وَرَآءِ, indecl., (Ḳ,) an adverbial noun of place or time: (Bḍ, &c.:) J mentions it in art. ورى, regarding the ء as substituted for ى; and this is the opinion of the Koofees, and of all writers on inflexion, though disapproved by F, who, however, mentions it again in art. ورى as though belonging to that art.: (TA:) *Behind:* and, contr., *before.* (Ḳ.) In like manner, الوَرَآءُ [*The location that is behind,* or *beyond;* and *the time past:* and, contr. *that is before,* or *preceding*]. (Ḳ.) Or it does not bear contr. meanings; but one meaning; namely, *what is concealed from one.* (Ḳ, art. ورى.) Or it is a homonym; [but not a word of contr. meanings; as it signifies *what is behind,* or *beyond, in respect of place,* and *what is before in respect of time*]. Fr. says, It is not allowable to say, of a man behind thee, that he is بَيْنَ يَدَيْكَ; nor of a man before thee, that he is وَرَآءَكَ; these expressions being only allowable [as synonymous] in cases relating to particular times of events or actions: thus one may say, وَرَآءَكَ بَرْدٌ شَدِيدٌ and بَيْنَ يَدَيْكَ برد شديد [meaning *Before thee is intense cold*]: each of these expressions is allowable because the intense cold is a thing that is coming; so, as it will overtake thee, it is, as it were, behind thee; and as thou wilt attain to the period thereof, it is, as it were, before thee. It is said in the Ḳur, [xviii. 78,] كَانَ وَرَآءَهُمْ مَلِكٌ *There was before them a king:* [because it has reference to a certain period, which might be said to be before them as they would attain to it, and behind them as it would overtake them: this passage Jelál-ed-Deen explains by saying, "there was behind them when they returned, and before them now, a king."] Of the same kind also is the phrase مِنْ وَرَائِهِ جَهَنَّمُ [Ḳur, xiv. 19,] *Before him is hell:* [for the same reason]. (TA.) — وَيَكْفُرُونَ بِمَا وَرَآءَهُ, [Ḳur, ii. 85,] signifies *And they disbelieve in what* [*hath been revealed*] *beside that:* syn. سِوَاهُ: (IAạr:) or it may mean *after that.* (Jel.) — وراء is masc. and fem. (TA.) Its dim. is وُرَيِّئَةٌ, (Ḳ,) accord. to those who hold the ء to be a radical letter, not substituted for ى; namely, the Baṣrees: accord. to others, وُرَيَّةٌ and وُرَىٌّ (TA.) — رَجُلٌ مَانِعٌ مَا وَرَآءَهُ — [See also art. ورى.] — وَرَاءَ ظَهْرِهِ: see زَبُونَةٌ. — وَرَآءٌ *A son's son,* or *son's offspring.* (Ḳ.) — وَرَآءٌ *Bulky, and thick in the* أَلْوَاح, or *shoulder-blades.* (AAF.)

ورب

1. وَرِبَ, aor. يَوْرَبُ, inf. n. وَرَبٌ, *It,* or *he,* (a root, origin, or stock, Ṣ, or a man, TA,) *was,* or *became, corrupt.* (Ṣ, Ḳ.)

2. وَرَّبَ, inf. n. تَوْرِيبٌ, [app., *He expressed himself respecting a thing equivocally,* or *ambiguously, by words objectionable in one sense, and allowable in another:* so thinks IbrD:] the inf. n. is thus explained: أَنْ تُوَرِّىَ عَنِ الشَّىْءِ بِالْمُعَارَضَاتِ وَالْمُبَاحَاتِ. (T, Ḳ, but in the latter, the و before the last word is omitted.)

3. وارب, inf. n. مُوَارَبَةٌ *He strove to outwit, deceive, beguile,* or *circumvent* [another]: syn. خَاتَلَ and دَاهَى. (Ḳ.) Accord. to IAth, it is from الوَرَبُ "the being corrupt:" or it may be from الارب "intelligence, &c.;" the أ being changed into و. The latter is the opinion of AM. (L.) — One of the sages says, مُوَارَبَةُ الأَرِيبِ جَهْلٌ وَعَنَآءٌ [*The striving to outwit the cunning,* or *intelligent,* or *sagacious, is ignorance and labour without profit*]. (TA.) [See art. أرب, where this saying, but with مؤاربة in the place of مواربة, is given as a trad.] — It is said in a trad., إِنْ بَايَعْتَهُمْ وَارَبُوكَ, i. e., خَادَعُوكَ, *If thou buy and sell with them, they will deceive thee,* or *endeavour to deceive the.* (IAth.)

وَرْبٌ The *hole of a wild beast:* pl. أَوْرَابٌ. (Ḳ, TA.) — وَرْبٌ The *space between two ribs;* مَا بَيْنَ الضِّلَعَيْنِ: (Ḳ:) but this (says SM) I find not in any other book than the Ḳ; and probably it should be ما بين إِصْبَعَيْنِ the *space between two fingers;* for we read in the L that ورب is said to signify ما بين الأَصَابِعِ: (TA:) pl. أَوْرَابٌ. (Ḳ, TA.) [See also أَرْبٌ.] — وَرْبٌ The *space measured by the extension of the thumb and fore-finger;* syn. فِتْرٌ: pl. أَوْرَابٌ. (Ḳ, TA.) = وَرْبٌ

A member; a limb: pl. أَوْرَابٌ. (Ḳ, TA.) ▾ وَرْبٌ [also] is a dial. from of إِرْبٌ, (Ḳ,) as signifying "a member, or limb." (TA.) The form of word commonly known, says AM, is إِرْبٌ; but I do not deny that ورب may be a dial. form, like as وِرْثٌ and إِرْثٌ are two words whereof one is a dial. form of the other. (TA.) — وَرْبٌ and ▾ وَرْبَةٌ The *podex:* syn. إِسْتٌ: pl. of the former أَوْرَابٌ. (Ḳ, TA.) — ▾ وَرْبَةٌ The *pit,* or *hollow, that is in the lower part of the side, i. e., the hypochondre,* or *flank.* (TA.) — وَرْبٌ The *mouth of the hole of a rat,* or *mouse,* (فَأْرَة,) *and of a scorpion:* pl. أَوْرَابٌ. (Ḳ.)

وُرْبٌ: see وَرْبٌ.

وَرْبَةٌ: see وَرْبٌ.

وَرِبٌ *Corrupt.* (Ḳ.) — عِرْقٌ وَرِبٌ *A corrupt root, origin,* or *stock.* (Ṣ, Ḳ.) Aboo-Dharrah El-Hudhalee says,

* إِنْ تَنْتَسِبْ تُنْسَبْ إِلَى عِرْقٍ وَرِبْ *

[*If thou mention thy lineage, thy lineage is traced up to a corrupt origin,* or *stock*]. (Ṣ.) — رَجُلٌ وَرِبٌ *A corrupt man.* (TA.) — وَرِبٌ A cloud *that is loose* (Ḳ) *and much broken.* (TA.)

مُوَرَّبٌ [i. q. مُؤَرَّبٌ] A member, or limb, *cut off entire.* (TA.)

ورث

1. وَرِثَ, aor. يَرِثُ, (Ṣ, Ḳ,) an instance of deviation from a constant rule, there being only the following verbs of the measure فَعِلَ which have the aorists of the measure يَفْعِلُ only, namely, وَرِثَ, وَثِقَ, وَرِعَ, وَرِمَ, وَرِىَ, وَفِقَ, وَلِىَ, and وَمِقَ, (Ibn-Málik and others,) and وَصِبَ: (TA, art. وصب:) the و falls out in يَرِثُ [&c.] because it occurs between ى and kesreh; and in those persons of the aor. which begin with ا and ت and ن because these letters are changed from ى, which is the original: (Ṣ:) inf. n. وِرْثٌ and إِرْثٌ, (Ṣ, Ḳ,) in which the و is changed into ا, (Ṣ,) and رِثَةٌ, (Ṣ, Ḳ,) in which the ة is a substitute for the [elided] و, (Ṣ,) and وِرَاثَةٌ (Ṣ, Ḳ,) [the most common form] and إِرَاثَةٌ, (TA,) and accord. to some مِيرَاثٌ, but this is an error, for مِفْعَالٌ is not one of the measures of inf. ns., (ISd,) [but it is used by some of the professors of practical law as an inf. n.,] and تُرَاثٌ: (Mṣb [but see وِرْثٌ below]:) *He inherited.* (Ṣ, Ḳ, &c.) You say وَرِثَ أَبَاهُ *He inherited* [*the property of*] *his father:* (Ṣ, Ḳ:) but the original phrase is وَرِثَ مَالَ أَبِيهِ *He inherited the property of his father.* (Mṣb.) Also وَرِثَ مِنْ أَبِيهِ (and عَنْهُ, A,) *He inherited of his father:* (Ḳ:) *or he inherited part of the property of his father.* (Mṣb.) And وَرِثَ الشَّىْءَ مِنْ أَبِيهِ *He inherited the thing of,* or *from, his father.* (Ṣ.) When you say وَرِثَ زَيْدٌ أَبَاهُ مَالًا [*Zeyd inherited of his father property*], the word مالا is a second objective complement, if the verb be doubly trans.; or it is a substitute of implication (بَدَلُ ٱشْتِمَالٍ) for زيد. (MF.) You say وَرِثْتُهُ مَالَهُ, and مَجْدَهُ, *I inherited his property,* and, ‡ *his glory:* and وَرِثْتُهُ عَنْهُ *I inherited it from him.* (TA.)

2. وَرَّثَهُ, inf. n. تَوْرِيثٌ, *He included him among the heirs of his property:* (Ṣ:) or *made him to be one of his heirs:* (TA:) [see also 4:] or وَرَّثَهُ مَالًا *he included him among his heirs, he not being one of them, and assigned him a portion:* (AZ, Mṣb:) [in like manner,] وَرَّثَ فِى مَالِهِ *he included among his heirs of his property one or more not of them.* (TA.) — وَرَّثْتُ فُلَانًا مِنْ فُلَانٍ *I made such a one to be the heir of such a one.* (TA.) See 4. — وَرَّثَ *He stirred* a fire, *in order that it might burn up,* or *blaze:* (Ḳ:) a dial. form of أَرَّثَ, q. v. (TA.)

4. اورثهُ الشَّىْءَ *He* (his father) *made him to inherit the thing.* (Ṣ.) — اورثهُ إِيرَاثًا حَسَنًا *He made him to have a goodly inheritance.* (TA.) اورثهُ الإِرْثَ, and ▾ وَرَّثَهُ إِيَّاهُ, and المِيرَاثَ, *He made him to inherit the heritage.* (A.) — اورثهُ and ▾ وَرَّثَهُ *He* (his father) *made him to be one of his heirs.* (Ḳ.) [See also 2.] — اورث وَلَدَهُ *He made his son sole heir.* (AZ.) — اورثهُ شَيْئًا ‡ *It occasioned him, as its result, a thing.* Ex. اورثه المَرَضُ ضَعْفًا ‡ *The disease occasioned him, as its result, weakness.* (TA.)

6. تَوَارَثُوهُ كَابِرًا عَنْ كَابِرٍ ‡ [*They inherited it by degrees, one great in dignity and nobility from another great in dignity and nobility*]. (Ṣ.) [See art. كبر.] — تَوَارَثَتْنِى الحَوَادِثُ (Bedr Ibn-'Ámir El-Hudhalee) ‡ *Misfortune took me by turns, as though they inherited me, one from another.* (TA.)

وَرْثٌ ‡ What is *fresh, juicy,* or *moist,* of things. (Ḳ.)

وِرْثٌ and ▾ إِرْثٌ [see 1] and ▾ تُرَاثٌ (in which the ت is originally و, Ṣ,) and مِيرَاثٌ (originally مِوْرَاثٌ, the و being changed to ى because of the kesreh immediately preceding it, Ṣ,) *What is inherited; an inheritance,* or *a heritage:* or, accord. to some, ورث and ميراث are used with reference to property, or wealth; and ارث with reference to rank or quality, nobility or eminence, reputation, or the like, in Arabic, حَسَبٌ: (M:) [the pl. of ميراث is مَوَارِيثُ.] [See also art. أرث.] — اُثْبُتُوا عَلَى مَشَاعِرِكُمْ هٰذِهِ فَإِنَّكُمْ عَلَى إِرْثٍ مِنْ إِرْثِ إِبْرٰهِيمَ ‡ *Remain ye steadfast in the observance of these your rites, or ceremonies; for ye act* [*therein*] *according to usage inherited from Abraham.* (TA, [app. from A'Obeyd].) [See also إِرْثٌ in art. أرث.] — لَهُمْ إِرْثُ مَجْدٍ ‡ *They have an inheritance of glory.* (TA.)

وُرْثَةٌ *Fire.* (L.)

وَارِثٌ *An heir:* pl. وُرَّاثٌ and وَرَثَةٌ. (Mṣb.) — It is said in a prayer (of Mohammad, TA) اَللّٰهُمَّ أَمْتِعْنِى بِسَمْعِى وَبَصَرِى وَٱجْعَلْهُ الوَارِثَ مِنِّى [*O God, cause me to enjoy my hearing and my sight, and make it* (i. e. the enjoyment that I pray for, TA) *survive me:* or,] *make it to continue with me until I die.* (Ḳ.) Or, accord. to another relation, which substitutes وَٱجْعَلْهُمَا for واجعله, *make them both to continue with me, sound, until I die.* Or, as some say, what is meant is the continuance and strength of those two faculties in old age, so that they may survive all the other powers: so says ISh. Some say, that by سَمْع is meant the remembering of what is heard, and the acting according thereto; and by بَصَر, the being admonished by what is seen, and the light of the heart, whereby one escapes from perplexity and darkness to the right course. (TA.) — الوَارِثُ (as an epithet applied to God, TA.) *He who remains after the creatures have perished.* (Ḳ.) He remains after everything beside Him has perished; and thus, what was the property of mankind, his servants, returns to Him. (TA.)

إِرْثٌ:
مِيرَاثٌ:
تُرَاثٌ: see وِرْثٌ, and 1.

مَوْرُوثٌ Property *inherited.* (Mṣb.)

المَجْدُ مُتَوَارَثٌ بَيْنَهُمْ ‡ *Glory is inherited among them.* (A.)

ورخ

1. وَرِخَ, aor. يَوْرَخُ, (Ṣ, L, Ḳ,) inf. n. وَرَخٌ; (Ṣ, L;) and ▾ تورّخ; (L;) *It* (dough) *was,* or *became, thin,* or *flaccid,* (Ṣ, L, Ḳ,) *by reason of the abundance of water in it.* (Ṣ, L.)

2. ورّخ الكِتَابَ بِيَوْمِ كَذَا *He inscribed the writing,* or *letter, with the date of such a day;* i. q. أَرَّخَهُ; (Ṣ, Ḳ*;) of which it is a dial. form. (Yaḳoob.)

4. اورخ *He made* dough *thin,* or *flaccid,* (Ṣ, L, Ḳ,) *by putting much water to it.* (L.)

5: see 1: — and 10.

10. استورخت الأَرْضُ, and ▾ تورّخت, *The land,* or *ground, became wet,* or *moist.* (Ḳ.)

وَرْخٌ *A kind of tree resembling the* مَرْخ *in its*

growth, (L, Ḳ,) except that it is dust-coloured, having slender leaves, like the leaves of the طَرْخُون, or larger. (L.)

أَرْضٌ وَرِخَةٌ Land having tangled and luxuriant herbage. (Ḳ.)

وَرِيخَةٌ Dough that is thin, or flaccid, (Ṣ, Ḳ,) by reason of the abundance of water in it. (Ṣ.) — Wet, or moist, land, or ground. (Ḳ.)

تَوَارِيخ, pl. of تَوْرِيخ : see تَأْرِيخ.

ورد

1. وَرَدَهُ, (Ṣ, M, L, Mṣb,) aor. يَرِدُ, (Ṣ, L, Mṣb,) inf. n. وُرُودٌ (M, L, Mṣb) and مَوْرِدٌ (L) and وِرْدٌ, (M, L, Ḳ,) or the last is a simple subst., (L, Mṣb,) *He* (a man, and a camel, &c., Mṣb) *came to it*, or *arrived at it*, (M, Mgh, L, Mṣb, Ḳ,) [*and repaired to it*,] namely a water (Ṣ, M, L, Mṣb, Ḳ) &c., (M, L, Ḳ,) whether he entered it or did not enter it; (M, Mgh, L, Mṣb, Ḳ;) as also وَرَدَ عَلَيْهِ, (M, L,) and ↓ تَوَرَّدَهُ, (M, L, Ḳ,) and ↓ اِسْتَوْرَدَهُ : (M, A, Mgh, L, Ḳ:) *he came to it* (namely a water) *to drink*: (L:) ‡ *he arrived at it* (namely a town or country or the like), whether he entered it or did not enter it: (Mgh, L:) it is allowed by common consent not necessarily to imply entering. (L.) [Hence, وَرَدَتِ الإِبِلُ, the objective complement مَآءً or المَآءَ being understood, *The camels came to water.*] — وَرَدَ, inf. n. وُرُودٌ, *He came; he was*, or *became, present.* (Ṣ, L.) — وَرَدَ عَلَيْنَا, inf. n. وُرُودٌ, † *He* (a man) *came to us.* (Mṣb.) — وَرَدَ الكِتَابُ (A, Mṣb,) inf. n. [وُرُودٌ and] مَوْرِدٌ (A,) ‡ *The letter came*, (A, Mṣb,) you say, وَرَدَ عَلَىَّ *to me*: (A.) — هُوَ يَتَوَرَّدُ ↓ المَهَالِكَ ‡ *He ventures upon*, or *goes into, places of destruction*]. (A.) — وَرَدَهَا, and ↓ اِسْتَوْرَدَ الضَّلَالَةَ ‡ [*He ran into error*]. (A.) — وَرَدَ عَلَيْهِ أَمْرٌ لَمْ يُطِقْهُ ‡ [*A thing befell him which he was unable to master*]. (A.) — وَرَدَ عَلَيْهِ *It contravened it; presented itself as an objection to it; opposed it.*] — [وَرَدَ, said of a word or phrase or the like, *It occurred.*] — وَرَدَتْهُ الحُمَّى, (aor. تَرِدُ, Mṣb, inf. n. وِرْدٌ, A) ‡ *The fever attacked him periodically.* (Ṣ, A, L, Mṣb.) — وُرِدَ ‡ *He suffered a periodical attack of fever.* (A, L, Mṣb.) = وَرُدَ, aor. ـُ, (Ṣ, Mṣb, Ḳ,) inf. n. وُرُودَةٌ; (Ṣ, L, Mṣb;) and ↓ اِيرَادٌ, originally اِوْرَادٌ, the و becoming ى because of the kesreh before it; (Ṣ, L, Ḳ;) ‡ *He* (a horse) *was*, or *became*, [*of a bright*, or *yellowish bay colour*;] *of a colour between that called* كُمَيْت and أَشْقَر : (Ṣ, L, Ḳ:) or, *of a red colour inclining to yellow.* (M, L, Mṣb.) — وُرُودُ الأَرْنَبَةِ see شَمَرَ and أَرْنَبَةٌ.

2. وَرَّدَ ثَوْبَهُ ‡ [*He dyed his garment*, or *piece of cloth, red*, or *of a rose-colour*]. (A.) — وَرَّدَتِ الشَّجَرَةُ, (AḤn, L, Ḳ,) inf. n. تَوْرِيدٌ; (Ḳ;) and وَرَدَتْ, aor. تَرِدُ; (Mṣb;) *The tree flowered*, or *blossomed.* (AḤn, L, Mṣb, Ḳ.) — وَرَّدَتْ ‡ *She* (a woman) *reddened her cheek with the dye of dyed cotton.* (L.)

3. وَارَدَهُ, (inf. n. مُوَارَدَةٌ, A,) *He came to water with him.* (L, Ḳ.) — بَيْنَ الشَّاعِرَيْنِ مُوَارَدَةٌ, and تَوَارُدٌ, ‡ [*Between the two poets is an agreement*, or *a coincidence, in ideas and expressions*; as though they both drew from the same source]. (A.) Similar to this is the phrase تَوَارُدُ الخَاطِرِ ‡ [*Agreement*, or *coincidence, of thought*, or *idea*]. (TA.)

4. اَوْرَدَهُ, and ↓ اِسْتَوْرَدَهُ, (Ḳ,) and ↓ تَوَرَّدَهُ, (ISd,) *He brought him to the watering-place.* (Ḳ.) — Also, the first and second of these verbs, *He brought him; made him to come*, or *to be present.* (Ṣ, L.) — [And the first, *He adduced it*, or *cited it*; namely, an evidence, a speech or saying, a word, &c. — *He set it forth*, or *expressed it*; namely, a meaning.] — اورده المَآءَ, (inf. n. اِيرَادٌ, A.) *He made him to come to the water.* (L, Mṣb.) [See an ex. voce حَمْضٌ.] — اورده الضَّلَالَةَ ‡ [*He made him to run into error.* (A.) — أَوْرَدَ عَلَيْهِ خَيْرًا [*He brought to him wealth, property*, or *what was good.*] (Mugh, in art. حطب.) — اورد عَلَيْهِ الخَبَرَ ‡ *He related to him the news.* (L.) — اورد الشَّىْءَ ‡ *He mentioned the thing.* (TA.) — أَوْرَدَ وَأَصْدَرَ ‡ *He began and compelled.* (TA, art. صدر.) — اورده واصدره *He brought it and he took it away.* (Har. p. 361.)

5: see 1, and 4, and 10. — تَوَرَّدَتِ الخَيْلُ البَلْدَةَ ‡ *The horses entered the town by little and little.* (Ṣ, L, Ḳ.*) = تورّد ‡ [*It became red, roseate*, or *rose-coloured*]: said of a woman's cheek. (A.)

6. تواردنا *We came to water together.* (A.)

10. استورد (ISd) and ↓ تورّد (Ḳ) *He desired to come to water.* (ISd, Ḳ.) [See an ex. of the part. n. voce حَمْضٌ.] — See 1 and 4.

11: see 1.

وَرْدٌ [coll. gen. n.] The *flower*, or *blossom*, of any tree (AḤn, L, Ḳ) or plant: (AḤn, L:) but its predominant application is to the *rose*, جُوجَم, (L, Ḳ,) the *well-known red flower* (TA) *which one smells*: (Ṣ, L, TA:) its colour varies in winter and summer: (L:) and it is of different kinds in the cultivated soil and in the desert and in the mountains: (AḤn, L:) n. un. with ة. (Ṣ, L.) Said to be an arabicized word. (Mṣb.)

وَرْدٌ ‡ A horse [*of a bright*, or *yellowish, bay colour*;] *of a colour between that called* كُمَيْت *and* أَشْقَر : (Ṣ, L, Ḳ:) a horse, (M, L, Mṣb,) or other thing, (M, L,) *of a red colour inclining to yellow*, (M, L, Mṣb,) beautiful in everything: (M, L:) fem. with ة: (Ṣ, L, Mṣb:) applied in the above sense to the sky, in the Ḳur, lv. 37: (L:) or it there means *roseate*, or *of a rose-colour*: (Zj, L:) pl. وُرْدٌ, (Ṣ, L, Ḳ,) like as جُونٌ is pl. of جَوْنٌ, (Ṣ,) and وِرَادٌ (Ṣ, L, Mṣb, Ḳ) and أَوْرَادٌ : (Ḳ:) but this last is unknown, and app. a mistake. (M, F, TA.) — وَرْدٌ ‡ A lion *of the colour termed* وَرْد : (Ṣ, A, L:) or *a lion*; as also ↓ مُتَوَرِّدٌ. (Ḳ.) — عَشِيَّةٌ وَرْدَةٌ ‡ *An evening when the horizon is red* (L, Ḳ) *at sunset*; which is a sign of drought: and in like manner the morning at sunrise. (L.) — لَيْلَةٌ وَرْدَةٌ ‡ *A night of which the beginning and end are red*; which is the case in a time of drought. (A.) — وَرْدٌ *Bold*, or *daring*; (Ḳ;) an epithet applied to a man; (TA;) as also ↓ وَارِدٌ. (Ḳ.) — وَرْدٌ *Saffron.* (Ḳ.) — الوَرْدُ الجَبَلِىُّ : see عَبَالٌ. — أَبُو الوَرْدِ ‡ *The penis*: (Ḳ:) so called because of its redness. (TA.)

وِرْدٌ *A coming to*, or *arriving at, water &c.*, whether one enters it or does not enter it; (Ṣ,* L, Mṣb, Ḳ;) *contr.* of صَدَرٌ. (Ṣ, L, Mṣb.) See also 1. — وِرْدٌ *Water to which one comes to drink.* (L.) — وِرْدٌ *The time of the day of coming to water, between the two periods of abstaining from water*: (L:) *a time*, or *turn, of coming to water.* (TA in art. حزب.) — وِرْدٌ *The arrival of the day of coming to water.* (L.) — وَرَدَتِ الإِبِلُ المَآءَ وِرْدًا, and أَوْرَادًا, and in like manner, الطَّيْرُ, *The camels*, and *the birds, came to the water in a herd*, or *in a flock*, and *in herds*, or *in flocks.* (L.) — وِرْدٌ *A company of men*, (Ṣ, L, Mṣb, Ḳ,) and *a number of camels*, and *of birds, &c.*, (L,) *coming to*, or *arriving at, water*; (Ṣ, L, Mṣb, Ḳ;) as also ↓ وَارِدَةٌ : (L, Mṣb, Ḳ:) the former originally an inf. n.: (Mṣb:) its pl. is أَوْرَادٌ. (L.) See also وَارِدٌ. — وِرْدٌ *A herd of camels.* (L.) — *A flock of birds.* (L, Ḳ.) — ‡ *An army*, (L, Ḳ,) so called as being likened to a herd of camels, or to a flock of birds. (L.) — *A portion*, or *share, of water.* (L, Ḳ.) — *Thirst.* (L.) — نَسُوقُ المُجْرِمِينَ إِلَى جَهَنَّمَ وِرْدًا [Ḳur, xix. 89,] † *We will drive the sinners to hell like beasts that come to water*: or, *thirsty*: (Beyḍ:) or, *walking and thirsty.* (Zj, L.) — وِرْدٌ ‡ The *day of a fever, when it attacks the patient periodically*: (Aṣ, Ṣ, L, Mṣb,* Ḳ*:) or *one of the names of fever*: (L, Ḳ:) but the former explanation is the more correct. (TA.) — وِرْدٌ † *A portion of the night when a man has to pray.* (L.) — وِرْدٌ ‡ *A section*, or *division*, (Ṣ, L, Ḳ,) *of the Ḳur-án*: (L, Ḳ:) *a set portion of recitation or the like*: (Mṣb:) *a certain portion of the Ḳur-án, as a seventh*, or *half a seventh, or the like*, (Mgh, L,) *which a person recites at a particular time*: (L:) *a set portion of the Ḳur-án*, or *of prayer; &c., of which a man imposes upon himself the recital on a particular occasion*, or *at a particular time*; *i. q.* حِزْبٌ *q. v.*: (Mgh, L:) pl. أَوْرَادٌ. (L, Mṣb.) Ex. قَرَأْتُ وِرْدِى [*I recited my set portion of the Ḳur-án, &c.*]: (Ṣ, L:) and لِفُلَانٍ كُلَّ لَيْلَةٍ وِرْدٌ

يَقْرَأُهُ مِنَ القُرْآنِ Such a one has every night a set portion of the Ḳur-án which he recites. (L.)

وُرْدَةٌ [A bright, or yellowish, bay colour;] a colour between that of a horse that is termed كُمَيْت and that of one termed أَشْقَر: (Ṣ, L:) or a red colour inclining to yellow. (L.)

بِنْتُ وَرْدَانَ, (Mṣb,) pl. بَنَاتُ وَرْدَانَ, (Ḳ,) A certain insect, (Mṣb, Ḳ,) well known, (Ḳ,) like the beetle, of a red colour, mostly found in baths and in privies. (Mṣb.)

الوَرِيدُ, and حَبْلُ الوَرِيدِ, [Each of the two carotid arteries: and sometimes applied to each of the two external jugular veins:] each of two veins asserted by the Arabs to be from the وَتِين [or aorta], on the right and left of the two sides of the neck, next the fore part, and thick: (Ṣ, L:) or the وريد is a certain vein, said to be the وَدَج [or external jugular vein]: or, by the side of the ودج: or, accord. to Fr, a certain vein between the windpipe and [the two sinews called] the عِلْبَاوَانِ, always pulsing; being one of the veins in which is the life; the blood not flowing in it, but only the soul, النفس [i. e., النَّفْس, not النَّفَس; for, accord. to the Arabs, the animal soul (الرُّوحُ الحَيَوَانِىُّ, as is said in the KT,) diffuses itself throughout the body, from the heart, by means of the pulsing veins, or arteries: see also وَدَجٌ]: (Mṣb:) or the وَرِيدَانِ are two veins in the neck, (AZ, L, Ḳ,) between the أَوْدَاج [or external jugular veins] and [the two parts of the neck called] the لِيتَانِ: in the camel, the وَدَجَانِ [or two external jugular veins]: (AZ, T:) or, accord. to AHeyth, and his is the correct explanation, two veins beneath the وَدَجَانِ, [see above,] which latter are two thick veins on the right and left of the pit between the clavicles; they (the former) are always pulsing, in man: the وريد is a vein in which the soul (النفس [see above]) flows, and in which the blood does not flow: and every pulsing vein, in which the life flows, is of those thus called: (T:) or the وريد is the vein in each side of the neck which swells out on an occasion of anger: (L:) or four veins in the head; of which two descend before the ears, and of which are the وريدان in the neck: or a certain vein beneath the tongue: and, in the upper half of the arm, the قَلِيق [or cephalic]: and, in the fore arm, the أَكْحَل [or median]: and, among those which separate in the outer side of the hand, the أَشَاجِع: and, in the belly of the fore arm, the رَوَاهِش: (T:) pl. أَوْرِدَةٌ [a pl. of pauc.] (M, Mṣb, Ḳ) and وُرُدٌ, (M, Mṣb,) like as بُرُدٌ is pl. of بَرِيدٌ, (Mṣb,) [and وُتُنٌ of وَتِينٌ, &c.,] or وُرُودٌ, (Ḳ,) [but this I think a mistake]. — رَجُلٌ مُنْتَفِخُ الوَرِيدِ [A man whose external jugular vein swells out;] a man of bad disposition or temper, prone to anger. (TA.)

وَرَّادٌ: see وَارِدٌ.

وَارِدٌ A man, and a camel, or other animal, (L,) coming to, or arriving at water, &c., whether he enter it or do not enter it; (L, Mṣb, Ḳ;) as also ↓ وَرَّادٌ: (L, CḲ:) pl. of the former, وُرَّادٌ, (Ṣ, L, Mṣb, Ḳ) and وَارِدُونَ: (L:) and of the latter, وَرَّادُونَ. (L.) See also وِرْدٌ. — إِنْ مِنْكُمْ إِلَّا وَارِدُهَا [Ḳur, xix. 72, There is not any of you that shall not come to it,] means, accord. to Th, that the Muslims shall come to hell with the unbelievers, but not enter it with them. (L.) — طَرِيقٌ وَارِدٌ ‡ A road, or way, by which people come to water: opposed to صَادِرٌ. (M, A, art. صدر.) See also مَوْرِدٌ. — مَا لَهُ صَادِرٌ وَلَا وَارِدٌ: see art. صدر. — وَارِدٌ A preceder. (L, Ḳ.) So (accord. to some, TA) in the Ḳur, xii. 19. (L.) — وَارِدٌ Courageous; (Ḳ;) bold; forward in affairs. (TA.) See also وِرْدٌ. — شَعْرٌ وَارِدٌ ‡ Long and lank hair: (L, Ḳ:) or hair so long as to reach the buttocks, (A,) of a woman. (L.) — وَارِدٌ ‡ Anything long. (L.) — أَرْنَبَةٌ وَارِدَةٌ ‡ The end, or tip, of a nose advancing over the middle of the mustaches: (A, L:) because the nose, when it is long, reaches to the water when the person drinks: and in like manner, a lip, and a gum. (L.) — فُلَانٌ وَارِدُ الأَرْنَبَةِ ‡ Such a one has a long end, or tip, to his nose. (Ṣ, L, Ḳ.) شَجَرَةٌ وَارِدَةُ الأَغْصَانِ ‡ A tree having pendulous branches. (L.) — See وِرْدٌ.

وَارِدَةٌ: see وِرْدٌ, وَارِدٌ, and مَوْرِدٌ.

إِيرَادٌ ‡ Income; revenue: pl. إِيرَادَاتٌ.]

مَوْرِدٌ A place of coming to water: (Mṣb:) a watering-place: (L:) and ↓ مَوْرِدَةٌ a road, or way, by which one comes to water; (L, Ḳ;) as also ↓ وَارِدَةٌ: (A, Ḳ:) pl. of the first (L) and second, (TA,) مَوَارِدُ; (L, TA;) and of the third, وَارِدَاتٌ. (TA.) — Hence, (A, TA,) مَوْرِدٌ and ↓ وَارِدٌ ‡ A road, or way; (Ṣ, L;) as also ↓ وَارِدَةٌ: (TA:) or the last, the middle and main part of a road; or a main road; or simply, a road; syn. جَادَّةٌ; (Ḳ;) as also مَوْرِدَةٌ: (L, Ḳ:) pls. as above. (A, TA.) — مَوَارِدُ أَمْرٍ ‡ [The ways leading to a thing: or the ways of commencing a thing]: (TA, art. رحب.) [See an ex., voce تَرَاحَبَ; and see its opposite, مَصَادِرُ أَمْرٍ, voce مَصْدَرٌ.] — [مَوْرِدٌ also signifies, agreeably with analogy, The time of coming to water: pl. مَوَارِدُ: see the last signification of ثُلَّةٌ in this lexicon: see also وِرْدٌ.] — مَوْرِدُ مَثَلٍ ‡ [The primary idea, or thing, signified by a parable or proverb: correlative of مَضْرِبُ مَثَلٍ: pl. مَوَارِدُ.] (TA, &c., passim.)

مَوْرِدَةٌ: see مَوْرِدٌ.

مَوْرُودٌ ‡ Attached by a fever periodically: (Ṣ, L:) or suffering a periodical attack of fever. (Mṣb.) — An Arab of the desert said to another, مَا أَمَارُ إِفْرَاقِ المَوْرُودِ [What is the sign of the convalescence of him who is attacked by a periodical fever?] and he answered, الرُّحَضَاءُ [The sweat which follows it; or copious sweat]. (Ṣ.)

مُوَرَّدٌ ‡ A shirt dyed of a rose-colour; of a less deep dye than that which is termed مُضَرَّجٌ: (Ṣ, L;) or dyed with saffron. (TA.) — خَدٌّ مُوَرَّدٌ ‡ A reddened cheek. (TA.) — رَجَعَ مُوَرَّدَ القَذَالِ ‡ He returned [with the back of his head] slapped, or thumped with the fist, [and rendered red]. (A.)

مُتَوَرِّدٌ: see وِرْدٌ.

ورس

1. وَرَسَ, inf. n. وُرُوسٌ, It (a plant) became green. (AA, A, Ḥn, M.) — See also 4. — وَرَسَ, (M, Ḳ,) aor. يَوْرُسُ, (Ḳ,) It (a rock, M, Ḳ, in water, Ḳ) became overspread with [the green substance called] طُحْلُب, so that it became green and smooth. (IDrd, M, Ḳ.) — See also 4.

2. وَرَّسَهُ, inf. n. تَوْرِيسٌ, He dyed it (a garment, or piece of cloth,) with وَرْس, q. v. (Ṣ, Ḳ.)

4. اورس المَكَانُ The place produced the plant called وَرْس. (Ṣ.) — اورس الرِّمْثُ The [trees called] رمث produced وَرْس, a thing yellow like the [garments termed] مُلَاء; as also ↓ وَرَسَ: so it is asserted, on trustworthy authority: (M:) or became yellow in their leaves, (Ṣ, Ḳ,) after attaining to maturity, (Ṣ,) and had upon them what was like yellow مُلَاء; (Ṣ, Ḳ;) and in like manner one says of a place, اورس المَكَانُ: (TA:) or became yellow in its fruit: (A:) — اورس الشَّجَرُ The trees put forth leaves; (Ḳ;) as also ↓ وَرَسَ. (IKṭṭ.)

وَرْسٌ A certain plant, (Ṣ, A, Mṣb, Ḳ,) of a yellow colour, (Ṣ, Mṣb,) resembling sesame, (A, Ḳ,) with which one dyes, (A, Mṣb,) and of which is made the [liniment called] غُمْرَة for the face, (Ṣ,) existing in El-Yemen, (Ṣ, Ḳ,) and nowhere else, (Ḳ,) being there sown; (Mṣb;) it is not wild, but is sown one year, and remains ten years, (AḤn, M,) or twenty years, (Ḳ,) without ceasing to be profitable, resembling sesame in its manner of growth; and when it dries, on its attaining to maturity, its pericarps (خَرَائِط) burst, and it is shaken, and the وَرْس shakes out from it: (AḤn, M,) it is useful for the [discolouration of the face termed] كَلَف, used as a liniment; and for the [leprous-like discolouration of the skin termed] بَهَق, [prepared] as a drink; and the wearing of a garment dyed with it strengthens the venereal faculty: (Ḳ:) or a certain yellow dye: or, as some say, a certain plant, of sweet odour: or, as is said in the قانون [of Ibn-Seenà, or Avicenna,] *a certain thing of an intensely red colour, resembling powdered saffron, brought from El-Yemen, and said to be scraped or rubbed off, or to fall off, from its trees:* (Mgh:) or, as some say, *a species of* كُرْكُم, q. v.: or, as some say, *resembling* كُرْكُم: (Mṣb:) or *a certain thing, yellow, like the* [*garments of the kind called*] مُلَآء, *that comes forth upon the* [*trees called*] رِمْث, *between the last part of summer and the first part of winter,* (M, TA,) *which, when it touches a garment, soils it:* (TA:) or *it also, sometimes,* [accord. to certain persons who seems to misapply the word, *is a substance which*] *pertains to the* [*trees called*] عَرْعَر *and* رِمْث, *and to other trees, above all in Abyssinia; but this is inferior to that first mentioned* (Ḳ, TA) *in virtue and properties: as to that of the* عرعر, *it is found between its rind and the main substance, when it dries up; and when it is rubbed, it rubs off; and there is no good in it; but* ورس [properly so called] *is adulterated with it: and as to that of the* رمث, *when it is the end of summer, and it has attained its utmost state, it becomes intensely yellow, so that what envelops it becomes yellow, and with this also one adulterates:* so says AḤn: (TA:) ورس is called in Persian اسپرك [إِسْپَرَك]; and in Turkish, آلاجهره. (TḲ.) [Freytag adds to what he has given on this word from the Ḳ, Ṣ, TḲ, as follows: "*Memecylon tinctorium.* Sprengel. hist. med., t. ii., p. 444, ed. tert. (ubi ورز scriptum est). Spreng. hist. rei herb., t. i., p. 258. Avicenn. p. ١٦٥."]

وَرِسٌ: see وَرِيسٌ.

وَرْسِىٌّ *A yellow* bowl: (A:) or a bowl *made of* نُضَار, (M,) which is a yellow wood: (TA:) or *of the best kind of those made of* نُضَار. (Lth, Ḳ.) — A pigeon that is *red inclining to yellowness:* (M:) or a pigeon *inclining to redness and yellowness.* (Ḳ.) — See also وَرِيسٌ.

وَرِيسٌ A garment *dyed with* وَرْس; as also ▾ وَرِسٌ and ▾ وَارِسٌ (M) and ▾ مُورَسٌ. (M, A.) You say, مِلْحَفَةٌ وَرِيسَةٌ, (so in some copies of the Ṣ and Ḳ) or ▾ وَرْسِيَّةٌ, (as in other copies of the Ṣ and Ḳ, and thus in a copy of the Mṣb,) [*An outer wrapping garment*] *dyed with* ورس; (Ṣ, Mṣb, Ḳ;) *i. q.* ▾ مُورَسَةٌ; (Ḳ;) which latter epithet is sometimes used. (Mṣb.) — See also وَارِسٌ.

وَارِسٌ applied to a place [*Producing the plant called* وَرْس]. (TA.) — Applied to a tree of the kind called رِمْث, *Producing* وَرْس, *a thing yellow like the* [*garments termed*] مُلَآء: (M:) or becoming yellow in the leaves, (Ṣ, Ḳ,) after attaining to maturity, (Ṣ,) and having upon it what is like yellow مُلَآء: (Ṣ, Ḳ:) or becoming yellow in its fruit: (A:) or, app., having وَرْس, like as تَامِرٌ signifies "possessing dates;" (AḤn;) and ▾ وَرِيسٌ likewise has the last of these significations: (TA:) ▾ مُورِسٌ also signifies the same as وَارِسٌ, applied to a tree of the kind abovementioned; (A, Ḳ;) but is very rare, though agreeable with analogy: (Ḳ:) it is said (M) one should not say مُورِسٌ; (Ṣ, M;) but it occurs in a poem of Ibn-Harmeh. (M.) — Applied to a tree [of any other kind], *Putting forth leaves.* (TA.) — Applied to a plant, *Becoming green.* (M.) You say also, صَخْرَةٌ وَارِسَةٌ بِالطُّحْلُبِ, *A rock overspread with the green substance called* طحلب, *so that it is green and smooth:* see 1]. (A.) — It also denotes intenseness of colour, in the phrase أَصْفَرُ وَارِسٌ *Yellow intensely bright.* (M.) And [in like manner] you say, جَمَلٌ وَارِسُ الحُمْرَةِ *A camel intensely red.* (Ṣgh.) And زَعْفَرَانٌ وَارِسٌ [app., *Bright-coloured saffron*]. (A.) See also وَرِيسٌ.

مُورِسٌ: see وَارِسٌ.

مُورَسٌ: see وَرِيسٌ, in two places.

ورش

1. وَرَشَ, (Ṣ, A, Ḳ,) aor. يَرِشُ, inf. n. وُرُوشٌ (Ḳ) and وَرْشٌ, (TA,) *He took,* or *reached,* or *took* or *reached with the hand,* or *with the extended hand,* (S, A, Ḳ,) food, (A, Ḳ,) or somewhat thereof, (Ṣ,) or a little thereof. (AZ.) — Also, (Ḳ,) inf. n. وَرْشٌ and وُرُوشٌ, (TA,) *He ate vehemently and greedily:* (Ibn-'Abbád, A, Ḳ:) but accord. to IAạr, رَوْشٌ, with the rá first, signifies the "eating much;" and وَرْشٌ, with the wáw first, the *eating little.* (TA.) — Also, (Ḳ,) inf. n. وَرْشٌ, (TA,) *He coveted; longed; yearned; eagerly desired; strove to acquire, obtain,* or *attain.* (Ibn-'Abbád, Ḳ.) You say, وَرَشَ إِلَيْهِ *He coveted it;* &c. (TḲ.) — وَرَشَ عَلَيْهِمْ, (A, Ḳ,) inf. n. وَرْشٌ, (TA,) *He came in to them uninvited when they were eating,* (A, Ḳ, TA,) *to get some of their food:* and when one has gone in to others while they were drinking, you say, وَغَلَ عَلَيْهِمْ: but see وَارِشٌ. (TA.) ═ وَرَشَ فُلَانًا بِفُلَانٍ *He incited such a one against such a one:* (Ibn-'Abbád, TA:) in the Ḳ, erroneously, وَرَشَ فُلَانٌ بِفُلَانٍ. (TA.) See also 2.

2. وَرَّشَ بَيْنَ القَوْمِ, (Ṣ,) inf. n. تَوْرِيشٌ, (Ṣ, Ḳ,) *He excited discord, dissension, disorder, strife, quarrelling,* or *animosity, between,* or *among, the people;* syn. حَرَّشَ; (Ṣ, Ḳ;) as also أَرَّشَ (Ṣ) [and هَرَّشَ]. See also 1, last signification.

وَرَشَانٌ *A certain bird,* (Ṣ, Mgh, Ḳ,) *of the pigeon-kind,* (AḤát, Mgh, Mṣb,) or *resembling the pigeon,* (TA,) *also called* سَاقُ حُرٍّ, (Ṣ, Mṣb, Ḳ,) *which is the male of the* قَمَارِىّ [or *kind of collared turtle-doves of which a single female is called* قُمْرِيَّةٌ (see قُمْرِىٌّ)], (Mṣb,) *of the birds of the desert,* (TA,) *the flesh of which is lighter than that of the* [*common*] *pigeon:* (Ḳ:) fem. with ة: (Ḳ:) pl. وَرَاشِينُ (Ṣ, Mgh, Mṣb, Ḳ) and وِرْشَانٌ, (Ṣ, Mṣb, Ḳ,) like as كِرْوَانٌ is a pl. of كَرَوَانٌ, contr. to rule. (Ṣ.) It is said in a proverb, بِعِلَّةِ الوَرَشَانِ تَأْكُلُ رُطَبَ المُشَانِ [*With the pretext of the warashán, thou eatest the fresh ripe dates of the* excellent *kind called* مشان]: (Ṣ, A, Ḳ:) said to him who pretends one thing and means another: (A, Ḳ:) originating from the fact that some people employed a slave belonging to them to guard the fresh ripe dates of their palm-trees, and he used to eat them, and, when reproved for his evil conduct, laid the blame upon the warashán; wherefore this was said to him. (Ṣgh.)

وَارِشٌ One *who comes in to a people uninvited, when they are eating;* like وَاغِلٌ in the case of beverage: (Ṣ:) and, accord. to some, *i. q.* وَاغِلٌ but others say, that وارش has the first signification only, relating to food: and that of *a sponger desiring food.* (TA.) See رَاشِنٌ and طُفَيْلِىٌّ.

ورط

1. وَرَطَهَا *He veiled, concealed, hid,* or *covered, her,* or *it,* or *them;* [to what the pronoun relates is not said; but I incline to think that the right reading is وَرَّطَهَا, and that the pronoun relates to camels; (see 2;)] as also ▾ اورطها: (L, TA:) from IAạr. (TA.)

2. وَرَّطَهُ, (Ṣ, Mṣb, Ḳ,) inf. n. تَوْرِيطٌ, (Ṣ, Mṣb,) *He made him to fall into what is termed* وَرْطَة [properly and also tropically, or in its primary sense and also in any of its subordinate senses]; as also ▾ اورطهُ, (Ṣ, Mṣb, Ḳ,) inf. n. إِيرَاطٌ: (Mṣb:) both signify † *he made him to fall into that from which he could not extricate himself:* (TA:) or *into that from which he could not easily extricate himself.* (Mṣb.) — ورّط إِبِلَهُ فِى إِبِلٍ أُخْرَى † *He hid,* or *concealed, his camels among other camels* [in order that they might escape the notice of the collector of the poor-rates]; as also ▾ اورط. (Ḳ.) [See also 1, and 3.]

3. وِرَاطٌ (Ṣ, Mṣb, TA) and مُوَارَطَةٌ (TA) [The act of *mutually making to fall into what is termed* وَرْطَة. ═ And hence,] † The act of *mutually deceiving, beguiling,* or *circumventing;* or *endeavouring to deceive, beguile,* or *circumvent:* (TA;) or the act of *deceiving, beguiling,* or *circumventing;* (Ṣ, Mṣb;) and the *acting,* or *advising,* or *counselling, dishonestly,* or *insincerely;* (Ṣ, Mṣb, TA;) and ▾ وَرْطٌ and ▾ وِرَاطَةٌ, the latter on the authority of J, [accord. to some

copies of the Ṣ, but in other copies وِرَاطٌ,] signify the same [as subsets.] (TA.) You say, لَا تُوَارِطْ جَارَكَ فَإِنَّ الوِرَاطَ يُورِدُ الأَوْرَاطَ † [*Do not thou practise mutual deceit with thy neighbour, or endeavour to deceiving him, &c., for the doing so brings upon its author things, or affairs, from which it is difficult to escape*]. (Z, TA.) And it is said in trad., لَا خِلَاطَ وَلَا وِرَاطَ, which is like his [Moḥammad's] saying, † *There shall be no putting together what is separate, nor separating what is put together*, from fear of the poor-rate: (Ṣ:) خلاط has been explained in its place: (TA:) وراط [has also been variously explained in that place, and, it is said,] signifies the *putting together what is separate*: and *the reverse*: (Ḳ:) or the *dispersing camels* (Ḳ, TA) *among other camels*: (TA:) or the *hiding camels among other camels*; (Th, Ḳ;) or *in a low, or depressed, piece of ground*; in order that the collector of the poor-rate may not see them: (Ḳ:) or the *making one another to fall into a* وَرْطَة, (TA,) *one saying to the collector of the poor-rate, "Such a one has that for which a poor-rate is due," when he has not*; (Ḳ, TA;) so accord. to IAạr: accord. to Ibn-Háni, it is from أَوْرَطَ الجَرِيرَ فِى عُنُقِ البَعِيرِ. (TA.) See 4.

4: see 2, in two places; and 1. — اورط الجَرِيرَ فِى عُنُقِ البَعِيرِ † *He put the end of the* جرير [q. v.] *of the camel into its ring, and then pulled it so as to throttle him*. (Ibn-Háni, Ḳ.)

5. تورّط فِى وَرْطَةٍ *He fell into what is termed* وَرْطَة [properly and also tropically, or in its primary sense, and also in any of its subordinate senses]. (Ṣ.) You say, تورّطتِ الغَنَمُ وَغَيْرُهَا *The sheep, or goats, &c., fell into mud from which they could not extricate themselves*; or *into a depressed piece of ground in which was no way directing to escape*: and hence the verb is used in relation to any straitness or difficulty. (Mṣb.) Thus you say, تورّط فُلَانٌ فِى الأَمْرِ † *Such a one undertook, or embarked in, the affair, and could not easily extricate himself*; and so ▼ استورط فيه: (Mṣb:) or the former signifies † *he fell into the affair, or case*: (Ḳ:) or † *he became entangled in the affair, and could not easily extricate himself from it*; (TA;) and so ▼ the latter: (Sh, Ḳ, TA:) and تورّط and ▼ استورط both signify *he stuck fast*: or † *he perished*; or *died*. (TA.)

10: see 5, in three places. — استورط مَعَ فُلَانٍ † *He behaved proudly, haughtily, or insolently, in speech, with such a one*. (TA.)

وِرْطٌ: see 3.

وَرْطَةٌ *Slime, or thin mud*, [in the CḲ, الرَّحْل is erroneously put for الوَحْل,] *into which sheep or goats fall, and from which they cannot extricate themselves*: (Mṣb, Ḳ:) this, or, as some say, what here next follows, is the primary signification: (Mṣb:) *a low, or depressed, piece of ground or land, in which is no way, or road*, (Ṣ, Mṣb, Ḳ,) *directing to escape*: (Mṣb:) this is said by A'Obeyd to be the primary signification: (Ṣ:) *a deep hollow, cavity, or pit, in the ground*: (TA:) *a deep hollow, cavity, or pit, formed for the purpose of a stratagem, such as may be in a mountain, occasioning difficulty to him who falls into it*: (Aṣ:) and hence, (TA,) *a well*: (Ḳ, TA:) and *anything that is* غَامِض [app. here meaning *low*, or *depressed*]: (Ḳ:) also, by derivation from the first of these significations, (Mṣb,) or from the second, (Ṣ, Mṣb,) [or some other,] † *perdition*; or *destruction*; or *death*: (Ṣ, Mṣb, Ḳ:) and † [*any embarrassing, or difficult, case, or affair*;] *any case, or affair, from which escape is difficult*: (Ḳ:) pl. [of pauc.] أَوْرَاطٌ, (Ṣ, IS,) the ة in the sing. being app. regarded as elided; (IS;) and [of mult.] وِرَاطٌ, (Ḳ,) and وَرَطَاتٌ. (TA.) — Also, ‡ The *podex*: or the *anus*: syn. إِسْتٌ. (Ḳ, TA.)

وِرَاطَةٌ: see 3.

[ورع &c.
See Supplement.]

وز

وَزٌّ a dial. var. of إِوَزٌّ, (Ṣ, Ḳ,) *A kind of water-fowl*; (Ṣ;) [the *goose*, or *geese*; and the *duck*, or *ducks*; but generally the former of these birds;] as also ▼ وَزِينٌ: (Ḳ:) n. un. of the former, وَزَّةٌ; (Mṣb, art. وز;) and of the latter, وَزِينَةٌ. (Ṣgh, TA.) See كُرْكِىّ.

وَزِينٌ and وَزِينَةٌ: see وَزٌّ.

أَرْضٌ مَوَزَّةٌ *A land abounding with the birds called* وَزّ; (Ḳ;) like مَأْوَزَّةٌ from إِوَزٌّ. (TA.)

وزأ

1. وَزَأَ, (Ṣ, Ḳ,) aor. يَزَأُ, (Ḳ,) inf. n. وَزْءٌ, (Ṣ,) *He dried flesh-meat*: (Ṣ, Ḳ:) or *he roasted and so dried it*. (TA.) — وَزَأَ القَوْمَ *He repelled one part of the people from another*. (Ḳ.) — وَزَأَ القَوْمُ *One part of the people repelled another part*. (TA.)

2. وَزَّأَ الوِعَآءَ, inf. n. تَوْزِئَةٌ and تَوْزِىءٌ, *He made tight the contents of the bag; or other repository*: syn. شَدَّ كَنْزَهُ. (AZ, Ṣ, Ḳ.) — وَزَّأَ, (Ṣ, Ḳ,) inf. n. تَوْزِىءٌ, (Ṣ,) *He filled a water-skin* (Ṣ, Ḳ) or other vessel. (TA.) — وَزَّأَتْ بِهِ, (Ṣ, Ḳ,) inf. n. تَوْزِئَةٌ, (Ṣ,) *She* (a mare, TA) or a camel, Ṣ, Ḳ,) *threw him* (i. e. her rider, TA,) *down prostrate*. (Ṣ, Ḳ.) — وزّاه *He made him bind himself by every oath*: (Ḳ:) or *by a hard, or severe, oath*. (L.)

5. توزّأ *It* (a water-skin, Ḳ, or other vessel, TA) *was filled, or became full*. (Ḳ.) — *He was, or became, filled with drink to satiety*. (Aṣ, Ṣ.)

وَزَأٌ *Strong-made*: (Ṣ, Ḳ:) or *a short, fat, strong-made*, man. (TA.)

وزب

1. وَزَبَ, aor. يَزِبُ, inf. n. وُزُوبٌ, *It* (water, Ḳ, or a thing, T,) *flowed*. (T, Ḳ.)

4. اوزب فِى الأَرْضِ ‡ *He went, or went away, or pursued his course, through the land*, (Ḳ,) like as does water. (TA.)

وَزَّابٌ ‡ *A clever thief*: (Ḳ:) so called because quick in his motions, like running water. (TA.)

مِيزَابٌ *A water-spout; a pipe or other channel that spouts forth water*; (TA, art. أزب;) *that by which water pours down from a high place*; (Towsheeḥ;) *a water-spout of wood, or the like, to convey away the water from the roof of a house*: (MF, art. زوب:) from وَزَبَ المَآءُ "the water flowed:" (Ḳ:) or a Persian term, arabicized; (Ṣ, Ḳ;) i. e., composed of the Persian words, (TA,) signifying "make water:" (Ḳ:) also written مِئْزَابٌ; and in this case its pl. is مَآزِيبُ: (Ṣ, Ḳ:) but if without ء, its pl. is مَيَازِيبُ, (Ṣ,) or مَوَازِيبُ; the latter agreeable with analogy, like مَوَاعِيدُ and مَوَازِينُ. (TA.) [See also arts. أزب and زوب. It has also two other forms, مِزْرَابٌ and مِرْزَابٌ.]

وزر

1. وَزَرَ, (A, Mgh, Ḳ,) aor. يَزِرُ, inf. n. وِزْرٌ, with kesr, (Ḳ,) *He bore, or carried, a heavy load, or burden*. (A, Mgh, Ḳ.) It is said in the Ḳur, [vi. 164, &c.,] وَلَا تَزِرُ وَازِرَةٌ وِزْرَ أُخْرَى *Nor shall any* [soul] *bearing* [a heavy burden] *bear the* [heavy] *burden of another* soul; (Ṣ;) i. e., its burden of sin: (Mgh, Mṣb:) meaning, that no one shall be punished for the sin of another; *nor shall any sinning soul bear the heavy burden of another soul*; every one shall be requited for his [own] deeds: (TA:) or *nor shall any sinning* [soul] *sin by the sin of another*. (Akh, Ṣ, TA.) — Hence, (Akh, Ṣ,) وَزَرَ, (Akh, Ṣ, A, Mṣb, Ḳ,) aor. يَزِرُ; and وَزِرَ, aor. يَوْزَرُ; (Akh, Ṣ, A, Mṣb, Ḳ;) and وُزِرَ (the same and A,) aor. يُوزَرُ; (Akh, Ṣ, Ḳ;) inf. n. وِزْرٌ and وَزْرٌ and وَزَرٌ and زِرَةٌ, (Ḳ,) or وِزْرَةٌ, accord. to Zj, as I have seen it [says IM] pointed and well written; (L;) ‡ *He sinned*: (Akh, Ṣ, A, Ḳ:) or *he bore* [*a burden of*] *sin*. (Mṣb.) See also 8. — وُزِرَ also signifies ‡ *He was charged with, or accused of, a sin*. (Ḳ,* TA.) — وَزَرَ لِلأَمِيرِ, (A,) and لِلسُّلْطَانِ, (Mṣb, [this I believe to be the right reading; but in the only copy of the Mṣb, that I have, I find it written السلطان;]) aor. يَزِرُ; (A, Mṣb;) inf. n. وِزَارَةٌ; (A;) and لِلْمَلِكِ; and ▼ توزّر لِلأَمِيرِ, (Ṣ,) or (Ḳ;) and ▼ وازره; (Ṣ, Ḳ;) ‡ *He was, or became*, وَزِير [*or vicegerent*] (Ṣ, A, Mṣb, Ḳ) *to the governor*, (Ṣ, A,) or *sultán*, (Mṣb,) or *king*. (Ḳ.)

3. وازرهُ *He bore* a burden *with him.* — [Hence,] وازر المَلِكَ أَعْبَآءَ المُلْكِ ‡ *He bore with the king* (حَامَلَهُ) *the burden of the regal office.* (A.) See also 1, last signification. — وازرهُ عَلَى الأَمْرِ, (TA,) inf. n. مُوَازَرَةٌ, (A, TA,) *He aided, assisted,* or *helped, him, and strengthened him, to do the thing:* originally آزَرَهُ: (A,* TA:) the former of these, وازره, is the more chaste. (TA.)

4. اوزرهُ *He appointed him a* وَزَر, (Ḳ, TA,) i. e., a *place of refuge to which to betake himself.* (TA.)

5: see 1, last signification.

8. إِتَّزَرَ, of the measure إِفْتَعَلَ, (Ṣ, Mṣb,) [originally إِوْتَزَرَ,] ‡ *He committed a* وِزْر, (Ṣ, Ḳ,) i. e., a *sin.* (Mṣb, TA.)

10. إِستوزرهُ ‡ *He took him,* or *chose him, as a* وَزِير [or *viceregent*]. (Ḳ.) You say, أُسْتُوزِرَ فُلَانٌ ‡ *Such a one was taken,* or *chosen, as a* وزير. (Ṣ, A.*)

وِزْرٌ *A heavy load* or *burden,* (A, Mgh, Ḳ,) *a bundle,* (Ṣ,) or *great bundle,* (Ḳ,) *that is carried on the back:* (Ṣ, Ḳ:) *a weight;* syn. ثِقْل: (Ṣ, [in which the syn. is written ثِقَل: so in two copies; and so app. accord. to A'Obeyd, who makes its pl. أَثْقَال:] and Mṣb [in which, in my copy, the syn. is written without syll. signs:] and Ḳ [in which it is written ثِقَل:]) pl. أَوْزَارٌ. (Mṣb, Ḳ.) — ‡ *A weapon; an instrument of war:* or *weapons; arms:* syn. سِلَاحٌ: (Ṣ, Mgh, Mṣb, Ḳ:) because heavy upon the wearer: (Mgh, Mṣb:) or أَوْزَار signifies the *burdens and instruments* of war, &c.; and the sing. is وِزْرٌ; (A'Obeyd, TA;) or it has no sing., accord. to some. (TA.) A poet says, (Ṣ,) namely El-Aạshà, (Mgh, TA.)

وَأَعْدَدْتُ لِلْحَرْبِ أَوْزَارَهَا
رِمَاحًا طِوَالًا وَخَيْلًا ذُكُورَا

[*And I prepared for the war its weapons and other apparatus; long lances and male horses*]. (Ṣ, Mgh, TA.) And it is said in the Ḳur, [xlvii. 5,] حَتَّى تَضَعَ الْحَرْبُ أَوْزَارَهَا, meaning, ‡ *Until the war terminates:* (Mgh, Mṣb:) because then the people thereof lay down their arms: (Mgh:) properly, *until the people of the war lay down their burdens:* (Mṣb:) *their weapons and burdens:* or, as some say, *their sins.* (Bḍ.) — ‡ *A sin:* (Ṣ, Bḍ, ubi supra, and Mṣb, Ḳ:) and [especially] *polytheism:* (Fr, Bḍ, TA:) pl. as above. (Bḍ, Mṣb, &c.) This is the sense in which it is most frequently used in the traditions. (IAth.)

وَزَرٌ *A mountain:* this is the primary signification: (Ṣ:) or *a mountain difficult of access,* or *strong:* (Ḳ, TḲ:) or *a mountain to which one betakes himself for refuge:* this is the primary signification. (Aboo-Is-ḥáḳ.) — *A place of refuge:* (Ṣ, Mṣb, Ḳ:) *any such place.* (Aboo-Is-ḥáḳ, Ḳ.) So in the Ḳur, lxxv. 11. (TA.) — See also وَزِير.

وَزِيرٌ i. q. مُوَازِرٌ [One *who bears* a burden or burdens *with another:* or one *who aids, assists* or *helps, and strengthens, another:* see 3:] (Ṣ, A, Ḳ:) like as أَكِيلٌ signifies i. q. مُؤَاكِلٌ, (Ṣ,) and جَلِيسٌ i. q. مُجَالِسٌ. (A.) — ‡ [*A vicegerent* of a king or the like: or *a confidential minister of state:* in English commonly written *vizier,* in imitation of the Turkish pronunciation; but properly, *wezeer:*] the *familiar* of the king, *who bears his master's burden, and aids him by his counsel:* (Ḳ:) or the وزير of the king is the *person who bears with him* (يُوَازِرُهُ, i. e. يُحَامِلُهُ,) *the burdens of the regal office:* not from مُوَازَرَةٌ, signifying the "act of aiding or the like," because the و in this latter word is substituted for ء, and the derivative from it of the measure فَعِيلٌ is أَزِيرٌ: (A:) ISd says, some hold that the و in وزير is substituted for ء; but Abu-l-'Abbás says, that this is not agreeable with analogy; for the substitution of ء for و in a word of this measure is rare, and that of و for ء is more strange: (TA:) the وزير is so called because he bears for the king the burden of administration: (Ṣ,* Mṣb:) or it is from ▼ وَزَرٌ, signifying "a mountain to which one has recourse to save himself from destruction:" so the وزير of the khaleefeh is *one upon whose counsel the khaleefeh relies in his affairs, and to whom he betakes himself for refuge* or *safety:* (Aboo-Is-ḥáḳ, TA:) pl. وُزَرَآءُ (A, Mṣb, Ḳ) and أَوْزَارٌ; (A, Ḳ;) the latter like أَشْرَافٌ and أَيْتَامٌ, (A, TA,) pls. of شَرِيفٌ and يَتِيمٌ. (TA.)

وِزَارَةٌ and وَزَارَةٌ The *condition,* or *office, of a* وَزِير: (Ṣ, Mṣb, Ḳ:) the former word is the more approved. (ISk, Mṣb.)

وَازِرٌ *Bearing,* or *carrying,* a heavy load, or burden. (A.) — [Hence,] also, (A,) and ▼ مَوْزُورٌ, (Ṣ, A, Mṣb, Ḳ,) ‡ *Sinning:* (Ṣ, A, Ḳ:) or *bearing* [*a burden of*] *sin.* (Mṣb.) مَأْزُورَاتٌ occurs in a trad., for مَوْزُورَاتٌ, the regular form, because it is there coupled with مَأْجُورَاتٌ, to which it is opposed. (Ṣ, Mgh, Mṣb, Ḳ.)

مَوْزُورٌ: see وَازِرٌ.

[وزع &c.

See Supplement.]

وس

R. Q. 1. وَسْوَسَ, [inf. n. وَسْوَسَةٌ and وِسْوَاسٌ, and simple subst. وَسْوَاسٌ, but see طَأْطَأَ,] *He spoke,* or *talked, indistinctly:* (TA:) [or *in a low, faint, gentle,* or *soft manner, with confusedness:* for] Aboo-Turáb is related to have said, that he heard Khaleefeh say, وَسْوَسَةٌ signifies the *speaking in a low, faint, gentle,* or *soft, manner, with confusedness:* or, accord. to one relation, it is [وَشْوَشَةٌ,] with ش. (TA.) [It is generally intrans., agreeable with the above explanations: but sometimes trans.; for you say,] وَسْوَسَ الرَّجُلَ *He spoke to the man with low, faint, gentle,* or *soft, speech.* (M.) — [Hence,] وَسْوَسَتْ إِلَيْهِ نَفْسُهُ, (Ṣ, M,* A,* Mṣb, Ḳ,*) and وَسْوَسَ إِلَيْهِ الشَّيْطَانُ, (Ṣ, A,* Mṣb, Ḳ,) and لَهُ, (Ṣ, Mṣb, Ḳ,) and فِيهِ, (TA,) or فِى صَدْرِهِ, (M,) inf. n. وَسْوَسَةٌ (Ṣ, M, A, Mṣb, Ḳ) and وِسْوَاسٌ, with kesr, (Ṣ, A, Mṣb, Ḳ,) and وَسْوَاسٌ, with fet-ḥ, is also allowable in the case of this and similar reduplicative verbs, (MF, voce طَأْطَأَ,) or this last is a simple subst., (Ṣ, Mṣb, Ḳ,) *His mind,* or *soul,* (Ṣ, M, A, &c.,) and *the devil,* (Ṣ, A, Mṣb, Ḳ,) *prompted,* or *suggested to him* [*something*], or *talked to him,* (Ṣ, M, Mṣb,) and [*in him,* or] *in his bosom:* (M:) or *suggested to him,* or *talked to him of,* (A,* Ḳ,) and *suggested in him,* or *talked in him of,* (TA,) *what was vain,* or *unprofitable, and destitute of good:* (A, Ḳ, TA:) and in like manner one says of the thoughts. (TA.) By the prep. ل by which it is made trans. in the Ḳur, in vii. 19, is meant إِلَى. (Ṣ, Mṣb.) You say also, وُسْوِسَ بِهِ [as though signifying properly *He had vain things suggested in him by the devil, so that his mind was disturbed thereby, and*] *his speech became confused, and he became stupified,* or *deprived of his reason.* (TA.) — [Hence also,] وَسْوَسَ الحَلْىُ, (M, A, Bḍ, in vii. 19,) inf. n. وَسْوَسَةٌ and وِسْوَاسٌ, (M,) ‡ *The woman's ornament sounded,* or *made a sound* or *sounds:* (M:) or *made a low,* or *gentle, sound;* or *a chinking.* (Bḍ, [who holds this to be a primary signification: but it is said in the A to be tropical.]) And وَسْوَسَ القَصَبُ ‡ [*The reeds made a low sound;* or *rustling*]. (A.) And سَمِعْتُ وَسْوَاسَهُ ‡ *I heard its low sounding,* or *its chinking;* or *its rustling*]. (A.) See also وَسْوَاسٌ.

وَسْوَسَةٌ: see 1; and وَسْوَاسٌ, in two places.

وَسْوَاسٌ a subst. from وَسْوَسَ; (Ṣ, Mṣb, Ḳ;) signifying, [*Speech,* or *talk, that is indistinct:* or *low, faint, gentle,* or *soft:* or *low,* &c., *and confused:* see 1. — And hence,] The soul's, or mind's, (Ṣ, M, Mṣb, Ḳ,) and the devil's, (Ḳ,) *prompting,* or *suggestion,* or *talk,* (Ṣ, M, Mṣb, Ḳ,) *of what is vain,* or *unprofitable, and destitute of good;* (Ḳ;) as also ▼ وَسْوَسَةٌ [used as subst., in which case its pl. is وَسَاوِسُ, occurring below]. (Ṣ, Ḳ.) — [And hence,] † *An evil,* or *unprofitable, idea, imagination,* or *thought, which bestirs itself in,* or *occurs to, the mind.* (Mṣb.) — And [by a metonymy,] † *A certain disease,* [i. e. *melancholia, in which is a doting in the imagination and judgment, a sort of delirium, vulgarly attributed to diabolical prompting* or *suggestion, but, it is said,*] *arising from a predominance of the black bile, attended with confusion of the intellect.* (Mṣb.) — [And from the primary signification seem to be derived those which here follow.] † The *low,* or *faintly heard, sound of the hunter and the dogs.* (Ṣ, Ḳ.) — † *A low* or *faint sound* [or *rustling*] of wind; as also ▼ وَسْوَسَةٌ. (M.) — ‡ The *sounds,* (Ṣ,) or *sound,* (M, Ḳ,) *of women's ornaments:* (Ṣ, M, Ḳ:) [the *chinking thereof:* see 1.] = Also, الوَسْوَاسُ *The devil;* (M, Ḳ;) *a name of the devil:* (Ṣ:) it occurs in verse 4 of the last chap. of the Ḳur; and is said to mean there ذُو الوَسْوَاسِ [*the prompter,* or *suggester, of what is vain,* or *unprofitable, and destitute of good.* (M.)

مَرَضٌ وَسْوَاسِىٌّ [*A disease of the nature of melancholia*]. (Ḳ in art. عشق.)

مُوَسْوَسٌ : see مُوَسْوِسٌ.

مُوَسْوِسٌ, with kesr, A man *subject to* وَسَاوِس [or *diabolical promptings, or suggestions, of vain,* or *unprofitable, things, and thereby confused in his intellect,* or *disordered in his mind*]: (M:) an act. part. n., applied as an epithet to a man, because he to whom it is applied talks to himself: and one also says مُوَسْوَسٌ [or مُوَسْوَسٌ إِلَيْهِ,] like المَغْضُوبُ عَلَيْهِمْ: (Mṣb.) or, accord. to I Aṭr, one should not say مُوَسْوَسٌ. (TA.)

وسب

1. وَسَبَتِ الأَرْضُ, aor. تَسِبُ, (inf. n. وَسْبٌ, TA;) and ▼ اوسبت; *The land became abundant in fresh herbage, such as is called* عُشْب, (Ṣ, Ḳ,) *and in dry herbage.* (TA.) — وَسِبَ, aor. يَوْسَبُ, inf. n. وَسَبٌ, *He,* or *it, was dirty:* (I Aṭr, Ḳ:) syn. with وَكِبَ and حَشِنَ. (TA.)

4: see 1.

وِسْبٌ *Wood that is put in the lower part of a well, when its earth is such as would pour in,* (Ḳ,) *and that prevents the earth from doing so:* called by the people of Egypt خَنْزِيرَة, and only of the wood of the sycamore fig-tree: (TA:) [the خنزيرة is a lining of planks, resembling a barrel; and the wood above mentioned is used in its construction because water does not rot it so quickly as it rots other kinds of wood:] pl. وُسُوبٌ. (Ḳ.) [Accord. to I Drd, of the dial. of El-Yemen. (Freytag.)]

وِسْبٌ *Plants; herbs; herbage:* (Ṣ, Ḳ:) or *abundance of herbage.* (M, in art. اسب.)

مُوسِبٌ ‡ A ram *abounding with wool:* (Ḳ:) likened to a land abounding with herbage. (TA.)

مِيسَابٌ Dates *such as are termed* مُجَزَّعٌ, [i. e., *half,* or *two-thirds, ripe*]: (Ḳ:) i. e., as applied to رُطَب, *vile,* or *bad.* (TA.)

وسج

1. وَسَجَ, (aor. يَسِجُ, Ḳ,) inf. n. وَسِيجٌ (Ṣ, Ḳ) and وَسْجٌ and وَسَجَانٌ; (L;) *He* (a camel) *went a certain pace;* (Ṣ, L, Ḳ;) [*more quick than that called* عَسْجٌ: the contr. is said in the TA, app. by a mistranscription: but see نَصَبٌ, and زَمَلٌ:] the first pace, accord. to En-Naḍr and Aṣ, is called الدَّبِيبُ; the next, العَنَقُ; the next, التَّزَيُّدُ; the next, الذَّمِيلُ; the next, العَسْجُ; and the next, الوَسْجُ: or *he went quickly,* or *swiftly.* (TA, L.)

4. اوسج *He incited, urged,* or *made,* a camel, *to go at the pace called* الوَسِيج. (Ṣ, Ḳ.)

جَمَلٌ وَسَّاجٌ عَسَّاجٌ *A quick,* or *swift, camel.* (Ḳ.) إِبِلٌ وُسُجٌ عُسُجٌ *Quick,* or *swift, camels.* (Ḳ.)

وسخ

1. وَسِخَ, aor. يَوْسَخُ (Ṣ, Ḳ) and يَاسَخُ and يَيْسَخُ, (Ḳ,) [the last two of which are irregular forms,] inf. n. وَسَخٌ; (L;) and ▼ إِتَّسَخَ and ▼ توسّخ (Ṣ, Ḳ) and ▼ استوسخ; (Ḳ;) *It* (a garment, Ṣ, L, Ḳ, and the skin, L, or some other thing, Mṣb) *was,* or *became, dirty, filthy,* (Ṣ, L, Ḳ,) *in consequence of its being seldom washed,* (L,) or *from want of care.* (Mṣb.)

2: see 4.

4. اوسخ (Ṣ, L, Ḳ) and ▼ وسّخ (L, Ḳ) *He,* or *it, made* a garment, (Ṣ, L, Ḳ,) and the skin, (L,) or some other thing, (Mṣb,) *dirty,* or *filthy.* (Ṣ, L, Ḳ.)

5: } see 1.
8: }
10: }

وَسَخٌ *Dirt, filth,* or *soil;* (Ṣ, L;) *what collects upon a garment,* or *the skin,* (L,) or *some other thing,* (Mṣb,) *in consequence of its being seldom washed,* (L,) or *from want of care:* (Mṣb:) pl. أَوْسَاخٌ. (Mṣb.) — لَا تَأْكُلْ أَوْسَاخَ النَّاسِ ‡ [*Live not thou upon the alms of men*]. (A.)

وَسِخٌ *Dirty,* or *filthy,* [*in consequence of being seldom washed,* or] *from want of care:* an epithet applied to a garment &c. (Mṣb.)

وسد

2. وسّدهُ وِسَادًا, or وِسَادَةً, (L, Ḳ,) and شَيْئًا, (Ṣ,) *He put a pillow,* (L, Ḳ,) and *a thing,* (Ṣ,) *beneath his* (another's) *head.* (Ṣ, L, Ḳ*.) [See an ex. in a verse cited voce ذَنُوبٌ: and another voce سَوَادٌ.]

4. اوسد فِى السَّيْرِ *He hastened,* or *was quick, in his pace.* (L, Ḳ.) — اوسدهُ, (Ṣ, L, Ḳ,) or اوسدهُ بِالصَّيْدِ, (Mṣb,) *He incited him* (a dog) *to the chase:* as also آسَدَهُ. (Ṣ, L, Mṣb, Ḳ.)

5. توسّد, (L, Ḳ,) and توسّد وِسَادًا, or وِسَادَةً, (L,) and شَيْئًا, (Ṣ,) *He put for himself a pillow,* (L, Ḳ,) and *a thing,* (Ṣ,) *beneath his head;* (Ṣ, L,) *he rested his head upon a pillow.* (L.) — توسّد ذِرَاعَهُ *He made his fore arm his pillow;* i. e., *lay upon his fore arm, putting it as a pillow.* (L.)

وِسَادٌ (Ṣ, L, Mṣb, Ḳ) and ▼ وِسَادَةٌ (Ṣ, A, L, Mṣb, Ḳ) and وُسَادَةٌ and وَسَادَةٌ, (Ḳ,) but some disallow the last two forms, (TA,) and إِسَادَةٌ, (L,) and أُسَادَةٌ, (Ḳ, art. أسد,) *A pillow,* or *cushion, upon which one rests his cheek* (Ṣ, A, L, Mṣb, Ḳ) or *head:* (L:) and the first, *a thing upon which one reclines,* or *rests:* (M, L, Ḳ:) or the first, only, signifies, *anything that is used as a pillow,* (A, Mṣb,) or *put beneath the head,* (L,) *whether of household-furniture,* (Mṣb,) or *stones,* (L,) or *earth* (A, L, Mṣb) *&c.:* (Mṣb:) pl. of the first, وُسُدٌ (Ṣ, Mṣb, Ḳ) and وُسْدٌ; (L, TA;) and of the second, وَسَائِدُ (Ṣ, L, Mṣb, Ḳ) and وِسَادَاتٌ. (Mṣb.) — إِنَّ وِسَادَكَ لَعَرِيضٌ ‡ [lit., *Verily thy pillow is wide:*] said by Moḥammad (L, Ḳ) to 'Adee Ibn-Ḥátim: (L:) alluding to his sleeping much; (L, Ḳ;) because he whose pillow is wide sleeps pleasantly: (Ḳ:) or to his sleeping night and day: (L:) or to his having a wide back to his neck, and a great head, indicating want of understanding. (L, Ḳ.) You say, هُوَ عَرِيضُ الوِسَادِ, meaning, *He is stupid, dull,* or *wanting in intelligence:* (Mṣb:) or *sleepy.* (TA, art. عرض.)

وِسَادَةٌ : see وِسَادٌ.

وسط

1. وَسَطَ القَوْمَ, aor. يَسِطُ, inf. n. وَسْطٌ (Ṣ, Mṣb, Ḳ) [and وُسُوطٌ (as shown below)] and سِطَةٌ, (Ṣ, Ḳ,) *He sat,* [or *was,* or *became,*] *in the middle,* or *midst, of the people,* or *company of men;* (Ḳ;) or *among them;* (TA;) *i. q.* ▼ توسّطهم; (Ṣ, Ḳ;) or ▼ توسّط بَيْنَهُمْ: (Mṣb:) and in like manner, وَسَطَ المَكَانَ [*he was,* or *became,* or *sat, in the middle,* or *midst, of the place*]: (Mṣb:) and وَسَطَ الشَّىْءَ, and ▼ وسّطه, and ▼ توسّطه, *he was,* or *became, in the middle,* or *midst, of the thing:* and [in like manner] وُسُوطُ الشَّمْسِ signifies ▼ تَوَسُّطُهَا السَّمَآءَ [*The sun's being,* or *becoming, in the middle,* or *midst, of the sky*]. (M.) — وَسَطَ الشَّىْءَ also signifies *He,* or *it, was,* or

became, in the best part of the thing, most remote from the two extremes. (TA.) And وَسَطَهُ *He alighted,* or *took up his abode, in,* or *among, the best,* or *most generous, thereof.* (M.) And وَسُطَ الرَّجُلُ قَوْمَهُ, and فِى قَوْمِهِ, inf. n. وَسَاطَةٌ, *The man occupied,* or *held, a middle place,* [meaning *the best place,* or *one of the best places,*] *among his people, in respect of truth and equity.* (Mṣb.) And وَسُطَ قَوْمَهُ فِى الحَسَبِ, aor. يَسِطُ, inf. n. سِطَةٌ, [*He held a middle,* or *good,* or *the best, rank among his people in regard of grounds of pretension to respect.*] (M.) And وَسُطَ فِى حَسَبِهِ, [aor. يَوْسُطُ,] inf. n. سِطَةٌ and وَسَاطَةٌ, [*He held a middle,* or *good,* or *the best, rank in regard of his grounds of pretension to respect;*] (M, TA;) and وَسَطَ signifies the same; (M;) and so does ▼ وسّط, (M, TA,) inf. n. تَوْسِيطٌ. (TA.) [See وَسَطٌ, below.]

2. وسّطهُ, (Ḳ,) inf. n. تَوْسِيطٌ, (Ṣ, Ḳ,) *He put it in the middle,* or *midst.* (Ṣ, Ḳ.) — And [so in the Ṣ, but in the Ḳ "or,"] *He cut it* [*in the middle,* or *midst,* i. e.] *in two halves.* (Ṣ, Ḳ.) [See the pass. part. n., below.] — [In the Ḳur, c. 5,] some read, فَوَسَّطْنَ بِهِ جَمْعًا [which may mean *And have put in the midst, thereby, a company* of the enemy: or *have divided in two halves, thereby, &c.*: or *have thereby become in the midst of a company* of the enemy]: (Ṣ, TA:) others read فَوَسَطْنَ. (TA.) See 1, first sentence. — وسّط فى حَسَبِهِ: see 1, last sentence.

5: see 1, first sentence, in four places. — توسّط بَيْنَ النَّاسِ *He mediated,* or *interceded, between the men,* or *people, for the purpose of accommodation;* from وَسُطَ الرَّجُلُ قَوْمَهُ and فِى قَوْمِهِ, explained above; (Mṣb;) or from وَسَاطَةٌ; (Ṣ;) *he made mediation,* or *intercession,* (عَمِلَ الوَسَاطَةَ,) *between them.* (Ḳ.) — توسّط also signifies *He took what was of a middle sort, between the good and the bad.* (Ḳ.)

وَسْطٌ, with the س quiescent, is an adv. n.; [as such written وَسْطَ, meaning *In the middle of; in the midst of;* or *among;*] (Ṣ, M, IB, Mgh, Ḳ;) and it is for this reason that it has its middle letter quiescent, (Ṣ, IB,) like بَيْنَ (IB) with which it is syn.; (IB, Mṣb;) [for] it may be used in any case in which بَيْنَ may be substituted for it; (Ṣ, IAth, Ḳ;) and, like بَيْنَ, it does not denote a part of the thing denoted by the noun to which it is prefixed, wherein differing from ▼ وَسَطٌ. (Ṣ, IB, Ḳ.) You say, جَلَسْتُ وَسْطَ القَوْمِ (Ṣ, IB, Mṣb) *I sat* [*in the middle of,* or *in the midst of,*] or *among, the people,* or *company of men,* (IB, Mṣb;) not being one of them. (IB.) And وَسْطَ رَأْسِهِ دُهْنٌ [*In the middle of his head is oil*]; not meaning a component part of the head. (IB.) And it is said in a trad. الجَالِسُ وَسْطَ الحَلْقَةِ مَلْعُونٌ [*The sitter in the midst of the ring is cursed*]: for he must of necessity turn his back towards some of those who surround him, and so displease them; wherefore they curse him and revile him. (IAth.) — It may not [properly] be used as a decl. n., (IB,) i. e. as an inchoative, (Mgh,) nor as an agent, nor as an objective complement; (IB, Mgh) &c.; thus, also, differing from ▼ وَسَطٌ; unless it have the adverbial particle [فِى] prefixed to it; in which case it has the sense of وَسَطٌ, and you say, فِى وَسْطِ رَأْسِهِ دُهْنٌ and جَلَسْتُ فِى وَسْطِ القَوْمِ [like as you say جَلَسْتُ وَسْطَ القَوْمِ and وَسْطَ رَأْسِهِ دُهْنٌ, explained above]: and sometimes it is used as a subst., preserving the quiescence [and the adverbial form], like as بَيْنَ is used as a subst., though virtually an adv. n., in cases like that where it is said in the Ḳur, [vi. 94,] لَقَدْ تَقَطَّعَ بَيْنَكُمْ [meaning مَا بَيْنَكُمْ, or, as explained in the Expos. of the Jel., وَصْلُكُمْ بَيْنَكُمْ]: (IB:) or وَسْطٌ is sometimes used for ▼ وَسَطٌ, improperly; (Ṣ;) or it may be so used; (Mṣb;) or it is so used by poetic license; (M;) or, as some say, each of them may take the place of the other; and this seems the most likely: (IAth:) or one says وَسْطٌ, with sukoon, only, of that whereof the component parts are separate, or distinct, (IAth, Ḳ*,) such as a number of men, and beasts of carriage, &c.; (IAth;) and ▼ وَسَطٌ, (IAth,) or both, (Ḳ,) of that whereof the component parts are united, (IAth, Ḳ*,) such as a house, and the head, (IAth,) or such as a ring: (Ḳ:) it is related, as on the authority of Th, that وَسَطُ ▼ الشَّىْءِ and وَسْطُهُ [both meaning *The middle,* or *midst, of the thing*] are said when the thing is solid; but when its component parts are separate, or distinct, the word is وَسْطٌ, with sukoon, exclusively. (M.)

وَسَطٌ [The *middle, midst,* or *middle part,* of a thing; i. e.,] properly, the *part of which several lateral,* or *outer, portions are equal;* as, for instance, the middle finger: but also meaning the *part which is surrounded,* or *enclosed, on its several sides, although unequally:* (Mṣb:) or the *part that is between the two sides* or *extremities* of a thing; (M, IB, Mgh, Ḳ;) [or the *part,* or *point, that is between every two opposite extremities* of a thing; and properly *when equidistant;*] as, for instance, the *centre* of a circle: (Mgh:) as also ▼ أَوْسَطٌ, (M, Ḳ,) which is [likewise] a subst., like أَفْكَلٌ and أَزْمَلٌ [but imperfectly decl. because originally an epithet]: (M:) وَسَطٌ has its middle letter with fet-ḥ in order that it may agree in measure with its contr., which is طَرَفٌ; the like agreement being frequent: (IB:) and it is only used in cases in which بَيْنَ may not be substituted for it, herein [and in other respects, mentioned in the next preceding paragraph,] differing from وَسْطٌ: (Ṣ, IB, Ḳ:) [respecting the similar and dissimilar usages of وَسْطٌ and وَسَطٌ, sufficient observations have been made in the next preceding paragraph, which see throughout, and more especially in its latter part:] the pl. of وَسَطٌ is أَوْسَاطٌ; and that of its syn. ▼ أَوْسَطُ is أَوَاسِطُ; or this may be a pl. of ▼ وَاسِطٌ, and originally وَوَاسِطُ. (M.) You say, جَلَسْتُ فِى وَسَطِ الدَّارِ [*I sat in the middle,* or *middle part, of the house*]; (Ṣ, Mgh, Mṣb;) because وَسَط is a subst. (Ṣ.) And اِتَّسَعَ وَسَطُهُ [*The middle,* or *middle part, thereof, became wide*]. (Mgh, Mṣb.) And ضَرَبْتُ وَسَطَ رَأْسِهِ [*I smote the middle,* or *middle part, of his head*]. (Mgh,* Mṣb.) And كَسَرْتُ وَسَطَ الرُّمْحِ [*I broke the middle,* or *middle part, of the spear*]. (IB.) And وَسَطُهُ خَيْرٌ مِنْ طَرَفِهِ [*The middle,* or *middle part, thereof is better than the extremity*]. (Mgh, Mṣb.) And خَيْرُ الأُمُورِ أَوْسَاطُهَا *The best of affairs,* or *actions,* or *cases, are such of them as are between two extremes.* (M. [See R. Q. 1, in art. حق.]) It is sometimes put in the accus. case as an adv. n.; as in the saying, جَلَسْتُ وَسَطَ الدَّارِ; but this is an instance of departure from the original usage; and [the meaning is جَلَسْتُ فِى وَسَطِ الدَّارِ signifying as explained above; so that] it is not here syn. with بَيْنَ, like as وَسْطٌ is. (IB.) — It is also used as an epithet: (IB, Mgh:) [as such signifying *Middle; intermediate; midway,* or *equidistant, between the two extremities* or *extremes; in place,* or *position;* but in this sense superseded in usage by ▼ أَوْسَطُ and ▼ وَاسِطٌ and ▼ مُتَوَسِّطٌ: and *in time;* but in this sense also superseded in usage by ▼ أَوْسَطُ:] *middling; of middle sort, kind,* or *rate;* (Mṣb;) as also ▼ أَوْسَطُ (Ṣ,* M, Mgh, Mṣb, Ḳ) and ▼ مُتَوَسِّطٌ (M, Mgh, Mṣb) and ▼ وَسُوطٌ (M, TA) [and ▼ وَسِيطٌ]; *between good and bad;* (Mṣb, TA;) as also ▼ أَوْسَطُ: (Mṣb:) *conforming,* or *conformable, to the just mean; just; equitable:* (Zj, Ṣ, Ḳ:) *good;* (Zj, M, Mṣb, Ḳ;) as also ▼ وَسِيطٌ: (M:) *most conforming,* or *conformable, to the just mean; most just; most equitable;* applied to what is so of a thing; (Ṣ, M, Ḳ;) whatever it be; (Ṣ, Ḳ;) as also ▼ أَوْسَطُ: (M:) *best;* (Mṣb;) as also ▼ أَوْسَطُ: (Ṣ,* Mṣb, Ḳ*:) *most generous:* (M:) and when used as an epithet, it is applied alike to a masc., fem., sing., dual, and pl., subst.: (Mgh:) the fem. of ▼ أَوْسَطُ is وُسْطَى; (Mgh, Mṣb;) and the pl. masc. أَوَاسِطُ; and pl. fem. وُسَطٌ. (Mṣb.) Hence, (Mṣb,) ▼ الإِصْبَعُ الوُسْطَى (Ṣ, Mṣb, Ḳ) *The middle finger.* (Mṣb.) And ▼ اليَوْمُ الأَوْسَطُ [*The middle day*]. (Mṣb.) And ▼ اللَّيْلَةُ الوُسْطَى [*The middle night*]. (Mṣb.) And ▼ العَشَرَةُ الأَوَاسِطُ, meaning *The* [*ten middle*] *days.* (Mṣb.) And العَشْرُ ▼ الوُسَطُ, meaning *The* [*ten middle nights*: not

‡ العَشْرُ الأَوْسَطُ; for this is a vulgar mistake, into which relaters of traditions have fallen; or it may be a mistake of transcription. (Mṣb.) And ‡ الصَّلٰوةُ الوُسْطَى, (M, Mgh, &c.,) mentioned in the Ḳur, [ii. 239,] (M, Ḳ,) meaning *The middle prayer* (Bḍ, TA) *between the other prayers,* (Bḍ,) or *between the prayers of the night and the day;* (TA;) or *the most excellent of them in particular:* (Bḍ:) i. e. *the prayer of the afternoon;* ('Alee Ibn-Abee-Tálib, I'Ab, and others, Mgh, Bḍ, Ḳ;) because the prophet said, on the day of the Aḥzáb, "they have diverted us from الصلوة الوسطى, the prayer of the afternoon:" (Bḍ:) or *the prayer of daybreak;* (also said to be on the authority of 'Alee, Mgh, Bḍ, Ḳ;) because it is between the prayers of the night and the day; (Bḍ;) for the saying of the prophet mentioned above does not contravene this and other assertions, since what is meant in the trad. is not what is meant in the Ḳur: (Ḳ:) or, (M, Ḳ,) accord. to Abu-l-Ḥasan, (M,) *the prayer of Friday;* (M, Ḳ;) because it is the most excellent of the prayers; (M;) and he who says otherwise errs, unless he trace up the assertion to the prophet: (M, Ḳ:) these three opinions are of the strongest authority; (B;) and the first is that which commonly obtains: (Mgh:) or *the prayer of noon;* (Mgh, Bḍ, Mṣb, Ḳ;) because it is in the middle of the day: (Bḍ:) or *the prayer of Friday on the day thereof;* but *on other days the prayer of noon:* (Ḳ, and also said to be on the authority of 'Alee:) or *the prayer of sunset:* (Mgh, Bḍ, Ḳ:) or *the prayer of nightfall:* (Bḍ, Ḳ:) or [*the night-prayer called*] الوِتْر: (Ḳ:) or *the prayer of the breaking of the fast:* (Ḳ:) or *the prayer of sacrifices:* (Ḳ:) or *the prayer of the period called the* ضُحَى: (Ḳ:) or *the prayer of the congregation:* (Ḳ:) or *the prayer of fear:* (Ḳ:) or *the prayers of nightfall and daybreak together:* (Ḳ, and said to be on the authorities of 'Omar and 'Othmán:) or *the prayers of daybreak and the afternoon together:* (Ḳ:) or *any of the five prayers;* because before it are two prayers and after it are two prayers: (Ḳ:) or *all the divinely-appointed prayers:* (Ḳ:) or *certain prayers not particularized:* (Ḳ:) or *prayer of middling length, between long and short.* (Ḳ.) Hence also, شَىْءٌ وَسَطٌ *A middling thing; a thing of middle sort or kind;* (Mṣb;) *between good and bad;* (Ṣ, Mṣb;) as also ‡ أَوْسَطُ: (Mṣb:) and in like manner it is applied to a male slave, and a female slave, (Mṣb,) and two male slaves, and two sheep or goats. (Mgh.) And مِنْ أَوْسَطِ ‡ مَا تُطْعِمُونَ أَهْلِيكُمْ, in the Ḳur, [v. 91,] *Of the middle sort of that which ye give for food to your families,* (Mgh, Mṣb,) *between what is prodigal and what is niggardly.* (Mgh.) And ‡ النَّمَطُ الأَوْسَطُ *The middle class of men:* occurring in a saying of 'Alee, cited in full in art. غط. (M.) And عَلِّمْنِى ‡ دِينًا وَسُوطًا *Teach thou to me a religion of the middle sort:* occurring in a saying of an Arab of the desert to El-Ḥasan, cited in full voce فَرْط. (M, TA.) And جَعَلْنَاكُمْ أُمَّةً وَسَطًا, in the Ḳur, [ii. 137,] (Ṣ, Mgh, Mṣb,) [*We have made you to be a nation*] *conforming,* or *conformable, to the just mean; just; equitable:* (Zj, Ṣ, IB, Bḍ, Ḳ:) or *good.* (Zj, Bḍ, Mṣb, Ḳ.) And مَرْعًى وَسَطٌ *Choice pasturage.* (M.) And رَجُلٌ وَسَطٌ *A good man;* as also ‡ وَسِيطٌ: (M:) or *a man having good grounds of pretension to respect.* (TA.) And فُلَانٌ وَسِيطٌ ‡ فِى قَوْمِهِ, (Ṣ, Ḳ*,) or بَيْنَهُمْ, (as in some copies of the Ḳ,) *Such a one is the best of his people* (‡ أَوْسَطُهُمْ) *in race, and the highest of them in station.* (Ṣ, Ḳ.) And فُلَانٌ وَسِيطُ ‡ الدَّارِ وَالحَسَبِ [*Such a one is of good quality,* or *of the best quality, in respect of tribe, and of grounds of pretension to honour*]. (Lth.) And هُوَ مِنْ وَسَطِ قَوْمِهِ, and ‡ مِنْ أَوْسَطِهِمْ, *He is of the best of his people.* (Mṣb.) And in like manner, هُوَ مِنْ وَسَطِ الشَّىْءِ, and ‡ مِنْ أَوْسَطِهِ, *It is of the best of the thing.* (Mṣb.) And قَالَ ‡ أَوْسَطُهُمْ in the Ḳur, lxviii. 28, *The best of them said:* (Jel:) or *the most rightly directed, of them, to the truth:* (Mṣb:) or it means ‡ أَوْسَطُهُمْ رَأْيًا [*the most remote, of them, from either extreme, in judgment*]; or سِنًّا [*in age*]. (Bḍ.)

وَسُوطٌ: see وَسَطٌ, as an epithet, in two places.

وَسِيطٌ: see وَسَطٌ, as an epithet, in five places. — *A mediator,* or *an intercessor, for the purpose of accommodation,* (O, Ḳ,) *between people,* (O,) or *between two persons engaged in mutual altercation* or *litigation.* (Ḳ.)

وَسَاطَةٌ [originally an inf. n.: (see 1:) — and hence, as a subst., *Mediation,* or *intercession*]. (Ṣ, Ḳ: see 5.) — وَسَاطَةُ الدَّنَانِيرِ *The best of deenárs.* (TA.)

[وَسِيطَةٌ *A mean,* or *means:* pl. وَسَائِطُ.]

وَاسِطٌ: see وَسَطٌ, as a subst., and also as an epithet. — وَاسِطُ الكُورِ, (Lth, Ṣ, Ḳ,) or الرَّحْلِ, (ISh, Az, M,) and ‡ وَاسِطَتُهُ, (Lth, M, Ḳ,) and ‡ مُوَسَّطَتُهُ, (Lḥ, M, [or perhaps ‡ مُوسِطَتُهُ, corresponding to ‡ مُؤْخِرَتُهُ,]) *The fore-part of the camel's saddle:* (Ṣ, Ḳ:) accord. to Lth, (Az, TA,) *the part, of the camel's saddle, which is between the* قَادِمَة *and the* آخِرَة; (Az, M, L;) but this is a mistake; (Az, L;) for the واسط of the camel's saddle is *one of the* شَرْخَانِ, (ISh, Az, L,) *which are its two extremities,* [or *upright pieces of wood,*] *like the* قَرَبُوسَانِ *of the horse's saddle,* (Az, L,) *between which the rider sits;* (ISh, Az, L;) *it is the extremity which is next to the head of the camel;* (Az, L;) *the tall fore-part next to the breast of the rider,* (ISh, Az, L,) *against which the breast of the rider sometimes strikes;* (TA, in art. نحز;) the آخِرَة being the extremity which is next to the tail of the camel; (Az, L;) the hinder part of the saddle, which is its tall and broad piece of wood that is against (تُحَاذِى) the head of the rider: (ISh, Az, L:) the former of these is not called واسط as being a middle part between the آخرة and the قادمة, as Lth says; nor has the camel's saddle any [part called] قادمة. (Az, L.) — الوَاسِطُ also signifies *The piece of wood that is in the middle, between the two pieces called the* عِضَادَتَانِ, *in the yoke that is upon the neck of a bull which draws a cart or the like.* (L in art. عضد.)

وَاسِطَةٌ The *jewel that is in the middle* of a قِلَادَة [or necklace], *which is the best* thereof; (Ṣ;) the *large pearl* (دُرَّة) *that is in the middle* thereof, *which is the most precious of the beads* thereof. (L.) — [In modern Arabic, *A means* of doing a thing. You say, بِوَاسِطَةِ كَذَا *By means of such a thing.* — Also, *An intermediary, interposer,* or *agent between parties; a go-between.*] — See also وَاسِطٌ. — هُوَ فِى وَاسِطَةٍ مِنَ العَيْشِ † *He is in a good condition of life.* (Er-Rághib, TA, in art. حف.)

أَوْسَطُ; fem. وُسْطَى; pl. masc. أَوَاسِطُ; pl. fem. وُسَطٌ: see وَسَطٌ, as a subst., in two places; and as an epithet, throughout.

مُوسَطٌ *What is in the middle* of a بَيْت [i. e. house, or tent, &c.], *particularly.* (Ibn-'Abbád, Ḳ.)

مُوسِطَةٌ, or مُوَسَّطَةٌ: see وَاسِطٌ.

قَتَلَ فُلَانًا مُوَسَّطًا *He slew such a one cut* [*in the middle,* or *midst,*] *in two halves.* (TA.) [This mode of slaughter, termed تَوْسِيط, was often practised under the rule of the Egyptian Sulṭáns; many instances thereof being mentioned by El-Maḳreezee and other historians. See De Sacy's Chrest. Ar., 2nd ed., vol. i. p. 468.]

مُتَوَسِّطٌ: see وَسَطٌ, as an epithet, in two places.

[وسع &c.

See Supplement.]

وش

R. Q. 1. [وَشْوَشَ, inf. n. وَشْوَشَةٌ, *He spoke in a low, faint, gentle,* or *soft, manner, with confusedness;* accord. to an explanation, given by Khaleefeh, of the inf. n.; or the word of which he gave that explanation was وَسْوَسَةٌ, with س: (see وَسْوَسَ:) or *he spoke confusedly, so as to be hardly intelligible:* or *he spoke in a low, faint, gentle,* or *soft, manner:* (see وَشْوَشَةٌ below: and see R. Q. 2:) in the present day it signifies *he whispered:* and وَشْوَشَهُ, *he whispered to him.*] — وَشْوَشْتُهُ, [or rather, app., وَشْوَشْتُهُ إِيَّاهُ,] *I gave or handed, it to him in a small quantity.* (Ḳ.)

R. Q. 2. تَوَشْوَشُوا *They were in a state of commotion, and spoke together one to another,* or *some of them to others, in a low, faint, gentle,* or *soft, manner.* (IDrd, Ḳ.)

وَشْوَاش : see وَشْوَش.

وَشْوَشَةٌ *Speech with confusedness,* (Ṣ, Ḳ,) *so as to be hardly intelligible:* (TA:) or *confused speech:* or *low, faint, gentle,* or *soft, speech:* or *such a word* or *saying.* (TA.) See R. Q. 1. — *Lightness, activity,* or *agility.* (Ḳ.)

وَشْوَشِىٌّ : see وَشْوَاش.

وَشْوَاش *Light, active,* or *agile;* (Lth, Ṣ, Ḳ;) applied to a man; (Ṣ;) and to an ostrich; (AA, Ḳ;) and so ▼ وَشْوَاشَةٌ applied to a she-camel; (Ḳ;) or this last, so applied, signifies *quick, and light* or *active* or *agile;* and so وَشْوَاش applied to a he-camel; and ▼ وَشْوَش applied to a he-camel and to a man. (TA.) You say also, رَجُلٌ وَشْوَشِىٌّ ▼ الذِّرَاعِ, meaning, نَشْنَشِيُّهُ, (Ḳ,) i. e., *A man slender in the* [*fore*] *arm, and light,* or *active, in work.* (AO, TA.)

وشب

وَشْبٌ [app. meaning *Fleshy*] is from the expression تَمْرَةٌ وَشْبَةٌ, (in one copy of the Ḳ, وَشْبَاءُ, TA,) *A date having a thick* لِحَآء [i. e. *pulp,* or *flesh*]. (Ḳ.) Of the dial. of El-Yemen. (TA.)

وِشْبٌ sing. of أَوْشَابٌ, (Ḳ,) which is the same as أَوْبَاشٌ (Ṣ, Ḳ) and أَشْوَابٌ, (TA,) [but see this last word, in art. شوب,] and signifies, *A medley,* or *mixed multitude;* (Ḳ;) or *sundry,* or *separate sorts* of people; (Ṣ;) *and young men of the baser sort.* (TA.) A term of dispraise only. (Marg. note in a copy of the Ṣ.)

وشج

1. وَشَجَتِ العُرُوقُ وَالأَغْصَانُ *The roots and branches became entangled together.* (Ṣ.) — وَشَجَ, aor. يَشِجُ, inf. n. وَشْجٌ and وَشِيجٌ, *It* (anything) *became entangled, intermixed, confused,* or *intricate.* (TA.) — وَشَجَتْ فِى قَلْبِهِ أُمُورٌ وَهُمُومٌ ‡ *Affairs, and griefs,* or *solicitudes, became perplexing in his heart.* (TA.) — قَدْ وَشَجَتْ بِكَ قَرَابَةُ فُلَانٍ, aor. تَشِجُ, Ḳ,) ‡ *The relationship of such a one to thee has become intricate;* (Ṣ, Ḳ, TA;) like as the roots and branches of trees become intricate. (TA.)

2. وشّج القَرَابَةَ, inf. n. تَوْشِيجٌ, ‡ *He* (God) *made the relationship intricate.* (Ṣ, Ḳ.) — وشّج اللّٰهُ بَيْنَهُمْ ‡ *God joined and mixed them together.* (TA.) — وشّج مَحْمِلًا *He laced together a* مَحْمِل [or basket in which grapes are carried to the drying-place] *with a leather thong,* or *the like,* (such as a شَرِيط, TA,) lest anything should fall from it. (Ḳ.)

وَشِيجٌ *Trees of which spears are made:* (Ṣ, Ḳ:) or *canes growing obliquely,* or, as in the M, *in an intricate manner:* or the *hardest of canes:* or, as a coll. gen. n., ‡ *spears;* n. un. with ة: (TA:) [See also عَجْلَةٌ:] or, originally, the *roots of canes:* and afterwards applied to signify *spears,* themselves; so called because of their intermingling when meeting together. (Ḥam, p. 165.) — تَطَاعَنُوا بِالوَشِيجِ ‡ *They thrust one another with the spears.* (A.) — أَلْقَتِ السَّنَةُ الوَشِيجَ *Drought destroyed the tangled trees,* or *their roots;* no moisture remaining in the earth. (TA, from a trad.) — وَشِيجٌ The *roots of the sinews.* (TA.) — وَشِيجٌ ‡ *Intricacy of relationship:* (Ṣ, Ḳ:) pl. وَشَائِجُ. (TA.) Ex. بَيْنَهُمْ وَشَائِجُ النَّسَبِ *There is an intricacy of relationship between them.* (TA.)

وَشِيجَةٌ The *root* (عِرْق) *of a tree.* (Ṣ, Ḳ.) — See وَاشِجَةٌ. — وَشِيجَةٌ [*An implement made of*] *fibres of the palm-tree* (لِيف) *twisted, and then tied* (or, as in some lexicons, *attached in the manner of a net,* TA,) *between two pieces of wood,* (or *a net between two pieces of wood,* TA,) *upon which reaped wheat &c. are carried.* (Ṣ, Ḳ.)

وَاشِجٌ Anything *entangled, intermixed, confused,* or *intricate.* (TA.)

وَاشِجَةٌ (Ṣ, Ḳ) and ▼ وَشِيجَةٌ (TA) ‡ *Intricate relationship;* or *intricate uterine relationship;* (Ṣ, Ḳ;) *and close.* (TA.) Ex. بَيْنَهُمْ وَاشِجَةُ رَحِمٍ *Between them is an intricate and close relationship.* (TA.)

أَمْرٌ مُوَشَّجٌ *An intricate,* or *a confused, affair.* (TA.)

وشح

2. وشّح المَرْأَةَ, inf. n. تَوْشِيحٌ, *He put on the woman a* وِشَاح, q. v. (Ṣ, Ḳ.) — See 5. — وشّحهُ وِشَاحًا ‡ *He struck him a blow upon the place of the* وِشَاح. (TA.)

5. توشّحت, (Ṣ, Ḳ,) and ▼ اتّشحت, (Ḳ,) *She* (a woman) *put on,* or *decked herself with, a* وِشَاح q. v. (Ṣ, Ḳ.) — توشّح بِثَوْبِهِ, (Ṣ, Ḳ, &c.,) and ▼ اتّشح بِهِ, (Mṣb,) ‡ *i. q.* تَقَلَّدَ: (Ḳ:) but MF disapproves of this explanation: (TA:) or *He put his garment under his right arm-pit, and threw it* [meaning *a portion of it*] *over his left shoulder,* like as the مُحْرِم does; (T, Mṣb;) like تَأَبَّطَ and اِضْطَبَعَ: (T:) or *he threw a portion of his garment over his left shoulder, and drew its extremity under his right arm, and tied the two extremities together in a knot upon his bosom.* (M.) Also, *He wrapped himself up in his garment.* (L.) — وشّحهُ ▼ الثَّوْبَ, as also أَتْشَحَهُ ‡ *He put on him the garment in the manner described in the explanation of the phrase* توشّح بِثَوْبِهِ. (M, L.) — توشّح بِسَيْفِهِ (Ṣ, Ḳ, &c.) ‡ *i. q.* تَقَلَّدَهُ: (Ḳ:) [or *i. q.*] توشّح بِحَمَائِلِ سَيْفِهِ *He put the suspensories of his sword over his left shoulder, leaving the right bare:* (T:) and توشّح بِنِجَادِهِ [signifies the same]. (A.) — توشّح بِلِجَامِهِ (L) ‡ *He threw the bit and bridle of his horse upon his shoulder, and put his arm through it, so that it became like a* وِشَاح. (Expos. of the Mo'allaḳát printed at Calcutta, p. 171.) [See the verse of Lebeed quoted below.] — توشّح امْرَأَةً ‡ *Inivit feminam:* (A, TA:) or *he embraced a woman round the neck, and turned her over.* (TA.)

8: see 5, in two places.

وِشَاحٌ : see إِشَاحٌ.

وِشَاحٌ and وُشَاحٌ, (Ṣ, Ḳ,) also written ▼ إِشَاحٌ and أُشَاحٌ, and by poetic licence ▼ وِشَحْنٌ, (Ṣ,) *An ornament worn by women,* (L,) [*consisting of*] *two series* (كِرْسَانِ) *of pearls and jewels strung* or *put together in regular order, which two series are disposed,* or *placed, contrariwise,* (يُخَالَفُ بَيْنَهُمَا,) *one of them being turned* (مَعْطُوف) *over the other* [*so that they cross each other*]: (L, Ḳ:) or *a thing woven of leather, and adorned with jewels, like a* قِلَادَة, *worn by a woman:* (Mṣb:) or *a wide* [*piece,* or *thing, of*] *leather,* (Ḳ,) or *a thing woven of leather, in a wide,* or *broad, form,* (Ṣ,) *and adorned with jewels, which a woman binds* (تَشُدُّهُ) *between her shoulders and her flanks:* (Lth, Ṣ, Mgh, Ḳ:) or *a* قِلَادَة *of the belly, which is sometimes long, so that the redundant portions of its two extremities are thrown over the shoulders:* (Mgh:) or *one of a pair of necklaces which a woman makes to hang down upon her sides; one upon her right side, and the other upon her left:* (W. 144:) [hence it seems to be of different kinds; one kind consisting of two ornaments resembling necklaces, one of which rests upon the right shoulder and against the left flank, the other resting upon the left shoulder and against the right flank; another kind seems, from an expression in the A, "a woman bearing a وِشَاح, and وِشَاحَيْن," to be one such ornament; another, an ornament resembling a necklace, thrown over the head, so as to rest upon the shoulders, crossing in front, and passing round the loins, and is tied or crossed in front, and of which the redundant portions are thrown over the shoulders: see also كَشْح:] pl. وُشُحٌ and أَوْشِحَةٌ (Ṣ, Ḳ) and وَشَائِحُ: (M, Ḳ:) the last thought by ISd to be formed as though from وِشَاحَة. (L.) — Lebeed says:

• وَلَقَدْ حَمَيْتُ الحَىَّ تَحْمِلُ شِكَّتِى •
• فُرُطٌ وِشَاحِى إِذْ غَدَوْتُ لِجَامُهَا •

[*And I have protected the tribe; a swift, outstripping, horse, whose bit and bridle were my* وشاح *when I went away, bearing my arms*: see توشّح بلجامه]: he relates his having gone forth as a scout for his people, mounted on his camel, with his horse by his side, and bearing its bit and bridle like a وشاح, so that he might bit the horse if he perceived the enemy. (L.) — وِشَاحٌ † *A bow*: (L:) [so called because of the manner in which it is worn]. — وِشَاحٌ (M) and ↓ وِشَاحَةٌ (M, Ḳ) † *A sword*: (M, Ḳ:) so called because of the manner in which it is worn: see 5. (M.) — غَرْثَى الوِشَاحِ, or هِىَ غَرْثَى الوِشَاحِ [and جَائِعَةُ الوِشَاحِ, and غَطْشَةُ الوِشَاحِ,] ‡ *She is slender in the belly and flanks*. (Ḳ.) [See also art. غرث.]

وِشَاحَةٌ: see وِشَاحٌ.

وَشْحَآءُ *A she-goat* (Ṣ, Ḳ) that is *black*, (L,) *with a white mark*, or *with two white marks, like a* وِشَاح; expl. by مُوَشَّحَةٌ بِبَيَاضٍ. (Ṣ, L, Ḳ.)

مُوَشَّحٌ ‡ A garment, and a cock, *having two marks like a* وِشَاح. (L.) — مُوَشَّحَةٌ ‡ A gazelle, and a sheep, and a bird, *having two streaks*, or *strips, one on each side*. (L.) [See صُلْصُلٌ.]

وشر

1. وَشَرَ, (Ṣ, Ḳ,) inf. n. وَشْرٌ, (TA,) *He sawed* a piece of wood with a مِيشَار; a dial. form of أَشَرَ; (Ṣ, Ḳ;) *i. q.* نَشَرَ. (Ḳ.) — وَشَرَتْ, aor. تَشِرُ, (Mṣb,) inf. n. وَشْرٌ, (Ṣ, Ḳ,) *She* (a woman) *sharpened* (Ṣ, Mṣb, Ḳ) her teeth, (Ṣ, Ḳ,) or her canine teeth, (Mṣb,) *and made* them *thin* [*and serrated*], (Ṣ, Mṣb, Ḳ,) meaning their edges: (TA:) [as also أَشَرَتْ.] See وَاشِرَةٌ.

10. اِسْتَوْشَرَتْ *She* (a woman) *asked for her* [*teeth or*] *canine teeth to be sharpened and made thin* [*and serrated*]. (Mṣb.)

وَشْرٌ a dial. form of أَشْرٌ [*A serration and a sharpness of the extremities* of the teeth]. (Ṣgh, Ḳ.)

وَاشِرَةٌ A woman *who sharpens and makes thin* [*and serrated*] *the* [*teeth, or*] *canine teeth*. (Mṣb.) It is said in a trad., لَعَنَ ٱللّٰهُ الوَاشِرَةَ وَالمُوتَشِرَةَ [*May God curse her who sharpens and makes thin and serrated the teeth, or the canine teeth, and her who orders one to do this, or who asks for it to be done*]. (Ṣ, TA.) An old woman does this in order to make herself like the young. (TA.)

مُوَشَّرُ العَضُدَيْنِ, applied to the beetle, [meaning, *Having the fore-shanks formed thin, and serrated*;] as also without ء. (Ḳ.)

مِئْشَارٌ, without ء, مِيشَار, *A saw*; a dial. form of مِئْشَار. (Ṣ,* Ḳ.)

مُوتَشِرَةٌ A woman *who orders one to sharpen teeth and to make them thin* [*and serrated*]: (L:) or *who asks for this to be done*; as also ↓ مُسْتَوْشِرَةٌ: (Ḳ:) if with ء, it is from أَشْرٌ, not وَشْرٌ; and if without ء, accord. to the regular way it should be مُتَّشِرَةٌ. (Ḳ.)

مُسْتَوْشِرَةٌ: see مُوتَشِرَةٌ.

[وشظ &c.

See Supplement.]

وص

2. وَصَّصَتْ, (AZ, TA,) or ↓ وَصْوَصَتْ, (M,) *She* (a girl, M,) *put on*, or *wore, her* نِقَاب [a kind of *face-veil*], (AZ, TA,) or *her* قِنَاع [a kind of *head-covering*], (M,) *in such a manner that nothing was seen but her eyes*: (AZ, M, TA:) تَرْصِيصٌ and تَوْصِيصٌ signify the same: (AZ, Ṣ, CḲ:) the former is of the dial. of Temeem: (AZ, TA:) or both the above verbs signify *she* (a woman) *contracted her* نقاب (Ḳ, TA) *so that it shewed nothing but her eyes*: (TA:) or وصوصت نقاب signifies *she* (a woman) *put her* نقاب *near to her eyes*. (Fr. TA.)

R. Q. 1. وَصْوَصَتْ: see 2, throughout. — وَصْوَصَ *He looked through a hole such as is termed* وَصْوَص. (Ḳ.) — *He* (a whelp) *opened his eyes*. (Ḳ.) = وَصْوَصَ عَيْنَهُ *He* (a man) *contracted his eye in order to obtain a sure view*. (IDrd, M.)

وَصْوَصٌ: see وَصَائِصُ.

وَصْوَصٌ, (Ṣ,) or ↓ وَصْوَاصٌ, (M,) or both, (Ḳ,) the latter on the authority of Lth, (TA,) *A hole in a veil or the like, of the size of the eye, through which one looks*. (Ṣ, M, Ḳ.) And وَصَاوِصُ, [the pl. of the former, or of either,] The *narrow parts of the apertures for the eyes of a* بُرْقُع [a kind of *woman's face-veil*]; (M, TA;) as also وَصَائِصُ. (TA.)

وَصْوَاصٌ: see وَصْوَصٌ. — *A small* بُرْقُع [a kind of *face-veil*]: (Ṣ, M:) pl وَصَاوِصُ (Ṣ,) signifying *small* بَرَاقِع *worn by a girl*. (Ḳ.) — بُرْقُعٌ وَصْوَاصٌ *A* بُرْقُع *that is contracted* [*so as to show nothing but the eyes*]. (M, TA.)

وصأ

1. وَصِئَ, as also صَئِىَ, (mentioned by Lb, TA,) *It* (a garment) *was, or became, dirty*. (Ḳ.)

وصب

1. وَصَبَ, aor. يَصِبُ, inf. n. وُصُوبٌ; (Ṣ, Ḳ;) and ↓ اوصب; (Ḳ;) *It continued; was constant*; (Ṣ, Ḳ;) *was fixed, settled, or firm*. (Ḳ.) — وَصَبَ لَبَنُ النَّاقَةِ † *The milk of the camel continued, or was constant*. (A.) — وَصِبَ, aor. يَوْصَبُ, inf. n. وَصَبٌ; (Ṣ, Ḳ, Mṣb;) and ↓ وصّب and ↓ اوصب and ↓ توصّب; (Ḳ;) *He* (a man, Ṣ,) *was, or became, diseased, ill*, or *sick*: (Ṣ, Ḳ:) or *in pain*: (Mṣb:) [or *in violent pain*: or *in continual*, or *constant, pain*: or *emaciated in body by reason of fatigue or disease*: or *in a state of excessive fatigue*: and, sometimes, *he suffered fatigue*, or *weariness, and languor*: see وَصَبٌ:] تَوْصِيبٌ is also explained as signifying the *being languid*: (TA:) and ↓ توصّب, as signifying *he felt*, or *experienced, pain in his body*. (A.) — وَصَبَ الشَّحْمُ ‡ *The fat* [in an animal] *continued*. (TA.) — وَصَبَ عَلَى الأَمْرِ, (Ṣ, Ḳ,) aor. يَصِبُ, [inf. n. وُصُوبٌ;] and وَصَبَ, aor. يَصِبُ; the latter aor. extr. [with respect to analogy]; (Kr;) like وَثِقَ, aor. يَثِقُ, and وَمِقَ, aor. يَمِقُ, &c.; but not mentioned by the lexicographers with these verbs; (TA;) [and ↓ اوصب; see below;] and ↓ واصب; (TA;) *i. q.* وَاظَبَ; *He kept, attended*, or *applied himself, constantly, perseveringly*, or *assiduously, to the thing*; (Ṣ, Ḳ;) *and managed it*, or *conducted it, well*. (Ḳ.) — وَصَبَ فِى مَالِهِ, and عَلَى ماله; and وَصِبَ; aors. as above; *He kept, attended*, or *applied himself, constantly to his property*, [meaning his camels &c.,] *and managed it well*. (Kr.) — اوصب ↓ القَوْمُ عَلَى الشَّىْءِ *The people kept, attended, or applied themselves, constantly, perseveringly, or assiduously, to the thing*. (Ṣ, Ḳ.)

2. وصّبهُ *He took care of him, tended him*, or *nursed him, in his sickness*: like مرّضه. (TA, from a trad.) — See 1.

3: see 1, and 4.

4. اوصبهُ *It* (a disease) *rendered him ill*, or *sick*. (TA.) See وَصِبَ. — اوصبهُ *He* (God) *afflicted him with a disease, sickness, or malady*. (Ṣ, Ḳ.) See وَصِبَ. — اوصب *He* (a man) *had diseased children born to him*. (Ḳ.) Accord. to IḲṭṭ, اوصب القَوْمُ *The people had their children wearied by disease*. (TA.) = اوصبت النَّاقَةُ الشَّحْمَ ‡ *The she-camel grew fat*, (Ḳ,) *and continued so*: (TA:) [explained in the Ḳ by نَبَتَ شَحْمُهَا, which is probably a mistake for ثَبَتَ; and if so, I prefer another reading of the phrase in the Ḳ, mentioned in the TA; namely, اوصب النَّاقَةَ الشَّحْمُ; i. e., *the she-camel was constantly fat*]. — اوصبت النَّاقَةُ, and ↓ واصبت, † *The she-camel yielded milk continually*, or *constantly*. (A.) — See 1.

5: see 1, in two places.

وَصْبٌ The *space between the third finger and the first finger*; or, lit., *what is between those two fingers*. (Ḳ.)

وَصَبٌ *A disease, sickness*, or *malady*: (Ṣ, Ḳ:) or *pain*: (Mṣb:) or *violent pain*: or *continual*, or *constant, pain*: or *continuance of pain*: (TA:) or *emaciation of the body by reason of fatigue* or *disease:* (IDrd:) or *excessive fatigue:* (Zj:) and, sometimes, *fatigue,* or *weariness, and languor:* (TA:) pl. أَوْصَابٌ. (K.)

وَصِبٌ (S, K) and ♦ وَاصِبٌ (TA) *Diseased; ill; sick:* (S, K:) or *in pain:* (Msb:) [or *in violent pain:* or *in continual,* or *constant pain:* &c.: see وَصَبٌ]: pl. of the former وَصَابَى and وِصَابٌ. (K.)

وَاصِبٌ: see وَصِبٌ. — عَذَابٌ وَاصِبٌ [Kur. xxxvii. 9,] *A continual, perpetual, constant,* or *fixed, punishment.* (Fr, TA.) — لَهُ الدِّينُ وَاصِبًا, [Kur, xvi. 54,] as Zj observes, is said to mean *To Him shall be rendered obedience perpetually,* or *constantly:* (Fr, S:) or it may mean *To Him shall be rendered obedience, whether man be content with that which he is commanded to do,* or *not;* or *whether it be easy to him,* or *not:* *to Him shall be rendered obedience, even if it be attended by excessive fatigue.* (TA.) — مَفَازَةٌ وَاصِبَةٌ *A desert far-extending,* [*as though*] *without end;* (S;) *that extends so far as scarcely to have an end;* (A;) *very far-extending.* (K.)

مُوصَبٌ *Afflicted* by God *with a disease, sickness,* or *malady.* (S.)

نَاقَةٌ مُوصِبَةٌ, and ♦ مُوَصِّبَةٌ [perhaps a mistake for مُوَاصِبَةٌ: see 4:] † *A she-camel that yields milk continually,* or *constantly.* (A.)

مُوَصَّبٌ *Having many pains* [or *diseases*]. (S, K.)

نَاقَةٌ مُوَصِّبَةٌ: see نَاقَةٌ مُوصِبَةٌ.

وصد

4. اوصد *He closed,* a door, or an entrance; syn. أَغْلَقَ; (S, M, A, L, K;) and أَطْبَقَ: (Msb, K:) as also آصَدَ. (S, L, K.) — See 10. — أُوصِدَ *It* (a door, or entrance) *became closed.* (S.) — اوصد *He covered,* or *covered over,* a cooking-pot. (M, A, L.) — وَقَعَ الجَبَلُ عَلَى بَابِ الكَهْفِ فَأَوْصَدَهُ *The mountain fell upon the entrance of the cavern, and stopped it up.* (L, from a trad.) See also أَوْطَدَ. — اوصدوا عَلَيْهِ ‡ *They straitened him, and imposed on him a difficulty which he was unable to bear.* (A.)

10. استوصد (S, A, L, K) and ♦ اوصد (A, K) *He made a fold, such as is called* وَصِيدَةٌ, (S, L,) or وَصِيدٌ, (K,) or *a* حَظِيرَة, *for his sheep* or *goats,* (A,) in a mountain. (S, L.)

وِصَادٌ (M, L,) as also إِصَادٌ, (L,) and ♦ وَصِيدٌ [see the Kur, xviii. 17,] (K,) *i. q.* مطبق: (M, L, K:) [in a copy of the M written مُطْبَقٌ: in the L, without any syll. signs: in the CK, مُطْبَقٌ: and in my MS. copy of the K, مُطَبَّقٌ: see the remarks on these words in art. أصد:]) or وِصَادٌ and إِصَادٌ are like طِبَاقٌ. (O.)

وَصِيدٌ *A court,* or *an open* or *a wide space in front of a house* or *dwelling,* or *extending from its sides:* (S, M, A, L, Msb, K:) as also أَصِيدٌ; q. v.: (L:) pl. وُصُدٌ and وَصَائِدُ. (TA.) — *A threshold* (Msb, K) *of a door* or *entrance.* (Msb.) — *A door,* or *entrance.* (A.) See وِصَادٌ. — It has the first of these meanings in the Kur, xviii. 17; (A, L, TA;) or the second: (TA:) or the third: (A, TA:) or it there means The *cavern of the Ashâb el-Kahf.* (K*, TA.) — Also, وَصِيدٌ, (K,) or ♦ وَصِيدَةٌ, (S, A, L,) [as also أَصِيدَةٌ,] *A fold* (حَظِيرَة) *for sheep* or *goats:* (A:) or *a house like a* حظيرة, *of stones, made in the mountains, for flocks* or *herds;* (L, K;) i. e., *for sheep* or *goats* &c.: (TA:) *an enclosure like a* حظيرة, *made for flocks* or *herds, excepting that it is of stones, and a* حظيرة [*is*] *of branches of trees:* (S, L:) F, misunderstanding this explanation, has erroneously said in the K, that وَصِيدٌ also signifies a حظيرة of branches of trees: (TA:) pl. وَصَائِدُ. (A.) — [*Snares,* or *traps,* for catching beasts of prey: see وَصَائِدُ in art. وصد.] — وَصِيدٌ Herbage *having the roots near together.* (S, L, K.) — وَصِيدٌ ‡ *Strait; straitened;* (K, TA;) as also ♦ مُوصَدٌ عَلَيْهِ. (A, TA.)

وَصِيدَةٌ: see وَصِيدٌ.

مُوصَدٌ A door, or entrance, *closed:* (L:) or *become closed.* (S.) — In the Kur, civ. 8, [and xc. 20,] مُوصَدَةٌ (as some read instead of مُؤْصَدَةٌ, L) signifies *Closed over.* (S, L.) — See وَصِيدٌ.

وصر

وِصْرٌ *A covenant, compact,* or *contract:* (S, K:) a dial. form of إِصْرٌ; like as they said إِرْثٌ and وِرْثٌ, and إِسَادَةٌ and وِسَادَةٌ. (S.) — Also, (S, A, K,) and ♦ وَصْرَةٌ (Lth, A, K) and ♦ وَصِيرَةٌ (K) and ♦ أُوْصُرٌ, (Lth, TS, L,) *A written statement of a purchase or sale, transfer, bargain,* or *contract:* (S, A, K, TA:) the first is from إِصْرٌ, and is generally used in this sense: pl. of the first, أَوْصَارٌ; and of the second, وَصَرَاتٌ: Lth says, that the second is an arabicized word; and others say, that the first and second are Persian words, arabicized. (TA.) One says, أَقْطَعَهُ الأَرْضَ وَكَتَبَ لَهُ الوِصْرَ, and الوَصْرَةَ, [*He made him a grant of the land to be held in fee, and wrote for him the statement of the transfer.*] (A.) And it is said in a trad., هٰذَا ٱشْتَرَى مِنِّى أَرْضًا وَقَبَضَ مِنِّى وِصْرَهَا فَلَا هُوَ يَرُدُّ عَلَىَّ الوِصْرَ وَلَا يُعْطِينِى الثَّمَنَ [*This man purchased of me some land* (or دَارًا *a house,* as in the TA) *and received of me the written statement of its sale, but he will not restore to me the written statement of the sale, nor will he give me the price*]. (S.)

وَصْرَةٌ:
وَصِيرَةٌ: } see وِصْرٌ.
أُوْصُرٌ:

[وصف &c.
See Supplement.]

وضأ

1. وَضُؤَ (S, K) aor. يَوْضُؤُ, inf. n. وَضَاءَةٌ; (TA;) and وَضِئَ, aor. يَوْضَأُ; (IO, &c.;) *He was,* or *became, fair, beautiful, neat,* or *clean.* (S, K.) — وَاضَأَهُ ♦ فَوَضَأَهُ, (S, K,) aor. of the latter يَضَأُ, (S,) dev. from rule, by which, as a verb of the class called افعال المغالبة, it should be like يَنْصُرُ, (TA,) *He vied with him for the honour of surpassing in fairness,* or *comeliness, and prevailed over him therein.* (S, K.)

2. وَضَّأَهُ [*He made him,* or *assisted him, to perform the ablution termed* وُضُوءٌ, or وَضُوءٌ. (M, TA.) [See an ex. voce قِسْطٌ.]

3: see 1.

5. تَوَضَّأَ, (S, K,) inf. n., [or rather quasi-inf. n., used for the regular inf. n. تَوَضُّؤٌ,] وُضُوءٌ, or وَضُوءٌ, or both, [see these two nouns below,] from وَضَاءَةٌ, (lit., *He made himself fair, beautiful, neat,* or *clean:* TA:) *He performed ablution,* لِلصَّلَاةِ *for,* or *preparatory to, prayer.* (S, K.) — It sometimes signifies *He washed some one* or *more of his members: he purified his hand,* or *hands, and mouth, by washing, from the foul smell of fat,* or *greasy, food: he washed his hand.* — Some say تَوَضَّيْتُ [for تَوَضَّأْتُ]; but this should not be said: (S:) it is of weak authority, or is viciously so pronounced: (K:) it is said to be of the dial. of Hudheyl. (TA.) — توضّأ, and توضّأت, *He* (a youth), *and she* (a girl), *arrived at the age of puberty.* (K.)

وَضِىءٌ: see إِضَاءٌ.

وَضُوءٌ: see وُضُوءٌ.

وُضُوءٌ signifies The *act of ablution,* &c. (S, K) (see 5); and ♦ وَضُوءٌ, the *water with which that act is performed,* or the *water that is prepared for that act,* (S, K, TA,) and is said to be also an inf. n., [or rather a quasi-inf. n., signifying the *act itself*]: (S, K:) or they are syn. words of two different dialects, each sometimes used as an inf. n., signifying the *act,* (though inf. ns. of the measure فَعُولٌ deviate from constant rule, TA,) and each sometimes as signifying the *water.* (S, K, TA.) AA says, that ♦ وَضُوءٌ signifies "the water with which one performs the ablution above mentioned;" and he knew not وُضُوءٌ [though it occurs in many traditions]: and A'Obeyd disallows وُضُوءٌ, and allows only ♦ وَضُوءٌ. (TA.)

وَضِىءٌ, (S, K,) pl. أَوْضِيَاءُ and وِضَاءٌ; (K;) and ♦ وُضَّاءٌ, [S, K; in the CK, erroneously, وَضَّاءٌ;]

pl. وُضَّاؤُونَ and وَضَاضِئُ ; (Ḳ;) and ▼ وَاضِئٌ, (Ḳ,) which is used in the future sense, accord. to Lḥ, [like an act. part. n., though from a neut. verb,] as in the ex. [mentioned in the Ḳ] مَا هُوَ بِوَاضِئٍ ; وَضِىٓءٌ being used in the present sense; (TA;) *Fair, beautiful, neat,* or *clean.* (Ṣ, Ḳ.) — In the following of En-Nábighah,

• فَهُنَّ إِضَآءٌ صَافِيَاتُ الغَلَائِلِ •

[*And they are fair, beautiful, neat, or clean; unsullied as to their inner garments*], ▼ إِضَآءٌ may be put for وِضَآءٌ. (TA.)

وَضَآءَةٌ *Fairness, beauty, neatness,* or *cleanness.* (Ṣ, Ḳ.)

وُضَّآءٌ and وَاضِئٌ : see وَضِىٓءٌ.

أَوْضَأُ *Fairer, neater,* or *cleaner.* (TA, from a trad.)

مِيضَأَةٌ, and, sometimes, ▼ مِيضَاةٌ, *A place in which, and from which, one performs the ablution termed* وضوء; (Ḳ;) [as also ▼ مُتَوَضَّأٌ:] *a* مِطْهَرَة (Ḳ: in the CḲ, مَطْهَرَة), meaning *that from which,* or *in which, one performs the said ablution:* (TA:) [*a tank for ablution,* accord. to present usage].

مِيضَاةٌ : see what precedes.

مُتَوَضَّأٌ : see مِيضَأَةٌ. *A privy;* or *place where one performs ablution.* (Ḳ, TA, voce مَذْهَب, &c.)

وضح

1. وَضَحَ, aor. يَضِحُ, inf. n. وُضُوحٌ (Ṣ, Mṣb, L, Ḳ) and ضِحَةٌ and ضَحَةٌ, (L, Ḳ,) the last with fet-ḥah because the guttural letter; (TA;) and ▼ اتّضح, (Ṣ, Mṣb, Ḳ,) and ▼ اوضح, and ▼ توضّح, (L, Ḳ;) *It* (an affair, أَمْرٌ, Ṣ, Ḳ, and a thing, شَىْءٌ, L,) *appeared; became apparent,* or *plainly apparent, overt, conspicuous, manifest, notorious, plain, obvious,* or *evident;* (Ṣ, L, Ḳ;) *became clear, unobscured, exposed to view, displayed, laid open, disclosed,* or *uncovered.* (Mṣb.) — ‡ *It* (language) *was perspicuous.* (The Lexicons, passim.) — توضّح ▼ مِلْكُ الطَّرِيقِ *The middle of the road became plainly apparent, obvious,* or *conspicuous.* (Ṣ.) — مِنْ أَيْنَ وَضَحَ الرَّاكِبُ, as AZ says, or, as others say, ▼ من اين اوضح, *Whence did the rider make his appearance?* (L.) Or وَضَحَ الرَّاكِبُ signifies *the rider came forth:* (ISd:) and ▼ من اين أَوْضَحْتَ *whence hast thou come forth?* (IAạr, Ṣ,) and [in like manner one says] من اين بَدَا وَضَحُكَ. (Ṣ.) = وَضَحَتِ الإِبِلُ ‡ بِاللَّبَنِ *i. q.* أَلْهَثَتْ. (Ḳ.) = وَضِحَ, aor. ـَ, inf. n. وَضَحٌ, [a verb of which the inf. n. is explained in the Mṣb by the word درن : if this be not a mistake of a copyist, it app. signifies *He,* or *it, was dirty;* or *was dirtied, soiled,* or *besmeared*].

2: see 4.

4. اوضحهُ, (Ṣ, Mṣb, Ḳ,) and اوضح عَنْهُ, (L,) inf. n. إِيضَاحٌ: (TA,) and ▼ وضّحهُ, (Ḳ,) inf. n. تَوْضِيحٌ; (TA;) *He rendered it apparent* or *plainly apparent, overt, conspicuous, manifest, notorious, plain, obvious,* or *evident;* (Ṣ, L, Ḳ;) *rendered it clear,* or *unobscured; exposed it to view; displayed it; laid it open; disclosed* or *uncovered it.* (Mṣb.) — *He rendered language perspicuous.* (The lexicons, passim.) — اوضحت الشَّجَّةُ فِى الرَّأْسِ *The wound upon the head laid bare the bone.* (Mṣb.) [See مُوضِحَةٌ.] — اوضح لَهُ الأَمْرَ, (Ṣ, Ḳ,) and الكَلَامَ, (Ṣ,) *He made the affair,* (Ṣ, Ḳ,) and *the language,* (Ṣ,) *plain,* or *clear, to him.* (Ṣ, Ḳ.) — See 1. — اوضح قَوْمًا *He saw a people.* (L.) — اوضح *He* (a man) *had white children born to him:* (Ṣ, L:) and in like manner one says [اوضحت] of a woman. (L.)

5. See 1. — توضّح [app., *He* (a sheep or goat) *had a whiteness predominant over other colours, overspreading generally his whole body:* or *in his breast and back and face*]. (L.)

8: see 1.

10. استوضح شَيْئًا *He put his hand over his eyes* (*in the sun,* L) *to try if he could see a thing,* (Ṣ, L, Ḳ,) *guarding his eyes with his hand from the rays of the sun:* as also اِسْتَكَفَّهُ and اِسْتَشْرَفَهُ. (L.) One says اِسْتَوْضِحْ عَنْهُ يَا فُلَانُ [*Try if thou canst see him,* or *it, by putting thy hand over thine eyes, O such a one*]. (Ṣ.) — استوضح السَّبِيلَ *He sought* or *endeavoured to see plainly* or *clearly the way:* syn. اِسْتَبَانَهُ (Beyḍ, vi. 55.) — استوضح الشَّمْسَ *He blinked at the sun;* syn. تَخَاوَصَ إِلَيْهَا. (A.) — استوضحهُ الأَمْرَ, (Ṣ, Ḳ,) and الكَلَامَ, (Ṣ,) *He asked him to make the affair,* (Ṣ, Ḳ,) and *the language,* (Ṣ,) *plain,* or *clear, to him.* (Ṣ, Ḳ.) — استوضح عَنِ الأَمْرِ *He inquired respecting the thing* or *affair; sought for information respecting it; inquired into it; investigated it.* (L.)

وَضَحٌ *Light, and whiteness,* (Ṣ,) of anything: (TA:) the *whiteness of daybreak,* or *dawn:* and *of the moon;* (Ḳ;) *and its light.* (TA.) — صُومُوا مِنَ الوَضَحِ إِلَى الوَضَحِ *Fast ye from new moon to new moon.* (IAth, from a trad.) — وَضَحٌ ‡ *Leprosy;* syn. بَرَصٌ. (Ṣ, Ḳ.) It is sometimes used in this sense, metonymically. (Ṣ.) — وَضَحٌ *A mark in a horse differing in colour from the generality of his coat.* You say بِالفَرَسِ وَضَحٌ *In the horse is such a mark.* (Ṣ.) — وَضَحٌ *A blaze,* or *white mark on a horse's forehead* or *face.* (Ḳ.) — *What is termed* تَحْجِيلٌ *in the legs of a horse.* (L, Ḳ.) And also applied to other varieties of colour. (L.) — فَرَسٌ ذُو أَوْضَاحٍ *A horse having a blaze and what is termed* تحجيل. (A.) — وَضَحٌ *Whiteness of the hair,* or *hoariness;* or *white,* or *hoary, hair.* (Ḳ.) — ‡ *Milk:* (L, Ḳ:) thought by ISd to be so called because of its whiteness: or *milk that has not been mixed with water:* (L:) or *that is just drawn.* (TA, art. زهر.) Aboo-Dhu-eyb says,

• عَقَّوْا بِسَهْمٍ فَلَمْ يَشْعُرْ بِهِ أَحَدٌ •
• ثُمَّ ٱسْتَفَاؤُوا وَقَالُوا حَبَّذَا الوَضَحُ •

[*They shot an arrow towards the sky, and no one knew of it: then they returned, and said, An excellent thing is milk*]: meaning, we would rather have milk than the blood of him who has killed our companion: they preferred that camels should be given them in compensation. (L.) [See also 2, in art. عقى.] — وَضَحٌ *A sound, whole* or *perfect,* [*silver coin, of the kind called*] دِرْهَم. (Ṣ, Ḳ.) دِرْهَمٌ وَضَحٌ *A clean, white dirhem:* pl. أَوْضَاحٌ. (TA.) — وَضَحٌ The *middle,* or *main part and middle,* of a road; the *part* of a road *along which one travels.* (Ṣ, Ḳ.) — وَضَحٌ *A woman's ornament* (حَلْىٌ) *of silver:* (A'Obeyd, Ḳ:) or, *of stones;* (El-Meshárik;) i. e. *of silver-stones:* (Towsheeḥ:) so called because of its whiteness: (TA:) pl. أَوْضَاحٌ: (Ḳ:) or أَوْضَاحٌ signifies *a kind of woman's ornament* (حَلْىٌ) *made of whole* [*silver coins such as are called*] دَرَاهِم: (Ṣ:) and (according to some, TA,) وَضَحٌ signifies *an anklet;* syn. خَلْخَالٌ. (Ḳ) — وَضَحٌ (Ḳ) or وَضَحُ الطَّرِيقَةِ, (L, but the latter word is there written طريقة,) *Small portions,* or *parts, of herbage;* (L, Ḳ;) *what has become white thereof:* (AḤn:) pl. أَوْضَاحٌ: (L:) or أَوْضَاحٌ مِنْ كَلَإٍ signifies *somewhat of herbage that has become white:* (Aṣ:) Az says, I have mostly heard the term وَضَحٌ, with respect to herbage, applied to the نَصِىّ *and* صِلِّيَان صَيْفِىّ *which is not a year old and has not become black:* and on another occasion he says, that it is the remains of the حَلِىّ and صِلِّيَان only. (L.) — وَضَحٌ *Whiteness predominating over other colours* in sheep or goats, *overspreading generally the whole body:* pl. أَوْضَاحٌ: (L:) or, *in the breast and back and face:* (T:) you say also ▼ لَهُ تَوْضِيحٌ. (L.) — مِنْ أَيْنَ بَدَا وَضَحُكَ: see 1. — وَضَحُ القَدَمِ *Whiteness of the hollow of the sole of the foot.* (L.)

وَضَحَةٌ *A she-ass.* (Ḳ.)

وَضِيحَةٌ *Camels*, or *camels and sheep*; syn. نَعَمٌ: pl. وَضَائِحُ. (L, Ḳ.)

وَضَّاحٌ: see وَاضِحٌ.

وَاضِحٌ and ↓ وَضَّاحٌ [but the latter has an intensive signification] *Apparent*, or *plainly apparent*; *overt*; *conspicuous*; *manifest*; *notorious*; *plain*; *obvious*; or *evident*; (L, Ḳ;) *clear*, or *unobscured*; *exposed to view*; *displayed*; *laid open*; *disclosed*, or *uncovered*. (So accord. to the explanation of the verb in the Mṣb.) — *Perspicuous* language. (The Lexicons passim.) — Also the ↓ latter, A man *of white*, or *fair, and beautiful, complexion*: (Ṣ, L, Ḳ:) *of beautiful and smiling countenance*. (L.) — See مُتَوَضِّحٌ. — Also the ↓ latter, ‡ *Leprous*. Hence Jedheemeh El-Abrash was called الوَضَّاحُ. (Ṣ.) — ↓ الوَضَّاحُ *The day*. (L, Ḳ.) The night is called الدَّهْمَانُ. (L.) — ↓ بِكْرُ الوَضَّاحِ *The prayer of morning*, or *daybreak*. The prayer of nightfall is called ثِنْىُ دَهْمَانَ. (L, Ḳ [but in the CḲ and a MS. copy of the Ḳ, for دَهْمَانَ we find دُهْمَانَ].) — ↓ عَظْمُ وَضَّاحٍ, (L, Ḳ,) and عُظَيْمُ وَضَّاحٍ, (L,) *A certain game* (*of the children of the Arabs of the desert*, L,) *in which children take a white bone and throw it in the darkness of night, and then disperse themselves in search of it*: (L, Ḳ:) *he who finds it wins*. (L.) [See more in art. عظم.] — ↓ هُوَ مِنْكَ أَدْنَى وَاضِحَةٍ *He is plainly apparent to thee, as though he had become white*. (Th.) — رَجُلٌ وَاضِحُ الحَسَبِ, and ↓ وَضَّاحُهُ, ‡ *A man as though he were conspicuous, clean, or pure, and white, with respect to rank or quality, nobility, reputation*, or *the like*. (L.) — In like manner one says, ↓ لَهُ النَّسَبُ الوَضَّاحُ ‡ *He is of conspicuous and pure race, or lineage*. (TA.) — وَاضِحٌ † An *illustrious* man. (Es-Saadee.) — [And so] ↓ أَوْضَاحٌ مِنَ النَّاسِ وَأَوْبَاشٌ [*Illustrious people, and mixed people of the baser sort*;] *companies of people of various tribes*. No sing. of اوضاح in this sense has been heard. (L.) — الوُضَّحُ [pl. of وَاضِحٌ] *The stars called* الكَوَاكِبُ الخُنَّسُ [namely, *Saturn, Jupiter, Mars, Venus, and Mercury*,] *when in conjunction with the bright stars of the Mansions of the Moon*. (L.)

وَاضِحَةٌ: see وَاضِحٌ. — صِيَامُ الأَوَاضِحِ, originally صِيَامُ الوَوَاضِحِ, (Hr, Ḳ,) pl. of وَاضِحَةٌ, (TA,) or الأَوْضَاحِ, (IAth,) *The fasting during the days of the white nights*: (Ḳ*, TA:) which was commanded by Mohammad: (Ḳ:) these are the 13th, 14th, and 15th, [of the lunar month]. (TA.) — الوَاضِحَةُ *The teeth that appear when one laughs*: (Ṣ, Ḳ:) an epithet in which the quality of subst. predominates: pl. ضَوَاحِكُ. (TA.) — See مُوضِحَةٌ.

أَوْضَحُ: see وَضَحٌ and وَاضِحٌ.

تَوْضِيحٌ inf. n. of 2, q. v. — And see وَضَحٌ at the end.

مُوضِحَةٌ (Ṣ, Ḳ) and ↓ وَاضِحَةٌ (TA) *A wound by which the head or face is broken, that shows the whiteness of the bone*: (Ṣ, Ḳ, TA:) or, *that removes the skin which is between the flesh and the bone*: the only kind of شَجَّة for which retaliation is allowed: for [some] other kinds there are assigned mulcts: and for this too is assigned a mulct, consisting of five camels: but a موضحة may also be *in other parts than the head* or *face*; and respecting this, a judge must give his sentence: pl. مَوَاضِحُ. (TA.) [See شَجَّةٌ.] — مَوَاضِحُ الحَقِّ i. q. مَبَايِنُهُ, q. v. (TA, in art. بين.) — مُوضِحَةٌ *A woman who brings forth white children*. (O, in TA, art. بيض.)

مُتَوَضِّحٌ and ↓ وَاضِحٌ A camel *that is white, but not intensely so*; (En-Naḍr, L, Ḳ;) *more white than such as is termed* أَعْيَصُ [app. a mistake for أَعْيَسُ] *and* أَصْهَبُ: (En-Naḍr, L:) also (the former accord. to the Ḳ, and the latter also accord. to the L) *of such a colour in the* أَقْرَاب [or *flanks*]. (L, Ḳ.) — مُتَوَضِّحٌ One *who is apparent*, or *plainly apparent*. (Ḳ.) — One *who shows himself openly in the road*, (Ṣ,) or *who goes along the middle*, or *main part and middle of the road*, (Ḳ,) *and does not enter a woody place or the like where he would be concealed*. (Ṣ, Ḳ.)

وضخ

1. وَضَخَ الدَّلْوَ, and ↓ اوضخها, *He nearly half-filled the bucket, so that it resembled one half-full*. (L, Ḳ.) [See also 4.]

3. واضخهُ, inf. n. مُوَاضَخَةٌ (Ṣ, Ḳ) and وِضَاخٌ, (Ḳ,) *He emulated*, or *imitated, him* (that is his companion) *in drawing water, doing as he did*. (Aṣ, Ks, Ṣ, Ḳ.) This is the original signification: afterwards used with reference to any two persons emulating each other. (Ks, Ṣ.) [Hence,] — ‡ *He emulated him*, or *imitated him, in running*; (L, Ḳ;) *and exerted himself excessively*, or *exceeded the usual bounds* or *degree, therein*: (L:) or [so in the L; in the Ḳ, and] *went, journeyed*, or *marched, like him*; or *kept pace with him in going, journeying*, or *marching*; (Ṣ, L, Ḳ;) *not a vehement rate*; (Ṣ, L;) as also واضخهُ السَّيْرَ. (L.) Az says, that مواضخة, as used by the Arabs, signifies emulation, although not with unusual exertion, or an exceeding of the usual bounds or degree, in running. (L.) [See also 6.]

4. اوضخ بِالدَّلْوِ *He drew water with the bucket and shook it about vehemently* [app. *so that it did not become*, or *remain full*]: or *he drew with it little water*. (L.) [See also 1.] — اوضخ لَهُ *He drew for him little*, or *a little, water*. (Ṣ, L, Ḳ.) — Also, اوضخت البِئْرُ *The well contained little water; its water became little*; (Ḳ;) water having been taken from it for irrigation. (TA.)

6. تواضخا *They* (two men standing together over a well, L) *emulated each other* [*in drawing water and*] *in watering*, or *irrigating*. (L, Ḳ.) — ‡ *They* (two horses) *emulated each other* [*in running*]: (L:) and تواضخت الإِبِلُ *the camels emulated one another in going, journeying*, or *marching*. (L, Ḳ*.) [See also 3.]

وَضُوخٌ *Water in a bucket resembling half* [*of the quantity that would fill it*]: (Ṣ, L, Ḳ:) or *what is less than the quantity that would fill it*. (L.)

وضر

1. وَضِرَ, (M, Mṣb, Ḳ,) said of a vessel, (TA,) and وَضِرَتْ, said of a bowl, (قَصْعَةٌ, Ṣ,) aor. يَوْضَرُ (Mṣb) and تَوْضَرُ, (Ṣ,) inf. n. وَضَرٌ, (Ṣ, Mṣb,) *It was*, or *became, dirty*, or *filthy*, (Ṣ, M, Mṣb, Ḳ,) *with grease or gravy*, or *the dripping that exudes from flesh-meat*, (Ṣ, M, Ḳ,) or *otherwise, with what is termed* وَضَرٌ. (M, Ḳ.)

2. وَضَّرَهُ [*He made it* (a vessel) *dirty*, or *filthy, with* وَضَر, i. e., *grease*, or *the like*]. — كَانَ نَقِىَّ العِرْضِ فَوَضَّرَهُ بِالدَّنَاءَةِ [*He was unsullied in honour, and he sullied it by baseness*]. (A.)

وَضَرٌ *Dirt*, or *filth*: (Ṣ, Mṣb): *and grease, gravy*, or *dripping that exudes from flesh-meat* or *from fat*: (Ṣ:) or the *dirt of grease or gravy*, or *of what exudes from flesh-meat*, and *of milk*: (M, A, Ḳ:) and (so in the M; but in the Ḳ, or) the *washings of a skin that is used for milk or for water*, and *of a bowl and the like*: (M, Ḳ:) [see عُشْبٌ voce خَضْرَآءُ الوَضَرِ:] and *remains of* هِنَآء [*or tar*] (AO, Ṣ, Ḳ) &c.: (AO, Ṣ:) [and *feculence* of clarified butter, adhering to the interior of a skin: see عَبَكَةٌ and عَبِقَةٌ:] and the *soil*, or *stain, of saffron and the like*; (Ḳ;) or *of* [*the perfume called*] خَلُوق, or *of* [*other*] *perfume having a colour*: and *a mark that remains from what is not perfume*: (TA:) pl. أَوْضَارٌ. (Ḳ.) — Also, The *odour*, (A,) or *what a man smells of the odour*, (AA, Ṣ, Ḳ,) *of food in a corrupt state*. (AA, Ṣ, A, Ḳ.) — You say also of a man, فِى أَخْلَاقِهِ وَضَرٌ ‡ *In his dispositions is foulness*. And هُوَ ذُو أَوْضَارٍ ‡ *He possesses foul qualities*. (A.)

وَضِرٌ *Dirty*, or *filthy*, (M, A, Mṣb, Ḳ,) *with grease, or gravy, or what exudes from flesh-meat,* or *otherwise, with what is termed* وَضَرٌ; (M, A, Ḳ;) applied to a vessel: (A:) fem. وَضِرَةٌ (M, A, Ḳ) and ▼ وَضْرَى; (M, Ḳ;) both applied to a woman; (M;) and the former, to a hand. (A.) See سَهِكٌ. — [Hence] الوَضْرَى (IAạr, Ḳ) and ▼ الوَضْرَآءُ (A, Ṣgh, Ḳ) *The anus;* syn. الإِسْتُ, (A, TA,) and القَنْدُورَةُ, (Ḳ, TA, [in the CḲ, القَنْدِيرَةُ, which is a mistranscription,]) both of which signify the same. (TA.) — [Hence also,] فُلَانٌ وَضِرُ الأَخْلَاقِ ‡ *Such a one is foul in dispositions.* (A.)

وَضْرَى and وَضْرَآءُ: see وَضِرٌ; the former in two places.

[وضع &c.

See Supplement.]

وط

1. وَطٌّ, [an inf. n., of which the verb is وَطَّ, aor., accord. to rule, ـِ, but accord. to the TḲ, ـُ,] The *crying* of the وَطْوَاط. (Ṣgh, Ḳ.) — The *creaking* of the [kind of vehicle called] مَحْمِل. (Ṣgh, Ḳ.)

R. Q. 1. وَطْوَطَةٌ, [inf. n. of وَطْوَطَ,] The *uttering speech,* or *words rapidly,* or *near together.* (Ḳ.) [See وَطْوَاطٌ.] — † The *being weak.* (Ḳ.)

R. Q. 2. تَوَطْوَطَ *He* (a child) *cried out.* (Ibn-'Abbád, Ṣgh, Ḳ.)

وُطُطٌ: see the last sentence of the next paragraph.

وَطْوَاطٌ The *bat;* syn. خُفَّاشٌ: (Aṣ, Ṣ, Ḳ:) or the *large* خُفَّاش: (Mṣb:) or the *swallow;* syn. خُطَّافٌ; (Ṣ, Mṣb;) this is thought by A'Obeyd to be, more probably than the first, the correct meaning; (Ṣ;) or the last may be right, but the first is that which is commonly known: (IB:) or it has the first signification, and also signifies *a species of the swallows* (خَطَاطِيف) *of the mountains,* (Ḳ, TA,) *black and likened to a species of the* خَشَاشِيف [or bats], *because of its* [*frequent*] *receding and turning aside* [*in its flight*]: (TA:) [Golius says, as on the authority of the Ḳ, "pcc. *genus montanum et vocale, quod* ǎrovs *dicitur;* i. e. the *swift*:] pl. وَطَاوِيطُ, (Mṣb,) or وَطَاوِطُ, (Ṣ,) or both, (Kr, Ḳ,) but the latter, which is irreg., only allowable in poetry, in cases of necessity. (Kr.) It is used in the first of these senses in the proverb, أَبْصَرُ فِى اللَّيْلِ مِنَ الوَطْوَاطِ [*More clear-sighted in the night than the bat*]. (Ṣ, Mṣb.) — *Clamorous;* (Lḥ, Ḳ;) applied to a man: (Lḥ:) and one *who utters his speech,* or *words, rapidly,* or *near together;* (Lḥ, Ḳ;) as though his voice were the voice of bats: so they assert it to mean: (Lḥ:) fem. with ة: (Ḳ:) and [in like manner] ▼ وَطْوَاطِىٌّ signifies *loquacious; a great talker; a babbler.* (Ḳ*, TA.) — † A man *weak in intellect and judgment:* (ISh:) or *weak* and *cowardly;* (A'Obeyd, Ṣ, Ḳ;) in the opinion of A'Obeyd, as being likened to the flying thing so called; (Ṣ;) as also ▼ وَطْوَاطِىٌّ: (Ḳ:) and ▼ وُطُطٌ, (IAạr, Ḳ,) of which وَطْوَاطٌ is the sing., (TA,) men (IAạr) *weak in intellects and bodies.* (IAạr, Ḳ.)

وَطْوَاطِىٌّ: see وَطْوَاطٌ, in two places.

وطأ

1. وَطِئَ, aor. يَطَأُ; (Ṣ, Ḳ;) the و falls out from the aor. of this verb, and from that of وَسِعَ, because they are transitive; for other verbs of the class فَعِلَ, having the aor. of the measure يَفْعَلُ, and the first radical letter infirm, are intransitive; and as these two differ from their class in being transitive, they are also made to differ in the aor.; (Ṣ;) or يَطَأُ was originally يَطِئُ, and therefore the و falls out from it; (TA;) inf. n. وَطْءٌ (TA) [and طِئَةٌ, q. v. infra]; and ▼ وَطَّأَ, (Ḳ, but this has an intensive signification, MF;) and ▼ تَوَطَّأَ (Ṣ, Ḳ) *He trod; trod upon;* (بِرِجْلِهِ *with his foot;* Ṣ) *trod under foot; trampled upon:* (Ṣ, Ḳ, TA:) or وَطِئَهُ signifies *he pressed,* or *bore, upon him,* or *it, with his hand* or *his foot.* (TA, in art. ثطأ.) [See also وَطْأَةٌ.] — طه, at the commencement of the 20th ch. of the Ḳur, is read by some طَهْ, and said to be for طَأْ, (the ه being substituted for ء,) and to signify *Tread upon the ground with the soles of both thy feet;* because Mohammad raised one of his feet in prayer. (TA.) — هُمْ يَطَؤُهُمُ الطَّرِيقُ ‡ *They* (i. e. the sons of such a one) *sojourn,* or *encamp, near the road, so that its passengers tread upon them* [*i. e., became their guests*]: (Sb, Ḳ:) a tropical phrase, in which الطريق is put for أَهْلُ الطَّرِيقِ; this being done to give greater force to the phrase, as it is one expressive of praise; for the road is a thing that is constant; whereas its passengers are sometimes upon it, and sometimes absent. (L.) [It means *They are a people who take up their abode near the road in order that many passengers may enjoy their hospitality.*] — [See also طَرِيقٌ.] — Of the same kind is the phrase أَخَذْنَا عَلَى الطَّرِيقِ الوَاطِئِ لِبَنِى فُلَانٍ ‡ [*We look to the road whose passengers tread on* (*i. e., make themselves the guests of,*) *the sons of such a one*]. (IJ.) — So too, مَرَرْنَا بِقَوْمٍ مَوْطُوئِينَ بِالطَّرِيقِ ‡ [*We passed by a people trod on* (*i. e., resorted to for their hospitality,*) *by the passengers of the road*]. (IJ.) — Also, يَا طَرِيقُ طَأْ بِنَا بَنِى فُلَانٍ ‡ *O road, bring us near to* [or, lit., *make us to tread on, i. e., make us the guests of,*] *the sons of such a one!* (IJ.) — وَطِئَ, (Ṣ, Ḳ,) aor. as above, (Ṣ,) *Inivit feminam.* (Ṣ, Ḳ.) — وَطَأَ, inf. n. طِئَةٌ, † *He trod under foot, and despised.* Ex. نَعُوذُ بِاللّٰهِ مِنْ طِئَةِ الذَّلِيلِ *We put our trust in God for protection from the vile person's treading us under foot, and despising us.* (Lḥ.) — وَطَأَ and ▼ وَطَّأَ (in MF's copy of the Ḳ واطأ) *He prepared, and made plain, smooth,* or *soft.* (Ḳ.) — وَطِيتُ, for وَطِئْتُ, is disallowed. (TA.) — وَطُؤَ, aor. يَوْطُؤُ, inf. n. وَطَآءٌ, [so in the TA: probably a mistake for وَطَاءَةٌ: see طِئَةٌ below:] *He* (a horse &c.) *was,* or *became, easy to ride upon.* (TA.) — وَطُؤَ, aor. يَوْطُؤُ, inf. n. وَطَاءَةٌ (Ṣ, Ḳ) and وُطُوءَةٌ (TA) and طَاءَةٌ (TA, as from the Ḳ) [and, app., طِئَةٌ, q. v. infra], *It* (a place, Ṣ) *was plain, level, smooth, soft,* or *easy to be travelled,* or *to walk,* or *ride* or *lie upon.* (Ṣ, Ḳ, TA.) = كُنْتُ أَطَأُ ذِكْرَهُ † *I used to conceal the mention of him,* or *it.* (TA, from a trad.)

2. See 1, in two places. — وَطَّأَ, inf. n. تَوْطِئَةٌ, *He made plain, level, smooth, soft,* or *easy to be travelled,* or *to walk* or *ride* or *lie upon.* (Ṣ, Ḳ.) *He made* a beast of carriage *easy to ride upon; trained,* or *broke,* it (M, voce رَاضَ.) — Also, (TA,) and ▼ تَوَطَّأَ, (L,) *He prepared* (L, ubi supra, and TA,) a bed, or a chamber. (TA.) — *He arranged,* or *facilitated,* an affair. (TA.) — وَطَّأَ [for وَطَّأْتُ] is disallowed. (Ṣ.) — وَطَّأَ *He* (i. e. God) *rendered* a land *plain, level, smooth, soft,* or *easy to walk* or *ride* or *lie upon.* (TA.) — Also, *He* (God,) *rendered* a land *depressed.* (Ḳ.) = See 4.

3. وَاطَأَهُ عَلَى أَمْرٍ, (AZ, Ṣ, Ḳ,) inf. n. مُوَاطَأَةٌ (Ṣ) and وِطَآءٌ; (TA;) and ▼ تَوَاطَأَهُ and ▼ تَوَطَّأَهُ; (Ḳ;) ‡ *He agreed,* or *concurred, with him respecting a thing.* (Ṣ, Ḳ.) The radical signification of واطأ is said to be *He trod in the footsteps of another:* and the signification of agreement is therefore figurative. (MF.) — فُلَانٌ يُوَاطِئُ ٱسْمُهُ ٱسْمِى ‡ [*Such a one's name agrees, or is the same, with mine*]. (Ṣ.) — لِيُوَاطِئُوا عِدَّةَ مَا حَرَّمَ اللّٰهُ ‡ [*That they may agree in the number of* (*the months*) *which God hath made sacred:* Ḳur, ix. 37]. (Ṣ.) — أَشَدُّ وِطَآءً, as some read, [in the Ḳur, lxxiii. 6,] signifies ‡ *More,* or *most, suitable;* (Ṣ;) [i. e., prayer, and the recitation of the Ḳur-án]: but some read وَطْئًا, in the sense of قِيَامًا: see نَاشِئَةٌ. (Ṣ, L.) See 4.

4. اوطأهُ غَيْرَهُ *He made another to tread,* or *trample, upon him.* (TA.) — اوطأهُ فَرَسَهُ *He made his horse to tread, or trample, upon him.* (Ḳ, TA.) — اوطأهُ الأَرْضَ *He made him to tread upon the ground.* (Mṣb.) — أَوْطَؤُوهُمْ † *They overcame them,* or *prevailed over them,* in a

contention, or dispute. (TA.) — In a trad. it is said, that the pastors of the camels, and the shepherds, boasted, one party over the other, and the former overcame the latter (اوطؤوهم). (TA.) The verb is used in this sense because it originally signifies, with the annexed pronoun, *they made* (others) *to tread*, or *trample, upon them:* (Ḳ, TA:) for him with whom you wrestle or fight, and whom you throw down, you trample upon, and make to be trampled upon by others. (TA.) — اوطأه العَشْوَةَ, (Ḳ,) and عَشْوَةً, (Ṣ, Ḳ,) *He made him to pursue a course without being rightly directed.* (Ḳ*, TA.) See art. عشو. — اوطأ فِى الشِّعْرِ, (Ṣ, Ḳ,) inf. n. إِيطَآءٌ; (TA;) and اوطأ الشِّعْرَ, and ▼ واطأ فيه, and ▼ وطّأه, and أَطَّأَهُ, and آطَأَهُ, (Ḳ,) in which last the و is changed into ا; (TA;) *He repeated a rhyme in a poem*, (Ṣ, Ḳ,) *using the same word in the same sense:* (Akh, Ḳ:) when the word is the same, but the meaning different, the repetition is not called ايطاء [but جِنَاسٌ تَامٌّ]. (TA.) This repetition (ايطاء) is deemed by Arabs a fault: or it is only deemed a fault if it occur two, or three, or more, times. (TA.)

5. See 1, 2, 3. — تَوَطَّيْتُ for تَوَطَّأْتُ is incorrect. (Ṣ.) — توطّأ *He, or it, was, or became, prepared.* (Ḳ.) [See also 8.]

6. تَوَاطَؤُوا † *They agreed together.* (Ṣ.) — تواطؤوا عَلَيْهِ † *They agreed together, or concurred, respecting it.* (TA.) [See 3.]

8. إِتَّطَأَ *It was prepared, and became plain, smooth*, or *soft.* (Ḳ.) [See also 5.] — إِتَّطَأَ العِشَآءُ (in a trad.) *The evening became completely dark:* [or *the period of nightfall fully came:*] also read إِيتَطَى, accord. to the dial. of the tribe of Ḳeys, and explained as signifying *the period of nightfall came.* The latter verb also signifies "concurrence, or concord, and agreement, with another." (TA.) — إِيتَطَأَ الشَّهْرُ [*About half the month has elapsed*]. This is said a day before the half, and a day after the half. (AZ.) — إِتَّطَأَ, (as in the CḲ,) or إِيتَطَأَ, (as in a MS. copy of the Ḳ,) measure إِفْتَعَلَ [in the TA written إِسْتَطَأَ, which is doubtless a mistake,] *It was right, and attained its full period; was perfect*, or *complete.* (Ḳ.)

10. استوطأ *He found*, or *deemed*, a thing *plain, level, smooth, soft*, or *easy to walk* or *ride* or *lie upon.* (Ḳ, TA.) — *He found*, or *deemed*, the thing on which he rode *smooth, soft*, or *easy to ride upon.* (Ṣ.)

وَطْءٌ and ▼ وَطَأٌ and ▼ مِيطَأٌ (measure مِفْعَلٌ, as shown in the TA; but in the CḲ, مِيطَأٌ;) *Depressed land*, or *low ground, between eminences* (نِشَازٌ [in the CḲ نَشَازٌ] and أَشْرَافٌ [in the CḲ إِشْرَافٌ]): (Ḳ:) نشاز, is pl. of نَشَزٌ, and اشراف is pl. of شَرَفٌ; and both signify "eminences." (TA.)

طَأَةٌ: see طِئَةٌ.

طِئَةٌ and ▼ طَأَةٌ (in both of which the final ة is a substitute for the incipient و, Ṣ) and ▼ وَطَآءَةٌ (Ṣ, Ḳ) and ▼ وَطُوءَةٌ (Ḳ) *Plainness, levelness, smoothness, softness*, or *state of being easy to walk* or *ride* or *lie upon.* (Ṣ, Ḳ, TA.)

وَطْأَةٌ [*A tread*, or *a treading.* — And hence,] ‡ *A pressure; oppression; affliction; violence:* (Ṣ, Ḳ:) or *a vehement assault*, or *punishment;* syn. أَخْذَةٌ شَدِيدَةٌ: (Ḳ:) also, *a hostile expedition* or *engagement; battle, fight*, or *slaughter.* (TA.) — اَللّٰهُمَّ اشْدُدْ وَطْأَتَكَ عَلَى مُضَرَ, in a trad., *O God, make thy punishment of Muḍar severe.* (Ṣ, TA.) — وَطِئَنَا العَدُوُّ وَطْأَةً شَدِيدَةً ‡ [*The enemy assaulted*, or *punished, us with a very vehement assault*, or *punishment*]. (TA.) آخِرُ وَطْأَةٍ وَطِئَهَا اللّٰهُ بِوَجٍّ, in a trad., ‡ *The last assault*, or *conflict, which God caused to befall* (*the unbelievers was*) *in Wejj* [a valley of Eṭ-Ṭáïf]. (TA.) — وَطْأَةٌ and ▼ مَوْطَأٌ (Ḳ) and ▼ مَوْطِئٌ (Ṣ, Ḳ) *A place on which the sole of the foot is placed; a footstep*, or *footprint.* (Ṣ, Ḳ.)

وَطَآءَةٌ: see وِطَآءٌ, and وَطْءٌ.

وِطَآءٌ (Ṣ, Ḳ) and ▼ وَطَآءٌ, (Ḳ,) the former is the word commonly known and approved; the latter disapproved by many; (TA;) The *contr. of* غِطَآءٌ (*a covering*); [*what is placed*, or *spread, beneath one, to sit* or *lie upon*]: (Ṣ, Ḳ:) pl. أَوْطِئَةٌ. (TA, in art. خور.)

وَطِىْءٌ *Plain, level, smooth, soft*, or *easy to be travelled*, or *to walk* or *ride* or *lie upon.* (Ṣ, Ḳ, TA.) — دَابَّةٌ وَطِىْءٌ (IAạr) *A beast easy to ride upon.* (TA.) — عَيْشٌ وَطِىْءٌ [*An easy life*]. (TA.) — وَطِىْءُ الخُلُقِ *Easy in nature*, or *dispositon.* (TA.)

وَطَآءَةٌ:
وَطُوءَةٌ: } see طِئَةٌ.

وَطِيئَةٌ *A certain kind of food*, (Ṣ) i. q. حَيْسَةٌ: (IAạr:) or *dates of which the stones are taken out, and which are kneaded with milk:* or *what is called* أَقِط, *with sugar:* (Ḳ:) or *a food of the Arabs, prepared with dates, which are put into a stone cooking-pot; then water is poured upon them, and clarified butter if there be any;* (*but no* اقط *is mixed up with them;*) *and then it is drunk, like* حيسة: (T:) or it is *like* حَيْس; *dates and* اقط *kneaded together with clarified butter:* (ISh:) or *a certain kind of food, also called* وَطِىْءٌ; *a thin* عَصِيدَة: when it is thickened, it is called نَفِيتَة; when a little more thick, نَفِيثَة; when a little thicker, نَفِيتَة; and when so thick that it may be chewed, عصيدة. (El-Mufaḍḍal.) — Also, (as some say, TA,) *A thing like* [*the kind of sack called*] *a* غِرَارَة: (Ṣ:) or *a* غرارة *containing dried meat* (قَدِيد) *and* كَعْك (Ḳ) *and other things:* (TA:) — أَخْرِجْ إِلَيْنَا ثَلَاثَ أُكَلٍ مِنْ وَطِيئَةٍ *Take forth and give us three cakes of bread from a* غرارة. (Ṣ, TA, from a trad.) — [See also وَاطِئَةٌ and مُوَطَّأٌ.]

وَاطِئَةٌ *Fallen dates.* (Ḳ.) An act. part. n. in the sense of a pass.: (Ḳ:) [such dates being so called] because they are trodden under foot. (TA.) Or [it is changed] from وَطَايَا, pl. of وَطِيئَة, [which is] from وَطْءٌ; [and such dates are] so called because their owner has despised them, or trampled upon them, (ذَلَّلها,) and spread them about, for those who may take them; wherefore they are not included in the conjectural estimate of the produce of the tree [made by the collector of the legal alms]. (TA.) — وَطْأَةٌ (Ḳ) [pl. of وَاطِئٌ] and وَاطِئَةٌ (Ṣ, Ḳ) *Travellers; wayfarers:* (Ṣ, Ḳ:) so called from their treading the road. (Ṣ.)

لَا يَتَوَضَّأُ مِنْ مَوْطَإٍ وضوء *One is not to perform* (i. e., to repeat it,) *on account of treading on filth in the road:* but this does not mean that one is not to wash off the filth. (TA, from a trad.) — See وَطْأَةٌ.

مَوْطِئٌ: see وَطْأَةٌ.

مِيطَأٌ: see وَطْءٌ.

آثَارٌ مَوْطُوءَةٌ (in a trad. respecting destiny) *Tracks trodden* [as it were] by past predestined events, good and evil. (TA, from a trad.)

وَطِىْءٌ ▼ مُوَطَّأُ الأَكْنَافِ, (Ḳ,) and الاكناف, (TA,) A man *of easy nature*, or *disposition, generous, and very hospitable:* or *one in whose vicinity his companion is possessed of power, authority*, or *dignity; not harmed, nor inconveniently situated.* (Ḳ.) — اَللّٰهُمَّ اجْعَلْهُ مُوَطَّأَ العَقِبِ † *O God, make him to be* (a Sulṭán, followed by many dependants, and) *one whose heels shall be trod upon:* (Ḳ*, TA:) an imprecation, occurring in a trad. respecting a man who had been secretly informed against to 'Omar, who said this with reference to the informer if a liar. (TA.)

وطب

وَطْبٌ *A skin* (سِقَآءٌ) *in which milk is put*, (Ṣ, Ḳ,) *specially used for that purpose:* (Ṣ:) or *a skin in which are put clarified butter and milk:* (Mejma' el-Biḥár, &c.:) it is *made of the skin of an animal such as is termed* جَذَعٌ, [*meaning a goat in its second year,*] or *what is above that* [*in age*]: (ISk, Ṣ, Ḳ:) the skin of a sucking kid, in which milk is put, is called شَكْوَةٌ; and that of one that is weaned, بَدْرَةٌ; and the like of a شكوة, in which clarified butter is put, عُكَّةٌ; and the like of a بدرة, مِسْأَدٌ: (ISk, Ṣ:) see also بَدْرَةٌ: pl. of pauc. أَوْطُبٌ, and of mult. وِطَابٌ (Ṣ) and أَوْطَابٌ, (dev. with respect to analogy, (TA,) [accord. to most grammarians; but not so accord. to Fr, because its first radical letter is و;] and pl. pl. (i. e. pl. of اوطب, TA,) أَوَاطِبُ. (Ḳ.) — وَطْبٌ ‡ *A hard, rough, rude,* or *coarse, man:* syn. رَجُلٌ جَافٍ. (Ṣ, Ḳ.) — وَطْبٌ ‡ *A large breast:* (Ḳ:) likened to the skin so called. (TA.) — صَفِرَتْ وِطَابُهُ ‡ *He died:* or *he was slain:* (Ḳ:) the body's becoming empty of the soul is compared to the skin's becoming empty of the milk: or the meaning is *his blood issued forth from his body:* or, as some say, *his skins became empty of their milk;* a hostile attack having been made upon his camels, and no milch camel remaining in his possession. (TA.) [See similar sayings voce رفد; and see Ḥam., p. 34.]

طبة, without teshdeed, [but whether طَبَةٌ or طِبَةٌ is meant is not said,] *A piece of skin,* or *hide:* thought by ISd to be perhaps from الوَطْبُ: but the word commonly known is طِبَّةٌ, with teshdeed, mentioned in art. طب. (TA.)

وَطْبَةٌ, occurring in a trad., accord. to one relation, and explained by En-Naḍr as signifying The *kind of food called* حَيْسٌ, *made of dates and* أَقِط *and clarified butter:* but said to be erroneous: accord. to another relation, وطبة, which is erroneous: accord. to another, وَطِيئَةٌ [q.v., app. the right reading]. (TA.) See حَيْسٌ.

وَطْبَاءُ ‡ A woman *having large breasts:* (Ṣ, Ḳ:) as though having a وَطْب; (Ṣ;) i. e., carrying a وطب of milk. (TA.)

وطث

1. وَطَثَ, (aor. يَطِثُ, Ḳ,) inf. n. وَطْثٌ, *He struck the ground vehemently with his foot:* (Ṣ, Ḳ:) or *he* (a camel) *struck vehemently with his foot:* (TA:) a dial. form of وَطَسَ, or viciously pronounced for the latter word: (Ṣ:) or the ث of وطث is a substitute for the س of وطس; and the meaning is *he broke:* (Yaḳoob:) or وَطَثَهُ, aor. يَطِثُهُ, inf. n. وَطْثٌ, signifies *he trod,* or *trampled, upon it so that he broke it.* (T.)

وطح

1. وَطَحَهُ, aor. يَطِحُ, (inf. n. طِحَةٌ, TA,) *He pushed him,* or *thrust him, with his hands, ungently, harshly,* or *violently.* (Ḳ.)

6. تواطح القَوْمُ *The people did evil,* or *mischief, one to another, by turns:* or *fought together.* (El-Umawee, Ṣ, Ḳ.) — تواطحت الإِبِلُ عَلَى الحَوْضِ, (TA,) or تواطحت الحَوْضَ, (Ḳ,) *The camels crowded,* or *pressed together, to the tank* or *cistern.* (Ḳ.)

وَطَحٌ [so in the Ṣ] and so written by Aboo-Sahl, but in the copies of the Ḳ وَطْحٌ, (TA,) *Dung* (عَرَّةٌ) or *mud that adheres to cloven hoofs, and to the claws,* or *talons of birds:* (Ṣ, Ḳ:) n. un. with ة. (TA.)

وطد

1. وَطَدَ, aor. يَطِدُ, inf. n. وَطْدٌ (Ṣ, L, Ḳ) and طِدَةٌ; (L, Ḳ;) and ▼ وطّد, (Ḳ,) inf. n. تَوْطِيدٌ; (Ṣ, L;) *He made a thing constant, firm, steady, steadfast, fast,* or *established.* (Ṣ, L, Ḳ.) — وَطَدَ, aor. يَطِدُ, inf. n. وَطْدٌ (Ṣ, L, Ḳ) and طِدَةٌ; (L, Ḳ;) and ▼ وطّد, (Ḳ,) inf. n. تَوْطِيدٌ; (Ṣ, L;) *He,* or *it, pressed upon* a thing *heavily;* syn. ثَقَّلَ. (Ṣ, L, Ḳ.) — وَطَدَهُ إِلَيْهِ *He drew and pressed him to him; hugged him.* (L, Ḳ*.) — وَطَدَ, inf. n. وَطْدٌ, *He pressed* a thing to another thing, *and made it fast.* (AA, L.) — وَطَدَهُ إِلَى الأَرْضِ *He pressed him to the ground* [*with his hand,* or *hands,* or *foot,* or *feet,*] *and kept him fixed upon it, preventing his moving:* (IAth, L:) *he trod upon him vehemently:* (Ṣ, L:) occurring in a trad. (L.) — وَطَدَ لَهُ مَنْزِلَةً ‡ *He prepared,* or *established,* (مَهَّدَ,) *for him a station;* (L, Ḳ;) as also ▼ وطّد. (TA.) — وَطَدَ الأَرْضَ *He closed up,* (Ḳ,) *and trod,* (TA,) *the ground, in order that it might become hard.* (Ḳ, TA.) — See 5. — وَطَدَ *He trod; trod upon; trod under foot; trampled upon;* a dial. form of وَطِئَ. (Ḳ.) — وَطَدْتُ عَلَى بَابِ الغَارِ الصَّخْرَ *I piled up the rocks at the entrance of the cave so as to stop it up with them.* (Ṣ, L.) See also 4.

2: see 1. — وطّد ٱللّٰهُ لِلسُّلْطَانِ مُلْكَهُ, as also اطّده, ‡ *God established,* or *confirmed, to the Sulṭán his dominion.* (L.) — وطّده *He beat it with the implement called* مِيطَدَةٌ. (A.)

4. وَقَعَ الجَبَلُ عَلَى بَابِ الكَهْفِ فَأَوْطَدَهُ *The mountain fell upon the entrance of the cavern, and stopped it up with its ruins.* Occurring in a trad. IAth says, One should only say وَطَدَهُ; or perhaps وطده is a dial. form. Another relation gives أَوْصَدَهُ. (L.) See also 1.

5. توطّد, (Ṣ, L, Ḳ,) and ▼ اتّطد; (L;) and ▼ وَطَدَ, (L, Ḳ,) inf. n. وَطْدٌ; (L;) *It became constant, firm, steady, steadfast, fast,* or *established.* (Ṣ*, L, Ḳ.)

8: see 5.

وَطْدَةٌ i. q. وَطْأَةٌ: so in the following words [of a trad.;] اللّٰهُمَّ ٱشْدُدْ وَطْدَتَكَ عَلَى مُضَرَ [*O God, make thy punishment of Muḍar severe!*] (Ḳ*, TA.) [See also وَطْأَةٌ.]

وَطِيدٌ and ▼ مَوْطُودٌ *Rendered constant, firm, steady, steadfast, fast,* or *established.* (L, Ḳ.) See also وَاطِدٌ. — وَطِيدٌ and مَوْطُودٌ *Pressed upon heavily;* syn. مُثَقَّلٌ. (L, Ḳ.)

وَطِيدَةٌ † *An established station which a man holds.* (Yaḳoob, L.)

وَطَائِدُ ‡ The *foundations,* or *bases,* or the *columns,* (قَوَاعِد,) of a building: (Ṣ, L, Ḳ:) the *columns* (أَسَاطِين) of a mosque. (A.) — فُلَانٌ مِنْ وَطَائِدِ الإِسْلَامِ ‡ [*Such a person is one of the columns of el-Islám.*] (A.) — وَطَائِدُ ‡ *The supports called* أَثَافِي of a cooking-pot: (A, Ḳ:) app. pl. of وَطِيدَةٌ. (TA.)

وَاطِدٌ *Constant, firm, steady, steadfast, fast, settled,* or *established;* as also, by transposition, طَادٍ [q. v. in art. طدو]. (Ṣ, L.) See also وَطِيدٌ, and مُتَوَاطِدٌ, and مُوطَدٌ.

مُوطَدٌ: see وَطِيدٌ, and مُوطَدٌ.

مِيطَدَةٌ *A wooden implement with which the foundations of a building &c. are compressed, in order that they may become hard.* (A, L, Ḳ.) — *A piece of wood with which a boring-instrument,* or *drill, is held:* [i. e., *a wooden socket which fits upon the top*]. (Ṣ, L.)

عِزٌّ مُوطَدٌ, and ▼ مَوْطُودٌ, and ▼ وَاطِدٌ, ‡ *Established,* or *confirmed, might,* or *glory.* (A.)

مُتَوَاطِدٌ *Continuous;* or *constant and uninterrupted;* (Ḳ;) as also ▼ وَاطِدٌ and طَادٍ. (TA.) — ‡ *Strong; vehement; hard.* (Ḳ, TA.)

وطر

وَطَرٌ *A want; an object of want* or *need:* (Zj, Ṣ, A, Mṣb, Ḳ:) or one *which one purposes to accomplish:* (Lth:) or *for which one is anxious,* (A, Ḳ,) or *desirous:* (Mṣb:) pl. أَوْطَارٌ. (Ṣ, A, Mṣb, Ḳ.) It has no verb. (Kh, Ṣ, Mṣb.) You say, قَضَيْتُ وَطَرِى *I accomplished,* or *obtained, my want,* &c. (A, Mṣb, Ḳ.) And قَضَيْتُ مِنْ كَذَا وَطَرِى *I accomplished my want of such a thing* [so as to have no further need of it: see Ḳur, xxxiii. 37, in two places]. (Lth.)

[وطس &c.

See Supplement.]

وظب

1. وَظَبَ عَلَى شَىْءٍ, (aor. يَظِبُ, Ḳ,) inf. n. وُظُوبٌ, (and وَظْبٌ, Mṣb,) *He continued, to do a thing; persevered in it:* (Lth, Lḥ, Ṣ, Ḳ:) or, (as also وَظِبَهُ, aor. and inf. n. as above, TA,) i. q. ▼ وَاظَبَ, [which is the more common,] inf. n. مُوَاظَبَةٌ, *he kept, attended,* or *applied himself, constantly, perseveringly,* or *assiduously, to a*

thing; he was, or became, intent upon it; (AZ, Lḥ, Ṣ, Ḳ;) ▼ واظب is said to be sometimes trans. without a preposition, like لَازَمَ; but Es-Saad denies this. (TA.) —— وَظَبَتِ الرَّوْضَةُ *The meadow was incessantly pastured on,* [*so that it became destitute of herbage*]. (TA.) See the pass. part. n. —— فُلَانٌ يُوظَبُ عَلَيْهِ, and ▼ يُوَاظَبُ عَلَيْهِ, [*Such a one is deprived of his property* (*his camels &c.*) *by successive misfortunes*]. (TA, [but for يوظب is there written يظلب.]) See the pass. part. n. —— وَظَبَ, inf. n. وَظْبٌ, *He trod; trod upon; trod under foot; trampled upon.* (Ḳ, TA.)

3: see 1. —— واظبهُ عَلَى خِدْمَةِ فُلَانٍ *He incited him, or urged him, to keep to, or continue in, the service of such a one.* (TA, from a trad.)

وَظْبَةٌ The *vulva* (حَيَاء, L, or جِهَاز, Ḳ,) *of a solid-hoofed animal.* (L, Ḳ.)

مُوَاظِبٌ, and ▼ وَاظِبٌ عَلَيْهِ, واظب على كَذَا, *Keeping, attending,* or *applying himself, constantly, perseveringly,* or *assiduously, to such a thing; intent upon it.* (Lḥ.)

مِيظَبٌ *i. q.* ظُرَرٌ, (Ḳ,) which is *a kind of stone.* (TA.)

رَجُلٌ مَوْظُوبٌ *A man deprived of his property* (مال [app. meaning *his camels &c.*]) *by successive misfortunes.* (Ṣ, Ḳ.) —— أَرْضٌ مَوْظُوبَةٌ *A land that has been pastured on by turns, so that there remains in it no herbage,* or *pasture.* (Ṣ, Ḳ.) In like manner, رَوْضَةٌ موظوبة: or *a meadow that has been incessantly pastured on.* And وَادٍ موظوب *A valley of which the herbage has been eaten by cattle &c., so that it has become barren,* or *bare.* (TA.)

وَاظِبٌ: see مُوَاظِبٌ.

[وظف &c.

See Supplement.]

وعب

1. وَعَبَهُ, aor. يَعِبُ, (inf. n. وَعْبٌ, Mṣb;) and ▼ اوعبهُ, (inf. n. إِيعَابٌ; Mṣb;) and ▼ استوعبهُ; (and ▼ توعّبهُ; TA, voce تَعَبْعَبَ;) *He took it altogether; took the whole of it.* (Ḳ, Mṣb.) See 4.

4: see 1. —— اوعبهُ (TA) and ▼ استوعبهُ (Ṣ, TA) *He extirpated it; eradicated it.* (Ṣ, TA.) —— اوعب and ▼ استوعب *He went to,* or *attained, the utmost limit in anything.* (TA.) —— اوعب الجِذْعَ ‡ *He extirpated the trunk of a palm-tree.* (Ḳ.) But this is a mistake: the right reading is اوعب الجَدْعَ *He made the mutilation* (of a nose, ear, hand, or lip) *to be radical,* or *total.* (TA.) See مُوعَبٌ. —— اوعب أَنْفَهُ *He cut off the whole of his nose.* (Ṣ, TA.) —— اوعبهُ *He cut off the whole of his tongue.* (TA.) —— اِسْتَرَطَ مَوْزَةً فَأَوْعَبَهَا *He swallowed a banana-fruit, and left nothing of it.* (Lḥ.) —— اوعب الشَّىْءَ فِى الشَّىْءِ, (Ḳ,) and ▼ وَعَبَهُ فيه, (Az,) *He put, inserted,* or *introduced, the whole of the thing into the* [*other*] *thing.* (Ḳ, Az, Mṣb.) —— اوعب فِى مَالِهِ *He lent,* or *paid in advance, of his property,* syn. أَسْلَفَ: (IM:) or *he was prodigal of his property;* syn. أَسْرَفَ: (IḲṭṭ:) or, as some say, *he expended his property in every way.* (TA.) —— اوعب القَوْمُ ‡ *The people collected themselves together; congregated:* (Ṣ, TA:) *they came all together.* (TA.) —— اوعب *He collected; gathered together; congregated.* (Ḳ.) —— اوعب بَنُو فُلَانٍ جَلَآءً فَلَمْ يَبْقَ بِبَلَدِهِمْ مِنْهُمْ أَحَدٌ ‡ [*The sons of such a one came all together, emigrating, so that there remained not in their country one of them*]. (ISk, Ṣ.) —— اوعب بَنُو فُلَانٍ لِبَنِى فُلَانٍ *The sons of such a one collected together a company for the sons of such a one.* (Lḥ.) —— اوعب القَوْمُ ‡ *The people went forth all together on a military expedition.* (TA.) —— اوعبوا النَّفَرَ *They* [*collected together the men, and*] *went forth all together on a military expedition.* (TA, from a trad.)

5: see 1.

10: see 1. —— استوعب الشَّىْءَ ‡ *It* (a place, or a vessel,) *was large enough to contain the thing; it held the thing,* or *received it into its capacity.* (TA.) —— النِّعْمَةُ الوَاحِدَةُ تَسْتَوْعِبُ جَمِيعَ عَمَلِ العَبْدِ يَوْمَ القِيَامَةِ ‡ *One favour* [*of God*] *will be equivalent to all the works of a man on the day of resurrection.* A trad. (TA.) —— اِسْتَوْعَبَ [generally signifies *He,* or *it, took, took in* or *comprised* or *comprehended* or *included,* or *took up* or *occupied, altogether, wholly,* or *universally;* or *took in the gross; engrossed:* like اِسْتَغْرَقَ]. See 1: and 4, in two places. إِذَا ٱسْتُوعِبَ جَدْعُهُ الدِّيَةُ, said in a trad. respecting the nose, *If the mutilation thereof be total, so that nothing be left of it, the* [*whole*] *price of blood* [*shall be paid*]: (Ṣ:) or, accord. to another relation, أُوعِبَ كُلُّهُ [*If*] *the whole of it be cut off.* (TA.)

طَرِيقٌ وَعْبٌ *A wide road.* (Ḳ.) You say, وَعْبٌ: and the pl. is وِعَابٌ. (TA.) —— وِعَابٌ *Wide places in a land.* (Ḳ.) Correctly, it is pl. of وَعْبٌ; but in the Moajam [el-Buldán] it is made a proper name of certain places. (TA.)

وَعِيبٌ An *ample* house, or tent. (Ḳ.) An *ample* vessel, that takes in the whole of what is put into it. (TA.) —— جَآءَ الفَرَسُ بِرَكْضٍ وَعِيبٍ *The horse came at his utmost rate.* (Ṣ, Ḳ.) —— وَعِيبٌ Pudendum mulieris *amplum.* (TA.)

هٰذَا أَوْعَبُ لِكَذَا *This is most proper,* or *fit, for the full giving, receiving,* or *the like, of such a thing:* syn. أَحْرَى لِاسْتِيفَائِهِ. (Ḳ.) This is taken from the following words of a trad. —— نَوْمَةٌ بَعْدَ الجِمَاعِ أَوْعَبُ لِلْمَآءِ *A sleep after coitus is most proper for the complete evacuation of the semen remaining in the penis.* (TA.)

جَدْعٌ مُوعَبٌ, (also written مُوعِبٌ, TA,) *A mutilation of the nose, ear, hand, or lip, by which it is extirpated.* One says, in reviling, جَدَعَهُ اللّٰهُ جَدْعًا موعبًا *May God mutilate him by an utter mutilation of the nose, &c.!* (Ṣ.)

جَاؤُوا مُوعِبِينَ ‡ *They came having collected together all that they could:* (Ṣ, Ḳ:) *they came all together, not one of them remaining behind.* (Mṣb.)

وعث

1. وَعِثَ, aor. ـَ, (inf. n. وَعْثٌ, TA,) and وَعُثَ, aor. ـُ, (inf. n. وُعُوثَةٌ and وَعَاثَةٌ, TA,) *It* (a road) *was difficult to travel,* (Ḳ,) *and arduous to ascend.* (TA.) —— وَعِثَ, aor. ـَ, inf. n. وَعْثٌ and وَعَثٌ; and وَعُثَ, aor. ـُ, inf. n. وُعُوثَةٌ; *It* (a road) *was soft, and like what is termed* وَعْثٌ. (ISd.) —— وَعِثَ *It* (dust) *was fine, and it* (land) *was soft, and loose, so that the feet of beasts of carriage sank in it.* (TA.) —— وَعِثَتْ يَدُهُ *His hand broke.* (Ḳ.)

2. وعّث, inf. n. تَوْعِيثٌ, *He withheld,* or *restrained, and turned,* or *diverted,* [another from a thing]. (Ḳ.) وعّثهُ عَنْ كَذَا *He turned him,* or *diverted him, from such a thing;* as also عوّثهُ. (Az.)

4. اوعث *He came upon a tract such as is called* وَعْثٌ: (Ṣ, Ḳ:) *he came upon an even and soft tract:* (A:) *he walked along a tract such as is called* وَعْثٌ. (Mṣb.) —— اوعث فِى مَالِهِ *He was prodigal of his wealth,* (ISk, Ṣ, Ḳ.) —— اوعث, inf. n. إِيعَاثٌ, *He confounded,* or *confused.* (TA.)

وَعْثٌ A place that is *even and soft,* (Ṣ, Ḳ,) *such as is termed* دَهْسٌ, (Ḳ,) or كَثِيرُ الدَّهْسِ, (Ṣ,) *in which the feet sink,* (Ṣ, Ḳ,) *and upon which it is troublesome to walk:* (Ṣ:) or sand *in which the feet of camels, &c., sink:* (ISd:) and [in like manner] ▼ وَعْثَآء signifies that *in which the hoofs of horses and the like, and the feet of camels, sink, consisting of fine sand, and what is termed* دَهَاس, *of small pebbles:* (Az, from Khálid Ibn-Kulthoom:) or وَعْثٌ signifies whatever is *soft and even:* (Aṣ:) or sand *that is not much in quantity:* or *a soft place:* pl. وُعْثٌ and وُعُوثٌ: and [in like manner] ▼ نَقًا مُوعِثٌ *an extended and gibbous tract of sand, which is soft, and in which the feet sink.* (TA.) —— Also وَعْثٌ and ▼ وَعِثٌ and ▼ مُوعِثٌ *A difficult road.* (Ḳ.) —— فِى الوُعُوثِ, and هُوَ يَمْشِى فِى الوَعْثِ, *He walks along a tract such as is called* دَهَاس, *(and along tracts of that kind,) in which walking is laborious.*

(TA.) — وَعْثٌ ‡ A bone *broken*, (Ṣ, Ḳ,) and *chipped*, or *notched*. (Ṣ.) — وَعْثٌ *Leanness*: (Ḳ:) *soft leanness*. (TA.) — وَعْثٌ *A corrupt and confused state* of an affair: pl. وُعُوثٌ. (L.) — وَعْثٌ ‡ Anything *inconvenient, troublesome, difficult*, or *toilsome*. (Mṣb.) — اِمْرَأَةٌ وَعْثَةٌ *A woman who is fat*, (Ḳ,) or *fleshy*; (Ṣ;) as though the fingers would sink into her, by reason of her softness and fleshiness. (TA.) امرأة وَعْثَةُ الأَرْدَافِ ‡ *A woman having soft buttocks*. (ISd.) Ru-beh says,

• تُمِيلُهَا أَعْجَازُهَا الأَوَاعِثُ •

[*Her soft buttocks make her to bend*]. Here اواعث may be pl. of وَعْثٌ, contr. to analogy; or it may be pl. of أَوْعُثٌ, which may be pl. of وَعْثٌ. (ISd.) ▼ وَعْثَاءُ also signifies the same as وَعْثٌ. (ISd.) — [For the prov.]

• عَلَى مَا خَيَّلَتْ وَعْثُ القَصِيمِ •

(TA,) [see 2, in art. خيل.]

وَعِثٌ: see وَعْثٌ.

وُعُوثٌ *Adversity; difficulty; distress; affliction; evil*. (TA.) — See وَعْثٌ.

وَعْثَاءُ ‡ *Inconvenience, trouble, difficulty*, or *toil*, (Ṣ, Ḳ,) of travel: (Ṣ:) or *severity of trouble, difficulty*, or *toil*, thereof. (A'Obeyd.) — Also the like with respect to crimes, sins, or the like: you say, رَكِبَ الوَعْثَاءَ meaning ‡ *He committed a crime, sin, fault*, or *act of disobedience*. (A'Obeyd.) — See وَعْثٌ.

مَوْعُوثٌ A man *deficient in rank* or *quality, nobility*, or *eminence, reputation* or *note* or *consideration*, or *what is termed* حَسَب. (Ṣ, Ḳ.)

مُوعِثٌ: see وَعْثٌ.

وعد

1. وَعَدَ, aor. يَعِدُ, inf. n. وَعْدٌ and عِدَةٌ, (Ṣ, L, Mṣb, Ḳ,) [in which the ة is a substitute for the elided و,] or the latter is a quasi-inf. n., (L,) and مَوْعِدٌ and مَوْعِدَةٌ, (L, Mṣb, Ḳ,) or the last is a quasi-inf. n., (L,) and مَوْعُودٌ and مَوْعُودَةٌ, (L, Ḳ,) the last two being instances of inf. ns. of the measures مَفْعُولٌ and مَفْعُولَةٌ, (L,) *He promised*. (TA.) It is trans. immediately, and by means of the prep. بِ; (L, Mṣb, Ḳ;) but some say that the ب is redundant in this case; and most of the lexicologists disallow it with this form of the verb, allowing it only with أَوْعَدَ. (TA.) It is also used with reference to good and evil: (Ṣ, L, Mṣb, Ḳ:) you say وَعَدَهُ خَيْرًا [*He promised him good*]: and وَعَدَهُ شَرًّا ‡ [*He threatened him with evil*]: (Fr, Fṣ, Ṣ, L, Mṣb, Ḳ, &c.:) and, [accord. to some,] وعده بِخَيْرٍ and بِشَرٍّ. (IKoot, Mṣb.) When neither good nor evil is mentioned, if you mean the former, you say وَعَدَ [*He promised good*]: and if you mean the latter, ▼ أَوْعَدَ, (Fr, T, Ṣ, L, Mṣb, Ḳ,) inf. n. إِيعَادٌ, with which وَعِيدٌ is syn., (Ṣ, L, Mṣb, Ḳ,) being one irregular inf. n., [or quasi-inf. n.,] (Mṣb,) [*He threatened*,] or *threatened with, evil*]; and ▼ أَوْعَدَهُ [*He threatened him, menaced him*, or *threatened him with evil*]; (Mṣb;) as also ▼ تَوَعَّدَهُ, (L, Mṣb,) inf. n. تَوَعُّدٌ; (Ṣ, L, Ḳ;) and ▼ اِتَّعَدَهُ. (L.) You also say ▼ اوعد خَيْرًا [*He promised good*]; (IAạr, T, ISd, Mṣb, Ḳ;) but this is extr.: (L:) and ▼ اوعد بِشَرٍّ [*He threatened*, or *threatened with, evil*]: (Ṣ, L, Mṣb, Ḳ:) when ب is introduced after this form of the verb, it relates only to evil: (Fṣ, Mṣb:) but you also say ▼ اوعده شَرًّا. (Mṣb.) — Failure of performance, with respect to a promise, the Arabs regard as a lie; but with regard to a threat, as generosity. A poet says,

• وَإِنِّى وَإِنْ أَوْعَدْتُهُ أَوْ وَعَدْتُهُ •
• لَمُخْلِفُ إِيعَادِى وَمُنْجِزُ مَوْعِدِى •

[*And verily I, if I threaten him* or *promise him, fail to perform my threat, but fulfil my promise*]. (Mṣb.) Nay, they do not apply the term خُلْف to the failure of performing a threat. (TA.) — يَوْمُنَا يَعِدُ بَرْدًا ‡ *Our day promises cold*. (L.) — وَعَدَتِ الأَرْضُ ‡ *The land promised good produce*. (A.) — وَاعَدَهُ فَوَعَدَهُ: see 3.

3. واعده, inf. n. مُوَاعَدَةٌ, *He promised him, the latter doing the same to him*. (Aboo-Mo'ádh, L.) — وَاعَدَهُ فَوَعَدَهُ *He vied with him in promising, and surpassed him therein, by promising more*. (L, Ḳ.*) — واعدهُ الوَقْتَ, and المَوْضِعَ, [*He appointed with him the time*, and *the place*]. (L, Ḳ.) أَوْعَدَنِى مَوْعِدًا is a vulgar mistake. (Aboo-Bekr, L.)

4: see 1 throughout. — اوعد, (A, L,) inf. n. إِيعَادٌ, (L,) in the sense of which وَعِيدٌ is also used [as a quasi-inf. n.], (Ṣ, A, L, Ḳ) ‡ *He* (a stallion-camel) *brayed*, (هَدَرَ, Ṣ, A, &c.) *on his being about to attack and fight with other camels*. (Ṣ, A, L.)

5: see 1.

6. تواعدوا and ▼ اِتَّعَدُوا signify the same, [*They promised one another*]: (Ḳ*, TA:) or the former relates to good, (Ṣ, Mṣb, Ḳ,) signifying *they promised one another something good*: (Ṣ, Mṣb,) and the latter, to evil, (Ṣ, L, Ḳ,) signifying *they threatened one another*: (L:) and this distinction is commonly admitted and observed. (TA.) — تَوَاعَدْنَا المَوْضِعَ, [and الوَقْتَ,] *We appointed mutually the place*, and *the time*]. (Mṣb.)

8. اِتَّعَدَ, (A,) [aor. يَتَّعِدُ,] inf. n. اِتِّعَادٌ, (Ṣ, L, Ḳ,) *He accepted a promise*: (Ṣ, A, L, Ḳ:) originally اِوْتَعَدَ; the و being changed into ت and then incorporated [into the augmentative ت]: some persons say اِئْتَعَدَ, aor. يَأْتَعِدُ, (inf. n. اِئْتِعَادٌ, TA) and pronounce the act. part. n. مُؤْتَعِدٌ, with ء; (Ṣ, L, Ḳ;) like as they say يَأْتَسِرُ: (Ṣ, L:) but [if they do not change the و into ت] they should say اِيتَعَدَ, and يَاتَعِدُ, and مُوتَعِدٌ, without ء. (IB, L.) — Also, *He confided in the promise of another*. (L.) — See also 1: — and 6.

وَعْدٌ and ▼ عِدَةٌ (in which latter the ة is a substitute for the [elided] و, Ṣ, L) and ▼ مَوْعِدٌ and ▼ مَوْعِدَةٌ and ▼ مَوْعُودٌ (A) and ▼ مَوْعُودَةٌ: (L:) see 1: *A promising; a promise*; (A, L;) meaning, *of something good*: (Ṣ, L, &c.:) pl. of the first, وُعُودٌ; (IJ, L;) or this has no pl.: (T, Ṣ, L, Mṣb:) and of the second, عِدَاتٌ: (T, Ṣ, L, Mṣb:) (and of the ▼ third, مَوَاعِدُ:] and of ▼ موعود, مَوَاعِيدُ. (L.) When عِدَةٌ is used as a prefixed n., [in a case of waṣl,] the ة is elided, (Fr, Ṣ, L,) and ى is substituted for it: (Fr, L:) a poet says,

• وَأَخْلَفُوكَ عِدَى الأَمْرِ الَّذِى وَعَدُوا •

[*And they have broken to thee the promise of the thing which they promised*]. (Fr, Ṣ, L.) — ▼ العِدَةُ ▼ عَطِيَّةٌ [*A promise is equivalent to a gift*]: i. e., it is base to break it as it is to take back a gift. A proverb. (TA.) — وَعَدَهُ عِدَةَ ▼ الثُّرَيَّا بِالقَمَرِ [*He promised him as the moon promises the Pleiades*]: for the moon and the Pleiades are in conjunction once in every month. Another proverb. (TA.) [Perhaps we may also read عِدَةَ الثُّرَيَّا القَمَرَ: see مِدَاد, in art. عد.] — إِخْلَافُ الوَعْدِ مِنْ أَخْلَاقِ الوَغْدِ [*The breaking of a promise is one of the natural habits of the mean and base*]. A saying of the Arabs. (MF.) — وَعْدٌ also signifies The *fulfilment of a promise*. Ex. مَتَى هٰذَا الوَعْدُ, in the Ḳur, [x. 49, &c.] means, *When shall be the fulfilment of this promise?* (L.) — Also, *a thing promised*. (TḲ, art. نجز.)

عِدَةٌ: see وَعْدٌ, and 1.

عِدِىٌّ *Of*, or *relating* or *belonging to, a promise*: rel. n. of عِدَةٌ, like زِنِىٌّ of زِنَةٌ, formed without restoring the و like as it is restored in [the rel. n. of] شِيَةٌ: [see art. شيو:] but Fr says عِدَوِىٌّ and زِنَوِىٌّ, like شِيَوِىٌّ. (Ṣ, L.)

وَعِيدٌ: see 1: *A threatening; a threat*: (Ṣ, L, Ḳ:) also written وَعِيدٌ. (TA.) See also 4.

الوَعِيدِيَّةُ *A certain sect of the* خَوَارِج, *who are extravagant in threatening; asserting that transgressors* [*who have been true believers*] *shall remain in hell for ever.* (TA.)

وَاعِدٌ ‡ A horse *that promises run after run.* (L, Ḳ.) —— ‡ A beast *that promises to be productive of good, and fortunate.* (L.) ‡ See an ex. in a verse cited voce مُصْدَق. —— ‡ A tree, or herbage, *promising good produce.* (A.) —— ‡ A cloud, *which, as it were, promises rain.* (L, Ḳ.) —— ‡ A day *which promises heat;* (L;) as also a year: (TA:) or *of which the commencement promises heat;* or *cold.* (Ṣ, L, Ḳ.) —— أَرْضٌ وَاعِدَةٌ ‡ *Land of which the herbage is hoped to prove good and productive,* (Aṣ, Ṣ, A, L, Ḳ,) *by reason of its first appearance.* (Aṣ, L.)

مَوْعِدٌ signifies *A covenant,* or *compact.* So, accord. to Mujáhid, in ch. xx. vv. 89 and 90, of the Ḳur-án. (L.) —— مَوْعِدٌ and مَوْعِدَةٌ: see 1, and وَعْدٌ. —— See also مِيعَادٌ.

مِيعَادٌ (Ṣ, A, L, Mṣb, Ḳ) and ▼ مَوْعِدٌ (Ṣ, A, L, Mṣb) *A time,* and *a place, of promise:* (Ṣ, A, L, Mṣb, Ḳ:) [and, *of appointment; an appointed time,* and *place*]. —— مِيعَادٌ *A mutual promising,* or *promise.* (Ṣ, Ḳ.)

مَوْعُودٌ and مَوْعُودَةٌ: see 1, and وَعْدٌ. —— اليَوْمُ الموعود [*The promised day;* meaning] *the day of resurrection.* (TA.) —— مَعْهُودٌ وَمَشْهُودٌ وَمَوْعُودٌ *Past and present and future:* the tenses of a verb. (Kh, in L, art. عهد.) —— مَوْعُودٌ is one of the inf. ns. which have pls. governing as verbs; its pl. being مَوَاعِيدُ.

Ex. مَوَاعِيدَ عُرْقُوبٍ أَخَاهُ بِيَثْرِبِ

[*As 'Orḳoob's promisings of his brother in Yethrib.*] (IJ, ISd.) See عُرْقُوبٌ.

وعر

1. وَعُرَ, (Ṣ, A, Mṣb, Ḳ,) aor. يَوْعُرُ; (TA;) and وَعَرَ, aor. يَعِرُ; (Mṣb, Ḳ;) and وَعِرَ, (Lḥ, A, Ḳ,) aor. يَوْعَرُ (Ḳ, TA) and يَعَرُ; (Lḥ, TA;) inf. n. وُعُورَةٌ (Ṣ, Mṣb, Ḳ) and وَعَارَةٌ, (Mṣb, Ḳ,) of the first (Mṣb, TA) and second; (TA;) and وَعْرٌ, (Mṣb, Ḳ,) of the first (TA) and second; (Mṣb, TA;) and وُعُورٌ, (Ḳ,) of the second only; (TA;) and وَعَرٌ, (Ḳ,) of the third; (TA;) *It* (a place, A, Ḳ, and a mountain, Ṣ, Mṣb,) *was,* or *became, rugged;* (A, Ḳ;) as also ▼ توعّر: (Ṣ,* A, Ḳ:) or *difficult.* (Mṣb.) —— [Hence,] ▼ توعّر ‡ *It* (an affair), and *he,* (a man,) *was,* or *became difficult,* or *hard.* (Ḳ,* TA.) You say, سَأَلْنَا فُلَانًا حَاجَةً فَتَوَعَّرَ عَلَيْنَا ‡ *We asked of such a one a thing wanted, and he was hard,* or *difficult, to us.* (Sgh, TA.) —— [Hence also,] وَعُرَ, inf. n. وَعَارَةٌ and وُعُورَةٌ, ‡ *It* (a thing) *was,* or *became, little,* or *scanty.* (Ḳ, TA.)

2. وعّره, inf. n. تَوْعِيرٌ, *He made it* (a place, Ḳ, and a mountain, Ṣ,) *rugged:* (Ṣ,* Ḳ:) [or *difficult.*]

4. اوعر بِهِ الطَّرِيقُ *The road became rugged to him:* or *brought him to a rugged land.* (Ḳ,* TA.) —— اوعر *He came,* or *lighted, upon a rugged place.* (A, Ḳ.) —— See also 10. —— ‡ *His* (a man's) *property became little,* or *scanty.* (Ḳ,* TA.) The man is thus likened to a rugged place without plants or herbage. (TA.) —— اوعره ‡ *He made it* (a thing, A, Ḳ,) *little,* or *scanty.* (Ṣ, A, Ḳ.)

5: see 1, in two places.

10. استوعره *He found it,* (Ṣ, Mṣb,) or *deemed it,* (Ḳ,) namely a place, (Mṣb,) or a road, (A, Ḳ,) or a thing, (Ṣ, Sgh,) *rugged,* (Ṣ,* Ḳ,) or *difficult;* (Mṣb;) as also ▼ اوعره. (Sgh, Ḳ.)

وَعْرٌ *Rugged; contr. of* سَهْلٌ: (A, Ḳ:) or *difficult:* (Mṣb:) applied to a place, (TA,) and a road, (A,) and a mountain: (Ṣ, Mṣb:) as also ▼ وَعِرٌ, (A, Ḳ, or, accord. to Aṣ, this latter is not allowable, (Ṣ,) and F's assertion, that this which is said in the Ṣ is nothing, being a negation of a negation without evidence, is a thing unheard of, MF,) and ▼ وَاعِرٌ and وَعِيرٌ and ▼ أَوْعَرُ: (Ḳ:) and *plain with ruggedness:* and a mountain *rugged, and difficult of ascent:* and a place *inspiring fear, and desolate:* (TA:) pl. أَوْعُرٌ, (Ḳ,) a pl. [of pauc.] of وَعْرٌ, (TA,) and وُعُورٌ, (A, Ḳ,) a pl. of mult. [of the same], (TA,) and وُعُورَةٌ, (A,) [of the same,] and أَوْعَارٌ, (A, Ḳ,) a pl. [of pauc.] of وَعِرٌ and وَعِيرٌ. (TA.) —— Applied to a place where a thing is sought, (مَطْلَبٌ, Ṣ, and Mṣb) † *Difficult* [*of access*]. (Mṣb.) —— Also, applied to a thing, ‡ *Little,* or *scanty.* (A, TA.) And you say, فُلَانٌ وَعْرُ المَعْرُوفِ, meaning, ‡ *Such a one has little goodness, beneficence,* or *kindness.* (Ṣ, A, Ḳ.) —— It is also an imitative sequent to قَلِيلٌ; (Ṣ, Ḳ;) [but in this case it is only a corroborative;] and to وَتْحٌ: (Ṣ:) and so is ▼ وَعِرٌ to مَعِرٌ, in the phrase شَعَرٌ مَعِرٌ وَعِرٌ, (Ḳ,) meaning, † *Little, scanty, hair.* (TA.)

وَعِرٌ: see وَعْرٌ, in two places.

وَعِيرٌ:
وَاعِرٌ: } see وَعْرٌ.
أَوْعَرُ:

وعز

1. وَعَزَ: see 4.

2: see 4.

4. اوعز إِلَيْهِ فِي كَذَا, (Ṣ, Ḳ,) or بِكَذَا, (Mgh,) inf. n. إِيعَازٌ, (Mgh, TA,) *He commanded,* or *ordered,* or *enjoined, him, respecting such a thing,* syn. تقدّم, (Ṣ, Mgh, Ḳ,) and أَمَرَ, (Mgh, Ḳ,) أَنْ يَفْعَلَ أَوْ يَتْرُكَ *that he should do* [it] or *not do* [it]; (Ḳ;) as also ▼ وعّز اليه, (Ṣ, Ḳ,*) inf. n. تَوْعِيزٌ; (Ṣ;) and (sometimes, Ṣ) ▼ وَعَزَ اليه, (Ṣ, Ḳ,*) inf. n. وَعْزٌ; (Ṣ;) which are also explained by قَدَّمَ [signifying the same as تَقَدَّمَ and أَمَرَ]: or the first and second are correct, accord. to ISk, but the last (وَعَزَ) is not allowable, accord. to him, nor is it, as related by AḤát, accord. to Aṣ. (TA.)

وعس]
See Supplement.]

وعظ

1. وَعَظَهُ, (Ṣ, Mṣb, Ḳ, &c.,) aor. يَعِظُ, (Mṣb, Ḳ,) inf. n. وَعْظٌ and عِظَةٌ, (Ṣ, Mṣb, Ḳ,) in which the ة is a substitute for the elided و, (TA,) and عَظَةٌ, (TA,) and مَوْعِظَةٌ, (Ḳ,) in which the ة is not to denote the fem. gender, because this is not real, (TA,) or this last is a simple subst., (Mṣb,) *He exhorted him, admonished him,* or *warned him; he put him in fear:* (IF:) *he exhorted him to obedience; commanded him to obey:* (Mṣb:) *he gave him good advice,* or *counsel;* and *reminded him of the results of affairs:* (Ṣ:) *he reminded him by informing him of that which should make the heart tender:* (Kh:) *he reminded him of that which should soften his heart, by the mention of reward and punishment.* (Ḳ.) It is said in the Ḳur, [xxxiv. 45,] إِنَّمَا أَعِظُكُمْ بِوَاحِدَةٍ *I only exhort you,* or *command you, to do one thing.* (Mṣb.) And you say, وُعِظَ بِغَيْرِهِ [*He was exhorted, admonished,* or *warned, by* the example of *another:* see 8]. (Ṣ.) [And وَعَظَ, alone, *He preached a sermon* or *sermons.*]

8. اِتَّعَظَ [*He became exhorted, admonished, warned,* or *put in fear:*] *he obeyed,* or *conformed to,* [*an exhortation to obedience,* or] *a command, and restrained himself:* (Mṣb:) *he accepted good advice,* and *the being reminded of the results of affairs:* (Ṣ:) *he became reminded of that which should soften his heart, by the mention of reward and punishment.* (Ḳ.) It is said, السَّعِيدُ مَنْ وُعِظَ بِغَيْرِهِ وَالشَّقِىُّ مَنْ ٱتَّعَظَ بِهِ غَيْرُهُ [*The happy is he who is exhorted,* or *admonished,* or *warned, by* the example of *another, and the unhappy is he by* the example of *whom another becomes exhorted,* or *admonished,* or *warned*]. (Ṣ, L.)

عِظَةٌ: see 1. —— [As a simple subst.,] it has for its pl. عِظَاتٌ: and is syn. with ▼ مَوْعِظَةٌ: (TA:) [the pl. of the latter is مَوَاعِظُ.] It is said in trad., لَأَجْعَلَنَّكَ عِظَةً *I will assuredly make thee a warning,* or *an example,* to others. (TA.) And in the Ḳur, [ii. 276,] فَمَنْ جَآءَهُ ▼ مَوْعِظَةٌ مِنْ رَبِّهِ [*But he to whom cometh an exhortation*, or *an admonition*, or *warning, from his Lord*]. (TA.) And ▼ القَتْلُ بِالمَوْعِظَةِ [*The slaying by way of warning*], mentioned in a trad., is when the innocent is slain in order that he who gives reason for suspicion may become warned. (TA.)

وَعَّاظٌ : see وَاعِظٌ.

وَاعِظٌ [*One who exhorts, admonishes, warns*, or *puts in fear* :] *one who exhorts to obedience; who commands to obey:* (Mṣb :) *one who gives good advice*, or *counsel;* [*who reminds of the results of affairs*; &c.: and *a preacher of a sermon* or *sermons*: see 1 :] and in like manner ▼ وَعَّاظٌ [*one who exhorts*, &c., *much*, or *frequently*]: (TA :) pl. of the former وُعَّاظٌ. (Mṣb, TA.)

مَوْعِظَةٌ : see 1 : — and عِظَةٌ, in three places.

[وعق &c.

See Supplement.]

وغب

1. وَغُبَ, aor. يَوْغُبُ, inf. n. وُغُوبَةٌ (and وَغَابَةٌ, IM and others), *He* (a camel) *was*, or *became, large, big*, or *bulky*. (Ṣ, Ḳ.)

وَغْبٌ *What is of a mean sort, of the utensils and furniture of a house*, or *tent*: (Ṣ, Ḳ :) pl. أَوْغَابٌ and وِغَابٌ : (Ḳ :) the former, of pauc.; the latter, of mult. (TA.) The اوغاب of a house, or tent, are the wooden bowl and the stone cooking-pot and the like: (Ṣ :) [as also أَوْقَاب]. — *A sack, such as is called* غِرَارَة : (Ḳ :) but this is included among the meaner sort of the utensils of a house, or tent; and is therefore not particularly mentioned by any of the lexicographers except T. (TA.) — وَغْبٌ (Aṣ, Ṣ, Ḳ) and وَغْبَةٌ (Th, Ḳ) *Stupid; foolish; of little sense*: (Ṣ, Ḳ :) *i. q.* لَغْبٌ, *a weak, stupid*, man: (TA, voce لغب :) pl. as above. (Ḳ, TA.) See also وَقْبٌ. — وَغْبٌ *Weak in body*: (as also وَغْدٌ : TA :) pl. as above. (Ḳ.) — وَغْبٌ *Base; mean; vile*: (as also وَغْدٌ : TA :) pl. as above. (Ḳ.) — وَغْبٌ *A large, big*, or *bulky*, camel: (Ṣ, Ḳ :) pl. as above: fem. with ة. (Ḳ.)

وغد

1. وَغُدَ, aor. ـُ, (Ṣ, Ḳ, &c.,) inf. n. وَغَادَةٌ, (L, Mṣb, Ḳ,) *He was*, or *became, a low*, or *ignoble, mean*, or *sordid, and weak person*, (Ṣ, Mṣb,) *who served for the food of his belly*: (Ṣ, L, Mṣb :) or *light*, (L,) *stupid, and weak* (L, Ḳ) *in intellect*, (L,) *low*, or *ignoble, and mean*, or *sordid*; (L, Ḳ ;) or *weak in body*: (L, Ḳ :) or *light in intellect*: or *weak as is a slave*. (Mṣb.) — وَغَدَ القَوْمَ, aor. يَغِدُ, (Ṣ, L,) inf. n. وَغْدٌ, (L,) *He served the people; acted as a servant to them*. (Ṣ, L.)

3. واغده, (L,) inf. n. مُوَاغَدَةٌ, (Ṣ, L, Ḳ,) *He* (a man) *did like as he* (another man) *did*: (L, Ḳ :) accord. to some, specially *in pace*, or *in going*, or *marching*; (L ;) *he went like him*; or *kept pace with him*: (Ṣ*, L :) and *he ran with him*; or *vied with him in running*: (Ḳ :) you say وَاغَدَتِ النَّاقَةُ الأُخْرَى *the she-camel went like*, or *kept pace with, the other*: (L :) and sometimes the term مُوَاغَدَةٌ is used in relation to a single she-camel, because one of her fore legs, and her hind legs, moves with (تُوَاغِدُ) the other. (Aṣ, Ṣ, L, Ḳ.)

وَغْدٌ *A low*, or *ignoble, mean*, or *sordid, and weak person*, (Ṣ, A, Mṣb :) *who serves for the food of his belly*: (Ṣ, A, L, Mṣb :) or *light*, (L,) *stupid, weak* (L, Ḳ) *in intellect*, (L,) *low*, or *ignoble, and mean*, or *sordid*: (L, Ḳ :) or *weak in body*: (L, Ḳ :) or *light in intellect*: (Mṣb :) or *weak; as is a slave*: (Umm-El-Heythem, Mṣb :) or *who eats and carries away*. (Expos. of the Lámeeyeh of Et-Tughráee.) — *A servant of a people*. (L, Ḳ.) — *A slave*. (L, Ḳ.) — *A boy*. (L, Ḳ.) — Pl. أَوْغَادٌ (A, L, Mṣb, Ḳ) and وُغْدَانٌ and وِغْدَانٌ. (L, Ḳ.) — *A certain arrow*, (Ṣ, A, L, Ḳ,) *of those used in the game called* المَيْسِر, (Ṣ, L,) *to which no portion*, or *share, pertains*. (Ṣ, A, L, Ḳ.) Accord. to the A, this is the original signification. (TA.) — The *fruit of the* بَاذِنْجَان. (L, Ḳ.) — المُوَاغَدَةُ *A certain game* (Ḳ) *of the Arabs, in which one player does like as the other does*. (TA.) — See also 3.

وغر

1. وَغَرَتْهُ الشَّمْسُ *The sun fell vehemently upon him*. (A.) — وَغَرَتِ الهَاجِرَةُ, (Ḳ,) aor. تَغِرُ, (Ḳ,* TA,) inf. n. وَغْرٌ, (TA,) *The summer-midday was*, or *became, intensely*, or *vehemently, hot*. (Ḳ,* TA.) — [Hence, (see وَغْرٌ,)] وَغِرَ صَدْرُهُ, (Ṣ, Mṣb, Ḳ,) aor. يَوْغَرُ (Ṣ, Mṣb,* Ḳ,*) and يِيغَرُ, with kesr to the first letter, (Fr, Ḳ,) [an irreg. form,] like يِيجَلُ ; (TA ;) and وَغَرَ, aor. يَغِرُ ; (Ḳ, TA ;) but يَوْغَرُ is more common than يَغِرُ ; (Aṣ, TA ;) inf. n. وَغَرٌ, (Ṣ, Mṣb, Ḳ,) of the former, (Ṣ, Mṣb,) and وَغْرٌ, (Ḳ,) [of the latter,] or وَغْرٌ is a simple subst., and the inf. n. is وَغَرٌ ; (Ṣ,* Mṣb, [but perhaps this is said because only the former of the two verbs is mentioned in the Ṣ and Mṣb] ;) *His bosom was*, or *became, affected with rancour, malevolence, malice*, or *spite, and enmity; and burned with wrath*, or *rage*; (Ṣ, A, Mṣb, Ḳ ;) عَلَى فُلَانٍ *against such a one*: (Ṣ, A :*) or *became filled with wrath*, or *rage*, (Mṣb, TA,) *and rancour, malevolence, malice*, or *spite*: (TA :) or *burned by reason of intense*, or *violent, wrath*, or *rage*: (TA :) and ▼ توغّر *he* (a man, TA,) *burned*, and *was*, or *became, hot, with wrath*, or *rage*. (Ḳ, TA.) You say also, وَغِرَ عَلَىَّ فُلَانٌ, aor. يَوْغَرُ, [see above, *Such a one became affected with rancour*, &c.; or *burned with wrath*, or *rage; against me*]. (Fr, TA.)

2 : see 4, in two places.

4. اوغروا *They entered upon the summer-midday when the heat was intense*, or *vehement*. (Ḳ, TA.) — اوغر المَآءَ *He heated the water*, (Ḳ, TA,) *by putting into it heated stones*: (TA :) or *i. q.* أَحْرَقَهُ : (TA :) — *He made the water to boil*. (Ṣ, Ḳ.) Sometimes, a live pig has its hair scalded off in it, and is then slaughtered: (Ṣ, Ḳ :) or, accord. to some lexicons, is then roasted. (TA.) This is done by certain Christians. (Ṣ, Ḳ.) You say أَوْغَرَ النَّصَارَى الخِنْزِيرَ *The Christians boiled some water, and scalded off the hair of a live pig in it, and then slaughtered it*. (A.) — اوغر اللَّبَنَ, *He made the milk what is termed* وَغِير *and* وَغِيرَة ; as also, ▼ وغّره, (Ṣ, Ḳ,) inf. n. تَوْغِيرٌ. (Ṣ.) — اوغره *He made him to be affected with rancour, malevolence, malice*, or *spite, and enmity, and to burn with wrath*, or *rage*: (Ḳ :) or *he made him to be affected with wrath*, or *rage*: (A :) [in like maner,] ▼ وغّره عَلَيْهِ, (TḲ,) inf. n. تَوْغِيرٌ, (Ḳ,) *he incited him to rancour, malevolence, malice*, or *spite, against him*. (Ḳ,* TḲ.) You say also, أَوْغَرْتُ صَدْرَهُ عَلَى فُلَانٍ *I made his bosom hot with wrath*, or *rage, against such a one*. (Ṣ.)

5 : see 1.

وَغْرٌ *Rancour, malevolence, malice*, or *spite, and enmity; and a burning with wrath*, or *rage*; (Ṣ, A, Ḳ ;) as also ▼ وَغَرٌ ; (A, Ḳ ;) or the latter is an inf. n., (Ṣ, TA,) but the former is a simple subst.: (TA :) or the *state of being filled with wrath*, or *rage*: (Mṣb :) from وَغْرَةٌ, explained below. (Ṣ.) You say, فِي صَدْرِهِ عَلَىَّ وَغْرٌ *In his bosom is rancour*, &c., *against me*. (Ṣ.) And ذَهَبَ وَغْرُ صَدْرِهِ *The rancour*, &c., *of his bosom departed*. And الهَدِيَّةُ تُذْهِبُ وَغْرَ الصَّدْرِ *The gift dispelleth the rancour, malevolence, malice*, or *spite, and the heat, of the bosom*. (TA.)

وَغَرٌ : see وَغْرٌ.

وَغْرَةٌ, (Ṣ, Ḳ,) and وَغْرَةُ حَرٍّ, (Mṣb,) *Intenseness*, or *vehemence, of heat*: (Mṣb, Ḳ :) or *of the burning thereof*, (Ṣ, TA,) *when the sun is in the meridian*. (TA.) You say, نَزَلْنَا فِي وَغْرَةِ القَيْظِ عَلَى مَآءِ كَذَا *We alighted during the intense midday heat at such a water*. (TA.)

وَغِيرٌ *Milk into which heated stones are thrown, and which is then drunk*: (Ḳ :) or (so accord. to the TA; but in the Ḳ, and) *milk boiled and cooked*: (Ḳ :) or *milk made hot with heated stones*; as also ▼ وَغِيرَةٌ : (Ṣ :) or the latter, or *pure milk alone, heated until it is thoroughly cooked*; and *sometimes clarified butter is put into it.* (ISd, TA.) —— Also, *Flesh-meat roasted upon heated stones:* (Lth, TA:) or *upon stones heated by the sun.* (L, Ḳ.)

وَغِيرٌ : see وَغِيرَةٌ.

هُوَ وَاغِرُ الصَّدْرِ *He has the bosom* [*affected with rancour, malevolence, malice,* or *spite, and enmity, and*] *burning with wrath,* or *rage;* عَلَىَّ *against me:* (TA:) or *filled with wrath,* or *rage.* (Mṣb.)

كَرِهَتِ الخَنَازِيرُ الحَمِيمَ المُوغَرَ *The pigs hated the boiled hot water.* A proverb. (TA.) See 4.

[وغل &c.

See Supplement.]

وفد

1. وَفَدَ عَلَيْهِ, (Ṣ, M, A, Ḳ,) [in the Mṣb, وَفِدَ, but this appears to be a mistake,] and إِلَيْهِ, (M, Ḳ,) aor. يَفِدُ, (M, Ḳ,) inf. n. وُفُودٌ (M, A, Ḳ) and وَفْدٌ (M, Ḳ) and وِفَادَةٌ, (M, A, Ḳ,) or this last is a simple subst., (Ṣ,) and إِفَادَةٌ, (M, Ḳ,) in which the و is changed into أ, (M,) *He came to him,* (Ṣ, M, A, Ḳ,) namely, to a king, (A,) or governor, (Ṣ, A,) or great man, ('Ináyeh,) *as an ambassador, envoy,* or *messenger;* (Ṣ, A;) or *to convey gifts, and to ask aid,* or *assistance:* ('Ináyeh:) or *he went forth to him,* namely, to a king, or governor. (Aṣ, L.)

2: see 4.

4. اوفدهُ عَلَيْهِ, (M, A, Ḳ,) and إِلَيْهِ, (Ṣ, M, Ḳ,) inf. n. إِيفَادٌ; (Ḳ;) and ▾ وفّدهُ إِلَيْهِ, (L,) inf. n. تَوْفِيدٌ; (Ḳ;) *He sent him to him,* (Ṣ, M, A, Ḳ,) namely, to a king, (A,) or governor, (Ṣ,) [or great man, *as an ambassador, envoy,* or *messenger;* or *to convey gifts, and to ask aid,* or *assistance:* see 1]. —— وفدهُ ▾ الأَمِيرُ إِلَى الأَمِيرِ الَّذِى فَوْقَهُ [*The governor, sent him as an envoy to the governor who was above him*]. (L.) —— مَا أَوْفَدَكَ عَلَيْنَا † [*What hath caused thee to come to us?*]. (TA.) —— بَيْنَمَا أَنَا فِى ضِيقٍ إِذْ أَوْفَدَ ٱللّٰهُ عَلَىَّ بِرَجُلٍ فَأَخْرَجَنِى مِنْهُ ‡ *While I was in difficulty, lo, God brought to me a man, and extricated me from it.* (A.) ═ اوفد عَلَى الشَّىْءِ, inf. n. إِيفَادٌ, ‡ *It rose up,* or *stood up, so as to be higher than the thing; overtopped it; overpeered it; overhung it; overlooked it.* (Ṣ, L, Ḳ*.) A poet (Ḥomeyd Ibn-Thór El-Hilálee, TA) says,

* تَرَى العِلَافِىَّ عَلَيْهَا مُوفِدَا *
* كَأَنَّ بُرْجًا فَوْقَهَا مُشَيَّدَا *

[*Thou seest the 'Iláfee saddle overtopping her, as though a high-raised tower were upon her.*] (Ṣ, L.) And one says of a horse, مَا أَحْسَنَ مَا أَوْفَدَ حَارِكُهُ *How beautiful is the prominence of his withers!* (Ṣ, L.) ▾ توفّد is also syn. with اوفد in the above sense. (Ḳ, TA.) —— اوفد, inf. n. إِيفَادٌ, ‡ *It* (a white antelope) *raised its head and erected its ears.* (L, Ḳ.) —— اوفد, inf. n. إِيفَادٌ, *He hastened,* or *went, quickly:* (Ṣ, L, Ḳ:) occurring in the poetry of Ibn-Aḥmar. (Ṣ, L.) —— اوفد, inf. n. إِيفَادٌ, ‡ *It rose,* or *became elevated.* (A, L, Ḳ.) —— اوفد ـه, ‡ *He raised,* or *elevated,* a thing. (L.)

5. توفّدت الإِبِلُ, and الطَّيْرُ, † *The camels,* and *the birds, strove to outgo,* or *outstrip, one another.* (L.) —— توفّدت الأَوْعَالُ فَوْقَ الجَبَلِ ‡ *The mountain-goats ascended upon the mountain.* (A.) —— See 4.

6. توافدنا عَلَيْهِ [*We came together as ambassadors,* or *envoys,* &c., *to him:* see 1]. (A.)

10. اِسْتَوْفَدَنِى † [app. *He asked,* or *desired, me to come*]. (TA.) ═ استوفد ‡ *He elevated himself, and made himself erect,* in his manner of sitting; (A;) a dial. form of استوفز [q. v.] (Ṣ.)

وَفْدٌ: see وَافِدٌ. —— الحَاجُّ وَفْدُ ٱللّٰهِ ‡ [*The pilgrims of Mekkeh are the ambassadors of God*]. (A.) —— وَفْدُ ٱللّٰهِ ثَلَاثَةٌ الغَازِى وَالحَاجُّ وَالمُعْتَمِرُ ‡ [*The ambassadors of God are three; the warrior, and the pilgrim of Mekkeh, and the performer of the ceremonies of the* عُمْرَة]. A tradition. (L*, El-Jámi' eṣ-Ṣagheer.) ═ وَفْدٌ The *upper part of an elevated long tract* (حَبْل: in some copies of the Ḳ, جَبَل:) *of sand.* (Ṣ, L, Ḳ.)

وِفَادَةٌ, subst. from وَفَدَ عَلَيْهِ, (Ṣ,) *A coming to a king,* (A,) or *governor,* (Ṣ, A,) [or *the like,*] *as an ambassador, envoy,* or *messenger,* [&c.: see 1]. (Ṣ, A.) —— لَهُ وِفَادَةٌ [a phrase of frequent occurrence in notices of companions of Moḥammad, meaning, *He had the honour of coming as an envoy to the Prophet*]. (TA, passim; and other works.)

وَافِدٌ *A man coming to a king,* (A,) or *governor,* (Ṣ, A,) [or *great man,*] *as an ambassador,* or *envoy,* or *messenger;* (Ṣ, A;) [or *to convey gifts, and to ask aid,* or *assistance:* see 1:] pl., (Ṣ, L,) or [rather] this first is a quasi-pl. n., (L,) ▾ وَفْدٌ (Ṣ, A, L, Ḳ) and وُفَّدٌ (Ḳ) and وُفَّادٌ; (A, Mṣb;) and pl. of وَفْدٌ, أَوْفَادٌ and وُفُودٌ: (Ṣ, L, Mṣb, Ḳ:) وَفْدٌ is also explained as signifying *a party that assembles together and comes to a country* or *town:* and *a party that repairs to princes,* or *governors, to visit, and to ask aid,* or *assistance,* or *some benefit,* &c.: (L:) and *a party that comes to a king respecting an affair of conquest,* or *for congratulation,* or *the like:* (Mgh:) and *a company chosen to go forth for the purpose of having an interview with great men:* (En-Nawawee:) and *a company of riders:* (Jel, xix. 88;) and *a company riding and honoured:* (Zj, in explanation of the same verse of the Ḳur-an:) but from the explanations in the Ḳ, and other lexicons, it seems to signify *a party coming, whether walking or riding, chosen for the purpose of having an interview with great men,* or *not:* the explanations of En-Nawawee and some others may be in accordance with general or conventional acceptations, and those of the rest may be proper, or literal. (TA.) —— وَافِدٌ ‡ A camel, (Ṣ, A, Ḳ,) or bird, (A,) or bird of the kind called القَطَا, (Ḳ,) *that precedes the others* (Ṣ, A, Ḳ) *in pace, and in coming to water.* (A.) —— الوَافِدَانِ (in the poetry of El-Aạsha, Ṣ, L) ‡ *The parts of the two cheeks which project when one chews, and which become depressed when one grows old.* (Ṣ, A, L, Ḳ.) One says of a very old man, غَابَ وَافِدَاهُ ‡ [*The middles of his cheeks have become depressed*]. (A.)

هُمْ عَلَى أَوْفَادٍ *They are upon a journey:* (L, Ḳ:) as also أَوْفَازٍ. (TA.)

مُوفَدٌ ‡ *Prominent,* or *elevated:* (A, L:) applied to a camel's hump, (A,) and to the pubes. (L.)

مُسْتَوْفِدٌ ‡ *Erecting himself, and not placing himself at his ease,* in his manner of sitting; (L;) i. q. مُسْتَوْفِزٌ. (L, Ḳ.)

وفر

1. وَفَرَ, (T, Ṣ, M, A, Mṣb, Ḳ,) aor. يَفِرُ; (T, Mṣb, Ḳ;*) and وَفُرَ, [aor. يَوْفُرُ;] (A, Ḳ;) inf. n. وُفُورٌ (T, Ṣ, M, Mṣb, Ḳ) and وَفْرٌ and فِرَةٌ, (M, Ḳ,) [all of the former,] or وَفْرٌ is inf. n. of the trans. v.; (Mṣb;) and وَفَارَةٌ, (Ḳ,) [which is of the latter;] *It* (a thing) *was,* or *became, full, complete, perfect, whole,* or *entire:* (Ṣ, Mṣb:) or *it* (a thing, TA, or property, M, Ḳ, and herbage, M, [and a collection of goods, or commodities, or household furniture and utensils,]) *was,* or *became, much, abundant, ample,* or *copious;* (T, M, A, Ḳ;) *not deficient:* (T:) or *it* (anything) *was,* or *became, generally,* or *universally, comprehensive:* [syn., in the last sense, عَمَّ, as is implied by an explanation of the epithet وَفْرٌ, by which this sense of the verb is indicated in the lexicons whence this signification is taken:] (M, A, Ḳ:) as also ▾ اتّفر, (Ḳ,) [and ▾ توفّر: see وَافِرٌ.] You say also of a branch, ▾ اِسْتَوْفَرَ وَرَقًا [*It was full of,* or *abounded with, leaves*]. (L, Ḳ, art. غدف.) —— وَفَرَ عِرْضُهُ, and وَفُرَ, (M, L,) inf. n. [of the former] وُفُورٌ, (M,) ‡ [*His honour, dignity,* or *estimation, was unimpaired;*] *he was honourable,* or *generous, not careless of his honour,* or *dignity,* or *estimation.* (M, L.) ═ وَفَرَهُ, (T, Ṣ, M, A, Mṣb, Ḳ,*) aor. يَفِرُهُ, (T, Mṣb,) inf. n. وَفْرٌ (T, Ṣ, M, Mṣb, Ḳ) and فِرَةٌ, (T, M,) and وَفْرَةٌ, (TA, as from the Ḳ, but wanting in the CḲ and in a MS. copy of the Ḳ,) *He made it full, without lack or defect, complete, perfect, whole,* or *entire;* (Ṣ, Mṣb;) as also ▾ وفّرهُ, inf. n. تَوْفِيرٌ;

(K;) and ▼ اوفرهُ, inf. n. إِيفَارٌ; and ▼ استوفرهُ: (Ṣ,* TA:) or, as also ▼ وفّرهُ, (T, M, A, K,) which latter is the usual form, (Lth, T,) *he made it much, abundant, ample,* or *copious;* (Lth, T, M, A, K;) *not deficient.* (Lth, T.) You say, وَفَرَ لَهُ مَالَهُ *He made his property much, abundant, ample,* or *copious.* (K,* TA.) And it is said in a trad., الحَمْدُ لِلّٰهِ الَّذِى لَا يَفِرُهُ المَنْعُ *Praise be to God, whom withholding doth not make to abound.* (TA.) You say also, ▼ وفّر الثَّوْبَ *He cut out the garment whole.* (M, K.) And ▼ وفّر السِّقَآءَ *He made the skin whole, without cutting off any redundance.* (M.) And ▼ وَفَّرْتُ لَهُ طَعَامَهُ, inf. n. تَوْفِيرٌ, *I made his food full,* or *complete, in quantity; not deficient.* (Mṣb.) And ▼ وَفَّرْتُ عَلَيْهِ حَقَّهُ فَاسْتَوْفَرَهُ *I gave him the whole of his right,* or *due, and so he received the whole of it;* syn. of the former verb with its objective complement and the prep., وَفَّيْتُهُ, (A, Mgh,) or أَعْطَيْتُهُ الجَمِيعَ; (Mṣb;) and of the latter verb with its objective complement, ▼ اِسْتَوْفَاهُ: (A, Mgh, K:) or both these verbs, thus used, signify the same, i. e., استوفاه, (Ṣ, K) [in the former of which we read, وفّر عَلَيْهِ حَقَّهُ تَوْفِيرًا وَاسْتَوْفَرَهُ أَيِ اسْتَوْفَاهُ; and in the latter, اِسْتَوْفَرَ عَلَيْهِ حَقَّهُ اِسْتَوْفَاهُ كَوَفَّرَهُ.] You also say, وَفَرَهُ عَطَآءَهُ, (M, K,) inf. n. وَفْرٌ, (TA,) *He restored,* or *returned to him his gift, being content with it,* (M, K,) or *deeming it little.* (M, TA.) And وَفَرَ اللّٰهُ حَظَّهُ مِنْ كَذَا *God made his lot,* or *share, of such a thing, full,* or *complete.* (T.) And ▼ وفّر شَعْرَهُ ‡ *He left his hair to become abundant and long.* (A, TA.) And وَفَرْتُ العِرْضَ, aor. أَفِرُهُ, (Mṣb,) inf. n. وَفْرٌ (Mṣb, TA) and فِرَةٌ; (TA [in my copy of the Mṣb, وفر, which is probably a mistranscription;]) and وَفَّرْتُهُ, in an intensive sense; (Mṣb;) *He preserved,* or *guarded, honour, dignity,* or *estimation.* (Mṣb.) And وَفَرَهُ عِرْضَهُ; (Ṣ, M, A, K;) and وفره عِرْضَهُ; (A;) and وَفَرَهُ لَهُ; (M;) or ▼ وفّره لَهُ, (K,) inf. n. تَوْفِيرٌ; (TA;) ‡ [*He preserved his honour, &c., unimpaired;*] *he spoke well of him, and did not find fault with him;* (A;) *he did not revile him;* (M, K;) as though he preserved it [namely his honour, &c.] to him abundant and good, not diminishing it by reviling. (M.) It is said in a proverb, تُوفَرُ وَتُحْمَدُ عَلَى كَذَا (Ṣ,* A,) ‡ *Thy honour,* or *dignity,* or *estimation, will be preserved,* or *guarded, and thou wilt be spoken well of, for such a thing:* (A:) from وَفَرْتُهُ عِرْضَهُ; and مَالَهُ: (Ṣ:) said by him to whom a thing is offered: and applied to a man who, when thou hast given to him a thing, returneth it to thee without discontent, or without esteeming it little. (Fr, Ṣ.)

2: see وَفَرَهُ, and what follows it in the same paragraph.

4: see وَفَرَهُ.

5: see وَفَرَ. — توفّر عَلَيْهِ ‡ *He was regardful of those things pertaining to him* (namely his companion, A) *which one is under an obligation to respect* or *honour;* (Ṣ, A, K;) *and held loving communion, commerce,* or *intercourse, with him.* (TA.) — توفّر عَلَى كَذَا ‡ *He turned his purpose,* or *intention,* or *strong determination* or *resolution,* (هِمَّتَهُ,) *toward such a thing.* (A, Mgh, Mṣb.)

8: see وَفَرَ.

10: see وَفَرَ: — and see وَفَرَهُ, in two places.

وَفْرٌ: see وُفُورٌ. — Also, [an inf. n. used as an epithet in which the quality of a subst. predominates] *Much,* or *abundant, property,* (Lth, T, Ṣ,) *of which nothing is deficient:* (Lth, T:) *what is much, abundant, ample,* or *copious,* of property, and of goods, or commodities, or household furniture and utensils; (M, A, K;) *whereof nothing is deficient:* (TA:) or *what is generally,* or *universally, comprehensive,* (عَامٌّ,) of anything: (M, A, K:) pl. وُفُورٌ. (M, K.) See also وَافِرٌ.

فِرَةٌ: see وُفُورٌ.

وَفْرَةٌ: see وُفُورٌ. — Also, *Hair collected together upon the head:* or *hair hanging down upon the ears:* or *hair extending beyond the lobe of the ear:* (M, K:) or *hair extending to the lobe of the ear:* (Ṣ:) or *hair* (T, Mgh, Mṣb) *such as is termed* جُمَّة, (T, A, Mgh,) *extending to the ears:* (T, A, Mgh, Mṣb:) it is said to be larger than what is termed جُمَّة; but this is a mistake: (M:) the order is this: first, the وَفْرَة; then, the جُمَّة; then, the لِمَّة: (Ṣ, M, K:) the second of these three is what extends beyond the ears; (M;) and the third is what descends upon the shoulder-joints: (Ṣ, M:) pl. وِفَارٌ. (M, K.)

وُفُورٌ and ▼ وَفْرٌ and ▼ وَفْرَةٌ and ▼ فِرَةٌ [are inf. ns., (see 1,) used as simple substs.,] all signify the same: (Ṣ, TA:) *Fulness, completeness, perfectness, wholeness,* or *entireness:* (Ṣ:) or *muchness, abundance, ampleness,* or *copiousness:* (TA:) and the second also, *richness;* or *competence.* (A, K.) You say, هٰذِهِ أَرْضٌ فِي نَبْتِهَا وَفْرٌ, (Ṣ,) and ▼ وَفْرَةٌ, (Ṣ, A,) and ▼ فِرَةٌ, (Ṣ, A, K,) i. e., وُفُورٌ, (Ṣ, A, TA,) *This is land in the herbage of which is fulness, &c.,* (Ṣ,) or *abundance;* (TA;) *the herbage of which has not been pastured upon.* (Ṣ, A, TA.) And هُوَ فِي وَفْرَةٍ مِنَ المَالِ [*He is in* possession of *abundance of property*]. (A.)

وَافِرٌ and ▼ مَوْفُورٌ and ▼ مُوَفَّرٌ and ▼ مُتَوَفِّرٌ [and ▼ وَفْرٌ and ▼ أَوْفَرُ] all signify the same: [i. e., *Full, without lack* or *defect, full-sized, complete, perfect, whole,* or *entire:* or *much, abundant, ample,* or *copious.*] (A, TA.) You say, مَالٌ وَافِرٌ, and نَبَاتٌ وَافِرٌ, &c., [*Full,* or *complete,* &c., or] *much,* or *abundant, property,* and *herbage,* &c., (TA.) And ▼ شَىْءٌ مَوْفُورٌ *A thing that is full, complete,* &c. (Ṣ.) And ▼ جَزَآءٌ مُوَفَّرٌ *A recompense of which nothing is deficient.* (TA.) And ▼ فُلَانٌ مُوَفَّرُ الشَّعَرِ ‡ *Such a one has his hair left to become abundant and long.* (TA.) And سِقَآءٌ ▼ أَوْفَرُ, (T, Ṣ, A, K,) and ▼ وَفْرٌ, (Ṣgh, K,) *A skin for milk,* or *water, made of hide of which nothing is deficient.* (T, Ṣ, A, K.) And in like manner, مَزَادَةٌ وَفْرَآءُ *A leather water-bag made of a complete skin;* (Ṣ, M, A, K;) *nothing thereof being deficient:* (Ṣ, TA:) also signifying *a leather water-bag filled* (M, K,* TA) *completely.* (M, TA.) And ▼ أَرْضٌ وَفْرَآءُ *Land in the herbage of which is abundance:* (M, K,* TA:) and *land of which the herbage has not been diminished.* (Ṣ, K.) And ▼ أُذُنٌ وَفْرَآءُ *An ear having a large lobe:* (M:) or *a large ear,* (K, TA,) *large in the lobe.* (TA.) You say also, ▼ هُمْ مُتَوَافِرُونَ *They are numerous.* (Ṣ, K.) — الوَافِرُ *The fourth metre* (بَحْر) *in prosody;* (M,* K;) *the measure of which consists of* مُفَاعَلَتُنْ *six times* [in its original state]: (Ṣgh, K:) or, [in practice,] مُفَاعَلَتُنْ مُفَاعَلَتُنْ فَعُولُنْ, *twice:* or مُفَاعَلَتُنْ مُفَاعَلَتُنْ, *twice:* (M, L:) so called because its feet are made full like those of the كَامِل, except that there is [in practice] an elision in their letters, so that it is not complete. (M, L.)

أَوْفَرُ, fem. وَفْرَآءُ, [pl. وُفْرٌ:] see وَافِرٌ.

مُوَفَّرٌ: see وَافِرٌ, in three places. — تَرَكْتُهُ عَلَى أَحْسَنِ مُوَفَّرٍ ‡ *I left him in the best state,* or *condition.* (TA.)

مَوْفُورٌ:
مُتَوَفِّرٌ:
مُتَوَافِرٌ: } see وَافِرٌ.

وفز

3. وافزهُ *He hastened with him; vied,* or *strove, with him in hastening;* or *made haste to be,* or *get, before him;* syn. عَاجَلَهُ. (A, TA.)

4. اوفزهُ *He hastened him.* (K.)

5. توفّز لِكَذَا *He prepared himself* (A, K) *for such a thing,* (A,) or لِلشَّرِّ *for evil,* or *mischief.* (K.) — Also, *He turned over and over upon his bed.* (A.) See also 10.

10. استوفز فِي قِعْدَتِهِ *He put himself in an upright posture, not at his ease, in his manner of sitting; he sat erect, not at his ease:* (Ṣ, Mgh, K:) or *he put down his knees* [*upon the ground*] *and raised his buttocks:* (Aboo-Mo'ádh, K:) or *he raised himself upon his legs,* or *feet, without*

having yet set himself firmly in a standing posture, but having prepared himself to leap, or spring, (Lth, Ḳ, TA,) or *to go away:* (Lth, TA:) or *he sat in a posture as though he desired to rise and stand up;* whether in the manner termed اقْعَآء [i. e. sitting upon the ground with the shanks erect], or otherwise. (MF.)

وَفْزٌ and ▼ وَفَزٌ *Haste:* pl. (of the latter, TA,) أَوْفَازٌ. (Ṣ, Ḳ.) You say, نَحْنُ عَلَى أَوْفَازٍ, (Ṣ, Ḳ,) and عَلَى وَفَزٍ, (Ḳ,) *We are in haste:* (K:) or *we are on a journey;* [like عَلَى أَوْفَادٍ;] *the time of our journeying has come.* (Ṣ, TA.) And لَقِيتُهُ عَلَى أَوْفَازٍ, and عَلَى وَفَزٍ, *I found him in a state of haste:* (Az, TA:) or *preparing* [*his apparatus for travel*]. (M, TA.)

وَفَزٌ: see وَفْزٌ.

وَفْزَةٌ *An upright posture in sitting, so that one is not at his ease.* (Lth, TA.) See 10.

مُتَوَفِّزٌ *Turning over and over upon the bed, scarcely sleeping:* (Ḳ,* TA:) mentioned by Z, and by Ṣgh in the O, on the authority of Ibn-'Abbád. (TA.)

مُسْتَوْفِزٌ act. part. n. of 10, q. v. One says, اِطْمَئِنَّ فَإِنِّى أَرَاكَ مُسْتَوْفِزًا [*Be thou at ease, for I see thee to be sitting in an upright and uneasy posture*]. (TA.)

وفض

1. وَفَضَ, (A, Mgh, Ḳ,) aor. يَفِضُ, (Ḳ,) inf. n. وَفْضٌ (A, Ḳ) and وَفَضٌ; (IDrd, Ḳ;) and ▼ اوفض, (Ṣ, Mgh, Ḳ,) and ▼ استوفض; (Ṣ, Ḳ;) *He ran:* (A, Mgh, Ḳ:) *he hastened,* or *went quickly.* (Ṣ, A, Mgh, Ḳ.) Hence, in the Ḳur. [lxx. 43,] ▼ كَأَنَّهُمْ إِلَى نُصُبٍ يُوفِضُونَ, or نَصْبٍ, *As though they were hastening,* or *going quickly, to a thing set up for worship.* (Fr, Ṣ, TA.) You say also وَفَضَتِ الإِبِلُ *The camels hastened,* or *went quickly:* (M:) or *went the pace termed* خَبَب. (Khaleefeh El-Ḥoseynee.) And *The camels became dispersed:* (AA:) and ▼ استوفضت *they became dispersed* (Ḳ, TA) *in their pasturing.* (TA.)

4. اوفض: see 1, in two places. — Also, *He made* a she-camel *to go the pace termed* خَبَب; as also اوضف. (Khaleefeh El-Ḥoseynee.) And *He dispersed* camels. (The same, and Ḳ.) See also 10. — اوفض لَهُ *He spread for him a carpet,* or *the like, by which to preserve himself from the ground;* (Ḳ, TA;) as also اوضر. (TA.)

10. استوفض: see 1, in two places. — Also, *He required,* or *commanded,* another *to hasten,* or *be quick,* or *he hastened, hurried,* or *urged,* him. (Ṣ, M, A, Ḳ, [but in the M; it seems to relate to camels, or an ostrich.]) — *He drove away* (Ṣ, M, Ḳ) camels, or an ostrich; as also ▼ اوفض: (M:) *he drove away,* or *expelled,* another *from his country:* (M:) *he banished* him. (Mgh, Ḳ.)

وَفْضٌ (Ṣ, M, Ḳ,) and ▼ وَفَضٌ (M, Ḳ) *Haste:* (Ṣ, M, Ḳ:) [like وَفْزٌ and وَفَزٌ:] pl. أَوْفَاضٌ. (Ḳ.) You say, جَآءَ عَلَى وَفْضٍ, and ▼ وَفَضٍ, and أَوْفَاضٍ, *He came in haste.* (M.) And لَقِيتُهُ عَلَى أَوْفَاضٍ *I found him in a state of haste:* (Ṣ, Ḳ:) like أَوْفَازٌ. (Ṣ.)

وَفَضٌ: see وَفْضٌ, in two places.

وَفْضَةٌ *A pastor's* [*bag of the kind called*] خَرِيطَة, *for his implements and provisions,* (M, Ḳ,) *which he carries therein.* (M.) — And hence, as being likened thereto, (M,) *A* [*quiver of the kind called*] جَعْبَة, (M, Ḳ,) or *a thing like the* جَعْبَة, (Ṣ,) *for arrows,* (M,) *of skins,* or *hides,* (Ṣ, M, Ḳ,) *in which is no wood:* (Ṣ, M:) or [*a quiver*] *smaller than the* جعبة, *having its upper and lower parts of equal size:* the جعبة is round and wide, and has a cover on the top, over its mouth: [see the latter word:] (ISh:) pl. وِفَاضٌ (Ṣ, M, A, Ḳ) and وَفَضَاتٌ. (A, TA.) — Also, *A thing like a quiver* (كِنَانَة), (Fr, M,) *of small size,* (Fr,) *in which a man of the class called* أَوْفَاض *puts his food.* (Fr, M.) — Also, The *small depression between the two mustaches, beneath the nose,* (Ḳ, TA,) *of a man.* (TA.)

أَوْفَاضٌ *Parties of men:* (A'Obeyd, Ṣ, Ḳ:) *a mixed multitude:* (A'Obeyd, M, Ḳ:) from وَفَضَتِ الإِبِلُ meaning "the camels became dispersed:" (AA:) or *poor, weak, defenceless people:* (L:) or *an assemblage,* (Ḳ,) or *a mixed multitude* or *collection,* (Ṣ,) *from various tribes, such as the* أَصْحَابُ الصُّفَّة: (A'Obeyd, Ṣ, Ḳ:) or *a company of whom every one has a* وَفْضَة *for his food,* (Fr, M, Ḳ,) i. e. a thing resembling a كِنَانَة, (Fr, M,) of small size, (Fr,) in which he puts his food; (Fr, M;) but this explanation is disapproved by A'Obeyd (TA) [and by ISd]: or الأَوْفَاض applies to *the persons called* أَهْلُ الصُّفَّة, (M,) who were a mixed multitude (A'Obeyd, M) from various tribes, (A'Obeyd,) consisting of ninety-three men. (TA.) [See صُفَّة.]

مِيفَاضٌ *Going quickly,* or *swiftly;* applied to a she-camel, (Ṣ, M, Ḳ,) and to an ostrich. (Ṣ, M.)

مُسْتَوْفِضٌ *Going quickly,* or *hastening, by reason of fright;* (Aṣ;) or *running away by reason of fright;* as though desiring his وَفْض, or running: (Ṣgh:) or *frightened.* (TA.)

[وفق, &c.
See Supplement.]

وقب

1. وَقَبَ الظَّلَامُ *The darkness came in upon the people.* (Ṣ, Ḳ*.) — So in the verse of the Ḳur. [cxiii. 3,] وَمِنْ شَرِّ غَاسِقٍ إِذَا وَقَبَ *And from the mischief of night when it cometh in upon men;* (Ṣ;) [for other explanations see غَاسِق in art. غسق.] — وَقَبَتِ الشَّمْسُ, (inf. n. وَقْبٌ and وُقُوبٌ, Ḳ,) ‡ *The sun set:* (Ṣ, Ḳ:) *entered its place* [of setting.] (Ṣ.) — وَقَبَ القَمَرُ, (inf. n. وُقُوبٌ, TA,) *The moon entered upon a state of eclipse;* (Ḳ;) *entered into the cone-shaped shade of the earth.* (TA.) — وَقَبَتْ عَيْنَاهُ (and simply وَقَبَ, TA,) *His eyes became sunk,* or *depressed, in his head.* (Ṣ.) — وَقَبَ, aor. يَقِبُ, inf. n. وَقْبٌ and وَقِيبٌ, *He* (a horse) *made a sound with his prepuce:* [in the Ṣ and Ḳ, the verb is not mentioned, but only the latter of the two inf. ns., which is explained as signifying "the sounding of a horse's prepuce:"] or *made a sound by the motion of his penis in its prepuce.* (TA.) — وَقَبَ, aor. يَقِبُ, inf. n. وَقْبٌ *It* (a thing) *entered:* (Ṣ:) but it is said in a marginal note in a copy of the Ṣ, that the inf. n. is correctly وُقُوبٌ, because the verb is intrans.: accord. to some, it signifies *he,* or *it, entered into a* وَقْب, q. v.; and in the Ḳ, وَقْبٌ is given as the inf. n. of the verb in this sense. (TA.) [In the CḲ, وَقْت is put by mistake for وَقْب.] — وَقَبَ, [aor. يَقِبُ,] inf. n. وَقْبٌ and وُقُوبٌ, *He,* or *it, became absent, hidden,* or *concealed.* (Ḳ.) — وَقَبَ [aor. يَقِبُ,] inf. n. وَقْبٌ, *He,* or *it, came; approached; advanced.* (Ḳ.)

4. اوقب النَّخْلُ *The palm-tree became rotten in the fruit-bearing stalks of its racemes.* (TA.) — اوقب *He* (Ḳ), or *it,* (a people, Ṣ,) *hungered; suffered hunger.* (Ṣ, Ḳ.) — اوقب شَيْئًا, (inf. n. إِيقَابٌ, TA,) *He put a thing into a* وَقْبَة, q. v.: (Fr, Ṣ, Ḳ:) or, as in some Lexicons, *into a* وَقْب. (TA.)

وَقْبٌ *A small hollow,* or *cavity,* (نُقْرَة,) *in which water collects,* in a mountain: (Ṣ:) or in a rock: as also ▼ وَقْبَة: (Ḳ:) or, accord. to some, وقب is a coll. gen. n., of which وقبة is the n. un.: (MF:) pl. أَوْقَابٌ: (TA:) or وَقْبٌ, accord. to the Ḳ, (but accord. to the TA ▼ وَقْبَة,) signifies *what is like a well, in a tract of hard and large stones that produce no plants, a fathom,* or *two fathoms, in depth,* (Ḳ,) *in which the rain-water stagnates.* (TA.) — The *cavity,* or *socket,* of the eye: (Ṣ:) *any cavity,* or *socket, in the body;* as that of the eye, and that of the shoulder-blade: (Ḳ:) pl. وُقُوبٌ and وِقَابٌ. (TA.) — The *pit,* or *cavity, above the eye* of a horse: (Ḳ:) pl. وُقُوبٌ and وِقَابٌ. (TA.) — The *hole into which enters the axle* of a pulley. (Ḳ.) — See also وَقْبَة. — *Stupid; foolish; of little sense:* (Ṣ, Ḳ:) like وَغْبٌ: (Ṣ:) an epithet of a man: pl. أَوْقَابٌ: (Ḳ, TA:) fem. with ة. (TA.) — So in the following trad. of El-Aḥnaf: إِيَّاكُمْ وَحَمِيَّةَ الأَوْقَابِ [*Beware of the care with which stupid people defend their rights:* a proverb]. (TA.) For الاوقاب, another relation substitutes الأَوْغَاب, meaning the same, or weak persons. (TA, art. وغب, on the authority of AA.) — See أَوْقَابٌ — A *despised*, or *contemptible*, *low*, *base*, or *ignoble*, man. (Th, Ḳ.)

قِبَةٌ The *thing that is in the belly, resembling the* فَحِث: (TA:) the إِنْفَحَة [a name given to the *stomach* of a sucking kid, &c.] *when it has grown large*, of a شَاة, [i.e., a sheep or goat or the like]: (Ḳ:) not in any animals but those termed شاء: (IAṣr:) mentioned before, in art. قب, [q.v., where it is also written قِبَّةٌ]. (TA.)

وَقْبَةٌ *A large aperture*, or *hole*, *in a wall, in which is shade:* (Ḳ:) pl. أَوْقَابٌ. — See وَقْبٌ. — وَقْبَةُ الثَّرِيدِ, (Ṣ, Ḳ,) and الدُّهْنِ, (Ḳ,) but the latter is a mistake, and the correct word is المُدْهُنِ, [a vase for ointment], (TA,) i.q. أُنْقُوعَتُهُ, [i.e., *its cavity* or *hollow*]. (Ṣ, Ḳ.) Lth says, that ▼ وَقْبٌ signifies *any cavity, hollow,* or *pit;* as that in a [stone of the kind called] فِهْرٌ, and in a مُدْهُن, or مُدْهُنَة, q.v. (TA.)

وُقْبِىٌّ *Fond of*, or *given to, the company of* أَوْقَاب, i.e., *stupid*, or *foolish, persons*. (Ḳ.)

أَوْقَابٌ [pl. of وَقْبٌ?] The *utensils and furniture, of the meaner sort, of a house*, or *tent:* (Ḳ, TA:) as also أَوْغَابٌ. (TA.)

ذَكَرٌ أَوْقَبُ *Multum penetrans in vulvam penis.* (Ḳ.) — رَكِيَّةٌ وَقْبَاءُ *A well of which the water sinks into the earth.* (TA.)

مِيقَبٌ i.q. وَدَعَةٌ [The *shell called cowry*]. (Ḳ.)

مِيقَابٌ A man *who drinks much of water:* (Ḳ:) or *of the beverage called* نَبِيذ. (L.) — مِيقَابٌ *A stupid*, or *foolish*, woman: or one *who gives birth to stupid*, or *foolish, children;* syn. مُحْمِقَةٌ. (Ḳ: [so in the CḲ: in a MS. copy, مُحَمَّقَةٌ, one *to whom stupidity*, or *folly, is imputed:* but the former is evidently the right reading; مِيقاب being an epithet similar to مِئْنَاثٌ and مِذْكَارٌ &c.]) — Also *Latam vulvam habens* mulier. (Ḳ.) — بَنُو المِيقَابِ a reproachful appellation, (Ḳ,) referring to the mother of the persons to whom it is applied. (TA.) — سَيْرُ المِيقَابِ *A journeying continued during a day and a night together.* (Ḳ.)

وقت

1. وَقَتَ, aor. يَقِتُ, inf. n. وَقْتٌ; and ▼ وَقَّتَ, inf. n. تَوْقِيتٌ; *He determined, defined*, or *limited*, a thing *as to time;* (IAth, L, Mṣb;) and *otherwise:* (L, Mṣb:) *he determined*, or *defined, times.* (Ṣ, Ḳ.) وَقَّتَهُ *He declared* [or *appointed*] *a time in which it should be done.* (Ṣ.) وَقَتَ اللّٰهُ الصَّلَاةَ, aor. يَقِتُ; and ▼ وَقَّتَهَا, *God hath determined*, or *defined, a time for prayer.* (Mṣb.) ▼ وقّت, as also أَقَّتَ, *He assigned*, or *appointed*, for a thing, *a particular time; he assigned*, or *appointed, a particular time for doing* a thing. (IAth, L.) وَقَّتَهُ ▼ لِيَوْمِ كَذَا [*I appointed him*, or *it, for such a day*]; like أَجَّلْتُهُ. (Ṣ.) — In the following words of the Ḳur. [lxxvii. 11,] وَإِذَا الرُّسُلُ أُقِّتَتْ ▼ اقتت, is a dial. form of وُقِّتَتْ, like as أُجُوهٌ is of وُجُوهٌ; (Ṣ;) and the meaning is *And when the Apostles shall have one* [*particular*] *time assigned to them* to decide between the people [to whom they have been sent to preach]: (Zj:) or, *shall be collected at their appointed time*, on the day of resurrection. (Fr.) This is the general reading: but there are other readings; namely, وُقِتَتْ, and وُقِّتَتْ, (Ṣ, TA,) and وُوقِتَتْ, which last is of the measure فُوعِلَتْ, from المُوَاقَتَةُ. (Ḳ.) — لَمْ يَقِتْ فِى الخَمْرِ حَدًّا *He* (Moḥammad) *did not determine*, or *define, for* [*drinking wine*,] *a castigation consisting of a certain number* [*of blows*, or *stripes*]. (TA, from a trad.) — وَقَتَ sometimes signifies *He* [i.e. God] *made* the entering upon the state of إِحْرَام in pilgrimage, and prayer at the commencement of its appointed time, *obligatory*, or *incumbent*, upon men. (TA.) — ▼ وَقَّتَ لِأَهْلِ المَدِينَةِ ذَا الحُلَيْفَةِ *He appointed, for the people of El-Medeeneh, Dhu-l-Ḥuleyfeh as the place where they should enter upon the state of* إِحْرَام. (TA, from a trad.)

2: see 1 throughout.

3. وَاقَتَهُ, inf. n. مُوَاقَتَةٌ, [*He made an appointment with him for a particular time*]. (Ḳ.)

وَقْتٌ (Ṣ, Ḳ) *A time;* or *space*, or *measure, of time*, (M, L, Ḳ, Mṣb,) *appointed for any affair; a season:* (Mṣb:) mostly used with respect to what is past: (M, Ḳ:) sometimes with respect to the future: (TA:) as also ▼ مِيقَاتٌ, (Ḳ, Mṣb:) or, accord. to some, there is a difference between these two words; the former having an absolute signification, and the latter signifying *a time appointed for the performance of some action:* [as in the Ṣ:] (TA:) pl. of the former أَوْقَاتٌ, and of the latter مَوَاقِيتُ. (Mṣb.) [Hence, وَقْتَئِذٍ *Then; at that time.*] — وَقْتٌ ‡ *A space*, or *measure, of local extension;* as a mile, &c. (Sb.)

مَوْقِتٌ, [of the measure] مَفْعِلٌ from الوَقْتُ: (Ṣ, Ḳ:) [it may therefore be an inf. n., or a noun of place, or a noun of time]. El-'Ajjáj says,

وَالجَامِعُ النَّاسَ لِيَوْمِ المَوْقِتِ

[*And He who congregateth mankind for the day of the appointment of a particular time*, or, *of the place of a certain event*, or, *of the time of a certain event;* i.e., for the day of resurrection]. (Ṣ.)

مِيقَاتٌ: see وَقْتٌ. — Also, *A place in which a certain action is appointed to be performed.* (Ṣ.) Ex. مِيقَاتُ الحَجِّ *The place where the pilgrims enter upon the state of* إِحْرَام: (Ṣ, Ḳ:) you say, هٰذَا مِيقَاتُ أَهْلِ الشَّامِ *This is the place where the people of Syria enter upon the state of* احرام. (Ṣ.) — [Also, *A place in which a meeting is appointed to take place at a particular time.* Ex.] الآخِرَةُ مِيقَاتُ الخَلْقِ [*The world to come is the place in which mankind are appointed to meet* after the resurrection]. (L.) — [Also, *That which determines the commencement*, or *the like, of a period &c.* Ex.] الهِلَالُ مِيقَاتُ الشَّهْرِ [*The crescent is that which determines the commencement of the month*]. (L.) — See also مُوَقَّتٌ.

مَوْقُوتٌ and ▼ مُوَقَّتٌ *Determined, defined, definite*, or *limited, as to time.* (L.) — وَقْتٌ مَوْقُوتٌ, and ▼ مُوَقَّتٌ, *A determined, defined, definite*, or *limited, time.* (Ḳ.) — إِنَّ الصَّلَاةَ كَانَتْ عَلَى المُؤْمِنِينَ كِتَابًا مَوْقُوتًا [Ḳur. iv. 104,] *For prayer is to the believers a prescript*, or *an appointment*, or *ordinance, ordained* [*to be performed*] *in the times* [*thereof*]. (Ṣ, Ḳ, &c.) — Also [مَوْقُوتٌ (see 1 and)] ▼ مُوَقَّتٌ *Determined, defined*, or *definite, as to its extreme limit, extent*, or *amount:* (L:) both signify anything *defined, definite*, or *limited.* (Mṣb.)

مُوَقَّتٌ: see مَوْقُوتٌ.

وقح

1. وَقُحَ, (Ṣ, Ḳ,) aor. يَوْقُحُ; (Ṣ;) and وَقِحَ, (Ḳ,) aor. يَوْقَحُ; (TA;) and وَقَحَ, (Ḳ,) aor. يَقِحُ; (TA;) inf. n. وَقَاحَةٌ and وُقُوحَةٌ, (Ṣ, Ḳ,) inf. ns. of the first, (TA,) and وَقَحٌ and وُقُحٌ, (Ṣ,) [also of the first,] and وَقْحٌ, so in [most of] the copies of the Ḳ, [but in the CḲ وُقُحٌ,] inf. n. of the second, (TA,) and قَحَةٌ and قِحَةٌ, (Ṣ, Ḳ,) in both of which the ة is a substitute for the [elided] و, (Ṣ,) and in the latter of which the fet-ḥah is put in the place of kesreh because of the guttural letter, both inf. ns. of the second and third; (TA;) and ▼ اوقح, and ▼ استوقح; (Ṣ, Ḳ;) *It* (a solid hoof, Ṣ, Ḳ, and a camel's foot, and the back, TA) *was*, or *became, hard.* (Ṣ, Ḳ.) — وَقُحَ, (Ṣ, Ḳ,) and وَقِحَ, and وَقَحَ, (Ḳ,) inf. n. وَقَاحَةٌ and قَحَةٌ and قِحَةٌ (Ṣ) and وَقَحٌ and وُقُوحٌ; (Lḥ;) and ▼ توقّح; (A;) *He* (a man) *had little shame:* (Ṣ, Ḳ:) *he was hard-faced, having little shame: he was bold to do bad, foul, or abominable, things, and cared not for them*, accord. to Bḍ and Z. (TA.)

2. وقّح, inf. n. تَوْقِيحٌ, *He repaired* a tank, or cistern, *with pieces of dry clay*, or *tough clay in which was no sand*, and (or, as is sometimes done, TA) *with broad and thin stones.* (Ḳ.) — وقّح, inf. n. تَوْقِيحٌ, *He rendered* a solid hoof

hard by means of melted fat, (Ṣ, Ḳ,) burning with the melted fat the places where the hoof was worn by treading, and the hairs next to the hoof. (TA.)

4 :
5 : } see 1.
10 :

وَقْحٌ and ▼ وَقَاحٌ ‡ A man *having little shame.* (Ṣ, A.) — وَقَاحُ الوَجْهِ, an epithet applied to a woman, (Ṣ,) without ة, as well as to a man, and وَقِحُ ▼ الوَجْهِ, applied to a man, ‡ *Hard-faced, having little shame;* (TA;) as also ▼ وَقْحَى applied to woman. (Mṣb.)

وَقَاحُ الذَّنَبِ † A man *patient in riding.* (IAạr, Ḳ.) [See ذَنَبٌ.] — وَقَاحٌ (Ṣ, Ḳ) and ▼ وَاقِحٌ (Ḳ,) A *hard* solid hoof, (Ṣ, Ḳ,) and camel's foot, and the back; the former an epithet both masc. and fem.: (TA:) pl. of the former وُقُحٌ, (Ṣ, Ḳ,) and وُقْحٌ. (TA.) فَرَسٌ وَقَاحٌ † *A hard and strong horse.* (Mṣb.) — See وَقِحٌ.

وَقِحٌ and وَقْحَى: see وَقْحٌ.

وَقَاحٌ: see وَاقِحٌ.

رَجُلٌ مُوَقَّحٌ ‡ *A man who has been tried* or *proved,* or *rendered experienced* or *expert* (Lḥ, Ṣ, Ḳ) *by trials which have befallen him;* as also مُوَقَّعٌ. (Lḥ, Ṣ.) — بَعِيرٌ مُوَقَّحٌ ‡ *A camel jaded by work.* (TA.)

وقد

1. وَقَدَتِ النَّارُ, aor. تَقِدُ, inf. n. وُقُودٌ (Ṣ, A, L, Mṣb, Ḳ) and وَقُودٌ, (Sb, Zj, L, Ḳ,) but this is a deviation [as to form] from the constant course of speech, and most hold that the former is an inf. n. and the latter a subst. signifying "fire-wood" [or "fuel"], though there are some instances of inf. ns. of the measure فَعُول, whereof قَبُول is one, (El-Baṣáïr, TA,) and وَقْدٌ (Ṣ, A, L, Mṣb, Ḳ) and وَقَدٌ and قِدَةٌ and وَقَدَانٌ (Ṣ, L, Ḳ) and وَقِيدٌ; (Ṣ, L;) and ▼ توقّدت, and ▼ اتّقدت, (Ṣ, L, Mṣb, Ḳ,) and ▼ استوقدت; (L, Mṣb, Ḳ;) *The fire burned; burned up; burned brightly* or *fiercely; blazed;* or *flamed;* syn. اِشْتَعَلَت; (Mṣb, art. شعل;) and هَاجَت; (L;) and سَطَعَت وَارْتَفَعَ لَهَبُهَا. (Bḍ, ii. 16.) — وَقَدَتْ بِكَ زِنَادِى † [*May my* زند *emit fire by thy means!*] a prayer, like وَرِيَتْ بك زنادى: (L:) [meaning, do thou aid, or help, me]. — وَقَدَ and ▼ توقّد *It* (anything) *shone,* or *glistened.* (L.) — توقّد ▼ قَلْبُهُ ‡ *His heart became excited with ardour,* or *eagerness.* (L.) — [And ▼ توقّد ‡ *He* (a man) *was,* or *became, clever, ingenious, acute, sharp,* or *penetrating.* (See وَقَّادٌ.)]

2: see 4.

4. اوقد النَّارَ, (Ṣ, A, L, Mṣb, Ḳ,) inf. n. إِيقَادٌ; (L, Mṣb;) and ▼ وقّدها, (L,) and ▼ توقّدها, (Ḳ,) and ▼ استوقدها; (Ṣ, L, Mṣb, Ḳ;) *He lighted,* or *kindled, the fire; made it to burn, to burn up, to burn brightly* or *fiercely, to blaze,* or *to flame;* syn. أَضْرَمَهَا; (Ḳ, art. ضرم;) and أَشْعَلَهَا; (TḲ;) *he raised the fire,* or *made it to burn up, with fire-wood,* or *fuel:* (A:) or the ▼ last signifies *he desired,* or *endeavoured, to kindle the fire, and to make it burn up,* or *burn brightly* or *fiercely, and blaze,* or *flame.* (Bḍ, ii. 16.) — كُلَّمَا أَوْقَدُوا نَارًا لِلْحَرْبِ أَطْفَأَهَا ٱللّٰهُ ‡ [*Whenever they kindle a fire for war, God extinguisheth it;* Ḳur. v. 69,] meaning, whenever they contrive a mischievous and deceitful plot, God annulleth it. (Mṣb.) — أَوْقَدْتُ لِلصِّبَا نَارًا [in some copies of the Ḳ, لِلصَّبِىِّ,] † *I relinquished silly and youthful conduct.* (L, Ḳ.) A poet says,

* صَحَوْتُ وَأَوْقَدْتُ لِلّهْوِ نَارَا *
* وَرَدَّ عَلَىَّ ٱلصِّبَا مَا ٱسْتَعَارَا *

† [*I recovered from intoxication, and relinquished vain and frivolous diversion; and youthfulness restored to me what it had borrowed*]. (L.) — أَبْعَدَ ٱللّٰهُ دَارَهُ وَأَوْقَدَ نَارًا أَثَرَهُ ‡ [*May God remove his dwelling far away, and*] *may He not bring him back,* or *restore him!* (L, Ḳ.) It was a custom of Arabs, when a man whose evil or mischief they feared removed from them, to light a fire behind him, that his evil or mischief might go with him. (L.)

5. See 1 and 4. — توقّد is also said of the odour of perfume, (Ṣ, A, Ḳ, in art. وهج,) meaning † *It was,* or *became, hot* [or strong]. (TḲ.)

8: see 1. — اتّقدت الشَّمْسُ [*The sun was,* or *became, burning,* or *fiercely burning*]. (M, Ḳ, in art. صقر, conj. 4, &c.)

10: see 1 and 4.

وَقْدٌ *Fire* itself. (A, L, Ḳ.) Ex. مَا أَعْظَمَ هٰذَا الوَقْدَ *How great is this fire!* (A.) — See also 1.

الوَقْدَةُ, (Ṣ, Ḳ,) or وَقْدَةُ الحَرِّ, (L,) ‡ *The greatest heat;* (Ṣ, L, Ḳ;) *which is a period of ten days,* or *of half a month.* (Ṣ, L.) — طَبَخَتْهُمْ وَقْدَةُ الصَّيْفِ ‡ [*The greatest heat of the summer affected them with a hot,* or *burning, fever*]. (A.) — وَقَدَاتُ سُهَيْلٍ: see the last paragraph of art. عدل.

وَقَدِى, fem. *Shining,* or *glistening.* (L.) — See also مِيقَادٌ.

وَقُودٌ *Fire-wood;* (S, L, Mṣb, Ḳ;) but it is only so called *when kindled;* (El-Ḥareeree, in De Sacy's Anthol. Gramm. Ar., p. 31 of the Arabic text;) as also وَقَادٌ and وَقِيدٌ: (Ḳ:) or *any fuel; anything with which fire is kindled,* or *made to burn, burn up, burn brightly* or *fiercely, blaze,* or *flame:* (L:) or *the blaze,* or *flame, of fire, which one sees.* (Lth, L.) — وَقُودُهَا ٱلنَّاسُ وَٱلْحِجَارَةُ [Ḳur. ii. 22; and lxvi. 6; *The fuel whereof shall be men and stones*]. (L.) — See also 1. In the Ḳur. lxxxv. 5, it is most properly rendered as an inf. n.; (Az, L;) and some in this case read الوُقُود. (Yaạḳoob, Ṣ, L.)

وَقَّادٌ *Shining,* or *shining brightly;* (L, Ḳ;) applied to a star. (L.) — وَقَّادٌ (L, Ḳ) and ▼ مُتَوَقِّدٌ (L) ‡ A heart, or mind, *quickly excited with ardour,* or *eagerness, in liveliness and acuteness* or *penetration.* (L, Ḳ.) — Also, both words, ‡ A man (L) *clever, ingenious, acute, sharp,* or *penetrating.* (L, Ḳ.)

غَائِرُ الوَاقِدَيْنِ ‡ *Blind:* (A:) by الواقدين are meant *the two eyes:* El-Aạshà says, accord. to one reading,

* رَأَتْ رَجُلًا غَائِرَ الوَاقِدَيْنِ *

but the reading commonly known is الوَافِدَيْنِ. (JK.)

مَوْقِدٌ (Ṣ, A, L, Mṣb) and ▼ مُسْتَوْقَدٌ (A, L) and ▼ مُوقَدٌ (JK) *A fire-place; a place in which fire is lighted.* (Ṣ, A,* L, Mṣb.) See an ex. voce حَسَّاسٌ.]

مُوقَدٌ: see مَوْقِدٌ.

زَنْدٌ مِيقَادٌ *A* زند *that quickly produces fire.* (A, L, Ḳ.) You also say زند وَقَدَى, i.e., مُتَوَقِّدَةٌ. (JK.)

مُتَوَقِّدٌ: see وَقَّادٌ.

مُسْتَوْقَدٌ: see مَوْقِدٌ.

وقذ

1. وَقَذَهُ, aor. يَقِذُ, (Ṣ, L, &c.,) inf. n. وَقْذٌ, (Ṣ, L, Ḳ, &c.,) *He beat him,* or *struck him, violently:* (L, Ḳ:) *he beat him until he became relaxed,* or *languid, and at the point of death:* (Ṣ, L, Mṣb:) or *he beat him so that he became at the point of death:* (A:) *he broke his skull, wounding the brain:* (L:) *he beat* or *struck, him upon the small protuberance above the back of the neck, so that the sound of the blow* or *blows reached the brain, and deprived him of reason:* (Aboo-Sa'eed, L:) *he beat him (a man) until he died.* (L.) — وَقَذَهُ بِالضَّرْبِ [*He killed him with beating*]. (ISk, L.) — وَقَذَ الشَّاةَ *He beat the ewe,* or *she-goat, to death with pieces of wood* [&c.: see وَقِيذٌ]. (L.) — وَقَذَهُ *He prostrated him.* (Ḳ.) — ضَرَبْتُ الحَيَّةَ حَتَّى وَقَذْتُهَا *I beat the serpent until I killed it.* (A.) — وَقَذَهُ † *It* (clemency, forbearance, or gravity,) *rendered him still, quiet,* or *tranquil:* (L, Ḳ:) *it* (the fear of God) *rendered him still, quiet,* or *tranquil, and had such an effect upon him as to prevent his*

committing an unlawful action. (L.) — وَقَذَهُ ‡ *It* (drowsiness, Ṣ, L, Mṣb) *overcame him:* (Ṣ, L, Ḳ:) or *made him to fall down.* (Mṣb.) — وَقَذَهُ † *He,* or *it, left him ill,* or *sick;* as also ♦ أَوْقَذَهُ. (Ḳ.) — وَقَذَهُ المَرَضُ, and الغَمُّ, † [*Disease, and grief, overcame him, or rendered him infirm, or caused him to be at the point of death*]. (L.) — وَقَذَتْهُ العِبَادَةُ ‡ [*Religious service rendered him infirm, or caused him to be at the point of death*]. (A) — وَقَذَتْنِى كَلِمَةٌ سَمِعْتُهَا ‡ [*A word, or sentence, that I heard, distressed me.*] (A.) — وُقِذَتْ ‡ *She* (a camel) *was milked against her wish, so that her milk became little.* (A.) — فِى قَلْبِى وَقْذَةٌ مِنْ ذٰلِكَ ‡ *In my heart is some distress remaining in consequence of that.* (A.)

4: see 1.

وَقِيذٌ *Beaten* [*violently:* or] *until he has become relaxed, or languid, and at the point of death:* [*&c.:* see 1:] as also ♦ مَوْقُوذٌ. (Mṣb.) — وَقِيذٌ (ISk, L, Ḳ) and ♦ مَوْقُوذَةٌ (Fr, ISk, Ṣ, L, Mṣb, Ḳ) A ewe, or she-goat, *beaten to death;* (Fr, ISk, L;) after which it is eaten: (ISk, L:) *killed with pieces of wood* (Ṣ, L, Mṣb, Ḳ) &c.; (Mṣb;) not legally slaughtered: (Fr, L, Mṣb:) *beaten to death with a staff,* or *stick;* (A, El-Baṣáïr;) or *with blunt stones:* (El-Baṣáïr:) the Arabs in the time of paganism killed beasts thus. (A.) — وَقِيذٌ *Prostrated.* (Ḳ.) [In the TA, السريع is erroneously put for الصَّرِيعُ.] — وَقِيذٌ † A man *in whom is no fat or strength;* مَا بِهِ طِرْقٌ. (Ṣ, L.) — وَقِيذٌ † *A slow, heavy man:* (L, Ḳ*:) as though his heaviness and weakness overcame him, or prostrated him, وَقَذَهُ. (L.) — وَقِيذٌ ‡ *Violently sick, and at the point of death;* as also ♦ مَوْقُوذٌ: (L, Ḳ:) *heavy,* (Lth, L,) *suffering from sickness that cleaves fast to him, and at the point of death:* (Lth, A, L;) *suffering from a swoon, and in such a state that it is not known whether he be dead or not.* (ISh, L.) — وَقِيذٌ ‡ *Ill, sick;* as also ♦ مُوقَذٌ. (TA.) — وَقَائِذُ *Stones spread about:* (L, Ḳ:) sing. وَقِيذَةٌ. (L.) — وَقِيذُ الجَوَانِحِ † *Grieved in the heart;* as though it were broken and weakened by grief. The جوانح [are the ribs that] enclose the heart. (L.)

مُوقَذٌ: see وَقِيذٌ.

مَوْقَذٌ *An extremity of the person,* (Ḳ,) or *place upon which a blow is severe,* (A,) as, (Ḳ,) or *namely,* (A,) *the elbow,* (A, L, Ḳ,) *and shoulder-joint,* (Ḳ,) or *extremity of the shoulder-joint,* (A, L,) *and knee, and ankle-bone:* pl. مَوَاقِذُ. (A, L, Ḳ.)

مَوْقُوذٌ and مَوْقُوذَةٌ: see وَقِيذٌ.

مُوَقَّذَةٌ A she-camel *suffering in her dugs from the effect of the rag with which they have been bound to prevent their being sucked,* (Ṣ, L, Ḳ,) *by reason of its tightness:* (L:) or *that has been sucked by her young one without its drawing her milk otherwise than scantily, by reason of the largeness of her udder, in consequence of which she suffers disease,* (Ṣ, L, Ḳ,) *and has a tumour* (Ṣ, L) *in her udder.* (L.)

وقر

1. وَقَرَ as syn. with أَوْقَرَ: and وَقَرَتِ النَّخْلَةُ as syn. with أَوْقَرَتْ: see 4. — [Hence,] وَقَرَ ٱللّٰهُ أُذُنَهُ, aor. يَقِرُهَا, (Ṣ, Mṣb, Ḳ,) inf. n. وَقْرٌ, (Ṣ, Mṣb,) ‡ *God made his ear heavy, or dull of hearing:* (Mṣb, Ḳ:*) or *deaf.* (Ṣ, Ḳ.) You say, اَللّٰهُمَّ قِرْ أُذُنَهُ ‡ *O God, make his ear heavy, or dull of hearing:* (A:) or *deaf.* (Ṣ.) — [Hence also,] وُقِرَتْ أُذُنُهُ, (ISk, Ṣ, TA,) aor. تُوقَرُ, inf. n. وَقْرٌ; (ISk, TA;) and وَقِرَتْ, aor. تَوْقَرُ; (Ṣ, Mṣb, TA;) and وَقَرَتْ, aor. تَقِرُ; (Mṣb, TA;) inf. n. وَقْرٌ, (Ṣ, Mṣb, TA,) which by rule should be وَقَرٌ, as inf. n. of وَقِرَتْ, (Ṣ, TA,) but which is regular as inf. n. of وَقَرَتْ; (TA;) ‡ *His ear was, or became, heavy, or dull of hearing:* (Mṣb, TA:*) or *deaf:* (Ṣ, TA:) but in the Ḳ we find, less properly, وَقَرَ and وَقِرَ, [as though signifying *he* (a man) *was, or became, dull of hearing:* or *deaf:*] inf. n. وَقْرٌ, which by rule should be وَقَرٌ; and وُقِرَ, like عُنِىَ. (TA.) You say also, وَقِرَتْ أُذُنِى عَنْهُ ‡ [*My ear was dull of hearing,* or *deaf, to* (lit. from) *him*]: (A:) and وَقِرَتْ عَنِ ٱسْتِمَاعِ كَلَامِهِ ‡ [*it was dull of hearing,* or *deaf, to* (lit. from) *the hearing of,* or *listening to, his speech*]. (A, TA: but in the latter, وَقَرَتْ.) — [Hence also,] وَقَرَ, aor. يَقِرُ, inf. n. وَقَارٌ, † *He,* or *it, was,* or *became, still,* or *motionless; rested;* syn. سَكَنَ. (TA.) So in the phrase وَقَرَ فِى القَلْبِ † *It* (a thing) *rested in the heart,* or *mind:* and وَقَرَ فِى صَدْرِهِ † *it* (a secret) *rested in his bosom:* occurring in a trad., accord. to different relations. (TA.) You say also, كَلَّمْتُهُ كَلِمَةً وَقَرَتْ فِى أُذُنِهِ ‡ *I spoke to him a speech which rested* (ثَبَتَتْ) *in his ear.* (Aṣ, A.) And وَقَرَ فِى السَّمْعِ وَوَعَاهُ القَلْبُ ‡ [*It rested in the ear; and the heart,* or *mind, kept it in memory*]. (A.) And وَقَرَ فِى قَلْبِهِ كَذَا ‡ *Such a thing came into his mind and left its impression remaining.* (A.) — [And hence,] وَقَرَ, aor. يَقِرُ; (Mṣb, Ḳ, TA;) and وَقُرَ, aor. يَوْقُرُ; (TA;) inf. n. وَقْرٌ, (Ḳ, TA,) of the former, (TA,) and وُقُورٌ, (Ḳ, TA,) of the latter; (TA;) ‡ *He* (a man, TA) *sat:* (Ḳ, TA:) or *he sat with* وَقَار [i. e. *gravity, &c.*]. (Mṣb.) — [Hence also,] وَقَرَ, aor. يَقِرُ; (Ṣ, Ḳ;) and وَقُرَ, aor. يَوْقُرُ; (Mṣb, Ḳ;) inf. n. وَقَارٌ, (Ṣ, Mṣb, Ḳ,) of the former, (Ṣ,) or of the latter, (Mṣb, Ḳ,) and قِرَةٌ, of the former, (Ṣ, Ḳ,) and وَقَارَةٌ, of the latter; (Ḳ;) *He was, or became, grave, staid, steady, sedate, or calm;* (Ṣ, Mṣb, Ḳ;) [see وَقَارٌ, below;] as also ♦ إِتَّقَرَ and ♦ تَوَقَّرَ: (Ḳ:) or this last, signifies *he showed, exhibited,* or *manifested, gravity, staidness, steadiness, sedateness,* or *calmness:* (KL:) [and also, agreeably with analogy, *he endeavoured,* or *he constrained himself, to be grave, &c.*] It is said in the Ḳur. [xxxiii. 33,] وَقِرْنَ فِى بُيُوتِكُنَّ [meaning, accord. to some, *And be ye grave, &c., in your houses,* or *chambers*]: (Ṣ, A:) or the meaning is, *and sit ye, &c.:* (TA:) and so another reading, وَقَرْنَ: (TA:) or this latter, (Ṣ,) or each of these two readings, (TA,) is from القَرَارُ, (Ṣ,) [i. e.,] from قَرَّ, aor. يَقَرُّ and يَقِرُّ, (TA;) and is a contraction of إِقْرَرْنَ [or إِقْرِرْنَ]. (Ṣ.)

2. وقّرهُ, inf. n. تَوْقِيرٌ, † *He made him* (a beast of carriage) *to be still,* or *quiet.* (Ḳ, TA.) — ‡ *He pronounced him,* or *held,* or *reckoned him, to be grave, staid, steady, sedate,* or *calm;* syn. of the inf. n. تَرْزِينٌ. (Ṣ.) — ‡ *He treated him, with honour, reverence, veneration,* or *respect;* (Ṣ, A, Ḳ, TA;) *did not hold him in light estimation.* (A, TA.)

4. اوقرهُ (inf. n. إِيقَارٌ, and قِرَةٌ, Ḳ, which latter is anomalous, TA,) *He loaded him:* (Ṣ, A, Mṣb, Ḳ:) or *loaded him heavily:* (A, Ḳ:) namely a camel, (Ṣ, Mṣb,) or a beast (Ḳ) or a mule, and an ass: (A:) [see وِقْرٌ, below: and ♦ وَقَرَهُ, aor. يَقِرُهُ, signifies the same; and its inf. n. seems to be وَقْرَى, q. v., as also, probably, وَقْرٌ: وَقَرَ, aor. يَقِرُ, is explained by Golius, as on the authority of Ibn-Maạroof, as signifying "gravavit, aggravavit."] You say, أَوْقَرَ الدَّابَّةَ قِرَةً شَدِيدَةً [*He loaded the beast of carriage severely*]. (TA.) And أَوْقَرَ رَاحِلَتَهُ ذَهَبًا *He loaded his riding-camel with a load,* or *heavy load, of gold.* (TA.) — اوقرهُ الدَّيْنُ ‡ *Debt burdened him,* or *burdened him heavily.* (Ṣ, A.*) — أَوْقَرَتِ النَّخْلَةُ, (Ṣ, A, Mṣb,) and ♦ وَقَرَتْ, (A,) *The palm-tree became laden,* or *heavily laden, with fruit;* (A;) *became abundant in fruit.* (Ṣ, Mṣb.) — And أَوْقَرَ, or أُوقِرَ, (accord. to different copies of the Ṣ, in art. دمر,) [or اوقر شَحْمًا or بِالشَّحْمِ,] said of a camel &c., *i. q.* دَمَّرَ بِالشَّحْمِ [*He was, or became, loaded, or overspread, with fat:* see دمّر]. (Ṣ, in that art.)

5: } see 1, last signification.
8: }

10. استوقر وِقْرَهُ طَعَامًا *He took,* or *received, his load,* or *heavy load, of wheat or other food.* (Ḳ.) — استوقرت الإِبِلُ, (Ḳ, TA,) or استوقرت الإِبِلُ شَحْمًا (A,) *The camels became fat;* (Ḳ;) [lit.] *carried fat:* (TA:) or *became heavy with fatness.* (A.)

وَقْرٌ *A heaviness in the ear;* (Ṣ, A, Ḳ;) a

heaviness, or *dulness, of hearing*: (Mṣb, TA:) or *deafness; entire loss of hearing.* (Ḳ, TA.) See 1.

وِقْرٌ *A load*, (Ṣ, A, Mṣb, Ḳ,) *in a general sense*, (A, Ḳ, TA,) *whether heavy or light or moderate*, (TA,) *of a mule and of an ass and of a camel*; (Mṣb;) or *mostly of a mule and of an ass*; that of a camel being mostly termed وَسْقٌ: (Ṣ, TA:) or *a heavy load*: (A, Ḳ:) or *a weight that is carried upon the back or head*: (TA:) pl. أَوْقَارٌ. (A, Ḳ.) You say, جَآءَ يَحْمِلُ وِقْرَهُ *He came carrying his load* [&c.]. (Ṣ.)

وَقْرٌ, or وُقْرٌ: see وَقُورٌ.

مَوْقُورٌ: see أُذُنٌ وَقِرَةٌ.

وَقْرَى: see مُوقَرٌ.

وَقَارٌ *Gravity, staidness, steadiness, calmness*; syn. رَزَانَةٌ, (Ṣ, Mṣb, Ḳ,) and حِلْمٌ, (Ṣ, Mṣb,) and سَكِينَةٌ, and وَدَاعَةٌ; (L, TA;) and ▼ تَيْقُورٌ is syn. with وَقَارٌ [in this sense], (Ṣ, Ḳ,) of the measure فَيْعُولٌ, (Ḳ,) originally وَيْقُورٌ, (Ṣ,) the و being changed into ت: (Ṣ, Ḳ:) [see 1:] or, accord. to some, it is syn. with تَوْقِيرٌ. (TA.) El-'Ajjáj says,

فَإِنْ يَكُنْ أَمْسَى البِلَى تَيْقُورِى •

i. e. امسى وَقَارِى. [*And if wear*, or *waste, hath become* the cause of *my gravity*, &c.: or, if it be syn. with تَوْقِيرِى, the cause of *making me still*, or *quiet*]. (Ṣ, TA.) Some make it to be of the measure تَفْعُولٌ, like تَذْنُوبٌ, &c. (TA.) — Also, The *greatness*, or *majesty*, of God: as in the Ḳur. lxxi. 12. (Ṣ. [See 1, in art. رجو.]) — See also وَقُورٌ.

وَقُورٌ (Ṣ, A, Ḳ) and ▼ وَقَارٌ, and ▼ وَقْرٌ, (Ḳ,) or ▼ وُقْرٌ, (L,) and ▼ مُتَوَقِّرٌ, (TA,) *Grave; staid; sedate; calm*: applied to a man: (Ṣ, A, Ḳ, TA:) and the first applied also to a woman: (Ḳ:) pl. of the first, وُقُرٌ, (A, TA,) applied to men, (A,) and to women. (TA.)

وَقِيرٌ ‡ *Heavily burdened with debt.* (TA.) — أُذُنٌ وَقِيرَةٌ: see مَوْقُورٌ.

جَنَانٌ وَاقِرٌ ‡ *A heart which fright does not make to flutter.* (A.)

وَقَارٌ: see تَيْقُورٌ.

مُوقَرٌ [*Laden*;] *having a load*: or [*heavily laden*;] *having a heavy load*: [as also ▼ مَوْقُورٌ:] applied to a man: (Ḳ:) and also [the former] applied to a woman, in the same sense: (TA:) or you apply to a woman the epithet مُوقَرَةٌ, meaning, *bearing a heavy burden.* (Fr, Ṣ, TA.) You say also ▼ دَابَّةٌ وَقْرَى, meaning ▼ مَوْقُورَةٌ [*A beast of carriage laden*: or *heavily laden*]: (Ḳ:) but ISd holds that ▼ وَقْرَى is used elliptically, for ذَاتُ وَقْرَى, and is an inf. n., of the measure فَعْلَى, like حَلْقَى and عَقْرَى. (TA.) [▼ مُوقُورٌ, in the same sense, is also applied to a ship; as in the Expos. of the Jel, ii. 159.] — نَخْلَةٌ مُوقَرَةٌ, (Ṣ, A, Ḳ,) and ▼ مُوقِرَةٌ, (Ṣ, Ḳ,) and ▼ مُوقَرٌ, (Ṣ, A, Ḳ,) like as one says, إِمْرَأَةٌ حَامِلٌ, (Ṣ,) and مُوقِرٌ, which is anomalous, (Ṣ, Ḳ,) and ▼ مِيقَارٌ, (Ḳ,) and ▼ مَوْقُورَةٌ, (A,) and ▼ مُوقِرَةٌ, (Ḳ,) *A palm-tree laden*, or *heavily laden, with fruit*; (A, Ḳ;) *abounding in fruit*: (Ṣ:) pl. [of the first, second, third, and fourth,] مَوَاقِرُ, (Ṣ, Ḳ,) and [of ميقار and موقورة,] مَوَاقِيرُ. (A.) — See also وَقِيرٌ.

مُوقِرٌ, and with ة: see مُوقَرٌ.

مُوَقَّرٌ pass. part. n. of 2, q. v. — نَخْلَةٌ مُوَقَّرَةٌ: see مُوقَرٌ.

مَوْقُورٌ, and with ة: see مُوقَرٌ. ═ ‡ A man [*dull of hearing*: or *deaf*. (Ṣ.) And أُذُنٌ مَوْقُورَةٌ ‡ *An ear dull of hearing*: or *deaf*: (ISk, A, TA:) as also ▼ وَقِرَةٌ, (A,) or ▼ وَقِيرَةٌ. (TA.)

مِيقَارٌ: see مُوقَرٌ.

مُتَوَقِّرٌ: see وَقُورٌ.

وقص

1. وَقَصَ عُنُقَهُ, (Ks, Ṣ, Ḳ,) and الشَّىْءَ, (A'Obeyd, TA,) aor. يَقِصُ, (Ks, Ṣ, Ḳ,) inf. n. وَقْصٌ, (Ks, Ṣ, Mgh,) *He broke his neck*, (Ks, Ṣ, Mgh, Ḳ,) and *the thing.* (A'Obeyd, TA.) You say also, وَقَصَتْ بِهِ رَاحِلَتُهُ [*His riding-camel*, or *she-camel, broke its neck*]: (Ṣ, Ḳ:) like as you say, خُذْ بِالخِطَامِ and وَقَصْتَ الخِطَامَ: (Ṣ:) and خُذْ: وَقَصَتِ النَّاقَةُ بِرَاكِبِهَا *The she-camel threw her rider and broke his neck.* (Mṣb.) And وُقِصَ *He had his neck broken*; (Ṣ, Ḳ;) said of a man: (Ṣ:) [and also] said of a camel, signifying, *he became diseased in his back, and without motion*: and in like manner said of the neck, and of the back. (Khálid Ibn-Jembeh.) And وَقَصْتُ رَأْسَهُ *I pressed*, or *squeezed, his head*; sometimes meaning, *so as to break the neck.* (TA.) — [Hence,] وَقَصَ الدَّيْنُ عُنُقَهُ ‡ *Debt* [*oppressed him as though it*] *broke his neck.* (TA.) — [Hence also,] الفَرَسُ يَقِصُ الإِكَامَ ‡ *The horse bruises the hills*, or *rising grounds*: (Ṣ, Ḳ:) or *breaks the summits thereof*: (A:) and in like manner one says of a she-camel. (TA.) — You say also, الدَّابَّةُ تَذُبُّ بِذَنَبِهَا فَتَقِصُ عَنْهَا الذُّبَابَ ‡ *The beast of carriage beats off from her with her tail, and kills, the flies.* (TA.) ═ وَقَصَتِ العُنُقُ *The neck broke*: thus the verb is intrans. as well as trans.: (Ḳ:) or, accord. to Ks, one does not say this: (Ṣ:) i. e., one only says of the neck وُقِصَتْ, using the pass. form. (TA.) ═ وَقِصَ, (Ṣ, Ḳ,) aor. يَوْقَصُ, (Ṣ,) inf. n. وَقَصٌ, (Ṣ, A, Mgh, Ḳ,) *He* (a man, Ṣ) *was short in the neck.* (Ṣ, A, Mgh, Ḳ.)

2. وقص عَلَى نَارِهِ, (Ṣ, A,) inf. n. تَوْقِيصٌ, (TA,) *He threw fragments*, or *broken pieces, of sticks upon his fire*: (Ṣ,* A:) or *he broke in pieces sticks upon his fire.* (TA.)

4. اوقصهُ *He* (God) *made him to be short in the neck.* (Ṣ, Ḳ.)

5. توقّص ‡ *He went a pace between that called* العَنَقُ *and that called* الخَبَبُ; (Ḳ;) *falling short of the latter, but exceeding the former, and removing his legs as in the pace called* الخبب, *excepting that they were nearer to the ground, and throwing himself* [*forward*]: (AO:) or *he trod vehemently in going*, (Ḳ, TA,) *with short steps*, (TA,) *as though breaking what was beneath him*: (Ḳ, TA:) or *he* (a horse) *bounded* (Aṣ, Ṣ, A) *in his running*, (Aṣ,) *making short steps*, (Aṣ, Ṣ, A,) *as though breaking his steps.* (A.) You say, مَرَّ فُلَانٌ يَتَوَقَّصُ بِهِ فَرَسُهُ *Such a one passed along, his horse bounding, and making short steps, with him.* (Ṣ.)

6. تواقص *He made himself like*, or *imitated, him who is short in the neck*: (Ḳ:) said of a man. (TA.) Hence, تَوَاقَصَ عَلَى بُرْدَتِهِ كَىْ لَا تَسْقُطَ *He bent and shortened himself to hold on his* بُرْدَة *with his neck, that it might not fall.* (TA, from a trad.)

وَقْصٌ: see what next follows.

وَقَصٌ ‡ *Fragments*, or *broken pieces, of sticks, which are thrown upon*, (Ṣ,) or *into*, (Ḳ,) *a fire*: (Ṣ, Ḳ:) or *small pieces of fire-wood with which a fire is made to burn more vehemently*; (A, TA;) as also وَقَشٌ: so, says Aboo-Turáb, I heard Mubtekir say. (TA.) ═ Also, sing. of أَوْقَاصٌ, as used in relation to the [tax called صَدَقَة; signifying ‡ *What is between one* فَرِيضَة *and the next* فَرِيضَة: (Ṣ, Ḳ:) *as, for instance, when camels amount in number to five, one sheep or goat is to be given for them; and nothing is to be given for such as exceed that number until they amount to ten*: thus, what is between the five and the ten is termed وَقَصٌ: (Ṣ:) sometimes pronounced ▼ وَقْصٌ: (Mṣb:) and in like manner, شَنَقٌ: (Ṣ:) or (accord. to some of the learned, Ṣ) وقص *relates to bulls and cows particularly*, (Ṣ, Mgh, Mṣb,) or *to these and to sheep and goats*, (Mṣb,) and شنق [q.v.] to camels: (Ṣ, Mgh, Mṣb:) both signifying *what is between one* فريضة *and the next*: (Ṣ, Mgh, Mṣb:*) or, accord. to Aboo-'Amr, (Mgh, L,) i.e. Esh-Sheybánee, (L,) وَقَصٌ signifies *camels for which it is incumbent to give sheep or goats in payment of the* صَدَقَة, (Mgh, L,) *when the camels are between five and twenty in number*; (L;) but some disapprove of this: (Mgh, L:) accord. to

IB, it signifies *sheep* or *goats taken in payment of the* صَدَقَة *for camels.* (L.) — You also say, صَارُوا أَوْقَاصًا † *They became scattered,* or *dispersed:* and أَتَانَا أَوْقَاصٌ مِنْ بَنِى فُلَانٍ † *There came to us separate portions of the tribe of the sons of such a one:* (Ibn-'Abbád, Ḳ:*) اوقاص in these cases being a pl., [namely of وَقْصٌ,] like أَسْبَابٌ, pl. of سَبَبٌ. (TA.)

وَقِيصَةٌ : } see مَوْقُوصٌ.
وَاقِصَةٌ :

أَوْقَصُ A man (Ṣ, Mgh) *short in the neck;* (Ṣ, A, Mgh, Ḳ;) *naturally so:* (TA:) or *having the neck inclining and short:* (A'Obeyd, TA:) fem. وَقْصَآءُ. (A, TA.) — خُذْ أَوْقَصَ الطَّرِيقَيْنِ ‡ *Take thou the nearer of the two ways:* (Ibn-'Abbád, Ḳ:*) or *shorter thereof.* (A, TA.)

مَوْقُوصٌ A man (Ṣ) *having his neck broken:* (Ṣ, Ḳ:) and so مَوْقُوصُ العُنُقِ: (A:) the fem. is with ة: and ▼ واقصة occurs in the sense of مَوْقُوصَةٌ in a trad. of 'Alee, in which he is said to have given judgment in the case of the قَارِصَة and the قَامِصَة and the ▼ وَاقِصَة, that the price of blood, or fine for homicide, should be paid in thirds; these being three girls, who were playing together, and mounted, one upon another; and the lowest pinched the middle one, who thereupon leaped off, so that the uppermost fell, and her neck broke; wherefore he imposed a third of the fine for the killing of the uppermost upon the lowest, and the like upon the middle one, annulling the third of the uppermost because she aided against herself: (Mgh, TA, in art. قرص, and Mṣb,) here, [accord. to those who hold that وَقَصَ is trans. only,] ▼ واقصة is like رَاضِيَةٌ, in the phrase عِيشَةٌ رَاضِيَةٌ; (TA, in art. قرص and in the present art.;) and is used in the place of موقوصة for the sake of agreement in form with the two other epithets: (Mgh, in art. قرص, and Mṣb:) ▼ وَقِيصَةٌ, also, signifies *having her neck broken;* and its pl. is وَقَائِصُ. (Meyd, as in Freytag's Lex., excepting that the pl. is there written وَقَايِصُ.) You say also عُنُقٌ مَوْقُوصَةٌ *A broken neck.* (Mṣb.) And مَوْقُوصٌ is also applied to a camel, signifying, *Become diseased in his back, and without motion.* (Khálid Ibn-Jembeh.)

[وقع, &c.

See Supplement.]

وكأ

1: see 8.

3. واكأ عَلَى يَدَيْهِ *He leaned upon his hands,* or *arms.* Mohammad was seen to do so when he raised and extended his hands in supplication to God. (IAth.)

4. أَوْكَأَهُ, (Ṣ, Ḳ,) inf. n. إِيكَآءٌ, (Ṣ,) *He set up for him a thing upon which to recline* (مُتَّكَأ.) (Ṣ, Ḳ.) — أَتْكَأَهُ, (in which ت is substituted for و,) inf. n. إِتْكَآءٌ, *He propped him up by a cushion or other thing whereon to recline; made him recline upon a cushion &c.* (AZ, TA.) — طَعَنَهُ حَتَّى أَتْكَأَهُ, (A,) or ضَرَبَهُ فَأَتْكَأَهُ, originally أَوْكَأَهُ, (Ṣ,) ‡ *He smote him,* (A,) or *pierced him,* (Ṣ,) *so that he made him fall in a reclining posture:* (Ṣ, A, Ḳ:*) or, *so that he threw him down upon his left side.* (Ḳ.) — See 3.

5: see 8.

8. اِتَّكَأَ *He sat in a firm,* or *settled, manner:* and *he sat leaning upon one of his sides:* (Mṣb, in art. تكأ:) the vulgar know it only in the latter sense: but it signifies *he leaned, rested,* or *stayed, his back,* or *his side, against,* or *upon, a thing:* and *he leaned, rested,* or *stayed, himself in any manner, upon a thing.* (IAth, in Mṣb, art. وكأ.) — اِتَّكَأَ عَلَى شَىْءٍ, (Ṣ,) and ▼ توكّأ, (Ṣ, Ḳ,) and ▼ اوكأ; (Ḳ;) and ▼ تَكِئَ, [in which ت is substituted for و,] aor. يَتْكَأُ, inf. n. تُكْأَةٌ; (Lth;) and ▼ وَكَأَ; (CḲ;) *He leaned,* or *reclined, upon a thing; supported, propped,* or *stayed, himself upon it.* (Ḳ.) — اِتَّكَأَ *He reclined* upon a cushion, &c. (TA.) — اِتَّكَأَ *He made for him* [i.e., app., for himself,] *a thing upon which to lean,* or *recline:* (CḲ, and a MS. copy of the Ḳ:) or *he made him to be a thing upon which to lean,* or *recline.* (TA.) [The latter seems to be wrong, unless the verb be read أَتْكَأَ.] — اِتَّكَأْنَا عِنْدَ فُلَانٍ ‡ *We ate a repast with,* or *at the abode of, such a one.* (TA.) — اِتَّكَأَتْ (MF) and ▼ تَوَكَّأَتْ (Ḳ) *She* (a camel) *was taken with the pains of labour, and cried out.* (Ḳ.) Accord. to Lth, تَوَكُّؤُ النَّاقَةِ signifies تصلّقها عند مخاضها: (TA:) [but it is evident that the right reading is تصلّقها; and the sense agreeable with the above explanation].

تُكَأَةٌ (in which ت is substituted for و, TA) *A staff,* or *stick,* (Ḳ,) *upon which one leans in walking; a walking-stick:* (TA:) *that upon which one leans or reclines.* (Ṣ, Ḳ.) — *One who reclines much.* (Ṣ, Ḳ.) — ‡ A *heavy* person [app., *in disposition*]. (TA.)

مُتَّكِئٌ act. part. n. of 8. — لَا آكُلُ مُتَّكِئًا *I* (said Mohammad) *eat not sitting in a firm,* or *settled, posture, cross-legged,* or *in such other similar manner as is adapted for much eating:* for he used to eat sitting upon his hams, with his shanks erect, so as to be ready to rise. The meaning is not [only] "inclining on one side," as the vulgar among students imagine. (Ḳ.)

مُتَّكَأٌ *A place in which one reclines:* (Ṣ:) *a chamber,* or *sitting-room.* (Akh, Ṣ.) — *That upon which one leans,* or *reclines, in eating, drinking,* or *talking.* (Zj.) — ‡ *Food,* or *a repast:* so called because people used to recline when they sat to eat: but the Muslims are forbidden to do so. [See مُتَّكِئٌ.] It is said to have this last meaning in the Ḳur. xii. 31. (TA.)

وكب

1. وَكَبَ, aor. يَكِبُ, inf. n. وُكُوبٌ (Ḳ) and وَكَبَانٌ (Ṣ) and وَكْبٌ (CḲ), *He walked, went,* or *marched along, in a leisurely manner,* (Ṣ, Ḳ,) or, as in some copies of the Ṣ, *in a grave and leisurely manner.* (TA.) See مَوْكِبٌ. — وَكَبَ *He* (an antelope) *proceeded at a quick pace,* (IḲṭṭ,) [*and with long steps:* see وُكُوبٌ]. [Thus the verb bears two contr. significations.] Hence the word ▼ مَوْكِبٌ (IḲṭṭ) [as meaning "a certain mode, or manner, of walking, &c."]. — وَكَبَ, inf. n. وَكْبٌ, *He,* or *it, stood erect; became erected, set up, raised,* or *reared:* (Ṣ, Ḳ:) *he stood.* (Ḳ.) — وَكَبَ عَلَى الأَمْرِ, and ▼ وَاكَبَ, (in a copy of the Ṣ, واكب, which is also mentioned in the sense here following by IḲṭṭ and IM, as stated in the TA,) *He kept, attended,* or *applied himself, constantly, perseveringly,* or *assiduously, to the thing,* or *affair.* (Ṣ, Ḳ.) — وَكَبَ; and ▼ وكّب inf. n. تَوْكِيبٌ; *It* (a date) *became black when ripe:* (Ḳ:) or وَكَبَ signifies, as below, "it (the skin, or a garment,) was dirty, or filthy;" and ▼ وكّب, *it* (a grape) *became black:* (TA: where it is said that this distinction [excepting that the second verb relates to the grape rather than the date] is meant in the Ḳ; the passage presenting what is termed لَفٌّ وَنَشْرٌ مُرَتَّبٌ:) or the latter verb signifies *it* (a grape or a date) *showed some degree of blackness.* (Az.) See مُوَكِّبٌ. — وَكِبَ, aor. يَوْكَبُ, inf. n. وَكَبٌ, *It* (the skin, or a garment,) *was dirty,* or *filthy.* (TA.) See وَكَبٌ.

2. وكّب, inf. n. تَوْكِيبٌ, [app., *He pursued a middle* or *just, way with respect to the* صِرَار; which is a *cord, or a piece of rag, that is bound over a she-camel's udder, or teats, to prevent her young one from sucking her*]. (Ḳ: the inf. n. is explained by the words المُقَارَبَةُ فِى الصِّرَارِ: written in the TA الاصرار; to which is there added, with kesr.) — See 1.

3. واكبهم (inf. n. مُوَاكَبَةٌ, TA,) *He marched,* or *journeyed,* or *kept pace, with them;* syn. سَايَرَهُمْ: or *he hastened with them, and strove to be before them;* syn. بَادَرَهُمْ: (Ḳ:) or *he rode with them* (Ṣ, Ḳ) *in their* مَوْكِب [or *procession*]: (TA:) and also, *he contended with them in a race or the like.* (Ṣ.) — See 1.

4. اوكب *He* (a camel) *kept to the mode of walking, &c.,* or *kept with* [*the kind of procession, called*] *a* مَوْكِب. (ISk, Ṣ, Ḳ: [but accord. to the Ḳ, the latter is the meaning intended; or, as said in the TA, *he kept with the procession of riders or camels;* for which,

however, SM knows no authority.) — اوكب *He* (a bird) *rose to fly*; ex., اوكب ثُمَّ طَارَ *he rose to fly, and then flew*: (Er-Riyáshee:) or *prepared to fly*; (Ṣ, Ḳ:) or *flapped his wings while falling.* (Ḳ.) — اوكبه *He made him angry.* (Ḳ.)

وَكَبٌ The *blackness of dates*; (Ḳ;) or *of grapes, &c.*, (T,) *when they become ripe.* (Ḳ, T.) Generally used with reference to grapes. (TA.) — *Dirt*, or *filth*, (Ḳ,) upon the skin or upon a garment. (TA.)

ظَبْيَةٌ وَكُوبٌ also *An antelope that keeps to its herd.* (TA.) — ظَبْيَةٌ وَكُوبٌ *An antelope proceeding at a quick pace, with long steps*; syn. اَلَّتِى تُعْنِقُ فِى سَيْرِهَا: (Ṣ:) and in like manner ↓ نَاقَةٌ مُوَاكِبَةٌ *a she-camel that proceeds in that manner*: (Ṣ, Ḳ:) see وَكَبَ: or the latter signifies *a she-camel that journeys*, or *marches*, or *keeps pace, with the* مَوْكِب: (Ḳ:) *that does not lag behind the* [*company of*] *riders.* (A.)

وَكَّابٌ A man (TA) *grieving*, or *mourning, much; very sorrowful, sad*, or *unhappy.* (Ḳ.)

وَاكِبَةٌ *i.q.* قَائِمَةٌ [app. signifying The *leg* of a quadruped]: (Ṣ, Ḳ:) from وَكَبَ "he stood." (TA.)

مَوْكِبٌ *A certain mode*, or *manner, of walking, marching, proceeding*, or *journeying.* (Ṣ.) See 1. — *A company* [or *procession*] *of men, riding* or *walking* [or *marching by slow degrees*, or *gradually*; or *in a grave manner, and by slow degrees*, or *gradually*]: (Ḳ:) or *a party of people riding upon camels, for the sake of pomp*, or *parade*, (Ṣ, Ḳ,) or *to go forth to the gardens* or *the like for amusement*: (TA:) and in like manner, *a company of horsemen*, or *a cavalcade*: (Ṣ:) pl. مَوَاكِبُ. (TA.) — سَارَ سَيْرَ المَوْكِبِ *He walked, marched*, or *journeyed* [*in the manner*, or *at the rate, of a ceremonious procession*, or *by slow degrees*, or] *without hastening.* (TA, from a trad.)

مُوَكِّبٌ A date (or grape, TA,) *becoming black, when ripe*: (Ḳ:) or a grape or date *in which the least blackness appears.* (Az.) — Also An unripe date *that is pricked with a thorn in order that it may ripen.* (AḤn.)

مُوَاكِبَةٌ: see وَكُوبٌ.

مَوْكُوبٌ: see 1.

وكت

1. وَكَتَ, aor. يَكِتُ, (inf. n. وَكْتٌ, *He*, or *it, made a mark*, or *impression*, or *left a mark.* (Ḳ.) You say وَكَتَ شَيْئًا *He*, or *it, made a mark*, or *impression*, or *left a mark, upon a thing.* (TḲ.) — وَكَتَ, aor. يَكِتُ, inf. n. وَكْتٌ; and ↓ وكّت, inf. n. تَوْكِيتٌ; *He filled* (Ḳ) a قِرْبَة, (Lḥ,) or a cup, or the like, as also وَكَّتَ. (Fr.) — وَكَتَ, aor. يَكِتُ, inf. n. وَكْتٌ, *He walked*, or *went, with short steps.* (Sh, Ḳ.) — *He* (a beast of carriage) *raised and put down his feet quickly.* (L.) — وَكَتَ المَشْىَ, inf. n. وَكْتٌ and وَكَتَانٌ, *He went*, or *walked, with short steps, but in a heavy and ugly manner.* (L.) — ↓ وكّت فِى سَيْرِهِ He went with a particular kind of pace. (L, from Kr.) — وَكَتَ الكِتَابَ, inf. n. وَكْتٌ, *He pointed*, or *dotted, the book, writing*, or *letter.* (L.)

2. وَكَّتَتِ البُسْرَةُ inf. n. تَوْكِيتٌ, *The date became speckled, by reason of its ripening.* (Ṣ, M, Ḳ.) — See 1.

وَكْتٌ, (Nh, &c.,) or وَكْتَةٌ, (L,) *A mark*, (L,) or *a small mark*, (Nh,) in a thing, *resembling a speck* (نقطة), *of a different colour from the thing itself*: (Nh, L:) pl. of the latter [or rather coll. gen. n., of which the latter is the n. un.] وَكْتٌ. (L.) — وَكْتٌ *A little; not much, a little thing.* (Sh, Ḳ.) — وَكْتٌ and وَكْتَةٌ *A speck that appears in a date by reason of its ripening.* (TA.) — وَكْتَةٌ *A speck* (نُقْطَة) in a thing: (Ḳ:) or *what resembles a* نُقْطَة in a thing: (Ṣ:) *a red speck*, or *spot, in the white of the eye, which, if neglected, becomes a* وَدْقَة: (ISd:) or *a white speck*, or *spot, in the black of the eye*: (TA:) you say, فِى عَيْنِهِ وكتةٌ [*In his eye is a speck, &c.*]. (Ṣ.) — فِى قَلْبِى وَكْتَةٌ مِمَّا قُلْتَ ‡ *On my heart is a slight impression made by what thou saidst.* (A.)

وُكْتَةٌ *i.q.* فُرْضَةُ زَنْدٍ (Ḳ: in the CḲ, فَرْضَة) [app., The *notch in a wooden instrument for striking fire*; as understood by Golius: but accord. to the TA, the *notch*, or *the like, in the joint called* زند *of a camel*].

وَكِيتٌ The *act of calumniating*, or *slandering*, syn. سِعَايَةٌ and وِشَايَةٌ, (Ḳ,) to one possessed of command, or power. (TA.)

رَجُلٌ وَكَّاتٌ, mentioned by Kr; thought by ISd to be from وَكَتَ المَشْىَ; [and therefore to signify *A man who walks, or goes, with short steps, but in a heavy and ugly manner*]; because were it by the phrase mentioned by Kr [i.e. وكّت فى سيره] it would be مُوَكِّتٌ. (TA.)

وَاكِتٌ, in a camel, *i.q.* نَاكِتٌ. (Ḳ.)

مَوْكُوتٌ ‡ *Changed in colour* (كَمِدٌ) *by reason of anxiety, or grief*: (Ḳ:) or *changed in colour* (كَمِدٌ), *and full of malevolence, and of anxiety*, or *grief.* (TA.) — عَيْنٌ مَوْكُوتَةٌ *An eye in which is a* وَكْتَة. (A, &c.)

بُسْرَةٌ مُوَكِّتَةٌ, and مُوَكِّتٌ, (the latter on the authority of Seer, TA) *A date speckled*, or *becoming speckled, by reason of its ripening.* (T, M, Ḳ.) When it is speckled in the part next the stalk, it is called مُذَنِّبَةٌ. (TA.) See بُسْرٌ.

وكث

10. استوكث *He ate of what is called* وكاث: (Ḳ:) *he hastened, and ate somewhat of that which is called* وكاث, *thereby to attain the period of the morning-meal called* الغَدَآء. (L.)

وِكَاثٌ and وُكَاثٌ *Food, aliment*, or *nutriment*, (غِذَآءٌ: so in some copies of the Ḳ, and in the TA: in the CḲ, غَدَآءٌ, or *a morning meal*:) *that is prepared*, or *taken, in haste*, (يُسْتَعْجَلُ بِهِ,) [*before the morning-meal called* غَدَآء: see 10]. (Ḳ.)

وكح

10. استوكحت الفِرَاخُ *The young birds became big, bulky*, or *coarse.* (Ṣ, Ḳ.)

وُكَّحٌ *Big, bulky*, or *coarse*, young birds: (Ḳ:) after the manner of a rel. n., as though pl. of وَاكِحٌ, or وَكُوحٌ, since it cannot be pl. of مُسْتَوْكِحٌ. (TA.)

وكد

1. وَكَدَ, aor. يَكِدُ, inf. n. وُكُودٌ, *He remained, continued, stayed, abode*, or *dwelt*, (L, Ḳ,) بِمَكَانٍ *in a place.* (L.) — See 2. — وَكَدَ أَمْرًا, (L, Ḳ,*) aor. يَكِدُ, inf. n. وَكْدٌ, (L,) *He aimed at a thing; sought, endeavoured after*, or *pursued, it; desired it; intended it*, or *purposed it*; syn. قَصَدَ (L, Ḳ) and طَلَبَ. (L.) See also below. — وَكَدَ وَكْدَهُ *He directed his course to*, or *towards, him*, or *it*; or *he pursued his* (another's) *course*; syn. قَصَدَ قَصْدَهُ; (Ṣ, L, Ḳ;) *doing as he did.* (L.) — وَكَدَ أَمْرًا, aor. and inf n. as above, also signifies *He laboured at, and endeavoured after, a thing.* (L.) — وَكَدَ, (L, Ḳ,) aor. يَكِدُ, inf. n. وَكْدٌ, (L,) *i.q.* أَصَابَ *He*, or *it, did*, or *went, right; attained* an object; *hit, struck, smote, affected, hurt, befell; &c.*]. (L, Ḳ.)

2. وكّد, (Ṣ, L,) inf. n. تَوْكِيدٌ; (Ṣ, Ḳ;) [and ↓ وَكَدَ as is implied in the Ḳ, but app. by the unintentional omission of the word وَكَّدَ;] and ↓ اوكد, inf. n. إِيكَادٌ; (Ṣ, L;) *He made* a horse's saddle, (Ṣ, L,) and a camel's, (L, Ḳ,) *firm, fast*, or *strong*; or *bound* or *tied* it *firmly, fastly*, or *strongly*; (Ṣ, L, Ḳ;) as also أَكَّدَ and آكَدَ: but more chaste with و. (Ṣ, L, Ḳ.*) — Also, *He confirmed, ratified*, or *corroborated*, a compact, a contract, a covenant, or an engagement; as also اكّد (Ṣ, L, Ḳ) and آكد: but, in this sense also, more chaste with و; (Ṣ, L;) or in this sense more approved with

أ : (L :) and in like manner وكد *he confirmed* an oath : you say, إِذَا عَقَدْتَ فَأَكِّدْ وَإِذَا حَلَفْتَ فَوَكِّدْ *When thou makest a contract, ratify; and when thou swearest, confirm.*

4 : see 2. — أَوْكَدَتَاهُ يَدَاهُ *His arms,* or *hands, exercised him with work.* From a trad., relating to a seeker of knowledge. (L.)

5. توكّد الأَمْرُ and تأكّد signify the same, [*The thing,* or *affair, became confirmed, ratified,* or *corroborated*]. (Ṣ, L, Ḳ.*)

وَكْدٌ *Desire; purpose; intention; aim; endeavour.* (L, Ḳ.) See also 1.

وُكْدٌ *Work; labour; exertion; endeavour.* (L, Ḳ.) Ex. مَا زَالَ ذٰلِكَ وُكْدِى *That ceased not to be my work,* (L, Ḳ,) *and endeavour.* (L.)

وِكَادٌ *A rope with which cows are tied on the occasion of milking.* (Ṣ, L.) — Also وِكَادٌ and إِكَادٌ sings. of وَكَائِدُ [and أَكَائِدُ], (IDrd, L, Ḳ,) [pls. deviating from the constant course of speech in relation to the sings.; see art. أكد;] signifying, (i.e. the pls.,) *Thongs,* or *straps, with which one binds* (L, Ḳ) *a camel's,* or *horse's saddle* : (L :) or *the thongs,* or *straps, by which the* قَرَبُوس *is bound to the two side-boards of a horse's saddle;* (IDrd, L ;) as also ▼ مَيَاكِيدُ and تَآكِيدُ and ▼ تَوَكِيدُ ; (Ḳ ;) or these are called مياكيد, but not تواكيد : (L :) and it [مياكيد] is a pl. that has no [proper] sing. (TA.)

مُوَاكِدَةٌ A she-camel *that strives,* or *exerts herself, in her progress, course,* or *pace.* (Ḳ.)

تَوَكِيدُ and مَيَاكِيدُ : see وِكَادٌ.

مُتَوَكِّدٌ بِأَمْرٍ, (L,) or لِأَمْرٍ, (Ḳ,) *Standing ready,* or *prepared, for a thing,* or *an affair* (L, Ḳ.)

وكر

1. وَكَرَ, aor. يَكِرُ, inf. n. وَكْرٌ (Ṣ, Ḳ) and وُكُورٌ, (Ḳ,) *He* (a bird) *came to the* وَكْر [or *nest*] : (Ḳ :) or *entered his* وَكْر. (Ṣ.) — وَكَرَ, (Mgh, Mṣb,) aor. يَكِرُ, (Mṣb,) *He* (a bird) *took for himself,* or *made,* or *prepared,* (اِتَّخَذَ,) a وَكْر ; (Mgh, Mṣb ;) as also ▼ وكّر, (A, Mgh, Mṣb, TA,) inf n. تَوْكِيرٌ ; (TA ;) but the latter has an intensive signification; (Mṣb ;) and ▼ اِتَّكَرَ. (Ḳ.) أَوْكَرَ in this sense is a mistake. (Mgh.) — وَكَرَ, aor. يَكِرُ ; (Ḳ ;) or ▼ وكّر, (A, L, Mṣb,) inf. n. تَوْكِيرٌ ; (Fr, Ṣ, L ;) *He made,* or *prepared, the food called* وَكِيرَة ; (Fr, Ṣ, A, L, Mṣb ;) لَهُمْ *for them.* (L, Ḳ.)

2 : see 1, in two places. — See also وَكِيرَةٌ, in two places.

8 : see 1.

وَكْرٌ The *nest* (عُشّ) of a bird ; (AA, Ṣ, A, Mṣb, Ḳ ;) *wherever it is ; in a mountain* or *a tree ;* (AA, Ṣ, Mṣb ;) *and so if the bird is not in it ;* (M, A, Ḳ ;) as also ▼ وَكْرَةٌ : (Ḳ :) the *place in which a bird lays its eggs, and has,* or *hatches, its young ; being a hole in a wall,* or *in a tree :* (T, TA :) the *place into which the bird enters ;* as also وَكْنٌ : (Aṣ, TA :) [see also عُشّ and سَرْبٌ :] pl. (of pauc., TA :) أَوْكُرٌ (Ḳ) and أَوْكَارٌ, (Ṣ, A, Mṣb, Ḳ,) and (of mult., TA) وُكُورٌ (Ṣ, Ḳ) and وِكَارٌ (Mṣb) and وُكُرٌ. (Ḳ.) You say, بُيُوتٌ كَأَوْكَارِ الطَّيْرِ [*Houses like the nests of birds*]. (A.) — ‡ [*A house :* as in the following saying,] مَا دَارَ فِى فِكْرِى نُزُولُكَ فِى وَكْرِى ‡ *Thine alighting at my house was not revolved in my mind*]. (A.) See also وَكِيرَةٌ. — The فرض [q. v.] of a زَنْدَة. (A, in art. فرض.)

نَاقَةٌ وَكَرَى : see جَمَّازٌ.

وَكْرَةٌ : see وَكْرٌ. — See also وَكِيرَةٌ.

وَكْرَةٌ : }
وَكِيرٌ : } see وَكِيرَةٌ.

وَكِيرَةٌ *Food that is prepared on account of the completion of a building ;* (Ṣ,* Mṣb,* Ḳ ;) as also ▼ وَكِيرٌ and ▼ وَكْرَةٌ and ▼ وَكَرَةٌ : (Ḳ :) *food which a man prepares on the occasion of building his* وَكْر [or *house*], or *buying it,* (A, TA,) *and to which he invites* [*others*] : (TA :) accord. to Fr, [*food*] *prepared by a woman among the requisites for a bride or a traveller* (فِى الجَهَازِ) ; sometimes, he says, called تَوْكِيرٌ : which latter word also signifies the *act of feeding* [*with the food called* وَكِيرَة]. (TA.)

وكز

1. وَكَزَهُ, (Ṣ, Mṣb,) aor. يَكِزُهُ, (Mṣb,) inf. n. وَكْزٌ, (Mṣb, Ḳ,) *He struck,* or *beat him,* (Ṣ, Mṣb,) [with anything,] as, for ex., with a staff, or stick : (TA :) or it signifies, (Mṣb,) or signifies also (Ṣ) *he struck,* or *beat, him with his fist upon his chin :* (Ṣ, Mṣb :) or, accord. to Ks, *i. q.* لَكَمَهُ ; (Mṣb ;) [i. e.] *he struck,* or *beat, him with his fist.* (A, Ḳ.) — *He pushed,* or *impelled,* or *repelled, him.* (Ṣ, Mṣb, Ḳ.) — *He pierced him* (Ks, Ḳ,* TḲ) with a spear. (TḲ.) — *He goaded him.* (TA.) — *He broke* his nose. (T, TA.)

وَكْزَةٌ *A blow with the fist.* (A.)

وَكَّازٌ One *who strikes,* or *beats, much with his fist.* (A.)

مُتَوَكِّزٌ بِأَمْرٍ *Standing ready,* or *prepared,* for a thing, or an affair. (L, art. وكد.)

وكس

1. وَكَسَ, aor. يَكِسُ, inf. n. وَكْسٌ, *It* (a thing, Ṣ, Mṣb) *was,* or *became, defective,* or *deficient ; it fell short ; it diminished,* or *decreased.* (Ṣ, A, Mṣb, Ḳ.) It is said in a trad., (Ṣ, Mṣb,) of Ibn-Mes'ood, (TA,) لَهَا مَهْرُ مِثْلِهَا لَا وَكْسَ وَلَا شَطَطَ *She shall have the dowry of her like : there shall be no falling short nor exceeding :* (Ṣ, A,* Mṣb,* TA :) or *there shall be no diminishing nor exceeding of the limit.* (Mgh.) [For] وَكَسَهُ, aor. and inf. n. as above, signifies *He rendered it defective,* or *deficient ; diminished it,* or *decreased it ;* (A, Mgh, Mṣb, Ḳ ;) as also ▼ وكّسهُ, (TḲ,) inf. n. تَوْكِيسٌ. (Ḳ, TḲ.) — *He made him* (a man) *to suffer loss ;* syn. نَقَصَهُ ; (Ṣ, TA ; as also ▼ وكّسهُ inf. n. تَوْكِيسٌ : (Ḳ,* TA :) or *he cheated,* or *defrauded him.* (IḲṭṭ, TA.) You say, وُكِسَ فِى تِجَارَتِهِ, (Ṣ, A, Mṣb, Ḳ,) inf. n. وَكْسٌ, (TA,) *He suffered loss,* (Ṣ, A, Mṣb, TA,) or *diminution of the price,* (TA,) [*in his traffic,* or *merchandise ;* as also ▼ أُوكِسَ, (Ṣ, A, Mṣb, Ḳ,) inf. n. إِيكَاسٌ ; (TA ;) and so وَكَسَ, aor. (Ḳ) and inf. n. (TA) as above. (Ḳ, TA.)

2. وكّسهُ, inf. n. تَوْكِيسٌ : see 1, in two places. — Also, *He reproved,* or *blamed, him,* or *did so severely ;* or *with the utmost severity ;* or *he reproached,* or *upbraided him.* (AA, Ḳ.)

4. أَوْكَسَ, (A,) or أَوْكَسَ مَالُهُ, (Ibn-'Abbád, Ḳ,) *His property went away.* (Ibn-'Abbád, A, Ḳ.) — أُوكِسَ فِى تِجَارَتِهِ : see 1.

أَوْكَسُ [*More,* and *most, defective,* or *deficient : less,* and *least, in value*]. The saying respecting the division of a building, يُنْظَرُ إِلَى صَاحِبِ الأَوْكَسِ means, *One shall look to see which is he whose place is of the less,* or *least, value.* (Mgh.) — A man *having a small portion,* or *little good fortune :* (A :) or *a low,* an *ignoble,* or a *mean,* or *sordid,* man. (Ibn-'Abbád, Ḳ.)

[وكع, &c.

See Supplement.]

ولب

1. وَلَبَ, aor. يَلِبُ, inf. n. وُلُوبٌ, *He entered* (Ḳ) into a house or tent, or into a tract, or quarter, or the like. (TA.) — وَلَبَ *He hastened* (Ḳ) in entering. (TA.) — وَلَبَ إِلَيْكَ الشَّىْءُ, aor. يَلِبُ, inf. n. وُلُوبٌ, *The thing,* of whatever kind it was, *came to thee,* or *reached thee.* (A'Obeyd, Ṣ.) In the copies of the Ḳ, وَلَبَ الشَّىْءَ وَإِلَيْكَ ; accord. to which, the verb, in the sense of وَصَلَ, there assigned to it, is trans. both immediately and by means of إِلَى : but the correct reading is ولب اليك الشىء, as above. In an old, and generally correct, copy of the Tahdheeb el-Af'ál of IḲṭṭ, it is said that ولب اليك الشّرّ signifies *The evil reached thee :*

syn. تَوَصَّلَ. (TA.) — وَلَبَ, inf. n. وُلُوبٌ and وَلْبٌ, *It* (corn or the like) *germinated in offsets around the older plants.* (IKtt.) — وَلَبَ بنو فُلَانٍ *The sons of such a one multiplied,* or *increased.* (IKtt.)

وَالِبٌ, *Going into a thing; entering into it.* (Esh-Sheybánee, Ṣ.)

وَالِبَةٌ The *offsets of the corn and the like:* (Ḳ:) so called because they enter into the roots of the parent-plants: (TA:) or *corn* or *the like growing from the roots of that which has preceded it:* (Ṣ:) pl. أَوَالِبُ. (TA.) — وَالِبَةٌ The *offspring* of camels, (IAạr, Ṣ,) and of sheep or goats, (IAạr, Ḳ,) and of cows, (Ḳ,) and of a people. (IAạr.)

تَوْلَبٌ: see art. تلب. Accord. to Suh, the ت is substituted for و, and the word is derived from والبة, the "offsets of corn and the like:" and Ibn-'Osfoor and IKtt assert the same. (TA.)

ولت

1. وَلَتَهُ حَقَّهُ, aor. يَلِتُ, inf. n. وَلْتٌ; and ♦ اولتهُ; *He diminished unto him his due,* or *right;* [or *defrauded him of part thereof*]: (Ḳ:) as also لَاتَهُ, and أَلَتَهُ, or أَلَّتَهُ. (TA.)

4: see 1.

ولث

1. وَلَثَتْنَا السَّمَآءُ, [aor. تَلِثُ,] inf. n. وَلْثٌ, *The sky wetted us with a little rain.* (TA.) — وَلَثَهُ, aor. يَلِثُ, (Ṣ,) inf. n. وَلْثٌ, (Ṣ, Ḳ,) *He beat, struck,* or *smote, him,* (AA, Ṣ, Ḳ,) with a staff, or stick, (AA, Ṣ,) *a little:* (Aṣ:) or *he beat him,* or *struck him, without wounding him.* (Aboo-Murrah El-Kusheyree.) — وَلَثَ لَهُ عَقْدًا *He made with him a covenant, compact,* or *contract, that was unintentional,* or *not firmly concluded,* or *settled.* (Ṣ.) وَلَثَ لَهُمْ, [aor. يَلِثُ,] inf. n. وَلْثٌ, *He gave them,* or *granted them, somewhat of a covenant, compact,* or *contract.* (TA.) — وَلَثَ, [aor. يَلِثُ?] inf. n. وَلْثٌ, *He concluded a covenant, compact,* or *contract.* (TA.) — وَلَثَ لَهُ, aor. يَلِثُ, inf. n. وَلْثٌ, *He made to him a weak promise.* (TA.) — وَلَثَ, inf. n. وَلْثٌ, فُلَانٌ لَنَا مِنْ أَمْرِنَا, *Such a one appointed the manner of somewhat of our affair for us;* syn. وَجَّهَ. (TA.) — وَلَثَ لِمَمْلُوكِهِ عِتْقًا, [aor. يَلِثُ, inf. n. وَلْثٌ,] *He promised his slave manumission after his death, saying, Thou art free after my death.* (ISh.)

وَلْثٌ *A little* of rain: (Ṣ, Ḳ:) ex. أَصَابَنَا وَلْثٌ مِنْ مَطَرٍ *A little rain fell upon us.* (Ṣ.) — وَلْثُ السَّحَابِ *A little rain.* (TA.) — وَلْثٌ *A covenant, compact,* or *contract, between a people, that happens unintentionally,* مِنْ غَيْرِ قَصْدٍ: (Ṣ:) or, *not firmly concluded,* or *settled:* (Ṣ, Ḳ:) or *somewhat,* or *a little,* of a covenant, compact, or contract: ex., in a trad., لَوْلَا وَلْثٌ لَكَ مِنَ العَهْدِ لَضَرَبْتُ عُنُقَكَ *Were it not for somewhat,* or *a little, of a covenant granted to thee, I had beheaded thee:* (TA:) or the *remainder* [or *what remains unfulfilled*] *of a covenant &c.:* (T:) or *a covenant &c. firmly concluded,* or *settled.* (TA.) — وَلْثٌ *A little* of anything that is much in quantity. (IAạr.) — وَلْثٌ *What remains, of dough, in a platter.* (Ḳ.) — *What remains, of water, in a* مُشْقُر. (Ḳ.) — *What remains, of the beverage called* نَبِيذ, *in the vessel.* (Ḳ.) — وَلْثٌ *A weak promise.* (Ḳ [See 1. In the CḲ, and in a MS. copy of the Ḳ, for الوَعْدُ is put الوَغْدُ.]) — You also say لَهُمْ وَلْثٌ ضَعِيفٌ, and وَلْثٌ مُحْكَمٌ, [*A weak promise has been made to them, and a firm promise*]. (TA.) — وَلْثٌ *A vestige,* or *trace, of ophthalmia.* (Ḳ.) — لَمْ أَرَ مِنْهُ إِلَّا وَلْثَةً ♦ *I saw not, of him,* or *it, aught save a small vestige,* or *trace.* (A.) — وَلْثٌ i.q. تَوْجِيهٌ; i.e., The *saying to a slave* (مَمْلُوك), *Thou art free after my death.* (Ḳ.)

وَلْثَةٌ: see وَلْثٌ. — عِنْدِى وَلْثَةٌ مِنْ خَبَرٍ *I have a little news.* (TA.)

شَرٌّ وَالِثٌ *A lasting,* or *constant, evil.* (Ḳ.) — دَيْنٌ وَالِثٌ, an expression used by Ru-beh, (TA,) *A burdensome debt:* (Ḳ:) or *a lasting,* or *constant, debt:* (IAạr:) or, as some say, *a debt by which one constantly binds himself* (يَتَقَلَّدُهُ), *as he does by a contract.* (L.) Aṣ disapproves of the expression. (TA.)

ولج

1. وَلَجَ, aor. يَلِجُ, inf. n. وُلُوجٌ and لِجَةٌ; and ♦ إِتَّلَجَ; (Ṣ, Ḳ;) and ♦ تولّج; (L;) *He,* or *it, entered.* (Ṣ, Ḳ.) You say وَلَجَ البَيْتَ, and ♦ اتّلجه, and ♦ تولّجهُ, *He entered the house.* (L.) And وَلَجَ الشَّىْءُ فِى غَيْرِهِ *The thing entered into another thing.* (Mṣb.) As is said in the Ṣ and L, Sb says that وَلَجَ has for its inf. n. وُلُوجٌ, which is of one of the measures of the inf. ns. of intrans. verbs, because the meaning [of وَلَجْتُ البَيْتَ] is وَلَجْتُ فِيهِ: and it is said in the M, that Sb holds the intermediate particle to be dropped: but Mohammad Ibn-Yezeed holds the verb to be trans. without an intermediate particle. MF observes, that Sb's words appear to make ولج a trans. verb, which no one asserts it to be: that if he mean that it has as its complement a noun in the acc. case as an adverbial noun of place, it is like دَخَلْتُ and other intrans. verbs: but if he mean that it governs a simple objective complement, like ضَرَبْتُ زَيْدًا, his opinion is not correct. (TA.)

4. اولج, (Ṣ, Ḳ,) inf. n. إِيلَاجٌ; (Mṣb;) and ♦ إِتَّلَجَ, as in the CḲ and in several MS. copies of the Ḳ) or أَتْلَجَ, (as in the L, and all the copies of the Ḳ consulted by SM, in this art., and in art. تلج,) in which ت is substituted for و, and this is the correct reading; (TA;) *He,* or *it, caused to enter; introduced; inserted.* (Ṣ, Ḳ.) — The expression in the Ḳur. [xxii. 60; and other chapters,] يُولِجُ ٱللَّيْلَ فِى ٱلنَّهَارِ وَيُولِجُ ٱلنَّهَارَ فِى ٱللَّيْلِ signifies *He maketh the night,* by increasing it, *to enter into,* [or *encroach upon,*] *the day, and maketh the day,* in like manner, *to enter into,* [or *encroach upon,*] *the night:* (Jel:) or *He increaseth the night with a part of the day, by taking from the latter and adding to the former, and in like manner increaseth the day with a part of the night.* (Ṣ.) — [اولج is often used for اولج ذكره; and hence as meaning *Inivit.*]

5: see 1.

8: see 1 and 4.

رَجُلٌ خُرَجَةٌ وُلَجَةٌ, (Ṣ,) and خَرَّاجٌ وَلَّاجٌ ♦, and خُرُوجٌ وَلُوجٌ ♦, (TA,) *A man frequently going,* or *coming, out and in.* (S, TA.) [This is the primary meaning: for others see art. خرج.]

وَلَجَةٌ *A place,* (Ṣ,) or *a cavern, in which passengers shelter themselves from rain &c.:* pl. أَوْلَاجٌ and وَلَجٌ, (S, Ḳ,) [or rather the latter, which is omitted in the CḲ, is a coll. gen. n., of which ولجة is the n. un.] or وُلُجٌ. (L.) — Also, *A bend,* or *place of bending, of a valley:* (IAạr:) pl. as above. (Ḳ.)

وَلَّاجٌ and وَلُوجٌ: see وُلَجَةٌ.

وَلِيجَةٌ *Anything that is introduced,* or *inserted, into a thing, and that does not belong to it:* any such thing is termed a وليجة of a thing. (A'Obeyd.) — هُوَ وَلِيجَتُهُمْ *He is an adherent to them;* (Ḳ;) *one who has entered,* or *become introduced,* or *included, among them,*] *and not belonging to them.* (TA.) Pl. وَلَائِجُ. (TA.) — وَلِيجَةٌ † *A particular,* or *special, intimate, friend,* or *associate,* of a man; syn. خَاصَّةٌ (Ṣ, Ḳ) and بِطَانَةٌ (Ṣ) and دَخِيلَةٌ: (Ḳ:) by these syns. A'Obeyd explains it in the Ḳur. ix. 16: and it is applied to one and to more than one: (TA:) or *one whom a person takes to rely upon, or to place confidence in, not being of his family:* (Ḳ:) and so some explain the word in the verse above referred to: (TA:) or it there signifies *an intimate friend who is one of the polytheists.* (Fr.)

وَالِجَةٌ i.q. دُبَيْلَةٌ, (Ḳ,) i.e., *A certain disease in the belly.* (TA.) *A pain that attacks a man;* or *a pain in a man;* وَجَعٌ يَأْخُذُ الإِنْسَانَ, (so in two copies of the Ṣ, and in the L,) or وَجَعٌ فِى الإِنْسَانِ: (so in the TA and a MS. copy of the Ḳ:) or *a pain that attacks the teeth;*

or *a pain in the teeth*; وَجَعٌ يَأْخُذُ الأَسْنَانَ, (so in a copy of the Ṣ,) or وَجَعٌ فِى الأَسْنَانِ. (So in the CK.)

أَوْلَجُ [*More, or most, penetrating*]: applied to language or discourse. [TA, in art. جمع: see an ex. voce مُجْمَعٌ.]

تَوْلَجٌ The *hiding place of a wild beast*, (or *antelope*, TA,) *among trees*, (Ṣ, Ḳ,) *into which he enters* (اَلَّذِى يَلِجُ فِيهِ); like دَوْلَجٌ: the ت, says Sb, is substituted for و, and the word is of the measure فَوْعَلٌ; for تَفْعَلٌ is scarcely found in Arabic as the measure of a subst., whereas فَوْعَلٌ is frequent. (Ṣ.)

مَوْلِجٌ *A place of entrance; a place into which one enters*: (TA:) pl. مَوَالِجُ. (Ṣ.) [See its contr. مَخْرَجٌ.]

مُوَلَّجٌ A man *attacked by the disease called* وَالِجَة, or دُبَيْلَة. (Ḳ, TA.)

ولح

وَلِيحَةٌ *A* [*sack of the kind called*] غِرَارَة: (Ṣ, L, Ḳ:) or *such as is called a* جُوَالِق: or *a large and wide* جوالق: (L:) and *a date-basket of palm-leaves*; syn. جُلَّةٌ: (Ṣ, L, Ḳ:) and *a sack or the like forming one half of a beast's load, in which are carried perfumes and clothes* (بَزّ) *and the like*: (L:) n. un. of وَلِيحٌ, pl. وَلَائِحُ. (Ṣ, L, Ḳ.)

ولد

1. وَلَدَتْ, (Ṣ, Ḳ, &c.,) aor. تَلِدُ, (L, Ḳ, &c.,) inf. n. وِلَادَةٌ and وِلَادٌ (Ṣ, A, L, Mṣb, Ḳ) and وَلَادَةٌ and وَلَادٌ, but each is more common with kesr, (Mṣb,) and إِلَادَةٌ and مَوْلِدٌ (L, Ḳ) and لِدَةٌ, (Ḳ,) [and app. مِيلَادٌ, like مِقْدَارٌ, (see an ex. voce تِلَادٌ, in art. تلد,)] *She* (a woman, Ṣ, L, or mother, L, or any animal having an ear, as distinguished from one having merely an ear-hole, (Mṣb,) *brought forth* a child, or young one; or children, young, or offspring. (Mṣb.) — Also, وَلَدَ, (aor. as above, Mṣb,) *He begot* a child, or young one; &c. (Th, L, Mṣb, Ḳ.) — أَرْضُ البَلْقَآءِ تَلِدُ الزَّعْفَرَانَ ‡ [*The land of El-Balkà produces saffron*]. (A.) — اَللَّيَالِى حَبَالَى لَيْسَ يُدْرَى مَا يَلِدْنَ ‡ [*The nights are pregnant: it is not known what they will bring forth*]. (A.) — [لَمْ يَلِدْهُ occurs in a verse cited voce رُبَّ, for لَمْ يَلِدْهُ; like لَمْ أَجِدْ for لَمْ أَجِدْ.]

2. وَلَّدَهَا, inf. n. تَوْلِيدٌ, *He assisted her* [namely a woman, A, L, Mṣb, and a ewe or she-goat, Ṣ, A, L, Mṣb, or other animal, Mṣb) *in bringing forth; delivered her of her child or young one*: (Ṣ, L, Mṣb, Ḳ*:) *he acted as a midwife to her*. (L.) — وَلَّدَهَا أَوْلَادًا *He made her to be the mother of children*. (MA.) See 4. — وَلَّدَهُ, (inf. n. تَوْلِيدٌ, Ḳ,) *He reared him; educated him; brought him up*. The Christians (as Th says, T, L) have corrupted, in the Gospel, God's saying to Jesus, on whom be peace! أَنْتَ نَبِيِّى وَأَنَا وَلَّدْتُكَ [in the CK, erroneously, وَلَدْتُكَ,] *Thou art my prophet, and I reared thee*: altering it thus, انت بُنَيِّى وانا وَلَدْتُكَ [*Thou art my little son, and I begot thee*]; attributing to Him a son. (T,* L, Ḳ.*) — وَلَّدَ ‡ *He innovated*, or *originated*, language, and a story or the like. (A.) † [*It* (a thing) *generated, engendered, produced*, or *originated*, another thing.]

4. اولدت, (inf. n. إِيلَادٌ, Mṣb,) *She* (a woman, Ṣ, L, Mṣb, and a ewe or goat, L) *attained to the time of bringing forth; was about to bring forth*. (Ṣ, L, Mṣb, Ḳ.*) — اولد القَوْمُ *The people attained to the time of* [*their having*] *children*. (IḲṭṭ.) — اولد الجَارِيَةَ *He made the girl to be the mother of a child*. (MA.) See 2.

5. تولّد الشَّىْءُ مِنَ الشَّىْءِ, (Ṣ,) or عَنْ غَيْرِهِ, (Mṣb,) † *The thing became generated*, or *engendered*, or *produced; it originated; from the other thing*. (Mṣb.) — تولّدت العَصَبِيَّةُ بَيْنَهُمْ ‡ [*Party-spirit originated, or became engendered, among them*]. (A.)

6. توالدوا *They multiplied*, or *became numerous*, [*by propagation*,] *and begot one another*; (Ṣ, L;) as also ↓ اِتَّلَدُوا. (TA.)

8: see 6.

10. استولدها *He rendered her pregnant; got her with child*. اولدها in this sense is not of established authority; and some expressly disallow it. (Mṣb.)

وُلْدٌ: see وَلَدٌ.

وُلْدُ رَجُلٍ, and ↓ وِلْدُهُ, *A man's people, tribe*, or *family*. So, accord. to some, in the Ḳur. lxxi. 20. (T.) — See وَلَدٌ.

وِلْدٌ: see وُلْدٌ, and وَلَدٌ.

وَلَدٌ (of the measure فَعَلٌ in the sense of the measure مَفْعُولٌ, Mṣb) and ↓ وُلْدٌ (Ṣ, A, L, Mṣb, Ḳ) and ↓ وِلْدٌ (Ṣ, L, Ḳ) and ↓ وَلْدٌ, (Ḳ,) each used alike as sing. and pl., (Ṣ, M, A, L, Ḳ,) and masc. and fem., (M, L, Mṣb,) *A child, son, daughter, youngling*, or *young one*; and *children, sons, daughters, offspring, young*, or *younglings; of any kind*: [often applied to *an unborn child*, &c.; *a fœtus*:] (M, L, Mṣb:) pl. [of pauc.] of وَلَدٌ, (M, L, Mṣb, TA,) and of وُلْدٌ, (M, L,) أَوْلَادٌ; (M, L, Mṣb, Ḳ;) and [pl. of pauc. of وَلَدٌ] وِلْدَةٌ and إِلْدَةٌ: (M, L, Ḳ:) and pl. of وَلَدٌ, وُلْدٌ, (Ṣ, M, L, Mṣb, Ḳ,*) like as أُسْدٌ is pl. of أَسَدٌ, (Ṣ, L, Mṣb,) in the dial. of the tribe of Ḳeys, (T, Mṣb,) who make وُلْدٌ singular. (T.) — وَلَدُكَ ↓ مَنْ دَمَّى عَقِبَيْكَ, a proverb, (T, Ṣ, L; but in the Ṣ, عَقِبَيْكَ;) of the Benoo-Asad, (Ṣ, L,) *Thy son is he who made thy two heels to be smeared with blood*; (TA;) i.e., whom thou thyself broughtest forth; (Ḳ, TA;) he is thy son really; not he whom thou hast taken from another, and adopted. (TA.) — مَا أَدْرِى أَىُّ وَلَدِ الرَّجُلِ هُوَ *I know not what man he is*. (Ṣ, Ḳ.)

لِدَةٌ, in which the ة is a substitute for the و that is elided from the beginning, for it is from الوِلَادَة, (Ṣ, L,) or, accord. to some, it is from لَدَى, q.v., (TA,) applied to a male and to a female, (TA, voce تِرْبٌ,) *i.q.* تِرْبٌ; (Ṣ, L, Ḳ;) meaning *One born at the same time with another; coëtanean*, or *a contemporary in birth* (TA) of a man: (Ṣ, L:) dual لِدَانِ; (Ṣ, L;) [but لدة occurs in a dual sense in the Jm and O and Ḳ, voce صَوْغٌ, q.v.;] pl. لِدَاتٌ and لِدُونَ: (Ṣ, L, Ḳ:) AHei and other expositors of the Tes-heel say, that words like لدة have the latter form of pl. when they become proper names. (TA.) The dim. [of the pl.] is وُلَيْدَاتٌ and وُلَيْدُونَ, (Ḳ,) because the formation of a dim. restores a word to its original form; (TA;) not لُدَيَّاتٌ and لُدَيُّونَ, as some of the Arabs erroneously make it: (Ḳ:) but this which F pronounces an error is accordant to the authority of the leading writers on inflexion, who say that by regarding the original form, and restoring it thereto, the word is made to depart from the meaning intended by it; for if its dim. were made وُلَيْدٌ, there would be no difference between it and the dim. of وَلَدٌ. (TA.) See also art. لدى. — See مِيلَادٌ.

وِلَادٌ and وَلَادٌ: see 1. — *Pregnancy*: (A, L, in which the former only is mentioned, and Mṣb:) the former is the more common. (Mṣb.)

وَلُودٌ [*Prolific; that breeds*, or *brings forth, plentifully*.] (Ṣ, Ḳ, art. أبد.) — See وَالِدٌ.

وَلِيدٌ (of the measure فَعِيلٌ in the sense of the measure مَفْعُولٌ, TA,) and ↓ مَوْلُودٌ signify the same, (T, L, Ḳ,) i.e., *A new-born child*: (M, L:) *a young infant*: (the former in the L, and the latter in the Mṣb:) the former, as well as the latter, masc.: (M, L:) or, accord. to some, the former is applied also to a female: as also ↓ وَلِيدَةٌ and ↓ مَوْلُودَةٌ: pl. of وليد, وِلْدَانٌ; and of وليدة, وَلَائِدُ. (L.) — الوَلِيدُ فِى الجَنَّةِ *The child that dies in early infancy, or that is prematurely born, is in paradise*. (L, from a trad.) — Also وَلِيدٌ *A boy*: (Ṣ, A, L, Ḳ:) *a youth*: (AHeyth, L:) ‡ *a boy who has arrived at the age when he is fit for service, before he attains to puberty*: (A, L:) *a youthful servant*; one is so called from the time of his birth until he attains to manhood: the servant of a man in paradise is a وليد always, never changing in age: (L:) *a slave;* (Ṣ, L, Ḳ;) or, as some say, one *born in servitude:* (TA:) fem. in these senses, with ة: (Ṣ, A, L, Ḳ:) a female slave is called وليدة even if aged: (L:) pl. (of the masc., Ṣ, L) وِلْدَانٌ (Ṣ, L, Ḳ) and وِلْدَةٌ; (L;) and (of the fem., Ṣ, L) وَلَائِدُ. (Ṣ, L, Ḳ.) — See also مُوَلَّدٌ. — أُمُّ الوَلِيدِ *The domestic hen.* (Ḳ.) — هُمْ فِى أَمْرٍ لَا يُنَادَى وَلِيدُهُ (Ṣ, L, Ḳ*) [*They are in a case,* or *an affair, wherein* (lit. whereof) *the boy,* or *servant-boy,* or *slave, will not be called out to*]: a proverb, (L,) originally meaning, they are in a case of difficulty or distress, such that the mother forgets her child, and does not call out to him: and afterwards applied to any case of difficulty or distress: (M, L:) or they are in a formidable case, in which children are not called out to, but those advanced in age: (AO, or Aṣ, M, L:) and sometimes it means, they are in such a state of abundance and affluence that if a وليد put forth his hand to take a thing he is not chidden away from it: (M, L:) or it is applied to a case of good and to one of evil, and means, they are so occupied with their case or affair that if a وليد put forth his hand to the most valuable of things he is not called out to for the purpose of chiding him: (Ḳ:) some say, that its original reference is to the running of horses; because a fleet and excellent horse goes without being called out to; and that it is secondarily applied to any case of great moment, and to any case of abundance. (Ṣ, L.) — One also says, فِى الأَرْضِ عُشْبٌ لَا يُنَادَى وَلِيدُهُ [*In the land is fresh herbage respecting which the servant-boy,* or *slave, will not be called out to*]; because it matters not in what part of such land the beasts are; the whole abounding with herbage: and جَاوُوا بِطَعَامٍ لَا يُنَادَى وَلِيدُهُ [*They brought food respecting which the servant-boy,* or *slave, would not be called out to*]; meaning, that one would not care what injury he might do to it, nor when he ate of it. (ISk, L.) — Muzarrid Eth-Thaạlebee says,

تَبَرَّأْتُ مِنْ شَتْمِ الرِّجَالِ بِتَوْبَةٍ
إِلَى ٱللّٰهِ مِنِّى لَا يُنَادَى وَلِيدُهَا

[*I have become clear of the vice of reviling men, by my turning unto God with repentance respecting which the servant* (myself) *will not be called out to*]; meaning, respecting which I shall not be questioned. (ISk, L.)

وَلِيدَةٌ: see وَلِيدٌ.

وُلُودِيَّةٌ, (IAạr, L, Ḳ,) an inf. n. which has no verb, (Th, L,) and وَلُودِيَّةٌ (Ḳ) and وَلِيدِيَّةٌ, which, accord. to Th, is the original form, and ↑ وِلَادَةٌ, (L,) *Infancy:* (IAạr, L, Ḳ:) *boyhood; girlhood: the state of a* وَلِيد or وَلِيدَة. (L.) Ex. فَعَلَ ذٰلِكَ فِى وُلُودِيَّتِهِ, and وَلُودِيَّتِهِ, *He did that in his infancy:* (El-Baṣáïr:) and فِى وَلِيدِيَّتِهِ *when he was a* وَلِيد. (L.) — وُلُودِيَّةٌ (L, Ḳ) and وَلُودِيَّةٌ (L) *Rudeness; coarseness; hardness; churlishness; deficiency in gentleness,* (L, Ḳ,) *and in knowledge of affairs:* (L:) *illiterateness.* (L.)

صُحْبَةُ فُلَانٍ وَلَّادَةٌ لِلْخَيْرِ ‡ [*The society of such a one is very productive of good.*] (A.)

وَالِدٌ and وَالِدَةٌ, (M, L, Ḳ) the former as a possessive epithet, and the latter as an act. part. n. (M, L.) A woman, and any pregnant animal, *having a child* or *young one,* or *children* or *young;* and *bringing forth.* (Th, M, L.) — Also وَالِدٌ *A father:* (Ṣ, L, Mṣb:) and *a mother;* (L;) as also وَالِدَةٌ; (Ṣ, L, Mṣb;) [which latter is the more common in this sense:] pl. of the former, وَالِدُونَ; and of the latter, وَالِدَاتٌ: (Mṣb:) the dual وَالِدَانِ signifies the *two parents;* the *father and mother.* (Ṣ, L, Mṣb.) — شَاةٌ وَالِدٌ *A pregnant ewe or goat;* (ISk, Ṣ, A, L, Mṣb, Ḳ;*) as also وَالِدَةٌ and ↑ وَلُودٌ: (L, Ḳ:) pl. وُلْدٌ, (as in the L, and most other lexicons, accord. to the TA, and in some copies of the Ḳ,) or وُلَّدٌ, (as in the A, and in other copies of the Ḳ,) each of which is correct. (TA.) — Also, *A prolific ewe* or *goat; that breeds,* or *brings forth, plentifully;* (Nh, L;) [as also ↑ وَلُودٌ: see Ṣ, Ḳ, art. أبد: see also an ex. of وَلُودٌ, applied to a woman, voce أَسْوَأُ مِنْ شَرٍّ.] — وَالِدٍ وَمَا وَلَدَ, occurring in a trad. respecting prayer for God's protection, [lit., *From the evil of a parent and what he hath begotten,*] is said to mean Iblees and the devils: (L:) or Adam and the true friends and the prophets and the martyrs and the believers whom he hath begotten. (El-Baṣáïr.)

مَوْلِدٌ The *place of birth* (T, Ṣ, M, A, Mṣb) of a man. (Ṣ, L, &c.) — See also مِيلَادٌ.

مُوَلِّدٌ [A woman, and] a ewe or she-goat, (L,) *about to bring forth:* (L, Ḳ:*) pl. مَوَالِدُ and مَوَالِيدُ. (L, Ḳ.)

مِيلَادٌ The *time of birth* (T, Ṣ, M, A, L, Mṣb, Ḳ) of a man; (Ṣ, L, &c.;) as also ↑ مَوْلِدٌ, (T, M, A, L, Mṣb, Ḳ,) and ↑ لِدَةٌ: (Ḳ:) but this last is mentioned only in the Ḳ, and requires proof. (TA.) — [See also 1, of which it is app. an inf. n.]

مَوْلُودٌ: see وَلِيدٌ.

رَجُلٌ مُوَلَّدٌ, (Ṣ, L, Mṣb,) and عَرَبِيَّةٌ مُوَلَّدَةٌ, (Ṣ, L,) *A man,* and *an Arab female, not of mere Arabian extraction:* (Ṣ, L, Mṣb:) or مُوَلَّدٌ (L) and its fem. مُوَلَّدَةٌ (M, L, Ḳ) signify a boy, or slave-boy, (L,) and a girl, or slave-girl, (M, L,) *born among the Arabs;* (M, L, Ḳ;) as also ↑ وَلِيدٌ (M, L) and وَلِيدَةٌ: (M, L, Ḳ:) or a boy, or slave-boy, and a girl, or slave-girl, *who has been born among the Arabs, and has grown up with their children, and been educated, disciplined,* or *bred, in their manner:* (A, L:) or the latter, مولّدة, signifies one *born in a country in* [and of] *which is only her father* or *her mother:* (ISh, L:) or one *born at thine own abode,* or *home;* (ISh, T, Ṣ, in art. تلد;) like تِلَادٌ: (Ṣ, art. تلد:) or *born in the territory of the Muslims.* (Mgh, art. تلد.) — شَاعِرٌ مُوَلَّدٌ ‡ [*A post-classical poet;*] *a poet of the last of the four classes; of the class next after the* إِسْلَامِيُّونَ; *also called* مُحْدَثٌ: (Mz, 49th نوع:) called by the former appellation [as well as the latter] because of his recent age. (L, Ḳ.) [It is difficult to mark the exact line of distinction between the Islámees and the Muwellads, so as always to be certain to which of these two classes a poet belongs. The latter are those born, not merely since the first corruption of the Arabic language, which happened in, or before, the age of Mohammad, (see Mz, 44th نوع,) but since the extensive corruption which happened after the Arabs had spread themselves, by their conquests, among foreigners, in consequence of which their language became simplified. This change took place in the latter half of the first century of the Flight. Hence the poetry of the Muwelleds is not cited as authoritative in lexicology or grammar, or as to the metres of verse, or rhymes. (See شَاهِدٌ.)] Ibn-Rasheeḳ mentions, as the most famous of the Muwelleds, El-Ḥasan (surnamed Aboo-Nuwás) Ḥabeeb, El-Boḥturee, Ibn-Er-Roomee, Ibn-El-Moạtezz, and El-Mutanebbee: [the first of whom died in the year of the Flight 195, or -6, or -8]. Aboo-'Amr Ibn-El-'Alà [who died in the year of the Flight 154, or -9,] termed El-Farezdaḳ and Jereer Muwelleds, in comparison with the Pagan poets and the Mukhaḍrams, though others call them Islámees. (Mz, 49th نوع.) — كَلَامٌ مُوَلَّدٌ ‡ [*Post-classical,*] or *innovated,* or *modern,* or *modernized, language;* (L;) *language which is not of the original dialect of the Arabs;* (A;) *language which is not genuine Arabic.* (Mṣb.) And simply مُوَلَّدٌ ‡ [*A post-classical phrase* or *word;*] *a modernism; an innovated,* or *a modern,* or *modernized, phrase* or *word; a phrase* or *word innovated by any of the Muwelleds, whose phrases* or *words are not cited as authoritative* [*in lexicology,* or *grammar,* or *as to the metres of verse,* or *rhymes:* see above]: the difference between it and the مَصْنُوع is, that the latter is given by its author as chaste (فصيح) Arabic; whereas this is the contrary [i.e., confessedly innovated]. (Mz, 21st نوع.) It is opposed to

لُغَةٌ. The lexicons passim.) — Also مُوَلَّدٌ, (L,) and its fem. with ة, (K,) ‡ *Anything innovated.* (L, K.) — كِتَابٌ مُوَلَّدٌ : ‡ *A forged writing.* (L, K.) — بَيِّنَةٌ مُوَلَّدَةٌ ‡ *Evidence not verified.* (L, K.)

مُوَلِّدَةٌ *A midwife.* (A, L, K.)

[ولس, &c.

See Supplement.]

ومأ

1. وَمَأَ إِلَيْهِ, (S, K,) aor. يَمَأُ, inf. n. وَمْءٌ; (S;) and ↓ اومأ, (S, K, which is the chaste word, MF,) inf. n. إِيمَآءٌ; (TA;) and ↓ وَمَّأَ; (K;) *He made a sign to him.* (K.) أَوْمَيْتُ [for أَوْمَأْتُ] is disallowed: (S:) [but see what follows in this paragraph]. Lth says, that الإيماء is *the making a sign with the head* or *the hand, as a sick man does with his head for the inclination and prostration in prayer:* (TA:) and اومأ برأسه sometimes signifies *He* [*made a sign with his head as though he*] *said "No:"* Akh cites this verse:

* إِذَا قَلَّ مَالُ المَرْءِ قَلَّ صَدِيقُهُ *
* وَ أَوْمَتْ إِلَيْهِ بِالعُيُونِ الأَصَابِعُ *

[*When the man's wealth becomes little, his friends become few; and the fingers, together with the eyes, make signs to him*]; in which اومت is for اومأت. (TA.) — [For a further explanation of اومأ, and the manner in which it is said to differ from اوبأ, see art. وبأ.]

2. وَمَّأَ: see 1. — ومّى بِالشَّىْءِ [for وَمَّأَ: as there is no such root as ومى:] *He took away the thing.* (TA.)

3. فُلَانٌ يُوَامِئُ فُلَانًا, and يُوَائِمُ, [*Such a one agrees, or vies, with such a one*]. These two verbs are of two different dialects, or the former is formed by transposition from the latter. (K, TA.) — ISh quotes,

* فَأَنَا الغَدَاةَ مُوَامِئُهُ *

meaning, accord. to Abu-l-Khattáb, "And I, in the morning, shall see him, or it:" syn. مُعَايِنُهُ. (TA.)

4: see 1.

10. استومى عَلَى الأَمْرِ [for استومأ: as there is no such root as ومى:] *He made himself master of the thing:* like استولى. (Fr.)

وَامِئَةٌ *A misfortune; calamity:* (S, K:) thought by ISd to be a subst. [not an act. part. n.] because no verb from which it could be derived is known. (TA.) — وَقَعَ فِى وَامِئَةٍ *He fell into a misfortune* or *calamity.* (S.) — ذَهَبَ ثَوْبِى فَمَا أَدْرِى مَا كَانَتْ وَامِئَتُهُ *My garment is lost, and I know not what misfortune has taken it away:* (M, K:) or, *who has taken it.* (Yaakoob, S.) The phrase without negation is also used. (L.) [See a similar phrase in art. لمأ.]

ومت

شَىْءٌ مَوْمُوتٌ *A thing that is known, and decided, or determined;* syn. مَعْرُوفٌ مُقَدَّرٌ. (K.)

ومد

1. وَمِدَتِ اللَّيْلَةُ, (S, L, K,) aor. تَوْمَدُ, inf. n. وَمَدٌ, (L,) *The night was, or became, one of* وَمَد, i.e., *intense heat, &c.,* as explained below. (S, L, K.*) One also says وَمِدَ اليَوْمُ: but the former is more common. (M, L.) — وَمِدَ عَلَيْهِ, (S,* M, A, L, K*,) aor. يَوْمَدُ, (K,) inf. n. وَمَدٌ, (M, L, K,) ‡ *He was angry with him;* (S, M, A, L, K;) *was incensed against him;* i. q. وَبِدَ, (S, L,) of which it is a dial. form. (S.)

وَمَدٌ *Intenseness of the heat of night;* as also ↓ وَمَدَةٌ: (S, L, K:) or *intense heat:* (CK:) or *sultriness;* i.e., *intense heat with stillness of the wind:* (Ks, T, L, K:) or *heat of whatever kind with stillness of the wind:* (M, L:) or *dew,* or *moisture, that comes during the greatest heat,* (M, A, L, K,) *from the direction of the sea,* (M, L, K,) *with stillness of the wind:* (M, L:) or *a dew,* or *moisture, that comes from the direction of the sea, when its vapour rises and is blown by the east wind, so that it falls upon the bordering regions like the dew of heaven, very noxious to men by reason of its offensive smell:* (T, L:) and وَمَدَةٌ *a dew, or moisture, from the sea, falling upon men in the intenseness of heat, when the wind is still:* (L:) *it comes during the greatest heat, from the direction of the sea, and falls upon men in the night;* (Lth, T, L;) *and sometimes in the days of autumn also.* (T, L.)

لَيْلَةٌ وَمِدٌ: (L, K:) and ↓ وَمِدَةٌ, (T, M, A, L, K,) which latter is the more common, (TA,) *A night of* وَمَد, i.e., *intense heat, &c.,* as explained above. (T, M, A, L, K.) One also says يَوْمٌ وَمِدٌ: but not so commonly. (M, L.) — هُوَ عَلَيْهِ وَمِدٌ ‡ *He is angry with him.* (A.)

وَمَدَةٌ: see وَمَدٌ.

وَمِدَةٌ: see وَمِدٌ.

ومض

1: see 4.

4. اومض *It* (lightning) *flashed, gleamed,* or *shone, slightly,* (S, A, Msb, K,) *not extending sideways in the adjacent tracts of cloud;* (S, K;) for when it does thus, it is termed خَفْوٌ; and when it extends high in the sky, without extending sideways to the right and left, it is termed عَقِيقَةٌ: (S:) it is also said of other things, beside lightning: (M:) and ↓ وَمَضَ, (S, M, A, Msb, K,) aor. يَمِضُ, (S, Msb, K,) inf. n. وَمِيضٌ and وَمْضٌ (S, M, A, K) and وَمَضَانٌ (S, A, K) and تَوْمَاضٌ, (M,) signifies the same; (S, M, A, Msb, K;) or *it* (lightning) *flashed faintly* or *weakly, and then disappeared, and then flashed again;* (IAar;) and is also, sometimes, said of fire, (M, TA,) and of anything of a clear [or bright] colour: (El-'Eyn:) or both verbs signify *it* (lightning) *gleamed,* or *shone.* (Ham, p. 785.) — Hence, أَوْمَضَتِ المَرْأَةُ ‡ *The woman smiled, so as to display her teeth:* the glistening of her front teeth being likened to the flashing of lightning. (A, TA.) — And ‡ *The woman stole a glance,* or *glances;* (S, M, K;) as also اومضت بِعَيْنِهَا: (A:) or this last, † *the woman looked,* or *gazed with widely opened eyes.* (L.) — And اومض لَهُ بِعَيْنِهِ † *He made a sign to him with his eye:* (M:) or اومض فُلَانٌ ‡ *such a one made a private,* or *secret, sign,* (K, TA,) إِلَىَّ *to me.* (TA.) = Also, *He saw the slight flashing,* or *gleaming,* or *shining, of lightning,* or *of fire.* (M, TA.)

وَمْضَةٌ [*A slight flash of lightning, &c.*] You say, شِمْتُ وَمْضَةَ بَرْقٍ كَنَبْضَةِ عِرْقٍ [*I looked at a slight flash of lightning, like a single pulsation of an artery, to see whither it tended, and where it might rain*]. (A, TA.)

بَرْقٌ وَمِيضٌ i. q. ↓ وَامِضٌ [*Lightning flashing, gleaming,* or *shining, slightly;* &c.: وميض in this case being app. an inf. n. used as an epithet.] (TA.)

وَامِضٌ: see what next precedes.

[ومق, &c.

See Supplement.]

ونب

2. ونّبه, inf. n. تَوْنِيبٌ, *He reprehended, reproved, blamed, chid,* or *reproached, him severely;* &c.: (K:) a dial. form of أَنَّبَهُ. (TA.)

[ونى, &c.

See Supplement.]

وهب

1. وَهَبَ لَهُ شَيْئًا, (aor. يَهَبُ, K; said to be originally يَوْهِبُ; which is changed into يَهِبُ because of the kesr; and then, into يَهَبُ because of the medial guttural letter; Msb, voce وسع;) inf. n. وَهْبٌ and وَهَبٌ and هِبَةٌ (S, K) and مَوْهِبٌ and مَوْهِبَةٌ, (Msb,) or the last two are substs., (S, K, &c.) *He gave him a thing;* properly, *as a free gift, disinterestedly, and not for any compensation.* (Msb, TA.) You should not say وَهَبْتُكَهُ [*he gave it to thee*], (K, &c.,) making

the verb doubly trans.: (TA:) or [this is allowable, as it is said that] AA has related this on the authority of an Arab of the desert: so in the Ḳ: but in the L, it is said that Seer' has related this, from 'Amr, (meaning Sb,) from an Arab of the desert. (TA.) En-Nawawee allows the expression وَهَبْتُ كَذَا مِنْهُ, meaning, *I gave such a thing to him, &c.*; (من being redundant, as in بِعْتُ كَذَا مِنْهُ "I sold such a thing to him;") as occurring in several trads. (MF.) — See 3. — وَهَبَنِى ٱللّٰهُ فِدَاكَ *May God make me* [or *give me as*] *thy ransom!* (IAạr, Ḳ.) وُهِبْتُ فِدَاكَ *May I be made* [or *given as*] *thy ransom!* Ibn-Umm-Ḳásim says, that وهب is one of the verbs which signify *He caused to be*, or *to become*: and he cites the above phrase from IAạr; and adds, that the verb is only used in the pret. tense. Others assert it to be rare. (TA.) — هَبْنِى فَعَلْتُ ذٰلِكَ *Suppose me*; syn. ظُنَّنِى; (AḤei, cited by Fei;) or *count me*, or *reckon me*; syn. أَحْسِبْنِى وَٱعْدُدْنِى; (M, Ḳ;) [or *grant me*;] *to have done that.* (M, Ḳ.*) هَبْ زَيْدًا مُنْطَلِقًا *Suppose Zeyd to be going away*, or *gone away*; syn. إِحْسِبْ. (So in two copies of the Ṣ: in another, أَحْسِبْ.) Thus this verb is doubly trans.: (Ṣ:) but it is not used in this sense in the pret., nor in the aor.: (Ṣ, Ḳ:) you do not say وَهَبْتُكَ فَعَلْتَ ذٰلِكَ [*I supposed thee to have done that*]: nor (as some assert, Mṣb,) do you say هَبْ أَنِّى فَعَلْتُ, (TA,) as say the vulgar, though what the grammarians say, respecting the class of verbs to which ظَنَنْتُ belongs, that أَنَّ and إِنَّ [with what follows them] may supply the place of the two objective complements, [as when you say ظننت إِنَّ ظَنَنْتُ أَنَّ زَيْدًا قَائِمٌ, and زَيْدًا لَقَائِمٌ, "I thought Zeyd to be standing,"] affords matter for controverting this. (Mṣb.)

3. وَاهَبَهُ ▼ فَوَهَبَهُ, aor. of the latter verb يَهِبُ and يَهَبُ, *He strove to surpass him in giving, freely*, or *disinterestedly, and he surpassed him therein.* (Ḳ.) [The former of the above aors., accord. to general opinion, is irregular; and the latter, regular; because the first radical letter is و; as in the case of وَاعَدَهُ فَوَعَدَهُ, aor. يَعِدُ: or, accord. to the rule laid down by Ks, the reverse is perhaps the case, because the medial radical letter is a guttural. See Lumsden's Ar. Gram., p. 171.]

4. اوهب لَهُ ٱلشَّىْءَ *He prepared*, or *made ready, the thing for him.* (Ḳ.) — أَوْهَبْتُكَ ٱلطَّعَامَ وَٱلشَّرَابَ *I prepared*, or *made ready, for thee the food and beverage, and abundance of them.* (Tahdheeb el-Af'ál.) But see this verb in an intrans. sense. — أَوْهَبَ ٱلطَّعَامُ ‡ *The food*, or *corn*, or *the like, became abundant and ample, so that some of it was given away.* (A.) — أَوْهَبْتُ لِأَمْرِ كَذَا ‡ *I became capable of such a thing and able to do it.* (A.) — أَوْهَبَ لَكَ ٱلشَّىْءُ ‡ *The thing was*, or *became, within thy power*, or *reach, so that thou mightest take it.* (Ḳ.*) Related on the authority of IAạr alone, who says, They did not say أَوْهَبْتُهُ لَكَ. (TA.) — أَوْهَبَ لَهُ ٱلشَّىْءُ *The thing was lasting to him.* (A'Obeyd, AZ, Ṣ, Ḳ.) J cites the following verse:

* عَظِيمُ ٱلقَفَا رِخْوُ ٱلخَوَاصِرِ أَوْهَبَتْ *
* لَهُ عَجْوَةٌ مَسْمُونَةٌ وَخَمِيرُ *

[*Large in the back of the neck, soft* (or *loose* or *flabby*) *in the flanks: dates of the best that El-Medeeneh produces, prepared with clarified butter, and leaven, are lasting* (*provisions*) *to him*]. But 'Alee Ibn-Ḥamzeh says, that this is a mistake, and that the right reading is أُرْهِنَتْ, meaning "are prepared, and continued." So in a marginal note in a copy of the Ṣ. (TA.) [So too in the margin of one of my MS. copies of the Ṣ.]

6. تواهبوا *They gave gifts, one to another.* (Ṣ, Ḳ.) — فِيهِمِ ٱلتَّوَاهُبُ [*They have a habit of mutually giving gifts*]. (TA.) — تَوَاهَبَهُ ٱلنَّاسُ بَيْنَهُمْ [*The people gave it; one to another*]. (TA.) — وَلَا ٱلتَّوَاهُبُ فِيمَا بَيْنَهُمْ ضَعَةٌ [*Nor is their mutual giving of what is* (*possessed*) *among them* (*from fear of*) *humiliation*]: i. e., they do not give by constraint. (TA, from a trad.)

8. إِتَّهَبَ (originally إِوْتَهَبَ, TA,) *He accepted a* هِبَة, *or gift.* (Ṣ, Mṣb.) اتّهبه *He accepted it* [*as a gift*]. (Ḳ.) إِتَّهَبْتُ مِنْكَ دِرْهَمًا [*I accepted from thee a dirhem, as a gift*]. (L.)

10. استوهب, (Ṣ,) or استوهب هِبَةً, (Mṣb,) *He asked for a* هبة, *or gift.* (Ṣ, Mṣb.) — استوهبهُ خَادِمًا [*He asked him to give him a servant.*] (Ḳ, art. خدم.)

هِبَةٌ and ▼ مَوْهِبَةٌ *A gift* (or *thing bestowed*); properly, *one that is freely and disinterestedly given, not for any compensation*; *a free*, or *disinterested, gift.* (L.) [In the Ḳ, the latter is explained as signifying simply *a gift.*] Pl. of the former هِبَاتٌ; and of the latter, مَوَاهِبُ. (A, &c.) — [A هِبَة is of two kinds: هِبَةُ صَدَقَةٍ *A free gift, for no requital*, or *compensation*: and هِبَةُ ثَوَابٍ *A gift for a requital*, or *compensation.* This distinction is made in law, &c.]

هِبَةٌ i.q. أَهْبَةٌ q.v. (Ḳ, in art. اهب.)

وَهُوبٌ:
وَهَّابٌ and وَهَّابَةٌ: } see وَاهِبٌ.

وَاهِبٌ and ▼ وَهُوبٌ (Ḳ) and ▼ وَهَّابٌ and ▼ وَهَّابَةٌ (Ṣ, Ḳ) epithets from وَهَبَ, ["he gave, &c.": the first signifies *Giving*; properly, *as a free gift, disinterestedly, and not for any compensation*: or *one who gives*; *&c.*:] the others are intensive epithets, [as is said in the Ṣ of the third and fourth,] signifying *one who gives liberally*, or *bountifully*; *&c.*: and in this sense ▼ ٱلْوَهَّابُ is used as an epithet of God; or, accord. to the Nh, it signifies *He who dispenses his bounties universally and perpetually, freely*, or *without constraint, and disinterestedly, for no compensation.* The ة in ▼ وهّابة is added to give more force to the intensiveness; as in عَلَّامَةٌ. (TA.)

مَوْهِب and ▼ مَوْهِبَةٌ substs. of وَهَبَ ["he gave, &c.;" signifying *A gift* (or *act of giving*): properly, *that is free and disinterested, not for any compensation*; *a free*, or *disinterested, donation*]. (Ṣ, Ḳ, &c.) See 1.

مُوهَبٌ A thing, such as food, *prepared, ready, at one's hand.* (Ṣ.)

وَادٍ مُوهِبُ ٱلحَطَبِ ‡ *A valley abounding with fire-wood.* (A.) — أَصْبَحَ فُلَانٌ مُوهِبًا *Such a one became prepared*, or *ready*, (مُعَدًّا; so in an excellent copy of the Ṣ: in another copy, مُعِدًّا:) *and able.* (Ṣ.)

مَوْهِبَةٌ: see هِبَةٌ. — ‡ *A cloud falling* [*in rain*] *in any place*: (Ḳ:) pl. مَوَاهِبُ: you say كَثُرَتِ ٱلمواهِبُ فِى ٱلأَرْضِ *The rains became abundant in the land.* (TA.) — مَوْهَبَةٌ and ▼ مَوْهِبَةٌ ‡ *A small pool of water left by a torrent*: or the former only is the correct word, and the meaning of which, as explained in the Ṣ, is *a small hollow*, or *cavity, in a mountain, in which water stagnates*: pl. مَوَاهِبُ: and in the T it is said that *a small cavity*, or *hollow, in a rock*, is called مَوْهَبَةٌ, with fet-ḥ, being extr. [with respect to rule]. (TA.)

مَوْهَبَةٌ: see مَوْهِبٌ and مَوْهِبَةٌ.

مَوْهُوبٌ *A thing given*; properly, *as a free gift, &c.*: see the verb. (Mṣb.) — مَوْهُوبٌ لَهُ *Having a thing given to him*; properly, *as a free gift, &c.* (Mṣb.) — مَوْهُوبٌ *A son*; *a child*; *offspring*: and *whatever is given to one by the Liberal*, or *Bountiful, Giver*, i.e., *by God.* An epithet in which the character of a subst. is predominant. (TA.)

وهت

1. وَهَتَهُ, aor. يَهِتُ, inf. n. وَهْتٌ, *He trod*, or *stamped upon it vehemently.* (L.) — *He pressed, compressed*, or *pressed against, him*; or *it*; syn. ضَغَطَهُ. (L, Ḳ.)

4. اوهت *It* (flesh-meat) *became stinking*: (Ṣ, Ḳ:) dial. form of ايهت. (TA.)

وَهْتَةٌ *A depressed*, or *low, piece of ground*: (Ḳ:) pl. [or rather coll. gen. n. of which it is the n. un.] وَهْتٌ. (TA.)

وهث

1. وَهَثَ فِى شَىْءٍ, aor. يَهِثُ, inf. n. وَهْثٌ, *He was persevering*, or *assiduous, in the thing.* (Ḳ.) —— وَهَثَ شَيْئًا, aor. يَهِثُ, inf. n. وَهْثٌ, *He trod*, or *trampled, vehemently upon a thing.* (Ḳ.)

5. تَوَهَّثَ فِى الأَمْرِ *He went*, or *penetrated, far into the affair.* (M, Ḳ.)

وَاهِثٌ One *throwing himself into destruction.* (TA.)

وهج

1. وَهَجَتِ النَّارُ, aor. تَهِجُ, inf. n. وَهْجٌ and وَهَجَانٌ; (Ṣ, L, Ḳ;) and وَهِجَت, [app. a mistake for وَهُجَت,] aor. تَوْهَجُ, [inf. n. وَهَجٌ;] (L;) *The fire burned*; syn. اِتَّقَدَت; (Ṣ, Ḳ, &c.;) and so ▾ توهّجت; (L;) syn. توقّدت; (Ṣ, L, Ḳ;) [or this last has an intensive sense, and signifies, as does the first accord. to the A, *it burned fiercely; glowed*]. —— Also, all these verbs, with the same inf. ns., *It* (the sun) *burned*, or *was hot: and it* (a fire) *burned from a distance.* (L.) —— Also, all the above verbs, with the same inf. ns., ‡ *It* (a day, and a night,) *was violently hot.* (L.)

2: see 4.

4. اوهج *He kindled* a fire; *made* it *to burn*; syn. أَوْقَدَ: (Ṣ, Ḳ;) [or *made* it *to burn fiercely*, or *to glow*:] in the M, ▾ وهّج. (L.)

5. توهّج: see 1. —— ‡ *It* (the odour of perfume) *was hot*, or *strong*; syn. توقّد. (Ṣ, Ḳ.) —— ‡ *It* (a jewel) *shone; glistened; glowed.* (Ṣ, Ḳ.) —— ‡ *It* (a day) *was violently hot.* (A.) —— ‡ *It* (heat) *was violent.* (A.)

يَوْمٌ وَهِجٌ, and ▾ وَهْجَانٌ, and لَيْلَةٌ وَهِجَةٌ, and ▾ وَهْجَانَةٌ, ‡ *A violently hot day, and night.* (L.)

وَهْجٌ and ▾ وَهِيجٌ The *burning*, or *heat*, of fire. (Ṣ, Ḳ.) [See 1.] —— Also, The *diffusion* (in a neut. sense) *of the odour* of perfume; and the *hot*, or *strong, odour*, thereof. (L.) —— Also, the latter, The *shining, glistening*, or *glowing*, of a jewel. (L.)

وَهْجَانٌ and وَهْجَانَةٌ: see وَهِجٌ.

وَهِيجٌ: see وَهْجٌ.

نَجْمٌ وَهَّاجٌ [*A fiercely burning*, or *glowing, star*]. (TA.) سِرَاجٌ وَهَّاجٌ [*A fiercely burning*, or *glowing, lamp*: Ḳur. lxxviii. 13:] i.e., the sun. (TA.)

مُتَوَهِّجَةٌ, as an epithet applied to a woman, *Hot in the pudendum*; expl. by حَارَّةُ المَتَاعِ. (L.)

وهد

وَهْدٌ (L) and وَهْدَةٌ (Aṣ, Ṣ, A, L) *A low*, or *depressed, place*; (Aṣ, Ṣ, A L;) *as though it were a hollow*, or *cavity, dug*, or *excavated*, for which the latter is also a name: (L:) and both words, *low*, or *depressed, ground*: (L, Ḳ:) pl. أَوْهُدٌ, (L, Ḳ,) a pl. [of pauc.] of the former, (TA,) and وِهَادٌ (Ṣ, A, L, Ḳ) and وُهْدَانٌ, or وِهْدَانٌ, (as in different copies of the Ḳ, the former being the reading in the TA,) and وَهْدٌ of وَهْدَةٌ: (Ṣ, L:) [or rather this last is a coll. gen. n., of which وَهْدَةٌ is the n. un.:] also وَهْدَةٌ *a hollow*, or *cavity*, or *deep hollow* or *cavity*, (هُوَّةٌ,) *in the ground*; (L, Ḳ;) and so أَرْضٌ وَهْدَةٌ, and مَكَانٌ وَهْدٌ: (L:) and *a round hollow excavated in the ground, deeper than what is called* غَائِطٌ, *not having abrupt sides, in width two and three spear's lengths, and not producing any herbage.* (L.) —— Also وَهْدَةٌ The *hollow, in the ground, in which the weaver puts his legs*, or *feet.* (Mgh.) —— Also, *i.q.* خُنْعُبَةٌ, (IAạr, L,) which latter, says Lth, signifies The *part where the mustaches divide.*

[وهر &c.

See Supplement.]

ويب

وَيْبٌ a word like وَيْلٌ (Ṣ, Ḳ) and وَيْحٌ and وَيْسٌ: these four words agree in form and meaning, and have no fifth; although some of the lexicologists differ, in holding that some of them relate to what is good, and others to the falling into destruction. Accord. to what is said by Z, in the Fáïḳ, ويب and ويح and ويس denote compassion: but ويل is used in reviling, and imprecating destruction. (MF.) IḲṭṭ says, in the Tahdheeb el-Af'ál, that the invariable verbs are nine in number: نِعْمَ and بِئْسَ and لَيْسَ and عَسَى and the verb of wonder and وَيْحَ زَيْدٍ and وَيْبَهُ and وَيْلَهُ and وَيْسَهُ; but that El-Mázinee asserts the last four to be inf. ns. (TA.) You say وَيْبٌ لِزَيْدٍ, (Ṣ, Ḳ,) and وَيْبَكَ, and وَيْبٌ لَكَ, and وَيْبًا لَهُ, and وَيْبٌ لَهُ, (Ḳ,) with the three different vowel-terminations, both in addressing a person and in speaking of one who is absent, (TA,) and وَيْبَهُ, and وَيْبَ غَيْرِهِ, (Ḳ,) [and وَيْبَ غَيْرِكَ, (see below,)] and وَيْبَ زَيْدٍ, (Ṣ, Ḳ,) and وَيْبُ زَيْدٍ, (TA,) [and وَيْبَ زَيْدٍ, (see below,)] and وَيْبَ فُلَانٍ on the authority of IAạr, (Ḳ,) who adds, except the بنو اسد, who, it appears, from his saying this, give fet-ḥ to the ب: (TA:) the meaning of all which is, May God make *woe* (ويل) to cleave *to thee!* [and *—to Zeyd! &c.*: or *Woe to thee!* &c.: but see what is said above.] (Ṣ, Ḳ.) Dhu-l-Khiraḳ Eṭ-Ṭuhawee uses ويب in the sense of ويل, addressing to a wolf the ejaculation وَيْبَ غَيْرِكَ, [which is therefore the same in meaning as وَيْبَكَ]: (TA:) but accord. to what is said by Z, in the Fáïḳ, وَيْبَكَ and وَيْبٌ لَكَ &c. signify *Mercy on thee!* or the like. (MF.) When ويب is put in the acc. case, it is so put as an inf. n. (Ṣ.) This is the opinion generally obtaining: the opinion that وَيْبَ is a verb is extraordinary. (TA.) When you use the prep. لِ, you [generally say] وَيْبٌ لِزَيْدٍ (or وَيْبًا لِزَيْدٍ, L): when you use لِ, it is more elegant to put ويب in the nom. case, as an inchoative, than in the acc. case: but when you use ويب as a prefixed noun, with its complement, the acc. is more elegant than the nom. case: [i.e., it is more elegant to say وَيْبَ زَيْدٍ than وَيْبُ زَيْدٍ.] (Ṣ, L.) Ks says, Some of the Arabs say وَيْبَكَ and وَيْبَ غَيْرِكَ; and some of them say وَيْبًا لِهٰذَا الأَمْرِ, like وَيْلًا لِزَيْدٍ, وَيْبًا لِزَيْدٍ. (TA.) —— (Ḳ,* TA) *i.q.* عَجَبًا لَهُ, [*I*] *wonder at*, or *with respect to, this thing!* (Ḳ,) and so وَيْبَهُ. (TA.)

وَيْبَةٌ *A measure consisting of twenty-two*, or *twenty-four*, أَمْدَاد (pl. of مُدّ), which see in art. مد. (Ḳ.) Not mentioned by J nor by IF; and IDrd doubted respecting it. In truth it is a post-classical word, used by the people of Syria and Egypt and Africa Proper. (TA.) [At present, the ويبة in Cairo is the sixth part of an إِرْدَبّ, which latter is equivalent, very nearly, to five English bushels.]

ويح

وَيْحٌ a word denoting compassion, or pity: (AZ, Aṣ, Ṣ, Ḳ:) وَيْلٌ denotes [an imprecation of] punishment; (Ṣ;) or [of] removal from good, or from prosperity: (AZ, Aṣ:) or [of] destruction: (AZ:) and وَيْسٌ denotes the same as ويح; (AZ;) or less than ويح: (Aṣ:) or ويح and ويس denote compassion, or pity, and admiration of one's beauty; as when you say of a child, وَيْحَهُ مَا أَمْلَحَهُ, and ويسه ما املحه, [*Mercy on him!* or the like: *how beautiful is he!*] (Kh) or, accord. to most of the lexicologists, ويل is a word said to, or of, any one who falls into destruction or trial, or misfortune, and on whom one does not wish God's mercy: and ويح is said to, or of, any one who falls into trial or misfortune, and for whom one wishes God's mercy, and his escape therefrom: the former word being so used in the Ḳur-án, and the latter by the Prophet: (T:) or ويل is said to, or of, him who falls into destruction: and ويح is a word by which one chides him who is at the point of falling into destruction: (Sb:) or ويح and ويل are syn., (Yz, En-Naḍr, Ṣ, Ibn-El-Faraj,) and ويس signifies the same: (Ibn-El-Faraj:) or ويح is a little softer, or more gentle, than ويل: (En-Naḍr:) [if so, وَيْحَهُ signifies *woe to him*: in the same, or in a milder, manner than وَيْلَهُ:] or the original of

وَىْ is ويح; sometimes ح being added to this latter word, and sometimes ل, and sometimes ب, and sometimes س; (Ḳ;) so that it becomes ويح and ويل and ويب and ويس. (TA.) [See ويل and ويب and ويس and وى.] You say وَيْحٌ لِزَيْدٍ [*Mercy on Zeyd! or woe to Zeyd!*]; putting ويح in the nom. case as an inchoative; (Ṣ, Ḳ;) and in like manner, وَيْلٌ لِزَيْدٍ: (Ṣ:) and also وَيْحًا لِزَيْدٍ; putting ويح in the acc. case because of a verb understood; (Ṣ, Ḳ;) as though you said أَلْزَمَهُ ٱللّٰهُ وَيْحًا [*May God make mercy, or woe, to attend him constantly!*]; and in like manner, وَيْلًا لِزَيْدٍ: (Ṣ:) or [it is put in the acc. case as an absolute complement of a verb understood, i.e., as an inf. n., and] the meaning is أَتَرَحَّمُهُ تَرَحُّمًا. [*I say, May God have mercy on him! emphatically*]: (Z, in the Fáïḳ:) you also say وَيْحَكَ, and وَيْحَ زَيْدٍ; (Ṣ, Ḳ;) making ويح a prefixed n.; (Ṣ;) and putting it in the acc. case again because of a verb understood; (Ṣ, Ḳ;) and in like manner, وَيْلَكَ, and وَيْلَ زَيْدٍ: (Ṣ:) and also وَيْحَمَا زَيْدٍ in the same sense. (Ḳ.)

ويس

وَيْسٌ a word used to denote compassion, or pity, and admiration of one's beauty; (M, Ḳ;) the object being a child; (Ḳ;) as when one says of a child, وَيْسَهُ مَا أَمْلَحَهُ [*Mercy on him!* or the like: *how beautiful is he!*]: (TA:) or وَيْسٌ and وَيْحٌ are used in the place of وَيْلٌ; (TA;) and وَيْسٌ لَهُ signifies وَيْلٌ لَهُ [*Woe to him!*]: (M, TA:) or, as some say, وَيْسٌ is a word denoting contempt; and has no verb; analogy forbidding that it should have one: (IJ, M:) Aboo-Turáb says, I heard Abu-s-Semeyda' say, وَيْسٌ and وَيْحٌ and وَيْلٌ have one meaning: (TA:) or وَيْسَكَ is not said except to children; and وَيْلَكَ is an expression in which is roughness and reproach; and ويح is a gentle and good expression. (AHát, TA.) See وَيْحٌ and وَيْلٌ and وَيْبٌ. — It also signifies *Poverty*. (ISk, M.) And one may say, if it be right to say so to one, وَيْسٌ لَهُ as meaning *Poverty be to him.* (ISk.) — Also, *What a man desires.* (M, Ḳ.) So in the phrase لَقِىَ وَيْسًا *He found*, or *met with*, or *experienced*, *what he desired*; (M, Ḳ;) accord. to an explanation given by IAạr; so that it means *much*: but in one place he says that this phrase signifies *he found*, &c., *what he did not desire*. (M.)

[ويل &c.

See Supplement.]

ى

The twenty-eighth letter of the alphabet: called يَآءٌ. It is one of the letters termed *soft*, or *weak*, and is a letter of prolongation and of augmentation. As a numeral it signifies *Ten*. ═ ى for يا frequently occurs in the phrase يَرَسُولَ ٱللّٰهِ, and in يَأَيُّهَا. — ى inserted to give fulness of sound to kesreh, see art. ا. — Used لِلْإِنْكَارِ, see الف الاستنكار in art. ا. — ى with sheddeh followed by ة converts a part. n. into a quasi-inf. n., as ٱلْمَضْرُوبِيَّةُ, "the being beaten." So, by the relative ى, يَآءُ ٱلنِّسْبَةِ, substs. and even particles are converted into abstract nouns of quality, as إِسْمِيَّةٌ and كَيْفِيَّةٌ. ═ يَا is the most common of vocative particles, used in calling to him who is near; [like *O!*]; and to him who is distant; [like *Ho there! Holloa!*]; and to him who is between near and distant; [like *ho! what ho!*]; (Ibn-el-Kátib, in the Káfiyeh, cited in TA, art. أَيَا.) Pronounced with imáleh, see art. إِمَّا. — يَالَ for يَا آلَ, see ل. — يَايَا and يَايَهْ, see art. أَيَا.

يأ

R.Q. 1. يَأْيَأَهُ, inf. n. يَأْيَأَةٌ and يَأْيَآءٌ, [respecting the form of which latter see فَأْفَأَ,] *He made a show of kindness, benignity,* or *favour to him.* (Ḳ.) — إِنَّمَا هُوَ يَأْيَآءٌ [*It is only making a show of kindness, &c.*: or, perhaps, *He is only one who makes a show of kindness, &c.*]. (L.) ═ يَأْيَأَ بِٱلْقَوْمِ *He called the people*: (Ḳ: so too in the L, and this is the correct meaning: TA:) or *he said to the people* يَأْيَأْ, *in order that they should assemble,* or *collect together.* (Ḳ) — يَأْيَأَ بِٱلْإِبِلِ *He called to the camels by the cry* أَىْ, (whence the verb is formed by transposition, TA,) *to quiet them.* (Ḳ.)

يَأْيَآءٌ The *cry,* or *crying, of the bird called* يُؤْيُؤٌ. (Ḳ.) — [See also the verb.] — See art. أَيَا.

يُؤْيُؤٌ *A certain bird* (Ṣ, Ḳ) *of prey,* (Ṣ,) *resembling the* [*kind of hawk called*] بَاشَق: (Ṣ, Ḳ:) it is *of the birds called* صُقُور, [pl. of صَقْرٌ,] as are also the بَازِى and the شَاهِين and the زُرَّق and the بَاشَق: (AHát in TA, in art. بشق:) accord. to Dmr, it is *a small bird, short-tailed, the temperament of which is, in comparison with that of the* باشق, *cold and moist; for it is more patient,* or *enduring, and heavier in motion*: the people of Egypt and Syria, he adds, call it جَلَمْ, on account of the lightness and swiftness of its wings: (TA:) pl. يَآئِى, and, in a verse, يَآئِى. (Ṣ.) — Also, accord. to AA, The *head,* or *uppermost part, of a vessel in which* كُحْل (*collyrium*) *is kept*: mentioned before as called بُوبُؤٌ, which is perhaps a mistake for يُؤْيُؤٌ. (TA.)

يأس

1. يَئِسَ, (Ṣ, M, A, Mṣb, Ḳ,) مِنَ ٱلشَّىْءِ, (Ṣ, A*, Mṣb,) aor. يَيْأَسُ and يَيْئِسُ, (Ṣ, M, Mṣb, Ḳ,) the latter of which is extr., (Sb, Ṣ, M, Ḳ,) like يَحْسِبُ, aor. of حَسِبَ, and يَنْعِمُ, aor. of نَعِمَ, (Aṣ, Ṣ, TA,) and is of the dial. of the higher classes of Muḍar, as are also the similar instances, but the former is of the dial. of the lower classes of the Muḍar; (AZ, Ṣ, Mṣb, TA;) or, as Sb says, accord. to his companions, the verb was originally of two forms, يَئِسَ, aor. يَيْأَسُ, and يَأَسَ, aor. يَيْئِسُ, and a compound [which is يَئِسَ having يَيْئِسُ for its aor.] was then formed from the two; but as to وَمِقَ, aor. يَمِقُ, and وَفِقَ, aor. يَفِقُ, and وَرِمَ, aor. يَرِمُ, and وَلِىَ, aor. يَلِى, and وَثِقَ, aor. يَثِقُ, and وَرِثَ, aor. يَرِثُ, in each of these only one form is allowable, with the kesr; (Ṣ, TA;) and some change the second ى of the aor. of يَئِسَ into ا, and say يَايَسُ and يَآسَ; (Mbr, Ṣ, TA;) and I'Ab reads, in the Ḳur. xii. 87, يِيْأَسُ, after the manner of the dial. of those who pronounce the first letter of the aor. with kesr excepting such as is with ى [for its first letter], (Ḳ, TA,) which dial. is that of Temeem and Ḳeys and Hudheyl and Asad; (Ks, Lh, TA;) the case of ى being made an exception by them because kesr with that letter is difficult of pronunciation; (Sb, TA;) but some of the Benoo-Kelb pronounce ى also with kesr, which is extr.; (Fr, Lh, TA;) and this is done in the instances of يِيْأَسُ and يِيْجَلُ because one ى is here strengthened by another; (Ḳ, TA;) [I find also, in a copy of the M, يَيْئِسُ, as an extr. form of the aor. of this verb, on the authority of Sb; but it is doubtless a mistranscription for يِيْأَسُ; and there is another evident mistranscription in a quotation from Sb immediately following in that copy, relating to aors. of the form of يِيْأَسُ, which has been rendered correctly above, in the present work, from the TA;] inf. n. يَأْسٌ (Ṣ, M, A, Mṣb, Ḳ) and يَأَسٌ, (TA,) or يَآسٌ, (as in a copy of the M,) and يَآسَةٌ; (Ibn-'Abbád, M, Ḳ, TA [but in a MS. copy of the Ḳ I find it written يَأْسَةٌ; and in the CḲ, يَأَسَةٌ;]) and إِيَاسٌ is also used as an inf. n. of this verb, though properly an inf. n. of 4; (Mṣb;) *He despaired of the thing;* syn. of the inf. n. قُنُوط, (Ṣ, A, Ḳ,) contr. of رَجَآءٌ: (M, A, Ḳ:) or *he cut off hope of the thing*: (A, Ḳ:*) or *his hope of the thing became cut off*: (Mgh:) and ↓ إِسْتَيْأَسَ signifies the same, (Ṣ, A, Ḳ,) in like manner followed by مِنْ; (Ṣ;) and so does ↓ إِتَّأَسَ, (Ṣ, Ḳ,) [originally إِيتَأَسَ,] of the measure إِفْتَعَلَ, but with incorporation [of the ى into the ت]. (Ṣ.) It is allowable to transpose the letters of يَئِسَ, so as to say أَيِسَ; but not those of the inf. n. (Mṣb.) There is not a word in the Arabic language commencing with ى followed by ء except يَئِسَ [and its derivatives] (IḲṭṭ) [and يَأْيَأَ and its derivatives, and words commencing with an augmentative ى followed by a radical ء]. The expression لَا يَأْسَ مِنْ طُولٍ, occurring in a description of Moḥammad, means that his stature was such as would not make [one] to despair of his height; for he was nearer to tallness than he was to shortness: (Ḳ,* TA:) يَأْسَ is here an indeterminate noun governed in

the accus. case by the negative لا: (TA:) or, accord. to one relation, the words are, لَا يَائِسَ مِنْ طُولٍ, [in the CK, erroneously, لا يايِسَ,] meaning, that his height was not despaired of; i.e., he who vied with him in tallness would not despair of him on account of his excessive height: (K, TA:) so that يَائِس is here in the sense of مَيْؤُوس, like مَآءٌ دَافِقٌ in the sense of مَدْفُوقٌ. (TA.) — [Hence,] يَئِسَتِ المَرْأَةُ *The woman was*, or *became, barren.* (Msb.) — يَئِسَ, (S, M, A, Msb, K,) aor. يَيْأَسُ and يَيْئِسُ, (M,) also signifies ‡ *He knew*; syn. عَلِمَ; (S, M, A, Msb, K;) in the dial. of En-Nakha'; (S, Msb;) or, accord. to El-Kelbee, (M,) or Ibn-El-Kelbee, (TA,) in the dial. of Wahbeel, a tribe of En-Nakha'; or, accord. to El-Kásim Ibn-Maan, of the dial. of Hawázin. (M, TA.) So in the Kur. [xiii. 30] أَفَلَمْ يَيْأَسِ الَّذِينَ آمَنُوا [*Do not then those who have believed know?*]: (S, M, Msb, K:) or, accord. to some of the lexicologists, *do not then those who have believed know with a knowledge wherewith they despair of its being otherwise than what they know?* or the meaning is, *do not then those who have believed despair* of the belief of those whom God has described as those who will not believe? (M, TA;) but I'Ab (M, TA) and 'Alee and others (TA) used to read أَفَلَمْ يَتَبَيَّنِ الَّذِينَ آمَنُوا; and I'Ab said that he thought that the writer had written يَيْأَسْ in a state of drowsiness. (M*, TA.) Soheym Ibn-Wetheel El-Yarboo'ee also uses the verb in this sense, in a verse cited in art. يسر, voce يَسَرَ, q.v. (S, M*). [Z says,] You say, قَدْ يَئِسْتُ أَنَّكَ رَجُلُ صِدْقٍ, meaning, ‡ *I have known* [*that thou art a good man*], because with eager desire is restlessness, and with the cessation thereof is quiet and tranquility; wherefore it is said, اليَأْسُ أَحَدُ الرَّاحَتَيْنِ [*Despair is one of the two states of rest.*] (A, TA.)

4. أَيْأَسَهُ, (S, M, A, Mgh, K,) inf. n. إِيَاسٌ, (L, Mgh, Msb,) of the same measure as كِتَابٌ, (Msb,) originally إِيْآسٌ, (L, Msb,) like إِيْعَاسٌ, (L,) and إِيمَانٌ, (Msb,) *He made him to despair*: (S, M, A, K:) or *to cut off hope*: (A:) or *to cease to have hope*: (Mgh:) مِنْ كَذَا of such a thing: (S:) as also ▼ آيَسَهُ [from أَيِسَ]. (Mgh, K.) — [Hence,] أَيْأَسَهَا اللّٰهُ *God made her to be,* or *become, barren.* (Msb.)

6: } 10: } see 1.

يَأْسٌ *Phthisis,* or *consumption*; syn. سُلٌّ; (M, K;) because he who is affected by it is despaired of; (M;) or [because] the first who was affected by it was اليَأْسُ, (K, TA,) or إِلْيَاسُ, (TA,) the son of Mudar the son of Nizár: (K, TA:) or, as Suh says, in the R, this disease was called دَآءُ اليَأْسِ, or دَآءُ يَاسٍ, because الياس the son of Mudar died of it. (TA.)

يَؤُسٌ: } يَؤُوسٌ: } see يَائِسٌ. يَئِسٌ: }

يَائِسٌ (M, Mgh, Msb) and ▼ يَئِسٌ (M) and ▼ يَؤُوسٌ (S, M, A, K) and ▼ يَؤُسٌ (M, K) *Despairing*: (S, M, A, Mgh, K:) but the third has an intensive signification, (Bd, xli. 49,) [and so the last.]

يَائِسَةٌ, *A barren* woman. (Msb.)

مَيْؤُوسٌ مِنْهُ *Despaired of.* (M, Mgh, Msb.*)

يب

2. خَرَّبُوهُ وَيَبَّبُوهُ [*They rendered it waste, and made it desolate*: see يَبَابٌ]. (A.)

يَبَابٌ *Vacant; in which there is nothing*; (Sh;) *in which there is no one.* (T.) أَرْضٌ يبابٌ *A land that is in a state of ruin,* or *waste, uninhabited, depopulated, deserted, desolate, in a state the contrary of flourishing*: (S, K:) *an uninhabited land,* accord. to some. (Msb.) خَرَابٌ يبابٌ: in this case, the latter word is merely an imitative sequent to the former: (Sh, Msb:) or it is not so; (S;) [and therefore the meaning is *A very desolate waste,* or *the like*; يباب being added to strengthen the signification of خراب: or merely *a waste,* or *the like*; يباب being an explicative adjunct]. دَارُهُمْ خَرَابٌ يَبَابٌ لَا حَارِسَ وَلَا بَابَ [*Their dwelling is desolate, vacant; there is (to it) neither guard nor door*]. (A.) حَوْضٌ يبابٌ *A tank,* or *cistern, that is empty; containing no water.* (A.) أَمْسَى مِنَ الأَنِيسِ يبابًا *It became devoid of inhabitants*: occurring in a verse of Ibn-Abee-Rabee'ah. (TA.)

يبس

1. يَبِسَ, aor. يَيْبَسُ (S, M, A, Msb, K) and يَابَسُ (K) and يَيْبِسُ, (S, M, Msb, K,) which latter is extr., (S, M, K,) so that it is like يَئِسَ, (TA,) inf. n. يُبْسٌ (S, M, Msb*) and يَبْسٌ (M, Msb,* TA) and يُبْسٌ (M) and يُبُوسَةٌ, (K [but not there said to be an inf. n., being only mentioned there in an explanation of the word يُبْسٌ, and accord. to general rule it would be an inf. n. of يَبُسَ, which is probably an obsolete form,]) *It was,* or *became, dry*; or *it dried,* or *dried up; after having been moist, humid, succulent,* or *the like*: (A, Msb, K:) or, [rather,] *it was,* or *became, dry*; or *it dried,* or *dried up*: and also, [but perhaps tropically,] *it was,* or *became, stiff, rigid, tough, firm, resisting pressure,* or *hard*: [*contr. of* رَطُبَ:] يُبْسٌ signifying the *contr. of* رُطُوبَة: (M:) يُبُوسَةٌ *is a quality which necessarily implies difficulty of assuming form and of becoming separated and of becoming united*: (KT:) and ▼ اِتَّبَسَ, (S, M, K,) of the measure اِفْتَعَلَ, (S,) the ى being changed into ت, (M,) as well as [its original form] اِيْتَبَسَ, (TA [there written اتّبس because it has the conjunction وَ prefixed to it]) aor. [of the former] يَتَّبِسُ and [of the latter] يَاتَبِسُ, (M,) signifies the same as يَبِسَ: (M, K:) or is quasi-pass. of ▼ يَبَّسَهُ [and therefore signifies *it became dried,* or *dried up*; &c.]; (Ibn-Es-Sarráj, S;) [as also ▼ تَيَبَّسَ, occurring in the TA, art. عكس.] You say, يَبِسَ النَّبَاتُ [*The plant,* or *herbage, became dry*; &c.] (S, K.) And يَبِسَتِ الأَرْضُ *The land lost its water and moisture; its water and moisture went away.* (M.) — [Hence, يَبِسَ طَبِيعَتُهُ † *He became costive.* And] يَبِسَ مَا بَيْنَهُمَا ‡ [*That* friendship *which was between them two became withered*; (see 2, and see also ثَرًى;) i.e.,] *they became disunited, each from the other; the bond of friendship that united them, each to the other, became severed*; syn. تَقَاطَعَا. (A, TA.) — Hence also, (M,) ▼ اِيبَسْ, (so in a copy of the M [agreeably with an explanation of its part. n. يَابِسٌ, q.v., and in a copy of the A written اِيْبَسْ,]) or أَيْبِسْ, [from أَيْبَسَ,] like أَكْرِمْ, (K,) ‡ *Be thou silent*; or *cease thou from speaking*: (M, A, K:) said to a man. (M.)

2. يَبَّسَهُ, (S, A, K;) inf. n. تَيْبِيسٌ, (S,) *He dried it; made it dry*; [&c.; see 1;] (S, A, K;) as also ▼ أَيْبَسَهُ. (M, A, K.) — [Hence the saying,] أُعِيذُكَ بِاللّٰهِ أَنْ تُيَبِّسَ رَحِمًا مَبْلُولَةً ‡ [*I pray that thou mayest be preserved by God from thy withering a freshened tie of relationship*]. (A, TA.) And لَا تُوبِسِ الثَّرَى بَيْنِي وَبَيْنَكَ ‡ [*Wither not the fresh and vigorous friendship, between me and thee*; i.e., *sever not thou the firm bond of friendship that unites me and thee*: see ثَرًى; and see also يَبِسَ مَا بَيْنَهُمَا]. (A, TA.)

3. يَابَسَهُ † *He treated him with dryness and hardness,* or *niggardliness*; syn. قَاسَحَهُ; (L, K, art. قسح;) i.e. عامله باليبس والشدّة. (TK, in that art.) [See يَابِسٌ.]

4. ايبست الأَرْضُ *The land had its plants* or *herbage,* (A,) or *its leguminous plants,* (Yaakoob, S, K,) *drying up,* or *dried up*: (Yaakoob, S, A, K:) or *became abundant in its dry plants* or *herbage.* (M.) — ايبست النَّاقَةُ *The she-camel became milkless.* (TA, voce وَجَبَتْ.) — ايبس القَوْمُ *The people journeyed in the land*: (K:) or *in the dry land*; (TA;) like as you say أَجْرَزُوا from الأَرْضُ الجُرُزُ. (S, TA.) — أَيْبِسْ: see 1, last signification. — ايبسهُ: see 2, in two places.

5: see 1.

8. يَاتَبِسَ and اِيتَبَسَ, aor. يَتَّبِسُ and اِتَّبَسَ: see 1.

يَبْسٌ: see 1: — and see يَابِسٌ, throughout.

يُبْسٌ: see 1: — and see يَابِسٌ, in two places.

يَبَسٌ: see 1: — and see يَابِسٌ, throughout.

يَبِسٌ: see يَابِسٌ.

يَبَاسٌ: see يَابِسٌ — يَبَاسِ, like قَطَامِ, [as a proper name,] *The pudendum*; syn. السَّوْءَةُ: or *the anus*; syn. الفُنْدُورَةُ; (Ḳ, TA [in one copy of the Ḳ, الفُنْدُورَةُ; and in the CḲ, القَنْدَوْرَةُ;]) i.e., الاِسْتُ: on the authority of IAạr. (TA.)

يَبُوسٌ: } see يَابِسٌ; for the latter, throughout.
يَبِيسٌ:

يَابِسٌ *Dry, or dried up, after having been moist, humid, succulent, or the like*: (A, Mṣb, Ḳ:) or, [rather,] *dry*, or *dried up*, or *exsiccated*: and also, [but perhaps tropically,] *stiff, rigid, tough, firm, resisting pressure*, or *hard*: [see 1:] (M:) pl. يُبْسٌ (M) and ▼ يَبْسٌ, which latter is like رَكْبٌ as pl. of رَاكِبٌ: (ISk, Ṣ, Mṣb:) and ▼ يُبْسٌ is a dial. form of يَبْسٌ: (A'Obeyd, Ṣ:) or يَبْسٌ is [rather] a quasi-pl. of يَابِسٌ, as is also ▼ يَبَسٌ: (M:) or this last is used by poetic license for يَبْسٌ: (TA:) also, (Ṣ, M,) ▼ يَبْسٌ signifies the same as يَابِسٌ, (Ṣ, M, Mṣb, Ḳ,) as also ▼ يُبْسٌ, (M,) and ▼ يَبِسٌ, (M, Ḳ,) and ▼ يَبِيسٌ, (Ḳ,) and ▼ يَبُوسٌ, (M,) and ▼ يَبَاسٌ, (TA,) and ▼ أَيْبَسُ: (Ḳ:) or ▼ يَبْسٌ signifies *dry from its origin, not having been known moist*: (Ḳ:) but ▼ يَبَسٌ is applied to a thing *dry after having been known to be moist*: (TA:) and as to the path of Moses, [to which the former of the last two epithets is applied in the Ḳur. xx. 79,] it had never been known as a path either moist or dry, for God only showed it to them created such; but the epithet is also read with sukoon to the ب, because, though it had not been a path, it was a place wherein had been water and which had dried up: (Ḳ, TA:) the latter reading is that of El-Ḥasan El-Baṣree: and El-Aạmash read the word with kesr to the ب: (TA:) Th [however] says, (Ṣ,) you say ▼ حَطَبٌ يَبَسٌ, *dry fire-wood*, as though it were so *naturally*: (Ṣ, Mṣb:) [and J says,] ▼ يَبَسٌ signifies a place *dry after having been moist*; and so in the instance in the Ḳur. mentioned above: (Ṣ:) [and Fei says,] it signifies a place *that has had in it water which has gone away*; or, as Az says, a path *in which is no moisture*: (Mṣb:) [and ISd says,] ▼ يَبْسٌ and ▼ يَبَسٌ signify a place that is *dry*: and in like manner, applied to land (أَرْض), *of which the water and pasturage have dried up*: and the latter, so applied, † *hard*; (M;) as also يَابِسٌ ‡ applied to a stone: (A:) ▼ يَبِيسٌ is [generally] applied to a plant, or herbage, as signifying *dry*, or *dried up*; (Ṣ, M, A, Mṣb, Ḳ;) as also [sometimes] يَابِسٌ; (M, Ḳ;) the former being of the measure فَعِيلٌ in the sense of the measure فَاعِلٌ: (Mṣb:) or it is so applied to herbs, or leguminous plants, of the sort termed أَحْرَار [that are eaten without being cooked, or that are slender and succulent, &c.], (Aṣ, Ḳ,) and of the sort termed ذُكُور [that are hard and thick, or thick and rough, &c.]; (Aṣ, TA;) and [so Aṣ, in the TA; and so in some copies of the Ḳ; but in the CḲ, or] those herbs and leguminous plants that become scattered when they dry up; (Aṣ, Ḳ;) as also ▼ يُبْسٌ and ▼ يَبْسٌ; (TA;) but not to what is dry of the حَلِىّ and صِلِّيَان and حَلَمَة. (Aṣ, TA.) — [Hence,] المَفْلُوجُ اليَابِسُ الشِّقِّ † *The palsied of whom the half is without sensation and without motion.* (Mgh.) And رَجُلٌ يَابِسٌ مِنَ السُّكْرِ (AḤn) app. meaning † *A man as though he were dead and dried up in consequence of much intoxication.* (M.) [And يَابِسُ الطَّبِيعَةِ † *Costive.*] And سَكْرَانُ يَابِسٌ † *Intoxicated so much as not to speak*; as though the wine had dried him up by its heat. (M.) And أَتَانٌ يَبْسَةٌ ▼ (IAạr, M) and ▼ يَبَسَةٌ (Th, M) † *A she-ass dry and lean.* (M.) And شَاةٌ يَبْسٌ ▼ and ▼ يَبَسٌ (AO, Ṣ, M, Ḳ) † *A ewe, or she-goat, without milk*: (AO, Ṣ, M, Ḳ:) or *whose milk has stopped, and her udder become dry.* (M.) And ▼ اِمْرَأَةٌ يَبَسَةٌ † *A woman who has no milk*: pl. يَبَسَاتٌ and أَيْبَاسٌ and [quasi-pl. n.] يَابِسٌ [like بَاقِرٌ and جَامِلٌ]. (TA, from the Moheet.) And ▼ عِرْقٌ يَبِيسٌ † [*A dry duct*], meaning, *penis.* (Lḥ, M.) And شَعَرٌ يَابِسٌ ‡ *Hair upon which no effect is produced by moistening with water nor with oil*; (A, TA*;) which is the worst sort thereof. (TA.) And ▼ يَبِيسُ المَآءِ ‡ *Dry sweat*: (M, A:) or [simply] *sweat.* (AA, Ṣ, Ḳ.) And رَجُلٌ يَابِسٌ and ▼ يَبِيسٌ ‡ *A man having little good*: (A:) and اِمْرَأَةٌ يَابِسَةٌ and ▼ يَبِيسٌ (A, TA) and ▼ يَبْسٌ (Ṣ, Ḳ, TA) ‡ *a woman having little good*: (A:) or *in whom is no good*: (Ḳ, TA:) or *who does not cause one to obtain any good.* (Ṣ.) And ▼ بَيْنَهُمَا ثَرًى أَيْبَسُ ‡ *Between them two is disunion.* (A, TA.)

أَيْبَسُ [comp. and superl. of يَابِسٌ]. — [Hence the saying,] أَيْبَسُ مِنَ الصَّخْرِ ‡ *Harder than rock.* (A.) — See also يَابِسٌ, near the beginning and at the end. — الأَيْبَسُ, as a subst., not an epithet, (AHeyth,) *The part of the shin-bone, in the middle of the shank, which, when pressed, pains one,* (AHeyth, Ḳ,) *and when it is broken, the leg is lost*: (AHeyth:) or الأَيْبَسَانِ signifies *the parts of the two shanks upon which is no flesh*: (Ṣ:) or *the parts of the two shanks* of a horse *upon which the flesh is dry, or tough*: (AO:) or *the shank-bones* (M, TA) *of the fore leg and hind leg*: (TA:) or *what appears of these*: (M, TA:) or *the parts above the* كَعْبَانِ and زَنْدَانِ [app. here meaning the *two ankles and wrists*]: (A:) pl. أَيَابِسُ: (Ṣ, Ḳ:) which is also applied to *such parts as are like the hock, or hough, and the shank.* (TA.) — Also, the pl., *Hard things upon which swords are tried.* (Ḳ.)

أَرْضٌ مُوبِسَةٌ [originally مُيْبِسَةٌ] *Land of which the plants, or herbage, are drying up, or dried up.* (A.)

رِيحٌ مِيبَاسٌ [*A very drying wind*]. (TA, voce تَكْبَاءُ.)

[يتم, &c.

See Supplement.]

يرنأ

Q. 1. يَرْنَأَ لِحْيَتَهُ (Ḳ, TA; in the CḲ, [erroneously,] تَرْنَأَ;) *He dyed his beard with* يُرَنَّأ. (Ḳ.) A strange verb as to its form, (Ḳ,) which [except in its final vowel] is that of an aorist, though it is a preterite. (TA.) Mentioned in the L in art. رنأ (q.v.), on the authority of IJ; and there also by ISd; and AḤei and others assert the ى to be augmentative. [If so, the verb is a quasi-quadriliteral-radical word.] F follows Ṣgh, in mentioning it here. (TA.)

يُرَنَّأ (Ṣ, Ḳ) and يُرُنَّأ and يُرَنَّاءُ (Ḳ) and يَرَنَّا (without ء) and (accord. to [the Bári', as mentioned in] the TA, art. رنأ,) يُرُنَّا and يَرَنَّأ and (accord. to MF, who omits the two forms here immediately preceding,) يَرَنَّاءُ and يُرَنَّا, without ء, (TA,) i.q. حِنَّاءٌ (Ṣ, Ḳ) [The *plant Lawsonia inermis*]. See also art. رنأ, where the word is written [erroneously in my opinion] يَرَنَّأ. Accord. to IB (not IJ [as in the CḲ]), the ء may only be omitted when the word is pronounced with ḍammeh to the ى. (TA.)

يسر

1. يَسُرَ, aor. يَيْسُرُ, [respecting the form of which see the same verb in a different sense below,] inf. n. يُسْرٌ and يَسَرٌ [and مَيْسُورٌ (see يُسْرٌ below)], *He was, or became, gentle, and tractable, submissive, manageable, or easy*; (M, Ḳ;) said of a man, and of a horse: (M:) and يَسِرَ [app. signifies the same: and] is said of speech, and of a thing or an affair; signifying, [when relating to the former,] *it was gentle*, or [when relating to the latter,] *easy*; like سَعِدَ الرَّجُلُ [as

syn. with سَعْدٌ], and نُحِسَ [as syn. with نَحِسَ]. (Bd, xvii. 30.) See also تيسّر — يَسَرَتْ, said of a woman: see أَيْسَرَتْ. ═ يَسُرَ, aor. ـُ, *It* (a thing) *was,* or *became, little in quantity:* (A, Mṣb:) *contemptible; paltry; of no weight* or *worth.* (A.) ═ يَسَرَنِى, aor. يَيْسِرُنِى, (AḤn, M, Ḳ,) inf. n. يَسْرٌ, (AḤn, M,) *He* (a man, AḤn, M) *came on,* or *from the direction of, my left hand.* (AḤn, M, Ḳ.) See also 3. ═ يَسَرَ, [aor. يَيْسِرُ, inf. n. يَسْرٌ,] *He divided* anything *into parts,* or *portions.* (TA.) You say, يَسَرْتُ النَّاقَةَ *I divided the flesh of the she-camel into parts* or *portions.* (TA.) And يَسَرُوا الجَزُورَ *They slaughtered the she-camel and divided its limbs,* (Ṣ,) or *portions,* (TA,) *among themselves;* (Ṣ, TA;) as also, accord. to Aboo-'Omar El-Jarmee, ↓ اِتَّسَرُوهَا, aor. يَتَّسِرُونَهَا, inf. n. اِتِّسَارٌ; and he adds that some people say, يَأْتَسِرُونَهَا, inf n. اِئْتِسَارٌ, with hemz; and هُمْ مُؤْتَسِرُونَ; like as they say in the case of اِتَّعَدَ. (Ṣ.) Soheym Ibn-Wetheel El-Yarboo'ee says,

أَقُولُ لَهُمْ بِالشِّعْبِ إِذْ يَيْسِرُونَنِى
أَلَمْ تَيْأَسُوا أَنِّى ٱبْنُ فَارِسِ زَهْدَمِ

[*I say to them, in the ravine, when they divide me among themselves,* deciding what shares they shall severally have in me, *Know ye not that I am the son of the rider of Zahdum,* and that ye may obtain a great ransom for me?] for capture had befallen him, and they played with [gaming-] arrows for him. (Ṣ, TA. [but in the latter, instead of تَيْأَسُوا, we find تَعْلَمُوا, which signifies the same.]) You say also, ↓ اِتَّسَرُوا, aor. يَتَّسِرُونَ and يَأْتَسِرُونَ; (Ḳ;) and ↓ تَيَاسَرُوا; (M, Ḳ;) *They divided among themselves the slaughtered camel.* (M, Ḳ.) — [Hence,] يَسَرَ, aor. يَيْسِرُ, (Ṣ, M, A, Mṣb, Ḳ,) in the [second] ى is not suppressed as it is in يَعِدُ and its coördinates [having و for the first radical], (Ṣ,) and يَيْسَرُ, like يَجْعَلُ, in the dial. of the Benoo-Asad, (TA,) inf. n. يَسْرٌ, (M, TA,) or مَيْسِرٌ, (A,) *He played at the game called* المَيْسِر; (M, Mṣb, Ḳ;) *he played with gaming-arrows.* (Ṣ, A, Mṣb.)

2. يَسَّرَهُ, (inf. n. تَيْسِيرٌ, M, &c.) *He* (God, A, Mṣb) *made it,* or *rendered it, easy; facilitated it.* (M, A, Mgh, Mṣb, Ḳ.) You say, يُسِّرَتْ عَلَيْهَا الوِلَادَةُ *The act of bringing forth was rendered easy to her.* (A.) — *He made his circumstances ample; he made his condition,* or *his way* or *course* [لِكَذَا *to such a thing*], *easy,* or *smooth:* (Sb, M:) *he accommodated, adapted,* or *disposed, him,* لِلْيُسْرَى [*to easy things,* or *affairs,* or *circumstances;* or *to the easier,* or *easiest, way*]: (Ṣ, A, [in the latter of which this is given as a proper, not tropical, signification:]) ‡ *he prepared,* or *made ready, him* or *it,* لِكَذَا *for such a thing.* (A [in which this signification is said to be tropical.]) تَيْسِير relates to both good and evil: (M, Ḳ:) as in the following instances in the Ḳur; [xcii. 7, 10;] فَسَنُيَسِّرُهُ لِلْيُسْرَى, and لِلْعُسْرَى, (M,) [*We will facilitate,* or *smooth, his way,* or] *We will accommodate him,* or *adapt him,* or *dispose him,* [*to a state of ease,* and *to a state of difficulty,* or (as explained in the TA, art. عسر,) *to punishment, and a difficult case:*] (Ṣ, A:) or *We will prepare him for paradise,* and *for hell:* (Jel:) or *We will prepare him to return to good,* or *righteous, conduct,* [and *to persevere in evil,* or *unrighteous, conduct;* the former leading to ease, and the latter to difficulty:] (Fr, TA:) or *We will prepare him for that habit of conduct which leads to ease,* such as the entering paradise, and *for that which leads to difficulty,* such as the entering hell: from يَسَّرَ الفَرَسَ, meaning, *he prepared the horse for riding, by saddling and bridling.* (Bḍ.) It is said in a trad. وَقَدْ يُسِّرَ لَهُ طَهُورٌ † *And water for ablution had been prepared and put for him.* (TA.) — يُسِّرَ الرَّجُلُ, (inf. n. تَيْسِيرٌ, Ḳ,) *The man's camels,* and *his sheep* or *goats, brought forth with ease,* (IAạr, M, Ḳ,) *and none of them perished.* (IAạr, M.) — يَسَّرَتِ الغَنَمُ *The sheep,* or *goats, abounded in milk,* (Ṣ, M, A, Ḳ,) and in like manner, الإِبِلُ *the camels,* (M,) *and* [so in the Ṣ, M, A, but in the Ḳ or] *in offspring:* (Ṣ, M, A, Ḳ:) and *they brought forth:* and *they were ready to bring forth:* and *they abounded.* (TA.) A poet (namely Aboo-Useydeh Ed-Debeeree, TA) says,

هُمَا سَيِّدَانَا يَزْعُمَانِ وَإِنَّمَا
يَسُودَانِنَا أَنْ يَسَّرَتْ غَنَمَاهُمَا

(Ṣ, M) *They two are our two chiefs, as they assert; but they are only our chiefs inasmuch as their sheep, or goats, abound in milk and in offspring.* (TA.) — See also أَيْسَرَتْ.

3. يَاسَرَهُ, [inf. n. مُيَاسَرَةٌ.] *He was gentle towards him; acted gently towards him; treated him with gentleness;* syn. لَايَنَهُ: (M, A, Ḳ:) *he was easy,* or *facile, with him;* syn. سَاهَلَهُ. (Ṣ, Ḳ.) Ex., cited by Th, from a poem: إِنْ يَاسَرْتَهُمْ يَسَرُوا *If thou treat them with gentleness, they become gentle.* (M.) And يَاسَرَ الشَّرِيكَ *He was easy,* or *facile, with the partner.* (TA, from a trad.) ═ ياسر, (inf. n. مُيَاسَرَةٌ, Ḳ,) *He took the left-hand side* or *direction;* (Ṣ, M, A, Mṣb, Ḳ;) as also ↓ تياسر; (Ṣ, Mṣb, Ḳ;) which latter is the *contr.* of تيامن: (Ḳ:) or ↓ تَيَاسَرُوا *they took the left-hand side* or *direction; contr. of* تَيَامَنُوا. (A.) You say, يَاسِرْ بِأَصْحَابِكَ *Take thou the left-hand side* or *direction with thy companions;* (Ṣ, A;) as also تَيَاسَرْ; but some disapprove of this latter. (Ṣ.) And يَاسَرَ بِالقَوْمِ *He took the left-hand side* or *direction with the people;* as also ↓ يَسَرَ بِهِمْ, aor. يَيْسِرُ; accord. to Sb. (M, TA.)

4. أَيْسَرَتْ *She* (a woman, M) *brought forth with ease; she had an easy birth;* (M, A, Ḳ;) as also ↓ يَسَّرَتْ, (M, IḲṭṭ,) which is in like manner said of a she-camel; (M;) or, as in the copies of the Ḳ, يَسَرَتْ, without teshdeed. (TA.) One says, in praying (M, A) for a pregnant woman, (A,) أَيْسَرَتْ وَأَذْكَرَتْ *May she have an easy birth,* (Lḥ, M, A,) *and may she bring forth a male child.* (Lḥ, M.) See the contr., أَعْسَرَتْ. ═ ايسر, (Ṣ, M, &c.,) aor. يُوسِرُ, in which the [radical] ى is changed into و because it is quiescent and preceded by ḍamm, (Ṣ,) inf. n. إِيسَارٌ (M, Mgh, Ḳ) and يُسْرٌ; (M, Ḳ;) accord. to Ḳr and Lḥ, but correctly the latter is a simple subst., (M,) *He became possessed of competence,* or *sufficiency;* or *of richness,* or *wealth,* or *opulence;* (Ṣ, M, Mgh, Mṣb, Ḳ;) *and abundance.* (Mṣb.) ═ أَيْمَنْتُ إِبِلِى وَأَيْسَرْتُهَا *I put my camels aside on the right hand and the left.* (A.)

5. تيسّر *It* (a thing, M, Mṣb) *was,* or *became, facilitated,* or *easy;* (M, A, Mṣb, Ḳ, TA;) *contr. of difficult, hard, strait,* or *intricate;* (TA;) as also ↓ استيسر. (M, A, Mṣb, Ḳ.) You say, أَخَذْنَا مَا تَيَسَّرَ, and ↓ مَا ٱسْتَيْسَرَ, *We took what was easy* [*of obtainment,* or *of attainment*]. (TA.) And it is said in a trad., respecting the eleemosinary tax called زَكَاة, وَيَجْعَلُ مَعَهَا شَاتَيْنِ إِنِ ٱسْتَيْسَرَتَا ↓ لَهُ أَوْ عِشْرِينَ دِرْهَمًا *And he shall put with it,* or *them, two sheep,* or *goats, if they be easy to him* [*to give*], *or twenty dirhems.* (TA.) And in the Ḳur, [ii. 192,] فَمَا ٱسْتَيْسَرَ ↓ مِنَ الهَدْيِ *What is easy* [*to give*], *of camels and kine and sheep or goats:* or, as some say, *either a camel or a cow or a sheep or goat.* (M, TA.) — Also, تيسّر لَهُ, (Ṣ, TA,) and ↓ استيسر له, (Ṣ, Ḳ, TA,) † *It* (a thing, or an affair, Ḳ) *was,* or *became, prepared,* or *made ready for him:* (Ṣ, Ḳ, TA:) [and *he prepared himself for it.*] It is said in a trad., قَدْ تَيَسَّرَا لِلْقِتَالِ † *They had both prepared themselves,* or *made themselves ready, for fight.* (TA, from a trad.) — تَيَسَّرَتِ البِلَادُ ‡ *The countries became abundant in herbage,* or *in the goods, conveniences,* or *comforts, of life.* (TA, from a trad.)

6. تَيَاسَرُوا [*They were gentle,* or *acted gently, one towards another; they treated one another with gentleness:* (see 3, of which it is the quasi-pass.)] *they were easy,* or *facile, one with another;* syn. تَسَاهَلُوا; (Ḳ,* TA;) تَيَاسُرٌ is the contr. of تَعَاسُرٌ. (Ṣ, art. عسر.) It is said in a trad., تَيَاسَرُوا فِى الصَّدَاقِ *Be ye easy,* or *facile, not exorbitant, one with another, with respect to dowry.* (TA.) ═ See also 3. ═ And see 1, latter part.

8: see 1, in two places.

10: see 5, in five places.

يُسُرٌ (TA) and ▾ يُسْرٌ, (M, A, K, TA,) [each an inf. n. (see 1) used as an epithet,] and يَاسِرٌ, (K, TA,) *Easy and gentle in tractableness, submissiveness, or manageableness*; applied to a man and to a horse: (TA:) or [simply] *easy; facile*; (M, A, K;) as also ▾ يُسْرٌ (TA) and يَسِيرٌ, (Msb), this last being syn. with هَيِّنٌ, (S, K,) and signifying *not difficult*, غَيْرُ عَسِيرٍ, (A,) and ▾ مَيْسُورٌ [respecting which see also عُسْرٌ, pl. مَيَاسِيرُ]. (A.) Hence, ▾ يُسُرَاتٌ, pl. of يُسْرَةٌ and يُسُرَةٌ, applied to the legs of a beast, signifies *Easy*: (M:) or *light*, or *active*, legs of a beast: (S, TA:) or *light*, or *active, and obedient*, legs of a beast of carriage: (A:) or the *legs* of a she-camel: and you say also, إِنَّ قَوَائِمَ هٰذَا الفَرَسِ يُسُرَاتٌ خِفَافٌ, meaning, *verily the legs of this horse are obedient* and *light* or *active*. (TA.) [Hence also,] وِلَادَةٌ يُسُرٌ [*An easy birth*, or *bringing forth*]. (A.) And وَلَدَتْ وَلَدَهَا يُسُرًا *She brought forth her child easily*: (M, K*:) said of a woman: (M:) or ▾ يَسَرًا. (CK.) And it is said in a trad., ▾ إِنَّ هٰذَا الدِّينَ يُسُرٌ *Verily this religion is easy; liberal; one having little straitness*. (TA.) You say also, ▾ خُذْ مَيْسُورَهُ وَدَعْ مَعْسُورَهُ [*Take thou what is easy thereof, and leave thou what is difficult*]. (A.) And ▾ مَيْسُورٌ is applied to a saying, or speech: (A:) so in the Kur. xvii. 30; meaning, *gentle*; (Bd, Jel;) *easy*: (Jel:) or ▾ قَوْلٌ مَيْسُورٌ means prayer for مَيْسُور, i.e., for يُسْر [q.v.]. (Bd.) — فَتْلٌ يُسُرٌ [The *twisting* a rope or cord *towards the left, by rolling it against the body from right to left*; or] the *twisting downwards, by extending the right hand towards the body* [*and so rolling the rope or cord downwards against the body or thigh*, which is the usual way of twisting]; (S, A*, K;) *contr. of* شُزْرٌ. (M, A, TA.) — طَعْنٌ يُسُرٌ The *thrusting*, or *piercing*, [*straight forward*; or] *opposite the face*: (S, M, K:) opposed to شُزْرٌ, which is from one's right and one's left. (TA.) See an ex. voce شَزَرَهُ.

يُسْرٌ [*Easiness; facility*;] *contr. of* عُسْرٌ; (S, M, Mgh, Msb, K;) as also ▾ يُسُرٌ; (S, Msb, TA;) [and ▾ يُسْرَى; (see 3, where it is variously explained;)] and ▾ مَيْسُورٌ is the *contr. of* مَعْسُورٌ, [and therefore signifies as above; or *easy; facile*;] (S;) or this last signifies, (accord. to the lexicologists, M,) what is *made easy*; or *facilitated*; or (accord. to Sb, M, [but see مَعْقُول,]) it is an inf. n. of the measure مَفْعُول, (M, K,) [used in the sense of يُسْر as explained above,] of the same kind as [its contr.] مَعْسُورٌ; and Abu-l-Hasan says, that this is the truth; for it has no unaugmented verb, and inf. ns. of this measure are not of verbs which are in use, but only of imaginary unaugmented triliteral-radical verbs, as in the case of مَجْلُودٌ, which is [really] from تَجَلَّدَ. (M.) For examples of يُسْرٌ, see عُسْرٌ. — Also, (accord. to the M; but in the K, or; and in both of these lexicons the signification here following is placed first;) and in like manner, ▾ يُسُرٌ, (K,) and ▾ يَسَارٌ, (S, M, Mgh, Msb, K,) and ▾ يَسَارَةٌ, (S, K,) and ▾ مَيْسَرَةٌ, and ▾ مَيْسُرَةٌ, (S, M, K,) of which last Sb says that it is like مَشْرُبَةٌ and مَسْرُبَةٌ in not being after the manner of the verb, [but after that of the simple substantive,] (M,) and ▾ مَيْسِرَةٌ, (K.) *Easiness* [*of circumstances*]; (M, K;) *competence*, or *sufficiency*; or *richness*, or *wealth*, or *opulence*; (S, M, Mgh, Msb, K;) *abundance*; (Msb;) [in these senses, also, *contr. of* عُسْرٌ;] and ▾ يُسْرَى signifies [*the same*; or] *easy things or affairs or circumstances*; *contr. of* عُسْرَى; as also ▾ مَيْسَرَةٌ. (TA, art. عسر.) You say also, ▾ أَنْظِرْنِى حَتَّى يَسَارِ [*Grant thou me a delay until* I shall be in a state of *easiness of circumstances*, &c.]; in which the last word is indecl., with kesr for its termination, because it is altered from the inf. n., which is المَيْسَرَةُ. (S.) In the Kur. [ii. 280,] some read, ▾ فَنَظِرَةٌ إِلَى مَيْسُرِهِ [*Then* let there be *a postponement*, or *delay, until his* being in a state of *easiness of circumstances*]: but Akh says, that this is not allowable; for there is no noun of the measure مَفْعُلٌ [of this kind]: as to مَكْرُمٌ and مَعُونٌ, [it is said that] they are pls. [virtually though not in the language of the grammarians] of مَكْرُمَةٌ and مَعُونَةٌ. (S.) [On this point, see مَأْلُكٌ, voce أَلُوكٌ.] — See also يُسْرٌ, in two places. — عُودُ يُسْرٍ: see عُودُ أُسْرٍ, in art. أسر.

يَسَرٌ: see يُسْرٌ. — *Made easy*, or *facilitated*; i.q. مُيَسَّرٌ: † *prepared*: (K:) or [the *game called*] المَيْسِرُ *prepared*: or, as some say, † *anything prepared*. (M.) — أَعْسَرُ يَسَرٌ A man *who works, or does anything, with both his hands* [*alike*]; *ambidextrous; ambidexter*: (S, M, Msb:) and ▾ أَعْسَرُ أَيْسَرُ occurs in a trad., accord. to one relation; but the former is the correct expression: (A'Obeyd:) and the fem. is عَسْرَاءُ يَسَرَةٌ: (M:) explained before, in art. عسر. (K.) — See also يَاسِرٌ, in six places.

يُسُرٌ: see يُسْرٌ, in two places.

يَسْرَةٌ: see يَسَارٌ, throughout.

يُسْرَى: see يُسْرٌ, in two places. — See also أَيْسَرُ. — See also يَسَارٌ, throughout.

يَسَارٌ: see يُسْرٌ, in two places. — Also, (S, M, Mgh, Msb, K, &c.,) and ▾ يِسَارٌ, (M, Msb, K,) the former of which is the more chaste, (ISk, IAmb, IF, M, Msb, K*,) or the latter is so, (IDrd, M, K,) or the latter is a variation used for the sake of assimilation to [its syn.] شِمَالٌ, (Sgh, TA,) or it is vulgar, (IKt, Msb,) and not allowable, (S,) or J is in error in disallowing it, (K,) or it is disapproved because the incipient ى with kesr is deemed difficult to pronounce, (M, TA,) but there are three other words commencing like it, namely, يِوَامٌ, an inf. n. of يَاوَمَهُ, though this is disallowed by some, and يِعَارٌ, pl. of يَعْرٌ, and يِسَافُ, a proper name of a man, also pronounced with fet-h [to the ى]; (TA;) and another form is ▾ يَسَّارٌ; (Sgh, K;) *contr. of* يَمِينٌ; (S, M, A, Mgh, Msb, K;) and so is ▾ يُسْرَى of يُمْنَى, (M, A, Mgh, Msb, K,) and يَسْرَةٌ of يَمْنَةٌ, (M, A, Msb, K,) and ▾ مَيْسَرَةٌ of مَيْمَنَةٌ, (A, Msb, K,) and ▾ أَيْسَرُ of أَيْمَنُ: (S:) ▾ يَسَارٌ and ▾ يُسْرَى signify The *left* [*hand, or arm, or foot, or leg, or*] *limb*: and the same two words, and ▾ يَسْرَةٌ and ▾ مَيْسَرَةٌ, the *left*, meaning the *left side* or *direction* or *relative location* or *place*: (Msb:) and ▾ أَيْسَرُ, the *left side*: or a person [or thing] *that is on the left side*: (Msb, art. يمن:) [and ▾ مَيْسَرَةٌ the *left wing* of an army:] the pl. of يَسَارٌ is يُسُرٌ (Lh, M, K) and يُسْرٌ, (K,) or يُسُرٌ; (AHn, M;) which last is [also] pl. of ▾ يُسْرَى; (TA;) [and the pl. of ▾ مَيْسَرَةٌ is مَيَاسِرُ.] You say, قَعَدَ فُلَانٌ ▾ يَسْرَةً *Such a one sat on the left side*. (S.) And قَعَدُوا يَمْنَةً وَ▾يَسْرَةً, (A, Msb*,) and عَلَى يَمِينٍ وَيَسَارٍ, and ▾ المَيْمَنَةِ وَالمَيْسَرَةِ, and ▾ اليُمْنَى وَاليُسْرَى, (A,) or يَمِينًا وَيَسَارًا, and عَنِ اليَمِينِ وَعَنِ اليَسَارِ, and المَيْمَنَةِ وَالمَيْسَرَةِ, and اليُمْنَى وَاليُسْرَى, meaning, *They sat on the right side and on the left*. (Msb.) And ▾ وَلَّاهُ مَيَاسِرَهُ [*He turned his left parts towards him*]. (A.)

يِسَارٌ: see يَسَارٌ.

يَسُورٌ: see يَاسِرٌ, in two places.

يَسِيرٌ: see يُسْرٌ. — *Little*, or *small, in quantity, petty*: (S, A, K:) *mean, contemptible; paltry; of no weight or worth*. (A.) — See also يَاسِرٌ.

يَسَارَةٌ: see يُسْرٌ.

يَسَّارٌ: see يَسَارٌ.

يَاسِرٌ: see يُسْرٌ, first signification. — [*Taking the left-hand side or direction*: or *coming on*, or *from the direction of, the left hand* of a person:] contr. of يَامِنٌ. (S.) — [*Dividing* a thing *into parts, or portions*.] — [Hence,] The *slaughterer of a camel*: (K, TA:) because he divides its flesh into portions: (TA:) the *person who superintends the division of the slaughtered camel* (M, K) *for the game called* المَيْسِرُ: (K:) pl. [يَاسِرُونَ and] أَيْسَارٌ: (M, K:) A'Obeyd says, I have heard them put يَاسِرٌ in the place of يَسَرٌ, [for the explanations of which see what follows,] and ▾ يَسَرٌ in the place of يَاسِرٌ, (M,) or ▾ يَسَرٌ and يَاسِرٌ signify the same: and the pl. is أَيْسَارٌ: (S, A:) يَاسِرٌ signifies [as explained above, and also] *a person who plays with gaming-arrows*, (S, Msb, TA,) [*at the* game called الْمَيْسِر,] *for a slaughtered camel;* because he is one of those who occasion the slaughter of the camel; and the pl. is [as above and] يَاسِرُونَ: (TA:) and ↓ يَسَرٌ, *i.q.* ضَرِيبٌ [which signifies *the same;* and the *person who is entrusted, as deputy, with the disposal of the arrows in the game above mentioned, and who shuffles them in the* رِبَابَة:] and, [as quasi-pl. of يَاسِرٌ, like as خَدَمٌ is of خَادِمٌ,] *a party assembled together at the game called* الْمَيْسِر: (M, K:) pl. أَيْسَارٌ: (M:) and ↓ يَسِرٌ and ↓ يَسُورٌ signify *one who contends with another at a game of hazard;* syn. قَامِرٌ: (K:) or ↓ يَسَرٌ and ↓ يَسُورٌ, and also يَاسِرٌ, are applied to *one who has,* or *to whom pertains, a gaming-arrow.* (IAar, TA.)

أَيْسَرُ [*More,* and *most, easy,* or *facile;* fem. يُسْرَى]. — See also يَسَارٌ.

مُوسِرٌ [originally مُيْسِرٌ,] *Possessing competence,* or *sufficiency;* or *rich,* or *wealthy,* or *opulent:* (M, K:) pl. مَيَاسِيرُ: (Sb, M, K:) [like مَفَالِيسُ, pl. of مُفْلِسٌ; and مَفَاطِيرُ, pl. of مُفْطِرٌ; as though the sing. were مِيسُورٌ:] but by rule it should be مُوسِرُونَ, for the masc., and مُوسِرَاتٌ for the fem. (Abu-l-Hasan, M.)

مَيْسَرٌ: see يُسْرٌ.

مَيْسِرٌ The *game,* or *play, with unfeathered and headless arrows;* (M, K;) the *game of hazard which the Arabs play with such arrows;* (S, Mgh, Msb;) *a game of the Arabs, played* [*by ten men,*] *with ten unfeathered and headless arrows:* they first slaughtered a camel, [bought on credit, (see below, in this paragraph,)] and divided it into ten portions, or, as some say, [agreeably with what follows,] into twenty-eight: the first arrow was called الفَذّ, and had [one notch and] one portion of the slaughtered camel: the second, التَّوْءَم, and had [two notches and] two portions: the third, الرَّقِيب, and had [three notches and] three portions: the fourth, الحِلْس, and had [four notches and] four portions: the fifth, النَّافِس, and had [five notches and] five portions; or, as some say, this was the fourth: the sixth, المُسْبِل, and had [six notches and] six portions: the seventh, المُعَلَّى, which was the highest of them, having [seven notches and] seven portions: the eighth and ninth and tenth were called المَنِيح and السَّفِيح and الوَغْد; and those three had no portions: [the players to whom these three fell had to pay for the slaughtered camel: (see المُسْبِل:) whence it appears, that if the camel was divided into ten portions, (see وَغْدٌ,) the game must have continued after all these were won, until it was seen whose were the eighth and ninth and tenth arrows; and it seems to be the general opinion that this was the case:] the camel being slaughtered, they collected together the ten arrows, and put them into the رِبَابَة, a thing resembling a quiver (كِنَانَة), and turned them round about or shuffled them (أَجَالُوهَا): [or they employed a person, whom they called حُرْضَة, to do this:] then they put them into the hand of the judge (الحَكَم), who took them forth one after another in the name of one after another of the party; [or they commissioned the حُرْضَة to do so;] and each took of the portions of the slaughtered camel according to his arrow; but those to whose lots fell the arrows without portions were obliged to pay the price of the slaughtered camel: with the flesh of which they afterwards fed the poor; and him who would not engage with them in the game they reproached, and called a بَرَم: (Sefeenet Er-Rághib, printed at Booláḳ; p. 637:) [see also عَشْرٌ, and ضَرِيبٌ, and رَقِيبٌ:] or *any game of hazard;* or *play for stakes, or wagers:* (K:) so that even the game of children with walnuts is included under this name by Mujáhid in his explanation of verse 216 of chap. ii. of the Kur.: (TA:) or *anything in which is risk, or hazard:* (Kull, p. 321:) or the *game of tricktrack, backgammon,* or *tables;* syn. نَرْدٌ: (Sgh, K:) and *chess* was called by 'Alee the مَيْسِر of the Persians, or foreigners: (TA:) or the *slaughtered camel for which they played:* for when they desired to play, they bought on credit a camel for slaughter, and slaughtered it, and divided it into twenty-eight portions, or ten portions; and when one [of the arrows] after another came forth [from the رِبَابَة] in the name of one man after another, the gain of him for whom came forth those to which belonged portions appeared, and the fine of him for whom came forth [any of the arrows called] the غُفْل: (K:) so called as though it were a place of division: and so used by the poet Lebeed, who speaks of a fat مَيْسِر. (TA.)

مَيْسَرَةٌ: see يُسْرٌ, in two places. — See also يَسَارٌ, in four places.

مَيْسُرَةٌ: }
مَيْسِرَةٌ: } see يُسْرٌ.

مُيَسَّرٌ *Prepared; disposed; made easy,* or *facile.* So in the following words of a trad.: فَكُلٌّ مُيَسَّرٌ لِمَا خُلِقَ لَهُ [*And every one is prepared, &c., for that for which he is created*]. (TA.) — *I.q.* زُمَاوَرْدٌ [q.v.]; (Mgh, K;) app. a post-classical word; so called because easily taken; (Mgh;) in Persian, called نُوَالَهْ [or نَوَالَهْ], (Mgh, K,) and in Egypt termed لُقْمَةُ القَاضِى. (TA.)

مُيْسِرٌ, applied to a man, (S, TA,) *Having numerous offspring of sheep* or *goats* [*and therefore much milk*]; (TA;) contr. of مُجْنِبٌ. (S, TA.)

مَيْسُورٌ: see يُسْرٌ, in three places: — and see also يُسْرٌ.

مَيَاسِيرُ She-camels *that bring forth easily.* (TA.)

يشب

يَشْبٌ *A well known stone;* [*jasper;* peculiarly *a whitish kind thereof, found in Mount Imaus:* (Golius, from Et-Teyfáshee:)] an arabicized word, from [the Persian] يَشْم, q.v. (K.)

يطب

4. مَا أَيْطَبَهُ: *i.q.* مَا أَطْيَبَهُ: (K:) a dial. form of the latter, or formed from it by transposition: (TA:) and in like manner أَيْطِبْ بِهِ, *i.q.* أَطْيِبْ بِهِ: [both signifying *How good, sweet, delicious,* or *pleasant, is he,* or *it*]. (TA, art. طيب.)

أَيْطَبُ *i.q.* أَطْيَبُ [*More,* or *most, good, sweet, delicious,* or *pleasant: and pure*]: a correct and chaste dial. form of the latter word. (Ex., from a trad., عَلَيْكُمْ بِالأَسْوَدِ مِنْهُ فَإِنَّهُ أَيْطَبُهُ *Keep ye to the black thereof;* (i.e., of the fruit of the أَرَاك;) *for it is the best of it.* But some deny its being a dial. form, [holding it to be formed by transposition]. (TA.) — أَقْبَلَتِ الشَّاةُ فِى أَيْطَبَتِهَا, and أَيْطِبَتِهَا, (the latter form from AZ, TA,) *The sheep,* or *goat, came in the vehemence of her lust for the male.* (K.) See also art. طيب.

[يعر, &c.

See Supplement.]

يفخ

1. يَفَخَهُ, (K,) aor. ـَ, because of the guttural letter, or ـِ, accord. to the common rule observed in the K, or ـُ, as though it were of the same class as وَعَدَ, (TA,) [the last is probably the most correct form, as يَأْفُخُهُ is the aor. of أَفَخَهُ, of which يَفَخَهُ is a dial. form,] *He,* or *it, hit him,* or *hurt him, on the part of his head called the* يَافُوخ. (K.)

يَافُوخٌ [The *top of the head;*] the *part where the anterior and posterior bones of the head meet:* [see يَأْفُوخٌ, of which it is a dial. form:] pl. يَوَافِيخُ. (TA.) ISd regards this form of pl. as an indication that the ى is a radical letter, and therefore mentions it in this art.; (TA;) [and F says the same in art. أفخ: but see that art.]. — مَسَّ بِيَافُوخِهِ السِّمَاكَ † [*He touched Spica Virginis,* or *Arcturus, with the top of his head*]. (A.) — وَطِئَ فُلَانٌ يَوَافِيخَ القَوْمِ † *Such a one had lordship and eminence given to him.* (A.) — صَدَعُوا يَافُوخَ اللَّيْلِ ‡ *i.q.* أَدْلَجُوا [*They journeyed in the night;* &c.] (A.) [See also art. أفخ.]

مَيْفُوخٌ *Hit*, or *hurt, on the part of his head called the* يَافُوخ. (Ḳ.)

[يفع, &c.
See Supplement.]

يقت

يَاقُوتٌ, [coll. gen. n., The *sapphire*, of whatever variety: the *ruby, oriental ruby*, or *red sapphire*, also called يَاقُوتٌ أَحْمَرُ; of which there are several varieties, whereof one is the *carbuncle*; also called يَاقُوتٌ جَمْرِىٌّ: the *sapphire*, commonly so called, or *blue sapphire*, also called يَاقُوتٌ أَزْرَقُ: and the *topaz, oriental topaz*, or *yellow sapphire*, also called يَاقُوتٌ أَصْفَرُ: the *jacinth*, or *hyacinth*, accord. to Golius, who observes, as on the authority of the Teyfáshee, that by this name are called *various gems of the East*; four species thereof being enumerated; the *red*, the *yellow*, or *gold-coloured*, the *blue*, or *azure*, and the *white*: that the *sapphire* and the *chrysolite* are also thus called: but that, by the word used absolutely, the *red jacinth*, or *hyacinth*, commonly called the *ruby*, is meant: which last remark is agreeable with modern usage:] *a well known gem*; (Ḳ;) of which there are many varieties, (TA,) the most excellent whereof is that called اليَاقُوتُ الأَحْمَرُ الرُّمَّانِىُّ, (Ḳ,) also called البَهْرَمَانِىُّ; [the *finest kind of ruby* or *carbuncle*;] said to be brought from Sarandeeb [or Ceylon]: it has the property of exhilarating, and of conjoining [separated friends]; (TA;) and is profitable for disturbance of the mind (occasioned by the black bile, TA) and palpitation, and weakness of the heart and stomach, if drunk; [being app. reduced to powder for that purpose, as is done with some other gems in the East;] and for congealment of the blood, if hung [upon the person]: (Ḳ:) it is a Persian word, (Ṣ,) arabicized: (Ṣ, Ḳ:) of the measure فَاعُولٌ: n. un. with ة; and pl. يَوَاقِيتُ. (Ṣ.)

يقظ

1. يَقِظَ, aor. ـَ, (Mṣb, Ḳ,) and يَقُظَ, aor. ـُ; (Lḥ, Ḳ;) and in the Mṣb is added يَقَظَ, i.e. like ضَرَبَ, which is strange; (TA;) [but this I do not find in my copy of the Mṣb;] inf. n. [of the first] يَقَظٌ (Mṣb, Ḳ) and يَقَظَةٌ, (Mṣb, TA,) or the latter is a simple subst., (Ṣ,) and [of the second] يَقَاظَةٌ; (Mṣb, Ḳ;) *He waked*, or *woke; did not sleep*, or *was not sleeping*. (Mṣb, Ḳ.) — See also 5.

2: See 4, throughout.

4. ايقظهُ (Ṣ, &c.) inf. n. إِيقَاظٌ, (TA,) *He awakened him*, (Ṣ, Mgh, Mṣb, Ḳ,) مِنْ نَوْمِهِ *from his sleep*; (Ṣ;) as also ▼ يقّظهُ, inf. n. تَيْقِيظٌ; (Ḳ;) and ▼ استيقظهُ. (TA.) — ‡ *He roused his attention*, لِلْأُمُورِ *to the things*, or *affairs*; (Mṣb;) as also يقّظهُ. (TA.) — ايقظ الغُبَارَ ‡ *He dispersed the dust*: (Lth:) and † *he raised the dust*; (Lth, Ṣ, Z;) as also ▼ يقّظهُ: (Lth, Ṣ:) or, accord. to Az, this is a mistranscription, for بَقَّطَ التُّرَابَ, inf. n. تَبْقِيطٌ. (TA.)

5. تيقّظ *He became awakened*; or *he awaked*, or *awoke*; (Ṣ, Mṣb, TA;) مِنْ نَوْمِهِ *from his sleep*; (TA;) as also ▼ استيقظ. (Ṣ, Mgh, Mṣb, Ḳ.) — ‡ *His attention became roused*, or *he had his attention roused*, لِلْأَمْرِ *to the thing*, or *affair*; (Mṣb,* TA;) as also ▼ استيقظ, and ▼ يَقِظَ: (Mṣb:) *he became vigilant, wary*, or *cautious*. (TA.) You say also, هُوَ يَسْتَيْقِظُ ▼ إِلَى صَوْتِهِ ‡ [*He has his attention roused at his voice*, to listen thereto]. (TA.)

10. استيقظ: see 5, in three places. — ‡ *It* (a woman's anklet or other ornament) *made a sound* or *sounds*: (Ḳ, TA:) like as one says [in the contr. case], نَامَ, meaning "its sound, or sounds, ceased," by reason of the fulness of the leg. (TA.) — استيقظهُ: see 4.

يَقْظٌ: see what next follows, in three places.

يَقِظٌ and ▼ يَقُظٌ and ▼ يَقْظَانُ A man *waking*, or *awake: not sleeping*: (Ḳ:) or the last has this signification; (Ṣ, Mṣb;) and its fem. is يَقْظَى: (O, Mṣb, Ḳ:) the pl. (Ḳ, &c.) of the first (IB, Mṣb) and second, (IB,) or of the first only, for the second has no broken pl., because of the rareness of فَعُلٌ as the measure of an epithet, (Sb, TA,) is أَيْقَاظٌ, (Sb, IB, Mṣb, Ḳ,) which is applied to women as well as to men; (O;) and the pl. of يقظان is يِقَاظٌ; (IB;) and the pl. of يقظى is يَقَاظَى. (Ḳ.) — And the first (ISk, Ṣ, Mṣb) and ▼ second (ISk, Ṣ) ‡ A man *vigilant, wary, cautious*, or *in a state of preparation*; (Ṣ, Mṣb;) *having his attention roused*: (Ṣ:) and *intelligent*: (Mṣb:) or a man *having his attention much roused, very vigilant, and possessing knowledge and intelligence*. (ISk.) [In the TA, each of these two epithets is said to be after the manner of the rel. n.; but they are both part. ns. from يَقِظَ as syn. with تيقّظ.] You say also, وَرَجُلٌ يَقْظَانُ الفِكْرِ ▼ مُتَيَقِّظُهُ and يَقِظُهُ and ▼ يَقُظُهُ ‡ [*A man vigilant in mind*]. (TA.) And إِنَّ فُلَانًا لَيَقِظٌ † [*Verily such a one is vigilant; not dull, heavy*, or *listless*; lit.] *light in head*. (AA.)

يَقْظَةٌ: see what next follows.

يَقَظَةٌ *A state of waking*, or *being awake*; (Ṣ, Mgh, Ḳ;) as also ▼ يَقْظَةٌ, occurring in the saying of the Et-Tihámee,

العَيْشُ نَوْمٌ وَالْمَنِيَّةُ يَقْظَةٌ *
وَالْمَرْءُ بَيْنَهُمَا خَيَالٌ سَارِى *

[*Life is a state of sleep, and death is a state of waking; and man between the two is a night journeying phantom*]; but most hold it to be used only by poetic license. (TA.)

يَقْظَانُ: see يَقِظٌ, in two places. — أَبُو اليَقْظَانِ *The domestic cock*. (Ḳ.)

مَا رَأَيْتُ أَيْقَظَ مِنْهُ ‡ [*I have not seen any more vigilant, wary*, or *cautious, than he*]. (TA.)

مُتَيَقِّظٌ: see يَقِظٌ.

[يقن, &c.
See Supplement.]

يلب

يَلَبٌ *Shields, of the kind called* تِرَسَةٌ, (Ḳ,) pl. of تُرْسٌ; or *of the kind called* دَرَقٌ, as is said in the R and M; which two kinds differ in this, that the درق, like the حَجَف, are of skin, or leather, without any wood or sinews (or nerves), whereas ترس is a more general appellation: (TA:) or *coats of defence*, syn. دُرُوعٌ, (Ḳ,) *of the fabric of El-Yemen*: (TA:) *made* [app. whether shields or coats of defence] *of skins*; (Ḳ;) i.e., *of the hides of camels*: (TA:) or *coats of defence* (دروع) *of the fabric of El-Yemen, made of skins sewed together*: a coll. gen. n., of which the n. un. is يَلَبَةٌ: 'Amr Ibn-Kulthoom says:

عَلَيْنَا البَيْضُ وَالْيَلَبُ اليَمَانِى *
وَأَسْيَافٌ يَقُمْنَ وَيَنْحَنِينَا *

[*Upon us (were) helmets, and leathern coats of defence of the fabric of El-Yemen, and swords that are straight* (so accord. to the above reading, of يَقُمْنَ, which I find in an excellent copy of the Ṣ: but some read يُقَمْنَ, which, I think, affords not so good a sense:) *and that curve*]: (Ṣ:) or *helmets made of camel's hides*: [see also أَلْبَةٌ and أَلَبٌ:] or [*head-coverings made of*] *plaited thongs of leather* (نُسُوعٌ) *woven together, which are put on the head in lieu of the helmet*: (TA:) or *skins which are sewed together, and worn on the head*, specially: (Ḳ:) or *skins which are worn beneath the* [*kind of coat called*] دِرْع, or [*beneath that of*] دِيبَاج; one of which is called يَلَبَةٌ: or *skins which are worn like the coats of defence called* دروع: or *skins of which such coats are made*: (TA:) or *any defensive coverings*, or *armour, of skins; not of iron*; and hence, *shields* (دَرَقٌ) [*of skins*] are thus called: a poet says,

عَلَيْهِمْ كُلُّ سَابِغَةٍ دِلَاصٍ *
وَفِى أَيْدِيهِمِ اليَلَبُ المُدَارُ *

[*Upon them (are, or were,) all (kinds of) ample coats of mail, smooth and glistening; and in their hands, round shields of skins*]: and يَلَبٌ, originally is a name of *that skin* [*of which such coverings are made*]: Aboo-Dahbal El-Jumaḥee says,

* دِرْعِى دِلَاصٌ شَكُّهَا شَكٌّ عَجَبْ *
* وَجَوْبُهَا القَاتِرُ مِنْ سَيْرِ اليَلَبْ *

[*My coat of mail is smooth and glistening: its cleaving* (or *sticking close*) *is an admirable cleaving: and its shield, of good dimensions, is of strips of skin:* so accord. to explanations in the Ṣ, in arts. شك and قتر: but I incline to think that جوبها here is the same as جَيْبُهَا; and that a word is understood, which makes the meaning to be *its opening at the neck and bosom, of good dimensions, is bordered with an edge of thongs*]: (Ṣ:) or simply *skin*, or *hide*. (Ḳ.) — Also *defensive coverings*, or *armour*, *of pieces of felt* (لُبُود), *with a stuffing of honey* (عَسَل) *and sand.* (Ḳ.) — Also, *Steel;* (Ḳ;) *pure iron:* (ISh, T, Ḳ:) n. un. يَلَبَةٌ. (TA.) Of this signification, the following hemistich is cited as an ex.,

* وَمِحْوَرٌ أُخْلِصَ مِنْ مَآءِ اليَلَبْ *

[*And a pulley-axis clearer* (*in its brightness*) *than the lustre of pure iron*, or *steel*]: but ISk says that it is by an Arab of the desert, who, hearing the verse of 'Amr Ibn-Kulthoom quoted above, erroneously supposed يلب to signify the *most excellent kind of iron;* and IDrd also asserts that the meaning assigned to it in this hemistich is founded upon a mistake. (TA.) See also أَلْبَةٌ. — Also, Anything *great, big,* or *large in size.* (Ḳ.)

[يمر, &c.
See Supplement.]

ينبت

يَنْبُوتٌ *A certain thorny kind of tree, not of the kind called* عِضَاه. Mentioned here by IM. See art. نبت. (TA.)

ينبث

يَنْبِيثٌ *A kind of sea-fish:* (IAạr, T:) different from the يَنْبُوتٌ: it is doubtful whether it be Arabic, or a foreign word introduced into the Arabic language. (T.) [See arts. بنث and نبث.]

يهت

4. ايهت (as also اوهت, TA) *It* (flesh-meat, Ḳ, or a wound, TA) *became stinking.* (AZ, Ḳ.)

يهمت

اليَهْمُوتُ *A name of the fish upon which is the earth:* erroneously written with ب [البهموت]: so says Esh-Shiháb in the 'Ináyeh. (MF, TA.) [See my translation of the 1001 Nights, note to the Introduction.]

يوح

يُوحُ, (so accord. to AHat, Mbr, AAF, Kr, Abu-l-'Ala El-Ma'arree, A,) [of the fem. gender, (see بُوحُ,)] indecl., and without the art. ال, (ISd,) accord. to IAmb بُوحُ, but this is a mistake originating from a corrupt transcription of the word, (IKh, IB, &c.,) and يُوحَ, also indecl. like بَرَاحِ, (TA) and يُوحَى, (IAth, Ḳ,) names of *The sun.* (Ṣ, art. بوح, Ḳ, &c.) [See بُوحُ.]

[يوم, &c.
See Supplement.]

END OF BOOK I.

SUPPLEMENT TO PARTS VII. AND VIII.

ق - ی

ق

قبس

قبوس *A sort of* طُنْبُور : see مَعَازِف.

قبع

1. قَبَعَ السِّقَآءَ : see خَنَثَ.

قَبِيعَةٌ [The *pommel* of a sword;] *the thing of silver* or *iron at the extremity of the hilt of a sword.* (Ṣ, Ḳ.)

قبل

1. قَبَلَ as syn. with ▾ أَقْبَلَ, q.v.: see أَدْبَرَ, in two places. — قَبَّحَ اللّٰهُ مَا قَبَلَ مِنْهُ وَمَا دَبَرَ : see دَبَرَ. — قَبِلَ *He took, received,* or *admitted, willingly,* or *with approbation; he accepted.* See قَبُولٌ. — قَبِلَتِ النَّعْلُ *The sandal had its* قِبَال *broken.* (TA in art. شسع.)

3. قَابَلَهُ *He faced,* or *fronted,* or *was opposite to* or *over against, him,* or *it.* (Ṣ,* Ḳ.) See also ▾ اِسْتَقْبَلَهُ *He,* or *it, corresponded to him,* or *it.* — قَابَلَهُ بِنَفْسِهِ [*He opposed himself to him*]. (TA, art. عرض.) See عَرَضَ لَهُ ; and see 4. — قَابَلَ كَذَا بِكَذَا *He requited such a thing with such a thing;* or *did,* or *gave, such a thing in return for such a thing;* as good for good, evil for evil, good for evil, or evil for good. (The Lexicons passim.) — *He counteracted such a thing with such a thing.* — *He compared such a thing* &c. — قُوبِلَ بِكَذَا *It was compensated,* or *requited, by,* or *with, such a thing:* see an ex. of the part. n. voce غُنْم. — قَابَلَ الشَّاةَ : see دَابَرَ الشاة. — فَرَسٌ مُقَابَلٌ مِنْ آفِقٍ وَآفِقَةٍ *A horse that is generous with respect to both parents.* (S in art. افق.)

4. أَقْبَلْتُهُ الشَّىْءَ *I made it to face the thing:* (Ṣ, Ḳ:) and ▾ قَابَلْتُهُ الشَّىْءَ app. signifies the same: see a verse of El-Aạshà voce اِرْتِسَام. — أَقْبَلَ بِهِ [*He turned it forward; contr. of* أَدْبَرَ بِهِ]. (Ṣ, Ḳ, art. دبر.) — أَقْبَلَ *He came, facing;* (JK, Ṣ,* Ḳ;*) *came forward; came on; advanced; contr. of* أَدْبَرَ. (Ṣ, Ḳ.) — أَقْبَلْتُ قِبَلَكَ [not قُبْلَكَ] *I advanced,* or *came, toward thee.* Like قَصَدْتُ قَصْدَكَ. (L, art. حرد.) See also Ḳur, ii. 172. — أَقْبَلَ عَلَيْهِ *He advanced,* or *approached, towards him,* or *it.* — أَقْبَلَ عَلَى إِنْسَانٍ, as though he desired no other person. (JK.) — اقبال The *advancing of fortune; contr. of* إِدْبَار. — الإِقْبَالُ فِى الدُّنْيَا [*Advance in the world,* or *in worldly circumstances*]. (Mgh in art. جد.) إِقْبَالٌ signifies The *being fortunate.* (KL.) — إِقْبَالٌ *i.q.* دَوْلَةٌ [*Good fortune;* &c.; see تَامِكٌ]: and عِزَّةٌ [*might;* &c.]. (Kull, p. 64.) — أَقْبَلَ عَلَيْهِ *He showed favour to him:* or, more properly, *he presented a favourable aspect to him;* or, accord. to general usage, *he met him kindly;* see بَشَّ لَهُ. — أَقْبَلَتْ عَلَيْهِ الدُّنْيَا, (A, art. فتح,) *The world favoured him.* — أَقْبَلَ عَلَى شَىْءٍ *He set about,* or *commenced, doing a thing.* (Ḳ, &c.) — See تَصَدَّدَ. — أَقْبَلَ عَلَيْهِ *He clave to it:* and *he took to, set about, began,* or *commenced it;* as also ▾ قَبِلَ عليه. (Ḳ.) — [أَقْبَلَ عَلَيْهِ بِالسَّيْفِ, and بِالعَصَا, and بِالسَّوْطِ *He advanced against him,* or *set upon him, with the sword,* and *with the staff* or *stick,* and *with the whip.*] — You say, أَقْبَلَ عَلَيْهِ بِالسَّوْطِ يَضْرِبُهُ [*He advanced against him,* or *set upon him, with the whip, striking him*]. (Ṣ in art. حول.) — See قَبَلَ and يُقْبِلُ بِالدَّلْوِ إِلَى البِئْرِ. — أَمْرُ فُلَانٍ الى إِقْبَالٍ : see أَدْبَرَ. — أَقْبِلْ عَلَيْهِ. — أَقْبِلْ عَلَى نَفْسِكَ : see Ḥar, p. ٥٠٨ : بِالتَّعْنِيفِ [*Betake,* or *apply, thyself to thine own affairs*]. (T, voce إِلَى.) — دَبَرَتْ لَهُ الرِّيحُ بَعْدَ مَا أَقْبَلَتْ : see دبر. — أَقْبَلَ [*He recovered,* or *regained, health;*] occurring in the Ḳ, as the explanation of أَقْبَلَ بَعْدَ هُزَالٍ . ثَابَ جِسْمُهُ. (Ḳ, art. ثوب.) (Ḳ, voce حَشَمَ.) — أَقْبَلَ, with reference to the slit ear of a she-camel: see أَدْبَرَ. — أَقْبِلْنَا بِذِمَّةٍ, app. a mistranscription for أَقْبَلْنَا : see ذِمَّةٌ.

6. تَقَابَلُوا *They faced,* or *confronted, one another:* see Ṣ in art. فقح.

8. اِقْتَبَلَهُ *He began it,* or *commenced it;* namely, an affair; (Ṣ,* Mgh, Ḳ;*) as also ▾ إِسْتَقْبَلَهُ. (Mgh.)

10. اِسْتَقْبَلَهُ : see اِسْتَدْبَرَهُ. *He faced him,* or *it.* (TA) *He turned his face towards him,* or *it.* — *He came before his face.* — *He went to meet him; he met him,* or *encountered him. He saw it before him: he looked forward to it: he saw it,* or *knew it, beforehand. He saw,* or *knew, at the beginning of it what he did not see,* or *know, at the end thereof.* — استقبلهُ بِأَمْرٍ (T, Ṣ, Ḳ, &c., in art. بده) *He met him,* or *encountered him, with a thing,* or *an affair,* or *an action.* (TḲ in art. بده.) — استقبلهُ بِمَا يَكْرَهُ (A, Ḳ, in art. بكت, &c.) *He encountered him with,* or, as it often means, *he accused him, to his face, of a thing that he disliked,* or *hated:* see بَكَّتَهُ; and the phrases ▾ قَابَلَهُ بِالكَذِبِ and البَهْتُ أَنْ تَسْتَقْبِلَ أَخَاكَ بِمَا لَيْسَ فِيهِ voce بَهَتَهُ ; and استقبلهُ بِالحَقِّ, voce قَرَحَهُ ; in both senses like لَقِيَهُ بِمَكْرُوهٍ. — اِسْتَقْبَلْتُهُ بِكَلَامٍ فِيهِ غِلْظَةٌ [*I encountered him,* or *confronted him, with speech in which was roughness*]. (JK, M, TA, art. جبه.) — اِسْتَقْبَلَهُ *He anticipated it;* namely, Ramaḍán, by fasting before its commencement. (TA.) — See 8.

قَبْلُ *Before; contr. of* بَعْدُ; (Ṣ, Ḳ, &c.;) an adv. n. of time; and, as some say, of place also; (MF, TA;) and of rank, or station. (TA.)

سَقَى إِبِلَهُ قَبَلًا [and بِالقَبَلِ] *He poured the water into the trough while his camels were drinking, so that it came upon them:* (T, TA:) or قَبَلٌ signifies a man's *bringing his camels to water, and drawing the water over their mouths, not having prepared for them aught* [*thereof*] *before that:* (Aṣ, TA:) and سَقَى عَلَى إِبِلِهِ قَبَلًا *he poured the water over the mouths of his camels:* (M, TA:) and ▾ أَقْبَلَ عَلَى إِبِلِهِ *he drew the water over the heads of his camels while they drank, when they had drunk what was in the trough,* (Lḥ, M, TA,) *not having prepared it before that:* and this is the most severe mode of watering. (Lḥ, TA.) See an ex. voce جَبًا, art. جبو and قِبَلٌ — جبى as opposed to دُبُرٌ: see the latter. — إِنَّ الحَقَّ بِقِبَلٍ *Verily the truth is manifest; where one sees it.* (TA, art. عجز.) — مِنْ ذِى قِبَلٍ: see إِذًا — أُنُف; and see قِبَلٌ; and مِنْ ذِى عَوْضٍ رَأَيْتُ الشِّعْرَى بِقِبَلٍ الخ: see M, art. دبر.

لَقِيتُهُ قِبَلًا *I met him face to face.* (JK.) — لَا أُكَلِّمُكَ إِلَى عَشْرٍ مِنْ ذِى قِبَلٍ ✝ *i. q.* من ذى قِبَلٍ, i. e. [*I will not speak to thee until ten* nights] *in what I* [*now*] *begin* [*of time*]: or the latter, *until ten* [*nights*] *which thou* [*now*] *beginnest:* and the former, *until ten* [*nights*] *of the days which thou* [*now*] *witnessest,* (Ḳ, TA,) i. e. *beginnest:* (TA:) or the latter, *of a time* [*now*] *begun;* or, *a future time.* (Mgh, Mṣb.) And أَتَيْتُ فُلَانًا مِنْ ذِى قِبَلٍ *i. q.* آنِفًا. (Lth in T, art. انف.) — قِبَلَ *Towards.* (Bḍ. ii. 172.) قِبَلُ شَيْءٍ *What is next to a thing:* you say, ذَهَبَ قِبَلَ السُّوقِ [*he went to the part next to the market*]. (TA.) لِى قِبَلَهُ مَالٌ *I have property in his hands;* i. e. *due,* or *owing, to me by him;* syn. عِنْدَهُ [q. v.] (Ḳ,* TA.) And لَنَا قِبَلَكَ حَاجَةٌ: (Ṣ in art. روى &c.:) see رَوِيَّةٌ (and عِنْدَ also). — هٰذَا الأَمْرُ مِنْ قِبَلِهِ *This thing, or affair, is from him;* syn. مِنْ عِنْدِهِ, meaning مِنْ لَدُنْهُ and مِنْ تِلْقَائِهِ. (Lth, TA.) يَتَكَلَّمُ مِنْ قِبَلِ أَنْفِهِ [*He speaks from* (i. e. *through*) *his nose*]. (JK and Ḳ, voce أَدْغَمُ.) — انشقّ من قِبَلِ نفسه *It* (a garment) *rent of itself.* (L, art. صوخ, &c.)

قُبُلٌ The *front,* or *fore part.* See Ḳur, xii. 26. The *former* or *first part:* see القُبُلُ — دَفْئِىٌّ. *The anterior pudendum* (فَرْج) [*vulva,* and *vagina,*] of a man or woman; (Mṣb;) opposite of الدُّبُرُ. (Ṣ, Ḳ.)

مَا لَهُ قِبْلَةٌ وَلَا دِبْرَةٌ, &c.: see دبر.

قُبْلِىٌّ: see دُبْرِىٌّ.

فُلَانٌ مَا — شِبْرٌ: see الشِّسْعِ and قِبَالُ الشِّبْرِ قِبَالٌ — دبر &c.: see يَدْرِى قِبَالَ الأَمْرِ مِنْ دِبَارِهِ; of the sandal: see زِمَامٌ.

قَبُولٌ *Favourable reception; acceptance; approbation:* (KL PṢ:) *love, and approbation,* and *inclination of the mind.* (TA.) عَلَى فُلَانٍ قَبُولٌ [*Approbation is bestowed upon such a one;*] *the mind accepts,* or *approves, such a one.* (Ṣ.) — قَبُولٌ *Goodliness, beauty, grace, comeliness,* or *pleasingness:* and [*beauty of*] *aspect* or *garb.* (Ḳ.) [And *Acceptableness.* عَلَيْهِ قَبُولٌ may be rendered *Upon him,* or *it, is an appearance of goodliness,* &c.]

قَبِيلٌ: see دَبِيرٌ — قَبِيلٌ *Kind, species, class, race.* مِنْ قَ *Of the kind,* &c. See قَبِيلَةٌ.

جَآءَ قُبَيْلُ *He came a little while ago;* syn. آنِفًا. (M in art. انف.)

قُبَالَتَهُ *Opposite to, in a position so as to face, him* or *it.* (Ḳ, &c.) See حِيَالٌ in art. حول. — قُبَالَةٌ The *direction, point, place,* or *tract,* in *front* of a thing; the *opposite direction* &c.

قَبِيلَةٌ *A body of men from one father and mother:* and ✝ قَبِيلٌ, without ة, *a body of men from several ancestors.* (Az in TA, art. سبط.) قَبِيلَةٌ — شَعْبٌ: see — *A mass of stone* or *rock at the mouth of a well.* (Ḳ and TA voce عُقَابٌ, q. v.) See قَابِلٌ.

عَامٌ قَابِلٌ, and ✝ مُقْبِلٌ, signify the same, [*A next-coming year*]. (Ṣ.) اللَّيْلَةُ المُقْبِلَةُ *i. q.* القَابِلَةُ [*The next night*]. (Ṣ, Ḳ.) See القَبَاقِبُ — قَابِلٌ لِكَذَا *Susceptible of such a thing.* — قَابِلٌ An arrow that wins [in the game of المَيْسِر]; (TA, art دبر;) *contr. of* دَابِرٌ, q. v. (Ṣ and TA, art. دبر.) — قَبَائِلُ of the head: see شَأْنٌ. — And ✝ قَبِيلَةٌ of a helmet: see قَابِلَةٌ — طِرَاقٌ *A wife.* (TA in art. عزب.)

قَابِلِيَّةٌ [*The quality of admitting* or *receiving; susceptibility*].

أَقْبَلُ لِلْمَوْعِظَةِ [*More,* or *most, inclined to accept admonition*]. (TA, art. رق.)

إِدْبَارَةٌ and its syn. إِقْبَالٌ: see 4; and see إِقْبَالَةٌ.

مُقْبِلٌ: see قَابِلٌ — [*I. q.* مُقْتَبَلٌ]. Ex. مُقْبِلَةٌ الشَّبَابِ (Ḳ, voce جَوَارِحُ,) and الرَّحِمِ. (TA, ibid.) See مُدْبِرٌ.

ثَغْرٌ بَارِدُ المُقَبَّلِ [*A mouth,* or *front teeth, cold,* or *cool, in the part that is kissed*]. (A, art. خصر, &c.)

المُقَابَلُ مِنَ المَنَازِلِ *contr. of* المُدَابَرُ, (M, art. دبر, q. v.) — مُقَابَلٌ *Noble, by the father's and mother's side:* (Ṣ, Ḳ, TA:) see an ex. voce طَابَ; and see إِزْدَوَجَا — مُقَابَلَةٌ applied to a ewe: see الجَبْرُ — دبر: see نَاقَةٌ مُقَابَلَةٌ مُدَابَرَةٌ — مُدَبَّرَةٌ جبر: see — فِى مُقَابَلَةِ كَذَا: والمُقَابَلَةُ *In comparison with such a thing:* see an ex. in art. غين in the Mṣb.

مُسْتَقْبَلٌ, with fet-ḥ to the ب, *Looked forward to, anticipated, begun.*

مُسْتَدْبِرٌ: see مُسْتَقْبَلُ المَجْدِ.

قبن

قَبَّانٌ *A steelyard:* see عَمُودُ المِيزَانِ.

قبو

قَبَآءٌ [*A kind of tunic, resembling the* قُفْطَان, *generally reaching to the middle of the shank, divided down the front, and made to overlap over the chest.* So in the present day. See also Dozy, Dict. des noms de vêtements, pp. 352-62.]

قتر

2. قَتَّرَهُ *He prostrated him upon his side,* عَلَى قُتْرِهِ [not على قُتْرَةٍ, as in the Ḳ]; (L;) *he threw him down upon one of his two sides,* عَلَى أَحَدِ قُتْرَيْهِ, having pierced him [with a spear]; (JK;) like قَطَّرَهُ.

اِبْنُ قِتْرَةَ *The* حَيَّة. (T in art. بنى.)

جَوْبٌ قَاتِرٌ *A shield of good dimensions.* (Ṣ.) See يَلَبٌ.

قتل

1. قَتَلَ الشَّىْءَ, inf. n. قَتْلٌ, † *He knew the thing; he was,* or *became, acquainted with it:* (Mṣb:) [or rather, *i. q.*] قَتَلَهُ عِلْمًا, (Bḍ in iv. 156, and TA,) and خُبْرًا, (Ḳ,) and بِعِلْمِهِ, (Bḍ, ubi supra,) *he knew it* (Bḍ, Ḳ, TA) *completely,* (TA,) or *thoroughly, very well,* or *superlatively well;* as also نَحَرَهُ عِلْمًا. (Bḍ.) See أَثْبَتَ الشَّىْءَ مَعْرِفَةً in art. ثبت.

2. قَتَّلَ: see a verse cited in art. عتب, conj. 4.

3. قَاتَلَهُ *He fought,* or *combated, him; contended with him in fight* or *conflict* or *battle.* قَاتَلَ عَلَى دِينِ ٱللّٰهِ: see 3 in art. ازى.

5. تَقَتَّلَتْ لَهُ means تَخَضَّعَتْ لَهُ وَتَذَلَّلَتْ حَتَّى عَشِقَهَا. (A.)

10. اِسْتَقْتَلَ [properly *He sought,* or *courted, slaughter;*] *i. q.* اِسْتَمَاتَ; (Ṣ, Ḳ;) meaning *he cared not for death,* by reason of his courage; (JM;) *he resigned and subjected himself to slaughter, and cared not for death.* (Mgh.)

قَتْلٌ: from this word is formed the pl. قُتُولٌ, on the authority of hearsay. (El-Jurjánee, in Mṣb, art. قصد.)

قَتَّالٌ [*Murderous; slaughterous; very deadly.*] You say حَيَّةٌ قَتَّالَةٌ [*A very deadly serpent*]. (TA in art. اصل.)

قَاتِلٌ *Deadly;* applied to a tree; (Ḳ in art. خمط;) and to poison. (TA in that art.)

مَقْتَلٌ *A* [*vital*] *place in a man* [*or an animal,* i. e.] *where a wound causes death;* (Ṣ, Mṣb;) as the temple: (Mṣb:) pl. مَقَاتِلُ. (Ṣ.)

حَوِّلْ إِلَىَّ وَجْهَكَ وَلِيَنِى مَقَاتِلَكَ means. (A.)

مُسْتَمِيتٌ: see مُسْتَقْتِلٌ.

قتن

1. قَتَنَ: see قَتُنَ.

قَنِيتٌ: see قَتِينٌ.

قحز

1. قَحَزَ *It* (an arrow) rose in the sky. (J Sh, in TA, art. شخص.)

قحف

قُحْفٌ: see جُمْجُمَةٌ, in two places; — and قُدٌّ. — *A glass bowl*; as also جُمْجُمَةٌ. (Az, TA in art. جمر.)

قحل

قَحُولٌ, applied to a man and to a horse, *i. q.* عَتِينٌ. (IAar in TA, art. عجر.)

إِنْقَحَلٌ; see إِنْزَهْو.

قحم

1. قحم نَفْسَهُ فِى الأُمُورِ and ♦تقحّم فيها and ♦اقتحم *He entered into affairs without consideration.* (A.)

5. تَقَحَّمَ *He experienced dearth, drought, or sterility.* See an ex. voce تَبِعَةٌ. — تَقَحَّمَ فِى الأَمْرِ بِلَا رَوِيَّةٍ [*He plunged, or rushed, into the affair without consideration*]. (Ḳ,* TA in art. علط.) See 1. — تَقَحَّمَ: see تَدَلَّتْ.

8. اِقْتَحَمَ. See 1. — Said of a young camel: see voce بُلَعٌ. — اِقْتَحَمَ الغَمَرَاتِ: see 1 in art. خوض. And اقتحم العَقَبَةَ: see عَقَبَةٌ.

قَحْمَةٌ, like قَحْبَةٌ, *An old woman.* See قَحْبٌ.

مُقْحَمٌ *Redundant; pleonastic; foisted in*: applied to a word and to a letter. — حَرْفٌ مُقْحَمَةٌ *A letter inserted without reason.* مُقْحَمَةٌ is also applied in like manner to a word. [In a copy of the Ṣ, in art. بهت, I find it written مُقْحِمَةٌ]: *i. q.* زَائِدَةٌ. (TA in art. بهت.)

قحو

أُقْحُوَانٌ: see بَابُونَجٌ. See also a verse cited voce تَنُّورٌ.

قدس

قَادُوسٌ (pl. قَوَادِيسُ) *An earthen or wooden pot of a water-wheel.* (PU.)

قدع

1. قَدَعَ فَرَسَهُ *He pulled in his horse by the bridle and bit, to stop him*; (Ṣ, Ḳ;) *he curbed, or restrained, him.* (Ṣ.) — هُوَ الفَحْلُ لَا يُقْدَعُ: see أَنْفٌ; and see قرع.

قدم

1. قَدَمَ القَوْمَ, aor. ـُ, inf. n. قَدْمٌ (Ṣ,* Mṣb, Ḳ) and قُدُومٌ; (Ḳ;) and ♦تَقَدَّمَهُمْ; (Ṣ,* Mṣb, Ḳ;) and ♦قَدَّمَهُمْ; and ♦اِسْتَقْدَمَهُمْ; (Ḳ:) *He became before the people*: (TA:) syn. سَبَقَهُمْ; (Mṣb;) *he preceded them; went before them; took precedence of them; headed them; led them, so as to serve as an example, or object of imitation.* — See أَمْهِرْ. — قَدِمَ البَلَدَ, aor. ـَ, inf. n. قُدُومٌ and مَقْدَمٌ, [*He came to, or arrived at, the town, &c.*] (Mṣb.) أَخَذَنِى مَا قَدُمَ وَمَا حَدُثَ: see art. حدث. — قَدِمَ عَلَى الأَمْرِ *i. q.* أَقْدَمَ عَلَيْهِ [*He advanced boldly to undertake the affair*]. (TA.) See an ex. in a verse voce مُضَافٌ. — See 6.

2. قَدَّمَ زَيْدًا إِلَى الحَائِطِ *He brought Zeyd near, or caused him to draw near, or to approach, to the wall.* (Mṣb.) — قَدَّمَهُ *He put it forward; offered it; proffered it.* — *He brought, and brought forward, him or it.* — قَدَّمَ لَهُ طَعَامًا *He proffered, offered, or presented to him, food.* — قَدَّمَ *He did* good or evil *previously, or beforehand*: (Bḍ, and Jel in xxxvi. 11; &c.:) *he laid up in store.* (Bḍ in xii. 48.) See زَلَّفَهُ. — قَدَّمَ *He made foremost; put, brought, or sent, forward; he advanced* him or it: *he promoted* him. — قَدَّمَهُ عَلَى غَيْرِهِ, inf. n. تَقْدِيمٌ, *He made him, or it, to be before, or have precedence of, another, in time*: and *in place*; i. e. *he placed, or put, him, or it, before another*; or *made him, or it, to precede another*: and *in rank, or dignity*; i. e. *he preferred him, or it, before another*; or *honoured, or esteemed, him, or it, above another.* (Kull, p. 104.) — قَدَّمَهُ لِكَذَا *He prepared it, or provided it beforehand, for such a thing.* See Ḳur, xii. 48. — قَدَّمَ عِنْدَ اللّٰهِ خَيْرًا *He prepared, or provided in store, for himself, good,* [i. e. *a reward,*] *with God.* (A and Mgh in art. حسب.) — قَدَّمَ لَهُ الثَّمَنَ *He paid him in advance, or beforehand, the price.* — قَدَّمَ أَنْ يَفْعَلَ كَذَا *He preferred doing such a thing*; syn. آثَرَ, i. e. فَضَّلَ. (M in art. أثر.) [Hence, قَدَّمَ العَجْزَ فِى الشَّىْءِ *He preferred backwardness with respect to the thing.*] (See قَدَّمَ and فَرَطَ; and see Kull, p. 279.) — قَدَّمَ syn. with تَقَدَّمَ, q. v.: like as أَخَّرَ is with تَأَخَّرَ: so in the Ḳur, xli. 1. (TA, art. أخر.) — قَدَّمَ [is trans. and intrans.: for its significations as an intrans. v., see its syn. تقدّم, and see 1:] as a trans. v. it is contr. of أَخَّرَ. (Mṣb, art. أخر.) — قَدَّمَهُ is syn. with بَدَأَ بِهِ. (Mgh and Mṣb in art. بدأ.) — قَدَّمَ: see تَقَدَّمَ. — See تَأَذَّنَ voce آذَنَ. — قَدَّمَ إِلَيْهِ فِى كَذَا: see أَفْرَطَ. — قَدَّمَ أَوْلَادًا and قَدَّمَتْهُمْ: see قَدَّمَهُ and ♦أَقْدَمَهُ *He urged him forward.* (Mo'allakát, 157.) — قَدَّمَ has تَقْدِمَةٌ for an inf. n.

4. أَقْدَمَ *He was bold, or audacious.* — أَقْدَمَ عَلَى الأَمْرِ *He ventured upon, or addressed himself to, the thing boldly, courageously, or daringly*; (Ṣ, Ḳ;) *he attempted it.* — أَقْدَمَ على قِرْنِهِ *He behaved boldly, courageously, or daringly, against his adversary*; (Mṣb;) *he attacked him.* — See 1. — أَقْدِمْ, (improperly إِقْدِمْ,) said to a horse, *Advance boldly!* (Ṣ.) So rendered voce أَهَابَ, and هَبْ.

5. تَقَدَّمَ *He was, or became, or went, before, or ahead; preceded; had, or took, precedence; contr. of* تَأَخَّرَ, q. v. See 1. — تَقَدَّمَ إِلَى الحَائِطِ *He drew near, or approached, to the wall.* (Mṣb.) — تَقَدَّمَ *He advanced; went forward, or onward.* (L, art. قود.) — تَقَدَّمَ عَلَى الحَقِّ: see Bḍ, xviii. 27. — تَقَدَّمَ *He became advanced, or promoted.* — تَقَدَّمَ مِنْهُ كَلَامٌ: see فَرَطَ: but the primary meaning is, *Speech proceeded from him previously.* — تَقَدَّمَ عَلَى غَيْرِهِ quasi-pass. of قَدَّمَهُ عَلَى غَيْرِهِ; *He, or it, was, or became, before, or had precedence of, another, in time*: and *in place*; i. e. *he, or it, was, or became, before another; preceded another; went before another*: and *in rank, or dignity*; i. e. *he, or it, was, or became, preferred before another*; or *honoured, or esteemed, above another*: in all these senses like تَقَدَّمَ غَيْرَهُ. See بَكَرَ. — تَقَدَّمَ فِى أَمْرٍ [*He was forward in an affair*] قَبْلَ فِعْلِهِ [*before doing it*]. (A'Obeyd, T in art. رمى.) — تَقَدَّمَ *i. q.* سَبَقَ; (Ḳ, art. سبق, &c.;) and *contr. of* تَأَخَّرَ. (TA, art. أخر.) — تَقَدَّمَ إِلَيْهِ فِى كَذَا, (Ḳ,) or بِكَذَا, (Mgh,) or both, (Mgh,) *He commanded, ordered, bade, charged, or enjoined, him respecting, or to do, such a thing*; (Mgh, Mṣb, Ḳ;) as also ♦قَدَّمَ, inf. n. تَقْدِيمٌ. (Mṣb.)

6. تَقَادَمَ is best rendered *It became old*: and ♦قَدُمَ *it was old.*

8. اِقْتَدَى بِهِ *He did as he did, following his example; or taking him as an example, an exemplar, a pattern, or an object of imitation.* (Mṣb.) *He followed his example, imitated him*; &c.

10. اِسْتَقْدَمَ *He went before.* — اِسْتَقْدَمَتْ رِحَالَتُكَ: see art. رحل.

قَدَمٌ The *human foot, from the ankle downwards.* (Mgh.) — لَهُ قَدَمٌ رَاسِخَةٌ فِى العِلْمِ: see art. رسخ. — عَلَى قَدَمٍ عَظِيمٍ *On an excellent foundation.* — فُلَانٌ عَلَى قَدَمِ فُلَانٍ *Such a one is successor of such a one.*

قِدَمٌ *Oldness; antiquity.* — *Existence, or duration, or time, without beginning; like* أَزَلٌ (Kull, p. 31; &c.) See أَزَلٌ. — عَلَى وَجْهِ الدَّهْرِ: قِدَمُ الدَّهْرِ means properly *the olden time; antiquity.* — عَلَى قِدَمِ الدَّهْرِ [*In,* or *from, old,* or *ancient, time; of old*]. (Ṣ, M, Ḳ, art. أس; in the first and last of which it is coupled with the like phrase.)

— مِنْ قُدُمٍ [*In front*]. (Ḳ, voce ظُنْبُوبٌ.)

قُدُمٌ: see أُخُرٌ.

قَادِمَةٌ as applied to a part of a camel's saddle is an improper word: the proper term is وَاسِطٌ.

قَدُومٌ *An adz;* [so in the present day, but pronounced قَدُّوم;] *a certain implement of the carpenter;* (Ṣ, Mgh, Mṣb;) *a* فَأْس *with which one hews, or forms or fashions by cutting.* (Ṣ.)

قَدِيمٌ *Ancient; old; to which no commencement is assigned.* — مَالٌ قَدِيمٌ *Old,* or *long-possessed, property.* (Ṣ, A, Mgh, Mṣb, all in art. تلد.) — قَدِيمٌ The *reputation* (حَسَبٌ) of a man or people. (TA, art. دثر.) See a verse in 1 of art. ثنى. — القَدِيمُ, as an epithet applied to God, *i. q.* القَدِيمُ الأَزَلِىُّ *The Ancient without beginning.*

القُدَّامُ *The location that is before.*

قَوَادِمُ: respecting the feathers thus called, see voce مَنَاكِبُ, and أَبْهَرُ.

المُقْدَمُ is here جَرِىْءُ المُقْدَمِ: see art. جرأ syn. with الإِقْدَامُ.

مِقْدَامٌ *Very bold or daring or courageous* (Ṣ, Ḳ,) *against the enemy;* (Ṣ;) as also مِقْدَامَةٌ. (Ṣ.) — مِقْدَامَةٌ: see voce مِعْزَابَةٌ. — [The pl.] مَقَادِمُ *Fronts; fore parts.* See an ex. voce أَعْثَرُ. — مَقَادِيمُ The *front of the forehead.* (JK.)

مُقَدَّمٌ *A provost, chief, head, director, conductor, or manager.* — مُقَدَّمٌ The *antecedent* (or *first proposition*) *in an enthymeme,* and (*first part*) *of a hypothetical proposition.* — مُقَدِّمَةٌ The *van,* or *vanguard,* of an army.

مُقَدِّمَةٌ The *ground whereon rests an inquiry* or *investigation:* and the *ground whereon rests the truth of an evidence* or *a demonstration:* and *a* [*premiss* or] *proposition which is made a part of a syllogism:* and المُقَدِّمَةُ الغَرِيبَةُ is *that* [*premiss*] *which is both actually and virtually suppressed in the syllogism; as when we say, A is equal to B, and B is equal to C, when it results that A is equal to C, by means of the* مُقَدِّمَة غَرِيبَة, *which is, every equal to the equal of a thing is equal to that thing.* (KT.)

مُتَقَدِّمٌ *Preceding: anterior; being,* or *lying, in advance of others.* — مُتَقَدِّمٌ فِى الأُمُورِ *Forward in affairs.*

المُسْتَقْدِمِينَ in the Ḳur, xv. 24: see Bḍ; and see its opposite, المُسْتَأْخِرِينَ.

قدو

قُدْوَةٌ and قِدْوَةٌ (Ṣ, Mṣb, Ḳ,) and قُدَوَةٌ (Ḳ,) *A pattern; an exemplar; an example; an object of imitation; one who is,* or *is to be, imitated.* (Ṣ, Mṣb, Ḳ, TA.) See إِسْوَةٌ.

قِدْيَةٌ: see قِدْوَةٌ.

قَادِيَةٌ The *first that come to one,* or *come upon one, of a company of men.* (TA in art. طحم.)

قذع

3. قَاذَعَهُ *He reviled him, being reviled by him;* and *vied with him in foul,* or *unseemly, speech* or *language.* (A, Ḳ.) See 3 in art. قدع.

قذف

1. قَذَفَ بِٱلْحِجَارَةِ وَغَيْرِهَا, aor. ـِ, inf. n. قَذْفٌ, *He threw stones, &c.* (Mṣb.) — قَذَفَ بِهِ *He cast it; cast it forth;* namely, an arrow, and a pebble, and speech, and anything. (Lth, TA.) It may sometimes be rendered *He shed it;* as, for instance, light into the heart, said of God. — يَقْذِفُ بِالحَقِّ (Ḳur, xxxiv. 47,) *He* (God) *uttereth truth.* (Zj, TA.) — قَذَفَ بِالسَّهْمِ *He shot the arrow.* (Lth, TA.) — قَذَفَ *He reproached, upbraided, reviled, vilified, defamed,* or *gave a bad name to,* a chaste woman: (MA:) *he reproached, upbraided,* &c. another; syn. شَتَمَ. (JK.) Used tropically, قَذَفَهُ is most correctly rendered ‡ *He cast at him an accusation:* but it is commonly used and expl. as syn. with شَتَمَهُ q. v. — قَذَفَ *He charged, reproached,* or *upbraided,* (رَمَى,) a chaste, or an honest, or a married, woman, *with adultery.* (Ṣ, Mṣb, Ḳ.) — قَذَفَهُ *He aspersed him, reviled him;* syn. شَتَمَهُ. (JK.) — قَذَفَهُ بِهِ *He reproached,* or *upbraided, him with it; he accused him of it.* (TA.) — Also, *i. q.* أَصَابَهُ بِهِ. (TA.) — وَيَقْذِفُونَ بِالغَيْبِ (Ḳur, xxxiv. 52,) *They uttering conjectures,* (Zj, TA,) or *uttering conjecture;* (Bḍ;) *speaking of that which was hidden* [*from them*], (Ksh,) *of that which had not become apparent to them.* (Bḍ.) — قُذِفَتْ بِاللَّحْمِ † *She* (a camel) *became fat and plump.* (TA, voce اُسْتُعْرِضَتْ.) — قَذَفَتْهُ القَوَاذِفُ: see طَوَّحَتْهُ الطَّوَائِحُ.

قُذُفٌ *Land in which is no pasturage wherein cattle may freely range.* (L, art. صح.)

قَذَّافٌ *i. q.* مَنْجَنِيقٌ: (Lth, Ḳ:) The *kind of instrument with which a thing is thrown so that it goes far;* n. un. with ة. (Aboo-Kheyreh, Ḳ.) See مِرْجَامٌ and مِرْجَمَةٌ. — قَذَّافَةٌ *A sling:* pl. قَذَّافَاتٌ. (MA.)

قَوَاذِفُ: see طَوَائِحُ; and طَوَّحَتْهُ الطَّوَائِحُ.

مَقَاذِفُ: see مَطَاوِحُ: *Places of perdition;* syn. مَهَالِكُ. (TA.)

قذل

القَذَالُ *The whole of the back of the head:* (Ṣ, Mṣb, Ḳ:) or the *part from the hollow of the back of the neck* (نُقْرَة القَفَا) *to the ear:* (El-Ghooree, Mgh:) [see القَمَحْدُوَةُ in art. قمحد:] and, in a horse, *the place where the* عِذَار *is tied, behind the forelock.* (Ṣ, Mṣb, Ḳ.)

قذى

1. قَذَّاهُ: see حَرَّضَهُ.

قَذًى *What falls into the eye;* (Ṣ, Ḳ;) *a little piece of wood, or dust, that falls into the eye:* (JK:) and *what falls into beverage;* (Ṣ, Ḳ;) *as flies, &c.;* (TA;) *what betakes itself* [or *is attracted*] *to the sides of a vessel, and clings thereto:* (AḤn, TA:) *dust, motes, or particles of rubbish, as of sticks and stalks and straws,* or *the like, that fall into the eye* or *into water and beverage:* (KL:) *any floating particles upon water, &c.:* [*scum:*] *dirt that falls into the eye;* (Mṣb;) *what collects in the inner angle of the eye;* (Ḥar, p. 65;) *what comes into the eye, such as a bit of straw, &c.:* (Id, p. 149:) [properly a coll. gen. n.:] قَذَاةٌ [the n. un.] *a thing that falls into the eye and pains it:* (Id, p. 259:) *a mote.* — أَغْضَى على قَذًى: see art. غضو.

قرش

1. قَرَشَ, aor. ـِ, inf. n. قَرْشٌ; and ▼ اِقْتَرَشَ and ▼ تَقَرَّشَ; *He gained, acquired,* or *earned,* and *collected,* for his family. (M.)

5 and 8: see 1.

قرص

قُرْصٌ *A round convex ornament* worn on the crown of the ṭarboosh. (See Modern Egypt. Appendix A.)

قرط

قُرْطٌ: see قِرَاطٌ.

قِرَاطٌ *A lamp,* or its *lighted wick:* syn. مِصْبَاحٌ or شُعْلَتُهُ: (Ḳ:) the *lighted wick* (شُعْلَة) *of a lamp;* (Ṣ;) and so ▼ قُرْطٌ. (L, art. صبح.)

قرطف

قُرْطُفٌ *A red garment, of the kind called* كِسَآء. See كَذَبَ, p. 2598c.

قرطل

قُرْطَالَةٌ *An ass's pannier, one of a pair.* See حُوَارَةٌ.

قرع

1. قَرَعَ in the sense of ضَرَبَ has مَقْرَعٌ for an inf. n. (Mgh, art. غمز.) — قَرَعَ فِى مَقْرَعِهِ i.q. ضَرَبَ فِى مَضْرَبِهِ. (TA in art. ضرب.) — قَرَعَ صَفَاتَهُ ‡ *He impugned his character; blamed* or *censured him; spoke against him.* (Mgh, art. غمز.) See مَغْمَزٌ. — قَرَعَ بَيْنَ ظُفْرِ إِبْهَامِهِ وَظُفْرِ سَبَّابَتِهِ *He fillipped with the nail of his thumb and that of his forefinger.* (Lth, Ḳ,* TA, art. قدع.) and أَنْفٌ: see هُوَ الفَحْلُ لَا يُقْرَعُ أَنْفُهُ. (زنجر.) — قَرَعَ أَنْفَهُ, inf. n. قَرْعٌ, † *He rejected him, repelled him,* or *turned him back;* namely a suitor in a case of marriage. (TA, in art. بضع.) See بُضْعٌ. — إِنَّ العَصَا قُرِعَتْ لِذِى الحِلْمِ: see Freytag's Arab. Prov. i. 55; and Ḥar, 656. — لَا يُقْرَعُ لَهُ العَصَا: see Freytag's Arab. Prov. ii. 543, and Ḥar, 655, in two places. — قَرَعَهُ بِعَصَا المَلَامَةِ: see عَصًا. — قَرَعْتُ رَأْسَهُ بِالعَصَا and بِالسَّيْفِ: see قَرَعَ لِأَمْرِهِ ظُنْبُوبَهُ and قَرَعَ ظُنْبُوبَ بَعِيرِهِ. — قَرَعْتُ سَاقَ: see قَرَعَ لِلْأَمْرِ سَاقَهُ: and ظنب: see art. &c.

2. قَرَّعَهُ *He reproached him for his crime or the like, saying to him, Thou didst so and so.* (TA, voce مُثَرِّبٌ.) — قَرَعَ *He took, got, or won, a bet, wager, or stake.* (L, in TA, voce نَدَبٌ.)

3. قَارَعَهُ: see its syn. سَاهَمَهُ.

4. أَقْرَعَ بَيْنَهُمْ *He ordered, or commanded, them to cast, or draw, lots, or to practise sortilege,* [*among themselves,*] for the thing (عَلَى الشَّىْءِ): (JM:) [see an ex. in the Mgh, in this art.:] or *he prepared, or disposed, them, for doing so,* for the thing (على الشىء): (Mṣb:) or *he cast, or drew, lots, or practised sortilege, among them.* (Ḳ.) The first explanation is generally preferable. See أَسْهَمَ بَيْنَهُمْ.

6. تَقَارَعَا: see هُمَا يَتَقَارَعَانِ الخَيْرَ وَالشَّرَّ.

حَبُّ القَرْعِ *Worms in the belly.* (TA, voce شهدانج.) But see دُودُ القَرَعِ. القرع is not a mistake for القرح: حَبُّ القَرَحِ is a corruption, found in medical books: حب القرع is a name of the tape-worm, because each joint of it resembles a grain, or seed, of the gourd. (IbrD.)

قَرَعٌ *Bare pieces of ground amid herbage.* (TA in art. خفى, from a trad.)

قُرْعَةٌ [*A lot* used in sortilege: *lots* collectively: *sortilege* itself. Used in all these senses in the present day, and app. in the classical times.] ضَرَبَ القُرْعَةَ *He shuffled, or cast, or drew, lots; performed a sortilege.*

قَرِيعٌ; pl. قَرْعَى: see an ex. of the pl. in a prov. cited voce اِسْتَنَّ. — هُوَ قَرِيعُ وَحْدِهِ: see وحد.

قَارِعَةُ الطَّرِيقِ *The higher, or highest, part of the road; the part that is trodden by the passengers;* [*the beaten way*]. (Mṣb.) In law books expl. as meaning أَطْرَافُ الطَّرِيقِ; opposed to its جَادَّة.

قَارِعَةٌ *A sudden calamity.* (Ḳ.) See also Bḍ, and Jel, in xiii. 31, and an ex. voce اِنْفَرَجَ.

مَقْرَعٌ: see مَغْمَزٌ.

مِقْرَعٌ: see مِضْرَبٌ.

مِقْرَعَةٌ *A whip: or anything with which one beats:* (Ḳ:) or *a thing with which a beast is beaten:* (Az, TA:) or *a piece of wood with which mules and asses are beaten:* (TA:) [*a cudgel:* often applied in the present day to *a cudgel made of the thick part of a palm-stick;* and this, when used in sport, has several splits made in the thicker end, to cause the blows to produce a loud sound:] pl. مَقَارِعُ. (TA.)

قرف

3. قَارَفَهُ *He was, or became, near to it;* meaning some base thing, or the like. (TA.) See قَرَفٌ.

قَرَفٌ The *mixing with others;* [and particularly *with others who are diseased* or *the like*]; a subst. from مُقَارَفَةٌ: (Ḳ:) the *being near to* [*a person,* or *persons,* or *a place, infected with*] *disease:* (Ṣ, TA:) the *being near to pestilence,* or *epidemic disease.* (T in art. تلف.) See تَلَفٌ.

اِتَّسَعَتْ signifies أَعْرَضَتِ القِرْفَةُ: (TA, art. عرض:) and اِتَّسَعَتْ قِرْفَتُهُ signifies كَثُرَ مَنْ يَتَّهِمُهُ. (TA, art. لبس.) See voce عَرَضٌ.

مَقْرَفٌ *A place of paring off:* see an ex. voce صَمْغٌ.

قرق

قِرْقٌ: see طُبْنَةٌ.

قرقع

قُرْقُعَةٌ (TA, art. نقض): properly فُرْقُعَةٌ, q. v.

قرم

1. قَرَمَ *It gnawed:* see عُثَّةٌ.

قَرْمٌ: see مُطَّعِبٌ.

قَرَمٌ: see شُورَى.

قُرْمَةٌ: see فُقْرَةٌ.

قِرَامٌ † *A kid.* (IAạr, in TA, art. عت.) — See مِقْرَمَةٌ.

مِقْرَمٌ: see مِقْرَمَةٌ.

مِقْرَمَةٌ *A coverlet of a bed;* (Mgh, in arts. قرم and حبس;) also called مِحْبَسٌ: (Id, in art. حبس:) or *a thin curtain,* accord. to some, *figured;* as also ↓ مِقْرَمٌ and ↓ قِرَامٌ: (Mṣb:) or this last, *a figured curtain.* (Mṣb.)

قرمص

قُرْمُوصٌ *A hollow which a man digs wherein to sit to protect himself from the cold.* (Mgh, art. ربض.) See an ex. voce رَبَضٌ.

قرمل

قَرْمَلٌ, pl. قَرَامِلُ: see سُفَّةٌ.

قرن

1. قَرَنَ شَيْئًا بِشَىْءٍ *He connected, coupled,* or *conjoined, a thing with a thing.* (Ṣ.)

3. قَارَنَهُ, (Ṣ,) inf. n. قِرَانٌ, (Ṣ, Ḳ,) and مُقَارَنَةٌ, (Ḳ,) *He associated with him; became his companion.* (Ṣ, Ḳ.)

4. أَقْرَنَ *He gave* of a thing *two by two.* (A'Obeyd in T, in art. بد, voce أَبَدَّ.) See أَبَدَّ. — أَقْرَنَ الشَّىْءَ, (Mṣb,) or بِالشَّىْءِ, (Ḳ,) [the latter more probably right,] *He was able and strong to do, or effect,* &c., *the thing;* (Mṣb, Ḳ;) *He had the requisite ability and strength for it.*

قِرْنٌ *One who opposes, or contends with, another, in science, or in fight,* &c.; (Mṣb;) *an opponent; a competitor; an adversary; an antagonist:* or one's *equal,* or *match, in courage,* (Ṣ, Ḳ,) or *generally,* one's *equal, match,* or *fellow.* (Ḳ.)

قَرْنٌ One's *equal in age;* syn. لِدَةٌ, (Ḳ,) or تِرْبٌ: with fet-ḥ when relating to age, and with kesr when relating to fighting and the like. (Ḥar, pp. 572, 64.) — قَرْنٌ, (JK, Mṣb,) or قَرْنٌ مِنَ النَّاسِ, (Ṣ,) [*A generation of men;*] *people of one time* (JK,* Ṣ, Ez-Zejjájee, Mṣb,) *succeeding another* قَرْن, (JK,) *among whom is a prophet,* or *class of learned men, whether its years be many or few.* (Ez-Zejjájee, Mṣb.) — قَرْنٌ The *part of the head* of *a human being which in an animal is the place whence the horn grows:* (Ḳ:) or the *side,* (Ṣ,) or *upper side,* (Ḳ,) *of the head:* (Ṣ, Ḳ:) or [more exactly the *temporal ridge* (see صُدْغٌ) i.e.] the *edge of the* هَامَة (which is the *middle and main part of the head* [i. e. *of the cranium*]), *on the right* and *on the left.* (Zj, in his "Khalḳ el-Insán.") — قُرُونٌ of the head: see a verse cited voce خَيْطٌ. — قُرُونٌ of horses: see أَجَمُّ. — قَرْنٌ of a solid hoof: see جُبَّةٌ. — قَرْنٌ of a desert, the *most elevated part.* (TA in art. جحف.) — قَرْنٌ أَعْفَرُ, as meaning *A spear-head,* see أَعْفَرُ. — قَرْنٌ *A pod, like that of the locust tree:* pl. قُرُونٌ. Occurring often in the work of AḤn on plants, and in the TA, &c. See غَافٌ. — قَرْنٌ [*A thing*] *in a she-camel, which is like the* عَفَل *in a woman;*

and which is cauterized with heated stones. (AA, TA, in art. عقل.) — قَرْنٌ *An issue of sweat*: pl. قُرُونٌ: see two ex. voce سَنَّ.

قَرْنٌ and ↑ قِرَانٌ *A cord of twisted bark which is bound upon the neck of each of the ploughing bulls* (Ḳ,* TA) *and to the middle of which is then bound the* لُومَة [*or whole apparatus of the plough*]. (TA.) See فَدَّانٌ. — [The pl.] أَقْرَانٌ *Sons of one mother from different men.* (TA, voce عَيْنٌ.) — قَرْنٌ: see جَعْبَةٌ.

قُرْنَةٌ The "*horn*" *of the uterus.*

قِرَانٌ: see قَرْنٌ.

أَبْرَمًا قَرُونًا: see بَرَمٌ.

قَرِينٌ *An associate; a comrade; a companion.* (Ṣ, Ḳ.) قَرِينَةٌ *A connexion; relation.* — قَرِينَةٌ [*A clause of rhyming prose, considered as connected with the similar clause preceding or following*; the two together being termed قرينتان]. (Ḥar, pp. 9, 23.) — Also, *A context*, in an absolute sense. — أَسْمَحَتْ قَرُونَتُهُ ↑ and قَرِينَتُهُ: see 1 in art. سمح.

قَرُونَةٌ: see قَرِينٌ.

أَقْرَنُ [*Horned; having horns*]. (Ṣ, voce كَرَّازٌ [which see]). See an ex. of the fem. قَرْنَآءُ, voce دَانَ in art. دين.

مِقْرَنٌ: see مِخْذَفٌ.

مُقْرَنٌ: see خَشْخَاشٌ.

قرنفل

حَبُّ القَرَنْفُلِ: see زَجَاجٌ.

قرى

1. قَرَى الضَّيْفَ is doubly trans.: see a verse cited voce قَوْهٌ.

8. اِقْتَرَى [meaning تَتَبَّعَ: see a verse of Aboo Dhu-eyb, voce خَافَةٌ, in art. خوف.] It also means *He investigated* a country or countries. (Ṣ,* Ḳ,* TA, all in art. قرى; and TA in art. قرو.) *He made much and diligent search.* (KL.) See also 10 in art. قرأ.

قِرًى *Entertainment for a guest; that with which a guest is entertained.* (Ṣ.) — *Water collected in a trough*, or *tank*, *for the drinking of beasts*: see بُيُوتٌ: thus explained in the M in art. بيت.

قَرِىٌّ *A place where water runs*, (T, Ṣ,) *to*, (T,) or *in*, or *into*, (Ṣ,) *meadows*, (T,) or *a meadow*. (Ṣ.) See شَيْخٌ (last sentence). — Pl. أَقْرِيَةٌ: see قَرْءٌ.

قَرْيَةٌ *A town*, or *village*; (Mṣb, TA;) *a small* بَلَد, *smaller than a* مَدِينَة: (MF, voce تَرْمَذ:) not well applied to a مَدِينَة unless qualified by an epithet denoting greatness. (TA in art. سيط.) See Bd, ii. 261.

نَاقَةٌ فِى قَرْوَتِهَا: see 4 in art. قرأ.

قَرِيَّةٌ [vulg. قَرْيَة The *yard of a ship*;] *a squared piece of wood upon the head of the mast of a ship.* (Az, TA in art. رنح.)

قَارِيَةٌ *A certain bird.* See خُضَارِىٌّ and قَنُوطٌ.

قَارٍ for قَارِئٌ, q.v.

نَاقَةٌ قَرْوَآءُ *A long-backed she-camel.* (IB, in TA, voce هِرْجَابٌ.)

مُقْرًى: see 2 in art. حجل.

مَقْرُوّ and مَقْرِىٌّ for مَقْرُوْءٌ: see art. قرأ.

قزدر

قَزْدِيرٌ: see قَصْدِيرٌ.

قزع

قُزَحٌ: see قَوْسُ قزع.

قزم

قزام: see أَحْصَنَ.

قسقس

قَسْقَاسٌ *I.q.* طُفَيْلِىٌّ. (IKh, TA, art. طفل.)

قسم

1. قَسَمَ and ↑ قَسَّمَ *He divided; parted; divided in parts or shares; distributed.* — قَسَمَ أَمْرَهُ, or قَسَّمَهُ ↑: see 3 in art. عدل.

2: see 1.

3. قَاسَمَهُ الشَّىْءَ *He divided with him the thing, each of them allotting to himself his share, or portion.* — قَاسَمَهُ بِاللّٰهِ *He swore to him by God.*

4. أَقْسَمَ عَلَيْهِ *He conjured him; he said* بِحَقِّكَ. (Mgh, art. طمر.)

5. تَقَسَّمَ *It* (a thing) *was*, or *became, divided*, or *distributed*. (MA.) See an ex. in a verse, voce شَتَّانَ.

7. اِنْقَسَمَ الَى أَقْسَامٍ كَثِيرَةٍ *It was divided into many parts.*

10. اِسْتَقْسَمَ *He sought to know what was allotted to him*, by means of the أَزْلَام, (Ṣ,* Mgh, and Ḥar, p. 465,) *and what was not allotted to him.* (Mgh, Ḥar.)

قِسْمٌ *A division*: (Mṣb:) and particularly (Mṣb) *a portion*, or *share*. (Ṣ, Mṣb, Ḳ.) Pl. أَقْسَامٌ. — لَيْسَ مِنْ أَقْسَامِ كَذَا *It is not a part of such a thing; it does not belong*, or *appertain, to such a thing; it is independent of such a thing.*

قَسَمٌ *A conjurement.* See أَقْسَمَ عَلَيْهِ. — *An oath* (Ṣ, Mṣb, Ḳ) *by God* [*&c.*]. (Mṣb, Ḳ.) *An asseveration.* — وَاوُ القَسَمِ *The* و *denoting an oath.*

قِسْمَةٌ is also used in the sense of مَقْسُومٌ [meaning *A thing*, or *collection of things, divided into portions*, or *shares*]: (Bd and Jel in liv. 28:) *a portion*, or *share*; like قِسْمٌ: (Mṣb:) [and *portions*, or *shares*; as in the phrase,] نُخْرِجُ طَرِيقًا مِنْ بَيْنِ قِسْمَةِ الأَرْضِ أَوِ الدَّارِ [*We will exclude a way*, or *passage, from among the portions*, or *shares, of the land*, or *the house*]. (Mgh in art. رفع.)

قَسَّامٌ *An officer of the Kádee, who divides inheritances.*

قسى

3. قَاسَاهُ *He endured it; struggled*, or *contended, with*, or *against, it; struggled*, or *contended, with*, or *against, its difficulty*, or *severity; he endured*, or *he struggled*, or *contended, with*, or *against, the difficulty*, or *trouble*, or *inconvenience, that he experienced from it* or *him*; [and so عَانَاهُ; for both of which see Ḥar, p. 564; and for the latter see شَاقَاهُ; and for both see also مُجَانَاةٌ]; syn. كَابَدَهُ, (Ṣ, Ḳ,) and عَالَجَ شِدَّتَهُ: (TA:) *he underwent difficulties, troubles*, or *inconveniences, in doing it.* (Mṣb in explanation of the syn. كَابَدَهُ.)

قُسِىٌّ pl. of قَوْسٌ.

قُسْوِىٌّ: see art. قوس.

قش

قَشٌّ *Stubble; stalk of corn, &c.; straw.* قَشُّ البَحْرِ *Seaweed.* قَشٌّ *Rushes of which mats are made.* حَصِيرَةُ قَشٍّ *A mat of rushes.*

قَشَّاشٌ: see رَمَّامٌ.

قشع

1. قَشَعَتِ الرِّيحُ السَّحَابَ *The wind removed*, or *cleared off, the clouds*; (Ṣ, Ḳ;) as also ↑ أَقْشَعَتْهُ. (Ḳ.)

4. أَقْشَعَ and ↑ اِنْقَشَعَ and ↑ تَقَشَّعَ *It* (a cloud) *became removed*, or *cleared off.* (Ṣ, Ḳ.) See 1.

5: } see 4.
7: }

قشف

1. قَشِفَ, inf. n. قَشَفٌ, *He was coarse in his*

living: this is the original signification: *he was neglectful of cleanliness:* (Mṣb:) *he was neglectful of washing and cleanliness; unfrequent in paying attention thereto; slovenly with respect to his person:* (M, Mṣb:) and ✝ تَقَشَّفَ signifies the like. (Mṣb.) — قَشِفَ, inf. n. قَشَفٌ, *He became sunburnt.* (M.)

5: see 1.

قشم

قَمْشٌ: see قُشَامَةٌ.

قصع

1. قَصَعَ: see an ex. voce صَارَّةٌ.

قَصْعَةٌ *A bowl not so large as a* جَفْنَة, *but next to it in size, that satisfies ten:* (Ṣ, voce صَحْفَة:) it is *a wooden bowl.* — قَصْعَةُ المَسَاكِينِ: see الثَّكَّة.

مُعَاقَصَة: see أَخَذْتُهُ مُقَاصَعَةً.

قصف

نَبَاتٌ قَصِيفٌ رَيَّانُ [*A weak,* or *fragile, sappy plant*]. (TA, in art. خرع.)

قصل

1. قَصَلَ: see خَصَلَ.

قَصَلٌ of wheat and barley: see جُرَامَةٌ.

قَصِيلٌ *Corn,* or *seed-produce,* (Ḳ,) or *barley,* (Mṣb,) *cut while green,* (Mṣb, Ḳ,) *for fodder.* (Mṣb.)

مِخْصَلٌ: see مِقْصَلٌ.

قصم

قَيْصُومٌ *Artemisia abrotanum,* or *southern-wood;* also called قَيْصُومٌ ذَكَرٌ: and قَيْصُومٌ أُنْثَى is applied to *santolina.*

قصى

2. قَصَّى: see قَصَّصَ.

5. تَقَصَّى: see تَقَصَّصَ. — تَقَصَّى شُرْبَ المَآءِ فلم يسئر منه شيئا [*He drank the water to the uttermost, not leaving any of it remaining*]. (TA, in art. شف.) — See 10.

10. اِسْتَقْصَى *He went to the utmost length,* or *point,* in a question, (Ḳ,) and in like manner you say, اِسْتَقْصَى الأَمْرَ and ✝ تَقَصَّاهُ. (TA.) — [*He exhausted* a subject. — *He proceeded to extremities. He was,* or *became, extreme,* in an action, &c.] — اِسْتَقْصَى مَسْأَلَتَهُ [*He went to the utmost point in questioning him,* or *asking him,*] respecting a thing, so as to draw forth the utmost that he possessed [of information respecting it]. (Ṣ, art. نص.) — اِسْتَقْصَى فِي المَسْأَلَةِ and ✝ تَقَصَّى (Ṣ, Ḳ) both signify the same; (Ṣ;) ‡ *He reached,* or *attained,* [*and elicited,* and *investigated,*] *the utmost* [*that was to be reached, &c.*] *in the question:* (Ḳ, TA:) and in like manner استقصى الأَمْرَ and ✝ تقصّاهُ (TA) ‡ [*He investigated,* or *searched, to the utmost the case,* or *affair;*] *he reached,* or *attained, the utmost of the case,* or *affair, in investigating it.* (MA in explanation of the former phrase.) — اِسْتَقْصَى عِلْمَهُ *He attained the utmost knowledge of it.* — اِسْتَقْصَى مَا عِنْدَ نَاقَتِهِ مِنَ السَّيْرِ [*He elicited,* or *exacted, the utmost of his she-camel's pace,* or *power of going on*]. (TA, art. نص.) — اِسْتِقْصَآءٌ, metonymically, signifies ‡ The *being niggardly, stingy,* or *avaricious.* (Az, TA in art. دنق.) — اِسْتَقْصَيْتُ المَكَانَ [?] *i. q.* اِسْتَغْذَيْتُهُ. (TA in art. عذى.)

حَاطُونَا القَصَآءَ and القَصَآءُ: and حُطْنِي القَصَا, &c.: see art. حوط, and see 1 in art. حبو.

قُصْيَا is like دُنْيَا and عُلْيَا, with و changed into ى. (ISd in TA, voce بُقْوَى.)

قض

قَضْقَاضٌ, (Ḳ,) and some say قَضْقَاضٌ, (TA,) The أُشْنَان *of Syria:* (Ḳ, TA:) or the *green, and lank* (سَبْط), *thereof:* (Ibn-'Abbád, TA:) or *a species of trees of the* [*kind called*] حَمْض, (AḤn, Ḳ, TA,) *slender and yellow.* (AḤn, TA.) See فِرْسٌ.

قضف

قَضِيفٌ *Lean,* or *light of flesh.* (TA in art. شلو.)

قضم

1. قَضِمَ *He crunched, nibbled* or *gnawed?* See خَضِمَ: and see also Freytag's Arab. Prov. ii. 245.

قَضَامٌ: } see خُضَامَةٌ.
مَقْضَمٌ: }

قَضِيمٌ as meaning *A skin* &c. has for pl. أَقْضِمَةٌ [a pl. of pauc.] and قُضُمٌ, and قَضَمٌ, accord. to Sb, is a quasi-pl. n., (TA,) and قَضَمٌ is a pl. [or quasi-pl. n.] thereof as meaning *a white skin upon which one writes.* (Ṣ, Ḳ.) See an ex. of قَضَمٌ voce عَسِيبٌ.

قضى

1. قَضَى *He finished* a thing *entirely, by word,* or *by deed.* This is the primary meaning. (Bḍ, ii. 111.) *By word, as in* وَقَضَى رَبُّكَ (Idem, ibid.) *And thy Lord hath commanded decisively.* (Idem, xvii. 24.) And *by deed, as in* فَقَضَاهُنَّ سَبْعَ سَمٰوَاتٍ [Ḳur, xli. 11, *And he completed them seven heavens*]. (Idem, ii. 11.) — And *He* (God) *desired* a thing *so as to necessitate its being.* (Idem, ii. 11.) — إِذَا قَضَى أَمْرًا, [Ḳur, ii. 111,] *When He* (God) *desireth a thing to be.* (Bḍ, Jel.) — [Thus it signifies *He decreed* a thing; *ordained* it; *pronounced* it; or *decided* it *judicially.*] — قَضَى عَلَيْهِ, aor. ـِ, inf. n. قَضَآءٌ &c., *He decided judicially,* or *judged, against him;* and بَيْنَ الخَصْمَيْنِ *between the two litigants.* (TA.) See قَدْرٌ. — [*He completed; accomplished;* or *fully performed;* a thing.] — قَضَى *He attained,* or *obtained,* or *accomplished,* his want. (Mṣb.) — [*He paid, discharged,* or *satisfied,* a debt, due, claim, or demand.] — قَضَيْتُهُ حَقَّهُ *I gave him* [*or paid him*] *his due,* (Mṣb,) *fully.* (Ḥar, p. 22.) — قَضَى عَنْهُ (Ṣ, Ḳ, in art. جزى, &c.) *He,* or *it, payed;* or *made,* or *gave,* or *rendered, satisfaction; for him.* (TḲ in that art.) And followed by شَيْئًا [*He paid a thing for him,* or *in his stead; gave,* or *rendered, it as a satisfaction;* lit. and fig.] (Ṣ, TA in that art., and Bḍ in ii. 45.) See جَزَى عَنْهُ; and see a verse cited voce دَانَ, in art. دين. — *He finished doing* a thing: *he finished* his prayer. (TA.) *He performed, fulfilled,* or *accomplished,* the pilgrimage, syn. أَدَّى, (Mṣb,) and the religious rites and ceremonies of the pilgrimage, (Bḍ, Jel in ii. 196,) syn. أَدَّى. (Jel, ibid, Mṣb.) — You also say, قَضَى بِهِ *He decreed it;* &c.; like حَكَمَ بِهِ: see an ex. voce سُلْطَانٌ. — قَوْلُهُ مِمَّا يَقْضِي العَجَبَ [*His saying* such a thing *is of the things that induce wonder in the utmost degree*]. (TA in art. جلب.) See Ḥar, p. 22. — وَقَضَيْنَا إِلَى بَنِي إِسرائِيلَ (Ḳur, xvii. 4): see إِلَى. — قَضْوٌ: see غَزْوٌ, and هَيُوٌ, and بُطْآنٌ; and see طَمِعَ in the Ṣ.

3. قَاضَاهُ *He cited him before a judge.* (TA.)

5: see 7.

6. تَقَاضَاهُ الدَّيْنَ *He took,* or *received, from him the debt.* (M, Ḳ.) — See 10. — And see تَشَارَيَا.

7. انقضى and ✝ تقضّى *It passed away; came to an end,* or *to nought; became cut off.* (Ḳ, TA.)

8. اِقْتَضَى كَذَا *It required such a thing: it required the inference of such a thing: it necessarily implied,* or *involved, such a thing as its consequence or concomitant; it required such a thing to be conceded; it necessitated such a thing.* — اِقْتَضَاهُ حَقَّهُ *He demanded of him his due.* (MA.) — اِقْتَضَيْتُ مِنْهُ حَقِّي *I took,* or *received, from him my due.* (Mgh, Mṣb.)

10. اِسْتَقْضَيْتُهُ *I demanded of him the giving* [*or payment*] *of my due,* (Mṣb, Ḳ,*) or *debt;* (Ḳ;) and in like manner ✝ تَقَاضَيْتُهُ دَيْنِي and بِدَيْنِي. (Mgh.)

قَضَآءٌ a term of the law; opposed to أَدَآءٌ, which see: and see an ex. cited voce ضَحْوٌ. —

A decree; an ordinance; a sentence, or *a judicial decision*. See عَوْدٌ, حُكْمٌ and دِينٌ. — قَضَآءٌ *The exercise of the office of a ḳádee*. [You say] القَضَآءُ جَمْرٌ [meaning, the *exercise of the* office of a ḳádee is one that often leads to hell]. (L, art. عود.)

قَضِيَّةٌ *A thing; an affair; a matter; a case; an event; an action:* significations well known, but not found by me in any classical writing, nor in any lexicon, excepting as implied when the word is used in explanations: syn. أَمْرٌ and شَأْنٌ. — *A case of law*. (L in art. جهد.) — قَضِيَّةٌ كُلِّيَّةٌ [*A universal or general prescript, rule, or canon*]. (Kull, voce قَاعِدَةٌ, p. 290; KT, in explanation of the same word.) — قَضِيَّةٌ in logic, *A proposition*.

مُقْتَضًى [*Exigence.*] — مُقْتَضَى اللَّفْظِ *That which the word, or expression, indicates*. (El-Fárábee, Mṣb, voce مَعْنًى.)

قطع

2. قَطَّعَهُ بِالضَّرْبِ *He mangled him with beating*. — تَقْطِيعٌ ‡ [*A griping, or cutting pain, in the bowels;*] i. q. مَغْصٌ *in the belly;* (Ṣ, Ḳ, TA;) as also تَقْضِيعٌ. (TA.) See also قُطْعٌ. — تَقْطِيعُ الصَّوْتِ (Ḳ in art. جدف) *A repeated interrupting of the voice in singing*. (TḲ in that art.) See جَدَفَ. — قَطَّعَ, inf. n. تَقْطِيعٌ, *He articulated*, or *spelled*, a word. — See تَقْطِيعٌ.

3. قَاطَعَهُ *He separated himself from him, with the latter's concurrence;* see فَارَزَهُ; and see اِنْقَطَعَ عَنْهُ. — قَاطَعَا *They disunited themselves, each from the other; severed the bond of friendship that united them, each to the other; contr. of* وَاصَلَا. (Ḳ.) See 6.

5. تَقَطَّعَ for قُطِّعَ: see Ṣ, voce خَطَرَ. — تَقَطَّعَ: see تَصَرَّمَ: *It* (a wound or ulcer) *became dissundered*, by putrefaction. — *It* (a garment, or a water-skin, &c.) *became ragged, tattered*, or *dissundered*, by rottenness. *It* (milk) *became decomposed; it curdled, clotted*, or *coagulated;* i. e. *separated into clots*.

6. تَقَاطَعَا [*They became disunited, each from the other; the bond of friendship that united them, each to the other, became severed*]; (A, art. يبس;) تَقَاطُعٌ signifies the *contr. of* تَوَاصُلٌ: (Ṣ:) see تَصَارَمُوا.

7. اِنْقَطَعَ بِهِ *He became disabled from prosecuting*, or *unable to proceed in*, or *prosecute, his journey*, (Ṣ, Mgh,) [*his means having failed him*, or] *his means of defraying the expense having gone, or his camel that bore him stopping with him from fatigue*, (Ṣ, Mgh,) *or breaking down or perishing*, (Mgh,) *or an event having befallen him so that he could not move*. (Ṣ.) — اِنْقَطَعَ فِى حُجَّتِهِ [*He was*, or *became, cut short*, or *stopped, in his argument*, or *plea*]. (TA, art. بلس.) — اِنْقَطَعَتْ قِرَاءَتُهُ is said when one is unable to perform [or continue] his recitation, or reading. (TA in art. عجم.) — اِنْقَطَعَ عَنِ الكَلَامِ [or مِنَ الكَلَامِ] (Ḳ in art. رجو) *He broke off*, or *ceased, from speech*]. (TA, art. بلت.) — انقطع الكَلَامُ *The speech stopped short*, or *broke off*. (TA.) — اِنْقَطَعَ عَنْهُ [*He broke off from him; separated*, or *disunited himself from him*]. See اِنْبَتَّ; and see قَاطَعَهُ here. — اِنْقَطَعَ *It became cut off, intercepted, interrupted; or stopped; was put an end to; or put a stop to; it stopped*, or *stopped short, it finished, it failed, it failed altogether; ceased; became extinct; was no longer produced; came to an end*. — *He cut himself off*, or *became detached*, or *he detached himself*, from worldly things, &c. — اِنْقَطَعَ وَسَكَتَ مُتَحَيِّرًا [*He was*, or *became, cut short, and was silent, being confounded*, or *perplexed, and unable to see his right course*]. (TA in art. بهت.) — اِنْقَطَعَ إِلَى فُلَانٍ ‡ *He made himself solely and peculiarly a companion, or an associate to such a one*. (TA.) And اِنْقَطَعَ إِلَيْهِ app. signifies † *He withdrew* from a person or persons, or a place, *to him*, or *it:* see بَاهَ إِلَيْهِ. — اِنْقَطَعَ فُؤَادُهُ: see اِنْذَعَفَ.

8. اِقْتَطَعَ [*He cut off for himself*] a piece from a thing: (Ṣ:) *took* a portion from another's property. (Mṣb.) — اِقْتَطَعَ جَدِيَّتَهُ: see 8 in art. قضب.

قُطْعٌ † *Pain in the belly*, and مَغْصٌ. (TA.) See 2.

قِطْعٌ, applied to an arrow: see مَقَاطِيعُ and بَرِىٌّ.

قِطْعَةٌ *A piece; bit; part*, or *portion, cut off, detached*, or *separated from the whole; a segment; a cutting; a slice; a slip; or the like: a piece*, or *portion*, or *parcel*, or *plot*, or *spot*, of land, ground, herbage, &c.: *a distinct quantity* or *number: somewhat*, or *some* of a number of things. — *A detached number* of locusts: see رِجْلٌ: and so of a herd or flock, &c.: and *a detached portion*. — قِطْعَةٌ, of poetry: see قَصِيدٌ: pl. قِطَعٌ, with which ▾ مُقَطَّعَاتٌ is syn.

ضَرَبَهُ بِقِطْعَتِهِ: see جُذْمُورٌ. — قِطْعَةٌ: see جِدْعَةٌ.

قَطِيعٌ *A herd, troop*, or *drove; a distinct collection* or *number;* of beasts, &c.; *a flock*, or *bevy*, of sheep, birds, &c.; *a party*, or *group*, or *collection*, of men, &c.; *a pack* of dogs. The term "herd" is applied to "a collective number" of camels by several good writers. We say a "flock" of sheep, and of geese; and "flock" or rather "herd" of goats; and a "herd" of oxen or kine, of camels, and of swine, and of antelopes; and a "swarm" of bees, &c. — قَطِيعٌ *A whip cut from the skin of a camel*. — قَطِيعَةٌ *A portion of land held in fee*. See Mgh, Mṣb. — قَطِيعَةٌ i. q. هِجْرَانٌ. (Ṣ, Ḳ.) And قَطِيعَةُ الرَّحِمِ [*The cutting*, or *forsaking*, or *abandoning, of kindred*, or *relations; contr. of* صِلَةُ الرَّحِمِ]. (Ḳ, voce حَالِقَةٌ.)

رَجُلٌ قَطَّاعٌ لِلْأُمُورِ (Ṣ, M, A, Ḳ, all in art. قضب); see قَضَّابَةٌ.

أَقْطَعُ اللِّسَانِ † *Unable to reply*. (AZ in TA, art. بكم.)

تَقْطِيعٌ *Conformation*, or *proportion*, of a man or beast; *lineament* of the face; *i. q.* قَدٌّ, of a man: (Ḳ:) and the *stature; or justness*, or *beauty, of the stature;* of a man; syn. قَامَةٌ: (Ḳ:) and the *cut, shape, fashion*, or *form*, of anything: see an ex. voce زَبَنٌ; and also voce قَدٌّ, where it is shown that, being an attribute of a thing as well as of a person, it does not always mean *stature* or *the like:* it signifies *cut, shape, fashion*, or *form:* and more commonly *conformation* or *proportion:* and hence, *beauty*, or *justness, of stature;* and simply *stature*, or *tallness:* pl. تَقَاطِيعُ, which is more commonly used than the sing. in the present day.

مَقْطَعٌ *A place of crossing*, or *traversing*, of a river [and a desert, &c.]: (Ḳ, TA:) pl. in this sense مَقَاطِعُ. (Ṣ.) — Also the *place of utterance* of a letter; like مَخْرَجٌ. — مَقْطَعُ الحَقِّ: see مَزَّةٌ. — قَهْوَةٌ لَذِيذَةُ المقطع: see جَلَآءٌ.

مَقْطَعَةٌ *A cause*, or *means, of cutting off*, or *stopping:* see مَحْسَمَةٌ.

ثِيَابٌ مُقَطَّعَةٌ [*Garments cut out of several pieces*] are *such as the shirt, and trowsers*, or *drawers, &c*. (Mgh in art. ثوب.) — دَرَاهِمُ مُقَطَّعَةٌ *Dirhems* [or *coins*] *that are* [*clipped*, or] *light of weight*, [or] *in which is adulterating alloy:* or, as some say, *much broken*. (Mgh.) — الحُرُوفُ المُقَطَّعَةُ *The letters of the alphabet:* so applied in an explanation of حُرُوفُ المُعْجَمِ, as syn. with this, in the Ṣ in art. عجم. See also قِطْعَةٌ. — See حَرْفٌ.

إِسْتِثْنَآءٌ مُنْقَطِعٌ *An exception in which the thing excepted is disunited in kind from that from which the exception is made; contr. of* مُتَّصِلٌ. — مُنْقَطِعٌ: see مُرْسَلٌ.

مَقَاطِيعُ *Heads of spears*, or *arrows;* syn. نِصَالٌ. (L, art. صلد.) See also قِطْعٌ.

قطف

قِطْفٌ A *bunch* of grapes, &c.: pl. قُطُوفٌ: see an ex. voce ذَلَّلَ. — قِطْفٌ i. q. مَقْطُوفٌ. (TA in art. بسط.) See بَسِيطٌ.

قَطَفٌ: see بَقْلٌ.

قَطَافٌ and قِطَافٌ The *time of gathering the crop of grapes:* (Ṣ, Mgh, Ḳ:) or the latter has this meaning; and the former is allowable accord. to Ks: (T, TA:) and the latter is also an inf. n., (Mgh,) or may be so, (Ks, T, TA,) meaning the *gathering of the crop of grapes:* (Mgh:) [or both have this meaning; for] you say, هٰذَا زَمَانُ القَطَافِ and القِطَافِ. (Mṣb.) See جَدَادٌ.

قَطِيفٌ a coll. gen. n. syn. with قَطَائِفُ, mentioned in the TA voce أُبْلُوجٌ, which see. — قَطِيفَةٌ *A villous,* or *nappy,* دِثَار [or *outer wrapping garment*]. (Ṣ, Mṣb, Ḳ.) See also رَاحُولَاتٌ.

قَطَائِفُ: see my 1001 Nights, note 23 to chap. viii. See also زَلَابِيَةٌ. In the TA, art. كنف, it is applied to كُنَافَةٌ.

مِقْطَفٌ (*vulg.* مَقْطَف) [pl. مَقَاطِفُ] A hand-basket, made of palm-leaves: *so called because originally used in gathering fruit.* (See also قُفَّةٌ and زَنْبِيل.)

قطن

1. قَطَنَ بِالمَكَانِ *He resided in the place.* (Mṣb.)

قَطْنُ syn. with قَطْ: see the latter.

قُطْنُ البَرْدِيِّ: see بَرْدِيٌّ.

قَطَنٌ The *part between the two hips,* or *haunches;* (Ṣ, Ḳ;) or the *downward* [or *lower*] *and even part of the back* of a man; (Mṣb;) the *lower portion of the loins.*

قِطْنَةٌ *i. q.* حَفِثٌ, as its description plainly shows; i.e., the *third stomach,* commonly called the *manyplies,* and by some the *millet, of a ruminant animal.* See رُمَّانَةٌ.

قِطْنِيَّةٌ and قُطْنِيَّةٌ [*Any kind of pulse,* or *seed of a leguminous plant that is cooked;* this is the general meaning, and includes almost all the particular definitions of the word]: pl. قَطَانِىُّ, (Ṣ, Mgh, Mṣb, Ḳ,) in the CḲ erroneously written with the article القَطَانِىُّ.

قَاطِنٌ *A resident.* (Mṣb.)

قَيْطُونٌ *A closet;* syn. مُخْدَعٌ; i.e., *a* [*small*] *chamber within a* [*large*] *chamber.* (L in art. سن.)

يَقْطِينٌ *A plant* (Ṣ, Ḳ) and *the like* (Ḳ) *that has no* سَاق [or *standing stem*]; (Ṣ, Ḳ;) *as the gourd-plant* and *the like:* (Ṣ:) *any tree* [or *plant*] *that spreads* [or *creeps*] *upon the ground, not rising upon a stem; such, for instance, as the colocynth;* but conventionally applied especially to the *gourd.* (Mṣb.) See سَطَّاحٌ.

قطو

قَطًا *Sand-grouse; pterocles melanogaster:* so Wilkinson, Anc[t] Egyp[ns], i. 250: see De Sacy's Chrest. Ar., 2nd ed., pp. 369, et seqq.

قَطْوَةٌ: see دَالِيَةٌ.

قَطَاةٌ, of a beast, The *croup,* or *rump, and what is between the hips,* or *haunches:* (Ḳ:) or [the *fore part of the croup;* i. e.] the *place where the* رِدْف *sits.* (Ṣ, Ḳ.) See أَدَلُّ مِنْ — .الغُرَابَانِ تَبَعٌ: see قَطَاةٌ.

قع

4. أَقَعَّ المَآءَ: see أَعَقَّ.

R. Q. 1. قَعْقَعَ: see an ex. voce شَنٌّ.

R. Q. 2. تَقَعْقَعَ *It made a sound,* or *noise; a "crepitus;" a succession of sharp,* or *harsh, sounds,* or *noises; a creaking, crackling, rustling, clattering, clashing, rattling,* &c.: see an ex. voce صَلَّ.

قَعْقَعَةُ السِّلَاحِ *The clash of arms.* — See عَقْعَقٌ. — قَعْقَعَةٌ *A gnashing of the teeth.*

مَآءٌ قُعٌّ or قُعٌّ: see عُقٌّ.

مَآءٌ قُعَاعٌ: see حُرَاقٌ and عُقٌّ.

خِمْسٌ قَعْقَاعٌ: see خِمْسٌ and حَثِيثٌ.

قعط

8. اِقْتَعَطَ: see اِعْتَجَرَ. — الاِقْتِعَاطُ and العِمَّةُ الطَّابِقِيَّةُ signify the same. (O, Ḳ, in art. طبق.)

قعف

7. انقعف: see انقعث; *He died.* (TA, art. قعص.)

قعى

4. أَقْعَى *It* (a star) *rose high, and then quitted not its place.* (TA, art. عرو.)

الإِقْعَآءُ: see عَقِبٌ.

قف

1. قَفَّتِ الأَرْضُ *The land had its herbs,* or *leguminous plants, dried up for want of water.* (A, TA, in art. حف.) [See also قَفَّتْ, said of land.] — قَفَّ: see R. Q. 2 in art. جف.

8. اِقْتِفَافٌ The *eating until nothing remains.* (Ḥam, p. 230.)

قَفٌّ: see غَفٌّ.

قُفٌّ *High ground,* (Mṣb, Ḳ,) *less than what is termed* جَبَل: (Mṣb:) or *a high portion of the* مَتْن *of the earth:* (Ṣ:) or *high and rugged ground, not amounting to what is termed* جَبَل. (Sh, TA.)

قُفَّةٌ (pl. قُفَفٌ) *A basket of the same kind as that called* مِقْطَف, *but larger; smaller than the* زَنْبِيل: *i. q.* مَرْجُونَةٌ. (TA in art. ضون.)

قَفِيفٌ: see قَبِيبٌ and جَفِيفٌ.

قفر

القَفْرُ اليَهُودِىُّ *Jews-pitch,* i.e. *asphaltum;* also called *mumia,* and in Arabic مُومِيَا: see De Sacy's Abd-allatif, p. 273: and see تِرْيَاقٌ and حُمَرٌ.

قَفُورٌ *i. q.* كَافُورٌ. (IDrd in TA, art. كفر.)

قفش

قَفْشٌ *A boot:* (M:) or *a short boot:* (IAạr, Ḳ, TA:) or *such as is cut, and not well made.* (Az, TA.)

قفل

4. أَقْفَلَ البَابَ *He locked the door.* (TḲ.) See also أَغْلَقَ.

قُفْلٌ: see فَرَاشٌ.

قَافِلٌ A *slender* horse. (TA, art. خشب.)

قَافِلَةٌ *A company, or an assemblage of persons, travelling together:* (El-Fárábee, Mṣb:) or *a company returning from a journey:* (Ṣ, Ḳ:) and *commencing a journey;* as auguring their return: (El-Fárábee, Mṣb, Ḳ:) he who restricts it to those returning from a journey errs: (El-Fárábee, Mṣb, in which see more:) *a caravan.*

قفو

1. قَفَا أَثَرَهُ and إِتَّرَهُ *He followed his track,* or *footsteps; tracked him.* (Ṣ, Mṣb.) — قَفَا فُلَانًا *He followed the footsteps of such a one.* (TA.) See قَصَّ أَثَرَهُ, which signifies the same, for a better explanation. See also قَفَوْتُ أَثَرَهُ.

قَفًا The *back of the neck.* (Ṣ, Mṣb, Ḳ.) — عَيْنَاهُ فِى قَفَاهُ is said of him who is put to flight, because he looks behind him, fearing pursuit.

(TA in art. انف.) And جَعَلَ أَنْفَهُ فِى قَفَاهُ : see أَنْفٌ. — [Also the *back* of the hand: and the *flat back* of a knife and the like.]

قَفِيَّةٌ : see دَوَآءٌ.

قَافِيَةٌ, by synecdoche, for ذُوقَافِيَةٍ, (IJ,) ‡ *A verse; a single verse of a poem.* (Akh, Az, TA.) — Also, [by a further extension of the proper signification,] *A* قَصِيدَة [or *an ode*, or *a poem*]. (Az, IJ, TA.)

قفز

قَاقُوزَةٌ and قَازُوزَةٌ : see طَاسٌ.

قل

1. قَلَّ, *It was, or became, few; small, or little, in number, quantity, or amount; scanty.* — هُوَ يَقِلُّ عَنْ كَذَا *He, or it, is smaller than, or too small for, such a thing;* syn. يَصْغُرُ. (TA.) — قَلَّ لَبَنُهَا *Her milk became little, or scanty; she became scant in her milk.* — قَلَّ خَيْرُهُ [*His good things, or wealth, and his beneficence, became few, or little; scanty, or wanting; he became poor;* and *he became niggardly*:] for قِلَّةُ خَيْرٍ signifies "poverty" and "niggardliness." (A, TA, in art. جحد.) And *It became scanty, or deficient, or wanting, in goodness.* — قَلَّ *He had few aiders:* see an ex. voce فَلَّ.

2. قَلَّلَهُ *He made it, or held it, to be little.* (Mṣb.) — *He showed it, or made it to appear, to be little, in quantity.* (TA.) — See 4.

4. أَقَلَّهُ *He lifted it, or raised it, from the ground; and carried it.* (Mṣb.) — أَقَلَّهُ الغَضَبُ † *Anger disquieted, or flurried, him.* (Mj, TA, in art. حمل.) And أُقِلَّ [alone] † *He was disquieted, or flurried, by anger.* (T, TA, in that art.) — أَقَلَّ مِنْهُ i. q. ↓ قَلَّلَهُ. (M.) — أَقَلَّ *He became poor:* (Ṣ, Mṣb:) or *he had little property.* (Ḳ.)

5. تَقَلَّلَ (Ḳ, art. نزر) *It became diminished, or rendered little or small in quantity.* (TḲ, same art.) — تَقَلَّلَهُ *He saw it, or deemed it, to be little in quantity.* (TA.)

10. اِسْتَقَلَّ *He was independent, or alone; with none to share, or participate, with him.* (TA.) [And اِسْتَقَلَّ بِنَفْسِهِ, *the same;* or (as shown by an explanation of the act. part. n. in the TA) *he managed his affairs, by himself alone, thoroughly, soundly, or vigorously.*] And هُوَ لَا يَسْتَقِلُّ بِهٰذَا *He is not able* [*by himself*] *to do this.* (TA.) — اِسْتَقَلَّ *He was independent of all others; absolute.* — اِسْتَقَلَّ *He* (a man) *rose, or raised himself,* with a burden: (JK:) and a bird in his flight. (JK, Ḳ.) — اُسْتُقِلَّ غَضَبًا *He* (a man) *became affected with a tremour, or trembling, by anger.* (JK.) — اِسْتَقَلَّ بِالشَّىْءِ i. q. اِسْتَبَدَّ بِهِ. (TA in art. حكو.)

قُلٌّ *Poverty:* see an ex. in a verse cited voce طَلَّاعٌ.

قُلُّ بْنُ قُلٍّ : see ضُلٌّ.

قُلَّةٌ *The top,* or *highest part,* of a mountain, &c. (Ṣ, Ḳ.) — *The top of the head and hump.* (Ḳ.) See a verse cited voce ظِلٌّ. — قلتان [app. قُلَّتَانِ, or rather قَلْتَانِ, from قلت] *The hollows of the two collar-bones* (الترقوتان). (TA, art. ترب.)

قِلَّةٌ [*Paucity; smallness; littleness; scantiness; want of due amount* of anything: as in قِلَّةُ مُبَالَاةٍ *want of due care:* or this phrase signifies *want of care:* also *fewness:* for] قِلَّةٌ sometimes signifies i. q. عَدَمٌ. (Mgh in art. حفظ.) — قِلَّةٌ may often be well rendered *Lack.*

قَلِيلٌ *Few; small, or little, in number, quantity,* or *amount; scanty.* — *A small quantity,* or *quantum,* or *number,* مِن مَالٍ وَغَيْرِهِ *of property,* or *cattle, &c.* — قَلِيلُ الخَيْرِ : [see art. خير, where an explanation is given equivalent to عَادِمٌ الخَيْرِ : and in like manner] قَلِيلُ الأَلَايَا is used to signify *Not making use of oaths at all.* (Mgh in art. حفظ.) It may be well rendered *Lacking, or destitute of, good,* or *wealth;* as well as *having little thereof:* it generally means *having little, or no, wealth, or good;* or *lacking,* or *destitute of, goodness or good things.* — قَلِيلٌ : see مُطْرِدٌ. — *Possessing little,* or *possessed in a small degree,* of anything.

قَلِيلَةٌ as a subst., *Little:* see كَثِيرَةٌ.

أَقَلُّ مَالًا وَوَلَدًا *Possessing,* or *possessor, of less* than another *in respect of wealth and children:* see an ex. (from the Ḳur xviii. 37) in art. ف.

مُسْتَقِلٌّ A writing *on a particular, peculiar,* or *special, subject.* — رِسَالَةٌ مُسْتَقِلَّةٌ *A monograph.* See also a verse cited voce عَنْتَرٌ. — مَعْنًى مُسْتَقِلٌّ بِهِ *An independent meaning.*

قلص

القَلَائِصُ, or القِلَاصُ, *Some small stars before* [i. e., *towards*] الثُّرَيَّا ; الدَّبَرَانُ *being between the Hyades and the Pleiades;*] *following* الثريّا. (Mir-át ez-Zemán.) Or *The Hyades.*

قلع

1. قَلَعَ and ↓ اِقْتَلَعَ *He pulled, plucked, tore, wrenched,* or *rooted, out,* or *up,* or *off; detached; removed from his or its place; displaced;* (Mṣb, Ḳ*;) *eradicated; uprooted; unrooted.* (Ḳ.) — تَقْلَعُ (Ḳ in art. جذو) and تقلعُ السَّيْرَ (TA in that art.) [app. for تَقْلَعُ فِى السَّيْرِ], said of she-camels, (Ḳ ib.) [app. *They raise their feet clear from the ground:* see قَلَعٌ and قَلْعٌ : the pret. seems to be قَلِعَ : so if تَقْلَعُ be the right reading: but in a copy of the Ḳ it seems to be تُقْلِعُ : see جَاذٍ, art. جذو.]

4. أَقْلَعَ *It* (rain) *left off.* (The lexicons passim.) *It cleared away;* syn. اِنْجَلَى. (TA.) — أَقْلَعَ عَنْهُ *He,* or *it, left him,* or *quitted him,* or *it.* (Mgh, Mṣb, Ḳ.) *He abstained,* or *desisted, from it.* (Ṣ.) — أَقْلَعَ *It* (hard fortune) *departed:* see an ex. voce إِبِدٌ. — أَقْلَعَتِ الحُمَّى *The fever passed away.*

5. تَقَلَّعَ فِى مَشْيِهِ *He walked as though he were descending a declivity.* (TA.)

7. اِنْقَلَعَ *It became pulled out,* or *up,* or *off; became removed from its place, displaced, eradicated, uprooted,* or *unrooted; it fell,* or *came, out.* You say, اِنْقَلَعَتْ أَسْنَانُهُ [*His teeth fell,* or *came, out.*] (TA, art. حس.)

8: see 1.

قَلَعَةٌ as meaning *Large stones:* see مِرْدًى.

قَلْعِىٌّ : see رَصَاصٌ and آنُكٌ ; in Turkish قَلَاىْ.

قُلُوعٌ is a quasi-inf. n. of the verb in the phrase أَقْلَعَتِ الحُمَّى : see صَلَّ.

مَقْلَعٌ : see an ex. voce صَمْغٌ.

مِقْلَاعٌ *A thing with which one throws a stone;* (Ṣ;) *a sling:* (PṢ:) so in the present day. — See also مِزْعَقٌ.

قلف

2: see 8.

8. اِقْتَلَفَ الظُّفُرَ *He pulled out the finger-nail by the root:* (Lth, TA:) and so ↓ قَلَّفَهُ, accord. to a usage of its pass. part. n. in the T, art. ظفر.

قُلْفَةٌ [also The *prepuce of the clitoris* of a woman;] *a piece of flesh between the* شُفْرَان *of a* woman, *which is cut off in circumcision.* (Mṣb, voce بَظْرٌ.)

أَقْلَفُ has also for pl. قُلْفَانٌ : see أَعْرَمُ.

قلفع

Q. 2. تَقَلْفَعَتْ عَنِ الكَمْءِ أَنْقَاضُهُ [*The crusts of earth broke up from over the truffle*]. (M, art. نقض.)

قلق

1. قَلِقَ, aor. ـَ, (M, Mṣb, TA,) inf. n. قَلَقٌ, (Ṣ, M, Mṣb, Ḳ,) *It was, or became, unsettled, unsteady,* *unfixed, loose, mobile, unquiet,* or *restless; it did not settle, become fixed* or *motionless* or *quiet* or *at rest,* or *it did not rest* or *remain* or *continue, in its place.* (TA.) *He,* or *it, became disquieted, disturbed, agitated, flurried,* or *in a state of unrest* or *commotion;* syn. اِنْزَعَجَ, (Ṣ, Ḳ, TA,) and اِضْطَرَبَ. (M, Mṣb.) — قَلِقَ إِلَيْهِ, or الى, لِقَائِهِ, see جَنْبَ.

2: see 4.

4. أَقْلَقَهُ *He,* or *it, disquieted him; disturbed him; agitated him; flurried him.* (Ṣ, Mṣb.) *He moved it,* a thing, from its place; as also ↑ قَلَّقَهُ. (M.)

قَلِقٌ *Unsteady; loose.* — عِبَارَةٌ قَلِقَةٌ *A loose expression.* (TA &c., passim.)

قَلَاقَةٌ *Looseness* in an expression. (TA &c., passim.)

قلم

قَلَمٌ and ↑ قَلْمَانٌ and ↑ قَلَمَانٌ: see جَلَمٌ. — *A writing-reed prepared for writing; a reed-pen.*

قَلَمَانٌ: see قَلَمٌ.

مُقَلَّمُ الظُّفُرِ and الأَظْفَارِ: see ظُفُرٌ.

قلمس

قَلَمَّسٌ: see نَاسِئٌ.

قلى and قلو

1. قَلَا and قَلَى *He fried* wheat; i.e. *roasted it in a* مِقْلًى [or *frying-pan* or *roasting-pan*]. (Mgh.) — قَلَى with يَقْلِى for its aor.: see أَبَى. — هُوَ يَقْلُو البُرَّ: see بَرَى. — قَلَى *He roasted in a frying-pan* (MA, KL) flesh-meat (MA) or anything: (KL:) and شَوَى signifies the same. (MA.) قَلَى البُرَّ بِالمِقْلَى and المِقْلَاةِ means شَوَاهُ [i.e. *he parched,* or *roasted, the wheat with the* مقلى]. (Mgh.) The aor. is يَقْلِى and يَقْلُو, and the inf. n. قَلْىٌ (MA, Mgh) and قَلْوٌ. (Mgh.)

قِلْىٌ *Potash;* as is shown by the explanations in the Ṣ, Ḳ, and TA. Hence our term "alkali." See حُرُضٌ.

مِقْلًى *A frying-pan;* i.q. طَاجِنٌ. (Mṣb in art. طجن.)

قم

1. قَمَّهُ: see 4; and قِمَّةٌ, in two places.

4. أَقَمَّ الفَحْلُ شَوْلَهُ and ↑ قَمَّتِ الشَّوْلُ: see أَشْمَلَ.

R.Q. 2. تَقَمْقَمْتُهُ *I took it,* or *devoured it, altogether.* (TA in art. عب.)

قُمَامَةٌ *Sweepings.* (Ṣ, Ḳ.)

مِقَمٌّ A man *who eats all that is upon the table.* (Ṣ, Ḳ.*) — مِقَمٌّ and مِقَمَّةٌ: see مِشْفَرٌ.

قُمْقُمٌ *A certain well-known vessel;* arabicized from كُمْكُمْ; (Ḳ, TA;) *a vessel of copper, in which water is heated;* also called مِحَمٌّ; and called by the people of Syria غَلَّايَةٌ; as also قُمْقُمَةٌ: (Mṣb:) or *a well-known vessel of copper, &c., in which water is heated, narrow in the head:* and hence, ‡ *a small vessel of copper* or *silver* or *china-ware, in which rose-water is put* [*for sprinkling, having a long and narrow neck, with a cover pierced with a hole* or *with several holes*]; (TA;) *the vessel of the perfumer:* and, with ة, *a vessel of brass, having two loop-shaped handles, which the traveller takes with him:* pl. قَمَاقِمُ. (Mṣb.)

قُمْقَامٌ: see حَلَمَةٌ and حَمْنَانٌ and طَبُّوعٌ.

قمع

1. قَمَعَهُ: see قَمَأَهُ.

قِمَعُ البُسْرِ *What sticks to the date, around its stalk:* (Mgh:) *the base of the date.* (Mgh, art. ذنب.) See ثُفْرُوقٌ. — See also a use of the pl. أَقْمَاع, voce دِرْدَارٌ. — قِمَعُ الأُذُنِ *The meatus of the ear:* see جُلْجُلَانٌ.

قمل

1. قَمِلَ: see تِينٌ.

4. أَقْمَلَ, said of the رِمْث: see حَنَطَ.

قُمَّلٌ i.q. سُوسٌ: or *a kind of* قُرَاد. (Jel, vii. 130.) See سَاسَ.

مُقْمِلٌ: see تِينٌ.

قمه

1. قَمَهَ, aor. ـَ, inf. n. قُمُوهٌ, i.q. قَمَحَ, q.v.

قن

قُنَّةٌ *An isolated mountain.* (Ḳ, voce جَبَلٌ.) See a verse cited in art. عز.

قِنَّةٌ *Galbanum:* so in the present day: see سَكْبِينَجٌ.

رَجُلٌ أُنَنَةٌ قُنَنَةٌ: see art. ان. The last word may perhaps be a mistranscription for قُنَّةٌ (from قن): but this I have not found in art. قن.

قِنِّيَّةٌ The *state,* or *condition, of slavery.*

قنبر

قُنَّابَرَى *A certain herb,* or *leguminous plant,* (بَقْلَةٌ,) *growing forth in the beginning of the* رَبِيع; a Nabathæan word; *called in Arabic* تَمْلُول [correctly تُمْلُول] *and* غُمْلُول; *eaten by men; and called in Pers.* بَرْغَشْت [correctly بَرْغُشْت]; *called by the people of Ghazneh* ثِرِنْد: (O:) correctly with teshdeed to the ن, though in most of the copies of the Ḳ without teshdeed; and with kesr to the ب, as in the Tekmileh. (TA.) See غُمْلُولٌ.

قنبع

1. قَنْبَعَ, said of seed-produce or corn: see أَحْنَقَ.

قُنْبُعٌ: see رَاكِبٌ, voce رُكْبَانُ السُّنْبُلِ.

قنر

قِنَوَّرٌ A *large, long-bodied* man. (Az, in TA, voce هِرْدَبَّةٌ.)

قنس

قَنْسٌ: see رَاسِنٌ.

قَوْنَسٌ The [*tapering*] *top of an iron helmet.* (Ḳ.) See دَنٌّ.

قنع

5. تَقَنَّعَ بِشَىْءٍ *He was content with a thing.* (Ḳ, voce تعصّب.)

قُنْعَانٌ [not قَنْعَانٌ, as in the CḲ] *With whom one is contented,* or *satisfied,* (Ṣ, Ḳ,) like ↑ مَقْنَعٌ, (Ṣ, Ḳ,) in respect of his judicial decision, or his evidence: (Ḳ:) used alike as masc. and fem. and sing. and pl. (Ṣ, Ḳ) and dual. (Ṣ.)

قِنَاعٌ *A woman's covering worn over the* خِمَار [or *head-covering*]; (Mṣb;) *a woman's head-covering, wider than the* ↑ مِقْنَعَة. (Ṣ, Ḳ.) — قِنَاعُ القَلْبِ *The integument of the heart; the pericardium.* (Mgh in art. خلع; and Ḳ.)

قَانِعٌ, as used in the Ḳur, xxii. 37, accord. to some, One *who asks,* or *begs.* (TA, art. عر.)

مَقْنَعٌ: see قُنْعَانٌ. — إِنَّ فِى ذٰلِكَ لَمَقْنَعًا [*Verily in that is a sufficiency*]. (Ṣ, M, in art. سود.)

مُقْنِعٌ: see صَافِحٌ.

مِقْنَعَةٌ [and مِقْنَعٌ, PṢ] *A woman's head-veil.* (MA, PṢ.)

قنفذ

مَا أَبْيَضُ شَطْرًا أَسْوَدُ ظَهْرًا يَمْشِى قَمَطْرًا وَيَبُولُ

قَطْرًا *What is white in one half, black in the back, that walks contractedly, and makes water in drops?* An enigma: to which the answer is, The قُنْفُذ [q.v.]. (L.) — قُنْفُذُ لَيْلٍ *One who sleeps not* [*during the night*]; because the قنفذ sleeps not: (L:) and *a calumniator; a slanderer;* (L, Ḳ;) as also أَنْقَدُ لَيْلٍ. (L.) — Also قُنْفُذٌ and قُنْفَذٌ The *rat,* or *mouse;* syn. فَأْرٌ: (Ḳ:) fem. with ة. (TA.) — قُنْفُذٌ † The *part behind the ear* of a camel, *whence the sweat exudes.* (Ṣ, L, Ḳ.) — And, with ة, † The *part of the head that is below that which is called the* قَمَحْدُوَة. (L.) — قُنْفُذ † *A place that produces tangled herbage:* (Ṣ, L, Ḳ:) *an elevated place abounding with trees:* AḤn says, that what is thus termed is in hard ground, between what is termed قُفّ and sand. (L.) — قُنْفُذُ رَمْلٍ † *Sand collected together,* (Aboo-Kheyreh, L, Ḳ,) *and elevated,* (Ḳ,) or *somewhat elevated:* (Aboo-Kheyreh, L:) or the *abundance of trees of sand:* or, as some say, قُنْفَذُ رَمْلٍ, with fet-ḥ, signifies *abundance and tallness of trees of sand.* (L.) — قُنْفُذٌ (L, Ḳ) and with ة (L) † *A tree in the midst of sand.* (L, Ḳ.) — قَنَافِذُ † *Mountains that are not long:* or *long and narrow tracts,* (أَحْبُل, L, Ḳ, TA: in the CḲ, أَجْبُل, or *mountains,*) of sand: (L, Ḳ:) or *hills with pointed heads* (نَبَك) *lying in the way,* or *road.* (Th, L, Ḳ.)

قنقل

قَنْقَلٌ *Half an* إِرْدَبّ. (T, voce إِرْدَبّ.) See كُرّ.

قنى and قنو

1. قَنِىَ الحَيَآءَ *He kept to the sense of shame,* or *modesty;* (Ṣ, Ḳ;) *he preserved it:* and i. q. اِسْتَحْيَى: and ↓ اِسْتَقْنَى *he kept to* [or *preserved*] *his sense of shame,* or *modesty.* (TA.) — قَنَا غَنَمًا, and ↓ اِقْتَنَى, *He took for himself, got,* or *acquired, sheep,* or *goats* [*for a permanent possession*], *not for sale.* (JK.) — قَنَا, aor. يَقْنُو, inf. n. قُنُوٌّ; a dial. var. of قَنَأَ, q.v. (TA.)

3. قَانَى: see قَانَأَ.

8. اِقْتَنَى *He gained, acquired,* or *got, for himself,* (Ṣ, Ḳ,) or *took for himself,* (Mgh,) property, or camels, &c., (Ṣ, Mgh,) *as a permanent stock, for propagation,* (Mgh,) *not for merchandise:* (Ṣ, Mgh:) *he made it to be in his possession, not to depart from his hand:* (TA:) *he acquired it for himself permanently,* or *for a permanence.* See 1.

10: see 1.

قَنًا of the nose: see شَمَمٌ. — قنا وشق a name given in Egypt to وُشَّق; also called أُشَّق and أُشَّج. (TA in art. اشق.)

قَنَاةٌ *A spear-shaft;* (Mgh;) *a spear* (T, Ṣ, Ḳ) *that is hollow, like a cane;* (Az, in TA;) *a spear with a head affixed to it.* (Mṣb.) — Hence, *A subterranean channel,* or *conduit, for water.* (Mgh.) — [And *A pipe.*] — قَنَاةُ الكُوزِ *The* بُلْبُل [or *spout*] *of the* كوز [or *mug*], *that pours forth the water.* (M, Ḳ, in art. بل.) — قَنَاةٌ, said to signify بَقَرَةٌ وَحْشِيَّةٌ: see قَنَاةٌ.

قِنْيَةٌ: see قِنْوَةٌ.

قِنْيَةٌ and ↓ قِنْوَةٌ Sheep, or goats, *taken for oneself, gotten,* or *acquired,* [*for a permanent possession,*] *not for sale.* (JK.)

أَقْنَى in the prov., خَلَاؤُكَ أَقْنَى لِحَيَائِكَ i. q. أَلْزَمُ [as meaning *Most preservative:* see that prov. in art. خلو, and see قَنِىَ الحَيَآءَ, above]. (Ṣ in art. خلو, and Meyd.)

مُقَانَاةٌ The *weaving with one thread white and one thread black.* (T, voce نِيرٌ.)

قهزب

قَهْزَبٌ *Short:* (Ḳ:) an epithet applied to a man. (TA.)

قهق

R. Q. 1. قَهْقَهَ *He uttered a reiterated* (Ḳ, TA) *and prolonged,* (TA,) or *a vehement, laughter:* (Ḳ:) or *he laughed, reiterating the sound of* قَهْ. (Ṣ, Mṣb, Ḳ.)

قَهْقَاهٌ: see حَقْحَاقٌ.

قهقب

قَهْقَبٌ *Big, bulky,* or *large in body;* as also قَهْقَمٌ: (Seer, L:) or the same as an epithet applied to a camel: (TA:) or *big, bulky,* or *large in body, and advanced in years;* as also قُهْقُبٌ, (Ḳ,) and قَرْهَبٌ. (TA.) — *Tall,* or *long, and having a capacious belly.* (Ḳ.) — *Hard, and strong,* or *robust.* (M.) — *I. q.* بَاذِنْجَانٌ; (IAar, Ḳ:) as also كَهْكَبٌ. (TA.)

قهقم

قَهْقَمٌ i. q. قَهْقَبٌ *Big; bulky; large in body.* (L.)

قهل

5. تَقَهَّلَ *He was,* or *became, unfrequent in washing and cleansing his person; slovenly with respect to his person.* (Ḳ.)

قهنب

قَهْنَبَانٌ: see what follows.

قَهْنَبٌ *Tall, and having a curving back, the upper part bending forward over the breast,* or *a bent and humped back,* or *a projecting breast and hollow back;* accord. to the different explanations of أَجْنَأُ: or *tall:* (Ḳ;) i. e., in an absolute sense; (TA;) as also ↓ قَهْنَبَانٌ. (Ḳ.) But AḤei and others assert that the ن is augmentative. (MF.)

مُقَهْنِبٌ *Always remaining at the water.* (Ḳ.)

قوى : see قو

قور

قَارَةٌ *A she-bear:* see an ex. in art. قطن (conj. 2).

قوط

قَوْطٌ: see an ex. in a verse cited voce رَاجِلَةٌ.

قوع

قَاعٌ *An even place;* (Ṣ, voce مَقَدٌّ;) *plain,* or *level, land,* (Ṣ, Mṣb,) *that produces nothing;* (IF, Mṣb;) *plain,* or *soft, land,* (أَرْضٌ سَهْلَةٌ,) *low, and free from mountains.* (Ḳ.) See also رَوْضَةٌ. Respecting its pls., see جَارٌ.

قوف

قُوفٌ of the ear, The *upper part:* or the *helix:* see سَكٌّ and أَسَكُّ and شَنَفٌ. Not to be confounded with فُوقٌ. — قُوفٌ and قَافٌ: see صُوفٌ.

قوق

قَاقٌ: see فَاقٌ, in two places. — القَافُ المَعْقُودَةُ: see art. قعد.

قُوقٌ: see نَاقٌ.

قول

1. قَالَ. The objective complement of قال, meaning *He said,* or what is termed مَقُولُ القَوْلِ, must be a complete proposition, or a word signifying at least one complete proposition, as كَلَامًا; or a word signifying a command or the like; or a word significant of a sound, termed اِسْمُ صَوْتٍ: it may be a verb; but cannot be an inf. n., as عِبَادَةٌ. (Gr.) [This is what is meant where] it is said in the Keshsháf, العِبَادَةُ لا تُقَالُ. (Kull, p. 327.) — قَالَ لَهُ signifies خَاطَبَ له; قَالَ عَنْهُ, رَوَى عنه; قَالَ عَلَيْهِ, اِفْتَرَى; قَالَ بِهِ, حَكَمَ به; and قَالَ فيه, اِجْتَهَدَ فيه. (Marg. note in Additions to a copy of the KT.) — تَرَكَ: see اِجْتَهَدَ فِيهِ, i.e. قَالَ فِيهِ فَمَا تَرَكَ. — قَالَ عَلَيْهِ, aor. ـُ, *He lied,* or *said what was false, against him.* (TA in art. تلو.) See تَقَوَّلَ. — قَالَ فِيهِ and عَنْهُ *He said of him,* or *it,* such a thing. — قَالَ بِكَذَا *He asserted his belief in such*

a thing, as a doctrine or the like: a well-known meaning. — قَالَتِ العَيْنَانِ *The eyes made a sign* [as though saying . . .]. (TA.) — قَالَ بِرَأْسِهِ *He made a sign with his head:* (TA:) or *a motion.* (Ḥam, p. 242.) — قَالَ بِيَدِهِ *He took* [*with his hand*]. (TA.) — قَالَ بِرِجْلِهِ *He walked,* or *struck* [*with his leg,* or *foot*]. (TA.) — قَالَ بِثَوْبِهِ *He raised his garment.* (TA.) — قَالَ بِالمَآءِ عَلَى يَدِهِ *He poured the water on his arm or hand.* (TA.) — قَالَ فِيهِ *He spoke against him; vituperated him.* — قَالَ شِعْرًا lit., *He said,* or *spoke,* or *put forth,* or *uttered,* or *gave utterance to,* or *recited, poetry; he spoke in verse; he poetized,* or *versified.* — قَالَ *He made a sign;* syn. أَوْمَأَ. (Ḥam, p. 601, where see other meanings: see also p. 242 of the same: and see Mgh.) قَالَ بِيَدِهِ [*He made a sign with his hand,* meaning to say . . .]. (A trad. cited voce خَطٌّ; and another voce حَرْفٌ.) Also, *He struck his hand* upon a thing. (Mgh.) See an ex. voce أَشْرَبَ.

5. تَقَوَّلَ عَلَيْهِ *He lied against him.* (Ḥar, p. 256.)

8. اِقْتَالَ عَلَيْهِ, (Ṣ,) or عَلَيْهِمْ, (Ḳ,) i. q. تَحَكَّمَ, (Ṣ,) or اِحْتَكَمَ. (Ḳ.) See مُقْتَال.

قَوْلٌ *A saying; something said:* and *speech,* or *diction.* — صَعُبَ عَلَيْهِ القَوْلُ [*Diction,* or *speech, was,* or *became, difficult to him*]. (Ḳ in art. جبل.)

قِيلٌ and ↓ مَقُولٌ: see زَعْمٌ.

قِيلٌ: see exs. voce أَصْبَحَ and voce صِرًى. — قِيلَةٌ [*A saying*]. (M, art. ابد.)

قَالَةٌ: see فُوهَةٌ, near the end.

قَوَّالٌ, &c., *Good in speech:* or *loquacious;* or *copious in speech; chaste,* or *perspicuous, in speech; and eloquent.* (Ḳ.) — اِبْنُ أَقْوَالٍ *The man who talks much.* (TA in art. بنى.)

مَقُولُ القَوْلِ *The thing said:* as كَذَا in the phrases يُقَالُ كَذَا and قَالَ كَذَا. See قَالَ.

مَقُولٌ: see قِيلٌ.

المَقُولَاتُ العَشْرُ, in logic, *The Ten Predicaments,* or *Categories;* namely, الجَوْهَرُ *Substance,* الكَمُّ *Quantity,* الكَيْفُ *Quality,* الإِضَافَةُ *Relation,* الأَيْنُ *Place,* or *where,* المَتَى *Time,* or *when,* الوَضْعُ *Collocation,* or *posture,* المِلْكُ *Possession,* or *having,* الفِعْلُ *Action,* or *doing,* and الاِنْفِعَالُ *Passion,* or *suffering.*

قوم

1. قَامَ *He stood still* (Ksh and Bḍ in ii. 19) *in his place.* (Ksh.) — قَامَتِ الدَّابَّةُ *The beast stopped* (Ṣ, Ḳ, TA) *from journeying,* (TA,) *from fatigue,* or *being jaded;* (Ṣ, TA;) i. q. انقطعت. (A.) And قَامَتْ عَلَيْهِ الدَّابَّةُ *His beast, being jaded, stopped with him, and moved not from its place.* (Mgh.) — قَامَ *He,* or *it, stood up,* or *erect;* syn. اِنْتَصَبَ. (Ḳ.) And hence, *He rose,* i.e. from sitting or reclining. — قَامَ بِاللَّيْلِ *He rose in the night* to pray. — قَامَ رَمَضَانَ *He passed the nights of Ramaḍán in prayer:* (El-'Alḳamee in a marginal note in a copy of the Jámi' eṣ-Ṣagheer, voce مَنْ:) or *he performed the prayers* [*of Ramaḍán*] *called* التَّرَاوِيح. (En-Nawawee, ibid.) — قَامَتِ الصَّلَاةُ *The people rose to prayer:* or *the time of their doing so came.* (TA.) — قَامَتِ السَّاعَةُ *The resurrection,* or *the time thereof, came to pass.* — قَامَتِ الشَّمْسُ وَكَادَ الظِّلُّ يَعْقِلُ [*The sun became high, and the shade almost disappeared, at mid-day*]. (JK.) — قَامَ عَلَيْهِ *He rose up against him:* see a verse cited voce حُوبٌ. — قَامَ بِالأَمْرِ *He undertook the affair; took,* or *imposed, it upon himself;* syn. تَكَفَّلَ بِهِ; and the epithet is قَائِمٌ and قَيِّمٌ: (Ḥam, p. 5:) [and] *he managed, conducted, ordered, regulated,* or *superintended, the affair;* syn. سَاسَهُ; (TA in art. سوس;) and قام عَلَيْهِ has this latter signification; and *he tended,* or *took care of, it,* or *him;* syn. سَاسَهُ and وَلِيَهُ: (Ḥam ubi supra:) [and] the former signifies *he attended to the affair;* [*occupied himself with it*]; (this should be the first explanation;) *was mindful of it; kept to it constantly,* or *steadily;* and is *contr. of* قَعَدَ عَنْهُ and تَقَاعَدَ: (JM, q. v.:) [or,] as *contr. of* قعد عنه and تقاعد عنه, *he acted vigorously in the affair;* as also ↓ أَقَامَهُ; syn. جَدَّ فِيهِ, and تَجَلَّدَ. (Bḍ in ii. 2.) — You say, قَامَ بِشَأْنِهِ *He undertook,* or *superintended,* or *managed, his affair,* or *affairs.* And you say, قَامَ بِاليَتِيمِ, (Mṣb in art. عول,) and بِالصَّبِيِّ, (Idem, art. كفل,) *He maintained the orphan,* and *the child;* syn. عَالَهُ and كَفَلَهُ: (Idem:) and قَامَ المَرْأَةَ, and عَلَيْهَا, *He undertook the maintenance of the woman;* or *he maintained her;* مَانَهَا [i. e. قَامَ بِكِفَايَتِهَا (Ṣ and Ḳ in art. مون)]; *and undertook,* or *managed, her affair,* or *affairs.* (Ḳ.) And الرِّجَالُ يَقُومُونَ عَلَى النِّسَآءِ *The men govern the women:* (Bḍ, iv. 38:) or *are mindful of them, and act well to them,* or *take care of them.* (TA.) — قَامَ بِعُذْرِى [*He undertook,* and *it served, to excuse me*]. (Mṣb and TA in art. عذر; &c.) — قَامَ بِهِ *He,* or *it, was supported,* or *sustained, by it; subsisted by it:* see the explanation of قِوَامٌ in the Mṣb. — قَامَ عَلَيْهِ كَذَا *It cost him such a thing, such a sum,* or *so much.* — قَامَ فِى نَفْسِهِ often signifies ثَبَتَ: so in أَنَّهُ كَذَا *It was,* or *became, established in his mind that it was so.* — قَامَ بِهِ قِيَامًا تَامًّا *He managed it perfectly.* — قَامَ يَفْعَلُ كَذَا *He began to do such a thing; he betook himself to doing such a thing.* (Zj, in TA, art. قدم.) — قَامَ المَآءُ † *The water congealed,* or *froze;* syn. جَمَدَ. (Ṣ, M, voce جَمَدَ.) — قَامَتْ عَيْنُهُ: see عَيْنٌ قَائِمَةٌ. — قَامَ قَائِمُ الظَّهِيرَةِ: see ظَهِيرَةٌ: there expl. from JK. — قَامَ وَقَعَدَ: see قَعَدَ; and أَقْعَدَهُ; and see an ex. voce سُدَّةٌ. — قَامَ has also for an inf. n. مَقَامٌ, agreeably with a general rule: see Bḍ in x. 72, &c.; and see مَرَامٌ in art. روم.

2. قَوَّمَهُ *He made it straight,* or *even;* namely, a crooked thing; as also ↓ أَقَامَهُ: (TḲ:) and *made it right,* or *in a right condition; direct,* or *rightly directed.* — قَوَّمَهُ بِكَذَا *He valued it,* or *rated it, as equal to,* or *worth, such a thing.* A phrase well known, and used in the present day. — قَوَّمَهُ *He set its price; assigned it its price; valued it;* (Ṣ,* Mṣb, Ḳ;) as also ↓ اِسْتَقَامَهُ. (Mṣb, Ḳ.) — قَوَّمْتُهُ فَتَقَوَّمَ ↓ i. q. عَدَّلْتُهُ فَتَعَدَّلَ. (Mṣb.) — قَوَّمَ *He made a writing, and an account,* or *a reckoning, accurate,* or *exact,* or *right.*

3. قَاوَمَهُ [*He rose against him, and withstood him,* or *opposed him, in contention;*] namely, his adversary. (Mgh in art. نهض.) — *It was equal,* or *equivalent, to it.* (Mṣb.) — قَاوَمَهُ فِى الحَرْبِ *He opposed him,* or *contended with him for equality, in war,* or *battle.* (MA.) — قَاوَمَهُ فِى حَاجَةٍ *He rose,* or *stood, with him* [or *assisted him*] *to accomplish some needful affair.* (IAth, TA.) — قَاوَمَهُ *It was equal,* or *equivalent, to it:* see Mṣb: syn. عَادَلَهُ, q. v. (TA in art. بوأ.) — يُقَاوِمُ السُّمُومَ [*It counteracts poisons*]. (TA, art. بلس.)

4. أَقَامَ *He set up, put up, set upright,* a thing. (Mṣb.) — أَقَامَهُ said of food, [*It sustained him, supported him*]. (Mṣb.) — أَقَامَ عَلَى خَطَرٍ *He stood to a bet, wager,* or *stake.* (TA, voce نَدْبٌ.) — أَقَامَ عَلَيْهِ الحَدَّ *He inflicted upon him the punishment termed* حَدّ. (Mgh, art. حد.) — أَقَامَ دَرْأَهُ: see درأ. — أَقَامَ لِلصَّلَاةِ, inf. n. إِقَامَةٌ, *He* (the مُبَلِّغ) recited *the form of words called* إِقَامَة, q. v. infra. — أَقَامَ *He remained, continued, stayed, tarried, resided, dwelt,* or *abode,* in a place: *he remained stationary.* — أَقَامَ الصَّلَاةَ, *He observed prayer:* or أَدَامَ فِعْلَهَا. (Ṣ, Mṣb.) See also Bḍ, and Jel ii. 2. — أَقَامَ فِعْلًا *He performed an action.* — See 1. — أَقَامَهُ عَلَى الطَّرِيقِ *He made him to keep to the road:* and لِلْقَصْدِ, *to the right way.* (L, art. لغد.) — See 10. — أَقَامَ الأَمْرَ *He put the affair*

into a right state; like نَظَّمَهُ: see the latter in the Mṣb. — أَقَامَهُ (Ḳ in art. عدل) *He made it to be conformable with that which is right;* namely, a judgment, a judicial decision. (TḲ in that art.) — See 2. — أَقَامَ بِهِ in the Ḥamáseh, p. 75, l. 9, app. signifies *He stood in his stead.* — أَقَامَ *He observed,* or *duly performed,* a religious, or moral, ordinance or duty. — أَقَامَ البَيِّنَةَ [*He established the evidence* or *proof;* and so اقام بها? the ب being redundant]. (Bḍ, iii. 68.) And [in like manner,] اقام حُجَّتَهُ *i. q.* أَثْبَتَهَا; (TA in art. ثبت;) and so, app., بِحُجَّتِهِ; the ب being redundant, as in an ex. voce خُطَّةٌ; but this is the only ex. that I know, and it is without explanation: Golius mentions the phrase أَقَامَ بِى عَلَيْكُمْ; but without indicating his authority. — أَقَامَ عَلَى حَالٍ *He abode, or continued, in a state,* or *condition;* and اقام على أَمْرٍ *the same;* and *he abode, continued, stayed,* or *waited, intent upon,* or *occupied in, an affair, a business,* or *a concern; he kept to it.*

5. تَقَوَّمَ *It subsisted:* see رُكْنٌ. — تَقَوَّمَ *It had a price; was valued.* — See 2.

6. تَقَاوَمُوهُ فِيمَا بَيْنَهُمْ *They valued it,* or *estimated its price, among them.* (TA.)

10. اِسْتَقَامَ *It became right; direct; in a right state; straight: even: tended towards the right, or desired, point, or object; had a right direction, or tendency; was regular.* — اِسْتَقَامَ عَلَى طَرِيقِ الحَقِّ (Ḳ, art. رشد) *He continued in the way of truth, or the right way;* as also ↑ أَقَامَ عَلَيْهِ? — لَمْ يَسْتَقِمِ الأَمْرُ *The affair was,* or *became, difficult:* see تَعَذَّرَ. — استقام لَهُ الأَمْرُ *The affair, or case, became in a right state for him;* syn. اِعْتَدَلَ. (Ṣ.) — اِسْتَقَامَ *He, or it, was,* or *became, right, direct, rightly directed, undeviating, straight,* or *even:* and *he,* or *it, stood right,* or *straight,* or *erect.* (MA, KL.) *He went right on, straight on,* or *undeviatingly:* (see ذَهَبَ:) whence اِسْتَقَامَ عَلَى الطَّرِيقَةِ *he went on undeviatingly in the way.* (See Ḳur lxxii. 16.) *He went right; pursued a right course; acted rightly,* or *justly.* See also سَدَّ, with which it is syn. *It* (an affair) *was direct in its tendency,* or *had a right tendency. It* (discourse, &c.) *had a right tenour.* — See 2.

قَوْمٌ [*A people, or body of persons composing a community:* and *people,* or *persons:*] *a company,* or *body,* [or party, (see what follows,)] *of men,* [properly] *without women:* (Ṣ, Mṣb, Ḳ, &c.:) or *of men and women together;* (Ḳ;) for the قوم of every man is his *party,* and his *kinsfolk,* or *tribe:* (TA:) or (Ḳ) sometimes *including women, as followers;* (Ṣ, Mṣb, Ḳ;) for the قوم of every prophet is of *men and women.* (Ṣ, Mṣb.) — قَوْمٌ opposed to نِسَآءٌ: see a verse cited voce سَوْفَ.

قَامَةٌ The *stature* of a man; his *height in a standing posture;* it is *a span* (شِبْر) *shorter than a* باع: (JK:) *tallness, height;* and *beauty,* or *justness, of stature.* (Ḳ.) — قَامَةٌ *A structure [or post] like the figure of a man, raised at the side of a well, whereon is placed the wood to which the pulley is attached:* pl. قَامٌ: (JK:) also called ↑ قَائِمَةٌ: see Ḳ, voce عَمُود: or قَامَةُ البَكْرَةِ signifies *the sheave* (بَكْرَة) *with its apparatus.* (Ṣ, Ḳ.)

دِينٌ قِيَمٌ *A right religion.* (Ḳur, vi. 162.) See دِرَّةٌ.

الرِّيَاحُ القُوَّمُ *The right* [*or cardinal*] *winds.* (Ṣ, voce نَكْبَاء.)

الدِّينُ القَيِّمُ (Ḳur ix. 36) *The right, correct,* or *true, reckoning.* (T in art. دين.) — قَيِّمُ الأَمْرِ *i. q.* ↑ مُقِيمُهُ and سَائِسُهُ: fem. قَيِّمَةٌ. (TA.) — قَيِّمٌ بِأَمْرٍ *A manager of an affair; i. q.* إِزَاؤُهُ. (Ṣ, Mṣb, art. ازى.) See قَامَ بِالأَمْرِ. — قَيِّمٌ *A manager, conductor, orderer, regulator,* or *superintendent,* of an affair: (TA:) *a manager, conductor,* &c., *of the affairs* of a people. (JK.) قَيِّمٌ عَلَى المَالِ *A good* [*manager and*] *tender of camels,* &c. (TA in art. بلو.)

قِيمَةٌ The *real value,* or *worth,* of a thing; its *equivalent;* differing from ثَمَنٌ, q. v. (MF in art. ثمن.)

قَوَامٌ *Stature,* and *goodly stature,* or *tallness,* of a man: (Ṣ:) *symmetry,* or *justness of proportion.* (Mṣb.) — قَوَامُ الأَمْرِ and قِوَامُهُ and قِيَامُهُ *The stay,* or *support, of the thing,* or *affair, whereby it subsists, and is managed and ordered.* (Mṣb.) And قِوَامٌ The *food that is a man's support;* (Mṣb;) [his *subsistence.*] — قِوَامٌ [The *main stay* of a thing.] — لَا قِوَامَ لَهُ بِهِ [*He has not power to withstand him.* (Ḳ, art. نجز.)

قِوَامٌ *Subsistence:* see رُكْنٌ and طَبْعٌ.

قِيَامٌ [*A state of purging,* or *flux of the belly:* used in this sense in the Ṣ, Ḳ, voce هَيْضَةٌ].

قَوِيمٌ: see صَوِيبٌ.

القَيُّومُ: see يَا قَيُّومُ in the last paragraph of art. شره, where I have rendered it on the authority of an explanation in the TA.

قَوَّامٌ One *who rises much,* or *often, in the night* to pray. (TA.) See صَوَّامٌ.

قَوْمِيَّةٌ is written with ḍamm in copies of the Ṣ, Ḳ, JK: in the CḲ, erroneously, قَوَمِيَّةٌ, in both senses. See voce مُتَشَمِّسٌ.

قَائِمٌ *Appearing; conspicuous;* [as though standing before one]: *said of a thing whether standing or thrown down.* (TA, in explanation of the phrase هٰذَا نُصْبُ عَيْنِى, art. نصب.) — قَائِمَةٌ, pl. قَوَائِمُ, *Leg of a horse,* &c. — عَيْنٌ قَائِمَةٌ *An eye* [*blind,* or *white and blind, but still whole:* or] *that has become white and blind, but not yet burst,* (AZ in L, art. سد,) or *sightless, but with the black still remaining.* (Mgh, Mṣb.) — قَائِمٌ and قَائِمَةٌ The *hilt* of a sword. (Mṣb.) — قَائِمَةٌ *A leg* of a table, and of a throne, or moveable seat, &c. (JK.) See also قَامَةٌ; and see قَوَمَةُ بَيْتِ النَّارِ. — إِسْنَادٌ (Ḳ, art. هربذ.) *The servants of the fire-temple.* (TA, same art.) — القَوَائِمُ *The winds.* So in a verse of Umeiyeh Ibn-Abi-ṣ-Ṣalt. (TA, voce سَدِرَ.) — قَوَائِمُ المَائِدَةِ [*The legs of the table*]. (Ḳ, art. عقر.) — قَطٌّ قَائِمٌ *A nibbing in which the pith and the exterior of the reed are made of equal length:* opposed to مُصَوَّبٌ. (TA in art. حرف.) — مَآءٌ قَائِمٌ *Frozen water.* And *stagnant water:* see حِبَاكٌ.

إِقَامَةٌ The *form of words chanted by the* مُبَلِّغ, not by the مُؤَذِّن, *consisting of the common words of the* أَذَان, *with the addition of* قَدْ قَامَتِ الصَّلَاةُ (*The time of prayer has come!*) *pronounced twice after* حَىَّ عَلَى الفَلَاحِ. See ثَوَّبَ.

مَقَامٌ The *place of the feet;* (Ḳ;) *a standing-place;* (Ṣ, Mṣb;) as also ↑ مُقَامٌ: (Ṣ:) or the latter, *a place of stationing:* (Mṣb:) and both, *a place of continuance, stay, residence,* or *abode:* (Ḳ:) [*a standing:*] and the latter, *a place of long continuance, stay, residence,* or *abode:* (Expos. of the Mo'allaḳát, Calc., p. 138:) and both, *continuance, stay, residence,* or *abode.* (Ṣ, Ḳ.)

مُقَامٌ: see مَقَامٌ.

مُقِيمٌ *Lasting; continuing:* (Bḍ, ix. 21:) *unceasing.* (Bḍ, ix. 69.) — أَخَذَهُ المُقِيمُ المُقْعِدُ: see art. قعد. — See قَيِّمٌ.

مَقَامَةٌ *A standing-place.* Hence, † *A sitting-place.* Hence, † The *persons sitting there.* Hence, † *An oration, or a discourse, or an exhortation,* (خُطْبَة او عِظَة,) *or the like, there delivered;* as also مَجْلِسٌ. (Mṭr, in De Sacy's ed. of El-Ḥareeree, p. 5.)

حَجَرٌ مُتَقَوِّمٌ (Ḳ, art. موس) *A precious stone.* (TA, same art.)

المِعَى المُسْتَقِيمُ *The rectum.*

تَقْوِيمَاتٌ [pl. of تَقْوِيمٌ] *Stellar calculations.* (TA, voce زِيجٌ.)

قوه

قُوهَةٌ : see فُوَّهَةٌ, last sentence.

قوى

1. قَوِىَ and ♦ تَقَوَّى (Ṣ, Ḳ) and ♦ اِقْتَوَى (Ḳ) *He became strong:* (Ṣ, Ḳ:) *vigorous, robust,* or *sturdy;* like اِشْتَدَّ, or the last signifies *he became excellent in strength.* (TA.) — قَوِىَ عَلَيْهِ *He had strength,* or *power, sufficient for it;* or *he had strength,* or *power, to endure it; he prevailed against it;* namely, travel, adversity, &c. And *He* or *it, prevailed over him,* or *it.* — See 4. — قَوِىَ is [said to be] originally قَوِوَ, because it is from القُوَّةُ: (I'Aḳ, p. 368:) but Lth holds قُوَّةٌ to be [anomalous,] originally قُوْيَةٌ. (TA.) I prefer the former opinion, and think it should be mentioned in art. قو, or I would rather head this art. قو or قوى, like غو or غوى. ISd holds قُوَّةٌ to be from قوو, like ثُوَّةٌ, q. v. from ثوو.

2. قَوَّاهُ : see شَدَّهُ — قَوَّانِى عَلَيْهِ : see 2 in art. طوق.

3. قَاوَاهُ *He vied with him, strove to surpass him, or contended with him for superiority,* (Ṣ, Ḳ,) *in strength:* (TA:) *i. q.* شَادَّهُ. (A, L in art. شد.)

4. أَقْوَتِ الدَّارُ *The house became empty, vacant,* or *unoccupied;* (Ṣ, Mgh, Mṣb, Ḳ;) as also ♦ قَوِيَتْ. (Ṣ, Ḳ.)

5. تَقَوَّى *He strengthened himself; made himself, or constrained himself to be, strong; affected,* or *endeavoured to acquire, strength.* See 1. — تَقَوَّى مِنَ الشَّىْءِ بِقَوْمِهِ : see تَمَنَّعَ.

8: see 1.

قُوَّةٌ *Strength, power, potency, might,* or *force; contr. of* ضَعْفٌ; (Ṣ, Ḳ;) in body, and in intellect: (TA:) *vigour, robustness,* or *sturdiness;* like شِدَّةٌ. — قُوَّةٌ *A strand;* i. e., *a single twist of a rope; a yarn; a distinct, and separately twisted, portion, of two or more which, being twisted together, compose the whole, of a rope,* and *of a string,* or *thread.* See also ثِنْىٌ. — *A faculty.* Ex. السَّمْعُ قُوَّةٌ فِى الأُذُنِ بِهَا تُدْرِكُ الأَصْوَاتَ [السمع *is a faculty in the ear by which it perceives sounds*]. (TA in art. سمع.) — بِالقُوَّةِ *Potentially,* or *virtually;* as opposed to بِالفِعْلِ, i. e. actually. — قُوَّةٌ لَفْظٍ : see لَيْتَ.

بِتٌّ قَوِيًّا, and قَاوِيًا, and مُقْوِيًا : see غَوِىٌّ and غَوِىٌّ in art. غو.

قيس

قَوَّاسٌ : see قَيَّاسٌ.

مَقِيسٌ (not مُقَيَّسٌ) *Consistent with analogy.*

قيص

مِقْوَصٌ : see مِقْيَصٌ.

قيض

1\. قَاضَ : }
7\. اِنْقَاضَ : } see انقاص, art. قيص.

مُنْقَاضٌ : see مُنْقَاصٌ.

قيظ

قَيْظِىٌّ : on the نِتَاج thus called see صَفَرِىٌّ.

قيق

قِيقَاءٌ, (Ḳ, voce تَلْتَلَةٌ; Ṣ, Ḳ, voce رَفَضٌ, and voce وَلِيعٌ; Ḳ, voce جُفٌّ; &c.,) or قِيقَاةٌ, (Ṣ, voce تَلْتَلَةٌ; and TA,) and قِيقَاةٌ, (TA,) or قِيقَاةٌ and قِيقَايَةٌ, (JK,) The *envelope* (قِشْرٌ, JK, or وِعَآءٌ, TA) *of the* طَلْع [or *spadix of the palm-tree*]; (JK, TA;) *which is made into a drinking-vessel, like the* تَلْتَلَة: (JK:) the قِيقَاء of the طَلْع is the *envelope* (غِشَآء) *that is with the* وَلِيع. (Ḳ, voce جُفٌّ.)

قِيقٌ and }
قُيَاقٌ : } see فَاقٌ.

قيقاء see voce حَرَبٌ and Ḳ, voce وَلِيعٌ and جُفٌّ.

قيل

1. قَالَ *He slept during midday:* (Mgh:) or *he stayed during midday.* (TA, art. هجر.) — قَيَّلَ : see another meaning, voce بَيَّتَ.

3. قَايَلَهُ البَيْعَ [*He dissolved, rescinded,* or *annulled, with him the sale*]. (A, art. رد.)

4. أَقَالَ ٱللّٰهُ عَثْرَتَكَ, and عِثَارَكَ, [*May God cancel thy slip, lapse, fault, wrong action,* or *mistake:* (A, art. عثر:) *may God raise thee from thy fall.* (Mṣb, art. قيل.) أَقَالَهُ عَثْرَتَهُ *He forgave him his slip, lapse,* or *fault.* (MA.)

5. تَقَيَّلَ أَبَاهُ : see تَقَيَّضَ and تَأَسَّلَ.

10. اِسْتَقَالَ البَيْعَ *He desired,* or *demanded, the rescinding of the sale,* or *purchase.* (MA.) And استقال العَثْرَةَ *He desired,* or *demanded, his passing over,* or *forgiving, the slip, lapse,* or *fault.* (MA.) See also Ḥar, p. 7. See also a verse cited voce عَثْرَةٌ.

قَائِلَةٌ : see غَائِرَةٌ.

مَقِيلٌ *A resting-place;* syn. مُسْتَقَرٌّ: hence, مَقِيلُ الحُبِّ [*the resting-place of love*] and مَقِيلُ الغَيْظِ [*the resting-place of wrath*], applied by El-Mutanebbee to *the heart.* (W, i. 112.) See an ex. (mistranslated) in De Sacy's Ar. Gr., sec. ed., ii. 165: the same, with a var., in Ibn-Aḳeel p. 210.

قين

قَيْنٌ The *part,* of a camel, *that is the place of the shackle,* or *hobble.* (Ḥam, p. 558.) See a verse of Dhu-r-Rummeh, voce دَانٍ.

ك

ك prefixed to a noun is called كَافُ التَّشْبِيهِ *The* ك *of comparison.* Respecting its being prefixed to pronouns, see أَنْ, suprà, p. 106. — إِجْعَلْ هٰذَا الشَّىْءَ كَأَنَّا وَاحِدًا *Make thou this thing to be [uniform, or] of one way,* or *mode,* or *manner.* (ISk, in TA, art. بأج.) — كَذٰلِكَ *The like thereof; such like;* and simply *such;* and *so.* — كَاْ and كَآءِ : see كَأَيِّنْ or كَأَيٍّ voce أَىٌّ. — كَمَا followed by a pret. often means *Like as when:* see an ex. in a verse cited above, p. 740. — كَمَا is often followed by a pret. in the sense of an aor.: see exs. in EM., pp. 41 & 214. — كَمَا أَنْتَ وَزَيْدًا [*Keep as,* or *where, thou art, and approach not Zeyd!* like مَكَانَكَ وَزَيْدًا]. Heard by Ks. (L, art. عند.) — كَمَا أَنْتَنِى *Wait for me where thou art!* Heard by Az from certain of the Benoo-Suleym. (L, art. عند.) — ك of allocution is varied like the pronominal affix of the sec. pers., accord. to the sex and number of the persons addressed: see exs. in the Ḳur, iii. 42 and xix. 21 (Flügel's ed., and Lees' Keshsháf), xii. 37, ii. 46, &c., and xii. 32. But sometimes the same form is used in addressing a number of persons as in addressing one man: see, for ex., Ḳur, iv. 96.

كبن

1. كَبَنَ : see صَمَنَ. — كَبَنَ الثَّوْبَ : see غَبَنَ.

كبا

كَبَا : said of a horse: see above, art. حَنَذَ, p. 656 *b*. — See also a phrase voce سَلَّةٌ. — كَبَا *He fell upon his face:* (Ḳ, TA:) or so كَبَا لِوَجْهِهِ: Ṣ, TA:) and كَبَا also signifies عَثَرَ [*he stumbled,* or *tripped*]. (TA.)

كت

R.Q. 1. كَتْكَتَ : see طَحْطَحَ.

كَتْكَتٌ The *coarse part of silk, and of tow, &c.*

كتب

كِتَابٌ (same as عَقْدٌ) *The ceremony* (not certificate) *of a marriage-contract.* كَتَبُوا كِتَابَهُ عَلَى فُلَانَةَ *They performed the ceremony of the contract of his marriage to such a woman* (*same as* عقدوا عَقْدَهُ). — أَهْلُ الكِتَابِ : see أَهْلٌ.

كتف

كَتِفٌ [The *shoulder-blade;*] *a wide bone behind the shoulder-joint.* (Mgh.) — [Hence, The *shoulder* itself.] See طُرَّةٌ and مُؤَرَّبٌ.

كُتْفَانٌ, as an epithet applied to the locust, see in TA, voce مُسَيَّحٌ. See also جَرَادٌ.

كِتَافٌ of a زِبِيل : see حَتِىٌّ.

كَتِيفَةٌ *i. q.* ضَبَّةٌ *A broad piece of iron.* A poet speaks of a wooden vessel of which a fracture is mended with a كتيفة. (Ṣ.)

كتل

2. كَتَّلَهُ, inf. n. تَكْتِيلٌ, *He made it* (أقط [&c.]) *into lumps,* or *compact pieces* or *portions.* (TA.) — And *He,* or *it, fattened him.* (Kr, TA.)

5. تَكَتَّلَ *It became compacted together in a mass; it became lumpy.* See قِيدَ, art. قود.

كُتْلَةٌ *A lump,* or *compact piece* or *portion,* (Ṣ, M,* Mṣb, Ḳ,) of a thing, (Mṣb,) or of gum, &c., (Ṣ,) or of dates, and of clay, &c.: (M, Ḳ:) *a piece,* or *portion,* of dates packed together in a receptacle: (Mgh:) and *a piece* of flesh-meat. (Ḳ.)

كتلة *i. q.* زِبِيلٌ. (TA in art. حصن.)

مِكْتَلٌ *A* زِنْبِيل, (Mṣb, Ḳ,) or *thing like a* زِنْبِيل, [or زَبِيل,] (Ṣ,) *holding fifteen measures of the quantity termed* صَاع; (Ṣ, Ḳ;) it is *a thing* [or *basket*] *made of palm-leaves, in which dates, &c., are carried.* (Mṣb.)

مُكَتَّلٌ *Round and compact;* (Ḳ;) applied to a head: (TA:) *short* (Ṣ, Ḳ, TA) *and strong:* (TA:) a man *thick in body,* (Ḳ, TA,) *compact therein, and inclining to shortness.* (TA.)

كتم

1. كَتَمَ, aor. ـُ, inf. n. كَتْمٌ [and كِتْمَانٌ], doubly trans., *He concealed,* or *suppressed,* a secret. (Mgh.) — كَتَمَ الرَّبْوَ : see a verse cited in the last paragraph of art. عور.

5. تَكَتَّمَ (Ḳ, art. دلس) *He* (a man) *concealed,* or *hid, himself.* (T, Ḳ, same art.)

6. تَكَاتَمُوا *They practised concealment, one with another:* see تَدَافَنُوا.

كَتُومٌ *A strict concealer of secrets.*

كَاتِمٌ meaning مَكْتُومٌ : see دَافِقٌ, in two places. — فِى كَاتِمِ السِّرِّ : see a verse cited in conj. 3 of art. عرض.

كتن

كَتَنٌ for كَتَّانٌ : see an ex. in a verse cited voce شَارِبٌ.

كج

كُجَّةٌ, see بُكْسَةٌ in the Ḳ and TA.

كحط

4. أَكْحَطَ : see أَقْحَطَ, in two places.

كحل

1. كَحَلَ † *He put out,* or *blinded,* an eye with a heated nail, &c.: see an ex. voce سَمَرَ.

8. مَا اكْتَحَلْتُ غِمَاضًا and غِمَاضًا &c.: see أَغْمَضَ. See also حَثَاثٌ.

10. اِسْتَكْحَلَ السَّهَرَ † [*He became sleepless;* as though he took sleeplessness as a collyrium]. (TA in art. حلس, from a trad.)

كَحْلٌ and كَحَلٌ (Ṣ, Ḳ) *A year of drought, barrenness, or dearth;* (Ṣ;) *a hard year.* (Ḳ.)

كُحَيْلٌ a proper name for *A horse of high breed;* as also ↑كُحَيْلَانٌ. (TA.) — كُحَيْلٌ *Tar* (قَطِرَان) in the dial. of El-Ḥijáz. (TA, voce غَرْبٌ; from the T.) See نِفْط.

كُحَيْلَانٌ : see كُحَيْلٌ.

عَيْنٌ كَحْلَآءُ *An eye that is black,* [or *black in the edges of the lids,*] *by nature, as though it had* كُحْل *applied to it.* (Mgh.) Not in the TA. [It seems to have both of these meanings.]

كَحْلَآءُ *A certain plant:* see Ḳ, voce شِنْجَار: *calendula arvensis:* see Delile, Flor. Aeg., no. 864.

الأَكْحَلُ *The median vein.* See أَبْجَلُ and وَرِيدٌ and أَبْهَرُ and الصَّافِنُ.

كدم

1. كَدَمَ *He bit with the fore part of the mouth.* (Ṣ, Mṣb, Ḳ.)

6. تَكَادُمُ الحُمُرِ [*The wild asses' biting one another with the fore part of the mouth*]. (TA in art. سحج.) See also تَسَانَّت.

كذبن

كَذْبَانُونَةٌ [Pers. كَدْبَانو] *An intelligent housewife, who is a good manager.* (Ḳ, art. هلج; but omitted in some copies.)

كذنق

كُذَيْنَق : see مِدَقٌّ, in art. دق.

كرز

3. فلان يُكَارِزُ عن الحق الى الباطل, inf. n. مُكَارَزَةٌ : *i. q.* يُعَاجِزُ, expl. in art. عجز. (TA, art. عجز.)

كرس

7. اِنْكَرَسَ فِى الشَّىْءِ *He entered into the thing and concealed himself.* (IḲṭṭ, in TA, art. نمس.)

كُرْسِىُّ الخَاتَمِ (T, Ḳ, art. بظر) *The bezel of the ring.* (TḲ.)

كُرْسَنَّةٌ, thus written: (TA:) [*Bitter vetch:*] see خَانِق.

كِرْسِنِىٌّ [or ↑كُرْسَنِىٌّ] *A sort of* حِمِّص. (The Minháj, in TA, art. حمص.)

كرش

كَرِشٌ or كِرْشٌ *The plant so named:* see رِقَّةٌ.

كرص

كَرِيصٌ *A kind of* أَقِط: see كَثٌّ.

مِكْرَصٌ : *i. q.* مِضْرَبٌ, q. v.

كرع

1. كَرَعَ فِى المَآءِ, and فِى الإِنَآءِ, *He put his mouth into the water, or into the vessel, and so drank.* (See عَبَّ.)

كِرَاعٌ : see عِدٌّ.

كُرَاعٌ : see ذِرَاعٌ, رَكَضَ, حُرَّةٌ, and بَدَنٌ.

كُرْسُوعٌ *The prominent extremity of the ulna, next to the little finger, at the wrist.* (Ṣ,* Ḳ.)

كرك

كُرْكِىٌّ The *Numidian crane; ardea virgo:* also called إِوَزٌّ عِرَاقِىٌّ, and وَزٌّ عِرَاقِىٌّ. See أَبُو غُرْنَيْق and العَيْزَار.

كرم

1. كَرُمَ, inf. n. كَرَمٌ, *It* (a thing) *was,* or *became, highly esteemed* or *prized* or *valued; excellent, precious, valuable,* or *rare:* (Mṣb:) followed by عَلَيْهِ: see 1 in art. فجع. — كَرُمَتْ أَرْضُهُ *His land yielded increase of its seed-produce,* (ISh, Ḳ,) *and its soil became good,* (ISh,) *being manured;* (ISh, Ḳ;) [or *it was,* or *became, generous,* or *good;* i. e., *productive,* or *fertile*]. — كَرُمْتُ عَلَيْهِ, (S, Ḳ, art. عز,) *I exceeded him in generosity, or nobleness.* (TḲ, voce عَزَّ.)

2. كَرَّمَهُ عَلَىَّ [*He honoured him above me*]. (Ḳur, xvii. 64.) — كَرَّمَهُ عَنْ كَذَا [*He preserved him from such a thing*]: see an ex. in a verse cited in art. عل (conj. 3): and see, here, 4 and 5. — كَرَّمَ *He highly regarded* a horse or the like. — See تَكْرِمَةٌ.

4. أَكْرَمَهُ *He treated him with honour, or courtesy.* — أَكْرَمَ, and ↑اِسْتَكْرَمَ, *He found a generous horse* (فَرَسًا كَرِيمًا). (TA in art. ربط.) See رَبَطَ. — أَكْرَمْتُ عَنْهُ عِرْضِى *I preserved myself from it.* (Ṣ in art. عرض. See also 2.)

5. تَكَرَّمَ عَنْهُ, and ↑تَكَارَمَ, *He shunned it; avoided it; kept, or removed, himself far from it; or preserved himself from it;* (Ḳ;) for instance, from foul speech. (TA in art. وقع.) — تَكَرَّمَ *He affected, or constrained himself, to be generous.* (Ṣ.)

6: see 5.

10. اِسْتَكْرَمَ الشَّىْءَ : see 10 in art. فره. — See also 4.

قِطْفُ ابْنِ الكَرْمِ *The* [i. e. *grapes,* or *bunch of grapes*]. (T in art. بنى.)

كَرْمٌ in a horse, &c., *generous quality.* See حَسَبٌ; and see كَرِيمٌ, and مَكْرُمَةٌ, and شَرِيفٌ.

ذُو الجَلَالِ وَالإِكْرَامِ (Ḳur, lv. 27) *Possessed of majesty,* or *greatness, and bounty:* (Jel:) or, *of absolute independence and universal bounty.* (Bḍ.)

العُرُوقُ الصُّفْرُ : see الكُرْكُمُ الصَّغِيرُ.

كَرِيمٌ *Generous; liberal; honourable; noble; high-born;* contr. of لَئِيمٌ. (Ḳ, &c.) — [A *generous,* a *noble,* a *high-bred,* a *well-born,* or an *excellent,* horse, &c.; *of generous, high,* or *good, breed* or *quality.*] — A thing *highly esteemed* or *prized* or *valued; excellent, precious, valuable,* or *rare.* (Mṣb.) — [أَرْضٌ كَرِيمَةٌ *Productive land.* See كَرُمَتْ أَرْضُهُ.] — بَعِيرٌ كَرِيمٌ عَلَى أَهْلِهِ [*A camel held in high estimation by his owner*]. (TA in art. دفع.) — [وَجْهُ اللّٰهِ الكَرِيمُ] means *The glorious face of God:* see an ex. voce سُبْحَةٌ. — كَرَائِمُ المَالِ (TA) or الأَمْوَالِ (Mgh, Mṣb) *Such as are held in high estimation, precious,* or *excellent, of cattle* or *other possessions;* (Mgh, Mṣb, TA;) the *choice,* or *best, thereof.* (Mgh, Mṣb.)

حُبًّا وَكَرَامَةً, see حُبٌّ. — لا ولا كَرَامَةً *No; nor a jar-cover:* i. e., *No:* (*I will not give thee,* or *I will not do, what thou requirest,*) *nor anything else.* See حُبٌّ; and see تَكْرِمَةٌ. — كَرَامَةٌ, the kind of miracle so called: pl. كَرَامَاتٌ; like the term χαρίσματα as used by St. Paul in 1 Cor. xii. 9: it may be well rendered *thaumaturgy:* and صَاحِبُ كَرَامَاتٍ *a thaumaturgus,* or *thaumaturgist:* see مُعْجِزَةٌ, and قَرَامَةٌ.

أَكْرَمُ in the sense of كَرِيمٌ, as in أَكْرَمُهُمْ أَبًا : see بَيَاضٌ.

تَكْرِمَةٌ, *syn.* with تَكْرِيمٌ; (Mgh;) subst. from كَرَّمَهُ; as also ↑كَرَامَةٌ. (Mṣb.)

مَكْرَمَةٌ *A means,* or *cause, of attaining honour.* (Mgh, Mṣb.)

مَكْرُمٌ : see أَلُوكٌ and يُسْرٌ.

مَكْرُمَةٌ *A generous,* or *honourable, quality* or *action.* (Mṣb, &c.) — عَلِىَ فِى المَكَارِمِ [*He became eminent in generous,* or *honourable, actions* or *practices* or *qualities* or *dispositions*]. (Mṣb in art. علو.) — مَكَارِمُ may often be rendered *Excellencies.*

أَرْضٌ مَكْرُمَةٌ and ↑كَرْمٌ; *Generous, good, land:* (Ḳ, TA:) [*good and fertile land:*] or *dunged and tilled land.* (TA.) And أَرْضٌ مَكْرُمَةٌ لِلنَّبَاتِ ‡ *Land producing good herbage* or *plants.* (Ṣ,

TA. [In some copies of the Ṣ, *good for herbage or plants.*])

كره

1. كَرِهَهُ [*He disliked, was displeased with, disapproved of, hated, him or it.*] الكَرَاهَةُ is the contr. of الرِّضَى and الإِرَادَةُ. (Marg. note in TA.) — كَرِهَهُ (Mgh, Mṣb), inf. n. كَرَاهَةٌ and كَرَاهِيَةٌ, (Mgh,) or كُرْهٌ and كَرْهٌ, (Mṣb,) *He did not desire it; he disapproved it,* or *was displeased* or *discontented with it;* (Mgh;) *he disliked it; disapproved it; hated it; contr. of* حَبَّهُ. (Mṣb.) — سَخِطَ : كَرِهَ and تَكَرَّهَ: see .

2. كَرَّهْتُ إِلَيْهِ الشَّىْءَ, inf. n. تَكْرِيهٌ, *I made the thing to be an object of dislike, disapprobation,* or *hatred, to him.* (Ṣ, Ḳ.*)

4. أَكْرَهْتُهُ عَلَى كَذَا *I made him to do such a thing against his will.* (Ṣ.)

5. تَكَرَّهَهُ *He showed,* or *expressed, dislike, disapprobation,* or *hatred, of it;* see تَأَجَّمَهُ and تَسَخَّطَهُ: and تَكَارَهَ عَلَيْهِ signifies the same; see قَنَعَ — تَكَرَّهَ *He expressed dislike, displeasure, disapprobation, discontent, or hatred.* (IbrD.) See examples in the Ḳ, voce أُخٌ, and voce أُفٌّ, &c. The above is the prevailing signification, and often occurs. — تَكَرَّهَهُ *i. q.* كَرِهَهُ, q. v. (Ḳ,* TA.) See also تَأَجَّمَهُ.

6: see 5.

كَرِيهٌ *Disliked, disapproved of, blamed,* or *hated; hateful, blameable, displeasing,* or *odious;* as also مَكْرُوهٌ.

البُغْضُ لَهُ signifies الكَرَاهِيَةُ لِلشَّىْءِ and عَدَمُ مُلَاءَمَتِهِ. (MF in art. ابى.)

كَارِهٌ *Unwilling:* see an ex. voce أَسَآءَ.

مَكْرُوهٌ *A thing that one dislikes, disapproves,* or *hates,* or *that one dislikes to do:* opposed to مَنْشَطٌ: (TA in art. نشط:) [*a thing,* or *an event, that is an object of dislike* or *hatred*].

مَكْرُوهٌ *Foul, abominable,* or *evil;* i. q. سَيِّئٌ; (Beyḍ, xvii. 40;) and شَرٌّ: (TA:) [*held in aversion*]. See كَرِيهٌ. — مَكَارِهُ, a pl. of مَكْرُوهٌ. — مَكَارِهُ الدَّهْرِ *The afflictions,* or *calamities, of fortune;* syn. نَوَازِلُهُ and شَدَائِدُهُ. (TA.) See also مَكْرَهٌ.

مُسْتَكْرَهٌ: see an ex. voce عَرْضٌ.

كرى

3. كَارَى عَلَى دَابَّةٍ *He employed a beast of carriage to carry for hire.* (IbrD.)

4. أَكْرَانِى دَارَهُ, and دَابَّتَهُ, *He let me his house, and his beast of carriage, on hire.* (Mgh.)

6: see 8.

8. اِكْتَرَى and اِسْتَكْرَى and تَكَارَى *He hired,* or *took on hire* a house, and a beast. (Mgh.)

10: see 8.

كَرًى or كَرًا *Drowsiness.* (Ṣ, Mṣb, Ḳ.)

كَرِىٌّ *One who lets a thing on hire;* (Mgh:) *one who lets beasts on hire.* (Mṣb.) See an ex. in a verse cited art. شمر, conj. 4. — And *One who is hired.* (Mgh, &c.) In one copy of the Mgh, المكترِى is put by mistake for المُكْتَرَى: i. q. مُكْرٍ: and مُكْتَرًى. (TA in art. حرم.)

كُرِىٌّ *Spherical:* see Ksh in ii. 20.

كُرِيَّةٌ *Sphericalness:* see Bḍ in ii. 20.

كَرَوْيَا [*Caraway-seed*] is of the measure فَعَوْلَل [and if so must be written كَرَوْيًا]: (Ḳ:) or it may be فَعَوْلَى: [but see what follows:] AḤn says that, if with medd, it is fem. [and therefore كَرَوْيَآء]: but it is not Arabic [and therefore, without medd, it is probably كَرَوْيَا]. (TA.)

كَرَوَانٌ: see ضُوَعٌ and قَبَجٌ.

مُكَارٍ *One who lets beasts of carriage, &c., on hire;* like كَرِىٌّ, q. v.; *an owner, and letter on hire, of asses* [&c.]. (KL.) See فَلَّاحٌ.

كسف

بَالٌ: see كَاسِفُ البَالِ.

كسق

كَوْسَقٌ i. q. كَوْسَجٌ. (M.)

كسل

2. كَسَّلَهُ, inf. n. تَكْسِيلٌ, said of satiety, *It rendered him heavy, sluggish, lazy, indolent,* or *torpid.* (TA.)

4. أَكْسَلَ عَنْهَا signifies أَوْلَجَ وَلَمْ يُنْزِلْ; [*Inivit sed non emisit;*] (IAạr, in TA, art. فهر;) [i. e., أَوْلَجَ ثُمَّ تَرَكَهَا وَلَمْ يُنْزِلْ].

كَسْلَانُ *Heavy, sluggish, lazy, indolent, torpid.* (Ḳ.)

مَكْسَلَةٌ: see an ex. voce كِظَّةٌ.

كسو

1. كَسَوْتُهُ سَيْفًا [*I invested him with a sword*]. (TA in art. غشو.)

5. تكسى: see تسقى.

كِسَآءٌ [*A garment*]. See عَبَآءَةٌ, and حِلْسٌ and مِسْحٌ. — ذُو كِسَآءٍ, as opposed to ذُو بُرْدٍ, † *A poor man.* (Ṣ, art. عج.) [The كساء was evidently a simple oblong piece of cloth; for الكِسَائِى is said to have been thus named because he wore a كساء while in the state of إِحْرَام; as is mentioned in the TA, art. كسو; but it seems to have been sometimes sewed in the manner of the عَبَآء, which see; and see also مِسْحٌ, and بُرْدٌ.] It is [properly] not one of the garments which are cut and sewed [but is a single piece]: (Mgh, art. قطع:) [*a wrapper,* or *wrapping garment, of a single piece*]. — رَكِبَ كِسَآءَهُ *He fell upon the back of his neck.* (IAạr, in TA, art. ردع.)

كَاسٍ *Having clothing:* see an ex. voce رُبَّ.

أَكْسَى: see بَصَلٌ.

كشف

1. كَشَفَهُ and كَشَفَ عَنْهُ *He uncovered it; unveiled it; laid it open; displayed it; exposed it to view; discovered it; detected it; revealed it; disclosed it.* — كَشَفَ عَنْهُ *He investigated, explored,* or *scrutinized, it; searched, examined,* or *inquired, into it.* — كَشَفَهُ *He removed it;* namely, a cover, or covering, or the like: and *he uncovered it, laid it open,* &c.; as also كَشَفَ عَنْهُ. — كَشَفَ شَيْئًا عَنْ شَىْءٍ *He removed, put off, took off,* or *stripped off, a thing from over,* or *from before, a thing which it covered or concealed.* (Ḳ.) — كَشَفَ *He removed, cleared away,* or *dispelled,* grief, or sorrow: see فَرَّجَ (of which it is an explanation in the Mṣb and Ḳ). — See 7.

3. كَاشَفَهُ, inf. n. مُكَاشَفَةٌ, [*He acted openly with him,* or *towards him;*] syn. of the inf. n. مُجَاهَرَةٌ. (Ḥar, p. 470.) *He,* or *it, appeared to him;* as also كَاشَفَ عَلَيْهِ; syn. ظهر له. (TA.) — كُوشِفَ بِمَا أَخْفَيْتُ *He became acquainted with, knew,* or *got knowledge of, what I concealed:* syn. إِطَّلَعَ عَلَيْهِ. (Ḥar. p. 686.) — مُكَاشَفَةٌ The *showing open enmity,* or *hostility, with any one.* (KL.) [I. e. كَاشَفَهُ alone, or] كاشفه بالعَدَاوَةِ signifies *He showed open enmity,* or *hostility, with him;* (Ṣ, MA, Ḳ;) and so كاشفه العَدَاوَةَ. (MA.) See صَفْحَةٌ. — [Also *Discovery,* or *revelation:* pl. مُكَاشَفَاتٌ: see Ḥájjee Khaleefeh, s. v.] — كَاشَفَهُ الحَرْبَ [*He made war with him openly*]. (Mṣb, art. نبذ.)

5. تَكَشَّفَ *He uncovered,* or *exposed, himself* in sitting. (TA, voce أَعْفَتْ.)

6. تَكَاشَفُوا *They revealed* their faults, or secrets, *one to another:* see تَقَاذَفُوا.

7. اِنْكَشَفَ عَنْهُ [*He,* or *it, withdrew,* or *became withdrawn,* or *removed* or *became removed, from him,* or *it,* or *from over it*]. — اِنْكَشَفَتْ said of a she-camel: see مُفَشَّنٌ. — اِنْكَشَفُوا [*They were*

routed, defeated, or *put to flight;* like ▼كُشِفُوا: the former is quasi-pass. of كَشَفَ, "he routed," &c.]. (Ḳ, voce جال in art. جول.) See also تَفْرِيجَة, in art. فرج.

كُشَّانٌ: see Ḥam, p. 49, l. 2.

مَكْشُوفٌ *Uncovered,* &c.; *overt.*

مُكَاشِفٌ [*A discoverer,* or *revealer:* thus I have rendered it voce عَيْنٌ.]

كشك

كَشْكٌ *Barley-water:* (Ḳ:) or *pounded wheat* or *barley:* a Persian word, arabicized. (Mgh.) Hence, كَشْكِيَّةٌ *A kind of broth.* (Mgh.)

كظم

1. كَظَمَ غَيْظَهُ *He repressed,* or *restrained, his wrath,* or *rage.* (Ḳ.) — كَظَمَ, aor. ـِ, inf. n. كُظُومٌ, *He restrained himself.* (TA.) — مَا يَكْظِمُ عَلَى جِرَّتِهِ: see جِرَّةٌ; and لَا يَكْظِمُ عَلَى جِرَّةٍ. — كَظَمَ عَلَى غَيْظِهِ *i. q.* كَظَمَ غَيْظَهُ. (TA.)

كَظَائِمُ [pl. of كِظَامَةٌ] *Subterranean conduits for water.* (TA in art. قنو.)

كعبر

كُعْبُرَةٌ and ▼كُعْبُورَةٌ *Anything compact* (Ḳ, TA) *and round:* (TA:) and the latter, *i.q.* عُقْدَةٌ [meaning *a knot,* or *a knob*]: (TA:) [pl. of the latter كَعَابِيرُ: see خُرُوٌ: see also أُخْرُمٌ].— Also The *seed-vessel* [i. e. *siliqua,* or *pod,*] of the radish and some other plants. (IAạr, TA voce إِسْحَارٌ.)

كُعْبُورَةٌ: see كُعْبُرَةٌ.

كعك

كَعْكٌ *A well-known bread;* (Ḳ;) *biscuit;* (MA;) or [*a kind of*] *dry bread:* (MA, TA:) now applied to *a sort of bread made in the form of a ring, hollow,* [*and generally containing some* دبس or *the like,*] *the best of which is brought from Syria, and given as a present.* (TA.)

كعل

كُعَلٌ: see ثُعَلٌ.

كعم

1. كَعَمَ البَعِيرَ: see عَكَمَ.

كِعَامٌ *A muzzle for a camel.* (PṢ.)

كِعَامَةٌ The *iron thing that embraces,* or *clasps,* (قَلْتَقِر,) *the muzzle of the horse.* (IDrd in his book on the Saddle and Bridle, p. 8.)

كف

1. كَفَّ الثَّوْبَ *He sewed the edge,* or *border, of the garment,* or *piece of cloth, the second time,* (Ṣ, Ḳ,) *after the* [*slight*] *sewing termed* المَلّ, (Ṣ,) or الشَّلّ. (Ḳ.) — [*He felled* (a seam or garment).] — كَفَّ عَنْهُ, aor. ـُ, *He refrained,* or *forbore, from it, as forbidden; abstained,* or *desisted, from it; left, relinquished,* or *forsook it:* (Mṣb:) [as also ▼انكفّ]. — كَفَّ عَنْهُ *He refrained, desisted, forbore, abstained,* or *held, from it.* (Ḳ, &c.) — كَفَّهُ عَنْهُ *He made him to refrain, forbear,* or *abstain, from it; averted him, turned him away* or *back, from it;* (Ḳ;) *prevented, hindered, held, withheld,* or *restrained, him from it.* (Mgh, Mṣb, TA.) — [كَفَّ بَيْنَهُمَا *He interposed as a restrainer between them two:* a phrase of frequent occurrence]. — كَفَّ مِنَ الشَّعَرِ (M, Ḳ, art. قصر) *He shortened the hair.* (M, ibid.)

3. كَافُّوا عَدُوَّهُمْ *i. q.* حَاجَزُوهُمْ, which see. — مُكَافَّةٌ signifies *i. q.* مُحَاجَزَةٌ, because it is a preventing, or an abstaining, from fighting. (Mgh.)

7: see 1.

كَفٌّ [generally The *hand:* sometimes, app., the *palm* only:] accord. to Az, the *palm with the fingers.* (Mṣb.) — [Hence, *A cake of the length and thickness of the hand:* thus in the present day. See عُجَّالٌ.] — كَفٌّ *A handful; what one takes with the hand,* or *grasps;* syn. قُبْضَةٌ. (Ṣ, art. قبض.) — [ضَرَبَهُ كَفًّا *He struck him a slap with the hand.*] — [كَفٌّ often signifies The *paw of a beast.*] — الكَفُّ الجَذْمَآءُ *The star α of Cetus.* — الكَفُّ الخَضِيبُ *The star β of Cassiopeia.*

كِفَّةٌ: see كُفَّةٌ.

كُفَّةٌ The *selvage,* i. e. *border,* or *side,* of a garment or piece of cloth, (Ṣ, Mṣb,) that has no هُدْب [or *end of unwoven threads*]: (Ṣ, voce طُرَّة:) or *what surrounds the skirt of a shirt:* or *whatever is oblong; as the* حَاشِيَة *of a garment or piece of cloth, and of sand:* and the *edge* of a thing. (Ḳ.)

كُفَّةٌ The *bezel,* or *collet,* i. e. the *part in which the stone is set,* of a signet-ring. (TA in art. ركب.) See كُرْسِيٌّ. — See also طَرْقٌ. — كِفَّةٌ *A scale* of a balance: (MA:) vulg. ▼كَفَّةٌ. (Ḳ.)

كَفَافٌ The *like* of a thing. (Ṣ, Ḳ.) — *Food,* or *sustenance, that renders one independent of others:* (Ṣ, Ḳ:) or *sufficient for one's want, not exceeding nor falling short.* (Mṣb.)

كِفَافٌ The *circuit, rim,* or *surrounding edge,* of a thing. (Ṣ, Ḳ.)

كِفَافَةٌ [app. a subst., not an inf. n.,] The *act,* or *art, of sewing in the manner termed* كَفّ; (TA;) contr. of شِلَالَةٌ. (TA in art. شل.)

نَاقَةٌ كَافَّةٌ *An old and weak she-camel.* (AO, TA in art. سدم.) — [مَا كَافَّةٌ The *restrictive* مَا, which is annexed to أَنَّ, إِنَّ, &c.: so called because it restrains the particle to which it is adjoined from exercising any government.] — كَافَّةٌ *Wholly.* (Bḍ and Jel in ii. 204.)

حَرْفُ مُكَافَاةٍ *A particle denoting compensation,* or *the complement of a condition;* like حَرْفُ جَزَآءٍ.

كفل

1. كَفَلَ بِالمَالِ *He was,* or *became, responsible, answerable, accountable, amenable, surety,* or *guarantee, for the property* (Mṣb) *owed by another person:* (IbrD:) [it may be rendered *he guaranteed the property.* See مَكْفُولٌ]. — كَفَلَ بِالنَّفْسِ *He was,* or *became, responsible, answerable, amenable,* or *surety, for another person,* (Mṣb,) i. e., *for the latter's appearance,* or *presence, to answer a suit.* (IbrD.)

كَفَلٌ The عَجُز [or *hinder part, posteriors, buttocks,* or *rump*]: (Mṣb, Ḳ:) or the رِدْف [or *hindermost part*] *thereof:* or the [*part called*] قَطَن. (Ḳ.)

كَفِيلٌ One who is *responsible, answerable, amenable,* or *a sponsor* or *surety.* (Ṣ, Ḳ, &c.)

كَفَالَةٌ *Responsibility; answerableness; amenability;* or *suretiship;* (Ṣ, Mgh, Mṣb, Ḳ;) the *conjoining of one responsibility* (ذِمَّة) *to another,* [i. e., the *conjoining one's own responsibility to that of another person,*] *with respect to the right of suit,* [*so that one person becomes liable to be sued for that which another owes*]; (Mgh;) *i. q.* ضَمَانٌ. (Ṣ, &c.)

مِكْفَالٌ A woman *large in the* كَفَل [or *hinder part,* or *posteriors*]. (TA in art. ثقل.)

مَكْفُولٌ app. signifies *Guaranteed,* or *pledged:* for, accord. to IḲṭṭ, as is said in the Mṣb, you say كَفَلْتُ بِالمَالِ as well as كَفَلْتُ المَالَ; meaning *I took upon myself the property; became responsible,* or *answerable, for it;* [or *I guaranteed it:*] or مَكْفُولٌ is better rendered *ensured by an acknowledgment of responsibility for it:* see an ex. voce مَرْهُونٌ.

كفن

5. تَكَفَّنُوا بِأَنْطَاعٍ [*They wrapped themselves with* انطاع *for grave-clothing*]. (TA, art. حنط.)

كفهر

4. اِكْفَهَرَّ, said of clouds: see a verse cited عَزَلَآءُ.

كفى

1. كَفَى He, or it, sufficed, or contented: hence كَفَانِى فُلَانٌ الأَمْرَ *Such a one sufficed me, or contented me, in respect of the affair;* i. e., by taking upon himself to perform it or accomplish it if good, or to prevent it or avert it if evil: and كَفَانِى شَهِيدًا *He sufficed me as, or for, a witness; or he suffices me as, or for, such:* and sometimes ب is redundantly prefixed to its agent, and sometimes to its objective complement; as in exs. cited in art. ب. See Ham, p. 152. كَفَى [*It sufficed, or satisfied, or contented,*] *it stood instead of another thing, or other things;* (Msb;) [as also كَفَى عَنْ غَيْرِهِ.] — كَفَى بِنَا for كَفَانَا &c. See W, pp. 5 and 6. — كَفَى, aor. يَكْفِى, inf. n. كِفَايَةٌ, also signifies مَنَعَ and دَفَعَ followed by مِنْ. (Har, p. 43, q.v.) [You say, كَفَاهُ الشَّرَّ *He repelled from him evil; and hence, he defended him therefrom; and he freed him therefrom:* said of God, and of a man, &c.]

8. اِكْتَفَى بِالشَّىْءِ *He was, or became, sufficed by the thing, so as to need nothing more; or content with it.* (Msb.)

كِفَايَةٌ *A sufficiency; enough; a thing that suffices, or contents, and enables one to obtain what one seeks.* (TA, art. بلغ.) — قَامَ بِكِفَايَتِهِ *He undertook his maintenance; he maintained him;* syn. مَانَهُ. (S, K, art. مون.)

أَكْفَى [*More, and most, satisfying*]. (Mgh, in art. جزأ.)

ككنج

كَاكَنَجٌ or كَاكْنَجٌ [Pers. كَاكْنَجْ]: see عُنَبٌ.

كل

1. كَلَّ *It* (the sight) *was, or became, dim, dull, or hebetated.* (K.) — *He* (a camel) *was, or became, fatigued, tired, or wearied.* (MA.) — كَلَّتِ الأَيْدِى *The hands, or arms, became weak;* syn. ضعفت [i.e. ضَعُفَتْ]. (Ham, 296.) — [كَلَّ عَنْ فِعْلٍ *He was fatigued, or weak, and so disabled, or incapacitated, from doing a thing;* like ضَعُفَ عَنْهُ and أَعْيَا عَنْهُ: see نُجْبٌ and عُرْسٌ.] — كَلَّتْ أَسْنَانُهُ, (K, art. ضرس,) inf. n. كَلَالٌ, (S, in that art.,) *His teeth were set on edge,* (TK, in that art.,) by eating, or drinking, what was acid, or sour. (S, K, in that art.) — كَلَّ *It* (a sword, &c.) *was blunt, and would not cut.* (K, &c.) — كَلَّتْهُنَّ for كُلُّهُنَّ: see Bd xxxi., last verse.

2. كَلَّلَ *He adorned a thing with gems or jewels.*

4. أَكَلَّ أَسْنَانَهُ [*It set his teeth on edge*]; said of acid, or sour, food or drink. (Ibn-'Abbád, in TA, art. ضرس.) See 1.

كَلٌّ *A burden;* syn. ثِقْلٌ: (S, Mgh, Msb, K:) *a person, or persons, whom one has to support;* syn. عَيِّلٌ, (K,) and عِيَالٌ: (S, Mgh, Msb, K:) applied to one and to more. (Msb.) See an ex. voce ذِمَّةٌ (last sentence but two).

كُلٌّ when preceded by a negative and followed by an exception, means *Any one;* as in the Kur, xxxviii. 13, إِنْ كُلٌّ إِلَّا كَذَّبَ الرُّسُلَ *There was not any one but accused the apostles of lying.* See also another ex. voce لَمَّا. — See بَعْضٌ. — هُوَ العَالِمُ كُلُّ العَالِمِ [lit. *He is the possessor of knowledge, the entirety of the possessor of knowledge,*] means that he is one who has attained to the utmost degree of the quality thus attributed to him. (Sb, K, TA.) — كُلَّمَا *Whatever.* — كُلَّمَا *Whenever; as often as; every time that; in proportion as.* — كُلَّمَنْ *Whoever.*

كِلَّةٌ [*musquito-curtain*]: see أَبُو دِثَارٍ and بَعُوضٌ.

كُلِّىٌّ *Relating to all or the whole; universal; total:* and often meaning *relating to the generality; general; contr. of* جُزْئِىٌّ. — And, as a subst., *A universal; that which comprises all* جُزْئِيَّات, *or particulars:* pl. كُلِّيَّاتٌ. — كُلِّيَّةٌ The *quality of relating to all or the whole; relation to all or the whole; universality; totality:* and often meaning the *quality of relating to the generality; generality.* — الكُلِّيَّاتُ الخَمْسُ, in logic, *The Five Predicables:* namely, الجِنْسُ *Genus,* النَّوْعُ *Species,* الفَصْلُ *Difference,* الخَاصَّةُ *Property,* and العَرَضُ *Accident.*

كَلِيلٌ *Weak, or faint, lightning* [app. likened to a blunt sword]. (TA in art. عمل.) — كَلِيلٌ لِسَانٌ كَلِيلٌ *A dull tongue; lacking sharpness.* (S.*) — ظُفُرٌ: see الظُّفُرُ.

وَرِثَ رَجُلًا كَلَالَةً, and عَنْ كَلَالَةٍ, *He was heir of a man who left neither parent nor offspring.* (IbrD.)

الإِكْلِيلُ *The 17th Mansion of the Moon;* (Kzw;) *the head of Scorpio.* (Aboo-l-Heythem, quoted in the TA, voce رَقِيبٌ.) — الإِكْلِيلُ *Three bright stars in* [*or rather before*] *the head of Scorpio,* [*namely* γ, η, *and* θ,] *disposed in a row, transversely.* — *The border of flesh round the nail:* (K:) in the TA, art. شظف, إِكْلِيلُ الظُّفُرِ.

مُكَلَّلٌ *Adorned with gems or jewels.* (L, art. نجد; a common meaning.)

كلف

1. كَلِفَ بِهِ *He became attached, addicted, given, or devoted, to it; or he attached, addicted, gave, or devoted, himself to it;* (S, Msb, K, TA;) *he loved it:* (Msb, TA:) [*he was fond of it:*] *he loved him,* [*or it,*] *vehemently.* (TA.) — كَلَفٌ, inf. n. of كَلِفَ: [*violent or intense love:*] see حُبٌّ; and see a verse cited in the first paragraph of that art.

2. كَلَّفَ نَفْسَهُ شَيْئًا *He tasked himself with a thing,* as also ▼ تَكَلَّفَ شَيْئًا. — كَلَّفَهُ أَمْرًا *He tasked him to do a thing; imposed upon him the task of doing a thing.* — So تَكْلِيفٌ The *imposition of a task or duty.* — *A task; compulsory work; a duty imposed.* — كَلَّفَهُ الأَمْرَ *He imposed upon him the thing, or affair;* syn. حَمَّلَهُ إِيَّاهُ. (Msb.) — كَلَّفَ نَفْسَهُ *He put himself to trouble or inconvenience;* like ▼ تَكَلَّفَ alone. — كَلَّفَهُ كَذَا *He imposed upon him the task of doing, or procuring, or bringing, such a thing.* — كَلَّفَهُ أَمْرًا *He imposed upon him a thing, or an affair, in spite of difficulty, trouble, or inconvenience:* (Msb:) *he ordered him to do a thing that was difficult, troublesome, or inconvenient, to him:* (S, K:) *he made, required, or constrained, him to do a thing; exacted of him the doing a thing;* meaning, *a thing that was difficult, troublesome, or inconvenient, to him:* (Kull, 123; and the Lexicons, passim.) See جَشَّمَهُ. — تَكْلِيفٌ *An imposition; a requisition; constraint, &c.*

5. تَكَلَّفَ أَمْرًا *He* [*undertook a thing, or an affair, as imposed upon him; or*] *took, or imposed, upon himself, or undertook, a thing, or an affair,* [*as a task, or*] *in spite of difficulty, trouble, or inconvenience;* (Msb;) syn. تَجَشَّمَهُ: (S, K:) *he constrained, or tasked, or exerted, himself, or took pains, or made an effort, to do a thing;* meaning, *a thing that was difficult, troublesome, or inconvenient, to him:* or *he affected, as a self-imposed task, the doing of a thing.* (The Lexicons, passim: see تغزّل: and see كَلَّفَهُ أَمْرًا.) — تكلّف صِفَةً *He affected, or endeavoured to acquire, a quality.* So in the explanations of verbs of the measure تَفَعَّلَ; as تَحَلَّمَ. (Sharh El-'Izzee, by Saad-od-Deen.) — Also, *He affected, or pretended to have, a quality, not having it.* So in the explanations of verbs of the measure تَفَاعَلَ, as تَجَاهَلَ: (idem:) [and sometimes in verbs of the measure تَفَعَّلَ also, as تَكَبَّرَ &c.]. And تَكَلَّفَ alone, *He exercised self-constraint, or put himself to trouble or inconvenience.* — تَكَلَّفَ *He affected* what was not

natural to him. — تَكَلَّفَ *He used forced efforts to do* a thing, and *to appear to have* a quality. *He affected, or endeavoured to do or acquire, &c.; he constrained himself to do, &c.; he applied himself, as to a task, to do a thing.* تكلّف الشَّجَاعَةَ *He made himself, or constrained himself to be, courageous; affected,* or *endeavoured to acquire,* or *characterize himself by, courage.* — تكلّف الشَّجَاعَةَ also, *He acted, or behaved, with forced courage; endeavoured to be courageous.* — تكلّف فِى عَرَبِيَّتِهِ *He used a forced, or affected, manner in his Arabic speech.* — تَكَلُّفٌ *A straining of a point* in lexicology. — تَعَقَّلَ signifies *He affected or endeavoured to acquire, intelligence;* explained by تكلّف العَقْلَ: and تَعَاقَلَ, he pretended to be intelligent, not being really so. (Ṣ, art. عقل.) تَكَلُّفٌ in a verb of the measure تَفَعَّلَ is as above explained, signifying a desire for the existence of an attribute in one's self: in a verb of the measure تَفَاعَلَ it is different, and means the pretending to be or to do something which in reality one is not or does not; as in the instance of تَجَاهَلَ, he pretended to be ignorant, not being so in reality. (Sharḥ El-'Izzee, by Saạd-ed-Deen.) تَكَلَّفَ كَذَا *He did so purposely.* — تَكَلَّفَ *He tasked himself.* — تَكَلَّفَ القَىْءَ *He vomited intentionally.* (TA, art. قى.)

كَلَفٌ [*A discolouration of the face, by*] *a thing that comes upon the face resembling sesame;* [by *freckles,* accord. to present usage:] and *a dingy redness that comes upon the face.* (Ṣ, Ḳ.)

كُلْفَةٌ *A difficulty,* or *difficult affair,* or *a duty,* or *an obligation, that one imposes upon himself;* (Ṣ, Ḳ;) or *a thing imposed upon one as difficult, troublesome,* or *inconvenient.* (Mṣb.) See حُبٌّ. — [*Constraint,*] *trouble, pain,* or *inconvenience.* (MA.)

كلم

3. كَالَمَهُ *i.q.* نَاطَقَهُ. (TA in art. نطق.)

5. تَكَلَّمَ عَنْهُ *He spoke for him;* syn. عَبَّرَ. (Ṣ, Mṣb, art. عبر.)

6. تَكَالَمَا *They spoke, talked,* or *discoursed, each with the other.* (Ṣ,* M.)

كَلِمَةٌ *A word:* (Kull, 301:) *an expression:* (Ḳ:) *a proposition: a sentence:* [*a saying:*] *an argument.* (Kull.) *An assertion: an expression of opinion.*

كَلَامٌ is a gen. n., applying to little and to much, or to few or many; (Ṣ, TA;) to what is a sing. and to what is a pl. (TA.) It may therefore be rendered *A saying, &c.;* and *sayings,* or *words:* see an ex. voce أَثْكَلُ, in art. ثكل. — كَلَامٌ *Speech; something spoken;* [*diction; language;*] *parlance; talk; discourse:* (Mṣb, &c.:) *a saying: a say: something said:* in grammar, *a sentence.* الكَلِمُ الطَّيِّبُ: see طَيِّبٌ. — كَلَامٌ: also, a quasi-inf. n. for تكليم, sometimes governing as a verb, [like the inf. n.,] accord. to some of the grammarians; as in the following ex.:

قالوا كلامك هندا وهى مصغية • يشفيك قلت صحيح ذاك لو كانا •

(Sharḥ Shudhoor edh-Dhahab.) See اِسْمُ مَصْدَرٍ. — عِلْمُ الكَلَامِ [*The theology of the Muslims;*] *a science in which one investigates the being and attributes of God, and the conditions of possible things with respect to creation and restitution, according to the rule of El-Islám;* which last restriction is for the exclusion of the theology of the philosophers. (KT.)

رَجُلٌ كَلِيمٌ, like سِكِّيتٌ [and حِدِّيثٌ] *i.q.* مِنْطِيقٌ. (Ibn-'Abbád, Z, TA.)

كُلْيَةٌ of a bow: see أَبْهَرُ. — of a مَزَادَة: see خُرْبَةٌ.

مُتَكَلِّمٌ *A Muslim theologian.* See عِلْمُ الكَلَامِ.

كلو

1. كَلَا, first pers. كَلَوْتُ, aor. يَكْلُو; and كَلَا, first pers. كَلَيْتُ, aor. يَكْلَا; inf. n., كِلَايَةٌ; see كَلَأَ.

الكُلَى: *the feathers* so called: see مَنَاكِبُ and أَبْهَرُ.

الكُلْيَتَانِ *A name of two stars on the ear of Taurus.* (See الكَلْبَانِ.)

كم

كَمْ: see its syn. كَأَيِّنْ or كَأَيٍّ voce أَىٌّ. — As an interrogative with the specificative suppressed, *What number? How many?* and, as in an ex. voce سَقْىٌ, virtually meaning *How much?* and so in an ex. voce مَسَافَةٌ and voce شِبْرٌ. Also *How long?* as in the Ḳur, ii. 161, &c.; a noun signifying a period of time being understood: see also an ex. voce عَسَفَ, and voce فَرَشَ.

كُمٌّ and كَمٌّ are both app. right: see قَدٌّ.

كِمٌّ *The calyx of a flower.* (Ḳ, &c.) — كِمٌّ *The envelope* [or *spathe*] *of the* طَلْع [or *spadix of a palm-tree*]: and the *covering* [or *calyx*] *of flowers* or *blossoms;* as also ♦ كِمَامَةٌ. (Ṣ, Mṣb, Ḳ.)

كُمَّةٌ *A* قَلَنْسُوَة: (TA in art. بطح:) or *a round* قلنسوة: (Ṣ, Ḳ:) pl. كِمَامٌ. (Ḳ,* TA in art. بطح.)

كِمَامَةٌ: see كِمٌّ.

كَمِّيَّةٌ *Quantum,* or *quantity,* as answering to "how many."

مُكَمَّمٌ *Covered over,* or *concealed* (مَسْتُور). (Ṣ, art. حصب.) See بُرْأَةٌ.

كُمْكَامٌ The *cancamum-tree:* see بُطْمٌ and ضِرْوٌ.

كمفطس

كَمَافِيطُوس [*χαμαίπιτυς, the ground-pine*]: see عَرْصَفٌ.

كمر

كَمَرٌ *A kind of belt with a receptacle for money.*

كمل

1. كَمَلَ *He,* or *it, was,* or *became, perfect;* and sometimes, *it was,* or *became, complete, entire, whole,* or *full;* which latter signification is more properly expressed by تَمَّ, which see.

كَامِلٌ *Complete* with respect to bodily vigour, having attained the usual term thereof. See لَيْثُ عِفِرِّينَ, art. عفر. Also *Consummate, perfect.*

نَقًا: عَيْنُ الكَمَالِ: see.

مُكَمِّلَاتٌ *Supererogatory acts of religious service.*

كمن

الكَمَانُ المُذَابُ, mentioned in the TA, in art. نبط, *i.q.* عِلْكُ الأَنْبَاطِ, which is applied as a لزوق to a wound.

كَامِنٌ *Latent.*

مَكْمَنٌ *A place of concealment, a lurking-place:* (Mgh, Mṣb:) pl. مَكَامِنُ. (Mṣb.)

كمه

أَرْضٌ كَمْهَآءُ *i.q.* مُغْمَةٌ and مِغْمَةٌ. (TA in art. غمه.)

كمى

كَمِىٌّ *A courageous* man: or one *wearing arms* or *armour:* (Ḳ:) or *a courageous man covered,* or *protected, by arms or armour;* (Ṣ;) *a courageous armed man.*

كن

كِنٌّ *A place of retreat* or *concealment;* such as a cave, and an excavated house or chamber: (Beyḍ, xvi. 83:) see بُرٌّ. — كِنٌّ *The shelter* of a wall: see دِفْءٌ. — *A thing that serves for veiling, covering,* or *protecting.* (Ṣ,* Mṣb,* K.) See ظِلٌّ, where I have thus rendered it.

كُنَّةٌ: see طَنَفٌ.

كِنَانَةٌ: see جَعْبَةٌ.

كَانُونٌ *A fire-place; a place in which fire is lighted.* (Ṣ, Ḳ.)

مَكْنُونُ القَائِلِ : see a verse of El-Aạshà in art. قيل.

مُسْتَكِنٌ : see فاعل مُسْتَقِرّ.

كنخب

كَنْخَبَةٌ *Confusion of speech, or discourse, by reason of errors, or mistakes.* (Yoo, Ḳ.) [App. an inf. n. of which the verb is كَنْخَبَ.]

كنس

كَنِيسٌ [*a kind of roast flesh-meat*]: see مَرْمُوض.

كنف

8. اِكْتَنَفَهُ القَوْمُ *The people were on his right and left.* (Mṣb.) — اِكْتَنَفَهُ *It bordered it on either side.*

كَنَفٌ *Vicinage* or *neighbourhood*, or *region* or *quarter* or *tract*, and *shadow* or *shelter* or *protection.* (Ḳ.) — كَنَفَا الإِنْسَانِ *The man's two sides, right and left.* (TA.)

كَنُوفٌ : see قَذُورٌ, in two places.

كَنِيفٌ : see زَرْبٌ.

كُنَافَةٌ *A kind of pastry*, resembling vermicelli, made of fine flour and water mixed in such proportions as to compose a thin paste, which is poured into a vessel whose bottom is pierced with numerous small holes: the vessel being then moved circuitously over a large round tray of tinned copper, beneath which is a fire, the paste runs in fine streams, is quickly but slightly baked, and swept off. For eating, it is slightly baked with clarified butter (سمن), and then sweetened with honey, or sometimes with treacle, or sugar. — كُنَافَةٌ *i.q.* Pers. رِشْتَهْ قَطَائِف [*Thread-ḳaṭáïf*]. (KL.) See إِطْرِيَةٌ.

كُنَافِىٌّ A maker or seller of كُنَافَة.

مُكَانِفٌ A she-camel *that lies down behind the other camels.* (Az, cited in L, art. روح.)

كنه

4. أَكْنَهَ : see an ex. in a verse cited voce مَعَسٌ.

كُنْهٌ : see فَصٌّ. — كُنْهٌ may often be rendered *Entity.*

كنى

1. كَنَى *He affixed a* كِنَايَة, meaning, with the Koofees, *a pronoun*, to a verb [&c.]: (TA in art. ريب :) but accord. to the usage of the verb in two instances in the M and Ḳ, voce رَابَ in art. ريب, it clearly means *he spoke allusively.* — كَنَى بِهِ عَنْ كَذَا, *He used it metonymically for such a word* or *phrase; he alluded thereby to such a thing.*

كُنْيَةٌ *A surname of relationship.*

كِنَايَةٌ *A metonymy:* see تَعْرِيضٌ; where the difference between these two words is explained. — Also, *An allusion.* (TA.) — Also, and ▼مُكَنًّى, accord. to De Sacy, in his Ar. Gr. i. 455, or ▼مُكَنٍّ, for I find its plural written in a copy of the Ṣ مُكَنِّيَات, *A pronoun;* see كَنَى.

مُكَنٍّ and مُكَنًّى : see كِنَايَةٌ.

كهب

كُهْبَةٌ, accord. to Ibn-El-Aạrábee, *Yellowness inclining to redness.* (TA, voce خُشْبَة.)

كهل

8. اِكْتَهَلَ, said of a plant, *It became tall and full-grown:* (TA:) or *it became of its full height, and blossomed:* (Ṣ:) see زَاخِرٌ.

كَهْلٌ *Of middle age*; or *between that age and the period when his hair has become intermixed with hoariness.* See شَبَابٌ; and شَيْخٌ and غُلَامٌ.

كُهُولَةٌ : see شَبَابٌ.

كَاهِلٌ [The *withers* of a horse, &c.] *i.q.* حَارِكٌ: or the *anterior portion of the upper part of the back, next the neck*, which is the *upper third part, containing six vertebræ:* or the *part between the two shoulder-blades:* or the *part where the neck is joined to the back-bone;* [the *base of the neck:* see ثَبَجٌ]. (Ḳ.)

كِهَانَةٌ *Divination; soothsaying.* (Ḳ, &c.)

كَاهِنٌ : see عَرَّافٌ and عَائِفٌ.

كو

كُوَّةٌ and كَوَّةٌ (Ṣ, Mṣb, Ḳ) and كَوٌّ (Ḳ) *A hole, or perforation, or an aperture*, (Ṣ, Mgh, Mṣb, Ḳ,) *in a wall* (Mṣb, Ḳ) or *chamber;* (Ṣ, Mgh;) [*a mural aperture;*] or the first and second, *a small one;* and the third, *a large one.* (Ḳ.) See also مِشْكَاةٌ.

كور

كارى [? كَارِىٌّ] *i.q.* غَرِيبٌ, applied to a man. (AA, in TA, voce غَرِيبٌ.)

كوع

كُوعٌ The *extremity of the radius*, or *bone of the fore-arm, next the thumb:* (Ṣ, Mṣb, Ḳ:) or the *protuberance formed thereby.*

كوف

5. تَكَوَّفَ : see تَشَأَّمَ.

كَافٌ *Same as* كُشّ (*because it is the name of the incipient letter of this word:* 1001 Nights ii. 304).

كُوفِيَّةٌ *A thing that is worn upon the head; so called because of its roundness, or its being round.* (TA.)

كوم

8. اِكْتَامَ *He walked upon the extremities of his toes, by choice.* (TA, voce حَارِقَةٌ, q.v.)

كون

1. كَانَ *He or it was.* A verb of the class called incomplete, (نَاقِصٌ,) because, with the agent which it comprises, or to which it relates, it cannot constitute a complete proposition; i.e., non-attributive. The other verbs of this class are, ظَلَّ, أَضْحَى, أَمْسَى, أَصْبَحَ, صَارَ, مَا دَامَ, مَا ٱنْفَكَّ, مَا فَتِئَ, مَا بَرِحَ, مَا زَالَ, بَاتَ, and لَيْسَ. Each of these governs its noun, or subject, in the nom. case, and its enunciative, or predicate, in the acc. case; as, كَانَ زَيْدٌ قَائِمًا *Zeyd was standing.* — (The ن in يَكُنْ and the like is often irregularly elided.) — كَانَ, divested of all signification of time, is often used as a copula. (See De Sacy's Gr. Ar. i. 196.) So too is كَائِنٌ; for هٰذَا كَائِنٌ زَيْدًا and هٰذَا زَيْدٌ signify the same. (Mughnee, voce أَنْ.) — كَانَ as a complete, i.e., an attributive, verb, see حَصَلَ, in three places.

5. تَكَوَّنَ *He, or it, received,* or *took, his,* or *its, being,* or *existence; came into existence; originated.*

10. اِسْتَكَانَ *He was,* or *became, lowly, humble, submissive,* or *in a state of abasement.* (Ḥar, p. 4, q.v.) See اِسْتَكَنَ in art. سكن : and see art. كين.

حَوْرٌ : see نَعُوذُ بِاللّٰهِ من الحَوْرِ بَعْدَ الكَوْنِ and كَوْرٌ.

كَيْنُونَةٌ : see شَاعَ.

مَكَانَةٌ *A particular place of being or existence.* See an ex. voce نَفْسٌ. — مَكَانَكَ وَزَيْدًا [*Keep where thou art and approach not Zeyd!*] Heard by Ks. (L, art. عند.) — *State,* or *condition.* [Bḍ, xi. 122, and xxxix. 40.] See art. مكن. — مَكَانٌ *i. q.* مَنْزِلَةٌ. (Bḍ, xii. 77.) — هٰذَا مَكَانٌ لِقَوْلِنَا كَذَا *This is a ground for our saying thus.* — أَصْبَحَ مَكَانَ كَذَا *It became as,* or *like, such a thing.* See a verse cited voce وَتْرٌ.

كوى

1. كَوَاهُ *He* (a veterinary, and any other, TA) *cauterized him;* i.e. *burned his skin; with an iron,* and *the like:* (Ḳ:) or *he burned him with fire.* (Mgh.)

كيس

كَيِّسٌ *Intelligent; ingenious, clever.* (S, Mṣb, Ḳ.) [Plur. كُوسَى :] also أَكْيَاسٌ. (Mṣb.)

أُمُّ كَيْسَانَ a metonymical name of *The knee,* in the dial. of El-Azd. (TA, art. ركب)

كيص

كِيصٌ : see دَنِيقٌ.

كيف

2. كَيَّفْتُهُ فَتَكَيَّفَ, used by the Muslim theologians, (Ḳ, TA,) verbs derived from كَيْفَ, (TA,) [signifying *I specified by the ascription of its quality* and *it became so specified,*] are formed in accordance with analogy, not heard from the Arabs. (Ḳ,* TA.)

5. تَكَيَّفَ : see what next precedes.

كَيْفِيَّةٌ *Quality as answering to "how?"; mode,* or *manner, of being.*

كَيْفُوفِيَّةٌ for كَيْفِيَّةٌ : see تَيْسِيَّةٌ.

كيل

8. اِكْتَالَ عَلَيْهِ and مِنْهُ : see عَلَى in the sense of مِنْ.

كَيْلٌ : see مِكْيَالٌ.

كَيَّالٌ [*A measurer* of corn and the like]. (A, art. بخس.)

مِكْيَالٌ *A measure with which corn is measured;* (Ṣ, Mṣb, Ḳ;) as also ▾ كَيْلٌ; (Mṣb;) *a measure of capacity.*

كين

10. اِسْتَكَانَ : see اِسْتَكَنَ in art. سكن : and see art. كون.

كَيْنٌ (also written كَيْنَةٌ, Ḳ, voce زَوْنَبٌ) : see بَظْرٌ.

كيه

كَيْهًا A *large,* or *bulky,* she-camel : see the last sentence in art. غذو.

ل

— ل. لَنَا فِى بَنِى فُلَانٍ دِمَآءٌ [*We have a claim, upon the sons of such a one, to blood, lit. bloods*]. (Ṣ in art. حبل.) — لَهُ أَنْ يَفْعَلَ كَذَا *He shall have a right to do such a thing:* see عَقَبَ. — رَأَيْتُ لَهُ بَرِيقًا *I saw it to have a glistening:* and سَمِعْتُ لَهُ صَوْتًا *I heard him,* or *it, to have a sound* proceeding from him, or it; or rather, *I heard a sound attributable,* or *to be attributed, to him,* or *it;* meaning, *I heard him,* or *it, utter* or *produce, a sound;* or *I heard in consequence of it,* &c. (see سَطَعَ). — لَهُ كَذَا often means *Such a thing appertains,* or *is attributable, to him,* or *it.* — مَا لَنَا أَلَّا نُقَاتِلَ, in the Ḳur ii. 247, [i.e. أَنْ لَا,] means *What object have we* (أَىُّ غَرَضٍ لَنَا) *in* (فِى) [*that we should not fight?* or, *in our*] *not fighting?* (Bḍ:) And مَا لَنَا أَلَّا نَتَوَكَّلَ عَلَى ٱللّٰهِ, in the same, xiv. 15, means *What excuse have we* (أَىُّ عُذْرٍ لَنَا) *in* (فِى) [*that we should not rely upon God?* or, *in our*] *not relying upon God?* (Bḍ.) مَا لَنَا أَنْ لَا نَفْعَلَ كَذَا [may be rendered *What reason,* or *motive, have we that we should not do such a thing?* or, *in that,* &c.? or *in our not doing* &c.? for] the original form of the phrase is مَا لَنَا فِى أَنْ لَا نَفْعَلَ كَذَا. (Mugh, voce أَنْ.) Often أَنْ is omitted, but meant to be understood: you say also, مَا لَكَ تَفْعَلُ كَذَا *What reason,* or *motive, hast thou that thou dost such a thing?* or *what aileth thee* &c.? It is often like مَا بَالُكَ. — غَرَّدَ بِصَوْتٍ لَهُ ضَعِيفٍ *It* (a bird) *warbled with a feeble voice peculiar to it.* — مَا لِى وَلِلْبَغْيِ بَعْضِكُمْ عَلَى بَعْضٍ: see بَغَى. مَا لِى أَرَاكَ تَفْعَلُ كَذَا *What hath happened to me that I see thee doing such a thing,* or *thus?* See an ex. in conj. 3 of art. بلو. — مَا لَكَ بِكَذَا: see a verse cited in art. علو. — أَنَا لَهَا *I am for it;* i.e., I am the man for it; meaning a war, or battle, حَرْبٌ, which is of the fem. gender. Often occurring in old Arabic stories. — ل in the sense of فِى: see Mṣb, voce عِدَّةٌ. — مَنْ لِى *Who is,* or *will be, for me, as aider,* or *helper,* or *defender,* or *surety?* For exs., see سُبْعٌ, and شَبْرٌ, and أُفًّا. — تَعْسًا لَهُ, and قُبْحًا لَهُ, and تَبًّا لَهُ, &c.: see the first word of each of these phrases. — مَنْ لِى بِكَذَا: see ب (near the end of the paragraph): and see also above. — ل in the sense of بَعْد: see an ex. voce أَفْطَرَ, and see other exs. in the Mṣb, art. فطر. — ل in the sense of بَعْدَ, or مِنْ وَقْتِ: see غَمَرَ. — لِلَيْلَةٍ خَلَتْ *When one night had passed;* i.e. *on the first day* of the month: ل in this case meaning عِنْدَ. — يَا لِلْفَلِيقَةِ *O come with succour to the calamity:* see فَلَقَ. — ل in the sense of عَلَى: see Ḳur xvii. 108-9, and xvii. 7, and xxxvii. 103: and see exs. voce قُوَّةٌ (last quarter). — ل in فِدًى لَكَ &c.: see art. فدى. — لَ used as a corroborative, (see Ṣ in art. لوم,) after لَوْ and لَوْلَا the conditional, and إِنْ, is sometimes difficult to express in English, except by emphasis in pronunciation; as in أَمَا إِنَّهُ لَرَجُلٌ كَرِيمٌ *Verily,* or *now surely, he* IS *a generous man.* This ex. occurs voce أَمَا. — لَ redundantly prefixed, for corroboration, to the ك of comparison: see a verse of Ṭarafeh voce ثِنْىٌ; and another similar instance in the Mugh, art. ل. — لَظَرُفَ زَيْدٌ means *How excellent,* or *elegant, in mind, manners, address, speech, person,* or *the like, is Zeyd!* syn. مَا أَظْرَفَهُ: and لَكَرُمَ عَمْرٌو *How generous,* &c., *is 'Amr!* syn. مَا أَكْرَمَهُ. (Mugh.) — لَنِعْمَ هُوَ *Excellent indeed is he,* or *it.* — مَا كَانَ لِيَفْعَلَ means, accord. to the Koofees, مَا كَانَ يَفْعَلُ; the ل being redundant, to corroborate the negation: accord. to the Baṣrees, مَا كَانَ قَاصِدًا لِأَنْ يَفْعَلَ. (Mugh.) See an ex. voce عَلَى as equivalent to فِى. — لَ in sentences beginning with إِنْ for إِنَّ: see p. 107, cols. 2 and 3: and see conj. 3 in art. قرأ. — ل of inception (لَامُ ٱلْإِبْتِدَآءِ): see exs. of this voce إِنَّ: and see De Sacy's Gr. Ar. ii. 582, &c. — لَ termed لَامُ ٱلْجَوَابِ is, I think, best rendered by *Then;* or *in that case:* see exs. voce أَمَّا. — لَ in لَعَمْرُ ٱللّٰهِ is [not a particle denoting swearing, but merely] a corroborative of the inchoative; the enunciative of which, i.e. قَسَمِى, or مَا أُقْسِمُ بِهِ, is understood. (Ṣ, art. عمر.) — يَا لَزَيْدٍ, and يَالَ زَيْدٍ, accord. to the Koofees, is a contraction of يَا آلَ زَيْدٍ. (Mugh, letter ل; and El-Ashmoonee on the Alfeeyeh, § الاستغاثة.) It seems that where the ل is not connected with the word following it, يَالَ is generally, if not always, for يَا آلَ; and so sometimes when it is connected. See يَالَ غُدَرَ, voce غَادِرٌ, and see عَجَبٌ. See also De Sacy's Gr. Ar., 2nd ed., i. 476, note.

لَا, the negative, does not necessarily restrict to the signification of future time a marfooạ aor. following it: in a case of this kind, مَا is often substituted for it in the explanation of a phrase; as in the instance of لَا يَعْرِفُ هِرًّا مِنْ بِرٍّ, in the TA, art. بر; and the aor. is more properly rendered by the present than by the future. — لَا رَجُلَ قَائِمٌ *There is not any man standing:* (Mugh:) but when the subst. and epithet are both simple words, and not separated, the latter may be used in three different ways; as in لَا رَجُلَ ظَرِيفَ and ظَرِيفًا and ظَرِيفٌ; otherwise it must be marfooạ or manṣoob, but not mebnee: this relates to لا used لِنَفْيِ ٱلْجِنْسِ. (Ibn-'Aḳeel, p. ١٠٦.) — لا, also, *Lest.* See رَكِبَهُ. — لَا لَهُ وَلَا عَلَيْهِ [*There is nothing due to him, nor anything to be demanded of him.* (Thus I have rendered this phrase, voce مَلِىٌّ, in three places.) For] when لا is a general negative, the context renders it allowable to suppress its subject, as in لَا عَلَيْكَ, for لَا بَأْسَ عَلَيْكَ; and sometimes the predicate, when known, is suppressed, as in لَا بَأْسَ. (Mṣb.) — لَاشَ, for لَا شَىْءَ: see art. لوش. — كَلَا وَلَا [*As the time occupied in saying* لَا وَلَا]. See an ex. in the TA, voce لَوْذَانٌ. — لَا وَلَا *Olive-oil:* in allusion to the words in the Ḳur xxiv. 35, occurring in a trad. —

لَا يَقْرَأْ, as a prohibition, and لا يَقْرَأُ as an enunciative with the same meaning: see a trad. thus commencing in the Jámi' es-Ṣagheer: and see the Ḳur lvi. 78: and see an ex. voce رَهْنٌ. — لَا أَغَرَّ وَلَا بَهِيمٌ : see بَهِيمٌ. — لَا in a case of pausation pronounced لَأْ: see art. ا (near the end).

لأك

1. لَأَكَ He sent. (Mṣb in art. الك.) — أَلْكِنِى إِلَيْهِ; and أَلَكْتُهُ: see art. الك.

10. اِسْتَلْأَكَ : see استألك.

مَلْأَكٌ : see مَأْلَكٌ.

لأل

لَأَّلٌ : see art. لؤ.

لَئَالَةٌ : see art. لؤ.

لِئَلَّا Lest; in order that not.

لأم

1. لَؤُمَ He was base, base-born, low, ignoble, ungenerous, mean, sordid; (Ṣ:) contr. of كَرُمَ. (Ḳ.) See لَئِيمٌ. — لَأَمَ : see also ظاهر.

3. لَاءَمْتُ بَيْنَ القَوْمِ, inf. n. مُلَاءَمَةٌ, I reconciled the people, (Ṣ, Mṣb,) and brought them together. (Ṣ.) — لَاءَمَهُ He was suited to him as a companion: see 5 in art. زوى. — لَاءَمَهُ It (food, T, and an affair, M) suited him. (T, M.) — And i. q. لَازَمَهُ. (T.) — And It coalesced, or united, with it.

8. اِلْتَأَمَ It (a wound, and a crack) became coalesced, consolidated, closed, or closed up: (Ṣ:) it (a hole, or rent,) became repaired. (Mṣb.) — اِلْتَأَمَا They (two things) agreed together, or became consistent. (Ṣ, Mṣb.) — اِلْتَأَمَ It drew, and stuck, together; coalesced; or consolidated. (Mgh.)

لُؤْمَةٌ : see لُؤَمَةٌ.

لُؤَمَةٌ, (Ṣ, Ḳ,) or † لُؤْمَةٌ, (M, IB,) The whole apparatus, or gear, of the plough: (AḤn, Ṣ, M, Ḳ:) or its iron [or share] and its wooden parts: (M:) or the سِنَّةٌ [or ploughshare] with which the earth is ploughed up, and which, when upon the plough, is termed عِيَانٌ, pl. عين: (IAạr, TA:) the سِكَّةٌ. (IB, TA.) See عِيَانٌ.

جَمِيعٌ : see رَجُلٌ جَمِيعُ اللَّأْمَةِ.

لَئِيمٌ Mean; ungenerous; sordid; ignoble; base; base-born; contr. of كَرِيمٌ. (Ḳ, &c.) See لَؤُمَ.

مَدَاقٌّ : see أَلْأَمُ الأُمُورِ.

أَلْأَمُ Baser, and basest; &c.: see an ex. voce زَكْمَةٌ.

اِسْتَلْأَمَ : see الاِجْتِمَاعُ i. q. المُلَاءَمَةُ.

لَفَتَ : See لُؤَامٌ i. q. رِيشٌ مُتَلَائِمٌ.

لأى

بَعْدَ لَأْىٍ After difficulty, &c. (Lth, TA.) See an ex. cited voce بَيَّنَ. — لَأْيًا With difficulty, trouble, labour, or exertion.

لبس

مُلَبَّسٌ pl. مُلَبَّسَاتٌ Sugared almonds, &c.

لبع

لَبْعًا : see ضَبْعٌ.

لبق

عَبِقٌ : see عَبِقَةٌ لَبِقَةٌ and عَبِقٌ لَبِقٌ.

عَذِقٌ : see لَبِقٌ بِالقُلُوبِ.

لَبَاقَةٌ : see إِنَاقَةٌ in art. انق.

لبك

1. لَبَكَهُ is like رَبَكَهُ.

لَبَكَةٌ : see عَبَكَةٌ.

لبلب

لَبْلَابٌ : see حِلْبَابٌ or حِلِبْلَابٌ.

لبن

بَنَاتُ لَبَنٍ [app. The small guts or intestines, in which originate the lacteals;] the intestines in which is the milk. (M, Ḳ.) See حَوِيَّةٌ, termed بَنَاتُ اللَّبَنِ. — لَبِنَةٌ [n. un. of لَبِنٌ]. (Az, in TA, art. عرس.)

لَبِنٌ Bricks; (T, Ṣ, M, Mgh, Mṣb, Ḳ;) crude, or unburnt, bricks. (MA.)

لِبْنَةٌ : see بَنِيقَةٌ.

لُبَانٌ [The frankincense-tree] is a tree of the kind called عضاه, having a fruit resembling the pistachio-nut, and a resin like the كُنْدُر, [which is said in the Ṣ and TA to be the same as the لُبَان,] when it concretes: (O and TA in art. سيع:) it is also, and more commonly, applied to the resin itself, i. e. frankincense, or olibanum: the tree that produces it is now known to be of the genus Boswellia, found in Ḥaḍramowt and other parts of Southern Arabia, and also in the opposite (eastern) region of Africa, and in India: it was formerly erroneously supposed to be the Juniperus Lycia. — حَصَى لُبَانٍ : see Ḳ, voce عَسَلٌ; and see art. حصى.

لِبَانٌ The sucking of milk or of the breast: (Ṣ, Mṣb, Ḳ:) see an ex. in a verse of El-Aạshà cited voce أَسْحَمُ: and see 1 in art. غذو.

لَبُونٌ : see لَقُوحٌ and بَكْرٌ. — اِبْنُ لَبُونٍ A male camel that has entered upon his third year: (Ṣ, Mgh, Ḳ:) or entering upon his third year: (Mṣb:) or in his second year. (Ḳ.)

عَسَلُ اللُّبْنَى i. q. المَيْعَةُ [now applied to Storax, or styrax] sometimes used for fumigation. (TA.) See art. عسل.

قُرْبِيُونٌ : see لُبَانَةٌ مَغْرِبِيَّةٌ.

لَبَنِيَّةٌ Food made with milk: so in modern Arabic: see خَطِيفَةٌ.

لُبَيْنَةٌ [A little milk: dim. of لَبَنَةٌ, n. un. of لَبَنٌ]: see رَثِيئَةٌ.

مِلْبَنٌ A thing like the مِحْمَل, upon which bricks (لَبِن) are carried from place to place. (M.) See فَشْغَاءُ.

لبى

2. لَبَّاهُ [inf. n. تَلْبِيَةٌ] He said to him لَبَّيْكَ. (MA.)

لَبَّيْكَ, and لَبَّيْهِ, and لَبَّىْ يَدَيْكَ : see art. لب.

لث

لِثَةٌ The gum. See art. لوث.

لثغ

لُثْغَةٌ The changing, in pronunciation, س into ث, or ر into غ or ل, (Ṣ, Ḳ, Mṣb,) and the like: (Mṣb:) or, one letter into another. (Az, in Mṣb, Ḳ.) Also, A word mispronounced; as when a word is said to be لُغَةٌ أَوْ لُثْغَةٌ a dialectal variant or a word mispronounced.

لثم

1. لَثَمَتِ الحِجَارَةُ خُفَّ البَعِيرِ The stones wounded the camel's foot, and made it bleed. (Ṣ.) — لَثَمَتْ She muffled herself with a لِثَام. (Ḳ.)

لِثَامٌ A kind of muffler for the mouth. (Ḳ.)

لثو

لَثًى : see عَبِيبَةٌ.

اَلْحُرُوفُ اللِّثَوِيَّةُ [*The gingival letters*:] these are ث, ذ, and ظ. (TA, commencement of باب الثاء.)

لج

1. لَجَّ فِى الأَمْرِ ***He kept, attended,*** or ***applied himself, constantly, perseveringly,*** or ***assiduously, to the thing***; ***he was persevering,*** or ***assiduous, in the affair.*** (Mṣb.)

لجف

لَجَفٌ : see قِصَابٌ.

لجم

4. أَلْجَمَ ***He bridled*** a beast; agreeably with an explanation in the Ḳ: and sometimes ***he bitted*** him; as expl. in the Mṣb.

5. تَلَجَّمَتْ : see 10 in art. ثفر.

لُجْمَةٌ : see لُجَمٌ.

لُجَمَةٌ and ▼لُجَامٌ ***A thing from which one augurs evil; an omen,*** or ***a bodement, of evil***: because it refrains one from a thing that he wants. (A, art. عطس.) ▼لُجَمٌ, which is originally the plural of both, is also used as a sing. (A, ibid, where see an ex.) See عَطَسَ and عُطُوسٌ.

لِجَامٌ [*A bit*; i. e., *the iron appurtenances of a bridle*]. To the لجام belong pieces of iron which are fastened one to another; as the فَأْسٌ, and the مِسْحَلٌ, and the عِضَادَتَانِ and its extremities of iron. (Az, in TA, voce قَيْقَبٌ.) The above explanation is incomplete: it means the *bridle,* or *headstall and reins, with the bit and other appurtenances*; like its Persian original, لِگَامٌ : see قُرْطٌ. It signifies The *piece of iron in the mouth of the horse*: thus, by extension, applied to *this with its thongs,* or *straps, and apparatus*: it comprises the شَكِيمَةٌ, which is the transverse piece of iron in the mouth; and the فَأْسٌ, which is the piece of iron standing up in the mouth; and the مِسْحَلٌ, which is the iron beneath the حَنَك; and the خُطَّافَانِ, which are two bent pieces of iron in the مِسْحَلٌ and the شكيمة, on the right and left; and the فَرَاشَتَانِ, which are two pieces of iron wherewith are fastened the extremities of the عِذَارَانِ; and the حَكَمَةٌ, which is the ring surrounding the مَرْسِنٌ and the حَنَك, of silver or iron or thong. (IDrd, in his Book on the Saddle and Bridle.) — See لُجْمَةٌ.

لجن

1. لَجِنَ : see لَجِدَ.

5. تَلَجَّنَ النَّبَاتُ : see تَلَزَّجَ.

لحظ

لَحْظٌ : see عَيْرٌ.

لحف

لِحَافٌ : see what follows.

مِلْحَفَةٌ *A* مُلَآءَةٌ *that is* سِمْطٌ [*not lined, nor stuffed*]: if lined or stuffed, the vulgar also call it by this name, but the Arabs do not know this: (L, TA:) and the same applies to the ▼لِحَاف: Az says, that لِحَافٌ and مِلْحَفٌ mean the same: like إِزَارٌ and مِئْزَرٌ, and قِرَامٌ and مِقْرَمٌ; and sometimes one says مِقْرَمَةٌ and مِلْحَفَةٌ; and it is the same whether the garment be سِمْط or *lined.* (TA.) He says also, [in another place,] that the Arabs apply the terms ▼لِحَافٌ and مِلْحَفَةٌ to *A night-wrapper* (إِزَارُ لَيْلٍ) *if it be* طَاقٌ وَاحِدٌ [*a single piece of stuff*; i. e. *not double, not lined nor faced, nor stuffed*]. (TA in art. سمط.) — See إِزَارٌ.

لحق

1. لَحِقَهُ and لَحِقَ بِهِ and ▼أَلْحَقَهُ *He reached him; overtook him; or came up with him.* (Ṣ, Mṣb, Ḳ.) — لَحِقَهُ *It* (grief, &c.) *overtook him; or ensued to him.* — Also, and لَحِقَ بِهِ *He overtook him; came up with him.* — لَحِقَ بِهِ *He became,* or *made himself, on a par,* or *as though on a par, with him.* See an ex. voce تَوَحَّشَ. — *It became adjoined,* or *annexed, to it.* — ▼ لُوحِقَ *It was firmly,* or *strongly, compacted* or *coherent* or *knit together*: and *its several parts were inserted one into another.* (TA.) — لَحِقَهُ الثَّمَنُ, inf. n. لُحُوقٌ, [*i. q.* أَدْرَكَهُ, i. e. The payment of] *the price was,* or *became, obligatory on him.* (Mṣb.) — لَحِقَتْ قُوَّتُهُ وَسِنُّهُ : see the last sentence of art. عون. — لَحِقَهُ has for its inf. n. لُحُوقٌ as well as لَحَاقٌ. (TA.)

3: see 1.

4. أَلْحَقَهُ بِهِ *He made him to reach, overtake,* or *come up with, him*; (Ṣ, Mṣb,* Ḳ;*) or *to follow him.* (Mṣb.) *He made it* (a punishment) *to* [*overtake him,* or] *befall him.* (Mṣb.) *He removed him to it*; namely, a place; lit., *caused him to reach it*: see an ex. voce خَافِقٌ. — *He affiliated him to him; announced him to be his son,* because of a mutual likeness. (Mṣb.) — أَلْحَقَهُ بِهِ *He classed him, as an adjunct, with him; put him on a par with him*; or *made him to be as though on a par with him.* See two exs. voce لَاطَ, in art. لبط. — See 1.

6. تَلَاحَقَتِ المَطَايَا *The saddle-camels overtook one another.* (Ṣ, Ḳ.) تَلَاحَقُوا *The last of them overtook,* or *came up with, the first of them.* (Ṣ, TA in art. درك.)

لُحُوقٌ *i. q.* لُزُومٌ and لُصُوقٌ. (TA.)

لَاحِقُ الأَطَالِ *Lean,* or *lank, in the sides.* (Ḥam, p. 496.) لَاحِقُ البَطْنِ *Lank in the belly.* (TA in art. رهف.)

إِلْحَاقٌ The *rendering a word quasi-coördinate to another word of which the radical letters are more in number than those of the former word. A letter which is added to a word for the purpose above mentioned.* See أَلِفُ الإِلْحَاقِ and أَلِفُ التَّكْثِيرِ in art. ا. — حَرْفُ إِلْحَاقٍ *A letter of adjunction,* or *quasi-coördination.*

مُلْحَقٌ, pl. مُلْحَقَاتٌ, *A word rendered quasi-radically coördinate to another word of which the radical letters are more in number than those of the former word.* — مُلْحَقٌ بِالرُّبَاعِيّ *A quasi-quadriliteral-radical word.* — See إِلْحَاقٌ.

مُتَلَاحِكٌ *i. q.* مُتَعَاوِنٌ بِرْذَوْنٌ. (TA in art. عون.)

لحم

4. أَلْحَمَ خَرْقَهُ [*He closed up the hole thereof* with a patch]; meaning a garment, or piece of cloth, and a skin, or hide. (TA in art. رقع.) — إِلْحَامٌ الجِرَاحَاتِ [*The consolidating of wounds*]. (Ḳ in art. سبع.) — أَلْحَمَهُ عِرْضَهُ : *He empowered him to revile, vilify,* or *censure, him*: (Ṣ, Ḳ, TA:) *he made his honour,* or *reputation, to be to him* [*as*] *a* ▼ لُحْمَة [*or hawk's portion of the quarry*]. (Ḥar, p. 392.) — أَلْحِمْ مَا أَسْدَيْتَ : see أَسْدَى.

6. تَلَاحَمَ *It was joined,* or *knit, together.* See Ḳ, voce مُزَفُورٌ.

8. اِلْتَحَمَ *It coalesced, consolidated, closed up,* or *became closely united.* (TA.)

تَمْرٌ لَهُ لَحْمٌ [*Dates having flesh*]. (Mṣb in art. حشف.) — لَحْمٌ : see ثَرِيدٌ, last sentence.

شَحْمٌ لَحِمٌ : see مَحِضٌ and شَحِمٌ.

لَحْمَةٌ and ▼ لُحْمَةٌ The *woof*; or the *threads that are woven into the* سَدًى, or *warp, of a piece of cloth.* (Mṣb, &c.)

لُحْمَةٌ : see 4, and لُحْمَةٌ شَابِكَةٌ — لُحْمَةٌ : see مُشْتَبِكٌ.

لَحَّامٌ *A butcher.* (Fr, TA in art. سطر.)

مَلَاحِمُ الفَرْجِ (Ḳ) *The narrow, or strait, parts of the pudendum muliebre:* (TA:) or rather, *the fleshy parts thereof:* the sing. مَلْحَمَةٌ signifying, accord. to analogy, *a place of much flesh:* see بِطَانٌ.

المُلْتَحِمَةُ [*The tunica albuginea, or white of the eye:* so in the present day]. (Ḳ, voce سَبَلٌ.)

بَازِلَةٌ : see شَجَّةٌ, and شَجَّةٌ مُتَلَاحِمَةٌ (voce بَازِلٌ).

لحن

1. لَحَنَ *He erred in speech; spoke incorrectly.* (Mṣb.) — لَحَنَ لَهُ *He said to him something which he (the latter) understood, but which was unintelligible to others:* (Az, Ṣ, Mṣb, Ḳ:) *he intimated to him something which he (the latter) alone understood.*

3. لَاحَنَهُمْ *i. q.* فَاطَنَهُمْ. (Ṣ, Ḳ.) See an ex. voce جَامِعٌ; and see my explanations of مُفَاطَنَةٌ.

لَحْنٌ The *meaning* of speech; its *intended sense or import:* (Ṣ, Ḳ, TA:) its *intent:* (TA:) [it is *direct:* and also *indirect:*] *an indication* thereof *whereby the person addressed is made to understand one's intent;* so says Az (Mṣb: [and the like is said in the TA on the authority of AHeyth:]) *an oblique,* or *ambiguous, mode* of speech: (Mṣb:) *an inclining* of speech *to obliqueness, or ambiguity, and equivocal allusion.* (Bḍ, in xlvii. 32.) — *A barbarism, an incorrect word.* — عَرَفْتُهُ فِى لَحْنِ كَلَامِهِ and فِى مِعْرَاضِ كلامه and فى نَحْوِ كلامه signify the same. (Mṣb in art. عرض.) See the last of these voce عَرُوضٌ. — لَحْنٌ *A modulated sound;* expl. as being مِنَ الأَصْوَاتِ المَصُوغَةِ المَوْضُوعَةِ: pl. أَلْحَانٌ and لُحُونٌ. (Ḳ.) You say, أَلْحَانُ الأَغَانِى [*The modulated sounds of songs*]. (Mgh.)

لحى

1. لُحِىَ : see a verse cited voce خَطَبَ. — لَحَاهُ ٱللّٰهُ : see شَرَاهُ.

5. تَلَحَّى, (Ṣ, Mgh,) and تلحّى بِعِمَامَتِهِ, (TA, art. عجر,) *He wound a part of his turban under his lower jaw:* (Ṣ, Mgh:) as also تَحَنَّكَ, q. v.

8. اِلْتَحَيْتُ اللَّحْمَ عَنِ العَظْمِ [*I peeled off the flesh from the bone*]. (O, Ḳ, in art. سلق.)

لَحْىٌ [not لِحْىٌ] The *jaw-bone;* (Mgh, Mṣb;) either *upper or lower:* (Mṣb:) and, in a man, (Mṣb,) the *part on which the beard grows.* (Ṣ, Mṣb, Ḳ.) — And sometimes *Either lateral portion of the lower jaw:* see ذَقَنٌ, and الفَنِيكُ.

لِحْيَةٌ : see ثِيلٌ — لِحْيَةُ التَّيْسِ is sometimes, by a synecdoche, put for the whole *person:* see a verse cited voce خُنْثٌ.

عَقَّ بِالشَّهْرِ : see مَسْحُ اللِّحَى.

لِحَآءٌ *Bark;* and in particular the *bark* of a plant, or of a tree, *of which ropes &c. are made.* — The لِحَآء of the date is [its *Pulp, pulpy pericarp,* or *flesh;* i. e.] the *part that clothes the* نَوَاة [or *stone*]. (TA.) — لِحَآءُ العِنَبِ [*The skin of grapes*]. (TA in art. شحم.)

لَوَاحِى الشَّيْبِ, for لَوَائِحُ الشيب, q. v.

لخق

لُخْقُوقٌ [*A sort of trench, or channel, made by water, which has worn and undermined its sides;*] *a place in which water flows, having sides worn and undermined thereby, and hollowed in the form of the river,* or *river-bed:* pl. لَخَاقِيقُ. (ISh, TA.)

لخى

أَلْخَى *Distorted in the mouth.* (CḲ; L, art. لخ, but written الخاء.)

لدم

مُلَدَّمٌ A garment, or piece of cloth, *patched,* or *pieced;* or *patched,* or *pieced, in several places;* like مُرَدَّمٌ. (Lth, T, in art. ردم.)

لدن

لَدْنٌ *Supple; lithe; limber; limp; pliant; pliable; flexible.*

مِنْ لَدُنْ *From the time of:* see a verse cited in art. عى, conj. 4. — هٰذَا الأَمْرُ مِنْ لَدُنْهُ *i. q.* مِنْ قِبَلِهِ, q. v. (Lth in TA, in art. قبل.)

لذع

1. لَذَعَ اللِّسَانَ [*It burned the tongue; was acrid*]. (Ṣ, Mṣb, art. حرف; &c.)

لَذْعُ البَرْدِ [*The hurting,* or *paining, of cold*]. (Ṣ, O, Ḳ, voce شَفِيفٌ.)

لز

3. لَازَّهُ *i. q.* ضَايَقَهُ. (TA, voce دَاقَّهُ.)

لِزٌّ *i. q.* زُوَيْنٌ. (A, Ḳ.) In the CḲ, وَلَزَزٌ قَبْنٌ is a mistake for وَاللِّزُّ الزُّوَيْنُ.

لزق

لِزْقُهُ and بِلِزْقِهِ *Close by his,* or *its, side.*

لزم

1. لَزِمَهُ *It necessarily,* or *inseparably, belonged,* or *pertained,* or *it clave,* or *adhered, to him,* or *it;* as also لَزِمَ لَهُ: *it* (disgrace, &c.) *attached to him.* — لَزِمَهُ أَمْرُ فُلَانٍ *The management of the affair,* or *affairs, of such a one was,* or *became, incumbent,* or *obligatory, upon him.* — لَزِمَ شَيْئًا *He kept close, clave, clave fast, clung,* or *held fast, to anything.* (Ṣ, Ḳ, &c.) And hence, *He preserved a thing:* see قَنِىَ. — See 3. — لَزِمَ الغَرِيمَ, and لَزِمَ بِهِ, and لَازَمَهُ ▼, *He adhered, kept, clave, clung,* or *held fast, to the debtor.* (Mṣb.) — لَزِمَ بَيْتَهُ *He kept,* or *clave, to his house* or *tent; did not quit it; was not found elsewhere.* (Kull, p. 318.) — لَزِمَهُ المَالُ *The* [*paying of the*] *money &c. behoved him, lay on him, was incumbent on him,* or *obligatory on him.* (Mṣb.)

3. لَازَمَهُ *He kept, confined himself, clave, clung, or held fast, to him, or it:* as also لَزِمَهُ ▼: *he held on,* or *continued, it.* See 1.

4. أَلْزَمَهُ شَيْئًا signifies *He necessitated him,* or *obliged him, to do,* and *to pay,* &c.; or *to suffer,* or *endure, a thing:* and hence, said of God, *He decreed,* or *appointed,* or *ordained, to him a thing.* And *He made him to cleave to a thing;* and *he made a thing to cleave to him.* See جَدَعَ. — أُلْزِمَ شَيْئًا لَا يُفَارِقُهُ [*He was made to cleave to a thing, not quitting it*]. (Ḳ.) — أَلْزَمَهُ ٱللّٰهُ الشَّرَّ *May God make evil to cleave to him:* or, *to attend him constantly:* or *decree evil to him.* — أَلْزَمْنَاهُ طَائِرَهُ فِى عُنُقِهِ, (Ḳur xvii. 14,) *We have decreed to him his happiness* or *his misery,* foreseeing that he would be obedient, or disobedient: (AM, in TA, art. طير:) or *we have made his works* and *what is decreed to him to cleave to him* like the طَوْق *upon his neck.* (Bḍ.) — أَلْزَمَهُ البَيِّنَةَ *He compelled him,* or *constrained him, to accept,* or *admit, the evidence,* or *proof.* (Jel xi. 30.) أَلْزَمَهُ المَالَ *He obliged him to pay the money &c.* أَلْزَمَهُ العَمَلَ *He obliged him to do the deed.* (Mṣb.) — أَلْزَمْتُهُ الذَّنْبَ, and الحَقَّ : see زَكَّ. — أَلْزِمْ نَعْلَيْكَ قَدَمَيْكَ [*Keep thou thy sandals upon thy feet*]. (From a trad. in the Jámi' eṣ-Ṣagheer.)

8. اِلْتَزَمَ *He took upon himself* an affair. (KL.) You say, اِلْتَزَمَهُ *He took it upon himself; charged himself with it; obliged himself to do it; became,* or *made himself, answerable for it by an inseparable obligation:* see بَآءَ. — اِلْتَزَمْتُ بِالمَالِ *i. q.* أَلْزَمْتُ بِهِ نَفْسِى, and تَكَفَّلْتُ

بِهِ, accord. to IAmb, or تَحَمَّلْتُ بِهِ, accord. to AZ; (Mṣb in art. كفل;) *I made myself answerable, responsible, or accountable, by an inseparable obligation, for the property:* see اِلْتَزَمَ — ضَمِنَ. المَالَ, and العَمَلَ, *He obliged himself, or took upon himself the obligation, to pay the money &c., and to do the deed.* (Mṣb.) — اِلْتَزَمَهُ *He kept, or restricted himself, to it;* i.e. an action, or usage, &c. — And *It was, or became, necessary for him, or obligatory upon him, to do it, or pay it,* &c.; or *to suffer it, or endure it.* — دَلَفَ لِالْتِزَامِى *He hastened to take me by the hand and embrace me:* see دَلَفَ. — اِلْتِزَامُ: i.q. لُزُومُ مَا لَا يَلْزَمُ: see below.

10. اِسْتَلْزَمَهُ *It necessarily required it or involved it.*

لَزُومٌ One *who keeps, cleaves, clings,* or *holds fast, much,* or *habitually,* لِشَىْءٍ *to a thing:* see an ex. in the Ḥam, p. 238, line 21.

لُزُومُ مَا لَا يَلْزَمُ *The imposing upon one's self what is not indispensable; or adhering to a mode of construction that is not necessarily to be followed:* as in the following instance in the خُطْبَة of the Ḳámoos: وَبَلَغُوا مِنَ الْمَقَاصِدِ قَاصِيَتَهَا وَمَلَكُوا مِنَ الْمَحَاسِنِ نَاصِيَتَهَا.

لَازِمٌ *Keeping, keeping close, cleaving,* &c.; *tenacious:* and *pertinacious.* — لَازِمٌ *A thing inseparable from another thing:* pl. لَوَازِمُ. (TA.) *Such as cleaves fast; inseparable:* as an epithet. — اِسْمٌ لَازِمٌ: see جَمْعٌ, as signifying "a plural." — لَوَازِمُ *Necessary,* or *inseparable, adjuncts, accompaniments, consequences,* or *results.*

أَلْزَمُ as syn. with أَلْقَى in the prov. خَلَاؤُكَ أَلْقَى لِحَيَائِكَ means *Most preservative:* see that prov. in art. خلو, and see قَنِىَ الحَيَآءَ, and لَزِمَ شَيْئًا.

لزن

لَزْنٌ: see أَسْلَفَ.

لس

لَسْلَسٌ: see سَلْسَلٌ.

لَسْلَسَةٌ: see سَلْسَلَةٌ.

مُلَسْلَسٌ: see مُسَلْسَلٌ and مُسَلْسَلٌ.

لسن

لَسَنٌ *Chasteness,* or *perspicuity,* or *clearness, of speech,* (Ṣ, Mṣb, Ḳ,) and *eloquence;* (Mṣb;) i.q. بَيَانٌ: or, as some say, the *quality of speaking well:* and *chasteness,* or *perspicuity,* or *eloquence, of speech, and sharpness of tongue.* (TA.)

لِسَانٌ of a sandal, The *thing* (هَنَة) *projecting in the fore part* thereof. (TA.) See مُسْرَدٌ. — لِسَانٌ The *tongue* [or *cock*] of a balance: see مِنْجَمٌ in the Ṣ and Ḳ. — لِسَانٌ *Information, news,* or *tidings;* syn. خَبَرٌ. (Ṣ in art. علو.) See a verse cited voce عُلْوٌ.

تَلَسُّنٌ: see خَلِيَّةٌ, voce خَلِىٌّ.

مُلَسَّنٌ, (Ṣ,) or with ة, (Ḳ,) A sandal *long and slender, like the form of the tongue:* (Ṣ, Ḳ:) or *having the extremity of its fore part like the extremity of the tongue.* (TA.)

لصق

3. لَاصَقَهُ *He associated with him.*

لَصِيقٌ *An associate; an adherent.*

مُلْصَقٌ i. q. دَعِىٌّ (TA;) as also مُلْصَقٌ (TA in art. لسق) and مُلَسَّقٌ: (Ḳ, and TA in that art.:) or [*a consociated alien;*] *one residing among a tribe of which he is not a member by lineage.* (TA.)

مُلْصَقٌ: see مُلْصَقٌ.

لط

لِطْلِطٌ: see دَلُوقٌ. — لِطْلِطٌ A she-camel *far advanced in age, and having lost her teeth.* (T, in L, voce كُحْكُحٌ.)

لطس

مِلْطَاسٌ *A pickaxe.* (TA.)

لطف

1. لَطُفَ *It* (a thing) *was small,* or *little;* (Ṣ, Mṣb, Ḳ, KL;) and *slender, thin,* or *fine:* (Ḳ, KL:) and *elegant,* or *graceful.* (KL.)

2. لَطَّفَ *It* (a medicine) *acted as an attenuant, and as an emollient.* — لَطَّفَهُ, inf. n. تَلْطِيفٌ, [*He made it slender*]. (A, and Ḳ, art. حشر; &c.)

3. لَاطَفَ *He caressed; treated with blandishment; soothed; coaxed; wheedled; cajoled:* i.q. بَارَّهُ. (Ṣ, Ḳ.) — لَاطَفَهُ also signifies *He spoke softly, gently,* or *blandly, to him.* (TA.) *He acted in a good manner with him:* (KL:) *manifested goodness towards him:* (PṢ:) *he acted towards him with goodness:* and *he did so, experiencing from him the same:* (TḲ:) or rather, as syn. with بَارَّهُ, *he behaved towards him with goodness and affection and gentleness, and regard for his circumstances;* or *did so, experiencing from him the same behaviour.*

4. أَلْطَفَهُ *He gave him a gift or present.* (TA.) — *He showed him kindness,* or *goodness,* and *affection and gentleness, and regard for his circumstances,* بِكَذَا [*by such a thing,* or *such an action,* &c.]. (Ṣ, Ḳ, TA.) Often occurring in the latter sense: but أَلْطَفَهُ بِكَذَا, expl. in the Ṣ and Ḳ by بَرَّهُ بِهِ, may mean *He presented him with such a thing;* like وَصَلَهُ بِهِ. — See أَلْطَفَهُ.

5. تَلَطَّفَ لِلْأَمْرِ i.q. تَرَفَّقَ: (Ṣ:) see طَبَّ. — *I.q.* تَكَلَّفَ اللُّطْفَ. (Bḍ xviii. 18.) — تَلَطَّفَ بِهِ *i.q.* تَرَفَّقَ. (Mgh in art. رفق.)

لُطْفٌ *Gentleness; graciousness; courtesy; civility:* (Ṣ, &c.:) see رِفْقٌ: and *delicacy of flavour,* &c.

لَطَفٌ *A gift,* or *present:* pl. أَلْطَافٌ. (MA.) — See لَطَفَةٌ.

لَطَفَةٌ *A present;* i. e. *a thing sent to another in token of courtesy or honour;* syn. هَدِيَّةٌ; (Ṣ, Ḳ;) as also لَطَفٌ, as stated by Z and others: pl. of the latter أَلْطَافٌ. (TA.)

لَطِيفٌ *Gentle, gracious, courteous,* or *benignant:* and also *subtle; knowing with respect to the subtilties, niceties, abstrusities,* or *obscurities, of things, affairs,* or *cases:* in both of these senses often applied to a man. And *Refined in manners,* &c. — *Obscure, recondite,* or *abstruse,* language. (Kull.) — See Ḥam, p. 455. — Applied to a medicine, &c., *Delicate:* see سُوسَنٌ.

لَطِيفَةٌ *A nice, subtile, subtilely excogitated, quaint, facetious,* or *witty, saying, expression,* or *allusion; a witticism; a quaint conceit.* — [*A nicety of language;*] *any indication of subtile meaning, apparent to the understanding, but not to be expressed;* as [matters of] the sciences of taste (عُلُوم الأَذْوَاق). (KT.)

الِانْطِلَافُ *Self-pollution,* by a woman: see جَلْدُ عُمَيْرَةَ in art. جلد.

لطم

2. لَطَّمَ *He slapped much, or violently.* See مُلَخَّصٌ, and see Ḳ, voce طَلَّمَ.

نَطِيحٌ: see لَطِيمَةٌ.

لَطِيمٌ: see نَطِيحٌ. — لَطِيمٌ *A small camel.* (TA, voce عَسْجَدٌ.) — زَوْمَلَةٌ see لَطِيمَةٌ. — *Small* weaned camels. (TA in art. عسجد.)

لعط

لُعْطَةٌ: see عُلْطَةٌ, in two places.

لعق

1. لَعِقَ *He licked* (Ṣ, Ḳ, TA) *his fingers:* (TA:) *he ate* a thing *with his finger* [*by taking* it *up therewith*]. (Mṣb.)

لَعُوقٌ *A linctus.*

مِلْعَقَةٌ [*A spoon;* vulgo مَعْلَقَةٌ;] *a well-known instrument.* (Mṣb.)

لعل

لَعَلَّ [*May-be; perhaps*]; a word denoting hope and fear. (Ḳ.) It governs the subject in the accus. case, and the predicate in the nom. See Ibn-'Aḳeel, ed. of Dieterici, p. 90; and see لَيْتَ. — لَعَلَّ, in its original and general acceptation, expresses hope; but in the word of God it [often] expresses certainty, and may be rendered *Verily.* (Jel, ii. 19.)

لعن

لُعْنَةٌ A man *who is much cursed.* (TA in art. خدع.)

لَعِينٌ The *base,* or *lower part, of a raceme of a palm-tree.* (TA in art. عهن.)

لعو

لَعًا, said to a camel when it stumbles: see تَعْسًا, voce تَعَسَ: and see the first paragraph of art. عول, last sentence but one.

لَعْوَةٌ *A hunting bitch.* (L, art. عقد.)

لغذ

3. لَاغَذَهُ *i.q.* ضَايَقَهُ. (TA, voce ذَاقَنَهُ.)

لغم

لُغَامٌ: see an ex. in a verse cited voce تَرَغَّمَ.

لغن

لُغْنُونٌ The *sides,* or *adjacent parts,* (النَّوَاحِى) *of the* لَهَاة, *impending* (مُشْرِفَة) *over the* حَلْق [or *throat*]; as also لُغَانِينُ: (JK:) see غُنْدُبَةٌ, and لُغْدٌ.

لُغْنُونَةٌ: see غُنْدُبَةٌ.

لغو

3. لَاغَاهُ *He jested,* or *joked, with him;* inf. n. مُلَاغَاةٌ. (A, TA.) You say, لَاغَاهُ فِى الْبَيْعِ. (A, TA, art. كيس.)

لَغْوٌ, applied to speech, &c., *Nought; of no account;* (M, Ḳ;) *unprofitable.* (M.) — الْيَمِينُ اللَّغْوُ: see KT, voce يَمِينٌ.

اللُّغَةُ *The genuine language* of the Arabs; which is *the classical language.*

لُغَوِىٌّ *Of,* or *relating to, the genuine language* of the Arabs. مَعْنًى لُغَوِىٌّ *A genuine lexicological meaning.*

لُغَيَّةٌ *A word of weak authority.* (TA, voce جِرَاب, et passim.)

لَاغٍ: see مَائِرٌ.

لف

1. لَفَّ *He folded,* or rather *wrapped; folded up,* or rather *wrapped up,* or *rolled up,* a thing in another thing. — لَفَّ الْعَدُوَّ [app. *He involved the enemy (in difficulty), or entangled him:*] said with reference to war, and excellence of judgment, and knowledge of the case of the enemy, and the subduing him, with the infliction of many wounds. (L, in TA, voce عَمْتَهُ.) But see عَمَتَ.

5: see 8.

8. اِلْتَفَّ *It* (herbage) *tangled; became confused, and caught,* one part to another: (Mṣb:) or *became luxuriant,* or *abundant;* (Ṣ;) *it* (a collection of trees) *became luxuriant,* or *abundant, and close together:* (AḤn:) [or *thickly intermixed:*] *it* (a thing) *became collected together, and dense;* (TA:) best rendered *tangled,* or *luxuriant,* or *abundant and dense.* — اِلْتَفَّ and ▼ تَلَفَّفَ *He wrapped,* or *enwrapped, himself* in, or with, a garment; (KL, PṢ;) *i.q.* اِشْتَمَلَ. (Mṣb.) — اِلْتَفَّ وَجْهُ الغُلَامِ means اِتَّصَلَتْ لِحْيَتُهُ [i. e. *The face of the young man became continuous,* or *uninterrupted, in its beard*]. (TA.) — اِلْتَفَّ *It* (an affair) *became complicated.*

لَفٌّ وَنَشْرٌ in rhetoric, [*Complication and explication, involution and evolution;* i.e., *a construction in which two or more words are mentioned, and, after them, two or more other words, as epithets, &c., referring to the former.* لف ونشر مُرَتَّبٌ, *Involution and evolution regularly disposed,* is when the order of the latter words agrees with that of those to which they refer. لف ونشر مَعْكُوسٌ, or مُشَوَّشٌ, *Involved,* or *disordered, involution and evolution,* is when the order of the latter words is contrary to that of those to which they refer]. (TA, passim.) See Ḥar, p. 383.

لَفَّةٌ *i.q.* لُقْمَةٌ: see صُفَّةٌ, last sentence.

لَفَّآءُ *A thick thigh:* see a verse voce تَسَاهَمُوا.

فُلَانٌ مِنْ لَفِيفِنَا وَضَفِيفِنَا: see art. ضف.

لِفَافَةٌ *A wrapper for the leg* or *foot &c.* (Ṣ, Ḳ.) — And *A pericarp;* a *glume,* and *the like;* *an envelope:* pl. لَفَائِفُ.

لَفِيفَةٌ *A lock* (خُصْلَةٌ) of hair. (Ṣ, voce خُصْلَةٌ.)

نَاقَةٌ مُلَفَّفَةُ السَّنَامِ [*A she-camel having the hump much enveloped with fur:* see اِلْتَفَّ وَجْهُ الغُلَامِ]. (Ibn-'Abbád, O, Ḳ, voce عُلْفُوفٌ. q.v.)

مُلْتَفُّ الخَلْقِ A man *having a well-knit frame; compact in make.* (L, art. مسد.)

لفط

3. لَافَطَهُ: see فَارَطَهُ.

لفع

اِشْتَمَلَ: see التَّلَفُّعُ.

لفق

1. لَفَقَ الثَّوْبَ *He joined and sewed together,* or *put together and sewed, the two oblong pieces of cloth of the garment;* (Ṣ, Mṣb, Ḳ;) and ▼ لَفَّقَ, inf. n. تَلْفِيقٌ, signifies the same, and is more common; or has an intensive signification. (TA.) — See also Ḥar, pp. 253 and 254. — ▼ تَلْفِيقٌ The *bringing,* or *putting, together.* (KL.) And The *making suitable,* or *conformable.* (KL.) — And The *speaking,* or *telling, what is untrue,* or *false:* (KL:) the *embellishing* [of speech] *with lies.* (Ḥar, p. 254.) — لَفَقَ *He felled* (a seam or garment).

2: see 1. — لَفَّقَ بَيْنَ الكَلَامِ, (JK, voce وَشَّعَ, &c.,) inf. n. تَلْفِيقٌ, (Ḳ, voce تَوْسِيعٌ, &c.,) *He interlarded,* or *embellished, the speech,* or *discourse, with falsehood:* see the pass. part. n. مُلَفَّقَةٌ: and see وَشَّعَ, and وَبَّقَ, and رَمَّقَ.

5. تَلَفَّقَ بِهِ: see تَأَفَّقَ.

لِفَاقَانِ *Two pieces which compose a* مُلَآءَة, (Mgh, Mṣb, TA, in art. ربط,) *being joined together,* (Mgh, TA, in that art.,) *by sewing* or *the like.* (TA in that art.)

لِفَاقٌ: see رَدِيمَةٌ.

أَحَادِيثُ مُلَفَّقَةٌ *Narrations,* or *stories, compounded,* or *combined, with falsehood; embellished* [or *interlarded*] *therewith:* and *put together.* (MA, Ḥar, p. 254.) — شُقَّةٌ مُلَفَّقَةٌ: see بَصِيرَةٌ.

لفم

لِفَامٌ *A kind of woman's face-veil.* See نِقَابٌ.

لفو

6. تَلَافَاهُ *i.q.* تَدَارَكَهُ [*He repaired it;* a meaning well known]; (Ṣ, Mṣb, Ḳ, TA;) namely, a short-coming; or failing, or falling short, of what

was requisite, or due; and an inconsistent act. (TA.) You say, هٰذَا أَمْرٌ لَا يُتَلَافَى [*This is an affair that will not be repaired*]. (TA.) And تَلَافَى أَمْرَهُمْ بِالصُّلْحِ [*He repaired their condition by peace, or reconciliation*]. (EM, p. 117.) See دقه.

لَفَاةٌ : see لَفَاتٌ.

لق

لَقٌّ *A fissure* in a rock. (AA, in TA, voce بَقَاقٌ.) —— لَقٌّ بَقٌّ and لَقْلَاقٌ بَقْبَاقٌ : see ثَتٌّ.

لقف

1. لَقِفَهُ *He seized it,* or *took it quickly;* (Ṣ, M, Ḳ;) namely, a thing thrown to him with the hand, or said to him. (M, TA.) See also last sentence of 1 in art. حنك.

5. تَلَقَّفَهُ مِنْ فِيهِ *He caught it and retained it quickly,* [i. e., what he said,] *from his mouth.* (TA.)

لقم

1. لَقِمَ لُقْمَةً, [aor. ـَ,] inf. n. لَقْمٌ, (JK, MṢ,) [*He gobbled a gobbet, or morsel, or mouthful,* or] *he swallowed the gobbet;* and so ↑ اِلْتَقَمَهَا. (Ṣ.) لَقِمَهُ, aor. ـَ, (Mṣb, K, &c.,) inf. n. لَقْمٌ, (JK, MA, Ḳ, MṢ, JM,) or لَقَمٌ (Mṣb, [app. a mistake,]) *He gobbled it;* i. e., *ate it quickly,* (Mṣb, Ḳ, TA,) as also ↑ اِلْتَقَمَهُ, (Mṣb, [see above,]) and *hastily; drew it with his mouth, and ate it quickly.* (TA.) —— لَقِمَ بِيَدِهِ *He put morsels into his mouth* (i. e., his own mouth) *with his hand.* See an ex. voce رَقَعَ. This seems to be the primary signification.

2. لَقَّمَهُ الطَّعَامَ and ↑ أَلْقَمَهُ إِيَّاهُ [*He fed with the food by the mouthful; put it into his mouth by the mouthful*]: (Mṣb:) or لَقَّمَهُ إِيَّاهُ and ↑ أَلْقَمَهُ إِيَّاهُ *he put a mouthful* [*of it*] *into his mouth.* (TA.) And لَقَّمَهُ and ↑ أَلْقَمَهُ [*He fed him by the mouthful; put mouthfuls into his mouth*]. (Ṣ.)

4. أَلْقَمَ *He put morsels into the mouth of* [such a one]. See 2. —— أَلْقَمْتُهُ الحَجَرَ † *I silenced him in an altercation.* (Mṣb.) —— أَلْقَمَهُ البِرْطِيلَ : see the latter word.

5. تَلَقَّمَ اللُّقْمَةَ *He swallowed the gobbet,* or *morsel,* or *mouthful, in a leisurely manner.* (Ṣ, TA.)

8: see 1. —— اِلْتَقَمَ فَاهَا فِى التَّقْبِيلِ [*He took her mouth within his lips in kissing*]. (Ṣ in art. كعم.) Hence the verb signifies †*It embraced,* or *clasped,* a thing: see an instance, voce مِحْضَنٌ.

لُقْمَةٌ *A morsel, gobbet,* or *mouthful: what is* [*swallowed,* or] *eaten quickly, at once,* of bread [&c.]; like as جُرْعَةٌ signifies what is swallowed at once in drinking: (Mṣb:) or *what is prepared to be* [*swallowed,* or] *eaten quickly* [*at once*]. (Ḳ, TA.) —— لُقْمَةُ القَاضِى, and لُقْمَةُ الخَلِيفَةِ : see زُمَاوَرْدٌ, art. ورد; and مُيَسَّرٌ.

لُقَمَاتُ القَاضِى *Same as* لُقَيْمَاتُ القَاضِى.

لقن

3. لَاقَنَهُ i. q. ضَايَقَهُ. (TA voce ذَاقَنَهُ.)

لَقَنٌ, arabicised from [the Persian] لَگَنْ [also written لَكَنْ], *A thing* [or basin] *resembling a* طَسْت, *of* صُفْر [or brass]. (TA.) See إِجَّانَةٌ.

لقى

1. لَقِيَهُ *He met him,* or *it.* (Mṣb.) —— And *He* [*met with,* or] *found him,* or *it.* (Mṣb.) You say, تَلْقَاهُمْ أُسْدًا [*Thou wilt find them lions*]. (Mughnee, voce إِنَّ.) See also لِقَآءٌ. —— لَقِيتُهُ and ↑ لَاقَيْتُهُ *I came near to him, facing him; came before his face, near to him.* (Ksh, in ii. 13.) —— لَقِيَهُ بِمَكْرُوهٍ (Ḳ in art. حبه, &c.) *He* [*encountered with him,* or] *said to him,* or *did to him, a thing disliked,* or *hated:* (TḲ in art. جبه:) like استقبله بما يكره.

2. لَقَّاهُ شَرًّا [*He made him to experience evil treatment*]. (TA in art. جدع, voce جَدَّعَ.) See below; and see مُلَقًّى. —— يُلَقَّوْنَ تَحِيَّةً *They shall be greeted with prayer for length of life, or everlasting existence.* (Bḍ in xxv. 75.)

3. لَاقَاهُ [*He met him face to face; had an interview with him;*] i. q. قَابَلَهُ. (TA.) See 1. —— لَاقَى *He experienced* pain &c. See an ex. voce دَبْرٌ; and voce آلٌ: like لَقِىَ, voce آلٌ. —— لَاقَى بَيْنَ طَرَفَىْ إِزَارِهِ وَشَدَّهُ [*He made the two ends of his* ازار *to meet, and tied it*]. (A, art. حجز.)

4. أَلْقَاهُ *He threw it where he would find it.* (Er-Rághib.) —— And hence, conventionally, *He threw it in any way:* (Er-Rághib:) *he threw it on the ground:* (Mgh:) [*he put it:*] أَلْقَيْتُ المَتَاعَ عَلَى الدَّابَّةِ *I put the goods upon the beast.* (Mṣb.) —— أَلْقَتْ وَلَدَهَا *She cast her young one,* or *her young.* —— أَلْقَى also signifies *He let fall* a thing, a curtain, &c. —— أَلْقَيْتُ إِلَيْهِ خَيْرًا † *I did good to him.* (TA.) And أَلْقَيْتُ إِلَيْهِ المَوَدَّةَ and بِالمَوَدَّةِ †[*I offered* or *tendered to him,* or *gave* or *granted him, love,* or *affection*]. (TA.) —— أَلْقَى عَلَيْهِ رَحْمَتَهُ †[*He made his love, &c., to fall,* or *light, upon him,* i.e. *he bestowed it upon him*]. (Ḳ, TA in art. رحم.) [See this and three similar exs. voce رَحْمَةٌ.] —— أَلْقَى إِلَيْهِ السَّلَامَ *He offered to him salutation,* or *submission:* see سَلَمٌ. —— شَرِبَ مَا أُلْقِىَ إِلَيْهِ : see art. شرب. —— أَلْقَيْتُ إِلَيْهِ القَوْلَ and بِالقَوْلِ *I told,* or *communicated, to him the saying.* (Mṣb.) —— أَلْقَى عَلَيْهِ شَرَاشِرَهُ : see art. شر. —— أَلْقَاهُ عَلَيْهِ *He put it into his mind; he suggested it:* القاه [thus used] is said of God and of the Devil. (Kull, p. 277, in explanation of الفيض. [See 1 in art. فَيْضٌ, last sentence but one.]) —— [And] *He dictated it;* (Mṣb;) namely, a writing to the writer. (Mṣb, in art. مل.) —— أَلْقَى إِلَىَّ سِرَّهُ [*He revealed to me his secret*]. (TA, art. سر.) —— لَا أُلْقِى إِلَيْهِ بَالًا : see art. بول. —— أَلْقَى بِنَفْسِهِ, said of night (اللَّيْلُ) : see رَبَضَ. —— أَلْقَى إِلَيْهِ كَلَامًا *He addressed to him speech.*

5. تَلَقَّاهُ مِنْهُ *He received it from him.* (TA.) —— تَلَقَّى i. q. تَلَقَّنَ. (Bḍ in l. 16.)

8. اِلْتَقَى مَسْلَكَاهَا [*Her vagina and rectum met together in one,* by the rending of the part between,] on the occasion of devirgination. (M, in art. اتم.)

10. اِسْتَلْقَى *He lay,* syn. نَامَ, (Ḳ,) upon the back of his neck. (JK, Ṣ, Ḳ.) And *It* (anything) *was* [or *lay*] *as though thrown down* or *extended.* (T, JK, TA.)

لَقًى *Muscles* of the flesh. (TA, art. ضيع.) —— لَقًى بَقًى : see بَقَاقٌ.

لِقَآءٌ The *facing* a thing: [*encountering it:*] and *meeting it, meeting with it,* or *finding it:* and *perceiving it by the sense, and by the sight.* (Er-Rághib, TA.) —— لِقَآءٌ : its predominant application is *Encounter,* i. e. *conflict, fight, battle,* or *war.* (Mgh.) —— يَوْمُ اللِّقَآءِ *The day of encounter* in fight &c.

بَيْعُ إِلْقَاءِ الحَجَرِ : see نَابَذَهُ, and art. لمس.

وَجَدْتُ هٰذَا مِنْ تِلْقَائِكَ *I experienced this from thee,* or *on thy part;* syn. مِنْ جِهَتِكَ and مِنْ قِبَلِكَ. (Mgh in art. قبل.) هٰذَا الأَمْرُ مِنْ تِلْقَائِهِ *This thing,* or *affair, is from him;* syn. مِنْ عِنْدِهِ; as also مِنْ قِبَلِهِ and مِنْ لَدُنْهُ. (Lth, in TA in art. قبل.) —— تِلْقَآءَ *In the direction that meets* or *faces.* (El-Khafájee, TA.) You say, تَوَجَّهَ تِلْقَآءَ فُلَانٍ [*He went towards such a one*], and تِلْقَآءَ النَّارِ [*in the direction of,* or *towards, the fire*]. (Ḳ.) And جلست تِلْقَآءَهُ *I sat over against him,* or *opposite to him.* (Ṣ.) And وَقَفَ تِلْقَآءَ البَيْتِ *He stopped facing the house.* (Mṣb.)

تَلْقَآءَ القِبْلَةِ — [*The direction of the Kibleh*]. (M, Ḳ, voce إِمَامٌ.) — See بَيْنَهُ.

مَلَاقِى الفَرْجِ [pl. of مَلْقًى,] *The narrow,* or *strait, parts of the pudendum muliebre.* (TA in art. لحم.) — ٱلْمَلَاقِى *The horizontal slabs in which is the aperture in a privy.*

مُلَقًّى *Greeted:* see بَلْهَنِيَةٌ, in art. بله.

لك

1. لَكَّهُ *He pushed him,* or *thrust him;* like صَكَّهُ and دَكَّهُ. (Aṣ, TA in art. دك.)

لِكَاكٌ *A pressing,* or *crowding:* see an ex. voce عَكَّةٌ.

لكز

لَكْزٌ [inf. n. of لَكَزَهُ] *i. q.* طَعْنٌ, like لَزٌّ. (TA, art. لز.)

لكم

لَكْمَةٌ *A blow with the fist.*

لكن

لُكْنَةٌ *An impotence, or impediment, or a difficulty, in speech* or *utterance;* (Mṣb;) *a barbarousness,* or *viciousness, and an impotence, or impediment, in speech:* (Ṣ:) or *the not speaking Arabic rightly, by reason of a barbarousness, or viciousness, in the tongue:* (Ḳ:) or *the interposing of* [*words of*] *a foreign language in one's speech.* (Mbr, TA.) See تَرْتَهَةٌ; and عُجْمَةٌ, with which it is syn.

لٰكِنْ, with the ن quiescent, has no government. — It means *But* after a negative proposition: *but not* after an affirmative: see إِلَّا.

لم

1. لَمَّ ٱللّٰهُ شَعَثَهُ *God rectified,* or *repaired, and consolidated, what was disorganized, disordered,* or *unsettled, of his affairs.* (Ṣ.)

2. لَمَّمَ *He made a* لِمَّة *of his hair.* (Z, TA in art. جمر.)

4. أَلَمَّ بِالقَوْمِ *He came to the people, and alighted at their abode as a guest.* (Mṣb.) See أَطَافَ. — And hence, أَلَمَّ بِالمَعْنَى † *He knew the meaning.* (Mṣb.) — And أَلَمَّ بِالذَّنْبِ † *He committed the sin,* or *offence.* (Mṣb.) — And أَلَمَّ *He,* or *it, visited covertly;* (Ḥam, p. 23;) or *in a light, slight,* or *hasty manner.* (Idem, pp. 385 and 815.) *It became near.* (Mṣb.) — *It happened.* (Ḥam, p. 385.) — أَلَمَّ بِهِ *He came to him.* (Ḥam, p. 127.) — *I. q.* زَارَهُ غِبًّا; as also أَلَمَّ عَلَيْهِ. (TA.)

8. اِلْتَمَّ *It was collected, accumulated.* — اِلْتَمُّوا *They collected themselves; congregated.*

لَمْ with an aor. following it is often to be rendered in English by the preterperfect: ex., لَمْ أَرَهُ مُذْ يَوْمَانِ *I have not seen him for two days.* — لَمْ يَضْرِبْ *He did not beat.* (Ṣ, &c.) See also لَمَّا. — أَلَمْ: see the latter half of art. أَلَا; and the former part of art. أَمَا. — لَمَّا as a particle of exception [is equivalent to our *But;* meaning both *except* and, after an oath or the like, *only,* or *nothing more than;* and] is put before a nominal proposition; as, إِنْ كُلُّ نَفْسٍ لَمَّا عَلَيْهَا حَافِظٌ [*There is not any soul but over it is a guardian,* (Ḳur lxxxvi. 4,)] accord. to those who pronounce the م with teshdeed: and before a verb which is literally, but not in meaning, a preterite; as in أَنْشُدُكَ ٱللّٰهَ لَمَّا فَعَلْتَ [*I conjure,* or *beg,* or *beseech, thee by God but that thou do* such a thing], i. e. مَا أَسْأَلُكَ إِلَّا فِعْلَكَ [*I do not ask of thee anything save thy doing such a thing*]. (Mughnee.) See its syn. إِلَّا. In the Ḳur xxxviii. 13, accord. to one reading, it occurs before a verb which is a preterite literally and in meaning. — لَمَّا, accord. to Ibn-Málik, is *syn. with* إِذْ: [and sometimes, like إِذْ, it means *Since,* or *because:*] one may say, لَمَّا أَكْرَمْتَنِى أَمْسِ أَكْرَمْتُكَ اليَوْمَ: but this is said to mean لَمَّا ثَبَتَ اليَوْمَ إِكْرَامُكَ لِى أَمْسِ أَكْرَمْتُكَ (Mughnee.) See also an ex. voce رَزَقَ. — لَمَّا يَضْرِبْ *He has not yet beaten.* (Ṣ, &c.) See also لَمْ.

لَمَمٌ *A slight insanity* or *diabolical possession;* (Mgh, Mṣb:) *a slight taint* or *infection of insanity.* See طَيْفٌ.

لَمَّةٌ *A touch,* or *somewhat* [*of a taint* or *an infection of insanity*], from the jinn. (S, Ḳ.) See لَمَمٌ.

لِمَّةٌ *Hair that descends below the lobe of the ear.* (Ṣ, Ḳ.) But see وَفْرَةٌ: and see a tropical use of it in a verse of Kumeyt cited in art. حف, p. 597 *c*.

مِلَمٌّ: see مِشَمٌّ.

مُلِمَّةٌ *A misfortune that befalls in the present world.* (Ṣ.) See an ex. in a verse cited voce حَجَا.

مُلَمَّمٌ A boy *having a* لِمَّة. (IDrd, TA, voce مُجَمَّمٌ.)

لمع

1. لَمَعَ *It* (lightning, &c.) *shone; shone brightly; gleamed; glistened.* (Ṣ, Mṣb, Ḳ.) — لَمَعَ بِيَدِهِ, (Ḳ, TA,) and بِثَوْبِهِ, (TA, S, Ḳ, &c., in art. خفق &c.,) and بِسَيْفِهِ, (TA,) *He signalled,* or *made a sign, with his hand* or *arm,* (Ḳ, TA,) and *with his garment,* and *with his sword;* or *did so for the purpose of information* or *warning;* by *raising it, and moving it about,* [or *waving it,* or *brandishing it,* i. e., *he waved it as a sign* or *signal,*] *in order that another might see it, and come to him;* as also ▾ أَلْمَعَ; but the former is the more approved; [*i. q.* Lat. *micuit;*] and sometimes the verb is used without the mention of the hand or arm [&c.]. (TA.) See a verse cited voce قَرْضٌ. — لَمَعَ بِسَيْفِهِ, (Ṣ, and Ḳ, art. لوح,) and بِثَوْبِهِ, (Ṣ, ibid, and S, Ḳ, &c., in art. خفق.) *He made a sign with his sword,* and *with his garment,* [*waving it about, to make it seen by some one whom he desired to see it*]. (Ṣ, Ḳ.)

4. أَلْمَعَ بِيَدِهِ, &c.: see 1.

8. اِلْتَمَسَهُ *He sought,* or *asked,* or *demanded, it.* (Ṣ, Ḳ.) *He sought it out.*

لُمْعَةٌ *A shining, glistening,* or *glossy, appearance,* [or *hue,*] *of the body:* (Ḳ:) *any colour different from another colour* [*in which it is*]; (TA;) [*a spot of colour*]. — [Primarily] *A portion* of herbage *beginning to dry up.* (Ṣ, Mṣb, Ḳ.)

تَلَامِيعُ: see إِبْرِيقٌ in the Ḳ, and my rendering in explaining the latter word, s.v.

لمق

لَمَاقٌ: see عَلَاقٌ, voce عُلْقَةٌ.

لن

لَنْ A particle denoting negation, rendering the aor. manṣoob, and restricting it to the future sense: not implying corroboration of the negation, nor its never-ending continuance; though Z asserts it to imply these. (Ḳ.) [Hence لَنْ يَضْرِبَ signifies simply *He will not beat:* not *he assuredly will not beat;* nor *he will never beat.*]

لنجر

لَنْجَرٌ *An anchoring-place, a harbour,* or *a port,* (مَرْسًى,) *for ships.* (TA.) Occurring in the Ḳ art. رسو. (TA.)

لهذم

لَهْذَمٌ *A sharp spear-head:* see an ex. in a verse of Zuheyr, cited voce زُجٌّ.

لهزم

لِهْزِمَةٌ accord. to different authorities, app. The

angle of the lower jaw: or the *ramus thereof:* or the *flesh upon the hinder part thereof.* See مَحْزُونٌ.

لهط

1. لُهِطَ بِهِ *He, or it, was cast,* or *thrown.* (TA in art. حشف.)

لهف

1. لَهِفَ عَلَيْهِ, (inf. n. لَهَفٌ, Ṣ,) and ▼ تَلَهَّفَ, *He grieved for it,* or *at it; regretted it;* syn. حَزِنَ and تَحَسَّرَ; (Ṣ, Ḳ;) meaning a thing that had escaped him after he been at the point of attaining it: (JK, TA:) or *he grieved for it,* or *at it;* or *regretted it;* and *was angry,* or *enraged, on account of it.* (TA.) But see تَحَسَّرَ; and see Ṣ, voce أَسِفَ. — تلهّف signifies *He felt,* or *expressed, grief, sorrow,* or *regret.*

5: see 1.

يَا لَهَفَ *O the grief!* see an ex. in art. خطأ, conj. 4.

لَهْفَةٌ *Greediness; voracity; eagerness.*

مَلْهُوفٌ *Greedy; ravenous; eager;* عَلَى or إِلَى *for* a thing.

لهم

4. أَلْهَمَهُ ٱللّٰهُ لِلْخَيْرِ [*God directed him by inspiration to that which was good,* or *to prosperity*]. (TA, art. وفق.) — أَلْهَمَهُ إِيَّاهُ *He suggested it to him;* (in the order of the words, *he suggested to him it;*) *he put it into his mind.*

8. اِلْتَهَمَ *He gulped.*

لَاهِمَّ and اللّٰهُمَّ: see اللّٰه.

لهو

1. لَهِيَ عَنْهُ, (Ṣ, Mṣb, Ḳ) and لَهَا عنه, (Mṣb, Ḳ,) *He became diverted from it, so as to forget it.* (Ṣ, Mṣb, Ḳ.) — See an ex. voce استأثر: and see عَنْ. — لَهَتْ إِلَى حَدِيثِهِ, inf. n. لَهْوٌ and لُهُوٌّ, *She* (a woman) *was,* or *became, cheered,* or *delighted,* and *pleased, with his discourse.* (M, Ḳ.) And so لَهَوْتُ بِحَدِيثِهِ. (T in art. رنو.)

4. أَلْهَانِي الشَّيْءُ *The thing diverted me;* syn. شَغَلَنِي. (Mṣb.) — أَلْهَاهُ بِالغِنَآءِ [*He diverted him by singing*]. (Ṣ, art. سمد.)

5. تَلَهَّى بِالشَّيْءِ i. q. تَعَلَّلَ: (TA:) and أُولِعَ بِهِ. (Mṣb.) — And تَلَهَّى *He diverted himself.* (TA.)

لَهْوٌ *Diversion; pastime; sport; play:* or especially, *such as is vain,* or *frivolous; idle sport:* (from various explanations:) *what occupies a man so as to divert him from that which would render him sad or solicitous, &c.:* (TA:) or *relief of the mind by means which wisdom does not require:* this [it is said] is the original signification: (Eṭ-Ṭarasoosee, Mṣb:) *a thing in which a man delights himself, and which occupies him so as to divert him, and then ceases.* (KT.) It has a more general application than لَعِبٌ: for ex., the hearing of musical instruments or the like is لَهْوٌ, but not لَعِبٌ. (TA.) — آلَةُ لَهْوٍ [*An instrument of diversion,* meaning, *of music*]. (Ḳ voce رَبَابٌ.)

لَهَاةٌ [The *uvula;*] the *red piece of flesh that hangs down from the upper* حَنَك. (Zj, in his Khalḳ el-Insán.) See also الأَسَالِيُّ, and شِقْشِقَةٌ. — اللَّهَاةُ [generally expl. as meaning *The uvula:* or] *what is between the end of the root of the tongue and the end of the* قَلْب [thus in all the copies of the Ḳ that I have seen, an evident mistranscription for قَلْت, i. e. *hollow*] *of the upper part of the mouth:* (Ḳ: [app. meaning *the arches,* or *pillars, of the soft palate;* agreeably with the next explanation here following:]) or *the furthest part of the mouth:* [see غُنَّةٌ:] and, of the he-camel, *the* شِقْشِقَة [i. e. *bursa faucium*]. (JK.) See also a usage of the pl., لَهَوَاتٌ, in the last explanation of قَلْتٌ.

لُهْوَةٌ *What is thrown,* [i. e. the *quantity of corn that is thrown,*] (Ṣ, Ḳ,) *by the grinder, with his hand,* (Ṣ,) *into the mouth of the mill* or *millstone.* (Ṣ, Ḳ.) And The *mouth* [*itself*] of the mill or mill-stone. (IḲṭṭ, TA; and Ṣ voce خُرْت.)

لو

لَوْ: see مَصْدَرِيَّةٌ. — It is used as an optative particle, لِلتَّمَنِّى. See Ḳur, ii. 162; and Jel, ibid. See also كَرَّةٌ. — لَوْ كَانَ هٰذَا لَكَانَ ذَاكَ *Had this been,* or *if this were, that had been,* or *would have been.* — صَلِّ وَلَوْ عَجَزْتَ عَنِ القِيَامِ means [*Pray thou though thou be unable to stand;* i. e.] *pray thou whether thou be able to stand* or *unable to do so.* (Mṣb in art. ان.) — See also exs. voce أَنَّ, and بَلْ. — لَوْ often begins a sentence ending with an aposiopesis. — لَوْ meaning أَنْ: see وَدَّ. — لَوْ تُسَوَّى بِهِمُ الأَرْضُ: see بِ as syn. with عَلَى. —

لَوٌّ The *word* لَوْ: see a prov. cited voce ذَنَبٌ (near the end of the paragraph). And see سَوْفَ.

لَوْ أَنَّ [*If*]. Ex. لَوْ أَنَّكَ قَائِمٌ لَقُمْتُ [*Hadst thou been standing, I had stood*]. (Ḳ, art. ان.) See Ḳur, xxxix. 58; &c.

لَوْلَا and لَوْمَا: see حَضَّهُ. — لَوْلَا فَعَلْتَ كَذَا means *Wherefore didst not thou such a thing?* and لَوْلَا تَفْعَلُ كَذَا means *Wherefore wilt not thou do such a thing?* and in like manner, لَوْمَا and أَلَّا and هَلَّا. See an ex. in the Ḳur, x. 98, explained in art. إِلَّا. — لَوْلَا هٰذَا لَكَانَ ذَاكَ *Had not this been,* or *but for this, that had been,* or *would have been.* — لَوْلَا is followed by a noun in the nom. case (as in the Ḳur, viii. 69), or by a verb, as in exs. above.

لَاتَ: see أَلَتَ.

لوص

مُلَوَّصٌ *The sweet food called* فالوذ: see مُزَعْفَرٌ.

لوع

لَوْعَةٌ *Ardour of love:* see حُبٌّ.

لوف

1. مَا عَاقَتْ وَلَا لَافَتْ: see 1 in art. عوق.

لوق

لَوِقٌ and لَيِّقٌ: see عَوِقٌ and عَيِّقٌ.

لوك

1. لَاكَ *He chewed* a morsel: (Ṣ, Ḳ, Mṣb:) or *chewed in the gentlest manner:* or *chewed* something hard; (Ḳ;) *rolling it about,* or *turning it round, in his mouth:* (TA:) [*he* (a child) *mumbled,* or *bit softly,* his finger]: (Ṣ, art. مرث:) *he* (a horse) *champed,* (Mṣb,) or *chewed,* the bit. (Lth in TA, art. الك.)

4. أَلِكْنِى إِلَيْهِ; and أَلِكْتُهُ; as though from أَلَاكَهُ: see art. الك.

5. مَا تَلَوَّكْتُ بِأَلُوكٍ: see أَلُوكٌ.

لوم

1. لَامَ, inf. n. لَوْمٌ, *He blamed, censured,* or *reprehended,* syn. عَذَلَ, (Ṣ, M, Mṣb, Ḳ,) a person, (Ṣ, Mṣb,) عَلَى كَذَا [for such a thing]. (Ṣ.)

4. أَلَامَ *He did a thing for which he should be blamed.* (Ṣ in art. جنف, and L and TA in art. ريب.)

5. تَلَوَّمَ i. q. تَكَلَّفَ اللَّوْمَ. (Ḥam, p. 356.)

لَائِمَةٌ *A thing for which the doer is blamed.* (TA.)

لون

2. لَوَّنَ i. q. ▼ تَلَوَّنَ *It became coloured.* (M.) — *It* (a palm-tree) *had dates which had become coloured.* (T.) — لَوَّنَ فِي الكَلَامِ [*He varied in speech*]. (Sgh, Ḳ, voce تَمَطَّطَ.)

5. تَلَوَّنَ *It became coloured.* (MA, KL.) See 1.

— *It became variegated*, or *diversified in colour*. — And hence, (see تغوّل,) *It varied in state*, or *condition; it was*, or *became, variable therein. He assumed various forms*, or *appearances*. — تَلَوَّنَ فُلَانٌ *Such a one varied in disposition*. (Mṣb.)

لَوْنٌ *Colour*: (Ṣ, Mṣb, Ḳ:) *distinctive quality* or *property*: (M, Ḳ:) *sort*, or *species*: (Ṣ, Ḳ:) *mood, disposition*, or *character*.

أَلْوَانُ الأَطْعِمَةِ [*Sorts*, or *species, of viands*]. (Ṣ in art. بأج.)

مُتَلَوِّنٌ *Varying*, or *variable, in dispositions*. — *Unsteady in disposition*. (Ḳ.)

لوى

1. لَوَى عَلَيْهِ *He waited for him*. (Mṣb.) — مَرَّ لَا يَلْوِى عَلَى أَحَدٍ *He went along, not pausing nor waiting for any one*. (Mṣb.) See the Ḳur-án, iii. 147. — لَوَاهُ بِدَيْنِهِ *i. q.* مَطَلَهُ. (Ṣ, Mṣb, Ḳ.) — لَوَى *He twisted* a thing; *turned* or *wreathed* it *round or about*: *contorted* it: *wound* it: *curled* it: *curved* it: or *bent* it. (Ḳ, &c.) And *He*, or *it, turned him* from his course; *made him to deviate*, or *swerve*. — لَوَى عَلَيْهِ *He went round it*, or *round about it*. (Bḍ, in liii. 20.) — لَوَى عَلَيْهِ أَمْرَهُ [*He made his case*, or *affair, difficult and intricate to him*: see إِلْتَوَى عَلَيْهِ]. (Ṣ, Ḳ, art. عوص.) — لَوَى خَبَرَهُ, † *He concealed his information*. (T, TA.) And لَوَى أَمْرَهُ عَنِّى ‡ *He concealed his affair from me*. (Ḳ, TA.)

4. أَلْوَى بِالكَلَامِ *He distorted, wrested*, or *wrung, the language*. (M, Ḳ.) [Hence, perhaps, فُلَانٌ يُلْوِى بِخَصْمِهِ, if the verb be correctly thus: see عُقْمِىٌّ, last sentence.]

5. تَلَوَّى *It twisted*, or *coiled, itself*: (KL:) *it became twisted*, or *coiled*: one says, تَلَوَّتِ الحَيَّةُ. (MA.) — تَلَوَّى مِنْ وَجَعِ الضَّرْبِ [*He writhed by reason of the pain of beating*]. (M, A, Ḳ, art. ضور.)

6. يَتَلَاوَيَانِ said of two serpents [*They twist together*]: see عَقَامٌ, last sentence.

8. إِلْتَوَى, neuter verb, *It twisted: wound: bent*. (Ḳ, &c.) — إِلْتَوَى عَلَيْهِ *It* (an affair) *became difficult*; or *difficult and intricate*. (TA.) — اِلْتَوَتْ عَلَىَّ حَاجَتِى *My want became difficult of attainment*. (TA.) — التوى عليه also *He acted*, or *behaved, perversely towards him*.

لِوَآءٌ *A banner*, or *standard*, syn. عَلَمٌ, (M, Mgh, Ḳ,) *of a commander*, (T,) or *of an army, less than the* رَايَة, *being a strip of cloth, twisted*, or *wound, and tied to a spear-shaft*. (Mgh.) See رِفَادَةٌ. Respecting the لِوَآء of the Kaabeh, see سَدَنَ and فَادَةٌ.

سَوَّآءُ لَوَّآءُ : see art. سوى.

اللَّوَا occurs in poetry for اللَّوَاتِى. (TA in art. شرف.)

أَلْوَى *Very contentious*. (Ḳ.) See an ex. voce مُسْتَمِرٌّ.

ليس

أَلْيَسُ : see the latter part of art. أَلَّا.

ليغ

1. لَاغَ, aor. يَلَاغُ, inf. n. لَيْغٌ : see an ex. in a verse cited voce تَزَنَّدَ.

ليف

لِيفٌ [The *membranous fibres that grow at the base of the branches of the palm-tree*:] the best sort is the لِيف of the cocoa-nut. (TA.) See شَرِيغٌ. — لِيف is used by Ibn-Muḳbil as meaning † *A she-camel's tail*. (TA in arts. شذب and شمل.)

ليق

1. مَا يَلِيقُ بِهِ *It is not suitable to him, does not befit him*, that he should do such a thing. (Mṣb.)

ليك

لَيْكَا, [i. e. لَيْكَ with an adjunct alif for the sake of the rhyme,] for إِلَيْكَ : see art. إِلَى, near the end.

ليل

لَيْلٌ : see نَهَارٌ. — بَنَاتُ اللَّيْلِ *Wishes*: (T, TA in art. بنى:) and *anxieties*. (TA ibid.) — إِبْنُ اللَّيْلِ *The thief*, or *robber*: (T in art. بنى:) and *the wayfarer*, or *traveller*. (Er-Rághib in TA in that art.) — أَخُو اللَّيْلِ *A nightfarer*: see a verse cited voce عَدَسَ.

لَيْلَةٌ *A night-journey*, or *night's journey*. — كَانَ كَذَا وَكَذَا ; and رَأَيْتُ اللَّيْلَةَ فِى مَنَامِى اللَّيْلَةَ ; and مَا أَشْبَهَ اللَّيْلَةَ بِالبَارِحَةِ : see above, p. 183 *a*.

أُمُّ لَيْلَى *Wine*: لَيْلَى signifying النَّشْوَةُ. (T in art. ام.)

نَهِرٌ لَيْلِىٌّ : see نَهِرٌ.

لَيَالٍ is pl. of لَيْلَاةٌ. (TA, voce أَرْضٌ.)

مُلَايَلَةٌ from اللَّيْلُ is like مُيَاوَمَةٌ from اليَوْمُ, and مُشَاهَرَةٌ from الشَّهْرُ, &c. (TA in art. ربع.)

لين

1. لَانَ, inf. n. لِينٌ [not لَيْنٌ as in the CḲ] and لَيَانٌ, (T, Ṣ, M, Ḳ,) *contr. of* خَشُنَ; (Ṣ, Ḳ in art. خشن, and TḲ;) *It was*, or *became, soft, as opposed to rough* or *harsh*; *smooth*; *plain*; *without asperities*; *fine to the touch*; *delicate*; *tender*; *supple*; *lithe*; *limber*; *pliant*; *pliable*; *flexible*; *ductile*; *malleable*; *soft*, or *flabby*; *lax*: and *he was*, or *became, soft*; *tender*; *pliant*; *gentle*; *bland*; or *mild*. Hence لَانَ جَانِبُهُ : see لَيِّنٌ. — لَانَ بَطْنُهُ *His bowels became relaxed*. — لَانَ *He relented*.

3. لَايَنَهُ بِالقَوْلِ *He soothed, coaxed*, or *wheedled, him with words*. (L, art. مسح.) — لَايَنَهُ [*He acted gently towards him*; (M, Ḳ;) *treated him with gentleness*, or *blandishment*; *soothed him*; *coaxed him*; *wheedled him*;] i. q. دَارَاهُ. (Ṣ, M, Mṣb, voce داراه.) — لَايَنَهُ *He was soft, tender, gentle, bland*, or *mild, towards him*. (M, Ḳ.)

4. أَلَانَ بَطْنَهُ [*It relaxed his bowels*]; said of medicine. (Ḳ in art. سهل.)

10. إِسْتَلَانَ : see its contr. استخشن.

لَانَ for الآنَ : see the latter in art. اين.

لِينُ العَيْشِ *Softness, delicateness*, or *easiness, of life*.

لِينَةٌ applied to *a palm-tree*: see art. لون; and see عَجْوَةٌ.

لَيِّنٌ — عَيْشٌ لَيِّنٌ *Soft, delicate*, or *easy, life*. — لَيِّنُ الجَانِبِ : see جَانِبٌ. — لَيِّنُ الأَعْطَافِ ; &c.: see art. عطف.

مُلَيِّنٌ A *lenitive*, or *laxative*, medicine.

ليه

لَاهُمَّ : see اللّٰهُ, and الحَمْدُ لَاهِ : and لَاهِ أَنْتَ : and art. ليه in the Ṣ; and see an ex. of لَاهُمَّ voce شَادِخَةٌ.

م

مَ for the interrogative مَا immediately following a prep.: see مَا in the Ṣ, Ḳ; and إِلَى last sentence. — مِ for مِنْ: see an ex., from a poet, voce رُبَّ. — مُ: see أَيْمُنُ اللّٰهِ &c.: see مُ ٱللّٰهِ. — مُ for أُمّ: see the latter.

مَا when following كُلّ or إِنَّ or أَيْنَ or أَنَّى, if having the signification of ٱلَّذِى, is written separately. (El-Ḥareeree, in De Sacy's Anthol. Gram. Ar., p. 67 of the Ar. text.) — مَا added to certain adverbial nouns is not merely redundant, but gives to them a conditional and general signification; as in أَيْنَمَا *Wherever;* and حَيْثُمَا *Wherever,* and *whenever;* &c.: see Ḳur, ii. 143, 145, &c.: and see De Sacy's Gram., i. 537 and 538. — مَا *While;* as in مَا دُمْتُ حَيًّا: and *as much as;* see Ḳur, lxiv. 16. — بِمَا *Because* بِمَا كَانُوا يَفْسُقُونَ *Because they did transgress;* or *for that they did transgress.* (Ḳur.) — مَعَ خَيْرٍ, for خَيْرٍ. See إِنَّكَ مَا وَخَيْرًا. — مَا is also added to a noun to denote the littleness of that which is signified by the noun; as in أَرْبٌ مَّا *Some little want.* (IAth in TA, art. ارب.) — مَا in أَمَّا and إِمَّا (of which latter إِمَّا لَا is an instance) I have mentioned in arts. أَمَّا and إِمَّا. — مَا أَنْتَ: see بَلَغَ: see بَالِغًا مَا بَلَغَ. — مَا أَنْتَ [*What art thou?*] means *what are thy qualities,* or *attributes?* (Ḥar, p. 155.) — مَا رَبُّ ٱلْعَالَمِينَ, in the Ḳur, xxvi. 22, means أَىُّ شَىْءٍ هُوَ. (Jel.) See also an ex. voce فِى. — مَا لَكَ signifies أَىُّ شَىْءٍ ثَبَتَ لَكَ (IbrD) and may be rendered *What aileth thee?* — شَىْءٌ مَّا *Some particular thing: something.* (See إِيهِ.) Also, *Any particular thing?* (IbrD.) See an ex. cited voce صَبَاحٌ. — فَتًى مَّا فُلَانٌ *An excellent youth is such a one.* (IbrD.) See Kull, p. 336. See also Bḍ, middle p. 42. — مَا is sometimes put for مَا دَامُوا, مَا دَامَ, and the like; i.e. *As long as:* see an ex. voce كَانَ, and التَّرْكُ, and جَلَّ. — ٱلشَّكْلُ إِلَى ٱلطُّولِ مَا هُوَ *The form inclines somewhat to length;* agreeably with a rendering voce عُقْرٌ: see De Sacy's Gr., sec. ed., i. 543 and 539: see also شَىْءٌ مَّا above: in the Ḳur xxxviii. 23, مَا is redundant, (Bḍ,) denoting vagueness and wonder, (Ksh, Bḍ,) or a corroborative of fewness: (Jel:) it means *somewhat* whether great or little in degree or importance. — مَا, the negative particle, followed by a pret., often requires the latter to be rendered in English by the preterperfect: ex. مَا رَأَيْتُهُ مُذْ يَوْمَانِ *I have not seen him for two days.* See De Sacy's Anthol. Gram. Ar., p. 253.

مأق

مَأْقٌ and مُؤْقٌ and مَأْقِى: see مَأْوِى.

مَأْقَةٌ *A sobbing;* i.e. *an affection like what is termed* فُوَاق, *as though it were breath heaved from the chest, on an occasion of weeping,* and *of being choked with weeping.* (Ṣ, Ḳ.)

مأن

1. مَأَنَهُمْ *He sustained them; bore the burden of,* or *undertook, their maintenance; he maintained them.* (Ṣ, Ḳ, arts. مأن and مون.) — مَأَنَ ٱلْقَوْمَ and مَأَنَهُمْ ♦ *He maintained,* or *sustained, the people,* or *party.* (M.)

2: see 1.

مَأْنَةٌ of the belly: see جَانِبَةٌ. — ٱلْمَأْنَتَانِ of the hump of a camel: see قَمَحْدُوَةٌ.

مَؤُونَةٌ *i. q.* قُوتٌ [*Food,* &c.]; (M;) a dial. var. of مَؤُونَةٌ ♦ (q.v.); as also مُونَةٌ: pl. مُؤَنٌ. (Mṣb.)

مَئِنَّةٌ: see art. ان, where will be found the explanations of this word given in the Ṣ and Ḳ in art. مأن.

مَؤُونَةٌ *A weight,* or *burden.* (Mgh, Mṣb.) See مِثْقَالٌ. — *Trouble, molestation,* or *embarrassment;* as also ♦ مُؤْنَةٌ: pl. of the former مَؤُونَاتٌ; and of the latter مُؤَنٌ. (MA.) — The *requisite means of subsistence.* (KL.) — مَؤُونَةُ ٱلْجِمَاعِ: see زَافِنَةٌ: it seems to mean *the pudendum muliebre considered as the means of* جِمَاع.

ماه

مَاهِيَّةٌ [The *quiddity,* or *essence,* or *substance,* of a thing;] *that whereby a thing is what it is.* (KT.) See also حَقِيقَةٌ, and جَوْهَرٌ, and ذَاتِيَّةٌ, and مَعْنًى.

مَيْهُنٌ: see بَنِينٌ, voce سَنَةٌ, in art. سنه.

مأى

1. مَأَى (like مَاءَ) *It* (a cat) *mewed.* (TA, voce مَاءَ, art. موأ.)

متع

1. مَتَعَ ٱلنَّهَارُ *The day became advanced, the sun being high,* (Ṣ, Ḳ,) *before the declining of the sun from the meridian.* (Ḳ.)

2. مَتَّعَهُ *He* (God) *made him to live.* (Bḍ in xi. 3.) — See مَلًّا. — مَتَّعَهَا *He gave her a gift after divorce.* (Ḳ.) And مَتَّعَهَا بِكَذَا *He gave her* (a divorced wife) *such a thing.* (Mṣb.)

5. تَمَتَّعَ بِهِ ♦ and ٱسْتَمْتَعَ ♦ and إِمْتَتَعَ are syn., signifying إِنْتَفَعَ بِهِ زَمَانًا طَوِيلًا; (Ḥam, p. ٣١٣;) [*He benefited,* or *profited by it; had the benefit, use,* or *enjoyment, of it; he enjoyed it;* accord. to the above authority, *for a long time;* but this restriction is not always meant.] You say, ٱسْتَمْتَعْتُ بِٱصْطِبَاحِ خَمْرٍ [*I enjoyed the drinking a morning-draught of wine*]: and بِٱلْإِصْغَآءِ إِلَى أَغَانِى جَارِيَةٍ [*the listening to the songs of a girl*].

(Mo'allaḳát, p. 169.) — تَمَتَّعَ *He became provided with* مَتَاع, *or utensils and furniture for the house, or tent.* (TA, voce تَبَتَّتَ, q. v.) — تَمَتَّعَ بِهِ i. q. عَاشَ. (Bḍ, Jel, xi. 68.) — تَمَتَّعَ generally signifies *He enjoyed it:* (MA:) so in many cases in the Ḳur, &c.

8: see 5.

10. إِسْتَمْتَعَ بِكَذَا, and † تَمَتَّعَ, *He benefited* or *profited by such a thing.* (Mṣb.) — See 5. — مُسْتَمْتَع: see مُلْبِس.

مُتْعَةٌ *Enjoyment;* a subst. in the sense of تَمَتُّع; (Ṣ, Mṣb, Ḳ;) syn. نَعْمَةٌ. (Jel, xlvi. 26.) See an ex., in a verse of Lebeed, voce فَرْطٌ. — مُتْعَةٌ *A gift to a divorced wife.* (Mṣb, Ḳ.) See أَوْلَيَا. — متعة الضُّحَى [i. e. مُتْعَة ?] i. q. مَتَاع. (TA voce فِيقَة, in art. فوق.)

مَتَاعٌ *Anything useful* or *advantageous;* as *goods:* such as the *utensils and furniture of a house or tent, or household-goods: any utensils,* or *apparatus: chattels: a commodity,* and *commodities;* (Mgh, &c.;) generally best rendered *goods, chattels, household-goods or chattels,* or *utensils and furniture.* — المَتَاعُ [signifies ‡ الفَرْجُ;] *a woman's pudendum:* (TA:) [see مُتَوَهِّجَة, in art. وهج: and] the *penis.* (Mgh.) — مَتَاعٌ also applies to *Food,* the *necessaries of life:* see two exs. voce حَفَفٌ. — مَتَاعٌ for a divorced wife, *A provision of necessaries, such as food and clothing and household-utensils* or *furniture:* see عُرْفٌ, and Bḍ in ii. 242: *i. q.* تَمْتِيعٌ. (Bḍ in ii. 237.) — مَتَاعٌ *i. q.* مَا يُتَمَتَّعُ بِهِ, and الإِسْتِمْتَاعُ; (Jel in iv. 79;) generally best rendered *Enjoyment,* in the Ḳur iv. 79 and ix. 38 and similar cases. See مُتْعَة.

متن

2. مَتَّنَهُ, inf. n. تَمْتِينٌ, *He made it,* or *rendered it, strong, stout, firm,* or *hard.* (TA.) — مَتَّنَ *He seasoned a skin with rob, or inspissated juice* (رُبّ). (Ḳ.)

مَتْنُ الظَّهْرِ is *The erector spinæ muscle, which consists of the sacro-lumbalis and longissimus dorsi and spinalis dorsi.* The مَتْنٌ is The *back:* (M, Mṣb:) or, as also † مَتْنَةٌ, (M,) or مَتْنَانِ, (T,) *two portions of firmly-bound flesh between which is the back-bone,* [or *that confine the back-bone,*] *rendered firm by being tied* (مَعْلُوبَتَانِ) *with,* or *by,* عَقَب [or *sinews,*] (T, M,) or the مَتْنَانِ are *the two sides of the back.* (M.) — مَتْنَا الظَّهْرِ *The two portions of flesh and sinew next the back-bone, on each side.* (Ṣ.) — مَتْنٌ [The *broad side,* or the *middle of the broad side, of the blade,* of a sword;] *the part in the middle of which is the* [*ridge called*] عَمُود, (En-Naḍr, in L, voce عَمُود,) or the *part in which is the* [*ridge called*] شُطْبَة, (Ḳ, voce سَفْسَقَة,) and شَطِيبَة, and عَمُود: (Ḳ, voce عَمُود:) or the *ridge* [*itself*] (عَيْر) *rising in the middle of a sword.* (T.) — مَتْنٌ The *hard and outer* or *apparent part* of anything: pl. مُتُونٌ and مِتَانٌ. (M.) — مَتْنٌ The *middle* of a bow, and of a spear. (Munjid of Kr.) — مَتْنٌ: see عَيْر. — مَتْنُ أُذُنِ الفَرَسِ The *part between two poles of a* بَيْت, or tent. (AZ in TA, art. ربع.) — مَتْنٌ *Elevated, and level, or plain, ground:* (M:) or *hard and elevated ground.* (Ṣ, Mṣb, Ḳ.) — مَتْنُ الفَرَسِ *One of the four bright stars in Pegasus, that* (a) *at the extremity of the neck:* see الفَرْغُ. — مَتْنٌ *i. q.* حَدِيثٌ and خَبَرٌ and أَثَرٌ, *A tradition of Mohammad, or of another, namely a companion of Mohammad, &c.* (IbrD.)

مَتْنَة: see مَتْنٌ.

مَتِينٌ *Strong; stout; firm; hard.* (Ṣ, Ḳ, Mṣb.) [*Well seasoned. Possessing any quality in a strong degree.*]

أَمْتَنُ حَلَاوَةً, *i. q.* أَشَدُّ حَلَاوَةً, *More sweet.* (TA, voce حَمْتٌ.)

تِمْتِينٌ: see تِمْتَانٌ.

تِمْتِينٌ (a subst., properly speaking, like تَنْبِيبٌ, q. v.) and † تِمْتَانٌ The *threads, or strings, of tents.* (Ḳ.)

متى

مَتَى signifies *When?* and *when* used to denote a condition: see أَنَّى and أَيْنَ. — حَتَّى مَتَى *Until when? how long?* and also *until the time when.* See Freytag's Arab. Prov. i. 382.

مثل

1. مَثَلَ aor. ـُ, inf. n. مُثُولٌ; (Ṣ, M, Ḳ, &c.;) and مَثُلَ; (M, Ḳ;) *He stood erect;* (Ṣ, M, Ḳ, &c.;) بَيْنَ يَدَيْهِ *before him.* (Ṣ, &c.) — مَثَلَ بِهِ, inf. n. مُثْلَةٌ, *He mutilated him; castrated him;* namely, a sheep or goat. (TA in art. دهن, from a trad.)

2. مَثَّلَ: see a verse of Kutheiyir in art. ورد, conj. 4. — مَثَّلَهُ: see شَبَّهَهُ.

3. مَاثَلَهُ *i. q.* شَابَهَهُ. (TA.)

4. أَمْثَلَهُ *He set it up:* from مَثَلَ "he stood erect." — *He set up* a butt or mark: see an ex. voce غَرَضٌ.

5. تَمَثَّلَ بِكَذَا [*He affected to be like, or imitated, such a thing;*] *i. q.* تَشَبَّهَ بِهِ. (TA, art. شبه.) — تَمَثَّلَ البَيْتَ and [more commonly] بِالبَيْتِ *He used,* or *applied, the verse as a proverb,* or *proverbially.* (MA.) — See تَشَبَّهَ.

6. تَمَاثَلَ *He became nearly in a sound,* or *healthy, state;* or *near to convalescence:* (Ḳ:) or *he became more like the sound,* or *healthy, than the unsound,* or *unhealthy, who is suffering from a chronic and pervading disease;* (TA;) or so تماثل لِلْبُرْءِ. (M.) Said also of a wound: (T, Ṣ in art. دمل:) and of a disease; like أَشْكَلَ. (TA, art. شكل.) — تَمَاثَلَا *i. q.* تَشَابَهَا. (M, Ḳ in art. سوى.)

8. إِمْتَثَلَ أَمْرَهُ *He followed his command, order, bidding,* or *injunction; did like as he commanded, ordered, &c.;* (Mgh;) *he obeyed his command, order, &c.* (Mṣb.)

مِثْلٌ *A like; a similar person* or *thing; match; fellow; an analogue.* (Ḳ, &c.) See نِدٌّ and voce بَدَلٌ. — *A likeness, resemblance,* or *semblance;* see شِبْهٌ. — *An equivalent; a requital.* — مِثْلَ, used as a denotative of state, means *Like.* Ex. مَرَّ مِثْلَ البَرْقِ *He passed like the lightning.* See an ex. in the Ḳur li. 23; and another, from Ṣakhr-el-Gheí, voce قَرْضٌ.

مَثَلٌ *i. q.* صِفَةٌ [as meaning *A description, condition, state, case, &c.*]; (Ṣ, Ḳ, &c.;) or وَصْفٌ [meaning the same]: (Mṣb:) or this is a mistake: (Mbr, AAF, TA:) or it may be a tropical signification: (MF, TA:) for in the language of the Arabs it means *a description by way of comparison:* (AAF, TA:) you say مثل زيد مثل فلان [*The description of Zeyd, by way of comparison,* or *the condition, &c., is that of such a one*]: it is from المِثَالُ and الحَذْوُ: (Mbr, TA:) it is metaphorically applied to *a condition, state,* or *case,* that is important, strange, or wonderful. (Ksh, Bḍ in ii. 16.) The phrase here given is more literally, and better, rendered, *The similitude of Zeyd is the similitude,* or *is that, of such a one;* for a similitude is a description by way of comparison. — You say also, جَعَلَهُ مَثَلًا لِكَذَا [*He made it* (an expression or the like) *to be descriptive, by way of comparison, of such a thing*]. (TA passim.) [And مَثَلُ كَذَا means *An expression denoting, by way of similitude, such a thing.*] — عَلَى المَثَلِ *As indicative of resemblance* to something. — See بَدَلٌ.

مِثَالٌ *Quality, mode, manner, fashion,* and *form;* (Mṣb;) *a model according to which another thing is made or proportioned; a pattern,* (مِقْدَار) *by which a thing is measured, proportioned, or cut out:* (T:) *an example of a class* of words, of a rule, &c. — مِنْ غَيْرِ سَبْقِ مِثَالٍ [*Without there having been any precedent*]. (Mṣb in art. قرح, &c.) — [*A bed:*] بَنَاتُ المِثَالِ *The daughters of the bed*; meaning *women*. (T in art. بنى.)

جوز مائل : see جوز.

تَمَاثِيلُ, in the following hemistich of Ibn-Aḥmar,

تَمَاثِيلُ قِرْطَاسٍ عَلَى هَبْهَبِيَّةٍ

signifies كُتُبٌ يَكْتُبُونَهَا. (L, in TA, voce هَبْهَبِىٌّ, as signifying a "light, or active," camel.)

مجر

1. مَجَرَ, app. an imitative sequent to فَجَرَ. See دعر.

مجل

1. مَجِلَتْ يَدُهُ *His hand became blistered,* or *vesicated, by much work.* (Mgh.)

مجمج

مَجْمَجَةٌ : see جَمْجَمَ and جَخْجَخَ.

مجن

1. مَجَنَ *He cared not for what he did* (Ṣ, Mgh, Ḳ*) *nor for what was said to him.* (Mgh, Ḳ.*) The epithet is مَاجِنٌ. (Ṣ, Mgh, Ḳ.)

عُقْبَةٌ مَجُونٌ [*A stage of a journey, or a march or journey from one halting-place to another,*] *that is far, or distant, or long.* (ISk in TA, voce بَاسِطَةٌ : but it is not quite clear in my copy of the TA whether it be مَجُونٌ or هَجُونٌ.)

مَجَّانٌ The *gift of a thing without price.* (IF, Mṣb.) — فَعَلْتُهُ مَجَّانًا *I did it without compensation.* (Mṣb.) هٰذَا الشَّىْءُ لَهُ مَجَّانًا *This thing is for him without an equivalent.* (El-Fárábee, Mṣb.)

مَاجِنٌ : see 1.

مجنق

1. مَجْنَقُوا : see art. جنق.

محت

مَحْتٌ and مَحْتَةٌ : see أَبْتٌ.

محق

1. مَحَقَ, aor. ـَ, inf. n. مَحْقٌ, *He rendered a* thing *deficient, and deprived it of its blessing, or increase:* or [*he annihilated, annulled,* or *obliterated,* it;] *he did away with* it *wholly, so that no trace thereof remained.* (Mṣb.) — أَعْمَدُ مِنْ كَيْلِ مُحِقٍّ, or مُحِقٍ : see عَمَدَ.

2: see 1.

الدُّعْمَاءُ, دَأْدَاءٌ : see لَيَالِى المُحَاقِ and.

محل

4. أَمْحَلَتِ النُّجُومُ *The stars set aurorally and brought no rain.* (Ṣ, Ḳ* in art. خوى.)

5. تَمَحَّلْتُ مَالًا بِغَيْرِ ثَمَنٍ *I laboured to acquire property without price:* (Mṣb:) or, accord. to Az, تَمَحَّلَ مَالًا means *he laboured,* and *exercised art* or *management, in seeking* [*to acquire*] *property.* (TA.) See also تَعَلَّتْ.

مَحْلٌ *Drought,* or *suspension of rain,* (Ṣ, Ḳ, Mṣb in art. جدب,) *and dryness of the earth* (Ṣ, Mṣb ubi suprà) *depriving it of herbage;* (Ṣ, TA;) and *i. q.* جَدْبٌ. (Ḳ.)

مَحَالَةٌ : see art. حول ; and see also فَوْهَاةٌ voce فَوْقَاةٌ , أَفْوَقُ voce أُفُوه, and قَبٌّ.

لَبَنٌ مُمَحَّلٌ *Sour milk upon which much fresh is milked:* see قَارِصٌ.

مُتَمَاحِلٌ : see وَدَاخٌ.

محن

مِحْنَةٌ *A trial,* (Ṣ, Mṣb, Ḳ,) or *trying affliction:* (Ṣ:) pl. مِحَنٌ. (Mṣb.)

مَحُونَةٌ (not مُحُونَةٌ): see art. حين.

محو

1. مَحَاهُ *He effaced, erased, rased, obliterated,* or *cancelled, it; removed,* or *did away with, its impression* or *trace.* (Ḳ.) — مَحَتِ الرِّيحُ السَّحَابَ *The wind made to pass away,* or *dispelled, the clouds.* (TA.) — مَحَا الصُّبْحُ اللَّيْلَ *Daybreak dispelled the night.* (TA.) — مَحَا اللّٰهُ عَنْهُ الأَسْقَامَ وَالذُّنُوبَ [*God removed from him diseases and sins; as though He cancelled them*]. (Mṣb in art. عفو.) — الإِحْسَانُ يَمْحُو الإِسَآءَةَ *Beneficence effaces, obliterates,* or *cancels, evil conduct.* (TA.)

مدن

مَيْدَانٌ : see art. ميد.

هُوَ ٱبْنُ مَدِينَتِهَا, said of a skilful guide: see بَجْدَةٌ.

مده

1. مَدَهَ : see مَدَحَ.

مدى

6. تَمَادَى فِى غَيِّهِ *He persevered in his error.* (Mṣb.)

مَدًى *The utmost extent, term, limit,* or *reach,* of a thing; syn. غَايَةٌ : (Ṣ, Mṣb, Ḳ:) *an extent, a distance; a space, an interval;* syn. مَسَافَةٌ : [meaning *a space that is,* or *that is to be, traversed*] and hence used in the sense before explained because extending to a غاية : (Z, in the Fáïḳ, quoted in the TA:) *a goal.* (The Lexicons passim.)

مُدْيَةٌ *A butcher's knife.* (Mgh.) See سِكِّينٌ.

مذق

مَذُوقٌ Milk *mixed with much water.* (TA in art. فضخ.)

مَمْذُوقُ النِّقْىِ [*Having diluted marrow*]; applied to a soft, or flabby, camel. (O, Ḳ in art. رك.) — عَيْشٌ مَمْذُوقٌ † *A turbid life.* (TA in art. سمر.)

مذقر

Q. 4. اِمْذَقَرَّتِ الإِبِلُ *The camels became dispersed.* (TA in art. صعر.)

مذى

4. أَمْذَى *Humorem tenuem e pene emisit* vir *propter lusum amatorium vel osculum.* (Mṣb, &c.)

مَذْىٌ *Humor tenuis qui propter lusum amatorium vel osculum e pene virili effluit; a discharge of a thin humour from the* ذَكَر, *occasioned by amorous toying* or *by kissing:* [app. *the prostatic fluid; a discharge from the prostate gland.*] (Ṣ, Mṣb, &c.)

مَذَّآءٌ app., Is *qui multum passus est seminis effluxum ex contactu feminæ aut osculo.* See مَزْكُوتٌ. See also أَمْذَى.

مَاذِىٌّ *Honey:* (Ḳ:) or *white honey:* (Ṣ, M:) or *fine,* or *thin, white honey.* (AA, TA.)

مر

مَرٌّ *A spade;* [so in the present day;] syn. مِسْحَاةٌ ; (M, Ḳ;) *with which one works in land of seed-produce:* (M and Ḳ, voce بَالٌ :) or the *handle thereof:* (M, Ḳ;) and in like manner, *of the* مِحْرَاثٌ [app. here meaning *fire-shovel*]: (M:) [see سِخِّينٌ] the *thing with which one works in earth,* or *mud.* (Ṣgh, TA.)

مُرَيْرَآءُ *An anæsthetic herb:* see سَكْرَةٌ.

مرز

مَرْزٌ [an inf. n.] *i. q.* غَمْزٌ; as also لَمْزٌ. (Fr in TA, art. لمز.)

مرس

مَرَاسَةٌ [*A wooden rake* or *harrow*:] *i.q.* مَلَاسَةٌ. (TA, art. صلع.)

مرطوط

مِرْطَرَاطٌ [*A sweet food*:] *i. q.* فَالُوذٌ; as also بِرْطَرَاطٌ. (TA in art. زع.)

مرع

1\. مَرُعَ and ♦أَمْرَعَ *It* (a valley) *abounded with herbage.* (Ṣ, Mṣb, Ḳ.)

4 : see 1.

مُرَعٌ, the bird so called: see an ex. voce بَلَغَ.

مرغ

2\. مَرَّغَ *He rolled,* or *turned over,* a beast of carriage, in the dust. (Ḳ.) —— مَرَّغَ *He smeared, seasoned, imbued,* or *soaked,* a mess of ثَرِيد, *with grease,* or *gravy,* or *dripping*; *i.q.* رَوَّغَ, and دَسَّمَ, and سَغْبَلَ. (TA in art. روغ.)

3\. مَارَغَهُ [*He rolled with him upon the ground,* or *in the dust*]; said of a man after his wrestling with another. (TA in art. رسغ.) See 3, in that art.

مرق

8\. اِمْتَرَقَ *He drew* a sword from its scabbard. (TA, voce اِهْتَلَبَ; and voce اِعْتَقَّ.)

مَرْقُ الإِهَابِ *The burying of the skin,* or *hide, in the earth, so that its hair may be removed, and it may become ready for tanning.* (Ḳ,* TA in art. افق.) See also فَلَقَ.

مَرَقٌ in grapes: see سُكَّرٌ. —— مَرَقٌ *Broth; gravy-soup;* and *any decoction.*

سَهْمٌ مَارِقٌ *An arrow of which the whole has passed through the animal at which it is shot.* (A, art. مرد.) See صَارِدٌ, and مُغْتَلِمٌ.

مُرَيْقٌ: see دُرِّىٌّ. —— مُرَيْقٌ in the Ḳ is a mistake for مُرَيْقٌ. (TA.) See also عُلَيْقٌ, in art. علو, in which مُرَيْقَةٌ is mentioned as the n. un.

مَمْرَقٌ *A kind of small lantern in the roof of a chamber, for the admission of air, generally octagonal, the sides of wooden lattice-work, and the top a cupola; a sky-light; any kind of window or aperture in a roof.*

مرن

1\. مَرَنَ *It was,* or *became smooth,* (Ṣ, M, Ḳ,) *with a degree of hardness.* (M, Ḳ.) Said of a camel's foot: see أَسْحَقَ. —— مَرَنَ عَلَى شَىْءٍ *He became accustomed, habituated,* or *inured, to a thing.* (Ḳ.)

2\. مَرَّنَهُ *He made it soft,* or *smooth,* لَيَّنَ. (Mṣb.)

مَارِنٌ The [*soft,* or *cartilagenous*] *part of the nose, beneath,* or *exclusive of, the bone.* (Zj, in his "Khalḳ el-Insán:" and the like is said in the Ṣ and Mṣb, and partially in the Ḳ.)

مرى

1\. الرِّيحُ تَمْرِى السَّحَابَ and ♦تَمْتَرِيهِ *The wind draws forth the clouds.* (M, TA.) See an ex. in a verse cited voce عَزْلَآءُ.

3\. مَارَاهُ, inf. n. مُمَارَاةٌ and مِرَآءٌ, *i. q.* جَادَلَهُ; (Ṣ, Ḳ;*) *He disputed with him,* or *did so obstinately, &c.*: (TA:) it is only *in opposing* [what has been said; not in commencing a disputation]. (Mṣb.)

6\. التَّمَارِى *The disputing,* or *contending, together.* (TA.) You say, هُمَا يَتَمَارَيَانِ بِالشِّعْرِ [*They two dispute,* or *contend, together, with verses* or *poetry*]. (TA in art. بده.)

8\. اِمْتَرَى *He doubted,* به *of it.* (Ḳur, xliii. 61.) —— See 1.

10\. اِسْتَمْرَأَتْهُ for اِسْتَمْرَتِ الإِبِلُ الحَمْضَ : see 1 in art. عدن.

مُرْوٌ *A certain plant*: see خَافُورٌ, and حَبَقٌ, and فَاخُورٌ.

مزر

مَزِيرٌ *Strong-hearted.* (Ṣ.) So I have rendered the fem. (with ة) in explaining بَلْهَآءُ: it seems there to mean *bold.*

مزق

2\. مَزَّقَ † *He scattered,* or *dispersed.* (Ḳur, xxxiv, 18; and Expos. of the Jeláleyn.) —— [مَزَّقَ, used tropically, may sometimes be rendered † *He mangled, rent much,* or *dissundered*; but more generally, † *he,* or *it, shattered, disorganized,* or *dissipated*; or † *he,* or *it, marred,* or *impaired*; being opposed to أَصْلَحَ, or to رَقَعَ or رَقَّعَ, in the sense of أَصْلَحَ, as in an ex. cited voce رَقَعَ; sometimes several of these renderings will be found to be appropriate in a single instance. You say, مَزَّقَ عِرْضَهُ † *He mangled, rent,* or *shattered,* or *marred, his honour,* or *reputation.* And مَزَّقَ عَقْلَهُ, and رَأْيَهُ, and أَمْرَهُ, † *It shattered,* or *disorganized* or *dissipated,* or *it marred* or *impaired, his intellect,* and *his judgment,* and *his state of affairs* or *circumstances.*] —— مَزَّقَهُ *He rent it,* or *tore it, much;* or *in several,* or *many, places. mangled,* or *dissundered, it*; and *cut it much*; &c. (TA.)

5\. تَمَزَّقَ عَلَيْهِ عَقْلُهُ † [*His intellect became shattered,* or *dissipated,* or *impaired*]. (TA in art. رقع.) And تَمَزَّقَ عَلَيْهِ رَأْيُهُ وَأَمْرُهُ † [*His judgment,* and *his state of affairs* or *circumstances, became shattered, disorganized, dissipated, marred,* or *impaired.* (A and TA in art. رقع.) See مَزَّقَ, of which تَمَزَّقَ is quasi-pass. —— تَمَزَّقُوا † *They became scattered,* or *dispersed.* (TA.) —— تَمَزَّقَ عِرْضُهُ † *His honour,* or *reputation, became mangled, rent,* or *shattered,* or *marred.*

مَزْقٌ The *rending, tearing,* or *slitting,* a garment and the like. (JK.)

مِزْقَةٌ *A piece torn off* of a garment (Ṣ, Ḳ*) &c. (Ḳ.)

مِزَاقٌ [A she-camel] *whose skin almost becomes rent in pieces by reason of her swiftness.* (O in art. عنسق.)

مزن

مُزْنٌ *Clouds* (Ḳ, and Ḥam, p. 564) *of any kind*: (Ḥam, ibid:) or *white clouds*: (Ṣ, Ḳ, and Ḥam, p. 53:) or *clouds containing water.* (Ḳ.)

اِبْنُ مَازِنٍ *The ant.* (TA in art. بنى.)

مزو and مزى

2\. تَمْزِيَةٌ The *praising,* or *eulogizing* [another]. (Ḳ, TA.) You say, مَزَّيْتُهُ عَلَيْهِ, syn. فَضَّلْتُهُ. (IAạr, TA.)

5\. تَمَزَّيْتَ عَلَيْنَا *Thou thoughtest,* or *hast thought, thyself superior to us in excellence*: and so تَفَضَّلْتَ. (TA.)

6\. تَمَازَوْا *i.q.* تَفَاضَلُوا. (TA.)

مَزِيَّةٌ *An excellent quality; an excellence.* (Ṣ, Mṣb, Ḳ.)

مسك

1\. يَمْسِكُ الرَّمَقَ : see art. رمق.

2\. مَسَّكَ بِالنَّارِ : see ثَقَّبَ.

4\. أَمْسَكَ *He retained; he withheld.* (Mṣb.) —— *He maintained*: *he was tenacious,* or *niggardly.* —— *He,* or **it, held fast* a thing: and *arrested it.* —— أَمْسَكَهُ *He held, retained, detained,* *restrained, stayed, confined, imprisoned,* or *withheld, him.* (Ḳ.) — أَمْسَكَ عَنِ الأَمْرِ *He held, refrained,* or *abstained, from the thing.* (Mṣb.) — أَمْسَكَهُ *He grasped it, clutched it, laid hold upon it;* or *seized it,* (قَبَضَ عَلَيْهِ) بِيَدِهِ *with his hand:* (Mṣb:) or *he took it;* or *took it with his hand,* (أَخَذَهُ,) namely, a rope, &c.: (Mgh:) or *he held,* or *clung, to it:* (TA:) [as also تَمَسَّكَ ↓ بِهِ]. Also, أَمْسَكَ بِهِ signifies [*the same;* or] *he laid hold upon,* or *seized, somewhat of his body,* or *what might detain him, as an arm or a hand, or a garment, and the like:* but أَمْسَقَهُ may signify *he withheld him,* or *restrained him, from acting according to his own free will.* (Mugh, art. ب.) — أَمْسَكَ بَطْنَهُ [*It bound,* or *confined, his belly* (or *bowels*)]: said of medicine. (Ṣ, O, Mṣb, Ḳ; all in art. عقل.) — الإِمْسَاكُ, in relation to تَحْجِيل: see an unusual application of it in art. طلق, conj. 4.

5: see 4 and 8. — تَمَسَّكَ بِحَبْلِهِ *He held fast by his covenant:* see أَعْصَمَ.

6. تَمَاسَكَ *He withheld,* or *restrained, himself:* (PṢ:) *he was able,* or *powerful;* as also تَمَالَكَ, q.v. (KL.) — مَا تَمَاسَكَ أَنْ فَعَلَ كَذَا *He could not restrain himself from doing so;* syn. مَا تَمَالَكَ. (Ṣ.) — تَمَاسَكَ *It held together.* — إِنَّهُ لَذُو تَمَاسُكٍ † *Verily he possesses intelligence.* (TA.) And مَا بِهِ تَمَاسُكٌ ‡ *There is no good in him.* (TA.) See مُسْكَةٌ.

8. اِمْتَسَكَ بِهِ *He clutched,* or *griped, him,* or *it;* i.q. تَمَسَّكَ ↓ بِهِ. (MA.)

10. اِسْتَمْسَكَ البَطْنُ [*The belly* (or *bowels*) *became bound,* or *confined*]. (TA in art. عقل.) — اِسْتَمْسَكَ بِهِ [sometimes] *He sought to lay hold upon it.* (Bḍ, in ii. 257.) — اِسْتَمْسَكَ: see an ex. voce صِرْعَةٌ.

مِسْكٌ [*Musk:* it is obtained from the musk-deer, moschus moschiferus; being found in the male animal, in a vesicle near the navel and prepuce.] It is masc. and fem. (IAmb, TA voce ذَكِىّ.)

مَسَكٌ *Tortoise-shell;* syn. ذَبْلٌ: (Ḳ:) *bracelets made of tortoise-shell* (ذَبْل), or *of* عاج [*ivory*]: (Ṣ, Mṣb:) *bracelets and anklets made of horn and of* عاج: n. un. with ة. (Ḳ.)

مُسْكَةٌ *Intelligence:* (Mṣb:) or *full intelligence,* (Ḳ, TA,) *and judgment; judgment and intelligence to which one has recourse;* as also مُسْكٌ, not ↓ مَسِيكٌ, as in the Ḳ; (TA;) i.q. تَمَاسُكٌ. (Mgh.) You say, لَيْسَ لَهُ مُسْكَةٌ *He has no intelligence.* (Mṣb.) — لَيْسَ بِهِ مُسْكَةٌ *He has no strength.* (Mṣb.)

مُسْكَانٌ: see art. سكن.

مِسَاكٌ or مَسَاكٌ A kind of *needles:* see مِدَادٌ.

مَسِيكٌ: see مُسْكَةٌ.

مَسَّاكَاتٌ [in the CḲ, art. روض, written مُسَّاكَات,] *Places, in land,* or *in the ground, to which the rain-water flows, and which retain it.* (TA.) See ضَابِطَةٌ.

مُمْسَكٌ, said of a horse, *white on both fore and hind leg on the same side:* see مُحَجَّلٌ.

مُتَمَاسِكٌ *Compact in the limbs,* (TA in art. بدن,) or *flesh.* (TA in this art.)

مسل

مَسَلٌ: see مَسِيلٌ, in art. سيل.

مسى

2. مَسَّاهُ بِكَذَا *He came to him in the evening with such a thing.* (TA, voce صَبَّحَ.)

4. أَمْسَى *He entered upon the* مَسَآء. (Mṣb.) — أَمْسَى as syn. with صَارَ: see an ex. voce نَشَطَ, in a verse of Himyán, and another voce عَسَى.

مُسْىٌ: see صُبْحٌ: أَتَيْتُهُ لِمُسْىِ خَامِسَةٍ.

مَسَآءٌ *Afternoon, counted from noon to sunset:* (Az, IKooṭ, Mgh, Mṣb, TA:) or, accord. to some, *to midnight:* (TA:) *contr. of* صَبَاح: (Ṣ, Ḳ, Mṣb, &c.:) and *evening, after sunset.* (Mgh.) — أَتَيْتُهُ ذَا مَسَآءٍ [*I came to him in the evening*]. (IAạr, TA, art. صبح.) See صَبَاحٌ. — أَتَيْتُهُ صَبَاحًا مَسَآءً: see صَبَاحٌ.

أُمْسِيَّةٌ: see أُصْبُوحَةٌ.

مُمْسًى a name for the مَسَآء; and the *time thereof;* and *the place thereof;* like as مُصْبَحٌ is a name for the صَبَاح; and the time thereof; and the place thereof. (Marg. note in a copy of the Ṣ, in art. صبح.)

مُسْتَمْسَكٌ *A place,* or *thing, to lay hold of:* see مَعَضٌ.

مش

R.Q. 2. تَمَشْمَشَتِ الإِبِلُ *The camels became dispersed.* (TA in art. صعر.)

مشق

1. مَشَقَ الخَطَّ *He elongated the handwriting:* or *was quick in it.* (M.)

2. تَمْشِيقٌ The act of *lacerating much:* see an ex. voce دَحِيقٌ.

كِتَابٌ مَشْقٌ *Writing with spaces,* or *gaps, and with elongated letters;* (JK;) [or *quick,* or *hasty, writing;* (see مَشَقَ;)] *contr. of* كِتَابٌ التَّحَاسِين. (Ḳ in art. حسن.)

مِشَاقٌ *Tow; oakum.*

مُشَاقَةٌ [the *hards,* or *hurds, of flax* or *hemp* and *any similar coarse fibres:* (see سَلَبٌ:) or *tow;* i.e.] *what falls from the combing of hair* and *flax* and *the like:* (Ṣ, Ḳ:) or *what is long:* or *not cleared:* (Ḳ:) or *what remains, of flax, after combing,* that is, *after it has been drawn through the* ↓ مِمْشَقَة, [or *heckle,*] *which is a thing like a comb, whereby the best becomes cleared, the broken particles and integuments, which constitute the* مُشَاقَة, *remaining.* (Mgh.)

مُشْقٌ *A certain sea-fish.* (Ḳ, voce مُدَّجٌ: in the CḲ, مُشَّقٌ.)

مِمْشَقَةٌ: see مُشَاقَةٌ.

مَمْشُوقٌ A man *light of flesh:* (Ḳ:) a horse *lean, lank, light of flesh, slender,* or *lank in the belly.* (S.) — مَمْشُوقَةٌ A damsel *tall and slender:* (Ḳ:) *slender:* or *perfect in make, and goodly,* or *beautiful:* (Mṣb:) or *goodly,* or *beautiful, in stature.* (Ṣ.)

مشل

2. تَمْشِيلٌ: see تَفْشِيلٌ.

مشن

1. مَشَنَ الأَدِيمَ *He pared,* or *removed the superficial part of, the hide.* (TA in art. ادم.)

6. تَمَاشَنَ *He wiped his hands together:* see طَرِيَانٌ.

مُوشَانٌ: see جُرَذٌ.

تِمْشَآءٌ: see تِبْيَانٌ, voce بَيَّنَ.

مشى

1. مَشَى *He walked, went,* or *went along;* (MA, KL;) [in its primary sense] *He went any pace upon his feet, afoot,* or *on foot; he footed;* whether *quickly* or *slowly:* (Mgh, Mṣb:) *he removed from place to place at pleasure:* (Er-Rághib:) *walked; went along, marched; travelled; trod; paced; stepped.* See 5. — مَشَى also signifies *He went on,* or *continued, in his course of action,* &c. (Mughnee voce أَنْ, in explanation of this verb as used in Ḳur xxxviii. 5.) — [مَشَى] † *It* (money) *passed; was,*

or became, current. — † *It* (a calumny) *was, or became, current.* See مِشْبَرٌ. — مَشَى بَطْنُهُ [*His belly became moved, or in motion; it discharged itself.*] (Ṣ, Ḳ, art. طلق; &c.)

2: see 4.

3. مَاشَاهُ *He walked, or went on foot, with him: he kept pace with him.* See an ex. voce الأَحْصَانِ.

4. أَمْشَى الدَّوَآءُ بَطْنَهُ (A, Ḳ, art. حدر,) [*The medicine moved, or purged, his bowels; made his belly to discharge itself:*] and مَشَّى ↑ البَطْنَ. (TA, art. طوس, &c.)

5. تَمَشَّى *i. q.* مَشَى: (TA:) [or, properly, and accord. to general usage, *he walked with slow steps:* so I have rendered it voce دَلَفَ, &c.:] *he walked heavily, with an effort.* (TḲ voce تَزَحَّفَ.) [One says in the present day, خَرَجْتُ تَمَشَّى *I went forth taking a walk;* and أَتْمَشَّى *He walked; walked about.*] — [Hence the saying,] تَمَشَّتْ فِيهِ حُمَيَّا الكَأْسِ [*The intoxicating influence of the cup of wine pervaded him,* or] *crept in him.* (TA.) See also تَفَشَّى.

6. تَمَاشَوْا *They walked, or went on foot, one towards, or to, another.* (TA.)

10. اِسْتَمْشَى بِالدَّوَآءِ [*He used the medicine as a laxative or purgative.* (IbrD.)] (Az in L, art. عقر.) — اِسْتَمْشَى بِهِ, referring to a plant, (Ḳ in art. صع,) *He drank its water* (i.e. *infusion* or *the like*) *for moving the bowels.* (TA ibid.)

مَشَّآءٌ [*That goes with energy; a good or strong goer;*] *strong to walk, or go, or go on foot.* (TA voce رَجِيلٌ.)

دَوَآءُ المَشِىِّ *Medicine that moves, or purges, the bowels.* (TA in art. طوس.)

مَاشِيَةٌ A she-camel *having numerous offspring.* (Ṣ, Mgh.) — Hence, and مَوَاشٍ, as ominous of good, *Camels,* and *cows,* and *sheep* or *goats that are for breeding and gain.* (Mgh.)

مَمْشًى *A passage, or way, by a place;* (TA;) [*a walking-place:* the gangway of a ship?]

مصع

4. أَمْصَعَتْ بِوَلَدِهَا *She* (a woman) *brought forth, or cast forth, her child with a single moan,* or *hard breathing* [or *with a single throe;*] like زَكَبَتْ بِهِ. (IAạr, L, art. حفد.)

مصل

مَصْلٌ [*A kind of* اقط]: see كَشْءٌ and عَبِيثٌ.

مضغ

مُضْغَةٌ *A piece, or bit, of flesh* (T, Ṣ, Ḳ), &c.: (T, Ḳ:) or *a morsel,* or *gobbet, of flesh,* i.e. *a piece of flesh such as a man puts into his mouth:* (Khálid Ibn-Jembeh, TA:) or *as much as is chewed* [*at once*]: (Mṣb:) and *such as the heart, and the tongue, of a man:* (TA:) and *a fœtus when it has become like a lump of flesh:* see Ḳur. xxii. 5; and see خَلِيقٌ.

مضف

مُضْفٌ: see سِيَرَآءُ.

مضى

1. مَضَى and تَمَضَّى ↑ *i. q.* تَقَدَّمَ [*He advanced, proceeded,* &c.]. (M.) — مَضَى *He, or it, passed; passed away; went;* or *went away.* (Ṣ, M, Mṣb, Ḳ.) — [*He went on.*] — مَضَى لَهُ, said of time: see تَشْبِيرٌ. — مَضَى فِى سَيْرِهِ *He advanced, or pressed onward, with a penetrative energy or force, or a sharpness and effectiveness, in his pace.*] — مَضَى الأَمْرُ, and القَوْلُ, † *The command, or order,* and *the saying, was effectual; had effect; was, or became, executed, or performed;* syn. نَفَذَ. (Mṣb, art نفذ.) — مَضَى فِى الأَمْرِ † *He acted* [or *went on,* and *did so*] *with penetrative energy, or with sharpness, vigour, and effectiveness, in the affair;* syn. نَفَذَ. (Ṣ, M, Ḳ.) See مَاضٍ فِى الأُمُورِ, below; and جَسَرَ. — مَضَى عَلَى الأَمْرِ *He executed, performed,* or *accomplished, the affair;* as also أَمْضَاهُ ↑: (Ṣ:) and *he kept,* or *applied himself, constantly,* or *perseveringly, to it.* (Mṣb.) — مَضَيْتُ على بَيْعِى and أَمْضَيْتُهُ ↑ *I effected,* or *executed, my sale.* (Ḳ.) — مَضَى *It* (a sword) *cut;* (M, Ḳ;) *penetrated; was sharp.*

4. أَمْضَاهُ [† *He made it* (i. e., a contract, sale, oath, &c.) *to take effect; executed it; performed it.*] — أَمْضَى الأَمْرَ: see مَضَى عَلَى الأَمْرِ. — أَمْضَى اليَمِينَ *He made the oath to be unconditional, without exception, absolutely* or *decisively* or *irreversibly binding.* (TḲ voce جَزْمٌ.) See جَزْمٌ. — أَمْضَى عَهْدَهُ † *He made his covenant, or contract, or the like, to have, or take, effect; executed or performed it.* (L, art. نفذ.) — أَمْضَى رَأْيًا *He formed,* or *gave, a decided opinion.* — أَمْضَى *He signed* a writing *with his name,* and so rendered it effective. — See 1.

5: see 1.

مَاضٍ فِى الأُمُورِ [† *Penetrating, sharp, energetic, or acting with penetrative energy,* or *vigorous, and effective, in the performing of affairs:* like شَمَشَعٌ, q. v. — مَاضٍ is coupled with the epithets مَاهِرٌ and جَادٌّ, &c., and implies penetration and skill, or proficiency in anything;] *excelling,* or *surpassing, in doing,* or *performing, a thing:* (KL from the "Destoor":) [it is also coupled with جَرِىءٌ and مُتَقَدِّمٌ, in the T, art. جهر. See also نَافِذٌ, its syn.] — أَمْرٌ مَاضٍ † *A command, or an order, that is effectual; that has effect; that is executed,* or *performed;* syn. نَافِذٌ. (L, art. نفذ.) — فَرَسٌ مَاضٍ † *A sharp, spirited, vigorous horse* [&c.]; contr. of بَلِيدٌ; (Lth, TA, voce نَدْبٌ;) *exerting,* or *having, a penetrative energy,* &c.: see مَضَى. — كَانَ ذٰلِكَ فِى الزَّمَنِ المَاضِى *That was in the time that is past;* contr. of المُسْتَقْبَل. (TA.)

إِمْضَآءٌ *A signature.*

تِمْضَآءٌ *One who performs affairs with energy and perseverance:* an intensive epithet: see صَمَيَانٌ.

مطق

5. تَمَطَّقَ *He tasted repeatedly,* or *smacked his lips:* see two explanations of this verb voce لَمَظَ.

مطل

1. مَطَلَهُ بِدَيْنِهِ, inf. n. مَطْلٌ, and مَاطَلَهُ ↑, inf. n. مِطَالٌ, *He delayed, or deferred, with him,* or *put him off, in the matter of his debt, by promising time after time to pay him.* (Mṣb.) See دَافَعَهُ and سَوَّفَهُ.

3: see 1.

مَطُولٌ *Much given to delaying, or deferring, with a creditor, or putting him off, in the matter of a debt, by promising time after time to pay him.* (Mṣb.)

مَمْطُولٌ Iron, or a sword, (Az, TA,) *beaten into a long shape:* (Az, Ḳ:) or anything *extended, elongated,* or *lengthened.* (Ṣ.)

مطى

1. مَطَا signifies *He drew,* or *pulled,* a thing; as, for instance, a well-rope: for] مَطَّ and مَدَّ and مَطَا are all one (Az and TA in art. مط.) See an ex. from Zuheyr, voce ثِنَايَةٌ.

5. تَمَطَّى *He stretched,* in a neuter sense: as also تَمَطَّطَ and تَمَدَّدَ.

مُطَآءٌ [for مُطَوَآءُ ?] *A stretching, through weariness,* &c.? (TA, art. ثاب.)

مَطِيَّةٌ *A camel:* (Mṣb:) *a camel, or beast, that one rides; a beast that goes with energy and speed:* (Ḳ:) or *a she-camel,* or *he-camel, that is used for riding;* (TA;) [and so *a horse,* &c.;] *a saddle-camel,* or *camel that one rides.* (KL.) — See two exs. of a metaphorical meaning voce زَعْبَرَ.

مُطَوَاءٌ The *stretching oneself by reason of fever.* (Aṣ in TA, voce بُرَحَاءُ.) — See ثُوَبَاءُ.

مع

مَعَ [generally thus in all cases] is a word, or noun, (Ṣ, Ḳ,) or particle, (Ḳ,) denoting concomitance, (Ṣ, Ḳ,) &c. (Ḳ.) It is said to denote the commencement of concomitance, though this is not invariably the case. (MF and TA, voce فِى.) — جِئْتُ مَعَ العَصْرِ means عِنْدَ العَصْرِ. (Mughnee.)

معس

8. اِمْتَعَسَ: see أَلْوَثُ.

معص

1. مَعِصَ: see مُغِصَ.

معق

1. مَعُقَ: see عَمُقَ.
4. مَا أَمْعَقَهَا: see عمق.
مَعِيقٌ: see عَمِيقٌ.

معك

مُتَمَعَّكُ الفَرَسِ (T, art. ردى) or الحِمَارِ (Ṣ, M, art. ردى) *The horses' or asses' place of rolling upon the ground.* See ردى.

معل

مَعْلٌ [not مَعِلٌ] *An agile, acute, clever,* man: see شَغْلٌ.

معن

4. أَمْعَنَ *He* (a horse) *went far,* (Ṣ, Mṣb, Ḳ,) in his run. (Ṣ, Mṣb.) — Hence, أَمْعَنَ فِى الطَّلَبِ *He went very far in search:* (Mṣb:) or *he went far,* or *to a great* or *an extraordinary length, therein.* (Mgh.) — امعن فِى الشَّىْءِ, (Ḥam p. 817,) or فِى الأَمْرِ, (MA, Ḳ, Ḥar p. 176,) *He went far,* (Ḳ, Ḥam, Ḥar,) or *deep,* or *beyond bounds,* (MA,) *in,* or *into, the thing,* or *affair.* (Ḥam, &c.) — أَمْعَنَ لِى بِحَقِّى: see أَذْعَنَ.

المَعْنُ *The drawing* of water.

معى

مِعًى *A narrow, depressed place.* (See طَأْطَأٌ.) — بَنَاتُ مِعًى *The* بَعْر. (T in art. بنى.) — المِعَى المُسْتَقِيمُ *The rectum.*

الأَمْعَآءُ *i. q.* الأَقْصَابُ; (AO: see voce قُصْبٌ;) *the guts;* i. e. *bowels,* or *intestines, into which the food passes from the stomach:* الحَشَا is the name of all the places of the food; and in the belly are the أَعْفَاج and the أَقْتَاب, to which the food passes after the stomach, and these are the lower امعاء; and all these are called the قُصْب: the حَوَايَا are all the امعاء that wind, or take a coiled, or circular, form. (Zj, in his "Khalḳ el-Insán.") — أَمْعَآءٌ: see a tropical signification (*water-holes*) of this pl. voce حَوِيَّةٌ.

مقط

مَاقِطٌ *A player with the ball.* (O in art. صوع.) See صَاعٌ, last sentence.

مقل

3. مَاقَلَهُ, inf. n. مُمَاقَلَةٌ *He vied with him in diving:* see غَامَسَهُ.

6. تَمَاقَلَا: see تَغَاطَسَا.

مُقْلٌ The *Theban palm; palma Thebaïca* of Pococke; the *cucifera* of Theophrastes. — Also The خُوص, or *leaves, of the tree thus called:* see صَمْغٌ. — See also نظر.

مَقْلَةٌ, for جُرْعَةٌ مَقْلَةٌ: see 3 in art. صفن.

مُقْلَةٌ The *ball,* or *globe,* or *bulb* (lit. *fat,* شَحْمَة), *of the eye,* i. e., the *eyeball, which comprises the white and the black.* (Khalḳ el-Insán of Zj; and Ṣ, Mṣb, Ḳ.)

مكر

1. مَكَرَ بِهِ *i. q.* خَدَعَهُ, (Mṣb, &c.,) see كَادَهُ.

مَكْرٌ [*Artifice; machination; stratagem; fraud; fraudulence; guile*].

مكن

2. مَكَّنَهُ *He gave him a place:* (Jel, vi. 6:) *he assigned him a place, and settled,* or *established, him.* (Bḍ, ibid, where see more.) You say also, مَكَّنَ لَهُ فِى مَنْزِلٍ [*He assigned,* or *gave, him a place in an abode*]. (Ṣ in art. بوأ.) — مَكَّنَهُ مِنْ شَىْءٍ, and ↓ أَمْكَنَهُ, *He made him to have mastery,* or *dominion,* or *ascendancy,* or *authority, and power, over a thing;* (Mṣb;) *put it in his power.* — مَكَّنَهُ مِنَ الشَّىْءِ, and ↓ أَمْكَنَهُ مِنْهُ, *He empowered him, enabled him,* or *rendered him able, to do the thing: he enabled him to have the thing within his power.* Ex. ↓ أَمْكَنَ يَدَيْهِ مِنْ رُكْبَتَيْهِ *He enabled his hands to take and grasp his knees:* from a trad. (Mgh.)

4. أَمْكَنَهُ مِنْ شَىْءٍ *He made him to have a thing within his power,* or *reach: enabled him to do, reach, get,* or *obtain, a thing.* See 2. — أَمْكَنَهُ *It was within his power,* or *reach; was possible,* or *practicable, to him.* — أَمْكَنَهُ *It became easy to him.* (Mṣb.) *It* (an object of the chase) *offered him an opportunity* to shoot it or capture it; or *became within his power,* or *reach.* — أَمْكِنِى, said to a woman, [meaning *Empower thou;* i. e. *grant thou access;*] occurs in a poem. (Ṣ, art. عرض.) — أَمْكَنَتْهُ *She granted him attainment.*

5. تَمَكَّنَ *i. q.* اِسْتَقَرَّ: (Mṣb, art. قر:) it is very often used in this sense, as meaning *He,* or *it, settled; became fixed,* or *established; it became fixed,* or *steady, in its place;* when said of a man, particularly implying *in authority and power:* see قَرَّ. — تَمَكَّنَ مِنْ شَىْءٍ, and ↓ اِسْتَمْكَنَ, *He became possessed of mastery,* or *dominion,* or *ascendancy,* or *authority, and power, over a thing; he was able to avail himself of it:* [*he was,* or *became, within reach of him,* or *it.*] (Mṣb.) — تَمَكَّنَ مِنْهُ *He assumed authority over him.*

10. اِسْتَمْكَنَ: see 5. — *He,* or *it, was,* or *became, firm.* It seems sometimes to mean *It* (a plant) *took firm root.*

مُكْنَةٌ, (Mṣb, TA,) with ḍamm, (TA,) *Power;* (Mṣb,* TA;) *ability;* (TA;) *strength.* (Mṣb.)

مَكِنَةٌ *i. q.* تَمَكُّنٌ. (Sh, TA.) — النَّاسُ عَلَى مَكِنَاتِهِمْ means على مَقَارِّهِمْ. (IAạr, TA.)

مَكَّانٌ: see مَصَّانٌ in art. مص.

مَكْنَانٌ: see رَيْحَةٌ.

مَكَانَةٌ *Greatness, and high rank* or *standing,* in the estimation of the Sulṭán: (Mṣb:) *an honourable place* in the estimation of a king. (Ḳ.)

جَلَسَ مُتَمَكِّنًا *He sat in a firm,* or *settled, posture;* as when one sits cross-legged.

مكو

مُكَّآءٌ *The bird so called,* because of its colour: see أَخْرَجُ.

مل

1. مَلَّهُ *He put it* (namely bread, or flesh-meat,) *into hot ashes,* [*to bake, or roast*]. (Ḳ, &c.) — مَلَّ الثَّوْبَ *He sewed,* or *tacked, the garment,* or *piece of cloth,* [*slightly,*] *previously to the* [*stronger*] *sewing termed* الكَفّ. (Ṣ.) See also شَلَّ. — مَلِلْتُ مِنْهُ & مَلِلْتُهُ, *I was averse from it;* (T;) *loathed it; was disgusted by it, with it,* or *at it;* (T, Ṣ, K;) [*was weary of it;*] *turned*

away from it with disgust. (T.) See سَئِمَ. —— مَلَّ مَلَالُكَ [*May thy disgust pass away, or cease*]: see أَضَلَّ ٱللّٰهُ ضَلَالَكَ.

4. أَمْلَلْتُ & أَمْلَيْتُ: see 4 in art. حظ. —— أَمَلَّ: see an ex. voce أَذَلَّ.

8. اِمْتَلَّ مِلَّتَهُ *He follows his way of religion:* see 8 in art. شرع.

مَلَّةٌ The *hollow that is made for baking bread: or the hot dust and ashes [in which the bread is baked].* (Mṣb.) —— *Hot ashes:* (Ṣ, Ḳ:) *ashes, and earth, in which fire is kindled.* (TA, art. خبز.) —— خُبْزُ مَلَّةٍ *Bread baked in hot ashes.* (Ṣ.) [It is generally made in the form of thick round cakes.]

مِلَّةٌ *A religion;* (Ṣ, Mṣb, Ḳ;) *a way of belief and practice in respect of religion.* (T, &c.) —— See 8.

مَلُولٌ *Conceiving [frequent] disgust.* (Mṣb.) See ذَوَّاقٌ.

مَلَالٌ: see 1.

مَلِيلٌ A man *burned by the sun;* as also مَمْلُولٌ. (TA.) See an ex. in a verse cited voce أَصْوَرُ; and see طَلْمَةٌ.

مَمْلُولٌ Flesh-meat *covered over in live coals.* (TA, art. عرض.) —— See مَلِيلٌ.

مُمْلُولٌ *An iron style with which one writes on tablets.* (Ḳ.) —— The *style, or bodkin, with which collyrium is applied to the eyes.* (Ṣ, Ḳ.) In the CḲ, incorrectly, مَمْلُولٌ: the former is found in MS. copies of the Ḳ, as well as in the Ṣ, and is right accord. to the TḲ.

ملع

مَلِيعٌ: see عُمْلُولٌ.

ملق

1. مَلَقَهُ *He flayed him* with a whip: like سَلَقَهُ. (TA in art. سلق.)

5. تَمَلَّقَهُ, (Ṣ, Ḳ,) and تَمَلَّقَ لَهُ, (Ṣ, Mṣb, K,) inf. n. تَمَلُّقٌ and تِمِلَّاقٌ, [like تِجِمَّالٌ and تِكِلَّامٌ, not تَمْلَاقٌ as in the CḲ,] *He behaved in a loving, or an affectionate, and a blandishing,* or *coaxing, manner to him.* (Ṣ, Mṣb,* Ḳ.) See a verse cited in art. رضو, conj. 5.

مَلِقَةٌ [*A swiftly-running mare*]. See عَبْرٌ بِهِ. مِلَاقٌ *Vehement in journeying, or in his pace;* i. q. مِلَاخٌ. (TA, voce مِلَاخٌ.)

مِمْلَقَةٌ *A harrow:* see مِمْلَسٌ.

ملك

1. مَلَكَهُ *He possessed it,* or *owned it,* [and particularly] *with ability to have it to himself exclusively:* (M, Ḳ:) [and *he exercised,* or *had, authority over it;* for] مُلْكٌ signifies the *exercise of authority to command and to forbid in respect of the generality of a people* [&c.]: (Er-Rághib, TA:) or the *having possession and command* or *authority:* and the *having power to exercise command* or *authority.* (TA.) مَلْكٌ, as inf. n. of مَلَكَهُ meaning *He possessed it,* is more common than مُلْكٌ and مِلْكٌ. —— مَلَكَ أَمْرَهُ [*He had the ruling,* or *ordering, of his affair,* or *case*] And مَلَكَ عَلَى ٱلنَّاسِ أَمْرَهُمْ *He had the dominion,* or *sovereignty,* or *ruling power, over the people.* (Mṣb.) ═ See 4.

2. مَلَّكَهُ *He made him to possess* a thing; (Ṣ, Ḳ;) as also أَمْلَكَهُ. (Ḳ.) —— *He made him king;* or *made him to have dominion, kingship,* or *rule.* (Mṣb, Ḳ.) —— يُمَلَّكُ ٱلرَّجُلُ أَمْرَهُ [*The man shall be made to have the ruling,* or *ordering, of his affair,* or *affairs,* or *case*]. (Sh, T in art. دين.)

3. مَالَكَ أُمَّهُ: see شَدَنَ.

4. مَلَكَ ٱلْعَجِينَ and أَمْلَكَهُ *He kneaded well the dough.* (Ṣ, Ḳ.) ═ See 2.

5. تَمَلَّكَ *He took possession of* a thing [*absolutely* or] *by force.* (Mṣb.)

6. مَا تَمَالَكَ أَنْ فَعَلَ *He could not restrain himself from doing;* (Mgh, Mṣb;) syn. مَا تَمَاسَكَ [q. v.] (Ṣ.)

مِلْكٌ: its pl. أَمْلَاكٌ, in common conventional language means [or rather includes] *Houses* and *lands.* (TA.) See its pl. pl. أَمْلَاكَاتٌ.

مُلْكٌ *Dominion; sovereignty; kingship; rule; mastership; ownership; possession; right of possession; authority; sway.* —— مُلْكُ ٱللّٰهِ *God's world of spirits; or invisible world.* (TA, art. شهد.) —— [مُلْكٌ (when distinguished from ملكوت) The *dominion that is apparent;* as that of the earth.]

مَلَكٌ *An angel:* see مَأْلَكٌ. —— مَلْكٌ *Water.* (Ṣ.)

مَلِكُ ٱلْأَمْلَاكِ *The king of kings.* See أَخْنَعُ.

مِلَاكُ ٱلْأَمْرِ and مَلَاكُهُ *That whereby the thing* &c. *subsists:* (Ṣ, KL:) *its* قِوَام [q. v.] *by whom,* or *by which, it is ruled,* or *ordered:* (Ḳ:) *its foundation;* syn. أَصْلُهُ: (KL:) *its support; that upon which it rests:* (T, TA:) it may be rendered *the cause,* or *means, of the subsistence of the thing;* &c.

مَلَاكٌ see مِلَاكٌ.

مَالِكٌ: see رَبٌّ. —— مَالِكُ ٱلْأَمْرِ *The possessor of command,* or *rule.* —— ٱلْمَالِكُ ٱلْكَبِيرُ *The Great Master, or Owner;* i.e., God; in contradistinction to ٱلْمَالِكُ ٱلصَّغِيرُ *the little master, or owner;* i. e., the human owner of a slave, &c. —— مَالِكٌ ٱلْحَزِينُ: (so in one copy of the Ṣ: in another, and the MA, and Ḳzw, مَالِكُ ٱلْحَزِينِ:) [*The heron:* or a species thereof] in Pers. بوتيمار; (MA;) *a certain bird, long in the neck and legs, called in Pers.* بو تيمار. (Ḳzw:) see سَبِيطَرٌ. —— أَبُو مَالِكٍ *Hunger.* (MF, art. جبر.) See also أَبٌ.

أَمْلَاكَاتٌ pl. of أَمْلَاكٌ pl. of مِلْكٌ *Goods,* or *chattels, of a bride:* see أَغْنَآءُ in art. غنى.

مَلَكَةٌ [*A faculty.*] *A quality firmly rooted in the mind.* (KT.)

مَلَكُوتُ ٱللّٰهِ *God's world of corporeal beings.* (TA, art. شهد.) Generally *The kingdom of God.*

مَلِيكٌ is also *syn. with* مَمْلُوكٌ; this is meant in the TA where it is said that مَلِكَةٌ in the saying لَنَا مُلُوكٌ وَلَيْسَ لَنَا مَلِكَةٌ [*We have kings of bees, but we have not slaves*] is pl. of ٱلْمَلِيكُ from ٱلْمَمْلُوكُ: it is also said in art. رغو in the TA, (see 4 in that art.) that مَلِيكَةٌ is syn. with مَمْلُوكَةٌ.

أَمْلَكُ: see شَرْطٌ and also أَمْلَأُ, and أَرْبٌ. —— مَا أَمْلَكَ شَدًّا وَلَا إِرْخَآءً: see شَدٌّ.

مَمْلَكَةٌ *A kingdom, or realm.* (Ṣ.)

مَمْلُوكٌ *A slave; a bondman;* syn. عَبْدٌ, (Ṣ,) or رَقِيقٌ. (TA.) In the present day, specially, *A white male slave.* (TA.) See مَرْبُوبٌ.

ملى

1. مُلِّيَ أَبَاهُ: see لَبِسَ in art. لبس. —— مُلِّيتُ فُلَانًا *I was made to live long with such a one.* (Ḥam, p. 412.) —— مَلَّاكَ ٱللّٰهُ حَبِيبَكَ *May God make thee to have enjoyment of thy friend* (مَتَّعَكَ بِهِ) *and to live long with him.* (Ṣ.) See لَبِسَ.

4. أَمْلَيْتُ and أَمْلَلْتُ: see 4 in art. حظ.

5. تَمَلَّى —— تَمَلَّى ٱلْعَيْشَ *He lived long.* (T.) —— تَمَلَّيْتُ عُمْرَهُ: see تَمَلَّى بِشَىْءٍ *He enjoyed a thing.* —— a verse of Ibn-Aḥmar cited voce أَبْلَى in art. بلو.

مَلِيًّا *A while:* (Mṣb:) or *a long time.* (Ṣ, Mṣb.)

من

1. مَنَّ عَلَيْهِ, (Ṣ, M, Mṣb, Ḳ,) aor. ـُ, (Mṣb,) inf. n. مَنٌّ (Ṣ, M, Mṣb, Ḳ) and مِنِّيفَى; (Ḳ;) and ▼ امتنّ; (Mṣb;) *He conferred*, or *bestowed, upon him, a favour*, or *benefit*. (Ṣ, M, Mṣb, Ḳ.) You say, مَنَّ عَلَيْهِ شَيْئًا, and بِشَىْءٍ, which latter is more common, and ▼ امتنّ عليه به *He conferred, or bestowed, a thing upon him as a favour*. (Mṣb.) — مَنَّ عَلَيْهِ, (Ṣ, M, Mṣb, Ḳ,) inf. n. مَنٌّ (T, Mṣb) or مِنَّةٌ; (Ṣ, Ḳ;) and ▼ امتنّ (Ṣ, M, Mṣb, Ḳ) and ▼ تمتّن; (M;) *He reproached him for a favour, or benefit, which he* (the former) *had conferred, or bestowed;* (M;) *he recounted his gifts or actions to him*. (Mṣb.) Ex., ▼ اِمْتَنَّ عَلَيْهَا بِمَا مَهَرَهَا [*He reproached her for the dowry he had given her*]. (Ḳ, art. مهر.) See Bḍ, ii. 264. See also an ex. in a verse cited voce سَوِفَ.

5: } see 1.
8: }

مَنْ [used for مَا in the sense of *What?* as in the following of El-Khansà,

* أَلَا مَنْ لِعَيْنِى لَا تَجِفُّ دُمُوعُهَا *

O! what aileth mine eye, that its tears dry not? quoted in the TA, art. فتأ.] — مَنْ: respecting its dual مَنَانْ and مَنَيْنْ, and its pl. مَنُونْ and مَنِينْ, see I'Aḳ, p. 319. — مَنْ لِى بِكَذَا: see ب (near the end of the paragraph).

مِنَ means زَيْدٌ أَعْقَلُ مِنْ أَنْ يَكْذِبَ — مِنْ الَّذِى يَكْذِبُ (Kull, p. 78) [i. e. *Zeyd is more reasonable than he who lies:* but, though this is the virtual meaning, the proper explanation, accord. to modern usage, is, that أَنْ is here for أَنَّ with the adjunct pronoun ه; for in a phrase of this kind, an adjunct pronoun is sometimes expressed; so that the aor. must be marfooa; and the literal meaning is, *Zeyd is more reasonable than that he will lie;* which is equivalent to saying, *Zeyd is too reasonable to lie.* It may be doubted, however, whether a phrase of this kind be of classical authority. The only other instance that I have found is هُوَ أَحْصَنُ مِنْ أَنْ يُرَامَ وَأَعَزُّ مِنْ أَنْ يُضَامَ, in the TA, voce أَلْ. Accord. to modern usage, one may say, أَنْتَ أَعْقَلُ مِنْ أَنَّكَ تَفْعَلُ كَذَا, which virtually means *Thou art too reasonable to do such a thing;* and here we cannot substitute الَّذِى for أَنَّ. See أَنْ for أَنَّ.] — see أَخْزَى ٱللّٰهُ ٱلْكَاذِبَ مِنِّى وَمِنْكَ — [أَىُّ see: أَسَدٌ — and لَقِيتُ مِنْهُ أَسَدًا — لَقِيتُ مِنْهُ — مِنْ — بحر see: رَأَيْتُ مِنْهُ بَحْرًا; and بَحْرًا in the sense of جَرَى مِنْهُ مَجْرَى — جَدٌّ: see عِنْدَ — كَذَا: see 1 in art. جرى — مِنْ and عَنْ, differences between: see مِنْ — عَنْ often means *Some.* — Often redundant: see 1 in art. عيض. — *Of*, or *among:* see two exs. voce فِى, latter part. — حُسَيْنٌ مِنِّى وَأَنَا مِنْهُ *Hoseyn and I are as one thing,* [as though each were a part of the other,] in respect of the love that is due to us, &c. (Commencement of a tradition in the Jámi' eṣ-Ṣagheer: thus explained in the Expos. of El-Munáwee.) See Ḥam, p. 139; and De Sacy's Gr. i. 492. — مَا أَنَا مِنْ دَدٍ وَلَا الدَّدُ مِنِّى: see art. دد. IbrD confirms my rendering of this saying. — يَتَعَرَّضُ إِلَى شَىْءٍ لَيْسَ مِنْهُ [*He applies himself to a thing not of his business to do*]. (TA, art. عش.) — لَيْسَ مِنَّا *He is not of our dispositions, nor of our way, course,* or *manner, of acting,* or *the like.* (TA, art. غش.) — لَيْسَ مِنِّى (Ḳur, ii. 250) *He is not of my followers:* (Bḍ, Jel:) or *he is not at one,* or *in union, with me.* (Bḍ. See 1 in art. طعم.) See a similar usage of مِن, voce عيض. — أَنَا مِنْهُ كَحَاقِنِ الإِهَالَةِ: see مِنْ — حاقن. — is used in the sense of فى in the phrase مِنْ يَوْمِ الجُمْعَةِ [*In*, or *on, the day of congregation*] in the Ḳur lxii. 9. (Ḳ, Jel.) So, too, in مِنْ يَوْمِهِ *In*, or *on, his*, meaning, *the same*, day: and مِنْ سَاعَتِهِ *In*, or *at, his*, meaning *the same, instant of time.* See also De Sacy's Gr., ii. 526.

أَيْمُنُ ٱللّٰهِ is for مُنَ ٱللّٰهِ.

مَنِىٌّ and المَنِىُّ, from مَنْ: see أَيُّ; and De Sacy's Anthol. Gr. Ar., pp. 374 and 401, and ١٦٣.

مَنٌّ: see رِطْلٌ.

مِنَّةٌ [*An obligation,* عَلَى أَحَدٍ *upon one*, and also لَهُ *to him.*] — *A favour, or benefit, conferred, or bestowed.* (M, Mṣb.) — Also an inf. n. See مَنَّ عَلَيْهِ.

لَا أَفْعَلُهُ أُخْرَى المَنُونِ *I will not do it till the end of time.* (Ṣ.) — مَنُونٌ is fem. and sing. and pl. (Fr, Ṣ.)

مَنِينٌ *The first* (or *main*) *rope of a well.* See كَرَبٌ.

مَنَّانٌ *Very bountiful* or *beneficent.* — Also [*Very reproachful for his gifts;*] *one who gives nothing without reproaching for it and making account of it:* an intensive epithet. (TA.)

اِمْتِنَانِىٌّ *Gratuitous; granted as a favour:* opposed to وُجُوبِىٌّ.

منجنق and منجن

مِنْجَنُونٌ, مَنْجَنُوقٌ, مَنْجَنُونٌ, مَنْجَنُوقٌ, and مَنْجَنِيقٌ: see art. جنق.

منع

1. مَنَعَ *He prevented, hindered, held back,* [*impeded, withheld, arrested, restrained, kept, debarred, precluded, inhibited, forbade, prohibited, interdicted:*] (MA, KL, &c.:) *he denied,* or *refused;* doubly trans.; (Ṣ, Ḳ, &c.:) مَنْعٌ is the *contr. of* إِعْطَآءٌ. (Ṣ, Mgh, Ḳ.) — مَنَعَهُ [*He protected it,* or *defended it,* or *guarded it,* (namely a place or the like) *from,* or *against, encroachment, invasion,* or *attack:*] *he protected, defended,* or *guarded, him.* (T in art. ذب.) — مَنَعَهُ العَطِيَّةَ [*He refused him the gift*]. (TA in art. حرم.) — حَرَمَهُ إِيَّاهُ *i. q.* مَنَعَهُ الشَّىْءَ [q. v.] (Ṣ in art. حرم.) — مَنَعَ الشَّىْءَ, inf. n. مَنَاعَةٌ, *i. q.* اِعْتَزَّ and تَعَسَّرَ. (TA.) See 8. — مَا مَنَعَكَ أَلَّا تَسْجُدَ (Ḳur vii. 11): see أَبَى.

3. مَانَعَهُ الشَّىْءَ *He disputed,* or *contested, with him the thing:* (Mṣb:) *he refused him the thing:* (TḲ:) *he endeavoured,* or *contended with him, to make him,* or *to entice him, to abstain from,* or *relinquish, the thing;* (TA;) [*he endeavoured to turn him away from the thing; to prevent his obtaining it* or *doing it; he prevented him from obtaining* or *doing the thing, being also prevented by him;* i. e. *he reciprocally prevented him,* &c.: and hence the meaning in the TA; and then that in the Mṣb:] مَانَعُوا عَدُوَّهُمْ signifies *i. q.* حَاجَزُوهُمْ: (TḲ, art. حجز:) see the latter. — تَمَنَّعَ عَلَى السَّنَةِ [*he resisted,* or *withstood, the year of dearth*]: said of an animal. (Ḳ.)

5. تَمَنَّعَ مِنَ الشَّىْءِ بِقَوْمِهِ and ▼ اِمْتَنَعَ *He became strengthened,* or *fortified, against the thing by his people,* or *party;* syn. تَقَوَّى. (Mṣb.) — تَمَنَّعَ عَنْهُ *He refrained, forbore,* or *abstained, from it, as being forbidden,* or *prohibited.* (Ḳ,* TA.) See 8. — تَمَنَّعَ بِهِ and ▼ اِمْتَنَعَ بِهِ *he protected,* or *defended, himself by it,* namely, a fortress; syn. اِحْتَمَى. (TA.)

6. تَمَانَعَا *i. q.* تَحَاجَزَا: (Ḳ, art. حجز:) see the latter.

8. اِمْتَنَعَ [*It was,* or *became, prevented from being; it necessarily was not.* You say يَمْتَنِعُ هٰذَا لِوُجُودِ ذَاكَ *This is prevented from being,* or *may not be,* or *necessarily is not, because of that's being.* And يَمْتَنِعُ أَنْ تَكُونَ هٰذَا *This may not be.*] — اِمْتَنَعَ *He refrained, forbore, abstained,* or *held back,* (Mṣb, Ḳ,) مِنَ الأَمْرِ *from the thing,* or *affair;* (Mṣb;) as also ▼ تَمَنَّعَ عَنْهُ: (TA:) *he did so voluntarily, of his own free will* or *choice; he refused:* you say, اِمْتَنَعَ عَنْهُ *he refrained,* &c., *from it voluntarily,* &c.; *refused it;* or *refused to do it.* (MF. in art. حصر.) See أَبَى. — اِمْتَنَعَ عَلَيْهِ *He,* or *it, opposed him; resisted him; withstood him; repugned him; was incompliant,* or

unyielding, to him; see أَبَى عَلَيْهِ. — اِمْتَنَعَ *It was,* or *became, inaccessible,* or *inapproachable;* like ▾مَنُعَ; syn. with حَصُنَ, q. v.: and also, *difficult of access,* as in an instance in art. أبى (last sentence of 4); and also عَرِسَ عَلَىَّ. — See 5.

مِنْعَةٌ: see مَنَعَةٌ.

مَنَعَةٌ *State,* and *power, of resistance;* lit. *a state of might of one's people* or *party, so that such as desires to do so will not prevail against him:* [or *a state of might in his people* or *party,* &c.; or *a state of might, and power of resistance, in his people* or *party:*] (Msb:) [*resistibility:* or simply *resistance:*] *inaccessibleness,* or *unapproachableness,* of a people; as also ▾مَنْعَةٌ and ▾مِنْعَةٌ. (TA.)

مَنُوعٌ One *who denies,* or *refuses to give;* as also ▾مَانِعٌ and ▾مَنَّاعٌ. (K.)

مَنِيعٌ, from مَنُعَ, [*Unapproachable; inaccessible:*] *difficult of access; fortified; strong:* (TK, voce وَزَرٌ:) [*defended,* or *protected, against attack:* like حَصِينٌ: *resistive; resisting attack;*] applied to a fortress. (Msb.) — قَوْمٌ مُنَعَاءُ [pl. of مَنِيعٌ] *An inaccessible,* or *unapproachable, people.* (TA.)

مَنَّاعٌ } مَانِعٌ } see مَنُوعٌ.

المُتَمَنِّعَانِ *The young she-camel and young she-kid:* because they resist the year of dearth by reason of their youthful vigour, &c. (K.)

مُمْتَنِعٌ *Resisting; resisting attack; unyielding; incompliant.*

منى

1. مَنَاهُ *He tried him; proved him.* (S, K.) You say, مَنَاهُ اللّٰهُ بِحُبِّهَا *God tried him by love of her.* (T.) And مُنِىَ بِكَذَا *He was tried by such a thing.* (T.) — مَنَى *He meditated* [a thing in his mind]; syn. قَدَّرَ. (Bd, ii. 73.) See أُمْنِيَّةٌ.

5. تَمَنَّاهُ *He wished,* or *desired, it.* (K, TA.) — التَّمَنِّى relates to that which is possible and to that which is impossible: whereas التَّرَجِّى relates only to what is possible. (I'Ak, p. 90.)

10. تُسْتَمْنَى, said of a she-camel: see 8 in art. سمو.

مَنًى: see مَنِيَّةٌ.

مُنْيَةٌ *A thing wished for* by a man: pl. مُنًى. (T.) This word and ▾أُمْنِيَّةٌ signify the same. (M, Mgh, Msb, K.) See an ex. in a verse cited voce أَوْ. — المُنْيَةٌ in the case of a covered she-camel, *The period by the end of which one knows whether she be pregnant or not.* (M.) — مُنْيَةٌ of a mare, *Twenty days.* (M, voce سُفُودٌ.)

مَنِيَّةٌ [*A decreed event. Fate; destiny:*] The *decree of death:* (IB:) or the *decreed term* [*of life,* or] *of a living being:* (Er-Rághib:) *death;* (S, M, K;) because it is decreed; (S, M;) as also ▾مَنًى: (M, K:) [properly a thing decreed: and hence the pl.] المَنَايَا signifies *the fates* or *decrees* [*of God*]. (T.) — مَنِيَّةٌ also means † *A man of courage upon his saddle:* (TA in art. حوى:) pl. مَنَايَا: see an ex. voce حَوِيَّةٌ.

أُمْنِيَّةٌ *An object of wish,* or *desire:* originally, *a thing that a man meditates* (يُقَدِّرُهُ) in his mind; from مَنَى signifying قَدَّرَ: and hence applied to a lie; and to what is wished, or desired, and what is read, or desired [pl. أَمَانِىُّ and أَمَانٍ]. (Bd in ii. 73.) See مُنْيَةٌ and حُجْوَى.

مه

لَيْسَ بِهِ مَهَاهٌ, (T in art. رمد,) or فِيهِ, (L in that art.,) *It has no goodness and lastingness.* (T and L in that art.)

مهد

4. أَمْهَدَتْ بِوَلَدِهَا *She* (a woman) *brought forth, or cast forth, her child with a single impulse.* (IAar, in L, art. خفد.) — أَمْهَدَتْ بِالوَلَدِ is *syn. with* أَسْهَدَتْ بِهِ; (IAar, O, TA in art. سهد;) and زَكَبَتْ بِهِ, &c. (IAar, L, in art. خفد.)

مهل

4. أَمْهَلَهُ *He acted gently, softly, or in a leisurely manner, towards, or with, him.* (K.) *He granted him some delay, or respite; let him alone, or left him, for a while.* (S, K.) [*In both senses*] *i. q.* أَرْوَدَهُ. (S, art. رود.) You say أَمْهِلْنِى حَتَّى أَفْعَلَ كَذَا *Grant thou me some delay that I may do such a thing; give me time to do such a thing.* See Har p. 164.

5. تَمَهَّلَ *He acted,* or *behaved, deliberately,* or *leisurely; without haste;* (S, Msb, K;) in an affair. (S, Msb.)

مَهْلٌ and ▾مَهَلٌ and ▾مُهْلَةٌ *Gentleness; a leisurely manner of acting or proceeding.* (Msb, K, &c.) — مَهْلًا *Act gently, softly,* or *leisurely.*

مَهَلٌ: see مَهْلٌ.

مُهْلَةٌ: see مَهْلٌ. — فِى الأَمْرِ مُهْلَةٌ *In the affair is a delay;* syn. تَأْخِيرٌ. (Msb.) — فِى مُهْلَةٍ *Leisurely; gently; by little and little.*

غُرْمُولٌ مُتَمَهِّلٌ *A hard penis:* see قَاسِبٌ.

مهم

مَفَازَةٌ مَهْمَةٌ *A far-extending* [or *desert,* &c.]. (S, K.) See اِصْمِيتٌ.

مهن

8. اِمْتَهَنَهُ *He used it for service and work:* (K:) *i. q.* اِبْتَذَلَهُ, q. v.: (S, Msb:) *He held it in mean estimation.* (Har, p. 65.)

مِهْنَةٌ [is syn. with عَمَلٌ and فِعْلٌ, and means *work, labour,* or] *service; ministration; performance of an office.* (S, &c.) — Also, The *clothes worn in service, or in the performance of business.* (Msb.)

مَهِينٌ *Contemptible; abject:* (S, K) *weak: having little judgment and discrimination.* (K.)

مهو

مَهْوٌ, applied to a sword, *Thin edged:* see an ex. voce خَشِيبَةٌ. — سَلْحٌ مَهْوٌ *Thin excrement.* (Skr in Carm. Hnds. p. 15.)

مَهًا † *Front teeth* (ثَغْرٌ) *that are clean, white, and lustrous* (*having much* مَآء): so in a verse of El-Aasha [cited voce رَفَّ]. (TA.)

مُمَهًّى Beverage, or wine, (شَرَابٌ,) *mixed with much water.* (IAar, in TA, art. حنذ.)

موا

مَآءٌ *Water.* — مَآءُ الظَّهْرِ [*The seminal fluid*]. (K, voce اِنْبَثَّ.) See Kur, lxxxvi. 6, 7, and see 4 in art. روق. — مَآءٌ *Lustre* [likened to water, and running water,] of the teeth, (IbrD,) &c.: see غَرْبٌ and ظَلْمٌ and دَرَزٌ. — مَآءٌ The *water* of a sword: see فِرِنْدٌ and رَوْنَقٌ: also its *lustre.* — سَيْفٌ كَثِيرُ المَآءِ [*A sword much diversified with wavy marks or streaks in its grain;* as are the swords of Damascus &c.] (TA voce إِبْرِيقٌ.) — بَنَاتُ المَآءِ *i. q.* الغَرَانِيقُ [*storks* or *cranes*]. (L, art. وضر.) See عِرْسٌ. — اِبْنُ المَآءِ is ‡ *A kind of bird;* pl. بَنَاتُ المَآءِ; (Mgh in art. بنى:) *the aquatic bird; the bird of the water.* (Msb in art. بنو.) — مَآءُ الشَّبَابِ: see شَبَابٌ. — مَآءُ الوَجْهِ: see حَقَنَ and تَشَهَّلَ. — مَآءُ الذَّهَبِ *Gold-wash* for gilding: and مَآءُ الفِضَّةِ *Silver-wash* for silvering: you say, طَلَاهُ بِمَآءِ الذَّهَبِ, and الفِضَّةِ *He washed it over with gold,* and *silver.* — مَآءٌ is used as a coll. gen. n., of which the n. un. is مَآءَةٌ; and therefore is sometimes made, as a pl., to have a pl. epithet: ex. مَآءٌ عِذَابٌ. (See عَذْبٌ). مَآءَةٌ signifies *A water;* or *some water.*

موق

موقٌ [*Stupidity;*] *foolishness with lack of understanding.* (Ṣ, Ḳ.) — *A kind of boot:* see جُرْمُوقٌ.

مول

5. تَمَوَّلَ *He became abundant in wealth.* (TA, art. ثمر).

مَالٌ *Whatever one possesses:* (Ḳ:) *property; wealth:*] accord. to Moḥammad [the Ḥanafee Imám), *whatever men possess, of dirhems,* or *deenárs,* or *gold,* or *silver,* or *wheat,* or *barley,* or *bread,* or *beasts,* or *garments or pieces of cloth,* or *weapons,* or *other things:* (Mgh:) [*property,* or *wealth:*] or originally *what one possesses of gold and silver:* then applied to *anything that one acquires and possesses of substantial things:* and mostly applied by the Arabs to *camels,* because these constitute most of their wealth: (IAth, TA:) and *animals.* (TA.) — مَالٌ *Camels or sheep or goats.* (Ṣ.) The مال of the people of the desert consists of what are termed نَعَمٌ, (T, Mṣb,) i.e. *Cattle, consisting of camels* or *neat* or *sheep* or *goats,* or *all these,* or *camels alone;* (Mṣb in art. نعم;) *herds,* or *flocks,* or *herds and flocks.* — مَالٌ *A square in arithmetic:* pl. أَمْوَالٌ. See جَذْرٌ. — رَجُلٌ مَالٌ, for ذُو مَالٍ. (L, art. صيد.)

مَالِىٌّ *Of,* or *relating to, property* or *wealth.*

موم

مُومٌ [*Pleurisy*]: see بِرْسَامٌ and حُمَامٌ.

مَوَامِى *Lands wherein is nothing:* see بَلُّوقَةٌ.

موه

2. مَوَّهَ *He silvered* or *gilded,* (Ṣ, Ḳ,) or *washed over with gold* or *silver,* (Mṣb,) a thing (Ṣ, Mṣb, Ḳ, TA) of brass (TA) or copper or iron. (Ṣ, Ḳ.) — *He* [*varnished* or] *embellished* falsehood *so as to give it the appearance of truth.* (TA.) *He falsified* information, عَلَيْهِ *to him,* in reply to a question. (Ḳ.) — *He involved in confusion,* or *doubt;* or *practised concealment* or *disguise;* or *he concealed* or *disguised:* (Ṣ, TA:) and *he deceived, deluded, beguiled, circumvented,* or *outwitted.* (TA.) — *He varnished,* or *embellished with a false colouring.*

4. أَمَاهَ *He* (a digger) *produced,* or *fetched out, water, by his labour* or *work;* syn. أَنْبَطَ المَآءَ; (Ṣ, Ḳ:) or *reached the water:* (Mṣb:) or *reached much water;* as also أَمْهَى. (AA, in TA, art. نبط.) — أَمَاهَ الرَّكِيَّةَ *He* (a man) *produced,* or *fetched out, by his labour,* or *work* [*in digging,*] *the water of the well;* syn. أَنْبَطَ مَآءَهَا: (Ṣ, Ḳ:) *He* (God) *made the water of the well to be much,* or *abundant.* (Mṣb.)

موى

مَاهَةٌ *Small-pox:* see آهَةٌ in art. اوه.

مَاوِيَّةٌ *A mirror;* so called in relation to water, because of its clearness, and because images are seen in it as they are in clear water: the م is a radical letter. (T in art. اوى.)

ميس

المَيْسَانُ One of the two stars called الهَنْعَةُ. The other [ع] is called الزِّرُّ. (El-Ḳazweenee.)

ميش

1. مَاشَ *He mixed hair with wool:* see طَرَقَ; and see Freytag's Arab. Prov. ii. 28. — مَاشَ الكَلَامَ i. q. طَارَقَهُ [*He practised various modes of speech*]. (TA in art. طرق.)

ميع

4. اماعهُ *He made it to flow.* (Mṣb.)

7. انماع *It flowed.* (Mṣb.)

مَائِعٌ Anything *in a melted state, fluid,* or *liquid:* opposed to جَامِدٌ. (Mṣb.)

مَيْعَةٌ *Briskness, liveliness,* or *sprightliness.* (Ṣ.) The *prime,* or *first part,* of youth, and of the day. (Ṣ, Ḳ.) The *first part* of the run of a horse: (Ṣ:) the *first part, and the briskness, liveliness,* or *sprightliness,* of a run, and of intoxication: or the *main part* of anything. (TA.) — And The *flowing of* anything poured out. (TA.)

ميل

1. مَالَ [*He,* or *it, inclined, leant, bent, propended, tended, declined, deviated,* or *deflected.*] — مَالَ مَعَهُ and مَايَلَهُ ♦ *He conformed with,* and *assisted,* or *aided, him.* (TA.) — مَالَ إِلَيْهِ *He loved him.* (TA.) — مَالَ عَلَيْهِ *He wronged him.* (TA.) *He was,* or *became, inimical to him.* — مَالَتِ الدَّابَّةُ مِنْ رِجْلِهَا (Ḳ, art. غمز,) *i. q.* ظَلَعَتْ [It *limped*]. (TA.)

2. مَيَّلَ بَيْنَ شَيْئَيْنِ *He wavered,* or *vacillated, between two things.* (Ṣ, MA.) See 10.

3. مَايَلَهُ *He inclined towards him reciprocally:* and مَايَلَا *they two inclined each towards the other.* (TḲ, art. هود.) See also مَالَ مَعَهُ in 1.

5. See 6. — تَمَيَّلَ بِالقَوْلِ *He vacillated in the saying:* see تَرَجَّحَ.

6. تَمَايَلَ فِي مِشْيَتِهِ [*He affected an inclining of his body,* or *a bending,* or *he inclined his body,* or *bent, from side to side, in his gait;* a meaning well known, and still common]; (Ṣ;) syn. تَثَنَّى. (Ḥar, p. 269.) — See تَرَابَغَ. — تَمَايَلَتْ فِى مِشْيَتِهَا and تَمَيَّدَتْ ♦ signify the same. (TA.) — تَمَايَلَ إِلَى الشَّىْءِ; and عَنْ طَرِيقِهِ: i.q. تَجَانَفَ [*He affected a deviation,* or *purposely deviated from his course,* &c.] (TA in art. جنف.)

10. استماله, and استمال بِقَلْبِهِ, (Ṣ, Ḳ,) *He inclined him,* and *his heart.* (Ḳ.) — اِسْتَمَالَهُ *He attracted him to himself;* or *sought to make him incline.* (MA.) — استمال is a quasi-pass. of مَيَّلَهُ ♦. (Ḳ,* TA.)

مِيلٌ as used by the Arabs, [*A mile:*] The *distance to which the eye reaches along land:* accord. to the ancient astronomers, *three thousand cubits:* accord to the moderns, *four thousand cubits:* but the difference is merely verbal; for they agree that its extent is ninety-six thousand digits; [about 5166 English feet;] each digit being the measure of six barley-corns, each placed with its belly next to another; but the ancients say that the cubit is thirty-two digits; which makes the mile three thousand cubits. (Mṣb, which see for more.) See also مُطْلَبٌ. — مِيلٌ *i.q.* مُلْمُولٌ, [*A style*]. (Ḳ.)

مَيْلٌ *Inclination; leaning; bent; propensity; tendency.*

مَيَلٌ *A natural wryness.* (Ṣ.)

مِيلَانٌ (?) of a مَحَالَة of a well: see ثِنَايَةٌ.

مَيَّالٌ [*i. q.* مُتَمَايِلٌ, *Inclining much*]. (A, art. فيد.) See سَيَّالٌ.

أَمْيَلُ *Swaying* on horseback: see an ex. of its pl. مِيلٌ in a verse cited voce أَشْعَلَ. — عِيَّةٌ مَيْلَآءُ: see قَفْدَآءُ.

امالة الأَلِف *The inclining of the sound of* ا, *when quiescent, after fet-ḥah, towards the sound of* ى; *so that the fet-ḥah, with that* ا, *composes a sound the same as that of the long "e" in the English word "there."* This is accordant with present usage; and I have not found any learned Arab who asserts otherwise. See also نَابٌ, and حَجَّاجٌ, and مَشُوبٌ.

ن

نأث

1. نَأَثَ عَنْهُ, aor. ـَ, (inf. n. نَأْثٌ, TA,) *He became distant, or far removed, from him, or it.* (K.) — نَأَثَ, aor. ـَ, inf. n. نَأْثٌ *He was slow, or tardy.* (TA.) — Also, inf. n. نَأْثٌ and مَنْأَثٌ, *He walked, or went,* syn. سَعَى, (K,) *at a slow pace.* (TA.)

4. انأثهُ, inf. n. إِنْآثٌ, *He removed him, or it, far off; put him, or it, at a distance.* (TA.)

سَيْرٌ مَنْأَثٌ [so accord. to a marginal note in the L, in the handwriting of SM] *A slow pace, or going, or journeying.* (TA.)

نأدل

نَئِدُلٌ *Calamity; incubus; nightmare:* see حَنْبَلٌ.

نئف

1. نَئِفَ *He disliked, disapproved, or hated.* (IAar, art. انف.)

نأى

1. نَأَى بِهِ [*He, or it, removed him; put or placed him at a distance, away, or far away.*] (S, art. طرح.) — نَأَى *He shrank* from a thing: see an ex. in a verse cited voce دَفَّ.

4. أَنْآهُ: see آنَاهُ in art. انى.

10. إِسْتَنْأَى: *i.q.* إِسْتَنْآهُ q. v. in art. نوأ.

نُؤْىٌ *A trench dug round a tent,* (S, K,) *or a barrier* [*raised*] *around it,* (T, IB, TA,) *to prevent the rain-water from entering it,* (S,) *or keep off a torrent.* (K.)

نبض

4. أَنْبَضَ فِى قَوْسِهِ *He made the string of his bow to vibrate, that it might twang.* (K.)

نبط

10. إِسْتَنْبَطَ *He drew forth, elicited, extracted, extorted:* see 4 in art. خرج. See also Bd, and Jel, iv. 85. It may sometimes be rendered *He excogitated.*

نبع

1. نَبَعَ *It* (water) *welled, or issued forth.* — نَبَأَ عليهم: see نَبَعَ عَلَيْهِمْ.

4. أَنْبَعَ *He* (God) *made, or caused,* water *to issue.* (Msb.)

نَبْعٌ *The tree so-called:* see an ex. of its n. un. in a verse cited voce تَخَوَّفَ and تَخَوَّفَ. — نَبْعَانِ: see شِرْيَانٌ and شَوْحَطٌ and فَتْخٌ. — نَبْعٌ The *two shafts* of a cart: so called because they were commonly made of wood of the tree called نَبْعٌ: see رَادَّةٌ.

اِنْبَعَ, irregularly formed from the augmented verb أَنْبَعَ: see an ex. in a couplet cited voce سَقَى.

نبق

نبق من الطريق and انباق denote *nearness* and *shortness in a way* (TA, art. عجل), like مُسْتَعْجِلَةٌ.

نَبِقٌ, properly *the fruit of the* سِدْر or *lote-tree*, is also applied to The *tree called* سِدْر *itself:* see دُوَمٌ. The fruit so called is a *drupe*, resembling the crab. — It seems to be also applied to *A drupe* absolutely, or *a drupe like that of the* سِدْر: see its dim., ▼ نُبَيْقَةٌ voce أَشْكَلُ: see also شِرْيَانٌ.

نبيق [app. نُبَيْقٌ] *A bad sort of dates, also called* خُبَيْقٌ. (TA in art. حبق.) — See نَبِقٌ.

نُبَيْقَةٌ of a grape-vine, *A* زَمَعَة *when it has grown large.* (ISh in TA, art. زمع.)

نبل

نَبْلٌ *Arrows:* (M:) or *Arabian arrows:* (T, S, Mgh, Msb, K:) for the sing. they say سَهْمٌ. (T.)

نُبْلٌ *Sharpness, acuteness,* or *sagacity;* syn. ذَكَآءٌ: and *generosity,* or *nobility;* syn. نَجَابَةٌ. (K.) — نُبْلٌ *Excellence;* (T, M;) syn. نَجَابَةٌ; and also ذَكَآءٌ. (M.) [Ex.],

كَفَى المَرْءَ نُبْلًا أَنْ تُعَدَّ مَعَايِبُهْ •

(MF, art. حبر.)

نبه

1. مَا نَبِهَ لَهُ *He did not know it;* or *know,* or *have knowledge, of it; was not cognizant of it;* or *did not understand it.* (K.) — نَبِهَ لِلْأَمْرِ *His attention became roused to the thing,* or *affair, after he had forgotten it.* (AZ, S.) — مَا نَبِهْتُ لَهُ: see مَا أَبِهْتُ لَهُ. — نَبَأَ عليهم: see نَبِهَ عَلَيْهِمْ. — نَبُهَ *He was, or became, eminent, celebrated, or well known.* (S, K,* TA.)

2. نَبَّهَهُ عَلَى الشَّىْءِ *He made him acquainted with the thing; informed him of it; gave him notice of it; notified it to him.* (S.) — نَبَّهَهُ لِلْأَمْرِ ‡ [*He roused his attention to the thing,* or *affair*]. (TA in art. يقظ.) — نَبَّهَهُ ‡ [*He roused him* from heedlessness or inadvertence: *he roused his attention.* (TA.)

5. تَنَبَّهَ عَلَى الشَّىْءِ *He became acquainted with the thing; became informed of it; had notice of it.* (S.) — تَنَبَّهَ لِلْأَمْرِ ‡ [*His attention became roused,* or *he had his attention roused, to the thing,* or *affair*]. (Msb and TA in art. يقظ.) — تَنَبَّهَ ‡ *He became vigilant, wary,* or *cautious.* (Msb, TA.) — تَنَبَّهَ and ▼ إِنْتَبَهَ ‡ *He became roused* from heedlessness or inadvertence; *his attention became roused;* or *he had his attention roused.* (TA.)

8: see 5.

نَبِيهٌ *Eminent, celebrated,* or *well known;* (Ṣ, Ḳ,* TA;) *contr. of* خَامِلٌ. (Ṣ, TA.)

كَلِمَةُ تَنْبِيهٍ *A word used to give notice,* to a person addressed, of something about to be said to him. (TA, voce هَا.) See also هَا termed تَنْبِيهٌ. It may generally be rendered *Now.*

نبى

1. نَبَا عَنِ الضَّرِيبَةِ *It* (a sword) *recoiled, or reverted,* [or *glanced off,* or *away,*] *from the thing struck with it, without penetrating, or without effect;* (TA;) *returned from it without cutting;* (Mṣb;) *took no effect upon it;* (Ṣ;) syn. كَلَّ. (Ḳ.) — نَبَا *It* (the edge of a sword) *would not cut; was blunt.* (TA.) — نَبَا عَنِ الشَّىْءِ *It* (the sight) *recoiled, or reverted, from the thing; was repelled by it;* (Ṣ,* Ḳ,* TA;) syn. تَجَافَى (TA) and كَلَّ. (Ḳ.) — نَبَا عَنِ الشَّىْءِ *It* (nature) *recoiled, flinched, shrank, or was averse, from the thing,* or *shunned it, and would not accept it.* (Mṣb.) — نَبَا جَنْبُهُ عَنِ الفِرَاشِ ‡ *His side did not rest,* or *was restless,* or *uneasy, upon the bed:* (Ḳ, TA:) *it shrank from it.* — نَبَا *It* (a saddle) *was unfirm,* or *unsteady; not firm,* or *steady, in its place.* (TA.)

نَبِىٌّ: see a verse voce رَتَمٌ.

نَبِيَّةٌ, *A thing like the* سُفْرَة, q.v., *made of palm-leaves, upon which flour or meal is sifted.* (I'Abbád, O, Ḳ.)

نتع

نُتُوعٌ The *gums* of trees; correctly نُتُوحٌ.

نتن

وَا نَتْنَاهُ and نَتْنًا لَهُ *Fye or shame on him* or *it!* See دَفْرٌ.

مُنْتِنٌ, originally مُنْتِينٌ or مُنْتَنٌ: see مُنْخِرٌ.

نثل

1. نَثَلَ *He cleansed an intestine:* see مُبْعَرٌ.

نَثُولٌ *A lean,* or *emaciated,* woman. (IAạr, TA, art. جمل.)

نَثِيلٌ The *dust,* or *earth, of the foundations of a house.* (TA, art. ثوب.)

نَثِيلَةُ بِئْرٍ *The earth that is around a well, that is seen from afar.* (Ṣ, art. جبو.)

نثى

1. نَثَيْتُ and نَثَوْتُ عَنْهُ خَبَرًا: see رثى.

6. تَنَاثَيْنَاهُ: see رثى.

أَنْثَى: see أَنْثَى.

نجع

1. نَجَعَ فِيهِ *It* (a discourse, Ṣ, Ḳ; and exhortation, Ṣ, Mṣb, Ḳ; and medicine, Ṣ, Mṣb; and fodder, Mṣb) *entered into him, and produced an effect upon him:* (Ṣ, Ḳ:) or *showed its effect* [*upon him*]. (Mṣb.) — *It* (medicine) *benefited him;* as also ▾ أَنْجَعَ and ▾ نَجَّعَ. (TA.) [And *It* (eating) *had an agreeable, a wholesome,* or *a beneficial, effect upon him:* so I have rendered it voce عَنَى.] — نَجَعَ said of food and of beverage, inf. n. نُجُوعٌ, *It was* [*wholesome,* or] *suitable,* or *it agreed.* (So accord. to an expl. of the inf. n. in the KL.)

2: } see 1.
4: }

8. إِنْتَجَعَ *He sought after herbage* (Ṣ, Mgh, Ḳ) *in its place:* (Ṣ, Ḳ:) or *went to seek after herbage in its place.* (Mṣb.) And انتجع بَلَدًا [*He sought after herbage in a district,* or *country*]. (Ḳ in art. حنك.)

نَجْعٌ for نَجَعٌ: see رِجْعَةٌ.

نُجْعَةٌ The *seeking after herbage* (Ṣ, Mgh, Ḳ) *in its place;* (Ṣ, Ḳ;) the *going to seek after herbage in its place.* (Mṣb.)

نَجِيعٌ *Effused blood:* see 2 in art. خوض.

مَنْجَعٌ, pl. مَنَاجِعُ *A desert:* see بَادِيَةٌ.

مُنْتَجَعٌ *A place where herbage is sought:* see مَحْضَرٌ.

نجف

نِجَافٌ of a door, *i. q.* دَرْوَنْد [a Persian word, *A bolt,* or *bar.*] (IAạr in L, art. رتج.)

نجل

طَعْنَةٌ نَجْلَآءُ *A wide wound with a spear or the like.* (TA.) See an ex. in a verse cited voce رُبَّ. — عَيْنٌ نَجْلَآءُ *A wide eye;* pl. عُيُونٌ نُجْلٌ. (TA.) See a verse in art. فرغ (conj. 4).

مِنْجَلٌ *A reaping-hook.* (Mgh; and Ṣ, Ḳ, voce مِعْضَدٌ.) *It has a toothed,* or *serrated, edge:* (A, art. حز; and Ḳ, art. اشر:) *and is sometimes plain.* (Ḳ, voce مِحَشٌّ, and M and L, voce سِنٌّ.) See مِخْلَبٌ and دَرْهَرَهَةٌ. — [*A reaping-hook:* or *a pruning-hook:* sometimes signifying the latter:] *an iron implement, having teeth, with which seed-produce is cut:* or one *with which the wood,* or *branch, is cut off from the tree, and cast down,* or *away.* (TA.)

طَخْمَآءُ: see تَجِيلٌ.

نجم

4. أَنْجَمَ *It* (rain, &c.) *left off.* (Ḳ.)

نَجْمٌ [*A star.* — Also, *An asterism,* or *constellation:* being applied autonomastically to] *the Pleiades.* (Ṣ.) — نُجُومٌ [like عُرُوقٌ] signifies also The *sprouts from the roots* [of a tree, or shrub], *before the* رَبِيع [meaning either *spring* or *autumn*], *the heads of which one sees like large needles, cleaving the ground.* (TA.) See عُسْلُوجٌ. — نَجْمٌ also signifies ‡ The *time when a payment falls due.* (Mṣb.) [Hence, app., an ex cited voce طَىٌّ.] — And hence, (Mṣb,) ‡ *An instalment;* syn. وَظِيفَةٌ. (Mgh, Mṣb.) See also عَزْلٌ. — نَجْمٌ and نَجْمَةٌ *A kind of plant, triticum repens* or *dogs' grass:* see ثِيلٌ.

مِنْجَمٌ The *beam of a balance;* (MA;) the *transverse piece of iron, in which is the tongue, of a balance.* (Ṣ, Ḳ.) See عَمُودُ المِيزَانِ.

نجو

1. نَجَا *Alvum dejecit;* (Mṣb, TA;) *ventumve per anum emisit:* (TA:) *he voided his ordure;* or *broke wind.* — نَجَا, inf. n. نَجَآءٌ, *He was quick,* or *swift,* and *outstripped.* (Ṣ.) See an ex. of the inf. n., voce غَوْلٌ. — نَجَا *He became safe,* or *secure; he escaped.* (Mṣb, &c.)

2: see 4.

4. أَنْجَاهُ and ▾ نَجَّاهُ *He saved him; rescued him; preserved him.* (Ḳ.)

10. إِسْتَنْجَى *He washed,* or *wiped with a stone* or *a piece of dry clay, the place* [*of exit*] *of his excrement.* (Mṣb.) = إِسْتَنْجَوْا: see 8 in art. سعر.

نَجْوٌ and نَجَآءٌ *A shower of rain.* — See شُؤْبُوبٌ and 1. — نجاء *A well of which the water is distant* [*from the mouth*]. (O, TA, voce قُرْبٌ.)

نَجْوَةٌ *An elevated piece of land.* (Mṣb.)

نَجِىٌّ: see نَجْوَى. — عُرْيَانُ النَّجِىِّ: see art. عرى.

نَجْوَى *Secret discourse between two persons or parties.* (TA.) — *A secret between two persons or parties;* as also ▾ نَجِىٌّ. (Ḳ*, TA.) — *A person, or persons, discoursing secretly, or telling secrets one with another.* (TA.)

مَنْجَاةٌ [*A cause, or means, of safety:* of the measure مَفْعَلَةٌ, originally مَنْجَوَةٌ; similar to مَفْلَحَةٌ, &c.]. (Ṣ.)

نَجِيثٌ a dial. var. of نَجُوثٌ: see دَوْكَةٌ.

نحز

1. نَحَزَ: see an ex. in a verse cited voce عَابِجٌ.

نَاحِزٌ: see نَاكِثٌ.

مِنْحَازٌ *A mortar;* syn. هَاوُونٌ. (Ḳ.)

نحس

5: see 10.

10. اِسْتَنْحَسْتُهُ عَنْ كَذَا and ↑ تَنَحَّسْتُهُ: see 10 in art. سنح.

نحف

نَحِيفٌ *Slender, slim, thin, spare, lean,* or *light of flesh.*

نحل

1. نَحَلَ جِسْمُهُ *His body became lean,* or *emaciated.* (Ṣ.)

نِحْلَةٌ *i. q.* فَرِيضَةٌ; or دِيَانَةٌ; and دِينٌ, as in the saying مَا نِحْلَتُكَ [*What is thy religion?*]. (TA.)

نحم

1. نَحَمَ, said of a horse, seems to be best rendered *He breathed pantingly,* or *hard, with a sound from the chest.* See 1 in art. ضبح.

نَحِيمٌ signifies *A sound* (صَوْتٌ) *from the chest* of the horse. (TA.)

نحو

1. نَحَا نَحْوَهُ *He went towards,* or *in the direction of, him* or *it.* (Mṣb, TA.) — Also, *He pursued his* (another's) *course, doing as he did;* or *purposed his purpose.* — See عَرَضَ عَرْضَهُ, and شَدَا شَدْوَهُ; and see قَصَدَهُ. — نَحَاهُ, inf. n. نَحْوٌ, signifies [also] *He purposed it,* or *intended it.* (MA.) — نَحَوْتُ جِلْدَ الْبَعِيرِ, and ↑ أَنْحَيْتُهُ, *I stripped off the skin of the camel.* (Mṣb, voce سَلَخَ). See 4.

2. نَحَّى *He put* a thing *aside,* or *away,* or *apart;* (Mṣb;) *removed* it *from its place,* (Mṣb, Ḳ, TA,) *placed* it *at a distance.* (TA.) — *He made* a person *to turn away,* or *withdraw,* or *retire,* from (عَنْ) an affair. — نَحَّى عَنْهُ الشَّىْءَ *He put aside,* or *away,* or *he warded off,* or *removed, from him the thing.* See 4.

4. أَنْحَى عَلَيْهِ [*He leant, bore,* or *pressed, upon him,* or *it,* with his body, hand, &c.:] i. q. اِعْتَمَدَ; as also ↑ نَحَا. (IAạr, TA.) — أَنْحَى عَلَى فُلَانٍ بِالسَّوْطِ [*He attacked such a one with the whip*], and بِالسَّيْفِ [*with the sword*]: and hence بِالتَّعْنِيفِ ‡ *he accosted him with harsh,* or *rough, behaviour;* syn. أَقْبَلَ عَلَيْهِ. (Ḥar, p. 508.) — أَنْحَى عَلَى الشَّىْءِ بِجَمِيعِ كَفِّهِ [*He seized the thing with his whole hand*]. (M, voce قَبَضَ [q. v.]). — أَنْحَيْتُ عَلَى حَلْقِهِ السِّكِّينَ *I applied the knife to,* or *put it across, his throat,* or *fauces;* syn. عَرَضْتُهُ: and in like manner you say, نحى عليه بشفرته [but whether by this be meant نَحَّى or نَحَا is doubtful. (TA.) — See 1.

5. تَنَحَّى *He,* or *it, removed; withdrew; went,* or *moved, away,* or *aside;* (Mṣb;) or *retired to a distance.* (TA.) — تَنَحَّى (TA, art. قعر,) signifies تكلّف ان يتكلّم كلامًا نَحْوِيًّا, i. e. تكلّف التكلّم على طريق النحاة. (IbrD.)

8. اِنْتَحَى *It fell, like a man's hand when he strikes with it upon his other hand;* (L, TA, in art. ترح:) and, in prostration, *he fell with his forehead to the ground, and rested upon his forehead, not upon the palms of his hands:* mentioned by Sh, from 'Abd-Eṣ-Ṣamad Ibn-Ḥassán, on the authority of some of the Arabs: so says Az. (L and TA in that art.)

نَحْوٌ The *like* of a thing: syn. مِثْلٌ. (TA.) — *Quantity,* &c.; syn. مِقْدَارٌ. (TA.) — *A division,* &c.; syn. قِسْمٌ. (TA.) — نَحْوَهُ: see نَحَا. — فِى نَحْوِ ثَلَاثٍ *About three.* نَحْوُ الثَّلَاثَةِ — عَرَفْتُهُ فِى نَحْوِ سَاعَاتٍ *In about three hours.* — فِى مِعْرَاضِ and فِى لَحْنِ كلامه and كَلَامِهِ كلامه signify the same. (Mṣb in art. عرض.) See the last of these, voce عَرُوضٌ. — اِتَّئِدْ عَلَى نَحْوِكَ, i. e. أَوْنُ عَلَى قَدْرِكَ [or مِقْدَارِكَ]: see art. اون.

نَحِىٌّ: see نِحْىٌ.

نِحْىٌ *A skin for holding liquids:* (Ḳ:) or *for clarified butter:* (Ṣ, Mṣb, Ḳ:) as also ↑ نَحْىٌ. (Ḳ.)

شَدِيدُ النَّاحِيَةِ †A *hardy* man. (TA, art. عرض.)

ذَاتُ النِّحْيَيْنِ. Respecting what is said of the woman thus named, and of خَوَّاتٌ, in the Ṣ, see شرد.

مُتَنَحٍّ *Going,* or *being, away* from (عَنْ) a place, person, or thing. — مُتَنَحًّى [*A place to which to turn away,* or *back,* from a thing; or *to which one removes, withdraws,* or *retires afar off*]. (Ḳ, voce مُنْكَصٌ.) See مُنْكَصٌ and مُنْحَرَفٌ.

نَاحِيَةٌ *i. q.* جَانِبٌ q. v., *A side; a lateral,* or *an outward,* or *adjacent, part* or *portion.* (Ḳ, &c.) — *An apartment* of a house. (Mgh, voce حَيِّزٌ.) And the pl., نَوَاحٍ, *The outer parts* or *regions* of an animal. The sing. may often be rendered *A part,* or *portion,* of a place. — نَاحِيَةٌ is of the measure فَاعِلَةٌ in the sense of the measure مَفْعُولَةٌ, [meaning مَنْحُوَّةٌ, *a part,* or *the like,* or *a point, towards which one goes,* or *directs himself; a point of direction;*] because one goes, or directs himself, towards it: (Mṣb:) best rendered as above; adding, or *part, region, district, quarter,* or *tract, considered with respect to its collocation or juxtaposition or direction,* or *considered as belonging to a whole: a vicinage,* or *neighbourhood:* and *a part of a country, a region, district, quarter,* or *tract, absolutely; a district; a province:* often best rendered *a side;* or *a region, district, quarter,* or *tract:* or *a part of a place, an apartment:* see حَيِّزٌ, in art. حوز. — Also *A limit, bound,* or *boundary:* see two tropical exs. of its pl. (نَوَاحٍ) voce حِنْوٌ, and another in a verse voce رَسُولٌ: or *a remote side;* syn. جَانِبٌ مُتَنَحٍّ: (Kz, in TA:) *a tract of land.* (KL.) See أُفُقٌ and جَانِبٌ. — عَلَى نَاحِيَةٍ *Beside, aside,* or *apart;* like عَلَى جَانِبٍ and عَلَى طَرَفٍ; and so نَاحِيَةً and فِى نَاحِيَةٍ, &c.: you say جَلَسَ فِى نَاحِيَةٍ مِنْهُمْ *He sat aside,* or *apart, from them:* and أَنَا فِى نَوَاحٍ مِنْ هٰذَا الأَمْرِ, expl. voce شَقٌّ. And فِى نَاحِيَةِ كَذَا *In the direction of such a thing:* see أَشْرَى. — هُوَ عَلَى نَاحِيَتِهِ *He is keeping to his own side, following his own course:* see جَدِيَّةٌ.

نخع

نُخَاعٌ *The spinal cord,* or *spinal marrow;* (Ṣ, Ḳ, &c.;) *what extends from the* هَامَة *through* (فِى) *the vertebræ to the end of the* ذَنَب, *like a cord of marrow.* (Zj in his "Khalḳ el-Insán.") See also شَلِيلٌ and البِخَاعُ.

أَخْنَعُ: see أَنْخَعُ.

نخف

نِخَافٌ *A boot:* (IAạr, Ḳ, TA:) or *a boot much patched.* (Az, TA.)

نخل

1: } see 8.
5: }

8. اِنْتَخَلَهُ *He cleared it* [or *sifted it*]; as also

نَخَلَهُ and ↓تَنَخَّلَهُ: (Ḳ [see سَفْسَفَهُ]:) or *he took the best of it* (Ṣ, Mṣb) *to the utmost*: (Ṣ:) or *he chose the best of it for himself.* (TA.)

نَخْلِىٌّ *A cultivator of palm-trees*: see عَطَّلٌ.

نُخَالٌ *Bran.*

نخو

1. نُخِىَ بِكَذَا: *He boasted of such a thing*: see زُهِىَ بِكَذَا.

نَخْوَةٌ *Pride; self-magnification; haughtiness.* (Ṣ, Mṣb, Ḳ.)

ندس

5. تَنَدَّسَ عَنِ الأَخْبَارِ *He sought to learn the news privily*: see تَحَدَّسَ and تَحَسَّسَ.

رِمَاحٌ نَوَادِسُ *Piercing spurs*: see a verse of El-Kumeyt cited voce غَارَةٌ, in art. غور.

ندف

1. نَدَفَ [*He separated and loosened* cotton *by means of a bow and a kind of wooden mallet, by striking the string of the bow with the mallet*: see حَلَجَ; and حَزَنَ] *he beat* cotton *with the* ↓مِنْدَف, (Ṣ, Mṣb,* Ḳ,) also called ↓مِنْدَفَة, i.e., *his wooden implement with which he strikes the bow-string, that it* [*the cotton*] *might become fine.* (Ḳ.)

مِنْدَفٌ and مِنْدَفَةٌ: see 1; and see مِحْزَنٌ and مِنْبَضٌ.

ندل

5. تَنَدَّلَ *He bound a* دَسْتَار [or مِنْدِيل i.e. *napkin or the like*] *upon his head.* (KL.) And ↓تَمَنْدَلَ بِمِنْدِيلٍ *He bound a* منديل *upon his head.* (Mgh.)

Q.Q. 2. تَمَنْدَلَ بِرَائِطَةٍ *He used a* رائطة [or رَيْطَة] *as a* مِنْدِيل. (TA in art. ريط from a trad.) — See 5.

مِنْدَلٌ app., *Hard steel* (ذَكَرٌ صُلْبٌ, *not penis rigens*). (Ḳ.) See ذَكَرٌ.

ندم

1. نَدِمَ عَلَى مَا فَعَلَ *He grieved for what he had done; regretted it; repented of it*: or *he disliked it.* (Mṣb.)

نَدِيمٌ *A companion in drinking; a cup-companion.* (Ṣ, Mṣb, Ḳ.) And hence, *Any convivial companion; a boon-companion.*

مَنْدَمٌ *Repentance*: an inf. n. of نَدِمَ; see an ex. in a verse of El-Ḳattál El-Kilábee, cited voce أَىٌّ.

ندى

1. نَدِىَ *It was, or became, moist, or moistened.* (Ṣ, Ḳ.) — مَا نَدِيَنِى مِنْهُ شَىْءٌ, (M,) or مَا نَدِيَنِى مِنْهُ شَىْءٌ أَكْرَهُهُ, (T,) [*A thing, or a thing that I dislike,*] *did not betide me or befall me* [*from him*]. (T, M.) And لَا يَنْدَاكَ مِنِّى شَىْءٌ تَكْرَهُهُ [*A thing that thou dislikest*] *shall not befall thee* [*from me*]. (M.) مَا نَدِيتُ كَفِّى لَهُ بِشَرٍّ [*My hand did not evil to him*]: and مَا نَدِيتُ بِشَىْءٍ تَكْرَهُهُ [*I did not a thing that thou dislikest*]. (T.) See also art. عرق, first par., last sentence but two. — سَأَلْتُهُ فَلَمْ يَنْدَ لِى بِشَىْءٍ [*I asked him, and he did not to me, or for me, anything*]. (TA, in art عنو.) — مَا تَنْدَى صَفَاتُهُ i. q. مَا يَبِضُّ حَجَرُهُ, q. v. (Ṣ, art. بض.) See also art. صفو.

2: see 5.

3. نَادَى عَلَيْهِ [*He made proclamation of him*] (Ṣ, A, Mṣb) بِالْإِفْلَاسِ (A) or أَنَّهُ أَفْلَسَ (Ṣ) or بِأَنَّهُ صَارَ مُفْلِسًا (Mṣb) [*that he had become bankrupt, or insolvent*]. — [نَادَى بِهِ *He proclaimed it; made proclamation of it*: a very common signification, but one which I have not found in any Lex.] — You say also نَادَى فِى النَّاسِ, meaning تَقَدَّمَ and أَعْلَمَ and تَأَذَّنَ. (Ṣ in art. اذن. See وَنُودُوا أَنْ تِلْكُمُ الجَنَّةُ (Ḳur vii. 41:) — [آذَنَهُ.] see أَنْ as a contraction of أَنَّ. — نَادَاهُ تُرَابُهُ: see نباته الارض. — نَادَاهُ *He called him; called to him; summoned him, or hailed him*: (Ṣ, Mṣb:) or, (T, M,) and نادى به, (M,) *he called out to him* (T, M) *with the loudest voice.* (T.)

5. تَنَدَّى [quasi-pass. of ↓نَدَّى, *It was moistened, by dew, or the like*; or] *i. q.* نَدِىَ [*it was, or became, moist*]; said of a place [&c.]: and *i. q.* تَرَوَّى. (TA.)

نِدَآءٌ signifies simply The *raising the voice;* not implying the expression of meaning by speech. (Er-Rághib, TA.) — حَرْفُ نِدَآءٍ *A particle of calling, or hailing, or invocation;* as يَا. — *A vocative particle.* — The *vocative form of speech.* — Also, agreeably with many other instances, like خَلْقٌ in the sense of مَخْلُوقٌ, an inf. n. used in the sense of a pass. part. n., meaning A person or thing *called;* the *object of a vocative particle,* syn. with ↓مُنَادًى.

نَدًى, originally, *Rain*: (Mṣb: [but generally it seems to signify *dew,* absolutely; or *day-dew.*] See a tropical usage in a verse of El-Kumeyt cited voce رِقْبَةٌ. — نَدًى *Bounty; liberality*: (Ṣ, M:) *a gift.* (T.) — نَدًى *Moisture* (Ṣ, Ḳ) of the earth; as also ↓نَدَاوَةٌ. (Ṣ.) — نَدًى is generally thus written: not نَدًا.

نَدِىٌّ *An assembly*: see a verse cited voce شَرَفٌ.

نُدُوَّةٌ and نَدَاوَةٌ *Moisture.* (Mṣb.) See نَدًى.

نِدَآءٌ: see مُنَادًى.

نرجس

دَابَّةٌ نَرْجِسِيَّةٌ *A beast of carriage whose whiteness inclines to yellowness* [like the narcissus]. (TA, art. قرطس.)

نرسن

نِرْسِيَانَةٌ *A species of dates.* (Ṣ, in art. رسو.)

نزع

1. نَزَعَ إِلَى أَهْلِهِ, (Ṣ, Ḳ,) aor. ـِ, (Ṣ,) inf. n. نِزَاعٌ (Ṣ, Ḳ) and نُزُوعٌ and نَزَاعَةٌ; (Ḳ;) and ↓نَازَعَ; (Ḳ;) *He yearned towards or for, longed for, or desired, his family.* (Ṣ,* Ḳ,* TA, PS). — نَزَعْتُ إِلَيْهِ inf. n. نِزَاعٌ, *I yearned towards, longed for, or desired, him or it*; syn. حَنَنْتُ. (Ḥam, p. 429.) See an ex. voce خَفَضَ. — Hence, نَزَعَ بِى إِلَيْهِ *It* (desire) *invited me to it.* (Ḥar, p. 606.) — نَزَعَ إِلَيْهِ *He inclined to it.* (Har, p. 234.) — نَزَعَ إِلَى عِرْقٍ كَرِيمٍ [*He inclined to a noble radical, or ancestral, or hereditary quality*; and in like manner, [لَئِيمٍ]: and نَزَعَ إِلَى أَعْرَاقِهِ and نَزَعَهَا [*he inclined to his radical, or ancestral, or hereditary, qualities*]: and نَزَعَتْ بِهِ أَعْرَاقُهُ [*his radical, or ancestral, or hereditary, qualities inclined him*]. (L, in TA.) — نَزَعَ إِلَى *It inclined by likeness.* (Mṣb.) — نَزَعَ أَبَاهُ (Ṣ, Mṣb, Ḳ,) فِى الشَّبَهِ (Ṣ,) and أَبِيهِ, (Ḳ,) *He resembled his father*: (Mṣb, Ḳ:) or *inclined to his father in likeness*; syn. ذَهَبَ: (Ṣ:) or *he took after his father; had a natural likeness to him.* — نُزُوعٌ signifies *Yearning*; and *natural inclining.* — نَزَعَ and ↓إِنْتَزَعَ *He pulled, plucked,* or *drew, out, or up, or off; removed from his or its place; displaced.* (Ṣ, Mṣb, Ḳ.) — نَزَعَ ثَوْبَهُ, (Mgh, in art. خلع,) and نَعْلَهُ, (Mgh and Mṣb in that art.,) *He pulled off his garment,* and *his sandal.* See, however, خَلَعَ.

— نَزَعَ, (Mṣb, TA,) aor. ـِ, (TA,) inf. n. نَزْعٌ (Mṣb, TA,) *He was at the point* [or *in the agony*] *of death;* meaning, *of having his soul drawn forth:* (Mṣb:) *he gave up his spirit;* as also ↓ نَازَعَ, inf. n. نِزَاعٌ. (TA.) — نَزَعَ فِى القَوْسِ *He drew the bow;* (Ṣ, Mṣb, Ḳ;) i. e., *its string;* or *he drew,* or *pulled, the string of the bow with the arrow.* (TA.) = تَنْزِعُهُ شَعْرَةٌ بَيْضَآءُ, relating to a horse: see أَسْفَى.

3. نَازَعَهُ الحَبْلَ *He contended with him in pulling the rope;* syn. جَاذَبَهُ إِيَّاهُ. Hence, نازعه فى كَذَا ‡ *He contended, disputed,* or *litigated, with him, respecting such a thing.* (Mgh.) — نَازَعَهُ الكَلَامَ ‡ *He disputed with him in,* or *respecting, words.* (TA.) — نَازَعَتْنِى نَفْسِى إِلَى هَوَاهَا, inf. n. نِزَاعٌ, *My soul strove with me to incline me to love her.* (TA.) See 1.

6. تَنَازَعْنَا الحَدِيثَ *We discoursed together; one with another.* (TA, art. هصر.) — تَنَازَعُوا الرَّجَزَ بَيْنَهُمْ (Ḳ, art. رجز,) *They recited verses,* or *poetry, of the metre termed* رَجَز *one with another;* as also تَعَاطَوْهُ. (TḲ, art. رجز.) — تَنَازُعٌ *The contending in altercation, disputing,* or *litigating, one with another:* (Ḳ:) or تَنَازَعُوا *they disagreed, one with another; held different ways* or *opinions.* (Mṣb.)

8. See 1. — إِنْتَزَعَ مِنْهُ حَقَّهُ *He wrested from him his right,* or *due.* — إِنْتَزَعَ حَدِيثَهُ: see اِقتضب.

نَزَعٌ *Baldness on each side of the forehead:* see جَلَحٌ; and غَمَمٌ.

نَزَعَةٌ *A baldness in the side of the forehead.* See صَدْمَةٌ.

بِئْرٌ نَزُوعٌ [*A deep well*] *i. q.* جَرُورٌ. (A, voce جرور.)

نُزَّعٌ is pl. of نَازِعٌ; as is also نُزَعٌ. (TA.) See an ex. in a verse cited voce بَابٌ.

نَزَّاعٌ *Dragging much,* or *forcibly:* see Ḳur, lxx. 16. — العِرْقُ نَزَّاعٌ (see Freytag's Arab. Prov., ii. 168) is probably similar to العِرْقُ دَسَّاسٌ, and means *The radical,* or *ancestral,* or *hereditary, quality is wont to return to its usual possessor:* or it may mean, *is wont to draw.*

أَنْزَعُ: see أَجْلَحُ.

مَنْزَعُ بِئْرٍ [*The bottom of a well; the place from which the water is drawn*]. (TA, art. متح.)

نزف

1. نَزَفَ *He entirely exhausted* (Ṣ, Mṣb, Ḳ) a well, (Mṣb,) or the water of a well. (Ṣ, Ḳ.)

مَنْزُوفٌ *Exhausted:* see an ex. voce ضَرِطَ.

نزق

نَزَقٌ *Lightness, and unsteadiness,* or *lightwittedness,* (Ṣ, Mṣb, Ḳ,) *on an occasion of anger;* (Ḳ;) *i. q.* سُرْعَةٌ; *lightness in any work, or action: hastiness, with foolishness or ignorance:* (JK, TA:) *hastiness, or sharpness, of temper; irascibility; passionateness:* a meaning deduced from various examples, and confirmed by present usage.

نَزِقٌ *Light, and unsteady,* or *lightwitted.* (Mṣb.) See also نَزِقٌ: and see شُنْذُوذٌ.

نَزِقَةٌ and ↓ نِزَاقٌ *A refractory* she-camel; *hard to be managed.* (Mṣb.)

نِزَاقٌ: see نَزِقَةٌ.

اللَّبُوَةُ أَنْزَقُ مِنَ الأَسَدِ [*The lioness is more impetuous than the lion*]. (Ṣ, voce سَبُعَةٌ.)

نزك

نَزْكٌ The *penis* (ذَكَر, Ṣ, Ḳ, i. e. قَضِيب, TA) of the ضَبّ (Ṣ, Ḳ) and of the وَرَل: (Ḳ: [in the CḲ, والورك is erroneously put for والوَرَلِ:) accord. to the assertion of the Arabs, (Ṣ,) it (Ṣ, Ḳ,) the former, (Ṣ,) as also the حِرْذَوْن, (Mṣb voce حرذون,) has two penes (نِزْكَانِ); (Ṣ, Ḳ, TA;) and the female has قُرْنَتَانِ, i. e. [two wombs] رَحِمَانِ. (TA.)

نزل

1. نَزَلَ المَكَانَ (Kull) and نَزَلَ بِالمَكَانِ (Mṣb in art. حل, &c.) *He alighted, descended and stopped* or *sojourned* or *abode* or *lodged* or *settled, in the place;* syn. حَلَّ فِيهِ. (Kull.) See حَلَّ. — نَزَلَ لَبَنُ الشَّاةِ [*The milk of the ewe descended into her udder; i. e. she secreted milk*]. (Ṣ, Ḳ, voce أَضْرَعَتْ.) — نَزَلَ مَنْزِلَ كَذَا *It took,* or *occupied, the place,* or *became in the position* or *condition, of such a thing:* see a verse cited voce أَنْ, near the end of the paragraph; and another voce حَبِيبٌ; and see مَنْزِلَةٌ. — نَزَلْتُ, الوَادِىَ, for فِى الوَادِى: see دَخَلْتُ البَيْتَ in art. دخل.

3. نَازَلَهُ *He alighted with him, each to oppose the other,* in war, or battle; inf. n. مُنَازَلَةٌ and نِزَالٌ. (Mṣb.) — نَازَلَهُ *He alighted with him.*

4. أَنْزَلَتْ *Her* (a camel's) *milk descended* [*into her udder*]: opposed to أَقْلَصَتْ. (TA, art. قلص.) — أَنْزَلَتِ اللَّبَنَ [i. e. اللِّبَأَ] *She* (a camel) *excerned the first milk,* or *biestings, into her udder; i. q.* أَبْسَقَتْ. (TA in art. بزق.) — *She excerned milk* [either *into,* or *from, the udder*]. أَنْزَلَتِ النَاقَةُ اللَّبَنَ مِنَ الضَّرْعِ [or فِى الضرع] — *The she-camel excerned the milk from* [or *into*] *the udder.* (TA, art. درأ.) — أَنْزَلَهُ *He lodged him; made him his guest;* or *gave him refuge* or *asylum;* syn. آوَاهُ; (Ṣ and Ḳ in art. اوى;) and ضَيَّفَهُ and أَضَافَهُ: (Mgh in art. ضيف:) [and *he lodged and entertained him;*] namely, a guest. (Mṣb.) *I. q.* أَثْوَاهُ مَنْزِلًا. (Fr in T in art. بوأ.) — أَنْزَلَهُ عَنْ كَذَا *He made him to resign,* or *relinquish, such a thing.* — أَنْزَلْتُ بِكَ حَاجَتِى [app. *I imposed my want upon thee*]. (Ṣ in art. عر.) And أَنْزَلَ حَاجَتَهُ على كريم. (TA.)

6. تَنَازَلَ *He descended gradually, by little and little.* — تنازل إِلَى أَحَدٍ *He humbled himself, condescended, to one.* — تنازل عَنِ المُلْكِ *He abdicated the kingdom.* — تنازل عَن شَىْءٍ *He desisted from a thing.* — تَنَازَلُوا *They alighted and ate by turns with different people; i. q.* تَنَاوَبُوا, q. v.

10. اِسْتَنْزَلَهُ *He made him,* or *caused him,* or *it, to descend.* (Mṣb.) — اِسْتَنْزَلَهُ عَنْ رَأْيِهِ [*He sought to make him resign,* or *relinquish, his opinion*]. (Bḍ, xii. 11.)

نُزُلٌ *Food* or *rations at a halt:* see سُكْنٌ, in two places.

نُزُلٌ *Food prepared for the guest.* (Mṣb.) See مُقَتَّةٌ.

أَرْضٌ نَزِلَةٌ: see حَشَادٌ.

نَزِيلٌ *A guest.* (Ṣ, Mgh, Mṣb,* Ḳ.) See also Ḥar, 353.

نَازِلٌ [*Alighting,* &c.,] has for pl. نُزُولٌ and نُزَّالٌ. (TA.)

نَازِلَةٌ *A defluxion:* pl. نَوَازِلُ. See سِلٌّ. — *A severe calamity* or *affliction,* (Ṣ, Mṣb, Ḳ,) *that befalls men.* (Ṣ, Mṣb.)

مَنْزِلٌ *A place of alighting* or *descending and stopping* or *sojourning* or *abiding* or *lodging* or *settling:* (Mgh:) *a place of settlement: an abode; a dwelling; a place where travellers alight in the desert;* syn. مَنْهَلٌ: a [*house,* or *mansion, such as is called*] دَارٌ: (Ṣ, Ḳ:) or, accord. to the فُقَهَآء, *less than a* دار, *and more than a* بَيْت [*or chamber*], *consisting of at least two chambers* (بَيْتَانِ) or *three.* (Mgh.) See also بَيْتٌ.

مَنْزِلَةٌ *A space which one traverses in journeying.* (TA, art. سير.) — مَنْزِلَةٌ, used unrestrictedly, *Station, standing, footing,* or *grade; honourable station* or *rank; a place of preferment.* — *A predicament in which one stands.* — كَلِمَةٌ بِمَنْزِلَةِ كَلِمَةٍ أُخْرَى *A word equivalent,* or *similar, to another word.* — [You say] يُسْتَعْمَلُ بِمَنْزِلَةِ كَذَا *It* (a word) *is used in the manner of such* [*another word*]; generally with respect to government, not necessarily with respect to meaning. (The lexicons passim.) — النَّازِلُ مِنَ الدِّينِ وَالدُّنْيَا مَنْزِلَةَ النُّورِ مِنَ العَيْنِ *Who is, in respect to religion and the world, as light to the eye.*

مُسْكِنٌ : see مَرْعًى مُنْزِلٌ.

نزه

2. نَزَّهَ اللّٰهَ *He declared God to be far removed,* or *free, from every impurity* or *imperfection,* or *from everything derogatory from his glory;* like سَبَّحَهُ and قَدَّسَهُ. — تَنْزِيهُ اللّٰهِ is *The declaring God to be far removed,* or *free,* [*from every imperfection or impurity,* or *from everything derogatory from his glory;* i. e.,] *from evil* [*of every kind*]; or *from the having anything like unto Him by participation of his essence or otherwise, and from defects that may not be imputed to Him.* (TA.)

5. تَنَزَّهَ عَنِ الأَقْذَارِ *He shunned, avoided,* or *kept* or *removed himself far from, unclean things;* (Ṣ,* Mgh, Mṣb;) *preserved himself therefrom.* (Mgh.) — تَنَزَّهَ, used absolutely, and said of a man, means *He shunned, avoided,* or *kept* or *removed himself far from, unclean things; kept aloof from, &c.;* or *from things occasioning blame.* (TA.) — تَنَزَّهَ is best rendered, when not used absolutely, *He removed himself,* or *kept, far,* or *aloof:* and with عَنْ following it, it may be rendered *he shunned,* or *avoided.* — تَنَزَّهَ عَنِ البَوْلِ [*He purified,* or *cleansed, himself from urine:* a meaning assigned in the TA, art. نزه, by an evident mistranscription, to استنزه]. (Mṣb in art. برأ: and a trad.) — Also, *He diverted,* or *recreated, himself;* or *took an airing;* in the country, or in a garden. — تَنَزَّهَ meaning *He went forth to the gardens* (Ṣ, Mṣb, Ḳ) *and* [*green fields,* or] *green plants,* and *meadows,* (Ḳ,) is a mistake, (Ṣ, Mṣb, Ḳ,) accord. to some; but IḲt holds it to be not so. (Mṣb)

نَزِهُ الخُلُقِ [in copies of the Ḳ الخَلْقِ] and نَزِهُ النَّفْسِ and ✝ نَزِيهُهُ [and ✝ نَازِهُهُ and ✝ نَزْهُهُ (see ظَلِفٌ)] *Who abstains from that which is indecorous,* &c. (Ḳ, TA.)

نَزْهٌ }
نَازِهٌ } see نَزِهُ الخُلُقِ.

نَزِيهٌ : see نَزِهُ الخُلُقِ. — نَزِيهٌ *A pious man;* or one *who abstains from unlawful things.* (TA.)

نزو

1. نَزَا عَلَى الأُنْثَى *He* (a solid-hoofed, or cloven-hoofed, animal, and a wild beast,) *leaped the female;* (Ṣ, &c.;) and so نَزَا alone, elliptically. — نَزَتْ حَنْجَرَتُهُ, said of a camel: see عَزَفَ.

نس

1. نَسَّ, aor. يَنِسُّ, *He went at a gentle pace.* (TA, art. خبز.)

R.Q. 1. نَسْنَسَتِ الرِّيحُ *The wind blew coldly:* see R.Q. 1 in art. سن.

رِيحٌ نَسْنَاسَةٌ *A cold wind:* see سَنْسَانَةٌ.

نسج

نَسِيجَةٌ, applied to a wind: see نَيِّحَةٌ, art. نوح.

نسع

نِسْعٌ *A plaited thong, serving for the nose-rein of a camel, &c.;* and sometimes *woven wide,* [*for a fore-girth,*] *placed on the breast of a camel.* (KL, TA.) See also نِسْعَةٌ.

نِسْعَةٌ *A kind of broad plaited fore-girth for a camel:* pl. نِسَعٌ and نُسْعٌ and أَنْسَاعٌ: (Ṣ:) or نِسْعٌ and نُسُوعٌ and أَنْسَاعٌ are pls. of نِسْعٌ, [a coll. gen. n.,] of which نِسْعَةٌ is the n. un. (Ḳ.) See عَظْمُ الرَّحْلِ, in art. عظم. — أَنْسَاعُ الطَّرِيقِ † *The furrows of the road, made by the beasts with their legs* [or *feet*] *in its surface.* (TA, voce شَرَكٌ.)

نسغ

مِنْسَغَةٌ *An instrument for pricking bread:* see مِرْقَمٌ.

نسف

1. نَسَفَتْهُ الرِّيحُ, (Mgh, Mṣb, TA,) aor. -ِ, (TA,) inf. n. نَسْفٌ; (Mṣb, TA;) and ✝ اِنْتَسَفَتْهُ, (TA,) *The wind carried it away;* (TA;) i. q. ذَرَتْهُ [q. v.]; (Mgh;) namely, dust. (Mgh, Mṣb.)

8: see 1.

مِنْسَفٌ *A vessel* (وِعَآء) *in which dates* [*and grain*] *are shaken to remove the dust, &c.* (TA in art. نفض.)

نسك

1. نَسَكَ *He worshipped:* used transitively. See an ex. in a verse of El-Aạshà, in the Ṣ, art. نصب. See 5.

4. أَنْسَكَ [app. *He washed and purified a garment*]. (TA voce إِجْتَابَ.)

5. تَنَسَّكَ *He devoted himself to religious exercises; applied himself to devotion;* (Ṣ, Mṣb, Ḳ;) as also ✝ نَسَكَ (Ṣ, Ḳ) and ✝ نَسُكَ: (Ḳ:) or the last, *he became a* نَاسِك. (Ṣ.)

نَسِيكَةٌ : see عَقِيقَةٌ.

مَنَاسِكُ الحَجِّ *The religious rites and ceremonies of the pilgrimage:* or *the places where those rites and ceremonies are performed.* (Mṣb.)

نسل

8. اِنْتَسَلَ said of camels' fur: see عَصِيرٌ.

نَسْلًا وَأَسْلًا is a form of imprecation against a man, like تَعْسًا وَنَكْسًا. (M, in art. اسل.)

نَسْلٌ *Progeny,* whether of man or beast. (The Lexicons passim.)

نسم

5. تَنَسَّمَ شَيْئًا *He sought, or endeavoured to get, or attain, a thing, with labour and perseverance:* i. q. تَطَلَّبَهُ. (IbrD.) — تَنَسَّمَ الخَبَرَ *He sought, searched,* or *inquired, for,* or *after, the news,* or *tidings;* (MA, KL;) [*as though endeavouring to scent it;*] so that he elicited it. (TA.)

نسم من الطريق, denoting *nearness and shortness of the way,* see نبق and مُسْتَعْجِلَةٌ.

نَسِيمٌ : see نَسَمٌ.

نَسَمَةٌ *A soul;* syn. نَفْسٌ, with sukoon: and نَسَمٌ *souls;* syn. نُفُوسٌ. (Mṣb.) — *A man.* (Ḳ.)

نَسِيمٌ *A gentle wind; a gentle gale; a breeze.* — The *commencement of any wind before it becomes strong:* (AḤn, M:) or *a pleasant wind:* (Ṣ:) or the *breath of the wind:* (Mṣb:) or the *breath of the wind when weak;* as also ✝ نَسَمٌ: or *a wind from which comes a weak breath:* pl. of both أَنْسَامٌ. (M.) — بَارِدُ النَّسِيمِ ‡ *One who chills people:* see ثَقِيلٌ. — نَسِيمٌ *Odour, scent, sweet or disagreeable:* see رَائِحَةٌ.

نَيْسَبٌ i. q. نَيْسَمٌ.

مَنْسِمٌ *The sole* (بَاطِن) *of the* خُفّ: or, *to a camel, the same as the* سُنْبُك *to the horse;* (Mṣb;) [i. e., *the toe,* or *nail,* or *edge of the fore part of the foot, of a camel:* see ظُفُرٌ:] the *extremity of the* خُفّ *of the camel* and *ostrich* and *elephant,* and *of the solid hoof:* or *each of the two nails* (ظُفْرَان) *of the camel, that are upon* [*each of*] *his fore-feet:* or it is, *to a she-camel, like the* ظُفُر *to a man:* (M:) or the خُفّ *of the camel,* (Ṣ, Ḳ,) and *of the ostrich.* (Aṣ, Ṣ.) — [Also, † The *toe* of a human being: see a verse cited voce جَذَا, art. جذو.]

نسى and نسو

1: see 6.

6. تَنَاسَاهُ *He pretended that he had forgotten it:* (Ṣ, KL,* TA:) and (TA) *he forgot it;* (MA, KL,* TA;) like ↑ نَسِيَهُ: (TA:) [or] *he constrained himself to dismiss it from his mind.* (MA.) — تَنُوسِىَ *It* (a word or the like) *was forgotten by degrees.* (Occurring often in the larger Lexicons.)

النَّسَا [vulg. عِرْقُ النَّسَا], app. *The sciatic vein;*] *the portion, in the thigh, of the vein* (عِرْق) *which, in the back, is called the* وَتِين, *and which extends to the shank, where it is called the* صَافِن: (IAth, TA, voce أَبْهَرُ:) or the صَافِن and the عرق النسا are *two branches of one* عِرْق [or *vein*]: (Ibn-Seenà, vol. i. book iii. p. 608: [where the opening of each of these to let blood is mentioned:]) [in a solid-hoofed animal,] النسا is *a vein* (عِرْق) *proceeding from the hip,* or *haunch, lying within each thigh, then passing by the hock, so as to reach the hoof: when the breast is fat, each of its thighs becomes cleft by two large portions of flesh, and the* نسا *runs between them, and is apparent.* (Ṣ.) [In the present day it seems to be applied by some to the *sciatic nerve:* and عِرْقُ النَّسَا, as also النَّسَا alone, often signifies *sciatica,* or *hip-gout:* see نِقْرِسٌ and also شَنِجٌ.]

مَنْسِيْنَهَا for مُنْسِيَنْهَا: see a verse cited voce عُقْبَةٌ.

نشف

1. نَشَفَ المَآءَ, aor. ـُ, (Mgh, Mṣb,) inf. n. نَشْفٌ, (Mṣb,) *He took* [or *absorbed*] *the water from the ground,* (Mgh, Mṣb,) or *from a pool,* (Mgh,) *with a piece of rag* or *some other thing* (Mgh, Mṣb) *of a similar kind.* (Mṣb.)

2. نَشَّفَتْ *She* (a camel) [*yielded frothy milk;*] *had* نُشَافَة. (Ṣ in art. رغو. [See 2 in that art.])

4. أَنْشَفَ الأَرْضَ المَآءَ [*It caused the earth to imbibe the water*], said of the سَمُوم. (Ḳ voce أُضْرُوب.)

مِنْشَفَةٌ (pl. مَنَاشِف) *A drying-towel; napkin.*

نشق

5: see 10.

10. اِسْتَنْشَقَ الرِّيحَ † [*He snuffed the wind*]: (TA, art. صخر:) *he snuffed, scented,* or *smelt, the wind;* as also ↑ تَنَشَّقَهَا. (Mṣb.) See 10 in art. شر.

نُشَاقَةٌ *What is taken* [or *ladled out*], *while hot, from a cooking-pot.* (TA.)

نصع

1. نَصَعَ *He,* or *it, purified.* (L.)

أَبْيَضُ نَاصِعٌ *Intensely white.*

نصف

4. أَنْصَفَهُ *He did justice to him:* (MA:) *he acted equitably with him:* (Mṣb:) *he gave him,* or *obtained for him, his right,* or *due,* from (مِنْ) another: see أَعْذَرَ. — إِنْصَافٌ The *giving what is right,* or *due:* (M:) or the *granting,* or *rendering, justice.* (KL, PṢ.) — أَنْصَفَهُ مِنْ ظَالِمِهِ [*He exacted justice for him from his wronger*]. (T voce ظَلَّمَ.)

8. إِنْتَصَفَ مِنْهُ *He exacted,* or *obtained, his right,* or *due, from him* (M, Ḳ) *completely, so that each of them became on a par with the other;* (Ḳ;) [i. e. *with equity*]. — إِنْتَصَفَ *It became halved:* (Mṣb:) [often said of the day-time (النَّهَار)].

طُبِخَ على النِّصْفِ, and أُصْلِحَ على النصف, *It* (wine) *was boiled until half of it had gone,* or *evaporated.* (TA, voce طَابَة.)

مَكَانٌ نَصَفٌ بَيْنَ مَكَانَيْنِ [*A place half-way, midway,* or *equidistant, between two places*]. (Mughnee in art. سَوَآءٌ.) — نَصَفٌ A *middle-aged woman or man:* (Ṣ, Ḳ:) or *forty-five years old;* or *fifty years old.* (Ḳ.) Dim. نُصَيْف.

نَصِيفٌ *A woman's muffler:* see خِمَارٌ.

نُصَيْفٌ, dim. of نَصَفٌ: see خُلَيْقٌ voce خَلَقٌ.

مُنَصَّفٌ *Expressed juice,* (Mgh, Mṣb,) or *wine,* or *beverage,* (Ḳ,) *cooked until half of it has gone* [*by evaporation*]. (Mgh, Mṣb, Ḳ.)

مُنَاصَفٌ *Not wholly ripe:* [*half-ripe:*] applied to the date. (TA, voce بُسْرٌ.)

أَنْصَافُ اللَّبِنِ [*Half-bricks,* or] *cut bricks, whereof the one is placed, in building, beside the whole brick, for the purpose of ornamentation.* (Mṣb in art. خرج.)

نصل

نَصْلٌ The *iron head* or *blade* (Mgh, Ḳ) of an arrow, (Ṣ, Mgh, Ḳ,) and of a spear, (Ṣ, Ḳ,) and of a sword, (Ṣ, Mgh, Mṣb, Ḳ,) and of a knife, (Ṣ, Mṣb,) and the like. (Mṣb.) — نَصْلٌ The *spun thread* of the spindle: (Ḳ:) see سُرْسُورٌ.

لِحْيَةٌ نَاصِلٌ *A very white beard.* (See العَنْقَآءُ, art. غرب.) — مَا بَلِلْتُ مِنْ فُلَانٍ بِأَفْوَقَ نَاصِلٍ: see بَلَّ and أَفْوَقُ in two places.

نصم

نُصْمَةٌ or نَصَمَةٌ *An idol:* see صَنَمٌ.

نصى

5. تَنَصَّى بَنِى فُلَانٍ: see تَذَرَّى.

نَصِىٌّ *A certain plant:* (Ṣ, TA:) Golius says, *a species of thistle;* but this seems to be inconsistent with the description of it: see رِيجَةٌ. — خَصِىٌّ نَصِىٌّ *Gelded, castrated.* The second word is an imitative sequent.

نَاصِيَةٌ properly, in the language of the [classical] Arabs, The *place where the hair grows in the fore part of the head:* and hence, the *hair of that part;* the *hair over the forehead;* (Az, TA;) [and this is the general meaning;) *i. q.* قُصَّةٌ and طُرَّةٌ. (Mṣb, art. قص.) The *forelock* of a horse. — نَاصِيَةُ بَنِى فُلَانٍ: see تَذَرَّى and ذِرْوَةٌ.

نضر

نُضَارٌ *A tree of which yellow cups* (أَقْدَاح) *are made.* (T, in TA, voce غَرَبٌ.) See وَرْسِىٌّ.

نضل

1. نَضَلَهُ *He overcame him,* or *surpassed him, in shooting.* (Ṣ, Mṣb, Ḳ.)

3. نَاضَلَهُ *He vied, competed,* or *contended for superiority, with him in shooting.* (Ṣ, Mṣb, Ḳ.) — نَاضَلَهُ, inf. n. نِضَالٌ: see بَيَّنَهُ. — نَاضَلَ عَنْهُ ‡ *He defended him, pleaded in defence of him,* or *repelled from him;* (Ḳ, TA;) *spoke in his defence, excusing him;* (Ṣ, TA;) *defended him,* &c., as above; (Ṣ;) *contended,* or *pleaded, in his defence;* (TA;) *defended him;* and *contended in his defence.* (Mṣb.)

نضو

1. نَضَا الخَيْلَ *He outstripped the* other *horses:* see تَجَرَّدَ.

نِضْوٌ *A lean,* or *emaciated,* camel: fem. with ة. (Ṣ, Mṣb, Ḳ.) نِضْوُ سَفَرٍ [*Lean,* or *emaciated by journeying*]; applied to a beast. (TA, in رجع.)

نطع

5. تَنَطَّعَ, (KL,) or تنطّع فى الكَلَامِ, (Ṣ, Ḳ,) *He went deeply, or far, in speech;* (KL;) syn. تَعَمَّقَ: (Ṣ, Ḳ:) *was exorbitant,* or *extravagant, therein:* (Ḳ:) or تنطّع signifies *he spoke with the extremity of his fauces;* [or *with a guttural voice;*] from النِّطَعُ signifying the upper غار in the mouth. (IAth.)

النِّطْعِيَّةُ and الحُرُوفُ النِّطْعِيَّةُ *Dental letters:* see ت.

نَطْعٌ, نِطْعٌ, نَطَعٌ } see نِطَعٌ.

نِطَعٌ and ▼ نِطْعٌ and نَطْعٌ and نَطَعٌ *A certain thing* (Munjid of Kr, Mgh, Mṣb, Ḳ) *that is spread* [*upon the ground to serve as a table for food,* and *for play at chess or the like,* and *to receive the head of a person when it is cut off*], (Munjid, Ḳ,) *made of leather;* (Munjid, Mgh, Mṣb, Ḳ;) *a piece of leather that is spread upon the ground for any of the purposes above mentioned.* — *The anterior part of the palate;* see غار.

نَطَّاعٌ *A man who makes* نُطُوع: and *who binds books.* (T, in TA, art. حط.)

نطف

نَطَفٌ *Earrings:* see a verse cited in art. سجد.

نُطْفَةٌ *Sperma* of a man (Ṣ, Mṣb, Ḳ) and of a woman. (Mṣb.)

نَاطِفٌ *A kind of sweetmeat;* (Mṣb;) *i. q.* قُبَّيْطَى. (Ṣ, Mṣb.)

نطق

1. نَطَقَ trans. by means of بِ: see Ḥam, p. 75. — نَطَقَ بِهِ means *he pronounced it,* or *articulated it.* — نَطَقَ, said of a bird or any animal: see Bḍ, xxvii. 16.

3. نَاطَقَهُ, inf. n. مُنَاطَقَةٌ, *He talked,* or *discoursed, with him;* syn. كَالَمَهُ, (TA,) followed by بِ before the subject of talk, &c. (TA in art. فرع.)

6. تَنَاطَقَا *They two talked,* or *discoursed, each with the other;* like تَقَاوَلَا. (TA.)

10. إِسْتَنْطَقَهُ *He desired him to speak;* (TA;) [*interrogated him:*] *he spoke to him until,* or *so that, he spoke.* (Mṣb.)

نِطَاقٌ The *bar* (مترس) of a door. (TA, art. لز.) — نِطَاقُ الجَوْزَآءِ *The Belt of Orion:* see الجَوْزَآءُ.

نِطَاقَةٌ *A ticket of price,* or *weight:* see بِطَاقَةٌ.

نَاطِقٌ — اطيار ناطقة *Singing birds.* — نَاطِقٌ an epithet applied to *A deenár.* — جَذْرٌ نَاطِقٌ *A rational root, in arithmetic;* opposed to جَذْرٌ أَصَمُّ. (Mgh, art. جذر.) — حَيَوَانٌ نَاطِقٌ *A rational animal.*

نَاطِقِيَّةٌ *Rationality.*

مَنْطِقٌ *Speech:* (Ṣ:) *Diction;* or *expression of ideas, or meanings, by voice and words.* (Ḳ, TA.)

مِنْطَقَةٌ *I. q.* حِيَاصَةٌ; (Mṣb;) *A kind of girdle, zone, or waist-belt, which is fastened round the waist with a buckle or clasp; worn by men and by women; and when worn by wealthy women generally adorned with jewels, &c., and having also two plates of silver or gold, also generally jewelled, which clasp together.* See إِبْزِيمٌ.

مِنْطِيقٌ *Eloquent:* (Ṣ, Ḳ:) or *able in speech; an able speaker.* (TA in art. فوه.)

الحِكْمَةُ المَنْطُوقُ بِهَا: see حِكْمَةٌ.

نطل

نَيْطَلٌ: see سَيْطَلٌ.

نطم

نَطْمَةٌ: see نَطْبَةٌ.

نطو

8. إِنْتَطَتِ المَفَازَةُ: see انتاطت, in art. نوط.

نَطَاةٌ *Distance,* or *far extent;* syn. بُعْدٌ. (TA.) See غَائِلٌ, in art. غول.

نَاطِيَةٌ *A female weaver:* pl. نَوَاطٍ. (TA in art. ذرع.)

نظف

10. إِسْتَنْظَفَ الذَّكَرَ مِنَ البَوْلِ: see استنقى.

نظم

1. نَظَمَ [*He pierced:*] *he pierced and knotted* a cord or rope: and *he* (a غَوَّاص) *pierced and plaited* [the leaves of] the مُقْل. (M.) — نَظَمَ *He strung* beads. (Mṣb.)

8. إِنْتَظَمَهُ *He transfixed,* or *transpierced, him;* (M;) *i. q.* اِخْتَلَّهُ. (Ṣ, M, Ḳ.) — إِنْتَظَمَ *It* (an affair [and language, &c.]) *was,* or *became, rightly* [or *regularly*] *ordered, arranged,* or *disposed.* (Mṣb.)

نَظْمٌ *What are strung,* of pearls and beads, &c. (M.) — النَّظْمُ: see الجَوْزَآءُ.

نِظَامٌ [*A standard* of a thing, *by which to regulate or adjust it.* See voce عِيَارٌ.] — ‡ The *cause,* or *means, of the subsistence,* of anything; or its *foundation,* or *support;* syn. مِلَاكٌ: (M, Ḳ:*) a tropical meaning. (TA) — † *A way, course, mode,* or *manner, of acting* or *conduct* or *the like: custom,* or *habit.* (M, Ḳ.) — لَيْسَ لِأَمْرِهِ نِظَامٌ † *His affair has not a right tendency.* (T.) And لَيْسَ لِأَمْرِهِمْ نِظَامٌ † *Their affair has not a right way,* or *method, of procedure, nor connexion, or coherence,* (مُتَعَلَّقٌ,) (M, TA,) *nor right tendency.* (TA.) And مَا زَالَ عَلَى نِظَامٍ وَاحِدٍ † *He ceased not to follow one custom, or manner of conduct.* (M, TA.) And أَحَادِيثُ لَا نِظَامَ لَهَا † [*Stories having no foundation,* or *no right tendency* or *tenour*]. (M and Ḳ in art. سطر.)

نَظَّامٌ and ▼ نَظِيمٌ *A composer of many verses,* or *of much poetry.* (TA.)

نَظِيمٌ: see نَظَّامٌ.

نعظ

1. نَعَظَ, aor. ـَ, inf. n. نَعْظٌ and نُعُوظٌ (Ṣ, Mṣb, Ḳ,) and نَعِظَ, (ISd, Ḳ,) *It* (the زُبّ, Ṣ, or ذَكَر, Mṣb, Ḳ,) *became erect,* (Ṣ, Mṣb, Ḳ), *by reason of carnal appetite;* (Mṣb;) as also ▼ انعظ. (M, TA.)

4. انعظ, (Mṣb, Ḳ,) inf. n. إِنْعَاظٌ, (Ṣ, Mṣb,) *He* (a man, Mṣb, Ḳ,) *became affected with carnal appetite:* (Ṣ, Mṣb, Ḳ:) and in like manner انعظت, said of a woman. (Mṣb, Ḳ.*) — *His penis became extended.* (M, in art. رول.) — انعظت *She* (a beast) *opened and contracted, alternately, her vulva;* (Ṣ, Ḳ;) and so ▼ انتعظت. (AO, Ḳ.) — See also 1. — انعظهُ *He caused it to become erect:* (Ṣ:) or *put it in motion:* (Mṣb:) namely his زُبّ, (Ṣ,) or ذَكَر. (Mṣb.)

8: see 4.

حِرٌ نَعِظٌ *A vulva excited by carnal appetite.* (Ḳ.)

نَاعُوظٌ *That excites erection of the penis.* (Ḳ.) شرب النَّاعُوظ [app. a mistranscription for شَرْبَةُ النَّاعُوظ] *Medicine which has that effect:* mentioned by Z and Ibn-'Abbád. (TA.)

نعق

1. نَعَقَ بِهِمْ إِلَى الفِتْنَةِ *He hallooed them on to fight, etc.:* see 10 in art. عو.

نَاعِقٌ *One who drives away the beasts, and cries out after them.* (TA in art. زعق.)

نَاعِقَآءُ : see عَانِقَآءُ.

نعل

1: } see 4.
2: }

4. أَنْعَلْتُ الخُفَّ and ♦ نَعَّلْتُهُ *I affixed a sole to the bottom of the* خُفّ [i. e. *boot*]: and hence, أَنْعَلْتُ الدَّابَّةَ and ♦ نَعَّلْتُهَا. (Msb.) See صِرْمٌ.

8. اِنْتَعَلَتْ ظِلَالَهَا : see ظِلٌّ.

نَعْلٌ [*A sandal: a sole:*] the *thing by which the foot is preserved*, or *protected, from the ground;* (K;) syn. حِذَآءٌ: and also applied to a تَاسُومَة [or *shoe*]. (Msb.) *What is now called* تَاسُومَة. (IAth, TA.) It often signifies only *a sole:* so in the S, K, Msb, &c., in art. خصف &c. — The *leathern shoe*, or *sandal*, of a camel; *which is attached by thongs*, or *straps, called* سَرَائِح (pl. of سَرِيحَةٌ) *to the* خَدَمَة or *plaited thong which surrounds the pastern:* see سَرِيحَةٌ and خَدَمَةٌ. — نَعْلٌ of a sword The *iron*, (Kr, S, K,) or *silver*, (S,) *thing* [or *shoe*] *at the lower end of the scabbard.* (Kr, S, K.) See غَاشِيَةٌ, and 2 in art. فرص. — نَعْلٌ meaning *A* حَرَّة, or *hard rugged tract of land*, &c.: see رَجُلٌ. — ‡ نَعْلٌ *A wife.* See عَتَبَة.

نَعَّالِيٌّ *One who takes care of the sandals* or *shoes* [*at the door of a bath or mosque*]. (TA in art. ثوب.)

نَاعِلٌ *Wearing*, or *having on the feet, sandals.*

نعم

1. نَعِمَ عَيْشُهُ *His life was*, or *became, plentiful and easy:* (Msb:) *was*, or *became, good*, or *pleasant.* (Mgh.) See عَوْقٌ. — نَعِمَ, aor. ـَ, is like فَضِلَ, aor. ـُ, and حَضِرَ, aor ـُ. See the latter. — عِمْ صَبَاحًا : see تَرِبَ, and اِنْعِمْ صَبَاحًا, and صَبَاحٌ. — نَعُمَ, inf. n. نُعُومَةٌ; (S, Msb;) and نَعِمَ; (S;) *It was*, or *became, soft*, or *tender*, (S, Msb,) *to the feet.* (Msb.)

2. نَعَّمَهُ, (S, Msb, K,) and ♦ نَاعَمَهُ, (S, K,) *He* (God, S, Msb,) *made him to enjoy*, or *lead, a plentiful, and a pleasant* or *an easy, and a soft*, or *delicate, state*, or *life; a state*, or *life*, of *ease and plenty.* (S, Msb, K.) — نَعَّمَهُ *He nourished well him*, or *it; pampered him.*

3: see 2.

4. أَنْعَمَ عَلَيْهِ بِشَىْءٍ *He conferred*, or *bestowed, upon him a thing as a favour.* See أَحْسَنَ. — أَنْعَمَ عَجْنَهُ *He kneaded it well, thoroughly*, or *soundly.* (TA, voce رَبَغَ.) — أَنْعَمَ الدَّقَّ *He bruised* or *powdered finely:* see دَقَّ. — أَنْعَمَ طَبْخَهُ *He cooked it well;* syn. أَجَادَ طَبْخَهُ. (IbrD.) The verb is often used in this sense. — أَنْعَمَ ٱللّٰهُ بِكَ عَيْنًا : see أَبْغَضَ.

5. تَنَعَّمَ *He enjoyed*, or *led, an easy, a pleasant, a soft*, or *a delicate, life, with ampleness of the means of subsistence; a life of ease and plenty.* (K.) — تَنَعَّمَ *It* (a tree) *became flourishing and fresh*, (TK, art. روى, &c.,) *luxuriant, succulent, sappy, soft, tender, and supple.* See رَوِىَ. — تَنَعَّمَ i. q. تَمَتَّعَ. (Msb.*)

نُعْمٌ contr. of بُؤْسٌ, (S,) [like ♦ نَعْمَآءُ and ♦ نُعْمَى and ♦ نَعْمَةٌ and ♦ نَعِيمٌ:] pl. أَنْعُمٌ. (S.) See نِعْمَةٌ.

نَعَمْ *Even so; yes; yea.* (Msb, &c.) See أَجَلْ and بَجَلْ.

نَعَمٌ *Pasturing* مَال [or *cattle*]; mostly applied to *camels*, and *neat*, and *sheep and goats:* or applied to *all these*, and to *camels when alone*, but neat and sheep or goats when alone are not thus termed; (Msb;) therefore, *cattle, consisting of camels or neat or sheep or goats*, or *all these*, or *camels alone.*

نِعْمَ الرَّجُلُ زَيْدٌ *Excellent*, or *most excellent*, or *excellent above all, is the man, Zeyd;* or [*very* or] *superlatively good*, &c. (Msb.) — See بِئْسَ.

نَعْمَةٌ *subst. of* تَنَعَّمَ (Msb, K) *in the sense of* تَرَفُّهٌ, (K,) or تَمَتُّعٌ: (Msb:) or *i. q.* تَنَعُّمٌ: (S: in F's smaller copy, تَنْعِيمٌ, an evident mistake:) i. e. *plentifulness, and pleasantness* or *easiness, and softness* or *delicacy, of life: ease and plenty.* — نَعْمَةٌ *A living in* [or rather *enjoyment of a life of*] *softness, daintiness*, or *delicacy*, and *ease, comfort*, or *affluence:* (KL:) *i. q.* ♦ نَعِيمٌ; (Msb;) and مُتْعَةٌ: (Jel in xliv. 26:) it is from التَّنَعُّمُ; and ♦ نِعْمَةٌ is from الإِنْعَامُ. (Ksh, cited in Kull, p. 364.) See نِعْمَةٌ: and see تُرْفَةٌ. — نَعْمَةُ الشَّبَابِ [*The flourishing freshness, softness, tenderness*, or *blooming loveliness* or *graces, of youth.* See عَيْعَبٌ.] — نَعْمَةٌ *Softness; tenderness; bloom;* or *flourishing freshness* (IbrD;) of a branch; and of youth, or youthfulness. (M, art. ملد; &c.)

نِعْمَةٌ and ♦ نُعْمَى and ♦ نَعْمَآءُ *A benefit; benefaction; favour; boon;* or *good:* (S, Msb:) *a blessing;* [*bounty; gratuity;*] or *what God bestows upon one:* and so ♦ نَعِيمٌ: (S:) [*grace of God:*] and ♦ نُعْمٌ and ♦ نَعْمَةٌ, with fet-h, [and ♦ نُعْمَى and ♦ نَعْمَآءُ and ♦ نُعْمٌ, *ease and plenty*,] *enjoyment;* (Msb;) [*welfare; well being; weal:*] ♦ نُعْمَى and ♦ نَعْمَآءُ are the *contr. of* بُؤْسَى and بَأْسَآءُ: (TA, art. بأس:) نَعْمَآءَ ♦ بَعْدَ ضَرَّآءَ, in the Kur [xi. 13,] is like health after sickness; and richness, or competence, after want. (Bd.) — نِعْمَةٌ *A blessing;* (S;) *a cause of happiness.* (K.) *A favour: a benefit; and the like.* (S.) — نِعْمَةٌ *Wealth*, or *property.* (K.) The first explanations given to it above are assigned in the K, not to this word, but to ♦ نَعِيمٌ and ♦ نُعْمَى. — نِعْمَةٌ with the article seems generally to signify *Wealth:* and without the article, *A benefit, benefaction, favour, boon*, or *blessing.*

نُعْمَةٌ The act of *rejoicing by a thing:* and the state of *rejoicing in a thing.* (KL.)

نُعْمَى *contr. of* بُؤْسَى; (S, TA in art. بأس;) and نَعْمَآءُ *contr. of* بَأْسَآءُ. (TA in that art.) — See نِعْمَةٌ.

نَعْمَآءُ : see نِعْمَةٌ.

نَعِيمٌ *Enjoyment;* [*delight; pleasure;*] as also ♦ نَعْمَةٌ, q. v.: (Msb:) *plenty and ease.* (K.) See نِعْمَةٌ.

نَعَامَةٌ The *blackness* of night. (S in art. سقط.) see an ex. voce سَقْطٌ. — نَعَامَةٌ *The ostrich:* it sometimes denotes the female. See مَخْزُومٌ and جَرَادٌ. — شَالَتْ نَعَامَتُهُمْ : see شَالَ, زَالَ, طَائِرٌ, and a verse voce إِمَّا. — اِبْنُ النَّعَامَةِ *The shank-bone:* and *a certain vein in the leg:* and *the middle*, or *beaten track, of the road:* and *the brisk, lively*, or *sprightly, horse:* and *the drawer of water* (السَّانِى) *who is at the head of the well.* (T in art. بنى.) — نَعَامَةٌ and نَعَامَتَانِ of a well: see زُرْنُوقٌ. — النَّعَائِمُ *Nine stars* [*of Sagittarius*], behind الشَّوْلَةُ, *four in the Milky Way*, [β, γ, δ, and ε,] called النَّعَائِمُ الوَارِدَةُ, *as though drinking: and four without the Milky Way*, [ζ, σ, τ, and φ,] *called* النَّعَائِمُ الصَّادِرَةُ, *as though returning from drinking; and the ninth*, [λ,] [*not mentioned by some*,] *high between them: each of the two fours forming the corners of a quadrilateral figure. The twentieth Mansion of the Moon.* (El-Kazweenee.)

عَيْشٌ نَاعِمٌ [*A plentiful and easy life.* See نَعِمَ عَيْشُهُ.] *A pleasant life.* (Mgh.) [*A soft*, or *delicate, life.*] — نَاعِمٌ *Soft*, or *tender:* applied to a plant or tree: (Mgh:) [*smooth; sleek.* And *i. q.* مُتَنَعِّمٌ.]

مُنَعَّلٌ, applied to a horse, white on the forelegs: see أَقْفَزُ.

أَنَاعِمُ, pl. pl. of نَعْمٌ: see a verse cited voce دَانٍ.

نعو

1. نَعَاهُ He announced his death: see a verse cited voce طُوبَالَةٌ.

نغ

نُغْنُغَةٌ: see غُنْدُبَةٌ, and نُغْنُغٌ.

النَّغَانِغُ Certain portions of flesh by the uvula. (O in art. علق.)

نغف

نَغَفَاتٌ Portions of dry mucus: see سَلِيلَةٌ.

نغق

نُغَاقٌ and نُعَاقٌ, of a crow, signify the same. (Lḥ in O, art. عوق.)

نغل

نَغِلٌ [in the CK نَغْلٌ] A hide vitiated, or rendered unsound, (Ṣ, Ḳ,) in the tanning. (Ḳ.)

إِبْنُ نُغَيْلَةَ The son of a female slave. (T in art. بنى.)

نغم

1. نَغَمَ, aor. ـِ and ـُ, He spoke in a low, gentle, or soft, voice or tone: (Ṣ, Mṣb:) [he spoke in an undertone:] he used such a voice in singing: (Ḳ:) or he modulated his voice, or made melody, in singing. (TḲ.) See جرس.

2. تَنْغِيمٌ: see شِينٌ.

5. تَنَغُّمٌ: see جَرْسٌ.

نَغْمَةٌ Gentle-toned speech; syn. جَرْسُ الكَلَامِ: (Mṣb:) and sweetness of voice, or melody, in recitation [and in singing]. (Ṣ, Mṣb.) — [Also, A musical sound, or note:] a melody: see طَرْقٌ: sweet sound: pl. نَغَمَاتٌ. (KL.)

مُنَاغَمَةٌ: see voce بَاغَمَةٌ.

نغو

3. نَاغَاهُ He interchanged speech with him, each of them addressing the other with a word or saying: (TA:) نَغَيْتُ إِلَيْهِ نَغْيَةً signifies I addressed to him a word or saying: and المُنَاغَاةُ signifies المُوَاجَهَةُ. (JḲ.)

نفع

1. نَفَعَهُ It profited him; availed him; was of use or benefit, or was useful or beneficial, to him. — يَنْفَعُ لِكَذَا: see an ex. voce جَدٌّ — نَفَعَهُ مِنْهُ and مِنْ كَذَا, It (a medicine) is good, beneficial, or profitable, as a remedy, for, or against, such a thing, meaning such a disease or the like.

2. نَفَّعَهُ, inf. n. تَنْفِيعٌ, He caused نفع to come to him. (TA.)

8. إِنْتَفَعَ بِهِ He benefited or profited by it; made use of it; had the use of it; enjoyed it; like تَمَتَّعَ بِهِ. See 10.

10. إِسْتَنْفَعَهُ He sought, or demanded, his profiting him, or being useful to him. (IAạr, TA.) — And إِسْتَنْفَعَ sometimes occurs in the sense of ✝ إِنْتَفَعَ. (TA.)

نَفْعٌ contr. of ضُرٌّ: (TA:) or a thing whereof one makes use for the attainment of good: (B:) or good: or a means of attaining one's desire. (Mṣb.)

مَنْفَعَةٌ [A cause, or means, of advantage, profit, utility; or benefit: and simply, advantage; profit, or profitableness; utility, use, usefulness; or benefit:] contr. of مَضَرَّةٌ. (Ṣ, art. ضر.)

نفق

1. نَفَقَتِ السُّوقُ The market became brisk, its goods selling much; syn. قَامَتْ. (Ḳ.) — نَفَقَ It was, or became, saleable; easy, or ready, of sale; or in much demand: see its syn. رَاجَ. — نَفَقَتْ It (a commodity, سِلْعَة,) was in much demand: and she (a woman) was demanded in marriage by many. (Mṣb.) — نَفِقَتِ الدَّرَاهِمُ, inf. n. نَفَقٌ, The dirhems passed away, came to an end, or became spent or exhausted; syn. نَفِدَت. (Mṣb.)

3. نَافَقَ He played the hypocrite in religion: (Ḳ, TA:) he pretended, to the Muslims, that he held the religion of El-Islám, concealing in his heart another religion than El-Islám. (Mṣb.) And نَافَقَ فُلَانًا He acted with such a one hypocritically. (TḲ in art. دهن. [But I have not found this elsewhere.]) And نَافَقَ فِي المَحَبَّةِ [He acted the hypocrite in respect of love]. (Ḥar, p. 505.) See خَانَ.

4. أَنْفَقَ He expended money: and he (God or a man) dispensed gifts.

5. تَنَفَّقَتِ الجَزُورُ [The slaughtered camel became dealt out, or dispensed]. (Ṣ, Ḳ in art. شيط.) — تَنَفُّقٌ: see Ḥar, p. 472. — تَنَفَّقَ It (a wound) cracked in its sides, and made, in the flesh, what resembled ✝ أَنْفَاق, i. e. holes in the ground, or subterranean excavations or habitations, pl. of نَفَقٌ. (TA in art. دسر.)

أَنْفَاقٌ — سَرَبٌ: see نَفَقٌ The holes of rats or mice. (Ṣ, TA in art. خفى:) see 1 in that art.: holes in the ground; or subterranean excavations or habitations; pl. of نَفَقٌ. (TA in art. دسر.) See 5. — Also Fresh olive-oil: see فَاقٌ in art. فوق: also mentioned in art. نفق in the TA.

نَفَقَةٌ What one expends, of money and the like, (Ḳ, TA,) upon himself and upon his family or household. (TA.)

نِيفَقٌ The part of a pair of drawers, or trousers, which is turned down at the top, and sewed, and through which the waistband, or string, passes. See نُقْبَةٌ.

نفل

2. نَفَّلَهُ, inf. n. تَنْفِيلٌ, He gave him spoil, (Ṣ, Mṣb,* Ḳ,) and a free and disinterested gift. (Mṣb, Ḳ.) And it is doubly trans.: see 2 in art. غنم.

نَفَلٌ Trifolium melilotus indica of Linn.: and medicago intertexta of Linn. (Delile, nos. 706, 730.) — نَفَلٌ: see غُنَيْمَةٌ.

نُفَلٌ: see تُسَعٌ.

نَافِلَةٌ: the pl., نَوَافِلُ, is explained in the TA, art. حرز, by زَوَائِدُ [Accessions, or additions]. — What accedes to, or exceeds, the original. (T.) A voluntary gift, by way of alms, or as a good work: (T:) a gift: (Ḳ:) or a gift عَنْ يَدٍ: (M:) a deed beyond what is incumbent, or obligatory. (M, Ḳ.) — نَافِلَةٌ Supererogatory prayer. (S, Mṣb.) See تَطَوُّعٌ.

نفى

1. نَفَاهُ He drove away, expelled, or banished, him, or it. (T, in TT.)

3. هٰذَا يُنَافِي هٰذَا This precludes the co-existence of this therewith; is inconsistent, or incompatible, with this.

6. تَنَافَيَا They two were incompatible.

8. إِنْتَفَى It was negative: contr. of ثَبَتَ and and وَجَبَ. (IbrD.) — إِنْتَفَى مِنْ شَيْءٍ He denied a thing; meaning an accusation or the like: syn. تَنَصَّحَ.

نُفَايَةٌ Refuse; i. e. what one rejects, of a thing, because of its badness: (Ṣ:) or refuse little in quantity: (T:) or the remains, and bad portion, of a thing: (M, Ḳ:) or, accord. to IAạr, *what is bad of wheat or food.* (M.)

فِعْلٌ مَنْفِىٌّ *A verb rendered negative* by its being preceded by مَا or the like; *contr. of* مُثْبَتٌ and مُوجَبٌ — كَلَامٌ مَنْفِىٌّ *A denied sentence; contr. of* مُثْبَتٌ and مُوجَبٌ; virtually the same as كَلَامٌ نَافٍ *a denying,* or *negative, sentence.*

نقع

1. نَقَعَ and ↑ اِسْتَنْقَعَ *It* (water) *remained,* or *stagnated,* or *collected,* in a hollow, or cavity: (Mgh:) or *remained long, and became altered:* (Mṣb:) or the former [and latter] *collected in a* مَنْقَع: (Ṣ:) or the latter [and former] *became yellow and altered.* (Ḳ.) — نَقَعَ and ↑ أَنْقَعَ [*He macerated, steeped,* or *soaked,* a medicine, *in water,*] *he left it in water until its colour became changed.* (Mṣb.)

4: }
10: } see 1.

نَقِيعٌ *An infusion;* meaning, *a beverage made by steeping something in water:* (Mṣb:) and *a mash.*

سَمٌّ نَاقِعٌ *Poison that takes effect;* (Ṣ, Ḳ;) *that kills:* (TA:) *that remains fixed,* (Abu-n-Naṣr, Ḳ, TA,) *and collects.* (Abu-Naṣr, TA.)

أَنْقَعُ *More,* or *most, thirst-quenching:* see an ex. under الحَاذُ, in art. حوذ; and another voce رَشَفَ.

أُنْقُوعَةٌ The *hollow,* or *depression, of* ثَرِيد, (Ṣ, A, Ḳ,) *in which the gravy collects.* (A, Ḳ.*)

مَنْقَعُ مَآءٍ, and ↑ مُسْتَنْقَعُ مَآءٍ, *A place where water remains and collects; where it collects and stagnates;* or *where it remains long, and becomes altered.* See نَقَعَ.

مُنْقَعُ البُرَمِ *Untwisted old thread which a woman spins a second time, and puts into the stone cooking-pots, because she has nothing but these [in which to deposit it].* (Ṣgh, Ḳ, TA. [From the Ḳ it would seem to be مُنْقَع alone: and in the CḲ, البُرامِ is erroneously put for البرام: Golius found it written البَرَام; and has wrongly explained it in his Appendix.]) — سَمٌّ مُنْقَعٌ *Poison made into a confection.* (Ṣ, Ḳ, TA.)

مُسْتَنْقَعٌ: see مَنْقَعٌ.

نقف

مِنْقَافٌ *A species of* وَدْع [or *cowry*]; (Ṣ, Ḳ*;) pl. مَنَاقِفُ: (TA in art. ودع: and thus in the M in art. دمل: in the T in that art. مَنَاقِيف: see دُمَّالٌ.) See بُوقٌ.

نقل

1. نَقَلَهُ *He related it, told it,* or *mentioned it,* from another; *he transmitted it; he transcribed it.* See 1 in art. حكى. نَقَلَ إِلَيْهِ حَدِيثًا [*He related to him a tradition*]. (Mṣb.) — نَقَلَهُ *He transferred it; shifted it; translated it; conveyed it. He discerned it,* or *took and mentioned it,* namely a word or phrase or signification, from (من) such a one; *he quoted it;* i. e. نَقَلَهُ إِلَى كِتَابِهِ مِنْ كِتَابٍ آخَرَ *he transferred it to his book from another book.*

5. تَنَقَّلَ بِالنُّقْلِ [and تنقّل alone] *He ate* نُقْل. (MA.) — Hence, تَنَقَّلَ بِالحَدِيثِ *He amused himself with talk;* like as one amuses himself with the eating of fruit after a meal: see تَفَكَّهَ.

8. اِنْتَقَلَ *He shifted, removed,* or *passed,* from one place, or time (as in an instance in the Ḳ voce أَسْوَعَ), or state, to another.

نَقْلُ الأَقْدَامِ *The shifting of the feet from place to place.* — بَآءُ النَّقْلِ i. q. بَآءُ التَّعْدِيَةِ *The* ب *that renders a verb trans.;* as in ذَهَبَ بِهِ. (Mughnee in art. ب.) — التَّآءُ لِلنَّقْلِ or الهَآءُ لِلنَّقْلِ means لِلنَّقْلِ مِنَ الوَصْفِيَّةِ إِلَى الاِسْمِيَّةِ, i. e. *The* ة that is added *for the transference* of a word *from the category of epithets to that of substantives;* as in خَلِيفَةٌ, accord. to some, and دَائِرَةٌ.

نُقْلٌ *Dried* and *other fruits* (such as *nuts, almonds, raisins, dried figs, dried dates,* &c.), [and *comfits:*] the *fruit* [*that is an accompaniment*] *of wine;* (MA in explanation of نُقْل [which is more common than نَقْل];) *fruit that is eaten with wine.* (KL in explanation of نُقْل.)

نَقَلٌ *Stones with trees.* (AZ and IḲṭṭ in TA, voce غَدَرٌ.)

مَنْقَلَةٌ i. q. مَرْحَلَةٌ (JK, Mṣb) مِنْ مَرَاحِلِ السَّفَرِ. (JK.)

مِنْقَلَةٌ *A thing upon which bricks are carried from place to place.* (O, voce شَبَحَةٌ.)

مُنَقِّلَةٌ: *A wound in the head,* by which bone is removed: see شَجَّةٌ.

المَنْقُولُ [*Discerned* knowledge; opposed to مَعْقُولٌ]: under this term are comprised the sciences of أُصُولُ الدِّينِ (also called عِلْمُ الكَلَامِ), الحَدِيثُ, and الفِقْهُ: all the other sciences are comprised under the term المَعْقُولُ; (IbrD;) i. e. *intellectual,* or *perceived by the intellect;* and *excogitated.*

نقلس

أَنْقَلِيسُ [*An eel*] i. q. [Pers.] مَارْ مَاهِى [and أَنْكَلِيسُ]. (En-Naḍr, in TA, voce جِرِّيثٌ.)

نقم

1. نَقَمَ عَلَيْهِ *He exacted vengeance upon him, punished him:* see an ex. voce ابدى in art. بدو. See 8.

8. إِنْتَقَمْتُ مِنْهُ *I took,* or *executed, vengeance on him,* or *inflicted penal retribution on him, for that which he had done:* (JK:) or *I punished him;* (Ṣ, Mṣb, Ḳ;) as also ↑ نَقَمْتُ مِنْهُ, (Mṣb, Ḳ,) and عَلَيْهِ, (TA,) aor. ـِ; (Mṣb, Ḳ;) and نَقِمْتُ. (Ḳ.) — See نِقْمَةٌ.

نِقْمَةٌ [and ↑ اِنْتِقَامٌ] *Vengeance;* or *penal retribution.* (JK.)

نقه

1. نَقَهَ *He recovered, but not completely, his health and strength:* (TA:) or *he became convalescent;* or *sound,* or *healthy; at the close of his disease:* (Ṣ:) or *sound,* or *healthy, but was yet weak.* (Ḳ.) See بَرِئَ.

نَقَاهَةٌ [*Convalescence;*] the *slight degree of health that immediately succeeds sickness.* (TA, art. برأ.)

نقى

2. نَقَّاهُ *He cleansed it; cleared it; picked it; purified it; removing from it what was bad.* (Mṣb, &c.)

10. اِسْتَنْقَى *He took extraordinary pains,* or *the utmost pains, in cleansing his body.* (Mgh.) You say also, اِسْتَنْقَى الذَّكَرَ مِنَ البَوْلِ (Ḳ, art. برأ,) [*He took extraordinary pains in cleansing the* ذكر *from urine:* or] *he cleansed the* ذكر *entirely from urine;* syn. اِسْتَنْظَفَهُ. (TA in that art.) — اِسْتِنْقَآءٌ: see voce اِسْتِبْرَآءٌ.

نِقْىٌ The *pith* of canes, or reeds: see دِهْنٌ. — *Somewhat of fat* in a camel. (TA in art. طعم.) — And *Marrow;* i. q. مُخٌّ. (TA voce صُهَارَةٌ.)

بَنَاتُ النَّقَى, or النَّقَا, *The* حُلْكَة [or حُلَكَة]; *to which the fingers* (بَنَان) *of virgins are likened:*

(T in art. بنى:) *a certain small reptile, that dwells in sand, resembling a fish, smooth, and having a mixture of whiteness and redness; called also* شَحْمَةُ النَّقَا. (TA.) See حُلَكَةٌ and شَحْمٌ. — نَقًا or نَقًى *An extended gibbous piece of sand.* (Ṣ,* Mṣb,* Ḳ.)

نُقَايَةٌ *The extract,* or *refuse,* of a thing: see عُصَارَةٌ.

مُنْقٍ, said of a sheep, *Becoming a little fat:* see سَاحٍ. — *A sieve,* syn. غِرْبَالٌ. (TA, art. دوس.)

مُنَقِّيَةٌ *A woman who trims the split palm-stalks in mat-making:* see شَطَبَ and شَاطِبَةٌ.

نكز

4. أَنْكَزَ: see مُنْكِدٌ and زَمَّةٌ.

مُنْكِزٌ: see مُنْكِدٌ.

نكع

نُكْعَةٌ, so written for نُكَعَةٌ or نَكَعَةٌ in the O and Ḳ, voce سُوقَةٌ, q. v., [The *head* of a plant.]

نكف

1. نَكِفَ مِنَ الشَّىْءِ, aor. ـَ, inf. n. نَكَفٌ; and نَكَفَ, aor. ـُ; and ↑ اِسْتَنْكَفَ; *He abstained from, or refused to do, the thing, from disdain and pride.* (Mṣb.)

5. تَنَكَّفَ بِمَوْضِعِ كَذَا [*He waited,* &c.,] i. q. تَلَبَّثَ. (TA in art. صقر, from the "Nawádir.")

10. اِسْتَنْكَفَ مِنْهُ (KL,* MA) *He disdained,* or *scorned, it; was ashamed of it.* (KL, MA.) See 1.

نُكَفَةٌ: see غُنْدُبَةٌ, and لُغْدٌ.

نكل

1. نَكَلَ, aor. يَنْكُلُ, see 1 in art. فضل.

اَلَّذِى يَنْكُلُ أَقْرَانَهُ signifies النِّكْلُ. (A, art. عض.) — See نَكَلَ.

نَكَلٌ and ↑ نِكْلٌ: see بَدَلٌ.

نَكَالٌ *Any punishment serving to give warning to others than the sufferer:* (M, Ḳ, TA:) or *that restrains the offender from repeating the offence.* (Bḍ, ii. 6.)

نكه

نَكْهَةٌ The *odour of the mouth.* (Ṣ, TA.)

نكى

1. نَكِىَ, aor. ـَ, inf. n. نَكًا, *He* (an enemy) *was defeated, and overcome.* (TA, art. نَكَا.)

نِكَايَةٌ The *inflicting injury* upon an enemy: (MA, KL:) *slaying and wounding* among the enemy: (Ṣ, Ḳ:) or *making much slaughter,* (MA,) or *a great,* or *vehement, slaughter* or *wounding,* (Mṣb,) [i. e. the *making havoch,*] among the enemy: (MA, Mṣb:) the *inflicting a routing and overthrow* among the enemy. (ISk, TA.)

نلج

نِيلَجٌ and نِيلَنْجٌ *Indigo-pigment:* see نَوُورٌ, art. نور.

نلك

نُلْكٌ A kind of medlar-tree, *Mespilus aronia.* See زُوبَةٌ.

نم

1. نَمَّ *He* [*uttered calumny:* or] *excited discord, or dissension, and made known discourse in a mischievous manner;* or *embellished speech with falsehood.* (M, Ḳ.) You say, نَمَّ بِهِ and عَلَيْهِ, inf. n. نَمٌّ and نَمِيمَةٌ and نَمِيمٌ, or this last is pl. of نَمِيمَةٌ, (M,) meaning, *He calumniated him;* or *misrepresented him.* — نَمَّ الحَدِيثَ *He made known, divulged,* or *told, conversation, in a malicious or mischievous manner, so as to occasion discord, dissension, or the like.* (TA, art. قت; and Mṣb.*)

R. Q. 1. نَمْنَمَ *He variegated* a thing: *he decorated* or *embellished* it. (Ṣ, Ḳ.)

نَمِيمَةٌ The *sound of the bow-string.* (Kr.) — نَمِيمَةٌ *Malicious and mischievous misrepresentation; calumny; slander;* (Ṣ, Ḳ;) the *embellishment of speech with falsehood.* (Kr.)

نَمَائِمُ The *sutures* of the skull; as resembling lines of writing; see شَأْنٌ.

نَمَّامٌ now commonly applied to *Wild thyme, thymus serpyllum:* see شَبَهَانٌ.

نَامَّةٌ *The artery in the head:* see أَبْهَرُ.

مُنَمْنَمٌ A garment, or piece of cloth, *figured with marks resembling writing, or otherwise.* See مُدَنَّرٌ.

نمص

أَنْمَصُ *Having no eyebrows.* (TA in art. نط.)

نمغ

نَمَاغَةٌ The *upper part of the head:* and also the *part that is in a state of commotion, of the* يَأْفُوخ *of a child, before it becomes hard.* (L, TA.) See also يَأْفُوخٌ.

نمل

2. نَمَّلَ الثَّوْبَ [*He mended a garment*] i. q. رَفَاهُ. (TA in art. لقط.)

5. تَنَمُّلٌ *A formication* or *stinging,* as of the torpedo fish: see "Abdollatiphi Hist. Aeg. Comp.," p. 82.

نَمْلُ سُلَيْمَانَ *Red ants:* see أَحْوَى, in art. حو.

أَنْمُلَةٌ (thus generally written, Mṣb) The *head* [or *end*] *of a finger;* (Ṣ, Mṣb;) i.e. (Mṣb) the *joint* (مَفْصِل) (Az, Mṣb) *in which is the nail:* (Az, Mṣb, Ḳ:) [i. e. the *ungual phalanx, with,* or *without, the flesh upon it:* (see قَصَبٌ:)] or *a joint,* or *an articulation,* (عُقْدَة) *of the fingers.* (Mṣb.)

نمى

1. نَمَى, aor. ـِ, inf. n. نَمَآءٌ, *It increased;* (M, Ḳ, Mgh, TA;) *multiplied; became plentiful,* or *abundant;* (Mṣb, TA;) said of a thing, (Mṣb,) of cattle, or wealth, (Ṣ, Mgh, TA,) &c. (TA.) — نَمَتِ الأَرْضُ *The land throve,* or *yielded increase.*

4. أَنْمَى الصَّيْدَ *The quarry died out of sight* of the sportsman: see أَصْمَى.

8. إِنْتَمَى إِلَيْهِ *He asserted his* [own] *relationship* [*of son*] *to him;* (Ṣ, Mṣb, Ḳ;) like إِعْتَزَى. (Ṣ and Mṣb in art. عزو.)

نَامِيَةٌ, of a grape-vine, The *shoot upon which are the bunches of grapes:* (M, Ḳ:) or the *eye,* or *bud, that breaks open so as to disclose its leaves and its berries:* (M:) or *its branches:* pl. نَوَامٍ. (T.)

نه

R. Q. 1. نَهْنَهَ بِهِ *He cried out to him,* or *at him,* namely, a beast of prey, *in order that he might forbear, refrain,* or *abstain.* (TA.)

نهق

النَّوَاهِقُ *The channels of the tears* of a horse. (M in art. سهر.)

نهك

1. نَهِكَ الشَّرَابَ *He consumed the beverage.* (Ḳ.) — نَهِكَهُ الدِّبَاغُ [*The tan wore it,* or *eroded it*], namely, a hide. (M and Ḳ, voce مُقَلْقَلٌ.) See مُقَلْقَلٌ.

8. اِنْتَهَكَ مَحَارِمَ ٱللّٰهِ [*He violated the sacred ordinances of God;*] *he did that which God had forbidden him to do.* (Ḥar, p. 18; where see more.) — اِنْتَهَكَ حُرْمَتَهُ *He violated* [his honour, &c.]. (MA.)

مَنْهُوكٌ *Affected with a constant, or chronic, pervading disease;* or *emaciated by disease, so as to be at the point of death.* (Ṣ, Ḳ.) — See مَسْلُوتٌ.

نهل

نَهَلٌ *A first drinking:* see عَلَلٌ.

مَنْهَلٌ *A watering-place;* i. e., *a spring to which camels come to water.* (Ṣ, Mṣb.)

نهم

1. نَهِمَ *He had an inordinate desire* or *appetite* (Ṣ, Mṣb, Ḳ) *for food.* (Ṣ, Ḳ.)

نَهِيمٌ *A chiding of camels.* (TA.)

طَرِيقٌ نَهَّامٌ *A road wherein is* [*heard*] *a chiding of camels:* (TA:) see حَنَّانٌ.

نهى

1. نَهَاهُ عَنْهُ *He forbade him it.* — لَا تُنْهَى وَلَا تُنْهَى: see art. سهى, in two places.

6: see 8.

8. اِنْتَهَى عَنْهُ, and ▼ تَنَاهَى, *He refrained, abstained,* or *desisted, from it, as forbidden; left, relinquished, or forsook it.* (Ṣ, Mṣb.) See an ex. of the latter voce سَوَادٌ. — اِنْتَهَى إِلَيْهِ *It ultimately reached,* or *extended,* and sometimes *it so pertained, to him,* or *it:* in the latter sense said of authority and the like: and simply, *it reached to him,* or *it.* — اِنْتَهَى إِلَيْهِ الخَبَرُ, and ▼ تَنَاهَى, *The information,* or *news, reached him.* (Ṣ.) — اِنْتَهَى إِلَى مَوْضِعٍ *He came at last,* or *ultimately, to a place.* So I have rendered it in explaining أَفْضَى. — اِنْتَهَى *It* (a thing, or an affair,) *attained the utmost possible point,* or *degree.* (Mṣb.) *It* (fruit, and the like) *attained its utmost state of growth.* — اِنْتَهَى *It is ended:* a word put to mark the end of a quotation.

رَكِبَ النُّهَى *He did that which he was forbidden to do.* (TA in art. ودع.)

نُهُوٌّ is anomalous, (TA,) like بُغُوٌّ.

نِهَايَةٌ The *utmost possible point,* or *degree:* (Mṣb:) and the *ultimate point,* or *element, to which a thing can be reduced* or *resolved:* its *utmost point* or *particular:* as also ▼ مُنْتَهًى. See فصّ. — نِهَايَةٌ فِى السَّخَآءِ [*Extreme in bounty,* or *munificence*]. (O and Ḳ, voce مِشْعَل.)

نَاهِيكَ بِأَخِينَا [*A person sufficing thee is our brother*]: the ب is added to denote emphatic praise. (Fr in TA, art. ب.) See also Ḥar, p. 28, and, more particularly, p. 91.

مُنْتَهًى *A place to which a person* or *thing comes at last; a journey's end; a goal; a destination,* or *place or state to which a person or thing is appointed to come; an end; an ultimate object:* see an ex. in a verse near the end of art. ب. See نِهَايَةٌ. — سِدْرَةُ المُنْتَهَى (Ḳur liii. 14) *The lote-tree of the ultimate point of access, in the Seventh Heaven:* see سدر.

نوح

الغُرَابُ النُّوحِىُّ [*The Noachian crow;*] an appellation applied in Egypt to the زاغ (or *rook*). (TA, art. زيغ.)

نوط

النَّوْطَةُ The *crop* of a bird: see الجِرِّيَّةُ.

نَوَّاطَة The *same as* نُوَّاعَةٌ. See رُجَّاحَةٌ.

نوع

5. تَنَوَّعَ, said of a branch of a tree: see تَنَوَّسَ. — تَنَوَّعَ *It became of various sorts,* or *species.* (Mṣb.)

نُوَّاعَةٌ *A child's swing, of rope.* See رُجَّاحَةٌ.

نوف

مُنِيفٌ *High; lofty;* applied to a mountain, and a building. (T.) You say also عِزٌّ مُنِيفٌ [*High nobility*]. (Ḳ in art. عيط.)

نوق

2. نَوَّقَ [*He broke,* or *trained,* a camel]. (TA, voce مُصْعَب.)

5. تَنَيَّقَ فِى مَطْعَمِهِ وَمَلْبَسِهِ, and تَنَوَّقَ, *He was nice and luxurious* (تَجَوَّدَ وَبَالَغَ) *in his diet and his apparel.* (JK, Ḳ.) Better explained voce تَأَنَّقَ. — تَنَوَّقَ: see تَأَنَّقَ and تَجَوَّدَ, and نِيقَةٌ.

نِيقٌ quasi-inf. n. of أَنَاقَ.

نَاقَةٌ — بَكْرٌ, and بَعِيرٌ, and قَلُوصٌ: see نَاقَةٌ: see رِحَالَةٌ. — أَيْنُقٌ pl. of أَيْنُقَاتٌ pl. of الحَذَّآءَ: نَاقَةٌ: see a verse cited voce مُشْمَهِرّ.

نِيقَةٌ a subst. from تَنَوَّقَ (IJ, Ṣ, Ḳ) as syn. with تَأَنُّقٌ (Ṣ) [and therefore signifying *Daintiness, nicety, exquisiteness, refinement,* or *scrupulous nicety and exactness;* and the *exceeding of what is usual* in a thing: or the *choosing what is excellent,* or *best, to be done, and doing admirably:* or the *doing firmly, solidly, soundly,* or *thoroughly, and skilfully:* or] the *exceeding what is usual* in a thing, *and making it good,* or *beautiful, and firm, solid, sound,* or *free from defect* or *imperfection.* (Ḥam, p. 625) See تَأَنُّقٌ.

نول

1. نَالَ, aor. يَنَالُ, has for inf. ns. نَالٌ and مَنَالٌ and مَنَالَةٌ. (TA.) — See 6.

3. نَاوَلَهُ شَيْئًا *He gave him a thing; presented,* or *offered, it to him; gave him it with his hand; handed it to him;* syn. عَاطَاهُ; (T;) *he gave him a thing with his extended hand.* (T, Ḳ.)

5. تَنَوَّلَ عَلَيْنَا بِشَىْءٍ يَسِيرٍ: see تَطَوَّلَ.

6. تَنَاوَلَ مَآءَ الحَوْضِ [*He reached, and drank of, the water of the drinking-trough*]: said of a camel. (Ṣ, art. نوش.) — تَنَاوَلَ مِنْ يَدِهِ شَيْئًا *He took from his hand a thing; took it with his hand from his* (another's) *hand;* syn. تَعَاطَاهُ. (T.) — [تَنَاوَلَ شَيْئًا *He reached a thing; took it with his hand; handed it to himself;*] *he took a thing with the extended hand;* (TḲ;) or simply *he took a thing; took it with his hand, took hold of it;* syn. أَخَذَهُ: (Ḳ:) best rendered, *he took,* or *reached,* or *reached and took, a thing, absolutely,* or *with the hand,* or *with the extended hand;* and in like manner, with the mouth, as in an instance voce زَمَّ, &c.; *he helped himself to it* (i. e. food). — تَنَاوَلَهُ بِالسَّيْفِ *He reached,* or *hit him, with the sword:* see نَفَحَهُ: and see تَشَاوَلُوا, and أَطَفَّ. — هُوَ قَرِيبُ المُتَنَاوَلِ and سَهْلُ المُتَنَاوَلِ [app. *He is one from whom it is easy to take,* or *receive, gifts, &c.*]. (TA.) — تَنَاوَلُوا الرِّمَاحَ: see 6 in art. ذوق. — تَنَاوَلَهُ بِمَا يَسُوؤُهُ [*He carped at him by saying,* or *taxed* or *charged him with, that which would grieve him*]. — تناوله بما ليس فيه [*He carped at him by saying,* or *taxed* or *charged him with, what was not in him*]. (TA, voce اِغْتَابَهُ.) — تَنَاوَلَهُ بِلِسَانِهِ *He carped at him with his tongue:* (IbrD:) as also ▼ نَالَهُ (TA, art. هلب.) — تناول شَيْئًا *It* (a noun, &c.) *applied to a thing.* — تَنَاوَلَ *It comprehended,* or *comprised:* post-classical in this sense, but commonly used. (MF, TA.) — تَنَاوَلَهُ بِمَا يُكْرَهُ *He taxed* or *charged him with,* or *accused him of a thing disliked,* or *hated.* See also art. نيل; see an explanation of اِغْتَابَهُ, and see ظَهْرٌ.

نَوَالٌ: see نَالٌ.

نَوَالٌ and ↓ نَائِلٌ (Ṣ, Ḳ) and ↓ نَالٌ (Ḳ) *A gift:* (Ṣ, Ḳ:) and *a benefit, or favour, obtained from a man.* (TA.) See two exs. of the first voce خَرْقٌ: and an ex. of the second voce عَرَبَةٌ. — نَوَالٌ is also used as an inf. n. See an ex., from El-Aạshà, voce لَيْسَ.

نَوَالٌ: see نَائِلٌ.

مِنْوَالٌ The *web-beam of a loom; the beam on which the web is rolled,* (Ṣ, Mṣb, in art. نول, and Ṣ, Ḳ, voce حَفَّةٌ,) *as it is woven.* (Mṣb.)

نام

1. نَامَتْ رِجْلُهُ † *I. q.* خَدِرَتْ [*His leg,* or *foot, became benumbed,* or *torpid*]. (TA in art. بسر.) — نَامَ † *It* (a woman's anklet) *ceased to sound,* by reason of the fulness of the leg: like as one says {in the contr. case], استيقظ. (TA in art. يقظ.) — نَامَ has for its inf. ns. نَوْمٌ and مَنَامٌ. (Mṣb.) — نَامَ الثَّوْبُ *i. q.* رَقَدَ [q. v.] (A, art. رقد.) — نَامَتِ السُّوقُ *i. q.* رَقَدَتْ [q. v.] (Th, in TA, art. رقد.) — نَامَ ‡ *He lay; as opposed to he sat and he stood.* See نَائِمٌ. — نَامَ عَنْ حَاجَتِهِ *He cared not for the object of his want, neglected it.* (Mṣb.)

2. نَوَّمَ and ↓ أَنَامَ † *It benumbed,* or *torpified:* see نَامَتْ رِجْلُهُ.

3. نَاوَمْتُهُ فِى شِعَارٍ وَاحِدٍ [*I slept with him in one under-garment*]. (Ṣ, art. شعر.)

4: see 2.

10. اِسْتَنَامَ إِلَيْهِ *He trusted to him, and became quiet, or easy, in mind; relied upon him.* (Ṣ, Ḳ.)

إِمْرَأَةٌ نَؤُومُ الضُّحَى *i. q.* رَقُودُ الضحى [which see]. (A, art. رقد.)

نَائِمٌ ‡ *Lying; as opposed to sitting and standing.* (Mgh.)

أَنْوَمُ [*More, or most, prone to sleep*]. (A, art. فهد.)

مَنَامٌ *Time of sleep.* (Jel, xxxix. 43.) See also 1.

نون

نُونَةٌ The *dimple in the chin of a young child:* (M, Ḳ:) see خُنْعُبَةٌ, and قَلْتَةٌ, and دَائِرَةٌ, and 2 in art. وسم.

نوه

1. نَاهَ بِهِ (Mṣb) and ↓ نَوَّهَ بِهِ (Ṣ, Mgh, Mṣb, Ḳ) *He rendered famous* (Ṣ, Mgh, Mṣb, Ḳ*) and *magnified;* (Mṣb;) and *rendered notorious;* (Mgh;) *it,* (Ṣ, Mṣb,) namely a person's name, (Ṣ,) or a thing, (Mṣb,) or *him.* (Mgh.)

2: see 1.

نوى

1. نَوَاهُ and ↓ اِنْتَوَاهُ *He intended it, purposed it, designed it, aimed at it, proposed it to himself as the object of his aim.*

8. اِنْتَوَى القَوْمُ مَنْزِلًا بِمَوْضِعِ كَذَا (Ṣ, Mṣb) *The people,* or *party, repaired,* or *betook themselves, to,* or *towards, a place of alighting* or *abode, in such a place.* (Mṣb.) See 1. — اِنْتَوَى *It* (a people, or company of men,) *removed from country to country,* or *town to town.* (TA.)

نَوًى *Date-stones:* they are often used as food for camels; (see إِبِلٌ نَوَوِيَّةٌ;) and for this purpose are bruised, and sometimes mixed with barley, and then moistened: see بَسِيسَةٌ. — نَوَاةٌ *What is cut off in the circumcision of a girl.* (Lḥ, in TA, voce عُذْرَةٌ.) The name shows that this is the prepuce of the *clitoris,* the end of which resembles the end of a date-stone. But see بَظْرٌ. — النَّوَى *What remains of the place of circumcision of a girl after that operation;* i. e. the بَظْر: (M:) or *the place of circumcision of a girl, which is what remains of her* بَظْر *when the* مُتْك *has been cut off.* (T.) — نَوًى *Pieces of gold, each of the weight of five dirhems.* (TA in art. جب.) — نَوًى The *tract,* or *region towards which one goes* (Ṣ) *in journeying,* whether *near* or *distant;* (Ṣ;) the *place that is the object of a journey:* (El-Ḳálee, TA:) [a traveller's *destination:*] the *course,* or *direction, that one pursues* (Ḳ, TA) in journeying and in acting or conduct: (TA:) see an ex. voce صَرْفٌ (third sentence), and عَقَرَ. It is of the fem. gender. (Ṣ.) See an ex. in some verses cited voce بَيْنٌ.

نِىٌّ and نَىٌّ: see art. نيأ.

نِيَّةٌ *An intention, an intent, a purpose, a design, an aim; a determination of the mind,* or *heart:* (Mṣb, TA:) this is the general meaning: (Mṣb:) the *direction that one takes* (Ṣ, Mṣb, Ḳ) *in a journey,* (Ṣ, Ḳ,) *near or distant,* (Ṣ,) and *in an action:* (Ḳ:) the *thing that one intends,* or *purposes,* or *aims at: an affair:* (Mṣb:) the *place to which one purposes journeying:* (Ṣ in art. زل:) see an ex. from a rájiz in art. زل, first paragraph: the *thing,* or *place, that one proposes to himself as the object of his aim,* in an action, or a journey: or the *thing,* or *place, that is the object of an action* or *journey:* see طِيَّةٌ and شُقَّةٌ. — نِيَّةٌ نَفْحٌ *i. q.* طَرُوحٌ and ضَرُوحٌ, &c. (O, art. ضرح.) — نِيَّةٌ بَعِيدَةٌ: see بَعِيدٌ, where the ة of the latter word has been accidentally omitted. It also often (or generally) means *A distant,* or *remote, thing,* or *place, that is the object of an action* or *journey:* &c.

أَنَا مُنْتَوٍ عَنْ هٰذَا الأَمْرِ *I. q.* مُتَرَيِّعٌ, q. v. (TA in art. ريع.)

نيك

1. نَاكَ النُّعَاسُ عَيْنَهُ, and نَاكَ المَطَرُ الأَرْضَ: see نَكَحَ.

نيل

1. نَالَ مِنْهُ *He defamed him.* (L, art. قبح.) — نَالَ مِنْ عِرْضِهِ *He defamed him.* (T, Ḳ, TA.) — نَالَ مِنْهُ *He harmed, hurt,* or *injured him,* namely, an enemy. (Mgh.) — نَالَهُ بِلِسَانِهِ is coupled in the Mṣb, art. قرص, with أَذَاهُ; and seems plainly to signify أَصَابَهُ, which, in this case, is the same as أَذَاهُ. And ↓ تَنَاوَلَهُ has a similar meaning. — نَالَ *He obtained,* or *attained.* (Ṣ, Ḳ.) نَالَ مِنْ عَدُوِّهِ *He attained* [or *obtained*] *the object of his aim,* or *desire, from his enemy.* (Mṣb.) — نَالَهُ, aor. يَنَالُ, *It reached him; came to him;* syn. وَصَلَ إِلَيْهِ. (M, art. نيل.) See also Bḍ, xxii. 38. — نَالَ لَكَ أَنْ تَفْعَلَ, aor. يَنِيلُ; see أَنَى. — نَالَهُ, first pers. نِلْتُهُ, and ↓ أَنَالَ لَكَ; inf. n. نَيْلٌ, *He obtained it; he attained it;* namely, the object of his wish, &c. (Ṣ, Ḳ, Mṣb, &c.)

4: see 1.

6. يَتَنَاوَلَانِ and هُمَا يَتَنَايَلَانِ signify the same. (TA.)

نَيْلٌ *Obtainment;* &c.: see 1.

إِنَالَةٌ The act of *giving;* (PṢ in art. نيل;) the *giving a gift.* (KL.) It seems properly to belong to art. نول.

نَيْلٌ (T, M, Ḳ) and ↓ نَائِلٌ (M, Ḳ) *What one obtains,* or *acquires,* (T, M, Ḳ,) *of the bounty of another;* like نَوَالٌ. (T.)

نيلج

See art. نلج.

ه

ه : the vowel of this pron. is sometimes, in a case of pause, transferred to the preceding letter: and this is always done in modern Arabic. — ه subjoined in هٰذِهْ, and the like: see أَبْيَضُ. — The هَا, termed تَنْبِيهٌ, is said by some to be used as an inceptive, without any meaning but inception. (See إِذَا.) See حَرْفُ تَنْبِيهٍ in art. نبه: and see an ex. voce لَا. When followed by a pronoun, as هُوَ, &c., it is best rendered *Lo.* — ه of pausation: see remarks on a verse cited voce حِينَ — بِهَا, in حَقًّا بِهَا, and many phrases syn. therewith, is app. for بِأَسْرِهِ. See حَقًّا.

هَءْ and هَآءِ: see art. هوأ.

هبخ

Q. Q. 3. اِهْبَنْبَخَ; (Ḳ;) and اِهْبَنْبَخَتْ, aor. يَهْبَنْبِخُ; inf. n. اِهْبِنْبَاخٌ; (TA;) *He,* (Ḳ,) and *she,* (TA,) *walked with an elegant and a proud and self-conceited gait, with an affected inclining of the body from side to side.* (Ḳ, TA.)

هَبَيَّخٌ, of the measure فَعَيَّلٌ, (Ṣ,) *A boy,* or *young man:* and هَبَيَّخَةٌ *a girl,* or *damsel:* both in the dial. of Ḥimyer. (L.) — Also, the former, *A soft boy,* or *young man:* (Ḳ:) or the former and latter, respectively, *a soft, thin-skinned, and plump, boy or young man,* (Ṣ,) *and girl or damsel:* (Ṣ, Ḳ:) or *a plump and goodly* young man, and woman: (L:) or the latter, *a tall and great* woman: (JK:) [and hence, app., applied as an epithet, in the sense of *long and large,* to a woman's train, in the following verse, quoted by Aṣ,]

* جَرَّتْ عَلَيْهِ الرِّيحُ ذَيْلًا أَنْبَخَا *
* جَرَّ العَرُوسِ ذَيْلَهَا الهَبَيَّخَا *

(L.) [*The wind dragged over it a train of dusky colour, and abounding with dust, like as the bride drags her long and large train.*] — Also, the latter, *A damsel suckling,* or *that suckles.* (M, Ḳ.) — Also, the former, *A stupid, and flabby, or flaccid,* man. (Ḳ.) — Also, a man *in whom is no good.* (Ḳ.) — Also, *A great valley.* (Ḳ) — And *A large river.* (Ḳ.)

هبع

هُبَعٌ, applied to a young camel: *a young camel brought forth in the end of the breeding-time.* (Ḳ, voce رُبَعٌ, q.v.) See بَلَغٌ.

هبل

1. هَبِلَتْ, inf. n. هَبَلٌ: see هَبِلَ.

8. اِهْتَبَلَ: see 5 in art. حفو. — *I. q.* تَحَيَّنَ. (TA.)

هَيْبَلِيٌّ *A Christian monk:* see أَبِيلٌ.

مَهْبِلٌ *The place of gestation:* see a verse cited voce مُحْبَلٌ.

هبو

1. هَبَا الرَّمَادُ, (JK, TA,) aor. يَهْبُو, (TA,) *The ashes became mixed with dust,* and extinguished: (JK, TA:) and هَبَا الجَمْرُ. (M, art. رمد.)

هَبْوَةٌ: see هَبَاءٌ.

هَبْوَةٌ *Dust rising,* or *spreading, in the sky like smoke.* (JK.)

هَبَاءٌ *The motes that are seen in the rays of the sun:* (TA:) see an ex. voce فَشَا.

هتك

1. هَتَكَ *He rent open.* (Ḳ, Ṣ.) — هَتَكَ اللّٰهُ سِتْرَهُ *God dishonour him:* see سِتْرٌ.

هَتَّاكٌ One *who rends frequently* tents and the like: see بَابٌ.

هَتَارَةٌ, for أَثَارَةٌ: see ثور.

هجع

5. تَهَجَّعَ *He slept.* (1001 Nights, ii. 321.)

هَجْعَةٌ †The *setting* of a star. (Ṣgh in TA, art. شرط.) See شَرَطٌ. — *A light sleep in the first part of the night.* (Ṣ.)

هجل

هُوجَلٌ, of a ship or boat, is smaller than the أَنْجَرُ. (O, TA, voce مَعَايِرُ.) — See De Sacy, Chrest. Arab., ii. 350.

هَجُولٌ *A fornicatress,* or *an adulteress:* pl. هَجَائِلُ. (JK.)

هجم

1. هَجَمَ عَلَيْهِ *He came upon him suddenly,* or *at unawares,* (Mgh, Mṣb, Ḳ,) or *came in to him without permission,* (Ḳ,) or *without asking permission:* (Mgh:) *he invaded, assaulted, assailed, attacked, attempted, or ventured upon, him or it:* *he pounced upon him or it.*

هَجْمَةٌ, or, accord. to Kz, هَزِيعٌ, *The third of the five divisions of the night.* (TA.) See خُدْرَةٌ, and يَعْفُورٌ. — As applied to camels, see عَائِضٌ and زِيَادَةٌ.

هجن

1. نَكَحَ فِي بَنِي فُلَانٍ وَهَجَّنَ أَوْلَادَهُمْ [*He married among the sons of such a one, and made their children to be base-born,* or *ignoble*]. (TA in art. بغل.)

هُجْنَةٌ [*Meanness of race,* in a horse]. (Ḳ, voce إِعْرَابٌ.)

هَجِينٌ *One whose father is free,* or *an Arab, and whose mother is a slave.* (Ṣ, Ḳ.) — *A* horse [*half-blooded*] *got by a stallion of generous race out of a mare not of such race:* (Ṣ:) or *got by an Arabian stallion out of a mare not of Arabian birth:* (Mṣb:) or *not of generous birth; a jade.* (Ḳ.)

هَاجِنٌ A girl *not arrived at puberty,* or a beast *not yet fit to be covered:* see an ex. voce جَلٌّ.

هجو

1. هَجَاهُ *He censured, dispraised, reviled,* or *satirized him,* (Ṣ, Mṣb, Ḳ,) *in verse.* (Mṣb, Ḳ.) — مَا هَجَوْتُ مِنْهُ شَيْئًا : see 1 in art. حجو.

3. هَاجَاهُ, inf. n. مُهَاجَاةٌ, *He contended with him in satirizing.* See 4 in art. فحم.

أُهْجُوَّةٌ, *Dispraise,* is like أُسْبُوبَةٌ, *contr. of* أُمْدُوحَةٌ.

هدف

10. إِسْتَهْدَفَ *He became a* هَدَف, or *butt.* (Ḥar, p. 65.) See رَتِيمَةٌ.

هَدَفٌ *A high* or *lofty building:* see صَدَفٌ.

هدل

1. هَدَلَ *He uttered a cry:* see هَدَرَ, in two places.

5. تَهَدَّلَ *It hung down;* [*it dangled;*] said of a branch of a tree, (Ṣ, TA,) and of fruit; *it hung loosely;* said of the former. (TA.)

مِشْفَرٌ أَهْدَلُ [*A camel's lip*] *flaccid,* or *pendulous.* (Ḳ, TA.)

هدم

1. هَدَمَ *He threw down, or pulled down,* a building; (Mṣb;) *pulled it to pieces; demolished* it; *destroyed* it: (Ḳ:) [the last two explanations are the most correct, as is shown by the phrase] نَقْضُ البِنَآءِ مِنْ غَيْرِ هَدْمٍ [*He took to pieces the building without demolishing, or destroying*]: (Ṣ, A, Mṣb, Ḳ,* in art. قوض:) *he ruined* [a building, &c.]; *reduced* [it] *to ruin.* (Ḥam, p. 31.)

6. تَهَادَمَتِ الحِيطَانُ [*The walls fell to ruin by degrees*]. (Ṣ in art. دعو.)

7. إِنْهَدَمَ *It became thrown down, pulled down, pulled to pieces, demolished,* or *destroyed:* and *it fell in ruins, or to pieces;* or *became a ruin.* — إِنْهَدَمَ الحَائِطُ مِنْ مَكَانِهِ مِنْ غَيْرِ هَدْمٍ [*The wall fell in ruins,* or *to pieces, from its place, without being pulled to pieces*]. (Lth, in TA, art. قيض.)

الدَّمُ الدَّمُ وَالهَدْمُ الهَدْمُ : see دَمٌ.

هَدَمٌ *Earth that is dug from a pit or well:* see حَفَرٌ.

هدمل

هِدَمْلَةٌ *Food and drink:* see بِطْحَلٌ.

هدن

هُدْنَةٌ عَلَى دَخَنٍ *An illusory truce:* see دُخَانٌ.

هدى

1. هَدَاهُ *He directed him,* or *guided him,* to the way; (Ḳ,* TA;) *directed him aright;* or *caused him to take, or follow, a right way* or *course* or *direction.* (Ḳ, TA.) See 8. — هَدَى العَرُوسَ *He sent* [or *conducted*] *the bride* (MA, KL) to her husband, (MA,) or to the house of her husband; (KL;) *i. q.* زَفَّهَا, (Ḳ in art. زف,) and so ✝ أَهْدَاهَا. (Mṣb in that art.) — يَهْدِى meaning يُؤَدِّى : see an ex. in a verse cited voce طَبْعٌ.

4: see 1.

6. تَهَادَنَا *They* (two parties who had been at war) *made a truce, each with the other.* (T, art. نبذ.)

8. اِهْتَدَى *He became rightly directed; followed a right direction;* (Ḳ;) *went aright;* as also ✝ هَدَى. (Ṣ.) — *He guided himself.* — *He went a right way; went aright.* — لَا يَهْتَدِى إِلَى جِهَةٍ *He cannot go aright; or knows not the way that he would pursue; or knows not in what direction to go:* sometimes said of a drunken man. — لَا يَهْتَدِى لِأَمْرِهِ means *He does not, or cannot, find the way to accomplish,* or *perform, his affair.* — اِهْتَدَى *He found,* (MA,) or *took* (KL,) *the right way* or *road.* (MA, KL.) — دَاهِيَةُ الغَبَرِ, by which دَاهِيَةٌ لَا يُهْتَدَى لَهَا is expl. in the Ṣ and O, means لَا يُهْتَدَى لِلنَّجَاةِ مِنْهَا, by which the same phrase is expl. in the JK: or it may be well rendered *A calamity in relation to which one knows not the right course to pursue.* — اِهْتَدَى also signifies *He continued to be rightly directed,* or *to follow a right direction:* and *he sought to be rightly directed,* or *to follow a right direction.* (TA.) — اِهِدَّى and اِهَدَّى, for اِهْتَدَى; like اِعِذَّرَ and اِعَذَّرَ, for اِعْتَذَرَ.

هُدًى *A way, course, method, mode,* or *manner, of acting,* or *conduct,* or *proceeding,* or *the like;* (Mṣb, Ḳ;) as also ✝ هِدْيَةٌ and ✝ هَدْيَةٌ: (Ḳ:) or to the second and third: and the first is pl. [or coll. gen. n.] of the last: (Ṣ:) and *a good way,* &c.: and *calm,* or *placid, deportment;* or *calmness,* or *placidity, of deportment:* (TA:) see also دَلٌّ. — هَدْيٌ [*Conduct, mode of life; manners*]. — See هَدِىٌّ.

هُوَ عَلَى هُدًى *He is following,* or *he follows, a right direction.* — الهُدَى *The Ḳur-án.* (Bḍ, Jel in lxxii. 13, &c.)

هَدْيَةٌ and هِدْيَةٌ : see هَدْىٌ.

هَدِيَّةٌ [n. un. of هَدِىٌّ] *A present;* i. e. *a thing sent to another in token of courtesy or honour;* (Mṣb;) such as is termed طَرِيفٌ and لَطَفٌ. (JK.) — هَدْىٌ and ✝ هَدِىٌّ [coll. gen. ns.] *What one brings as an offering to Mekkeh,* (Ḳ,) *or to the Kaabeh,* (Beyḍ, v. 2,) *or to the Ḥaram,* (Ṣ, Mgh,) *consisting of camels* (Lth, Ṣ, Mgh, Mṣb) *or other beasts,* (Lth,) namely *kine or sheep or goats,* (Mgh,) *to be sacrificed,* (TA,) *and of goods or commodities:* (Lth:) n. un. with ة. (Ṣ, &c.) — Also, *Camels,* absolutely. (TA.) — هَدِىٌّ also *One who is entitled to respect,* or *honour,* or *protection:* so in a verse cited voce اِسْتَبَاءَ. (ISk in T in art. بوأ.)

هَادٍ : see an ex. of its pl. هَوَادِى meaning *Necks* of horses, voce تَالٍ. — هَادِيَةٌ The *fore part of the neck of a horse.* (Ḳ in art. سلف.)

أَخَذَ هَادِىَ الرَّحَى فَجَعَلَ يُدِيرُهَا — [*He took the handle of the mill, and began to turn it*]. (Ḳ, art. هبز.)

أَهْدَى مِنْ دُعَيْمِيصِ الرَّمْلِ *More expert,* &c.: see art. دعمص.

المَهْدِىُّ, meaning *The directed* by God to the truth, is a proper name, and the name of him of whose coming at the end of time the happy tidings have been announced. (TA.) [It is always so pronounced by the Arabs in the present day: not المَهْدِى.]

هذ

1. هَذَّ بِسَلْحِهِ *He ejected his excrement.* (TA, art. تر.)

هذى

1. هَذَى *He talked nonsense; he raved,* or *talked irrationally, foolishly,* or *deliriously;* (JK, Ḳ;) *by reason of disease or some other cause.* (Ḳ.) — هَذَى بِهِ *He talked irrationally,* &c., *with him.* (TA.) — And *He mentioned him, or it, in his irrational,* &c., *talk.* (TA.)

3. قَعَدَ يُهَاذِى أَصْحَابَهُ [*He sat talking irrationally,* &c., *with his companions*]. (TA.) — سَمِعْتُهُمْ يَتَهَاذَوْنَ [*I heard them talking together irrationally,* &c.] (TA.)

شَرَابٌ هَاذٍ ‡ [*Beverage causing delirious,* or *irrational, talk.*] (TA.)

هر

1. هَرَّ, inf. n. هِرٌّ, *He drove sheep or goats:*

(IAạr, in Ṣ, Ḳ, voce بِرٌ :) or *he called* them. (Yoo, in TA, ibid.)

هرجل

هِرْجَالٌ, pl. هَرَاجِيل, *A tall, long-bodied,* or *bulky, she-camel:* (TA:) see هِرْجَاب.

هرح

أَرَاحَ : see هَرَاحَ.

هرس

هَرَاسٌ *A certain thorny* or *prickly tree,* (Ṣ, Ḳ, TA,) *the thorns* or *prickles of which are like the* حَسَك, (TA,) *and its fruit is like the* نَبِق : n. un. with ة. (Ḳ, TA.) See قُطْبٌ.

هرشف

هِرْشَفَّةٌ *A piece of rag with which water is dried up from the ground.* (TA, art. جف.) — See هِرْشَبَّةٌ.

هرطل

هِرْطَالٌ *A large long-bodied* man. (Az, in TA, voce هِرْدَبَّةٌ.)

هرق

1. هَرِقْ عَلَى خَمْرِكَ [*Pour* water *upon thy wine;* i.e.,] *quiet thine anger.* (T.) See also Freytag's Arab. Prov., ii. 875; also the same, ii. 877. — هَرِقْ عَنَّا مِنْ رُوبَةِ اللَّيْلِ : see رُوبَةٌ.

4. أَهْرِقْ عَنْكَ مِنَ الظَّهِيرَةِ, *i. q.* أَبْرِدْ, q. v. (IAạr, in TA, art. فيح.) See 4 in art. روق. — هَرَاقَهُ and أَهْرَاقَهُ and ↓ هَرَقَهُ, aor. ـَ, inf. n. هَرْقٌ, *He poured it out,* or *forth:* see 4 in art. روق. — هَرِيقُوا عَنْكُمْ أَوَّلَ اللَّيْلِ, (in the Ḳ, erroneously, عَلَيْكُمْ,) *Alight ye in the first of the night:* (TA:) or *disburden yourselves* (أَنْزِلُوا عنكم): or *relieve,* or *rest, yourselves;* which seems to be generally meant by هريقوا عنكم.

هُرَاقَةٌ and إِهْرَاقَةٌ *The seminal fluid* of a man: see إِرَاقَةٌ, in art. روق.

هرل

Q.Q. 1. هَرْوَلَ *He walked quickly:* (Mṣb:) [*he went a kind of trotting pace between a walk and a run;* see رَمَلَ;] هَرْوَلَةٌ is not so quick as خَبَبٌ [*an amble*]; (Mṣb;) and is *between* مَشْىٌ [*a walk*] *and* عَدْوٌ [*a run*]: (Ṣ, Mṣb, Ḳ:) it is *a kind of* عَدْو: (Ṣ:) or *quicker than* عَنَق: or *a quick walk.* (Ḳ.)

هرم

1. هَرِمَ *He became extremely aged;* (Ḳ;) *old and infirm;* (Mṣb;) *decrepit;* or *a weak old man.*

هَرِمٌ *The mind:* see 6 in art. رق.

هرن

كُرٌّ : see الكُرُّ الهَارُونِىُّ.

هرنصن

The هرنصانة, (Ḳ,) i. e. هِرْنَصَانَةٌ, (TA,) or هِرِنْصَانَةٌ, (so in the CḲ, and in my MS. copy of the Ḳ,) with kesr, (Ḳ,) and the ر quiescent, and with kesr to the ن, (TA,) is *A certain worm,* (Ḳ,) accord. to IAạr; said by others to be (TA) what is *called the* سُرْفَة [which is very variously described]. (Ḳ, TA.) See دُخْلُل.

هرى

هُرْىٌ *A granary:* see نِبْرٌ.

هزر

هَزَوَّرٌ *A strong* boy or young man: and a *weak* old man: as also حَزَوَّرٌ: pl. هَزَاوِرَةٌ. (Abu-ṭ-Ṭeiyib, in TA, art. حزر.)

هزع

هَجْمَةٌ : see هَزِيعٌ.

هزل

1. هَزَلَ is *contr. of* جَدَّ. (Ṣ, Mgh, Ḳ.) You say, هَزَلَ, aor. ـِ, inf. n. هَزْلٌ; (Ṣ, Mṣb, Ḳ;) and هَزِلَ, aor. ـَ, (Ḳ,) inf. n. as above; (TA;) and ↓ هَازَلَ; (Ḳ;) *He jested,* or *joked;* (Mṣb;) or *was not serious,* or *in earnest;* (TA;) فِى كَلَامِهِ *in his speech;* (Mṣb, TA;) and فِى الأَمْرِ *in the affair.* (TA.)

3. هَازَلَ *He jested,* or *joked.* (Ḳ.) See 1.

هُزَالٌ *Leanness, meagreness, emaciation: contr. of fatness.* (Ṣ, Ḳ.)

هَزْلَى, pl. of هَزِيلٌ *Lean, meagre, emaciated.* (Ḳ, voce خَشَبٌ.)

مَهْزُولٌ : see two exs. in a verse cited voce عِرْضٌ.

هزم

7. إِنْهَزَمَ *It* (an army) *was routed, discomfited, defeated,* or *put to flight.* (Ḳ, &c.) See حَاصَ, in art. حيص; and إِنْحَازَ, in art. حوز; from both of which it is distinguished.

هَزْمَةٌ The [*purring,* or] *sound of the throat* of a cat. (TA.) — The *pit between the two collar-bones.* (TA, art. ترب.) — [The *pit* above a horse's eye.] (Ḳ, voce وَقْبٌ.) See also خَنْعَبَةٌ, and قَلْتَةٌ: and see عَقْمٌ, where it seems to mean *a stricture:* it generally and properly signifies *a depression,* or *dint:* or *a pit,* or *small hollow, resembling a dint:* see also غَيْبٌ.

مَهْزُومُ الصَّدْرِ *Depressed of breast,* i. e., apparently, *illiberal, niggardly:* see حَوْضٌ.

هشم

1. هَشَمَهُ *He crushed it.*

2. هَشَّمَهُ, inf. n. تَهْشِيمٌ, *He broke it* [*much,* or *so crushed it*]; (TA;) namely, a dry thing, and anything hollow, such as the head, and the like. (TA in art. شدخ.)

5. تَهَشَّمَ *It* (a plant, or herbage,) *became* هَشِيم, i. e. *dry, and broken in pieces.*

هَشِيمٌ A plant *that is dry, and breaks,* or *is broken, in pieces.* (Ṣ, Mṣb, Ḳ.)

هَاشِمَةٌ *A wound in the head which breaks the bone:* see شَجَّةٌ.

كُرٌّ : see الكُرُّ الهَاشِمِىُّ.

هضم

1. هَضَمَ لَهُ : see تَخَوَّفَهُ. — هَضَمَهُ and إِهْتَضَمَهُ : see هَضَمَ مِنْ مَالِهِ.

5: see 7.

7. إِنْهَضَمَ *It* (a thing) *melted,* or *dissolved, after being congealed.* (JK.) — إِنْهَضَمَتِ الثَّمَرَةُ, and ↓ تَهَضَّمَتْ, *The fruit broke;* or *became broken,* or *crushed;* syn. تَشَدَّخَتْ; (TA;) and *became mellow, so as to be easy of digestion.* See also بَوْغ. — إِنْهَضَمَ, said of food, (MA,) *It was,* or *became, digestible,* or *easy of digestion.* (MA, KL.) — إِنْهِضَامٌ of the زَوْر [app. *Depression*]. (Ḳ in art. جنف. [There coupled with دُخُولٌ.]) See also صَقَلٌ.

8: see 1. — إِهْتَضَمَ الشَّجَرَ مِنْ أَعْلَاهُ (Ḳ voce شَعَبَ) *He cropped the tops of the shrubs:* see شَعَبَ.

هَضَرٌ *Contraction of the sides,* (Ṣ, Ḳ,) *and lankness of the belly, and smallness of the flank:* (Ḳ:) in a horse it is a fault. (Ṣ.)

هَاضُومٌ : see هَضُومٌ.

هَاضُومٌ *Any medicine* [or *other thing* (see حَاطُومٌ)] *that is a digestive of food;* as also هَضُومٌ; (Ḳ;) *i. q.* جُوَارِشُ. (Ṣ.)

هطل

1. هَطَلَ *It* (water) *poured:* see its inf. n. voce سَكْبٌ.

هف

هِفٌّ *Certain small fish,* which are dried: see سُمَيْكَاءُ.

هفو

1. هفا, said of the heart, *It fluttered,* or *palpitated;* and, as Z says, *was flurried* by reason of grief, or of beating. (TA.) See 1, in art. فهو.

هَفْوَةٌ *A slip, lapse, fault,* or *fall into wrong-doing;* pl. هَفَوَاتٌ. (TA.)

هق

هَقْهَاقٌ see : قَرَبٌ هَقْهَاقٌ.

هقر

هِقْوَرٌ *A large, long-bodied* man. (Az, in TA, voce هِزَوْبَّةٌ.)

هقع

الهَقْعَةُ *Three small stars* [λ, φ 1, *and* φ 2, *of Orion,*] *forming the points of a triangle, in the head of* الجَوْزَاءُ *The 5th Mansion of the Moon.* (El-Ḳazweenee.) [This is accord. to those who make نَوْءٌ to signify the "auroral setting:" accord. to those who make it to signify the "auroral rising," these stars compose الهَنْعَةُ, q. v.; and الهَقْعَةُ seems to consist of o 1 and o 2 *of Orion.*]

هك

1. هَكَّ : see سَكَّ.

هَاكٌّ : see فَاكٌّ.

هَكَّاكٌ : see فَكَّاكٌ.

هل

4. أَهْلَلْنَا هِلَالَ شَهْرِ كَذَا : see سَلَخَ.

10. إِسْتَهَلَّ : see a verse cited at the close of the first paragraph of art. خبعك. — See also a verse cited voce أَلْأَ. — See مُسْتَهَلٌّ.

هَلْ may be originally هَلُو or هَلَى or هَلَّ : (Akh, in Ṣ, voce بل :) see بَلْ. — هَلْ followed by إِلَى : see the latter. — حَيَّ هَلَ : see حى. — هَلَّا : see حَضَّةٌ and عَزَّ, latter part, and لَوْلَا, and أَلَّا.

هَلَّةٌ : see بَلَّةٌ.

الهِلَالُ *The new moon;* or *the moon when it is termed* هِلَال : it may be explained as meaning, generally, *the moon when near the sun,* or *moon a little after or before the change.* — See سَنَا.

مُسْتَهَلُّ الشَّهْرِ *The first night of the lunar month.* (Mṣb.)

هلف

أَحَصُّ see يَوْمٌ هِلَّوْفٌ.

هلك

1. هَلَكَ, inf. n. هَلَاكٌ &c., (Ṣ, Ḳ, &c.,) *He,* or *it, perished, came to nought, came to an end, passed away, was not, was no more,* or *became non-existent* or *annihilated:* (KL, PṢ in explanation of هَلَاكٌ, &c.:) or *fell:* or *became in a bad,* or *corrupt, state; became corrupted, vitiated, marred,* or *spoiled:* or *went away, no one knew whither:* (Mgh in explanation of هَلَاكٌ:) *he died.* (Ḳ.) — هَلَكَتْ أَرْضُهُ *His land had its herbage dried up by drought:* see جَرِبَ.

2. وَادِي تُهُلِّكَ *I. q.* تُضُلِّلَ.

4. أَهْلَكَهُ *He destroyed, made an end of,* or *caused to perish* or *come to an end, made away, did away with,* or *brought to nought, him,* or *it; took away his life.*

6. تَهَالَكَ غَمًّا [app. *He perished gradually by reason of grief.*] (A, art. سوس : see 1 in that art.) — تَهَالَكَ عَلَيْهِ *He was vehemently eager for it.* (TA.) — تَهَالَكَ فِيهِ *He strove, laboured, toiled,* or *exerted himself, in it,* namely in running; as also ‡ إِهْتَلَكَ. (TA.) *He strove, laboured, toiled,* or *exerted himself, and hastened, in it,* namely an affair; as also ‡ استهلك فيه. (TA.) — تَهَالَكَتْ said of a she-camel, *i. q.* عَشِقَتْ [*She vehemently desired the stallion*]. (AA, TA in art. عشق.)

8 : see 6.

10. إِسْتَهْلَكَ properly signifies *He sought,* or *courted, destruction;* like إِسْتَمَاتَ : see مُسْتَمِيتٌ : and see an ex. voce شَرْشَرَةٌ. — إِسْتَهْلَكَ فِي كَذَا *He* (a man) *distressed, troubled,* or *fatigued, himself in,* or *respecting, such a thing.* (TA.) See also 6.

هَلَكَةٌ *The drying up of the plants,* or *herbage.* (AḤn, TA.) See هَلَاكٌ.

هَلَاكٌ [*Perdition; destruction; a state of perdition* or *destruction; a lost state;*] *death.* (Ḳ.) — هَلَاكٌ and ‡ هَلَكَةٌ are syn. (Ṣ, Mṣb, Ḳ.) — إِرْتَبَكَ فِي الهَلَكَاتِ *He stuck fast in cases of perdition:* see art. ربك.

هَالِكٌ *Dead;* or *dying.* (Bḍ, Jel in xii. 85.) — هَالِكٌ sometimes means *Subject to perish;* as in the Ḳur, xxviii. last verse.

أَلُوكٌ : see مَهْلَكٌ.

مَهْلَكٌ *Death:* see a verse cited voce سَهْوٌ.

مَهْلَكَةٌ *A cause of perdition,* or *of death.* (TA in art. بخل.) — ‡ *A place of perdition* or *death:* and *a desert:* (KL:) or *a* [*desert,* or *such as is termed*] مَفَازَةٌ; (Ṣ, Ḳ, TA;) because persons perish therein; (Z, TA;) or because it urges [or leads] to perdition. (TA.) See جَادَّةٌ.

هُوَ مُسْتَهْلِكٌ إِلَى كَذَا *i. q.* مُسْتَمِيتٌ [q. v.]. (TA, art. موت, from the A.) — مُسْتَهْلِكُ الوِرْدِ *A road that destroys him who seeks water, by reason of its far extent.* (O.)

هلم

هَلُمَّ *i. q.* تَعَالَ, *Come.* (Ṣ, Ḳ, &c.) — It is intrans.; as in هَلُمَّ إِلَيْنَا *Come to us.* And trans. also; as in هَلُمَّ شُهَدَاءَكُمْ *Cause your witnesses to come; bring your witnesses.* (Mṣb.) — هَلُمَّ جَرًّا *At thine ease:* see 1 in art. جر.

هم

1. هَمَّ. *He purposed,* or *intended,* a thing. هَمٌّ denotes more than إِرَادَةٌ, and less than عَزْمٌ. (Ḳull, p. 382.) — لَا مَهَمَّةَ وَلَا مَكَادَةَ : see art. كود. — هَمَّ بِالشَّىْءِ [*He meditated, proposed to himself, purposed,* or *intended, to do the thing;*] *he desired to do the thing,* (Ṣ, Mṣb,) *without doing it;* (Mṣb;) *he endeavoured to do the thing.* (Ṣ.) — هَمَّ بِالأَمْرِ *He intended the affair,* or *purposed it;* or *he desired it.* (Mgh.) — هَمَّ بِهِ فِى نَفْسِهِ [aor. ـُ] *He intended it, meant it, desired it,* or *determined upon it, in his mind.* (TA.) See also a verse cited voce زَتْرٌ. — هَمَّ بِالبُكَاءِ [*He was about,* or *ready, to weep;* like أَرَادَ البُكَاءَ, q. v.], and تَهَيَّأَ لِلْبُكَاءِ. (A, art. جهش, &c.) — هَمَّ بِالسُّقُوطِ [*It threatened to fall*], said of a

wall. (Ṣ, in art. وهى, &c.) — هَمَّهُ and ↑ أَهَمَّهُ *It disquieted him;* (Mṣb;) *caused him care,* or *anxiety.* — لَا يُهِمُّهُ إِلَّا بَطْنُهُ [*Nothing causes him care,* or *anxiety, but his belly*]. (Ṣ in art. بطن.)

4. أَهَمَّهُ *It rendered him anxious;* (MA;) *disquieted him,* and *grieved him.* (Mgh.) See عَنَّاهُ.

7. إِنْهَمَّ: see a verse cited in art. ب, p. 144.

8. إِهْتَمَّ بِالْأَمْرِ *He was grieved,* and *disquieted, by the affair,* or *case:* (TA:) you say إِهْتَمَّ لَهُ بِأَمْرِهِ *he was grieved for him by his affair,* or *case.* (Ṣ.) [*He was,* or *became, anxious, disquieted,* or *grieved,* by it.] — *He minded,* or *attended to, the affair:* (MA:) *undertook,* or *superintended,* or *managed, the affair.* (Mṣb.) See عُنِىَ, in art. عنى. — إِهْتَمَّ لَهُ *He cared for, minded,* or *regarded, him,* or *it.* (Ḥar, p. 94.) — إِهْتَمَّ بَلَدَ كَذَا i.q. إِعْتَسَّهُ. (TA in art. عس.)

هَمَّ for هَمَا for أَمَا before an oath: see the last.

هَمٌّ and ↑ هِمَّةٌ *Purpose,* or *intention;* syn. أَوَّلُ العَزِيمَةِ and أَوَّلُ العَزْمِ. (Mṣb.) See Ḥar, p. 345, and a verse cited voce طَلَّاع. — Also the ↑latter, *Strong determination* or *resolution.* (Mṣb.) — هَمٌّ *An object,* or *a thing intended* or *meant* or *desired* or *determined upon, in the mind.* (Ḳ,* TA.) See an ex. voce حَمٌّ and سَمٌّ: you say, هَمُّهُ كَذَا *His object is such a thing.* — هَمٌّ [*Anxiety;* or *disquietude,* or *trouble, of mind; solicitude; care:* or *grief,* or *sorrow:*] *distress,* or *disquietude, affecting the heart* or *mind, by reason of some harm,* or *annoyance, that is expected to happen;* differing from غَمٌّ, which signifies "distress, or disquietude, affecting the heart or mind, by reason of what has happened:" or both, as some say, signify the same [namely *distress,* or *disquietude, of mind*]: the difference is asserted by 'Iyáḍ and others. (TA in art. غم.) — هَمُّهُ بَطْنُهُ [*His object of care,* or *of anxiety, is his belly*]. (Ḳ in art. بطن.) And لَا هَمَّ لَهُ إِلَّا بَطْنُهُ [*He has no object of care,* or *of anxiety, but his belly*]. (TA in that art.) — هَمُّكَ مَا عَنَاكَ means هَمُّكَ مَا هَمَّكَ: and also signifies اذابك. (JK.) See also Freytag's Arab. Prov. ii. 880.

هِمٌّ *A decrepit, old, and weak,* or *extremely aged,* man. (Ṣ, Mṣb, Ḳ.)

هَمَّةٌ: see هِمَّةٌ.

هِمَّةٌ *A thing that one meditates, purposes,* or *intends to do;* or *that one desires to do;* or *endeavours to do; a purpose; an intention;* or *an object of desire,* or *of endeavour;* as also ↑ هَمَّةٌ. (JK, Ḳ.) — هِمَّةٌ [*Ambition;* particularly *of a high kind;*] *a faculty firmly rooted in the soul, seeking high things, and fleeing from base things.* (Ibn-Kemál, in TA.) See بَعِيدٌ, and هَمٌّ — هِمَّةٌ [*Mind; purpose; aspiration; desire; ambition; enterprise; emprise.*] — هِمَّةٌ عَالِيَةٌ *High purpose; ambition.*

هُمَامٌ *An aspiring king:* (Ṣ, Ḳ:) *a magnanimous,* i. e. *courageous and liberal, chief.* (Ḳ.)

هُمْهَامٌ *A wild bird of the crow kind:* see صُرَدٌ.

هَامَّةٌ, pl. هَوَامُّ, *Any venomous creeping thing* or *reptile* or *the like, that may be killed; such as the scorpion, and the serpent:* and ‡ *a louse:* (Mgh:) *what has deadly venom; as the scorpion:* (Az, Mṣb:) and sometimes, *what is noxious:* (Mṣb:) *any reptile or the like, from the louse to the serpent;* (AḤát, Mṣb:) but its application to the louse is tropical: (Mṣb:) *any venomous or noxious reptile or the like; such as the scorpion, and the serpent:* the *like of serpents and scorpions;* because they creep (تَهِمُّ, i.e. تَدِبُّ). (JK.)

مُهِمٌّ *A difficult, an arduous, a distressing,* or *an afflictive affair,* or *business:* syn. أَمْرٌ شَدِيدٌ: (Ṣ:) and مُهِمَّاتٌ signifies أُمُورٌ شِدَادٌ, (JK,) *affairs of difficulty:* and, *of importance.*

بَرَدٌ مُنْهَمٌّ [app. *Dissolving hail-stones*]. (Mughnee and Ḳ, in explanations of ب.) See a verse in explanation of ب used redundantly, p. 144.

هجد

هَمْدَةٌ *A trance:* so rendered voce رَقْدَةٌ.

همرجل

هَمَرْجَلٌ A *bulky* she-camel. (IAạr, TA, voce شَمَرْدَلٌ.)

همش

8. إِهْتِمَاشٌ The *intermingling,* or *interpenetrating.* (KL.) — And the *proceeding slowly.* (KL.) See قَرْتَنٌ.

همل

1. هَمَلَ, aor. ـُ, inf. n. هَمَلَانٌ; and ↑ إِنْهَمَلَ; *It* (water) *overflowed, and poured forth.* (Mgh.) — تُهْمَلُ عَلَى رُؤُوسِهَا وَظُهُورِهَا; so in a copy of the Ḳ, voce وَسُوطٌ: in other copies of the Ḳ, يُحْمَلُ or تُحْمَلُ: if the first be correct, the meaning is probably Camels *left without rein and without burden;* and this is agreeable with the context.

4. أَهْمَلَ المَاشِيَةَ *He sent* [or *left*] *the cattle to pasture* [*by themselves,*] *without a pastor, by night and by day.* (Mṣb.) — أَهْمَلَهُ *He left it, let it alone,* or *neglected it, intentionally* or *from forgetting:* (Mṣb:) or *he left it,* or *let it alone,* expl. by خَلَّى بَيْنَهُ وَبَيْنَ نَفْسِهِ: (Ṣ, O, Ḳ:) or *he left it,* or *neglected it, and did not make use of it.* (Ḳ.) — أَهْمَلَ عَبْدَهُ (Ṣ, Ḳ, in art. سمع) *He left his slave without work,* or *occupation:* (PṢ:) *he left him to himself, uncontrolled.*

7. إِنْهَمَكَ فِى الأَمْرِ *He exerted himself, strove,* or *laboured, in the affair,* (Ṣ, Mṣb,) *and persisted,* or *persevered, in it.* (Ṣ, Mṣb, Ḳ.) — إِنْهَمَكَ فِى البَاطِلِ *He obstinately persevered in vain or false affairs.*

هَمَّالٌ Applied to the eye or eyes, *Flowing abundantly with tears:* see a verse cited voce عَلَقٌ.

مُهْمَلٌ *Having no government.* (TA, art. on the particle ف.) — لَفْظٌ مُهْمَلٌ *A word that has no grammatical government; contr. of* عَامِلٌ. (IbrD.)

هن

هَنٌ and هَنٌ *A thing:* and *a penis:* and the *vulva of a woman:* (KL:) or the former is pl. [or coll. gen. n.] of ↑ هَنَةٌ, which signifies *a small,* or *little, thing:* (MA:) or this last signifies *a thing,* (KL,) as does هَنٌ: (Ḳ, KL:) [but the former meaning I have found to be very common, and I think it the more approvable. ↑ هَنَةٌ may be rendered *something, somewhat:*] it denotes anything. (TA.)

هَنَةٌ: see هَنٌ.

هنبر

هِنْبِرٌ *A light,* or an *active,* ass. (IAạr, in TA, voce يَعْفُورٌ.)

هنع

الهَنْعَةُ *Two white stars,* [γ *and* ξ *of Gemini,*] *between which is the space of the length of a whip, in the Milky Way; one of which is called* الزَّرُّ, *the other* المَيْسَانُ. — *The 6th Mansion of the Moon.* (El-Ḳazweenee) — Or *The three stars* [λ, ϕ *1, and* ϕ *2,*] *in the face of Orion.* (Idem, descr. of Orion.) [The former accord. to those who make نَوْءٌ to signify the "auroral setting:" the latter accord. to those who make it to signify the "auroral rising:" accord. to those who make it to have the first of these two significations, the three stars in the face of Orion compose الهَقْعَةُ, q. v.] See التَّحَايِى, in art. حى.

هنم

Q. Q. 1. هَيْنَمَ *He concealed*, or *kept secret*, a story; syn. أَسَرَّ. (A, art. جهر.)

هوع

هَيْعُوعَةٌ, originally هَيْوُعُوعَةٌ: see شَاعَ.

هول

مَهُولٌ *Terrible*. (TA.)

نَارُ الْمُهَوِّلِ: see نَارٌ.

هوم

2. هَوَّمَ *He slept*. (TA, voce نَامَ.)

هَامَةٌ The *head*: (Ṣ, Ḳ:) or the *part between the two edges of the head*: or the *middle*, and *main part, of the head*, [see قَرْنٌ, and صَدًى, in several places,] of anything: (TA:) or the *upper part of the head, in which are the* نَاصِيَة *and the* قُصَّة, *which mean the fore part of the hair of the forehead; in it is the* مفرق, *which is the* فرق *of the head, between the two sides, extending to the* دَائِرَة. (AZ, TA.) See also two explanations voce جُمْجُمَةٌ. — هَامَةٌ The *crown*, or *top, of the head*. See قَمَحْدُوَةٌ, and اِعْتَجَرَ. — هَامٌ meaning *Headmen*, or *chiefs*: see a verse cited in art. غلصم. — بَنَاتُ الْهَامِ *The marrow of the brain*. (TA.) — أُمُّ الْهَامِ (Ḳ in art. دمغ) app. *i. q.* أُمُّ الدِّمَاغِ and أُمُّ الرَّأْسِ: see أُمٌّ and دِمَاغٌ. — هَامَةٌ *An owl: a certain night-bird*, (Ṣ, Ḳ,) *that frequents the burial-places, of small size*, (TA,) *i. q.* صَدًى: (Ṣ, Ḳ:) or *i. q.* بُومَةٌ: (TA:) pl. [or coll. gen. n.] هَامٌ. (Ṣ.) See بُومٌ; and see also أَخْرُ.

هون

1. هَانَ, inf. n. هَوَانٌ and هُونٌ (Mṣb, Ḳ) and مَهَانَةٌ, (Ḳ,) *He, or it, was*, or *became, low, base, vile, abject, mean, paltry, contemptible, despicable, ignominious, inglorious*, and *weak*; syn. ذَلَّ, (Mṣb, Ḳ,) and حَقُرَ, (Mṣb,) and ضَعُفَ. (TA.) — هَانَ عَلَيْهِ [*It was of light estimation to him*]. *It* (a thing) *was* [*easy and*] *light to him*. (TA.) — هَانَ also, *He, or it, was*, or *became, gentle*, and *easy*. (Mṣb.)

2. هَوَّنَهُ عَلَيْهِ *He* (God) *made it easy and light to him*. (Ḳ,* TA.) — هَوِّنِ الْأَمْرَ وَلَا تَحْزَنْ لَهُ [*Make thou the case*, or *affair, light*, or *easy*; i. e., *regard it lightly; and do not grieve for it*]. (TA, art. خفض.)

4. أَهَانَهُ, and ▼ تَهَاوَنَ بِهِ, and ▼ اِسْتَهَانَ بِهِ, *He held him in light*, or *little*, or *mean, estimation*, or *in contempt; despised him; made light of him* or *it*. (Ṣ, Ḳ, &c.) — أَهَانَهُ *He lowered*, or *abased, him; debased him; rendered him abject, vile, mean, paltry, contemptible, despicable*, or *ignominious*.

6: } see 4.
10: }

هَيْنٌ and ▼ هَيِّنٌ *Easy*: (Ṣ, Mṣb, Ḳ:) and the latter *of light estimation, paltry, despicable*. (Ḳ,* TA.)

على هِينَتِك *at their ease*.

هَيِّنٌ: see هَيْنٌ.

أَهْوَنُ in the sense of هَيِّنٌ: see أَكْبَرُ. See also an ex. voce بَصِيرَةٌ; and another voce بَعْرٌ.

بَعِيرٌ مُهَانٌ عَلَى أَهْلِهِ [*A camel held in mean estimation by his owner*]. (TA, art. دفع.)

هوى

1. هَوَى بِهِ *He made it to fall down*: see an ex. in a verse of Ru-beh, cited voce رِيَاغٌ, in art. ريغ. — See 4. — هَوَتْ أُذُنُهُ *His ears heard a confused*, or *humming*, or *singing, sound*. (Ḳ.) — هَوَتْ أُمُّهُ is used to express wonder; like as when one says, قَاتَلَهُ اللّٰهُ مَا أَسْمَعَهُ. (IB, in TA, art. ام.)

4. أَهْوَى إِلَى الشَّىْءِ بِيَدِهِ *He extended*, or *stretched forth, his arm*, or *hand, to the thing to take it*; it being near: if it be distant, you say, ▼ هَوَى إِلَيْهِ, without ا. (Mṣb.) And أَهْوَى إِلَى سَيْفِهِ *He reached his sword; took it with his hand*, or *with his extended hand*; or *took hold of it*. (Mṣb.) And أَهْوَيْتُ بِالشَّىْءِ [in my copy of the Mṣb, erroneously, إِلَى الشَّىْءِ] *I made a sign with the thing*. (Aṣ, Ṣ.)

5. تَهَوَّهَ: see آهَةٌ, in art. اوه.

7. اِنْهَوَى: see اِنْغَوَى, in art. غو.

هَاهُ and هَاهٌ: see آهٍ, in art. اوه.

الْهَوَى *Love*, and *attachment*: then, *inclination of the soul, or mind, to a thing*: then, *blameable inclination*; as when one says, اِتَّبَعَ هَوَاهُ [*He followed his evil inclination*]; and هُوَ مِنْ أَهْلِ الْأَهْوَاءِ [see below]. (Mṣb.) See also حُبٌّ. — هَوًى Also signifies *Beloved* [or *an object of love*]. (Ḳ, Ḥam, p. 546.) [Being originally an inf. n., it may be used alike as sing. and pl. See an ex. in a verse cited in the first paragraph of art. زين: and see an ex. voce شَكْلٌ. — الْهَوَى *The inclination of the soul to that in which the animal appetites take delight, without any lawful invitation thereto*; (KT;) [*natural desire*:] *love, and desire*; generally, *such as is not praiseworthy*: (Mgh:) I render it, *love*, or *desirous love*. — [Its pl.] أَهْوَاءٌ also signifies *Opinions declining*, or *swerving, from the right way*, or *from the truth*. (Bḍ, ii. 114.) [Hence,] أَهْلُ الْأَهْوَاءِ [*The people of erroneous opinions*]. (T, in art. سمع; &c.)

هُوَّةٌ *A deep hollow in the ground*: (Ṣ, JK, M, Mṣb, Ḳ:) or *a hollow*, or *cavity, in the ground*; *a pit*: (Mṣb:) or *a descent in the ground*: (Ḳ:) or *a deep hollow, cavity, or pit*; as also ▼ مَهْوَاةٌ: or *a low*, or *depressed, place in the ground*. (TA.) — اِجْعَلِ الْأَمْرَ هُوَّةً وَاحِدَةً *Make thou the affair*, or *case*, [*uniform*, or] *one uniform thing*. (Fr in TA, in art. بأج.)

هَوَاءٌ *A vacancy; a vacuity; a vacant*, or *an empty, space*. (Mgh.) — *A vacant*, or *an empty, thing*. (Mṣb.)

هَوِىٌّ and هُوِىٌّ: see 4, (last sentence), in art. سلم.

هَاوَنٌ, said to be thus, with fet-ḥ to the و, originally هَاوُونٌ, [*A mortar*;] the *thing in which one pounds, or bruises*: pl. هَوَاوِينُ. (Mṣb.)

هَاوِيَةٌ *An abyss; a depth*, or *deep place, of which the bottom cannot be reached*. (JK, TA.)

مَهْوَى الرَّكِيَّةِ [*The cavity of the well*]. (Ḳ, voce إِزَاءٌ.) — See مَهْوَاةٌ.

مَهْوَاةٌ: see هُوَّةٌ. — The *space between two mountains*; (Ṣ, Mṣb;) and *the like*; as also ▼ مَهْوًى: (Ṣ:) *a pit*, or *hollow, dug*, or *excavated*. (Mṣb.)

مُهَيًّا *i. q.* زُمَاوَرْدٌ. (MF, art. ورد.)

هيف

5. تَهَيَّفَ, (Ṣ, Ḳ,) said of a man, (Ṣ,) is from الْهَيْفُ [the hot south-west wind], like تَشَتَّى from الشِّتَآءُ. (Ṣ, Ḳ.) See an ex. voce مَصْقُولٌ.

الْهَيْفُ: respecting the wind thus called, see نَكْبَآءُ.

رِيحٌ مِهْيَافٌ [*A very thirsty wind*]. (TA, voce نَكْبَآءُ.)

هيق

هَيْقَةٌ A female ostrich. (A, art. زمر.)

هيل

7. إِنْهَالَ It (sand, &c.) poured down. (Ṣ, Ḳ.) — إِنْهَدَمَ الجِدَارُ وَٱنْهَالَ [The wall fell in ruins, or to pieces, or became a ruin, and broke, or crumbled down]. (Ḳ in art. قيض.) So rendered voce إِنْقَاضَ, art. فيض.

هَيْلٌ inf. n. of هَالَ: see حَثَا. — هَيْلٌ and ▼ هَائِلٌ Sand that will not remain steady in its place, but falls down. (JK.)

هَيُولَى and هُيُولَى: wrongly mentioned in art. هول. See مَادَّةٌ.

مَهِيلٌ: see كَثِيبٌ.

هيم

2. هَيَّمَهُ: see هُيُومٌ.

هُيَامٌ: see an ex. in a verse of Lebeed, voce أَصْلٌ.

هُيَامٌ: see هُبٌّ.

هُيُومٌ [The being bewildered, or distracted, by amorous desire;] the pursuing a heedless, or an inconsiderate course, or going at random, heedlessly, or without consideration, or certain aim, by reason of amorous desire: and تَهْيَامٌ the [being so, or] doing so, much. (TA.) You say, of love [or amorous desire], ▼ هَيَّمَهُ, inf. n. تَهْيِيمٌ. (TA.) — An affection like insanity arising from amorous desire: (JK:) bewilderment, or distraction, by amorous desire. (KL.)

هَيْمَانُ A man loving intensely, or very passionately or fondly: (TA:) and so applied to a heart: see شَنِقٌ. — هَيْمَانُ A thirsty camel: fem. هَيْمَى: pl. هِيمٌ. (Jel, lvi. 55.)

مُهَيَّمٌ: see voce قَتٌّ.

هين

1. هَانَ لَهُ, aor. يَهِينُ, He treated him with gentleness, or blandishment; syn. دَارَاهُ. (Aboo-Is-ḥáḳ, in TA, art. عن; but only the imp., هِنْ لَهُ, is there mentioned, said to be with kesr.) See عَزَّ, near the end, p. 2031, and the distinction there made between هِنْ and هُنْ.

هيه

هَيَةَ and هِيهِ and هِيهٍ: see إِيهٍ and إِيهِ and إِيهَ

هَيْهَاتَ كَذَا Far, or far from being believed or from the truth, is such a thing; as also هَيْهَاتَ لِكَذَا: or the latter means remoteness, or remoteness from being believed or from the truth, is to be attributed to such a thing: هَيْهَاتَ followed by لِ means بَعُدَ, (Jel, in xxiii. 38,) or بُعْدٌ الصِّحَّةُ or التَّصْدِيقُ: (Bḍ, ibid:) or البُعْدُ: (Bḍ, ibid, TA:) and without لِ after it, it denotes the pronouncing [a thing] remote. (TA.) See أَيْهَاتَ. — هَيْهَاتَ denotes one's deeming a thing remote, or improbable, and despairing of it; and means مَا أَبْعَدَ [Very far, &c.], or بَعُدَ جِدًّا [How far, &c.]; implying more than بَعُدَ, though we render it by this word. (Kull, p. 382.)

هى

ابن هَيَّانَ and إِبْنُ هَيٍّ The low, ignoble, mean, contemptible, man. (T in art. بنى.)

و

وَ: you say, سَارَ زَيْدٌ وَعَمْرٌو, using و as a conjunction; rather than سِرْتُ وَزَيْدًا وَعَمْرًا: and, using و as [a prep.] denoting concomitance; rather than وَزَيْدٌ. (I'Aḳ, p. 161.) — مَا أُمِّى وَأُمُّهُ; and مَا أَنَا وَطَلَبُ الوَحْشِ: see أُمٌّ: and see another ex. in a verse cited voce حَلِمَ. In the Ḳur, ii. 121 some read وَإِسْمَعِيلَ; and others وإِسْمٰعِيلُ. In مَا لَكَ وَزَيْدًا, the و denotes concomitance; *What hast thou in common*, or *to do, with Zeyd?* or it is for وَ in مَا لَكَ وَلِزَيْدٍ. — وَهُوَ لَكَ: see حَمْدٌ. — الوَاوُ لِمُطْلَقِ الجَمْعِ [*The* و *denoting unrestricted conjunction*, not necessarily implying simultaneousness nor relative order]. (I'Aḳ, p. 254.)

وَا generally means *Alas!* see وَا حَرَبًا, and the last verse voce حَتَّى. — وَا زَيْدَاهُ *Alas, Zeyd!* — وَا دَفْرَاهُ, and وَا نَتْنَاهُ, *Alas, stench!* meaning *Alas, what an abominable thing!* See دَفْرٌ; and أَبٌ.

وأر

1\. The verse of Lebeed,

تَسْلُبُ الكَانِسَ لَمْ يُوأَرْ بِهَا
شُعْبَةَ السَّاقِ إِذَا الظِّلُّ عَقَلْ

means *She carries off from the gazelle entering his covert, he not being frightened by her, the branch of the trunk of the tree* above him, *when the shade contracts*, or *decreases*, or *goes away, at midday:* he is describing his swift she-camel.

10\. إِسْتَوْأَرَ *He hasted in the darkness;* as also اسْتَاوَر. (Ḳ, art. أور.)

وأل

1\. وَأَلَ: see آلَ, in art. اول, in two places.

أَوَّلُ *First*, and *former; preceding all others, and preceding another.* See art. أول. — أَوَائِلُ السُّوَرِ *The first parts*, or *beginnings, of the chapters of the Ḳur-án.* — جَآءَ فِى أَوَائِلِ القَوْمِ *He came among the first comers of the people.* (Mṣb.) — And الأَوَائِلُ *The people of former ages;* as also الأَوَّلُونَ. — لَقِيتُهُ عَامًا أَوَّلَ means *I met him [in a former year,] before this year, though by several years.* ('Alee El-Ḳári, in his Expos. of the Ḳ, from Seer; cited in the margin of a copy of the Ḳ; art. اول.) See عَامٌ.

وأم

3\. See art. ومأ.

وِئَامٌ The *being mutually near; mutually agreeing.* (T, voce تَوْمٌ.)

التُّوَءمَانُ, *The herb so called:* see art. تأم.

وأى

1\. وَأَى as syn. with وَعَدَ; imperative إِهْ, with the ه of silence added; fem. corroborated form of the imperative إِنَّ; of which last, see a curious ex. in the end of article حَرْفُ الأَلِفِ, in the Mughnee.

وبر

1\. وُبِرَتِ النَّخْلَةُ [*The palm-tree was fecundated:*] i. q. أُبِرَتْ, i. e. أُلْقِحَتْ. (Aboo-'Amr Ibn-El-'Alà, in L, art. أبر.) See art. أبر.

4\. أَوْبَرُوا عَلَى شَىْءٍ i. q. اوصبوا عليه, q. v. (TA, art. وصب.)

مَأْبُورَةٌ i. q. نَخْلَةٌ مَوْبُورَةٌ. (Aboo-'Amr Ibn-El-'Alà, *l. c.*)

وبش

وَبْشٌ *A whiteness on the nails:* see زِنْجِيرٌ.

وبل

1\. وَبَلَ *He* (a horse) *ran vehemently:* see an ex. in a verse cited voce دَامَ, in art. دوم.

وَبْلٌ *Violent rain, consisting of large drops;* as also ▼ وَابِلٌ; (Ḳ;) *a heavy rain.*

بَلَةٌ: see إِبَالَةٌ.

وَبَلَةٌ: see أَبَلَةٌ.

وَبَالٌ *An evil result.* (Mṣb.)

وَبِيلَةٌ: see إِبَالَةٌ.

وَابِلٌ: see وَبْلٌ.

وَابِلَةٌ The *extremity [in which is the glenoid cavity]* of the scapula: and the *portion of flesh* [or *muscle*] of the scapula. (IAạr, T.) See مَرْدَغَةٌ, and also صَدَفٌ; and more particularly إِنْفِرَاكٌ.

وبه

1\. وَبِهْتُ, and مَا وَبِهْتُ لَهُ: see مَا أَبِهْتُ له.

وبى

1\. وَبِئَتِ الأَرْضُ and وَبُؤَتِ الأَرْضُ: see وبئ.

4\. مَاءٌ لَا يُوبِى: see وبأ.

وتر

وَتَرَةٌ The *vein* (عِرْقٌ [meaning the *frenum*]) *that is in the inner side* (بَاطِن) *of the glans of the penis.* (Ṣ, Ḳ, and Zj, in his "Khalḳ el-Insán.")

ثَأْرٌ: see voce مَوْتُورٌ.

وتن

الوَتِينُ [*The aorta:* or *the aorta descendens:*] *a certain vein* [or *artery*] *adhering to the inner side of the backbone all along, which supplies all the* [*other*] *veins* [*or arteries*] *with blood, and irrigates the flesh, being the river of the body:* or *a certain thick white vein resembling a cane:* [this last is the description given by Zj in his "Khalḳ el-Insán:"] or [*the aorta ascendens;*] *the* نِيَاط *of the heart:* or *a certain white vein within the back of the neck: it is said to draw up* [*its supply*] *from the heart, and in it is the blood.* — Also, *the* خِلْب, q. v.: pl. أَوْتِنَةٌ and وُتْنٌ: (M:) *i. q.* نِيَاطُ القَلْبِ. (Bḍ, and Jel, lxix. 45.) See أَبْهَرُ.

وتى

3. وَاتَاهُ عَلَى الأَمْرِ, inf. n. مُوَاتَاةٌ and وِتَآءٌ, *i. q.* طَاوَعَهُ; a dial. var. of the verb with ء [i. e. آتَاهُ, q. v., and of وَاطَأَهُ also]. (TA.) See 3 in art. عدو.

4. أَوْتَى: see وَتٌّ.

مستوتى, or مُسْتَوْتٍ *A mare desirous of the stallion:* see مُسْتَأْتٍ in art. اتى.

وثر

التَّوَاثِيرُ *i. q.* أَعْوَانُ الرَّجُلِ. (TA, in art. امل.)

وثق

1. وَثُقَ *It was,* or *became, firm, stable, fast,* or *strong;* (Mṣb;) *i. q.* أُحْكِمَ (Ṣ, Mgh, Ḳ) [or اِسْتَحْكَمَ, q. v.]. — وَثِقَ بِهِ *He trusted,* or *confided, in him.* (Ṣ, Mgh, Mṣb, Ḳ.)

4. أَوْثَقَهُ *He made it firm, stable, fast,* or *strong.* (Mṣb.) — *He bound,* or *tied, him,* or *it, firmly, fast,* or *strongly,* in a bond. (Ṣ, Ḳ, TḲ.) See شَدَّهُ.

5. تَوَثَّقَتِ العُقْدَةُ [*The knot became firm,* or *fast*]. (A, in art. ارب.)

10. اِسْتَوْثَقَ مِنْهُ [*He secured himself against him,* by a bond or the like, or absolutely:] *he took,* or *received, a bond* (وَثِيقَة) *from him.* (Ṣ, Ḳ.) — أُكْتُبُوهُ اسْتِيثَاقًا وَدَفْعًا لِلنِّزَاعِ [*Write ye it,* (namely, the debt,) *for the creditor's self-securing, and for preventing contention*]. (Jel, ii. 282.) See اِسْتَظْهَرَ. — اِسْتَوْثَقَ مِنَ البَابِ *He closed the door firmly.* (MA.) — اِسْتَوْثَقَ مِنْ أُمُورِهِ: see اِسْتَوْثَقَ مِنَ المَالِ. — أَعْتَبَ: see استوثج. — اِسْتَوْثَقَ بِهِ *He confided in him.*

ثِقَةٌ *Trusty; trustworthy; honest:* applied as an epithet alike to a man and a woman, and to two or more men or women: pl. ثِقَاتٌ (Mṣb.) — بِهِ ثِقَتِي *In him is my trust,* or *confidence.* (TA.) — لَسْتُ مِنْهُ عَلَى ثِقَةٍ *I am not confident,* or *sure, of it.* Occurring in the Ṣ, art. ضمر, &c. See an ex. voce شَهْرٌ (last sentence). — أَخْذٌ بِالثِّقَةِ: see أَخٌ. — أَخُو ثِقَةٍ: see أَخَذَ, and see my explanation of إِحْتَاطَ.

الوَثِيقَةُ فِي الأَمْرِ *The doing the thing firmly; and taking the sure method,* or *way;* expl. by إِحْكَامُهُ والأَخْذُ بِالثِّقَةِ. (TA.) — وَثِيقَةٌ *A bond, security,* or *writing of obligation for the payment of a debt or the like:* pl. وَثَائِقُ. Ex., كِتْبَةُ الوَثَائِقِ (Bḍ, ii. 282,) *The mode of writing bonds.* — *A pledge.* — وَثِيقَةٌ *i. q.* دُرْجَةٌ, q. v.

أَخَذَ الأَمْرَ بِالأَوْثَقِ *He set about the affair in the surest,* or *firmest, manner.* (TA.)

مَوْثِقٌ and مِيثَاقٌ *A compact; a contract; a covenant; an agreement; a league; a treaty; an engagement; a bond; an obligation; a promise.* (Ṣ, Ḳ, &c.)

مِيثَاقٌ: see مَوْثِقٌ; and Jel, &c., in ii. 60 and 87.

مَوْثُوقٌ بِهِ *In whom* [*and in which*] *trust,* or *confidence, is placed.* (Mgh.)

مُوَثَّقَةُ الخَلْقِ A she-camel *rendered firm, strong,* or *compact, in make.* (Ṣ.)

وثم

وَثِيمَةٌ *Broken stones.* (TA, art. جرم.) See جَرَامٌ.

وثن

وَثَنٌ *An idol:* see صَنَمٌ and عَثَنٌ and عَنَنٌ.

وثى

وَثْيٌ: see وَثْءٌ.

وجع

1. وَجِعَ رَأْسَهُ *He had a pain in his head:* see أَلِمَ.

4. أَوْجَعَهُ *He,* or *it, pained him;* or *caused him pain,* or *aching.* (Ḳ, MA, TA.)

5. تَوَجَّعَ *He expressed,* or *manifested, pain, affliction, distress, grief,* or *sorrow;* [*complained; moaned;* or] *uttered lamentation,* or *complaint;* (PṢ;) syn. تَأَلَّمَ. (Ṣ, art. ألم) and تَفَجَّعَ (Ṣ, art. فجع; and Ḳ) and تَشَكَّى (Mṣb, Ḳ) and تَأَوَّهَ (Mṣb, art. اوه) and أَهَّ (Ṣ, art. أه) and تَحَزَّنَ. (Ḳ, art. حزن.) — تَوَجَّعَ لَهُ مِنْ كَذَا [*He was pained for him,* or *he lamented for him, on account of such a thing*]; *he pitied him for such a thing.* (Ṣ, Mṣb, Ḳ.) — تَوَجَّعَ لِلْمُصِيبَةِ [*He lamented for the affliction,* or *calamity*]. (Ḳ, art. فجع.) — تَوَجَّعَ إِلَيْهِ من كَذَا *He lamented, complained,* or *expressed pain,* or *grief, to him, on account of such a thing.*

وَجَعٌ *A disease,* or *malady,* (Ṣ, Mṣb, Ḳ, TA,) *of any kind,* (Mṣb,) *causing pain.* (TA.) — وَجَعُ المَفَاصِلِ *Pain of the joints;* i. e. *arthritis:* see نِقْرِسٌ.

جِعَةٌ *The* نبيذ, *or beverage, made from barley:* see مِزْرٌ.

الوَجْعَاءُ *The anus:* see a verse cited voce أَفْدَعُ.

وجن

وَجْنَةٌ The *ball,* or *elevated part, of the cheek.* (Ṣ, Mṣb, Ḳ.)

وجه

2. وَجَّهْتِ سِجَافَتَهُ and هَتَكْتِ سِدَافَتَهُ; i. e. أَخَذْتِ وَجْهَهَا, بِسِتْرَهِ: see arts. سجف and سدف, and جوه, conj. 2.

3. وَاجَهَهُ, inf. n. مُوَاجَهَةٌ, *He faced him; confronted him; encountered him; met him face to face* (Ṣ, Ḳ, Mṣb.) *He confronted him, accosted him,* or *encountered him, with speech,* or *words,* or *with his face.* (Lth, JK, TA.)

4. أَوْجَهَ *He repelled,* or *rejected,* an asker, or a beggar. (T.) — See جوه.

5. تَوَجَّهَ *He tended, repaired,* or *betook himself,* to, or towards, him, or it, *either in a direct course, or indirectly.* (IJ, in M and L, art. قصد.) — أَحْمَقُ مَا يَتَوَجَّهُ *A stupid man, who does not accomplish his affair well.* (JK.)

8. لَمْ يَتَّجِهْ لِشَيْءٍ (Ṣ, Ḳ, art. بور; and M, Ḳ, art. بلد; &c.) *He did not apply himself rightly to anything; he knew not the right course to pursue;* like لَمْ يَهْتَدِ. See also أَحْمَقُ مَا يَتَوَجَّهُ; and see بَائِرٌ and غُمِّيَ. — اِتَّجَهَ لَهُ رَأْيٌ *i. q.* سَنَحَ. (Ṣ, TA.) See سَنَحَ, in two places. — اِتَّجَهَ إِلَى الصِّحَّةِ *He became convalescent.*

وَجْهٌ — أَسْلَمْتُ وَجْهِي لِلّٰهِ *I resigned,* or *resign, myself to God:* i. e., *I became,* or *become, a*

Muslim: وجه is here used for the whole because it is the most noble part: (Jel, ii. 106:) or ذاتى *my course.* (TA.) — مِنْ كُلِّ وَجْهٍ *In every respect; considered from every point of view.* — الوَجْهُ أَنْ يَكُونَ كَذَا *The* [*proper* or *reasonable*] *way is that it should be thus:* or *the valid and obvious* [*way*]. (Mṣb.) See تُرْعَةٌ. — وَجْهٌ *A course, a purpose, or an object,* which one is pursuing; *a direction* in which one is going or looking, &c.; as also ▼ جِهَةٌ. — *The way of* a thing. (TA.) — لَيْسَ لِكَلَامِكَ وَجْهٌ *There is no truth,* or *correctness, in thy saying.* (TA.) — وَجْهٌ *Brightness* [of intellect]. (L, voce كَدَّ.) — لِوَجْهِ ٱللّٰهِ (Ḳur, lxxvi. 9) *For the sake of God;* or *to obtain the countenance* or *favour of God.* (Ḳull, p. 378.) See فِى ذَاتِ ٱللّٰهِ in art. ذو. — لَوْكَانَ كَذَا لَكَانَ وَجْهًا *Were it so, it were reasonable.* — لَا وَجْهَ لَهُ, said of a phrase, &c., *There is no reasonable way of accounting for it.* — لَيْسَ بِالوَجْهِ same as لَيْسَ بِوَجِيهٍ ? *Not of respectable, or esteemed, or high, authority:* (said of a word or phrase, &c.:) or *it is not the proper way.* — إِبْتِغَاءَ وَجْهِ ٱللّٰهِ *From a desire of God's recompense:* (Ḳur, ii. 274; and Expos. of the Jeláleyn:) or *countenance,* meaning *favour.* There are several similar phrases in the Ḳur, where وجه is explained in the same sense of ثَوَاب in the Expos. of the Jeláleyn. — حَبَسَهُ عَنْ وَجْهِهِ [*He withheld him, or restrained him, from his course, purpose, or object*]. (Ṣ, art. الت.) — صَرَفَ الشَّىْءَ عَنْ وَجْهِهِ *He turned the thing away, or back, from its course,* عَنْ سَنَنِهِ. (TA.) — خَرَجَ وَجْهُهُ (Ṣ, A, L, art. مرد; and L voce استعلج;) [for خَرَجَ نَبَاتُ وَجْهِهِ, *The hair of his face grew forth*]. — وَجْهُ الدَّهْرِ *The beginning of time,* (Ḳ,) and نَهَارٍ *of day.* (TA.) — رَوَاهُ عَلَى وَجْهِهِ, (Ṣ, Ḳ, art. قص,) and حَدَّثَ بِهِ عَلَى وَجْهِهِ: (Mṣb, art. قص:) see قَصَّ, in two places. — أَتَيْتُ الأَمْرَ مِنْ وَجْهِهِ, &c., and جِهَتِهِ: see مَأْتَى. — وَجْهٌ *The drift* of speech. (Ḳ, Kull, p. 378.) — مَضَى عَلَى وَجْهِهِ [*He went at random, heedlessly, headlong,* or *in a heedless,* or *headlong, course,* or *manner;* and so ذَهَبَ عَلَى وَجْهِهِ]: see رَكِبَ رَأْسَهُ in art. ركب. — ذَهَبَ عَلَى وَجْهِهِ حَيْثُ شَآءَ [*He went away at random whither he would*]. (TA in art. سوم.) — بَلَّتْ مَطِيَّتُهُ عَلَى أُطْلُبُوا — أَبَلَّتْ and وَجْهِهَا: see 1 in art. بل. — الحَوَائِجَ إِلَى حِسَانِ الوُجُوهِ *Make ye petition, for the things that ye want, to persons of good rank* or *station.* (El-Ḥasan El-Muäddib, in TA, art. نضر.) — وَجْهٌ † *Consideration and regard.* See 3 in art. اسو. — وَجْهٌ and ▼ جِهَةٌ *The place towards which one goes:* (Munjid of Kr:) or the *place, region, quarter, part,* or *point, towards which a person,* or *thing, goes, tends,* or *is directed:* so I have rendered ▼ جِهَةٌ: see صُقْعٌ, and ▼ جِهَةٌ: مُسْمُوخٌ signifies *any place towards which one looks* or *goes;* as also ▼ وِجْهَةٌ: (Har, p. 373:) the *place,* or *point, of the tendency* or *direction* or *bearing* of anything: whence ▼ جِهَةَ كَذَا *in the direction of such a thing:* and ▼ لِجِهَةٍ *towards one quarter.* — Hence, وَجْهُ الطَّرِيقِ *The point,* or *place, to which the way,* or *road, leads:* see ذُنَابَةٌ. And in like manner, وَجْهُ أَمْرٍ and ▼ جِهَتُهُ *The end,* or *result, of an affair, to which it leads,* or *tends.* — رَمَوْا وَجْهًا وَاحِدًا [*They shot in one direction*]. (M voce رشق.) — وَجْهُ الضُّحَى *The first,* or *beginning, of the* ضُحَى. (TA voce رَوْنَق, q. v.) — وَجْهٌ *A chief* of a people or party. (Ḳ.) — أَتَوْا مِنْ وَجْهِهِمْ: see فَوْز. — وَجْهٌ i. q. طَرِيقَةٌ [meaning The *mode,* or *manner,* of a thing]. (KL.) — مَا أَدْرِى مَا وَجْهُهُ *I know not what is its meaning.* — أَخَذَ وَجْهَهَا [app. *He degraded her; took away her grade:* and hence *he took her maidenhead:* see وَجَّهْتِ بِسَجَافَتِهِ].

مِنْ جِهَةِ كَذَا — جِهَةٌ: see وَجْهٌ throughout. *In respect of,* or *with reference to, such a thing:* and *by reason,* or *on account,* or *because, of such a thing.* — الجِهَاتُ السِّتُّ *The six relative points* or *directions* or *locations;* namely, above, below, before, behind, right, and left.

وِجْهَةٌ: see وَجْهٌ. — *A way, mode,* or *manner, of acting,* &c.

وَجِيهٌ *Worthy of regard.*

أَوْجَهُ *More, and most, worthy of regard.*

تَوْجِيهٌ: see وَلَثٌ. — التَّوْجِيهُ i. q. التَّوْرِيَةُ.

مُتَوَجَّهٌ *A place towards which one tends, repairs,* or *betakes himself.*

وجى

1. وَجِىَ and ▼ تَوَجَّى [said of a man, or of a horse or the like, or of a camel] *His foot,* or *hoof,* or فِرْسِن, *was,* or *became, attenuated, and chafed,* or *abraded:* (TA:) or *he* (a horse) *experienced a pain in his hoof.* (Ṣ.)

5: see 1.

وحج

مُوحَجٌ: transp. for مُوجَحٌ.

وحف

5. تَوَحَّفَ quasi-pass. of أَتْحَفَهُ: see تُحْفَةٌ.

8. إِتَّحَفَهُ: see art. تحف.

وُحْفَةٌ and وُحَفَةٌ, said to be the originals of تُحْفَةٌ and تُحَفَةٌ: see تُحْفَةٌ.

وحل

وَحْلٌ (Ṣ, Mṣb, Ḳ) and وَحَلٌ (Mṣb, Ḳ) *Slime, mire,* or *thin mud,* (Ṣ, Mṣb, Ḳ,) *in which beast of carriage stick.* (Ḳ.)

وحم

1. وَحِمَتْ *She was incompliant to the male:* see an ex. voce شَغَبَ.

وحن

جِنَةٌ: see إِحْنَةٌ.

وحى

4. أَوْحَى إِلَيْهِ *He* (God) *revealed to him;* or *spake,* or *made known, to him by revelation* — Also, *He suggested to him;* or *put into his mind.* (Mughnee voce أَنْ.)

وَحِىٌّ *Hasty;* (Ḳ;) *quick;* (Ṣ, Mgh, Mṣb, Ḳ; applied in this sense to death. (Ṣ, Mgh, Mṣb.)

الوَحَاءَ الوَحَاءَ [Make thou] *haste;* or *haste to be first,* or *before,* or *beforehand: haste;* &c. (Ṣ, TA.)

فِى أَوْحَى مُدَّةٍ *In the shortest period:* see an ex. in the first paragraph of art. ثقف.

وخف

1. وَخَفَهُ *He beat it* (namely خِطْمِىّ, IDrd, Ḳ, and in like manner سَوِيق, IDrd) *with his hand, and moistened it in a* طَسْت [or basin], (TA,) *until it became viscous,* or *cohesive,* (Ḳ, TA,) *and became* [*fit for*] *food;* (TA;) as also ▼ أَوْخَفَهُ (Ḳ) and ▼ وَخَّفَهُ. (TA.)

2: see 1.

4: see 1.

وخم

5: see 10.

10. إِسْتَوْخَمَهُ *He found it* (food) *to be unwholesome;* as also ▼ تَوَخَّمَهُ: (JK, Ḳ:) *he found it* (a land) *to be insalubrious:* (TA:) *he found it* (a country or town) *to disagree with*

its inhabitants. (Ṣ, Mṣb.) — مَا أَسْتَوْخِمُ أَنْ : see 5 in art. أَصْحَبَكَ — جدب.

وَخْمٌ *A heavy person* (Ḳ) [i.e., *dull*].

وَخَمٌ *A tainted condition of the air, engendering pestilential diseases.* (TA.)

وَخِيمٌ *Unwholesome* food: (Mgh:) *unsuitable food.* (Ḳ.)

وخى

3. وَاخَاهُ: see آخَاهُ.

5. تَوَخَّاهُ *He sought it, aimed at it,* or *purposed it:* (Ṣ, Mgh, Mṣb, Ḳ:) and *he sought it,* &c., *exclusively of,* or *in preference to, any other thing.* (Mgh.)

ودع

1. وَدُعَ, (Ṣ, Ḳ,) inf. n. وَدْعٌ and دَعَةٌ, (TA,) *He* (a man, Ṣ,) or *it,* (a thing, TA,) *became still, quiet,* or *at rest;* (Ṣ, Ḳ, TA;) as also ▼ اِتَّدَعَ, (Ḳ, TA,) [quasi-] inf. n. تُدْعَةٌ and تَوَدُّعٌ. (TA.) You say to a man, ▼ اِتَّدِعْ and ▼ تَوَدَّعْ meaning *Be thou grave, staid, steady, sedate,* or *calm.* (TA.) See also 1; and art. وذر. — وَدُعَ and وَدَعَ, inf. n. وَدَاعَةٌ, *He was,* or *became, in a state of ease, and ampleness of the means* or *circumstances of life.* (Mṣb.) — دَعْ: see an ex. voce آذَى: it may be rendered, in different cases, *Leave thou,* or *let alone,* or *say nothing of:* see بَلْهَ. — دَعْنِى مِنْ كَذَا *Let me alone and cease from such a thing:* and *exempt thou me,* or *excuse me, from such a thing.* — دَعْ عَنْكَ كَذَا *Dismiss thou from thee such a thing.* See عَنْكَ. — دَعْ مَا يَرِيبُكَ إِلَى مَا لَا يَرِيبُكَ: see art. سوى. — دَعْ مَا زَيْدٌ: see رِبِّى in art. ربب. — وَدَعَ used as a pret.: see an ex. voce زَائِلَةٌ, in art. زول.

2. وَدَّعَهُ, (MA,) inf. n. تَوْدِيعٌ, (PṢ,) *He bade farewell to him.* (MA, PṢ.)

3. وَادَعَهُ, inf. n. مُوَادَعَةٌ, and subst. وِدَاعٌ, *He made peace* or *reconciled himself, with him:* (Mṣb:) [the inf. n.] مُوَادَعَةٌ is *syn. with* مُصَالَحَةٌ because it is مُتَارَكَةٌ [*a mutual leaving,* or *leaving unmolested*]. (Mgh.) — مُوَادَعَةٌ is also syn. with تَرْكٌ; as also ▼ دَعَةٌ: (TA:) so that وَادَعَهُ signifies *He left him:* but more correctly, *he left him, being left by him;* like تَارَكَهُ, and خَالَاهُ; and this is the primary meaning.

5: see 1.

6. تَوَادَعَا *They two made peace,* or *became reconciled, each with the other.* (Ḳ.)

7: see 1.

8. اِتَّدَعَ: see 1: *he acted,* or *proceeded, with moderation, without haste* or *hurry,* in his pace or journeying. (M in art. اون.)

10. اِسْتَوْدَعَهُ مَالًا *He intrusted him with property; intrusted to him property; gave property to him in trust,* or *as a deposit.* (Mṣb.) And اِسْتَوْدَعَهُ وَدِيعَةً *He asked him to keep, preserve, guard,* or *take care of, a deposit.* (Ḳ.)

دَعَةٌ *Ease; repose; freedom from trouble or inconvenience, and toil or fatigue; tranquillity;* syn. خَفْضٌ (Ṣ, Mgh, Ḳ, TA) and رَاحَةٌ (Mgh, Mṣb, TA) and سُكُونٌ; (TA;) and *ampleness of circumstances* (سَعَةٌ) in life: (Ḳ:) or دَعَةٌ is syn. with راحة and سكون; but خَفْضٌ signifies "ampleness of the circumstances" (سَعَةٌ) of life, and "plentifulness and pleasantness" thereof: [see an ex. of both, voce خَفْضٌ]. (El-Marzookee and MF, art. خفض.) — See 1 and 3.

وَدَعَةٌ *A cowry; Cypræa:* see an ex. cited voce سَرٌّ.

وَدِيعَةٌ *A thing committed to the trust and care of a person; a trust; a deposit.* (Mgh, Mṣb.) See 10.

وَدَاعٌ [*Gravity, steadiness:*] i. q. سَكِينَةٌ, [like ▼ مَوْدُوعٌ,] as also وَقَارٌ. (Ṣ, L, in art. سكن.) — And *Valediction.* (Ṣ, Mṣb.)

مِيدَعٌ and مِيدَعَةٌ *A garment,* or *piece of cloth, used as a repository for clothes.* (TA.)

مَوْدُوعٌ: see وَدَاعٌ, and see a verse cited voce مَصْدَقٌ.

مُسْتَوْدَعٌ *A depository:* see a verse cited voce ظِلٌّ.

ودق

وَدْقٌ *Rain,* (Ṣ, Ḳ, TA,) whether *violent* or *gentle:* (TA:) or *violent rain.* (MF in art. قهب.)

وَدِيقٌ: see 10 in art. قرأ.

مُتَوَدِّقٌ: occurring in the TA, art. قهب; from الوَدْقُ, meaning *Violent rain.* (MF.)

ودك

وَدَكٌ *Grease,* or *gravy:* i. e. the *oily matter that is produced from flesh-meat;* (TA;) or the *dripping that exudes from flesh-meat* and *from fat.* (Mgh, Mṣb.)

ودن

مَوْدُونٌ: see مَطْلُولٌ.

ودى

1. وَدَى القَتِيلَ *He gave the bloodwit to the heir,* or *next of kin, of the slain person.* (Mṣb.)

3. وَادَاهُ inf. n. مُوَادَاةٌ, *He took* [*from him*] *the* دِيَة. (TA.) See 3 in art. عدو.

4. أَوْدَى بِهِ *It destroyed him;* (T;) *it removed him,* or *took him away:* (M, Ḳ:) said of death [&c.]. (T, M, Ḳ.) See an ex. in art. بلو, conj. 8, and another voce أَزْلَمُ. — أَوْدَى: see a verse cited voce قَلَبَةٌ. — أَوْدَى العَيْرُ إِلَّا ضَرِطًا: see ضَرِطَ.

دِيَةٌ *Bloodwit; a fine for bloodshed,* i. e., *homicide;* consisting of a hundred camels. — دِيَاتُ جِرَاحَاتٍ [*Fines for wounds*]. (Ṣ, M, TA, &c., in art. شنق.)

وَدِىٌّ *Small* فَسِيل, q. v.; (Ṣ, Mṣb, Ḳ;) *shoots,* or *offsets, cut off from palm-trees and planted:* (Mgh:) *young palm-trees.* (TA.)

وَادٍ [*A valley; a water-course,* or *torrent-bed:* and sometimes *a river;*] *a space intervening,* (M, Mṣb, Ḳ,) i. e. *any such space,* (M, Mṣb,) *between mountains or hills;* (M, Mṣb, Ḳ;) *through which a torrent runs forth* [*occasionally* or *constantly*]: (Mṣb:) for which reason it is thus called. (M, Mgh, TA.) — حَلَّ بِوَادِيهِ i. q. بَاعَ عَلَى بَيْعِهِ in one of the senses explained in art. بيع; i. e., ‡ *He superseded him,* &c.

تَوْدِيَةٌ; pl. تَوَادٍ, in the accus. case, by poetic licence, تَوَادِيًا: see a verse cited voce خِلْفٌ.

وذم

4. أَوْذَمَ حَجًّا: see an ex. voce دَسِرٌ.

وذم [app. وَذَمٌ] The *villosity* of a tripe. (TA, art. ترب.)

ورع

1. وَرِعَ *Piety:* or *pious fear:* syn. تَقْوَى: (Ḳ:) and *abstinence from unlawful things.* (TA.) — هُوَ وَرَعٌ ضَرَعٌ: see ضَرَعٌ.

ورف

1. وَرَفَ, and its inf. n. وَرِيفٌ: see رَفَّ, in two places.

ورق

وَرِقٌ *Silver,* whether coined or not: (AO,

TA:) or *coined dirhems*; (Ṣ, Ḳ;) *coined silver.* (Mgh.) See عَيْنٌ.

أَوْرَاق, pl. of وَرَقٌ, meaning أَحْدَاث: see قَعْبٌ.

وُرْقَةٌ *Ash-colour.* (Mṣb.) See سُمْرَةٌ.

وَرِقَةٌ and وَرِيقَةٌ: see وَارِقٌ.

شَجَرٌ وَارِقٌ *Trees having leaves:* (Mṣb:) [or *leafy trees; trees having many leaves;* for] شَجَرَةٌ وَارِقَةٌ (TA) and ▼ وَرِقَةٌ and ▼ وَرِيقَةٌ (Ṣ, Ḳ, TA) signify *a tree having many leaves.* (Ṣ, Ḳ, TA.) And شَجَرَةٌ وَارِقَةُ الظِّلَالِ [*A tree having leafy coverings* or *shades*]. (Ḳ in art. غيل.)

أَوْرَقُ, applied to a camel, *White inclining to black;* i. e. *of a dusky white hue:* or rather, simply, *duskish;* or *dusky;* (Ṣ, Ḳ;) or *of a colour like that of ashes.* (T, Mgh, Mṣb.) See أَحْمَرُ and خُطْبَانِىٌّ — أَوْرَقُ *Ashes.* (Ḳ.) See an ex. a verse cited voce عِنَّةٌ, last sentence.

ورك

وَرِكٌ *What is above the thigh;* [the *haunch;* or *hip;* and often signifying only the *hip-bone;* and the *hip* as meaning the *joint of the thigh?*] (Ṣ, Ḳ, &c.)

مُوَرِّكٌ of a camel's saddle: see 8 in art. عقل.

ورل

وَرَلٌ: see ضَبٌّ: there are two species: وَرَلُ البَحْرِ *the* ورل *of the river; the monitor of the Nile; lacerta Nilotica:* (see Forskål, Descr. Animalium, p. 13:) and وَرَلُ الأَرْضِ *the* ورل *of the land; the land monitor; lacerta scincus:* vulg. pronounced وَرَن.

ورم

1. وَرِمَ أَنْفُهُ ‡ *He became enraged:* see أَنْفٌ.

4. أَوْرَمَهُ meaning أَرْغَمَهُ *He angered him:* see شَرَاهُ.

وَرَمٌ, a coll. gen. n., *Swellings, or tumours:* n. un. with ة. The n. un. occurs in the TA, art. جعر, &c.

وره

وَرْهَاءُ الرَّخَمِ: see رَخَمٌ.

ورى

1. وَرَى, aor. يَرِى, inf. n. وَرْىٌ [and وُرِىٌّ and رِيَةٌ, Ḳ]; and وَرِىَ, aor. يَرِى; and ▼ أَوْرَى; *It* (a زند) *produced its fire.* (Mṣb.) — وَرِيَتْ بِكَ زِنَادِى, or وَرَتْ: see art. زند, and see وَقَدَ and خَيَّابٌ: see قَدْحٌ لَا يُورِى — . راى and زَهَرَ.

2. وَرَّى بِشَىْءٍ عَنْ شَىْءٍ [*He pretended, or made believe, a thing, instead of a thing* which he meant: as is shown by the explanation of a trad. in the TA]. (Ṣ, art. عرض; save that the inf. n. is there mentioned instead of the pret.) — وَرَّى عَنْ كَذَا, inf. n. تَوْرِيَةٌ, *He alluded to such a thing equivocally, or ambiguously; equivocated respecting it: he meant such a thing and pretended another.* (M, Ḳ.) التورية is also called الإِيهَامُ and التَّوْجِيهُ and التَّخْيِيلُ: (Kull, p. 113:) and signifies The *using a word, an expression, or a phrase, which has an obvious meaning, and intending thereby another meaning, to which it applies, but which is contrary to the obvious one.* (Mṣb.) See مِعْرَاضٌ. — See 4.

3. وَارَاهُ *He hid it, concealed it, or covered it.* (Ṣ, Mṣb, Ḳ, &c.)

4. أَوْرَى and ▼ وَرَّى and ▼ اِسْتَوْرَى *He made* his زند *to produce fire.* (Ṣ, Ḳ.) — See 1.

10: see 4.

وَرْىٌ *Purulent matter in the interior of the body:* or [*an abscess;* or] *a severe ulcer that discharges purulent matter and blood.* (M, Ḳ, TA.) وَرْيًا وَقُحَابًا: see قُحَابٌ.

رِيَةٌ: see رِئَةٌ, in art. رأى.

وَرَائِى كَذَا *Behind me is such a thing,* as though it were a burden upon my back. — مِنْ وَرَاءِ وَرَاءِ *From behind a thing covering,* or *concealing.* (TA.) — فُلَانٌ مِنْ وَرَاءِ فُلَانٍ *Such a one is an aider of such a one:* or *a follower.* (Ḥam, p. 206.) — اَللّٰهُ مِنْ وَرَائِكَ *God is seeking after thee,* and *watching,* or *lying in wait, for thee.* (Ḥam, p. 206.) See also an ex. in the first paragraph of art. قتل.

التَّوْرَاةُ *The Book of the Law revealed to Moses.* (Bḍ, iii. 2; &c.)

وزع

الوَزَعَةُ i. q. أَعْوَانُ الرَّجُلِ. (TA in art. امل.)

وَازِعٌ: see فَارِغٌ.

وزغ

4. أَوْزَغَتِ الطَّعْنَةُ بِالدَّمِ: see أَزْغَلَتْ.

وَزَغَةٌ *A certain reptile* (دُوَيْبَّةٌ); (Ṣ;) i. q. بُرْصٌ [*a lizard of the species called gecko, of a leprous hue,* as its name برص indicates]; (TA, art. برص;) and i. q. سَامٌّ أَبْرَصَ: (JK, M, Ḳ:) or سامّ ابرص is a name of *the large* وَزَغ; (A and Mṣb, both in art. برص;) or is *of the large* وَزَغ. (Ṣ and Ḳ, both in art. برص.)

وزن

1. وَزَنَ *It* (a thing) *was heavy:* (Mṣb:) or *outweighed,* or *preponderated;* syn. رَجَحَ. (TA.)

3. هٰذَا يُوَازِنُ هٰذَا *This is equiponderant to this.* (Ṣ.)

8. اِتَّزَنَهُ *He took it,* or *received it, by weight.* (Ṣ,* Mgh, Mṣb, Ḳ.*) See an ex. voce سَنْجَةٌ.

الوَزْنُ *A certain star in the left fore leg of Centaurus.* (Kzw.) See حَضَارِ.

زِنِىٌّ, rel. n. of زِنَةٌ. (Ṣ, art. وعد, q. v., voce عِدَةٌ.)

وَازِنٌ: see رَاجِحٌ: *heavy:* (Mṣb:) or *of full weight:* (KL:) pl. وُزَّنٌ: see زَالٌّ. You say, دِرْهَمٌ وَازِنٌ (Ṣ) *A full, or complete, dirhem:* (so in a copy of the Ṣ:) [*a dirhem of full weight:*] *a heavy dirhem.* (PṢ.)

وَزَّانٌ *A weigher.* (TA, in art. قسط.)

مِيزَانٌ *A weighing-instrument;* (TA;) *a balance; a pair of scales.* — The *weight* of a thing. (Ḳ, &c.) See مِثْقَالٌ.

وزى

3. وَازَاهُ, inf. n. مُوَازَاةٌ: see آزَاهُ. See also 3 in art. قرأ.

السَّجْعُ المُتَوَازِى *A variety of rhyming prose:* see سَجْعٌ.

وسط

وَسُوطٌ *A middle-sized tent of goats' hair:* see مِظَلَّةٌ.

وسع

1. وَسِعَ الإِنَاءُ المَتَاعَ [*The vessel was sufficient in its capacity* or *dimensions,* or *sufficiently capacious,* or *large, for the goods*]; and المَكَانُ القَوْمَ [*the place for the company of men*]. (Mṣb.) لَا يَسَعُكَ ان تَفْعَلَ كَذَا *It is not in thy power,* or *proper for thee,* (MA,) or *allowable for thee,* (Mgh, Mṣb,) *to do such a thing.* (MA, Mgh, Mṣb.) — وَسَعَ عَلَيْهِ رِزْقَهُ, aor. يَوْسَعُ; and ▼ أَوْسَعَهُ, and ▼ وَسَّعَهُ; *He* (God) *made his means of subsistence ample and abundant.* (Mṣb.)

2. وَسَّعَ *He made wide, broad, spacious, roomy,* or *ample.* — وَسَّعَ لَهُ فِى المَجْلِسِ *He made room,* or *ample space, for him in the sitting-place.* (Ṣ, art. فسح.) — [And so] تَوَسَّعُوا ↑ فِى المَجْلِسِ *They made room,* or *ample space,* [*one for another,*] *in the sitting-place.* (Ṣ, art. فسح.) — وَسَّعَ عَلَيْهِ, for وَسَّعَ عَلَيْهِ رِزْقَهُ, *He* (God) *amplified, enlarged,* or *made ample* or *plentiful, his means of subsistence;* contr. of ضَيَّقَ. — See 1, and 4.

4. أَوْسَعَهُ الشَّىْءَ [*He made,* or *rendered, the thing ample,* or *free from straitness, to him;*] *he made the thing sufficient for him;* syn. جَعَلَهُ يَسَعُهُ: (TA:) [*he gave him sufficiently of the thing; or largely thereof.*] — اللّٰهُمَّ أَوْسِعْنَا رَحْمَتَكَ *O God, make thy mercy sufficient for us;* syn. اِجْعَلْهَا تَسَعُنَا. (TA.) — أَوْسَعَهُ أَمْرَهُ [*He made,* or *rendered, his state,* or *case,* or *affair, ample,* or *free from straitness, to him*]. (Ṣ, art. فرش.) See فَرَشَهُ. — أَوْسَعُوا لِلرَّجُلِ *They made room,* or *ample space, for the man,* in a place of standing or of sitting. (Mṣb, voce فَرَجَ.) — أَوْسَعَ عَلَيْهِ, (Ṣ, Ḳ,) and ↑ وَسَّعَ, (Ḳ,) *He* (God) *enriched him;* or *rendered him free from want.* (Ṣ, Ḳ.) — See 1.

5. تَوَسَّعَ [*He became,* or *made himself, ample,* or *abundant, in his circumstances;* or *in his means of subsistence;* for توسّع فِى عَيْشِهِ;] i. q. تَرَفَّغَ. (Ṣ, in art. رفغ.) — تَوَسَّعَ *He took a wide, an ample,* or *a large, range,* فِى أَمْرٍ, in an affair. — تَوَسَّعَ فِى السَّخَآءِ † [*He took a wide,* or *an ample range,* or *was profuse, in bounty,* or *munificence*]. (Ṣ, Ḳ, in art. خرق.) — *It expanded itself, spread out, dilated, widened.* — *He expatiated.* One says, توسّع فِى الدَّارِ, and لَهُ سَاحَةٌ يتوسّع فِيهَا. (TA, voce تركّح.) — *He strode,* in walking. — تَوَسَّعُوا فِيهِ حَتَّى أَطْلَقُوهُ عَلَى كَذَا *They extended its* (a word's) *signification,* or *amplified in respect of it,* or rather, *took an extended range in using it, so that they applied it to such a thing.* (The lexicons, &c., passim.) — تَوَسَّعَ: see تَبَقَّرَ.

8. اِتَّسَعَ *It* (a man's state, or condition, &c.) *became free from straitness,* or *unstraitened.* — اِتَّسَعَ عَيْشُهُ [*His means,* or *circumstances, of life became ample,* or *plentiful*]. (Mṣb, art. نعم.) — اِتَّسَعَ *It widened, became wide, dilated,* or *expanded.* — اِتَّسَعَ بَطْنُهُ *His belly became wide,* or *distended.* — اِتَّسَعَ لِأَمْرٍ *He was capable of doing a thing.* An instance occurs in the TA, voce أَوْهَبَ. — اِتِّسَاعُ البِئْرِ i. q. جِرَابُهَا [*The interior of the well*]. (Ḳ, art. جرب.) See also 5, in art. عقد. — اِتَّسَعَ الخَرْقُ عَلَى الرَّاقِعِ *The hole was wide to the pitcher:* see خرق. — اِتِّسَاعٌ *Extension of the signification* of a word or phrase: *an amplification.* (The lexicons, &c., passim.)

سَعَةٌ *Width; breadth; extent,* or *space, from side to side.* See سَدِيلٌ. — سَعَةُ العَيْشِ *Ampleness of the means,* or *circumstances, of life; an unstraitened,* or *a plentiful, state of life.* — سَعَةٌ [*Ample scope for action, &c.:* and *a state in which is ample scope for action, &c.:* see نَفَسٌ, and مِعْرَاضٌ:] *richness,* or *wealthiness,* or *competence:* and *capacity,* or *power,* or *ability:* (Ṣ, Ḳ:) and *plentifulness* and [consequently] *easiness* of life. (TA.) — سَعَةُ الصَّدْرِ i. q. سَعَةُ الخُلُقِ. (Ḥar, p. 194.) — لَكَ عَنْهُ سَعَةٌ: see رُدْحَةٌ. — يَجُوزُ فِى السَّعَةِ *It is allowable absolutely, in other cases than those of poetical necessity.* (IbrD.)

وَسَاعٌ A horse *wide in step:* (Ṣ, Ḳ:) or i. q. جَوَادٌ. (Ḳ.)

وَسِيعٌ, pl. وِسَاعٌ: see أَرِيضٌ in art. أرض.

عَيْشٌ وَاسِعٌ *A life ample in its means* or *circumstances; unstraitened,* or *plentiful.* — وَاسِعٌ *Having power,* or *ability:* (Bḍ, iv. 129:) or rather, *having ample power or ability; powerful.* See Ḥam, p. 609. — نَفْسٌ وَاسِعٌ: see رَابِطٌ. — خُلُقٌ وَاسِعٌ † *A large,* or *liberal, disposition:* see بَارِحٌ. — وَاسِعُ الخُلُقِ ‡ *Large,* or *liberal, in disposition.* — وَاسِعُ الصَّدْرِ: see مُجَمَّرٌ. — وَاسِعُ الجَرْىِ (Ṣ voce سَهْبٌ, applied to a horse,) *Wide-stepping* [*in running*]. (So expl. in the PṢ.)

أَوْسَعُ *Wider,* or *widest:* see 3 in art. خلط.

مُوَسَّعٌ عَلَيْهِ *Amply,* or *abundantly, provided with the means of subsistence.*

مُتَّسَعٌ *Width; extent; ampleness of space,* and *of quantity:* properly *a place of width,* or *spaciousness.* See نُفْسَةٌ and مُنْبَسَطٌ.

وسق

وَسْقٌ *A camel's load:* see وِقْرٌ.

وَسِيقَةٌ *A mob of driven cattle:* see سَيِّقَةٌ and مِعْتَاقٌ.

وسل

1: } see 5.
2: }

5. تَوَسَّلَ بِالدَّلْوِ إِلَى المَآءِ [*He sought to get at,* or *obtain, the water by means of the bucket*]. (M in art. دلو.) — تَوَسَّلَ إِلَيْهِ بِكَذَا *He sought to bring himself near to him, or to approach to him, to gain access to him, or to advance himself in his favour, by such a thing:* (Mṣb, &c.:) so too ↑ وَسَّلَ; (Ṣ, Ḳ;) and ↑ وَسَلَ, aor. يَسِلُ. (Mṣb.)

وَسِيلَةٌ *A means of access to a thing;* (IAth;) *a means of becoming near to a thing:* (IAth, Mṣb:) these are the primary significations: (IAth:) *a means of becoming near to,* or *intimate with,* or *of ingratiating oneself with, another:* (Ṣ:) *honourable rank* or *station with a king: degree: affinity:* (Ḳ:) *a tie,* or *connexion:* (TA:) it may be rendered *a means of access, nearness, intimacy, ingratiating oneself, attachment,* or *connexion:* and also, *of attainment,* or *accomplishment.*

وسم

1. وَسَمَ الثَّوْبَ [*He marked,* or *put a mark on, the garment, &c.*]; said of a trader, or dealer. (JK in art. رقم.) — وَسَمَهُ بِالهِجَآءِ [*He branded him,* or *stigmatized him, with satire*]. (TA.) See a hemistich cited voce شَكِىٌّ. — وَسَمَهُ *He marked it* [in any manner]. (Mṣb.) — وَسَمَهُ بِالقَوْلِ ‡ *He stigmatized him,* or *set a mark upon him whereby he should be known, by something said.* (TA in art. علط.) — وَسَمْتُ الكِتَابَ [*I put a superscription,* or *title, to the book,* or *writing.*] (TA in art. عنو.) — وَسُمَ, inf. n. وَسَامَةٌ (Ṣ, Mṣb, Ḳ) and وَسَامٌ, (Ṣ, Ḳ,) *He* (a man, Ṣ) *was beautiful in face:* (Ṣ, Mṣb:) or *bore the impress,* or *stamp, of beauty.* (Ḳ.)

5. تَوَسَّمْتُ فِيهِ الخَيْرَ i. q. تَفَرَّسْتُهُ; (Ṣ;) [*I discovered,* or *perceived, in him good,* or *goodness, by right opinion formed from its outward signs;*] originally, *I knew its real existence in him by its outward sign.* (MF.) See also Ḥar, pp. 30, 46, 76. — تَوَسَّمَ *He examined deliberately in order to know the real state or character of a thing by the external sign thereof.* (Bḍ, xv. 75.) — *He perceived* a thing *by forming a correct opinion from its outward signs.* (TḲ.)

سِمَةٌ *A brand,* or *mark* or *figure made with a hot iron, upon an animal.* (Ḳ.) And i. q. عَلَامَةٌ [*A mark, sign, badge, token, symptom, &c.*]. (Mṣb.) And The عُنْوَان [or *title*] of a book or writing. (TA in art. علو.) See also سِيمَةٌ and سِيمَى in art. سوم.

وَسْمَةٌ [now applied to *Woad*]: i. q. عِظْلِمٌ, *with which one tinges* or *dyes* [*the hands, &c.*]: (Ṣ:) *a certain plant, with the leaves of which one tinges* or *dyes* [*the hands, &c.*]; and said to be the عِظْلِم: (Mṣb:) the *leaves of the* نيل [or *indigo-plant*]: or *a plant* [*of another species* (TA)] *with the leaves of which one tinges* or *dyes* [*the hands, &c.*] (Ḳ.)

الوَسْمِىُّ: on the rain thus called, see نَوْءٌ.

مَوْسِمٌ [*A periodical festival: a fair:*] i. q. عِيدٌ. (Mṣb, art. عود.) — مَوْسِمُ الحَاجِّ *The fair, and place of meeting, of the pilgrims.* (Mgh.)

مِيسَمٌ *A brand*, or *mark made with a hot iron.* (TA, voce جِدَادٌ.) — [Originally] *A branding*, or *cauterizing, instrument* [or *iron*]; (Ṣ, Ḳ;) *a marking instrument.* (Mṣb.) — *An impress*, or *a character, of beauty.* (Ṣ, Ḳ.) See an ex. in a verse cited voce أَثَرٌ.

وسى

3. وَاسَى: see آسَيْتُهُ, throughout.

4. أَوْسَى, originally أَسْوَى: see إِسْتَوَى.

6. تَوَاسَوْا: see its syn. تَآسَوْا.

وشظ

وَشِيظٌ [thus without ة]: see صَمِيمٌ.

وشع

وَشِيعَةٌ *A ball of spun thread.* (AA, TA in art. سحل.)

وشق

8. إِتَّشَقَ: see تَجَبْجَبَ.

وَشِيقَةٌ: see جُبْجُبَةٌ.

وشك

3. يُوشِكُ أَنْ يَكُونَ *It will soon be:* (Ṣ, Mṣb, Ḳ, TA:) or *it is near to being.* (Mṣb, TA.)

وَشْكَانُ an anomalous inf. n., or perhaps a simple subst.: see 1 in art. شنأ.

وَشِيكًا *Quickly*, or *speedily.* (IB, TA.) See an ex. in a verse cited voce تَارَةٌ.

وشل

وَشَلٌ: applied to water: see an ex. voce سَجْعٌ; and another in a verse cited voce وَقْلٌ; and another voce رَاشِحٌ.

وَشُولٌ A she-camel *whose milk lasts throughout the year.* (IAạr., in TA, art. شكر.)

وشم

4. أَوْشَمَ فِيهِ, said of hoariness, *It became abundant*, or *spread:* see 5 in art. سنم.

8. إِتَّشَمَتْ بِالنَّؤُورِ [*She tattooed herself with smoke-black*]. (T, art. نور.)

وَشْمٌ *Tattoo:* see أُسَفٌ and قُرْحٌ.

وَاشِمَةٌ *A female tattooer.* See رَجَعَ, latter part of the paragraph.

مُوَشَّمٌ [*Tattooed*]: see a verse cited voce طَفْلٌ.

وشى

1. وَشَى, inf. n. وَشْىٌ, *He variegated*, or *figured*, a piece of cloth, or a garment; (Mgh, Mṣb,* Ḳ;) and *embellished it.* (Ḳ.) — وَشَى بِهِ إِلَى السُّلْطَانِ, (Ṣ, Ḳ,) or عِنْدَ السُّلْطَانِ, (Mṣb,) *He calumniated*, or *misrepresented, him to the Sultán.* (Ṣ, Mṣb, Ḳ.)

شِيَةٌ *Any colour differing from the main colour of a horse, &c.; a colour differing from the rest*, (Ṣ,) or *from that which generally pervades a thing.* — لَا شِيَةَ فِيهِ *It is of one generally pervading colour, in which is no other colour.* — شِيَةٌ [also] *A mark, sign, symptom*, or *token, by which a thing is known;* syn. عَلَامَةٌ; (Mṣb;) and مَخِيلَةٌ, which see.

وَشْىٌ, originally an inf. n., *A kind of variegated, or figured, cloth, or garment.* (Mgh, Mṣb.*) — وَشْىٌ The *variegation, figured work, or figuring*, of a garment; *making* it *party-coloured.* — وَشْىٌ sometimes signifies *A natural diversity of colours:* see رُمْلَةٌ. — وَشْىٌ of a sword: see فِرِنْدٌ.

شِيَوِىٌّ: see what next follows.

وَشَوِىٌّ rel. n. of شِيَةٌ, the rad. و being restored; (Ṣ in the present art.;) and so ▼ شِيَوِىٌّ, like عِدَوِىٌّ [of عِدَةٌ]. (Ṣ in art. وعد.)

قَوْلٌ مُوَشًّى بِهِ [*A saying misrepresented*]. (TA in art. قت, in an explanation of قَوْلٌ مَقْتُوتٌ.) — مُوَشًّى is used by Aboo-Dhu-eyb to signify *A musical reed-pipe.* (TA, art. نوب.)

وصف

1. وَصُفَ *He attained to the proper age for service.* (Ḳ.) See an ex. in the Ḳ, voce مُغْلَدُونَ.

4. أَوْصَفَ and ▼ إِسْتَوْصَفَ *He* (a boy) *became of full stature, and fit for service.* (Mgh.)

8. إِتَّصَفَ بِالعِلْمِ [*He was*, or *became, characterized*, or *he characterized himself, by knowledge*, or *science*]. (Mṣb in art. أهل.)

10: see 4.

صِفَةٌ *A quality; an attribute; a property;* or *a description*, as meaning the *aggregate of the qualities or attributes or properties* of a thing; or the *state, condition*, or *case*, of a thing. So explained voce صِنْفٌ, and voce صُورَةٌ. See its syn. حَالٌ. — صِفَةٌ in grammar, *The same as* نَعْتٌ, *An epithet.* (Ḳ.) — *A word denoting an attribute* (مَعْنًى) *and a substance* (ذَات). Under this term are comprised the اسم فاعل, the اسم مفعول, the صفة مشبّهة, and the افعل التفضيل. (I'Aḳ, sect. الصفة المشبّهة باسم الفاعل.) — صِفَةٌ مُشَبَّهَةٌ [*A simple epithet*]; *an epithet resembling an* اسم فاعل. — صِفَةٌ غَالِبَةٌ *An epithet in which the substantive character predominates.* — صِفَةٌ, as a general term for an attributive word, is also applied by Lth and other old writers to *An adverbial n. of place or time*, and to *a preposition.* It is so applied in the L and TA, art. عنل, &c. It was applied to the former by Fr, (T, voce ظَرْفٌ,) and to the latter also. (L, TA, ubi supra.)

بَيْعُ المُوَاصَفَةِ: see 3 in art. روض.

وصل

1. وَصَلَهُ, and وَصَلَ إِلَيْهِ, *He, or it, arrived at, came to, reached, attained, him, or it;* (Ṣ, Ḳ, &c.;) as also ▼ تَوَصَّلَ إِلَيْهِ. (M.) — وَصَلَ رَحِمَهُ *He made close his ties of relationship by behaving with goodness and affection, &c., to kindred:* see صِلَةُ الرَّحِمِ. — وَصَلَهُ and ▼ وَاصَلَهُ *He had, or held, close, or loving, communion, commerce, or intercourse, with him.* (Mṣb, Ḳ.) — وَصَلَهُ, inf. n. وَصْلٌ and صِلَةٌ; and ▼ وَاصَلَهُ, inf. n. مُوَاصَلَةٌ and وِصَالٌ; are said with relation to love, whether chaste or unchaste. (M, Ḳ.) — And وَصَلَ حَبْلَهُ, inf. n. وَصْلٌ and صِلَةٌ; and ▼ وَاصَلَ حَبْلَهُ: [*He made close his bond of love, by affectionate conduct*]. (M.) — وَصَلَهُ *He gave him property.* (TA.) And وَصَلَهُ بِجَائِزَةٍ [*He gave him a gift*]. (Ḳ in art. جوز.) — وَصَلَ *He connected*, or *conjoined*, a word *with a following word, not pausing after the former; he made no interruption.*

2. وَصَّلَهُ, inf. n. تَوْصِيلٌ, *He joined*, or *connected, much: he made* a string *to have many joinings.* (TA: the latter from an explanation of the pass. part. n.) — وَصَّلَهُ إِلَيْهِ *He made it to reach it*, or *him:* syn. أَنْهَاهُ إِلَيْهِ, and أَبْلَغَهُ

إِيَّاهُ; like إِلَيْهِ ↑ أَوْصَلَهُ [q. v.]. (TA.) See an ex. voce غَفَلَ.

3. See 1. — وَاصَلَ الصِّيَامَ, inf. n. مُوَاصَلَةٌ and وِصَالٌ, *He continued the fasting uninterruptedly.* (TA.) — وَاصَلَ: see وَاتَرَ. — وَاصَلَ المَرْأَةَ *He held communion, or commerce, of love with the woman.* — وَاصَلَا *Contr. of* قَاطَعَا. (Ḳ in art. قطع.)

4. أَوْصَلَهُ *He made,* or *caused, him,* or *it, to reach; he caused to come, brought, conveyed,* or *delivered, him,* or *it;* (Ṣ,* M, Ḳ,*;) إِلَيْهِ *to him,* or *it;* as also ↑ وَصَّلَهُ. (M.) See أَدَّاهُ.

5. تَوَصَّلَ إِلَيْهِ *He applied himself with gentleness, or courtesy, to obtain access, or nearness, to him.* (Ṣ.) See 1.

8. اِتَّصَلَ بِهِ *It communicated with it.* (Modern usage.)

وَصْلٌ *Union* [of companions or friends or lovers]; *contr. of* فِرَاقٌ (T, Ṣ, voce بَيْنٌ) or *of* فُرْقَةٌ (Mṣb, ibid.) or *of* فَصْلٌ (Bd in vi. 94) or *of* هِجْرَانٌ. (Ṣ.) — فِى الوَصْلِ وَالوَقْفِ *In the case of connexion with a following word and in the case of a pause.*

وِصْلٌ and ↑ وُصْلٌ *A limb:* see فَخِذٌ and فَعْمٌ; and see also Ḥar, p. 346. Between every فَصْلَانِ [or rather between every فَصْل and the فَصْل next to it] is a وِصْل. (O, Ḳ, in art. فصل.)

وُصْلٌ: see وِصْلٌ.

صِلَةُ الرَّحِمِ ‡ *The* [*making close one's ties of relationship by*] *behaving with kindness,* or *goodness and affection and gentleness, and considerateness,* or *regard for their circumstances, to kindred,* or *relations, even though remote,* or *evil-doers:* and قَطْعُ الرَّحِمِ signifies the contr. (IAth, TA.) — صِلَةٌ *A gift for which no compensation is to be made; a free gift; a gratuity;* like هِبَةٌ and صَدَقَةٌ. (Marg. note in a copy of the KT.) — صِلَةٌ The *connexion* of a verb *with the objective complement,* whether immediate or by means of a preposition. — صِلَةٌ The *complement of a* مَوْصُول [or *conjunct*], (I have thus rendered it voce أَلْ,) whether the latter be a particle or a noun. (I'Aḳ, sect. المَوْصُول.) — [The term صِلَةٌ is also applied in the Mṣb, art. أذن, to لَهُ in the phrase مَأْذُونٌ لَهُ.] Often applied to the connective prep. by which a verb or act. part. n. is transitive, together with the noun or pronoun governed by it; as to لَهُ in أَذِنَ لَهُ: and that prep. alone is called حَرْفُ الصِّلَةِ. Also, to a prep. by which a pass. verb or part. n. is connected with its subject, together with that subject; as لَهُ in أُذِنَ لَهُ. In this case it is an inf. n. in the sense of a pass. part. n., namely, of مَوْصُول. (IbrD.) — [صِلَةٌ *A connective* word or phrase: as يَكَدْ is said to be in the phrase لَمْ يَكَدْ يَرَاهَا: see art. كود. In this case it is an inf. n. used in the sense of an act. part. n.] It is used in this sense especially with reference to cases in the Ḳur-án. (MF, art. كود.)

وُصْلَةٌ: see عُلْقَةٌ: *A means of connexion,* or *attachment:* see ذَرِيعَةٌ.

مَوْصِلٌ *A joint, or place of juncture.*

مَوْصُولٌ, in grammar, [*A conjunct*]. This is of two kinds; مَوْصُولٌ حَرْفِىٌّ and مَوْصُولٌ إِسْمِىٌّ. The former term [or *conjunct particle*] is applied to the infinitive particles أَنْ, أَنَّ, كَىْ, لَوْ, and مَا. The latter term [or *conjunct noun*] (I have thus rendered it voce أَلْ, and voce إِنْ, and voce إِنَّ) is applied to the conjunctive nouns الَّذِى, and its fem. الَّتِى, and مَنْ, and مَا, and ذُو in the dial. of Ṭeiyi, and to أَلْ, which last some incorrectly hold to be a conjunct particle, and others assert to be a determinative particle and not a conjunct, and to ذَا after the interrogative مَا or مَنْ. (I'Aḳ, sect. المَوْصُول.)

اِسْتِثْنَآءٌ مُتَّصِلٌ *An exception in which the thing excepted is united in kind to that from which the exception is made; contr. of* مُنْقَطِعٌ.

وصى

2. وَصَّاهُ and ↑ أَوْصَاهُ *He enjoined him; charged him; bade him; ordered him:* (Ḳ, &c.:) *he commanded him,* بِكَذَا, *to do such a thing.* (Mṣb.)

4. أَوْصَى لَهُ بِالثُّلُثِ *He bequeathed to him the third* of the property. (MA.) — أَوْصَى *He made his will.* — See 2.

6. تَوَاصَوْا *They enjoined, charged, bade, ordered,* or *commanded, one another.* See an ex. voce تَبَاعَثُوا.

وَصِىٌّ *A person commissioned; a commissioned agent:* (Ḳ:) *an executor appointed by a will.*

وَصِيَّةٌ *An injunction, a charge, bidding, order,* or *command:* (Ḳ:) *an admonition, with an endeavour to persuade:* and *a command:* its place may be supplied by any word in which is the meaning of أَمْرٌ. (Mṣb.) — And *A will,* or *testament.* (Ḳ,* TA.)

وضع

1. وَضَعَهُ *He put it,* or *laid it,* (KL,* PṢ,) in, or on, a place: (PṢ:) *he put it,* or *threw it, down* from his hand: (TA:) *contr. of* رَفَعَهُ: (Mgh:) syn. حَطَّهُ: (Ḳ,* TA, in art. حط:) but it has a more general sense than this last. (Er-Rághib, Kull.) — وَضَعَ *He put down* a thing: contr. of رَفَعَ. (Ḳ, voce نَصَبَ.) — وَضَعَتْ *She brought forth.* — وَضَعَ لَهُ *He appointed to him,* or *for him,* a sign, or token, &c.: see Mṣb in art. علم. — وَضَعَ عَلَيْهِ *He imposed upon him* a fine, or tax, &c. — وَضَعَ *He remitted* a tax or the like; *did not exact* it. (Mgh, Mṣb, in art. جوح.) — وَضَعُوا الحَرْبَ ‡ [*They gave over,* or *relinquished, war;*] *they made peace;* opposed to رَفَعُوهَا. (Ḥam, pp. 179 and 180.) — وَضَعَ مِنْهُ, (Ṣ,) or عَنْهُ, (Ḳ,) *He lowered his grade, rank, condition,* (Ṣ, Ḳ,) or *estimation.* (Ḳ.) — وُضِعَ فِى تِجَارَتِهِ *He lost,* or *suffered loss or diminution, in his traffic;* (Ṣ, Mgh, Mṣb, Ḳ;) *did not gain in it;* (Mgh;) as also ↑ أُوضِعَ. (Mgh.) — وَضَعَ *He forged* (a word:) *he forged* (poetry, على in the name of). (Mz, 8th نوع.) — وَضَعَ لَفْظًا لِشَىْءٍ *He applied* or *assigned* or *appropriated a word,* or *phrase, to denote,* or *signify, a thing.* (Kull, 371, &c.) See also إِزَآءٌ. — وَضَعْتُ عَلَيْهِ الشَّىْءَ app. signifies *I made the thing according to his,* or *its, measure.* See قَدَرْتُ.

2. فِى فُلَانٍ تَوْضِيعٌ: see طُرْقَةٌ.

4. See 1. — مِنْ أَيْنَ أَوْضَعَ الرَّاكِبُ i. q. مِن اين أَوْضَحَ. (T, in L, art. وضح.)

6. تَوَاضَعَ *He was,* or *became, lowly, humble, submissive,* or *in a state of abasement:* (Mṣb:) or *he lowered, humbled,* or *abased, himself.* (Ṣ, Ḳ.) — تَوَاضَعَا الرُّهُونَ *They two laid bets, wagers,* or *stakes, each with the other;* syn. تَرَاهَنَا. (TA, art. رهن.) — تَوَاضَعَتِ الأَرْضُ ‡ *The land was lower than that which was next to it.* (TA.)

8. اِتَّضَعَتْ أَرْكَانُهُ: see R. Q. 2 in art. ضع.

وَضْعٌ, as one of the ten predicaments, or categories, *Collocation,* or *posture.* — Also The *constitution* of a thing; its *conformation;* its *make.* And i. q. فَنٌّ, meaning *A mode,* or *manner,* &c.

ضَعَةٌ perhaps an inf. n. of وَضَعَتْ, meaning "she brought forth:" see 1, third sentence, in art. قرأ.

وَضِيعٌ *Low, ignoble, vile,* or *mean; of no rank,* or *estimation.* (Mṣb.)

هُوَ مَوْضِعُ سِرِّى *He is the depository of my secret,* or *secrets.* — مَوْضِعُهُ الرَّفْعُ *Same as* مَحَلُّهُ الرفع. — مَوْضِعٌ The *proper application,* or *meaning*, of a word. (Bḍ, iv. 48 and v. 45.) See 1 in art. حرف. And The *case in which a word is to be used*: see Ṣ, art. on the particle ف. — And The *proper place* of a thing. — *Ground*; as when one says, "a ground for, or of, belief, trust, accusation," &c. And The *proper object* of an action, &c.: as in the phrase فُلَانٌ مَوْضِعٌ لِلْإِكْرَامِ *Such a one is a proper object of honouring.*

مَوْضُوعٌ *A certain pace of a beast*; *contr. of* مَرْفُوعٌ. (Ṣ in art. رفع.) — مَوْضُوعٌ as an inf. n., signifying a certain manner of going of a beast: see رَفَعَ البَعِيرُ. — مَوْضُوعٌ, in logic, † *A subject, as opposed to a predicate*: and † *a substance, as opposed to an accident*: in each sense, *contr. of* مَحْمُولٌ. — † The *subject* of a book or the like. — See أَصْوَاتٌ مَصُوغَةٌ — مَصْنُوعٌ. مَوْضُوعَةٌ: see art. صوغ.

مُوَاضَعَةٌ [when used as a conv. term in lexicology] *i. q.* إِصْطِلَاحٌ [when so used]. (Mz, 1st نوع.)

أَكَمَةٌ مُتَوَاضِعَةٌ [† *A low hill*]. (Ṣ in art. خشع.)

وضف

4. أَوْضَفَ النَّاقَةَ *He made the she-camel to go the pace termed* خَبَب; like أَوْفَضَهَا. (Khaleefeh El-Ḥoseynee, in TA, art. وفض.)

وضن

وَضِينٌ *A girth* (بِطَان) *wide, woven of thongs or hair, or only of skin*; (M, Ḳ;) *said to be adapted for the* رَحْل *and the* هَوْدَج; the بِطَان being peculiarly for the قَتَب: (M:) or *it is for the* هَوْدَج, *like the* بِطَان *for the* قَتَب *and the* تَصْدِير *for the* رَحْل *and the* حِزَام *for the* سَرْج; and *both* [but to what this refers is doubtful] *are like the* نِسْع, *except that they are of thongs woven one upon another, doubly* or *more.* (Ṣ.)

مِيضَنَةٌ *i. q.* قُفَّةٌ i. e. مَرْجُونَةٌ. (TA in art. ضون.)

وطس

1. وَطَسَ: see طَاسَ in art. طوس.

وطن

2. وَطَّنَ نَفْسَهُ عَلَى الأَمْرِ *He disposed and subjected his mind, or himself, to do the thing*; syn. مَهَّدَهَا لِفِعْلِهِ وَذَلَّلَهَا. (Mṣb.) — وطّن نفسه على الشَّىْءِ, and لَهُ, *He induced, or persuaded, himself to do the thing*; syn. حَمَلَهَا عَلَيْهِ. (ISd, in TA.) See also 5 and 10.

4: see 10.

5. تَوَطَّنَتْ نَفْسُهُ عَلَى الشَّىْءِ, and لَهُ, *He undertook the thing, and submitted to it*; syn. تَحَمَّلَتْ وَذَلَّتْ لَهُ (ISd, in TA) [see also 2 and 10] *his mind, or he, became disposed and subjected to do the thing*; syn. تَمَهَّدَتْ. (Ḳ [in the CḲ, for تَوَطَّنَهَا تَمَهَّدَهَا, is put تَوَطَّنَهَا تَمَهَّدَهَا].)

10. إِسْتَوْطَنَ *He took for himself as a home*, or *settled place of abode*, (Ṣ, Mṣb, Ḳ,) a country; (Ṣ, Mṣb;) as also ↓ أَوْطَنَ (Ṣ, Mṣb, Ḳ) and ↓ وَطَّنَ (Ṣ, Ḳ) or ↓ تَوَطَّنَ. (Mṣb.)

وَطَنٌ The *place of abode* or *residence* (Ṣ, Mgh, Ḳ) of a man: (Ṣ, Mgh:) a man's *settled place of abode*; his *place of constant residence*; his *dwelling*; his *home*. (Mṣb.)

وظف

2. وَظَّفَ عَلَيْهِ العَمَلَ *He appointed him the work.* (Mṣb.) — وَظَّفَ عَلَيْهِمُ الخَرَاجَ [*He assessed them their rates of the* خراج]. (Mgh in art. قسط.)

وَظِيفٌ, in every quadruped, *What is above the* رُسْغ [or *pastern*], *to the joint of the* سَاق: in the fore-leg of a horse, *what is beneath the knee, to the* جُبَّة; and in the hind-leg, *what is between the* كعب [or *hock*] *and the* جُبَّة: accord. to IAar, in a camel, *from the* رُسْغ [or *pastern*], *to the knee* in the fore-leg, and in the hind-leg *to the* عُرْقُوب [or *hock*]: (M, TT:) [the *shank*, fore and hind]. — See جُبَّةٌ, and رُكْبَةٌ, and حَوْشَبٌ. — In a horse, *What corresponds to the* كُرَاع *in an ox or a sheep or goat*; *or the slender part of the leg.* (Ḳ, voce كراع.) (The مَوْصِلُ الوظيف is *The joint between which and the hoof is the slender part called the* رُسْغ. (Ḳ, art. رسغ.) The *slender part of the* ذراع *and* سَاق *in a horse, camel, &c.* (Ṣ, Ḳ.) That which is broad, in the hind-leg, is preferred; and that which is gibbous in the fore-leg. (Ṣ.) [In art. جُبَّة, the place where the سَاق and وظيف meet is mentioned.] The arm (ذِرَاع) of a camel, [&c.,] is above the وظيف. (Ḳ, voce ذِرَاع.) The وظيف evidently signifies what anatomists call the *metacarpus* (in the fore-leg) and the *metatarsus* (in the hind-leg): see ركبة and كَعْبٌ. In general it seems to signify the *slender part of the shank, next the pastern*: and this, accord. to the explanation of مُسْتَدَقّ in the M and Ḳ, is the meaning assigned to it in the Ṣ and Ḳ. See also ذِرَاع.] — The *bone of the* سَاق. (L, art. زج.) — مَوْصِلُ الوَظِيفِ *The fetlock-joint.* (Ṣ, Ḳ, voce رُسْغ.)

وَظِيفَةٌ *A daily allowance*, or *portion*, *of food, or the like.* (Ṣ, Ḳ.) — وَظِيفَةٌ also *An appointed part-payment*, or *instalment*, *due at a particular period.* (Mgh, Mṣb, in art. نجم.) — وَظِيفَةٌ مِنْ خَرَاجِ الأَرْضِ [*An assessed rate of the land-tax*]. Ṣ, voce طَسْق.)

وع

قُرَانِقُ: see وَعْوَعٌ.

وعس

1. فَحَدَهُ i. q. حَنَّكَهُ وَعَسَهُ الدَّهْرُ and عَرَكَهُ and &c. (IAạr, TA, in art. حنك.)

وعق

عُوَاقٌ: see وُعَاقٌ.

عَوِيقٌ: see وَعِيقٌ.

وعل

وَعِلٌ *A mountain-goat*: (Ḳ, &c.:) see ثَيْتَلٌ; also أَلْبٌ; and أُرْوِيَّةٌ and شَبْرٌ.

وُعُولٌ as meaning *Noble* persons: and *strong* men: see two exs. voce تَحْتَ.

وعى

1. وَعَاهُ *He kept it in mind, and considered it.* (Mṣb.) — وَعَى الحَدِيثَ *He kept*, or *retained, the narration in his mind*, or *memory*; or *knew it*, or *learned it, by heart*; and *studied it until he knew it.* (Mṣb.) — وَعَى, aor. ـَ, *He heeded*; *paid attention to.*

4. أَوْعَاهُ الحَدِيثَ *He made him to retain the narration in his memory*; or *to know it*, or *learn it, by heart.* (TA, in art. زكت.)

وِعَآءٌ *A* [*bag*, or *wallet*, or] *receptacle*, *for travelling-provisions, and for goods or utensils, &c.*: (Ṣ, MA:) *a vessel* (?). — وِعَآءُ القَلْبِ [*The pericardium*]. (TA, voce فُؤَادٌ.) — بَثَثْتُ لَهُ مَا فِى وِعَائِى † *I showed him what was in my heart.* (Er-Rághib, TA, in art. شكو and شكى.) — حَرْفُ الوِعَآءِ [*The adverbial particle* فِى]. (IB, in TA, art. وسط.)

وغل

4. أَوْغَلْتُهَا, for أَوْغَلْتُ فِيهَا : see a verse cited voce غَمْرٌ.

وَاغِلٌ : see وَارِشٌ, شَطَنَ, and طَفَا.

وغم

وَغْمٌ, said of food : see فَغْمٌ.

وفض

2. وَفَّضَ الرَّحَى He put a وِفَاض [or skin] beneath the [hand-]mill. (M, in art. ثفل.)

4. أَوْفَضَ : see أَوْفَضَ.

وِفَاضٌ : see 2, and ثِفَالٌ.

وفق

1. وَفُقَ أَمْرُهُ His affair, or case, was right, agreeable with what was wished, or desired. (A, TA.)

2. وَفَّقَ أَمْرَهُ [He accomodated, adapted, or disposed, his affair to its object; directed it to a right issue;] prospered it. (TK.) — وَفَّقَهُ لِأَمْرٍ He disposed him, or adapted him, to a thing; he disposed him, or made him fit, for a thing. — وَفَّقَهُ ٱللّٰهُ God accommodated him, adapted him, or disposed him, or directed him, to the right course; syn. سَدَّدَهُ: (Msb:) God made him to take, or follow, a right way, course, or direction, [in an affair]: or directed him by inspiration to that which was good, or to prosperity. (TA.) — وَفَّقَهُ لِلسَّدَادِ [He accommodated, adapted, disposed, or directed him, to that which was right]. (K, art. سد.) — وَفَّقَ بين الشَّيْئَيْنِ He effected an agreement, a harmony, a reconciliation, an accommodation, or an adjustment, between the two things. (MA.) And وَفَّقْتُ بَيْنَ القَوْمِ [I effected an agreement, a harmony, &c., between the people, or party; made peace between them]. (Msb, in art. صلح; &c.)

3. وَافَقَهُ He, or it, was conformable, or did conformably, to him, or it; was as he, or it, was, or did as he, or it, did: coincided with him, or it: it suited him, or it: it matched it; tallied with it. — وَافَقَهُ عَلَى أَمْرٍ i. q. اِتَّفَقَ ♦ مَعَهُ عَلَيْهِ, He agreed with him, or was of one mind or opinion with him, upon, or respecting, a thing, or an affair. (TA.) — [وَافَقَهُ is best rendered He agreed, consented, accorded, or was of one mind or opinion, with him: and he complied with him, or it (see طَاوَعَهُ): and he coincided with him, suited him, or it; it matched it, &c.] — وَافَقَ العَذَابُ الذَّنْبَ [The punishment agreed, or corresponded with the sin, crime, or offence]. (TA.) — وَافَقَ It was suitable, or convenient. — See مُشَاكَلَةٌ in art. شكل, conj. 3. — وَافَقَهُ He encountered him; syn. with صَادَفَهُ, q. v.

4. أَوْفَقَ أَمْرَهُ He found his affair, or case, agreeable with his wish, or desire. (TA.)

8. اِتَّفَقَ It happened; chanced. So used in the K, art. لفت, and in many other works. — اِتَّفَقَ مَعَهُ عَلَى أَمْرٍ : see 3.

تَوْفِيقٌ A certain legal document: a pleading. See مَحْضَرٌ.

إِتِّفَاقِيٌّ Casual.

وفى

1. وَفَى بِالعَهْدِ and بِالوَعْدِ [He fulfilled, performed, kept, or was faithful to, the compact, or covenant, and the promise]: act. part. n. وَفِيٌّ; pl. أَوْفِيَاءُ. (Msb.) — وَفَآءٌ signifies The being faithful to an engagement, or promise: see 1, last sentence, in art. رعى. — وَفَاهُ He paid it: see an ex. (فِي ثَوْبَىْ أَبِي أَنْ أَفِيَهُ) voce ثَوْبٌ.

2. وَفَّاهُ حَقَّهُ and ♦ اوفاهُ and ♦ وافاهُ and ♦ توفّاهُ and ♦ استوفاهُ He paid, or rendered, to him fully, or completely, his right, or due. (K. [In the CK, أَوْفاهُ is erroneously put for وَافَاهُ.])

3. وَافَى بِهِ He brought it: see a verse cited in art. سجد. — See 2.

4. أَوْفَى عَلَيْهِ He looked upon it, looked upon it from above, looked down upon it; got a view of it; or saw it; syn. أَشْرَفَ عَلَيْهِ, (S, Msb, K, TA,) and اِطَّلَعَ; and اوفى فيه [likewise] signifies اشرف. (TA.) — See 2.

5. تَوَفَّاهُ ٱللّٰهُ God took his soul, (S, K,) [either at death, or in sleep. See the Kur-án, vi. 60]: or caused him to die. (Msb.) — See 2 and 10.

10. اِسْتَوْفَاهُ and ♦ تَوَفَّاهُ He [exacted,] took, or received, it fully, or wholly. (Mgh.) See an ex. voce عَلَى. — See 2. — اِسْتَوْفَى [He completed] so many years of his age. (A, O, in TA, voce احفر.)

وَفِيٌّ : see وَفَى. — وَفِيُّ العَهْدِ [A fulfiller, performer, or keeper, of the compact, or covenant. (TA, voce إِلٌّ.)

وقع

1. وَقَعَ الأَمْرُ The thing, or affair, [fell, befell,] happened; took place; came to pass; became [executed, performed, or] realized; syn. حَصَلَ. (TA.) — وَقَعَ فِي He lighted, or came, upon a thing or place; and he became in a place. — وَقَعُوا فِي السَّنَيَاتِ البِيضِ [They lapsed into the years of scantiness of herbage]. (K in art. سنه, q. v.) — وَقَعَ إِلَيْهِ It chanced, or happened, to come to him, or it: and, said of a thing borne by water, it drifted to it, namely, a place. — وَقَعَ عَلَيْهِ It fell, lay, or closed, upon it, or against it. — وَقَعَ بِالأَمْرِ He originated the thing, or event, and made it to befall. (TA.) — وَقَعَ He fell into a snare, or the like: he became insnared. — وَقَعَ فِي أَرْضٍ فَلَاةٍ i. q. صَارَ فِيهَا [He was, or became, meaning he found himself, came to be, or chanced to be, in a desert, or waterless, land]; (Msb:) and فِي رَوْضَةٍ [in a meadow, or garden]: (T, S, in art. انق:) [or he lighted upon, &c.; from the lighting of a bird]. — يَقَعُ followed by عَلَى, often signifies It (a garment, &c., or a portion thereof,) lies against or upon a certain part of the body, &c. — وَقَعَ بِهِمْ and ♦ أَوْقَعَ بِهِمْ He made much slaughter among them: (Msb:) or he fought them vehemently: (K:) or he fell upon them in fight: (PS:) both mean the same: (S:) he made an onslaught upon them: اوقع بِالعَدُوِّ he made an assault, or a sudden assault, upon the enemy. (MA.) — وَقَعَ فِيهِ, inf. n. وَقِيعَةٌ, He spoke evil of him, behind his back, or in his absence, or otherwise, saying of him what would grieve him if he heard it; (S;) slandered him. — He reviled, vilified, or vituperated, him; charged him with a vice, fault, or the like; defamed him; or detracted from his reputation. (Msb.) — وَقَعَ مَوْقِعًا مِنْ كِفَايَتِهِ [and مِنْ حَاجَتِهِ, (see K, art. فقر,)] It supplied, or sufficed for, his need; syn. أَغْنَى غَنَاءَهُ. (Msb.) وَقَعَ مَوْقِعًا signifies It stood in stead, or in some stead: see فَقِيرٌ, in the K; and see Bd, and Jel, ix. 60: مَوْقِعًا عَظِيمًا, in great stead. — لَمْ يَقَعْ مِنْهُ مَوْقِعًا [It did not stand with him in any stead]. (S, K, voce تَسَخَّطَ, end of art. سخط.) [You say] وَقَعَ مِنْهُ الأَمْرُ مَوْقِعًا حَسَنًا أَوْ سَيِّئًا The thing stood with him [in good stead, or (if the expression be allowable) in evil stead]; syn. ثَبَتَ لَدَيْهِ. (TA.) — وَقَعَ مَوْقِعًا مِنَ الحَاجَةِ [It supplied, or sufficed for, what was needed]. (Bd, ix. 60.) — قُحَاحٌ : see بِقُحَاحِ قُرْتِكَ and وَقَعْتُ بِقُرْتِكَ. — يَقَعُ عَلَى كَذَا It (a word) applies to such a thing.

2. وَقَّعَ فِي الكِتَابِ, (MA, TA,) inf. n. تَوْقِيعٌ, (KL, TA,) [as commonly used in the present day,] He signed the writing [for the purpose of giving effect to it, either beneath, or by endorsing it]: (MA, KL:) [but as generally used in earlier, though post-classical, times,] he annexed to the writing, after it had been finished, for the

Sulṭán or the administrator of affairs, to whom it had been submitted, something [*for the purpose of giving effect thereto*]; *as, for instance, when a complaint is submitted to the Sulṭán or to the administrator, and one writes beneath the writing or on the back thereof,* "*Let the affair,* or *case, of this person be looked into, and let his right,* or *due, be fully exacted for this person:*" or, accord. to Az, *he wrote, upon the writing, a concise abstract, omitting redundances, of the objects of want* [*petitioned for therein*]: from تَوْقِيعُ الدَّبَرِ ظَهْرَ البَعِيرِ ["the gall's, or sore's, marking the back of the camel"]; as though the مُوَقِّع upon the writing marked, upon the case respecting which the writing was written, that which confirmed it, and rendered its execution obligatory: (TA:) تَوْقِيعٌ also signifies such a writing itself (مَا يُوَقَّعُ فِى كِتَابٍ; Ṣ, Ḳ, TA;) and its pl. is تَوْقِيعَاتٌ: (TA:) it is said to be an Islámic term; not old Arabic. (TA.) [Also *He made an entry of a note or postil or the like,* or *entries of notes, &c., in the writing,* or *book:* see an ex. voce ضعف. — وقع به *He blamed him; reproved him angrily,* or *severely.* (TA.) — See 4.

3. وَاقَعَ الأَمْرَ † *He threw himself* [or *plunged*] *into the affair: he fell into the affair: he fell into the affair, subjecting himself to difficulty.* (MA.) And † *He fell to the thing;* such as eating, and drinking, and the like: see 3 in art. فتك, for an instance of this, as well as a similar, meaning. — وَاقَعَ الأُمُورَ, inf. n. مُوَاقَعَةٌ and وِقَاعٌ, app., *He was near to doing,* or *experiencing, the affairs,* or *events;* syn. دَانَاهَا. (TA.) — وَاقَعَ شَيْئًا also means *He experienced the occurrence of a thing; he met with a thing;* i.e., something occurred. — وَاقَعَ شَيْئًا *same as* وَقَعَ فِى شَىْءٍ; *He fell into a thing.* (Ḳur, xviii. 51, and Expos. of the Jeláleyn.) — وَاقَعَهَا *He compressed her.* (MA.) — وَاقَعَ بِهِمْ [*He engaged with them in fight,* or *conflict*]. (Ṣ.)

4. أَوْقَعَ الأَمْرَ, inf. n. إِيقَاعٌ, (with which ▾ تَوْقِيعٌ is syn., as is shown in the TA,) *He made the thing,* or *affair, to happen, to take place, to come to pass,* or *to become executed* or *performed* or *realized.* — أَوْقَعَهُ *He caused him to fall into a snare,* or *the like; he ensnared him.* — أَوْقَعَ بِهِمْ: see 1. — أَوْقَعَ فِيهِمْ شَرًّا *He caused evil to befall them; occasioned them evil.* — أَوْقَعَ بِهِ [*He punished him*]. (A, art. عذر.) — See 1. — أَوْقَعَ فِى قَلْبِهِ *He put into his heart,* or *mind.* — أَوْقَعَ بَيْنَ القَوْمِ, (L, art. أرش,) or أَوْقَعَ بَيْنَهُمُ الشَّرَّ (TA, in that art.) *i. q.* أَرَّشَ. (L, TA, in that art.) — أَوْقَعَ *He made a verb transitive.*

5. تَوَقَّعَهُ and ▾ اِسْتَوْقَعَهُ *He expected it; looked for its coming to pass,* or *being.* (Ṣ, Ḳ.)

10: see 5.

وَقْعٌ: see 8, in art. حذو.

وَقْعَةٌ *An onslaught; a shock in battle:* (Ṣ:) or *such as is repeatedly made.* (Ḳ.)

وَقِيعَةٌ *The wisp of wool, &c., with which one tars a mangy camel:* see رِبْذَةٌ.

وَقَّاعٌ فِى الشَّرِّ [app., *One who is wont to make others fall into evil,* or *mischief*]. (Ḳ, voce مُنْدَاصٌ, q. v., in art. ديص.)

وَاقِعٌ *Actually occurring.* — *An event; a fact; a case.* — فِى ٱلْوَاقِعِ *In fact; in reality.*

إِيقَاعٌ, in music, *A cadence.*

مَوْقِعُ إِثْمٍ *An occasion* (lit., *a place*) *of falling into sin.* — وَقَعَ مَوْقِعًا: see وَقَعَ, in three places: lit., *It fell in a place of falling,* or *where it should fall:* sometimes app. meaning *it had an effect.*] — It is said of a half of a date given as alms, لَا يَتَبَيَّنُ لَهُ مَوْقِعٌ عَلَى الجَائِعِ كَمَا لَا يَتَبَيَّنُ عَلَى الشَّبْعَانِ إِذَا أَكَلَهُ [app., *There appears not, of it, any effect upon the hungry,* &c.]. (O, in art. وقع, in explanation of a trad. mentioned there and in the Mṣb.) See وَقَعَ عَلَى, voce مُوَاقِعَةٌ.

مُوقِعٌ *An efficient.*

مُوَقَّعٌ *Tried, experienced:* see مُوَقَّحٌ.

وقف

1. وَقَفَ *He was,* or *became, still,* or *stationary;* (Mṣb;) [*he stood still;*] *he continued standing:* (Ḳ:) and [simply] *he stood;* contr. of جَلَسَ. (TA.) — وَقَفَ الدَّابَّةَ, inf. n. وَقْفٌ, *He made the beast to be,* or *become, still,* or *motionless.* (Mṣb.) — وَقَفَ عَلَيْهِ *He stopped,* or *paused, upon coming to him,* or *it; he stopped,* or *paused, at it;* or *where he,* or *it, was.* — وَقَفَ عَلَى شَىْءٍ *He paused at, and paid attention to, a thing.* — وَقَفَ عَلَيْهِ *He comprehended it,* namely, a meaning: *he understood it.* (TA. [Or, correctly, وُقِفَ, for it is there altered.]) — *He met with it;* namely, a word or the like, in reading: often occurring in this sense. — وَقَفَ عَلَيْهِ *He saw it:* and *he was introduced into it, and knew what was in it.* (TA.) *He was made to know it surely.* See Bḍ, vi. 27 and 30. — وَقَفْتُهُ على ذَنْبِهِ *I made him acquainted with,* or *made him to know, his crime, sin, fault, or the like;* (Ṣ, K:) and so ▾ أَوْقَفْتُهُ عَلَيْهِ, q. v. (Mgh.) — وَقَفَ, aor. ِ, inf. n. وُقُوفٌ, *He withstood, resisted:* governing by عَنْ. — وَقَفَهُ and ▾ أَوْقَفَهُ and ▾ وَقَّفَهُ [*He bequeathed it,* or *gave it, unalienably:*] the first of these is the most chaste: the last is disapproved and rare. (TA, art. حبس.) See مُؤَبَّد.

2. وَقَّفَهُ عَلَى الأَمْرِ [*He made him to pause,* or *wait, at the thing,* or *affair*]. (Ḳ, TA, in art. ثبط.) See the quasi-pass. تَوَقَّفَ; and see ثَبَّطَهُ. — وَقَّفَهُ, inf. n. تَوْقِيفٌ *He taught him the places of pausing, in reading.* (Mgh.) And hence, *He made him to know* a thing. (Mgh.) — وَقَّفَهُ عَلَى الشَّىْءِ, meaning عَرَّفَهُ إِيَّاهُ, *He made him acquainted with the thing; informed him of it; gave him notice of it;* though often occurring, for وَقَفَهُ عَلَيْهِ, seems to be post-classical. It is used in this sense, or as meaning *He* (God) *revealed to him the thing,* in many places in the Mz, 1st نوع: as, for ex., in the following instance, cited from IF, وَقَّفَ ٱللّٰهُ آدَمَ عَلَى مَا شَآءَ أَنْ يُعَلِّمَهُ إِيَّاهُ [*God taught,* or *revealed to, Adam what He pleased to teach him*]. — وَقَّفَ الحَدِيثَ, (JK,) inf. n. تَوْقِيفٌ, (Ḳ,) *He explained the tradition;* syn. بَيَّنَهُ. (JK, Ḳ.*) — تَوْقِيفٌ, as a legal term: see نَصٌّ عَلَى شَىْءٍ مَّا. — See 1.

3. وَاقَفَ *He stood* with another *in a competition; was a partner* in a match, &c.: see رَسِيلٌ.

4: see 1. — أَوْقَفَهُ عَلَى شَىْءٍ *He acquainted him with a thing.* — أوقفته على ذَنْبِهِ: see وَقَفْتُهُ, which is the expression commonly known.

5. تَوَقَّفَ عَلَى الشَّىْءِ ‡ *He paused,* or *waited, at the thing;* syn. تَلَبَّثَ. (IDrd, Ḳ, TA.) (Accord. to some copies of the Ḳ, تَثَبَّتَ.] You say, تَوَقَّفْتُ عَلَى هٰذَا الأَمْرِ ‡ *I paused,* or *waited, at this thing,* or *affair.* (TA.) And تَوَقَّفَ عَلَى جَوَابِ كَلَامِهِ ‡ [*He paused,* or *waited, at the reply to his speech*]. (TA.) And hence, تَوَقَّفَ عَلَى السَّمَاعِ *He limited,* or *restricted, himself to what had been heard* [from the Arabs, with respect to a construction, &c.]; *did not transgress it,* or *overstep it.* See مُتَوَقِّفٌ. — تَوَقَّفَ فِيهِ † *He paused upon it; he hesitated,* or *deliberated, respecting it.* Of very frequent occurrence. — تَوَقَّفَ عَنِ الأَمْرِ † *He held, refrained,* or *abstained, from the thing,* or *affair.* (Mṣb.) — تَوَقَّفَ عَلَى كَذَا *It* (for instance, an

opinion or a judgment, and the truth of an evidence or a demonstration, and the result of an inquiry or investigation) *rested, was founded* or *grounded, depended,* or *was dependent, upon such a thing.* You say, of knowledge, يَتَوَقَّفُ حُصُولُهُ عَلَى كَذَا *Its origination rests upon such a thing;* as, for instance, speculation.

وَقْفٌ *An entailed,* or *unalienable, legacy* or *gift; a mortmain.* See أَرْقَبَ. —— الوُقُوفُ بِعَرَفَاتَ *The halting* of the pilgrims *at* Mount *'Arafát.*

حَبِطَ مَوْقِفُ الفَرَسِ *The horse's belly was inflated:* see حَبِطَ.

مَوْقُوفٌ عَلَى حَدِّ كُفْرٍ *Brought to the verge of infidelity:* see حَدٌّ.

أَنَا مُتَوَقِّفٌ فِى هٰذَا [*I am pausing,* or *hesitating, respecting this;*] *I do not form,* or *give, a decided opinion* (لَا أُمْضِى رَأْيًا) *respecting this.* (TA.)

وقى

1. وَقَاهُ ٱللّٰهُ ٱلسُّوْءَ *God preserved him from evil.* (Mṣb.) See a verse cited voce نَقَشَ. —— وَقَاكَ ٱللّٰهُ كُلَّ مَحْذُورٍ *God preserve thee from all fear:* see مَحْذُورٌ. —— قِ, or قِهْ, and تَوَقَّ, are imperatives [meaning *Be thou cautious*]. (JK.) —— قِ عَلَى ظَلْعِكَ: see ظَلَعَ. —— وَقَاهُ and ▼ اِتَّقَاهُ both signify *He was cautious of it;* syn. حَذِرَهُ. (K.)

5. تَوَقَّاهُ (and, accord. to a usage in the K, art. حرز, also تَوَقَّى مِنْهُ) *He guarded against it; was cautious of it;* syn. تَحَرَّزَ منه and اِحْتَرَزَ منه. (Ṣ, K,* art. حرز.) —— تَبَقَّهْ وَتَوَقَّهْ: see 4 in art. بقى.

8. اِتَّقَى *He preserved,* or *guarded, himself exceedingly,* or *extraordinarily:* (Ksh, Bḍ in ii. 1:) *he put a thing between him and another to preserve him,* or *guard him.* (Ḥam, p. 350.) —— In the conventional language of the law, *He preserved,* or *guarded, himself exceedingly,* or *extraordinarily,* (Ksh, Bḍ, ubi supra,) *from sin, of commission* or *of omission,* (Ksh,) [or] *from what would harm him in the world to come.* (Bḍ, who describes three degrees.) It may often be rendered *He was pious;* or *careful of his religious duties.* —— اِتَّقَى عَلَيْهِمْ وَحَذِرَ [*He guarded himself against them in an extraordinary degree, and was cautious,* or *wary*]. (JK, TA, in art. خشى.) See 1. —— يَتَقِى, for يَتَّقِى: see art. تقى: and see a verse of Khufáf Ibn-Nudbeh, (quoted in the Ṣ, in art. وقى,) cited voce أَثْرٌ. —— يَتَقْ for يَتَّقِ: see a verse cited voce مُتَأَوِّبٌ.

وَقِىٌّ *Cautious, guarding himself from sin, &c.:* see تَقِىٌّ.

وَقِيَّةٌ *Property by means of which one preserves himself:* pl. وَقِيَّاتٌ. (TA.) See a verse cited voce مُحْبَلٌ.

وِقَايَةٌ *Excess of preserving* or *guarding.* (Ksh, Bḍ in ii. 1.) —— *A preservative.*

وَاقٍ A saddle *that does not gall the back.* (Ṣ, K.)

وَاقِيَةٌ used as an inf. n., like بَاقِيَةٌ: see Ḥar, p. 136. —— وَاقِيَةٌ as meaning *one preserver:* see an ex. voce بَاقِيَةٌ.

أُوقِيَّةٌ *An ounce:* see رِطْلٌ, in two places.

وك

وَكٌّ and عَكٌّ: see art. عك.

وكظ

وَاكَظَ and مُوَاكِظٌ i. q. وَاظَبَ and مُوَاظِبٌ: وَاكِظٌ عَلَى كَذَا *Attending assiduously to such a thing; intent upon it.* (Lḥ, in TA, art. وظب.)

وكع

وَكَعَةٌ pl. of وَكِيعٌ, like as خَبَثَةٌ is of خَبِيثٌ, *Base:* see a verse cited voce أَحْصَنَ.

وكف

1. وَكَفَ said of water from the eyes: see a verse cited voce رَسَمَ. One of its inf. ns. is وَكَفَانٌ. (K, voce جَدٌّ.)

2. وَكَّفَ عَلَى الخُبْزِ [*It was made to drip upon bread*]; said of fat melting and dripping. (TA in art. جمل.) —— وَكَّفَ and ▼ أَوْكَفَ: see أَكَّفَ and آكَفَ.

4: see 2.

وَكْفٌ: see an ex. in a verse cited voce خَيْطَةٌ.

وَكِيفٌ, inf. n. of 1: see رَسَمَ.

وكل

1. وَكَلَهُ إِلَى رَأْيِهِ, inf. n. وَكْلٌ and وُكُولٌ, *He left him to his opinion,* or *judgment.* (TA.) And وَكَلْتُهُ إِلَى نَفْسِهِ, aor. يَكِلُ, inf. n. وُكُولٌ, [*I left him to himself;*] *I did not manage his affair, nor aid him.* (Mṣb.) And كِلْنِى إِلَى كَذَا *Leave thou me to manage such a thing.* (TA.) —— وَكَلْتُهُ إِلَى دِينِهِ [*I left him to his religion, not interfering with him therein*]. (Ṣ, Mṣb, K, voce دِينَتُهُ.)

2. وَكَّلَهُ بِشَىْءٍ *He appointed him,* or *intrusted him, as his commissioned agent, factor,* or *deputy, with the management,* or *disposal, of a thing.* —— وَكَّلْتُ بِفُلَانٍ *I associated a* وَكِيل [or *factor,* &c.] *with such a one.* (T in art. ب.)

5. تَوَكَّلَ عَلَيْهِ, and ▼ اِتَّكَلَ عليه, *He relied upon him;* (Ṣ, Mṣb;) *and confided in him:* (Mṣb:) *he submitted himself to him.* (K.) —— تَوَكَّلَ بِالأَمْرِ *He became responsible to him for the management of the affair.* (TA.) —— تَوَكَّلَ لَهُ بِهِ *He became responsible to him for it.* (TA.) —— تَوَكَّلَ فِى أَمْرٍ *He became* وَكِيل *in an affair.* —— تَوَكَّلَ بِمَالِ أَحَدٍ *He became administrator of one's property.*

6. تَوَاكَلَهُ *He deserted him,* or *it:* i. q. تركه: see two exs. voce سَدِرَ.

8: see 5. —— مُتَّكَلٌ is used as an inf. n. of اِتَّكَلَ.

وَكَلٌ and ▼ وُكَلَةٌ and ▼ تُكَلَةٌ *An impotent man,* (Ṣ, K,) *who commits his affair to another.* (Ṣ.)

وُكَلَةٌ: } see وَكَلٌ
تُكَلَةٌ: }

وَكِيلٌ *A witness;* syn. شَهِيدٌ. (Jel, ii. 66; and iv. 169.) —— *A commissioned agent; a factor; a deputy.*

وَكَالَةٌ, for دَارُ الوَكَالَةِ, *A factory:* pl. وَكَائِلُ.

وكن

وُكْنَةٌ certainly means, sometimes, A bird's *nest,* wherever it be: see an ex. in the first paragraph of art. غدو.

وكى

وِكَآءٌ *A tie:* see an ex. voce اِسْتٌ, in art. سته. —— The *tie,* (Ṣ, Mgh, Mṣb, K,) which is a cord, (Mṣb,) *of the head* (Ṣ, Mṣb) *of the* قِرْبَة, (Ṣ, Mgh, Mṣb, K,) *&c.* (K.)

ول

R. Q. 1. وَلْوَلَتْ *She* (a woman) *wailed,* or *raised her voice with weeping.* (Ḥar, p. 395.)

ولس

3. وَالَسَ *He acted perfidiously,* or *practised fraud:* see دَالَسَ.

وَلْس *Treachery*: see دَلْس.

ولع

2. وَلَّعَهُ بِهِ [*i. q.* أَوْلَعَهُ بِهِ]: (Ḳ, art. غرو:) *He made him to be desirous, or fond, of it.* See أَغْرَاهُ بِهِ.

4. أَوْلَعَهُ بِكَذَا *He, or it, rendered him eagerly desirous of such a thing; or fond of it.* (MA.) — أُولِعَ بِهِ *i. q.* أُغْرِىَ بِهِ. (Ḳ.) — أُولِعَ بِهِ *He became attached to it, or fond of it;* [*was devoted, or addicted, to it; was eagerly desirous of it;*] *he adhered, clung, or clave, to it; or loved it;* (Mṣb;) *i. q.* أُغْرِىَ بِهِ. (Ṣ.) See this last, and أُغْرِمَ بِهِ.

وَلْع *Lying*: see شَهْل.

وَلَعٌ and وُلُوعٌ *Eager desire* [بِشَىْءٍ *for a thing*]; syn. حِرْصٌ: (Ḥar, p. 607:) *fondness* [for it]; *attachment* [to it]: (L, Mṣb, TA:) *i. q.* غَرَامٌ. (Ṣ, Ḳ, in art. غرم.)

وَلِيع and وَلِيعَة of the طَلْع: see ضَحْك.

مُوَلَّع *Marked, in oblong shapes, with black and white:* (Ṣ:) *or, with other colours.* (Aṣ, Ṣ.) See also مُلَمَّع.

ولغ

1. وَلَغَ *He* (a dog) *lapped.* (Ṣ, Mṣb, Ḳ.) See an ex. voce مَخْشُوم.

ولف

الوَلْف *The common cyclamen*: see بَخُورُ مَرْيَمَ.

وِلَاف, for إِلَاف: see أَلِفَهُ.

ولم

وَلِيمَة *A repast prepared on the occasion of a wedding:* (T, Ṣ, M, Mgh, Mṣb, Ḳ:) or, *on any occasion.* (M, Mgh, Ḳ.)

وله

1. وَلِهَ *His reason departed,* or *he became bereft of his reason* or *intellect, in consequence of grief;* (Ḳ;) or *of joy, or grief;* (Mṣb;) or *of intense grief;* (Ṣ, Mgh;) or *of the loss of the beloved:* (TA:) or *he grieved, or sorrowed:* (Ḳ:) and *he became confounded, or perplexed, and unable to see his right course,* (Ṣ, Ḳ, TA,) *by reason of intense grief:* (S, TA:) and *he feared.* (Ḳ.) See also أَلِهَ, in two places. — وَلِهَ إِلَى أُمِّهِ *He* (an infant) *yearned for his mother.* (TA.) And وَلِهَ إِلَيْهِ is app. syn. with أَلِهَ إِلَيْهِ, q.v.

وَلَه *Distraction* in love: see حُبّ.

وَالِه [*Bereft of the beloved:*] *i. q.* ثَاكِل. (TA, art. طرب.) And *Distracted.*

ولى

1. وَلِيَهُ, (Ṣ, Mṣb, Ḳ,) and وَلِىَ عَلَيْهِ, (Mṣb, Ḳ,) inf. n. وِلَايَةٌ (Ṣ, Mṣb, Ḳ,) and وَلَايَةٌ, (Ḳ,) or the former is a simple subst., (TA,) and signifies the office, and authority, (Ḳ,) *He held command or authority over it; had charge of it; presided over it, or superintended it,* (namely a thing, Ṣ, Mṣb, Ḳ, and a country, province, town, or the like, Ṣ, Mṣb,) *as a prefect, commander, governor, lord, prince, king, administrator, or manager;* (Ḳ, TA;) *i. q.* ✝ تَوَلَّاهُ. (Mṣb.) — وَلِىَ كَذَا *He performed the act or office of doing such a thing; he did such a thing himself.*

2. وَلَّى *He caused to turn away, or back.* (Ḳur-án, ch. ii. v. 136.) — *He caused to turn towards,* with acc. (Idem, ch. ii. v. 139.) — *He turned away, or departed.* (TA.) — وَلَّى عَنْهُ *He turned away from, avoided, shunned, and left, him or it.* (Mṣb.) — وَلَّتِ الحَرْبُ [*The war declined*]. (A, Ḳ, in art. سفر.) — وَلَّى هَارِبًا *He went back, or retreated, fleeing.* (Ṣ.) — وَلَّيْتُهُ ظَهْرِى *I placed him behind me, and betook myself to defending him.* (TA in art. شزن.) — More commonly *I turned my back upon him, or it:* see Ḥar, p. 564. — وَلَّى اللَّيْلُ لِيَذْهَبَ *The night* [*declined,* i. e.] *retreated to depart;* syn. أَدْبَرَ. (T in art. دبر.) — وَلَّى أَمْرُ القَوْمِ لِفَسَادٍ *The case of the people, or party, declined, or became reduced to a bad state;* syn. أَدْبَرَ. (M in art. دبر.) — وَلَّى كِبَرًا, and وَلَّى alone, both of frequent occurrence in the lexicons, &c., [*He became in a declining state by reason of age.*] شَيْخٌ وَلَّى said of a man is *syn. with* دَبَرَ; as also وَلَّى (S in art. دبر.) See also two exs., p. 75, col. 3. — التَّوْلِيَةُ, like الإِدْبَارُ, properly signifies *Retrogression;* and hence, like this English word, tropically, *declension.* — وَلَّاهُ أَمْرًا *He set him over the thing; appointed him superintendent of it; or set him to do it;* as also ✝ أَوْلَاهُ إِيَّاهُ. — وَلَّاهُ دُبُرَهُ and وَلَّى دُبُرَهُ; see دُبُر, and see three phrases voce ذَنَب.

3. وَالَاهُ *It was next, or adjacent, to it.* Said of one place or tract with respect to another. — وَالَى *He made a consecution, or succession, of one to the other;* (Ṣ, Ḳ;) بَيْنَهُمَا *between them two;* (Ṣ;) or بَيْنَ الأَمْرَيْنِ *between the two things or affairs; he made a successive connexion, or no interruption.* (Ḳ.) And والاه *He made it consecutive, successive, or uninterrupted, in its progressions, or gradations, or the like;* syn. تَابَعَهُ [which see]. (Mṣb.) — وَالَاهُ, (MA,) inf. n. مُوَالَاةٌ, (Ṣ, KL, TA,) *He befriended him, or was friendly to him.* (Ṣ, MA, KL, TA.) See شَايَعَهُ.

4. أَوْلَى *He gave:* and *he made near.* (KL.) — أَوْلَاهُ مَعْرُوفًا *He did to him, or conferred upon him, a benefit, or favour;* syn. أَسْدَاهُ إِلَيْهِ; *as though he made it cleave to him, being next to him:* or *he put him in possession of it.* (TA.) You say also, أَوْلَاهُ ذُلًّا [*He brought upon him abasement, or ignominy*], (Ṣ, Ḳ, in art. خسف,) and الذُّلَّ وَالهَوَانَ. (Mṣb in that art., voce خَسْف, q. v.)

5. تَوَلَّى *He turned himself,* الى *towards.* (Jel, ii. 139.) *He turned away* (Idem, xix. 50; and Ṣ, Mṣb) عَنْهُ *from him, or it.* (Ṣ.) — تَوَلَّى *He turned the back to another:* see a verse in art. فيل, conj. 1. — تَوَلَّى أَمْرًا *He took upon himself an affair.* — تَوَلَّى كِبْرَهُ *He took upon himself, or undertook, the main part thereof;* syn. تَحَمَّلَ مُعْظَمَهُ. (Jel, xxiv. ii.) — تَوَلَّاهُ: see وَلِيَهُ.

10. إِسْتَوْلَى عَلَيْهِ *He mastered, or gained the mastery over, him or it;* (Mṣb;) *he got it in his hand, possession, or power.* (TA.) — إِسْتَوْلَتْ عَلَيْهِ الحُجَّةُ [*The argument, allegation, or plea, overcame him*]. (L in art. بهت.)

وَلِىٌّ *The manager of a thing, or of the affairs* of another: (Mṣb:) the *guardian,* or *manager of the affairs, and maintainer,* of an orphan: the *guardian* of a woman, *who affiances* her, *and independently of whom marriage cannot be contracted* by her. (TA.) The *executor* of a deceased person: (Bḍ, xvii. 35:) the *heir* of a deceased person. (Bḍ, Jel, ibid.) The *heir* [or *next-of-kin*] of a slain person, (Bḍ, Jel, xvii. 35,) *who has the management of the affairs after the death* of that person. (Bḍ, ibid.) And the slayer's *next-of-kin, who is answerable for him.* — وَلِىُّ عَهْدٍ and وِلَايَةُ عَهْدٍ: see art. عهد. — وَلِىُّ اللّٰهِ may be rendered *The friend of God:* or وَلِىّ has the meaning of an act. part. n., i. e. the *constant obeyer* [of God]: or that of a pass. part. n., i. e. [the *favourite* of God;] the *object of the constant beneficence and favours* of God. (TA.) See عَدُوّ. — اللّٰهُ وَلِىُّ الحَمْدِ signifies both مُسْتَحِقُّهُ and صَاحِبُهُ. (IbrD.) — وَلِىّ, pl. أَوْلِيَاء *A saint, &c.* — وَلِىّ The *rain after the* وَسْمِىّ. (TA in art. عنو.)

وَلَآءٌ *Relationship:* so in the phrase بَيْنَهُمَا وَلَآءٌ [*Between them two is relationship*]. (JM.) —— Also used for وَلَآءٌ: أَصْحَابُ وَلَآءٍ: see a verse cited voce عَيْرٌ. —— وَلَآءٌ The *right to the inheritance of the property left by an emancipated slave.*

وِلَايَةٌ: see وَلِىٌّ.

وَالٍ *A prefect, governor, ruler, king, regent, judge, magistrate, &c.* See مَعُونَةٌ.

فُلَانٌ أَوْلَى بِكَذَا *Such a one is more,* or *most, entitled to such a thing; has a better,* or *the best, right,* or *title,* or *claim, to it; is more,* or *most, deserving,* or *worthy, of it; is more,* or *most, competent to it; is more,* or *most, fit for it;* syn. أَحَقُّ بِهِ. (Mṣb.) But see أَحَقُّ. See also an ex. voce أُولُو, from the Ḳur, viii., last verse, and xxxiii. 6. —— أَوْلَى بِشَىْءٍ *More worthy,* or *deserving, of a thing. More fit, apt,* or *proper, for a thing.* —— بِالطَّرِيقِ الأَوْلَى *A fortiori:* see طَرِيقٌ.

مَوْلًى *A lord,* or *chief;* syn. سَيِّدٌ. (TA in the addenda.) —— The *son of a paternal uncle:* (Ṣ, Mṣb:) or *a relation,* (Ḳ,) *such as a son of a paternal uncle* (IAạr, Ḳ) and *the like,* (Ḳ,) [i.e.] and *such as a son of a sister.* (IAạr, TA.) —— And *A freedman;* (Ṣ, Mṣb, Ḳ;) so called because he is in the condition of the son of a paternal uncle; *being one* [*under the patronage of his emancipator,* i.e.,] *whom the emancipator is bound to aid, and whose property he inherits if he dies having no* [*natural or other legal*] *heir.* (TA.) And (Ḳ) *a slave:* (M, Ḳ:) fem. with ة. (M.)

مَوَالِيَا, vulg. مَوَّال (not مَوَّالِيَا) *A kind of short poem,* generally of five lines, of which all but the penultimate end with the same rhyme: see note 5 to ch. xxvi. of my "1001 Nights."

ومى

2. وَمَّى and ↓ اِسْتَوْمَى: see وَمَأَ.

10: see 2.

مَوَامٍ *Lands wherein is nothing.* (A'Obeyd, TA, in art. بلق.) The pl., when indeterminate, is thus, not مَوَامِى. See a verse in art. عرى, conj. 12. [This is a correction of art. موم, to which this word, and also the verb, belong: for there is no such root as ومى.]

ونى

1. وَنَى فِيهِ *He entered upon a thing languidly;* and عَنْهُ *He passed from it:* see عَنْ.

6. تَوَانَى *He was,* or *became, languid, remiss, weak, feeble,* or *faint,* (T, Ṣ, M, MA, Mṣb, Ḳ,*) in actions, and affairs, (T,) in respect of an object of his want, (Ṣ,) or in an affair. (MA, Mṣb.) —— تَوَانَى فِى الأَمْرِ *He flagged,* or *was remiss, in the affair;* (Mṣb;) i.q. قَصَّرَ. (Ṣ.)

وَنَاةٌ *A woman languid,* or *gentle,* or *grave in deportment, &c.:* see أَنَاةٌ.

مِينَآءٌ *A port:* see an ex. in a verse cited voce شُحُونٌ: it is masc.; its ء being a substitute for ى: or it is an ancient Egyptian word in origin.

وهر

تَيْهُورٌ, originally وَيْهُورٌ: see تهر

وهف

خُذْ مَا أَوْهَفَ *Take what is easily attainable; what offers itself without difficulty.* (AA, in TA, voce انتدب.)

وهق

6. تَوَاهَقَتْ أَخْفَافُهَا: see مِغْلَاةٌ.

الوَهَقُ *The lasso.* —— مِغْلَاةُ الوَهَقِ: see مِغْلَاةٌ, art. غلو.

وهل

لَقِيتُهُ أَوَّلَ وَهْلَةٍ *I met him the first thing:* see صَوْلَةٌ.

وهم

1. وَهِمَ فِى الحِسَابِ, (Ṣ, Mgh, Mṣb, Ḳ,) aor. يَوْهَمُ, inf. n. وَهَمٌ, (Ṣ, Mṣb,) *He committed an error,* or *a mistake, in the reckoning,* or *calculation;* (Ṣ, Mgh, Mṣb, Ḳ;) as also ↓ أَوْهَمَ فِيهِ: (Mgh, Mṣb:) and *committed an inadvertence therein.* (Ṣ.) [And in like manner, فِى قَوْلِهِ *in his saying.*] It is said in a trad. of 'Alee, قَالَ الشَّاهِدَانِ أَوْهَمْنَا ↓ إِنَّمَا السَّارِقُ هٰذَا or وَهِمْنَا accord. to different readings [*The two witnesses said, We have committed a mistake,* or *misconception: the thief is only this*]. (Mgh.) —— وَهَمْتُ الشَّىْءَ, (Mgh, Mṣb,*) aor. أَهِمُ, inf. n. وَهْمٌ, (Mgh,) [*I thought of the thing;*] *the thing occurred in my mind.* (Mgh, Mṣb.*) And وَهَمْتُ إِلَى الشَّىْءِ, (Mṣb,) or فِى الشَّىْءِ, (Ṣ, Ḳ,) aor. as above, (Ṣ, Mṣb, Ḳ,) and so the inf. n., (Ṣ, Mṣb,) *I thought of the thing,* (Ṣ, Mṣb, Ḳ,) *while desiring to think of another thing.* (S, Mṣb.)

2: see 4.

4. أَوْهَمَهُ *He made him to think* [or *imagine a thing*]; as also ↓ وَهَّمَهُ. (Ṣ, Ḳ.) أَوْهَمَهُ كَذَا *He made him to think,* or *suspect, such a thing.* (MA.) —— See 8. —— أَوْهَمَ: see وَهِمَ. —— أَوْهَمَ فِيهِ also signifies *He doubted respecting it.* (Mgh.)

5. تَوَهَّمَ is properly rendered *He presumed, surmised, fancied,* or *supposed* a thing: and تَوَهُّمًا, *upon presumption, surmise,* or *supposition;* and *suppositively:* see وَهْمٌ; and خَالَ and خَالَ. —— تَوَهَّمَ *He thought;* (Ṣ, Ḳ;) *he imagined* a thing: (TA:) *he doubted:* see an ex., in a verse of 'Antarah, cited voce مُتَرَدَّمٌ.

8. اِتَّهَمَهُ بِكَذَا (Mṣb, Ḳ) and اِتَّهَمَهُ بِهِ (AZ, Ḳ) and ↓ أَوْهَمَهُ بِهِ (Ḳ) *He made him an object of imputation,* or *suspected him, of such a thing; he imputed to him such a thing.* (Mṣb, Ḳ, TA.) See art. تهم. —— اِتَّهَمَهُ بِكَذَا, as also اِتَّهَمَهُ بكذا, and ↓ أَوْهَمَهُ بكذا, *He suspected him of such a thing;* i.e., of a thing that was attributed to him. (Marg. note in Ḳ.) [This is the signification commonly obtaining. See an ex. in the TA, voce سِخَاب. —— Also, the second, *He accused him of such a thing.*]

وَهْمٌ *A thought,* or *an idea, occurring in the mind:* (Mgh, Mṣb,* Ḳ:*) pl. أَوْهَامٌ: (Mṣb:) or *of the two extremes* [or *different opinions* or *ideas*] *between which one wavers, that which is outweighed* [*in probability*]. (Ḳ.) *An* [*indecisive*] *opinion* or *idea outweighed in probability* [or *formed from evidence outweighed in probability; a presumption; a surmise; a fancy; a supposition*]: opposed to ظَنٌّ, q.v. (Kull, p. 376.) —— Also *Doubt,* or *suspicion:* but for this I have found no authority; though it is well known, and plainly indicated in the Mṣb, in art. خيل; voce خَيَّلَ, q.v. in this Lex. —— Also The *object of a thought,* or *of an idea, occurring in the mind.* (Mgh.) And The *mind* itself, or *intellect;* syn. عَقْلٌ. (MF, TA.) In modern Arabic it signifies *An imagination, a fancy, a chimera,* and *a conjecture.*

وهن

1. وَهَنَ *He was,* or *became, weak,* or *infirm, in an affair,* and *in operation,* and *in body;* (Mṣb:) and so said of a bone: (Bḍ, and Jel in xix. 3:) and *he was,* or *became, languid, languid and faint,* or *lax in the joints;* (TA, Bḍ in iii. 140;) *enervated, unnerved,* or *broken in energy;* (Bḍ, ubi suprà;) *cowardly.* (TA, Jel in iii. 140.) —— See also 4.

2: see 4.

4. أَوْهَنَهُ *He, or it, weakened him:* [*rendered him languid, languid and faint,* or *lax in the joints; enervated him, unnerved him,* or *broke his energy; rendered him cowardly:* (see وَهَنَ :)] (Ṣ, Mṣb, Ḳ:) and ↓ وَهَّنَهُ, (Ṣ, Mgh, Mṣb, Ḳ,) but the former is the better, (Mṣb,) and ↓ وَهَنَهُ. (Ṣ, Ḳ.)

وَهْنٌ The *period about midnight;* (Ṣ, Ḳ;) or the *time after an hour,* or *a short period,* (سَاعَة,) *of the night:* (JK, Ḳ, TA:) or *when the night is departing.* (Ṣ.) See إِنْىٌ.

عِرْقُ الوَاهِنَةِ *The cephalic vein:* see قَلِيق.

وَهْنَانَةٌ *I. q.* وَنَاةٌ, q. v.; and see أَنَاةٌ.

تَوْهُونٌ *Weak, languid, unable to rise:* see عُدَوَآة.

وهى

1. وَهَى *It was, or became, much slit,* or *rent.* (Mṣb.) — *It was,* or *became, lax, flaccid,* or *flabby:* (Mṣb:) or *weak;* said of a rope, (Mgh,) or other thing: or *it fell.* (Mṣb.) See وَاهٍ. — وَهِىَ *It was,* or *became, uncompact, unsound,* or *weak.* — وَهَى أَمْرُهُ [*His affair,* or *case, was,* or *became, in a weak,* or *an unsound, state*]. (TA, art. نغض, &c.)

وَاهٍ *Lax; weak; frail; wanting in strength, compactness, firmness,* or *toughness; unsubstantial; unsound.* See an ex. in the Ṣ, voce أُنْشُوطَةٌ, where it is applied to love, or affection. — وَاهًا : see an ex. voce نُغْبَةٌ; and see آهِ, in art. اوه, in two places.

ويل

وَيْلٌ لَهُ and وَيْلًا لَهُ and وَيْلَةٌ *Woe to him!* [See عَوْلَك]. *Perdition befall him! Punishment befall him!* (Kull, p. 377.) See voce وَيْبٌ, and voce وَيْحٌ, and وَيْسٌ.

وَيْهًا [an imperative verbal noun, which may be rendered *On!*] a word of incitement. (Ṣ, Ḳ.) One also says to a man, and to a horse, يَا وَيْهَاهْ [*Ho! On!*]. (A'Obeyd in TA in art ايه.) See أَيَّهَ. — وَيْهَكَ : see أَيْهَكَ in art. ايه. I have not found this anywhere but in that art. in the Ḳ, and doubt its correctness.

ى

يتم

4. أَيْتَمَهُ [*He made him fatherless*]. (TA in art. ايم.) See an ex. in art. ايم, conj. 2.

يتن

وَلَدَتْهُ يَتْنًا *She brought him forth feet foremost.* (M.) In Fresnel's three copies of the Aghánee, (see his "Seconde lettre sur l'Histoire des Arabes avant l'Islamisme," Journal Asiatique, 3rd Series, no. 16,) erroneously written نينا.

يثم

أَيْثَمُ and تِيثَمُ [for تَأْثَمُ and آثَمُ]: see أَثِمَ.

يد

يَدٌ The *arm, from the shoulder-joint to the extremities of the fingers.* (Mṣb.) — [The *fore-leg* of a horse, &c.] — يَدٌ بَيْضَآءُ: see أَبْيَضُ, in two places, near the end of the paragraph. — يَدٌ A *sleeve:* see R. Q. 1 in art. ردن. — يَدُ القَوْسِ: see رِجْلٌ, in two places. — أَعْطَاهُ عَنْ يَدٍ. — ثَمَانِيَةٌ: see الأَيْدِى for طِوَالُ الأَيْدِ. — عَنْ يَدٍ, as occurring in the Ḳur, ix., 29, *He gave it in acknowledgement of the superiority of the receiver;* that the power (يَدٌ) of the latter was superior to that of the giver: or, *because of favour received;* or, *from subjection and abasement:* (M:) or, *from compulsion:* (A 'Obeyd, T:) or, *obediently:* or, *walking with it; not riding, nor sending it:* or, *in ready money.* (TA.) — أَسْلَمَ عَلَى يَدَىْ فُلَانٍ *He became a Muslim by the advice and persuasion of such a one.* (Marg. note in a copy of the Jámi' eṣ-Ṣagheer, on a trad. commencing مَنْ أَسْلَمَ.) — أَخَذْتُ عِنْدَهُ يَدًا: see art. اخذ. — لِفُلَانٍ عِنْدِى يَدٌ *I owe such a one a benefit.* — عَلَى يَدِهِ *By his agency,* or *means.* See the corresponding expression in Hebrew, in Ps. lxiii. 11, Jer. xviii. 21, and Ezek. xxxv. 5, in the phrase "to pour out (the blood of) a person by means of the sword." — وَلَا تُلْقُوا بِأَيْدِيكُمْ إِلَى التَّهْلُكَةِ (Ḳur, ii. 191): see ب (used redundantly) — لَا آتِيهِ يَدَ الدَّهْرِ, and يَدَ المُسْنَدِ, *I will not come to him, or do it, ever; I will never do it.* (IAạr, in L, voce مُسْنَدٌ.) See أَبَدٌ and جَدًّا. — عَلَى يَدَىْ: see الخَيْرِ وَالْيُمْنِ. — بِعْتُهُ يَدًا بِيَدٍ: see نَاجِزٌ. — You say, also, بَايَعْتُهُ يَدًا بِيَدٍ, the two nouns being only thus used, as a denotative of state, *I contracted a sale with him for ready money;* i. q. بِالتَّعْجِيلِ وَالنَّقْدِ. (Mgh.) — عَلَىَّ يَدِىَّ [or يَدَىَّ ?] لَكَ أَنْ يَكُونَ كَذَا is like لك ان يكون كذا. (Aboo-Sahl El-Harawee, TA in art. حبق.) — أُتِىَ عَلَى يَدِ فُلَانٍ: see ذَاتُ يَدَيْنِ and أَوَّلُ ذِى يَدَيْنِ: see art. أتى. — تَحْتَ يَدِهِ *Under his authority.* — يَدٌ ذو. — † *Generosity.* (A, voce شَبْرٌ)

مَيْدِىٌّ A gazelle *whose fore-leg is caught in a snare:* see مَرْجُولٌ.

يربع

الجَارُ اليَرْبُوعِىُّ: see الجار البَرَاقِشِىُّ, in art. برقش.

يرع

يَرَاعٌ *A firefly:* see حُبَاحِبٌ.

يرق

يَرَقَانٌ *Saffron.* (Sgh, in TA, art. شعر.) — See أَرَقَانٌ.

يرم

يَرْمِىٌّ and أَيْرَمِىٌّ *A sign-stone:* see إِرَمٌ.

يزن

يَزَنِىٌّ and أَيْزَنِىٌّ, applied to a spear: see أَزَانِىٌّ, in art. زأن.

يشم

4. مَا أَيْشَمَهُ *How unlucky!* a vulgarism: see 4 in art. شأم.

يفع

يَفَعٌ: }
يَفَعَةٌ: } see يَافِعٌ
يَفَاعٌ: }

يَافِعٌ and ▼ يَفَعَةٌ A boy *grown up,* (Mṣb, TA,) *grown tall;* (Ḥam, p. 354 et seq., Ḥar, p. 189;) as also ▼ يَفَاعٌ and ▼ يَفَعٌ. (Ḥam, ibid.) See an ex. voce خَبَاةٌ; and شَادِخٌ and مُطَبِّخٌ.

وَلَدُ المُيَافَعَةِ [*The offspring of fornication,* or *adultery*].

يقن

1. يَقِنَهُ, (Ṣ, Mṣb, Ḳ,) and يَقِنَ بِهِ; (Mṣb;) and ▼ أَيْقَنَهُ, (Ṣ, Ḳ,) and ▼ ايقن بِهِ; (Ḳ;) and ▼ تَيَقَّنَهُ; and ▼ اِسْتَيْقَنَهُ, (Ṣ, Mṣb, Ḳ,) and ▼ استيقن بِهِ; (Ḳ;) all signify the same; (Ṣ;) *He knew it; he was,* or *became, certain,* or *sure,* or *he made sure, of it;* syn. عَلِمَهُ; (Mṣb, Ḳ;) *intuitively,* and *inferentially;* (Mṣb;) [see 1 in art. علم;] and تَحَقَّقَهُ. (Ḳ.)

4: }
5: } see 1.
10: }

يَقِينٌ is of the measure فَعِيلٌ in the sense of the measure فَاعِلٌ, signifying *Sure,* or *certain,* and *manifest*. (Mṣb.) — And *knowledge*, or *certainty*; [see ظَنٌّ;] *instinctive* and *inferential*. (Mṣb.) — عَيْنُ اليَقِينِ : see عَيْنٌ (latter part). — حَقُّ اليَقِينِ and الحَقُّ اليَقِينُ : see جَامِعٌ; where the two words are said to have the same meaning: and Bḍ and Jel in lvi. 95; in the latter of which, اليقين in حَقُّ اليَقِينِ is expressly said to be an epithet: see also Ḥam, p. 335.

يم

2. يَمَّمَ : see أَمَّمَ. And يَمَّمَ المَرِيضَ and المَيِّتَ : see Mgh in art. أَمَّ.

5. تَيَمَّمَ : see صَعِيدٌ and art. ام. — تَيَمَّمَ *i. q.* قَصَدَ قَصْدًا. يَمَامَةٌ (TA in art. ام.)

المُشَرَّكَةُ : see الفَرِيضَةُ اليَمِّيَّةُ.

يَمَامٌ : see حَمَامٌ.

يمر

يَامُورٌ The *male of the* أَيِّل [or *mountain goat*: not ايل]. (M, TT.)

يمن

1. يُمِنَ, (T, M, Ḳ,) and يَمِنَ, (M, Ḳ,) *He was prosperous; fortunate; lucky*. (T, M, Ḳ.)

3. يَامَنَ : see 3 in art. شأم in two places.

4. أَيْمَنَهُ *He made it to incline towards the right*: see an ex. voce سِنٌّ (near the end of the paragraph). — أَيْمَنَ : see أَشْأَمَ in two places. — أَيْمَنَتْ إِبِلِى : see أَيْسَرَتْ.

5. تَيَمَّنَ *He was placed on his right side in the grave*. (TA, voce عَلْبَى.) — تَيَمَّنَ بِهِ *i. q.* تَبَرَّكَ بِهِ [q. v.]. (Ṣ.) — فُلَانٌ يُتَيَمَّنُ بِرَأْيِهِ, i. e. يُتَبَرَّكُ بِهِ, (T,) app. *One is fortunate in, or derives a blessing from, his counsel*. — *He augured good by it, or from it; or looked for good fortune, or a blessing, from it*; syn. تَبَرَّكَ بِهِ: (Mgh, Mṣb, &c.:) opposed to تَشَآءَمَ بِهِ, in the Ḳ, art. طير; and in Bḍ, xvii. 14; and well known. — تَيَمَّنَ بِكَلِمَةٍ [*He augured good from the word*], (Ḥar, p. 488,) and بِكَلَامٍ. (Mṣb. in art. فأل.)

6. تَيَامَنَ : see تَشَأَمَ. — تَيَامَنُوا : see 3 in art. يسر.

يُمْنٌ *Prosperity: good fortune; good luck; auspiciousness*; (T, Ṣ, M, Ḳ;) *contr. of* شُؤْمٌ, (M,) and of نَحْسٌ. (L, art. سعد.)

يُمْنَةٌ : its pl. seems to be يُمَنٌ. See بُرْدٌ.

اليَمِينُ *The location that is on the right*. — يَمِينٌ also, The *south*. See سَرْحٌ. — يَمِينٌ also signifies *A covenant* (Bḍ, and Jel in lxviii. 39) *confirmed by an oath*. (Bḍ, ibid.) يَمِينُ ٱللّٰهِ *The oath by attestation of God*: see أَيْمُ ٱللّٰهِ, and عَهْدُ ٱللّٰهِ. — حَلَفْتُ يَمِينًا [*I swore*, or *have sworn, an oath*]. (T, Ṣ, M, voce أَمِينٌ, which see. You say, يَمِينَ ٱللّٰهِ لَا أَفْعَلُ (as in some copies of the Ṣ [meaning, حَلَفْتُ يَمِينَ ٱللّٰهِ]): or يَمِينُ ٱللّٰهِ (as in other copies [meaning, يَمِينُ ٱللّٰهِ قَسَمِى]). See a similar form of oath voce حَرَامٌ. — يَمِينًا صَادِقَةً لَأَفْعَلَنَّ : see زَعْمَةٌ.

يَمَانٍ *A garment of Yemen*: see a verse voce تَسْهِيمٌ.

يَمَانِىٌّ and يَمَانُونَ : see تِهَامِىٌّ.

يَامِنٌ : see يَاسِرٌ.

أَيْمَنُ [The *right, as opposed to the left*; see Ḳur, xix. 53, xx. 82, and xxviii. 30;] *contr. of* أَيْسَرُ; and [in like manner] ↓ مَيْمَنَةٌ is *contr. of* مَيْسَرَةٌ. (Ṣ.) — أَيْمَنُ, *contr. of* أَشْأَمُ, as signifying The *right*, opposed to the *left*: and as signifying *Lucky*, or *auspicious*: pl. أَيَامِنُ. See أَشْأَمُ. — It is also used in the sense of يُمْنٌ: see أَشْأَمُ. — Also *More*, and *most, lucky*, or *auspicious*, or *happy*: see 8 in art. ذل.

أَيْمُنٌ, used only in swearing, is a sing. noun, not a particle, nor pl. of يَمِينٌ: and is derived from يُمْنٌ. (Mughnee.)

الأَيَامِنُ : see an ex. of this word, voce ثَابِرٌ.

مَيْمَنَةٌ The *right wing* of an army. See أَيْمَنُ.

مَيْمُونٌ *Fortunate; happy*; (T, M, MA, KL;) *blest*. (T.) See an ex. voce عَرِيكَةٌ.

تَيَمُّنٌ The *having* [or *receiving*] a *blessing*. (KL.)

تَيَمُّنًا for تَأَمُّنًا : see أُمْنَةٌ.

ينم

يَنَمَةٌ : see حَلَمَةٌ.

يوم

يَوْمٌ *A time, whether night or day*: (Mṣb;) *time absolutely, whether night or not, little or not*: this is the proper signification; (Kull, p. 390:) and *day*, meaning the *period from the rising of the sun to its setting*; (Lth, TA;) the *time when the sun is above the earth*: this is the common conventional acceptation: (Kull, ubi suprà:) and the *period from the second* [or *true*] *dawn to sunset*: (Mṣb, Kull:) this is the legal acceptation: (Kull:) and *a civil day*; the *period of the revolution of the greatest firmament*. (Kull.) — Also, *An accident*, or *event*; syn. كَوْنٌ and كَائِنَةٌ. Ex., نِعْمَ ٱلْأَخُ فُلَانٌ فِى اليَوْمِ إِذَا نَزَلَ بِنَا *Excellent is the brother, such a one, in the case of the accident, when it befalls us*. (T.) — See نَهَارٌ. — يَأْتِينَا يَوْمَ يَوْمَ *He comes to us day after day*, i. e., *every day*: (Sharḥ esh-Shudhoor:) and يَوْمٌ يَوْمٌ. (In a verse cited by IJ. in Mz, sect. on the حَقِيقَة and مَجَاز.) — يَوْمٌ *A day-journey*, or *day's journey*. — *A day*, as in our phrase "he won the day;" meaning *contest, fight*, or *battle*: I render it *a day* [*of conflict*]. — أَيَّامُ العَرَبِ *The* [*days*, (agreeably with an English, as well as Arabian, usage,) meaning] *conflicts* (وَقَائِع) *of the Arabs*. (ISk, T.) — ابْنُ يَوْمِهِ *He who thinks* [*only of the present day*,] *not of the morrow*. (Er-Rághib, in TA, art. بنى.) — يَوْمُ الشَّكِّ : see شَكٌّ. — بَيْنَ الأَيَّامِ and فِيمَا بَيْنَ الأَيَّامِ : see نَدْرَةٌ, in two places.

يَوْمِيَّةٌ *A day's wages*.

مُيَاوَمَةٌ from اليَوْمُ is like مُلَايَلَةٌ from اللَّيْلُ, and مُشَاهَرَةٌ from الشَّهْرُ, &c. (TA, in art. ربع.) See مُسَاوَعَةٌ.

يى

2. يَيَّيْتُ يَآءً حَسَنَةً [*I wrote a beautiful* ى]. (TA, in art. حى.)

END OF THE SUPPLEMENT.